THE REIGN OF
HENRY THE FIFTH

BY

JAMES HAMILTON WYLIE

VOLUME I
(1413—1415)

GREENWOOD PRESS, PUBLISHERS
NEW YORK   1968

First published, 1914

Reprinted with the permission of the
Cambridge University Press.

First Greenwood reprinting, 1968

Library of Congress catalogue card number: 69-10175

Printed in the United States of America

PREFACE

I HAVE to acknowledge my indebtedness to the publications of many fellow-workers in the same field, though in the case of two of them their results have unfortunately reached me too late for insertion in this volume. These are Mr C. L. Kingsford, who, in his *English Historical Literature in the Fifteenth Century*, has conclusively proved the dependence of Tito Livio on *The Brut*, and Professor Otto Cartellieri of Heidelberg, who, in his *Beiträge* (IV) *zur Geschichte der Herzöge von Burgund*, has, for the first time, published the full text of the Conventions of 1414 with the Duke of Burgundy.

But, after all, my chief gratitude will always be due to the spirit of liberality in my country as embodied in the Library of the British Museum, where facilities for the highest and most lasting of human enjoyments are open freely to all comers from every country in the world.

J. H. W.

LONDON
October, 1913.

CONTENTS

CHAPTER I

CORONATION

HENRY IV died on March 20, 1413[1], and his eldest son Henry V at once took possession of the throne at the age of 25[2]. On the following day he issued the usual order from the Palace at Westminster that no one was to leave the country without special permission[3], together with a call to the sheriffs to proclaim the King's Peace[4] in the capital and all the counties throughout England, asserting that the succession had devolved upon him[5] and pronouncing the usual threats of imprisonment[6] against all who should assemble "excessive meetings[7]" or cause riot, disturbance or insurrection. Justices of the Peace were at once appointed[8], and the king's brother John[9] and the Earl of Westmoreland[10] were continued in their respective offices as Wardens of the East and West Marches of Scotland while the captive King of Scots[11] and the Duke of Albany's

---

[1] See App. A.   [2] See App. B.

[3] Black Book of Adm. i. 282, March 21, 1413.

[4] Cf. "stablished his pees," Brut, ii. 534.

[5] Rym. ix. 1; Nicolas, Chron. of Hist. 303.

[6] For similar proclamations of Edward I, II, III, though not in such full details, see Rym. ii. 1; iii. 1; iv. 24. None such appear to have been issued on the accession of Richard II or Henry IV.

[7] In the proclamation of Henry VI, where the phrasing is almost identical, the words are *conventicula illicita*, Rym. x. 254. For commission appointed on April 3, 1413, to enquire into illegal meetings at Nottingham, see Pat. 1 H. V, i. 27 d.

[8] Pat. 1 H. V, i. 34 d, 35 d, 36 d, March 21, 1413.

[9] Doyle, i. 150; Wylie, iv. 471.

[10] Rot. Scot. ii. 203, 204; Ord. Priv. Co. ii. 126; Rym. ix. 102; Goodwin 15.

[11] See App. C. Claus. 1 H. V, 38, March 21, 1413; Rym. ix. 2; Cal. Doc. Scot. iv. 169; J. T. T. Brown, 93; Lawson, xix.; Wylie, ii. 403; not March 20 as Cowan, i. 167. For payments for expenses of the King of Scots, the "Master of ffyth" and Griffin, son of Owain in the Tower, see Iss. Roll, 1 H. V, Pasch. and Mich., June 27; July 7, 17; Oct. 2, 10, 21, 25, 29; Dec. 1, 4, 9, 11, 1413; Jan. 25, Feb. 22nd (*bis*), 1414; Cal. Doc. Scot. iv. 170, 171; Devon, 324; also to Simon Campe, sub-constable of the Tower, for same, Exch. Accts. 406/21, 22. He was deputy for the Duke of York on July 4, 1413. D. K. Rept. liii. App. I, p. 30.

son Murdach together with Griffith[1] the son of Owen Glendower were brought for safer custody to the Tower. All these arrangements were made on the day after the late king's death and then after following his father's body to Canterbury[2] the new king began to prepare for his coming coronation.

On April 2, 1413[3], the Earl of Warwick (Richard Beauchamp)[4] was appointed to act as Steward of England at the ceremony[5] in the absence of the Duke of Clarence[6], the

[1] His fellow-prisoner, Owen ap Griffith ap Richard (Wylie, ii. 403, note 1), was pardoned on May 29, 1413, Pat. 1 H. V, i. 20. For Rhys ap Griffith, committed to the Tower Jan. 23, 1417, see Claus. 4 H. V, 9.

[2] Waurin, ii. 162; Wylie, iv. 113. Cf. And to Cauntilbur men hym bere, Lydgate in Jul. E. iv. f. 7; Petegrue, 594; called "Cameterbury" in Harl. MS. 4205; lythe in Cauntreburye, Greg. Chron. 53; per aquam transportatus, Usk, 119 [298]. For 22/- paid for wine offered to the King at Blean by the citizens of Canterbury in primo adventu suo, though this may of course possibly refer to his subsequent visits in June and July, see Hist. MSS. 9th Rept. p. 138, from Canterbury City Records, 1413.

Belloc (166) thinks that the body was "lashed upon the deck with other cargo." I can find no ground for his theory that Windsor was "too kingly" for him to have been buried there.

[3] Pat. 1 H. V, i. 28, 36; Rym. ix. 3; Cal. Rot. Pat. 260; Harcourt, 190, 200.

[4] The heading of the earliest Issue Roll of Henry V (i.e. 1 H. V, Pasch.) shows Master John Oudeby, clerk, "Ex parte Richard Earl of Warwick *Camar.*" Oudeby died on March 7, 1414, not 1413, as Wylie, ii. 109, 110. See inscription on his brass at Flamstead, near Dunstable in Clutterbuck, i. 365, showing that he was appointed to the living by the Earl of Warwick on March 20, 1407. He was also Rector of Braughby (? Wragby) in the diocese of Lincoln. For Flamstead as one of the possessions of the Earl of Warwick in 1402 see Feudal Aids, ii. 444. Oudeby's successor at Flamstead was appointed on March 8, 1414. For John Oudeby, canon of Lichfield in 2 H. V, see Inq. ad Quod Damn. 369; do. List. ii. 742, i.e. the prebend of Bishopshill which he had held since 1380. Le Neve, i. 589. In the Subsidy Roll of 1412, Johannes Oudeby, clericus, owns property in London yielding 5s. 2d. per annum, Archaeol. Journ. xliv. 73. The headings of the Receipt and Issue Rolls for 3 H. V (i.e. from March 31, 1415 to Sept. 29, 1415), also 5 H. V (in duplicate, i.e. April 11, 1417 to March 27, 1418), have Nicholas Calton, clerk, ex parte Richard, Earl of Warwick, *Camar.* Calton held the prebend of Eaton (Southwell), Nov. 7, 1408, became Archdeacon of Taunton on Sept. 1, 1416, and died in 1440. Le Neve, iii. 421.

[5] For the Steward or Seneschal of England (originally the *dapifer* or sewer who waited at the King's Table) as "Master of the Ceremonies at any great pageant," see Harcourt, 191. The office was attached to the Earldom of Leicester by virtue of the barony of Hinckley, Doyle, ii. 336-340; Harcourt, 176, 183, 188, 200, where it is identical with the office of Chief Justiciary of England, which carried the right of presiding at the trial of a peer—called grand juge d'Engleterre, juge greigneur—the office being claimed by Henry IV ainsi comme son père (i.e. John of Gaunt) et ses prédécesseurs. It is said to have been merged in the Crown, temp. H. IV, Perkins, 87; cf. Wylie, i. 29. For supposition that S. S. Collar means "Senescallus," see Foss; Hackington, 77; Macklin, 149; Druitt, 189; Mayo, i. pp. xlv, l.

[6] Henry of Bolingbroke inherited the office from his father as Earl of Leicester (not Lancaster as Wylie, i. 33); Doyle, ii. 316, but on becoming King in Oct. 1399, he bestowed it on his son Thomas (Wylie, i. 29; Doyle, i. 397), who held it till his death. He is called Steward of England in French Rolls, 1 H. V, 4, 12, 23, 26, Aug. 23, Nov. 25, 1413; Jan. 23, March 15, 1414. Also Rym. ix. 239 (May 8, 1415); ibid. ix. 462 (July 10, 1417); Rot. Norm. 244 (Feb. 8, 1418).

After his death at Beaugé (not in the castle of Beaufort, as Poulson, Holderness, 72) on March 22, 1421, the Stewardship was never again regranted except for particular occasions. Harcourt (191, 362) quotes printed Patent Rolls (i.e. Cal. Rot. Pat. 238, 243;

duties of the Constable being undertaken by Henry Lord
Fitzhugh[1]. The king stayed at Sutton[2] near Chiswick
from April 2 to April 5. On the 6th he was at Kingston[3]
and on the 7th he was conducted with a great riding[4]
through London to the Tower where on the following day
he conferred the order of knighthood[5] on some 50 candidates[6] who took the customary bath[7] and watched their
arms through the night in the old Norman Chapel of
St John[8] in the great white tower. These included the
young Earl of March[9] and his brother Roger[10], Richard
Lord le Despenser[11] and John Holland[12] son of the Earl
of Huntingdon whose fathers had risen in the cause of
Richard II and paid the penalty at the block 13 years
before. The new knights with a great rout of lords escorted
the young king in state[13] through the Cheap to the Palace at
Westminster and he was crowned by Archbishop Arundel
on Passion Sunday, April 9, 1413[14], in the Abbey Church

Cal. Pat. Hy IV, i. 69, 78, 152, 371, 507, 524, 529, 530, 566) to show that he was called
Steward of England in Nov. 2, 3, 14, 1399; March 5, June 1, 1400; May 16, June 27,
July 4, 16, 1401. He regards the statement in Year Book 1 H. IV, fol. 1, that the office
of steward was vacant in Jan. 1400 and that the Earl of D—— (? Devonshire) was then
appointed pro tem. to preside at the trial of the Earl of Huntingdon (see Wylie, i. 102)
as an "unmitigated error," an "atrocious blunder," etc. and the corresponding statement
in Ann. 337 as "quite untrue" (p. 428), believing the whole entry to be a forgery dating
from about 1499 (pp. 420, 433).
    [1] Dugd. Baronage, i. 404.
    [2] See Wylie, iv. 12. For timber, stone, lead and other sufficient *stuffura* for repairing
the manor of Sutton, see Pat. 3 H. V, i. 16 d, April 17, 1415.
    [3] Exch. Accts. 406/2, 5; Vita, 18; Pauli, v. 76; Ramsay, i. 163.
    [4] Chron. Lond. 95; Anstis, Obs. 39, App. 24.
    [5] Rym. ix. 3 (May 12, 1415) refers to stuff for vesture "encontre votre coronation,"
also for lords and squires to take the order of knighthood "à même le temps."
    [6] Exch. Accts. 406/15. Shaw (i. 129) gives the names of eight of them.
    [7] In 1423 such knights are called "Chevaliers de Bath," Rot. Parl. iv. 228; Anstis,
Obs. 27; cf. "Knyghtis of the Bathe," Greg. Chron. 165; Fab. 565.
    [8] For picture of it see Bayley, 107; Britton and Bayley, 28; Knight, London, ii. 220;
Ros, 22.
    [9] Doyle, ii. 470.
    [10] For their robes, contra coronationem suam, see Anstis, Obs. App. 25, where the list
includes the brother of the Earl of Huntingdon, John Phelip, John Rothenhale and [blank]
West, esquires.
    [11] Born 1396, Wylie, iv. 423. Shaw (i. 129) thinks that he is "wrongly called Lord"
because of his father's attainder; see Comp. Peer. iii. 93. E. Hardy (i. 28) imagines him
to have been "consigned to a continental convent."
    [12] Born 1394, Doyle, ii. 229.
    [13] Vita, 20.
    [14] Eulog. iii. 421; Usk, 120; Chron. Giles, 3; Wals. ii. 390; Strecche, 265; Ber-
mondsey, 484; Exch. Accts. 406/21 (5); Iss. Roll, 5 H. V, Apr. 21, 1417; MS. Bodl.
496, f. 2246; Elmham, Lib. Metr. 82, 95; do. Mon. Aug. 72. Not April 5, as Duchesne,
819; nor April 8th, as Shaw, 127; nor April 10, as Chambers' Encycl. v. 647; Church,
47; nor Aug. 9, 1412, as Rastell, 247, which seems to be a haunting date for Henry V
(see Wylie, iii. 323); nor 1408, as Watson, 104; nor 1414, as Croyl. Hist. 499.

where a stage[1] or scaffold draped with cloth of gold had
been erected between the high altar and the choir that all
might see the details of the day[2].

After the ceremony the minstrelsy struck up[3] and the
king was ushered to the Coronation Feast[4] in the Great
Hall of the adjoining Palace where he was seated on the
marble chair[5] on the dais at the upper or gable end detached
by some feet from all immediate company and one who was
present tells how he looked like an angel[6] as he sat so
comely and gracious beneath the cloth of estate[7] amidst
the noise and whiffling of the waits in their coloured long-
cloth gowns[8] aloft and the din and clamour of the guests
below. Queen Joan had sent two panniers of Brittany
lampreys; two Sussex does had come in from Sir John
Pelham; William Croisier[9] presented a large pike[10] and the
conduit in the Palace Yard ran with red Gascon and Rhine
wine[11].

The *menu* of King Henry's coronation feast is still
preserved[12] and it shows that as at his father's coronation[13]
there was plenty to the most and to the least[14]. The guests
were kept quite busy over three full courses[15] any one of

[1] Greg. Chron. 165; Lethaby, 22. For the stage for the coronation of Henry IV, see
ibid. 219.
[2] Devon, 321. For representation of the coronation carved on the north side of
Henry V's Chantry in Westminster Abbey, see Keepe, 154; Gough, II. ii. 69; Neale,
ii. 94; Carter, ii. 35; Le Keux, 40; Knight, London, iv. 142; Stanley, 60; W. Jones,
210; Archaeologia, iii. 189, where it is called a picture; F. Bond, 192; do. Guide, 21,
who supposes that it represents his coronation in France.
[3] Antiq. Repert. ii. 288.
[4] For 13s. 4d. paid to 4 garciones going to Westminster to prepare couches and other
necessaries for the Coronation Feast, see Exch. Accts. 406/21, 30. On that Sunday,
£971 was spent out of a total of £1168 for the week. Ramsay, i. 164/317; Antiquary,
viii. 98.
[5] Stow, vi. 49; Halle, 105.
[6] Memorials, 65.
[7] For picture of a king sitting at a separate table under a canopy with side tables at
right angles and a cupbearer kneeling, see Montfaucon, ii. 334.
[8] Wardrobe Accts. 406/26.
[9] Or Croyser, Wylie, iii. 322, note 1; Gaunt Reg. ii. 371.
[10] For payments to bearers for delivering 1 lws (i.e. pike), see Exch. Accts. 406/21, 30.
[11] For 114s. 9½d. paid on this account, see ibid. 406/21, 22.
[12] Cookry, 4, 5.
[13] Two Cookery Books, 57; Brayley and Britton, 293. For his marriage feast at Win
chester, see Two Cookery Books, pp. xiii, 58; Strutt, Man. ii. 100; Wylie, ii. 288 n.
[14] Chauc. Squire's Tale, 10614.
[15] For pulmenta (pottage) fercula meliora and fercula grossa, see Mann. and Meals,
ii. 40. For specimens of 2, 3, or 6-course dinners, see ibid. i. 164, 165, 166, 170, 277;
Menagier, ii. 91–100. For Archbishop Nevil's banquet at Cawood, Jan. 16, 1466, see
Wheater, 214; Purey-Cust, ii. 126.
A modest public dinner in London in the 14th century, with all extravagance cut

which with its multitude of messes[1] would have very severely tried the capacity of a modern stomach, in which respect even in those days Englishmen held a lead which was the admiration of all countries and nations of the world[2]. And when we know as we do the recipes for producing some of these culinary marvels[3] and find among them such concoctions as a white-meat[4] or blandesory[5] made of hen-brawn ground with rice and milk of almonds[6] or flampets[7] of fat pork and figs boiled in small ale with cheese fried in clean grease and then baked in a coffin of paste and coloured with the yolk of eggs we get a curious peep into some of the possibilities of the mediaeval digestion[8].

Each course had also its special subtleties[9] in confectionery known as warners[10] because they foretold the coming heavier fare. These gastronomic triumphs were made of sugar, paste, or jelly[11] worked up into antelopes or gilded eagles or swans and cygnets sitting on green stocks with scriptures or subscriptions[12] in pastry coming out of their mouths calling upon the new king to "keep the law and guard the *foi*" and "have pit*ee* on the commonal*tee*" with such saws[13] as "out of *court* be banished *tort*" or "one and

down, consisted [of 3 courses, viz. (1) bread, beer and wine, (2) pottage and grosse char, and (3) double roast in one dish, cheese and no more (*sauns pluis*), Lib. Cust. 227. For commyn brede and grete fleshis and chese of the bugle, see Secreta, 178. For a dinner given to the Abbot of Châtillon-sur-Seine et ses gens on July 3, 1412, see Vidier, 372, where the cost = 29s. 6d., excluding belle chiere et garnison d'ostel.

[1] Mès, Menagier, i. 6; ii. 91, where there are 4 or 5 messes to each course or assiette. Cf. Wright, Dom. Man. 162.

[2] Antiq. Repert. ii. 291*.

[3] Bonis, I. cxxxi.

[4] Greg. Chron. 169.

[5] Forme of Cury, 26, 100, 118; English Cookery, viii.

[6] Cookry, 105.

[7] Forme of Cury, 54, 82; Greg. Chron. 141, 169.

[8] For abundance at feasts, see Bouchot, 53. e.g. at Milan in 1386 at the marriage of Lionel, Duke of Clarence, with Yolande, daughter of Gian Galeazzo Visconti. See Athenaeum, June 28, 1902. There is plenty of evidence that this heaped abundance prevailed not only at "feasts of solemnity," but among more homely guests according to the "English guise." Mann. and Meals, i. 169, 170.

[9] Mann. and Meals, i. 169, 175; Greg. Chron. 141, 169; Jusserand, Lit. Hist. 263; MacCracken, p. xxv.

[10] Two Cookery Books, x.; Forme of Cury, 154.

[11] Mann. and Meals, i. 151. [12] Mann. and Meals, i. 169.

[13] "Thenez la ley, gardez la fey"; "Eyez pité des comunalté"; "Hors de Court soit bannez tort"; "Un sauvez plus, Maynteyn Dieu"; Cookry, 4, 5, probably "Un sanz pluis" as Devon, 339; Nicolas, Navy, ii. 446; cf. "en un sanz plus," Kal. and Inv. ii. 100 on one of the King's rings. Fab. 587.

no more" with "God before[1]" and others suited to that
notable and honourable day.   If contrasts are to be drawn
with our modern banquets it is certain from a perusal of
the cautions given in the treatises which aimed at teaching
courtesy[2] that our forefathers in the 15th century were
much behind us as regards the etiquette of the table.   For
side by side with precepts against loud supping, fidgetting
with the feet, playing with the knife, or overfilling the
spoon and dropping sauce and pottage on the breast, they
abound in cautions against scrambling for the best portions
in the dip-charger, making sops of bitten bread, licking
plates with the tongue, blowing in the cup, leaving fat in
the ale or wine, spreading butter or cheese with the thumb
or wiping the knife or hands or even the teeth on the table
cloth or other still more shocking enormities.   It is true
that they also contain rules that silence must be kept in
the lord's presence[3], forbidding loud speech save only of the
lord and such as he spoke to and requiring such low communication in the hall that the chief officer's voice be heard
above that of all the others, but these can only have been
counsels of perfection and we know that as a fact the
English of that day had a reputation for fighting like devils
and eating like wolves[4].   To these singularities must be
added the presence of horses in the hall[5], for besides the
well authenticated entry of Dymock[6] the mounted champion
armed as St George with his challenge to all who would
dispute the new king's title, there is good evidence that
dishes for the high table were brought in by servants on
horseback who must have acquired special skill in balancing

[1] Henry V, 3, 6, 165; Speght, 36; Melusine, 107, 128, translating "Dieu avant" in
Arras, 120; cf. "Deo prævio," Rym. ix. 793; "God to-forn," Lydg. Troy Book, 45,
342, 401.
[2] e.g. Mann. and Meals; Add. MS. 37969; Hazlitt, Remains, Vol. iii.; Secreta;
Jusserand, Lit. Hist., etc.; passim.
[3] Add. MS. 37969/6.
[4] Kempe, 21.
[5] Vita, 22, 23, where all the nobles are said to be on horseback.   Called large war-
horses in W. Jones, 209.
[6] For the claim of John Dymmok before the coronation of Richard II, see Legg,
Coronation Records, 140, 159.   For his entrance at the Coronation Feast of Henry IV,
see Ann. 288; Kingsford, Chron. xxxvi. 49 (where he is called Thomas); Harcourt, 182.
Also Philip Dymmok at the Coronation of Henry VI, Nov. 6, 1429, Pol. Songs, 11. xxxiv.
147; Greg. Chron. 168.   For picture, see Wright and Smith, 2.   For Scrivelsby Court,
near Horncastle, the home of the Dymokes since 1380 (Ing. p. Mort. iv. 29), see Perkins,
128, 137.

themselves with the steaming messes held in both hands[1],
while the marshal rode about with his tipstaffs to keep a
passage clear for circulation[2] among the crowds of persons
who were not seated with the guests[3]. When the feast was
done the minstrelsy led the way[4] and the royal procession
filed out with the king bringing up the rear according to
the maxim that "ever the better the latter[5]." But throughout the whole the king was moody and was believed to
have eaten nothing at the banquet or even for three
days after[6], and a Frenchman who was present at the
coronation service in the Abbey reported that the English
were by no means agreed in accepting their new king but
that large numbers said that the crown should have come
to the Earl of March and he inferred that it would be no
reign of peace but a reign of civil war[7]. The late king on
his death-bed had foreseen that discord might arise between
Henry and his brother the Duke of Clarence[8], and this fear
finds echo in a singular poem[9] in which all who are wise
are urged to stand with the new king and keep the crown
unbroken, for if they quarrel among themselves the flower
of chivalry will end and other lands that hate us will spy
our feebleness and fall upon us on every hand and take the
crown from the right heir and seize our towns and castles
beyond the sea and our very lives and our kingdom will be
gone[10]. Surely we have been chastised enough already, says
the poet, but God will only burn the rod if we show that we

---

[1] For picture, see Schultz, 458; do. Häusl. Leben, 301; also fancy picture in Viollet-
le-Duc, Mobilier, i. 365. Viennent à cheval, Weale, Van Eyck, lxiv.; also of heralds
and minstrels, ibid. lxv. For the Coronation Feast of Charles VI at Rheims in 1380, see
Louandre, i. 176.

[2] Fabyan, 586.

[3] In Brut, ii. 427 the Coronation Feast of Queen Catherine in 1421 is "opyn to alle
pepull, straungeris and other that wold come."

[4] Chauc. Squire's Tale, 10582.

[5] Riley, Mem. 651; Lel. Coll. vi. 7–14, from Archbishop Nevil's feast, temp. Ed. IV.
For "established rule that the lord of the banquet should remain till every guest had
taken leave," see E. Hardy, ii. 183.

[6] Prout fide dignorum asseruere testimonia, Vita, 24; Pauli, v. 76.

[7] St Denys, iv. 770; Ramsay, i. 164; Wylie, iv. 104.

[8] This is recorded on the authority of the Earl of Ormonde. Kingsford, Biogr. 80;
do. First Life, pp. xxvii, 14.

[9] Kail, 50–55; but the editor's attempts to fix the exact dates of the first 12 pieces in
successive years of the reign of Henry IV seem to me to be purely fanciful.

[10] Byzonde the see and we had nouzt, but all oure ennemies so neyze us were thouz
all here gold were hider brouzt I wold set hit at lytel store oure enemys wold coke therfore with ordynaunce and habergeoun wyn that and wel more oure londes oure lyves, the
reme, the crowne. Kail, 51.

have at last learnt to be wise[1]. If Englishmen who have made
mastery throughout the world and have made heathen and
Christian alike to quake should now raise strife with one
another they will not only lose the bloom of their great
renown but stry their own nest and the conqueror will be
ill-paid in the lives of the good men that will be lost while
other kingdoms will laugh us to scorn and say that God is
sending vengeance on us for our sins.

But though this feeling may have been present in many
hearts it found as yet no open vent, and when Dymock's
challenge was cried in the middle of the feast no adverse
voice was raised[2]. Thus the prelude passed in outward
universal joy and on the Friday following the Prior of
Lewes wrote from London to the Abbot at Cluni that the
new king had succeeded to his father's throne "with the
unanimous will and consent of all the lords and prelates
and with the universal acclaim of the whole nation[3]." And
so in order that the new reign might open if possible with
a clean sheet a general pardon[4] was offered to all who had
been concerned in rebellions in England, Wales or Ireland,
provided that they sued for it before July 6[5], and even
Scotland was included in the general terms.

Yet the heavens had their warning signs for those who
cared to read them and the Coronation was deeply marked
in the English mind by a long remembered blizzard which
lasted for two days[6], covering up the hills and burying men
and beasts and houses deep in snow[7]. Some said that the

---

[1] Kail,'54.

[2] Waurin, ii. 162; Tyrrell, i. 283; Brougham, 52. Pauli (v. 76) thinks that no one
thought of the claim of the Earl of March; also Lingard, iii. 235. Milman (viii. 221)
more truly says that "Henry's title was by no means generally acknowledged," though
the lines in Pol. Songs, ii. 119 seem to refer to subsequent events and not to Henry's
accession as Ramsay, i. 161.

[3] For his letter dated April 14, 1413, see Duckett, i. 256.

[4] Memorials, 67; Vita, 17. Carte (ii. 674) thinks that this was "according to the
practice of former kings of England," but this does not seem to be borne out by the docu-
'ments printed in Rymer.

[5] Rym. ix. 3, called June 24th in Usk, 120, 299. For payments to messengers
carrying these proclamations to the Sheriffs, see Iss. Roll, 1 H. V, Pasch., May 4, 1413.
The date was subsequently extended to Aug. 8, 1413, Rym. ix. 4. For proclamation to
this effect in London, ordered on June 18, 1413, see Letter Book I, 119.

[6] Strecche, 265a, who says that there had not been such hail in the country since
the days of the British king Leyer or Lear, who built Leicester (Leyercestram), see
T. F. Johnson, 4.

[7] Usk, 120; Ott. 273; Wals. ii. 290; Hypodig. 437; Elmham, Lib. Metr. 95;
Hard. 371; Fabyan, 577; "a ful trobly wet day," Chron. Lond. 95; "a grete raynye
day," Short Chron. 54; "tempestates et procellæ," Redman, 12; "a sore ruggie and

coming reign would be cold and stern, but the hopeful ones
saw in the omen a forecast that the new king would stop
the frost of vice and let the calm, still fruits of virtue
bloom, so that his people might say that the winter was
past and the rain was over and gone[1].

But for all their hopes the year seemed fraught with
mischief. The summer was one of excessive heat; sickness was abroad throughout the country and many persons
died[2]. During the long drought fires broke out in various
parts of England[3]. At Norwich a great part of the city
was burnt down, the convent of the Black Friars being
wrecked in the general ruin[4]. Tewkesbury also suffered
frightfully from a similar disaster[5], and when the king
visited the town in the spring of the following year[6] he
increased his growing popularity by contributing handsomely
to relieve the prevailing distress[7]. On Sept. 1 England
was visited by a great tempest of hail[8]. On Sept. 8[9] the
village of Robertsbridge in Sussex was set on fire by
lightning, and on Dec. 28 a violent thunderstorm broke
over the southern coast which wrecked the church of
St Giles at Winchelsea, shattering the belfry and fusing
the bells[10]. Our neighbours also did not escape this visitation as appears from the annals of other countries. At
Bruges a great conflagration started on July 26, 1413,
which destroyed 1500 houses[11]. In Paris the sittings of

tempestuous day," Holinsh. iii. 543; W. Jones, 307. For a modern fancy picture of
the snow, showing the King entering the Abbey by a Norman doorway, see Bradley, 97.
  [1] Song of Solomon, ii. 11. Murray-Smith (60) regards it as "emblematic of the
purity of his ideals, etc."
  [2] Wals. ii. 297; Hypodig. 446.
  [3] Capgr. De Illustr. 112.
  [4] Ott. 273; Wals. ii. 290; Hypodig. 438; Capgr. Chron. 303; Stow, Chron. 344;
Monast. viii. 1487; Blomefield, iii. 126.
  [5] Elmham, Lib. Metr. 96.
  [6] For documents dated at Tewkesbury, April 2, 1414, see Rym. ix. 120; Ewald, xliv.
552; Rapin, Acta Regia, ii. 126; Chancery Warrants, Ser. 1. 1364/8.
  [7] Rym. ix. 188. Noscere si vultis inopes quos ipse refovit Hoc patet in multis ut
Thewekisburia novit, Memorials, xxxvi. 67.
  [8] Chron. Lond. 95.   [9] Eulog. iii. 421.
  [10] For the devilish smell in a thunderstorm, see Wylie, i. 279; cf. odore foetidissimo
(St Denys, vi. 110) of the storm at Essonnes, near Corbeil, in 1417; une puanteur
merveilleuse, Juv. 535. "Also ther an horryble ayere, No wyght almost myght the
savoure abyde," Stone, 100 (1467); "All a-stonyed he stode so hit stongke," Pol.-Relig.
Po. 116.
  [11] J. Meyer, 240 a. On Sept. 9, 1413, St Mary's Church at Sluys was struck, ibid.
For a great fire at Basle, July 5, 1417, when 250 houses were burnt, see Basler Chron.
v. 150, 226, 227. For a fire at Beaune (Côte d'Or) in 1401, which raged for three days

the Parliament could only be held from 6 to 9 o'clock in the morning[1], while on the other hand the fierce heat ripened the grapes in the neighbouring vineyards so that the vintage was gathered a full month before the usual time[2]. In Italy a spell of unusual heat is recorded during the middle of June[3], and in Normandy the crops of corn, wine and fruit yielded plentiful harvests in the autumn[4]. This surplus heat was followed by searching winds in the following spring[5] which brought on an epidemic of chin-cough[6] called "the thumps[7]." In Paris no business could be done in the courts for the lawyers had all lost their voices, the priests were laid up and no one went to church[8] and the Registrar of the Parliament entered a piteous account in his journal[9] of how he had to keep to his house for 16 days and could not sleep at night for racking pains in his head, shoulders, legs, arms, ribs, kidneys, stomach and all over him. No climate in Europe escaped, from Lombardy to Holland[10], though England appears to have been singularly immune. In Switzerland everybody went

and nearly destroyed the whole town, see Garnier, 310, after which the source de l'Aigue was brought into the town for a water supply.

[1] Pour les très excessives chaleurs qui sont et plus grans que l'en ne vit onques maiz, Baye, ii. 117. Excessivissimi calores, ibid. 307 ; St Denys, v. 80 ; Aubert, Org. 238.

[2] i.e. by August 16, Bourgeois, 43. For the good vintage at Arles in Aug. 1414, see Boysset, 393 : fon granda sason de vin en Arle et resteron pluros vinhas a vendemiar per fauta de vaisela.

[3] i.e. from June 10th to 21st, 1413, Twinger, 618.

[4] Cochon, 338 ; Coville, 338.

[5] i.e. February and March, 1414. St Denys, v. 282 ; Juv. 493. Cf. Quid de aere dicam? qui supra solitum turbulentus pro calore frigora, pro sereno nubila, pro blandâ aestatis suavitate horridam hyemis exhibet effigiem, Clemanges, Epist. 336 (written in 1414). For storm at Dordrecht and flooding of large tracts in Holland, when 10 villages were destroyed with their inhabitants on Nov. 19th, 1412, see Clemanges, Ep. 336. For flooding of the Loire at Orleans, Feb. 5, 1414, see Lottin, i. 182. For flood at Münster-eifel, near Bonn, in 1416 when 150 people were drowned, see Hegel, ii. 143.

[6] Coqueluche, Choisy, 315 ; Montlezun, iv. 167 ; Daniel, iii. 861 ; Devienne, Artois, iii. 49 ; Mazas, Vies, 551 ; Ollier, 5 ; Bearne, 267 ; grande maladie de ryeume par tus-serie, Cochon, 338, who says that only 1 in 40 escaped and many died. Périaux, 167 ; tousserie, April 26, 1404 ; May 5, 1414, Aubert, Org. 172 ; la toux, Leroux de Lincy, I. xli. For tussis at Cologne in 1414, see Hegel, ii. 197. For 1414 as an année de peste, see Coyecque, i. 103. Among the French victims was the Lord of Aumont, who had been the Keeper of the Oriflamme, Kellot, 95. For the "Quhew" (i.e. cough), see Bower, iv. 1212, with theories as to its climatic causes, i.e. a dry, cold winter followed by a rainy spring and autumn.

[7] le tac, le horion, Baye, ii: 172, 187 ; Bourgeois, 618 ; Leroux de Lincy, I. xlii. In Godefroy, iv. 497, horion=gros rhume. Cf. coups et horions, Juv. 366 ; Lecesne, 156 ; donez lui des bons horions sur le dos, Romania, xxxii. 62.

[8] Cf. die phaffen wurden ouch als kranck daz man bresten hat an gottes-dienste, Basler Chron. v. 148.

[9] Baye, ii. 172, 175, May 1-19, 1414.

[10] Basler Chron. v. 148.

about coughing and running and many had to take to their
beds[1]. At Tournai the worst time was during Lent[2].
There men called the thing the "Heuke[3]" or the jacket,
and when business people got it on them they went
whooping about the streets[4]. Not many died but several
became deaf and they would joke one another by shouting
"Not got it off yet[5]?"

[1] Yederman jung und alte faste hüstig und flüssig das die lute zu bete niederlagent,
Basler Chron. v. 148 (i.e. at Schaffhausen).
[2] Le ont porte en ce quaresme, Pay Bas, 345, i.e. from Feb. to May 1414, ibid. 343.
[3] La Heuquette, J. Meyer, 242; Vinchant, iv. 48.
[4]   Od on toussir et rouquier
         Tous les jours de rue en rue. Pays Bas, 345.
[5]   Les gens en degatoient le ung l'aultre:
         "Vous estes sortis de la heuquette?" Pays Bas, 344.

CHAPTER II

RECONSTRUCTION

IT will be remembered that while the late king was nearing his end a Parliament had been called to meet at Westminster on Feb. 3, 1413[1]. Although we have no record of a formal opening it is certain that the members actually assembled, that petitions were presented[2], and that tenths and fifteenths were granted[3], but when the king died this parliament was *ipso facto* dissolved[4]. The members[5] however being still at Westminster took the opportunity to express their delight at the accession of the new king and in view of possible claims by the Earl of March many of the lords hastened to Kennington[6] to take the oath of allegiance even before the coronation[7], though they guarded themselves with a protest that their action should not be appealed to hereafter as a precedent. But

[1] Rot. Parl. iv. 9; Wylie, iv. 102.

[2] e.g. in a petition presented in November, 1414, Thomas Paunfeld says that he "persuede diverse billes before oure liege lord kyng Henry the fourthe and his worshipeful Lordes and Cões, in his Parlement holden at Westminster the x day of Feüer the xiiij yer of his Regne," Rot. Parl. iv. 57.

[3] Rec. Roll, 1 H. V, Pasch., July 14, 1413, refers to tenths and fifteenths granted by laity to Henry IV *ultimo*. For reference to purveyance "stabled in Statute the xiiii. year of the regne" of H. IV, see Letter Book I, 297.

[4] Stubbs (iii. 83) treats the first parliament of H. V as a continuation of the last parliament of H. IV, quoting Rot. Parl. ix. 9 for a statement that the wages of members were paid from Feb. 3 to June 9, 1413, but the passage distinctly says that the parliament of Feb. 3 "fuist dissolvé" by the death of Henry IV. See also Ramsay, i. 162; Letter Book I, 113, note. Reference to Claus. 1 H. V, 12 d, June 9, 1413, and Prynne, 498–501, will show that the expenses of members were not paid from Feb. 3, but from May 15, 1413, which is rightly called "a new Parliament" in Gairdner, Lollardy, i. 71; Church, 43.

[5] Not of a parliament summoned by Henry V as supposed by Towle, 249.

[6] Firent leur homage a Kenyngton (March xxi, anno primo), Hoccleve, Min. Po. 39; Mason, 13.

[7] Tit. Liv. 5; Vita, 16; Duck, 21.

> Quem flexo proceres regem venerantur orantes
> Poplite testanturque hilari sua gaudia gestu. Ocland, H. i.

when they raised the question as to how their expenses were to be met it appeared that there was no precedent for this either and they seem to have had to pay their own way back home themselves[1]. On March 22, 1413[2], writs were issued calling a Parliament to meet at Westminster[3] three weeks after Easter[4] and in the meantime some important changes took place among the holders of the offices of state.

A recent writer has supposed that the new king "took into his confidence the ministers of his father[5]" but to this view some notable exceptions must be recorded. On the very first day of the new reign Archbishop Arundel resigned the Chancellorship[6]. Henry had in vain tried to dislodge him during his father's lifetime[7] and his first official act on coming to the throne was to replace him by appointing his uncle Bishop Henry Beaufort to be Chancellor of England and Keeper of the Great Seal[8]. On the same day the Archbishop gave up the castle of Queen-

---

[1] Rot. Parl. ix. 9; Cotton, 536; Goodwin, 7. Church (47) sees evidence in this that the new king "had a will of his own."

[2] Claus. 1 H. V, 37 d; Dugd. Summons, 388; Goodwin, 4; Letter Book I. pp. xviii, 113.

[3] Dep. Keep. 2nd Rept. App. II. p. 185. For payments to messengers carrying writs to sheriffs, bishops, etc. together with commissions of the peace, see Iss. Roll, 1 H. V, Pasch. May 4, 1413.

[4] In 1413, Easter Day fell on April 23, Bond, 380; Itin. 398.

[5] Gairdner, 88.

[6] Campbell, Chancellors, i. 369; Foss, iv. 186, 192; Stubbs, iii. 81; Ransom, 143.

[7] Ord. Priv. Co. iii. 186; Wylie, iv. 88; Tout, 262, who thinks that this was "the only thing which Henry did that showed any spirit of revenge." Dale (170) feels that "it would be agreeable to believe that Henry's distrust of the Archbishop arose partly from the fact that he had been the promoter of the Act *De Haeretico Comburendo.*" Benham (Winchester, 142) supposes that Bishop Beaufort opposed the statute and favoured Oldcastle; but see Wylie, iii. 302. Radford (Cardinal, 105) thinks that Archbishop Arundel's resignation in 1410 was caused by his "arbitrary enforcement of the ecclesiastical constitutions on Lollardy" (i.e. the Constitutions of 1407, Wylie, iii. 426). For supposed feud between the Archbishop and the Beauforts, see Kingsford, 61, who thinks that the former "represented the old baronial and constitutional party, while the Beauforts were the leaders of the Court party" or supporters of Prince Henry (p. 64). In Hassell, 219, the Prince of Wales with the Beauforts opposes Archbishop Arundel and the greater nobles with the Duke of Clarence. In C. R. L. Fletcher, 312, the Beauforts turn to the rising sun of the Prince of Wales. Oman (Pol. Hist. 219, 220) considers the supposed quarrel to be "almost as obscure as it is uninteresting." Radford (18) thinks that "there *may* have been personal grounds or there *may* have been political etc." but that "the whole situation was intricate." Lodge (326) calls it "an obscure intrigue." For supposition that Henry's "close friendship with the Beaufort family led him in 1410 into a breach with his father," see Fletcher-Walker, 7, imagining (p. 10) that *Bishop* Beaufort (probably meaning his brother *Thomas* Beaufort, Wylie, iv. 51) ceased to be Chancellor "when that young man (i.e. Prince Henry) quarrelled with his father in 1411."

[8] Claus. 1 H. V; Rot. Parl. iv. 3; Dugd. Chron. Ser. 56. On Jan. 24, 1414, the Great Seal was deposited in the Treasury in a leathern bag, Kal. and Inv. ii. 91.

borough which was now granted to Gilbert Umfraville for life[1]. John Wakering still remained Keeper of the Chancery Rolls[2] and John Prophet Keeper of the Privy Seal[3]. At the same time the Earl of Arundel was appointed Treasurer[4] in place of Sir John Pelham[5], and the customers and controllers from the various ports were ordered to appear before him in the Exchequer on May 7[6] bringing their books, tallies, monies and securities. On March 22[7] he succeeded the king as Warden of the Cinq Ports and Constable of Dover[8] with power to repair the castle walls[9], towers, chapel, belfry and glass windows and to overhaul all vestments, books, ornaments, bows, arrows, cross-bows, quarrels and other artillery[10]. On May 7[11] the king's brother

---

[1] Pat. 1 H. V, i. 29; ibid. iv. 19 (March 21, Nov. 16, 1413), where he is not yet called Earl of Kyme. See Wylie, iv. 63, note 8.

[2] Iss. Roll, 1 H. V, Mich. (Oct. 17, 1413). For his appointment on March 2, 1405, see Newcourt, i. 340; Hennessy, 379; Wylie, iii. 301, note 2; not 1404 as Archaeologia Cantiana, xiii. 382. For confirmation of 2 pipes of red Gascon wine granted to him when he was a clerk in our chancery, see Pat. 1 H. V, 2, 3, 4; Claus. 1 H. V, 31, April 5, 1413; Wylie, iv. 206. For writ signed "Waker." Nov. 5, 1414, see Escheators Inquisitions, Ser. 1. 1008. In Rec. Roll, 3 H. V, Pasch., June 27, 1415, he receives £40. 14*s.* for cannsis (? canvas) as *late* Clerk of the Rolls. In the Leicester Parliament (1414) he was a Receiver of Petitions (Rot. Parl. iv. 16, where he is called *Sire* John Wakering).

[3] Claus. 1 H. V, 26, June 28, 1413. For his appointment, Oct. 4, 1406, see Wylie, iv. 310. For £120 (i.e. 20*s.* per day, from March 20 to July 18, 1413) paid to him as Keeper of the Privy Seal, see Iss. Roll, 1 H. V, Pasch., July 24, 1413; also ibid. Mich. Oct. 27, 1413; Jan. 25, Feb. 22, 1414.

[4] i.e. March 21, 1413, Pat. 1 H. V, i. 37; Cal. Rot. Pat. 260; Devon, 323; Doyle, i. 74; Pells, Rec. Roll, 1 H. V, Pasch.; do. Iss. Roll, 1 H. V, Mich. (heading). The earliest extant Pell Rolls (both Issue and Receipt) for the reign date from Easter 1413, and there is no entry on either earlier than May 4, 1413, where the Issue Roll refers to a pair of budges with letters delivered to Thomas Arundel, Treasurer of England. For £96. 12*s.* 5½*d.* paid to him for attendance at the Council, see Iss. Roll, 1 H. V, Mich., Dec. 4, 1413. For his presence at Windsor and Guildford, see Iss. Roll, 1 H. V, Pasch., July 17, 1413. In Devon, 336 (Oct. 30, 1414) he is Treasurer of England, £7. 11*s. od.* being paid for dining the Chancellor, Treasurer, Lords of the Council, Justices and other officers of the King's Court at Westminster at the election of the Sheriffs and Escheators of counties. He is still Treasurer of England on May 25, 27, 30, and June 5, 1415, Ord. Priv. Co. ii. 167; Rym. ix. 257, 260, 262. For 100 marks p.a. paid to him pro feodo suo in the office of Treasurer together with an increment of £300 p. a., see Iss. Roll 3 H. V, Pasch., April 24, 1415. For £108. 15*s.* as his allowance from May 12 to July 31, 1415, see Iss. Roll, 3 H. V, Pasch., May 18, 1415. Malden (70) thinks that Henry appointed him Treasurer "so as not to break entirely with the Arundel interest."

[5] Ramsay, i. 162; Wylie, iv. 51, note 3; not Henry Lord Scrope, as Dugd. Chron. Ser. 56; Dict. Nat. Biogr. li. 13.

[6] In quindena Paschae, Iss. Roll, 1 H. V, Pasch., May 4, June 9, 1413, where payments to the messengers are recorded.

[7] Pat. 1 H. V, i. 37.

[8] In Iss. Roll, 1 H. V, Mich. Feb. 22, 1414, he receives £73. 4*s.* 5½*d.* as Keeper of the King's castle at Dover to pay his men.

[9] The murage granted in 1412 (see Wylie, iv. 86) was continued with the addition of 1*d.* in the £, upon all goods entering the town, Pat. 1 H. V, i. 24, April 13, 1413.

[10] Pat. 1 H. V, i. 1; Priv. Seal, 658/1.

[11] Pat. 1 H. V, iii. 44; Comp. Peer. iv. 44; Doyle, ii. 22.

Humphrey was appointed Chamberlain of England[1], Henry Lord Fitzhugh being the king's Chamberlain[2].

Henry's panegyrists never tire of ringing his praises for selecting sober counsellors and dismissing corrupt judges[3], and his first judicial appointment was made on the very day of his accession when William Lasingby[4] was made chief Baron of the Exchequer[5] but as John Cokayn[6] whom he replaced still continued on the list of judges[7] we

[1] Exch. Accts. 406/21, 27; Finke, Acta, i. 382, Aug. 1414; Ancient Corrdce. xliii. 174, June 15, 1415; cf. Magni Camerarii Anglie, Vickers, 429, 455. Grant Chambellan dengleterre, ibid. 434. For documents signed "H" (i.e. Humphrey) "Chambellan d'Engleterre," see Rym. ix. 3, March 12, 1413; Ord. Priv. Co. ii. 140, 169, 338; Rym. ix. 189, 238, 253, Dec. 10, 13, 1414; April 29, May 15, 26, June 15, 1415; see also Sloane MS. 4600, ff. 298, 306, 311, April 21, May 23, 1415.

[2] Rym. ix. 13, 385, May 24, 1413; Sept. 4, 1416; Rot. Parl. iv. 218. For £31. 7s. 9d. wages (+robes=53s. 4d.) paid to him as sub-camar. regis for Michaelmas Term, 1413, see Exch. Accts. 406/21, 27. In Pat. 1 H. V, i. 30, May 24, 1413, he is Camerarius Regis; also Cal. Rot. Pat. 260; Chancery Warrants, Ser. 1, 1364/10, June 8, 1413; Finke, Forsch. 256; Camerarius Noster, Ordonnances, xi. 112; Rot. Norm. 153, 244, Sept. 8, 1417, Feb. 8, 1418; Rym. ix. 626, 627, 628, Oct. 26, 1418; Bréquigny, 43, Jan. 3, 1419; Ewald, xli. 705; Rym. ix. 833, 848, Jan. 1, Feb. 15, 1420; Ewald, xlii. 334, 339. Chambellan du roy, Rym. ix. 501, Oct. 13, 1417; vostre Tresorer et Chamberlein, Rym. ix. 425, 490; nostre Chamb., Chancery Warrants, Ser. 1. 1364/60, June 5, 1418; Grand Chambellan, Oct. 5, 1422, Farin, 147; Chéruel, App. 67; called Lord Chamberlain of the King's Household in Dugd. Bar. i. 404. For £100 p. a. granted to him, July 24, 1414, see Pat. 2 H. V, ii. 30. For confirmation to him of custody of the castles of John Lord Darcy, see Pat. 1 H. V, v. 14, Feb. 21, 1414. In July 1414 he was a custos pacis at Ripon for enforcing the Lollard Statute, Pat. 2 H. V, ii. 32 d. For two books by Richard Heremita, i.e. Richard Rolle, the Hermit of Hampole, and other legacies left to him by Henry Lord Scrope, June 23, 1415, see Rym. ix. 274, 276. King Henry V made him one of the executors of his will, dated July 24, 1415, leaving him all his furred robes and gowns, with all his trussing-beds and 500 marks in money, Rym. ix. 291, where he is "camerarius noster." Among the English at Constance are Henry and William Visii (i.e. Fitzhugh), camerarii regis Angliae, Mansi, xxviii. 64. In 1415 (Duc. Lanc. Accts. various 27/6) Henry Fitzhugh is Constable of Pickering Castle and Master Forester of Pickering Forest. For custody of St Leonard's Hospital at York vacant by the death of William de fferiby, granted to Robert (i.e. the future Bishop of London, Wylie, ii. 221, note 6), son of Henry Fitzhugh, kt., see Pat. 2 H. V, iii. 11, May 15, 1415.

[3] Tit. Liv. 5; First Life, 20; Harpsfeld, Hist. 587; Malcolm, 76. Cf. qu'il vorrait estre conseillez par les pluis sages et discretes de son Roialme, Rot. Par. iv. 3.

[4] Iss. Roll, 1 H. V, Mich., Nov. 8, 1413, refers to him as appointed on March 21st last. Foss (iv. 206) supposes him to be identical with William Lasingby, who had been involved in the treason of the Earl of Northumberland, and whose lands were forfeited but subsequently restored by Henry IV, Rot. Parl. iii. 605, 606, 655.

[5] For pictures of the Court of Exchequer, see Archaeologia, xxxix. p. 361 (temp. H. VI); Pulling, 94 (temp. H. VII).

[6] Wylie, ii. 339. For his purchase of the manor of Bury-Hatley or Hatley-Port, now Cockayne-Hatley, near Biggleswade, see Fuller, Worthies, i. 118; Cockayne, i. 7, ii. 22, who supposes him to have been buried there, but no trace of his tomb now exists, though Lysons (Bedfordshire, p. 92) refers to "an altar tomb stripped of its brass plates" in the church. For supposition that he was buried at Polesworth, near Tamworth, see Cox, ii. 383.

[7] e.g. in Iss. Roll, 1 H. V, Mich., Oct. 27, 1413. He is on commissions for gaol delivery of Newgate, Nov. 7, 1413, Letter Book I, 120; also 1414, 1415, 1416, 1417, 1418, 1420, 1422, ibid. 131, 145, 168, 191, 212, 240, 265. His will is dated Feb. 1428 (6 H. VI). He married Ida, daughter of Thomas Grey, Lord of Ruthen, and is said

must look elsewhere for evidence if this reputed scrupulousness in regard to judicial purity is to be sustained and at least one of the early changes on the bench is in puzzling contradiction to the claim.

No English reader can approach the new reign with his judgment quite unwarped. As he sits waiting for the opening, the curtain which is shortly to be lifted has been pictured for him by a magic hand and with a resistless spell[1]. His view is filled with visions of Falstaff rebuked[2], Gascoigne advanced and the scapegrace king turned from his former self to mock the expectation of the world. In a previous work[3] I have done my best to stand by the venerable story of the Prince and the Judge. And I would gladly do the like for Shakespeare's noble sequel in which the regenerate king commits to the judge's hand the unstained sword that he had used to bear, but this part of the legend cannot possibly hold its ground. For though William Gascoigne received his summons[4] to the forthcoming parliament as Chief Justice of the King's Bench[5], yet within a week afterwards he had been superseded and henceforward drops into semi-obscurity[6]. On March 29, 1413[7], his place was filled by the elevation of William

to have been present (or even killed) at the battle of Shrewsbury in 1403 (Ann. 369), but this is probably a confusion with his brother Edmund. For his effigy in the church at Ashbourne wearing the coif, see Wylie, ii. 339, note 2, though the identity is doubted in Planché, Ashbourne, 377, who regards it as the figure of his father, John Cokayne (d. 1373); also S. Glover, ii. 34, who calls it "an old man in a close cap."

[1] Dale, 173; "the historian from whose verdict there is no appeal," Historians' Hist. xviii. 526; "a hold on the popular imagination beyond the power of sober historical evidence to destroy," Workman, i. 268. For Shakespeare's sources, see Kingsford, First Life, pp. l, lvi.

[2] See App. D.

[3] Wylie, iv. 94–99, where "Consignment" on p. 98, note 4, should be "Controlment"; see Harcourt, 56; Scargill-Bird, 259.

[4] Dated March 22, 1413. Dugd. Summons, 389; Goodwin, 5; Tyler, ii. 10.

[5] For picture of the Court of King's Bench (temp. Henry VI) showing prisoners chained by the leg, see Archaeologia, xxxix. p. 359; Besant, Survey, i. 221.

[6] Stubbs (iii. 82) attributes his removal to the fact that he was "an old man who had been long in office." Kingsford (91) thinks that he was over 70 years old and that his age is enough to account for his resignation, but he was really only about 63; see Wylie, ii. 180. Ramsay (i. 163) regards it as a prompt dismissal, and thinks that the later gifts were an *eirenikon*.

[7] Pat. 1 H. V, i. 25; Claus. 1 H. V, 33; Wylie, iv. 97, note 4; Cal. Rot. Pat. 260, where Hankford is granted 2 robes and 180 marks p. a.; Foss, iv. 169, where the controversy as to the date of Gascoigne's death is well summed up and finally disposed of. The last payment to Gascoigne is enrolled on July 7, 1413, where he is called *late* Chief Justice of the King's Bench, Devon, 322; see also Pauli, v. 77; Stubbs, iii. 81. In Pat. 2 H. V, i. 33, dated May 19, 1414, William Gascoigne and W. Waldeby are referred to as *late* justices in York Gaol.

Hankford[1] one of the puisne judges of the Court of Common Pleas[2], but Gascoigne himself lived on for years in his native home in Wharfedale[3], taking occasional duties on quests, special assizes or gaol-deliveries[4]. Together with his brother Richard he was appointed[5] by the new king a Justice of the Peace for Northumberland, Cumberland and the three Ridings of Yorkshire. On May 15, 1413[6], he was commissioned together with others to enquire into a complaint made by Henry Lord Scrope that in the previous reign a chaplain named John Newark and other disturbers of the peace had broken into his close and houses at Faxflete by night, carried off his wife Joan[7], entered his castle at Sandal near Wakefield and robbed him of goods valued at £5000. When the Lollard Statute was passed in 1414 Gascoigne was one of the justices appointed to enforce it in the districts about Beverley and Ripon[8] and in the same year the king favoured him with a grant of some fat bucks and does from the forests of Pontefract[9] and Galtres[10]. In the summer of 1415[11] he was a member of a commission in Yorkshire charged to inquire into the carrying-off of Murdach Earl of Fife while on his way to the Border, and in the same year he lent £40[12] to help to meet the cost of the coming expedition into France, being also commissioned[13] to array the forces of the West Riding for the

---

[1] Called Haukford or Hawkesford in Ewald, 40; Gidley, 55. In Rot. Parl. iv. 7, Hankford is Chief Justice *in praesenti parliamento*, i.e. before June 9, 1413. In Dugd. Chron. Ser. 56, he is Chief Justice on Jan. 29, 1414 from Pat. 1 H. V, 33. On March 21, 1413, he was appointed a Justice of the Peace for Surrey, Pat. 1 H. V, i. 35 d. He represented his native county (i.e. Devonshire, Wylie, iv. 97) in the Westminster Parliament in 1414, Return Parl. i. 283; also in 1423, ibid. i. 305. For his monument in the church at Monkleigh, near Bideford, see Wylie, iv. 97. On March 11, Oct. 27, 1421, he is patron of the church at Horwood, near Barnstaple, Lacy, pp. 8, 11; also of Creacombe, near Tiverton, March 20, 1422, ibid. 48. For possessions of Richard Hankeford in Cornwall, Devon and Somerset, see Inq. p. Mort. iv. 44 (7 H. V, 1419–20); Staff. Reg. 122, 143. On July 21, 1404, he is patron of Norton, near Taunton, Holmes, Reg. (Bowet), p. 52. For his epitaph, see Fuller, Worthies, i. 281.

[2] Campbell, Chief Justices, i. 139; Foss, iv. 324. For picture of the Court of Common Pleas (temp. H. VI), see Pulling, frontispiece; Archaeologia, xxxix. p. 360, from the original at Whaddon House, near Stony Stratford, Lipscomb, iii. 498; Clinch, 258.

[3] Cf. armiger in comitatu Eboraci natus, Raine, Hist. iii. 290; Wylie, ii. 180.

[4] Pat. 3 H. V, ii. 5 d, March 18, 1416.

[5] Pat. 1 H. V, i. 35 d, 36 d.

[6] Pat. 1 H. V, ii. 24 d.

[7] Wylie, iii. 284, note 5.

[8] Pat. 2 H. V, ii. 32 d.

[9] Tyler, i. 380; Ewald, 40.

[10] Called 2 deymes (i.e. fallow deer) de graes and 2 deymes de fermeson every year from the forest of Gastres (*sic*), Priv. Seal, 659/134, Nov. 17, 1413.

[11] Pat. 3 H. V, i. 3 d, July 6, 1415.

[12] Lent on June 6, 1415. Rec. Roll 3 H. V, Pasch., June 6, 22, 1415.

[13] Rym. ix. 253 [255], May 29, 1415.

defence of the coasts against possible attack while the king was away. On Dec. 12, 1415[1], he was appointed together with Thomas Cumberworth[2] and others to report on the belongings of Lord Zouche who had just died. On Feb. 12, 1416[3], he was engaged on a gaol-delivery at Bristol and on August 8 of the same year[4] he served on a commission in reference to a claim to property in dispute between the Earls of Huntingdon and Westmoreland. He made his will on Dec. 15, 1419[5], and died two days later[6]. His body was buried in his parish church at Harewood in Wharfedale where his effigy may be seen to this day[7].

The other judges were all continued in office[8]. Sir William Thirning received his patent as Chief Justice of Common Pleas[9] on May 2, 1413[10], but he resigned his post within a few weeks, made his will on May 28[11], and died

[1] Priv. Seal Writs, 1423/1204.

[2] For Thomas Cumberworth, see Wylie, ii. 234. He was appointed a Justice of the Peace for Lincolnshire on March 21, 1413, Pat. 1 H. V, i. 34 d. On July 6, Oct. 28, Nov. 9, 1416, he is sheriff of Lincolnshire, Rec. Roll 4 H. V, Pasch., Mich. (i.e. from Dec. 1, 1415, to Nov. 30, 1416, also in 1430, Sheriffs' Lists 79). On Sept. 3, 1416, he was a commissioner for the arrest of a Lincolnshire squire named John Mouter who was committed to the Tower under an order dated Feb. 3, 1417, Claus. 4 H. V, 9; Cal. Pat. H. V, ii. 82. On April 1, 1418, Thomas Cumberworth is on a commission of array for Lincolnshire, Pat. 6 H. V, 31 d. On July 3, 1420, he was appointed a J.P. for Lindsey, Pat. 8 H. V, 20 d.

[3] Pat. 3 H. V, ii. 11 d.

[4] Pat. 4 H. V, 7 d.

[5] Wylie, ii. 180, note 3. It was proved on Dec. 23, 1419. Palmer, Yarm, 17; Purey-Cust, ii. 243, who gives his arms from York Minster, ibid. ii. 205.

[6] i.e. Dec. 17, 1419, not 1413 as Scrope, 265.

[7] Gough, ii. 37; Weiss, i. 144; Campbell, Chief Justices, i. 137; Kingsford, 90; Aubrey, i. 37; Cassell, i. 503 (altered); Pulling, 17. For a document relating to his purchase of the wardship of young Stephen Scrope, circ. 1409, containing his signature and that of John Fastolf the lad's step-father, still existing at Castlecombe near Chippenham, see Scrope, 264. For William, son of Wm. Gascoigne and of Johanna his wife as tenant of lands of Stephen le Scrop defunct, see Memoranda Rolls, K. R. 3–4 H. V, 31, Nov. 6, 1415.

[8] Vita, 26; Iss. Roll 1 H. V, Mich., Oct. 27, 1413, names W. Hankford, Hugh Huls (or Holes, Pat. 2 H. V, i. 39 d), R. Tyrwhit, R. Norton, R. Hull (or Hill, Foss, 346), J. Culpeper and J. Cockayne. For manor of Trembethow in the parish of Lelant in St Ives Bay (Cornwall) as the seat of John Hals (Cal. Pat. H. V, i. 8, 16; Foss, 358), Justice of Common Pleas temp. H. V, sold by him to Godolphin, see J. H. Matthews, 46; Staff. Reg. 239, 354.

[9] For John Hotoft, Chief Clerk of the Court of Common Pleas, see Rec. Roll 3 H. V, Pasch., July 8, 1415, cf. Wylie, iii. 322, note 1. For John Hotot, appointed a Scholar of King's Hall at Cambridge in 1415, que le dit Johan n'est pas bien apris en la science de Gramaire non obstant, see Exch. Accts. 348/29.

[10] Pat. 1 H. V, i. 36; Foss, iv. 190, 208, 212.

[11] Wylie, ii. 37, note 1; Gibbons, 140, proved July 21, 1413, at Melchbourne near Higham Ferrers. In it he leaves bequests to the parson of Edenham near Bourne (Lincs.) for tithes omitted while he dwelt there. He desires to be buried in St James' Abbey (? at Northampton), leaving 100 marks to be spent in the great Newark there. There is a reference to him in Iss. Roll 1 H. V, Mich., July 7, 1413. For his widow Joan, see Claus. 6 H. V, 1 d, March 11, 1419.

very shortly after.   His place was filled on June 26, 1413[1],
by the promotion of a Yorkshireman Richard Norton[2] of
Norton Conyers[3] near Ripon, then one of the puisne judges
of the same court[4].

[1] Pat. 1 H. V, ii. 36; Cal. Rot. Pat. 261; Iss. Roll 1 H. V, Mich., Oct. 27, 1413.
[2] Rot. Parl. iv. 59; Pat. 2 H. V, i. 14 d, June 28, 1414.   In Iss. Roll 1 H. V, Pasch.,
July 4, 1413, he is called one of the late King's sergeants, also Bibl. Top. Brit. II. App.
No. x. 75*.   In Pat. 2 H. V, i. 12 d, 24 d, June 20, 28, 1414, he is one of the King's
justices.   For grant to him of 2 casks of Gascon wine as Chief Justice of Common Pleas,
see Pat. 2 H. V, i. 20, May 20, 1414.   On May 4, 1414, he was appointed an executor
under the will of Master John Newton, Treasurer of York Minster, who left him a gilt
cup, quam olim habui de domino Cantuariensi, Test. Ebor. i. 367, 368, 370, where he
is called "justiciarius."   On June 23, 1415, Henry Lord Scrope made him a supervisor
of his will, leaving him a silver cup, 5 marks in money and a good gown of Baudekyn de
Cipre, Rym. ix. 277.   For white Baudekyn, see Rym. ix. 278, 280.   For baudequin de
Chypre, see Fagniez, Inventaires, xxviii. 99, called cloth of gold in Littlehales, II. x.;
tissue de soie fabriqué à Bagdad, Monget, i. 48; cf. Wylie, ii. 436; iv. 335.   In 1415 he
has custody of the lands of Milo Stapleton during the minority of his son and heir Milo,
Rec. Roll 3 H. V, Pasch., May 14, 1415.   For Miles Stapleton, kt., of Ingham near
Norwich and Bedale (Yorks.), see Stapleton, Lib. de Ant. Leg. clxxxviii., clxxxix.; Wylie,
ii. 224, note 4; iv. 328.   For Norton's place on a commission to try rebels in 1405, see
Wylie, ii. 230, 231.   He was the son of Adam Conyers who took the name of Norton,
Dict. Nat. Biog. xli. 217 d, and he married Elizabeth daughter of John Tempest of
Studley, Foss, Dict. 487.   He died Dec. 20, 1420, Surtees, Durham, i. clxiii.; Foss, iv.
207.   For his brass at Wath near Ripon, see Macklin, 173; Druitt, 227.   For Richard
Norton, a king's messenger of Receipt of Exchequer, see Iss. Roll 3 H. V, Pasch.,
April 19, May 1, 1415.
[3] Test. Ebor., i. 364.   For chantry founded by him in the church at Norton Conyers
in 9 H. V (1421), see Inq. ad Quod Damn. (List), ii. 744.
[4] Pat. 1 H. V, i. 25; Cal. Rot. Pat. 260.

CHAPTER III

PARLIAMENT AT WESTMINSTER

AFTER his coronation the king remained for two days at Westminster. On April 10, 1413, he went to Sutton[1] where he stayed till April 13. On the following day he was at Uxbridge[2] and on the 15th at Langley. By May 14 he had moved to Kennington and on the next morning[3] he attended the opening of his first Parliament in the Painted Chamber[4] of the Palace at Westminster.

Thirty-eight secular barons had been summoned, the list being in all respects identical with that issued by the late king[5], except that the name of Thomas Nevil Lord Furnival now disappears, he having died six years before[6], though

---

[1] See Wylie, iv. 12, 548.

[2] Woxbrigge, Exch. Accts. 406/24, 5. For 6s. 8d. paid to Nicholas Talbot hospit' dni pro pejoracione domus, ibid. 406/21, m. 30.

[3] Rot. Parl. iv. 3; Ott. 273; Wals. ii. 290; Hypodig. 438; Goodwin, 5; Pauli, v. 77; Stubbs, iii. 83; Tyler, ii. 6. Not May 14, as Gairdner, Lollardy, i. 71.

[4] Otherwise called St Edward's Chamber, from a tradition that Edward the Confessor died in it, the Great Chamber, or the King's Chamber, Barnard, 338; Lethaby, 258. It was called *camera depicta* from the wall paintings or "histories" (Lethaby, 259) representing the coronation of Edward the Confessor and various biblical subjects, painted by Master Walter of Durham circ. 1267, Walcott, Westminster, 210; Woltmann, i. 384; do. (Colvin), i. 399; Wright and Smith, pp. 6, 409; Gent. Mag., ii. 391 (1819); Lethaby, 258, 266; Cust, Cat., 133; Archaeologia, l. 5; Burlington Mag., vii. 263; cf. in cujus parietibus sunt omnes historiæ bellicæ totius bibliæ ineffabiliter depictæ, Simeonis, 5 (written in 1322); Lethaby, 263, who gives an account of the subjects. For an account of it in Sept. 1819, see Neale, ii. 60. For a specimen of the paintings copied by Stothard in that year now in the library of the Society of Antiquaries, copies of which by Crocker are now in the University Galleries at Oxford, see Barnard, 337, Plate LXXV; Lethaby, 260. For pictures of armed men from it, see Knight, London, vi. 122; Roujoux, ii. 99; also tapestry, Wright and Smith, 407. For pictures of it both exterior and interior with tapestry and hangings in 1800, see J. T. Smith, 45, 48, 50, and Plates (1807, 1809); Wright and Smith, 141; also after the fire in 1834 with vaults underneath, see Besant, Westminster, 41, 44, 47.

[5] Dugd. Summons, 386-9.

[6] i.e. in March, 1407, Wylie, ii. 113. Not 1406, as Purey-Cust, i. 171. For Furnival arms in York Minster, see ibid. i. 169. For his wife Joan, daughter of William de Furnivale, see Baildon, Site, 29.

summons had continued to issue automatically for his appearance in the three Parliaments that had met since his death. One new name however is added, viz. that of the Earl Marshal John Mowbray[1]. He was now nearly 24 years of age and had just received his lands within a few days of the late king's death[2]. He was thus able to take his place of honour at the coronation ceremonies[3] of the new king, where his presence would be an indication to the country that the bitter feud that had caused the banishment of both their fathers at Coventry[4] had been appeased in the persons of the sons and that the great family of Mowbray had at length tacitly acknowledged the usurpation of the house of Lancaster as a fact beyond recall[5]. The writs to archbishops, bishops, abbots and judges present no new feature except that a summons was now first addressed to William Lodington[6] who had just been made a King's serjeant[7] and was soon afterwards appointed a judge of Common Pleas[8].

According to the returns now extant[9] 74 knights of the shire assembled, representing 37 counties[10], while 182

[1] Pat. 2 H. V, i. 9, July 3, 1414, refers to his mother Elizabeth (i.e. Fitzalan, Doyle, ii. 582), Duchess of Norfolk, as the wife of Gerard Usflete (or Ousefleet). They had jointly sued Richard Housewyf of Rothley for a debt of £40, temp. Henry IV, Priv. Seal 658/11, April 6, 1413. In Claud. C. x. p. 285, quoted in Bree, 67, she is now (circ. 1415) the wife of Gerard Usflete, kt., spelt "Usseflete" in Pat. 4 H. V, 19 d, July 17, 1416, where he is on a commission to enquire into a charge of taking hares, rabbits, pheasants, and partridges from a warren at Ampthill (Beds.); or Ursflett, MS. Bodl. 7440 (i.e. Glover's Agincourt Roll), see Nicolas, 402; not "Ufflet," as Brook, 23; also "Urseflete" in Exch. Accts. 45/1. For his arms in York Minster, see Purey-Cust, ii. 417.

[2] Claus. 1 H. V, 23, April 11, 1413; Pat. 1 H. V, iv. 14, Nov. 24, 1413, shows that he had proved his age. Cf. Dict. Nat. Biogr., xxxix. 221; Wylie, ii. 30, note 3.

[3] He received a silver-gilt alms dish valued at 25 marks for his coronation fee, Rym. ix. 3.

[4] For the lists at Gosford Green, see Reader, 19; Royal Visits, 6; M. D. Harris, 131; called "that singular affair" in Harcourt, 185. For account of it, see Brett, 46. For picture of the banishment from Harl. MS. 4380, f. 148, see S. A. Smith, 404. For Milan armour ordered by Henry of Bolingbroke for these lists, see J. S. D. Scott, i. 214; Wylie, iv. 139. For fancy picture of the combat, see Cassell, i. 438.

[5] Goldwin Smith, i. 256.

[6] Dugd. Summons, 390.

[7] Dugd. Chron. Ser. 57, from Liberate Roll 1 H. V, m. 6.

[8] i.e. June 16, 1415, Foss, iv. 206, from Dugd. Orig., 46; Chron. Ser., 58. He died in 1419. For his brass at Gunby near Spilsby in Lincolnshire, see Cambridge Camden Society.

[9] Return Parl. i. 278–80, though it is obvious that the absence of a return is not always evidence of the absence of members, e.g. the names of members elected for the City of London in the Parliaments of 1410, 1411, and 1414 appear in Letter Book I, 81, 95, 121, though not found in Return Parl. i. 274, 276.

[10] In Cleop. C. iv. 116, the number of counties in England is given as 36½. For 37 shires and 110 cities and boroughs represented in the "Model Parliament" of 1295, see C. R. L. Fletcher, 202.

burgesses came up from 89 cities and boroughs[1]. No new
names of any note occur in the lists, but Alderman Drew
Barentin[2] the goldsmith was there as a representative of the
City of London, Roger Leche sat for Derbyshire[3], John
Doreward for Essex[4], Thomas Chaucer (who still retained the
office of Chief Butler[5]) for Oxfordshire, John Leventhorpe[6]

[1] The claim of Colchester to exemption from sending representatives was confirmed
on May 25, 1413, Pat. 1 H. V, v. 19.
[2] When an apprentice his Christian name had been enrolled by mistake as Andrew,
Letter Book I, pp. viii, 6; Riley, Mem. 553. In Rec. Roll 3 H. V, Mich., Dec. 23, 1415,
he farms the agistment (i.e. fees for pasturing) in Watlington Park near Thame which
was near to his property at Haseley, see Wylie, ii. 478, note 6. In Exch. Accts. 46/38
he is referred to as dead after Nov. 19, 1416, his widow being named Christian or Christina
(Claus. 4 H. V, 15; 8 H. V, 17, May 22, 1420, where she is to receive her dower. She
did her homage Nov. 17, 1416, Claus. 4 H. V, 10, 15). For intermarriage of the Baren-
tins of Haseley with the Sussex family of Lewknor, see W. D. Cooper, 134. For Richard
Bronte, appointed parker of Ryxburgh (i.e. Princes Risborough near Aylesbury) in place
of William Leukenore, see Priv. Seal 664/698, Nov. 10, 1416. For action brought by
Reynold Barantyn against William Randolf, executor of Drew Barantyn, see Early Chanc.
Proc. i. 10; also against Nicholas Wotton, late mayor of London (i.e. 1415–16), re lands
of Drew Barantyn in London, ibid. i. 20. Drew Barentyn left no son and his widow was
officially examined *per ubera et ventrem* by women in the presence of certain knights to
certify that she was not pregnant. After which the heir was declared to be his nephew
Reginald the son of his brother Thomas, who took the oath of fealty on Aug. 16, 1416
(Priv. Seal 665/706; Claus. 6 H. V, 3, 18, June 5, 1418, Feb. 14, 1419). For Reginald
Barentyn esquire of Oxfordshire (Hardy and Page, i. 178), collector of tenths and fifteenths
in that county, see Rec. Roll 3 H. V, Pasch., May 4, 1415; 6 H. V, Mich., Feb. 13, 1419.
For his brass at Chalgrove near Wallingford (1441), see Macklin, 156. Besides his estates
in Bucks. and Oxon. Drew Barentin owned property in Staining Lane, known as the Jews'
Garden or burying place (Stow, Kingsford, i. 301), or Jewen Garden (now Jewin Street),
at the west end of St Giles' Church in Cripplegate and a hospitium and shops in Alders-
gate, Inq. p. Mort. iv. 23. Both he and his wife were buried in the parish church of
St John Zachary (or Sacharies, Stow, Kingsford, i. 303, 305; ii. 141) at the corner of
Foster Lane and Maiden Lane, one of the churches that was not rebuilt after the fire
(Stow, iii. 96, 120). His house was near the church and adjoined the Goldsmiths'
Hall.
[3] Wylie, iv. 478. On March 21, 1413, he was appointed a Justice of the Peace for
Staffordshire and Derbyshire, Pat. 1 H. V, i. 35 d. He also represented Derbyshire in
the Westminster Parliament in Nov. 1414, Return Parl. i. 283. On May 29, 1415, he
was a commissioner for arraying the forces of Derbyshire, Rym. ix. 253 [255]. For arms
of Leche of Chatsworth, see Lysons, Magn. Brit. v. cxxxiv.
[4] Wylie, iv. 424, not Dorewood, as Manning, 24; Mowbray, i. 115, 116, 125; Dasent,
pp. xxiii, 125. Called Durward in Rym. ix. 253 [255], where he is a commissioner for
arraying the forces of Essex on May 29, 1415; also Nicolas, App. 18, where he lends
money to the king. For John son of William Doreward (Essex), see Claus. 4 H. V, 22 d,
May 14, 1416. He died in 1420 (8 H. V), Inq. p. Mort. iv. 81. In 1415 he owned the
manor of Bocking near Braintree, Inq. Ad Quod Damn. (List), ii. 743. For his widow
Isabel, see Claus. 8 H. V, 1, March 10, 1420, where he is *defunctus*; also March 3, 1421,
ibid. m. 2.
[5] See App. E.
[6] Return Parl. i. 279; Clutterbuck, I, xxvi. He came from the neighbourhood of
Bradford in the West Riding of Yorkshire and bought the manor of Shingey or Shingle
near Sawbridgeworth about 1392, Chauncy, 181 (not 1420, as Cussans, Braughing, 82),
where he died on May 27, 1433, Weever, 549; Chauncy, 178; Clutterbuck, iii. 206;
Cussans, Braughing, 94. For his brass in Sawbridgeworth church, see Gough, II. ii. 104;
Macklin, 156; Wylie, iv. 116, note 7. It contains a shield with the royal arms of England which is not to be taken as an evidence that he belonged to the family of Plantagenet,
as Bray, Beauties, vii. 214; Cussans, Braughing, 82, which is rightly called "a whimsical

for Hertfordshire and Thomas Rempston[1] the younger for Notts., while Alexander Lound[2] who had crushed the Earl of Northumberland at Bramham Moor[3] again appeared for Yorkshire. Bristol chose merchants as its members, Northampton and Southampton were respectively represented by a dyster[4], a maltman and an armourer,

mistake" by Waller. It is merely an indication that he was in the King's service (i.e. as Receiver General), see Wylie, iv. 480. For other examples, see Gent. Mag. 1840, N.S. xiii. 140; see also tomb of Witasse de Gitry at Senlis with 3 fleurs de lys in the belt as a King's sergeant, Willemin, ii. 160. For blazon of "Leyvynthorpe," see Harl. MS. 4205, f. 35. In Rec. Roll 7 H. V, Mich., Feb. 3, 1420, John Leventhorpe is connected with loans from the hundred of Braughing (Herts.). For references to him in connection with Essex, see Pat. 6 H. V, 14 d. For John Lalesbury parson of Storteford, John de Leventhorpe esquire, and others in a suit *re* the manor of Thorley near Bishop Stortford, see Early Chanc. Proc. i. 19. For Leventhorpe's suit in connection with riots at Wednesbury (Staffs.), see ibid. i. 27. For an action at Maldon (Essex) on Oct. 7, 1437, by John Leventhorpe and his wife Catharine against John Dale Prior of Leghis (i.e. Little Leighs near Chelmsford), see Maldon Town Records, Bundle 423/no. 2, in Essex Herald, April 18, 1905, though Leventhorpe died in 1433 (*ut sup.*) and his wife Catharine on Oct. 5th or 15th, 1431, Clutterbuck, iii. 208, called Aug. 29, 1431, in Chauncy, 181, or Oct. 5, 1437, in Cussans, Braughing, 94, who calls her the daughter of John Hotost (p. 82, or Hotoft, see P. 18, note 9; Inq. p. Mort. iv. 216, 226), though her father's name is usually given as Twitchet, Chauncy, 181; Clutterbuck, iii. 208. Their son John Leventhorpe married Joan Barrington who died in 1448. For mandate to the Abbot of Westminster (May 24, 1443) to deliver up to him 2 coffers containing evidences touching inheritance of the Duchy of Lancaster which his father had delivered to Abbot Richard Harowden by command of Henry V, see Hist. MSS. Report, iv. 190.

[1] Wylie, ii. 481, note 2, not Rempton, as Belleval, 361. For his retinue (8 + 24) at Southampton in July 1415, see Exch. Accts. 45/5; Nicolas, Agincourt, 383. They are mostly yeomen from Notts. and Derbyshire, Claus. 4 H. V, 13, where they are shipped in the *Marye de Harflet* in 1416. He was present at the siege of Rouen in 1418, Rym. ix. 595–6, and was chamberlain to the Duke of Bedford in France in 1424, Beaurepaire, Administration, 171, 224. For drowning of his father Thomas Rempston in 1406, see Wylie, ii. 480—not 7 H. IV (i.e. 1405) as Bree, 78, quoting Harl. MS. 235, p. 266, where he is called Remton; Ros (296) thinks that he "had been in his barge to the court at Westminster to solicit a reprieve for a State prisoner under sentence of death" but gives no reference.

[2] For confirmation of grant to him (40 marks p. a.), see Iss. Roll 1 H. V, Mich., Dec. 1, 1413; also 2 casks of red Gascon wine, Pat. 1 H. V, iii. 7; Claus. 1 H. V, 8, June 12, 1413. For authority to the Sheriff of Yorkshire to pay money to him and Henry Lound, John Mosdale (Constable of Scarborough, Wylie, ii. 276), John Selby, and John Skipton, see Rym. ix. 248, May 16, 1415. For indenture with him dated May 13, 20, 23, 1415, to serve with the king in France with 2 + 6, see Rym. ix. 244, 250; Exch. Accts. 45/5 (4); Nicolas, Agincourt, 381; two of whom fell ill at Harfleur, Exch. Accts. 45/1. For indenture April 29, 1415, and retinue of Henry Lound (3 archers only), see Exch. Accts. 45/5, 46/40; Nicolas, 381, in handwriting of Sir Simon d'Ewes (1602–1650) in which he is joined with John Clement, Robert Helion, William Burgoyne, John Asto (*sic*) (= Aske, Nicolas, Agincourt, 375), and Robert Ashfelde, see Harl. Charters, 43, E. 39. He is called Londe in Nicolas, 350, but Lound in Fifty Wills, 52, where, under the will of Roger Salvayn of York, Oct. 26, 1420, he is to have a black gown furred with funes (i.e. foynes = weasels, Wylie, iv. 345), cf. pro novo epitogo de viridi velvetto de mottele pulverisat' et furrat' cum foygnes, Harcourt, 445, and a habergoun of Mylen (i.e. Milan). For ung hauberjon d'acier de Milan, see Toulgoët-Treanna, 116. For Alexander Lound of South Cave near Hull in list of Yorkshire gentry (1433), see Fuller, Worthies, ii. 523.

[3] Wylie, iii. 155.

[4] Cf. Wylie, ii. 413.

and Wallingford[1] sent up Lewis John[2] the vintner[3] who
was now one of the collectors of customs for the port of
London[4].

At the opening of the session the Chancellor, Bishop
Beaufort, discoursed to the assembled members from the
text[5]: "Stable counsel before deed[6]." The new king's
policy, he said, would be, as his dead father had urged, to
foster his friends and fight his foes and he now sought their
advice so that he might do what was best for himself and
for the realm. Let the knights, citizens and burgesses
therefore meet in their usual place in the Chapter-House[7]
of the adjoining Abbey at 7 o'clock on the following
morning to choose their Speaker and the king would see
him at 8.

On the next day the Commons met accordingly and
chose William Stourton[8] one of the representatives for the

---

[1] Return Parl., i. 278.
[2] Wylie, iv. 93. In Pat. 1 H. V, v. 12; Claus. 1 H. V, 3, Jan. 1, 1414, Ludovicus
Johan has married Alesia, widow of Francis Court, knight (who is *defunctus* in Claus.
1 H. V, 18, Sept. 18, 1413; Priv. Seal 659/161, Dec. 7, 1413, see Wylie, iv. 417) without permission, but is pardoned on payment of 5 marks, his son Thomas being then under
age.   In Pat. 2 H. V, ii. 31, the custody of the manors of Lockerley and Tytherley in
West Hampshire, which had been granted to Sir Francis Court and his wife Joan on
Nov. 3, 1402 (Cal. Pat. H. IV, i. 49; Inq. p. Mort. iv. 129), is granted to Lewis John on
Oct. 6, 1414, to reckon from Dec. 7, 1414.   In Claus. 1 H. V, 2, Feb. 15, 1414, Ludovicus John goes bail in £40 for Drew Barentin, William Waldern, and others who have
bought goods captured from Genoese under letters of marque.   In the Westminster
Parliament, Nov. 1414, Lodowicus Jon' is one of the representatives of Southampton
county (i.e. Hampshire), Return Parl. i. 283.   In Nov. 1414 he was allowed to retain
his possessions in England as a freeman of London (*Frank Homme de Loundres*) in spite
of the statute of 1401 (Wylie, i. 171), both his father and mother being Welsh, the
same privilege being granted also to John Montgomery and John Stiward, esquires.
[3] For £224. 0s. 22½d. (*sic*) and £81. 0s. 14d. (*sic*) for wine bought from him, see Iss.
Roll 1 H. V, Pasch. and Mich., May 31, 1413, Feb. 19, 1414, Exch. Accts. 406/21 (1).
For his claim (40 marks) for wine supplied to Henry IV still unpaid in Nov. 1414, see
Rot. Parl. iv. 37; Cotton, Abridg. 540.
[4] In Rec. Roll 1 H. V, Mich., Feb. 16, March 8, 1414, he is *late* collector.
[5] Called "the *absurd* practice of opening Parliament with a political speech introduced
by a Scripture text," Foss, iv. 359.
[6] Ecclesiasticus, xxxvii. 16 (20), "Biforn alle deed stable counseil." "A stedfast
council go bifore ech dede," Scotichron. iv. 1188, 1190, 1191, where the reference is given
as Eccles. xxxi. with two readings, viz. "Ante actum concilium stabili" and "Ante
omnem actum præcedat te concilium stabile." Cf. Conc. iii. 380, "stabili," Rot. Parl.
iv. 3; "stabilire," Cotton, 534. Cf. "He shal his wittis stable," Gower in Urry, Chaucer,
541; "that formeth and stabelyth Kinges," Brampton, 35 (written in 1414); "the foundation and stablyng of the foresaid Almshouse," Stow, London, iii. 4; "the lawe ystablid,"
Secreta, 135, 178; "stablyt and confermyd," ibid. 140, 147; "ordeyned and stabled,"
Lett. Bk. I, 294.
[7] It had been set apart for them in 1333 and is called their *ancient* place of meeting
in 1377, J. T. Smith, 141, 226.
[8] For account of him, see Mowbray, 98–166.

county of Dorset[1] whose lands lay on the border of Dorset-shire, Wiltshire and Somerset[2]. In 1402 he had been Steward of Wales; he appeared as a representative of Wiltshire in one of the Great Councils held in the reign of Henry IV[3], and he was one of those substantial west-countrymen to whom the Duke of York had applied for a loan when matters were desperate at Carmarthen in 1404[4]. He now protested before the king that he had but small estate and little knowledge and that he was bodily too weak for the office of Speaker. Henry however insisted that he should take it up as his fellows had chosen him and he accordingly accepted as his duty required. But his pro-testation soon proved to have been based on real grounds for on June 3[5] the Commons reported that he was lying in his bed so ill that he could no longer retain his post and John Doreward was appointed Speaker in his stead. He was afterwards removed to his home at Stourton[6] in the ex-treme western border of Wiltshire where he died on Sept. 18, 1413[7], and was buried in the neighbouring Carthusian Priory at Witham[8].

[1] He sat for Dorsetshire in 1410 and 1413, Return Parl. i. 274, 278; also Somerset, 1401–2; and Wilts. 1407, Mowbray, i. 114, 117.
[2] For list of his manors in Dorset, Hampshire, Somerset, and Wilts., see Inq. p. Mort. iv. 5. He owned Broadway, Olore Magna (near Weymouth) and Buckhorn Weston (near Shaftesbury), Hutchins, ii. 486; iv. 116, and had married in 1397 Elizabeth daughter of Sir John Moigne of Maddington (Wilts.) and Great Easton near Dunmow, Manning, 54; Mowbray, i. 98, 105.
[3] i.e. in 1403, Ord. Priv. Co. ii. 87.
[4] Wylie, i. 457; Ord. Priv. Co. i. 273; Mowbray, i. 110.
[5] Rot. Parl. iv. 5; Cotton, 535.
[6] For picture of Stourton House in 1674, see Hoare, iv. Addenda; Aubrey, 390, Plate XXXVII; Jackson, Leland, 63; Mowbray, i. 24, 171, 514. It adjoined the 6 springs of the Stour, 3 of which are in Somersetshire and 3 in Wilts., which appear heraldically in the arms of the family, Aubrey, 380, Plate XXXVI; Mowbray, i. 3. The house was burnt down in 1720. For a huge bone (2 ft. long) formerly kept there but destroyed when the museum was burnt down in 1867, probably a fossil from the adjoining oolite formation, but attributed to one of the giants of the house of Stourton or an elephant brought into Britain by the Romans, see Aubrey, 390; Hoare, iv. Addenda, p. 7; Gent. Mag., May 1826, p. 497; Mowbray, i. 6.
[7] Mowbray, i. 98, 165; Hoare, Mere Hundred, i. 48–9 (not 1403, as ibid. 44). For his will dated July 20, 1410, proved Sept. 22, 1413, see Mowbray, 98, 165–6, in which he desired to be buried in the cloister at Witham naked except for a linen cloth to cover him—absque herceo sive aliquo alio apparatu, and with 5 wax candles burning at his funeral.
[8] i.e. Witham Friary near Frome, Collinson, ii. 232–6; Lewis, Topogr. Dict. iv. 631; Wakeman, 171; called Witham in Selwood in Rym. ix. 307; Wills of Kings, 217. For grants to it of the alien priories of Spetisbury (near Blandford) and Monks Toft (near Norwich) by Henry V, and Warmington (near Banbury) by Henry VI, see Monast. vi. 1; vii. 1046; Collinson, ii. 233.

On May 22[1] the Commons prayed the king to secure better tranquillity against rioting in the country, having special regard to a recent disturbance raised by the townsfolk of Cirencester against their Abbot[2] and they reminded him how graciously his father had formerly promised to grant this request though the king himself would know how ill that promise had been kept.

It will be remembered that in the struggle of 1404[3] a sum of £12,000 per annum had been earmarked as a first charge upon the revenue of the country to pay for the cost of the Royal Household and again when Henry IV was for the moment set aside in 1406[4] he had been allowed to keep £6000 per annum to meet his personal expenses while the income tax granted in 1411[5] for his separate use was still being collected at the time of his death[6]. But the futility of the whole arrangement is proved by the fact that he died in debt[7] and that his executors[8] were unable to pay any of his bequests and consequently declined to administer his estate. Whereupon arose the danger that all his assets would have to be realised to satisfy the actual demands of his creditors. In order to save the risk of such a scandal and to rescue the late king's soul from so grave a peril[9] a valuation was made according to which the new king agreed

---

[1] Rot. Parl. iv. 4.

[2] For several townsmen of Cirencester bound under penalties of £40 not to do any wrong (*malum*) to their Abbot, see Claus. 1 H. V, 38 d, April 13, 1413. For commission of enquiry under Chief Justice Hankford, Gilbert Talbot of Irchenfield and others dated June 12, 1413, see Pat. 1 H. V, i. 20 d. For temporalities granted to William Best, a Canon of the Augustinians of St Mary, Cirencester, elected Abbot, see Rym. ix. 351, May 21, 1416.

[3] Wylie, i. 412; Oman, Polit. Hist. 188.

[4] Wylie, ii. 477.   [5] Wylie, iv. 42.

[6] Rec. Roll 1 H. V, Pasch., June 9, 1413. For payments to messengers in reference to the collection of it, see Iss. Roll 1 H. V, Mich., Oct. 17, 1413.

[7] Not that "he had carefully hoarded gold," as Belloc, 164. For £868. 14s. 3½d. due for wine to Thomas Chaucer, Lewis John and John Snypston, and £447. 17s. 10d. for wine, cloth, &c. to Mark Le Feyre, none of whom had been able to get their money by Nov. 1414, see Rot. Parl. iv. 37, 40; Cotton, Abridg. 540. For other accounts for spices, peltry, &c., see Rot. Parl. iv. 67, 75, 76, Nov. 1415 and March 1416.

[8] i.e. Archbishop Bowet, Bishop Langley, Sir John Pelham, Robert Waterton and John Leventhorpe, with King Henry V and Archbishop Arundel as supervisors, Rym. ix. 9, 10; Rot. Parl. iv. 5, 37, 40, 75, 76, 323; Cotton, 535, 540; Goodwin, 6; Cal. Pat. H. VI, i. 188. In the first will the Prince was made sole executor, Wylie, iii. 235. For subsequent appointment of Archbishop Chichele and Bishop Beaufort to supervise the executors' accounts and give a release, see Rym. ix. 140, June 16, 1414.

[9] Rot. Parl. iv. 40. Cf. summa excrescens (i.e. after the estate had been taxed to its full value) debitis solutis in salutem animæ suæ converteretur, Denifle Auct. ii. 255, where the English nation in the University of Paris administers the will of one of its members who had died intestate and sine hærede in 1418.

to pay £16,666. 13*s*. 4*d*.[1] to the executors in four annual instalments and in return to keep all his father's effects in his own hands, it being understood that household debts should be paid first as the late king had expressly enjoined[2] and that legacies should be considered subsequently if anything remained over. There is a fine picturesqueness about this filial act which would seem to be an earnest of that real heart-conversion of the new king which was believed to have whipped the old offending Adam out of him, but the brightness of the deed is dimmed when we discover that he only paid a quarter of the stipulated sum to the executors[3] and never even cleared off his own previously contracted liabilities[4] though it is evident that he must have been immensely the gainer by the will transaction even if he had fulfilled his engagement to the letter.

It was perhaps in connection with this dramatic bargain that the Commons now agreed to allow a fixed sum of £10,000[5] to be allotted every year for the expenses of the

---

[1] Pat. 1 H. V, ii. 14; Rym. ix. 9, May 15, 1413; Rot. Parl. iv. 37, 40.

[2] Mea solve debita, Strecche 264 b; debita patris tui fideliter solvas, Capgr. de Illustr. 110; Church, 43; Wylie, iv. 105.

[3] Rot. Parl. iv. 172, 324 shows that at his death in 1422, 19,000 marks were still due by him to his father's executors, also Cal. Pat. H. VI, i. 158, Oct. 20, 1423. For receipt for £4000 given by Archbishop Bowet as one of them dated May 15, 1414 (enrolled July 19, 1414, Devon, 334), see Dep. Keep. 45th Rept. p. 317 from Excheq. Treas. of Receipt Box 13, no. 384. For payments to creditors of Thomas More *late* custos hospit. (or garderobæ) regis, see Iss. Roll 7 H. V, Mich., Nov. 22, 30, 1419; Feb. 22, 1420.

[4] Ord. Priv. Co. ii. 315; Wylie, iii. 325. For £260 paid to Benet Spine, a merchant of Bordeaux on May 29, 1415, for advances made to him when Prince of Wales, see Rot. Vasc. 3 H. V, 3; Gesta xvii. from Priv. Seal 3 H. V; also £826. 13*s*. 4*d*. repaid to Bishop Beaufort on Jan. 27, 1414, Devon, 329. For payments to creditors of Simon Bache (Rym. ix. 357; Wylie, iv. 378) and John Ikelington as treasurers of Henry when Prince of Wales (Cal. Pat. H. V, i. 329), see Iss. Roll 7 H. V, Pasch. and Mich., May 1, 1419, Feb. 19, 1420. In Pat. 2 H. V, i. 19, May 29, 1414, Simon Bache is jam defunctus. For references to him as *late* Treasurer of the Hostel to the King when he was Prince of Wales, see Iss. Roll 3 H. V, Mich., Dec. 20, 1415; Pat. 4 H. V, 17; Priv. Seal 664/653, May 15, 1416 (also Ikelington). For his brass at Knebworth (Herts.), of which he was Rector (Cussans, Broadwater, 123), see Clutterbuck, ii. 381; Cussans, 116; Macklin, 147; also Transactions of Monumental Brass Society, iii. 106. He died May 19, 1414, having held the prebends of Tachbrook (Lichfield), Spaldwick or Sanctæ Crucis (Lincoln), and Caddington Minor (St Paul's), the latter since July 25, 1406, Cal. Pat. H. IV, iii. 215; Hennessy, 19, xxvii; Le Neve, i. 628; ii. 200, 372. For John Bache, priest, instituted to the parish of Oldbury near Birmingham, Aug. 18, 1401, see Bund, 380.

[5] Rot. Parl. iv. 5; Priv. Seal 5 H. V (870). Cf. "notwithstanding the preferrence [or preferrement] of £10,000 granted unto us," Chancery Warrants, Ser. 1. 1364/43, 46, 50, 57, 63, 67, 73. This is said to have been less than a third of the late king's expenditure, Ramsay, i. 165; Cotton (535) translates it as if it were for the payment of annuities alone, but though the wording is obscure, a comparison with Rot. Parl. iii. 528 shows that this item was not meant to be included. Iss. Roll 1 H. V; Mich., Jan. 27, 1414, records payment of £8000 to the king.

Royal Hostel, Chamber and Wardrobe, the Keeper of the Great Wardrobe being Thomas Carnika[1] who had been the king's General Receiver when he was Prince of Wales[2]. His official duties were largely performed by his deputy John Dalton[3] and two months later he was made Dean of Wells[4], but he died on September 16, 1413[5], and was succeeded as Keeper of the Great Wardrobe by an esquire John Spenser[6] who had been controller of Henry's Household as Prince of Wales and whose appointment is dated October 1, 1413[7].

The next point that exercised the attention of the Commons was the old trouble about expelling foreigners and they prayed that the law[8] might be strictly enforced; to which the king offered no objection provided that they

---

[1] For £1000 borrowed for the king's expenses per Thomas Carnika (or Karnika) the king's wardrober, see Rec. Roll 1 H. V, Pasch., May 13, 1413. For his appointment on March 21, 1413, with a salary of £20 per annum, see Pat. 1 H. V, i. 26; Iss. Roll 1 H. V, Pasch., May 4, 20, 1413, where he is called Clerk of the Great Wardrobe. Called Carvica in For. Accts. p. 105, which refers to his account as Keeper of the Great Wardrobe in 1 H. V (1413-14).

[2] Iss. Roll 3 H. V, Pasch., May 1, 1415. For Thomas Carnyca, clerk, in 1400 (2 H. IV) see Hardy-Page, i. 170. For payments to Hotspur as Warden of Berwick in 1401-2 per manus Thomæ Carnika, see Rec. Roll (Auditors)—a fragment entered as 3 H. V in Public Record Office Catalogue—but really belonging to 3 H. IV. He is called *John* Carnyka in Exch. Accts. 106/24 (2), where he is custos of the Great Wardrobe in Oct. 1413.

[3] For Carnika's and Dalton's account (£6981) for bed-furniture, pellure, and cloth for liveries, see Exch. Accts. K.R. 406/15. For receipt by Treasurer from John Dalton, clerk to Thomas Carnyka, for certain lands 1 H. V, see Exch. Accts. K.R. 335/11.

[4] i.e. on the promotion of Richard Courtenay to be Bishop of Norwich, Le Neve, i. 152, where he is called Karneke.

[5] Exch. Accts. 406/15; Angl. Sacr. i. 589; Monast. ii. 283. For William Tiller, one of his executors, see Rec. Roll 3 H. V, Pasch., July 5, 1415. In For. Accts. 3 H. V he is *late* Keeper of the Wardrobe. For payments to Robert Frampton (see Wylie, iii. 233) for attending in London to audit and complete Carnika's account and for superintending domains of the Duchy of Cornwall for 3 years, see Iss. Roll 3 H. V, Pasch., May 1, 1415. For Robert Frampton, an auditor for the Earl of Stafford, May 6, 1403, see Clark, Great Waltham, 12. In the Subsidy Roll of 1412 he owns property in London yielding 60s. per annum, Archaeol. Journ. xlv. 69. Carnika was succeeded as Dean of Wells on Nov. 8, 1413, by Walter Medford (or Metford, Angl. Sacr. ii. 589) who died in 1423. For his will dated Dec. 15, 1421, proved July 14, 1423, see Le Neve, i. 152. Medford appears as Archdeacon of Dorset (appointed Aug. 20, 1397, Le Neve, ii. 639); Treasurer of St Paul's, Feb. 12, 1401 (Le Neve, ii. 354); Chancellor of Salisbury, Sept. 26, 1402 (ibid. 650); Archdeacon of Salisbury, Dec. 14, 1404 (ibid. 624); and Archdeacon of Berkshire, Dec. 1404 (ibid. 634). He held prebends at St Paul's in 1417, 1418 (ibid. i. 372, 427). He attended the Council at Constance, and on Dec. 7, 1417, was appointed Papal Collector in England for the new Pope, Martin V, Letter Book I, 193. For a document dated London Feb. 20, 1420 (i.e. 1421), in which he is Dean or Provost of the Collegiate Church of St Cybi at Holyhead (Wylie, ii. 66), see Harl. MS. 862, f. 78 b. In this he appoints Walter Swafham Archdeacon of Bangor (since 1398, Le Neve, i. 113) and Thomas Howell Archdeacon of Anglesey (d. 1427, ibid. i. 114) as his attorneys.

[6] Wylie, iv. 542.

[7] Pat. 1 H. V, iii. 12; Rym. ix. 271; Iss. Roll 1 H. V, Mich., Oct. 25, 1413, where he is called Clerk of the Great Wardrobe, also Rec. Roll 3 H. V, Pasch., Sept. 3, 1415.

[8] Wylie, i. 411; ii. 425.

did not infringe his prerogative and left him to make exceptions when he liked. Under the grip of this expulsion fever all Welshmen and Irishmen were ordered to return to their own country before Michaelmas 1413[1], exceptions being allowed in the case of those Irishmen who had taken either Oxford or Cambridge degrees or who were sergeants or apprentices of the law, but Irish "chamber deacons[2]" (i.e. private chaplains having benefices in Ireland but licensed to beg in England) were required to void and help in the defence of their own country. On the other hand the usual order had been issued on the first day of the reign[3] that no English trader should leave the country without express permission first received. On June 9, 1413[4], the Commons voted the subsidy for four years at the rate of 43s. 4d. on every sack of wool and every 240 pelts and 100s. on every last of hides exported from the country, foreign merchants[5] paying an extra 6s. 8d. in each case. The tonnage remained at 3s. and the poundage at 1s. and both were granted for one year only. The boroughs and counties voted their tenths and fifteenths[6]

---

[1] See proclamation dated Sept. 6, 1413, in Claus. 1 H. V, 21 d. The latest date for their leaving England was subsequently extended to Christmas 1413, see Cal. Pat. H. V, i. 122, Nov. 8, 1413, showing many exemptions granted on payment of various sums of money to Irish drapers, tailors, brewers, chaplains, slaters, labourers, and fruiterers living at Bristol, Coventry, Dunstable, Glaston, Harwich, Leicester, London, Lostwithiel, and Steventon. Also many Welshmen at Alcester, Bristol, Shrewsbury and Stoke, including Welsh parsons beneficed at Hemingby (Lincs.), Moulsoe (Bucks.), Quinton (Gloucestershire), Stewkley (Bucks.), a barber and a whitetawyer at Bristol. On Oct. 16, 1413, the Mayor and Aldermen of London passed an ordinance that in future no one should be an Alderman unless he was born in England and his father was an Englishman, Letter Book I. 117.

[2] Rot. Parl. iv. 13; Stat. ii. 173; Cotton, 537; Fuller, Eccl. Hist., Bk. IV, p. 166; Richey, 225; Tyler, ii. 241; O'Flanagan, i. 81; H. F. Berry, 560; Murray, Dict. s.v.; called "Irish beggars" in A. Wood, Hist., i. 557; "lawless Irishmen" in Hook, v. 134.

[3] Claus. 1 H. V, 36, March 21, 1413; Iss. Roll 1 H. V, Pasch., May 4, 1413. For order dated Sept. 10, 1413, forbidding Lombards to leave London for abroad, see Claus. 1 H. V, 16.

[4] Rot. Parl. iv. 6; Rapin, i. 505; Goodwin, 6. Church (60) thinks that they granted "a tax on stoneware" (!) which is possibly a mistake for "stapleware," as Cotton, 535.

[5] On Nov. 25, 1413, foreign merchants and the Hansers of the Gildehalla Teutonicorum received the usual confirmation of their chartered privileges on paying 40 marks into the Exchequer, Rym. ix. 77. For the Aula Teutonicorum in London see Pauli, Pict. 180; Wylie, ii. 72; called Gildalla Theutonicorum, Loftie, i. 173; the Haunce of Almain, ibid. i. 172; Highe Duchmen of Pruse, Pol. Songs, ii. 169. For picture of it on the waterside, see Hazlitt, Companies, 165.

[6] Dep. Keep. 2nd Rept., App. II, p. 185; Usk, 120; J. E. T. Rogers, 101. Not a fifteenth and a half, as Carte, ii. 675. For commissioners appointed July 5, 1413, pro una quintadecima integra levand' in London, see Letter Book I, 119. For collectors of first half of fifteenth and tenth granted by the laity *anno primo*, see Rec. Roll 1 H. V, Mich., Nov. 14, 1413; ibid. 3 H. V, Pasch., July 17, 1415.

respectively, Northumberland and Cumberland being again specially excused from payment as they had been for the last dozen years on account of invasions by the Scots and the burning and plundering of Alnwick, Berwick and Warkworth[1].

Among the petitions[2] sent up one relates to an old grievance in regard to the excessive charges made by archdeacons[3] and other officials in the bishops' courts in connection with the proving of wills[4]. The question had been often brought up in the three preceding reigns[5]. It was now claimed that the legal fee for probate of a will was 2s. 6d.[6] but that the officials often ran it up to £10, £20, £40 or sometimes even £100. The bishops undertook to find a remedy, but when the next Parliament met they were still asking for further delay[7]. In October 1414 the Convocation of Canterbury under the direction of Archbishop Chichele arranged for a sliding scale of charges increasing from 1s. up to £20 according to the value of the estate[8] but it was not till the spring of 1416 that a remedy was enacted by statute[9] after which rules were drawn up

---

[1] Pat. 1 H. V, i. 11, 13, June 3, 1413; cf. Wylie, i. 192, 299, 406; ii. 116, 433; iii. 119. For similar exemptions (including Westmoreland) on Dec. 8, 1414, see Cal. Doc. Scot., iv. 172, also in the Parliament of Nov. 1415, see ibid. p. 174; Pat. 3 H. V, ii. 21, 27, Nov. 13, 26, 1415, where Newcastle is specially exempted on account of repairs to ruined fortifications, capture of shipping, and fatigue in guarding against surprises (*insidias*) by the Scots. For Newcastle harassed by Scottish balingers, see Ord. Priv. Co. ii. 186, Dec. 2, 1415; Pat. 4 H. V, 11, Nov. 20, 1416.

[2] Rot. Parl. iv. 8, 9.

[3] For the Archdeacon as the Bishop's Eye, see Haitze, i. 423.

[4] For incroyables abus que les officialités tolèrent dans l'exécution des testaments, see Synod of Rheims (1408) in Jadart, 184. For requirement of the bishops in 1236 that the parish priest should be present when a will is made, see Conc. i. 638. For claim of the bishops to distribute the property of intestates barred by Statute of 1357 in favour of "next friends," see Stat. i. 351; Grose, Intestacy, 120. At Sandwich the estates of persons who died intestate were administered by the mayor and jurats, Boys, 524; Grose, 128.

[5] Rot. Parl. ii. 130, 230, 313; iii. 25, 43; Stat. i. 351.

[6] Said to be 8d. in Rot. Parl. iii. 43 b, cf. Wylie, iii. 236, note 2; ibid. ii. 208, note 8. For maximum fee for sealing and engrossing wills (*leur seel et escriture*) in the Church Courts in France, see Aubert, Comp. 149. In a provincial synod held in the Black Friars at Perth, July 16, 1420, the universal existing practice in regard to the administration of wills was found to be that the estate was divided into 3 parts, (1) going to the widow if any, (2) to the children if any, and (3) the remainder to be used for funeral expenses including masses (*pro exequiis et animâ defuncti*), paying 1s. in the £ to the Bishop for confirmation, Conc. iii. 397.

[7] Rot. Parl. iv. 17. Ramsay (i. 165) thinks that the king "refused to cut down the charges."

[8] Usk, 123.

[9] Rot. Parl. iv. 84; Stat. ii. 195.

requiring a systematic inventory[1] of the deceased's effects, a proper audit and formal release of the executors and fixing 5s. as the maximum charge for insinuation[2]. And while on the question of bishops' courts the Commons complained that cases of lechery and adultery were punished with a 40s. fine, that the country was poor and that offenders could not afford to pay so much and ought to get off with a flogging instead[3]. In this case also the king undertook to bear the grievance in mind and to have the bishops' attention called to it forthwith[4].

Another curious complaint was directed against an old custom[5] which had long prevailed in regard to the perils of shipmancraft[6] and had been often appealed against. If a death occurred on board a ship whether from the fall of a stone[7], or the snap of a rope[8], sprit[9] or mast, or if anyone fell overboard and was drowned, the ship itself was presumed to have caused the mischief and was forfeited as

[1] In 1287 a Synod at Exeter required that the executors should make an inventory of the deceased's property within 15 days of the funeral before proceeding to administration which was to be completed in 12 months, Conc. ii. 155. Cf. faire l'inventaire des meubles (in 1396), see Fagniez, Jurisprudence, 36; "ovesque le Inventorie" (in 1415), Rot. Parl. iv. 84. For inventory of goods of Thomas Bitton, Bishop of Exeter, who died in 1307, see Ellacombe; also of Archbishop Bowet, who died Oct. 20, 1423, see Raine, Historians, iii. 296, where 53s. 4d. is paid to a clerk of the Chapter at York for registration. The earliest extant inventory in connection with wills proved in the Chancellor's Court at Oxford dates from 1443, Griffiths, xiii. For inventories of goods at death at St Jean d'Angély, Oct. 1, Nov. 2, 1412, see Aussy, Reg. iii. 47, 49; also of Nicholas Flamel in Paris (1418), see Le Villain, Flamel, 218; also of John Fastolf at Caister (1459), see Amyot, 239–272; Paston Letters, i. 467; also of Helewese Samar at Chatham Hall near Chelmsford, see Chatham Hall Rolls, Apr. 20, 1308, including live stock, standing crops, farm implements, and household furniture. For 16s. paid pour grossoier le testament et l'inventaire out of a total expenditure of £34. 7s. 6d. for a funeral in Paris in 1380, see Douet d'Arc, Enterrement, 139.

[2] i.e. registration, Du Cange s.v. For Archbishop Chichele's order super approbatione testamentorum, dated July 1, 1416, see Conc. iii. 377; Lyndwood, 71; Duck, 73. Cf. de probacon', approbacon' et insinuacon' ac administracon' bonorum etc., Challoner Smith, I. ix. For portatio, insinuatio et probatio testamentorum, see ibid. I. xiii. For 28 boxes of inventories of testators' goods which executors were bound to exhibit to the officers of the Archbishop of Canterbury, see Fifty Wills, p. viii. At Maldon in Essex the executors under the will of John Wellys were sued in the town court on June 9, 1421, for non-payment of tithes, to which they make answer that everything connected with the will has been submitted to arbitrators who settled all matters and fecerunt scribere in registro, Maldon Rolls, 13/2.

[3] Guthrie, ii. 448. Æneus Sylvius noted that in England fornicators had to do penance by walking naked through the streets with a candle in their hand.

[4] Not that he "curbed the power of the Church," as Gesta, p. xxvii.

[5] Rot. Parl. ii. 372 (temp. Ed. III). Une possession quele les rois d'Engleterre ont euz d'auncienté, ibid. iii. 121.

[6] Kail, 62.

[7] Par l'eschier d'une pier, Rot. Parl. iv. 492.

[8] Ibid. iii. 444.

[9] Laud, Troy Book, 373.

a deodand[1] to the king or the feudal lord within whose domain the accident occurred, the proceeds being dispensed as alms through regularly appointed officers[2], while if any money was found on the dead man half of it was to go for the repose of his soul and the other half to his relations, his shoes, knife and girdle passing as perquisites to the watchman and his breeches to the boatswain both of whom were responsible for the disposal of the body[3]. The rule was probably of very primitive origin, the ship like dumb animals[4] or inanimate objects[5] such as sticks, tubs, anchors, ladders or windmills, being held responsible for the damage

[1] For deodands or banes (i.e. slayers, Murray, Dict., s.v.), see Letter Book B, xv, xvi. They were not finally abolished till 1846 when they were declared by statute to be "unreasonable and inconvenient."

[2] Rym. ix. 163.

[3] Black Book of Admiralty, i. 85, 153; iii. 183.

[4] For a donkey tried, condemned and hanged at Dijon in 1405 for having caused the death of a child, see Archives historiques, artistiques et littéraires, i. 117, where the hanging cost 2½ francs. For the hanging of a bull in 1313, see Sorel, 272; Périaux, 164; also at Cantry near Beauvais in 1499, Duranville, Pont de l'Arche, 35. For a cock publicly burnt at Basle in 1474 for laying an egg, such eggs being regarded as peculiarly diabolical and supposed to contain serpents, Sorel, 283. For the cursing of rats, moles, frogs, flies, crows, caterpillars, field mice, and other pests, ibid. 285, 287, 288; Rittiez, Palais, 47. For pigs dressed in men's clothes and burned, hung or buried alive for killing children, after being imprisoned and formally tried, see Louandre, i. 181; Sorel, 269, 277, who gives an instance (p. 275) in 1386 where the pig was first cut across the snout and fitted with a man's mask, the proceedings being justified by reference to the Levitical law. For a pig hung by the hams (*garés*, i.e. *jarret*) on the bridge at Pont de l'Arche in 1408, see Duranville, 33. For pigs condemned by the skevins at Abbeville in 1313, 1378, 1414, 1480, then drawn through the streets and hung up by the hind foot au son de 3 cloches, see Comité de Travaux Historiques (1899), p. 23, where 60 sous are paid to the hangman for the execution. For a pig hung for killing a child at Vaudreuil near Louviers Oct. 16, 1408, see Périaux, 163, from Cochon. For a cow burnt in 1349 for worrying a child, see Périaux, 164. For another case at Auffay near Dieppe, see C. Beaurepaire, Notes, ii. 95. For arms of the lordship of Auffay with picture of the ruined castle, see Sarrazin, Jeanne d'Arc, 132, 133, quoting D'Estaintot, Recherches sur Auffray, p. 75.

[5] For 6s. 8d. paid by John Day and John Smyth from the value of half-a-cartload of arrows which caused the death of Rose Parkyn, see Rec. Roll 3 H. V, Pasch., June 15, 1415. Also 13s. 4d. paid by the Abbot of the Cistercians at Kirkstead (Monast., v. 465) near Tattershall, from the value of a windmill (*molendini ventritici*) which caused the death of William Cowper of Covenham near Louth, ibid. May 2, 1415. For a stick that caused a death at Leicester sold as a deodand and the proceeds given to charity, see Bateson, i. 364, 368, and when a child was killed by falling into a tub of hot grout (*gruth*) the tub was sold for 3d. and the grout for 5d., ibid. i. 368; also a ladder from which a man had fallen (4d.), ibid. i. 375. For horses valued at 20s. and 6s. 8d. respectively as deodands to the king in 1415 because they had caused the death of a man and a child *ex casu fortuito*, see Ad Quod Damn. 371. For the bell of St Mark's in Florence pronounced seditious and carried through the city on a donkey's back, see Rittiez, Palais, 48. On Aug. 5, 1417, the *Mary Knight* of Danzig got on a shoal called the "Rantesbourne Shelpe" in the Thames opposite the "Lymehostes" (i.e. Limehouse) near West Greenwich and the pilot or lodesman (*conductor*) who had been taken on at Harwich was killed while standing on an anchor which hung from the bows as he was driving a spike (*spek*) to slack the knot in a rope. He fell and struck his forehead against the fluke and the jury found that the anchor had caused his death, assessing its value at £3, Riley, Mem., 655; Letter Book I, 185.

done by it according to the ancient precepts of the Levitical
law.   It had doubtless often operated humanely in securing
immunity from risks for all on board, but it was liable to
result in excessive hardship.   A shipowner[1] for instance
might have paid £500 for his vessel[2] and then have to
forfeit both hull and freight owing to the foolhardiness of
some drunken loon[3] who got killed in a chance-medley[4] or
fell overboard through no fault of anybody but himself.
Such obsolete regulations tended to check all enterprise on
the part of the shipping interest and the supply of bottoms
was becoming far too small for the increased requirements
of England's rapidly expanding trade especially in the port of
London.   The king promised consideration[5] but as the very
same request came up again some 20 or 30 years later[6] it is
clear that the consideration did not result in much.

Reforms were allowed in the matter of purveyance[7], the
king's caters[8] being henceforward bound to reckon eight
bushels of corn to the quarter instead of exacting nine as
had been their custom previously.   The vat when filled
was not to be heaped[9] but shaved even[10] with a strickle or

---

[1] Cf. "les owynours," Rot. Parl. iv. 12; "awner," ibid. v. 55; "Then commeth oure
owner lyke a lorde," Reliq. Antiq. 2; Clowes, i. 343.

[2] Rot. Parl. ii. 94.

[3] Par yveresse, Rot. Parl. ii. 346; Bree, 254, from Harl. MS. 21, p. 90; de sa folie,
Rot. Parl. iii. 94.

[4] Ascun foitz p chaud melle ascun occist autrui en mesme tielx vesselx, Rot. Parl. iv.
12; tue par ascun autre, ibid. iv. 492; debates, frayes et aultres misgovernaunces, ibid.
v. 55.   For chance medley or chaud medley, see Stephens, Commentaries, iv. 42; cf.
Chauff medley (Kingsford, Chron. 54).   At that medle or mellé, Laud Troy Book,
373, 482.

[5] Church (48) thinks that the request was refused.

[6] Rot. Parl. iv. 492; v. 55 (1442).

[7] For summary of the Statutes dealing with Purveyance from 1330 onwards, see
Letter Book I, 288–298, dated Feb. 20, 1424.

[8] See Letter Book I, xliv. 288, 294, 295, where they are also called "takers"; cf.
"lorrible nom le heignous noun de parveiours des vitailles," "that odyouse name pur-
veour be chaunged and cald Catour or Buyer," Stat. i. 371 (1362); Halliwell, s.v. *Acater*,
Cater, *Taker*.   For yeoman of the king's Acatry, see Early Chanc. Proc. i. 46; Murray,
Dict., s.v. *Acatery*.   For "Cator," see Archaeol. xxviii. 14; Freeman, Exeter, 164.

[9] Token 25 quarters of corne for 20 quarters for as mochell as thei mesured every
bushell heped, Letter Book I, 288.   For boisseaus rais v. boisseaux combles, foulés v.
non foulés, mensuram calcatam et impulsam, see Delisle, Agric. 541; Aussy, Reg. iii.
224; cf. setiers combles, Affre, Aveyron, i. 225.   For the heaped bushel made illegal by
Statutes of 1834, 1835, see Statutes at Large, lxxiv. 142; lxxv. 322.   For the "bushel of
Sudbury measure by hepe," see Barham, 158.   For standard weights and measures defined
12 H. VII, see Stat. ii. 637, all ultimately based on the sterling or pennyweight (or 20th
part of an ounce) which must weigh "32 cornes of dry wheat that growe in the middes of
the eare of the whete according to the olde lawe of the land," Wylie, iv. 44.   The carat
was originally a pea-pod (*siliqua*).   For Hanse Carat, goldsmith in Paris 1392, see Add.
Ch. 2092.

[10] Rasee et nient coumblé, Rot. Parl. ii. 269; iii. 281, 291; iv. 81; v. 103.   Euene

strike[1] so that the bushel would stand on the top. No charge was to be made for meting[2] and the carriage must be paid readily in hand[3]. So the first Parliament of Henry V ended pleasantly after a session extending over 25 days[4] and at its close the usual feast took place in Westminster Hall on Whitsunday, June 11, 1413, the cost of which amounted to £151. 16s. 1½d.[5]

The Southern Convocation which was dissolved on May 8th, 1413, granted one tenth[6] as did also the Northern Province at York on July 28th, messengers having been already despatched[7] to the Archbishop of Canterbury and a number of bishops and others asking for loans for immediate use though it took quite three years to get the money actually in[8].

But though the proceedings passed off quite amicably within the Parliament, outside there was a belated flicker of an old trouble about the "maumet" that had long threatened the peace of England. From the very beginning of the new reign emissaries had been abroad supplied with money in abundance to work up the tradition that Richard II was still alive. On April 14, 1413[9], an order was put out for the apprehension of a Scottish knight, Sir Andrew Hake (a conspirator of long standing[10]), a Yorkshire squire named Henry Talbot, a yeoman named John Whitelock[11], and two

---

mesure mett and wyzt, Kail, 63. For razer as a measure, e.g. of wheat, beans, meal or apples, see Godefroy, Cotgrave, s.v. *Rasier*; Monast., vii. 668; Surtees, i. 129; A. Lambert, 476; G. Newman, 22. Cf. onze rès d'avoyne, Tuetey, Test. 53; mesure rase, Godefroy, s.v. *Ras*.

[1] Lib. Alb. 362; Halliwell, 818. For picture of the use of it in Paris 1528, see Lacroix, 285. Cf. "take hem by mesure striken," Letter Book I, 289, 292; "striken and not heped," ibid. 295; "striked," Cotton, Abridg. 547; "a strik of corn," Coventry Leet, i. 27; 20 strike of oats, Cent. Dict., s.v.

[2] In Caxton, Dial. 44, Paulyn the metar of corn hath so much moten of corn and mestalyn that he may no more forage. For the "coren metere" at Ghent, see Vigne, Recherches, 53, Plates 12, 15, with their arms showing cornshovels; also Vigne, Vade Mecum, 38, Plate 103, showing the bushel and strike.

[3] Letter Book I, 297; Rot. Parl. iv. 14; Stat. ii. 174. For payments to messengers carrying proclamations to this effect, see Devon, 324, Oct. 10, 1413.

[4] The writs of expenses vary from 26 days (Middlesex) to 42 days (Cumberland), Prynne, 498–501.

[5] Exch. Accts. 406/21, 7.   [6] Usk, 120; Cal. Pat. H. V, i. 287.

[7] Devon, 323, July 17, 1413; Iss. Roll 1 H. V, Mich., Oct. 2, 1413.

[8] Rec. Roll 3 H. V, Pasch. and Mich., July 17, Dec. 12, 20, 23, 1415; Rec. Roll 4 H. V, Pasch., June 5, 1416.

[9] Pat. 1 H. V, i. 27 d; Cal. Pat. H. V, i. 35.

[10] For his connection with the conspiracy against Henry IV in 1399, see Letter Book I, p. 4.

[11] Called "Whitlok," Cal. Pat. H. V, i. 35; "Wyghtlok," Pat. 2 H. V, i. 29; "Whitelocke," Stow, i. 88.

chaplains together with any gold or silver that might be
found upon them. On June 7, 1413[1], a manifesto was
found posted on the church doors of the Abbeys at Westminster and Bermondsey, of St Thomas' Hospital in Southwark[2] and in other places elsewhere. It was addressed to
the members of the parliament by John Whitelock who
had been for many years a devoted adherent of King
Richard II[3] and had firmly convinced himself that his old
master was veritably "in the warde and kepyng of the
Duke of Albany[4]." Of this he offered to take his oath
on the Gospels or on God's body and if that did not
settle the question he declared himself ready to be shut up
in any honest prison in England till he had proved his
words provided that he was guaranteed "sufficient living"
while he was there and was not murdered or left to die of
cold and hunger. If his evidence should prove true he
asked no more than "a free issue out of prison and my
name of a true man"; but if it was found to be false he
was willing to suffer the vilest death "that may be ordeined
for me," adding, " I betake[5] the devil ever to lie in helle,
body and soul without departyng but that persone that was
sumtyme kyng Richard be alive in Scotland." Now if he
had kept all this vapouring for his own private friends, he
might have died in his bed, but for the last seven years he
had been exploited all over England and Wales and after a
short visit to Scotland he had just made his way back accompanied by Sir Andrew Hake. But even before the late
king's death Whitelock had been already run to earth and he

---

[1] Dep. Keep. 53rd Rept. (1892), App. I. 29, from Indictments in the King's Bench,
Trinity Term, 1413.

[2] Goodwin, 3, from Term Trin. Midd.; Guthrie, ii. 448.

[3] He calls himself " yoman with Kyng Richard the time of xxx[ti] wynter," i.e. since
1383, Dep. Keep. 53rd Rept. (1892), App. I. 29. The mention of "Kyng Henry *and his
sones*" shows that the document was drawn up during the lifetime of Henry IV.

[4] Qui in domo dicti ducis detinetur.

[5] Cf. I betake (i.e. commit) my soul unto God, Fifty Wills, 104; Gower, Conf. Am.
192; Nicholson and Burn, i. 94; Pollard, 85; G. W. Taylor, 103; je donne et envoye
mon esprit, Chalvet, 239; Champollion-Figeac, 129; Héricault, i. 89. Cf. god betaght
(i.e. dead), Chancery Warrants, Ser. I. 1364/51, 53; Gower, Conf. Am. 408; Townley
Myst. 13; Wylie, i. 430, note 4; or God bitaught (1379), Wickham's Register in Palaeographical Society, Ser. II. Plate 198. The Fadyr of hevyn beteche I the, Pol. Relig.
Po. 130; suche a wounde thei hym betaujht, Laud Troy Book, 203; Gower, Conf. Am.
415; I the beteche, Laud Troy Book, 486; Halliwell, i. 169; bytaujt Jason a riche ring,
Laud Troy Book, 28; cf. granted betakyn and lette, Benham, 57; I betake you all to
the fiend, York Play, 319; Wycliffe, 146; Townley Myst. 18; I the betake my yonge
daughter here, Chauc. (S.), iii. 160.

and his comrades had been in sanctuary at Westminster since March 14, 1413, where they were still sheltered when the manifesto appeared.   Within a short time however they gave in and were transferred to the Tower[1], and on July 8, 1413[2], an order was issued to the Constable to bring up John Whitelock together with Thomas Clerk, Elias Kynet, kt.[3] and Andrew Porter for trial on the Tuesday following (July 11), when a jury was sworn[4] and a true bill of indictment returned with the result that the knight was set at liberty[5] but the other two were remitted to the Tower.   Whitelock afterwards managed to escape through the connivance of a warder named Richard Bathe and remained for a time at large with Sir Andrew Hake and several others who had accompanied him from Scotland, but the sub-constable of the Tower, Simon Campe[6], was fined 1000 marks and degraded from his office while the warder Bathe who was afterwards captured was drawn, hanged and quartered at Leicester whence his head was sent to London in May, 1414, to be fixed on one of the gates of the Tower[7].

---

[1] For order dated June 13, 1413, for the detention of Thomas Whitlok and Thomas Clerk in the Tower, see Claus. 1 H. V, 21.

[2] Claus. 1 H. V, 21.   For a document "de Billa Wightlock," see Sotheby Catalogue of Phillipp's MSS. p. 90, Lot 532, sold April 26, 1911.

[3] Called Lynet in Goodwin, 4, quoting Term Trin. Rot. xvii. Surrey.

[4] For their names, see Dep. Keep. 53rd Rep. App. 1. 28.

[5] For order for his liberation addressed on July 28, 1413, to Sir Robert Morley as Keeper of the Tower, see Claus. 1 H. V, 22.

[6] See page 1, note 11 ; not the Duke of York, as Goodwin, 4.   He is called Simeon Campe in Exch. Accts. 406/21, mm. 21, 22.   The fine was remitted on May 24, 1414, Pat. 2 H. V, i. 29 ; Cal. Pat. H. V, i. 191, where Campe is called Lieutenant for Edward Duke of York, Constable of the Tower.

[7] Stow, Chron., 345; ibid., London, Bk. i. 88 (i. 58, ed. Kingsford), where he is called the porter.

CHAPTER IV

CALAIS

CALAIS was to benefit by the change of reign. The new king had himself had some personal experience of the difficulty of maintaining the garrison there in efficiency and his administration as Captain of Calais when Prince of Wales had been bitterly attacked[1]. He now annulled and cancelled all grants that had been made in connection with the place by his two predecessors and took the whole of the revenues of Calais and the Marches into his own hands except that some large obligations entered into with his brother the Duke of Clarence remained undisturbed, on the understanding that he should still continue to pay £600 per annum for these privileges as heretofore, and forasmuch as the proportion of English amongst the population of Calais was steadily decreasing[2] and their position was becoming every year more precarious in presence of a growing settlement of Frenchmen and others[3] it was decided to enforce rigorously the orders made at the time of the capture in the days of Edward III whereby the freedom of the town was to be restricted to Englishmen only[4]. All foreigners (including of course Frenchmen) residing in Calais were to pay one-fifth of their property[5] for the privilege of residence; mixed marriages were to be forbidden except by special

---

[1] Sandeman, 17; Wylie, iv. 89.

[2] Not that the native population had been ousted, as supposed by Sandeman, p. 3.

[3] For natives of Holland, Zealand, Brabant and Flanders living at Calais in 1414, see Exch. Accts. 187/4.

[4] Rym. ix. 40; Carte, Rolles, ii. 208, July 15, 1413; Dep. Keep. 44th Rept. 544; Sandeman, 102. For confirmation of liberties to the inhabitants of Calais June 3, 1413, see Fr. Roll 1 H. V, 28–35. For the Mayor, Aldermen, burgesses and commonalty of Calais, see Priv. Seal 660/205, March 1414; also Wylie, iii. 68.

[5] Not $\frac{1}{15}$th, as Sandeman, 98.

permission¹, and all houses must be roofed with slate or tiles to minimise the risk of fire. Robert Thorley² was reinstated as Treasurer of Calais and on May 16, 1413³, he and Sir William Bardolf were commissioned to enquire as to victuals, artillery and other stuff in the town and the neighbouring fortresses. On June 7, 1413⁴, John Ormesby who was the king's carpenter and lived in Boulogne St.⁵ was ordered to provide carpenters⁶ and during the year

¹ For licence (in spite of the recent order) granted to Richard Crosse, a soldier whose wife Joan was the child of Flemish parents, but had been taken to Sandwich in infancy and had spent most of her subsequent life at Calais, see Pat. 2 H. V, ii. 32, July 28, 1414.
² Wylie, iv. 552. He had been imprisoned in Oct. 1412, ibid. iv. 89. For his account from Dec. 28, 1409, to May 29, 1412, see For. Accts. 4 H. V, 14 d, showing that he was reappointed Treasurer on Oct. 27, 1409, in succession to Richard Merlaw or Marlow (Wylie, ii. 110; iii. 306; Letter Book I, 28). The account (in which he is called both Thorley and Throley) shows an expenditure of £43,581. 17s. 5d. during 2½ years, and if to this be added £88,487. 17s. 9½d. spent in the previous 2½ years (see Wylie, iii. 67, note) we arrive at a total of £132,069. 15s. 2½d. spent in 5 years and 2 months. Ramsay, i. 319 (Antiquary, viii.), estimates an annual expenditure of £25,000 at Calais for a garrison of 773 men during the reign of Henry V. For repair of a panel in the Great Hall in the Market-place at Calais temp. Ric' M'lawe, see Exch. Accts. 187/6, which contains particulars of expenditure of £11,536. 19s. 1d. made by Robt. Thorley during the time Henry was Captain of Calais as Prince of Wales, i.e. from March 18, 1410 (Wylie, iii. 306, not 1409, as Lavisse-Rambaud, iii. 393), till Oct. 20, 1412 (Wylie, iv. 89); also £5170. 0s. 2½d. received by Robert Thorley between Aug. 6, 1413, and Aug. 6, 1417, showing payments for 21 cementers, 32 carpenters, as well as smiths, tilers, plumbers, bakers, &c. Thorley's account shows that he kept two books, one called *"Registrum de redditibus custumarum et assise"* and the other *"Rentale Regis in villa Cales,"* with a separate silver seal for the Scunnage (i.e. Skevinage, Eschevinage, Scabinage, Eskevinagium, l'Eskivenage, Skabinagium, Rot. Parl. iii. 500; Rym. x. 490; Du Cange, s.v.; Wylie, iii. 210, note 8), now St Pierre (Dillon, 303-329, 376). For John Montgomery appointed bailiff of "le Eskenage" at Calais v. John Kyghley, see Priv. Seal 658/59, June 16, 1413; Ewald, xliv. 544, 552, who supposes it to mean "the assize of wine, ale, beer and bread." For John Bernard, *late* Treasurer of Calais (i.e. before Nov. 15, 1412, Wylie, iii. 306, note 7), see Rec. Roll 1 H. V, Pasch., Mich., May 31, Nov. 7, 1413; ibid. 3 H. V, Pasch., May 6, 1415. In Rec. Roll 1 H. V, Mich., Dec. 11, 1413, Jan. 27, 1414, Robert Thorley is *late* Treasurer of Calais; also Rec. Roll 3 H. V, Pasch., June 14, 1415, which shows £221. 0s. 19d. (*sic*) paid for passage and repassage of 100 men-of-arms and 300 archers. For retinue (5 + 13) of the Treasurer of Calais in 1415, see Excerpt. Hist. 26.
³ Carte, Rolles, ii. 207.
⁴ Fr. Roll 1 H. V, 3.
⁵ Called Boloinstreet or Boloignstreet in Exch. Accts. 187/3, which contains a detailed account for building and repairing his house dated Aug. 3, 1412, showing wages of cementers (at 6d. to 8d. per day) with charges for timber (5s. the piece), beams, braces, summers (2s. a piece), puncheons, posts, resons, chimneys, a penthouse (or pentice, Halliwell, 615; Baildon, Site, 98; or pentise, E. T. Bradley, 381), a porch with porchstones, brickstones (3s. 4d. per 1000), gables, an autee (?), sloshornes (not slofhoues, as Wylie, iii. 307), and husblase (not houseflax, as Wylie, iii. 306), ? from blaese = torch, lantern, Bosworth-Toller, s.v.
⁶ For payments to Thomas Clopton, master-carpenter, and 32 carpenters at 8d. per day at Calais from Aug. 6, 1413, see Exch. Accts. 187/6. For payments to carpenters at Dunster for making cippes (? door posts, cf. cippus = stocks, Halliwell, i. 250), bordes, trestles, windows and doors, also iron to make twists (2 twistez pro hostio), hooks, &c., les rakkes in porta, and 2 hooks and 3 large nails for said rakkes, see Lyte, 119. For assers, tables, planchebord, elmenbord, oakenbord, slittyngwerk and quarters, somers

large payments are recorded to Richard Threll[1] as victualler[2], for corn[3], cattle[4], pigs[5], schonen herrings[6], Portuguese wine[7] and salted meat. The Duke of Clarence was Captain of Calais[8] and Guînes[9] with William Lord Zouche of Harring-

(i.e. wall-plates, see Cotgr., s.v. *Summer*; Halliwell, ii. 827), and bemys, giestes (i.e. joists, Halliwell, i. 399), and rafters, braces, wynbemes (i.e. window-beams), and cross andrewes, see Rackham, 36, 39. For plaunchebourde, quarterbourde, ieese and rafters see Feuillerat, 122.

[1] For his appointment, March 22, 1413, see Fr. Roll 1 H. V, 1, where he is called "Trele," but "Thelle" in Rec. Roll 8 H. V, Pasch., July 9, 1415; or "Threl" in Iss. Roll 4 H. V, Pasch., May 27, 1416, where he receives £33. 6s. 8d. for victualling Sangatte; or "Threll" in Iss. Roll 3 H. V, Pasch., April 24, 1415 (where he receives £10 for buying planks pro estuffamento), and May 18, 1415 (with payments to him for providing corn and £128 for 32 casks of Gascon wine bought from Guerrys Darrengorsa of Bordeaux); also Exch. Accts. 328/6; Iss. Roll 3 H. V, Mich., Nov. 4, 1415; Rec. Roll 3 H. V, Mich., Nov. 4, 1415; Exch. Accts. 187/6, which shows £2377. 4s. 5½d. paid to him (Richard Threll) inter alia for chains, anchors, belts, haspes, hakes, bendis, virrolls (i.e. ferules), gemels (i.e. hinges), pickoises all made of iron, besides spring locks, plate locks, stock locks and hanging locks (cerur' pendul') for doors and gates.

[2] Threll succeeded Richard Clitherow as victualler, Exch. Accts. 187/6, where he is *nuper* emptor victualium, Wylie, ii. 114, note 1; iii. 306. For "vittler," see Cotton and Dallas, iv. 76; "vychelere," ibid. v. 24.

[3] e.g. for 300 quarters of wheat at 5s. 8d. the quarter, Iss. Roll 1 H. V, Mich., Oct. 17, Nov. 8, 1413; Jan. 27, 1414.

[4] For 100 Welsh cattle (£67. 13s. 4d.) including 3s. 4d. for bringing them to London, also £60 for 93 Welsh cattle killed and salted in London and sent over to Calais together with 5 marks for slaughtering and £6. 8s. for salting cattle in Calais, also salt-meat sent over from Arundel in a balinger and £15 paid to the Countess of Arundel for hire of a balinger to carry pigs, cattle, &c., including wages for men-of-arms, archers and crew, see Iss. Roll 1 H. V, Mich., Feb. 16, 19, 22, 1414. For John Yonge varlet summoned from Arundel in great haste and staying 14 days in London advising as to victualling and artillery at Calais, see Iss. Roll 1 H. V, Mich., Oct. 21, Dec. —, 1413.

[5] For hogs salted for garrisons, see Clarke, 173; cf. lart c'est à dire char salle, Meun, 141; baquons et lart et char salle, Priorat, 277.

[6] For the Schonentide, see Wylie, ii. 68; cf. les parties de Scone, Rot. Parl. ii. 306; iii. 63. Cf. as thikke as heryng fletes, Laud Troy Book, 198; Kempe, 25. For heringman, heringfrowe, see C. G. A. Schmidt, 28; heryng fletes in here scole (or skull, i.e. shoal, Halliwell, ii. 716), Laud Troy Book, 418; au temps de herengison, Regnault, 27; herring-fare, Halliwell, i. 446.

[7] For 30 casks of Portuguese sweet wine at £5 per cask bought of John Martin, 2 lasts of herrings de scone £14, with portage and wharfage (40d.), 9 quarters of salt for salting cattle infra quandam navem versus Cales (36s.), see Iss. Roll 1 H. V, Mich., Feb. 20, 22, 1414.

[8] Carte, Rolles, i. 209, Nov. 2, 1413. For grants to him of tithes and fisheries of Frétun, Calkwell (i.e. Coquelles, Wylie, iii. 161, note 3), Galimot, &c., see ibid. March 21, 1414. Not that the Earl of Warwick succeeded the Prince of Wales directly as Captain of Calais, as Sandeman, 11.

[9] Wylie, iii. 161, 164; Carte, Rolles, i. 210, 211, Aug. 21, 23, 27, 29, Nov. 25, Dec. 16, 1413; Jan. 10, 23, 24, Feb. 5, 8, 13, March 15, 1414; Priv. Seal Bills 1114/29, 30, 32, 33; 1115/2, 4, 7, 10, 11, 12, 14, 16, 17, 21; Ord. Priv. Co. ii. 145, Feb. 15, 1415; Fr. Roll 1 H. V, 4 (where Thomas Norreys parson of Gatcombe in the Isle of Wight is with him); also Fr. Roll 4 H. V, 4, 6, Feb. 2, 1417. For Thomas Corbet of Essex going to Guînes in the service of the Duke of Clarence, Captain of Guînes, see Pat. 2 H. V, i. 13, June 17, 1414. He is still Captain of Guînes in Fr. Roll 6 H. V, 3, Jan. 7, 1419. For £3342. 10s. 6d. paid to him as Captain of Guînes, also £7662. 0s. 12d. (*sic*) for the garrison of 60+60 from Aug. 6, 1413, to April 23, 1414, see Exch. Accts. 187/6, which records clearing the moat at Guînes and a long ditch apud le Pynfold juxta le Turnepyk near the gate of the castle, and refers also to a lodge near the Mill Tower, a new watchhouse and garecte (i.e. watchtower, guérite, Murray, Dict., s.v. *Garret*) between the

worth near Uppingham as his Lieutenant[1]. On Feb. 3, 1414[2], Richard Beauchamp Earl of Warwick[3] was appointed Captain of Calais and Governor of the Marches of Picardy. He was received at Calais with great distinction, kissing the cross at his entrance into the town[4] and soon afterwards he took part in a three days' tournament in the Park Hay

---

"ffanetour" and the first tower, together with payments to two sawyers for sawing 1065 feet de planchour bord'. For 100 men as the garrison of Guînes in 1415, see Excerpt. Hist. 26. In Fr. Roll 4 H. V, 3, Feb. 28, 1417, Robert Gray, fishmonger of London, is provider of victuals to the castle of Guînes.

[1] For £8089. 5s. 5d. paid to Dns. William la Souche (Wylie, iv. 236, 238) for wages from Aug. 6, 1413, to Aug. 6, 1414, see Exch. Accts. 187/6. He appears as Lieutenant of the town of Calais on May 1, July 8, Oct. 15, 19, Nov. 28, Dec. 16, 1413; Jan. 10, 23, 1414, in Fr. Roll 1 H. V, 10, 12, 13, 22, 25, 37; Priv. Seal Bills 1114/42, 1115/9, 28, 40. On Oct. 19, 1413, Henry Pay is in his service as waterbailiff of Calais, ibid. 1115/28; Fr. Roll 1 H. V, 1; Carte, Rolles, i. 212. For confirmation of this office to him, see Pat. 1 H. V, i. 14, June 12, 1413. For safe-conduct granted to deputies of Flanders by William la Zouche, Lord of Totnes and Harringworth, dated 1413, see Barante, iii. 143. Lord Zouche died on Nov. 3, 1415, Inq. p. Mort. iv. 15; Dugd. Bar. i. 692, where Totnes Castle in Devonshire is among his possessions. In Claus. 3 H. V, 4, Feb. 13, 1416, he is *defunctus*, also Pat. 6 H. V, 11, Feb. 20, 1419; Claus. 6 H. V, 20, May 2, 1418, where his widow Elizabeth who died in 1425 (Inq. p. Mort. iv. 99) is married to William Garnall. In Pat. 3 H. V, ii. 18, Dec. 13, 1415, Ralph Earl of Westmoreland is granted the custody of the lands of his son William held per servitium militare; also Pat. 8 H. V, 15, July 12, 1420, when the boy was 13 years of age (Dugd. i. 692). For the king as guardian of William Lord de Zouche, see Early Chanc. Proc. i. 30.

[2] Fr. Roll 1 H. V, 10; Carte, Rolles, i. 210, 211, though he already appears as Captain of Calais on Jan. 31, 1414, Rym. ix. 111, not that he was appointed on July 18, 1414, as Ord. Priv. Co. ii. 147, or June 19, 1415, as Dugd. Bar. i. 244; Goodwin, 64; Hunter, 29; Demotier, 81, where the appointment is to last till Feb. 3, 1417 (or June 29, 1415, as Sloane MS. 4600, ff. 265, 267, 278), which probably represents his return from Constance (i.e. before May 21, 27, 1415), on which days he was present at council meetings in London at the Blackfriars and the Tower, Rym. ix. 319; Ord. Priv. Co. ii. 167; Dict. Nat. Biogr. iv. 30; Add. MS. 24062, f. 147. He is called Captain of Calais on April 21, 1415, Rym. ix. 224 (not April 24, as Lenz, 71), though this will not justify the inference that he had already returned from Constance by that date. During his absence his place was filled by a lieutenant, viz. William Lisle jun., knight, who was appointed on Nov. 16, 1414, Rym. ix. 178, 179, 201; Dep. Keep. 44th Rept. p. 556, and in Feb. 1415 it is stated that there is at present no Captain in the Marches of Calais, Ord. Priv. Co. ii. 147, though on Feb. 6 and June 5, 1415, Lisle is officially called Lieutenant for the Earl of Warwick, Rym. ix. 201, 260. In Feb. 1417 Lisle was still at Calais, Ord. Priv. Co. ii. 209, though soon after that date he was succeeded as Lieutenant by William Bardolph, Rym. ix. 314, Oct. 7, 1415. On April 1, 1413, the custody of the castle of Calais was entrusted to Thomas Beaufort, Earl of Dorset, Fr. Roll 1 H. V, 1; Carte, Rolles, ii. 212. For payments to him for wages of 40+20 as Captain of Calais, see Exch. Accts. 187/6, ? temp. H. IV (see Wylie, iii. 306), where his appointment is dated July 1, 1408. On Sept. 7, 1409, he was about to start for Calais, Letter Book I, 73. The Earl of Warwick is "ore Capitain du Calays" in 3 H. V (1415-16) in Sloane MS. 4600, f. 296, from Calig. D. 5, where he petitions the Chancellor, Bp. Beaufort, for £100 per annum and a guarantee for the wages of the garrison at Calais. In Sept. 1417 he is still Captain of Calais though actually taking part in the siege of Caen, Rym. ix. 490; Rot. Norm. 153.

[3] In 1411 (12 H. IV) he had been retained in the service of the Prince of Wales for life, Sloane MS. 4600, f. 282, and he was present at the suppression of Oldcastle's rising in Fickett's Field in Jan. 1414, Rous, 365.

[4] See pictures from Cotton MS. Jul. E. iv. Art. 6, in Strutt, Manners, ii. Plates XXXI, XXXII; Carysfort, Pag. xxv, xxvi; Green, ii. 518.

at Guînes at each of which he handsomely unhorsed the champion who ventured to accept his challenge[1].

It has been estimated that during the reign of Henry V the numbers of the garrison at Calais amounted on an average to 150 men-of-arms and 300 archers[2] and a controller's account written on June 8, 1418[3], shows that the numbers were constantly changing. On the Earl of Warwick's appointment it had been stipulated that in war time there should be 240 + 274[4], of whom 140 and 150 respectively were to be mounted, together with 4 mounted scourers[5], 40 balisters, 33 carpenters, 20 cementers and masons besides artillery and other mechanical craftsmen[6]. The above numbers appear to have been actually maintained in 1416[7] and payments running for three years from Aug. 6, 1414[8], give the figure at 460, i.e. 230 of each arm, while yet another account shows that 30 + 500 were garrisoned in the town[9], 30 + 20 in the Castle and 18 on the Rushbank[10], each force being under its own separate captain. On July 19, 1413, a Yorkshireman Roger Salvayn[11]

---

[1] Rous, 366; Strutt, Manners, ii. Plates xxxv, xxxvi, xxxvii; Carysfort, Pag. xxix, xxx, xxxi; Brett, 59; but if the dates there given, viz. Jan. 6, 7, 8, are correct, the meetings must have been after his return from Constance.

[2] Rym. ix. 223. Called "thordinarie nombre," Excerpt. Hist. 26.

[3] i.e. by William Caston or Caxton, Exch. Accts. 187/6.

[4] Sloane MS. 4600, ff. 265, 267, where the figures vary somewhat; cf. Goodwin, 64, where the archers amount to 334.

[5] Skurat' or scuratores at 1s. 6d. per day.

[6] Excerpt. Hist. 26 adds 1 plumber, 1 tiler, 1 yeoman artiller and 1 purveyor of stuff.

[7] Exch. Accts. 187/6, where £4154. 17s. 8d. is paid for them anno 4.

[8] Ibid., where the amount paid is £2500.

[9] i.e. 3 knights (at 2s. per day), 26 "men of armys" (at 1s.), 300 archers (at 8d.) and 200 foot (at 6d.), Excerpt. Hist. 26, though Sandeman, 21, gives only 387 for the town and castle.

[10] Excerpt. Hist. 26. In Exch. Accts. 187/10, April 9, 1413, the garrison consists of 16 balistars or men-of-arms who must be English born.

[11] Fr. Roll 1 H. V, 23. He is called Treasurer, ibid. 1 H. V, 10, Nov. 28, 1415; also Rec. Roll 3 H. V, Pasch., June 21, July 5, 1415; Rec. and Iss. Roll 3 H. V, Mich., Dec. 3, 1415; Iss. Roll 4 H. V, Pasch., May 27, June 4, July 6, 1416; do. 6 H. V, Pasch., May 2, June 20, 1418; Iss. Roll 7 H. V, Pasch. and Mich., May 5, 12, Oct. 13, Nov. 7, 30, Dec. 4, 1419; Jan. 20, Feb. 17, 1420; also Iss. Roll 8 H. V, Pasch., May 11, 23, 24, June 10, 1420; July 22, 1418, in Exch. Accts. 187/13; Rec. Roll 7 H. V, Mich., Pasch., Jan. 20, May 2, 1420, but *late* Treasurer in Rec. Roll 4 H. V, Pasch., June 4, 1416, though this entry is a subsequent insertion. During this time his attorney in England is Robert Thresk (Iss. Roll 6 H. V, Pasch., May 6, 12, 1418; Rec. Roll 6 H. V, Pasch. and Mich., May 9, June 20, July 1, Nov. 22, 1418; Iss. Roll 7 H. V, Mich., Oct. 13, 1419), who had been a Remembrancer of the Exchequer since March 21, 1413 (Pat. 1 H. V, i. 29). For 40 marks paid to Robert Thresk for parchment, see Rec. Roll 3 H. V, Pasch., July 9, 1415. In Rec. Roll (Auditors), March 2, 1416, he is Remembrancer to J. Kirkeby Marshal of the Exchequer, cf. Iss. Roll 5 H. V, Mich., Dec. 15, 1417. For 25s. paid to Roger Salvayn as a squire of the king's chamber before

was appointed to succeed Robert Thorley[1] as Treasurer of Calais and before Aug. 6, 1413[2], £4666. 13s. 4d. had been paid to him from the revenues of the Duchy of Cornwall[3] for wages to the garrison[4] while further sums amounting to £2539. 8s. 9½d. followed within the next six months[5]. John Gerard[6] was still Captain of the Lancaster Tower on

Oct. 31, 1413, see Q. R. Accts. 406/21, 27, though he had been in the service of Hotspur and had carried his defiance before the Battle of Shrewsbury (1403), Wylie, i. 361; Harl. MS. 293 (78), which contains a sixteenth century copy of the defiance. For £100 left to him in Henry V's will in 1415, see Rym. ix. 291. For a cask of wine given to him by the king at Harfleur in Sept. 1415, probably because he was on the sick list, see Hunter, 47. For his retinue (3 + 12) in 1417, see Iss. Roll 5 H. V, Pasch., Apr. 29, 1417; Rym. ix. 595. In Rec. Roll 7 H. V, Mich., Nov. 16, 1419, he and Lewis John are farmers of the King's Change (*cambii regis*). For grant to him and Lewis John as changers (*escambius*) or firmarii cambii regis, Rec. Roll 7 & 8 H. V, Pasch., May 1, 1419, July 3, 1420, of the exchange of all money going to Rome from Aug. 13, 1417, to Sept. 29, 1419, on payment of £200 p. a., see Pat. 5 H. V, 1; Priv. Seal 5 H. V, 876, Feb. 18, 1418; Rec. Roll 6 H. V, Mich., Nov. 8, 1418. For various journeys made by him from Normandy to Picardy, 5 & 7 H. V, see For. Accts. P. R. O. p. 80; Exch. Accts. 49/14, where his wife Mathilda is his executrix.

For his will (where he is Roger Salvayn *knight* of York), dated Oct. 26, 1420, proved May 1422 (or March 7, 1422, Surtees, iv. 118), see Fifty Wills, 52, in which he desires to be buried in the church of the Grey Friars at York, leaving to his brother Thomas the "place at Duffield" that he had bought of John Fulthorpe. For account of his brother Gerard Salvayn in connection with his estate, see Exch. Accts. 187/7, including £37 for removing his body from London to York and for trentals of masses there, also 20 marks paid to two chaplains celebrating mass for his soul at North Duffield (Wylie, ii. 253), £10 to a bishop ad disponend' expeditionem animae suae, £20 to domina Mathilda Salvayn and £4 to his daughter Alice. In the account John Orwell (Wylie, iii. 59) and Robert Day are mentioned as having been Roger's deputies as Treasurer of Calais. For Roger Salvayn's account as Treasurer of Calais from the day on which he took up his appointment (Aug. 1, 1413), see Exch. Accts. 187/6, showing that he received 10s. per day while in England, arrived at Calais Dec. 22, 1413, and that from Dec. 12, 1415, to July 12, 1416, he was in England collecting money at certain customs ports (i.e. Hull, Boston, Lynn and Ipswich), which yielded him altogether £23,000. Bishop Beaufort, writing from Bruges on Sept. 4, 1417, notes that when he was at Calais the wife of Roger Salvayn spoke with him regarding the office of Treasurer of Calais from which her husband claimed to have been discharged and asking for his formal quittance as she is still keeping together all that belongs to the Treasury at her own cost, Ord. Priv. Co. ii. 234; Gilliodts van Severen, 359, where the letter is wrongly dated 1415. For his account as Treasurer of Calais on May 11, 1416, see Exch. Accts. 187/5. He is called Salvan in Iss. Roll 5 H. V, Mich., Dec. 7, 15, 1417; or le Sylvan, Surtees, iv. 114. In Rec. Roll 8 H. V, Mich., Jan. 21, 1421, he is referred to as *late* Treasurer of Calais, his attorney being Robt. Cawood in Iss. Roll 8 H. V, Mich., Oct. 15, Nov. 1420; March 11, 1421. For his accounts as Treasurer of Calais, 6 to 9 H. V, see Exch. Accts. 187/13.

For John Salvayn, Treasurer of the Household, see Iss. Roll 6 H. V, Pasch., May 13, 1418.

For John Salvayn of York (or of Warwick), going to France in comitiva of the Duke of Bedford, see French Roll 8 H. V, 8, Apr. 19, 1420.

[1] Page 38, note 2.
[2] Iss. Roll 1 H. V, Mich., Dec. 4, 1413.   [3] See Appendix F.
[4] For 53s. 4d. paid for an iron chest for Calais to keep wages in, see Iss. Roll 1 H. V, Mich., Jan. 27, 1414. In Nov. 1414 the garrisons in Picardy petition that their wages may be paid in the Exchequer at Calais instead of requiring them to cross to England. Rot. Parl. iv. 55.
[5] Viz. £1716. 12s. 9d. and £822. 16s. 0½d. Iss. Roll 1 H. V, Mich., Dec. 11, 1413, and Feb. 22, 1414.
[6] Wylie, iii. 58, note 4; Priv. Seal Bills 1114/56, June 28, 1413; ibid. 1115/11, 13,

the Rushbank[1] and John Lardner[2] remained for a time in command at Oye[3] but by Feb. 22, 1414, he had been replaced by John Bastyner who received £1265. 0s. 10¼d. to pay the garrison early in the year 1414[4] while £645. 15s. 8¾d. went to Ralph Rochford[5] to pay his men at Hammes[6].

23, Oct. 29, 1413, Jan. 30, Feb. 11, 1414; Iss. Roll 1 H. V, Mich., Jan. 27, 1414; Fr. Roll 1 H. V, 10; Carte, Rolles, i. 211; Pat. 6 H. V, 20, Aug. 5, 1418; Fr. Roll 6 H. V, 3, 7, 52, June 30, July 2, 29, 1418, Feb. 22, 1419; Fr. Roll 8 H. V, 2, 3, 7, 9, Nov. 19, 1420, Jan. 26, May 20, 1421. For £1226 paid to him from Aug. 6, 1413, to Aug. 6, 1417, see Exch. Accts. 187/6. For his appointment by John Earl of Somerset, on June 6, 1405, to succeed John Toty, deceased (Wylie, iv. 143, note 3), confirmed by Henry IV, Jan. 2, 1406, and by Henry V, April 12, 1415, see Rym. ix. 218.

[1] For its position see Demotier, 112; Wylie, iii. 58; called "towre of Risebanke," Excerpt. Hist. 26; Ellis, Orig. Lett. Vol. II. Frontispiece (1546), not "the *town* of Rysbank" as Sandeman, 6, though called "Rysbank a great tower," ibid. 32, 37. It is still called "Risban," see map in Demotier, 402; Joanne, Nord, 80; Ardouin-Dumazet, xviii. 34. For view of Calais with the Lancaster Tower, see Zeiller, Pt. II. 14; Lennel, 12 (1544). For Rysbank repaired cum faget' spinarum garbis arundinum et seggis, see Exch. Accts. 187/6 which has also a reference to "batell' regis vocat' le feribot," i.e. for crossing the Paradise or harbour, Sandeman, 40. For le lieu appellé Paradis qe est bien près les fosses de la ville, see Stat. ii. 108; cf. niefs au dit lieu de paradys pour y reposer, also les Baekenes devant la port, ibid. For "risshebotes," see Riley, Mem. 676; Letter Book I, 169.

[2] Priv. Seal Bills 1114/50, 1115/3, 22; Carte, Rolles, ii. 207, 209, 211, June 3, Nov. 23, 1413; March 8, 1414; Early Chanc. Proc. i. 33; Wylie, iii. 59, note 6.

[3] For Oye fortified in 1347, see Harbaville, ii. 199. For account of it, see Desrues, 127; not "caya" as Rym. ix. 635; nor "Vye" as Bree, 147, from Cleopatra, F. iv.

[4] Iss. Roll 1 H. V, Mich., Feb. 22, 1414. Yet on Aug. 2, 1415, Lardner is still called Warden of Oye with a peace staff of 4 + 20 rising to 40 + 20 (sic) in time of war in Sloane MS. 4600, ff. 266, 268, though ibid. 265, 267, 281 has William Del Hoo, kt. as Custos of Oye in 11 H. IV, who may be the same as William del Hay, esquire, retained 10 H. IV with Geoffrey Arden to serve the Prince for life, ibid. 12. On Feb. 4, 1415, Nicholas Horton (? Hooton) is Custos of Oye with a garrison of 4 + 20, also French Roll 6 H. V, 5, 6, July 21, 1418; ibid. 8 H. V, 4, Oct. 21, 1420; Carte, Rolles, ii. 236, 241. For indenture with him, July 22, 1418, see Exch. Accts. 187/10, 13, where the peace garrison = 2 + 2, but 10 + 10 in time of war. For payments to Lardner as Captain of Oye for 20 + 40 from Aug. 6, 1413, to April 23, 1414, and onwards till Aug. 7, 1417, see Exch. Accts. 187/6, also for 2 + 6 and 6 balisters. He died before July 21, 1418, on which day Nicholas Hooton was appointed to succeed him, Exch. Accts. 187/10; Carte, Rolles, ii. 241. For Richard Hyman (or Heyman), as one of his executors, Jan. 25, 1423, see Carte, Rolles, ii. 252; Ord. Prov. Co. ii. 345.

[5] Wylie, ii. 56, note 3. He is Captain of Hammes on May 10, June 5, 20, July 6, 17, Aug. 5, Oct. 9, 15, 21, 24, 1413; Jan. 23, Feb. 22, 1414, Pat. 1 H. V, ii. 9; v. 24; Priv. Seal Bills 1114/34, 44, 47, 53, 55; 1115/15, 38, 39; Iss. Roll 1 H. V, Mich., Feb. 22, 1414; Carte, Rolles, i. 207, 208, 210; on July 18, Oct. 8, 21, 1413, he is going over sea to Picardy, Fr. Roll 1 H. V, 16, 23; Priv. Seal Bills 1115/15. For £3024. 7s. 1¼d., paid to him for wages of 30 + 20 at Hammes, see Exch. Accts. 187/6, but in Sloane MS. 4600, ff. 268, 280, his retinue at Hammes on July 6, 1413, is 30 + 50. In 1415 the garrison = 41, Excerpt. Hist. 26. For grant to Rochford of 20 marks p.a., see Iss. Roll 6 H. V, Pasch., March 9, 1418. In Iss. Roll 4 H. V, Mich., Feb. 20, 1417, he is dapifer regis. He was sheriff of Lincolnshire in 1404, 1407, 1409, Sheriffs Lists, 79; Wylie, ii. 228, 401. For grant to him on April 1, 1415, from lands of John Beaufort, late Earl of Somerset, see Iss. Roll 5 H. V, Mich., Feb. 10, 1418. For the family of Rochefort at Walpole near Wisbech, see Blomefield, ix. 108.

[6] For plan of Hammes, see Dillon, 301; "in inaccessible marshes," Sandeman, 34. Exch. Accts. 187/6 has payments for repairing belfry (campanil') of the castle at Hammes, also putting 5 doors with 10 hengles (i.e. hinges, Murray's Dict., s.v.) and 5 stone windows and a gunhole in the tower between the barbican and the watchhouse, also for raising a causey between the castle turnpike and the "pennes" (barriers) with timber

William Swinburn[1] was still Captain of Marck[2] with
Edmund Wyse[3] as his lieutenant and John Vale[4], who had
previously been Receiver at Calais[5], received 100 marks
in connection with his command in the newly captured
castle of Balinghem[6] near Ardres.

During the last reign complaints had been frequent in
regard to the misuse of funds in the administration of Calais
and the fortresses on the March, even Henry himself not
having escaped charges of malpractice during his tenure of
office as captain there[7] and it was apparently with a view
to clearing the air as a warning to future captains and

of the lintel (*lyntell*) and carriage from a place called "le stones." Letter Book I, 29
shows that Thomas Swinburn was Captain of Hammes on Feb. 29, 1404, not that he
was appointed on March 14, 1405, on which day he appointed a deputy there on his
departure for Bordeaux, see Wylie, ii. 56, note.

[1] Wylie, ii. 89, note 6; iv. 74, note 3; Fr. Roll 1 H. V, 15, 21; Carte, Rolles, i. 209;
Priv. Seal Bills 1114/49; 1115/19, 20, 27; July 5, 15, Oct. 20, Dec. 5, 1413; Sloane
MS. 4600, ff. 265, 267. For £974. 2*s*. 8*d*. paid to him as Captain of Marck when Robert
Thorley was Treasurer of Calais (see page 38), also £2153. 8*s*. 2*d*. for wages of 20 + 20
at Marck from Aug. 6, 1413, to Aug. 6, 1414, see Exch. Accts. 187/6. He is still
Captain of Marck on Sept. 6, 1418, Deputy Keepers Rept. xliv. 697. For money lent by
him in Feb. 1417, see Iss. Roll 4 H. V, Mich., Feb. 20, 1417. For his retinue (5 + 14)
at Southampton in July, 1417, see Gesta, 269. He was present at the siege of Rouen in
1418, Rym. ix. 595. For land lately acquired from William Swynbourne, esquire, and
his wife Philippa by Gilbert Umfraville and others, see Pat. 8 H. V, 12, Nov. 28, 1420.
For 200 crowns paid by the Jurade of Bordeaux to the proctor of Wilham Swyntborna,
March 22, 1416, see Jurade, 336. He was brother and executor to Thomas Swinburn,
knight, late Mayor of Bordeaux, Wylie, iii. 99 (not Strimburn, as Ribadieu, Châteaux,
380), from whom that city had bought the castle of Ornon (Jurade, 41, 86; Drouyn,
Guienne, i. p. l.; Wylie, iii. 273) in the parish of Gradignan, south of Bordeaux, Beaurein,
ii. 342, where Henry Bowet has permission to sell the castle of Ornon to Bordeaux
in 1406. For William Swinburn and the executors of Sir Thomas Swinburn, see Jurade,
288, Nov. 23, 1415. For one of them, Thomas Barton (Wylie, iii. 98, note 6) going
to Aquitaine on July 14, 1413, see Priv. Seal 658/73; Rot. Vasc. 1 H. V, 10. For Sir
Thomas Swynburne, kt. and Elizabeth Tryvet his wife as patrons of the living of Otter-
hampton near Bridgwater, Nov. 17, Dec. 15, 1406, see Holmes, Reg. 64, 65. In Rot.
Vasc. 3 H. V, 2, Aug. 29, 1415, Thos. is *late* constable of Fronsak. For les procureurs
de l'eretey de mossenhor Thomas Swyntborna, see Jurade, 346 (1416). For William
Swynbourne, M.P. for Essex in Nov. 1414, see Return Parl. i. 283.

[2] For Marck, see Wylie, ii. 89, called "Marc" in Sandeman, 34, who regards it as a
"strongly fortified *town*." For confirmation of privileges to the inhabitants of Marck,
see Fr. Roll 1 H. V, 34, 35, June 30, 1413.

[3] Priv. Seal Bills 1115/19; Fr. Roll 1 H. V, 16, Dec. 5, 1413, see Wylie, iii. 59,
note 6.

[4] Iss. Roll 1 H. V, Pasch., July 4, 1413.

[5] Wylie, iii. 306; Exch. Accts. 187/6.

[6] Wylie, iii. 60; iv. 72; called Balinghem in Harbaville, ii. 186; Ardouin-Dumazet,
xviii. 297; Joanne and Cochery, s.v., but Bevelinghen in Bonaparte, ii. 69; St Denys, iii.
551; Balinghin on map of 1544, in Vaillonet, Plate x; Baveling' on a seal, 1348, in
Demay, i. 78, not Banellingham as Rym. ix. 490; nor Banelinghen as Henry, 80. Exch.
Accts. 187/6 contains payments to Roger Salvayn (see page 41), for custody of Bave-
linghem from Aug. 6, 1414, to Aug. 6, 1417, with 4 + 24 (half mounted and half pedit')
and 12 balisters. For garrison = 13 + 14 and 12 balisters, July 16, 1421, see Exch. Accts.
187/10.

[7] Page 37, note 1.

governors that an enquiry was held before the Earl of Arundel as Treasurer of England and William Lord Zouche as Lieutenant for the Earl of Warwick. The enquiry was opened at Calais on Aug. 24, 1414, and evidence was submitted to a jury of 12 burgesses all of whom possess genuine English names[1], and much valuable statistical matter is consequently now available in the documents which still exist and relate to these transactions[2]. The evidence submitted had reference to alleged frauds committed during the time of the four victuallers[3] who held office at Calais when Henry IV was king. These were Reginald Curteys[4](twice), Robert Thorley[5], Richard Marlow[6] and Richard Clitherow[7] and the captains mentioned are John Beaufort Earl of Somerset (1401–1410)[8] and the Prince of Wales (1410–1413)[9]. The items in question are arranged under the headings of the various commodities such as malt, barley, beans, oats, salt (both white and coarse[10]), sea-coal[11], billets (at 3s. 4d. per 1000), bows (2s. each)[12], bowstrings (8d. per dozen), arrows with heads (2s. per sheaf), lances without heads (1s. 8d. to 2s. each),

[1] Viz. Thomas Somerford, John Watford, John Amery, William Elnar, John Bristowe, Richard Baker, Roger Best, Edmund Fraunceys, Thomas Frankeleyn, Robert Louthe, Robert Nicholl and John Stanley, junr.

[2] Exch. Accts. 187/3, 4.

[3] For the victualler and purveyor at Calais, see Sandeman, 88.

[4] Wylie, iv. 231, Jan. 20, 1400.

[5] Page 38, note 2.

[6] Wylie, ii. 110.

[7] Page 39, note 3.

[8] Appointed March 23, 1401, Carte, Rolles, ii. 181; Sandeman, 11; Wylie, i. 206; Doyle, iii. 343.   For his death at 37 years of age, see Oman, Pol. Hist. 219.   For reference to inquisition after his death held in Middlesex, June 28, 1410, see Iss. Roll 3 H. V, Mich., Oct. 28, 1415; ibid. 4 H. V, Pasch., May 14, 1416; ibid. 5 H. V, Mich., Feb. 10, 1418; ibid. 8 H. V, Pasch., May 11, 1420; Devon, 343, showing that he died on Palm Sunday, 11 H. IV (i.e. March 16, 1410, Walcott, Cant. 51; Wylie, iii. 304), not 1419, as Hassell, 221.   For his brother Bishop Beaufort, as one of the executors of his will, see Iss. Roll 3 H. V, Pasch., April 12, 1415; For. Accts. 4 H. V, 14 d; Exch. Accts. 187/6. For the Bishop's dispute with John Doreward in regard to the will, see Pat. 4 H. V, 19 d, July 28, 1416.

[9] Appointed March 18, 1410, Carte, Rolles, ii. 199; Sandeman, 11; Wylie, iii. 306.

[10] Sal gross'.   For gros sel (or sel gris) and sel menu, see Fréville, i. 293; sel blanc de Languedoc, Spont, 431; Cotgr., s.v.; sel noir de Guérande (Brittany), Spont, 430; sel de Poitou or de Ponant (i.e. black or grey salt), Fréville, i. 293, i.e. for Marennes, Arvert, Oléron and Ré, Spont, 430, 431.   In Le Quesnoy black salt costs 20 to 25 sols the load (*charge*), but white costs 5 livres, i.e. 4 or 5 times as much, the white being much the heavier, Spont, 433.   For salt albi, see Amyot, 278.

[11] For carbones maritimi to be sent from Newcastle to London, see Pat. 3 H. V, ii. 21, Dec. 5, 1415; charbon de mier imported at Sandwich, Boys, 556; 4 quarters of "see cole" 8d., Aubrey, ii. 58, from books of the Brewers' Company, 1425.

[12] Cf. Wylie, iv. 230.   For £70 paid for timber and £9 paid for 300 bowstaves, see Iss. Roll 1 H. V, Mich., Dec. 1, 1413.

lance-heads (7*d.* to 1*s.* each), fir spars[1] at 3*d.* to 6*d.* each, iron at 6*s.* 8*d.* the cwt.[2], and quick lime[3] (8*d.* to 1*s.* per quarter). Besides this there are winches[4], haucepies[5], hendriks for stretching the arblasts (*p' balist' tendend'*), winchards and quarrels for the springalds, iron plates for winging (*pro pennacione*) bolts, lathnails[6], gut for housetiles (*nerff' pur housetile*), coarse gut (*nerff' gross'*), grease[7] and glue. The account also contains particulars of the revenues of the place with lists of the tenants of hostels, cottages, shops, rooms, cellars[8] &c. in many of the streets[9].

[1] Sparr' de ffir', cf. bothe sparre and rafter, Lydg., Troy Book, 140, Cotgrave, s.v. For sparrys (21*s.* the 100), see Maldon Rolls, 12*s.* 6*d.*; for scipplancken, sparren, middelhouten, posten, rebben, stylen, scraghen, corbulen, spillen, sloven, stansoeuen, wrangen, &c., see Gilliodts van Severen, Invent. iv. 172.

[2] Centena, called 108 lbs. in Du Cange, s.v.

[3] Cals' ustum, cf. pour estaindre chaux et mellier o sablon, Darne, 87. For "lyme and ston," see Kail, 66; murs de pers et de chaux, Burtt, 56.

[4] For winches used in building Dunster Church in 1444, see Lyte, 134.

[5] Wylie, iii. 41, Haucepy, Murray's Dict., s.v.; haussepiez, Darne, 41; cf. poudres, canons hauchepiez et tous aultres abillements pour la guerre, Bréquigny, 117; arbalêtes d'un pied et leurs haussepieds, Bonis, I. cxii; un hauspie a parer arbalaistres, Port, 328; hausspee a tandre, ibid. 329; spelt Hanespeces, Hanespeces, or Hausepeces in For. Accts. 3 H. V (? neck-pieces); hauchepied, A. Martin, i. 151 (1336); = marchepied (stirrup or stretcher) pour tendre avec le pied les grosses arbalestes à tour, Godefroy, s.v. For aucepis, a wolf trap for jerking a noose with the foot, see York, 34, possibly chausse-pieds, i.e. slippers.

[6] Cf. Lyte, Dunster, 118; clou a latter, Monget, ii. 12. For clou chestival or quetiveil, Godefroy, s.v. clou a lath (Aussy, Reg. iii. 111 = lath Cotgr., s.v.); cf. in peciis meremii vocatis lates, Hist. MSS. 15th Rept. App. Pt x. p. 144; clou renfoncé (thick), grant clou a coustre (= rib, Cotgr., s.v. or coulter, Cotgr.), les doubliers et les noes (i.e. noues = gutter, Littré, s.v.; Godefroy, s.v. noe) de la salle, Darne, 62. For bordnales, see Baildon, Star Chamber, 28; traversnails, ibid. 29; lednails, ibid. 30. For 1 cratnail (i.e. cartnail), 6*d.* in 1383, see Scrope, 163. For 16*s.* 11*d.* pro clerostis (cloutnails) brodis (brads) et lynoes (lining nails), Walcott, Vestiges, 52. For clou a latte, do. a chaussier, do. a plomb, Brièle, iii. 43.

[7] Silig' (? smigma). For cras (i.e. grease) at Rouen in 1315, see Chéruel, Commun, i. 320.

[8] Sufsalle (*sic*). Cf. de quodam celario et warderoba et celario sub iisdem (1253), G. F. Turner, 18, 27. For John Chambre al. John del celer, Ewald, xliv. 616. For celarium below the moothouse at Colchester to be fitted with decent windows and used as a woolmarket, Benham, 6, 12. Cf. at celer door, York, 100; hath in hir celer drinkes ful divers, Lydg., Troy Book, 145. Cf. thy sillers disclose, Secreta, 142. For a sellar, 2 solers and a latrine (1361), see Exeter Deeds no. 906; also sellers and sollers, ibid. no. 1623.

[9] e.g. Foresters Street, John Geralds (or Heralds) Street, Woodport Street, Boleyngate (al. Bolengate, see p. 38, note 5) Street, Begins (al. Bogines) Street, St Nicoll (i.e. Nicholas) Street, Richardoredhalle Street, Mesondew (i.e. Maisondieu) Street (in quo tenetur hospicium artillar' Dni Regis), Old Staple Court Street, Friars Street, Parsons Street, Bert Street, the Watchhouse, the Bolenwell, &c.

CHAPTER V

ITINERARY

THE king had spent the first three months of his reign chiefly at Westminster or Kennington[1], going down to Langley[2] on April 15, 1413[3], whither he summoned the new Chief Justice and his colleagues to confer with him when Easter was over[4]. We find him staying at Kennington till May 27, 1413, and he was there again in the early days of June. After the rising of the Parliament[5] he left Kennington with many of his lords on June 13 and travelled by Dartford[6], Rochester (June 14) and Ospringe (June 15) to Canterbury[7], the harness of the officers of his household having been sent down beforehand from Lambeth as far as Faversham by barge[8]. The party arrived at Canterbury on June 16[9] and on the following day the king gave a funeral feast in honour of his dead father, the cost of which is entered at £127. 7s. 2½d.[10] not including £5. 14s. 8d.[11]

---

[1] Rym. ix. 13.
[2] For the Manor of Kings (or Childs or Chiltern) Langley near Watford, see Clutter-buck, i. 433; R. Gee, 10; Cussans (Cashio), 86; Lewis, iii. 24. The remains known as King John's Bakehouse, shown in Clutterbuck, i. 433, are really a portion of the Priory buildings, the only remains of the Palace being "the merest fragment on the left of the road leading up the hill from the village." J. Evans, 308, 309. For Queen Joan at Langley on Feb. 23, 1411, see Pat. 1 H. V, i. 33. For fancy picture of the Palace, see Knight, Shakespeare Richard II, p. 124, called "an ideal elevation" in R. Gee, 10.
[3] Exch. Accts. 406/21, m. 5.
[4] For payments to messengers to William Hankford and his *socii* to come before the King at Langley in crastino Clauc. Pasch., see Iss. Roll 1 H. V, Pasch., May 4, 1413.
[5] Page 34.
[6] For 13s. 4d. paid to William Chaunderell for destruction of his garden, and 6s. 8d. to John Horner pro conculcatione domorum at Dartford, see Exch. Accts. 406/21, m. 30.
[7] For 13s. 4d. paid to Philip Cranbourne going to Canterbury for herbergage for the King and divers other lords of England, see ibid.
[8] Exch. Accts. 406/21, m. 22.
[9] For documents dated at Canterbury, June 16, 1413, see Priv. Seal 658/54; Fr. Roll 1 H. V, i. 33; Carte, Rolles, ii. 212; Ewald, xliv. 543, 552.
[10] Festum exequiarum regis defuncti, Exch. Accts. 406/21, m. 7.
[11] Ibid., m. 19.

paid for 1320 gallons of wine which had been previously forwarded by way of Leeds. On Trinity Sunday (June 18)[1] he attended a solemn service in the Cathedral at the grave in Beckett's Crown behind the high altar, where a hearse[2] had been put up at the cost of £100 on which candles and wax torches burned night and day[3] while 90 banners were displayed about it painted with the arms of all the kings of Christendom together with multitudes of fanes[4], getons and valances all gay with various devices[5]. The day finished up with a Trinity feast which cost the Exchequer £98. 16s. 3d.[6] and two days later[7] Archbishop Bowet founded a chantry[8] in the Minster at York for two priests who were to receive a yearly stipend of £6. 13s. 4d. each to sing for the souls of King Henry IV and Bishop Beaufort, their maintenance to be covered by appropriating the revenues of the parish church of Walton-on-Thames.

On June 19 the king set out from Canterbury, returning by Sittingbourne, Newington[9] and Rochester (June 20) to Kennington where he stayed from June 21 to 25[10]. On

---

[1] Rot. Vasc. 1 H. V, 12; Priv. Seal Bills 1114/52; Rym. ix. 27; Capgr. 303; Stow, Chron. 344; Wylie, iv. 114.

[2] For picture of a hearse with candles at the funeral of the Archbishop of Bari at Constance, see Richental (Prokhorof), 25.

[3] For £100 paid to a waxchandler for a hearse to be made and placed within Christ Church, Canterbury, for the vigil of Trinity with wax lights and other apparatus and 20 torches to burn round it, with 53s. 4d. paid for cloth for covering the barrier round it (*barr' pro hercia*), see Iss. Roll 1 H. V, Pasch., May 20, June 27, 1413.

[4] Fanez, Rym. ix. 3.

[5] Iss. Roll 1 H. V, Pasch., May 20, 1413, has £60 paid for making and painting 90 vexilla cum toto estuffamento pro eisdem (6s. 8d. each), 50 gytons with various arms and valances painted with ymagines to be placed in the hearse for the anniversary of Henry IV at Trinity next *now* in the Abbey of Christ Church at Canterbury. In Devon, 326, Nov. 15, 1413, the cost of the banners is given at 16s. 8d. each, and the getons at 3s.

[6] Exch. Accts. 406/21, m. 7.

[7] i.e. June 20, 1413, Pat. 1 H. V, 2, 19; Cal. Rot. Pat. 261; not Oct. 24, 1413, as Fabr. Rolls, 274.

[8] W. Page, 12, i.e. the Chantry of All Hallows on the south side of the Presbytery close to Bowet's tomb, Stevens, i. 60, 74; Drake, 519; Manning and Bray, ii. 770; but as the name of Richard Pitts, who was Archdeacon of Cleveland, March 11, 1411, to 1414 (Le Neve, iii. 147), when he became Treasurer of York Minster (Drake, 568), appears among the list of officials, it is probable that he really supplied the funds.

[9] For 6s. 8d. each paid to John Britiller hospitant' regem et familiam and Gilbert Atte Chitter at Waltham for his houses *defractis* while entertaining the king's *familia*, also 20d. paid to John Trigg at Newenton pro pejoracione vessellamentorum, see Exch. Accts. 406/21, m. 30.

[10] Though there is a document dated at Westminster, June 23, 1413, in Priv. Seal 658/55.

June 26[1] he was rowed up the river in his barge to Sutton[2] where a council was held on June 29[3] which advised that he should remain in the neighbourhood of London during the summer so that he might the more readily deal with any pressing business as soon as news of it should come in. In spite of this advice however he left Sutton on July 3, slept at Windsor on July 4, travelled down again by Dartford, Rochester and Ospringe (July 5) for another visit to Canterbury, where he passed the night on July 6 and 7[4]. The purpose of this second journey was probably purely devotional in order to visit the shrine of St Thomas on the great Translation Festival (July 7) and make in person the offering of a golden head inwrought with pearls and precious stones which he had ordered at a cost of £160[5] together with two golden candlesticks weighing 18 marks troy[6]. On the following day he started to return, slept at Faversham on July 8 and 9, was at Rochester on July 10 and passed through Dartford on the 11th to Westminster where he transacted business for a few days. On July 17[7] he was at the Lodge in Windsor Park where he rusticated with his falconers[8] and feuterers[9]

---

[1] Exch. Accts. 406/21, m. 8.

[2] For the King's barge passing between Sutton and Shene, see Exch. Accts. 406/21, m. 23. For payments before Oct. 31, 1413, to William Godeman (who had succeeded Robert Atte Were, Wylie, iv. 29, 213) as Master of the King's barge and a crew of 16 bargemen for passages to Sutton, Westminster, Lambeth and Rotherhithe, see Exch. Accts. 406/21, m. 21. In do. m. 22 Robert Atte Were is *defunctus*. For extracts relating to the King's barge, see Lega Weekes, 167. For payments to John Freeman, the ferryman at Datchet, see Exch. Accts. 406/21, mm. 22, 30. Cf. Wylie, iv. 203.

[3] Ord. Priv. Co. ii. pp. xii, 125.

[4] Exch. Accts. 406/21, m. 8. Not that Rochester was the farthest point reached, as Ramsay, i. 167.

[5] Devon, 322.

[6] Pat. 2 H. V, ii. 38.

[7] apud Logen de Windsor, Iss. Roll 1 H. V, Pasch., July 17, 1413; Exch. Accts. 406/21, m. 2, probably in the Little Park to the east of the castle, Tighe and Davis, i. 75, 369; Archaeologia, xxvi. 277.

[8] For his falconers, see Exch. Accts. 406/21, m. 32. For Robert Morton esquire, keeper of the King's falcons, see Iss. Roll 1 H. V, Mich., Oct. 10, 1413.

[9] For Roger Kent, Feuterer de Buckehoundes, see Pat. 1 H. V, ii. 33. For feuterer (i.e. dog keeper), see Halliwell, 355; Ogilvie, Dict. i. 744; not tenterer, as Wylie, iii. 245; York, p. xxii. For veltrars, see York, 105, 144; or veautrers (valtrarii), G. F. Turner, s.v.; not veantrer, as Rot. Parl. v. 167; cf. Tho veloter two caste of brede he rase, Two lesshe of grehoundes yf that he have, Manners and Meals, i. 320, ii. 127. Called men who held the hounds in slips or couples, York, 72, 107, 162; Godefroy, s.v. vautroi; Cotgr., s.v. vaultre, valtri; G. F. Turner, 151; veltre, veltris, veltrehus, vertragus, York, 142, 199; Prompt. Parv., s.v. grehounde (gresehounde), veltraga, vertagus; Fuller, Worthies, ii. 4, who derives it from velt (i.e. field) and rach (i.e. brach); not boarhounds, as Littré, s.v. vautri al. veltre, viautre. For account of William Brocas, Master of the King's "buk-hundes," on July 5, 1449, see Cal. Pat. P.R.O. H. VI, iv. 241, showing ½d. per day each

for the rest of the month with the exception of a short visit to Kingston on the 21st[1]. On Aug. 1[2] he watched a wrestling match in Windsor Forest[3], and on the same day he sent to the monks at Westminster[4] a huge stag which had just fallen to his cross-bow[5]. From Aug. 2 to 11 he was at Henley-on-the-Heath[6] and from Aug. 15 to Sept. 23 his time was mainly spent at Windsor[7] where he was present at the consecration of Bishop Courtenay on Sept. 17[8]. From Sept. 24 to Oct. 8 he was at Guildford[9] whither 1200 marks in money were sent down to him[10] for the expenses of the household[11]. On Oct. 9, 1413, he was

for food for 30 hounds (i.e. 24 running dogs and 6 greyhounds), wages of 1 yeoman vautrer (2*d.* per day), and 2 yeomen called berners (1½*d.* per day).

[1] For 3*s.* 8*d.* paid to John Harlande at Kingston, pro occupatione domorum, see Exch. Accts. 406/21, m. 30.

[2] Exch. Accts. 406/21, m. 23.

[3] For description of Windsor Forest, see J. C. Cox, 287–300.

[4] For 8 fallow deer from Windsor Forest given by Henry III to the Abbey where the huntsman blew 2 menees (Halliwell, ii. 549) on his horn at the high altar when delivering them, see York, 177.

[5] Memorials, 71. For the cross-bow used in hunting the deer, see Gaston Phoebus in Gallwey, 43, 49, 78, 79, with dogs retrieving bolts, ibid. 33.

[6] For documents dated at Henley, Aug. 11, 1413, see Priv. Seal 628/81; also Aug. 28, 1415, ibid. 628/88; Pat. 1 H. V, iii. 6; iv. 25. For repairs to Henley-on-the-Heath in 1413, see Exch. Accts. 502/29, including tiles for pointing rooms brought from Aldborough (i.e. Albury) and Guildford, also for sowding (i.e. soldering) defects in a gutter.

[7] He was at Windsor Aug. 15, 18, 20, 22, 27, 1413, Exch. Accts. 406/21, m. 19; Rym. ix. 46; also Sept. 16, 17, 18, 20, 1413, Pat. 1 H. V, iii. 17, 18; v. 17; Claus. 1 H. V, 18, 22 d; Fr. Roll 1 H. V, 22; Cotton MS. Calig. D. 5, f. 1. For messengers sent from Windsor Park with tallies and letters of the Treasurer of England to the customers of Southampton, see Exch. Accts. 406/21, m. 32 d. For a document dated at Westminster on Aug. 19, 1413, see Rot. Scot. ii. 207.

[8] Stubbs, Reg. 85; Mowbray, 165.

[9] For 21*s.* 8*d.* paid for damage to house and vessels at Guildford, see Exch. Accts. 406/21, m. 30. For 2*s.* 4*d.* paid to John Feriby for travelling 7 days from the court at Guildford to London, Windsor, Sutton, Kennington, Westminster, Eltham and Merton, see ibid. m. 23. In Rec. Roll 1 H. V, Mich., Nov. 8, 1413, John Feriby (or Fearby, Wylie, ii. 476, note 8) and John Wake are farmers of the subsidy and of ulnage of cloth in Norfolk, Suffolk, Essex and Herts.; called Fereby et socii in Rec. Roll 3 H. V, Mich., Nov. 8, 1415.

[10] For payment to Robert Burton sent to Guildford with 1200 marks to be delivered to the King and the Treasurer of the Household there, see Iss. Roll 1 H. V, Mich., Oct. 2, 1413. The Earl of Arundel as Treasurer of England was there also, Exch. Accts. 406/21, m. 12, Oct. 2, 1413, which records £200 received from him at Guildford.

[11] For compotus of Thomas More, Treasurer of the Royal Household (appointed May 28, 1401, Cal. Pat. H. IV, i. 445) from March 23, 1413, to Oct. 31, 1413, when he was succeeded by Roger Leche, kt., see Exch. Accts. 406/21, during which time the total expenditure = £8600. 17*s.* 0*d.*, including £6. 10*s.* 1*d.* given in alms at the daily mass. On April 4, 1413, Thomas de Brounflete, knight, late Treasurer of the Household to Henry IV (Wylie, ii. 475, note 13; iii. 284, note 5), handed over to Thomas More, now Treasurer of the Hostel to Henry V, jewels and vessels the exact weights of which are all recorded, including deep chargers (?dip-chargers, Wylie, iv. 198, 210), candelabra, a large pot (*cacabus*, see Wylie, iv. 198), ladles and chaufrons, see Exch. Accts. 406/17. For inventory of dishes, &c., valued at £976. 10*s.* 0½*d.*, see ibid. 406/20. For Thomas More, clerk, *late* Keeper of the Wardrobe, see Iss. Roll 3 H. V, Mich., Feb. 20, 23,

at the Abbey at Chertsey and from Oct. 10 till the end of that month at the Augustinian Priory at Merton[1], after which the Court appears to have removed to Kennington[2] and thence to Eltham[3] for the winter.

1415, which refers *inter alia* to supplies of pike, flounders and other fish, faggots, talwood, &c. (for tallwodde and smallwodde, see Essex Herald, 28/3/05). In Pat. 4 H. V, 17, June 1, 1416, More is *nuper* Thesaurarius; also Iss. Roll 6 H. V, Pasch., Mich., June 20, 1418; Feb. 14, 1419. For wages (£31. 7s. 9d.) and robes (53s. 4d.) to Thomas More as Treasurer of King's Household for Michaelmas Term, 1413, see Exch. Accts. 406/21, m. 27. On June 1, 1416, he is *late* Treasurer of the King's Hostel, Rym. ix. 357. For references to him as holding the same office, see Wylie, i. 301 (Oct. 22, 1403); Pat. 1 H. V, i. 28, April 12, 1413; Cal. Rot. Pat. 260; Iss. Roll 1 H. V, Pasch., May 4, 1413; Rec. Roll 1 H. V, Pasch., Sept. 18, 1413. Thomas More was Dean of St Paul's (so called in Pat. 3 H. V, i. 31, June 25, 1415) from Jan. 1407 till his death in Dec. 1421, Le Neve, ii. 312. He had before held the prebends of Chamberlainewood (St Paul's) in 1390, Aylesbury (Linc.) in 1395, and Leicester St Margaret (Linc.) in 1399, ibid. 168, 374, 395. On Nov. 3, 1398, he was made Archdeacon of Colchester, ibid. 340. He rebuilt the chapel in the Pardonchurchyard (or Pardonchurchhaugh, Benham-Welch, 59) on the north side of St Paul's, and was himself buried there on Jan. 4, 1422, Stow, 122 (ed. 1876), called the Charnel Chapel, i.e. over the charnelhouse, where two brotherhoods were founded in 1379, Knight, London, iv. 222. More had likewise added the cloister in which was afterwards painted the picture of the Dance of Death known as the Dance of Paul's, with Lydgate's verses (MacCracken, xii; Benham, 10), translated from those in the cemetery of the Innocents near the Halles in Paris. For permission to him to found a chantry dedicated to St Anne and St Thomas the Martyr for 3 chaplains in the chapel called "Pardonchirchehawe," see Pat. 3 H. V, ii. 31. It was destroyed temp. Ed. VI, the materials being used in building Somerset House, when the bones were removed to Finsbury, where they formed a bone-hill (now Bunhill Fields), Benham-Welch, 59. In 1421 More was received *in fraternitatem* at St Albans, and his executors contributed 26s. ad opera hujus ecclesiae, Amundesham, i. 65.

[1] Exch. Accts. 406/21, mm. 9–17. For John Romeney, elected Prior of Merton, see Pat. 1 H. V, i. 28, May 1, 1413. For money delivered to the King at Merton, see Iss. Roll 1 H. V, Mich., Oct. 17, 1413. For reference to the Treasurer of England at Merton, see ibid. Oct. 21, 1413, with an entry on the same day of 71s. 8d. +£6. 2s. 1d. for breakfast at Westminster (one day) for the Chancellor, Treasurer and other Lords of the Council, together with the Justices and barons for electing sheriffs, escheators and Justices of the Peace.

[2] For an indenture dated at Kennington, Nov. 1, 1413, see Exch. Accts. 406/18.

[3] For reference to the Treasurer at Eltham and 7s. 8d. paid to a malemaker (Wylie, iv. 274) for 4 pairs of budgets (bowges) to carry a certain sum of money from Westminster Abbey to Eltham with all speed, see Iss. Roll 1 H. V, Mich., Nov. 8, 1413; Feb. 16, 22, 1414; also for the Keeper of the Wardrobe at Eltham, ibid. Dec. 9, 1413.

CHAPTER VI

SCOTLAND

NEGOTIATIONS that had been pending with Scotland during the closing months of the late reign[1] were allowed to proceed and safe-conducts were issued for Walter Forrester Bishop of Brechin[2], Clerk of the Rolls of Scotland[3], and others who were coming to treat for the release of King James.

On April 12, 1413[4], an order was made out for the liberation of Sir James Douglas and 24 other Scots[5] from the Tower, the list including John of Alwa or Alway[6], Robert Scrimgeour, who had been macer to King Robert III[7], Dougall Drummond, chaplain to King James, who became the medium of further negotiations[8], and John Wells, afterwards the king's confidential servant to whom

---

[1] For a safe-conduct dated Feb. 7, 1413, see Rot. Scot. ii. 202 ; Exch. Roll Scot. iv. p. lxxvii.

[2] Rym. ix. 5, 48; Rot. Scot. ii. 204, 207; Cal. Doc. Scot. iv. 169, April 16, 1413.

[3] i.e. from 1410 to 1425, Exch. Roll Scot. iv. 127, 132, 134, 159, 160, 166, 185, 191, 208, 214, 234, 240, 261, 267, 284, 290, 306, 310, 332, 337, 352, 358, 373, 379.

[4] Claus. 1 H. V, 37 ; Rym. ix. 5.

[5] For order for them to be committed to the Tower per John Drax, dated April 2, 1413 (called Apr. 8 in Cal. Doc. Scot. iv. 169), see Claus. 1 H. V, 36. For order for their release, April 14, 1413, see Rym. ix. 5.

[6] Possibly Alva near Alloa; called "Aulway" in Cal. Doc. Scot. iv. 169, 180. In 1416–17 he is a servant to John Lyon (or Lyouns, ibid. p. 176). He was Clerk of the Cocket at Haddington in 1431, Exch. Roll Scot. iv. 391, 530, 591.

[7] Cal. Doc. Scot. iv. 470 and *passim*. For portrait of Robert III from Newbattle Abbey, see Cowan, i. 141; for fancy picture of him, Jonston, Inscriptiones, i; Pinkerton, Iconographia. For his seal (conventional), see Anderson, Diplomata, Plate LX; Pinkerton. For his medal with sword, sceptre, orb, crown and motto: *His ornari aut mori*, see Anderson, Diplomata, Plate CLXXVI. He is called "the old and valetudinary king" in D. Stewart, 61, who dates his death March 29, 1405, instead of April 4, 1406; see Wylie, ii. 390; Lawson, xvi; Rait, Scotland, 109.

[8] Exch. Roll Scot. iv. pp. lxxxv, 339, 344, 345, 347.

he entrusted the care of his little daughters Margaret and Elizabeth[1]. The balance of the Earl of Douglas' ransom[2] was likewise paid off and on Aug. 26, 1413[3], a permit was issued for him to cross from France and have an interview with King Henry.

But during those months events were happening which kept English vigilance from being ever lulled to sleep.

The truce with Scotland had still five years to run and would not formally expire till Easter 1418[4], but in view of the prevailing temper it was now decided that if satisfactory terms could not be arranged for the future outlook, the forces of Lancashire, Yorkshire, Nottingham, Lincoln and Derby should be placed at the disposal of the Wardens of the Marches to strengthen their position and enable them to insist effectually upon compliance with all necessary demands. An immediate instalment of 50 men-of-arms and 100 archers was despatched to the East March with £455 assigned to pay their wages while a force of half that strength was sent to Carlisle[5]. The Earl of Westmoreland received £939. 17s. 6½d.[6] to pay his troops on the West March and sums amounting to £1950. 10s. 8d.[7] were sent as wages for the garrison at Berwick to the king's brother John[8], to whom grants were made of manors and fishing rights on the Scottish side of the Tweed[9]. Robert Umfraville was summoned to appear before the Council at Westminster by the middle of August 1413[10] in order to arrange for the future custody of Roxburgh which had been granted to him for six years in 1411 with an allowance of

---

[1] Exch. Roll Scot. iv. pp. ci, 411, 437, 438, 473, 508.

[2] Viz. 700 marks, Rym. ix. 718; Rot. Scot. ii. 205. For meetings at Cawthorpe (near Louth) and Raby to discuss ransoms in 1413, see Rym. ix. 49; Rot. Scot. ii. 204, 208. Barrett (108) seems to think that the Earl of Douglas was set free immediately after the battle of Shrewsbury, but his whole account of the battle is uncritical and unreliable.

[3] Rym. ix. 48; Rot. Scot. ii. 207; Chancery Warrants, Ser. i. 1364/1; Michel, Ecossais, i. 113.

[4] Wylie, ii. 393; iii. 281.

[5] Ord. Priv. Co. ii. 133.

[6] i.e. £625 for wages from March 21, 1413, Iss. Roll 1 H. V, Pasch., July 24, 1413, and £314. 17s. 6½d., ibid. Mich., Nov. 15, 1413.

[7] Viz. £1325. 10s. 8d., Iss. Roll 1 H. V, Pasch., July 24, 1413 (not £1335 as Devon, 323), + £625 Iss. Roll 1 H. V, Mich., Nov. 15, 1413.

[8] For his appointment as keeper of the town and castle of Berwick, see Pat. 1 H. V, iii. 41, June 12, 1413.

[9] Rot. Scot. ii. 207.

[10] Ord. Priv. Co. ii. 135.

£1200 per annum in war-time and 1000 marks in time of
peace[1]. Half of this amount was still in arrears but before
the king had been a year on the throne the annual allowance
had been paid up in full[2] and on May 24, 1414[3], an order
was sent out for stone-cutters, carpenters and labourers to
repair the castle, arrangements being at the same time
made for the carriage of corn, beer and provisions for
victualling the garrison. The traders of Berwick[4] were in
the meantime to be kept in good humour by a ten-years
renewal of their privileges whereby the rate of duty was
reduced on wool grown between Teviotdale and the
Coquet[5]. On July 19, 1413[6], Robert Umfraville and
Robert Ogle were appointed to negotiate on behalf of the
king of England; on Aug. 7[7] three Scottish knights[8] were
commissioned by the Duke of Albany, who was then at
Doune Castle on the Teith, to meet them on the Border
and on Sept. 26, 1413, a truce with Scotland was proclaimed
to last till June 1, 1414[9], and it was while these negotiations
were going on that the safe-conduct was issued[10] for the Earl
of Douglas to come by land to Calais with 40 persons,
cross thence to any of the Cinq Ports and return to France
or Flanders.

Communications had been for some time passing
between the Dukes of Albany and Burgundy and when
Henry IV was dying, a Scottish knight named John Bothwell[11]
was with the latter from whom he brought back a handsome
chamber[12] of Arras as a present to the Duke of Albany in

---

[1] Wylie, iii. 280; Ord. Priv. Co. ii. 133, 134.

[2] Viz. £166. 13s. 4d. + £366. 13s. 4d. + £133. 6s. 8d., Iss. Roll 1 H. V, Pasch.,
Mich., July 4, 1413, Feb. 22, 1414; Cal. Rot. Scot. iv. 170.

[3] Rot. Scot. ii. 211.

[4] For fresh letters issued to Robert Umfraville as Chamberlain and Customer of
Berwick on April 6, 1415, to replace those which he had lost dated June 17, 1404, when
he was appointed to succeed Gerard Heron, kt., *defunctus* on payment of £40 p. a., see
Rot. Scot. ii. 213.

[5] Rot. Scot. ii. 206.   [6] Rym. ix. 40; Rot. Scot. ii. 206.

[7] Rym. ix. 45; Kal. and Inv. ii. 89; Goodwin, 11.

[8] Viz. Patrick Dunbar of Bail, son of the Scottish Earl of March (Exch. Roll Scot.
iv. 250), William Hay of Locherwart or Lochorward (ibid. iv. 76, 115), and William
Borthwick (ibid. iv. 115, 144, 224).

[9] Rym. ix. 60.

[10] Viz. on Aug. 26, 1413, see p. 53, n. 3. For belief that this safe-conduct was not
used, see Dict. Nat. Biogr. xv. 265.

[11] Called Boutheville in Laborde, i. 97; cf. Bothville, Cal. Doc. Scot. iv. 128,
131, 134.

[12] Une chambre de tapisserie de haute lisse, Michel, Ecossais, i. 114. For chambres
de tapisserie, see Bulletin de la Soc. archéol. de Touraine, i. 259. Cf. chambres, tapis,

Scotland.   It is not surprising therefore to find that during
the spring and summer of this year the Earl of Douglas had
been in Paris in company with the Earl of Orkney[1] where he
formed an alliance with the Duke of Burgundy on April 2,
1413[2], whereby he agreed to bring 4000 Scots to the service
of the Duke in Artois or Flanders, as might be arranged, the
Duke of Burgundy on his side undertaking to land 300 men
in Scotland if required, and it is probable that the Earl of
Douglas now seized the opportunity of putting himself right
with the dominant Armagnacs who were just reasserting
themselves against the violence of the Cabochians, while
his ally the Duke of Burgundy was at that very moment
being driven from power in the capital.   In the meantime
the Duke of Albany had bestirred himself on behalf of his
eldest son, the captive Murdach, and sent his second son
John Earl of Buchan[3], then Chamberlain of Scotland[4], accompanied by his chaplain John Busby to England in the
autumn of 1413 to arrange if possible for his release[5].   On
July 16, 1413[6], passports were issued for William Cockburn[7],
John Sinclair and others to visit England.   Others again
such as Robert Maxwell of Calderwood[8] and Master
Robert Lany (or Lanyn) Provost of St Andrews[9] followed

carreaux d'ouvrage, Deschamps, viii. 137; une chambre blanche de satino à devise de
faucons et autres oiseaulx volans garniz de 6 tappiz de Guinec to cost 4000 liv. tourn.,
Lecoy de la Marche, Manuscrits, 179.
    [1] Wylie, ii. 395/2, 399/1; not 1412, as Bower, ii. 447; Maxwell, i. 141; Rait,
Quair, 17, supposes that he was "tutor" (i.e. instructor) to King James, and remained
with him throughout.
    [2] Gachard, 44; not April 11, as Plancher, iii. 373; nor 1412, as Michel, Ecossais,
i. 113; Beaumont, i. 306.
    [3] Not eldest son, as Maxwell, i. 140; called "Bughan" in Rym. ix. 244, or
"Bogham," Rym. ix. 48; Rot. Scot. ii. 208; cf. Wylie, ii. 264. He had been made
Earl of Buchan in 1408, being then about 28 years of age, Pinkerton, Iconographia,
who gives a fancy picture of him from a private collection near Chambord (Loir et Cher).
For his marriage in 1413 (contracted in July 1410, Maxwell, i. 140) with Elizabeth,
daughter of Archibald Earl of Douglas, see Douglas, Peerage, i. 266; Exch. Roll Scot.
iv. p. clxxxiii; but cf. Wylie, ii. 382, note 6.
    [4] Exch. Roll Scot. iv. pp. l, clxxxii, 261, 262 (June 27, 1416), 326, 327. For his
account as Chamberlain of Scotland rendered at Perth on July 28, 1420, by his deputy
John Forster of Corstorphine, see ibid. pp. 332–336.
    [5] Rym. ix. 48; Rot. Scot. ii. 207, Sept. 1, 1413. For safe conduct, dated July 6, 1413,
for Alexander Carnys Provost of Lincluden and Master Gilbert Kaime or Cavane till
Nov. 1, 1413, see Priv. Seal 658/72; Rym. ix. 30; Cal. Doc. Scot. iv. 169.
    [6] Rym. ix. 40; Rot. Scot. ii. 206, 207.
    [7] He was customer of Haddington and was absent in England on July 3, 1413, Exch.
Roll Scot. iv. 177. For his death in 1419 see Bower, iv. 1212.
    [8] Near Kilbride in Lanarkshire, Exch. Roll Scot. iv. 238.
    [9] Ibid. iv. 142, 163, 211, 223, 238; called "Langue" in Menteith, i. 245.

in November[1] and on Dec. 19, 1413[2], Sir William Douglas of Drumlanrig[3], Alexander Scheles of Peebles[4] and John Wells were all in London and had personal interviews with King Henry about the release of the Scottish King James who, as we have seen, was then lodged in the Tower[5].   On Aug. 3, 1413[6], an order was issued to deliver him and Murdach to the custody of the constable of Windsor[7] but both were back again in the Tower by Oct. 31, 1413[8].   In the following year the release of King James seemed so near at hand[9] that 5000 marks out of the money expected for his deliverance was earmarked for payment of the wages of the garrison at Calais[10] but in spite of protracted negotiations his actual release was really as far off as ever and on Feb. 22, 1415[11], he was sent to the dreary flats at

---

[1] For their safe-conducts dated Nov. 13, 1413, Feb. 11, May 8, June 28, July 20, 1414, see Rym. ix. 71, 113, 125, 145; Rot. Scot. ii. 209, 210, 211; Exch. Roll Scot. iv. pp. lxxi, lxxviii. For £120 paid to them in 1414 for expenses of two journeys to England pro liberatione domini nostri regis see ibid. iv. 211. For safe-conduct dated Oct. 10, 1413, for Sir J. Drummond of Concraig (near Crieff) coming to England, see Cal. Doc. Scot. iv. 170.   [2] Rym. ix. 79, 80; Rot. Scot. ii. 209.

[3] For safe-conduct for his return dated Feb. 8, 1414, see Rot. Scot. ii. 209. For permission dated Oct. 15, 1414, for him to come to Berwick to fight with John Clifford kt., see ibid. ii. 212; Rym. ix. 161, subsequently altered to Carlisle Dec. 16, 1414, ibid. ix. 192.

[4] Exch. Roll Scot. iv. 23.   [5] Page 1, note 11.

[6] Rym. ix. 44; Cal. Doc. Scot. iv. 170; J. T. T. Brown, 93; Tighe and Davis, i. 278, who think that King James was at Windsor for 11 years.

[7] On May 7, 1413, Sir John Stanley is referred to as Constable of Windsor Castle, Pat. 1 H. V, iii. 44; cf. A. W. Moore, i. 211; Wylie, ii. 292; and on his departure for Ireland John Wyntershull was appointed as his lieutenant Sept. 5, 1413, in place of John Horsey *exoneratus*, Pat. 1 H. V, iii. 12 d; Tighe and Davis, i. 283, who quote Ashmole MS. 1115, f. 38 b, for Robert Wythele as seneschal (i.e. steward) of Windsor with John Hagdoun and William Tyler, bailiffs in 1 H. V. For John Hargrove appointed parker of Windsor *vice* Thomas Walton deceased see Pat. 1 H. V, i. 23, May 14, 1413. Stanley died in Ireland on Jan. 18, 1414, and on Jan. 28 John Waterton the Master of the King's destrers was appointed to succeed him as Constable of Windsor with custody of the parks, Pat. 1 H. V, v. 25; Cal. Rot. Pat. H. V, i. 155; For. Accts. 4 H. V, m. 12.

[8] For payments to Roger Leche keeper of the wardrobe (see page 50, note 11), for expenses of the King of Scots together with Murdach and Griffin in the Tower, Feb. 22, Oct. 20, Nov. 9, 1414, see Cal. Doc. Scot. iv. 171, 172; J. T. T. Brown, 94; also from Oct. 1, 1414, to Feb. 23, 1415, at 20s. per day per William Hoodleston or Hudleston, see Exch. Accts. 406/29; Rym. ix. 189, Dec. 8, 1414.

[9] For safe-conduct, May 8, 1414, for John Porter (Wylie, ii. 399, note 5) coming from Scotland to see Murdach of Fyfe, see Rym. ix. 125. For instructions from the Duke of Albany dated at Falkirk May 26, 1414, to Robert Maxwell and Provost Lany (see page 55) to treat for the release of Murdach, see Menteith, i. 245, from "Cotton Library" turned into English—not that he was released shortly after Aug. 3, 1413, as Cowan, i. 167, who seems to doubt (p. 159) whether Albany had been a party to the negotiations.

[10] Gesta, 82, from Privy Seal Writs, State Paper Office, Bundle 9.

[11] Cal. Pat. H. V, i. 286, 352, where he is to be kept in certain places, to be agreed upon. See also Iss. Roll 3 H. V, Mich., Dec. 14, 1415; Devon, 343; Rym. ix. 203; Wylie, ii. 403; not 1414, as Cowan i. 167 (who seems to suppose that Pelham "resided at Windsor"); Lawson, xix. For payment to Pelham for food and clothing for King James from Feb. 2, 1415, to Dec. 30, 1415, see Rec. Roll 3 H. V, Mich., Dec. 12, 1415.

Pevensey under the charge of Sir John Pelham who received £700 per annum for his maintenance[1], being retransferred to the Tower after King Henry's return from Agincourt[2]. During this time good feeling certainly existed between the two sovereigns for we know that the prisoner James had presented Henry with three palfreys[3], and on Jan. 30, 1416[4], described him as "more gracious than he could say or write" while still urging that the Duke of Albany should do his duty for his deliverance.

[1] For his expenses from Dec. 19, 1415, to Jan. 28, 1416, see Iss. Roll 4 H. V, Pasch., April 30, Aug. 10, 1416. For John Pelham's park at Herstmonceux, see Ad Quod Damn. 368. For his will dated at Robertsbridge, Feb. 8, 1429 (not 1428 as Wylie, ii. 112), where he died on Feb. 12 following, see Collins, viii. 106; Inq. p. Mort. iv. 121. For value of his manors in Sussex with inventory dated Sept. 29, 1403, see Collins, viii. 97. On March 21, 1413, he was appointed a Justice of the Peace for Surrey and Sussex, Pat. 1 H. V, i. 35 d. He was commissioned to array the forces of Sussex on May 29, 1415, Rym. ix. 253 [255]; Pat. 3 H. V, ii. 37; Collins, viii. 103, and on Oct. 24, 1415, he was on a drainage commission for Peasemarch, Rye, Farleigh (i.e. Fairlight) and Pett, Pat. 3 H. V, i. 17 d.

[2] On Jan. 28, 1416, he was placed under the charge of Sir William Bourchier, Constable of the Tower, at a cost of 13s. 4d. per day, Devon, 345, March 18, 1416. For his expenses in the Tower at 13s. 4d. per day from Jan. 28, 1416, to Dec. 12, 1416, on which day Roger Aston the Lt-Governor was *exoneratus*, see For. Accts. 6 H. V, 20; Cal. Doc. Scot. iv. 175; Iss. Roll 4 H. V, Mich., Nov. 4, 1416; Add. MS. 24513, f. 13, where Roger Aston, kt., Lieutenant for William Bourchier Constable of the Tower, received payment on Aug. 10, 1416, on account of King James who had been in his custody since Jan. 24, 1416. For a letter from him to the city of Perth written in London, Aug. 8, 1416, see Menteith, i. 287.

[3] i.e. between 1414 and 1416, see Exch. Accts. 106/24 (1) where they are called "Bayard Kyng, Lyard Kyng and Blaunche Kyng." Also 2 palfreys, one of which was called "Dun Wodevyle," were given by King Henry to the Earl of Fyfe with 3 laton saddles and bits and reins (capistr').

[4] Menteith, i. 285, 286; Exch. Roll Scot. iv. p. lxxviii; Maxwell, i. 142; Lang, i. 292; Wylie, ii. 403, note 3; not 1417 as J. T. T. Brown, 94. The letters were sent to Scotland by John Lyon "belufit chapellayn" who was in London on Jan. 20, 1416, on which day a safe-conduct was issued for his return to Scotland available till April 1, 1416, Rot. Scot. ii. 215. For a curious quarrel as to priority of knowledge about these letters, see Burnett, 9, 15–19. If "Stratford Aw" from which they are written means Stratford on Avon James was apparently staying at the college there (see Monast. viii. 1471), if Stratford Abbey as Lawson, xxi, xc; Wylie, ii. 403, note 3, it is to be noted that this house was known as Stratford Langthorne (Monast. v. 586) which has been sometimes confused with St Leonard's nunnery at Bromley; called Stratford at Bow, Lysons, Environs, ii. 59; Monast. iv. 119; Ashbee, p. 3; called domus de S—juxta civitatem Londonii juxta stratam publicam situata, which was sunk in poverty temp. H. IV, V. Add. MS. 24062, f. 150.

CHAPTER VII

IRELAND

On June 8, 1413[1], Sir John Stanley was for the second time[2] made Lieutenant of Ireland in place of the king's brother the absentee Duke of Clarence[3]. The appointment was to last for six years on the understanding that he should receive 4000 marks (£2666. 13s. 4d.) for the first year and £2000 per annum afterwards, for the defence of the country over and above the cost of transport of his troops and baggage[4]. On June 19, 1413[5], orders were sent to the mayors of Liverpool and Lancaster arranging for the shipment of 1000 horses for him at ports in Lancashire and Cheshire, and on July 15, he was still preparing to start[6]. On Sept. 6, 1413[7], a proclamation was issued requiring that all Irishmen should return to their own land to

[1] Pat. 1 H. V, ii. 15; iii. 19, 34; iv. 36; Cal. Rot. Pat. 261; Ord. Priv. Co. ii. 231; Ramsay, i. 167. He is called Lieutenant of Ireland on July 13, 15, 27; Oct. 6, 24, 1413, in Priv. Seal Bills 1114/3, 43, 46; 1115/24, 35; for two payments to him of £1333. 6s. 8d. each on June 27 and Nov. 15, 1413, respectively, see Iss. Roll 1 H. V, Pasch. and Mich., on which latter date he is called Lieutenant of Ireland for *three* years.

[2] Wylie, i. 223–227. For account of him see ibid. ii. 289–293. He was the second son of William Stanley knight of Stourton in Wirral (Cheshire) who died in June 1398. William Stanley's grandson Thomas married Maud the only daughter of John Arderne kt. of Elford near Lichfield, for whose monument, see Earwaker, i. 323, 324, 328; Wylie, Notes, 113. For a pedigree of the Stanleys, originally from Stoneley in Staffordshire (Sleigh, 185), see Earwaker, i. 328; ii. 602. For their arms (3 stags' heads), see Vict. Co. Hist. Lancs. iii. 158, with bibliography. For "the Eagle sitting on a Roote, A swathed Infant holding in her foot," see Drayton, 31. This appears on the stall-plate of his grandson Sir Thomas Stanley, K.G. (d. 1459), Hope, Plate LXII; also of Sir Thomas Stanley, K.G. (d. 1504), ibid. Plate LXXXVI.

[3] Wylie, iv. 551. For arrears to be paid to him from the death of Henry IV till the arrival of Sir John Stanley, see Claus. 1 H. V, 16, July 14, 1413. On Oct. 1, 1413, the Duke of Clarence is still called Lieutenant of Ireland in Claus. 1 H. V, 14, 17.

[4] For £120 paid for shipping his men, see Iss. Roll 1 H. V, Pasch., June 27, 1413.

[5] Pat. 1 H. V, i. 19 d. For 4 small iron guns and 4094 lbs. of gunpowder delivered to him, see Ord. Priv. Co. ii. 341.

[6] Profecturus, Pat. 1 H. V, ii. 1.

[7] Claus. 1 H. V, 21 d.

defend it, and later in the same month, Stanley sailed from
Chester for his new command. On Oct. 1[1] he landed at
Clontarf on the north shore of Dublin Bay and a Parliament was held at Dublin on Nov. 6[2]. The new Lieutenant
was certainly at Dublin on Oct. 25 and Nov. 19[3], and
he spent his Christmas and held his New Year's Feast at
Ardee[4] in County Louth, but he died on Jan. 18, 1414[5],
killed, as the native bards believed, by the stinging virulence
of their lampoons[6]. His wife Isabel the heiress of Knowsley[7]
followed him to the grave nine months later[8] and they were
buried side by side in the chapel of the tower that he had
built by the waterside at Liverpool[9].

John Stanley left indeed no pleasant memory among
the English settlers in Ireland who complained that he
enriched himself by his extortions and did not pay his way[10].
The Irish had been lately giving trouble[11] and the native
annals record victories for them in County Wexford[12] under
Art McMorough Lord of Leinster, by the O'Byrnes over
the English of Dublin and by Murrough O'Connor Lord of
Offaly (now King's County) at Killeagha[13] in the Barony of
Fore near Oldcastle in County Meath. So on the day of
Stanley's death[14] three war-governors were deputed to act
in the king's name until the appointment of his successor.

[1] Marleburgh, 218; Sanford-Townsend, 93; D'Alton, 85; called Sept. 25 in Holinsh.
76, who calls it "Clawcarfe"; though For. Accts. 8 H. V, m. 30, records charges for the
Red Cog taking him from Chester to Dublin in *August*, 1413, William Turbuk being the
Constable of Chester though not mentioned in list of Constables in Ormerod, i. 224.

[2] i.e. Monday after All Saints, Cal. Rot. Hib. i. 203.

[3] Cal. Pat. H. VI, i. pp. 96, 99, 157.

[4] Anstis, i. 39. For documents dated there on Dec. 25, 1413, and June 1, 1414,
allowing a murage for building the town walls, see Cal. Rot. Hib. i. 202, 203. For confirmation of privileges to Athirde (Atrium Dei—called Athird in Holinsh. i. 76), see Pat.
2 H. V, ii. 9, Oct. 20, 1414.

[5] Marleburgh, 218; Gilbert, Viceroys, 301; not Jan. 8, as Beltz, xvii, clvii; nor
Jan. 6, as Earwaker, ii. 602; nor Jan. 6, 1413, as R. Cox, i. 149. In Pat. 1 H. V, ii.
4, Feb. 14, 1414; Cal. Rot. Hib. i. 203, he is *nuper* loc. ten. Hib.

[6] Four Masters, iv. 819; Gilbert, Viceroys, 301. For native Irish writers of the
fifteenth century, see Olden, 281.

[7] Wylie, ii. 290.

[8] She died Oct. 26, 1414, Earwaker, i. 328; Langton, i. 105, from inquisition held
at Ormskirk on June 5, 1415, where she is called "Issabella."

[9] T. H. Turner, iii. 421; Vict. Co. Hist. Lancs. iii. 159; Baines, ii. 307, with view
of it in 1680; Wylie, ii. 292.

[10] Gilbert, Viceroys, 302, 568; riens ou poy, H. F. Berry, 568, where the settlers
complain in 1421 that his heirs are graundement enriches e enhansez and ought to be
made to pay his debts.

[11] Holinsh. i. 76.

[12] Called Conta Reagh, Four Masters, iv. 815.

[13] Cill Eochain, ibid.   [14] Cal. Rot. Hib. i. 203.

These were Christopher Holywood, Sir Edward Perrers[1], and Janico Dartas[2], who was still constable of Dublin[3], while the chancellor, Thomas Cranley[4] Archbishop of Dublin, took formal charge of the government as Justiciar or Lord Justice of Ireland[5], John Bermingham[6] a Judge of the Irish Bench undertaking the duties during his temporary absence in England[7]. Cranley however soon

[1] For grant to him dated March 28, Sept. 13, 1414, of custody of two parts of the lands of the late John Darcy in Ireland during the minority of Philip the son and heir, see Cal. Rot. Hib. i. 204, 205; Rot. Select. 52. For Perrers' previous appointments in 1407 and 1409, see Wylie, iii. 163, 170. For his appearance before the Barons of the Exchequer in Dublin Nov. 2, 1415, and Dec. 10, 1417, see Rot. Select. 52. In Claus. 4 H. V, 15 (Aug. 27, 1416), also Exch. Accts. 247/7, 10 (1420) where he is called Edward Pers, kt., he is Constable of the castle of Wicklow [*Wynkynlo inter Obrynnes* (i.e. O'Byrnes, Wylie, ii. 145) *situata*], where his son John is also mentioned. On June 26, 1417, he was one of those who signed the memorial to the English government urging that John Talbot should not leave Ireland, Orig. Lett. Ser. II. i. 63.

[2] For grants to him of 100 marks p. a. from the customs of Drogheda, £40 p. a. from the fee farm of Dublin, and 1s. per day (Wylie, iii. 166, note 1) confirmed on April 21, 1413, see Pat. 1 H. V, iii. 20, 30; Rot. Parl. iv. 161; Memoranda Roll K. R. 3–4 H. V, 41, May 3, 1415; Gesta, 126, June 5, 1418; Carte, Rolles, i. 264; Dep. Keep. Rept. xli. 693; Pat. 6 H. V, 20, July 20, 1418; Claus. 6 H. V, 3, Sept. 23, 1418; also of the manor and town of Esker, see Priv. Seal 658/76, July 17, 1413; for arrears pardoned to him Dec. 25, 1413, see Rot. Select. 41. This manor was regranted to him for life together with Newcastle of Lyons and Tassagard (i.e. Saggard) from Sept. 16, 1420, see Pat. 8 H. V, 1, Feb. 18, 1421 (i.e. after the death of Sir John Dabridgecourt), Wylie, iii. 167; D'Alton, 649. For permission to him and his wife Elizabeth to accept lands at Killaghyr (co. Louth) from two chaplains, see Cal. Rot. Hib. i. 204, dated July 14, 1414. For his muster (10 + 30) at Southampton in 1415, see Exch. Accts. 46/3 (8); Sloane MS. 4600, pp. 265, 267, 278; not Dartus as Hunter, 54, nor Daytas as Nicolas, Agincourt, 378. For permission dated Dec. 9, 1416, for him to export 600 barrels of wheat from Ireland to England, Harfleur, Bordeaux and Bayonne, see Pat. 4 H. V, 7. In Priv. Seal Writs 3 H. V he is Seneschal of Ulster and Custos of Greencastle and Carlingford. On March 25, 27, 1417, he is going to England, Cal. Rot. Hib. i. 214. For 2 trotters and 2 palfreys in the king's stables called Lyard Janico, Bayard Janico, &c., as gifts from him, see For. Accts. 3 H. V; Exch. Accts. 106/24 (1), where he receives a horse called Lyard Mortimer. For English earls interceding for him after he had fought a duel, cf. Gesta, 126, note, who refers to his obit (Nov. 20) in Book of Holy Trinity, Dublin. He was with the king at Louviers in June 1418, Rym. ix. 595; Chancery Warrants, Ser. I. 1364/63 ("which yet is abydyng with us"); and he took part in the siege of Rouen in the same year, Rym. ix. 596; Gesta, 125; J. Page, 9 (who calls him "Janygo," cf. "Iemco," or "Ienyco the Squyere," Brut, ii. 396). For hospitium de Arthas at Bordeaux, see Carte, Rolles, i. 348, where the praepositura Umbrarie (i.e. the Ombrière, Wylie, iii. 75) at Bordeaux, is granted to him Sept. 14, 1400, see Exch. Accts. 187/12. For grants to Sampson Dartas Apr. 19, 1414, see Cal. Rot. Hib. i. 205. For Robert Dartays in Essex and Herts., see Pat. 3 H. V, ii. 10 d.

[3] Pat. 1 H. V, 32; Wylie, iii. 86.

[4] Not "Crawley" as R. Cox, i. 149; Lascelles, i. 27 (who supposes that he was Lieutenant of Ireland); Tyler, ii. 355.

[5] Holinsh. i. 76. On Jan. 19, Oct. 18, 1414, he is Justic' Hibernie, Rot. Select. 40, 44; Cal. Rot. Hib. i. 205, though said to have been appointed on Jan. 22, 1414, in Marleburgh, 218. On Nov. 13, 1414, he is *nuper* Justic', Cal. Rot. Hib. i. 206, called Governor in Gilbert, Viceroys, 302.

[6] Cal. Rot. Hib. i. 203.

[7] He had been appointed Chancellor of Ireland on April 20, 1413, being in England at the time, Pat. 1 H. V, iii. 21; Wylie, iii. 161 (where the word "settled" should be altered). For a palfrey, "Lyard Develyn," given by him to the king, see Exch. Accts. 106/24 (1).

returned[1] and at once marched out from Tristeldermot with prayers and a religious procession and slew 100 of the O'Mores and the O'Dempseys at Kilkea[2] in the valley of the Barrow, repairs being about the same time ordered for the dilapidated walls at Naas[3]. On Feb. 13, 1414[4], the Treasurer, Lawrence Merbury[5], left for England to lay the state of Ireland before the Council and to seek a remedy with the result that on Feb. 24, 1414[6], the great John Talbot[7] Lord of Furnival and Hallamshire was appointed Lieutenant of Ireland for six years though he did not actually take up his command in the country till nearly nine months later, and pending his arrival a force of 60 men-of-arms and 300 archers was sent over for the protection of the settlers under Thomas, Earl of Desmond[8].

On the day on which John Talbot received his appointment as Lieutenant, Hugh Burgh[9] was made Treasurer of Ireland in place of Lawrence Merbury who was again appointed Chancellor of Ireland on March 2, 1414[10]. On Feb. 25, 1414[11], a Parliament met in Dublin and sat for

[1] He was in Dublin on March 16, May 28, July 12, 1414, Rot. Select. 42; Cal. Rot. Hib. i. 209. [2] Marleburgh, 219; called Kilka in Holinsh. ii. 76.
[3] For murage for 20 years granted for this purpose from May 24, 1414, see Cal. Rot. Hib. i. 206.
[4] On this day William Tynbegh was appointed to act as his deputy during his absence, Cal. Rot. Hib. i. 203; Cal. Pat. H. VI, i. 99.
[5] For grant to him of the manor, castle and domain of Tallagharn in South Wales (i.e. Laugharne near Carmarthen) dated June 9, 1413, see Pat. 1 H. V, i. 22; Cal. Rot. Pat. 260; also of the manors of Crumlin and Chapelizod near Dublin, the latter on March 11, 1415, see Cal. Rot. Hib. i. 206; D'Alton, 545, 696. For allowance of £40 p. a. (Wylie, ii. 133, note 3) continued to him June 12, 1413, see Pat. 1 H. V, i. 8. For will of his former colleague Edward Noon, kt. (Roy. Lett. i. 76; Wylie, ii. 133), dated at Shelfang (? Shelfhanger near Diss in Norfolk), proved at Lambeth in 1413, see Genealogist, vi. 132. For Lawrence son of Thomas Merbury in Ireland, see Pat. 3 H. V, i. 21; ii. 26, May 3, Nov. 5, 1415.
[6] Pat. 1 H. V, v. 13; Cal. Rot. Hib. i. 206, 212; Doyle, iii. 309; cf. Devon, 335; Sanford-Townsend, i. 245; not 1413, as Gilbert, Viceroys, 304; O'Flanagan, i. 80. For £100 paid to him as Lieutenant of Ireland, see Devon, 335, July 19, 1414.
[7] Called "John Talbot de Halomshire Sire de Furnivall" in Rot. Parl. iv. 161; Add. MS. 24513, f. 13.
[8] He is stated to be about to cross on April 21, Dec. 18, 1413, in Pat. 1 H. V, iii. 18 d; v. 30; Priv. Seal Bills 1115/8, 18; Four Masters, iv. 815, where the Earl of Ormonde (i.e. James Butler the 4th Earl) also comes from the King of England. In Pat. 1 H. V, iv. 4, Thomas Abbot of Keynsham near Bristol is going to Ireland on Dec. 18, 1413, with R (*sic*) Earl of Desmond, and on Sept. 12, 1413, the Earl of Desmond granted to him the advowson of the church of Dungarvan, Cal. Rot. Hib. i. 204.
[9] Pat. 1 H. V, iv. 2. He was still Treasurer on Sept. 18, 1414; Jan. 7, 11, May 23, 1415; Cal. Rot. Hib. i. 209, 211; also in 1420 (8 H. V), Exch. Accts. 247/14. On Oct. 18, 1414, he was going to England on business of John Talbot, Cal. Rot. Hib. i. 205. For the manors of Esker, Saggart and Crumlin granted to him in 1416, see D'Alton, 649, 723.
[10] Chancery Warrants, Ser. 1. 364/4; Pat. 1 H. V, v. 16; Cal. Rot. Hib. i. 205, 207; Wylie, iii. 162, 170. He was still Chancellor in 1420, Exch. Accts. 247/7, 8.
[11] Marleburgh, 218; Holinsh. i. 76.

15 days but refused to grant a tallage. On March 6, 1414[1], Edward Perrers was appointed Marshal of the armed forces of Ireland but the only outcome of the preparations would appear to have been a serious defeat of the settlers by the O'Connors in County Meath where Thomas Mareward Baron of Skreen[2] was killed[3] and Christopher Fleming and Janico Dartas[4] were taken prisoners.

But as a rule the Irish records are of little interest at this time. The king's thoughts were elsewhere and Ireland was left to fight her own battles by herself. The Carmelites of Leighlin received their usual allowance for keeping the bridge over the Barrow against the Irish, and the land-owners of County Carlow[5] had to be compensated for the losses inflicted on them by their remorseless neighbours. Here and there some favoured Englishman[6] receives a betterment in recognition of his services in Dublin, while others are appointed to petty offices as waterbailiffs, gaugers[7] or spigurnels[8]. Some Irishmen were allowed the *libertas Angliae*[9] (i.e. to come under English law) with permission, in spite of English statutes[10], to hold

[1] Cal. Rot. Hib. i. 203.
[2] For the manor of Santry granted to him as one of the possessions of the family of Feipo or Phepoe into which he married (Wylie, ii. 133, note 4), see D'Alton, 253.
[3] Four Masters, iv. 815; Moore, iii. 153; Wylie, ii. 133. In Marleburgh, 219; Holinsh. ii. 76; the engagement is dated May 10, 1414, but this must be too early, for Mareward is still referred to in a document dated July 17, 1414, in Cal. Rot. Hib. i. 204. On April 12, 1415, he is *late* Baron of Skreen (ibid. 210), and his death is referred to in a document dated Dec. 18, 1415 (ibid. 215), where his wife is called Joan and his son Thomas is under age. This son signed the protest of June 26, 1417, as Baron of Skreen, Orig. Lett. Ser. II. i. 63.
[4] Called John Dardis in Marleburgh, 219. On the arrival of John Talbot his grants (see page 60, note 2) were all suspended as having been p'chaces sinistrement et p faux suggestion, and not restored to him till Nov. 16, 1417, Rot. Parl. iv. 161.
[5] Wylie, ii. 127; e.g. Robert Vale, Lord of Castletown (? either Black Castle near Leighlin Bridge or Ballymoon near Bagenalstown), received 20 marks p. a. for his losses through the Irish, Pat. 2 H. V, iii. 5, June 25, 1414.
[6] e.g. increase of 40s. p. a. granted on April 14, 1414, to John Corryngham, clerk, Treasurer of the Exchequer of Ireland, Cal. Rot. Hib. i. 204. On Jan. 18, 1416, he was appointed Keeper of the Palace in the castle at Dublin and Clerk of the Works of the Castle, Gilbert, 569.
[7] Priv. Seal 659/106; Cal. Rot. Hib. i. 213.
[8] i.e. sealer of writs (*obsignator*), Du Cange, vi. 649; Cent. Dict., s.v.; Purey-Cust, ii. 158; Blount, s.v., considers it to be a proper name. For John Morker spigurnell de Cancellar' Regis, see Iss. Roll 1 H. V, Mich., Dec. 1, 1413. For spigurnellus Cancellar', see Pat. 1 H. V, i. 15, June 22, 1413. Also for the Duchy of Cornwall, For. Accts. 5 H. V.
[9] For grants to Nicholas McKynnyla (July 13, 1414) and Robert O'Croghan (Jan. 28, 1415) to be of free status and quit *ab omni servitute Hibernicali*, see Cal. Rot. Hib. i. 203.
[10] For order of adjourned Parliament that met at Westminster May 8, 1416, that no one of the Irish nation should be an Archbishop, Bishop, Abbot or Prior, or hold a benefice in Ireland, see Stat. ii. 197; H. F. Berry, 560; not 1417 as O'Flanagan, i. 85.

benefices[1] or to be received into religious houses. Permits
of absence were granted to Irish labourers and others to
reside away from their country[2] while English merchants[3]
were authorised to import English cloth and salt, bringing
away Irish fish and Irish corn in return.

We have seen above that John Talbot was appointed
Lieutenant of Ireland[4] on Feb. 24, 1414, though on Nov. 16
of the previous year the records contain an order committing
him to the Tower[5]. So far I have not been able to find
any explanation of this fact unless it be in connection with
certain "discords, dissensions and debates" that had arisen
between him and the Earl of Arundel about some land in
Shropshire[6] and it may be that Talbot's appointment to the
government of a country where his kinsmen had long held
land[7] was a sort of diplomatic ostracism intended to nip
the possibility of a Talbot-Arundel feud which might have
developed into political venom such as was sapping the life-
blood of France beyond the Channel. It has been suggested[8] however that Talbot's imprisonment may have
been connected with Oldcastle's rising and the date of the
warrant would at first sight seem to lend some probability
to this view. But that he could have shown no real
sympathy with this movement is obvious from the fact that
just when it had reached its most dangerous climax he was

---

[1] For John Martell, a native of Ireland, warden of the Free Chapel at Cork, a
scholar in the University of Oxford, see Pat. 4 H. V, 3, March 26, 1417. Tyler
(ii. 232) thinks that "no Irishman in those days was ever promoted to an ordinary
benefice."

[2] Pat. 1 H. V, iv. 34. For permission dated April 1, 1414, for John, son of Richard,
chaplain, to be absent from Ireland for 7 years, also to Gilbert Alneth (July 11, 1414),
clerk, physician to the Duke of Clarence, for 2 years, see Cal. Rot. Hib. i. 204, and
John Pedwell, prebendary of Tipperkevin, Dublin, going to Rome on private business,
ibid. i. 205, Sept. 14, 1414.

[3] e.g. Robert Russell of Bristol, Pat. 2 H. V, iii. 7 d, Feb. 12, 1415. For the
"Trinitee de Bristol" carrying wine, salt, cloth, &c., to Ireland, see Claus. 1 H. V, 36,
April 5, 1413.

[4] "Lyeutenant of Irland," Secreta, 133; Gilbert, Account, 119.

[5] Claus. 1 H. V, 14; Dugdale, i. 328.

[6] i.e. a close called Pokmore which the Abbot of Wenlock had let to John Talbot to
farm; see order dated Feb. 1, 1414, to the escheator of Salop to take it over for the
king, Claus. 1 H. V, 12; called "le comune de Poukesmere" in Chancery Warrants,
Ser. 1. 1364/9; Gesta, xxviii, where a writ dated June 3, 1414, from the King to the
Chancellor directs that the case shall be decided in the courts.

[7] For Malahide on the coast near Dublin, granted to Richard Talbot in 1174, see
D'Alton, 191, 199. For Thomas Talbot, who had been in those parts since the time of
Richard II, see Orig. Lett. Ser. 1. i. 63; also Richard Talbot, of Meath, ibid.

[8] Dict. Nat. Biogr. v. 319.

considered safe enough to be appointed a commissioner for the trial of the rebel Lollards in Shropshire[1].

In view of his approaching departure for Ireland he took out letters of attorney on May 14, 1414[2], but at least six months more elapsed before he actually sailed[3]. On Sept. 26[4], Archbishop Cranley crossed again to England in person and it was evident that Talbot's departure could not now be longer delayed. Official payments had been made to the new Viceroy before July 19, 1414[5]. Orders had been issued on Aug. 18[6] to provide shipping for his passage. Harbingers[7] and purveyors had been appointed to provide corn, barley, bread, fuel, wine, beer, fish, flesh, poultry and all things necessary for his hostel[8] while tilers, stonecutters and carpenters were busy renovating and repairing Dublin Castle for his reception[9]. He landed at Dalkey on Nov. 10, 1414[10], and three days later[11] he was ceremoniously received by Archbishop Cranley in the Lady Chapel of Trinity Church in Dublin[12]. Letters of protection were made out for him in England on Dec. 4, 1414[13], and we have still a note of the wages paid to the

[1] Pat. 1 H. V, v. 23 dors. Jan. 11, 1414, where he is called John Talbot of Halumshire; also on July 28, 1414, to enforce the Leicester statute against the Lollards, Pat. 2 H. V, ii. 32 d.

[2] Pat. 2 H. V, i. 37. For Sir John Aston, clerk, and Robert Dyke going to Ireland in the service of John Talbot, knight, see Pat. 2 H. V, i. 33, May 10, 1414.

[3] For order dated May 21, 1414, to him and William Roos of Hamlake to arrest William Laverok of Chesterfield, see Pat. 2 H. V, i. 19 d. For tomb of William Roos at Bottesford with SS collar, see Eller, 25, 365; Wylie, ii. 180, note; also that of his wife Margaret, who was a daughter of John Lord Arundel, Eller, 366. She died July 3, 1439; Comp. Peer. vi. 402. For will of Beatrice (see Wylie, ii. 179, note 1), Lady de Roos, dated Jan. 26, 1414, proved May 16, 1415, see Palmer, Yarm, 17. For Roos arms in York Minster, also at Kirkham Priory near Malton (Yorks.), founded by Walter l'Espec, see Purey-Cust, i. 236; ii. 252. For pictures of Kirkham, see Archaeologia, xxi. 160; Monast. vi. 207.

[4] Cal. Rot. Hib. i. 209.

[5] Devon, 335.

[6] Cal. Rot. Hib. i. 208.

[7] Herberger, ibid. Nov. 13, 1414. Cf. herbegier, harbesher, herbarjour, Halliwell, i. 434, 445.

[8] Cal. Rot. Hib. i. 208, 209, Sept. 18, Dec. 8, 1414.

[9] Ibid. 209, Oct. 11, 1414.

[10] Marleburgh, 219; Holinsh. ii. 76; D'Alton, 889; not September, as Four Masters, iv. 821; nor 1415, as Loch Cé, ii. 145, which says that he plundered many of the bards of Erin.

[11] i.e. Nov. 13; not 30, as Gilbert, Viceroys, 304, who thinks that he was then in his 41st year, but he was certainly much younger, Wylie, iii. 111, note 7. In D.N.B. lv. 319, he is supposed to have been born in 1388. His elder brother Gilbert was born in 1379, Wylie, ii. 19.

[12] Cal. Rot. Hib. i. 206.

[13] Pat. 2 H. V, ii. 2.

troops who came over with him from Dec. 5, 1414, to Feb. 20, 1415[1]. One of the objects of the new appointment had been "the keeping of the sea[2]" and for this purpose he was accompanied by some of the king's ships. On Dec. 10, 1414[3], a knight named John Keghley and an esquire John Brigg were appointed Admirals of Ireland and on Jan. 1, 1415[4], Robert Bowland was made a Marshal of the Admiralty in Ireland for life.

John Talbot's administration was marked at the outset by a burst of restless activity and during the year that saw the capture of Harfleur and the victory of Agincourt he was hosting the wild Irish and the rebel English as far from the capital as he dared. He rebuilt the broken bridge over the Barrow at Athy[5], spoiled the Walshes of Sleave Breathnagh in the west of County Kilkenny and plundered Brinemore in West Meath[6]. Twice he raided the O'Mores of Leix[7], staying six days in their country and each time burning the crops and wasting the land. He took the strongholds of Shenneigh and Colindragh[8] and set free many English prisoners. After the second visit O'More came to terms, gave up his son as a hostage for good behaviour and served in person with the English force in their attack upon the O'Connors[9] and MacMahons in Louth[10].

[1] In comitiva dn̄i de Talbot, Exch. Accts. 44/24. For £2166. 3s. 4d. (i.e. £1333. 6s. 8d.+£832. 16s. 8d.) paid to him for wages from Jan. 30 to Dec. 31, 1415, see Rec. Roll 3 H. V, Pasch., June 25, 1415; also Ord. Priv. Co. ii. 179, where the amount is totalled as £2445. 12s. 4½d.; see also Cleop. F. iii. f. 141; Ord. Priv. Co. ii. 198; Orig. Lett. Ser. ii. i. 54.

[2] For payment recorded Oct. 4, 1414, for repair of the Cog John going with Dominus Talbot pro salva custodia maris, see William Catton's account in For. Accts. 8 H. V.

[3] Cal. Rot. Hib. i. 206. For Admirals of Ireland from Wicklow Head to Lepers Island (Leperisylond, probably the same as Slepesyland in Wylie, iii. 166), see Pat. 2 H. V, ii. 22; Cal. Rot. Pat. 263, where "Wykyngloue (i.e. Wicklow) Head" becomes Wikinglande. Cf. Nicolas, Navy, ii. 534.

[4] Cal. Rot. Hib. i. 206.

[5] Moore, iii. 154; Gilbert, Viceroys, 305. Not Athenry, as Dict. Nat. Biogr. lv. 319.

[6] Four Masters, iv. 821.

[7] Now Queen's County, called Layse or Laies in Orig. Lett. Ser. ii. i. 56; or "the Morthes of Leys" in Secreta, 203. Cf. R. Cox, i. 150.

[8] For Collyndrogh, Cullintraugh or Colyntagh in Co. Meath or Co. Carlow, see Inquisitionum Repertorium, Index, s.v.; Cal. Rot. Hib. i. 139, 160. The name may perhaps still survive in the Barony of Cullinagh near Abbey Leix in Queen's County. Shenneigh is identified as Shean in D'Alton, 30.

[9] For various indentures between John Talbot and the Irish leaders O'Connor, O'Brien, &c., still extant, see D'Alton, 201.

[10] Or Uriel, Wylie, ii. 146. Called "the parts of Ulnestre" in Orig. Lett. Ser. ii. i. 56; D'Alton, 30.

Here the new Viceroy made a great impression by cutting his way for six miles through a dense forest and carrying off great numbers of cows, horses and small cattle, thereby for the moment striking amazement into the Irish chiefs, one of whom named Maurice O'Keating submitted at Whitsuntide at Lissenhall[1] near Malahide with a rope round his neck and his sword's point held against his throat[2], while Arthur MacMorough of Kildare sent an envoy[3] to England in the summer of 1415 signifying his willingness to do homage, his son Gerald Caelmanach following later on the same errand[4]. But nothing really permanent came of it, for in spite of a mandate[5] to the new bishop[6] to treat for terms the English in Meath were again attacked in 1416 by the O'Connors of Offaly who captured arms and horses and took many prisoners[7], while MacMorough slew or captured 340 of the settlers in County Wexford, taking hostages before he would consent to terms of peace. Meanwhile the interests of the Viceroy's family were not allowed to suffer, for besides the appointment of his brother Richard as Archbishop of Dublin to be presently related, Talbots with various Christian names constantly appear as holders of many positions of profit[8].

---

[1] Lassenhall, Cal. Rot. Hib. i. 226; D'Alton, 327.

[2] Orig. Lett. Ser. II. i. 59; Tyler, ii. 238, who dates it in 1417.

[3] Viz. John Down, the Cistercian Abbot of Dusk or Dousk in Co. Kilkenny (= Vallis S. Salvatoris or Vallis Dei), Dublin St Mary's, ii. 218, 226, 228, 231.

[4] For his safe-conduct, dated July 24, 1415, see Rym. ix. 287. For Donough, son of Art MacMurragh, King of Leinster, sent to the Tower by John Talbot, see Gilbert, Viceroys, 311; O'Flanagan, 83, who gives neither date nor authority. He is called Arthur MacMurgh captayne of Iryshmen in laynystere in Secreta, 186; or Art Mac-Murdhadha, Loch Cé, ii. 147. For his death in 1417, see Four Masters, iv. 831, where he is Art, son of Murtagh, son of Maurice, Lord of Leinster. For leynestere, or laynester, whych is the v[e] part of Irlande, see Secreta, 181, 184, the other parts being Thomon (or Thomond, of which the Obrenys, or O'Breens, Wylie, ii. 145, are princes in 1422), Connaght and Monstre (the Bourkenys), Uriel (the McMahons), and Ulnestre (O'Neyle-boy), Secreta, 203.

[5] Cal. Rot. Hib. i. 209, March 10, 1415.

[6] i.e. Edward Dauntsey or Dantsey, who had been Archdeacon of Cornwall since July 13, 1396, Le Neve, i. 398; Staff. Reg. 80. He was appointed Bishop of Meath, April 11, 1413 (Pat. 1 H. V, i. 28; Cotton, iii. 113; Gams, 229), in succession to Robert Montague or Montan, who died May 24, 1412, Eubel, i. 355. Dauntsey received the temporalities on Feb. 13, 1415, Cal. Rot. Hib. 208, 215, and held the bishopric till his death on Jan. 4, 1430.

[7] Four Masters, iv. 829.

[8] e.g. £20 p. a. granted to Thomas Talbot, junr, Feb. 21, 1415, Cal. Rot. Hib. i. 208. Walter Talbot is made Marshal in County Wexford, Jan. 18, 1416, ibid. i. 211, and Thomas Talbot is appointed Coroner for County Kilkenny, Feb. 18, 1416, ibid. i. 212. For Thomas Talbot, Knight, as attorney for the viceroy's brother, Gilbert, Lord Talbot, then in England, see ibid. i. 211, Jan. 14, 1416. For John Talbot, Kt., going to Ireland on Oct. 10, 1415, see Pat. 3 H. V, ii. 23. For the tomb of Richard

Apart from the time spent in Dublin John Talbot was frequently found at Trim, Naas, Tristeldermot, Ardbrakan, Ardee, Lusk and Tallaght[1] but though he accomplished in a short time more than had been done in Ireland for many years past yet he could not get payment for his men who took to promiscuous plundering to find sustenance for themselves and their horses. Again and again important personages crossed to England[2] to ask for men, money, ships and guns, but no satisfaction could be obtained from the English Treasury as all available funds were wanted for the conquest of the crown of France, and at length when Agincourt was won and King Henry had come back in triumph, John Talbot recrossed to press his claims in person at Westminster. He sailed from Clontarf on Feb. 7, 1416[3], and took part in the reception of King Sigismund on his landing at Dover in May of the same year[4]. He left the government of Ireland again in the hands of Archbishop Cranley[5] who took the oath as his deputy in Dublin on Feb. 14[6]. During Talbot's absence his wife bore him a son at Finglas[7] on June 19, 1416[8]. But the child, who was named Thomas, died on August 10 following and was buried in the church of the Black Friars in Dublin.

Archbishop Cranley called a Parliament at Trim on May 11, 1416, which sat for 11 days and granted a subsidy of 400 marks and life went on in Ireland very much as usual. The archbishop crossed for the last time to England on April 30, 1417, commissioned to represent the desperate

Talbot, a burgess, in the Cathedral at Kilkenny, see Carrigan, iii. 152, who dates his death as 1408 (?), but 1415 in Holinsh. ii. 76, where he is *Robert* Talbot, "a right noble man that walled the suburbs of Kilkenny."

[1] Cal. Rot. Hib. i. 206–211 has documents dated at Trim, Jan. 7; Feb. 13, 16; March 1, 9, 10, 11, 29; April 12; Nov. 12; Dec. 2, 18, 19, 1415. Naas, Feb. 26; May 12; June 10, 26; July 9; Aug. 1, 1415. Tristeldermot, Feb. 22, 23, 24, 1415. Ardbrakan, Feb. 28; March 14, 21; April 22, 24; Aug. 8, 28; Sept. 28; Nov. 13, 1415. Ardee, Sept. 8, 13, 18; Oct. 5, 6, 10, 18, 23, 24; Dec. 8, 1415; Jan. 23, 1416. Lusk, Nov. 2, 1415. Tallaght, Dec. 21, 29, 1415. See also Cal. Pat. H. VI, i. 99.

[2] e.g. Hugh Burgh, the Treasurer, p. 61, note 9; Cal. Rot. Hib. 211, May 23, 1415. Bishop Dauntsey, ibid. Nov. 12, 1415.

[3] Cal. Rot. Hib. i. 212; not 1415, as O'Flanagan, i. 80. There is no ground for supposing that he was present at Agincourt, as Nicolas, 127; Towle, 325, the retinue (20 + 53) given in Nicolas, 345, at Southampton in Aug. 1415, being that of his brother Gilbert.

[4] Ord. Priv. Co. ii. 194.

[5] Gilbert, Viceroys, 306.

[6] Cal. Rot. Hib. i. 212.

[7] A few miles to the north-west of Dublin, D'Alton, 376.

[8] Not 1414, as Gilbert, 306.

condition of the country, in spite of some opposition on the part of the Talbot faction[1]. But he was now 80 years old[2] and he died at Faringdon in Berkshire on May 25, 1417[3]. His body was carried to Oxford and buried in the chapel of the New College of which he had been Warden 20 years before[4], and the college still possesses several of his books, some of which he had bought at Liverpool and Chester on landing from Dublin[5]. He is described by a contemporary as beautiful and courteous, tall of stature and of a sanguine complexion[6] and with a high capacity for wit[7], and his memory was cherished among the English at Dublin as that of a kindly, honest administrator who paid his way reasonably without oppressive extortion[8]. He was succeeded as archbishop by John Talbot's brother Richard who was made Archbishop of Dublin on Dec. 20, 1417[9].

He had previously been beneficed in the diocese of St David's[10], had been vicar of Ludlow[11], Radnor and Henllys[12] near Newport in Monmouthshire, had held prebends in connection with the cathedrals of Hereford[13] and York[14], had been Precentor of Hereford[15] and had lately been appointed Dean of Chichester[16]. He crossed to Ireland

[1] For refusal of the Chancellor, Laurence Merbury, to affix the Great Seal of Ireland to his commission, see Gilbert, 310; H. F. Berry, 567.

[2] He was born in 1337, Dict. Nat. Biogr. xiii. 17.

[3] Gams, 218; Pits, 597.

[4] For his brass with epitaph, see Waller; Ware, i. 337; Wood, Antiq. i. 201, where he is said to be dressed in his "formalities"; Druitt, 79. He had also been the first Warden of Wickham's College at Winchester, Wylie, iii. 162, note 1, but resigned May 12, 1389, Leach, 66, 67, 128. For picture of him in Thomas Chandler's MS. at New College, Oxford, see Archaeologia, liii. 232; Leach, 216.

[5] e.g. on July 2, 16, 1408, from a priest or from Friar Richard Torbok (see p. 59, note 1) at Chester, or from a bookseller in Liverpool, Coxe, New College MSS. xxxvii, xxxviii, xci, civ, cxii, cxxii, where he is called "Cranle."

[6] Marleburgh, 219. Non modo ingenio verum etiam calamo utpote bonis instructus artibus plurimum invaluit, Leland, Commentarii, 269, who says that he wrote an elegant Latin poem (consisting of 106 lines) to the king, whom he supposes to have been King Henry III (!), Lascelles, i. 27, v. 35; D'Alton, Archbishops, 152; Gilbert, Viceroys, 303; O'Flanagan, i. 80.

[7] O'Flanagan, i. 83.

[8] Gouverna benignement et honestement, H. F. Berry, 568.

[9] Gams, 218; Eubel, i. 237; Lib. Metr. 163; D'Alton, 153; O'Flanagan, i. 86; quoting for his consecration The White Book of Christ Church, compiled in the 16th century by Thomas Fitch, sub-prior.

[10] Cotton, ii. 16.

[11] Which he resigned in 1407, Reg. Mascal, f. 26.

[12] Called Hentles in Pat. 1 H. V, i. 27, where he exchanges to it from Radnor on July 21, 1413.

[13] i.e. Putson Major since June 6, 1401, Le Neve, i. 526.

[14] i.e. Fridaythorpe, in Oct. 1412, ibid. iii. 187.

[15] Since June 9, 1407, ibid. i. 486; O'Flanagan, i. 86.

[16] i.e. in 1415, Le Neve, i. 256.

on May 2, 1418[1], and retained the archbishopric till his death which happened on Aug. 15, 1449[2]. On Feb. 26, 1417[3], a petition was presented to the Council at Westminster that all persons born in Ireland should return thither to take their share in the defence of the country as they had been required to do more than three years previously[4]; to which the king replied that the matter should be attended to when Lord Furnival's term of office had expired. But the situation could not brook such delay and before a month was out the necessary order was issued in the most peremptory terms[5]. For the next two years the records show that John Talbot's allowance of £2000 per annum as Viceroy of Ireland was punctually paid[6] though he did not actually return to his command till April 14, 1418[7], and even then made no long stay in the country. We know that he was at Swords on Jan. 5, 1419[8], but later in the same year he sailed from Ireland for the campaign in France, leaving the government in the hands of his brother Richard[9] who received £500 per annum from the Irish Exchequer as Lord Justiciar of Ireland[10] in addition to his emoluments as archbishop. John Talbot never actually returned to Ireland[11] and after his departure tongues were freely let loose against his extortion and rapacity which spared neither saint nor sanctuary[12]. He still formally

---

[1] Pat. 6 H. V, 29, where he is going to Ireland in comitiva Johannis Talbot.

[2] H. Cotton, ii. 16; Elmham, Lib. Metr. 163.

[3] Ord. Priv. Co. ii. 219.   [4] Page 29.

[5] Iss. Roll 4 H. V, Mich., March 18, 1417.

[6] Iss. Roll 4 H. V, Pasch., Mich., May 11, 1416, March 9, 1417; also £1042. 16s. 5d., ibid. 5 H. V, Mich., March 5, 1418, and payments are still made to him as Custos of Ireland in Iss. Roll 6 H. V, Pasch., April 4, 8, 1418, and *passim*; do. 7 H. V, Pasch., Mich., May 1, 5, 21; June 1; Aug. 26; Dec. 5, 1419; also March 8, 1420, where he is called *Gilbert* Talbot.

[7] Called a leave of absence for 10 years in Gilbert, Viceroys, 311; D'Alton, 201, supposes that he was at the siege of Caen in Sept. 1417, but this is probably a confusion with his brother Gilbert. For letters of protection, April 4, 1418, for him going to Ireland, and letters of general attorney, April 12, 1418, see Pat. 6 H. V, 28, 29; though from H. F. Berry he would appear to have been present at a Parliament held in Dublin on Jan. 27, 1417 (4 H. V).

[8] Rot. Select. 40; also on July 21, 1419, Cal. Pat. H. VI, i. 99.

[9] Dict. Nat. Biogr. lv. 319; O'Flanagan, i. 86.

[10] He was appointed Justiciar on March 6, 1420, Exch. Accts. 247/9; and sworn in office as Justic' ter' Hib' on March 9, 1420; ibid. 247/10. He is still so named on Oct. 28, 1422; Gilbert, 569.

[11] He actually ceased office on Feb. 24, 1420, Exch. Accts. 247/7. In Iss. Roll 8 H. V, Mich., Jan. 30, 1421, he is *late* Lieutenant of Ireland. In Rot. Parl. iv. 161, July 12, 1421, he is *ore* enhabitant en Engleterre. He was present at a Council at Westminster on Nov. 5, 1422, Ord. Priv. Co. iii. p. 6.

[12] Gilbert, 310, 570; O'Flanagan, i. 83; saunz poy ou rien paier, H. F. Berry, 570.

retained the name of viceroy till he was succeeded in office on Feb. 10, 1420[1], by James Butler, 4th Earl of Ormond.

I have already endeavoured to show how entirely misinformed the English settlers were as to the real habits and character of their neighbours whom they persisted in speaking of as the "wild Irish[2]" and a recently published account[3] of the personal experiences of a southern traveller who journeyed into the very heart of the country supplies so many authentic details of the highest interest in regard to this question that I am tempted to digress here into a short abstract of its contents[4]. Raymond of Perillos[5] was a native of the county of Roussillon, which, though on the northern side of the Pyrenees, then formed part of the Kingdom of Aragon. But his father had been personally attached to the Kings of France and he himself had been brought up at the court in Paris, where he had been one of the chamberlains to Charles VI[6]. In 1390 he was created Viscount of Perillos[7], a fortress in the Corbières close to the frontier of Languedoc, where the remains of a castle may be seen to this day[8]. He was also Lord of Roda[9] and

---

[1] Exch. Accts. 247/10, 13; not 1419, as Lodge, Peerage, iv; nor 1407, as Ware, Hist. and Antiq. ii. 88 (W. Harris, edn. 1764); H. L. Ward, ii. 492; R. Cox, i. 152.

[2] Wylie, ii. Chap. xlvi. Cf. "des Escos sauvages," "des Hirlandois sauvaiges," Lannoy, Œuvres, 169, 171, who visited the Purgatory in Ireland in 1430.

[3] i.e. by A. Jeanroy. Portions of it were translated into Latin by the Irish controversialist O'Sullivan Beare, and published in his History in 1621.

[4] For a previous short account of this episode, see Wylie, ii. 168.

[5] For an account of him, see Anselme, vii. 758; Gazanyola, 257; Jeanroy-Vignaux, pp. xiv–xviii, who finds no mention of him later than 1405 (p. xviii) and refers to his supposed burial in the Grey Friars Church at Perpignan (pp. xxii, lix); but he had an interview with King Sigismund at Perpignan in 1416 to press for confirmation of some disputed rights which his brother Michael d'Estienne (called Michael Stephani Arragonensis or de Insulâ in Gall. Christ. iii. 1689), Archbishop of Embrun (1379–1427, Eubel, i. 243; Sauret, 167), claimed in connection with the mines of Argentière and Freyssinières in Dauphiny, Comba, 282. For Ponzetuo de Perillos, nephew of the Archbishop, see A. Leroux, 173, Feb. 14, 1418.

[6] Jeu era son servido e camerlene (i.e. of Charles VI) et fory de son payre que me avia noyrit, Jeanroy, 53. Cf. camerarius regis Francie, Carte, Rolles, ii. 174.

[7] Called Perillaux in Rym. viii. 14; Anselme, vii. 759; Perilleu, Carte, Rolles, ii. 174; Perellos, Demay, ii. 51; D. M. J. Henry, ii. 36, where he is captain-general of Roussillon at Perpignan; Periglios, Wolff, Panormita, 45; Perilleux, O'Connor, 52; Perhilos, Healy, 663; Perelhos, Delehaye, 38; Pereliosus, Valla, 1044, 1056, where he is inter primos Catalanorum procerum; called Don Raimondo de Perellos, Faraglia, 188; Raymundo de Perellis, or Don Ramon de Perellis, Ametller y Vinyas, i. 47, 64; Raimondo Periglios, Giannone, ii. 308; Don Ramon de Perellos gobernador de los Condades de Rosellon y Cerdaña, Zurita, ii. 98; Raimondo Periglios Catalano huomo de multa autorita, Summonte, ii. 590.

[8] Joanne, s.v. Perillos; Jeanroy, xiii.

[9] He calls himself Vesconte de Perelhos et de Roda et Senhor de la baronia de Serret, Castellane, 51, 72; Jeanroy, 3, 54. Roda is called Rodes in Rym. viii. 14; Carte, Rolles,

Céret[1]. He was a great traveller and had often been imprisoned both by Christians and Saracens[2] and when King John I of Aragon died in 1395, his restless spirit formed a resolve to visit the famous Purgatory at Lough Derg[3] in Ireland to try if he could find the spirit of his dead sovereign there and see what pains he was enduring[4]. With this purpose in his mind he went to Avignon where he had an interview with Pope Benedict XIII and two Cardinals who all advised him not to tempt God and deceive himself[5] but to remember the fate of the many former venturers to whom the Purgatory had proved their grave. But his mind was quite made up and after obtaining the Papal blessing he left Avignon with his nephew and his three sons[6] on Sept. 8, 1397[7], and was well received on his arrival in Paris. A safe-conduct[8] had been already procured from King Richard II and after full deliberation Raymond made his way across from Calais and landed at Dover[9] on Nov. 1, 1397. He was sure of a welcome in this country, for the long truce had just been signed[10] with France after the recent royal marriage between King Richard and the French king's daughter Isabel[11]; one of the members of Raymond's company being Enguerrand Lord of Coucy[12] whose wife Isabel had come over as governess to the young bride and was now the greatest lady at the English court[13].

ii. 174, or Rodda in Anselme, vii. 758, who places it at the entrance to Cerdagna coming from Roussillon. In Jeanroy-Vignaux, p. xv, it is petite ville de Catalogne, probably Roda near Vich. For Lois de Perellos, Vicomte de Roda, see Vidal, 370; not that he was a knight of Rhodes, as Gilbert, Viceroys, 275; O'Connor, 62, 98; Félice, 57; Healy, 663. For Pons Périlleux (or de Perilloniis, Sauret, 167), son of the Viscount of Rodez (*sic*), who went bail for Guillaume Meuillon when he was imprisoned in the castle of Caillé at Cagliari in Sardinia, see Meuillon, 18. For seal of Pons de Perellos, chamberlain to the king and the Duke of Burgundy, Feb. 20, 1406, see Demay, ii. 51; called Perilleux in La Barre, Mem. ii. 120 (1410).

[1] For his connection with Céret (Pyrénées Orientales), see Jeanroy, 15.
[2] Castellane, 54.   [3] See App. G.
[4] Jeanroy-Vignaux, pp. xvii, xxi, 11; Castellane, 55.
[5] Ne volgnes temptar dieu ne enganar me meteys, Castellane, 59, 67.
[6] Castellane, 67; Jeanroy-Vignaux, 20.
[7] Not 1398, as stated in the MS., see Jeanroy-Vignaux, pp. xvii, 2, 11; Castellane, 53, 56.
[8] Dated Sept. 6, 1397, Rym. viii. 14; Carte, Rolles, ii. 174; Delehaye, 38; not Sept. 7, as Krapp, 25, 32; Félice, 57; nor 1328, as O'Sullivan, 22.
[9] He calls the cliff "lo cap de Garalh," Jeanroy-Vignaux, 53.
[10] Comensan lo matremoni avian faytas treyas de xxx ans, Jeanroy-Vignaux, 12; Castellane, 57; really 28 years, Wylie, i. 84; Dict. Nat. Biogr. xlviii. 151; Rym. vii. 820.
[11] See App. H.
[12] Traison, 25, 26, 163, 165; Wylie, i. 85; P. Meyer, Entrevue, 218; though called Courcy, ibid. 218, 223.
[13] La major doma que forsen entorn la regina d'Englaterra, i.e. Isabel (d. 1437) daughter of Jean Duke of Lorraine, second wife of Enguerrand de Couci, Anselme, v. 514; viii.

Travelling by Canterbury to London Raymond found that King Richard was at Woodstock[1], whither he straightway went and received a most friendly reception during a stay extending over 10 days. The manor of Woodstock, which he calls Got[2], then formed a part of the Queen's dower[3] and Raymond describes the park as a vast enclosure like the Bois de Vincennes near Paris in which the king had a fine strong hostel[4] with large rooms within eight miles of Oxford, which the English call "Estancfort." Hiring a ship at Chester[5] he touched at Holyhead[6], visited Anglesey which he describes as "very populous[7]" and then after some days sailing landed at Dublin[8]. Here he had an interview with the Viceroy, Roger Mortimer, Earl of March[9], who did his best to dissuade him from his purpose but finding that he could not prevail he provided him with

545; Mas-Latrie, 1590; Wylie, i. 85 ; his first wife, whom he married in 1383, being Isabel daughter of Edward III, King of England, Stubbs, Germ. 149; Maulde la Clavière, i. 12.

[1] For documents dated at Woodstock Nov. 17, 20, 1397, see Rym. viii. 25, 26.

[2] Called "un parc nommé Houdescot près de la cité d'Oucsenefort," in Salmon, 53. This cannot be Stamford, as Castellane, 57.

[3] Wylie, ii. 284. Cf.

> Before the chambre window of the Quene
> At Wodestok upon the grene I lay.

Clanvowe in Chauc. (S), vii. 358, from the Cuckoo and the Nightingale, written circa 1403, by John (not Thomas, as Wylie, iii. 261), father of Thomas Clanvowe (Kittredge, 17), when he was old and "unlusty," Chauc. (S) vii. pp. lix, 348. Cf. this tretise made Sir Johan Clanvowe kny3t the laste viage that he made over the greate See in whiche he dyede, Coxe, Univ. Coll. MS. vii. For £20 per annum from the farm of the castle and cantred of Builth granted to Thomas Clanvowe temp. R. II and H. IV, confirmed May 25, 1414, see Pat. 2 H. V, ii. 34, which seems to show that the knight did not die in 1410 as supposed, see Wylie, iii. 297, note 1. The place called "Yosex," at which his will is dated, is Yazor near Hereford (called Yavesore, Feudal Aids, ii. 391, 394, 397; Yavelhouere, Robinson, Mansions, 317). For will of Peryne Clanvowe dated 1422, in which she is to be buried beside her husband at Zasore, see Fifty Wills, p. 49; Clinch, Costume, 57. He was Sheriff of Herefordshire in 1397, Sheriffs' Lists, 60; Wylie, iv. 184. In Copinger, Heraldry, p. 22, Thomas Clanvowe kt. grants his family coat of arms in 11 H. IV (1409/10) to his cousin William Criketot. For John Clanvowe or Clabowe, who was living in 1424, see Inq. p. Mort. iv. 94, 95, where he owns Michaelchurch in Herefordshire. The name appears as Clanbowe or Clavenogh temp. Ed. III, Duncumb, ii. 286, where they are owners of Cusop near Hay.

[4] For view of the manor-house at Woodstock taken in 1714, see Macfarlane-Thomson, ii. 57; Craik-Macfarlane, i. 481; Marshall, 136.

[5] Xistier, Sesterscire, Jeanroy-Vignaux, 13; Castellane, 57.

[6] Olyet, ibid., cf. 'Arripay for Henry Pay, Wylie, ii. 324; C. R. L. Fletcher, 309, 317.

[7] La yla d'Arman que foc del rey de C. cavalhiers en lo temps del rey Artus e es be poblada, Jeanroy-Vignaux, 13; Castellane, 58.

[8] This I take to be the meaning of davant la ciutat de Beboi que es asses gran ciutat, ibid. Castellane (58) suggests Ballivir in Armagh, which is quite impossible; O'Sullivan, 22, translates it as "Dubhlinnam." It may perhaps be Malahide or Baldoyle. For Baldoyle as a landing place, see Wylie, ii. 125; called Beldoyle in D'Alton, 170.

[9] Not Richard, as Krapp, 26. Nor Richard Plantagenet, as Félice, 58. He was appointed Lieutenant of Ireland Apr. 24, 1397, Doyle, ii. 469; Wylie, i. 3.

an escort of 100 men-of-arms under the command of two
cousins, Thomas and John Talbot, the latter of whom understood the Irish language and was able to act as interpreter[1]
to the party.   Thus accompanied Raymond started in
November 1397 for Armagh[2] where he presented his
credentials to Archbishop John Colton[3] whom he says the
people regarded as a pope.   The archbishop, who had only
just returned from his visitation to Derry[4], tried to frighten
him off from the journey but he gave him the sacrament
with his own hand[5] and met him again a week later at
Dundalk[6], which he describes as a city as big as Puigcerda
or Tarragona.   Here he received a safe-conduct to an Irish
chief called O'Neil[7], but as soon as they were actually in
the country of the wild Irish the escort turned back and
Raymond's little party went on their way alone.   The Irish
chief however sent to meet the travellers with a present of
meat and salt and two spongy buns[8] which were as black
as a coal and as soft as paste though they proved pretty
palatable nevertheless.   So they made their way to
Termon[9] on the north bank of Lough Erne, where they
had to leave their horses and travel the rest of the way on
foot to the Priory which was five miles away.   Arrived at
the monastery in Lough Derg[10] they found the Prior who
uttered the usual warning against tempting God and
pointed to the graves of other foolhardy travellers who
had ventured the risk to their cost, but Raymond's mind
was not to be shaken and after hearing a requiem mass he
handed to his nephew a will that he had previously drawn

---

[1] Que sabia la lenga de Yrlonda que era mon trocheman.   Castellane, 59, names also
an esquire Johan Dimi as a member of the party.

[2] Armanach, ibid.

[3] Called Archbishop of *Ireland* in Krapp, 26, 42.

[4] Wylie, ii. 161–5.

[5] Presi de sa ma nostre Senhor, Jeanroy-Vignaux, 14 ; Castellane, 60.

[6] Diondani, Dundela, ibid.; not Drogheda, as Wylie, ii. 168.

[7] O'Sullivan Beare, 22; = O'Nellum regem, Krapp, 26; Félice, 58.   For O'Nell
Captayn of Iryshemen of Ulvestere, see Secreta, 186; or O'Neyle, ibid. 203.

[8] Fougasses, see Cotgr., s.v. *Fouace*; in Godefroy Fouacier = patissier.

[9] i.e. Termon Dubheoc or Daveog (now Termon Magrath on Drumawark Hill near
Pettigo, O'Connor, 46, 51, 63, 129), the Magraths being the Termons or erenaghs (i.e.
guardians) of this sanctuary.   Vila appelade Processio, i.e. Protectio or Sanctuary which
is the meaning of Termon or Tearmuin, O'Sullivan Beare, 22.   For termon-lands, see
O'Connor, 47 ; Wylie, ii. 161.

[10] Lotherge stagnum rubeum, Delehaye, 48.   The monastery stood on Saints' Island
(H. L. D. Ward, 491; Krapp, 35; Delehaye, 47, 58), which was connected with the
shore by a bridge, O'Connor, 64, 80, 81, 84 (with picture).   It was established there by
the Austin Canons in the eleventh century and destroyed in the seventeenth.

up and having arranged with the monks to bury his body
where they liked he kissed them and said farewell as one
who might never come back again to them alive.   Then
they stepped into a boat made out of a hollowed tree-trunk[1]
and were put across about half-a-mile of water[2] to the
island where Raymond went down into the pit[3].

What he saw there is only a repetition of the account
given nearly 200 years before by the English monks Henry
of Sawtrey and Jocelyn, translations of which into French
and English had long been circulating to stimulate the
curious all over Europe.   He adds however as special
personal items that he saw and talked with King John of
Aragon and was surprised that he had so much punishment
laid upon him for he had always regarded him as a just
king[4], while to his great surprise he met also his own niece
Aldosa de Queralt[5] who had died since he started from
home and was now having a very hot time in the Hole for
painting her face and generally playing the coquette, also
a Franciscan whom he knew named Francis Delpueg from
the Grey Friars at Gerona who had now to do his punishment for carrying off a nun[6].

On his return Raymond was received by King O'Neil
with all kindness at Armagh, where he stayed long enough
and had his eyes open wide enough to tell us what he
actually saw.   O'Neil he reports as the greatest of the chiefs
in that part of the country.   He owned 3000 horses and
had 90[7] mounted warriors who rode with saddles and wore
coats of mail with belts and iron basnets and gorgets of
mail[8].   They were armed with swords and short lances,
while the rest of the fighting men carried long, sharp,
straight knives[9] and small bows with which they did great
execution though they were only three feet long.   Nobody
whether king, bishop, abbot, lord or knight wore shoes[10],

---

[1] Una barca d'un fust cavat car autras barcas non y avia, Castellane, 65 ; navicellam,
Delehaye, 47.
[2] Krapp, 53 ; or a mile, Delehaye, 47.
[3] "This pytte or hole," Krapp, 41.   See App. G.
[4] Jeanroy-Vignaux, 33; Castellane, 69.
[5] Called "Aldonsa Carolea a cousin of his," in Krapp, 26; Félice, 58.
[6] Por una monga que trayssa du monestier.
[7] Or 40, Jeanroy-Vignaux, 16.
[8] Gorgeyta de malha et capelinas redondas de ferr', ibid. 16; Castellane, 61.
[9] Los cotelhs son lonxz et estregz et talho fort be.
[10] Ne porto caixssas, ni sabatis nè porto bragas.

breeks or hose and they rushed to battle with a war-whoop like the Turks.   Both men and women went naked except for their frieze cloaks[1], and all alike, even the queen's damsels themselves, showed every part of the body[2] with as little shame as we should show our faces[3], and he adds "they are the finest men and the prettiest women that I have seen in any part of the world."   Bread, wine and oats were un-known as they sowed no corn and reared no vines[4], though as regards this statement he must certainly have been mistaken[5].   The cattle shared the houses with their owners[6] and were fed on grass and holly-leaves[7] just bruised to crush the spines and as the pasture failed the homes were changed to keep up with the beasts.   The people lived mostly on beef[8], the great lords drinking milk, the others beef-brose[9] and the poor folks nothing but water[10]. Raymond spent Christmas Day with the chief and was present at the feast where all were seated on the rushes. The meat was carried in on poles like a bier[11] and O'Neil wiped his mouth with the most dainty plants, asking with much curiosity about the manners of the Kings of France, Aragon and Castile but maintaining that his own were the best and most perfect in the world.   So far from taking any harm Raymond, like other pilgrims, had everywhere received much help[12] from these strange people, whom he had been led to regard as savages who had no government and whom no one could trust[13].   After leaving O'Neil he spent New

---

[1] Mantels de flissa, Wylie, ii. 149, note 10.   For panni Hibernie de Galway (or Galewych), see Pat. 5 H. V, 4, 5; Cal. Rot. Pat. 266.

[2] Mostro los partz vergonhozas tant los femmes quant los homes.

[3] Mostravo tot quant avien au tan pauca di virgonha coma de mostra la cara (visage), Jeanroy-Vignaux, 17; Castellane, 63.

[4] Els no semeno negun blat ne' non reculthisso pont de vy.

[5] See Wylie, ii. 150.

[6] Los hostals son comunement pres dels buous, Castellane, 64.

[7] La fuelha dels agreffols (i.e. acrifolium, Jeanroy, Glossary; Castellane, 64, who calls it the wild gooseberry), called Steckpalmen in Du Cange, s.v., or an unknown tree of evil omen, Lewis and Short, s.v.

[8] Pannier, 22, 139.   [9] Del broet de la carn.

[10] James Yonge in 1422 testifies to "the grete abstynence that owre Irysh enemys supportyth in metes and drynkes," Secreta, 176.

[11] Coma hom porta semals (une civière).

[12] No fazian mal, ajudo mot a endresser los peleris.

[13] Gens salvatges lasquals non avian regimen en que negus se degnas fizar, Jeanroy-Vignaux, 13; Pannier, 22, 139; iretges salvatges (i.e. Irois sauvages), Perillos, 60; Pannier, 22; wylde Yrische, Pol. Songs, ii. 188; Pauli, Hertzberg, 50; not hérétiques sauvages, as Castellane. 60, who quite needlessly supposes that some Wycliffites may have been at work amo~~t them.

Year's Day in a castle belonging to the Countess of March[1]
and then sailed from Dundalk[2] back to Holyhead, found
King Richard and his queen at the Abbey at Lilleshall[3] in
Shropshire, and after paying his respects crossed from Dover
homewards.　For the next seven months he stayed about
the French court and was present at the fêtes given to
King Wenzel[4] when he visited Rheims in the spring of
1398[5].　On his return he wrote an account of his journey
in his native Catalan which is still to be seen in the Public
Library at Toulouse.　He reappears in 1420 as Admiral of
Aragon[6] in which year he joined in the attack made on
Naples by King Alfonso V.

　　One or two other visitors have also left us scanty
fragments of information as to Ireland in that same age.
On September 20, 1409[7], a Durham man named William
of Stranton[8] went down into St Patrick's Hole, being conducted over the place by the Yorkshire saint, John of
Bridlington, and the Cornish saint, Ive of Quethiock near
Liskeard, or according to another account by Saint Hilda of
Whitby, whose shrines he had often visited, but his story
reads like a mere moralising sermon against the prevailing
vices of his day[9] such as dressiness[10], drunkenness, lechery
and swearing.　Among the victims in the Hole Stranton
found his own sister and her lover whose marriage he had

---

[1] Jeanroy-Vignaux, 52; Castellane, 71.　For a story that he was stabbed at the
Purgatory by one of his companions, a knight named Ugolino, and that his ghost still
walks the countryside, see O'Connor, 106.

[2] Daneli.

[3] Liquesiel fort bela abadia de monges negres (i.e. Austin or Black Canons), not
Liquefiel, usually supposed to be Lichfield.　For a document dated at Lilleshall Jan. 25,
1398, see Rym. viii. 32.　For Henry IV at Lilleshall in 1402, 1403, see Wylie, iv. 481.

[4] L'Emperador de Alamanha que era adonc lo rey de Boemia.

[5] For Wenzel's arrival at Rheims, March 22, 1398 (not 1397, as Castellane, 53), see
St Denys, ii. 564; Jeanroy-Vignaux, p. xvii.

[6] Navarrette, i. 442; Faraglia, 188.　For a picture of him in the Monastery at Montserrat near Barcelona, see Jeanroy, xv, quoting Zurita, Book 10, chap. 50.　For views of
Montserrat, see Piferrer, ii. 242, 246, 250.

[7] Krapp, 35, 56, 58; H. L. D. Ward, ii. 484; Delehaye, 38; sometimes called
April 11, 1406, H. L. D. Ward, ii. 487; or 1407, Aubrey, ii. 59; or May 3, 1409, O'Connor, 99.

[8] Usually called Staunton, H. L. D. Ward, ii. 484; Frati, Tradizioni, p. 60; Wylie,
ii. 169.　He came from Stranton near Hartlepool, Krapp, 55, who publishes the text
from MS. Royal 17 B. xliii, described in H. L. D. Ward, ii. 484, but without any details
of the journey.

[9] Félice, 66, with summary, pp. 60–70.

[10] Wylie, ii. 444, note 2; H. L. D. Ward, ii. 489; Krapp, 36, who refers (p. 40) to a
similar condemnation at a visit by Edmund Liversedge, not yet published.

prevented, and his uncle[1] a parson who had neglected the
duties of his parish, together with plenty of vainglorious
bishops, fraudulent executors who "tokyn the dedis goodes
to here owne use[2]," negligent priests who let the rain and
snow get in to the roof of their chancels where God's body
should be sacred[3], parents who would not flog their children
and worldly prioresses who had entered religion for pomp
and pride to have ease of their bodies and abundance of
riches, living like empresses with rings on their fingers,
silver and overgilt girdles at their waists, buckles on their
shoes and other such nice vanities[4], all of whom were taking
their appropriate punishments in the raging and tearing
torment of the fiery place.   But again there is no question
of any wild or terrifying population without, and when in
his farewell word at parting St John of Bridlington bids
the pilgrim to dread nought of the way as he passed homewards[5] his fear is directed against the possibility of the
sight of evil spirits and not to attacks by savage tribes.

Yet another peep into this fascinating mediaeval hell[6] is
afforded by a letter written by a Florentine, Antonio Mannini,
who had been mixed up in the intrigues of the reign of
Richard II.   In 1411 he found himself in Dublin with time
on his hands and, falling in with a Hungarian knight
Lawrence Rátholdi who was on his way to the Purgatory,
he resolved to make use of his opportunity and try the
adventure himself.   Accordingly he left Dublin on Sept. 25,
1411[7], and after what he calls three weeks[8] on a dangerous
road he reached Lough Derg on Nov. 4.   The lake he
describes as lying amidst very high mountains and he gives
particulars of the Priory with exact dimensions of the island
and the chapel.   At the Priory he made his confession and
for the usual three days[9] tasted nothing but bread and water.
On Nov. 7[10] he rose before dawn and after further confession

---

[1] Thi eme that was person of suche a place, Krapp, 69.   For "eme" or "em," see
Laud Troy Bk. 9, 176, 211, 258; Weever, 478; Wylie, ii. 403.
[2] Krapp, 65.
[3] Ibid. 70.   [4] Ibid. 75, 76.
[5] Ibid. 77.
[6] Al misterioso Pozzo, Frati, 140.
[7] Frati, 156; do. Tradizioni, 58.
[8] Called 3½ months, d'aller et retour, in Delehaye, 41.
[9] Il digiuno consueto, Frati, 156; called 15 days by Grissafary in 1353, Wylie, ii. 166;
O'Connor, 85, 99; also by Rátholdi, pro ut moris est, Delehaye, 47.
[10] Delehaye, 38.

and mass he was rowed across by one of the canons in the little boat made out of a hollowed tree-trunk[1] in which there was only room for four. The day was calm and the canon plied the oars and when they got within half a bow-shot of the island[2] a big bird like a heron and as black as a coal with not a feather on its back and only four or five on each wing rose and fluttered about the boat. Mannini wanted to know what it was but the canon, speaking in Latin, said: "Nothing! nothing! Don't ask! don't ask[3]!" and then went on to tell him that it was a demon that had tempted St Patrick. They called it "corva[4]" and scared it away by blowing on a horn. Arrived at the chapel the visitor stripped to his shirt and put on a long white cloak like a deacon's dalmatic, took a cross in his hand and lay with beating heart[5] and eyes closed while they chanted over him the office for the dead. By the time this was over he was so weak that he could not stand, but at last they got him on his feet and down he went into the Hole. How long he stayed there he does not know but he thinks it was five hours or possibly 24. He only knows that in the darkness he saw an enormous black spider as large as the palm of your hand, and as the ugly thing came near him he grasped his cross quite tightly in the right hand and fell asleep and when they came to wake him they thought that he was dead[6]. He came to himself however and waited while his Hungarian friend took his turn on Nov. 11[7] as to which he testifies that Rátholdi came through quite well and behaved himself as a good knight should[8]. The two returned together to Dublin where Mannini wrote a letter on Feb. 25, 1412[9], to a Florentine merchant[10] in London

---

[1] In uno piccolo batello, Frati, 156; fatto come un taglio d'un albero vuoto e pur forza cavato, do. Tradizioni, 58.

[2] i.e. Station Island, see O'Connor, 54, 64, 114. For a visit to it on March 29, 1905, see Félice, 14.

[3] Nihil, nihil est! non quæritis! non quæritis! Frati, 157.

[4] Demon cornu hibernicè nuncupatus, Delehaye, 48.

[5] 'l cuore mi comincio a ritremare e a battere, Frati, 159.

[6] Mi trovo sanza ninno spirito o sanza aliture, Frati, 160.

[7] Delehaye, 50. For certificate dated Thursday after Martinmas from Matthew, Prior of the Purgatory, see Krapp, 35, not the Prior of St Matthew, as ibid. 58, 59.

[8] E portossi come buono cavalieri, Frati, 162; exivit incolumis et jocundus, Krapp, 34.

[9] Frati, 154–62, not Feb. 11, 1411, as ibid. 140; do. Tradizioni, p. 57.

[10] i.e. Corso di Giovanni Rustichi, of whom nothing is known except that he was imprisoned at Piacenza in 1424.

in which he told him that he was not allowed to write down what he had seen or to speak of it except in confession but that he would tell him all about it when they met. And so we lose sight of him altogether except that we know that he did not get back from Ireland until nearly two years later[1]. He subsequently returned to Florence and died there in 1431[2]. His letter, which was carried to England by Rátholdi together with others addressed to two Englishmen whom he calls "Nortona" and "Giovanni Berlintona[3]," somehow came into the hands of the youngest of his four brothers[4], Salvastro Mannini, who entered it up in a commonplace book which has fortunately survived until this day[5].

His companion, Lawrence Taar[6] or Rátholdi from Pásztóth[7], was a great traveller and linguist[8] who had been brought up from childhood at the Hungarian court where he was now head sewer and dispenser[9] to King Sigismund who together with his queen Barbara gave him a general letter of safe-conduct on Jan. 10, 1409[10], to cover him in his proposed journey in search of knightly adventures including visits to Compostella and the Irish Purgatory. How he had fared in the first part of his programme we do not know, but in Sept. 1411, as we have seen, he had recently arrived in Dublin with a herald and a train of followers[11] where he was received as a personage of distinction and paid visits of devotion to the relics of St Patrick, St Columba and St Bridget, specially venerating the famous Jesus staff in the Cathedral of the Holy Trinity with which St Patrick had driven all the snakes out of

---

[1] He left Ireland on Oct. 12, 1413, Frati, 154, 162.

[2] Salutati, iii. 499.

[3] Frati, 155.

[4] He had four brothers, viz. Alamanno (d. 1423), Luigi, Niccolò and Salvastro. His father's name was Alamanno di Zucchero detto Mannino, Salutati, iii. 620.

[5] Salutati, iii. 499, where it is described as Cod. Magliab. xxv. 595, c. 423 (Carlo Strozzi), probably a MS. of Antonio Magliabecchi in the Laurentian Library at Florence.

[6] L. L. Kropf, in Catholic Home Annual, N.Y. 1897, p. 72; Delehaye, 91.

[7] i.e. Pásztö near Gyongyös in the County of Heves, Krapp, 35; called Tar Lörincz, Laurentius Taar, Sobole Ratholdi in Irodalomtörténeöi Közlemények, 1896, p. 402; Kropf, Pászthói, 716; Wylie, ii. 169. For a church dedicated to St Michael in villa tua propria, see Delehaye, 53.

[8] Omnes mundi partes pro majori noviter visitavit, Delehaye, 44; variis ydiomatibus eruditum, ibid. 51; ebraici, greci et latini ydiomatibus, ibid. 58.

[9] Magister dapiferorum reginalium Hungare, Delehaye, 40, 57, 58; supremus dispensator, ibid. 46; Kropf, Pászthói, 718, 725, 730.

[10] Dated in castro nostro S^{ti} Georgii, Jan. 10, 1408 (i.e. 1409), in Delehaye, 46, though called 1408 in H. L. D. Ward, ii. 489; Krapp, 34; Félice, 59.

[11] Delehaye, 45.

Ireland[1].   He was honourably received by the Archbishop
of Armagh[2], but the description of his journey is a blank,
and when he reached the Saints' Island he got the usual
warning from the Prior and took the usual bread-and-water
discipline[3].   He was struck with the abundance of trout
and salmon in the Lough and when the Prior and one of
the canons rowed him over in the skiff he saw the same
diabolical bird like a ragged heron[4], hooting like an owl.
He likewise gives the dimensions of the island which he
found crowded with ravenous choughs, kites, owls and
vultures and other satanic fowl[5], nesting and chattering
in their old ancestral homes among the thorns and prickly
bushes with which the place was overgrown.   Having
changed his clothes and put on three albs and a new pair
of breeches[6] he lay flat on the ground while the Prior
recited the litany of the dead, and as they opened the
door they sang the *Dies Irae* and sprinkled him with holy
water and so they locked him in.   Round his neck he had
four pieces of the True Cross, some little pieces of three of
the Holy Coats[7] and other precious relics and stones, and
he carried a book of the seven psalms and a candle (*sereum*)
which had to be cut into nine pieces as the roof was so low[8].

Once in the Hole Owen's trite old visions came to him
with the accustomed "admirable regularity[9]," and so his experience provides us with nothing new[10] except that he
went a mile down before he reached the Purgatory and
that he saw a number of his own relations in the flames as
well as the souls of St Nicholas, of an Englishman whom
he calls Eugene or O'Brian[11] and of his own compatriot
George Krisszafàn[12], whose visit to that awful place some

[1] Krapp, 34; clensit from al venemouse bestis, Secreta, 202.
[2] i.e. Nicholas Fleming (May 1, 1404—June, 1415), H. Cotton, iii. 16.
[3] Sub mensura panis et aquæ, Delehaye, 47.
[4] Ardee dispennatæ, Delehaye, 48.
[5] Capis, coredulis (quasi cor edens, Du Cange, s.v.), &c.
[6] Nudus et jejunus exceptis rosetis et uno femorali, Delehaye, 58.
[7] Cum particulis trium tunicarum Jhesu Christi, Delehaye, 50.
[8] Propter stricturam spelunce, ibid.; Krapp, 34.
[9] Félice, 9.
[10] For analysis of his account from Royal MS. 10 B. ix. ff. 36–44, described in H. L. D.
Ward, ii. 489, see Krapp, 33–36, with text in Delehaye, 45.   For several MSS., see
O'Connor, 106.
[11] Delehaye, 58.
[12] Krapp, 35; Delehaye, 36, 58; Georgius Grifani or Krisszafàn, Kropf, Pászthói, 716,
726; called György Crissafan, Toldy in Szazadok, v. 231, 247; or Cussafan, M. Denis,

60 years before has been already described[1]. Back again
in Dublin he received a final certificate from Archbishop
Fleming[2] and supplied particulars of his adventure to
a notary named James Yonge[3] who drew up the colourless
account as we have it now. To this however he appended
a personal note to the effect that he had paid the visit in
order to see the wonders of Ireland and to report on them
to his master Sigismund. Asked as to whether he had
convinced himself that Purgatory was an actual reality, as
the soul was usually supposed to be invisible, impassive
and incorporeal, or whether, when he saw these visions, he
was "out of the body," he could only say "God knows!"
but he rather thought he must have been "in the body"
all along, for he lit nine separate bits of his candle and saw
them burn away before he got out of the place himself.

Lawrence still continued high in Sigismund's service
and was employed by him to negotiate at Venice on
Jan. 20, 1413[4], but the report of his visit had a singularly
unfortunate reaction on his master's character and a century
later a tradition was afloat that Rátholdi had seen Sigismund
himself down there in a red-hot bath and a bed of fire[5] getting
purged of his sin by the ladies whom he had led astray in
his lifetime.

2445, where the year is wrongly given as 1343, and Archbishop Fitzralph's letter is dated
at Dromiskin near Dundalk; Crissiphani, in O'Connor, 95. For suggestion that this is
the Neapolitan form of Christopher, see Kropf, ut sup.

[1] i.e. in 1353, Wylie, ii. 166.

[2] Dated at Dromiskin, Dec. 27, 1411, Delehaye, 57, in which he styles himself
Primas Hibernie.

[3] Notarius imperialis et hujus memorialis compilator, Delehaye, 56, 58; Krapp, 35.
For William Yonge, Archdeacon of Meath since 1407, see H. Cotton, iii. 127. He became Chancellor of Ireland in 1422 (1 H. VI), Rot. Pat. Hib. i. 224; O'Flanagan, i. 84.

[4] Kropf, Pászthói, 730.

[5] Tinodi, 358, who had read the account "in an old song" now lost, but possibly=
Thurocsi, Lat. Chron. Sig., see Kropf, Pászthói, 725; Wylie, Constance, 20.

CHAPTER VIII

SPAIN AND PORTUGAL

AMBASSADORS were already on their way to England from Ferdinand I[1] who besides being Regent of Castile[2] for his young nephew Juan II[3] had just succeeded by election to the disputed throne of Aragon. His uncle Martin I, King of Aragon, called the Humane[4], had had only one son, known as Martin King of Sicily[5], but that son had died on July 25, 1409[6], and by the advice of Vincent Ferrer King Martin of Aragon had married a

[1] El Honesto, Courteault, Archives, 134, 152. For picture of him see Fages, i. 397.

[2] Cum sitis unus de tutoribus carissimi nepotis nostri Johannis regis Castelle et Legionis (see letter of Henry V to Ferdinand in Add. MS. 24,062, f. 150 b), i.e. under the will of his brother, Henry III, dated Dec. 24, 1406, whereby he arranged for a council of regency, in which his wife Catherine and his brother Ferdinand were to occupy the chief places; Daumet, Alliance, 69. For poem by Ruy Paez de Ribera to Catherine and Ferdinand as Regent for Don Juan, see Baena, i. 292. For poems of Alfonso Alvarez de Villasandino on the sickness and death of Henry III (d. Dec. 25, 1406, Gamez, 429, 430; Staindl, 527; Lodge, 475; Wylie, ii. 330), see Baena, i. 61, 64; ii. 287. For poems addressed to Catherine as madre de nuestro señor el rey Don Juan see Baena, i. 65, 313.

[3] Rym. ix. 134. For picture of him see Heiss, Monedas, i. 83. For his coins see ibid. i. 91–97, Plates 11, 12. For his monument (d. 1454) in the Charterhouse at Miraflores near Bourgos see Carderara, xlviii; also his second wife Isabel of Portugal (d. 1496), daughter of the Infante Juan, to whom he was married at Madrigal in 1447 (Carderara, cxxiii). For poems on his birth (March 6, 1405, Beaucourt, i. 302; Wylie, ii. 329) by Friar Diego de Valencia, Francisco Imperial (a Genoese living in Seville), Bartholomé Garcia de Cordova (a friar in the monastery of Freydeval, i.e. Fres-del-Val or Frex del Val, near Bourgos, see Los Rios, 799, 803), Don Mosse (surgeon to his father, Henry III, Baena, ii. 318), and his secretary, Ferrant Manuel de Lando (who celebrates the tournament held at Valladolid on March 7, 1405, in honour of the event, and who died after 1449, Baena, ii. 75, 277), see Baena, i. 199, 208, 217, 219, 278. In Harl. MS. 431, f. 126, is a letter from Henry IV, dated Sept. 12, 1408, addressed to him as King of Castile.

[4] El Humano, P. Bofarull, ii. 294; M. A. S. Hume, 255. For altar frontal with his arms and those of his first wife, Maria de Luna, who died in 1407, see Burlington Magazine, vii. 142. For his registers (248 vols.) see Courteault, 150, 151.

[5] For his coins see Heiss, ii. 23, 185, 230, 353, 420; Plates 72, 79, 90, 98, 105, 117, 141.

[6] Anselme, i. 289; P. Bofarull, Generacion, 312; Heiss, Monedas, ii. 23, 35; iii. 33; Grande Encycl. xxiii. 330; called July 24, 1409, in Historians' Hist. x. 106 (not 1412, as Heiss, Monedas, i. 88). For his will dated in Castro Calleri (i.e. Caillé) at Cagliari in Sardinia July 25, 1409 (not 1410, as Meuillon, 18), see Starrabba, 9. For 16th century map of Sardinia see Belleforest, Cosmogr. ii. 825. For a plan of Cagliari, ibid. ii. 832; Münster, 284; called "Culle" in Bouvier, Descript. 67.

second wife[1] in the hope of averting the danger of a disputed succession. But he was a stout torpid man[2] and in broken health at 55 years of age[3]. He put himself into the hands of the nuns of Valdonzella[4] near Barcelona, who plied him with what they considered the right sort of fare to suit his case[5], without consulting the doctors[6]. On May 29, 1410, he ate roast goose[7] and garlic, which proved too heating[8], and in two days afterwards he was dead[9].

A vivid description of that death-scene still remains. Intriguers (men and women) came and went in the room seeking promises for their favourite candidates, but the only witness of the last agony was the court fool, who joked on to keep his dying master alive till he saw his soul pass up from his feet, flit like a little shadow across his stomach and finally flicker out at his lips and vanish clean away[10]. Martin I was buried in the cathedral at Barcelona on June 19, 1410, Pope Benedict XIII being present at the

---

[1] i.e. Margaret de Pratis, in Aug. 1409, Alpartil, 196; Eubel, Bullarium, vii. 553. For her Register, 1412–1421 see Courteault, Archives, 151.

[2] Carderara, xxxix; adipibus torpidum...incommodâ habitudine corporis, Valla, 1040, 1041; nimium pinguis, Alpartil, 196.

[3] Called 52 in Tolra de Bordas, 24.

[4] Vallis Puellarum, Surita, Indices, 407; Gamez, 449; in valle Donzellae non procul a muris Barcelonae, Valla, 1040; Valdoncellus, Bayle, 165, 198; Marineo, 865.

[5] For usus rerum faecundantium see Kymer, 556.

[6] Quae quotidie citra medicorum conscientiam cibariis ad Venerem quam ad salutem aptioribus inferciebant unguentisque oblinebant, Valla, 1040, who says that a lot of this sort of stuff was found in the convent.

[7] For "gos farced," i.e. with parsley, swine's grease, mutton suet, boiled together with chopped eggs, pepper, ginger, cinnamon, saffron, salted grapes or onions, cloves, and a little boiled pork, see Two Cookery Books, 44, 81, 109.

> But a fatt goos whan it is newe slayn
> In disshis of gold a morsel agreable
> Is sewid up atte kingis table
> Swymmyng on lyve in watris cristallyn
> Tendre rostid requeerith to have good wyn.
>   Pol. Relig. Po. 23.

[8] Cf. Ne mangés espices et aulx (i.e. garlic) et teles viandes qui engendres mauvaises chaleurs et perilleux esmovemens, i.e. Gerson's advice to his sisters, Jadart, 134. For avoidance of sauces and hashes advised by Vincent Ferrer see Bayle, 354. For buvrages et potages pour malades see Ménagier, ii. 237.

[9] i.e. May 31, 1410; Gams, Kirchengesch. i. 295; Finke, Acta, i. 9; Gamez, 474; D. M. J. Henry, ii. 31; Blancas, 217; do. Inscriptiones, 34; Viciana, iii. 160; Papon, iii. 311; P. Bofarull, 296; Touron, iii. 45; Fages, ii. 3; do. Notes, 152; Tolra de Bordas, 24; Lavisse-Rambaud, 469; Alpartil, 247; called May 30 in Arenijs, 647; Schirrmacher, vi. 181; not May 21st, as Gazanyola, 256; Vidal, 258.

[10] Valla, 1040, who had the story from the fool when he was a rich old man, 84 years of age, and still kept up his craft (necdum a scurrando vacans). Valla also notes (1041) that there was a total eclipse of the moon in the month in which King Martin died, but this took place on March 21, 1410; Oppolzer, 365. For this reference I am indebted to my friend, Mr C. T. Whitmell, of Leeds.

funeral[1], but in 1416 his body was removed to the burial place of the Kings of Aragon in the great Cistercian Abbey at Poblet[2] near Tarragona. He left behind no lawful child[3] and very soon six claimants[4] were in the field, each pushing his pretensions with threatening zeal.

Within a year[5] after the king's death the Archbishop of Saragossa[6] was assassinated and the whole country was filled with the fiercest internal discord[7], every man carrying a sword or a dagger, whether at home, in church or in council, always at hand for use in private feuds[8]. For two years there was no recognised ruler in the land till the position at length became intolerable and the Estates of the provinces of Aragon, Catalonia and Valencia met and elected three arbiters each, to whom was delegated the task of choosing a king. These nine commissioners[9], mostly lawyers and churchmen, including the Archbishop of Tarragona[10], the Bishop of Huesca and the brothers Boniface[11] and Vincent Ferrer, met on March 16, 1412[12], in the castle at Caspe[13] near the confines of the three provinces, where they listened to representatives and proctors of the different claimants for 30 days[14], and after being further locked up for

[1] He afterwards went to Montserrat and thence to Tarragona, leaving for Saragossa on Nov. 5, 1410, Arenijs, 648.

[2] Marineo, 865; Viciana, iii. 160; P. Bofarull, ii. 294; Monfar, ii. 346. For his epitaph see Piferrer, ii. 397. For account of Poblet or Poboleda see Piferrer, ii. 351-446.

[3] El qual no descana hijo ni hija, Guzman, 34. For his bastard children see Beccario, Spigolature.

[4] Gamez, 474; P. Bofarull, ii. 296; Janer, 5; Fages, ii. 8, 16 (with illustration); do. Notes, 228; called 4 in Gams, Kirchengesch. i. 295; or 5 in Blancas, 218; Cavanilles, iv. 60. For their names see Papon, iii. 312; D. M. J. Henry, ii. 34; E. A. Schmidt, Aragonien, 322.

[5] Not within a month, as Valla, 1043.

[6] i.e. Garcia Fernandez de Heredia, Archbishop from Oct. 5, 1383, killed June 1, 1411; Gams, 20; called Garsias in Marineo, 860; Alpartil, 201.

[7] Magis atque magis indies ad vim spectare res videbantur, omnia plena motus, timoris, turbationum et periculorum, Valla, 1041.

[8] Valla, 1060.

[9] Quam nos altres non persones hi erem per elegir rey, Ferrier, i. (Sermons) 38; P. Bofarull, ii. 299; Monfar, ii. 419, 424, 439; Cavanilles, iv. 71; Blancas, 236-239; Valla, 1040; Marineo, 866; Viciana, iii. 160; Surita, ii. 4; Mariana, ii. 214; Teoli, 75; Llorente, 140; A. Butler, i. 431; Bayle, 190, 201; Fages, ii. 11; App. xxxviii; do. Notes, 229.

[10] i.e. Pedro (called Francis in Valla, 1047) Sagarriga, translated from Lerida, July 12, 1407, died Dec. 31, 1418, Gams, 44, 77; Eubel, i. 294, 505.

[11] Petreius, 27, where he is unus de *septem* regentibus regni Valenciae (*sic*).

[12] Janer, 57; P. Bofarull, ii. 302.

[13] Al castel de Casp, Ferrier, i. (Sermons) 38; Guzman, 44, 45; Surita, ii. 25; not in the Cortes, as Grande Encycl. iii. 529. For ruins of the castle with the hall called after St Vincent Ferrer, now a yard (préau) for women from appel de justice, see Fages, ii. 22; do. Notes, 228. [14] Viciana, iii. 161.

eight days in secret deliberation they delivered their judgment on June 24, 1412[1]. By this decision, which is known as
the "Compromise of Caspe[2]," they directed that Ferdinand,
the Regent of Castile, should henceforward be king of a
united Aragon[3]. On June 28[4], an altar was set up outside
the western door of the church in the castle yard at Caspe
and benches were placed for the commissioners, and
there at the head of the great double flight of steps[5]
Ferdinand was declared King of Aragon[6], as a personage
accepted of all[7], by the mouth of Vincent Ferrer[8], who
preached to the assembled crowds from the text: "Let us
be glad and rejoice and give honour to him, for the marriage
of the Lamb is come[9]." As he commended the decision
with all the force of his matchless eloquence the multitude
who thronged the square to the very housetops shouted:
"Viva nostre Rey et Senyor Don Ferrando![10]" The
banner of Aragon was then unfurled before the altar amidst
shouts again and again renewed; the bells rang out; the
fifes and horns took up the joy and the streets were filled
with dancers day and night[11].

In this success it is certain that Ferdinand received
the active support of Pope Benedict XIII, who afterwards

---

[1] Nauclerus, 1043, 1044; Blancas, 242, 488; do. Inscriptiones, 35; Janer, 69;
Cavanilles, iv. 74. For their declaration see Janer, 171, 173.

[2] Called el Parlamento de Caspe in Guzman, 44; or Congreso de Caspe, Heiss,
Monedas, ii. 25; el Fallo de Caspe, C. Soler (quoted in Fages, Notes, 241). For a
picture of it in the Palacio de la Diputación at Madrid (Quadrado, 406), see Fages,
ii. 20.

[3] Valla, 1047; Historians' Hist. x. 120.

[4] Janer, 86, 175, 176; Cavanilles, iv. 76; not June 14, as Gazanyola, 256; nor
June 29, as Valla, 1047; Boyssel, 391; Fages, ii. 19; nor June 30, as Guzman, 45;
nor July 25, as Viciana, iii. 166; nor 1411, as Tolra de Bordas, 24; nor 1414, as Grätz,
iv. 221.

[5] For picture of the church see Fages (edn. 1901), i. 415.

[6] His full title was King of Aragon, Sicily, Valencia, Majorca, Sardinia and Corsica,
Count of Barcelona, Roussillon and Cerdagne, Duke of Athens and Neopatras (in
Phthiotis, Grande Encycl. iv. 445), Rym. ix. 293, 295; cf. cum Rex Aragoniae
nuncupatur Cataloniae quoque Princeps subintelligitur, Valla, 1041; Monfar, ii. 340,
549, 560, 591; Surita, Indices, 405; Lodge, 478; Blancas, Inscriptiones, 34.

[7] De consensu totius populi, Add. MS. 24,062, f. 150; Viciana, iii. 162; E. A. Schmidt,
Aragonien, 326. For a letter to him written at Constance June 9, 1417, see Mart. Anec.
i. 1750, in which the writer says that there would have been no peace in Aragon but for
his auctoritatis pondus et consilii.

[8] Yo pronouncii la sentencia en Casp, Ferrier, i. (Sermons) 35.

[9] Rev. xix. 7; Janer, 71, 177. The full text of the sermon is lost (Finke, 32), but
Mariana (ii. 217) supplies the substance of it from his own imagination. Cf. Cavanilles,
iv. 77; Touron, iii. 75; Bayle, 205; Fages, Notes, 256.

[10] Cf. nobile Infante Don Ferrando, Baena, 66, 239, 292, 307.

[11] Valla, 1048; muy grande alagria, Guzman, 45.

threw out the taunt that he had made him[1] and could unmake him again ; but the real hero to whom the country owed its rescue from anarchy was the great Dominican Friar afterwards canonised as St Vincent Ferrer[2], and it is one of the penalties of his commanding influence in an ultra-credulous age that his record is so overlaid with childish miracles as to leave the true picture of the real man in a hopeless confusion of absurdities.

For certainly there is no personage, whose life was passed in strenuous effort in those distant days, whose fame has been so cruelly wounded in the house of his friends. From the day of his death down to the present time his biographers[3] have worked him as a patchwork of thaumaturgics, relying upon "immemorial traditions[4]" as if they were sober facts and paying less heed to the actual verities of human life than to a mistaken regard for the "edification of the faithful[5]." Indeed it would seem as though the more babyish the reputed miracle the more greedily has it been swallowed. Their hero cures the blind before he is born[6] ; he makes an eight-months' infant come down from its betrayed mother's breast to walk along a crowded church

---

[1] Me qui te feci, Marineo, 867 ; Mariana, 937 (edn. 1592) ; Tolra de Bordas, 30.

[2] For bibliography of works on him see Fages, Notes, pp. i–lx ; for a representation of him by Fra Angelico in the predella of the Crucifixion in the chapter-house of the convent of St Mark at Florence see Marchese, i. 216, who questions the identity. For fancy pictures of him see Teoli, Frontispiece ; Fages, I. cxxxii ; Schedel, 265.

[3] For his biographers see Bayle, pp. xxi–xxiv; Fages, i. App. pp. lxxxvi–cxxxiii. The industry and patience displayed in this latest life cannot but command respect, but the book is only one more proof of the incurably uncritical trend of the hagiologist mind. In his preface (I. p. x) P. Fages declares that it is idle to try and reduce his hero to human proportions, and seems to think that he has added to our stock of reliable proof by quoting from Teyxidor, who was an inmate of the Black Friars at Valencia in the 18th century (p. iv). In Fages, Notes, 235, Viciana is quoted as a contemporary author, though he did not publish his chronicle till 1563. For a criticism of the book (which was written in response to an urgent call for a really worthy biography of the saint by P. Meyer in Romania, x. p. 229), see Ec. des Chartes, lvii. 461, where it is called ouvrage mal digéré ; le verbiage, le mauvais goût, l'absence de critique gâtaient le fruit d'abondantes recherches ; cf. hat beiden Teilen genügen wollen, dem Forscher und dem Beter, Finke, 25. Previous to the canonisation, though the stories of miracles were in the air, yet they were accepted with much greater reserve, e.g. *si vera memorantur* miraculis clarus, Valla, 1047 ; *dicitur* quod claret multis miraculis, Alpartil, 308. Finke, 35, regards the Naples' depositions as die dürftigsten weil offizielsten. In dealing with similar testimony in regard to the visions and marvels of Ermine, who died Aug. 25, 1396, Gerson has some highly interesting comments ; e.g. multa insuper ibidem (i.e. in the certified testimony) ponuntur pro miraculis quae naturaliter salvari possint, and he thinks that the statements should be published, because some people are so ignorant and others so obstinately credulous (tam ob pravam eruditionem multorum quam propter obstinatam quorundam credulitatem), Jadart, 178.

[4] Pradel, 5.   [5] Bayle, 354.

[6] Fages, i. 12.

and single out her seducer[1], while a dishonest taverner pours a bottle of his diluted wine into the saint's scapular only to find the water separating from the wine as soon as it touches the holy man's garment[2].   In a pelting storm at Graus he waves his hand and at once the sun comes out[3]. If the crows caw or the mules bray when he is preaching, he has only to motion to them and they are still[4], and when 1000 thirsty people follow him about, they all drink from his half-cask of wine and yet it keeps as full as ever[5]. When a child had been killed and cut up and baked in an oven and served up in a dish, he makes it come to life again, open its eyes and give its father a kiss, and you may still see the oven at Morella, where it all happened[6].   And thus the real life-purpose of this wondrous man who preached as never man had preached since the days of the Apostles[7], who swayed whole nations, reconciled the feuds of contending towns and factions[8] and saved his country from the most embittered of civil wars, is lost in a cloud of fatiguing and unprofitable puerilities.

Yet for years he pursued one fixed, devoted course of life.   He lived with Pope Benedict at Avignon[9] and with kings at the courts of Aragon and Castile without becoming entangled either in royal or papal intrigues.   He spent his life in harmonising discords[10] but there is no evidence that he ever made an enemy, except it were the saintly Gerson who chid him mildly for coquetting with the Flagellants[11]. With honours offered on every hand he chose the life of

---

[1] For a picture of the scene see Teoli, 65.

[2] Bayle, 226 ; Fages, ii. 58.   [3] Ibid. ii. 59.

[4] Ibid. ii. 59, 60.

[5] Ibid. ii. 91, 92, where he also feeds 4000 people in the Charterhouse of Scala Caeli near Conflans, in August, 1415.

[6] Ibid. ii. 72.   For a picture of the miracle see ibid. (2nd edn.), ii. 53.   For the attestations see ibid. i. App. xxxvii.

[7] Despuys que les Apostles mortz foran non fou vist in auzit home si automens predicant, Boysset, 362; Magnus predicator ad populum, Alpartil, 405.

[8] Bayle, 155 ; Fages, ii. 32 ; Pradel, 46.

[9] i.e. from 1394 to 1399, Fages, Notes, pp. 90, 99; Alpartil, 396–403.

[10] For letter from Benedict XIII to him in 1414 to make peace if possible between the Counts of Foix and Armagnac see Eubel, Avign. 183.   For picture of him reconciling enemies see Fages (2nd edn.), i. 249; e.g. between the clergy and town of Valencia in reference to the university in 1411, Fages, i. 3, 277.   Not that he founded the university, as Bayle, 171 ; Pradel, 72, which was really founded in 1209.   For bull of Alexander VI (1492–1503), see Llorente, 143.

[11] Antonio, ii. 207 ; Fages, i. App. lvi ; Notes, 133, with postscript by Pierre d'Ailli, from Hardt, vol. ii. p. 252.   For Gerson's treatise against the Flagellants see Tritheim, Cat. 135.

voluntary poverty[1] and to the last he was plain " Brother Vincent[2] " to the throngs of listeners who marvelled at the power of his mighty tongue.

In accordance with the compromise Ferdinand was proclaimed King of Aragon at Saragossa[3] on Sept. 3, 1412[4], thus uniting for the moment all northern and eastern Spain from Alicante to Finisterre, with the exception of Navarre, under the personal influence of one controlling will[5]. But the new king had still to fight his way to general acceptance in his own domain and one at least of his fellow-competitors, James (or Jaime) the Luckless[6], Count of Urgel[7] in Catalonia, a youngish man of commanding presence[8] who had married the Infanta Isabella[9], sister to the late King Martin, did not easily acquiesce in the decision of the electors at Caspe. He accordingly got together 2000 French horsemen as mercenaries, who entered the country from Andorra[10], and he engaged in a compact with the Duke of Clarence[11], who was wintering idly with a large force of English troops at Bordeaux[12]. According to this the English duke undertook to bring 1000 lances and 3000 archers in person to his assistance[13] if his father would allow him, or if he could not actually come himself he would send 500 men-of-arms and 3000 archers by Midsummer Day 1413[14], the Count of Urgel

---

[1] Nyder, Formicarius, in Fages, i. App. cxviii.

[2] "Fray Vicente," Guzman, 42; Bayle, i. 144; Fages, i. 221, App. xvi; "Maestro Vicente," Surita, ii. 73; "Mestre Vincens," Rouquette, 410; Thomas, 241; Affre, Rodez, 45; Annales du Midi, iv. 382, 384; Petit Thalamus, 452; "Maestre Vicent," Finke, 32; Guzman, 61; Bayle, 104; "Maestro Fray Vycente," Baena, i. 281 (from Ferrant Manuel de Lando); "Frayre Vinsens," Boyssel, 362; Romania, xxi. 549; "Frater Vincentius de Valencia," Glassberger, 228.

[3] For Saragossa as urbs antiquissima, see Rożmital, 103.

[4] Mariana, ii. 218; Schirrmacher, vi. 189; Marineo, 866; Touron, iii. 57.

[5] Quod utriusque regni unus ipse gubernaculum fuerat, Valla, 1064.

[6] El Desdichado, P. Bofarull, ii. 295; Monfar, ii. 325; Janer, 5, 56, 170. For his descent from Alfonso, King of Aragon, who died in 1336, see Lodge, 549.

[7] For coins of the county of Urgel see Heiss, Monedas, ii. 175, Plate 97.

[8] Juvenis eximiâ specie corporis, Valla, 1037.

[9] i.e. in 1405, Vidal, 40; Lodge, 483, 549.

[10] Monfar, ii. 462. For his application for French and Navarrese mercenaries, see Cavanilles, iv. 81.

[11] Called Orthomas duque de Clarencia in Surita, ii. 37; cf. Mariana, ii. 219; Schirrmacher, vi. 191.

[12] Que habian passado al reino de Francia con muy poderosa ejercito en favor de los duques de Orleans y Berri contra Carlos (*sic*) delfin de Francia, Surita, ii. 37, 39; cf. Wylie, iv. 85.

[13] Not ad capessendum regnum, as Valla, 1060, who confuses the English king (Henry IV) with Henry V.

[14] Surita, ii. 37; Schirrmacher, vi. 191; Monfar, ii. 461.

promising to give him his sister in marriage[1] and make him King of Sicily[2] in the event of their ultimate success. But owing to the death of Henry IV and the return of the Duke of Clarence to England more help was promised than was really brought[3] and only 700 Gascon troops[4] actually crossed the mountains under the command of Don Antonio de Luna[5]. These entered Huesca and some of them effected an entrance into Lerida[6] by stealth, but when a trumpeter in the town, being a heavy drinker like the rest of his class, got out of bed in the night[7] and played a call on his bugle for a joke they thought they were discovered and decamped out of the town in a panic. In the end they were driven back disastrously[8] and the Count of Urgel surrendered on Oct. 30, 1413[9], after sustaining a ten weeks' siege at Balaguer[10]. He was sentenced to imprisonment for life in the fortress of Xativa near Valencia, where he was ultimately assassinated on June 1, 1433[11]. After this pronounced success Ferdinand was formally accepted as King of Aragon by the Cortes at Saragossa in Jan. 1414[12]

[1] Great confusion centres round this point. Janer (90) speaks of envoys sent to England to arrange a marriage between a daughter of King Ferdinand (*sic*) and a son of the Duke of Clarence. In Monfar (ii. 462) the Duke of Clarence is himself to marry Isabel, the daughter of the Count of Urgel. In Surita, ii. 60, Clarence is called the Duke of York.

[2] Goodwin, 9; Monfar, ii. 461. This was one of the titles of the Kings of Aragon, see Rym. ix. 622; p. 85, note 6.

[3] Valla, 1060.

[4] Called 400 Gascons in Guzman, 43; Valla, 1043, 1044; Schirrmacher, vi. 187; or 350 men-of-arms and 400 archers in Surita, ii. 39; or 600 English and Gascons, E. A. Schmidt, Aragonien, 329.

[5] Valla, 1044, 1056, says they were under Raymond Pereliosus (i.e. of Perillos); also Monfar, ii. 414, 455; Schirrmacher, vi. 187. For Mosen Ponce de Perellos as envoy to the Count of Urgel see Guzman, 46; Monfar, ii. 448, 525.

[6] For account of Lerida see Piferrer ii. 313, 335.

[7] Ejus rei gratia qua solent qui saepius bibunt, quod genus est in primis tubicinum; Valla, 1059.

[8] Goodwin, 10; Guthrie, ii. 451, who supposes that Ferdinand was dead and Martin alive. Fages, ii. 24, thinks that they retired after a regiment had been cut up on July 10, 1413.

[9] Surita, ii. 42, 52; Mariana, ii. 220; Schirrmacher, vi. 192; Finke, Acta, i. 311; Gamez, 474; or Oct. 31, as Janer, 96; Monfar, ii. 529, 531, 535. In Cavanilles, iv. 83, 84, the siege lasts from Aug. 15 to Oct. 29, 1413; called from Aug. 10 to Oct. 26, 1413, in Fages, Notes, 245.

[10] For account of Balaguer and the ruin wrought to its buildings by the siege see Piferrer, ii. 335, 336. In Valla, 1061, it is oppidum situ et opere et arce tutissimum. For coins of Balaguer see Heiss, Monedas, ii. 137, Plate 88. For a letter of Ferdinand to Vincent Ferrer dated Lerida, Nov. 30, 1413, announcing the fall of Balaguer and inviting him to his coronation at Saragossa, see Fages, ii. 276, App. ii.

[11] Guzman, 52; Surita, ii. 43; Marineo, 867; Valla, 1062; M. A. S. Hume, 256, 257; E. A. Schmidt, Aragonien, 330, who quotes Carbonell, 111, for his sentence; Heiss, Monedas, ii. 175, 176, who gives the year as 1435, ibid. 26.

[12] Janer, 97, 179.

and crowned in the old cathedral of San Salvador[1] in the same city by the Bishop of Huesca[2] on Feb. 11 following[3].

Before this great settlement had been achieved King Ferdinand had tried to interest the Duke of York[4] in his quarrel, who sent a representative[5] to meet him at Balaguer, but as the English duke was a grandson of King Pedro the Cruel[6] and hinted at the revival of dormant claims to the throne of Castile himself[7], there was little prospect of successful negotiation in that quarter.

On hearing the news of Henry V's accession, King Ferdinand had sent letters to him desiring a league with England since his elevation to the throne of Aragon[8], and a continuation of the truce with Castile, and on receiving an encouraging reply he despatched envoys to England on this business. On May 22, 1413[9], the Lieutenant of Calais, William Lord Zouche of Harringworth[10],

[1] Known as La Seo (i.e. sedes), Alpartil, pp. xxv, 202 ; Marineo, 865 (of the Cathedral at Barcelona). For additions and repairs made to it by Benedict XIII in 1412 see Quadrado, 428–437. For le seo = Ecclesia major de Valentia, see Quetif, i. 691 ; Fages, Notes, 174. Fages (ii. 79) places the coronation at the Palace Aljaferia des Maures, now a barrack.

[2] i.e. Dominic Ram (Aug. 20, 1410—Sept. 13, 1414), afterwards Archbishop of Tarragona (Viciana, iii. 166 ; Guzman, 54) and Cardinal of Porto (March 3, 1443) till his death on April 25, 1445 ; Gams, pp. ix, 37; Eubel, ii. 6; called "Osciensis" in Alpartil, 202.

[3] Bofarull, ii. 307 ; Mariana, 933 ; Blancas, 243 ; E. A. Schmidt, Aragonien, 327, 330 ; Historians' Hist. x. 107 ; Fages, Notes, 247 ; called Feb. 10 in Viciana, 166 ; or Feb. 16, Surita, ii. 55. Not Jan. 1414, as Cavanilles, iv. 86. For odes on the coronation see Baena, i. 67, 68 ; also play attributed to Enrique de Villena, F. Wolf, 582.

[4] Called Eduardo Duque de Ayork in Surita, ii. 37, 47, who supposes him to have first favoured the Count of Urgel, together with the Marquis of Dorset (el Conde de Orset) ; cf. Monfar, ii. 461.

[5] Called Juan de Monforte in Surita, ii. 47.

[6] Called the

> Glorie of Spaine,
> Whom fortune held so high in majestee.
> Chaucer, Monk's Tale, 14,685.

[7] Surita, ii. 37, 47. His father, Edmund of Langley, had married in 1372 (not 1369, as J. Evans, 305) Doña Isabel (b. circ. 1355), 3rd daughter of Pedro the Cruel (d. 1369) (not Henry, as Percy MS. 78 in Armitage-Smith, 467) ; Wals. i. 313; ii. 194. She died Nov. 23, 1393, and was buried in the Priory Church at Langley, Ann. 344 ; Doyle, iii. 742 ; Comp. Peer. iv. 120; viii. 213 ; Lingard, iii. 99; York, xxiii. For a reference to her property in Kent see Memoranda Roll K.R. 3–4 H. V, Rot. 2, Nov. 28, 1415. Her remains, together with those of her husband and their monument, were removed to the parish church at King's Langley, circ. 1574, where they were examined on Nov. 22, 1877; J. Evans, 321–328. For the tomb see Sandford, 377 ; Gough, ii. 11 ; R. Gee, 12 ; Knight, Shakespeare, Richard II, p. 115; J. Evans, 311 ; Wylie, iv. 202.

[8] For an undated letter from Henry V to Ferdinand see Add. MS. 24,062, f. 150. In this he refers to a letter written by Ferdinand dated apud Conchen civitatem (i.e. Cuenca, Eubel, i. 208) in March last (? 1413) to the effect that he desired a league with England since his elevation to the throne of Aragon. The letter was brought by Henry's squire, J— S— (possibly John Sturminster ; see Wylie, iii. 285, note 7).

[9] Rym. ix. 2 ; Carte, Rolles, ii. 207.   [10] Page 40, note 1.

was commissioned to interview these envoys at the Strait
and verify their credentials[1]. They then sped onwards,
broke their journey at Canterbury[2] and had an interview
with King Henry at Westminster.

Disputes were constantly arising in regard to the capture
and detention of Biscayan shipping and the arrival of King
Ferdinand's envoys afforded an opportunity for improving
the relations between England and Castile. In the previous
winter, arrangements had been made that all English claims
against Castile should be presented at Bayonne before
Easter 1413[3] and a copy of the peace concluded between
the two countries in the late reign[4] was now produced from
the Privy Council Office and submitted afresh for re-
examination, and before the end of the year Archdeacon
Juan Roderici[5] arrived in England as an ambassador from
the Castilian court at Toro[6]. On Jan. 3, 1414, John
Hovingham, Archdeacon of Durham[7], was deputed to

[1] For £13 paid to a lawyer, Doctor Ralph Greenhurst, sent to Picardy to communicate with ambassadors of the King of Aragon at Calais, see Iss. Roll 1 H. V,
Pasch., May 20, 1413. For Ralph Greenhurst's appointment as a notary in the Chancery,
confirmed April 22, 1413, see Pat. 1 H. V, i. 24. For messengers to Calais with
passports for Francis de Pawe, knight, and Lodewic de Pastelhon, Doctor of Laws, see
Iss. Roll 1 H. V, Pasch., May 31, 1413.
[2] For their expenses at Canterbury (£10), together with those of envoys from the
Duke of Burgundy, see Iss. Roll 1 H. V, Pasch., June 27, 1413; Exch. Accts. 406/21(2).
[3] Letter Book I, p. 111; Rym. viii. 771.
[4] Wylie, iii. 285. It was deposited in the Exchequer on May 19, 1413, by Robert
Fry, clerk of the Council, and delivered to Master Thomas Felde on June 27, by
whom it was returned on July 10, 1413, Kal. and Inv. ii. 88.
[5] In Rym. ix. 80, 160, he is called Archdeacon de Gordonio (? Logroño), or Cordova
in Carte, Rolles, ii. 211.
[6] For his appointment as ambassador at Toro, Aug. 18, 1413, see Rym. ix. 105.
For account of Toro see Quadrado, 611.
[7] i.e. since Nov., 1408. His appointment was confirmed on April 12, 1409, Le Neve,
iii. 303, where he is called Honingham. On Oct. 23, 1413, he was appointed a notary
in the Chancery, vice Ralph Greenhurst (see *supra*, note 1), deceased, Pat. 1 H. V,
iv. 11; see also Cal. Pat. H. V, i. 185, May 24, 1414. For Master John Hovingham,
Doctor of Laws, appearing in the Admiralty Court in appeal of John Saunders, see
Pat. 2 H. V, i. 14, July 1, 1414. He is called John Ovyngham, ibid. i. 29 (May 22, 1414);
ii. 30 (July 28, 1414); Onyngham, Conc. iii. 374; Honyngham, Rym. ix. 208, 214;
Gibbons, Linc. 125; Honigscham, Dacher, 23; Mansi, xxviii. 633; Henyngham, Chron.
Lond. 98; Henningham, Finke, Forsch. 256. He is called clericus Eboracensis in
Rym. ix. 214, which makes it probable that the name is derived from Hovingham
near York, rather than Honingham near Norwich. In Pat. 3 H. V, i. 11, June 26,
1415, he holds the prebend of Skypwyk in the collegiate church of Howden. For
fragments of his seal attached to receipts (dated May 3, Oct. 1, 1416, May 8, 1417),
for his annuity of 50 marks p.a. granted to him Oct. 23, 1413, see Exch. Accts. 215/1, 3.
For his large private mark as a public notary, i.e. a triangle and emblems of the
Trinity with "Hovingham" written along the bottom step of the base of a cross, see
Cotton MS. Calig. D. v. f. 140; Rym. ix. 214, May 14, 1414. For two notaries' signs
in 1328 see Aussy, Registres, 46, 47. For his will in which he is Rector of Walde-
grave (i.e. Walgrave near Northampton), dated June 12, 1417, and proved at the Old
Temple, London, Dec. 15, 1417, see Gibbons, Linc. 125. In this he desires to be

confer with him, and on Jan. 17 a safe-conduct was issued
for a messenger[1] bringing letters from Queen Catherine[2]
and the Constable of Castile[3] with the result that on Jan. 28,
1414[4], a truce between England and Castile was signed in
London[5] to last for one year from Feb. 2, 1414, and arrangements were made for a subsequent meeting to be held at
Bayonne or Fuenterrabia[6] on July 1, following. When that
day arrived Thomas Field (or Felde), Dean of Hereford[7],

buried in the conventual church of St Bartholomew (i.e. in West Smithfield, Letter Book
I, 14) if he should die in London, or in "my parish" church of Easington near Durham
if he should die in the diocese of Durham. From this we learn that he was born at
Easington, that his father was named William, that he had a hostel (hospitium) in
London, and that Roger Walden, late Bishop of London (Wylie, iii. 123–128), was his
benefactor. He leaves legacies for prisoners in Ludgate, Newgate, and the Fleet, for
poor women in the archdeaconry of Newton, for his parishioners at Walgrave, with
£5 for making a vestment for the high altar of St Peter at Walgrave, and £5 to the
Minster at York, where his father and mother are buried. He refers to payment of
forgotten tithes, and to books lent to be copied but not returned, viz. Tabula Juris,
a Bible, a Portiforium (York use), Gorham on Matthew, Speculum curatorum, missals,
sermons written by the late Prior of St Bartholomew's, Bartholomew de Casibus, etc.

    [1] Viz. Raphael Sinola, Proctor of the Constable of Castile, French Roll 1 H. V, 12 ;
Carte, Rolles, ii. 210.
    [2] See p. 82, note 2 ; Wylie, ii. 330 ; she is called grande de corps, tres grosse,
blanchie et colorée et par la taille et le maintien semblait autant un homme qu'une
femme. Elle eut une grande maladie de paralysie après laquelle elle ne fut pas bien
déliée de la langue ni du corps, Guzman in Puymaigre, Cour, i. 213. For account of
Fernan Perez de Guzman see ibid. i. 191–216 ; with doubts as to his authorship of the
chronicle of Juan II, see ibid. 209 ; Kelly, 102. Catherine is called "a capricious,
arrogant and bigoted young woman" in Graetz, iv. 209. For her death at Valladolid at
the age of 50 in 1418, see Puymaigre, i. 213. For a horse in the stud of Henry IV called
Bayard Despenser, the gift of the Queen of Spain, Apr. 8, 1410 or 1411, also Grisell
Mendosa, see Add. MS. 24,513, f. 4 a.
    [3] For poems addressed to Ruy Lopes Duvalos and Alvaro de Luna as constables of
Castile at the beginning of the 15th century, see Baena, i. 73, 74, 76, 159, 160, 175.
    [4] Rym. ix. 110 ; Kal. and Inv. ii. 91 ; J. Dumont, II. pt. ii. 11 ; Goodwin, 35 ;
Guthrie, ii. 455.
    [5] For order (Feb. 12, 1414) for proclamation of it in London see Letter Book I, 123 ;
Rym. ix. 115. It was confirmed April 18, 1414, Rym. ix. 122.
    [6] Called "Fountrabis in frountera Ispanica," Mirot-Déprez, lxi. 27. For pictures of
it see Surita, ii. 156 ; P. H. Lalanne, 77, where the Basque name is Ondarrabia or
Ondur-Ibaia, i.e. river waif, épave de rivière. For pillage and burning of it in 1412 by
Navarrese and French under Amanieu d'Albret, see ibid. 85.
    [7] He is Dean of Hereford on May 28, 1406, Cal. Pat. H. IV, iii. 198, though said
not to have been installed till 1407 in Le Neve, i. 476, who refers to his will dated
at Maidstone July 29, 1419, proved Nov. 26, 1419. In 1417 he was one of the
Chancellors of Archbishop Chichele (Conc. iii. 348), and on March 24, 1419, he was
appointed one of the proctors of the Chapter of Canterbury in regard to their property
in France (Lit. Cantuar. iii. 138). For a letter written by Thomas Felde to the Abbot of
St Albans see Harl. MS. 431/42, in which he asks for promotion for a priest, W— B—, to
the vacant vicarage of Bygrave, near Baldock, in Hertfordshire (which belonged to the
Abbot, Clutterbuck, i. App. 5 ; iii. 492), according to a promise made by his relative,
Philip Thornbury, before he went to Gascony with the Duke of Clarence (i.e. in 1412,
Wylie, iv. 84). The request appears to have been unsuccessful, for Thomas Chalgrove
was appointed Rector on May 1, 1415, on the death of Robert Marshton (Clutterbuck,
iii. 494 ; Cussans, Odsay, 54). Philip Thornbury, kt., was M.P. for Herts. in 1417 and
1421, Clutterbuck, i. p. xxxvi ; Return Parl. i. 289, 299. His father, Sir John Thornbury,
had crenellated the manor-house of Bygrave in 1387, Clutterbuck, iii. 492.

and Jean Bordili[1], Archdeacon of Médoc[2], were empowered in conjunction with Sir John Blount to effect
a settlement of claims[3] put forward by Castile and Leon
between the accession of Henry V and Candlemas 1414[4]
and to arrange for a further prolongation of the truce[5]
and a final peace, if possible. By July 1, 1414[6], their
chests were packed and sealed and they left London on
July 27[7] for Spain, viâ Dartmouth and Bayonne[8], carrying
with them King Henry's confirmation of the previous truce
sealed with the great seal of England in white wax, which
they delivered to the Castilian representatives[9] at Bayonne
on Nov. 27, 1414, and at a formal meeting at Fuenterrabia
it was decided to prolong the truce till Feb. 2, 1416[10].
During the interval the question of a permanent alliance

[1] Rym. ix. 113. For his previous employment with Blount in 1411 see Rym. viii. 702.
For order dated July 12, 1415, to collectors of customs at Hull to pay him £171. 16s. 8d.
as remainder of his claim for going on embassy to communicate with the King of Castile,
"apud ffount Rabie," see Claus. 3 H. V, 17 ; called "Front Arabiez" in Bouvier,
Descript. 125.

[2] Rym. ix. 146, 180.

[3] For a Spanish ship, of which Fernandus Alfonsus is master, sent to England to
Henry IV by "our dearest aunt queen of Spain" (i.e. Catherine), ordered to be detained
to see which goods are Spanish and which belong to Genoese or our other enemies, see
Pat. 1 H. V, 1. 27 d, March 23, 1413. For order dated May 17, 1413, for release from
Southampton of two ships, viz. Seynt Pere de Seynt Mayo en Biskey and Saint Pere,
with 100 quintals of iron captured by the Gabriel de la Tour, see Claus. 1 H. V, 21.
For two ships each called Ste Marie de Ispanñ, whose masters were Sancinus Lopus
(i.e. Sanzio Lopez) and John de la Sowe, together with a barge called the Trinity of
Spain, with cargoes of Rochelle wine belonging to Richard Garner, now in sanctuary at
Westminster, see Pat. 1 H. V, i. 25 d, May 6, 1413.

[4] For order to the Abbots of Bewlee and Tychiff (i.e. Beaulieu and Titchfield) to
repair a large ship belonging to the King of Spain, then lying at Southampton, see
Iss. Roll 1 H. V, Mich., Feb. 20, 1414. For carpenters, artificers, and labourers to
make and repair a ship of Spain now at Southampton, see Pat. 1 H. V, v. 22 d, Feb. 8,
1414. For a letter of Henry V to John King of Castile, "our brother," see Add. MS.
24,062, f. 151. It complains that on St Thomas' Day, anno primo (i.e. Dec. 21, 1413),
Martin G——, a merchant of Castile, seized John H——, an English merchant, with
his ship, the Catherine of Bristol, and goods valued at £400, in the port of Lisbon,
which John, by way of reprisal, afterwards seized Martin and a ship laden with iron as
he was touching at an English port. This seizure was sanctioned in an Admiralty court,
and afterwards, i.e. a little before June 24 last (probably 1414), Martin seized goods
belonging to Henry D—— de R—— in comitatu Suthamptonie and John Ff——, of
Bristol, in a town of Spain called B—— (? Bilbao), for which the latter claims restitution.

[5] For appointment of Fernando Pedro de Avala, kt., and two doctors, viz. Gonsalvo
Morvac and John Velasci, of Cuellar, to meet English representatives and arrange prolongation of truce, see Rym. ix. 135, dated Salamanca, June 2, 1414.

[6] Rym. ix. 146, 147.

[7] Exch. Accts. 321/22, which gives their expenses, with six men and three horses,
from that date till their return to London on March 5, 1415, see Mirot-Déprez, lxi. 27.

[8] Rym. ix. 152.

[9] Ibid. ix. 180.

[10] For order dated Feb. 24, 1415, to the Sheriffs of London, etc., to proclaim this
extension, see Rym. ix. 204 (Letter Book I, p. 163). For reference to las bones treubas
et suffrensa de guerra existing between England and Castile on Aug. 28, 29, 1415, and
Feb. 24, 1416, see Jurade, 242, 243, 331.

was kept constantly under review, and on his return to London Master Field[1] repeatedly borrowed documents bearing upon previous relations with Castile from the Exchequer at Westminster[2], with the result that before Candlemas 1416 had arrived the king's officers at Bordeaux were authorised to arrange for a further extension[3] and while this question was being studied three envoys arrived in England with important proposals from King Ferdinand in regard to Aragon.

These were Master Felipe Malla[4] and two knights named Juan Fabra of Valencia and Berenguer Claver[5]. They arrived at Southampton on July 21, 1415[6], instructed to negotiate an alliance between the kingdoms of England and Aragon, and to open up proposals for a marriage between Henry and King Ferdinand's eldest daughter Donna Maria[7]. They brought with them two coursers and a jennet as presents for the English king[8] with whom they had many opportunities of personal intercourse[9],

---

[1] For £108. 8s. 8d. paid to him as balance for his mission to Spain, see Rec. Roll 3 H. V, Pasch., July 1, 1415.

[2] e.g. on May 4, 1415, he borrowed a document from the Exchequer having to do with an alliance made with Pedro, King of Castile, in the days of Edward III (possibly the convention of Sept. 23, 1366, Rym. vi. 514), Kal. and Inv. ii. 21. This paper he returned on May 8, 1415, borrowing it again on May 10, and returning it on June 17, Kal. and Inv. ii. 93. On Oct. 8, 1415, he handed to the Treasurer a hanaper containing four documents confirming and prolonging the truce between England and Castile, ibid. ii. 94.

[3] Rym. ix. 328, Jan. 13, 1416, appoints the seneschal (John Tiptoft), the constable of Bordeaux (William Clifford), the Mayor of Bordeaux (John St John), and two lawyers (Bertrand d'Asta and Arnold de Meana) as commissioners for the negotiations.

[4] Surita, ii. 74; or Malia, Valla, 1066; or Medalia, Rym. ix. 546; St Denys, vi. 176; Maedalia, Finke, Forsch. 185; Madalia, St Denys, v. 720; Goodwin, 178. Not Pierre, as Postel, 92. He had studied law and theology at the Universities of Barcelona (where he afterwards obtained a canonry in the Cathedral), Lerida and Paris, Fromme, 19, 20. He was one of the representatives of the King of Aragon at Constance, where he arrived on Jan. 4, 1417 (Finke, Forsch. 185; Fromme, 43), and took a prominent part in the negotiations, Bofarull-y-Sans, *passim*. He conferred with Sigismund at Narbonne on Dec. 9, 1415, St Denys, v. 720. He was now a canon and penitencer of the Cathedral at Barcelona, St Denys, vi. 176. For penitencer or penitentiary, see Cent Dict., s.v.; Murray, Dict., s.v.; Halliwell, ii. 614; Chaucer (S), iv. 630; Wylie, ii. 342, note 3. For penitenciarius appointed to hear confessions, etc., in the church at Bath, see Holmes, Reg. 22 (1401).

[5] Surita, ii. 67.

[6] For their expenses in England from July 21 to Sept. 15, 1415, see For. Accts. 3 H. V; also £7. 15s. 3d. paid on the same account, Iss. Roll 3 H. V, Mich., Dec. 23, 1415; also £12. 6s. 10d. paid in July, 1415, by the Treasurer of the King's Household for their expenses during 16 days in July, 1415, Exch. Accts. 406/29.

[7] Usk, 125; la mayor de las hijas del rey, Surita, ii. 67, 75; Fromme, 5. For Ferdinand's two daughters, Maria and Leonora (Eleanor), see Mariana, ii. 225.

[8] Among the horses listed in John Waterton's account (1414–1416) occur Bayard Arragon (*bis*) and Morell Arragon.

[9] Satis et abunde experimento comprobavi vestram serenitatem virtutis amore

carrying away with them a charming impression of his kindness and condescension and general treatability[1].

The visit of these envoys is of more than usual interest as their bill of expenses is fortunately still preserved[2], giving full details of where they stayed and what they ate from day to day[3]. It was made out by a clerk named Nicholas Harewood[4], acting on behalf of John Waterton, who began his entries at Winchester on July 21 and ended them at Southampton on Sept. 16, 1415. The king was at this time at Southampton preparing to cross to France, and the envoys probably had an interview with him immediately on their landing. Leaving Winchester on July 22 they travelled by Basingstoke, Hertfordbridge, Windsor and Brentford[5] to London which they reached in the evening of July 24[6]. Here they stayed six days and on July 31 we find them at Dartford on their way to Canterbury, apparently to pay a visit to the shrine. Stopping at Rochester on July 31 they reached Canterbury on the following evening, having halted to bait at Ospringe. The next day (August 2) they started to return, dined at Sittingbourne, slept at Rochester, halted again at Dartford, and were back in London for supper on August 3, proving conclusively that in the summer at any rate the pilgrimage could be managed in two days and one night on the road[7]. After two days they took the road again on August 5 and travelled by Kingston, Guildford, Farnham,

---

flagrantem, regiâ humanitate, condescencione benivolâ tractabilem se precibus omnibus in eam confugientibus, Rym. ix. 546.

[1] Cf. bonere and tretabil, Secreta, 211.

[2] Exch. Accts. 321/32; Mirot-Déprez, lxi. 29; printed in Kirk, Analogues. See App. H.

[3] An interesting record of the daily expenses at Dunster Castle for the year ending June 27, 1406, has been published (Lyte, 114–119), and forms a fitting companion to this roll as indicating west-country prices at about the same period. See App. I.

[4] He was one of the executors of John Waterton in 1421, Ord. Priv. Co. ii. 279.

[5] Called Baynford or Braineforde, Lysons, Environs, ii. 41, 45, 67; Lewis, i. 357.

[6] In For. Accts. 5 H. V, the journey from London to Southampton and back is done in 4 days.

[7] In 1360 King John of France halted for the night six times on the road between Dover and London, sleeping at Dover, Canterbury, Ospringe, Rochester (after dining at Sittingbourne), Dartford, and Eltham, Douet d'Arcq, Argenterie, 282. For halting-places of Queen Joan in 1403, see Wylie, ii. 437, note 4, where Wickham possibly means East Wickham near Bexley Heath. For "Scheteres hylde" (Shooters Hill) in via versus Cantuariam, see Arderne, xxvii. For map of the pilgrim road in 1675 by John Ogilby (b. 1600, d. 1675), see Beryn, where Shinglewell is not marked. It is called Singlewell in Littlehales, 3. For la haute chymyne entre Canterbury et London, see Orthographia, xiv. from Add. MS. 17,716.

Alton and Alresford[1], arriving at Southwick on August 8. Here they stayed (probably at the Priory[2]) till August 12, when they paid another visit to Winchester, remaining there till August 23. Starting again on August 24 they journeyed a second time to London, stayed there from August 27 till Sept. 1, were back at Winchester by Sept. 4 and reached Southampton on Sept. 7. Here the account goes on till it closes on Sept. 16, 1415, on which day they probably set sail again for their own country.

John Waterton, whose name is appended to their account, had been appointed[3], together with Master John Kempe[4], to return with them and negotiate with King Ferdinand who was expected to be at Perpignan before the winter. Waterton and Kempe left London on Sept. 8[5], and joined the envoys at Southampton, where they waited till they had the wind at will[6]. All sailed together from Southampton early in October[7] and reached Bayonne after a fifteen days' passage. After this we lose sight of them till Dec. 5, 1415[8], on which day they had an interview with King Ferdinand at Perpignan in the stormy time that preceded his final breach with the Pope. According to their instructions[9] the two Englishmen were to draw attention to the fact that Henry was still unmarried, and if they found any readiness to consider a match for Ferdinand's daughter, Maria, they were to say that it was a very difficult matter[10] which would require much deliberation, though they were

---

[1] Called Alford and Alsforde in the document; also Aldford, Alreford, Alsford in Woodward, ii. 26, 27, 35.

[2] For the Priory of the Black (or Austin) Canons at Southwick see Lel. Itin. iii. 94. For their seal see Pedrick, p. 127, Plate xxxviii; and arms, Vict. Co. Hist. (Hants.), iii. 162, with a picture of the village. For Queen Elizabeth's stay there in 1591, see Nichols, Progresses, iii. 122. For the Prior's chair (13th century), see Cassell, i. 448.

[3] i.e. on July 25, 1415, Rym. ix. 293; Usk, 125, 307.

[4] Hook, v. 193. Nicholas Harewood had received £20 of the money spent on the ambassadors per manus magistri Johannis Kempe clerici.

[5] For their expenses (£492) from that date till their return to London on June 13, 1416 (278 days), see Exch. Accts. 321/33; For. Accts. 3 H. V; do. (P.R.O.), p. 80; Mirot-Déprez, lxi. 29. They took 20 horses with them, and their voyage out from Southampton in the John Baptist of Bayonne took 15 days, the return journey in the same ship occupying 22 days at sea.

[6] Cf. Lydg. Troy Book, 30; when thei hadde wedur, ibid. 97, 106; par fortune de vent, Lannoy, Œuvres, 176; if the wind be not your friend, Speght, 357.

[7] For £20 paid for expenses of envoys of the King of Aragon, who are about to depart *in proximo*, see Iss. Roll 4 H. V, Pasch., Sept. 2, 1415.

[8] Surita, ii. 75, where Waterton is called Juan Gut Trunton.

[9] Dated at Southampton, July 28, 1415, Rym. ix. 295; cf. Gesta, 8; Chron. Giles, 9, where reference is made to the liber evidentiarum regalium et recordorum.

[10] Perquam ardua materia, Rym. ix. 296.

authorised to explain that King Henry was not averse to considering it. They were to add, however, that he had two noble brothers (i.e. the Dukes of Bedford[1] and Gloucester) not yet wived (*nondum conjugatos*), either of whom might be had if terms could be arranged, and for this purpose they were to ask for a dower of 200,000 crowns with the lady which might be beaten down to 160,000, according as circumstances should shape[2]. They were authorised also to negotiate an alliance with Aragon, provided that the French and Scots were not included, but it is likely that no definite arrangement was made, for Ferdinand was then a dying man and had but a few weeks to live. As to the marriage project it was found that Maria had already been betrothed to Juan, the young king of Castile[3], though he was somewhat younger than herself.

Knowing that King Henry was a prince of great weight, great valour and great wealth[4], King Ferdinand tried to secure him by offering his second daughter, Leonora, to the king of Castile but the arrangement could not be worked out, and after Ferdinand's death, which happened on April 2, 1416[5], the English envoys returned and were back in London by June 13, 1416; but six months later[6], when other envoys were despatched to Constance, they were authorised to continue negotiations for an alliance with the representatives of Alfonso V[7], who was Ferdinand's son and successor. In the end Maria married the king of Castile at Medina del Campo on Oct. 20, 1418[8], and Leonora[9] married Duarte, who afterwards became king of Portugal[10].

[1] In Waurin, iii. 114 [76] he is grant de corps et gros de membrez sage et hardy en armes.
[2] Prout res exigit, Rym. ix. 296. For similar bargaining in regard to the marriage of Hans, Duke of Sulzbach, at Ribe (Higgins, i. 60, 143; ii. 280), see Wylie, ii. 435, note 7.
[3] There is no evidence to show that she was allowed any personal choice in the matter, as supposed by D. M. J. Henry, ii. 43. She died at Villacastin near Avila in 1445, Heiss, Monedas, ii. 26.
[4] Muy poderoso principe y de gran valor y muy rico, Surita, ii. 75, who refers to the capture of Harfleur, but not to the battle of Agincourt. Cf. Fromme, 33.
[5] i.e. at Igualada near Barcelona, Encycl. Brit., s.v. *Ferdinand*.
[6] Rym. ix. 410, Dec. 2, 1416.
[7] In Rym. ix. 622 (Sept. 24, 1418), Alfonso, King of Aragon and Sicily, has granted (on Aug. 30, 1417) protection for 3 years to all English merchants and their ships, and King Henry now grants the same terms for Castilians.
[8] Heiss, Monedas, i. 88; not 1420, as Weale, Van Eyck, 15.
[9] Not Maria, as Heiss, Monedas, ii. 26, quoting Florez y Bofarull. Leonora died at Toledo on Feb. 19, 1445.
[10] Duarte, pp. xv, xvi, 1, where she is called "Rainha Dona Leonor sua molher." Cf. Mas Latrie, 1738.

With Portugal also King Henry was endeavouring to continue on terms of friendship, and early in July, 1413, arrangements were pending for the departure of William Porter "on secret business" to King João[1]. He was accompanied by Arundel Herald and the two sailed together in one of the king's ships, the *Marie de la Tour*[2], for Bordeaux whence they would proceed in another vessel to Lisbon. But in the meantime two Portuguese envoys were on their way to England from King João at Santarem[3] to secure confirmation of the treaties made with Henry's two predecessors, and as their credentials were made out at Lisbon on July 25, 1413[4], it is evident that the two parties must have crossed each other on the voyage. The Portuguese envoys were a knight named João Valasci of Almada on the south shore of the Tagus, and João Alvari, Dean of Viseu[5]. They landed in England about the end of August, 1413[6], and after some delay had an interview with the king at Windsor[7]. It is certain that these envoys made a prolonged stay in England, and when at length the principals started for Dover they had a further long wait[8] before they got under way, and even then some of their men remained behind in London[9]. The purpose of their visit is now for the first time explained by the publication of a document still preserved in the library of the Vatican, which shows that at this very time the king of Portugal was applying to Pope John XXIII for a dispensation for a marriage between the English king and his youngest

---

[1] For his arms at Constance, see Richental (Sorg), 100.

[2] Iss. Roll 1 H. V, Pasch., May 31, July 4, 1413. For £10 paid for victualling her on this account, see ibid., Mich., Dec. 1, 1413.

[3] Rym. ix. 27, June 21, 1413; Goodwin, 11.

[4] Cott. MS. Vesp. C. xii. 129.

[5] Kal. and Inv. ii. 88. The former appears as Vacques, Vas (Wylie, ii. 335, note 5), Vaques (Iss. Roll 1 H. V, Mich., Feb. 22, 1414), Vasques (Rym. ix. 664; Halle, 86; Grafton, i. 530), Valusci (Bréquigny, 43; Carte, Rolles, i. 271; Ewald, xli. 705) or Naâsq'Dalmadnã, Vesp. C. xii. 129; called "Johannes de Vasques de Allamond" in Redman, 55. Cf. Puiseux, Rouen, 171.

[6] For £47. 17s. 7½d. paid on their account from Sept. 1 to Oct. 8, 1413, see Exch. Accts. 407/21, 23.

[7] For payment to messengers from Kennington to Windsor Park pro hospitatione extraneorum de Portugal, see Exch. Accts. 406/21, 30. For reference to John Vaques Dalmadan, kt., with a doctor and his other knights from Portugal coming to the king's presence, see Iss. Roll 1 H. V, Mich., Nov. 8, 1413; Jan. 27, 1414.

[8] Ibidem per longum tempus attendentes, Iss. Roll 1 H. V, Mich., Feb. 22, 1414.

[9] For 10 marks paid to men remaining in London after the departure of John Vages (*sic*), see ibid. Jan. 27, 1414.

daughter Isabel[1], then a girl of 16 years of age[2]. The Pope, who was then at Florence, granted the necessary dispensation on Oct. 21, 1413[3], but the project came to nothing and Isabel was reserved for quite another destiny. Seventeen years later she became the wife of Philip the Good, Duke of Burgundy[4], and her marriage was the occasion of two notable events, one of which was the founding of the famous Order of the Golden Fleece[5], and the other the painting of her portrait by Jan Van Eyck[6], who was one of the envoys despatched to Lisbon by Duke Philip to negotiate preliminaries at her father's court[7]. This picture has now unfortunately disappeared[8] but other representations of her still remain[9], and later in her life she was described as a short plump brunette with jet black eyes that smelt of garlic[10]. She lived to a good old age and died on Dec. 17, 1471[11]. Two years afterwards her body was buried with that of her husband in the Charter-house at Dijon[12].

[1] Called Elisabeth officially, Barante, iv. 293; cf. Weale, Van Eyck, lv, lix, lxii, lxiv, lxv, lxvi; Eubel, Bullarium, vii. 458, June 8, 1412.
[2] She was born Feb. 21, 1397, Weale, Van Eyck, 12.
[3] Papal Letters, vi. 412.
[4] He married her as his third wife at Bruges on Jan. 10, 1430, Barante, iv. 290, 293. Not at Sluis on Jan. 7, 1430, as Weale, Van Eyck, pp. xxii, 12, which was the date of the "espousailles," ibid. lxxi. Not 1429, as Azurara, i. 11, 301; Grande Encycl. xxvi. 673. For his motto, "Autre n'aray tant que je vivray" from Dynter, see Montille, 145, who regards it as expressing son attachement inébranlable à la Duchesse.
[5] Barante, iv. 293.
[6] Called one of the brothers in Lecoy de la Marche, Manuscrit, 198. For Herbert van Eyck (1366–1426) and Jan (b. circ. 1386, d. July 9, 1441), see Michiels; Weale, pp. 2, 16. For Jan van Eyck in the service of Jean sans Pitié in 1422, see F. Denis, 87; Weale, 8; called wan Eych in Villeneuve-Bargemont, i. 384. Cf. firent paindre bien au vif la figure de madame l'infante Elizabeth, Weale, lix, where Jan is "excellent maistre en art de painture." For portraits sent to lovers, see Bouchot, 63.
[7] Wylie, ii. 332, note 4.
[8] It passed afterwards into the possession of Margaret of Austria, Regent of the Netherlands at Malines, and was described in the inventories of her collection in 1516, 1524; Kämmerer, 46, who calls Isabel la belle Portugaloise. For a supposed copy of it at Tournai, see Weale, 180. It was painted at Aviz in Jan. 1429, and sent to the Duke on Feb. 12; Weale, Van Eyck, lviii, lx, who thinks there were 2 portraits (p. 15).
[9] e.g. Montfaucon, III. iii. 226, Plate xli; also ibid. 260, from the Chapter-house of the Carthusians at Montregnault near Noyon, founded by her in 1448. For picture of her in the hospital at Beaune, see ibid. 118. For brass in the Cathedral at Basle (1450) representing her with her husband Philip and their son Charles the Bold, showing the motto "Autre n'aury," see Creeny, 29. For her arms in a modern window in the Hôtel Dieu at Beaune, see Montille, 147.
[10] Me semblait que ses yeux trop noirs avaient une odeur d'ail, Darmesteter, Marguerites, 113, translated as "a scent of garlick about her," by M. Tomlinson.
[11] Morillot, 35, 39, 42, 51, from her epitaph in the Charterhouse at Yosnay near Béthune (Pas de Calais), whence the body was removed on Dec. 28, 1473, not that she died on Dec. 12, 1472, as Azurara, i. 11.
[12] For reception of the bodies at Dijon on Feb. 8, 1474, see Maillard de Chambure,

After the visit of the Portuguese to England the course of trade between the two countries flowed amicably on without let or interruption[1] and in Feb. 1415 it was a generally recognised fact that Portugal was one of England's close allies[2].

151.   For their epitaphs, see Morillot, 47, 48, where she is fille de roy et du sang d'Engleterre.   For plan of the vault made in 1766, showing the position of both the coffins before the demolition of the church in 1792, see Morillot, 6.

[1] On Dec. 5, 1413, John Edwakere, a Bristol merchant, exports 100 quarters of wheat to Portugal, Fr. Roll 1 H. V, 14; not 1100 quarters, as Carte, Rolles, ii. 210.   For 300 quarters of wheat going to Portugal in the Margaret of London, see French Roll 1 H. V, 4, March 12, 1414; also 50 quarters from Chichester and Sandwich, Fr. Roll 1 H. V, 13, Dec. 10, 1413.   For permission to export 400 lances to John, King of Portugal, see Rym. ix. 160, Sept. 26, 1414; also 350 lances and harness for 6 men-of-arms, ibid. ix. 195, Jan. 20, 1415.   For £201. 10s. 2d. paid to Oliver Martin, a Portuguese merchant, for 9 pipes of Algarve wine at £4 per pipe for the king's store, see Devon, 328, Dec. 11, 1418.   For £15. 16s. 6d. (+46/8 wharfage) paid for wine to Alfred Martin of Portugal, see Iss. Roll 1 H. V, Mich., Feb. 20, 22, 1414.   For payment to winedrawer for removing 60 casks of Portuguese wine from London to Westminster, see Iss. Roll 1 H. V, Mich., Feb. 22, 1414.   For English vessels with cargoes of wax, oil and fruit from Portugal for Bristol, Dartmouth and Lynn, see Rot. Parl. iv. 89 (1415).

[2] Jure mutui foederis et amoris, St Denys, v. 412.   Ils estoient alliés ensemble avec les Anglois, Juv. 501; pour ce que ilz sont aliez avecques eulx, Bouvier, Descript. 22, 126.

CHAPTER IX

BRITTANY

In spite of frequent threatenings the relations between England and Brittany had for some long time remained externally peaceful. It is true that there had been periodical outbreaks of piracy and interruptions of trade and that our people regarded the Bretons as "the greatest rovers and the greatest thieves[1]," but truces had been continued on both sides as their dates expired and commissioners had crossed the water from time to time for personal conference so that differences had been adjusted by the exercise of mutual forbearance[2]. Thus on July 6, 1411[3], a truce had been concluded between the two countries to last for two years and trade continued in its usual course[4] and before the year was out a representative of each side had been appointed, viz. Henry, Lord of Le Juch[5], on behalf of the Duke of Brittany, and Ralph Greenhurst[6] on behalf of the

[1] Pol. Songs, ii. 164; Wylie, iv. 35.
[2] For a barche or neff dont Guillo Bintie estoit garde taken from the English, which went on the rocks at Penmarch, see Blanchard, ii. 38, where the goods are to be restored in May, 1407, by the men of Guérande near St Nazaire. At that time 120 English were released on paying their cautions (Blanchard, ii. 45, 47, 49) at Jersey. Some of their names appear as Trordelay, Toudrelay, Parcar, Boirroill (?Burrell), Evan, Millefort (Milford), Cradol (?Cradock), Lay, Young, Clerk, Peppin, &c. For goods seized on a ship of Guérande by men of Rye and Winchelsea, see Early Chanc. Proc. i. 39.
[3] Blanchard, ii. 155. For a truce for 1 year and 10 months signed in London, temp. H. IV, see Ramet, ii. 44.
[4] For wheat exported to Brittany by an Englishman, John Cantel, on April 16, 1407, see Blanchard, ii. 23; also lead for the tower of the castle of Cesson, near St Brieuc, ibid. For safe-conducts (June, 1407) for English merchants, see Blanchard, ii. 62, where their names appear as Berthelot (?Bartlet), King, Hoskin, Foldo, Qualton (Walton), Hellesmez (?Ellesmere or Elsmie), Crasquelle (Creswell), and Parquier (Parker).
[5] i.e. near Douarnenez (Finistère); not "Inch," as Rym. viii. 712; ix. 81, 82, 85, 123; Cal. Pat. H. V, i. 224; Goodwin, 33, 34. He was nominated on Oct. 27, 1411, Blanchard, ii. 154.
[6] Appointed Dec. 28, 1411, Rym. viii. 712. Not Svenhurst, see Blanchard, ii. 154. On May 22 and July 14, 1413, he acted as protonotary in the negotiations with the Duke of Burgundy at Calais, Rym. ix. 12, 34, 41, and died before Oct. 23, 1413; see page 91, note 7.

king of England, with a view to arranging a ten years'
truce dating from Jan. 1412[1]. These envoys met and
agreed upon a release of prisoners on both sides, and by
a subsequent order[2] it was arranged that the Lord of
Le Juch should come to England and Sir John Blount,
the Deputy Admiral[3], should cross to Brittany for further
settlement of details, and on July 3, 1412, a treaty of
alliance between the two countries had been arranged in
London by Richard Lord Grey of Codnor and the Lord
of Châteaugiron[4], acting as plenipotentiaries for their respective sovereigns.

Soon after the accession of Henry V a commission was
appointed[5] by the Duke of Brittany to treat for a renewal
of the ten years' truce. The Breton commissioners were
the Lord of Le Juch and Master Paul de l'Hôpital, Sir
John Dabridgecourt[6] and Archdeacon Hovingham[7] being
appointed to meet them as the representatives of England
on Dec. 14, 1413[8]. After several communications had
passed, an understanding was arrived at on Jan. 3, 1414[9],
whereby the Duke of Brittany undertook not to help King
Henry's enemies, the island of Bréhat[10] being expressly
excluded from the settlement. The truce was confirmed
on April 18, 1414[11], and it was further arranged that
commissioners should meet in Guernsey on May 1, 1414,
to deal finally with all complaints of infraction during the
late reign[12].

---

[1] See letters of Henry IV, Dec. 21, 1411, in Blanchard, ii. 166.
[2] Viz. Feb. 21, 1412, Lobineau, ii. 895; Wylie, iv. 26, note 6.
[3] Ibid. iii. 302.
[4] Appointed May 10, 1412, Blanchard, ii. 158.
[5] i.e. on Aug. 10, 1413, Rym. ix. 81, from Ancenis on the Loire, Blanchard, ii. 169,
where Henri du Juch and Master Paul de l'Hôpital are the Breton representatives for
recovering ships, goods, men and money detained by the English.
[6] Wylie, iii. 167. For Aubercicourt (ibid. iv. 420), formerly Abrecicort, see
Duthilloeul, 48; not Ambrafficourt, as J. T. Smith, 245; nor Ambreticour, as Topham, 22.
For Nicholas Vaberiggecourt (or Vabrushcourt), kt., and his wife Elizabeth in 1390, see
Boys, 154.
[7] Page 91.
[8] Rym. ix. 79; Kal. and Inv. ii. 92; Carte, Rolles, ii. 209, 210.
[9] Rym. ix. 80, 112, 123, 143, 144, 309; J. Dumont, II. ii. 2. For order to arrest
late bailiffs of Weymouth and to restore a balinger to the ambassadors of the Duke of
Brittany, see Iss. Roll 1 H. V, Mich., Feb. 19, 1414. For enquiry as to breaches of
truce with Flanders and Brittany, see Pat. 1 H. V, 5, 21 d, Feb. 12, 1414.
[10] Called Bryacke in Bree, 83, from Harl. MS. 235. See Wylie, iii. 102.
[11] Rym. ix. 123.
[12] Ibid. ix. 80–88, 114, 116; J. Dumont, II. ii. 2; Goodwin, 33, 34.

On June 26, 1414[1], a Norfolk knight (John Colvil[2])
and a Devonshire lawyer (Master Richard Hals[3]) were
instructed to proceed to Brittany and take over ships and
cargoes that had been captured since the truce began.
They had an interview with the Duke of Brittany at
Savenay, near Nantes, on Oct. 12, 1414[4], and on Oct. 17[5]
an indenture was drawn up whereby it was agreed that
prisoners[6] captured since Jan. 3, 1414, should be restored
together with many barges, crayers and balingers from
Bridgwater, Exeter, Saltash, Bristol and Lowestoft, the
value of the plundered cargoes being minutely inventoried
in items such as 2 pipes of cider (3 francs), 18 large panes
of cloth (1 franc), 4 sailors' hutches[7], 6 flock beds[8] and
palliasses, 3 rundles[9] of wheat, a small silver monstrance[10]
($2\frac{1}{2}$ francs), several portages or loads of salt both by
Morlaix and Lannion measure (at 35s. the portage) and
casks of Angevin, Gascon and Rochelle wine (at from 8
to 10 crowns the cask), 2 iron hauberks, 12 doz. settes
(i.e. arrows), quantities of bows, lances, basnets, capellines[11],
Olonne and Josselin[12] cloth, and 40 gold nobles, all captured

---

[1] Rym. ix. 143, 144; Blanchard, ii. 183.   The appointment was ordered during the
Leicester Parliament, i.e. before May 29, 1414, Rot. Parl. iv. 88.

[2] For order dated July 14, 1414, to secure ships and sailors at the ports of London,
Southampton, Poole, and Weymouth for the passage of John Colvyll, knight, to
Brittany, see Pat. 2 H. V, ii. 30 d; For. Accts. P.R.O. p. 80; For. Accts. 5 H. V.
For £28. 3s. 1d. paid to him for embassy to Duke of Brittany from July 19, 1414, to
Dec. 1, 1414, see Iss. Roll 8 H. V, Pasch., May 23, 1420.   In Claus. 6 H. V, 8 d, he is
called John Colvill of Norfolk; not Cambridgeshire, as Wylie, iii. 369.   He came from
Walsoken near Lynn, Blomefield, ix. 124, where his death is dated 1425.   For his lands
at Walpole, see ibid. 102.   For Gild or Fraternity to be founded in the chapel of the
Trinity juxta fossatam called the Stathedyk in Walsoken near Wisbech by Geoffrey
Colvyll esquire and others, see Pat. 2 H. V, iii. 10, Feb. 2, 1415.

[3] He was Treasurer of Exeter Cathedral from Sept. 27, 1400, and died May 18,
1417, Le Neve, i. 415; Staff. Reg. 121.   For his will dated at Exeter, May 1, 1417,
proved May 25, 1417, see Staff. Reg. 416.

[4] Cal. Pat. H. V, i. 224.

[5] Rym. ix. 163, 194.   For acte d'estimation, see Ramet, ii. 44, from the archives at
Nantes.

[6] Including Thomas Molington of London, John William of Fowey, John Smith and
William Lawrence of Calais, and William Russell of Benestowe.

[7] For 1 huche (6s.), in 1412, see St Germain, 446; 1 petite hucheste (3s.), ibid. 456.
For 1 huche (1478), see C. Beaurepaire, Notes, ii. 18; una hucheta de fust, Jurade, ii. 60;
une huche en bois de quesne, C. Beaurepaire, Mélanges, 153; "whutche," Caxton,
Dial. 18.

[8] Litz de bourre, cf. Cotgr., s.v. Bureau; Littré, s.v. Bure; C. A. Costa de Beaure-
garde, 162; 1 cousee (mattress) plaine de boure, St Germain, 448.   For carting flocks
(cariage de beuer) at Bordeaux, see Rot. Parl. iv. 77.

[9] Rondelles.   Cf. rundlet, Wylie, iv. 360.   [10] Monstre d'argent.

[11] Cotgrave, s.v.; Halliwell, i. 231.

[12] Jouselin, Fr. Roll 2 H. V, m. 4; not "Jonoclin," as Rym. ix. 165.   For view of
the Castle at Josselin see Grande Encycl. xxi. 209.

about Mid-Lent 1414, one of the Breton pirates[1] being
Hervé Duchastel who had already had some experience
of the inside of English prisons[2]. The whole claim
amounted to 2114 crowns which had to be paid before
Candlemas next[3]. But the English on their side had
also much to answer for[4] and so, when all claims had been
discussed, an indenture was drawn up balancing the account
as between the two parties on Oct. 17, 1414. A few days
later[5] Colvil was presented by the Duke of Brittany with
a gold cup which had belonged to his brother Giles, who
had lately died during the siege of Bourges[6]. At the
opening of the New Year (1415) a clerk of the Admiralty
named John Chamberlain[7] was preparing to cross over to
pay and receive money according to the terms of the
decision, though he appears not to have actually started
till Midsummer 1415[8], and on Aug. 23 following John
Hovingham and Simon Flete left London on a further
embassy to the Duke. They sailed from Topsham near
Exeter with a suite of 8 men and 12 horses and were back
in London by Dec. 7, 1415[9]. Thus there was a chance of
quieter times for traders in the channel, and the bay-salt[10]

---

[1] Prenneurs, Rym. ix. 164.

[2] Wylie, i. 436.

[3] Rym. ix. 166. For order for restitution to Wm. Olinthon, a merchant of Herteford, for 25 tuns of wine captured by Bretons from Guérande, see Cal. Pat. H. V, i. 224 (Feb. 1, 1415). For picture of Guérande (Loire Inf.) with the Church of St Aubin, see Touchard-Lafosse, IV. iii. 368.

[4] e.g. for a ship of Le Conquet called St Mark, captured from the Bretons and taken to the port of Hamele (i.e. Hamble near Netley in Southampton Water), see Pat. 1 H. V, iii. 27 d. For commission (April 14, 1413) appointed to sit at Fowey as to Breton ships seized by Fowey and Dartmouth men and taken to Winchelsea and Rye, see Claus. 1 H. V, 32; Pat. 1 H. V, i. 26. For commission to release a Breton vessel detained by the bailiffs of Fowey, see Iss. Roll 1 H. V, Mich., Jan. 27, 1414.

[5] i.e. Oct. 23, 1414, Lobineau, ii. 925; Blanchard, ii. 183.

[6] i.e. at Cosne, July 19, 1412; Cagny, 71, 74; Wylie, iv. 78; called July 25 in Bibl. de l'Ecole des Chartes, xlvii. 531; or July 12, Trévédy, 9. For statement that he was buried in the Cathedral at Nantes see Travers, i. 508; C. Barthélemy, Bretaigne, 172. For picture of the church of St Aignan at Cosne, see Touchard-Lafosse, iii. 157.

[7] Rot. Parl. iv. 88; Rym. ix. 194, Dec. 31, 1414.

[8] Blanchard, ii. 191, June 25, 1415, where he is called Chambrel'.

[9] For payments to John Hovingham as ambassador to the Duke of Brittany, in certis secretis negociis, from August 23 to Dec. 7, 1415, see Rec. Roll (Auditors) 3 H. V, Mich., Feb. 8, 1416; Iss. Roll 4 H. V, Pasch., July 8, 1416; Exch. Accts. 321/31; Mirot-Déprez, lxi. 29.

[10] For 3000 quarters of salt bought from Breton traders at Dartmouth for London merchants, see Claus. 1 H. V, 30, June 2, 1413. For 800 quarters of salt from Brittany captured by Dartmouth men, temp. H. IV, see Claus. 1 H. V, 19, Aug. 12, 1413. For a ship called the St Catherine from Portugal to Bruges with salt from the Bay captured en une contree de la mer appelé Belin (i.e. Bélon) and brought to Blavnez (i.e. Blavet, now Port-Louis near Lorient), see Blanchard, ii. 203, June 13, 1406. For bay-salt, see

and lampreys[1] passed across more freely, though Breton rovers[2] still lay in wait in St Matthew's Roads[3] for the wine ships passing up from La Rochelle and Bordeaux.

During the latter part of the preceding reign exasperating relations had been accumulating with the Genoese, who had captured vessels sailing from London with cargoes of wool, and when Henry came to the throne claims had been lodged against them amounting to £24,000. On March 21, 1413, letters of marque[4] had been issued authorising certain London traders to retaliate upon Genoese vessels at sea until cargoes to the amount of £10,000 had been captured, and it was not long before plenty of plunder was brought in and sold in English ports for what it would fetch[5]. On July 10, 1413[6], Bishop Chichele and others were commissioned to report to the Council on these difficulties, and in the spring of 1414 the Doge of Genoa sent envoys[7]

Kingsford, 226. It was named not from the Bay of Biscay, as ibid. 343, but from the Bay of Bourgneuf; see Black Book of the Admiralty, i. 132; Wylie, iii. 47; called Bourgneuf en Rais in Blanchard, ii. 205, i.e. the Pays de Retz, with Rezé as its chief town opposite to Nantes, the district to the south of the estuary of the Loire. Cf. le pays de la baye lequel croist tres plus grand de sel que il ne fait en autre d' (? ledit) terrouer de Guerrande et que en iceli a tres bons havres et est franc de charges et devoir, Blanchard, iii. 38, where Guérande is grandement peuplé de gens. For sel noir de Guérande, see Spont, 430. For plusseurs terres frostes (i.e. abandonnées, désertes, Godefroy, s.v.; cf. frostes et inhabitées, Blanchard, ii. 257) appellées baulles (=pièce de toile grossière, Godefroy, s.v. *Baule*) convenables a faire salines ou terrouer nantoys, en celui de Guerrande et en la ripvière de Loyre, see Blanchard, ii. 253. Cf. terres frostes, baules et croyssements (i.e. silt), ibid. For picture of the marais salants at Noirmoutier, see Robuchon, Poitou, xi, also in the Charente Inférieure near Rochefort, see Joanne, ii. 870. For mercatores patrie Britannie et de la Baye, see Cal. Rot. Hib. 213. For un voyage a la Baye from Rouen in 1400, see C. Beaurepaire, Notes, iii. 266, who supposes it to be Quimperlé. For sel de la Baye, sel de Brouge (near Rochefort), see Fréville, i. 293.

[1] In 1466 the Bohemians with Rożmital saw 400 lampreys pulled out of the Loire at Nantes at one time, Rożmital, 49. For lampreys at Orleans, see Cuissard, 126.
[2] Cf. Roveres sur la meere, Rot. Parl. iv. 376.
[3] i.e. off Brest; not *trade* de St Matheu, as Rot. Parl. iv. 90.
[4] Pat. 1 H. V, iii. 21. Cf. une marque, reprensaille et autre nouvelletés, Gilliodts van Severen, 341; Rot. Parl. iv. 51.
[5] Claus. 1 H. V, 2 (Feb. 15, 1414), where Drew Barentin, William Waldern and others to whom the letters of marque had been issued find bail in £40 for having bought goods captured from the Genoese. See also Early Chanc. Proc. i. 28, where the goods had been bought by Lawrence de Platea and Bartholomew de Boniface, merchants of Pemound (Piedmont) and Plesance (Placentia). For safe-conducts Feb. 24, 1419, for Lawrence de Platea and Jacobus de Cambyan de Pemount, mercatores coming to England to trade, see Fr. Roll 6 H. V, 3.
[6] Ord. Priv. Co. ii. 132.
[7] Viz. Benedict Buccanègra, Bishop of Ventimiglia (Stella, 1248; Gams, 827; Eubel, i. 560, where he is supposed to have died in 1411), and Adam Otræmarinis. For their safe-conducts issued April 3, 1414, see Rym. ix. 120. For safe-conducts dated Aug. 20, Nov. 28, 1414, for the Bishop and Janot Lamelin, ambassadors from the Doge and Communitas of Genoa, see Rym. ix. 157, 181; Carte, Rolles, ii. 217; Dep. Keep. 44th Rept. 557.

to London to effect a settlement. At the first interview the Genoese maintained that the goods they had captured belonged to Florentine merchants with whom they were at war[1], asserting that they really had a claim against us for £17,000, against which we counterclaimed for £13,000, but this was afterwards reduced to £8000 and under reasonable treatment there seemed to be a prospect of a peaceable settlement.

About the same time Thomas de la Croix[2] came across[3] from the Lord of Milan, whereupon the creditors of the late Earl of Kent[4] took advantage of the opportunity to press for payment of the dowry that had been promised with his sister-in-law, Lucy Visconti, on her marriage six years before[5].

Other outlying interests had been safeguarded by the arrival in London of envoys from the High Master of the Teutonic Knights[6], and John Kington, who had often been employed in negotiations with the Order in the preceding reign[7] but had now become a monk at Canterbury[8], was summoned from his retirement to give the benefit of his advice in consultation[9]. At the same time the settlers in the English factories in Holland secured a confirmation[10] of the privilege of electing their own governors which had been granted to them during the late reign[11].

---

[1] Ord. Priv. Co. ii. 257, where the document is undated.
[2] Wylie, iii. 172; Wenck, 113; called "Thomas de la Crosse" in Rec. Roll 3 H. V, Pasch., June 10, 1415. For £40 paid to him for bringing horses to England from abroad, see do. 4 H. V, Mich., Nov. 4, 1416.
[3] For his safe-conduct dated March 9, 1414, see Priv. Seal 659/194; Rym. ix. 118; Carte, Rolles, ii. 211.
[4] Rym. ix. 121; Wylie, iii. 104.
[5] For grant of 4 casks of wine to her, May 18, 1409, see Rym. x. 315, confirmed Oct. 28, 1413, by Henry V, as carissimæ *sorori* suæ Lucie des Viscontes, see Claus. 1 H. V, 11. For her betrothal, May 25, 1406 (not March, as Wylie, ii. 40, note 2), see Wenck, Lucia, 45; Engl. Hist. Rev. (1897), xii. p. 252. For her marriage, see Wenck, 6, do. Lucia, 8; Holt, Langley, 235, 268, 323, 336; Knight, London, i. 118.
[6] "Mestre de Pruce," Ord. Priv. Co. ii. 132.   [7] Wylie, iv. 475.
[8] Ore moigne, Priv. Seal 658/80, July 29, 1413; qui habitum religionis assumpsit, Stone, 7, 185, showing that he was admitted to the monastery of Christ Church, Canterbury, in 1408, and died there on Oct. 18, 1416, being buried in the infirmary chapel. Stone, who calls him Kynton, describes him as: inceptor legum, vir magnus et potens in seculo magnaeque famae et officii in curia Henrici quarti et ipsius protonotarius; also as Chancellor to Queen Joan and often ambassador for Henry IV, extra regnum Angliae. See Wylie, ii. 71; iv. 1, 5, 7, 10, 13.
[9] For £36 paid to him coming from Canterbury to the King at Westminster, see Devon, 334, July 16, 1414.
[10] Rym. ix. 68.   [11] i.e. in 1407, Wylie, ii. 68, note 1.

CHAPTER X

WALES

In the autumn of 1413 Hugh Huls[1] and the new Chief Justice Hankford[2] were despatched to North and South Wales respectively to hold quests[3] in reference to those persons who had been implicated in the rebellions of the late reign, with a view to an extension of the pardons offered at the king's accession[4]. Special commissioners were also afoot in various parts of Wales[5], and on Sept. 6, 1413[6], a proclamation was issued requiring all Welshmen to return to their own country and defend it before the coming Christmas. With the new year the Earl of Arundel appears as the King's Lieutenant for North and South Wales[7], while he and Edward Charleton, Lord of Powys[8], continued

[1] Iss. Roll 1 H. V, Mich., Feb. 22, 1414. For payment to Roger Horton, sergeant-at-law, helping Hugh Huls in commission for rebellion in North Wales, see ibid. Dec. 9, 1413. For brass of Hugh Huls or Holes at Watford, see Cussans, Cashio, 191; Druitt, 227; Macklin, 173; Wylie, ii. 183, note 2. He died at Oxey near Watford, July 2, 1415, Clutterbuck, i. 246.

[2] Page 17, note 1. For commission to William Hankford and John Russell to enquire into rebellions in South Wales, July 12, 1413, see Pat. 1 H. V, iii. 31 d. For £20 paid to Thomas Conelly, King's Attorney in the King's Bench, who was in comitiva of the Chief Justice, see Iss. Roll 1 H. V, Mich., Oct. 21, 1413.

[3] Cf. that haldeth questes or assize, Kail, 36; Halliwell, ii. 658.

[4] Page 8, note 5.

[5] e.g. John St John, kt., John Greyndore, kt. and others appointed June 12, 1413, to enquire into rebellions in Kidwelly, Caerkennyn, Brecknock, Hay, Ogmore and Ebboth, Pat. 1 H. V, iii. 39 d. For reference to dower in St Clears of Margaret, widow of Ll. ap Morgan (who had died a rebel), now wife of Raulyn Greyndour, see Priv. Seal 658/58, June 26, 1413.

[6] Claus. 1 H. V, 21 d. For exceptions in the case of John Lewis, chaplain and Griffith ap Hopkin, see Priv. Seal 659/172, Dec. 22, 1413.

[7] Iss. Roll 1 H. V, Mich., Jan. 25, 1414.

[8] For £120 paid to him for wages of 10 men-of-arms and 20 archers at Monmouth (apud Montho in Wales) from Jan. 1 anno primo (i.e. 1414 but probably meant for 1413) till April 1st following, see Iss. Roll 1 H. V, Mich., Dec. 4, 1413; Pat. 1 H. V, iv. 38, Nov. 7, 1413. For other references to him see Pat. 2 H. V, ii. 3, Dec. 10, 1414. For

to hold enquiries as to the treasons of the past[1]. On July 16, 1414[2], the Duke of York is Justiciar in South Wales with power to appoint an acting deputy, and in accordance with the prevailing conciliatory spirit pardons were freely granted[3] and forfeited lands restored[4] on payment of the fines imposed. Thus the men of Anglesey were fined 800 marks, while fines of 500 marks apiece were imposed on the men of Flint and Carnarvon and 300 marks on those of Merioneth, all to be payable within terms varying from six to eight years according to the ability of each county[5]. In Carmarthenshire an interesting correction had afterwards to be made when it was discovered that lands had escheated to the king which by Welsh law were not escheatable[6], and the claim was ultimately allowed as valid after the county had already paid £1000 into the Exchequer. On Sept. 22, 1413[7], Thomas Barneby was appointed Chamberlain of North Wales, but he was succeeded by Thomas Walton on July 24, 1414[8]; William Venables of Kinderton was Constable

his custody of lands quæ fuerunt Alianoræ late countess of March (Wylie, ii. 36), see Rec. Roll 1 H. V, Pasch., June 9, 1413. For expenses, July 3, 1405, of a varlet of the Countess of March coming to Dunster with letters to Hugh Luttrell, see Lyte, 117. She died Dec. 23, 1405.

[1] Pat. 1 H. V, iii. 41 d, July 18, 1413; do. v. 16 d, Feb. 27, 1414.
[2] Pat. 2 H. V, ii. 34; Dict. Nat. Biogr. xlv. 403.
[3] e.g. to Meredith Boule, Meredith ap Eynon ap Gwyllim and William ap Tudor (the friend of Owen Glendower, Wylie, i. 215; ii. 15), Pat. 1 H. V, ii. 31; Priv. Seal 658/55, June 23, 1413, where forfeited lands are restored in Gowerland and the diocese of St David's. For pardons to Henry Don of South Wales (Wylie, i. 447; the then representative of the Cheshire family of Done of Utkinton was called John, Dep. Keep. 36th Report, 154, 155; Ormerod, ii. 244;—not Henry, as Owen and Blakeway, i. 182), Morgan ap David ap Jevan ap Mauric', Griffith ap Meredith ap Henry and Jevan Gwyn ap Gwyllym dated May 6, 29; June 8, 12, 30, 1413, see Pat. 1 H. V, i. mm. 12, 15, 20, 23, 29; also to Ll. ap Madok Dew, Pat. 3 H. V, i. 16, May 15, 1415; and to Thomas Vaghan and William ap Thomas ap Prune in South Wales, Pat. 4 H. V, 3, March 15, 1417. For order dated June 26, 1415, for John Matthews a canon of St John the Evangelist at Carmarthen, then a prisoner in the Tower, to be handed over to the Abbot of Waltham, see Rym. ix. 282. For payment to Stephen Drax the king's sergeant-at-arms for bringing Christopher Rys (arrested by him) to the king's person at Southampton, by letter dated Easter, 1413 (sic), see Iss. Roll 3 H. V, Pasch., May 1, 1415.
[4] For lands of John Astewyk in the hundred of Aylesmere (i.e. Ellesmere, Salop) forfeited for rebellion, see Pat. 2 H. V, i. 15. For land of John Astewick in Lincs. 40 Ed. III, see Inq. p. Mort. ii. 303.
[5] Pat. 1 H. V, iv. 15, Nov. 30, 1413; ibid. 2 H. V, i. 21, May 18, 1414.
[6] Non escheatabiles, Pat. 3 H. V, ii. 21, Nov. 12, 1415.
[7] Pat. 1 H. V, iii. 28. For his previous term of office, see Wylie, ii. 12. In 1420 he is constable of Carnarvon, For. Accts. 8 H. V, 1, where two French knights, viz. Ralph de Gall and Colard Blosset, were imprisoned. Gall was sent to London with John Helegh as Barneby's lieutenant and left Carnarvon with 4 varlets and 6 horses on April 1, 1420, arriving in London on April 16th, and Blosset started with Gilbert Rachedale on Oct. 21, 1420, arriving on Oct. 26. Both were sent to the king in Normandy under writ dated Oct. 15, 1420.
[8] Pat. 2 H. V, ii. 35.

of Chester[1]; on Oct. 17, 1413[2], a naturalised Welshman, Rys ap Thomas, was appointed Steward of Cardigan; the ruined walls of Carmarthen were ordered to be repaired[3] and 120 men-of-arms and 240 archers were to be distributed to strengthen garrisons in various parts of Wales, wages for them being sent down at intervals[4] at the rate of 1s. and 6d. each per day respectively. At Chester the dilapidated walls of the cathedral[5] told of the general prevailing distress, while subsidies that should have been paid up by the clergy more than 12 years ago were still outstanding as arrears and showed no prospect of being ever collected in such districts as the archdeaconries of St David's and Carnarvon[6].

But the dominant fact is the cessation of all effective resistance on the part of the arch-fugitive, Owen Glendower[7], whose career was now nearly at an end. His last days have long been shrouded in impenetrable mystery. In England he was believed to be starving in the open, having

---

[1] Priv. Seal 658/84, Aug. 18, 1413, with a reference to the time when Oweyn de Glendurdy lay in the country near Chester with large numbers of Welsh rebels, i.e. in 1403, see Wylie, ii. 2, 291. For his previous appointment Nov. 18, 1399, see Wylie, ii. 188, note 6.

[2] Pat. 1 H. V, iii. 11. For confirmation of letters patent declaring him to be the king's liegeman, see ibid. i. 9, June 13, 1413.

[3] Pat. 3 H. V, i. 27, May 8, 1415.

[4] e.g. £333. 6s. 8d. (June 9, 1413) + £333. 13s. 4d. (July 4) + £84. 6s. 8d. (July 17) + £173. 6s. 8d. (Oct. 20) + £115. 6s. 8d. (Nov. 15) + £533. 6s. 8d. (Dec. 4) + £260 (Jan. 25, 1414) per manus Thomas Strange and John Clifford esquires, Iss. Roll 1 H. V, Pasch., Mich., *passim*.

[5] For permission to the Dean and Canons to collect alms because their church and college were ruinosa et debilitata, see Pat. 2 H. V, iii. 9, Jan. 28, 1415.

[6] For pardon to the Abbot of Vale Royal as collector of $\frac{7}{20}$ths granted by the clergy of the Southern Province at St Paul's on June 26, 1401, see Conc. iii. 254 (for $\frac{1}{10}$ths granted by the clergy anno 2, see Rec. Roll 6 H. V, Mich., Nov. 11, 1418), of which he was still unable to get in £51. 2s. 6d. from the archdeaconries in Carnarvon and St David's, see Pat. 2 H. V, i. 16, 20.

[7] The Welshmen called him Sion Hendy o Went-Iscoed, Archaeol. Cambr. i. 47. He is called Howinus Glyndour armiger Wallicus in Strecche, 264 a; cf. Glandoure, Rot. Parl. v. 104; Glendour, ibid. v. 139; Glendourde, ibid. iv. 440 (1433), where the same name is given to his grandfather whose wife was called Elizabeth; Glendurdy, ibid. v. 107; Glyndourdrye, ibid. v. 470, 524; Ewyn Glendor, Petegrue, 594; not Glandover, as Lavisse-Rambaud, iii. 391. For other varieties of spelling, see Wylie, i. 142, note 2; iii. 271, note 2. For supposition that he was a squire to Richard II (which should be Henry IV, Wylie, i. 143), see Rowlatt, 29; Oman, Hist. 214; Low-Pulling, 504; Arnold-Forster, 228; Historians' Hist. xviii. 517; E. Hardy, I. pp. iv, 1, who makes him go with Richard II to Ireland and present at his surrender at Flint. B. E. Warner (102) calls him a "romantic half-barbarian," "a veneered courtier," a poet, "a gentleman but not a soldier nor a diplomatist" (103). In Goldwin Smith (i. 248) he is "a formidable though somewhat bombastic personage." C. R. L. Fletcher, 310, thinks that he was "a statesman as well as a Welsh thief." For picture of his house near Glyn Dyfrdwy, see L. J. Roberts, 27. For his seal, see Archaeologia, xxv. 616, 619; Macfarlane-Thomson, i. 540; Cassell, i. 510; E. Hardy, ii. 31; Kingsford, 32; Durham, 22; Wylie, i. 143, note 3.

no settled home but roaming the mountains by day and hiding away at night[1]. At one time he wanders in the solitary Berwyns, where the Abbot of Valle Crucis[2] near Llangollen met him and told him that he had risen 100 years before his time[3]. Another version finds him on the top of Laughton Hope[4], better known as Robin Hood's Butts, or the Sugarloaf, near Weobley in Herefordshire. At other times he was disguised as a reaper with a sickle lurking in the caves and thickets of Snowdon with Meredith, his only surviving son[5]. His eldest son Griffith, who had been captured near Usk in the spring of 1405[6], died during his imprisonment in the Tower[7]. His daughter Catherine[8], the widow of Edmund Mortimer[9], and her three little girls who had fallen into the hands of the English at the capture of Harlech in 1409[10] had all died in London before the year 1413 was out, and were buried in the church of St Swithin's in Candlewick Street[11], while a further symptom of the

[1] Sub divo semper larem fovit in montibus latens, Strecche, 264 b.   E. Hardy (ii. 297) saw "no appearance of probability" in these accounts. Cf.

> And made me eat both gravel, durt, and mud,
> And last of all my dung, my flesh, my blood,
> Or starve for hunger in the barren field.

Mirror for Magistrates, 302 ; W. F. Trench, 43 ; Wylie, iii. 269.

[2] For account of Valle Crucis, see Archaeol. Cambr. i. 17-32 with picture in Frontispiece; also A. G. Bradley, 54 ; L. J. Roberts, Frontispiece ; E. Hardy, i. 238 ; Wylie, iii. 141.

[3] Ellis Griffith in Hist. MSS. in Welsh Language, 1. pp. xii, 214 ; A. G. Bradley, 280.

[4] Harl. MS. 35 quoted in First Life, pp. vii, 191 ; see Duncumb, Grimsworth, 73.

[5] Usk, 119, 298 ; Wylie, iii. 269.

[6] Usk, 103, 282, who gives a clear account of the capture (Wylie, ii. 171), showing that Griffith was planning an attack on Usk when the garrison of the castle under Lord Grey of Codnor and John Greindour rushed out and pursued him, capturing him at Monkswood about a mile and a half to the north-west of Usk on the opposite side of the river. Large numbers of the Welsh were slain including the Abbot of the Cistercians at Lantarnam (not Llanthony, as Usk, 282) near Caerleon (Lel. Coll. i. 104; Itin. v. 13 ; Coxe, 118 ; Monast. v. 728), called Abbas Glamorgan, i.e. the district of the Morgan family, in Scotichron. iv. 1204, where he is called John Powel an Austin Canon killed at Brinbiga apud aquam de Uske. About 300 of the captives were beheaded near the pound (prope Pinfaldum, i.e. the pinfold) in front of Usk Castle. The news reached Venice where it was regarded as an intervention of Providence (espreso miracholo de Dio) and a great blow to France, Morosini, i. 195, where Owen is called el re de Galo (not Portogalo) and the English are supposed to have numbered 15,000. For a plan of Usk with a picture of the castle keep, see Coxe, 124, 135.

[7] The statement in Usk, 103, 282, would seem to imply that he died in 1411, which cannot be right, see page 2, note 1. He is called Griffith ap Vechan ap Owen commonly called Balff in Hardy, i. 148, who refers to a "respectable family" claiming descent from him in Ireland possibly the Balfes of Fydorfe, co. Meath, Foster, Collect. Geneal. (Funeral Certificates of Ireland), p. 10.

[8] She is so called in Iss. Roll 1 H. V, Mich., Feb. 19, 22, 1414 ; Wylie, iii. 266, note 5 ; not Jane, as A. G. Bradley, 105 ; nor Eva, as E. Hardy, i. 161, 214 and *passim*.

[9] Not Edward, as E. Hardy, i. 14.

[10] Usk, 119, 298 ; Wylie, i. 344 ; iii. 266.

[11] Though not named among the monuments in Stow, Bk. ii. 191; do. Kingsford, i. 224.

growing sense of security in Wales is furnished by the
issue of an order to the Carmelites at Ludlow on July 5,
1417[1], to replace the image of the Virgin with its rich
decorations in the chapel at Pilleth in Radnorshire, which
had been entrusted to their keeping at the time of the
disaster in which Mortimer had been captured in 1402[2].

Before the king set sail for France in August, 1415, he
authorised Gilbert Talbot[3] to negotiate with the fallen
Glendower in case he should be willing to sue for pardon[4],
and six months later negotiations were in progress with his
son Meredith on the understanding that Owen should
be pardoned if he came to ask it[5]. But all such offers
were unavailing, for about that time he was past human
aid. Four years of want and hardship[6] had worn out his
strength, and in the spring of 1416[7] he finished his miserable life without a struggle[8]. His people buried him at
night, but when the fact became known, some loyalists
removed the body and to this day no one knows the spot
where it was really laid[9]. Hence have arisen the stories
that he lies at Bangor, or at the home of one of his married
daughters either at Monnington[10] or Kentchurch[11] in Herefordshire, or that he died in a wood in Glamorganshire,

For £5 + £14. 0s. 11d. + 33s. 4d. paid for their funerals, see Iss. Roll r H. V, Mich.,
Dec. 1, 1413, Jan. 27, Feb. 19, 22, 1414; Devon, 327.

[1] Priv. Seal 5 H. V, 834.

[2] Wylie, i. 282.

[3] Not of Grafton near Bromsgrove, as A. G. Bradley, 303, which manor was not
granted to the Talbots till 1486, Nash, i. 158. For supposition that Davy Holbache
was joined with Gilbert Talbot in this matter, see Pennant, Wales, 368. For £20 paid
to John Southern of Mitton near Whalley (Lancs.) pro secretis agendis in Wales, see
Iss. Roll 3 H. V, Mich., Oct. 15, 1415.

[4] Rym. ix. 283, July 5, 1415; Pennant, Wales, 368; Usk, 313.

[5] Si se ad gratias petendum obtulerit, Rym. ix. 330, Feb. 24, 1416; Tyler, i. 244;
A. G. Bradley, 304.

[6] Viluit sors Oweni, Usk, 104; Tit. Liv. 4; First Life, 10.

[7] Called shortly before Feb. 1416 in Oman, Pol. Hist. 238; L. J. Roberts, viii; or
Sept. 20, 1415, Pennant, Wales, 368; Owen and Blakeway, i. 206; Beaumont, i. 241;
Oman, Pol. Hist. 260; Hassell, 218; Low-Pulling, 504, repeating the haunting date for
which there is no authority, Wylie, iii. 270, note 5.

[8] Sine conflictu devenit ad suum finem, Strecche, 264. b. For supposition that he
was then 62 years of age, see Wylie, iii. 271; called 63 in Yonge, 236. In L. J. Roberts
(p. vii) his birth is dated 1359.

[9] Usk, 129, 313, who fixes the date as the year of Agincourt, i.e. the year ending
March 19, 1416, Wylie, iii. 270, note 3.

[10] For picture of Monnington with the flat stone at the entrance to the church, see
A. G. Bradley, 308.

[11] Not Ewyas, as Kingsford, 58. For picture of Kentchurch Court whose owner John
Skidmore, or Scudamore, married Owen's daughter Alice, see A. G. Bradley, 314. The
small Flemish picture of a monk now at Kentchurch (W. Coxe, 338) has been supposed
to represent the bard Sion Kent or John à Kent who was present at an Eisteddfod, temp.

while patriots long imagined that he had only lain down in his armour with his warriors in a cave[1] where he was sleeping on till England should be self-abased—all of which stately fancies seem to point to the belief that he never really bowed to the conqueror, but died with his fortunes broken but his spirit unsubdued. At any rate no record now remains of any pardon received or submission accepted. His forfeited estates which had passed to the Beauforts[2] were never allowed to return, and when in more settled times his daughter Alice put in a claim for recovering a portion of them by writ of formedon[3], the claim was stopped and her father was repeatedly referred to as a traitor[4]. His son Meredith received his pardon on April 30, 1417[5], and took service with the English in France in 1419[6], and two years later he was received into complete favour, on the principle that the son shall not bear the father's iniquity[7].

For many of the particulars of the last days of Owen Glendower we are indebted to the querulous and chatty chronicle of Adam of Usk[8], who had direct personal intercourse with him, having joined him after crossing from Brittany to Barmouth in 1406, and when Owen had thrown over the Roman obedience and intended to make the Welsh Church once more independent of the see of Canterbury, Adam was selected to be Bishop of Llandaff[9], though he

---

Ed. III, Iolo MSS. 492. For his poems, see ibid. 676, 682. For supposition that it represents Owen Glendower himself, see C. J. Robinson, 153, who gives a picture of the house in 1774.

[1] Called Og of Dinas in the vale of Gwent in A. G. Bradley, 302.

[2] e.g. to John Earl of Somerset, Nov. 8, 1414, Rot. Parl. iv. 440; see also ibid. v. 470 (1461), 524 (1464), 607 (1467).

[3] i.e. per formam doni "which was the remedy for a tenant in tail on a discontinuance," Stephens, Blackstone, i. 162, cf. Murray, s.v. A. G. Bradley (306) states that "a few years after his death Parliament passed a law for the benefit of his heirs," which seems to be a reference to Rot. Parl. iv. 377 (1431), which contains a proviso: "so that this be not prejudiciel to any of the heirs of the blode of the said Owen (meaning probably Meredith who had submitted), as touching any tailled land."

[4] e.g. in 1433, 1444, 1449, Rot. Parl. iv. 440; v. 104, 139.

[5] Pat. 5 H. V, 35, where he is called Meredith ap Owain de Wall', the negotiation being transacted through Gilbert Talbot. Cf. Rym. ix. 330; Cal. Pat. H. V, i. 404; ii. 89.

[6] Cal. Rot. Pat. 7 H. V, p. 267; cf. regi famulatus est, Tit. Liv. 4; was taken into service with the Prince, First Life, 10.

[7] i.e. April 8, 1421, Pat. 9 H. V, i. 27; Cal. Pat. H. V, ii. 335; A. G. Bradley, 306.

[8] Oman (R. II.–R III. 500) calls him "a strange flighty being."

[9] For authority for his installation granted by Benedict XIII on April 26, 1407, see Eubel, Provisiones, 426, where he is called Adam of Wesk. The permission for Adam's installation was issued by Griffin Yonge, Bishop of Bangor, whom Benedict had on that day designated Bishop of St David's in order to free the Welsh Church from "the oppression of the English," Eubel, i. 430; do. Gesch. pp. 265, 266.

never actually held the post.   For, as he says, he only pretended to become Owen's man while secretly arranging to
desert him[1], as after two years he actually did, escaping by
night to the castle of Welshpool where he spent three
dreary years under the protection of Lord Powys from 1408
to 1411[2].   But at length Archbishop Arundel took him back
into favour and gave him the living of Merstham[3] near
Reigate, where he gathered servants, books, clothes and
household goods and blessed God like Job for ever[4].   He
died at Usk, his native place, where he made his will on
Jan. 20, 1430[5], and a brass in the parish church still
preserves his memory[6].

Thus had resistance quite died down, and with it died
all hope of the revival of independence for the Welsh
Church and nation and the establishment of separate Welsh
universities[7] which once had seemed a possibility of the
insurrection, and "the rebellion time[8]" could soon be
spoken of as a thing of the past.

The general pacification of the country is strongly
evidenced by the employment of many Welshmen in
positions of trust under the English government[9] and it
is significant to find many Welsh squires[10] as well as 500

[1] Usk, 117, 295.   [2] Ibid. 118, 296.

[3] Though his name does not appear in the list of rectors in Manning and Bray, ii. 263.

[4] Usk, 119, 297.

[5] It was proved Mar. 26, 1430, see Challoner Smith, ii. 541, from Register Luffenham,
f. 13, now in Somerset House, with text in Eng. Hist. Rev. (1903), xviii. 316;
Usk, xxix.

[6] For this brass, see Usk, xxxi, with facsimiles in Archaeologia, ii. 20 (1773);
Camden, Britannia (Gough's edition), ii. 487; W. Coxe, 418.

[7] See Wylie, ii. 313.   It is now known that as a sequel to these efforts Benedict XIII,
on April 15, 1407, granted power to Griffin Yonge, who had before been Archdeacon of
Merioneth (Le Neve, i. 116), but now appears as Bishop of Bangor, to found a studium
generale in any place that Owen should select, and that on April 26, 1407, Griffin
renounced the Roman obedience and received from Benedict power to enquire as to the
position of the see of St David's which had been for long subject to the archbishops of
Canterbury *per oppressionem Anglicorum*, Eubel, i. 130; do. Zur. Gesch. pp. 265, 266.
Griffin Yonge is called priest of the diocese of Lichfield in Papal Lett. vi. 502, where
he obtains the see of Bangor from Benedict XIII, i.e. before Feb. 14, 1407, Eubel,
Provisiones, 426; Papal Lett. vi. 137.   On July 28, 1414, John XXIII declared at
Bologna that Lewis Bifort had been lawfully Bishop of Bangor all the time, though at
that date he had no hope of again securing the see as Griffin Yonge was then in actual
possession.   Griffin appears to have been appointed Bishop of Ross in Scotland in 1418
(Gams, 241; Eubel, i. 446), and on Feb. 1, 1423, Bishop of Hippo (Eubel, i. 288; do.
Provisiones, 426).

[8] Sloane MS. 4600, ff. 298, 311.

[9] In Monmouthshire in 1417 the coroner is Morgan ap Rosser and the deputy-sheriff
is Morgan ap Jevan ap Jankyn, Ord. Priv. Co. ii. 215.

[10] For specimens see Exch. Accts. 45/1, where the following names of Welsh squires
occur, i.e. Yewan ap Griffith ap Madduck (*sic*) ap Meredith, Howel Dewgh (i.e. Dhu)

archers from South Wales with genuine Welsh names[1] fighting side by side with Englishmen at Agincourt[2], though there is also evidence that some Welsh gentlemen fought with the French on the opposite side.

It may be argued that this is only a proof of Welsh adaptability and indeed it is expressly recorded by a compatriot that when they saw their cause was lost they took to living like Englishmen[3]. They tilled the ground, moved into the towns, made money and kept it, rode in hauberks, wore shoes[4], slept under blankets, and tried to pass as English rather than Welsh[5]. Thus money broke them down and the fear of losing what they had, for it is only the haveless that can afford to be dreadless, and only the empty wayfarer that can whistle in the face of the robber[6]. To many an ardent spirit this tame submission after 15 years of struggle seemed a return to slavery[7] and some said that it was God's judgment on them because they gave up going to church and took to haunting dice and taverns[8]. Others attributed the failure to their internal dissensions. So long as they heard their weekly mass all went well, but when they lapsed into pride and all vanities and vices, God abandoned them to their fate[9]. There were of course whole districts filled with irreconcileables, and

de Kery, Thomas ap Griffith Goch, Deyvw (i.e. Dhu) ap Philip, Griffith ap Llfi. (? Llewellyn), John ap Meredith, all amongst the archers in the retinue of the Earl of Arundel probably from his tenantry in Yale and Bromfield and the neighbourhood of Oswestry.

[1] Wylie, Notes, 135. For fame of the Welsh archers, see Rym. v. 9; Lingard, iii. 123; and their skill with the long bow (1150), see Giraldus, vi. 54; Oman, 559; do. Art of War, 98; Morris, 15, 16, of the men of Gwent, whose tactics were adopted by Edward I. For Roger le Walsshman and John le Walsshman in the retinue of John Savage at Calais in 1419, see Exch. Accts. 49/22.

[2] Wylie, Notes, 135. John Merbury received £435 for their wages from William Botiller at Hereford on June 6, 1415, but a warrant dated 10 H. V (i.e. 1422) calls on the sheriff of Hereford to distrain Merbury's goods for not accounting for the money, ibid. where John Merbury is *late* our Chamberlain in South Wales.

[3] More Anglicorum, Usk.

[4] Cf. nudati semper tibiis (alle with bare legges), Higden, i. 403; nudis pedibus ambulant, Girald. vi. 181, v. calceati peditant (=gooth i-hosed and i-schod) in Higden, i. 410. See also Cleaveland, ii. 90; Historians' Hist. xviii. 518; Wylie, iv. 334.

[5] Higden, i. 410.

[6] Causæ sunt divitiæ, timor damni nos retrahit, nil habens nil metuit, Wright, Feudal Manuals, 152, from MS. temp. H. VI, in possession of T. L. Duncomb Jones Parry, Madrin Castle, Pwllheli.

[7] In exterminium et servitutem redacti sunt, Scotichron. iv. 1193; sub servitute tributaria (p. 1202); jacet sub gente saxonicâ squalida et oppressa (p. 1206).

[8] Scotichron. iv. 1204, where they are held up as a warning to the Scots.

[9] Pluscard, 352, who refers to the resistance preached by Abbot Powell in Glamorgan.

bands of plunderers still straggled across the border, masked[1] in the forests of Shropshire, Hereford and even Gloucestershire to trap any English they could waylay and carry them off to the mountains where the king's writ did not run.

But though these desperadoes could well be left to a process of gradual extinction, yet was race hatred still unquenched and keen as ever, and 30 years after the last embers of the struggle had sparked out the Welshmen held the English "nothing in favour[2]," while the English in the Welsh and border-towns petitioned "to avale[3] the Welshmen's pomp and pride" by the enforcement of those statutes that had been passed in the first heat of the strife, and that Welshmen might be "bounden and arted[4] to do such labours and services by right as they have used to do of old time[5]"; and so no office in Wales might be held by any Englishman who had married a wife "of the friendship or alliance of Owen[6]," while no Welshman might become a denizen lest he should thereby acquire the privilege of serving on a jury "to the utter destruction of all Englishmen" in the Principality[7].

[1] Mussiez, Musciez, Rot. Parl. iv. 52; Stat. ii. 188; cf. les faces bien muchiez, Pastoralet, 748; mucées, Monstr. 402; Le Fèvre, i. 294; Wylie, iii. 90, note 2.
[2] Rot. Parl. v. 104 (1444).
[3] Cf. "avaled and descended," Lydg. Nightingale, 11.
[4] Halliwell, s.v. *Arte.*
[5] Rot. Parl. v. 139 (1447).
[6] Ibid. iv. 233, 377, 440.
[7] Ibid. v. 104.

CHAPTER XI

AQUITAINE

It will be remembered that after the accommodation with the French before Bourges in July, 1412[1], a large force of English[2] under the Duke of Clarence[3] had moved southward to winter at Bordeaux[4]. They laid siege to Talmont[5] and reduced every fortress[6] within 20 leagues of Bordeaux with the single exception of Marmande[7], plundering and pillaging at the expense of loyalists and enemies alike[8] and doing an infinite amount of damage even in the very suburbs of Bordeaux[9]. Supplies were sent out to them from England[10] to meet immediate needs and some instalments of

[1] Wylie, iv. 79.

[2] Ibid. iv. 75, 85; called 10,000 to 12,000 in Cagny, 76; or 8000 in Mont St Michel, i. 19; Henty, 82; à grand effort et puissance de gens d'armes et de traict, Vaissète (Molinier), x. 1960.

[3] For 2000 marks p. a. granted to him on June 14, 1413, see Iss. Roll 4 H. V, Pasch., May 14, 27, 1416. He had already custody of the lands of Henry, son of John Beaufort, late Earl of Somerset, whose widow Margaret he had married in 1412, Cal. Pat. H. IV, iv. 423; Wylie, iii. 305; iv. 76. In Rym. ix. 463, July 10, 1417, he has also custody of the lands of Thomas, son of Mons. Maurice Russel, kt.

[4] For plan of Bordeaux, see Drouyn, Guienne, Plate 150; do. Bordeaux, ad fin. For 15th century picture of Bordeaux, see Froissart (Johnes), ii. 195. For view and plan in 1666, see Lopès, ii. 49; Desrues, 236 (17th century). For view showing castle, cathedral, etc., see De Witt, 317. For fancy picture of Bordeaux, ibid. 231. It is called urbs amplissima in 1466, Rozmital, 61. For views of the cathedral at Bordeaux, see Lopès, i. 104, 130; Frontispiece; Grande Encycl. vi. 386; Bourassé, Cath. 580; Loth, 86. For the detached bell-tower (campanile sive pinnaculum novum), see Belleforest, Cosmogr. ii. 382. It was projected in 1429 and built in 1440 by Archbishop Pey Berland, Lopès, i. 176, 177, 179; ii. 305; Drouyn, Bordeaux, 387. For Bordeaux in the 14th century, see Ribadieu, Châteaux, 557.

[5] For wood to make les emparas (i.e. fencing, Godefroy, Cotgrave, s.v. *Emparence*) of 2 guns for the siege, see Jurade, 35.

[6] For obsidium de D— by the Duke of Clarence in Gascony, see Nasmyth, 373.

[7] Ordonnances, x. 226, where exemptions from *péage* are granted to it similar to those of Condom, Agen and Villeneuve. It is situated above La Réole on the Garonne (Lot et Garonne) and was captured by the French from Bernard de Lesparre in 1403, Samazeuilh, i. 449.

[8] Douet d'Arcq, i. 364; pillant gastant et conquérant forteresses et pais, Ec. des Chartes, vii. 60, Jan., Feb., 1413.

[9] Las ballegas, Jurade, 9, 12, 24, 26, 214 and *passim*; cf. comonzaron de hacer la guerra cruelmente en Gascuña, Surita, ii. 37, 39.

[10] For 100 quarters of oats sent to Thomas, Duke of Clarence, as Lieutenant of Aquitaine in the Catherine of Bayonne, see Claus. 1 H. V, 32, April 18, 1413.

the indemnity were paid up by the French dukes who had originally called them in[1], but the yield from such sources was altogether inadequate and so as Lieutenant of Aquitaine[2] the duke summoned the Estates of the Bordelais[3] to ask for means to feed his men, whom he conveniently assumed to have been sent over for the protection of Guienne. These meetings were usually summoned by the crier with a trumpet[4] and were held in the chapter-house of St Seurin[5]. They were attended by the royal officers such as the Seneschal[6], the Judge of Gascony[7], and the members of the King's Council, the Archbishop, the Dean and some of the clergy of Bordeaux, the Town Clerk and representatives of the Jurade, the Council of 30, the Council of 300 and a sprinkling of lawyers and bachelors. On this occasion the Estates pleaded poverty but agreed in the end to submit to a tax on wine[8] and other commodities, to be levied for a year dating from May 15, 1413[9]. The incidence of the tax was extended also to Bayonne, Dax[10],

[1] Wylie, iv. 81, 83.

[2] For his appointment July 11, 1412, see ibid. iv. 76; Rym. viii. 758; Carte, Rolles, i. 195; Bellecombe, 40, 42; Doyle, i. 397; not July 12, as Ducarel, Misc. 30; do. Postscript, 7. For confirmation of the appointment in April, 1413, see Venuti, 187, quoting De Brousse, De Primatu Aquitaniæ; not that the Duke of York remained Lieutenant till July 22, 1413, as Doyle, iii. 744. For a letter dated Bordeaux, May 5, 1414, from the Jurade to the Duke of Clarence's Chamberlain, William Marny, see Jurade, 6.

[3] i.e. Bordeaux and the district round, including Bourg, Libourne and St Emilion, Jurade, 234

[4] Cf. Duplès-Agier, I. xvii.

[5] Jurade, 152. For extract from old book of Chronicles of St Severin, see Harl. MS. 4763, ff. 169–172; Cotton MS. Tiberius, B. 12, ff. 138–141. For the collegiate church of St Seurin, or St Severin, see Lopès, i. 243, 249, 251, 312, 320; ii. 7, 8, 9, 112; Drouyn, Bordeaux, 28; Baurein, ii. 191, 192; Mâle, 415. For pictures, see A. Laborde, II. Pl. cxxi; with the bishop's throne, Kraus, II. i. 485. It contained the tombs of SS. Veronica, Severin and Fort (Baurein, i. 380), and was a place of pilgrimage (Tanon, 502; Grande Encycl. vii. 387; Robert, 134), the water there being considered effectual in curing diseases of the eyes, Lopès, ii. 11. For legendary history of St Seurin, see Brutails, xxv. For a 16th century plan of Bordeaux showing the Bourg of St Seurin, outside the walls to the south-west, and the seigneurie de St Seurin with its claims to independent jurisdiction, see Brutails, lviii; Lavisse, Etudes, 277–283; Braun-Hohenberg, Théâtre, i. 10 (10th century); Zeiler, x. 20. For sanctuary at St Seurin, Ste Croix and the cathedral, see Drouyn, Bordeaux, 151.

[6] For view that the Seneschal was really the head official who kept the country, raised taxes, called out troops and administered justice, the King's Lieutenant being a military chief with fonctions extraordinaires et passagères, see Bellecombe, 16, 37.

[7] For the Juge de Gascoyne, see Baurein, iv. 260.

[8] For officium gaugeti (i.e. gauging, gaugeage, Rym. xiii. 127), turragii (? tronagii) et portagii at Bordeaux, see Rym. ix. 408. For the English king's right to 30s. on every tun of wine at Bordeaux, see Baurein, iv. 238.

[9] Rym. ix. 32.

[10] For Dax with its wooden bridge over the Adour (*Dura*) in 1466, see Rożmital, 61, where it lies sub montibus altissimis (i.e. the Pyrenees) qui nivibus nunquam liquescentibus semper albent.

St Sever[1] and the Landes[2], but the Duke of Clarence did not remain in the country long enough to see it gathered in. Immediately on receiving the news of his father's death[3] he took prompt steps for returning to England. He chartered eight ships that were lying at Bordeaux belonging to some English traders, viz. Richard Merlawe[4] and Walter Gawtron[5] of London and Edmund Arnold of Dartmouth[6], to convey some of his troops with their harness and other belongings, Sir John Colvil being made governor and captain for the voyage[7]. Sailing from Bordeaux on April 6,

---

[1] For assizes held at Bordeaux, Bazas, St Sever and Dax, all subordinate to the Seneschal of Aquitaine, see Bellecombe, 16. For the diocese of Bazas, see ibid. 118, 119; for the sénéchaussée of Bazas, ibid. 193.

[2] For Mathieu de Gournay as Senescallus Landarum, Nov. 24, 1405, see Carte, Rolles i. 190; Bellecombe, 36.

[3] Wals. ii. 290; Hypodig. 438; Capgr. 303; Wylie, iv. 86, note 3. Add. Ch. 64 shows that he was still at Bordeaux on April 14, 1413. In Exch. Accts. 186/2 is a document dated Jan. 6, 1413 (which ought to mean 1414), signed "J. du Pont par Mons. le Duc" as Lieutenant of Guienne. J. du Pont was keeper of the royal seal at Bordeaux on Dec. 1, 1413, receiving officium executorie regalis, Rot. Vasc. 1 H. V, 3; Carte, Rolles, i. 197; Wylie, iii. 108, note 5. Rot. Vasc. 6 H. V, 2, May 20, 1418; Carte, Rolles, i. 202, grants to John de Pount, Esquire, officium scribarie and of clerk of the court and the provosty of the Ombrière (Wylie, iii. 75) in the city of Bordeaux vacant by the death of Bernard de St Paul. For the manor of Aber near Bangor (Carnarvon) granted to John du Pont, July 30, 1417, see Pat. 5 H. V, 18; Priv. Seal 5 H. V (849).

[4] Or Marlow, Wylie, ii. 110; iii. 66. He was mayor of London in 1409-10, Letter Book I, 78; also in 1417-18, ibid. 190. In Rec. Roll 6 H. V, Pasch., Mich., April 5, May 25, Oct. 22, 1418, he is mayor and escheator of London, see also Fab. 583. He was succeeded by William Sevenoke in Nov. 1418 (Letter Book I, 206), who is mayor in Pat. 6 H. V, 16 d, Dec. 1, 1418, also in Claus. 6 H. V, 13, Nov. 1, 1418, where Merlawe is *late* mayor. For his gifts to the church of St Michael, Queenhithe, near Thames St., see Stow, Book iii. 212; do. Kingsford, ii. 5. For his will dated Sept. 18, 1420, enrolled May 12, 1422, see Sharpe, ii. 428; Stow, Kingsford, ii. 357.

[5] He was a draper and a member of the Common Council in 1410 (Letter Book I, 88, 104, 117), one of the representatives of the City of London in the Parliaments of 1410, 1413, 1427 and 1429 (ibid. I, 81, 109, 113; Return Parl. i. 279, 313, 316), and a representative of Middlesex in 1417 and 1423 (ibid. i. 290, 306; Loftie, ii. 397).

[6] In Pat. 1 H. V, i. 27 d, April 25, 1413; Iss. Roll 1 H. V, Pasch., May 4, 1413, he and John Hawley are customers for Exeter. In Rec. Roll 1 H. V, Pasch., July 14, 1413, he is referred to as *late* collector of customs for Exeter and Dartmouth, also Rec. Roll 1 H. V, Mich., Nov. 8, 1413, where he is called *Edward*; do. 2 H. V, Pasch., May 6, 8, 1414. In Rec. Roll 4 H. V, Pasch., June 27, 1416; Iss. Roll 4 H. V, Pasch., July 24, 1416, both are again collectors of customs and subsidy at Exeter and Dartmouth. Arnold represented Dartmouth in the Westminster Parliament in 1414, Return Parl. i. 283. For messenger sent to Dartmouth for him to answer in the Exchequer, see Iss. Roll 4 H. V, Mich., Nov. 9, 1416; cf. Wylie, iv. 74, note 3. In Claus. 4 H. V, 6, Feb. 6, 1417, he is water-bailiff of Dartmouth and is called Edmund Arnaud Gascoign (i.e. a Gascon), do. 5 H. V, 16 d. For £20 paid to him for repair of a ship called Cordewer of Lisbon (Lusshebone) with a portage of 250 dol., see Iss. Roll 7 H. V, May 24, 27, 1419. In Priv. Seal 5 H. V (585), Aug. 23, 1417, Robert Staunford genre de la femme de Esmon Arnold of Dartmouth is an outlaw. For Robert Stamford's suit against Edmund Arnold for a murderous assault on him when searching Arnold's ship on behalf of the king's searcher at Dartmouth, see Early Chanc. Proc. i. 32.

[7] For the Christopher of Hull acting as Admiral (Admiralx de tout la Flete d'Engleterre adoncq la esteantz) to a fleet of wine ships sailing from Bordeaux in April, 1416, in

1413, they overtook two Prussian hulks at Belle Isle off the coast of Brittany. These were laden with wine from La Rochelle[1], and Colvil straightway sent an esquire and two masters to board them and require them to produce their charters[2]. But the next day the strangers showed fight and delivered a regular attack[3] in which many of the English were killed. However, by God's help, both the Prussian ships were ultimately overmastered and brought safely into Poole and Southampton[4] to await the decision of the Admiral's court.

The Duke of Clarence was received in London[5] with "joy and great pleasaunce[6]" and on July 14, 1413[7], the King granted him a pension of 2000 marks per annum which was to be continued to his male heirs. He brought over with him John Count of Angoulême[8], the youngest brother of the Duke of Orleans, and others of the hostages[9] that had

---

which the masters of all the vessels were sworn before the constable at Bordeaux to stand by each other in case of attack, see Rot. Parl. iv. 86, 103 ; Nicolas, Navy, ii. 414 ; Simon, ii. 14. The ships scattered and the Christopher was captured by Genoese à grant anientisement et velany a tout le Naveye d'Engleterre.

[1] For Rochelle wine, see Simon, i. 273, who thinks that the wine ships reached England from Gascony twice a year, i.e. before Christmas and before Easter (p. 264).

[2] Chartres de lour affrettementz, called bills of lading in Clowes, i. 370 ; Simon, ii. 12.

[3] Orgoilousement come gentz de guerre.

[4] They were still there on June 9, 1413, Rot. Parl. iv. 12 ; Claus. 1 H. V, 24 d, 26, 29, June 14, July 4, 13, 1413 ; Nicolas, Navy, ii. 404.

[5] S'en retourna par Bordeaulx en Angleterre, Mont St Michel, i. 19. For permission for 22 casks of wine bought in Gascony for Thomas of Lancaster to enter London free of customs, see Claus. 1 H. V, 21, June 7, 1413.

[6] Hardyng, 373 ; festoie honourablement, Waurin, ii. 163.

[7] Pat. 1 H. V, iii. 18 ; Iss. Roll 1 H. V, Mich., Jan. 27, Feb. 22, 1414 ; do. 3 H. V, Pasch., April 11, 1415. For £500 p. a. granted to him and his wife, Margaret, half of which was advanced on July 19, 1414, see Devon, 334 ; Iss. Roll 3 H. V, Pasch., Apr. 26, 1415 ; also payment to her of £400 p. a. granted to her by Henry IV, see Iss. Roll 1 H. V, Pasch., July 24, 1413, together with custody of the lands of Bertram Monboucher (Inq. p. Mort. iv. 7, 100 ; Wylie, i. 214) deceased, which was granted to him on Nov. 2, 1414, Pat. 2 H. V, ii. 16, but subsequently vacated because of other grants made to the Duke of Clarence, May 18, 1417. He is in receipt of £1846. 13s. 4d. p. a. in Iss. Roll 5 H. V, Mich., Nov. 30, Dec. 27, 1417 ; do. 6 H. V, Pasch., April 5, 1418 and *passim* ; do. 7 H. V, Pasch., May 12, 1419 ; do. 8 H. V, Pasch., Mich., May 11, Oct. 29, Nov. 8, Dec. 14, 1420. For 2000 marks p. a. paid to him and his wife Margaret from possessions of her late husband, John Earl of Somerset (cf. Wylie, iii. 305 ; iv. 76, custody of which was granted to him on June 14, 1413, Iss. Roll 5 H. V, Mich., Feb. 10, 1418 ; do. 8 H. V, Pasch., May 11, 1420), see Iss. Roll 3 H. V, Mich., Oct. 28, Dec. 23, 1415 ; Devon, 343 ; also Rec. Roll 3 H. V, Mich., Oct. 28, 1415 ; Iss. Roll 4 H. V, Mich., Nov. 9, 23, 1416.

[8] In R. L. Stevenson, 184, he is "laid by the heels for an unpatriotic treaty."

[9] Biondi, 104 ; Duchesne, 819. Add. Charter, 59, shows that some hostages were still detained at Fronsac on Jan. 25, 1414. For the names of 6 hostages who came to England with the Count of Angoulême, see Maulde la Clavière, i. 34, from Pat. Roll, May 31, 1423 (? not in Cal. Pat. H. VI), i.e. the letter of the Duke of Orleans written at Bolingbroke on that date in Champollion-Figeac, 318 ; Dupont Ferrier, 34 ; Wylie, iv. 81, note 4, omitting Essor de Pontbriant and reading "Coutellier" for Bouteiller.

been delivered up at Buzançais[1] as caution[2] for payment of the large sums due to him from the French dukes who had called him across in the previous year. On his departure the defence of Aquitaine was entrusted to the King's uncle, Thomas Beaufort[3], Earl of Dorset[4], and to the Duke of York[5], both of whom remained in the country[6] after the Duke of Clarence had left. On July 22, 1413[7], the Earl of Dorset, who had been[8] marshal to the Duke of Clarence, was appointed Lieutenant of Aquitaine for six months with

---

[1] Wylie, iv. 82; called "Bousanssoys" in Add. Ch. 58. For the Duke of Clarence at Buzançais and Villedieu on the Indre, see Toulgoët-Treanna, 120, where he has interviews with envoys sent by the Bishop of Poitiers to secure protection for Poitou from invasion by the English; also ibid. 122, where the Duke gives 120 crowns on Nov. 16, 1412, to a secretary of the Duke of Orleans for his expenses in drawing up the treaty, his own chamberlain, William Marny (cf. Wylie, iv. 74, note 2), receiving 650 crowns from the Duke of Berry. For the negotiations, see Molandon, 613; Maulde la Clavière, i. 32; Dupont Ferrier, 34. Not that the Count of Angoulême was captured at Agincourt, as Windecke, 89 (die *zwy* jungen herrn von Urlianze); Guzman, 61; Heuterus, 203; Joubert, 5; Touchard-Lafosse, 82.

[2] Cf. comme caution d'une somme d'argent, from letter of the Duke of Orleans dated Paris, March 7, 1415, in Report on Fœdera, App. 2, 243.

[3] Called John Branford, Duke of Exeter, in Eulog. iii. 420, but he was not created Duke of Exeter till Nov. 18, 1416, Doyle, i. 710; Complete Peerage, iii. 297; Black Book of Admiralty, i. 347, though he is so called in the king's will dated July 24, 1415, Rym. ix. 293. Halle's statement (p. 55) that he was "well learned and sent into Italy by his father intending to have been a priest" is probably a mere literary fiction introduced to embellish an imaginary speech, though it is accepted by Holinsh. iii. 546; Biondi, 110.

[4] He was created Earl of Dorset on July 5, 1412, Dugd. ii. 125; Doyle, i. 615, 710; Wylie, iv. 73, note 9; not 1411, as Comp. Peerage, iii. 147; not Earl of Worcester, as Grey Friars Chron. 13. In Wills of Kings, 264, he is said to have been created Earl of Le Perche in 1409.

[5] For his previous appointment as Lieutenant of Aquitaine, dated Aug. 28, 1401, see Carte, Rolles, i. 187; Bellecombe, 40; York, p. xxx; Doyle, iii. 189; Wylie, i. 124; iv. 231, 232; not 1400, as Doyle, iii. 744, who supposes that he held the office till July 22, 1413. Privy Seal Bills 1114/52; Rym. ix. 27, dated June 18, 1413, shows that he was then staying in Aquitaine for a year for the defence of that country; called Mossenhor de Horc in Petite Chronique, 65, where 1415 should be 1413. For 5 casks of Gascon wine bought for the use of the Duke of York at Bordeaux, see Claus. 1 H. V, 16, Oct. 16, 1413; cf. Waurin, ii. 162, where he is called brother to Henry IV. In Rym. 180, Nov. 24, 1414, he is still Warden of the Channel Islands; cf. Wylie, iii. 48. On Feb. 1, 1414, he was at Fotheringhay, where he appointed James Quoquerell bailiff of Guernsey, which appointment was confirmed by the king on Feb. 28, 1415, Pat. 2 H. V, iii. 3. For letter of John Lisle, dated July 26 [1406], to the Privy Council, see Roy. Lett. ii. 115, stating that the Lord of Langon (near Fougeray, Ille et Vilaine) in Brittany has landed 2000 armed men in Alderney and is plundering and speaks of going to the Isle of Wight. For the castle of Gurry (i.e. Gorey) in Jersey, see French Roll 6 H. V, 3.

[6] Page 90, note 4. Rot. Vasc. 1 H. V, 15, May 13, 1413, refers to the Earl of Dorset as being then in Aquitaine for safe custody of the same, also May 13, July 8, 17, 1413, in Priv. Seal Bills 1114/6, 41, 45.

[7] Jurade, 1; Carte, Rolles, i. 197; Rym. ix. 42, which contains an enumeration of his powers similar to those of the Duke of Clarence (see page 117, note 2); cf. Doyle, i. 615, 710; Bellecombe, 42; Venuti, 188, quoting P. Louvet, Hist. de Guienne. The Earl of Dorset is called Lieutenant of Aquitaine in Priv. Seal Bills 1115/2, 25, Oct. 25, 1413; Feb. 8, 1414.

[8] Soc. Archéologique de Touraine, xii. 245–250, Oct. 20, 1412, where he is also Admiral of England and Ireland.

a retinue of 240 men-of-arms and 1200 archers[1] and among his secretaries was a clerk who bore the interesting name of Philip Caxton[2].

The Earl of Dorset was instructed to receive the homage of all the king's lieges on the spot[3] and take from them an oath that they would be "good English[4]," commissioners being appointed to enquire into the tenure of all property held there under grants issued in previous reigns[5]. A troublesome dispute had recently arisen in Bayonne. The late king had granted to Charles Beaumont[6], the castellan of Mauléon, the right to levy a toll at Guissen[7] upon all traffic passing the gorts[8] or wears[9] in the Adour[10].

[1] Rot. Vasc. 1 H. V, 8; Ord. Priv. Co. ii. 129. For their pay for 6 months from April 6, 1413, see Pat. 2 H. V, iii. 14, Feb. 16, 1415; Iss. Roll 5 H. V, Mich., Feb. 1, 1418. For their muster at Bordeaux on Aug. 1, 1413, see Calig. D. 5, f. 1. In Iss. Roll 3 H. V, Mich., Jan. 23, 1416, the Earl of Dorset receives £32. 13s. 4d. (as part payment of arrears of £5397. 4s. 4d.) for these troops per manus Philippi Caxston, clerk; also £1000, ibid. 6 H. V, Mich., Feb. 23, 1419.

[2] For wages paid to the garrison of Harfleur through Philip Caxton as attorney for the Duke of Exeter, see Iss. Roll 4 H. V, Mich., Nov. 30, 1416; Exch. Accts. 328/6, Nov. 17, 1416. In Iss. Roll 5 H. V, Pasch., June 21, 1417, he is a servant of the Duke of Exeter, also general attorney for the Duke, ibid. Mich., Feb. 1, 1418. For account of William Caston (sic), controller of Calais, see Exch. Accts. 187/6, 5 H. V. The name appears as Caxtona in Jurade, 39. For similar terminations, cf. Boxtona, ibid. 43 (i.e. Peter Buckton, Wylie, iii. 99. For his wife Cecily and his sons Peter, Ralph and William, see Test. Ebor. i. 360. For his muster of 117 archers in 1400–1, see Yeatman, ii. 138 from P. R. O. B. 55, no. 15, which contains also musters of Thomas Stanley, Ralph Green (3+6 Staffordshire), John Cokayne (0+12) etc.); also Swyntborna, Jurade, 8, 137, 336 (i.e. William Swinburn, page 44, note 1); Holma (i.e. Holme), Jurade, 8; Diepa (i.e. Dieppe), ibid. 251; Andria (i.e. Andrew), ibid. 3, March 27, 1414, where one of the Jurats is mestre Johan Andria, mestre de l'escole.

[3] For homage done to the Black Prince in Aquitaine in 1363, see Rouquette, 64.

[4] Rym. ix. 28; Ord. Priv. Co. ii. 128, June 26, 1413; cf. "bons Anglos," Jurade, 180.

[5] Rym. ix. 71.

[6] Carte, Rolles, i. 193, Aug. 28, 1409; Rym. viii. 576, 580; Devon, 401. For confirmation to him of the bailliage of Labourd, the district round Bayonne, and the castellanery of Mauléon on June 29, 1413, see Rot. Vasc. 1 H. V, 9; Carte, Rolles, i. 196, 197, June 29, July 12, 1413; also Feb. 5, 1416, Rym. ix. 330; Wylie, iii. 72, note 10. In Devon, 330, he is called the son of King Charles III of Navarre to whom a grant of 250 marks p. a. was confirmed by Henry V on June 29, 1413, £40 of which was paid through Charles Beaumont before Jan. 27, 1414.

[7] Probably Guiche near Bayonne. For its position, see Wylie, iii. 72, reading Peyrehorade for Peire Hurade and Sorde for Sordes.

[8] i.e. eel-traps. For "repailler et nouvellement faire la gorce" in the Eden at Carlisle in 1416, see Rot. Parl. iv. 92; cf. une gorz, ibid. iv. 243; gors, kydeux, etc., ibid. iv. 8. For fishgarths, see R. Davies, York Records, 81; cf. Murray, Dict., s.v. Gorce, where it means an eddy or whirlpool. For Londoners' complaints against gors (or gours, Rot. Parl. iv. 30), fishgarths, wears, stakes and millstanks in the Thames, Medway and Lee, Nov. 1414, see Rot. Parl. iv. 35; Cotton, Abridg. 539.

[9] For stagnorum cum piscar' in mare vocat' les weres at Watchet, see For. Accts. 4 H. V, 12; cf. wers, millponds and kydelx, Benham, 115; Letter Book I, p. 58; Wylie, ii. 479; Black Book of Admiralty, i. 77, where it is urged that the fishery should be cried "common to all people." For assize of nets in the Thames, see Letter Book I, 44, 53. For false kidells in the Thames burnt temp. Ed. I, see Letter Book A, viii. For nace (i.e. nasse), see Ducange, v. 570.

[10] Not "le Don," as Wylie, iii. 72, note 7.

Naturally the citizens of Bayonne resented this new impost on their corn[1], wine, cloth, leather, iron and other necessaries of life, and they were joined by the people of Dax and St Sever who were also sufferers by the oppressive *péage*[2]. The new king undertook at once to enquire into the grievance and commissioned his judges in Guienne to report on the matter before May 1 of the following year[3], and at the same time an order was issued to prevent the building of a stone castle in the neighbourhood of Bayonne which the burgesses asserted would be a menace to their rights[4].

The new Lieutenant still retained his office of Admiral of England, Ireland, Aquitaine and Picardy[5], but his duties in this respect were discharged by deputy[6] and various other changes occur in the administration of Guienne coinciding with the opening of the new reign. Thus on March 23, 1413[7], William Clifford[8] was appointed to succeed William Faringdon[9] as Constable of

---

[1] For 200 quarters of wheat exported from Southampton to Bayonne, see Rot. Vasc. 1 H. V, 1, March 11, 1414.

[2] For pedagium, droit seigneurial, see Ordonnances, x. 226; cf. Gabellas, pedagia, theolonia, Prato, 351, 357.

[3] For names of the commissioners appointed to conduct the enquiry, see Rym. ix. 30, 152, July 12, 1413, July 10, 1414, viz. John Bordili, judge of the High Council (see page 93), Thomas Field, Dean of Hereford, Guilhem de Cerpat, judge of the High Council of Bordeaux and Bertrand de Asta, judge of the Court of Appeals of Gascony (Wylie, iii. 71, note 3). For Bertrand de Asta, Doctor in decretis and Master Johannes de Bordili at Bordeaux, Feb. 8, 1414, see Rym. ix. 113.

[4] Rym. ix. 47, Aug. 23, 1413.

[5] Wylie, i. 376, note 6, where July 7 should be July 27 (Doyle, i. 613). For confirmation, see Pat. 1 H. V, i. 12; Cal. Rot. Pat. 260; Iss. Roll 1 H. V, Mich., Feb. 19, 1414; Nicolas, Navy, ii. 404; Black Book of Admiralty, 1. pp. xxi, 360. For Admiralty Ordinances (Vesp. B. xxii. f. 17, now in show case at the British Museum as a specimen of English illumination work) probably written for him, see Black Book Adm. 1. p. xix; G. F. Warner, Reproductions, 11. Plate xvii; do. Illuminated MSS. Plate 43. On April 21, 1419, he signs himself Admiral of England, Guienne and Ireland, Ord. Priv. Co. ii. 248, where his deputy is John Hunt, not Hart, as Black Book, 1. p. xx. He was succeeded by the Duke of Bedford on July 26, 1426, Cal. Pat. H. VI, i. 349; Ord. Priv. Co. iii. 207; Doyle, i. 151; not "two years before his death," as Black Book Adm. 1. p. xxi, which happened circ. Jan. 1, 1427, Dict. Nat. Biogr. iv. 56. In Pat. 2 H. V, ii. 32 d, July, 1414, he is custos pacis for Lynn. In Pat. 2 H. V, i. 14, July 1, 1414, his lieutenant in the Admiralty court is Master Henry Poole.

[6] In For. Accts. 8 H. V, m. 29, Thomas Talbot is Admiral of England on Dec. 30, 1414, Feb. 20, 1415.

[7] Carte, Rolles, i. 196; Baurein, iv. 289.

[8] For confirmation June 10, 1413, of an annuity of £50 granted to him when he was in the retinue of Henry IV, see Pat. 1 H. V, i. 18; Iss. Roll 1 H. V, Mich., Oct. 21, 1413; Feb. 22, 1414; also of £40 p. a. granted Oct. 28, 1399, Cal. Pat. H. V, i. 254.

[9] Wylie, iv. 86, note 7. For a reference to William Faryngdon (*sic*) as Constable of Bordeaux on Aug. 13, 1412, see Exch. Accts. 186/2. In Rot. Vasc. 3 H. V, 2, Aug. 29, 1415, he is *late* constable. For William ffarington (*sic*), collector of tenths and fifteenths in Lancashire, see Rec. Roll 3 H. V, Pasch., July 16, 1415. For account of William

Bordeaux[1] with John Bowet as controller[2] and Stephen French[3] as provost of the castle[4]. Clifford, however, did not leave England till July 3, 1413[5], his duties being performed in the meantime by the deputy-constable John Fastolf[6]. When he did sail he took with him a sum of £5600 to be paid over to the Earl of Dorset[7] on his arrival. On July 19, 1413[8], Clifford received the additional

---

ffaringdon (*sic*) as Constable of Bordeaux from Oct. 1401 to Nov. 16, 1413, when William Clifford's account begins, see For. Accts. 5 H. V; Wylie, iii. 274, 275. His deputy was John Burnaby. The account is all quite legible and shows a total receipt of £111,289. 14s. 3¼d. nigr. which is equivalent to £14,838. 12s. 7d. sterling English (i.e. allowing 1d. sterling English as equal to 7½d. black). The expenses = £116,057. 14s. 6½d. black, or £15,474. 7s. 3½d. sterling English, and the difference is given as £4768. 0s. 3¼d. black or £635. 14s. 8¼d. English sterling. For his receipt for wages Nov. 20, 1412, see Demay, Invent. i. 376, showing "William ffarngdoyn" on his seal, though spelt Faryngton in Cal. Pat. H. V, i. 33, 223. For monetam auri et argenti ac etiam monetam nigram (monoye noire), see Rym. viii. 141 ; Ducarel, Misc. 30 ; do. Postscript, 6, 8. For 1 sterling = 5 denarii bonorum Burdegaliæ, see Rym. ix. 431.

[1] For instructions to William Clifford as Constable of Bordeaux dated Windsor, Sept. 20, 1413, see Cotton MS. Calig. D. v. 6, 1. For his account as Constable of Bordeaux 1–6 H. V, see Exch. Accts. 186/1–6, 187/1, of which 186/1 contains 69 documents (1416–1417) chiefly receipts for wages from sergeants-at-arms, captains, lawyers, etc. (of which the latest appears to be dated Sept. 30, 1417), with seals attached much mutilated, and signatures of the recipients written on the documents. 186/2 has 112 documents mostly of 1413/14 ; 186/3 has 28 chiefly of 1415 ; 186/4 has 66 dated 1415/16 ; 186/5 has 42 dated 1418 in bad condition. Clifford is Constable of Bordeaux, Sept. 15, 1414, Jurade, ii. 270 ; May 28, 1416, ibid. 348 ; Aug. 15, 1416, Rym. ix. 382 ; Feb. 18, 1417, Ord. Priv. Co. ii. 206 ; March 24, 1418, Rot. Vasc. 6 H. V, 2 ; Carte, Rolles, i. 202, where he is granted the præpositura and scribaria of Libourne.

[2] For confirmation of appointment of John Bowet (Wylie, ii. 350 n.) as controller of the castle of Bordeaux in place of John Skelton, see Pat. 1 H. V, i. 13, June 5, 1413. Bowet is still controller on Aug. 13, 1418, and March 7, 1420, Exch. Accts. 186/1, 187/9.

[3] In Priv. Seal 658/40, June 3, 1413, he is Provost de humbrer (i.e. the Ombrière, Wylie, iii. 75), or præpositus Umbrarie, Rot. Vasc. 1 H. V, ii. 10, Nov. 14, 1413, where he is appointed *July* 3, 1413 ; not of Bayonne, as Carte, Rolles, i. 196. For the Prevot de l'Ombrière (a royal judge, Baurein, iv. 258), les officiers royaulx et autres habitans en le chasteau de Bourdeaux in 1414, see Jurade, 7.

[4] For 18th century view of the Ombrière which has now entirely disappeared, showing the Rue Poitevine, see Gironde, xii. 124 ; called rua peytabine, see Wylie, iii. 108, note 3 ; Jurade, ii. 37, 39 ; Lopès, i. 329 (with picture) ; Baurein, iv. 28. For rue de Londres, ibid. iv. 59. For the Free Chapel of St Thomas in the Castle at Bordeaux, see Priv. Seal 665/706. For squaquerium castri regis Umbrerie in the hall of which the King's Council sat, see Baurein, iv. 262 ; Jurade, ii. 8. For "shadwe or owmbre," Lydgate, Burgh, 13.

[5] Rym. ix. 29 ; Priv. Seal Bills 1114/54.

[6] Wylie, iv. 86 ; Add. Ch. 256, Oct. 19, 1413, where he gives a receipt to the Duke of Orleans for 765 gold crowns (of 18 sols each) being part of 1365 gold crowns (= £277. 10s. English). The document is witnessed by Aimery de Robinsart, an English knight who is called the "canonier."

[7] Iss. Roll 1 H. V, Pasch., Aug. 14, 1413.

[8] Carte, Rolles, i. 196 ; Ord. Priv. Co. ii. 134 ; Baurein, iv. 289. For his account beginning from that date, see Exch. Accts. 187/1. For £558 paid to him as custos of Fronsac, see Iss. Roll 5 H. V, Pasch., May 25, 1417. He is still captain of Fronsac, ibid. Mich., Oct. 21, 1417, where Peter Clifford is also named as keeping the castle ; also Priv. Seal 866, Oct. 29, 1417, and Rot. Vasc. 5 H. V, 3, Oct. 29, 1417, where he receives lands of La Libarde (i.e. La Barde), Puyon (i.e. Poyanne in the Landes, not Pujols, as Carte, i. 201), Quançon and Balizac near St Symporien ; also Pat. 5 H. V, 19, Nov. 10, 1417 ; Rot. Vasc. 5 H. V, 3, Nov. 16, 1417 ; Iss. Roll 5 H. V, Mich., Dec. 27, 1417.

appointment of captain of Fronsac for eight years with an allowance of 1000 marks per annum[1].

On April 1, 1413[2], John St John[3] of Fonmon Castle[4] near Barry in Glamorganshire was appointed mayor of Bordeaux[5] and soon after his appointment he left Bordeaux for England with the expectation of being back at the latest by Midsummer 1414[6], but on his arrival in London he suddenly found himself overwhelmed with business[7] and his duties had to be undertaken by a wealthy citizen, Bernard de St Abit[8], who acted as sub-mayor during his prolonged absence. The mayor himself did not actually return till Sunday May 26, 1415[9], and made his appearance in the Jurade on June 3, bringing with him a letter from King Henry written at Westminster as far back as the previous Oct. 15, regretting that so far he had done little for Bordeaux but promising them relief shortly (*refreschament deintz brieff*) in the shape of some guns and a master gunner to handle them[10].

[1] For payment of £333. 6s. 8d. to him as captain of Frounsak, see Iss. Roll 1 H. V, Pasch., July 17, 1413; see also ibid. Mich., Nov. 15, 1413; Pat. 1 H. V, iii. 19 d, Sept. 28, 1413; Priv. Seal Bills 1114/36, Sept. 14, 1413; Sloane MS. 4600, 268, 281. He was still captain of Fronsac on Jan. 22, 1415, Guinodie, iii. 182; also Jan. 26, 1417, Iss. Roll 4 H. V, Mich. For payments to him for wages of Lincoln and Notts. men, see Iss. Roll 6 H. V, Pasch., May 9, 1418. For letters of general attorney for him staying abroad dated July 20, 1416, see Rot. Vasc. 4 H. V, 18; or letters of protection, July 16, 1416, Carte, Rolles, i. 200.

[2] Carte, Rolles, i. 196; Pat. 1 H. V, iii. 19 d; Rot. Vasc. 1 H. V, 4, Oct. 19, 1413.

[3] Called John Sent John in Iss. Roll 1 H. V, Pasch., Aug. 14, 1413; Pat. 2 H. V, ii. 29, July 15, 17, 1414; not "John Seint," as Guthrie, ii. 468; Cotton MSS. Catalogue, 456. For John Sent John, kt. of Co. Northants. owing £10 to Nicholas Wymbyssch, clerk, see Claus. 8 H. V, 1 d, Feb. 28, 1421.

[4] Rot. Vasc. 4 H. V, 18; Carte, Rolles, i. 309; G. T. Clark, Genealogies, 429. See page 94, note 3.

[5] Jurade, 187. In Rym. ix. 152, July 10, 1414, he is mayor of Bordeaux. For instructions to him as mayor of Bordeaux, dated at Windsor, Sept. 20, 1413, see Calig. D. v. f. 1 (this page is now destroyed), i.e. touching the governance of the Earl of Dorset, the King's Lieutenant in Guienne, also Dec. 15, 1416, see Rym. ix. 419. He is still mayor of Bordeaux on Jan. 18, Sept. 1, 1418, Rym. ix. 597, 625; Jan. 18, Dec. 20, 1418, Rot. Vasc. 6 H. V, i. 2; Sept. 26, 1419, Ord. Priv. Co. ii. 263, 264, 266; Exch. Accts. 187/12, i.e. between March 27, 1418, and Aug. 14, 1419; June 3, 1420, Carte, Rolles, i. 203. For confirmation of grant of 40 marks to him, see Pat. 2 H. V, ii. 29, July 15, 17, 1414. For a letter of Henry V dated at Gisors, Sept. 26, 1419, in which he is mayor of Bordeaux, see Baurein, iv. 240.

[6] In Privy Seal Bills 1115/26, 37, Oct. 5, 26, 1413, he is referred to as going to Aquitaine. On Feb. 14, 1415, he was still expected at Bordeaux, Jurade, 118.

[7] Jurade, 187.

[8] Or Avit, Jurade, 3, 26, 40, 49, 51, 89, 94 and *passim*, where he is still deputy mayor on March 27, June 15, July 24, Oct. 31, Nov. 17, 1414. He resigned his office as sub-mayor on June 3, 1415, and was succeeded on June 5 by Johan den Freychen (de Fraxina, i.e. Ash, Jurade, 172, 174, 183), who had given up the office before July 26, 1415, Jurade, 206, where he is "sobz mayer qui fo."   [9] Jurade, 171.

[10] Maistre trehour d'icelle, Jurade, 187, cf. Godefroy, s.v. *Traieur* (i.e. Tireur).

Ever since the accession of the new king there had been much talk at Bordeaux of sending a deputation from the Jurade to England to congratulate him and secure the usual confirmation of their privileges[1]. It is not possible to say when the project first came up for discussion as the Bordeaux Council Book for the first year of the new reign is now lost, but more than a year after the coronation, viz. on May 15, 1414[2], it was at length decided that such a deputation should be sent as soon as possible. The question was mooted on July 21, 1414, when an election to replace 12 retiring members of the Jurade took place in a conclave at the Common House[3] whither they had been summoned in the usual way by the bellman[4] in their scarlet and sanguine gowns[5], after hearing a Mass of the Holy Spirit in the adjoining church of St Eloi[6], and the matter came up again at subsequent meetings held on July 24 and 28[7], but nothing decisive came of it. At length on Oct. 31, 1414, they got as far as nominating the deputy-mayor, Bernard de St Abit, and a Dominican friar named William Faure[8] to go to England as representatives, but one thing or another kept coming in the way to prevent their departure. Either they were afraid they might be arrested and detained if they found themselves in London without the Earl of Dorset's hearth-money[9] or the necessary expense (1½ nobles per day) was objected to because the town was so very poor[10], and so they appear either as "going to start" (Jan. 26, 1415) or "not yet started" (March 26) or still talking "sobre lo boiatge d'Anglaterra" (March 11)[11], and the question was postponed in meeting after meeting till the July elections were over. Then the Jurade inclined to save

[1] For privileges of Bordeaux, see Simon, ii. 177, 178; Wylie, iii. 73.
[2] Jurade, 12.
[3] For the Maison Commune at Rodez and Millau in Rouergue, see Rouquette, 154, 217, 223, 406; also at Clermont-Ferrand, Noces, 220.
[4] Au son de la campana se cum es acostumat, Jurade, 17.
[5] For 2⅔ ells of scarlet and sanguin allowed to each member for livery, see Jurade, 39.
[6] En lur conclavi, Jurade, 40, 333, 335; en la meyson cominan de Sant Ylegi or Ilegi, ibid. 12, 26, 234, 334, i.e. near the Porte du Cahernan or Cayffernan on the east side of the city, Drouyn, Bordeaux, 56.
[7] Jurade, 47, 68.
[8] Ibid. 89, 115, 125.
[9] Ibid. 115, Feb. 9, 1415. For feu = maison or ménage, see Dognon, Instit. 619.
[10] Jurade, 125, March 13, 1415.
[11] Also March 23; April 3, 17; May 4, 22, 29, 31; July 4, 11, 26, 27; Aug. 23, 1415, Jurade, 111, 122, 131, 135, 140, 153, 156, 160, 170, 191, 196, 211, 216, 234.

expense by foregoing the luxury of a formal deputation altogether and authorised Arnold William Lamfort to go instead[1], and on July 26, 1415, the question was to be definitely settled one way or another within a se'nnight[2]. Whereupon they borrowed enough money[3] to make the thing a certainty and on Nov. 12 it was settled that the mayor was to have 2 nobles a day during the voyage, which sum was raised to 6 francs on Nov. 23, 1415, together with 8 ells of scarlet for his livery and 60 crowns for his fur[4]. It was intended that he should sail in the *Nicholas de Sent Johan* of Bayonne[5] but at the last moment the master of that ship was arrested at the instance of the Queen of Castile on a charge of carrying pirated goods and receiving $\frac{1}{3}$rd of their value as his share of the plunder[6]. At last, after the sub-mayor, John Estene, had been authorised to act as his deputy in his absence[7], the people of Bordeaux were assembled by sound of trumpet to say good-bye to their mayor[8] and John St John started again for England. Accompanied by the town clerk he sailed in a balinger[9] for Bristol on Dec. 7, 1415[10], for a formal interview with the king, after taking an oath that neither of them would transact any other business in England with the town's money. They were to have allowances of 500 and 400 francs respectively to last them for 100 days[11] and they took with them 200 casks of good wine, 100 for the king and 100 to be distributed as presents among the lords of the court[12] in the hope that they might thereby specially mollify the Earl of Dorset and secure his good word for the town as occasion should arise[13], for according to the latest accounts he and his men were grumbling heavily at not being paid as they had expected[14].

---

[1] Jurade, 200, 201, July 17, 19, 20, 1415.
[2] Ibid. 209, 215.
[3] e.g. 360 francs from Benet Spina, Jurade, 301, 302.
[4] Per sas furraduras, Jurade, 287, 288.
[5] Jurade, 289.   [6] Ibid. 293.
[7] Ibid. 323.   [8] Ibid. 288.
[9] For los baleneys de la ciutat (i.e. Bordeaux), see Ribadieu, 107.
[10] Jurade, 292, 293.
[11] Ibid. 289.
[12] Ibid. 254, 263, 264, 266, 286, 289; Baurein, iv. 242; not that they took this wine to the king *in Normandy*, as Simon, ii. 179.
[13] Que ed fos content de la bila et ed fos bon senor et amie a la ciutat si cum besont es, Jurade, 286.
[14] Murmuren fort quar no es estat paquet, ibid. 257, Sept. 3, 1415.

For soon after the Earl had arrived in Guienne to take up his command he had assembled the Estates of the Bordelais and the Landes who met in Parliament at Bordeaux on Feb. 26, 1414[1], and voted a hearth-tax[2] of 2 francs per household[3] to pay his salary and the wages of his men for 3 months. The tax was expected to realise 25,000 gold crowns from the whole Duchy[4], the share of the district around Bordeaux being fixed at 10,000 crowns[5], whereof the city itself was to raise 1500 while an additional 2000 francs was promised by the Estates of Bayonne, Dax, the Landes, and St Sever. But needy as he was, the Earl had to go home penniless, and the minute-book of the Town Council at Bordeaux is dotted all over for the next 12 months with appeals from him to get the money collected and promises from them to collect it "as shortly as possible[6]."

It was therefore a matter of ordinary municipal prudence that the mayor and town clerk of Bordeaux should not arrive in London with empty hands, and they were accordingly authorised to compound with the Earl, if they could induce him to accept 1000 gold francs in full settlement of his claim[7]. The voyage was performed in safety, and on Feb. 24, 1416[8], mayor St John wrote from London to the

---

[1] Jurade, 294.

[2] Fouatge, fogatge, ibid. 329. For a fogatge or folgnatge réal at St Flour, see Boudet, 49, 76: For a fouage called for from the estates of Guienne in a letter from Henry V, dated at Mantes, Oct. 11, 1419, see Ord. Priv. Co. ii. 265.

[3] Los dos ffranxs per fuc, Jurade, 2, 12, 46, 232. For fouage of 10 sous par feu voted by Rouergue in 1367 to the infant son of the Black Prince, see Rouquette, 91; also 2 sterlings per feu imposed by the Black Prince in 1365, ibid. 95; ⅓ of a franc per feu, ibid. 370; 10 sous in Angoulême in 1368, ibid. 128, 137, 138; 2 francs per feu at Montpellier in 1379, ibid. 309. It was claimed as a substitute for military service, ibid. 124. For assiette de feux at Caen in 1371, see Mem. Soc. Ant. Norm. xi. 205. For fouage at Cordes (Languedoc), i.e. 6 francs par feu in 1382, see Portal, Cordes, 59, where feu = ménage possédant au moins 10 livres de revenu (p. 61), cf. Viollet, iii. 512; or maison habitable et habitée (lo tet cubert), Barrière-Flavy, 7, where there is a distinction between feu gentil payable to the local lord and feu comtal payable to the Count of Foix (p. 6). In 1385 the number of feux at Foix was 600 (ibid. 10, 16 with names) and at Tarascon 179 (p. 50). In the 14th century the number at Cintegabelle on the Ariège was over 1100, do. Cintegabelle, 7. For a fouage at Angers in 1355, see Godard-Faultrier, ii. 317, 318; in the Bourbonnais 1367–76 to repair the walls of Souvigny, see Gélis-Didot, 16; also in Forez granted to Anne Dauphine, dowager duchess of Bourbon in 1411, La Mure, ii. 210; do. at Arques (= 10s. par feu) in 1399, 1403, Coville, Recherches, 407; Deville, Arques, 178, 369, 406; do. (4 groats par feu) at Bourg-en-Bresse in 1424, Brossard, 157.

[4] Jurade, 88.

[5] Ibid. 230.

[6] e.g. Jurade, 4, 5, 49, 78, 104, 193, 214, 232, 234.

[7] Ibid. 303, i.e. at 20 sous the franc, Wylie, iv. 307.

[8] The letter had been read in Bordeaux by March 5, Jurade, 329.

Jurade reporting that he had found the Earl much incensed[1]; that he demanded at least half of the 29,000 crowns that he claimed, insisting on the payment of 6000 at once[2]. 600 crowns would be advanced by Benet Spin (or Spina)[3], a Bordeaux merchant then in London, on the security[4] of the vessels, and others had promised to find 1200 more by Whitsuntide, but nevertheless it was expected that all the ships would be detained, so the mayor advised that it would be best to keep in with the Earl who was just then in great favour at the court[5]. The King he reported was pleased with the wine[6] and excused himself for not sending the promised guns, but his answer as to the privileges of Bordeaux was still delayed. All the lords likewise had had their presents except two, and to meet possible requirements 40 more casks[7] were asked for, to be forwarded by the first ship that sailed. The mayor himself prolonged his visit far beyond the stipulated 100 days and we know that he was still here on Oct. 19, 1416[8], on which day he was stated to be about to leave England to undertake the safe-keeping of Bordeaux.

This little episode stands out with some clearness against the general confusion of darkness that surrounds the details of the English administration of Aquitaine, but some few facts may also be regarded as established in connection with events that were occurring in that country in the meantime. While the Duke of Clarence was raiding and plundering to keep his soldiery in food[9], complaints

---

[1] Fort turbat contra la ciutat.
[2] The payment of this amount together with 3000 or 4000 crowns more was authorised by the Jurade on March 7, 1416, Jurade, 333, 334.
[3] Called Benedeyt Espina in Jurade, 193, 232; or Benedictus Espyne in Rot. Vasc. 3 H. V, 1, July 8, 1415, where he receives officium executorie sigilli nostri et contrasigilli. For a letter written to him from Bordeaux by Piquard Oliver on July 27, 1415, see Jurade, 217.
[4] Chavissensa; see Godefroy, s.v. *Chevissance*.
[5] The king ama lodeit senhor (Dorset) et aujourn d'uy que se gouverna par son concelh. He was in England at the arrival of Sigismund in May, 1416, Noblesse, 15. For a letter from the Earl of Dorset written at Harfleur thanking Bordeaux for the bel donne et present of 40 pipes of wine, see Jurade, 344, where he says that mon estet et exploite sont bon, Dieu merci.
[6] For order to the customers of London to remit the duty on 200 barrels of wine for the king and 10 each for the Dukes of Clarence, Bedford and Gloucester and Bishop Beaufort, see Claus. 3 H. V, 2, Feb. 1, 1416, where it is given by the citizens of Bordeaux through their mayor John Seint John.
[7] Said to be specially to propitiate the Earl of Dorset, in Simon, ii. 179.
[8] Rot. Vasc. 4 H. V, 18, or Aug. 15 in Carte, Rolles, i. 200.
[9] Page 116.

went up in heaps to Paris, but the Dauphin only laughed believing that the English meant no real harm to him[1]. All France was in turmoil. The Cabochians were wreaking vengeance on the Armagnacs in Paris and in the south the Armagnacs declined in disgust to fight for a lily-garden[2] in which they were only to be rooted out as nettles[3] or plucked up as noxious weeds[4], so that they often donned the red cross of England[5] and openly joined hands with their country's enemies[6]. On Feb. 13, 1413[7], Bernard Count of Armagnac[8] and Charles d'Albret[9], the Constable of France, made a treaty with the Duke of Clarence who promised to lend them 500 men-of-arms and 200 archers to help them in their attack upon the Count of Foix[10], and in accordance with this many French and English forces combined for the capture of the castle of Biron[11].

In this confusion of allegiance it is no wonder that the Gascon lords turned French or English just as occasion suited, and town and country alike became a prey to plundering bands known as roadmen or tinkers[12], who

---

[1] Et ne s'en fait que moquer, Ec. des Chartes, vii. 61.
[2] Cf. creu ou jardin semé de fleur de lys, Chalvet, 9; Champollion-Figeac, Poésies, 6.
[3] Juv. 479. For the nettle as a device of the Duke of Orleans, see Add. Charters, 2429 (Sept. 30, 1413) and 2433.
[4] St Denys, v. 42; Barante, iii. 53; Michelet, v. 304.
[5] Coville, 332, 338; H. Martin, v. 526; Barante, iii. 58.
[6] St Denys, v. 64; qui (i.e. Armagnacs) era rebele al rey de Fransa, Esquerrier, 67. For 1500 gold crowns paid to Hodgkin chamber-squire to the Duke of Clarence who had come from Bordeaux with 16 men-of-arms and 212 archers and taken service with the Duke of Orleans from Aug. 1 to Nov. 1, 1413, besides similar services rendered before, see Add. Ch. 63, April 6, 1414; do. 66; cf. Ribadieu, 105.
[7] Gaujal, ii. 276; iv. 545, from archives of Nérac near Agen, now at Pau.
[8] Vaissète, ix. 1015. For account of him, see Samazeuilh, Nérac, 110–115.
[9] For treaty with the English concluded by Charles d'Albret in the name of the King of France, see Raymond, iv. 15, E. 60 (1412-19).
[10] i.e. John I, who succeeded his father Archambaud de Grailli in 1412, Flourac, 45; Vaissète (Molinier), ix. 1015; Wylie, iii. 79, note 7; not 1414 as Samazeuilh, Nérac, 193; Cadier, 159. His brother Gaston, Captal de Buch, remained faithful to the English, see Dognon, 451; Baurein, iii. 289–300, 344–356, 405; Ribadieu, Châteaux, 167, where the Captalat de Buch includes the parishes of La Teste, Gujan and Cazau to the south of the Bassin d'Arcachon. For feud between counts of Foix and Armagnac, see Bonal, 519; Gaujal, ii. 275; Rouquette, 55, 261; Flourac, 49, 51; cf. la guerre deus comtes, Jurade, 100, May 29, 1415; called ennemi héréditaire in Barrière-Flavy, Cintegabelle, 6; Dognon, 451.
[11] i.e. near Monpazier (Dordogne), Raymond, iv. 15 (E. 59); called Lobiron in Petite Chron. 65; more probable than Biron near Pons (Charente Inf.) as suggested, ibid. p. 71.
[12] Routiers, roteralhas payroliers (or chaudronniers, Godefroy, s.v. *Pairoliers*) et gens meschantas, ribaudas gens et pauco valents, Verms, 593; los rotiers de Fransa, Esquerrier, 67; vils ramas de soldats de toutes les nations surtout de Gascons et d'Anglais, Montlezun, iii. 375. For routiers in Rouergue, 1366-70, see Rouquette, 100, 234, 252–258, 260; called rétiers in Affre, Rodez, B.B. 3. For derivation from *rota* (i.e. chamber), see Rouquette, 255, quoting Villandrando; also Ducange, s.v. *Rota*; or from *route* (i.e.

took the cattle and sheep as they grazed and even the very boots and jackets of those who consented to pay black-mail[1] in order to secure a temporary sufferance[2] till some stronger robber should come to drive their oppressor out. As an illustration we may take the two towns of Langon[3] and St Macaire[4] which were on opposite banks of the Garonne. Both lay within the English portion of Gascony, but the former was of the English obedience[5] and the latter of the French[6], and each town seized every available opportunity to harass the other. In 1411 the Langon men captured the town and castle of St Macaire after bringing up engines that shot stones and viretons[7]. Three years later St Macaire and its neighbour La Réole[8] were reported to be almost deserted, and the report adds that, though they had both lately been strong and populous towns[9], such few inhabitants as still remained were unable to find food enough to eat.

Guillaume Amanieu de Madaillan[10], Lord of Lesparre

compagnie), see Lavallée, 13. For rois des compagnons, or compagnies, see Labroue, Livre, 382, 385; service de la chevauchée, ibid. 15; gens des compagnies, Vaissète, iv. 438; gens de compaigne, Cagny, 84, note; grandes compagnies, chef de bandes, etc., Duplés-Agier, I. xxiv; called "irregular regulars" in M. Bernard, 95. For condottieri (leaders of companies) in Italy, see Yriarte, 92; called "late comers," Morant, ii. 288. For hommes d'armes chascun ove son pillard at the siege of Mortagne on the north shore of the Gironde, see Frois. ix. 509 quoted in Labroue, Livre, 13.

[1] Patigeneran, Jurade, 226, 227.

[2] For sufferantia a bellicis actibus (i.e. trieuve ou souffrance de guerre), see Rym. ii. 685, 715; iii. 192; Ducange, s.v.; cf. soufferte ou abstinence de guerre, Rym. ix. 692. For la suffreanc, see De la Ville le Roulx, 168; =respite in Cotgr., s.v. *Souffrance*. For sufreda per pati o suffrensa o autramens, see Magen, 331; paticium seu suffrancium, Aussy, 28; Tholin, Inventaire, 10. For sueffra, soufferta, see Rouquette, 258, 267, 350, 352, 364; sufferte, Labroue, Livre, 30; suffrensa, Jurade, 252.

[3] For view and plan of Langon, see Drouyn, Guienne, ii. 68, Plates 78, 80. It was granted by Henry V to Menaud de Fabas in lieu of a payment of 5000 francs, Raymond, iv. 45 (E. 187). On Jan. 11, 1406, the Count of Armagnac had occupied Langon in the name of the King of France after the Jurade of the place had refused to surrender to Bernard d'Albret, Lord of Auros, seneschal of the Bordelais, Bazadais and Les Landes, who had required them to take an oath to the King of France, Gironde, x. 71.

[4] For view of St Macaire, see Virac, 3, 392; Drouyn, Guienne, ii. 106, Plates 84–91.

[5] De l'autra hobediensa, Magen, 320.

[6] Virac, 95, 96.

[7] Gironde, x. 73; Virac, 97.

[8] For La Réole, see Drouyn, Guienne, i. 128; Plates 43–61. For grans mortalités et pestilences at St Macaire and La Réole, see Gironde, x. 560. For the salin at La Réole for the sale of salt brought up the Garonne in boats, see Pérouse, 90. For territory of La Réole attacked by the men of Libourne and St Emilion in 1415, see Ribadieu, 111.

[9] Grandement peuplées et garnis de riches gens, see report of the Duke of Berry, Dec. 20, 1414, Gironde, x. 560, where each town is allowed 50 livres to repair its fortifications. In Ribadieu, 106, St Macaire, Rions, La Réole, Bazas, Budos and Noaillan fall to the French in 1377.

[10] See Wylie, ii. 424; called Amenoil in Sloane MS. 4600, f. 579, where he is charged with the defence of Guienne. For account of the castle of Madaillan near Agen, see

and Rauzan[1], had died and a dispute had arisen about the lordship of Lesparre[2] which was claimed by Bernard de Lesparre[3], Lord of La Barde[4]. Hitherto the family of Lesparre had been staunch for the English connection[5], but now Amanieu's widow, Joan of Armagnac[6], a clever and powerful woman[7], declared her intention of marrying the Count of Foix and of betrothing her daughter to his son, thus bringing Médoc under French influence and menacing the very city of Bordeaux. To check this move orders were issued on May 31, 1415, to seize the lordship into King Henry's hands until the dispute should be settled[8]. The matter was still under the consideration of the Council at Westminster on Feb. 25, 1416[9], and on Aug. 15 following[10] it was decided that Joan should be proceeded against if she still refused to give up her late husband's will, but on July 24, 1417, she ceded the castles of Lesparre and Breuil[11] together with other property[12] to the Constable of Bordeaux for ever in return for a payment of £2200[13].

Tholin, 181–184. It was just outside the jurisdiction of the seneschal of Agen, ibid. 154, 173–178. In Rot. Vasc. 5 H. V, 4 the hospitium de Madalhan had come to Bernard de Lesparre defectu heredum.

[1] i.e. since 1392, Baurein, i. 152. For account of Rauzan near Libourne, see Drouyn, i. 83, Plates 28, 30; Ribadieu, Châteaux, 91, 397.

[2] For account of the Honor of Lesparre (called Sparre in J. T. Smith, 170), see Baurein, i. 229; Ribadieu, Châteaux, 33. For picture of the ruined donjon, see Joanne, iv. 2156. On Oct. 8, 1417, the Captain of Lesparre is William Ays de Barry, Rot. Vasc. 5 H. V, 6, m. 3.

[3] Baurein, i. 154. For grant to him, temp. Richard II, of the castle of Marmande (Lot et Garonne) cum peagio ibidem if he could take it from the enemy (it was captured from him by the French in 1403, Andrieu, i. 148), and the seneschalcy of the Agenais with £100 p. a. from the customs between Aiguillon (at the confluence of the Lot and the Garonne) and Bordeaux, confirmed by Henry IV and V, see Rym. ix. 245, May 13, 1415; Carte, Rolles, i. 185, 199; Baurein, i. 379. For his defence of Blaye in the English obedience in 1406, see Wylie, iii. 79, 82. For his visit to England in 1410, see Baurein, i. 380.

[4] i.e. on the south shore of the Gironde below Bordeaux.

[5] Wylie, ii. 424.

[6] She was the daughter of Jean III, Count of Armagnac, and Margaret, Countess of Comminges, and had married Amanieu on Feb. 19, 1409, Jurade, i. 416.

[7] Famme subtile et de grande puissance, Jurade, 186. She is called Domina de Lesparre et Roazan in Rot. Vasc. 3 H. V, 2, July 10, 1415; also Jurade, 195, where in a letter dated at Lesparre, July 7, 1415, she protests her loyalty to the king of England and denies the rumours as to her daughter's marriage.

[8] Jurade, 239.

[9] Ord. Priv. Co. ii. 245.

[10] Rym. ix. 382.

[11] Bruelhe, Ribadieu, Châteaux, 32.

[12] i.e. Carcans, Roison (? Rauzan), Pinons, Quançon, and Balizac, Rot. Vasc. 5 H. V, 6; Carte, Rolles, i. 201; Rym. x. 472, 474; Cal. Dipl. Doc. 318.

[13] Iss. Roll 5 H. V, Mich., Oct. 4, 1417, where Clifford is called *Richard*. He was to draw his 1000 marks p. a. (see p. 124) from the revenues of Lesparre, but on Dec. 20,

In 1414[1] Bernard de Lesparre was captured by the Count of Foix at Mauvezin[2] in Bigorre and imprisoned at Foix, only regaining his liberty on undertaking to pay a ransom of 8300 gold crowns, for which he had to give substantial hostages[3]. He was certainly at Bordeaux on Aug. 29, 1415[4], and in England in 1417 where he received 12,000 gold crowns in consideration of the surrender of his claims to the castles of Lesparre and Breuil[5], which afterwards became a valuable English asset[6]. Bernard was again at Bordeaux on June 18, 1418[7], but the terms of his ransom-money proved ultimately too onerous to be carried out and he returned to his captivity in 1421[8]. The story is infinitely complicated and known to us only by accidental glimpses, but the singular part of it comes out in the fact that whereas in the north of France the Armagnacs are the pronounced opponents of the English, in the south they lend their aid to a partisan of England[9] because of his feud with their southern enemy, the Count of Foix, and in the same spirit when hard pressed by the Burgundians in Paris they give active help to the English in Guienne. And the English on their side were not slow to take full advantage of their opportunity.

1418, that sum was still unpaid by Jean de Fronsak, the tenant (*occupator*) of the castle, though the late Lady of Lesparre, Jeanne d'Armagnac, had left valuable pieces of arras (*pannos de Aracio*) and other hustlements (*hustillamenta*) as pledges that it should be paid, Rot. Vasc. 6 H. V, 2. On Oct. 29, 1417, Clifford received a grant of the lands of La Barde and Poyanne near Montfort-en-Chalosse, Carte, Rolles, i. 202.

[1] Baurein, i. 153; Flourac, 52 ; Gaufreteau, 8, 68.
[2] Near La Barthe (Hautes Pyrénées).
[3] For a letter from his hostages written on Nov. 27, 1414, at Orthez in Béarn, see Jurade, pp. vii, 14, 97. For deliberation at Bordeaux as to his ransom on May 18, 1414, see Baurein, i. 154.
[4] Baurein, i. 380.
[5] For his receipts for 5000 crowns dated London, May 24, 1417, and 7000 crowns dated Southampton, June 12, 1417, see Cal. Dipl. Doc. 308 where he receives also the parish of Carcans for life on July 24, 1417. For charter whereby he resigned his claims deposited in the Exchequer on Oct. 12, 1419, see Kal. and Inv. ii. 100. For a trapper (or horsecloth, cf. "trappures," Chaucer, Knight's Tale, 2501 ; Godefroy, s.v. *Trapier*) of cloth of gold pledged by him with Henry V, see Delpit, 221; Kal. and Inv. ii. 97, Feb. 8, 1418.
[6] For Lespant qui modo dicitur Lesparra, see Bouillons, 482. For castrum et villa de Sparre granted to John Tiptoft, see Rym. ix. 914, June 21, 1420. For the jurisdiction committed to John Ratcliff, July 13, 1423, see Carte, Rolles, i. 205. For rights in la terre de Lesparre claimed by Charles de Beaumont on behalf of his wife in 1419, see Rym. ix. 741.
[7] Rym. ix. 597.
[8] He died circa 1433, Baurein, i. 379, 381, but certainly before Dec. 14, 1439, ibid. i. 155.
[9] Verms, 592.

To the north of the Dordogne the district of Périgord
had lately had a chequered history.   Just before Henry IV
began his reign in England the Count of Périgord, Archambaud VI, had been declared a rebel and banished by the
King of France[1].   His estates were then confiscated[2] and
bestowed upon the Duke of Orleans[3], whereupon he repaired
to England and did homage to Henry IV, joining in his
expedition into Scotland in the summer of 1400[4].   In
the following year he returned to Guienne with the Earl
of Rutland[5], and his presence produced years of confusion
according to the varying fortunes of the two contending
sides.   Thus in 1404 the French captured Courbefy[6] in
the mountains of the Limousin and afterwards spread
southward along the valley of the Dordogne, when the
Duke of Orleans made his great effort in Périgord.   In
1406[7] they seized Limeuil, Moruscle[8], Paunat[9], Campagne,
Montréal, Mussidan and Thenon.   In 1407 the English
seized and burned Nontron[10] to the north of Périgueux,
but in 1408 the whole county is treated as a domain
of France[11] and little remained to the English save some

---

[1] i.e. July 19, 1399, Anselme, iii. 74; Mas Latrie, 1660; Jarry, 219; Cosneau,
Connétable, 485. He was besieged by Boucicaut at Montignac from Aug. 5, 1398,
Dessalles, ii. 375; not Dec. 24, 1393, as Anselme, vi. 319.

[2] For Périgord Blanc, i.e. the valleys of the Isle and the Dordogne (comprising the
arrondissements of Périgueux, Ribérac and Bergerac), see Labroue, Livre, vii. 425.

[3] i.e. on Jan. 23, 1400, Dessalles, iii. 35, 36; Lodge, 321; Wylie, iv. 69, note 6; not
1399 as Anselme, iii. 237.   Périgord was sold by Charles, Duke of Orleans, on March 4,
1437, to Jean de Bretagne, Count of Penthièvre, Anselme, iii. 74. For earlier negotiations
between Jean, Count of Armagnac, and the Duke of Orleans for the purchase of Périgord,
see Affre, Rodez, B. B. 3.

[4] Dessalles, ii. 394; Wylie, i. 135.

[5] Who was appointed Lieutenant of Aquitaine, Aug. 28, 1401, Carte, Rolles, i. 187;
Ord. Priv. Co. i. 181; Rym. viii. 222; Doyle, iii. 189 (not 1400 as ibid. 744); Wylie,
i. 124; iv. 231; Dessalles, ii. 397, where his baggage was lost in a Spanish ship at
Bordeaux.

[6] In the commune of St Nicholas near Châlus (Haute Vienne), A. Thomas, Etats, ii.
307; Wylie, i. 388; ii. 316; called "Corbeffin" in Jurade, ii. 113; Samazeuilh, 450;
"Corbefin" in Chronographia, iii. 241; "Courbafy" in Dessalles, ii. 397, where the
attacking force under Charles d'Albret consists of 1200 men-of-arms and 300 crossbowmen, Périgueux supplying rams and catapults; or "Corbesin" in Martial, 5, where
it rhymes with Limousin.

[7] Not 1405 as Labroue, Livre, 302.

[8] Called Maruscles in Jurade, i. 507; Marusclas, St Denys, iii. 420, 422; Moruscle,
Dessalles, ii. 415; supposed to be identical with Mareuil (? Mareuil-sur-Belle near Nontron)
in Labroue, Livre, 302.

[9] Not Paunac as Wylie, iii. 76; called Pénac in Dessalles, ii. 406.   For Campagne,
St Exupéry, Carlux (near Sarlat, seized by the English in 1405 but yielded again to the
French, Dessalles, ii. 400, 408), Leyrat (in the commune of Ales on the south bank of the
Dordogne, Labroue, Livre, 218) and Bigaroque (in the commune of Caux on the north bank
above Limeuil) which fell into the hands of the English again in 1408, see Dessalles, ii. 409.

[10] Dessalles, ii. 408.   [11] Ibid. ii. 409.

disputed towns, such as Condat[1] and Bergerac[2] on the north bank of the Dordogne[3]. But now, encouraged by the arrival of the Duke of Clarence, Count Archambaud again pushed forward and the English became masters of Villamblard, Grignols[4] (near Mussidan), Ribérac, and even approached Périgueux[5] by Chancelade and Château L'Evêque[6], and after the English victory at Agincourt the fortunes of the deposed Count[7] continued to rise. He captured Auberoche[8] and held it undisputed till his death, which happened in 1430 at Le Change on the Auvézère[9].

After the departure of the Duke of Clarence the Earl of Dorset[10] continued offensive operations northward. Advancing into Angoumois he captured Ribérac[11], Aubeterre[12], Montandre[13], and Barbezieux[14], crossed the Charente under the guidance of the Armagnac governor

---

[1] Near Vayrac (Dordogne); not Condat at the confluence of the Isle and the Dordogne, see Guinodie, I. vii; Guadet, Atlas. In 1411 it had been granted to Sir Thomas Swinburn as Captain of Fronsac, and in 1414 was granted to Hugues de Bernard de Guienne, Dessalles, ii. 412, 414. On July 11, 1417, Condat (called Condak or Cundak, Rym. iv. 43, edn. 1830) and Barbanne de Lussac (Gironde) are named among the lands belonging to the hospitium de Madalhan which are not to be returned to Bernard de Lesparre (see p. 131, note 2) because they had been granted to Nicholas Bowet, most of which lands were then in the hands of the French.

[2] For Bergerac granted to John of Gaunt, Oct. 8, 1370, see Armitage Smith, 199, who refers (p. 201) to the arms of Bergerac in the Coucher Book of the Duchy of Lancaster. See also Gaunt Reg. i. 4, 83, 289, where he is seignour de Bragerac.

[3] In 1411 the English occupy Carlux, Bigaroque, Comarque (on the Garonne near Agen), Marzac and Pestillac (near Puy l'Evêque) in the valleys of the Lot and Dordogne, Dessalles, ii. 412; also Allas de Berbiguières near St Cyprien, which was still in their possession in Nov. 1414, when 12,000 liv. were to be raised to buy it back, C. Portal, Cordes, 60, 62.

[4] For plan of the castle, see Labroue, Livre, 271.

[5] For a 16th century plan of Périgueux, see Belleforest, Cosmogr. ii. 202.

[6] Dessalles, ii. 414.

[7] Mazas, Vies, v. 617, supposes that he was actually present at Agincourt on the English side.

[8] Dessalles, ii. 415.

[9] Labroue, Livre, 376. For his will dated at Auberoche on Sept. 22, 1424, with the names of his executors, see Raymond, iv. 177 (E. 640).

[10] Called the Duke of Clarence in Ribadieu, 105, who adds the Captal de Buch, the Sire de Duras and many burgesses of Bordeaux.

[11] Ribadieu, 105.

[12] For the Lord of Duras and a force of Anglo-Gascons besieged by the Duke of Bourbon in Aubeterre and Marusclas, see Ribadieu, 105.

[13] Cagny, 72; Ribadieu, 105. For banner made for siege of Montandre, see Jurade, 60, July 28, 1414.

[14] For 2 boites de fil to make cordes d'arbalestes and some viretons sent from Paris to Barbezil and for the defence of the bridge of Taillebourg, see Aussy, Reg. iii. 74, though on Aug. 30, 1413, payments are recorded to Jean des Aies (or Deshaies) Captain of Châteauneuf for guarding the bridges over the Charente, ibid. iii. 75, 167, also 700 crowns spent on the garrison for preventing the English from crossing, ibid. iii. 62.

of Châteauneuf[1] and laid siege to Taillebourg[2], meeting with little serious opposition and paying everywhere for what his troops took. Favoured by sympathisers in the town[3] the Earl captured Soubise[4] on the southern side of the estuary as a preliminary to a great attack upon Rochefort. But it was soon evident that the English were not to be allowed to have it all their own way. The town of St Jean d'Angély prepared resolutely to face them. The townsmen set to work to strengthen their defences[5], demolished all buildings that lay outside the town[6], arranged to watch the walls night and day[7], and quartered from 60 to 80 men-of-arms within the walls upon whose fidelity they could well rely[8]. Seven guns with 2 rundlets (*rondelles*) of powder, together with arrows, pavises and other artillery[9], were sent to them from Paris to be distributed amongst the townsmen for their defence, and in July 1413[10] a large force under Jacques, Lord of Heilli[11], started from the capital "to smash the English

[1] Coville, 334.

[2] Ribadieu, 105. For Taillebourg incorporated into the domain of the King of France in 1410, see Massiou, iii. 255.

[3] St Denys, v. 226.

[4] For documents of the Earl of Dorset dated Sales en Marempne, June 23, 24, 1413, see Exch. Accts. 186/2, i.e. Marennes, in quibus existunt salinæ, Ducange, s.v. *Maritimæ*. For the salterns at Marennes (Charente Inférieure) with the church of St Pierre de Sales, see Bourricaud, 99; Grande Encycl. xxiii. 57. In 1310 the neighbouring town of Breuil is called Brolium in Marennia, Bourricaud, 100, 113. In Aussy, Reg. iii. 6, an aid of 1000 fr. is to be levied in the Chastellenie of St Jean d'Angély to repay the mayor and skevins for advances made to defend the country against the English faisant guerre en pays de Xaintonge et Guienne oultre la rivière de Charente where they détiennent et gastent plusieurs pais, villes, et forteresses comme l'isle de Marennes, Soubise, Barbezil, Pont L'Abbé et plusieurs autres (dated Paris, Oct. 5, 1415). For a meeting of the Estates at Pons pour la délivrance de Sablonceaux, see ibid. iii. 120. For payment to the Earl of Dorset's herald for bringing news of the capture of Sotzbisa, see Jurade, ii. 27, June 15, 1414; not that it was captured in 1412 or 1415, as Petite Chron. 65, 76.

[5] For repair of their bridges and walls including 2000 tiles, see Aussy, Reg. iii. 113.

[6] Ibid. iii. 59, June 14, 1413.

[7] For an order of the mayor to this effect dated June 1413, see ibid. iii. 55.

[8] Qui soient seurs à la couronne, ibid. iii. 58, June 16, 1413. For payment for them since the capture of Soubise, see ibid. iii. 62.

[9] i.e. 99 pavez, 39 doz. bowstrings in wooden chests, 155 butts (*botes*) of thread to make cordes d'arbalestes, 1800 arrows ferrées et barbées, 1 pipe de broches a faloz (lanterns), 8 faloz singles and 2 doubles à deux chandelles, 50 boxes of trait de viretons and chaussetrappes barbues, 16 lances, 14 of which were ferrés and 2 sans fers, ibid. iii. 71, where the mayor gives a receipt for certaine artilherie on Aug. 24, 1413. A subsequent inventory of them was taken on Jan. 8, 1416, ibid. p. 73. For the conseil du roy dining at the mayor's hostel, see ibid. 121, July 17, 1413.

[10] Coville, 334, from Bibl. Nat. fr. 20437, f. 57.

[11] For his seal Jan. 23, 1408, see Demay, Invent. i. 485, where he is "sign' de Heilly" and Captain of Beauquesne near Doullens in Picardy; also Sept. 18, 1410, ibid. i. 486, where he is Marshal to the Duke of Guienne and "Sire de Helly et de Pas," i.e. Heilly on the Ancre near Corbie and Pas-en-Artois near Doullens; also Feb. 4, 1413, ibid., where

and chase them out of the country[1]." But they were intercepted by an English force which slaughtered 8000 of them[2] and carried off their leader, the Lord of Soubise and Taillebourg[3], as a prisoner to Bordeaux[4], together with the mayor of La Rochelle[5] and the captains of Rochefort, Royan, Talmont, St Jean d'Angély[6], the Lord of Viville[7], and many more[8].

But this run of success was checked when the Armagnacs gained the upper hand in Paris and availed themselves of a temporary calm in the capital to make a vigorous effort to recover lost ground in Aquitaine. The English garrison at Soubise had made use of the position as a base from which to harass La Rochelle and plunder the shipping that passed in and out of the roads. But while a portion of them were away at Bordeaux the Duke of Bourbon collected a force of 1300 men-of-arms and 800 archers[9] at Niort, moved down by St Jean d'Angély[10] and Taillebourg[11] to Saintes and promptly seized his opportunity. Borrowing scaling-ladders from La Rochelle he divided his forces into three bands and delivered an attack on

he is Captain of Talmont in Saintonge. On June 6, 1413, he is Marshal of Guienne, Aussy, Reg. iii. 58, 62, 71.

[1] Ruer jus les diz Angloys et les cassier hors du pais, Coville, 334, from a letter written by the Lord of Heilli at Parthenay, July 22, 1413, not July 27, 1412, as Cagny, 72, note.

[2] Chron. Lond. 95.

[3] i.e. Jean de Parthenay-Larchevêque, Aussy, Reg. iii. 27, 241; Barbot, 274. He was the son of Louis, Lord of Taillebourg, who died in 1395, Aussy, Reg. ii. 261. In Aussy, Reg. iii. 90, 92, Jan. 9, 1414, the Lord of Soubise a esté prins et détenu est en dures et fortes prison at Bordeaux, where he was still a prisoner on Oct. 16, 1414, Finot, Paix, 28, 73.

[4] St Denys, v. 67.

[5] i.e. Regnaud Gerard, Aussy, 27; Barbot, 270, 273. For seal of the mayor of La Rochelle, see De Witte, 391. The captain of La Rochelle in 1414 was an Orleanist, François Gringnaux, who had been captain of Talmont in 1409. For a letter of his dated Blois, Aug. 13, 1418, see Delaville Le Roulx, 190. For a 15th century picture of La Rochelle, see De Witte, 389; also a plan (17th century), Zeiler, vii. 56.

[6] Aussy, 27. For plan of the town, see do., Reg., Frontispiece.

[7] For £20 paid to William Cofusec, squire to Thomas Earl of Dorset, for bringing news of the capture of the Lords of Viville and other Frenchmen ordinat' p' rescussu castri de Montendre and other castles, see Iss. Roll 1 H. V, Pasch., Aug. 14, 1413.

[8] Juv. 480; Le Laboureur, 375; Baye, ii. 113; Coville, 200; Perrens, Democr. ii. 211. For 100 casks of La Rochelle wine sent to England for ransom of John Lord of La Leigne in the commune of Condac, i.e. near Ruffec (Angoumois) in Saintonge, taken prisoner by John Radcliffe, see Rym. ix. 172, Nov. 7, 1414.

[9] Called 6000 men in Ribadieu, 105, who places the expedition in 1414–15. The Duke's arrival "for the defence of the country" was announced at Bergerac on Oct. 11, 1413, Charrier, i. 171. On Jan. 28, 1414, he is called chief of the army of Guienne, Anselme, i. 303; Belleval, 108, 273.

[10] Juv. 487; Ribadieu (105) assumes that it had been captured by the English because it was in their possession in 1442. For 17th century view of it, see Zeiler, x. 34.

[11] Le Fèvre, i. 73.

Soubise on Nov. 22, 1413[1]. The garrison at the time
consisted of 500 or 600 English and Gascon troops[2] under
a captain named Blount[3]. At first they refused to believe
that the Duke of Bourbon was in earnest and reminded
him of the help they had actually rendered to him in the
previous year. But circumstances had changed since then
and the Duke now saw his chance. A sudden *sortie* from
the town made him at first recoil, but renewing his attack
on the following day he forced an entrance, slaughtered
300 of the garrison and took the rest of them prisoners[4].
He then rased the walls of Soubise, filled in the ditch and
gave up the town and its inhabitants to pillage. Taillebourg also fell into his hands and its castle was demolished[5],
and then after making an ineffectual attack on the English
garrisons at Aubeterre (on the Dronne), Barbezieux, and
Marusclas[6], he returned to Paris on Jan. 22, 1414[7], where
he was fêted amidst general rejoicing and his gallant deeds
and elegant dress[8] were the talk of the great Parisian
ladies[9]. Further preparations were soon made for following up his victories and a force was ordered to assemble to
meet him at Périgueux on Feb. 22, 1414[10]. On Dec. 1,
1414[11], he was made Captain-general of Languedoc in the
Armagnac interest, to which was added a few weeks later[12]
the provocative title of Captain-general of Guienne beyond
the Dordogne. Fired with the thirst for future glory he
founded a brotherhood or order of chivalry on New Year's

---

[1] St Denys, v. 224; not 1412 as Le Fèvre, i. 73.

[2] Juv. 487; Massiou, iii. 257.

[3] Chron. Lond. 95; Le Fèvre, i. 74. For a dispute between John Blount and a jurat
at Bordeaux before May 5, 1414, see Jurade, ii. 8.

[4] Bourricaud, 39, with account of Soubise, p. 125.

[5] Aussy, Reg. iii. 106, Feb. 3, 1414; also ibid. 155 (1416).

[6] Ribadieu, 105.

[7] St Denys, v. 236; Le Fèvre, i. 74. For a valet de chariot of the Duke of Bourbon
at St Jean d'Angély and a valet of a Lombard there with the bastard of Bourbon, see
Aussy, Reg. iii. 94, Nov. 30, Dec. 5, 1413.

[8] For picture of him in a jacket with long trailing sleeves, pointed shoes and a large
circlet of jewels in his hat, see Montfaucon, iii. 261; La Mure, ii. 120, from L'Armorial
de Guillaume Revel, f. 17, or Armorial d'Auvergne by Gilles le Bouvier, herald to his
father-in-law the Duke of Berry; also in S. Harding.

[9] Dieu scet comment le duc Jehan estoit en bruit entre les dames et damoiselles,
Le Fèvre, i. 117. He is called jeune, vaillant et bon, La Mure, ii. 152; vaillant
chevalereux et bon, Godefroy, Charles VI, 751.

[10] For summons to join it received at Bergerac on Feb. 20, 1414, see Charrier, i. 172,
where he is called "monsgr. de Borbo."

[11] Vaissète, iv. 437; Huillard-Bréholles, ii. 197. For his previous appointment to
the same office on June 12, 1404, see Anselme, i. 303; Allier, Ancien Bourbonnais, ii. 4.

[12] i.e. June 18, 1415, La Mure, ii. 130.

Day, 1415[1], the company of which was to consist of 13 knights and 3 squires[2], and every Sunday[3] each member was to wear on his left leg a badge with a prisoner's chain worked in gold or silver until he had fought and conquered an Englishman in a fight to the utterance[4] on English soil[5]. By this no doubt they understood the soil of Guienne, and with this view he was again on the warpath in the spring of 1415. At the head of a force of 6000 men-of-arms he advanced through Saintonge. By April 16, 1415[6], he had reached Pons and was threatening an attack on Blaye, little thinking that before the year was out he would be himself a prisoner in England in grim reality.

On the very day on which the Duke of Bourbon entered Paris the Earl of Dorset's six months term of office expired as Lieutenant of Aquitaine. Loans had been called for from bishops, abbots, and lay lords to help his expenses[7]; goods had been shipped to him in bales and chests from London[8]; but the pay of his troops was still largely in arrear[9] and he appears to have been in no hurry to depart, for we know that he was at the Pipolin[10] at Bordeaux in November and December 1413 and Feb. 1, 1414[11], and he is still called Lieutenant of Aquitaine on Feb. 8 and April 30, 1414[12].

[1] Douet d'Arcq, i. 370; not 1414, as Béraud, ii. 57, who gives the text of his cartel of defiance which he calls " cette fanfaronnade " (p. 59); cf. "un acte de folie," Touchard-Lafosse, i. 663.

[2] Huillard-Bréholles, Rançon, 40, who calls it "une manifestation bizarre."

[3] Not that they were to challenge the English every Sunday, as Depeyre, 235.

[4] Cf. "unto outrance," Lydg. Troy Book, 20 ; "brought him to outrance," ibid. 435; "at outrance of Fortune," ibid. 389 ; Halliwell, ii. 593 ; J. Coke, 75.

[5] Allier, Ancien Bourbonnais, ii. 17.

[6] Jurade, 147, where Blaye applies to Bordeaux for help in artillery and powder.

[7] Iss. Roll 1 H. V, Pasch., July 17, 1413.

[8] In Claus. 1 H. V, 11, Sept. 24, 1413, his attorney Thomas Noble, clerk, ships to him from London for his use at Bordeaux 2 bales with 13 short-cloths *sine grano* and 3 pieces of Welsh frieze, and 2 chests (cistas) with 3 ells of scarlet, 8 ells of broad-cloth *sine grano*, 3 pairs of shoes and other harness by the *Thomas* of London, of which Thomas Newport is master.

[9] Page 121, note 1. Pat. 2 H. V, iii. 14 shows that £5397. 6s. 4½d. was still due to him as wages for his men from April 6 to Oct. 6, 1413, and that an arrangement was made on Feb. 16, 1415, that of this amount £2000 should be paid up in March 1415, £1333. 6s. 8d. at Michaelmas 1415, and £730. 13s. 0½d. at Michaelmas 1416. For £1031. 6s. 8d. paid to him as part payment of £5397. 6s. 4½d. still due for wages, see Iss. Roll 8 H. V, Pasch., May 23, 1420, where he is Duke of Exeter.

[10] For hospitium vocatum Pipolin, see Carte, Rolles, i. 227. It was otherwise called Po Paulini or de Podio Paulini, ibid. i. 41, 75, 164; or Puy Paulin, Drouyn, Guienne, i. 67 ; ii. 257, 266, 450 ; Ribadieu, Châteaux, 13; or Puch Paulin, Drouyn, Bordeaux, 101, 460, who shows its position on the site of the old Roman wall, eastern side.

[11] Exch. Accts. 186/2 ; also documents dated there Nov. 15, Dec. 22, 1415, where it is called Pepoulyn.

[12] See page 120, note 7 ; Exch. Accts. 186/2.

He afterwards made a tour southwards to gather in such sums as he could from the taxation in Gascony. On March 25, 1414[1], he was at St Sever[2] on the Adour and on April 5[3] at Bayonne, from both of which places he wrote letters to Bordeaux urging the Jurade to collect the hearth-tax, of the proceeds of which he had so far received but little. He passed 10 days at Bordeaux during the early part of May pressing for the collection, but the burgesses pleaded that such a thing was impossible on account of the poverty and misery produced by the prevalence of the fever[4], all but 4 or 5 of the jurats being unable to leave their beds[5], and the town records afford some curious first-hand glimpses into the prevailing views on the subject of mediaeval physic.

At Bordeaux, as in most other places, the doctors were appointed by the town[6], who paid their fees[7] and required them to appear together with the apothecaries[8] in the church of St Eloi to take an oath at the altar that they would not poison their patients[9], but on this occasion all

---

[1] Jurade, ii. 2.　　　　　　　　[2] Formerly Cap de Gascogne.
[3] Jurade, ii. 4.
[4] Febrion, Jurade, ii. 4. For epidemics at Bordeaux, Aug. 8, 1415, and generally, see Jurade, ii. pp. v, 226. For deaths at La Réole, see p. 130, note 8.
[5] Lez autres ne se poudient bougier de leurs liz.
[6] For a médecin municipal at St Flour (Auvergne), hired at 2 fr. 10 sols per month for emergencies to tend the poor, see Boudet-Grand, 42. For the médecin publique at Collioure in Roussillon, in 1372, see Chauliac, lxvi. For phisicus appointed for Modon and Koroni in the Morea, see Sathas, iii. 25. At Troyes there was only one physician in 1406, an Italian from Alessandria, and he was paid by the town, where the civil population was reckoned at 13,000, without counting the priests and religious, Boutiot, ii. 315. For a physicien pensionnaire and chirurgien assermenté who takes an oath de bien et loyalment visiter les malades at Tournai in 1416, see Vandenbroeck, pp. v, 127. For a free apothicairerie at Orleans garnie de drogues pour les pauvres, with a medicus and a surgeon to visit them, founded under the will of Henri de Vistre in 1407, see Lottin, i. 175. For oath of the barber-surgeons, see Chauliac, lx.
[7] For two physicians receiving 80 francs p. a. between them paid by the town of Bordeaux, see Jurade, ii. 33, 42, 58, 59. On July 26, 1415, Pey Harben, Bachelor in Medicine, is to have 25 fr. p. a. Cf. annua pro tali capientes præmia facto, Astesan, 540, quoted in Coyecque, i. 97.
[8] For oath of los metges (veterinary surgeons) et los botiqueys, see Jurade, ii. 212.
[9] Jurade, ii. 43. For popular belief that every surgeon was a thief, a murderer or a swindler, see Arderne, pp. xxii, xxv; cf. Wylie, ii. 181, note. For a satire on médecins, see Gebhart, Conteurs, 264. Cf.

     S'est cele science del mains (i.e. chirurgie)
     Mès ele a si hardies mains
     Qu' ele n'espargne null gent
     Dont ele puist avoir argent
     Mais il cunchient (moquent) mainte gent
     Que deniers et de l'argent
     Qu'ils recoivent de lor poisons
     Font il a Paris granz mesons. Andeli, xxv. 47.

the doctors died[1], and on the recommendation of an apothe-
cary[2] named James Ram it became necessary to send to
Montpellier[3] for others, one of whom appears to have
seriously advocated rooting up all vegetation and driving
the whole population away on pain of death. At the usual
preliminary examination by the town authorities[4] prior to
his appointment he undertook to defend 13 theses, some
of which are obvious enough, such as that food is necessary
to preserve life[5] and that a human body cannot stand up
under the pressure of a hard compact mass like a form of
stone or metal. On Dec. 10, 1414, a doctor[6] was appointed
in Bordeaux who was prepared to prove among other propositions that a practitioner ought to have all his senses
perfect, as "medical speculation[7]" has only to do with things
discoverable by the senses, boldly asserting in defiance both
of the prevailing theory and practice that it has nothing
whatever to do with astrology, though there are certain
diseases whose causes cannot be foreseen but which come
by the judgment of God and can very seldom be cured, in
which case if there is any suspicion of infection in a place
the only plan is to clear out altogether[8].

The death of Cardinal Uguccione on July 14, 1412[9],
had caused a vacancy in the see of Bordeaux. He
had been Archbishop since 1385[10]. As he had died in

---

[1] Jurade, 25, June 2, 1414. For 18 medesis, fizisias, surgias and megas at Montauban,
circ. 1350, see Bonis, I. cxvii.

[2] For ypothecarius, see Magen, 350.

[3] For Montpellier as the fons originalis medicinæ, see Fournier, Statuts, ii. 162.
For documents relating to the University of Montpellier from 1137 to 1494 A.D., see
ibid. ii. 1–300. For Montpellier and Salerno as medical schools, see Sandys, 606. For
inventory of goods belonging to the Faculty of Medicine in the University of Paris,
Nov. 22, 1395, see Vallet de Viriville, Instruction 362. At Dijon in 1407 it was ordered
that no one should practise medicine unless he had a licence from a studium generale.

[4] For towns appointing médecins after examination, see Chauliac, li.

[5] By which he means the blood made up of 4 liquids. Jurade, ii. 26, where the
passage appears to be tantalizingly corrupt.

[6] i.e. John de la Puyada, Jurade, ii. 98.

[7] Medicalis speculatio. Cf. experientia quæ potissimé in facto medicinali res est
magistra, Fournier, ii. 162. For the two parts of medicine, i.e. practical and theoretical,
see Jurade, 25.

[8] In locum alium a tali clade alienum commigrare, Clamenges, ii. 90. For la fuite
as a remedy against plague, see Boudet-Grand, 27. Cf. Fleen wykked eyerys, eschewe
the presence of enfect placys, Lydg. Burgh, 41. Cf. Wylie, ii. 409, note 2 ; iii. 33, 110.

[9] Papal Lett. vi. 365 ; Eubel, i. 25 ; Souchon, ii. 115, 278 ; though called Aug. 14 in
Lopès, ii. 286, from Archives Depart. G, 240 ; Gams, 520 ; Wylie, iii. 367 ; not Aug. 19
as Jurade, ii. 36, where he is "Mossenhor lo Cardinall que ffo" ; nor 1411 as Ehrle,
Perpignan, vii. 641.

[10] He had previously been a canon of the Cathedral at Bordeaux (Devienne, Eglise,
72), and was made Cardinal-Priest of the Quatuor Coronati in 1405. He was Bishop of

Rome[1] the Pope claimed the right to appoint his successor and the see remained vacant for nearly a year. At length on June 26, 1413[2], the uncertainty was ended by the appointment of David de Montferrand, a young man only 26 years of age, but described as of baronial race both on his father's and his mother's side. He was a native of the Bordelais[3], and in spite of his youth he had been Dean of St Seurin for the last 9 years[4] and Bishop of Dax since 1408[5]. On June 20, 1414, the Estates of the Bordelais met in the chapel of the new Archbishop's Palace at Bordeaux, but they were summoned by the seneschal, Galhar Durfort[6],

Faenza in 1378 (Gams, 672; Eubel, i. 255), and was translated to Benevento in 1383 (Gams, 672; Eubel, i. 37; do. Provisiones, 430).

[1] He was buried in the church of Santa Maria Nuova in Rome, Wylie, iii. 367; not beside John XXIII as Devienne, Eglise, 72—probably misunderstanding "soubs Jean XXIII" in Lopès, ii. 286—who was buried in the Baptistery at Florence. For his epitaph written by Pey Berland, see Wylie, iii. 367, note 6. For Pey Berland's birthplace in the parish of Avensan near Castelnau in Médoc, see Lopès, ii. 302 (with the chapel of St Raphael), which is the actual building in which he was born, Baurein, ii. 81. For his seal, his arms and his medal, see Lopès, ii. 291, 306, 312. For bas-relief of his consecration in the church at Avensan where his father is buried, see Baurein, ii. 79. For his mother's tomb in the neighbouring church at Moulis, see ibid.; Lopès, ii. 291. He is called fils d'un simple villageois (Gaufreteau, 10), though the poverty of his parents has been doubted. He founded a mass in St Michael's Church at Bordeaux in memory of Master Raymond de Bruges (a little to the north of Bordeaux, Gironde, xi. 50; Baurein, ii. 79, 80, 178), qui me instruxit ad scribendum, Lopès, ii. 294, 295. On June 1, 1413, he received a canonry and prebend in Bordeaux Cathedral, being then a chaplain at the White Friars in Bordeaux and curé of Bouliac, Baurein, ii. 80; Devienne, Eglise, 76; Gironde, viii. 327 (where the bull is countersigned by Poggio in Rome); called Bouillac in Ribadieu, La Guyenne, 167. For picture of the church of Bouliac near Bordeaux see Lopès, ii. 296; Grande Encycl. vii. 687. For Pey Berland's handwriting, March 4, 1420, when he is still curé of Bouliac and canon of Bordeaux, see Gironde, vii. 412. For his death (Jan. 17, 1458), and his tomb in the cathedral, see Lopès, i. 217, 218; ii. 310, 314.

[2] Papal Lett. vi. 453. Called Nov. 16, 1413, in Gall. Christ. ii. 840, or June 23rd in Eubel, i. 155, who supposes him to have been identical with Jean de Montferrand, one of the cathedral canons (Devienne, Eglise, 72) who had been appointed Archbishop by Gregory XII on July 1, 1409, but had died on Aug. 12, 1410 (Wylie, iii. 364, note 6). For order of the King's Council refusing to recognise him, dated Sept. 22, 1409, see Lopès, ii. 285, with a similar resolution of the Chapter on the same date in Devienne, Eglise, 72. Archbishop David held the see till his death on Oct. 16, 1430, Gams, 520.

[3] Pagi Burdigalensis, Gall. Christ. ii. 840; called of Toledo in Gaufreteau, 8.

[4] i.e. since Feb. 25, 1404, Brutails, xxvii.

[5] Gams, 544; Gall. Christ. ii. 840, though not in Eubel, i. 97.

[6] See Wylie, ii. 55. He is called senescallus Vascon' in Rot. Vasc. 3 H. V, 3, June 2, 1415. He was Lord of Duras (Lot et Garonne; for view of Duras, see Drouyn, Guienne, Plate 78; Labroue, 135, 136) in the valley of the Dropt, and of Blanquefort in Médoc, between Marmande and Villeneuve (see Drouyn, Guienne, ii. 38, Plates 72–77). Andrieu (i. 149) thinks that he served under the Duke of Orleans in the French attack on Guienne in 1406. For a small fragment of his seal, see Exch. Accts. 186/2, where he is "Gualhard Durffort"; also ibid. 186/3, Dec. 10, 14, 1414; Feb. 5, 1415, with seal well preserved showing a helmet and plume. In Jurade, 270, 275 (Sept. 15, Oct. 14, 1414) he is nostre car senhor (i.e. Lord of Bordeaux). For letters dated June 14, 1415, addressed to him by the Count of Armagnac as "car oncle," see ibid. 51, 181, 227. In Rym. ix. 259, June 2, 1415; Baurein, i. 154; ii. 169, he receives a grant of the hospitium de

and the Earl of Dorset seems not to have been present[1]. He was certainly back in London by July 14, 1414[2], on which day he was about to take up his quarters with the king in the Palace at Westminster, the parishes of Stratford[3] and Ham having been allotted to him for his maintenance. On July 25, 1414[4], he wrote another urgent letter to the Jurade asking for the proceeds of the hearthtax which had been promised by the previous Easter. Three weeks later (i.e. on August 17) the king himself wrote in the same strain urging that his uncle had actually advanced 4000 crowns of his own money but had received no provision at all from them for carrying on the government of the Duchy, though he had placed complete reliance on their promises. This letter was received in Bordeaux on Oct. 11, 1414[5], but produced no more effect than the other, and on Oct. 15[6], the king pressed them with another reminder for the payment of the Earl's claim which amounted to 29,000 crowns[7]. The Earl of Dorset did not return to his command at Bordeaux and no one was appointed to succeed him till May 8, 1415[8], when Sir John Tiptot was formally appointed Seneschal of Aquitaine[9].

But in the meantime the successes gained by the Duke of Bourbon in the previous year had put heart into the harassing attack to which the English were exposed on

---

Livran in potestate de Lesparre in Lower Médoc, forfeited by the rebellion of the daughters of Fauquet, Lord of La Trau (near Bazas, Ribadieu, Châteaux, 223), where William Bruere is still captain on Jan. 8, 1414, Exch. Accts. 186/2; Anstis, i. 198; Wylie, iii. 72, note 5.

[1] Jurade, 28.

[2] Rym. ix. 154. On July 17, 1414, one of his retinue, John of Douazit, was made Baron of Douazit near Mugron, ibid. ix. 155; Carte, Rolles, i. 198, 216, 220, 235, 237.

[3] Then called Stratford in West Ham or Stratford Langthorne, Monast. vi. 587.

[4] Jurade, 87, Sept. 29, 1414, on which day the letter was presented to the Jurade by the Earl's butler, whose name is given as Hoton Expenser (i.e. probably Spenser or Despenser, Jurade, 94).

[5] Jurade, 88.

[6] Ibid. 187.

[7] Page 128.

[8] Rot. Vasc. 3 H. V, i. 2; Rym. ix. 240; Jurade, 234; Baurein, i. 380; Bellecombe, 33; Blore, 43, where there is a writ dated Oct. 20, 1415 (not Aug. 16th as Carte, Rolles, i. 199), to William Clifford, constable of Bordeaux, to pay his wages from May 8, 1415. For a similar writ, dated March 24, 1416, see Exch. Accts. 186/4 with a fragment of the seal of England.

[9] Rym. ix. 262, where he is senescallus Ducatus Aquitaniæ. In a letter written in London, June 8, 1415, "Mossenhor Johan Tiptot" is "ordenet de nostre senescaut," Jurade, 193. In 1408 he had been Seneschal of the Landes (not Lannes as Carte, Rolles, i. 191) and constable of Dax, Wylie, iii. 72, note 6 (not 1417 as Bellecombe, 36).

their northern front. At Bergerac[1], which was regarded
as the key of Gascony[2] on the north bank of the Dordogne,
a pact[3] or sufferance[4] had been assured to the semi-loyal
townsmen by the Duke of Clarence and was continued by
the Earl of Dorset[5], but they were hard pressed by Bertrand
d'Abzac who was in command of the neighbouring fortress
of Castelnau[6]. At Candlemas 1414 their pact with the
English was prolonged for 4 years, for which they paid
25 casks of white wine and claret[7], but when the Duke of
Bourbon was laying his plans for attacking us in the spring
of 1414 they received their summons to contribute to his

[1] For the Jurade at Bergerac, whose numbers varied from 25 to 40 chosen by the consuls
from the most notable men of the town, see Charrier, i. pp. vii–ix. For fancy picture of
Bergerac in 1346, see Labroue, 48. For plan of the town at the end of the Middle Ages,
do. Livre, 145. It is called "Bergerat" in Bouvier, Description, 35.

[2] Frois. Bk. iv. ch. 1, quoted in Labroue, Livre, 21.

[3] For "pats" = pactum, conventio, see Lamothe, ii. 147; Rouquette, 256, 259, 325;
or "pati," Jurade, 252, 265; Boudet, 39, 103, 168, 261; "patis," Charrier, i. 139, 141,
162, 163, 166, 170, 181. For appatiser = contraindre les habitans d'un pays à nourrir des
troupes, see M. Bernard, 98; "appatysed unto our lord the king," Black Book of Adm.
i. 469; Nicolas, Agincourt, App. 38; Wylie, ii. 317. He pateysed the contre (= il
prenoit a pasti partout), Coudrette, 91, 247; shal never more patyse you, Arras, 304;
patiz or trybut, ibid. 301; for som patyse, ibid. 324; appatice, Archaeologia, xvii. 215.
In Magen, 251, la finanssa facha = ont pactisé; cf. far e tractor pati, ibid. 328 (1353).
For patis, paatiz, apatis (i.e. money paid as a protection against molestation), see Cosneau,
84; Lavisse, 100; Delisle, Agric. 643; C. Portal, Insurrections, 463; Ribadieu, 104;
do. Guienne, 164; Quicherat, 15; Rouquette, 275, 326; appatissement, Labroue,
Livre, 28; pactionner, ibid.; pastum pecunialem, triennium pastum, St Denys, vi. 162.
For pasticium dated Beaulieu, Oct. 20, 1412 (Wylie, iv. 81), see Soc. Archéol. de
Touraine, xii. 245, where the Abbot of Cormery on the Indre (nr. Montbazon, Indre et
Loire) undertakes to pay a patis (*nos pastissare fuimus compulsi*) of 300 crowns and
3½ pipes of salt on condition that the English would spare the Abbey, but as the salt
could not be procured, another 50 crowns was accepted instead by John Blount representing the Earl of Dorset. The dormitory, cloister and chapter-house at Cormery had
been destroyed before May 22, 1411, per hostes regni, ibid. xii. 243; Bourassé, 386.
For pictures of the Abbey of Cormery, first rebuilt after its destruction by the English in
the middle of the fourteenth century, see A. Noel, 43; Bourassé, 309. For money raised
in Languedoc in 1407 de quoi rompre le patis concluded with the English, see C. Portal,
72, 74.

[4] Page 130, note 2.

[5] Referred to in Charrier, i. 181 (Aug. 5, 1414).

[6] i.e. Nov. 30, 1413, Charrier, i. 171, 180, 181. On July 29, 1405, the Count of
Clermont had spent 15,000 francs on the siege of Castelnau (Wylie, iii. 76), but when
he applied to Bergerac for help to "deliver" it from the English, together with Badefols
on the left bank of the Dordogne (for plan of the castle at Badefols, which dominated the
shipping, see Labroue, Livre, 15, 71), which he had just seized (Dessalles, ii. 399), the
Jurade at Bergerac replied that they were too poor and could not let him have a penny,
assigning as a reason that Castelnau was not in the seneschalcy of Périgord, being really
in that of Sarlat (Charrier, i. 141, 145, 158). At that time Bergerac was anti-English,
and had been so since 1339 (Labroue, 29). On April 9, 1405, it was threatened by
Ramonet de Sort, a captain of companies in the English service (ibid. 119), and on
Aug. 23, 1405, its fortifications were to be strengthened in anticipation of an attack by
the English (Charrier, i. 142), who on Sept. 15, 1405, tried to cross the Dordogne in
cuirbouly boats (guatarras de quer bulhit), but failed owing to the strong flood, in which
one of their lighters was swept away, Charrier, i. 144; Labroue, 118.

[7] Charrier, i. 182, Aug. 24, 1414; where the wine is valued at 7 francs the cask.

force, and by Nov. 11, 1414, they had openly gone French[1] and refused admission to any one in the obedience of the King of England unless he left his sword and knife behind him before entering within the gates[2]. A few weeks however produced a further change of front, and on Jan. 15, 1415[3], they had arranged another pact with the English to last for a year, according to which they paid 11 pipes of wine and 7 abnals of French oil to secure the friendship[4] of the wife of the Seneschal[5] and the Constable of Fronsac. This pact however availed them little in view of the fact that Marshal Boucicaut, who had been appointed Governor of Languedoc and Périgord[6] with special directions to attack the English, was pressing them hard for a tax of 1 franc per hearth[7] to pay for the deliverance of Castelnau and would take no excuse, so that they had to borrow 100 francs from any one who would lend on the security of a tax levied on wine sold in their taverns[8], and even this did not save them from having their cattle raided by the French when Boucicaut was withdrawn to repel the invaders in Normandy[9], and so, when their pact with the English expired, they obtained a further renewal of it till May 1, 1416[10], taking care however to send a message to Paris denying a rumour

---

[1] Los quals eran frances coma nos, Charrier, i. 186.

[2] Los glavis e las espazas, Labroue, 119; Charrier, i. 186. For a similar order at Liège (i.e. culteaus aultres que petis cuteaus qu'on dist coutel taille-pain), see Henaux, i. 559. For Ardres in 1396, see P. Meyer, Entrevue, 212. For Dijon in 1400, see Gouvenain, i. 25. Cf. inermes exceptis de gladio et cultello, Rym. ix. 262. For order at Rouen (Nov. 6, 1410) that no stranger is to carry armeure, couteaux, espées ou dagues, see C. Beaurepaire, Invent. Rouen, 42; also at Tournai (Nov. 5, 1413), Vandenbroeck, 103. For permission to carry them at Perpignan during feuds or bandositats, see Vidal, 368 (=puguen portar dagua o coltell sens alguna pena). At Coventry in 1421 every hosteler is to warn his geastys to leave hur wepons within hur Innes, except a knight or a squire that may have a sword born aftur hym, Cov. Leet, i. 29; also in London, 1409, 1416, Letter Book I, xxviii. 72, 160. Cf. Wylie, ii. 4, note 1. For son cousteau à taillier pain, see Longnon, 3.

[3] Labroue, 119.

[4] Per estar amieco, Charrier, i. 187, where abnal is explained as "ancienne mesure."

[5] i.e. Monsieur de Duras. See p. 141, note 6.

[6] i.e. on Feb. 4, 1413, Vaissète, iv. 453; called 1414 in Thalamus, 459; Vaissète (edn. Molinier), x. 1960. He was at Montpellier on Jan. 28, 1413; at Béziers, Jan. 31, 1413 (Charrier, i. 188), and arrived at Toulouse on March 28, 1413 (Vaissète, x. 1963), where he remained till the following midsummer. On July 15, 1414, he was at Balma, near Toulouse (ibid. x. 1972).

[7] Plus riguoroza foguatge, un tal de 1 franc per fut, per paguar la buga (or vugas) in a letter from Boucicaut received on Jan. 28, 1415, and another dated Feb. 11, 1415, in the former of which he requires the money to be sent to Sarlat within 8 days, Charrier, i. 192, 197. He was at Sarlat on Feb. 5, 1415, ibid. i. 188.

[8] Pougèzes, Charrier, i. 162, 164, 188, 189, 195.

[9] Charrier, i. 198, Aug. 10, 1415.

[10] Ibid. i. 199, 201, Dec. 15, 1415.

that had got abroad that the place was English[1]. At the same time the towns of Condom[2], Port Ste. Marie, and others in the Agenais petitioned to be included in the same " sufferta[3]."

And during all this time the territorial lords on the whole of the fringe of the English possessions were constantly in a state of suspended allegiance, each fighting for his own hand with his pack of *routiers*[4], or paid pillagers, who took the right of marque[5] under a nominal obedience indifferently to the French or English king[6] with true Gascon instability[7], according as either rôle offered the richer prospect of plunder[8]. But the people in the towns, to whom the notions of patriotism or nationality were alike unknown[9], had the feeling that their chartered rights would on the whole be best preserved by siding with the more distant power[10]. These as a rule managed to go English, but in any case they usually had to pay their blood-money to one rule or the other and sometimes to both, if their houses, wine, corn, cattle, rye, or even the very boots, cloaks, capes and petticoats they had on[11] were to remain unplundered by the companies of raveners who roamed the country in the pay of the highest bidder. Typical evidence of the living facts of this unstable time may be gleaned from a perusal of the recently published records of Bergerac[12] and a further illustration may be found in the story of the town of Limeuil[13] at the junction of the Dordogne and the Vézère. It had

---

[1] Que la vila era Angleza, Charrier, i. 202, Jan. 7, 1416.

[2] For the diocese of Condom with archdeaconries and parishes, see Bellecombe, 106–117. For the seneschaussée of Condom, ibid. 147–159.

[3] For a letter from the Count of Armagnac, written at Gages near Rodez on Nov. 28, 1415, asking that these places in the Agenais may be included in the sufferta, see Charrier, i. 181.

[4] Page 129, note 12. On May 15, 1416, the men of St Jean d'Angély decided to hire Spanish crossbowmen to protect them against " gens d'armes qui pillent et robbent le pays," Aussy, 28.

[5] " Prend marque," " le droit de marque," Labroue, Livre, 24.

[6] For les Anglais d'Angleterre und les Anglais de France, see ibid. 395.

[7] Telle est la nation des gascons; ils ne sont point estables, Froiss. Bk. iii. ch. 2 in Rouquette, 320; indifférent sur leur nationalité, ibid. 319; légiers de teste, Bouvier, Descript. 13, 42.   [8] Labroue, Livre, 380, 389, 391.

[9] Lodge, 516; presque vides de sens, Rouquette, 166, 241, App. V. Cf. l'idée de la patrie est toute moderne, Rocher, v. 386; le baronnage ne connaissait que le droit féodal, son horizon ne s'étendait guère au delà de ses domaines de sa province, ibid. 387.

[10] Baurein, iv. 233; qui les gênait le moins, Rouquette, 240.

[11] Labroue, Livre, 10, 16.

[12] For the lords of Bergerac, see Labroue, Livre, 47–66. For brigandage at Bergerac, see ibid. 10.

[13] Ibid. 27.

long been a brigands'-nest[1] when in 1405 Jean de Beaufort drove his father out of it and then went to Bordeaux with his father-in-law, Raymond de Montaut, Lord of Mussidan[2], to ally himself with the English, with whose sanction he seized Brantôme[3] which was only recovered by the French after a severe siege in 1406[4]. In the same campaign they attacked Limeuil, which capitulated to them on Feb. 10, 1406[5], but was recaptured by the English before Martinmas in the same year[6], only to be again retaken for the French by the Constable d'Albret in 1409[7], when Jean de Beaufort was driven into banishment. After Agincourt he was still in the pay of the English[8], but was assassinated on July 3, 1420[9].

[1] Labroue, Livre, 15, 221.
[2] Jean de Beaufort had married Raymond's daughter Margaret, Anselme, vi. 320. Raymond died in 1406. For account of him, see Anselme, iv. 448; vi. 222, 321; Carte, Rolles, i. 154. For his widow, Mariota or Maria (Rym. ix. 409, 431), see Wylie, iii. 78; Ribadieu, Châteaux, 379, where she is Chatelaine de Vayres on the south bank of the Dordogne below Fronsac. For Mossenhor Amanio de Muyssida, see Labroue, Livre, 234, 407, 408, 410.
[3] Dessalles, ii. 400.
[4] Wylie, iii. 75, though Gauluet's muster to join in the attack is dated Aug. 25, 1405. See Guessard, 448.
[5] Wylie, iii. 76.
[6] Labroue, Livre, 218, though not admitted in Dessalles, ii. 398.
[7] Together with Bigaroque (otherwise called Roc), near Tremolat, Labroue, Livre, 224.
[8] For 200 crowns paid to Jean, Lord of Gramont (*sic*), Mussidan and Blaye, see Exch. Accts. 186/1, Nov. 13, 1416. For his seal (a lion rampant on a shield surmounted by a helmet with branched plume), ibid. 186/3, Jan. 8, 1415.
[9] Anselme, v. 330.

CHAPTER XII

PREPARATIONS

DURING the first year of the new reign large sums of money had been paid into the Treasury by the numerous insurgents and traitors who had sued for pardon in accordance with the promises of the recent proclamation[1], as well as by absentee owners of land in Wales and Ireland, to prevent the confiscation of their property, and double fees had been exacted[2] for the re-issue or confirmation of grants. The whole of these incomings however had to be appropriated for the king's use and other sources had to be found to meet the charges required for the resumption of hostilities against the French. The Londoners were all for fight; the Lombards[3] and the citizens were ready to accommodate with loans[4]; and the bishops, abbots, and wealthy laymen also responded readily to appeals. On July 7, 1413, £2000 was lent by Richard Whitington[5] and a few days afterwards £1000 by John Hende[6], and £2000 by the London citizens collectively[7]. Bishop Beaufort lent £1333. 6s. 8d., while

[1] Page 8.

[2] Usk, 120.

[3] For £400 repaid to Bernerdyn Lombard, see Iss. Roll 1 H. V, Pasch., July 24, 1413.

[4] Regi succursum plebs animosa dedit, Elmham, Lib. Metr. 104.

[5] He was still Mayor of the Staple at Calais, Iss. Roll 1 H. V, Pasch., July 7, 1413, when he lent £2000 which was repaid on Nov. 15, 1413. For £1000 paid to him, see Iss. Roll 1 H. V, Pasch., July 7, 1413. Oman (Pol. Hist. 205) thinks that Henry was so penniless "that he borrowed £6000 from Whittington," etc.

[6] Rec. Roll 1 H. V, Pasch., July 14, 17, 1413, which was repaid on July 24 and Sept. 18, 1413, Iss. Roll 1 H. V, Pasch. In Claus. 6 H. V, 13, Nov. 1, 1418, John Hende is dead, but his widow Elizabeth survives owning tenements with shop, solar, seler, etc. given to her by Adam Francis, kt. (Wylie, iii. 286, note 4), though there is no mention of this in his will, Sharpe, ii. 171.

[7] Iss. Roll 1 H. V, Pasch., July 24, 1413, where the Mayor is called *John* Waldern, but his real name was William (Letter Book I, 108) and he is so called in Rec. Roll 1 H. V, Mich., Oct. 27, 1413. The money was repaid on July 24, 1413; see Iss. Roll 1 H. V, Pasch.

other bishops and abbots and many laymen came forward with various temporary loans[1], most of which were repaid before 3 months were out[2].

But indeed the young king needed no extra spur in the direction of fight, and the return of his brother from Bordeaux marks a turning point in the whole policy of England. As Prince of Wales he had accepted presents from the party of the Duke of Burgundy[3] and had steadily favoured negotiations with him[4]; but his father had formed an alliance with the Orleanists a year before his death, under a promise on their part that the old limits of Aquitaine should be restored and that Normandy should return to the English allegiance, which it had renounced since the days of King John[5]. In this policy the son had seemed to acquiesce[6], though at the very same moment he was corresponding in terms of perfect friendship with the Duke of Burgundy[7]. We have already seen[8] how King Henry IV sent an immense English force to help the Orleanists in 1412 only to find himself thrown over by them and fooled with promises of impossible compensation, and so the new king had stepped into a field of action ready made to his taste. His father's policy was discredited and the Orleanist alliance was naturally abandoned. He had told his Parliament that he would foster foreign friends and fight foreign foes[9], and it could be no secret which were the friends he meant to foster and the foes he meant to fight.

---

[1] e.g. Bishop Bubwith, Hugh Lord Burnell, and Sir Thomas Brook (Wylie, iii. 293) each lent £333. 6s. 8d.; the Bishops of Ely, Lincoln and Worcester, £200 each; the Bishops of Chichester and Exeter, £133. 6s. 6d. each; the Bishops of Chester, Hereford and London, £100 each; besides various sums from the Abbots of St Albans and Bury St Edmunds (£100 each), Glastonbury and Waltham (£63. 13s. 4d.). For £160 advanced by the Earl of Arundel, see Rec. Roll 1 H. V, Pasch., July 14, 1413.

[2] e.g. Aug. 14, Sept. 18, 1413, Iss. Roll 1 H. V, Pasch., Mich., Jan. 23, 1414.

[3] Exch. Accts. 45/22 (2).

[4] Vita, 10; Tit. Liv. 4; Juv. 497, who represents that in 1414 the King and the Duke of Bedford favoured the Burgundians, while the Dukes of Clarence, Gloucester and York inclined to the Armagnacs. Cf. Michelet, vi. 9; Wylie, iv. 89.

[5] Wals. Hypodig. 4.

[6] For a letter from the Earl of Arundel to the Duke of Burgundy, dated May 31, 1412, excusing himself for supporting the Armagnacs on the ground that he did so by command of the King *and the Prince of Wales*, see Beaucourt, i. 252.

[7] For his letter to the Duke of Burgundy dated from "Schafort" (? Hertford), May 22, 1412, with the Duke's reply dated from before Bourges (June 14, 1412), in which he expresses his grante, bonne et parfaite amictié *en especial avec vous* and urges a marriage with his daughter Anne (Wylie, iv. 36, 64), see Beaucourt, i. 132, quoting Moreau, 1424, No. 55.

[8] Wylie, iv. ch. XCIII.

[9] Page 24.

On May 10, 1413[1], a passport had been issued for William Boumyer[2], governor of the Duke of Burgundy's great city of Arras, to come to England and confer. A month later[3] Master Ralph Lemaire[4], Provost of St Donatian's at Bruges and Chancellor of Flanders[5], crossed over for a similar purpose. Both these envoys landed at Dover about June 19, and arrived at Canterbury just after the king had paid his ceremonial visit to his father's tomb as described in a previous chapter[6]. They stayed at Canterbury till June 26[7], and when the Council met at Sutton on June 29[8] four notable Englishmen of the highest rank had been selected to negotiate for an alliance with the Duke of Burgundy. These were Henry Chichele Bishop of St Davids[9], Richard Beauchamp Earl of Warwick[10], William Lord Zouche of Harringworth, Lieutenant of Calais[11], and Henry Lord Scrope of Masham[12]. Their commission was dated July 14, 1413[13]; they left London on July 29 or 30, crossed direct to Calais, where they met the Duke's representatives on Sept. 28[14], and were not back in England again till the middle

---

[1] Fr. Roll 1 H. V, 37; Rym. ix. 7; Rapin, Acta Regia, ii. 122.

[2] Or Bonmyer; not Boninger, as Carte, Rolles, ii. 207.

[3] June 13, 14, 1413, Rym. ix. 27; Carte, Rolles, ii. 207; called June 4, 1413, in Coussemaker, 176.

[4] Or Major, Rym. ix. 56. He left Paris during the Cabochian Terror in May, 1413 (Monstr. ii. 362), where he seems to be an Armagnac. He was sent as an envoy to Tournai in November and December, 1417, and on April 5, 1418, Vandenbroeck, 143, 147, 149, 160.

[5] Fr. Roll 1 H. V, 4.

[6] Page 47.

[7] Page 91, note 2. For their expenses (£15. 8s. 0d.) at Dover and Canterbury, June 19 to 26, 1413, see Exch. Accts. 406/21, 2, where they are called ambassadors of France, ex parte ducis Burgundie. For 26s. 8d. paid to John Vowe, of London, for damage to his house and vessels while entertaining the King's *familia* who were waiting for *extranei ducis Burgundie*, see Exch. Accts. 406/21, 30.

[8] Page 49.

[9] Called De Buscop van Zinte Dauyds, de grave van waerwyc ende eenen rudder (ritter) gheheeten de heere Scroupe, Gilliodts van Severen, iv. 255.

[10] For pardon to him of all debts etc., dated May 27, 1413, see Pat. 1 H. V, i. 24.

[11] Carte, Rolles, ii. 210; page 40, note 1.

[12] Not Richard, as Croyl. 500; nor Thomas, as J. S. Fletcher, i. 126. He is called Scrob or Scroub in Strecche, 265, 266; not "Stroul" or "Srool," as Waurin, i. 179; nor "Scroph," as Mézeray, ii. 565; nor "le Schrof," as Coussemaker, 176; nor Robert Scrooph, as Mazas, Vies, v. 554, 569. In Rot. Parl. iv. 64 he is called le Scrop de Masham de Faxflete; not "Faxflot," as Stow, 346. Cf. Wylie, iii. 284, note 5. In Ad Quod Damn. 373, he is dominus de Masham (not "Marsham," as Sandford, 279; nor "Mersham," as Church, 65), and his lands include the Manor of Upsall. Cf. Wylie, ii. 198, note 1.

[13] Rym. ix. 34, 57; Carte, Rolles, ii. 208; Rapin, i. 506; Acta Regia, ii. 123; Goodwin, 13; Ramsay, i. 170; Coussemaker, 176.

[14] Ibid. 177, from Archives du Nord.

of October[1]. They were empowered to redress infringements of the truce with Flanders, as to which they entered into an agreement with envoys of the Duke of Burgundy at Calais on Oct. 7, 1413[2], and they were also to approach the King of France[3], offering to meet any envoys whom he might appoint with a view to securing a more friendly understanding[4].

For already the old provocations were in full blast[5]. On July 14, 1413[6], the levies of Hampshire and the Isle of Wight were called upon to be in readiness to repel an expected invasion by the French, but instead of waiting for invasion three English armed barges under Richard Hawkwood[7] put across the Channel in the same

---

[1] Rym. ix. 56; Dumont, II. i. 359. For payments to Bishop Chichele (£86. 13s. 4d., July 29 to Oct. 16, 1413), to the Earl of Warwick (£121. 3s. 0d., July 22 to Oct. 14, 1413), and Henry, Lord Le Scrope (£64, from July 30 to Oct. 20, 1413), see Iss. Roll 1 H. V, Mich., Nov. 15, 1413. Exch. Accts. 321/14 shows that Scrope left London on July 30, 1413, on a journey to Calais and Lollingham (i.e. Leulinghen. Cf. Wylie, i. 205, note 2; iii. 290, note 10; called Loulynĝhm in Cotton MS. Tiberius, B. 12, f. 50; Lelingueham, St Denys, ii. 74; Leulinghem, Coussemaker, 110; see Harbaville, ii. 66; Johanne, Nord, 76) with other ambassadors, to treat with ambassadors of France and Flanders for continuation of the truce made temp. H. IV. Scrope had already received £112 for his expenses to Lollingham and back, Iss. Roll 1 H. V, Pasch., July 17, 1413, which also shows £186. 13s. 4d. each to Bishop Chichele and the Earl of Warwick, and £56 apiece to Richard Holme and Ralph Greenhurst (see page 91, note 1) in their company (*comitiva*) respectively, going to Lollyngham to meet ambassadors of the King of France for continuation of the truce. Scrope afterwards received £176 more, his suite (*familia*) returning in company with the Earl of Warwick on Oct. 20, 1413; Ramsay, i. 171; Mirot-Déprez, lxi. 25. In Add. MS. 24062, f. 150 *b* is an undated letter from King Henry to Charles, King of France, referring to the expiration of the treaty on Jan. 1 last and suggesting a conference as to repairing injuries done on both sides since that date. The bearer of the letter is called "G. roy d'armes."

[2] For the original of this agreement with portions of the seals of the Bp. of St Davids, Wm Lord Zouche and Richard Holme, see Sotheby, Catalogue of Phillipps MSS., April 26, 1911, p. 90, lot 531; Coussemaker, 177, from Archives du Nord, B. 562. The Flemish ambassadors are Willelmus Castellanus Furnensis (i.e. the Châtelain of Furnes) and Thierry Gherbode; cf. Morosini, i. 189, note; Wylie, ii. 100, note 1. For account of Gherbode, see Coussemaker, 27–39, showing that he died Jan. 14, 1421, and is buried at Werwicq, near Ypres. For analysis of his correspondence in the Archives at Lille, from 1385–1420, see Coussemaker, *passim*; Finot, Paix, 4.

[3] Ord. Priv. Co. ii. 130. [4] Rym. ix. 38.
[5] St Denys, v. 285. [6] Pat. 1 H. V, ii. 1 dors.
[7] Or Hakewood, Pat. 1 H. V, iii. 19, July 26, 1413. He was probably a connection of the great Sir John Hawkwood, who died March 16, 1394 (Morant, ii. 288; Dict. Nat. Biogr. xxv. 241), though I have not found any actual proof of this. For Sir John Hawkwood's son, John, born in Italy (called Giovanni Augud junior), see Temple-Leader, 303, 309, 361. He was naturalised as an Englishman, Nov. 3, 1407, Cal. Pat. H. IV, iii. 276. For John Hawkewode who served as a man-of-arms in the muster of Duke Humphrey at Agincourt, see Wylie, Notes, 127. For fresco of John Hawkwood in the Cathedral at Florence (Joannes Acutus), painted by Paolo Uccello in 1436, see Yriarte, Condottiere, 104, 113; Marcotti, Frontispiece; Temple-Leader, do., 292, 294, 296; Bibl. Top. Britt. vi. 44; Venturi, Storia, vii (1), 336. It was originally painted above the place where the tomb was to be erected, but was transferred to canvas and set up in its present position at the west end of the church, circ. 1845, Temple-Leader, 296. He was variously called Haccoude (Froissart), Augut, Augud, Haukkodue or Hauto, Morant, ii. 288; Temple-Leader, 293, 294, 303; or Haukwode, Gaunt Reg. ii. 299;

month[1]. The force landed and burnt St Aubin[2], which was strongly held by the one-eyed Burgundian leader Robert de la Heuse[3], who sallied out against them. They however drove him back into the town but lost their leader[4] in the skirmish. On Aug. 14[5] they made a dash to capture Dieppe[6] but were again baffled, though they afterwards succeeded in effecting a landing at Tréport, where they plundered the Abbey of St Michael[7] and slew many of the monks. After this they over-ran the country for 10 miles round[8], burning many villages and carrying batches of prisoners back to England.

These irritating incidents were still in the making when the four above-named English envoys set out on their mission of peace, but though they went through the form of negotiating with the French at Leulinghen there was apparently little heart in the business, and there is evidence that other negotiations on "certain secret articles and matters" had been proceeding with representatives of the Duke of Burgundy[9] at the same time and place, while in Paris it was believed that an actual alliance had been already concluded between the English and the Duke[10], who held

not Haakwood, as Monnier, i. 30. For his tomb at Sible Hedingham, his native place, to which his body was removed, see Temple-Leader, 307; Bibl. Top. Britt. vi. Frontispiece. For account of Paolo Uccello (1396–1479), see Yriarte, Florence, 313, who gives the Sant Egidio picture; Venturi, Storia, vii (1), 332.

[1] Monstr. ii. 376; Le Fèvre, i. 88; Duchesne, 819; Goodwin, 4; Guthrie, ii. 448.

[2] Roncière, ii. 213 (from Chartres Royales MS. fr. 25709, f. 697 in Bibl. Nat.), dates this after July 1415, but it seems to fit in better here.

[3] Cagny, 79; or le Borgne, Anselme, vii. 756, where he is Lord of Vantes and Castellan of Bellencombre, near Dieppe. For his seal (1387), see Demay, Invent. i. 493. He had been appointed Provost of Paris on March 21, 1413, being then absent in Picardy, Bourgeois, 616; Pannier, 393; Wylie, ii. 300, note 2. He returned to Paris on Aug. 9, 1414, but on the fall of the Cabochians in the same month, he was deposed in favour of the Armagnac, Tanneguy du Chastel, Bourgeois, 617. For La Heuse on the Roll of Battle Abbey, see Brut, ii. 537. For arms of the Lords of La Heuse, near Longueville (Seine Inf.), see Sarrazin, Jeanne d'Arc, 134.

[4] Called miles famosus de genere regis, St Denys, v. 68; Juv. 480.

[5] F. Bouquet, ii. 15.

[6] For a sixteenth century plan of Dieppe, see Belleforest, Cosmogr. ii. 106. For pictures of the castle and the church of St Jacques, see D. Turner, i. 11; Cotman and Turner, i. 35; Bordeaux, 1. i. 59, 60.

[7] For the Abbey, see Gall. Christ. xi. 244; Coquelin, *passim*.

[8] G. Dupont, 507; Coville, Recherches, 392, from MS. fr. 25709, f. 671.

[9] For payment to Richard Norton, messenger, sent to Calais with passports for Waleran, Count of St Pol, and John Bishop of Tournai (i.e. Jean de Thoisy, from 1410 till his death, June 2, 1433, Gams, 251; Eubel, i. 517), to meet with "our ambassadors," see Iss. Roll 1 H. V, Pasch., July 7, 1413. For commission of Count Waleran and the Bishop of Tournai, dated Aug. 22, 1413, i.e. the day before the Duke of Burgundy's flight from Paris, see Rym. ix. 58.

[10] Juv. 478. In Cochon, 273, the Duke is supposed to have met King Henry in

at that time the dominating influence in the capital. But on Aug. 23, 1413, the Duke of Burgundy fled from Paris, and on Sept. 15 the English envoys met him at Bruges[1] and remained there with an escort of 200 mounted men at his expense till Sept. 19[2]. On Thursday, Oct. 19[3], some of them had another interview with him at Lille[4], at which it was proposed that the English king[5] should marry one of the Duke's daughters, receiving with her the fortresses of Cherbourg, Le Crotoy and Caen[6], but the arrival of envoys from Paris[7] on Nov. 5 put an end to this project, and on Nov. 16, 1413, the Duke denied that he had ever entertained it[8]. This however did not interrupt his friendly intercourse, for an esquire whose name appears as William Rabek[9] was certainly in London as an ambassador on his behalf during the ensuing winter, while on Nov. 25, 1413[10], special protection was extended to the wine-ships on their way to Flanders, and on Jan. 29, 1414, passports were issued for the Duke's representatives[11] to cross and hold personal interviews with the English king, as a result of which it was arranged that claims arising out of breaches of the truce between England and Flanders would be favourably considered if presented at Calais before May 15, 1414[12].

person at Calais (*Karlès*) et là firent leur apointement et aliances ensembles, which is a confusion with the events of 1416.

[1] Barante, iii. 83; Gilliodts van Severen, Invent. iv. 255.

[2] The Duke of Burgundy's total expenses for the year amounted to £15,998. 2s. 6d., including £710. 10s. 7d., the cost of the English envoys' journey from Calais and back, Itin. 401, 402, 403.

[3] Ibid. 402, 403.

[4] Monstr. 293; Le Fèvre, i. 118, 120; J. Mayer, 241; Duchesne, 820; Duck, 35.

[5] Or one of his brothers, John or Humphrey, according to Brando, 160.

[6] D. Sauvage, 223. St Denys (v. 353) adds Chinon in Touraine, at the junction of the Vienne and the Loire. Chinon and Le Crotoy were in the hands of the Duke of Burgundy in 1414, but were to be delivered up to the French King by the Treaty of Arras (Sept. 4, 1414), Monstr. 345; St Denys, v. 386, 388, 422.

[7] i.e. the Bishop of Evreux, the Admiral of France and others, Itin. 403; Monstr. ii. 412; Le Fèvre, i. 124.

[8] St Denys, v. 218; called Nov. 26 in Barante, iii. 91. For visit of the Duke of Brittany and his brother the Count of Richmond to Paris in 1413, to thwart the marriage of Henry V with a daughter of Burgundy, see Paradin, 570.

[9] For references to him, see Iss. Roll 1 H. V, Mich., Jan. 27, Feb. 19, 22, 1414. Called Rabecque in Coussemaker, 176.

[10] Carte, Rolles, ii. 209; Rym. ix. 72.

[11] i.e. Ralph le Maire, Peter Lord of Viesville near Charleroi, John Lord of Roubaix, and William de Halewyn, Lord of Dunkirk, Carte, Rolles, ii. 210; Rym. ix. 112; also March 6, 1414, Carte, Rolles, ii. 211; Lettenhove, Flandre, iii. 83.

[12] Rym. ix. 114, 116.

But at this stage it is of more lasting interest to follow the course of King Henry's four negotiators in regard to the policy of France. A truce at the moment existed between the two countries that would expire on Dec. 31, 1413, and on the very day before the Duke of Burgundy fled from Paris, commissioners had been appointed[1] to meet the English envoys and discuss the prospects of the future. These made their way at once to Boulogne and held repeated conferences with Bishop Chichele and his colleagues at Leulinghen from Sept. 1, 1413[2], onwards. The conversations were carried on in Latin and the documents were subsequently drafted in the same language, though the Frenchmen protested that this should not be taken as a precedent for ousting French from its accustomed place in diplomacy. The French were requested to take note that their king would have to make good all breaches of the truce made with Richard II in 1396[3], while the English would be willing on their part to do the like. To this the French replied that their instructions did not refer to the truce of 1396 but to those made during the reign of Henry IV, especially in regard to the capture of Balinghem in the previous year[4].

The English then reopened all the ancient history about the claims of Edward III to the French crown in right of his mother Isabel, to which the French returned a learned and sufficient reply, taking their ammunition from a treatise drawn up some 12 years before[5] when the French king had deliberately challenged the claim by granting the Duchy of Guienne to his son and heir as a preliminary to a coming attack on Aquitaine. This manifesto had been originally put forward in the name of some members of the University of Paris[6], but it was actually composed by the learned humanist, Jean de Montreuil[7], who had had a large experience of public affairs as secretary to the French king, the

---

[1] For their appointment, Aug. 22, 1413, see Rym. ix. 58.
[2] Report on Fœdera, App. D. 76.
[3] Wylie, i. 84.		[4] Ibid. iv. 72.
[5] i.e. in 1402, ibid. i. 155; not in 1410, as Thomas, 25. In Anselme, ii. 522, the grant is dated Jan. 14, 1400.
[6] A. Thomas, 24.
[7] For letters of Salutato to him, dated July 2, 1395, July 14, 1396, see Salutati, iii. 71, 143, who addresses him as vir insignis in cunctisque venerationis honoribus excolende; see also Wylie, iii. 24 n., 25 n., 88 n., 99 n., 340 n.

Dauphin and the Dukes of Berry, Burgundy and Orleans[1], and in the course of his many travels had visited our country in 1394[2]. This famous treatise is still preserved in the National Library in Paris[3], and it formed the basis of all subsequent agitations[4] down to the time when we were finally expelled from France. It challenged the right of the English kings to be Dukes of Aquitaine, and therefore every step in the negotiations of Brétigny and Calais, justifying the action of Charles V with all that followed from it, and from the Frenchman's point of view it showed up the baselessness of Edward III's claim, relying on much erudite pedantry about Pharamond and the Salic law[5] to establish the female bar[6]. The English on their side worked on such evidence as they found in certain "most beautiful and notable books" which they brought with them to the meeting[7]. Then the question turned on the treaty signed at Brétigny in 1360[8], by which it was claimed that the French should deliver up some lands in Guienne and elsewhere if the English withdrew their garrisons from certain places not claimed as ever having belonged to the English crown, and then both sides went seriously to work

[1] A. Thomas, 7.
[2] Wylie, ii. 389.
[3] Bibl. Nat. MS. fr. 21381; Thomas, 23. It was rewritten in Latin by its author in the autumn of 1415, and dedicated to Jean de Thoisy, Bishop of Tournai (Bibl. Nat. MS. 10920, 10921, 18337; Thomas, 19), when the English army was marching from Harfleur to Agincourt, and again in French in the following year (i.e. Sept. 24, 1416, Thomas, 22, from MS. Vat. Reg. 894; Champion, Chron. Mart. p. x, who quotes G. Corrozet, Trésor des Histoires de France (1603), p. 120; Chronique Martiniane, Vol. II), when there was hope of getting help from King Sigismund. See also Grudé, i. 556; Paquot, ii. 263.
[4] e.g. by Juvenal des Ursins in 1445, Bibl. Nat. MS. fr. 17512; Thomas, 28; by Robert Blondel in his Oratio Historialis in 1458; Blondel, i. 164, 235; ii. p. xiii; do. Des Droits de la Couronne de France, i. 295; and by an unknown writer in 1463, Thomas, 29.
[5] Loy salique, lex salica, Thomas, 25. For treatise of Bishop Beckington in refutation of the Salic Law, see Collinson, iii. 384, written while he was Dean of the Court of Arches, which office he certainly held when he was present at the trial of Wm Taylor in the hostry of the Black Friars on Feb. 11, 1423, Conc. iii. 407; Bekynton, I. p. xx; though in Hennessy (312) he is supposed to have been appointed in 1430. For his admission as one of Wickham's scholars at Winchester in 1403 or 1404, see Bekynton, I. xvi, cxviii. For his clerical appointments, see Hennessy, xxxiv. For his collection of documents bearing on the claim of the English kings to the crown of France (i.e. Cotton MS. Tiberius, B. 12; Harl. MS. 4763), see Angl. Sacr. i. 573; Bekynton, I. p. xi. For Pharamundus, see J. Coke, 112.
[6] Henry V, 1, 2, 42.
[7] Lesquelz les Anglois portent communement avecques eulx quant ils doyvent assembler avec les François pour traicter, Thomas, 20, referring to chronicles written by "Maistre Jehan Boor, un grant historien des Angloiz (p. 26)," i.e. probably the Brut.
[8] Vita, 28.

quoting historical evidence to prove that the terms of the treaty had never been fully carried out, each party blaming the other for the non-fulfilment of the conditions.

Thus nothing could be concluded but another patchwork truce for the district lying between Nieuport and the mouth of the Somme, which was agreed to on Sept. 25[1], to last for 8 months, i.e. from Oct. 1, 1413, till June 1, 1414[2], while a further general truce was accorded on Oct. 16[3] to last till the following Easter[4]. The English wished each side to be allowed to help its own allies, but the French objected and were only pacified when two separate copies were drawn up, one containing such a clause and the other omitting it, the question in dispute being reserved for final confirmation at Boulogne and Calais respectively by Nov. 1[5]. On Oct. 8, 1413[6], passports were issued for Guillaume Boisratier[7], Archbishop of Bourges[8], and the Gascon Charles d'Albret[9], Constable of France[10], to cross to England and confer

---

[1] Goodwin, 14, from Bishop Beckington's Register, Cotton MS. Tiberius, B. 12, f. 48; Sismondi, xii. 399; Spencer, 29.

[2] Rym. ix. 58; Report on Fœd. App. D. 77. For confirmation dated Oct. 16, 21, 1413, see Carte, Rolles, ii. 209; Rym. ix. 68. For payments to messengers for proclaiming it at Calais, see Devon, 325, Oct. 17, 1413. It was further confirmed by the Bishop of Durham and the Archbishop of Bourges on Jan. 29, 1414 (Carte, Rolles, ii. 211), and proclaimed on Jan. 31, 1414 (ibid. 212).

[3] Fr. Roll 1 H. V, 19, 20.

[4] Monstr. ii. 391; Le Fèvre, i. 105; Isambert, vii. 408.

[5] Report on Fœd. App. D. 77.

[6] Rym. ix. 60; Carte, Rolles, ii. 209; Fr. Roll 1 H. V, 22, where the safe-conduct is for John, Archbishop of Sens.

[7] Waurin, ii. 169. He attended as a member of the Council in Paris in Jan. and Feb. 1413, and on May 24, 26, Aug. 3, Sept. 5, 18, 1413, Bibl. de l'Ec. des Chartes, vi. 288; Baye, 115, 129, 140; Ordonnances, x. 70, 140; St Denys, v. 168; Rym. ix. 55. He was confessor to Queen Isabel (Monstr. ii. 353; D. Sauvage, 215; Paradin, 565), and had been marked down for vengeance by the Cabochians in May 1413, Le Fèvre, i. 81. He was Chancellor to the Duke of Berry (Mazas, Vies, v. 562, who quotes Thaumas de la Thaumassière, Bk. iv, for statement that he was a native of Bourges).

[8] Not *Thomas*, Archbishop of *Bruges*, as Church, 55. He had previously been Bishop of Mende in the Cevennes, but had been translated to Bourges on May 12, 1409, Gall. Christ. i. 101; ii. 86, 87; Gams, 524 (not 1410 nor Oct. 21, 1408, as Thaumas, ii. 87, 102), but did not actually enter into possession till May 18, 1410, on his return from the Council of Pisa. He held the archbishopric till his death on July 19, 1421, Gall. Christ. ii. 87; Ordonnances, x. 27, 140. For his epitaph in the Cathedral at Bourges, see Thaumas, ii. 87. For his chapel there with fragments of a window, see E. Beaurepaire, Vitraux, 24.

[9] He was Lord of Labrit or Lebret in the Landes, called La Byrt in Tit. Liv. 14; Vita, 54; or La Britte, Rym. ix. 188. See Wylie, ii. 319, note 10. Cf. Et pour d'Alebret le bon Charles, Thomassy, 171; dum in Anglia legationis regis Franciæ officio fungeretur, St Denys, v. 534.

[10] Appointed Feb. 7, 1403, Anselme, vi. 207; not 1402, as Thibault, 314; deprived by the Cabochians in 1413, St Denys, v. 64, but restored in the same year, ibid. v. 158; Monstr. ii. 403; Le Fèvre, i. 78, 80, 109; Fenin, 35; Perrens, ii. 245. For disputes about the office between him and the Burgundian, Waleran Count of St Pol, see Fenin, 586.

further.   Their commission was made out in Paris on
Nov. 11, 1413[1]; they reached England on Dec. 6[2], but
they do not appear to have arrived in London till Dec. 19[3].
They were lodged in Bishop Langley's hostel[4] and had
an audience with the king in person at Westminster.   On
Jan. 10, 1414[5], Bishop Langley and the Earl of Warwick
were appointed to treat with them, and on Jan. 23[6], fresh
safe-conducts were issued for them to last till the end
of February.   On Jan. 24[7] an understanding was arrived
at to recommend a truce for 12 months from Feb. 2, 1414[8],
and an English herald[9] was sent over to Paris to discuss
claims for breaches committed in the past.   The English
wished the treaty to be drawn up in Latin as the most
convenient language for all, but the visitors held out for
French as had been the custom with their forefathers[10].
Not to fall out over words it was arranged that the document should be engrossed[11] both in French and Latin in
parallel columns, and as it was hoped that it would be
binding on the allies of both parties, viz. the Emperor

---

[1] Rym. ix. 70.

[2] Their expenses in England date from Dec. 6, 1413, Rym. ix. 188.

[3] Chron. Lond. 97; not October, as Rapin, i. 506.

[4] In Iss. Roll 3 H. V, Pasch., May 18, 1415, is an entry of £15. 17s. 4d. for sheep
bought for expenses of Lord de Brett and other ambassadors hospitat' in hostel of the
Bishop of Durham; also 6s. 8d. paid to John Brom sent in all haste to John Wilcotes, kt.,
assigned to order and provide for ambassadors of the King of France until they come to
the King's presence.   For John Brome, garcio of King's chamber at Harfleur, see ibid.
Sept. 2, 1415.   For a horse and money left to him in the King's will at Southampton,
see Rym. ix. 291.

[5] Rym. ix. 88; Carte, Rolles, ii. 210.   There is no evidence that Marshal Boucicaut
was with them, as supposed in Mazas, Vies, v. 510, 557.

[6] Rym. ix. 90; Carte, Rolles, ii. 210.

[7] Rym. ix. 91, 101, 102, 110, 198, 206, 224, 226; Dumont, II. ii. 4; Rapin, Acta
Regia, ii. 125; Goodwin, 35; Caro, Kanzlei, 117; Mirot, Fusoris, 146.   For reference
(April 29, 1414) to two letters in the Exchequer (cf. Kal. and Inv. ii. 216) recording
truce with France for 1 year from Feb. 1414, see Delpit, 216.

[8] St Denys, v. 280.   Copies were deposited in the Treasury at Westminster on
April 29, 1414, Kal. and Inv. ii. 9.   For order dated Jan. 29, 1414, to proclaim the
truce in Aquitaine, see Rot. Vasc. 1 H. V, 1.   In Exch. Accts. 186/2, April 30, 1414,
the Earl of Dorset orders 7 crowns to be paid to 2 clerks for copying the truce (les
trèves), and 6 crowns to a herald for proclaiming it, with 1 crown to the trompettes and
payments to sergeants-at-arms going to all the garrisons to announce it.

[9] Called G—— king of arms in Henry's undated letter to the King of France (Add.
MS. 24062, f. 150), in which he admits that his subjects have violated the truce with
France made during his father's time, but which expired on Jan. 1 last.

[10] Cf. non latino quod a nostris jam Galliarum curiis repudiatum est.   Neque enim aut
principes nostri aut hii qui cancellis eorum præsunt latinæ quippiam eloquentia didicerunt
etc., Clamenges, Epist. p. 58; see Wylie, i. 440; ii. 390; iii. 21.   For Latin as "the most
stedfaste langage," see Secreta, 146.

[11] For wages of scribes at 5d. per day, see Iss. Roll 1 H. V, Pasch., Mich., July 14,
1413, Feb. 22, 1414.   For £5 paid clericis scribentibus rotulos scaccarii, see Exch. Rolls
Scot. iv. 288, 289, 309.

Sigismund, King Wenzel, the Kings of Aragon, Castile, Navarre, Portugal, Denmark and Scotland, the Dukes of Brabant and Gueldres, Duke Louis of Bavaria, the Count of Holland and the Doge of Genoa, it looked as if at last a long spell of peace was really about to settle over Europe both by land and sea.

On Jan. 28, 1414[1], Henry Lord Scrope[2], Hugh Mortimer[3], and Master Henry Ware[4] were about to cross the Channel in company with the French envoys to continue negotiations in Paris, taking with them copies of previous treaties for reference[5], but they do not appear to have started till a fortnight later. On Jan. 29, 1414[6], orders were given to charter ships at Southampton, Poole, Weymouth, and the Camber at Rye[7] to convey the French envoys back, and in the middle of February[8] further directions were given to provide horses[9] and shipping[10] for their voyage either by way of Dover, Southampton, Poole, Weymouth, or Melcombe. At length the whole party, both Englishmen and Frenchmen, reached Paris, which they entered on March 4, 1414[11], where the truce was ratified on March 10 following[12].

Acting on the long prevalent belief that a lasting peace between the two countries could only be secured "by way

---

[1] Rym. ix. 102 ; Carte, Rolles, ii. 211.

[2] He was absent from Jan. 29 to May 4, 1414, Ramsay, i. 173 from Enrolled Household Accts.

[3] Wylie, iv. 498. On March 21, 1413, he was appointed a Justice of the Peace for Buckinghamshire and Worcestershire, Pat. 1 H. V, i. 34 d ; Cal. Pat. H. V, i. 416, 425. For Thomas Mortimer, esquire, sheriff and escheator of Northants and Rutland in 1413, see Rec. Roll 1 H. V, Pasch., Mich., May 4, Oct. 2, 1413. On July 12, 1414, Thomas Mortimer is commissioned together with Ralph Green and others to enquire into claims of men of Benyfeld (i.e. Benefield, near Oundle), Pat. 2 H. V, ii. 39 d.

[4] For Henry Ware's account going to Paris in the company of Henry le Scrop, from Feb. 2 to May 2, 1414, in a ffarescost de Cales, see Exch. Accts. 321/15 ; Mirot-Déprez, lxi. 26. For payments of £100 each to Scrope and Mortimer, and £50 to Ware for embassy to France, see Iss. Roll 1 H. V, Mich., Jan. 25, 1414.

[5] For payment of 6s. 8d. each to 5 scribes in the Privy Seal Office for copying them out, see Devon, 331, Feb. 10, 1414. They are called "old truces with foreign countries" in Hoccleve, Min. Po. lx.

[6] Rym. ix. 104 ; Pat. 1 H. V, v. 24 d.

[7] Wylie, ii. 104. For la Caumbre or Cambre at Rye, see Bree, 173, 174, 176 ; Oppenheim, Accts. 31. For position of it, see Burrows, 195.

[8] For £1634. 0s. 11½d. paid for expenses of the French envoys from Dec. 6, 1413, to Feb. 13, 1414, see Rym. ix. 188.

[9] For order for horses to convey the French ambassadors from London to Dover or Southampton, see Pat. 1 H. V, v. 29 d, Jan. 23, 1414.

[10] For payment for ships and sailors, including the Great Marie de la Tour which would afterwards proceed to La Rochelle, see Iss. Roll 1 H. V, Mich., Jan. 27, 1414 ; Devon, 327.

[11] St Denys, v. 228.   [12] Rym. ix. 119.

of marriage[1]," the English envoys were empowered to arrange a match between King Henry and the French King's youngest daughter Catherine, who was now nearly 12 years of age[2]. On August 31[3] of the preceding year, the Duke of York[4] had arrived in Paris from Bordeaux to broach this same marriage question, though many people thought that he had really come to report on the divisions that were distracting the lords of France[5]. The French king however received him with great distinction, and the young princess was introduced with state ceremony. Dressed in a gown of silk interwoven with gold she stood surrounded with her suite of ladies, pranked with gems and ouches[6]. The Duke of York was entertained about the Court in Paris till Candlemas, 1414[7], during which time he received some instalments on account of the money still due to him under the settlement made at Buzançais in 1412[8], and when the new year turned he received handsome new-gifts, among which was a gold hanap with a golden bear as a fretlet, given to him by the Duke of Berry[9], who also

---

[1] Wylie, iv. 36. For St Brigit's revelation, see Marryat, i. 296.

[2] She was born in the Hostel of St Pol on Oct. 27, 1401, Anselme, i. 115; Beaucourt, i. 3; Cosneau, 103; Mas Latrie, 152; Strickland, ii. 106, who gives the story from Choisy that she and her sister Michelle were found in rags in the Hostel of St Pol and removed to the convent at Poissy; Cousinot, 153; Swallow, Catherine, 7; Thibault, 290; Vallet de Viviville, i. 236; not 1400, as Wills of Kings, 244; Belleval, 13; nor that she was born before the king's madness began, as Æn. Sylv. Comm. 154. She was the twelfth child (though called 13th in St Denys, v. 160) and the youngest daughter, Barante, iii. 83; not the eldest, as J. R. Green, 263. She died in the Abbey at Bermondsey on Jan. 3, 1437, Strickland, ii. 155; Ramsay, i. 494; Dict. Nat. Biogr. lvii. 291; called Jan. 2 in Wills of Kings, 244; not June 4, 1438, as Mont St Michel, i. 15 note; Grande Encycl. ix. 840. For commission, dated March 26, 1437, for executing her will, see Rym. x. 662; Rot. Parl. iv. 505. For removal of her body from St Nicholas' Chapel in Westminster Abbey to Henry V's Chantry in 1878, see T. Wright, Views, North Ambulatory; Hialt, 75. For a romance about her love for Owen Tudor, whose blood goes back "au grand Calloüiador" and who has escaped to Paris to ask help against Henry V, after making his last stand at Milford, see Baudot de Juilli, Caterine, 11, 56 and *passim*.

[3] Goodwin, 14. He was present at the fêtes held on Oct. 1, 1413, in connection with the marriage of Queen ⌐abel's brother, Louis Duke of Bavaria, with Catherine of Alençon, widow of Pierre de Navarre, Cosneau, Connétable, 29. For a gold paternoster given by the Duke of York on Sept. 14, 1413, to the Duke of Berry, who gave it away again on Oct. 7, 1413, see Guiffrey, i. 300.

[4] St Denys, v. 158; called the Earl of Rutland in Monstr. ii. 403; not that they were two different men who both came, as Le Fèvre, i. 118; J. Meyer, 241; D. Sauvage, 220; called Duc de Yrot, Conte de Rotelan, Pays-Bas, 353; not the Earl of Warwick, as Le Laboureur, 902.

[5] Juv. 487.　　　　　　　　[6] For "nouche," see Rym. ix. 276; Wylie, iv. 355.

[7] Juv. 493, though in St Denys, v. 228, he is said to have left Paris about the end of Nov. 1413.

[8] For a receipt given by him to the Duke of Berry on Oct. 3, 1413, for 1500 crowns, as part of 6000 still due to him, see Toulgoët-Treanna, 121; Wylie, iv. 83; Archiv. Nat. K. K. 250, f. 10ᵛᵒ, quoted in Guiffrey, i. 208.

[9] Guiffrey, i. 208; also a gold rosary with 28 beads (boutons), ibid. 92.

presented him with a large uncut diamond[1], and a spine
from the Crown of Thorns, enclosed in a crystal cross[2].
On his return to London he had had a glowing tale to tell
of the Princess Catherine's lovely figure, her beauty, and
her general suitability[3], and the English envoys were now
authorised to make a definite proposal for her hand, King
Henry agreeing to await her father's decision till May 1,
1414, or even later, if desired[4].

But yet through all these months the English king
never ceased to keep an ear open to friendly intercourse
with the traitor Duke of Burgundy, while the duplicity
with which the whole tissue of his diplomacy was penetrated
is proved to the hilt by the fact that, while he was fooling
the Armagnacs in Paris with the outward semblance of a
desire for peace, he was storing vast quantities of material
in deliberate preparation for war. The London fletchers[5]
supplied arrows by the score and the hundred; bowyers[6]
were pressed to make and mend bows and bowstaves[7];

---

[1] Poinctu, non fait, Guiffrey, i. 128.

[2] Guiffrey, i. 32, who confuses him with his brother, the Earl of Cambridge.

[3] Formâ pulchritudine et aptitudine, St Denys, v. 160; puella pulcherrima, ibid. 228.
> Sa belle fille aux blons loriaux
> Et alla a sy fresche couleur
> Qu'avoir doibt ami de valour.   Pastoralet, 757.
> Et fu belle que flour de may.   Ibid. 846.

[4] Rym. ix. 104; Carte, Rolles, ii. 211.

[5] For fletcher or fflecher, see Iss. Roll 1 H. V, Mich., Feb. 19, 1414; Cal. Doc. Scot.
iv. 176; Letter Book I, 25, 99; Wylie, iv. 272; or fflexoner, Iss. Roll 3 H. V, Pasch.,
May 18, 1415, showing £10 and £6 paid to Stephen Fflexoner and Alexander Atte
Wood (bower) respectively; or setter (Cl. 8 H. V, 16 d), i.e. arrowsmith, Wylie, ii. 93.
For names of 11 flecchers and 1 stringer in London, see Iss. Roll 7 H. V, Pasch., Mich.,
June 1, 1419, Feb. 22, 1420.

[6] For order to Nicholas Frost, bowyer, dated April 20, 1415, see Rym. ix. 224; also
£10 paid to Henry Bower for making bows pro stauro regis, Iss. Roll 3 H. V, Pasch.,
April 16, 27, 1415. For "bower," see Iss. Roll 1 H. V, Mich., Feb. 22, 1414; Wylie,
iv. 269; bowiere, Pat. 6 H. V, 24; Letter Book I, 65, 173; bowman, Exch. Rolls Scot.
iii. 713; bogener, Schmidt, 28; bowmaker, Caxton, Dial. 36, where he makes "bows
and arwes the arblasters shote."

[7] For meremium vocatum Bowestaves, see Rym. ix. 224. In 1413 the price paid for
bowstaves was 60s. per 100. For £52 paid for 1200 (i.e. £4. 6s. 8d. per 100), see Iss.
Roll 1 H. V, Mich., Nov. 8, 1413. In Rot. Parl. vi. 156 (1472–1475) they were to be
sold at 40s. per 100, and such as were called the wrak, i.e. "not good ne able to make of
but childern bowes," at 10s. to 13s. 4d. per 100, the bowyers selling them at 8d., 10d.
or 1s. each for a yeoman. For bows at 1s. 3d. each, arrows at 1s. 9d. per sheaf, and
strings at 6s. per gross, see Devon, 318; Fortescue (Plummer), 283. For £28. 6s. 8d.
paid for 1000 bowstaves (or £2. 16s. 8d. per 100) to John Cowbill, esterling, and 5s. for
carriage to the Tower, see Iss. Roll 1 H. V, Pasch., Aug. 14, 1413. For carriage of
bowestaffes from Styles wharf to Pountenys yn, see ibid. Mich., Feb. 22, 1414. For a
round bow (2s. 4d.), 8 bolts (14d.), 2 doz. strings (13d.), with a cardboard hutch for
keeping bows (12d.) and a leather case for bolts (3s. 4d.), see Baildon, Wardrobe, 499
(1394). For bois à faire arcs et arbalestres shipped from Pera, see Bouvier, Descr. 93.

arrows[1], strings[2], and brimstone[3] were packed in barrels[4] and stored in vast quantities[5] in Pountney's Inn[6] in the lane leading from Candlewick St.[7] to the Old Swan[8]. On

[1] For £37. 10s. paid for 500 garb of arrows bought from Stephen Seler, fflecher, of London, i.e. at 1s. 6d. per garb, see Iss. Roll 1 H. V, Pasch., Aug. 14, 1413. For £121. 13s. 4d. paid for arrows bought of Stephen Fleccher, see Rec. Roll 3 H. V, Pasch., June 25, 1415. For 2000 sayettes (or saietes, Fréville, ii. 280; settes, Wylie, iv. 361) at 12 sols per dozen, at Lille, in 1359, see La Fons-Melicocq, 19; do. Artillerie, 5. Cf. quarreaux i trestrent et saetes, Le Marchant, 181.

[2] For hand bowes each garnished with 3 strings, and 400 lbs. of thread made of sinews for to make strenges for bowes for a stown (i.e. stone), see Caxton, Fayt, ii. 25; Wylie, iii. 58, note 1. The strings were made of gut (cf. cordes a boyau, Meun, 143, translating *funibus nervinis*) or, in emergency, of horsehair, or even of woman's hair (se felz cordes faillent on doit prendre crins de chevaulx ou les cheveuls des Femmes, Christine, Chas. V, p. 270), Clarke, 175. Cf.

> Coues et traces de cheval
> Por rapaxoillier arbaletes
> De corde s'on n'ai autres prates
> Chevoz de fomes tot sanz dote. Priorat, 282.

For stringers, see Pat. 3 H. V, i. 25; 5 H. V, 17, Sept. 1, 1417; Wylie, iv. 277; or strengers, Letter Book I, 144, 157. For bowstrings sold by spicers (épiciers) at Orléans in 1419, see Cuissard, 145. For arkes, setes et cordes pur les arkes, see Romania, xxxii. 58.

[3] For £166. 13s. 4d. and £40 paid to Philip de Albertis for 19 barrels and 14 butts of sulphur for the king's stores, see Iss. Roll 1 H. V, Mich., Nov. 8, 1413, Feb. 22, 1414, together with 17s. 3d. for carriage to Pountney's Inn, see ibid. Dec. 1, 1413, Jan. 27, 1414, where the original has "Bromstone," not "Bromstons" as Devon, 326.

[4] Nervos arcuum doliis plenis, Strecche, 266; saectes barellés, Delisle, Agric. 489. Cf. bowes and arowes in chestes were take, Harflet, Bodl. 70.

[5] After the death of the Earl of Arundel in Sept. 1415, the remainder of the stores were transferred to a hostel in Mincing Lane and ultimately to the Tower, Iss. Roll 3 H. V, Mich., Feb. 29, 1416, where it is called Mincheon Lane from the Minchuns or nuns of St Helens in Bishopsgate, Stow, 50.

[6] Called Pountenays hyn, Pountenysyn, Poundenayshyn, Iss. Roll 1 H. V, Mich., Nov. 8, 1413, Feb. 30, 1414. It was called after John Poultney or Pulteney, or Putteney (Kingsford, Chron. 10; Greg. Chron. 78, 79, where he is Mayor of London in 1331, 1332, 1334 and 1337), al. Pountney or Pontenay, a Leicestershire man from Poultney, near Lutterworth (see Nichols, Leicestershire, iv. 316). For his life and pedigree, see H. B. Wilson, 25, 222. In his will, dated Nov. 14, 1349, he leaves 53s. 4d. to prisoners in Newgate, ibid. 32. In 1347 he founded the College of St Lawrence Poultney in his house in Candlewick St. (Benham-Welch, 15), which was pulled down in 1600, Fabyan, 419, 422, 441, 444; Fox-Bourne, 49; Newcourt, i. 388; Pennant, London, 351; Tyler, i. 258; Aungier, Chroniques, 64; Bridgett, ii. 155.

[7] For a chantry in the Church of St Laurence de Pountney juxta Candlewykke Strete, see Ad Quod Damn. 372; do. ii. 743 (P.R.O.).

[8] It lay between Suffolk Lane and Lawrence Pountney Inn, to the north side of Thames St., and was quite distinct from the Coldharbour or Coleharbour which adjoined the Steelyard on the water-side in Dowgate, close to All Hallows the Less, or All Hallows on the Cellars, to the south of Thames St., H. B. Wilson, 180 (see Hollar's map (1647) in J. E. Price, 60; also map in Loftie, i. 50). For picture of it, circ. 1600, see Besant, Survey (Tudors), p. 134. Not in East Cheap as Sanford, 181; Kingsford, 69, 87; though wrongly identified with it by Stow, Bk. ii. 206; J. Foster, xxii; Ramsay, i. 127; Kingsford, Chron. 316. It was granted by Henry IV to the Prince of Wales for life in 1410, Pennant, London, 351; Pauli, Pictures, 422; and was known to Londoners as "therber," Kingsford, Chron. 168, i.e. the inn, Wylie, iii. 304, note 4; cf. "herberow," Caxton, Dial. 5. For "harbour" as a translation of hospitium nocturnum, see First Life, 50, 62. For the Coleharbour at Sandwich, see Boys, 790. For a fanciful derivation from "coluber" as a tortuous winding ascent, see Archaeologia, xxxvii. 123.

Pountneys Inn was granted to the Heralds by Richard III when he incorporated them into a college (for grant dated March 2, 1484, see Antiq. Report, i. 162, i.e. of

May 10, 1413[1], an order had been issued that no bows,
arrows, arms, or artilleries were to be sold to the Scots
or other foreign enemies, and on June 8[2], a fletcher
named Nicholas Mynot was appointed keeper of the king's
arrows in the Tower, where smiths[3] were kept sweating at
the forges making guns, other guns being also wrought at
Bristol[4] and elsewhere, and forwarded on carts[5] to London.
Towers and scaling ladders[6] were constructed, engines were
built for battering and mining walls, also pontoons for
bridging rivers[7], and vangs[8], brooms[9], crows, beaks,
tribuls, caltraps, iron hawes[10], pegs, wooden plugs[11], and
tampons[12] for the guns were bought in great quantities

Cold Harbour in the parish of All Saints), but it reverted to the crown in 1485, Stow,
ii. 206. In the time of Henry VIII it was called the Manor of the Rose on Lawrence
Pountney Hill, see Henry VIII, 1, 2, 153. For remains of it with the crypt ("recently
destroyed," Benham-Welch, 23), see H. B. Wilson, 194. For Merchant Taylors' School
built on part of the site, see Stow, i. 169.

[1] Claus. 1 H. V, 31 d.

[2] Pat. 1 H. V, i. 12, where he has his livery and a house in the Tower, between that
of the Clerk of the Works and the Wakefield Tower; see also Cal. Pat. H. IV, i. p. 156.
Cf. garde de nos settes, Priv. Seal 658/45. For 620 garb of arrows bought of him at
1s. 6d. per garb, and 20 garb at 2s., with payments of £41. 13s. 9d. and £33. 3s. 4d. for
same, see Rec. Roll 3 H. V, Pasch., June 25, 1415. For other purchases from him see
Iss. Roll 7 H. V, Pasch., June 1, 1419.

[3] Artifices ingenii conspicuos, Strecche, 266 a. For fabri wanted for making guns
and ironwork in the Tower, see Pat. 1 H. V, v. 24 d, Feb. 12, 1414. For £22 paid to
William Marsh, the king's smith in the Tower, see Iss. Roll 1 H. V, Mich., Oct. 10,
1413. Called William Atte Mersh in Iss. Roll 7 H. V, Pasch., May 18, 1419; also Cal.
Rot. Pat. H. V, i. 346, June 6, 1415, where he is to take 40 smiths across the sea.

[4] For £107. 10s. 8d. paid to John Stevens (Wylie, iv. 546) for making a large cannon
at Bristol, see Devon, 332, Feb. 20, 1414.

[5] For order for horses, oxen, carts and waggons (*plaustra*) to bring guns and other
necessaries from Bristol to London, see Pat. 1 H. V, iii. 19, Sept. 1, 1413; Rym. ix. 49.
For 2 carts drawn by 6 horses each to carry 2 gros canons gettans pierres, 4 petits canons
gettans plommes et 2 grosses grilles de fer in 1377, see Lacabane, 34, 46. For short
carts with 3 horses each, see Caxton, Fayt, ii. 21.

[6] Gesta, 25. For 24 great ladders with double steps, strong enough to carry 4 men-
of-arms, see Caxton, Fayt, Bk. ii. ch. 28, where the ladders are from 26 to 40 ft. long
and fitted with 3 pulleys at the upper end.

[7] Vita, 34, where all these preparations are placed in 1414.

[8] i.e. spades, Ducange, vi. 1410; Wylie, iv. 231. For £20 pro emptione vangar' et
tribul' see Iss. Roll 7 H. V, Pasch., July 10, 1419. Cf. corbels, vanz (not vauz) and
besches, Blk. Bk. of Adm. ii. 200.

[9] Cf. pro scopis ad mundand' ecclesiam (1460), Jackson, 209.

[10] For 40s. paid pro vangis, scopis, tribulis et hawes de ferro bought for the king's
use, pro certis secretis causis regem ad hoc moventibus, see Iss. Roll 1 H. V, Mich.,
Oct. 10, 1413.

[11] Cf. 16 pieces de gros merrein pour fair iiij quevals pour les iiij gros canons,
Bréard, 71.

[12] Cf. 200 tappons de bois pour mettre et ferir dans les canons (1382), Bréard, 71;
also 70 grans chevilles de fer pour ferir à force les tappons dedens les canons, ibid. 70;
for 10,000 tappons, to be placed between the charge of powder and the gun-stone, see
Lottin, i. 186. Called a wad in Clowes, i. 366, or tampyne, i.e. a bung for a cask,
Man. and Meals, i. 121. For turners to make tampons from elm-wood, see Caxton,
Fayt, ii. 26. For tampons pour traire pierres de canons at 25s. per 100 (1404), see La
Fons.-Melicocq. 26. For tampons de mespliers (i.e. medlar), see ibid. 10.

"for secret reasons known to the king." Oaks were felled[1] at Langley and Eltham; nails were bought from the nailers and cords and cables from the ropers[2], and wainscots[3], oarpieces[4], and boards[5] were stored by the thousand for building, fitting, and repairing ships[6], while galleys and other vessels of all nationalities were seized on the high seas and pressed into the general service[7]. Painters[8] were hired in London and the suburbs, and the craftsmen of the mistery of armourers fetched armour by land and sea[9]. Tapicers, both men and women, were full of orders for cloth[10], and crowds of turners and joiners[11] were helding[12] axes, lances, picks, and mattocks, while the shieldmakers were fixing up linden shields[13] with skins and horn and glue. The king's pavilioner, John Cony[14], gathered in workers to make and mend tents; sea-coal was bought at Newcastle at 6s. 6d. the chaldron[15], and cargoes of osmund, copper, flax, pitch and squaregood[16] or woodash

---

[1] For July as the right month for felling trees, see Christine, Livre des Faits, 271 (=de ces arbres on doit faire aès).

[2] For roper, see Pat. 2 H. V, i. 9; Maldon Rolls, 12/6; Cotton and Dallas, iv. 60; Wylie, iv. 276.

[3] For £26. 13s. 4d. paid for 2000 wainscots at 20 marks per 1000, see Iss. Roll 1 H. V, Mich., Jan. 25, 1414.

[4] Orepeces, Exch. Accts. 44/24.

[5] For weldichebordes (4d. each) and botineholtbordes for repair of Porchester Castle (1321–1338), see Archaeol. Inst. (Winchester), 38, 42.

[6] For purchase of timber, boards, iron, pitch, tar, bolts, cords, cables and other things to mend and repair the king's ships, see Pat. 1 H. V, iii. 30 d, July 22, 1413, where William Catton is keeper of the king's ships.

[7] Chomo fu fato de moltre altre choche e nave de tute generacion dizente de Christiantade, Morosini, ii. 58. For apprehension in Venice lest their galleys should be seized on their arrival in London, see Ven. State Papers, i. 56, 57, Aug. 19, 1415.

[8] Operarios et artifices ad misteram picture pertinentes, Pat. 1 H. V, v. 36 d, Jan. 13, 1414.

[9] Pat. 2 H. V, i. 19, April 22, 1414.

[10] For order to John Stout, tapicer, see Pat. 2 H. V, i. 19, April 26, 1414. For the tapicers or tapsers of London, see Letter Book I, 115, 150, 153, 207; Wylie, iv. 278.

[11] For 100 lances without heads bought for 50s. from John Wyndmer, joiner, see Rec. Roll 3 H. V, Pasch., June 22, 1415; also £25 for 1000, ibid. May 1, 1415.

[12] For £15 paid to John Bower (or Bowyer), tourner, for helding (i.e. bending, Stratmann, 334; Halliwell, i. 443; Murray, Dict., s.v. *Hield*) axes, see Iss. Roll 3 H. V, Pasch., April 16, 22, 1415.

[13] Cf. mæremium vocat' lynde (see Stratmann, 401) in an order to Richard Isak, sheldmaker, Pat. 2 H. V, ii. 19 d.

[14] Or Conyn; not Covyn as Rym. ix. 200, where there is an order to him dated Feb. 5, 1415. Cf. Priv. Seal 658/52, June 13, 1413.

[15] Exch. Q. R. Accts. 44/23; see p. 45, note 11. For 1 qr. de carbon marin' (2s.), temp. William of Wickham, see Walcott, Prices, 85; also 61 qrs. carbon (40s. 8d.), ibid. For busche et charbon, see Deschamps, viii. 104, 137, 187. For coal mines (13th and 14th century) at Boussages in Languedoc, see Bulletin hist. du Comité de Travaux historiques (1899), p. 326.

[16] Cf. squarkynnyd (i.e. burnt), Halliwell, ii. 791.

came in from Danzig and other Hanse towns on the
Baltic.

The above are some of the items which abound in the
Exchequer accounts of the year, but the general list is well
summed up by a contemporary writer[1] in a single passage,
in which he specifies the stores accumulated at Windsor
and elsewhere as comprising hauberks, helmets, shields,
corslets, bucklers, lance-heads, gauntlets of plate, swords,
bows, many thousands of arrows, casks full of bowstrings,
axes, saws, wedges, hammers, forks, mattocks[2], hoes, spades,
caltraps, and other tools for felling and splitting wood and
mining walls.

[1] Strecche, f. 266.   In Bouvier, 428, Henry takes with him stores de traict, de bom-
bardes, de toute artillerie, de vivres outre qu'il en venoit tous les jours d'Angleterre par
mer très largement.

[2] Fossoria, cf. Ducange, s.v.

CHAPTER XIII

THE CABOCHIANS

BUT while these preparations were pressing on in England events had passed in Paris which demand a short consideration here if we are rightly to grasp the full meaning of the national disaster which subsequently overwhelmed our unhappy neighbours in France.

Large areas of that country had long been accustomed to the meetings of local bodies periodically convened to legalise the taxation which might be levied by feudal superiors in the districts or sub-districts and other areas over which they claimed sway. These were known as councils of the Three Estates[1] and were composed of representatives of the whole population of the areas in question, regarded as three groups or arms[2], viz. the clergy, the nobles and the people, the latter being usually synonymous with the Commons or burgesses of the towns, otherwise known as the Third Estate[3]. A modern writer has described this last group by the comprehensive name of non-nobles[4], but they called themselves the "upper hand[5]," the "good men[6]," or the "superiors" who paid the representatives they sent[7] up, as distinguished from the "small folk[8]" who had as yet no part or lot in the matter.

[1] See App. J.

[2] For the 3 bracos of Aragon and Valencia in 1412, see Viciana, iii. 160; cf. brachia ecclesiastica, patricia, plebeia, Valla, 1043. For bras ecclesiastique, militaire et royal (i.e. the towns) in the Cortes of Catalonia see D. M. J. Henry, ii. 43.

[3] Misnamed "la nation entière moins la noblesse et le clergé" by Thierry, see Ménorval, II. p. iv; clergé noblesse et tiers état, A. Thomas, i. 10, 29, 30; Raymond, iii. 58 (of Béarn). For the 13 "bonnes villes" that formed the tiers état in the Provincial Estates of Lower Auvergne see Tardieu, Clermont, i. 474; do. Dictionnaire, 35, 36; Thomas, ii. 56; Mazure, 235; Michel, ii. 340.

[4] Les non-nobles, Duruy, i. 312.

[5] For main majeure (including the mercadors), main moyenne and main mineure as classes among the burgesses at Perpignan see Vidal, 81, 266; tam majoribus quam minoribus, Benham, 46. For superiores v. mediocres see Wylie, iii. 204, note 4. For majores v. mediocres at Wells in 1407 see Holmes, 71.

[6] Probi homines, prud'hommes de la cité, Dognon, Instit. 196, 198; boshoms, proshomes, solempnials personas, Magen, viii. 208, 320.

[7] Tant de bouche que autrement, A. Thomas, i. 49.

[8] Le menu peuple, le pauvre peuple, plebeii, roturiers, Dognon, Instit. 155, 157, 193; Débat, 42; la gent menuda, Magen, 257; le menu commun, Bourgeois, 615, 616; Wylie, iv. 137, note 6; called "le quatrième état sans nom" in Ménorval, II. pp. iv, viii.

As to the origin of these assemblies, which were usually held in some religious building[1], much variety of opinion has long prevailed, but there can be no question as to their universality in the beginning of the 15th century and so omnipresent is the institution that it has been averred with much probability of truth that every province[2], county, seneschalcy[3] and bailiwick[4] had its states, though of course the smaller the area the more insignificant would be the assembly and the more ineffectual the check. Such at least is the fact in regard to Central and Southern France, but in the north the sectional states had largely fallen into disuse, and in place of them larger assemblies known as States General had been summoned at intervals[5] for the last 100 years to meet in Paris from the whole vast area known as Languedoil[6]. Writers on the English Constitution were long ago struck with their resemblance to our English Parliament[7], by which name indeed they are not unfrequently designated[8] and their origin and functions have proved a very fascinating subject for researchers[9], from whose conclusions it appears to be established that the earliest meetings of the States General date no further back than 1302[10] and that they met spasmodically at subsequent dates[11]; that they were usually called together to

[1] A. Thomas, ii. 52; e.g. in the Black Friars at Clermont, Rivière, i. 311. For picture of a meeting temp. Charles VII, see Wallon, 524, from MS. 1450 Bibl. de l'Arsenal, Paris.

[2] "Etats particuliers des provinces," Rivière, i. 309.

[3] For assemblées de seneschaussée originating since 1302, see Dognon, 195, 205.

[4] For Estates of the bailiwicks of Dijon and Auxois meeting at Dijon and Semur, see Plancher, iii. 465.

[5] Sans périodicité, Grande Encycl. xvi. 514.

[6] For États Généraux de la Langue d'Oyl, see Bailly, i. 142; Coville-Lavisse, 340; Delachenal, Chas. V, i. 120, 249, 341, 389; Mirot, 47.

[7] Fortescue (Plummer), 113; cf. Thatcher-Schwill, Middle Ages, 507. For the Model Parliament of 1295 see Tout, Advanced Hist. 191.

[8] Omnium Galliarum (*sic*) concio magna quam Parliamentum nominant, Tit. Liv. 83; parlement général, Blanchard, iii. 328 (of the 3 Estates of Brittany); Parliamentum, Wals, ii. 336 (of the Estates of Normandy); son Parlement, N. Travers, i. 520; Rouquette, 134. For the English Parliament called "The Three Estates of the Realm" in 1431, see Rot. Parl. iv. 371; Bekynton, ii. 264 (1434).

[9] For bibliography of the subject see Viollet, Instit. iii. 245.

[10] i.e. notables of Languedoil and Languedoc convoked in Paris by Philippe-le-Bel against the pretensions of Pope Boniface VIII, April 10, 1302, Michel, ii. 263; Picot, i. 191; do. Documents, pp. viii, 1; A. Thomas, 21; Duruy, i. 343; Rambaud, i. 268; Hallam, 118; Musson, xlii; Fréville, Commune, i. 251; Duruy, i. 334; A. Gasquet, i. 168; Galton, 15.

[11] e.g. 1303, 1308, 1317, 1351, 1355, 1356, 1357, Picot, Documents, *passim*; Desjardins; Mirot, 6. For meetings in 1314 and 1338 see Rittiez, Hôtel de Ville, 103, 113. For meetings of Etats généraux de la langue d'oil, Nov. 4, 1356, and April 1357, see Michel, ii. 316, 323; Dureau de la Malle, 41.

lighten the difficulties of some embarrassed ruler in times of stress[1], and that they had little actual power except as a safety valve for dangerous effervescence[2], in which case they loudly voiced the pent-up discontent and their meetings were often followed by passionate outbursts of revolutionary violence[3]. So now with the periodical distress in France came once more the periodical attempt at remedy, and when all other means had been exhausted in the search for funds it was determined once again to try the effect of a meeting of the States General in Paris.

No such meeting had been held for the last 30 years[4], and the session which opened in the Hostel of St Paul on Jan. 30, 1413[5], resulted in some pretty plain speaking. When the king asked for a "good big tax[6]" the demand was met by a roll as thick as a man's arm petitioning against the extortions of the royal officers who were eating up the people, coming in poor and going out rich and despoiling the country for wages and gifts[7] to keep them in wantonness and luxury[8], while the people starved. The goods of such men, said the petitioners, ought to be seized until they had been brought to account, and if the king wanted money he could get it by laying a tax of 1000 francs apiece upon some 1600 of the richest persons in the country[9]. No wonder that it was getting to be regarded as an act of treason to summon the Estates, for their meetings clearly

---

[1] Dans des vues purement personelles, Boulé, i. 280.
[2] Pour se concilier l'opinion publique, Grande Encycl. xvi. 524.
[3] e.g. the Jacquerie in 1358 and the Maillotins in 1382.
[4] Picot, i. 250, 254; or even since 1369, Grande Encycl. xvi. 514, 515, where the meetings of 1381, 1382 are regarded as "assemblées de notables." For the meetings in Nov. 1380, see Mirot, 29.
[5] Bibl. de l'Ec. des Chartes, vi. 279; Barante, iii. 22; Picot, i. 254; Schmidt, ii. 232; Desjardins, 115; Meindre, iii. 53; Batiffol, 187; not 1415, as Lavisse-Rambaud, iii. 135; nor 1412, as Marle, 27.
[6] Une bonne grosse taille, Capefigue, iv. 12; Perrens, Democratie, ii. 195; Picot, i. 255; Bibl. de l'Ec. des Chartes, vi. 279.
[7] Gens de néant non avanciez par importunitez et puissance d'argent et autrement— trop d'officiers qui ont trop grans gaiges et dons et si gastent tout, Ec. des Chartes, vi. 282, from complaint of the clergy of the provinces of Rheims, Sens, Rouen, Bourges and Lyons presented on Feb. 3, 1413. For remonstrance delivered on the same day by the city and University of Paris see Moranvillé, Remontrances, 420; cf. exactiones fere quotidianas quæ in luxum atque in pompam magnatorum populis esurientibus imponuntur, Clamenges, Ep. p. 335 (written in 1414).
[8] Quid in verbo, in cultu, in gestu, in epularum excessu, vestium deformitate, mores effæminatissimos, quid in omni genere et gradu luxum inauditum omnia consumentem atque pervastantem, Clamenges, Ep. p. 192.
[9] Raymond, iv. 16 (E. 61) from a copy in the Archives at Pau, Barante, iii. 35.

tended "to lessen the authority of the king[1]." But in the present instance it was only another case of "words said, soon dead[2]," and the sittings closed on Feb. 24, 1413[3], with no better result than to lay bare the bitterness of the existing ill-will at a time when division meant nothing less than national destruction. In Guienne the Duke of Clarence[4] was waiting his opportunity to pounce; the coasts of Normandy were ravaged by an English fleet; the plains of Picardy lay open to attack from the English at Calais and even Rheims began to fear that they might fasten on the rich wide field of Champagne and none would be able to hold it against them[5]. And with all this crushing need no money was in sight, no corn, no stores, no supplies[6], while the very air was filled with apprehensions of coming disaster.

This year a Carmelite in Paris had a dream in which he saw the new English king aloft in great pomp on one of the great towers of Notre Dame banning the king of France, who was surrounded by his people clad in black and seated on a stone in the parvis below[7]. A year ago the young Dauphin Louis[8] had been hailed as the restorer and comforter of France, whose noble nature was her only hope, her refuge and her remedy[9], but he was now turning a deaf ear to his instructors and heeding neither bit nor curb[10] but shaping surely for a petty life[11]. Young as he was the fact could not be concealed that he was growing

---

[1] Comines, quoted in Lannoy, Œuvres, lxxxiii.

[2] Voix oye (i.e. ouïe) est tost perie, Cochon, 264; Perrens, ii. 203.

[3] Desjardins, 123.

[4] Not the Duke of Lancaster, as Bibl. de l'Ec. des Chartes, vi. 278; Desjardins, 115.

[5] Bibl. de l'Ec. des Chartes, vi. 281, 283.

[6] Nullum superesse fiscum, nullum aerarium, nullam curam rei frumentariæ, nullas ad dubios rerum eventus in urbibus munitiones, nullam in opibus annonam repositam, Clamenges, Ep. p. 191.

[7] Juv. 478; Michelet, v. 303; H. Martin, v. 539; Coville, 207; Lavallée, Jean Sans Peur, 268.

[8] Not Charles, as Towle, 281. For fancy picture of Louis, see Mézeray, ii. 572; S. E. Harding.

[9] Tuam ingenuissimam naturam, Clamenges, Epist. p. 154; tu spes una, tu remedium, tu malorum refugium es, ibid. p. 155; spem remedii, spem salutis et præsidii hujus desolatissimi regni, ibid. p. 268; see also Christine de Pisan's dedication in her Livre de la Paix, Bibl. Nat. MS. 7398, f. 22; Wylie, iv. 78, note 8, written in 1412 (called 1413 in S. Scrope, p. xvii); Pannier, Joyaux, xxvi. 217, where the Dauphin is un homme meur, très sage et pesant en œuvre et en fait, though only 15 years old.

[10] Clamenges, Epist. p. 268.

[11] A mener vie sy petite que son corps estoit en trez grand péril et dangier d'entrer et cheoir en débilité et feblesse de maladie (written May 2, 1413), Bibl. de l'Ecole des Chartes, vi. 61; Pannier, Joyaux, xxvi. 210.

fat and clumsy[1] and too fond of dress and finery, dancing while his friends were dying and turning night into day[2] to the strike of organs[3] and the taboring of the drum[4] and all such other means whereby the devil could kindle and blow the fire of lechery[5], so that Frenchmen who loved him well[6] still feared the prospect of another mad reign[7], when they heard how readily he wept[8] or swooned and spat up blood[9]. They cautioned him against idle flatterers, praised the marriage state and warned him that it was not safe for a prince to be too much alone or too freely given to carnal pleasures[10]. But above all he must not raise those whom nature meant to be low[11], for a rivulet in flood does more damage than a big river in steady flow[12]. To such men he must give no office or authority, for these things belong by right to burgesses of ancient line[13]. For how should a lout who barely knows his paternoster[14] and has little enough sense to govern himself[15] be set to govern others? "Egad,"

---

[1] Croist et augmente en corpulence de sa personne, Douet d'Arcq, i. 325, April 3, 1410; suffisament grand et gros de corps, pesans et tardif et po agile, Baye, ii. 235; Norm. Chron. 247; Ménorval, ii. 44.

[2] Sa condition estoit d'emploier la nuit à veiller et po faire et le jour a dormir, Baye, ii. 232.

[3] Moult grant plaisir avoit à sons d'orgues lesquelx entre ces autres oblectations mondains hantoit diligemment, Baye, ii. 231. For "noys of organes" see Misyn, 10.

[4] St Denys, v. 234; Juv. 487. For the tombar, tymbre, tabour, tabal see Vidal, Perpignan, 313, with picture of fife and drum. For picture of tabour see Willemin, i. 64, pl. 106 from the Abbey at Bon-Port near Pont de l'Arche.

[5] Chaucer, Pardoner's Tale, 12,413.

[6] Le peuple qui de bon cuer fin l'aime, Christine de Pisan in her Prayer to the Virgin written in 1414, Thomassy, 174; Koch, 82; not 1404, as Pisan, III. p. ii.

[7] St Denys, v. 16, 28, 80; Michelet, v. 294; H. Martin, v. 531; Perrens, ii. 210; Coville, 20, 181, 203, 332; Brachet, 58.

[8] Monstr. ii. 354; Ordonnances, x. 176; Le Fèvre, i. 82; Paradin, 565.

[9] St Denys, v. 80; Juv. 481; Barante, iii. 61. Cf. de statu tenui ducis Guienne, St Denys, iii. 266; cf. her herte blode spitte, Lydg. Troy Book, 402, 466.

[10] Ne te passionum absorbeat impetus nec juveniles tibi dominentur concupiscentiæ, ne te frangat et enervet libido vana atque inepta dissolvat lætitia, etc., Clamenges, Epist. p. 158. See also Christine de Pisan in Thomassy, 159.

[11] Thomassy, 162; Lenient, Satire, 255. Cf. Quelle folie...rebellion contre vos mageurs es estas ou Dieu vous a esleuz, devez estre humble soubz seigneurie de greigneurs et loyaument faire voz ouvrages, from Christine, Livre de la Paix, Viollet, 169; c'est grant folie de avancer et edifier ung homme vicieux de basse condition que ne surhaulchast jà ceulx qui par nature doivent estre bas, cf. Gerson in Michelet, v. 323; Lannoy, pp. lxxxi, 370.

[12] Le ruissel qui court par l'abondance de la pluye va plus orgueilleusement que celuy qui vient de la fontaine et court toujours, Lannoy, 370.

[13] For la haute bourgeoisie, see Delaunay, 30.

[14] Cf. Wylie, ii. 490.

[15] Cf. Les assemblées de gens du commun peuple qui n'ont pas eu ne n'ont sens n'entendement de discerner et de pressentir le bien du mal, Ordonnances, x. 211.

cried the mocking Christine, who lived right through those dreadful days[1], "no government could well be worse, for these fools are proud, however low. And what else could you expect when a jobbard[2] suddenly finds himself the master? He cocks his bristles, manages his pike, growls and swears and thinks he knows his business only too well[3]. Just look at their meetings. It is real sport to watch them there[4]. The biggest fool leads off with one foot forward and the other behind, his hands at his sides and his apron on, and when it is over they come out as stupid as sheep and as savage as boars; no respect for prince or princess, lord or master[5]. Gentry is cheap and must be swept away. And how they love to kill and slaughter, to smash the rich man's coffers and stave his casks of wine[6]. To arm this riff-raff[7] and teach them war is just to pick the rod that will be used to thrash you[8]. If fighting must be done, it should be by men who do naught else but fight[9]. No! let the little commons stick to their work[10]. Give them peace and justice and salute them kindly in the street[11], but don't let them wear outrageous gowns broidered with devices fit for gentlefolks. Punish all swearing and blasphemy; stop all silly meetings in one another's houses; and, as idleness is the mother of vice, set searchers to catch these wanton birds who do naught but haunt taverns, and

[1] Je Christine qui ay pleuré unze ans en abbaye close où j'ay tousjours puis demouré, Quicherat, Procès, v. 4; Wallon, 427, from her poem finished July 31, 1429.

[2] Malostru, i.e. mal instruit, see Cent Ballades, 63, 226; Lak of discrecioun sett Jobbardis upon stoolis which hath distroied many a comounte, Pol. Relig. Po. 40; see also Halliwell, ii. 485; Godefroy, s.v. *Jobard*; Murray, Dict., s.v. *Jobard*; Wright, Dict., s.v. *Jobbernowl*.

[3] Thomassy, lxxii. 163.

[4] For picture (14th cent.) of le démagogue qui prèche au peuple, see Dehaines, 545.

[5] Cf. n'avoit aucune révérence aux princes ny autres personnes, Paradin, 566.

[6] Thomassy, xxxiv (not lxxiii, as Wylie, iv. 138 note).

[7] Hazlitt, iv. 41; Clay, 13; Halliwell, ii. 684.

[8] Thomassy, 167.

[9] Und streiten sol die ritterschaft hert für die anderen vorgenant (i.e. the clergy and the workers), Wolkenstein, 102. For protest against this view, see St Denys, v. 548.

[10] For le menu commun, see Bourgeois, 615, 616; Wylie, iv. 137, note 6. Wer zu der arbeit ist geborn, der arbeit durch getrauen hort, &c., Wolkenstein, 82.

[11] O ses greigneurs soit humblement
Entre esgaulx familierement
Entre ses mendres amiable
Et entre dames honourable. Petit, 12, 130; Sauvage, 294.
Car humble est un grant noblesse
Ce me semble et bien aimable
Vers toutes gens et convenable. Petit, 123.

clap them into prison if they don't mind their business on the worky-days[1]."

But all this *bourgeois* indignation[2] only blazed up after Paris had passed through the furnace of the great "commotion[3]." On April 28, 1413[4], the Cabochians burst into the Hostel de Guienne in the Rue St Antoine[5], got the Dauphin into their power[6] and threw the Duke of Bar[7] and others into prison. Some days later[8] they forced themselves pell-mell into the presence of the king and made him don the white bonnet[9], entered the queen's

---

[1] Thomassy, 169; cf.
      Complicibus coeunt scissor, sutorque putator
      Cedentes operi plures de plebe creati. Blondel, i. 22.
      Avec eulx mainent savatiers
      Et cousturiers et vignerons
      Et daultres lessans leurs mestiers
      Plus que nommer n'en daignerons. Ibid. i. 105.

[2] Cf. cette muse bourgeoise (i.e. Christine), Lenient, 372.

[3] En certaines *motions*, Wassebourg, 461:
      Nulla timenda magis est pestis turbine plebis
      Ista lues agrum Francum fœdat luteossa. Blondel, i. 24.
      Nulle peste n'est tant doubteuse
      Comme de peuple *commotion*
      Qui toute France a fait boeuse
      Et partout mis sedicion. Ibid. i. 108.

[4] Rym. ix. 52; Baye, ii. 108, 304; Isambert, vii. 402; Ordonnances, x. 175; St Denys, v. 20, 170, 258; Monstr. ii. 449; Le Fèvre, i. 119; Bibl. de l'Ec. des Chartes, vii. 62; Cousinot, 146; Gaguin, ccl; Crevier, iii. 363; H. Martin, v. 531; Sismondi, xii. 407; Perrens, Democr. ii. 209; Coville, 185; Barante, iii. 44; Valois, Conseil, 129; not April 21st, as Sauley, 17.

[5] Coville-Lavisse, 344.

[6] St Denys, v. 104–106; Monstr. ii. 346; Le Fèvre, i. 77; quasi in custodiam conjecti, Bucelin, 375. For declaration of the Dauphin that this was all done without his consent, see Gouvenain, i. 4.

[7] Not Béarn, as Goodwin, 11, 12; nor Berg, as Allgem. deutsche Biogr. xix. 503. i.e. Edward formerly Marquis of Pont à Mousson (Pontmous, Pontamouss, Lacomblet, iv. 115); Anselme, v. 513; Belleval, 141; Harl. MS. 782; Servais, ii. 298; Würth-Paquet, 221, where the marquisate is granted on July 12, 1417, to Adolph Duke of Berg, époux d'une Duchesse de Bar. He had just succeeded to the title on the death of his father Robert Duke of Bar, April 12, 1411, Mas Latrie, 1553; Renard, 69; Clouët, iii. 532. He was Lord of Cassel near Hazebrouck, which came to him from his mother Yolande of Flanders, A. Duchesne, Dreux, Bar-le-Duc, 56; Renard, 252, 254.

[8] i.e. May 22nd according to Baye, ii. 112, 304; Bourgeois, 30; Bouvier, 425; or May 12th, St Denys, v. 40; cf. quâdam alterâ die, St Denys, v. 174, 258; "depuis," Ordonnances, x. 176; Mém. Soc. de l'Hist. de Paris, iv. 163; postridie, Rym. ix. 52; the week before Ascension (i.e. June 1st), Bourgeois, 613; called May 20th in Riezler, iii. 224; Allgem. deutsche Biogr. xix. 504.

[9] St Denys, v. 38, 52; Juv. 478; Bourgeois, 31; Le Laboureur, ii. 864, 867, 871; Gerson, iv. 660; Monstr. ii. 349, 350; Le Fèvre, i. 78; Cochon, 265; Isambert, vii. 282; J. Meyer, 240; Duchesne, 820; Daniel, iii. 852; Rapin, i. 506; Acta Regia, ii. 120; Michelet, v. 300; H. Martin, v. 533; Sismondi, xii. 416, 418; Thierry, I. lxv; do. Essai, 57; Schwab, 447; Vallet de Viriville, i. 9; Beaucourt, i. 13; Ramsay, i. 130; Coville, 193, 198. The white bonnet (not a white scarf as Gairdner, 93) was borrowed from the men of Ghent, Lettenhove, Flandre, iii. 80; Barante, iii. 50; Lavallé, Jean Sans Peur, 193, 197, 209; Wright, France, i. 465, 466; Ménorval, ii. 47. In the insurrection of Etienne Marcel, in 1358 (Duruy, i. 370; Picot, i. 76), the Dauphin (afterwards Charles V)

apartments, flung her brother Ludwig, Duke of Ingolstadt, who was captain of the Bastille, into prison in the round tower of the Louvre[1], and many others, including several of the queen's ladies, into the dungeons of the Palais[2]. Then having secured unrestrained possession of the capital they wreaked a red fool-fury on the Armagnacs with their gallows and their Seine[3], culminating in the execution of Pierre des Essars[4], formerly Provost of Paris[5] and Grand Master of the king's finance, whom they tied to a cart-tail, dragged through the streets on a hurdle and beheaded at the Halles on July 14, 1413[6].

It was amidst this outburst of mob-frenzy that King Charles VI accepted the famous Cabochian ordinance[7] which was solemnly published in the Parliament on May 26, 27, 1413[8]. It was meant to effect a radical reform in the administration of the finances of the country and modern students of French constitutional history have combined to chant its praises as a model of good sense and conservative moderation[9]. But it proved but a passing

was forced to wear the Paris colours, the red and blue cap (called red and green in Hoffbauer, St Paul, ii. 11).

[1] Bourgeois, 615; Capefigue, iv. 23; Meindre, iii. 64; Allgem. deutsche Biogr. xix. 504; Babeau, 39.

[2] Not that they threw the Dauphin into prison, as Mazas, Cours, ii. 171.

[3] Monstr. ii. 362; les Parisiens en faisoient mourir et noyer journellement sans ordre ne ordonnance, Le Fèvre, i. 84; qui faisoient prison privée, prenoient, tuoient, meurtrissoient, noioient par nuit sans quelconque ordre et forme de procez et par corruption d'argent, Gerson, iv. 659; pilleries, meurtres, roberiez et aultres deliz, Bibl. de l'Ec. des Chartes, vii. 67; puis les faire noyer et pendre, Martial, 15; D. Sauvage, 217; Paradin, 566; though Coville (Lavisse), 352, thinks that ils furent violents et maladroits *sans commettre de grands excès.*

[4] See Wylie, ii. 61, note 6; i.e. on July 1, 1413, Anselme, viii. 554, 556, where he is Lord of Thieux, La Motte, Tilly and Villerval; also Brièle, iii. 36.

[5] For seal of the Prévôté de Paris see Monget, i. 4.

[6] Gaulthier, v. 28; not July 1st, as Barante, iii. 60; Lavillegille, 71; Maillard, 82. His headless body hung for 3 years on the great stone gibbet of Montfaucon, Mézeray, ii. 563; D. Sauvage, 217. Haggard, 78, 95, calls him a "greedy and savage villain" and a "bold rascal."

[7] For summary of the Ordonnance Cabochienne (or Cabochine, Godefroy, i. 764) see Picot, i. 271–296; Desjardins, 125; Nouvelle Revue (1891), 378–380; Boulé, i. 311–336; Bailly, i. 158; Rambaud, i. 247. For the Grande Ordonnance of 1357 under Etienne Marcel, see Hallam, 122; Duruy, i. 369; Grande Encycl. xvi. 514.

[8] Rittiez, Hôtel de Ville, 199; Aubert, Organisation, 199; called May 21st in Sismondi, xii. 419; or May 25th in Chéruel, Administration, i. 89; Finot, Paix, 8.

[9] Cf. ces ordonnances étaient bonnes et sages, Barante, iii. 57; un vaste plan de réforme embrassant tous les besoins de l'Etat, Péchenart, 53; un monument de prévoyance et d'administration, Capefigue, iv. 15; ce beau code de réforme administrative si sage et modéré, A. Thierry in Grande Encycl. xvi. 515; that great reform charter, Historians' Hist. xi. 168; sage dans ses principales dispositions, Boutiot, ii. 343; monument remarquable d'administration, Lavallée, i. 374; véritable code administratif, Lavisse-Rambaud, iii. 136; grande charte de réforme, Duruy, i. 419; ni révolutionnaire ni

flash[1], and for the men of its own day it was streaked with blood and nicknamed[2] from a brutal grallocher called Simon, or Simonet, Caboche[3], the hated leader of a "pack of butchers." At any rate it left no lasting mark and has to-day merely an antiquarian interest[4]. For the Paris *bourgeoisie* with the University at their head[5] were like the weathercock that turns with every wind[6]. They soon tired of the strife and denounced the Cabochians as "sons of iniquity[7]," though only a short while before they had excused their atrocities on the ground that they had put pity for their country before all else[8]. On Aug. 4, 1413[9], another "sheep's-clothing peace[10]," known as the Fourth Peace or

novatrice elle n'avait rien de démocratique, Coville (Lavisse), 348; conservatrice et non révolutionnaire, Clamageron, i. 460; sa sagesse incontestable, Meindre, iii. 61; la belle et sage ordonnance, Viollet, Textes, 155; une remarquable tentative constitutionnelle, Viollet, Institutions, iii. 203; ordonnance admirable, Ménorval, ii. 49.

[1] Cet éclair passager de l'esprit démocratique, Puiseux, Docteurs, 28; demeura stérile, Meindre, iii. 61.

[2] Schmidt, ii. 237.

[3] Simon le Coustailler dictus Caboche boum, Rym. ix. 55; not Jean, or Janot, as Paradin, 562, 567, 568; Lobineau, i. 530. See App. K.

[4] N'a qu'un intérêt de curiosité, Rambaud, i. 247.

[5] For reaction in the University of Paris see Aubert, Comp. 200. For a later appeal to the clergy not to meddle with popular risings cf.

> O clergie plain de sapience
> Qui avez divine science
> Et sanz mouvrir commun de ville
> Car telle chose est trop subtille.   Regnier, 60.

Legrand (14) thinks that la plupart des clercs et des dignitaires de l'université sortaient du peuple and were therefore les premiers promoteurs des modifications d'opinions et de croyances.

[6] St Denys, v. 154; Daniel, iii. 861; cf.

> A fane that turneth in al windes.   Melusine, 298.
> Folwe the wynd as doth the fane.   Kail, 8.
> The comoun peple chaungeth as a phane
> Today thei wexe and to-morwe wane
> As doth the mone thei be so flaskysable
> Who trusteth them schul fynd them ful unstable.
> Lydg. Troy Bk. 116.

> Helas! he qu' esse de commun
> Comment il est tantot tourné
> Adès a l'autre, adès a l'un,
> Ainsi que le vent est mené.   Martial de Paris, i. 30.

[7] Bibl. de l'Ec. des Chartes, vii. 97.

[8] See letter from the people of Paris to the people of Noyon, ibid. vii. 63; Perrens, ii. 218.

[9] St Denys, v. 128, 178, 260; Juv. 485, 490; Baye, ii. 118, 125; Bibl. de l'Ec. des Chartes, vii. 67; Cousinot, 149; Bourgeois, 614; Brando, 162; Barante, iii. 72; Riezler, iii. 221; Coville, 355; not September, as Monstr. ii. 398.

[10] Paix fourrée, Perrens, ii. 242; Coville, 5, 341, 350; Thomassy, Gerson, 216; pacem ovinis pellibus circumtectam, St Denys, v. 82; vulpinis pellibus involutam, ibid. 122. For supposition that the phrase refers to the Cabochians see Steyert, in La Mure, ii. 124; but see Cotgr., s.v. Cf. Godefroy, s.v. *Forrer* (=garnir de faux cheveux), also ibid. Complément, ix. 652; Littré, 1708; Jervis, 198; Wylie, iv. 31; "une paix telle-quelle," Dreux du Radier, iii. 143; "paix boiteuse," Valois, iv. 109. For account of the fool who

the Peace of Pontoise[1], was announced with bell-ringing and processions[2], whereat the Cabochians fled from Paris[3], the Duke of Berry returned[4] and the reins were once again in the hands of the Armagnacs. Straightway the Duke of Bar[5] and Duke Ludwig were released unharmed from their prisons and the latter, who had already married one rich French wife[6], very soon obtained a further solatium by marrying[7] another, viz. Catherine the young widow of Peter of Evreux, the younger son of Charles II, king of Navarre, whereby Ludwig acquired the title of Count of Mortain. But just as he had effected this second marriage with a French heiress his father died[8], and soon afterwards[9] he returned to Ingolstadt, whither he had sent many mule-loads of good things from France including jewels, pearls, enamels, crystal- and goldsmiths'-work reputed to be worth 5 million gulden[10], some of which were used to build the church of Our Lady in that town, and with the rest he lived " French fashion[11]," in riot and licentiousness, his exactions bearing so heavily on the religious houses in his own country that he was excommunicated on Sept. 5, 1433[12], and remained so till his death in 1447[13].

The fall of the Cabochians was marked by a triumphal

bought a pax and furred it (la fit fourrer) see Juv. 443; Dreux du Radier, iii. 144; which Guizot (ii. 244) explains as l'enfoncait dans sa fourrure; cf. "this is the cloak of peace," R. Black, ii. 265.

[1] Pax quarta appellata, J. Meyer, 241 *a*; Paradin, 566; D. Sauvage, 218; Mézeray, ii. 564, who thinks it was brought about par un coup presque miraculeux; Daniel, iii. 854.

[2] Monstr. ii. 399.

[3] Tyrrell, 288 [168], thinks that the butchers were driven out by the carpenters (see Ménorval, ii. 51); also Cassel, i. 524, who gives a fancy picture of "the battle."

[4] For payment dated Aug. 9, 1413, for satin moyen vermeil to make un grant estandart for him pour chevaucher vers la ville de Paris, see Toulgoët-Treanna, 105.

[5] News of his release reached his brother the Cardinal of Bar on Sept. 8, 1413, Wassebourg, 467; Roussel, i. 353.

[6] i.e. Anne daughter of Jean de Bourbon Count of La Marche and Vendôme, Häutl, 124.

[7] i.e. at the Hostel of St Pol on Oct. 1, 1413, H. Sauvage, 237; page 158, note 3. Cf. ein wip hette von Franckenrich, Basler Chron. v. 155.

[8] i.e. Stephen III, Duke of Bavaria and Lord of Ingolstadt, Windecke, 7, who died on Oct. 2, 1413, Brachet, 4 (with pedigree); or Sept. 26, Häutl, 123.

[9] He was knighted by Charles VI at the siege of Soissons on May 21, 1414, Monstr. 335; and was down with the flux at the siege of Arras in Aug. 1414, Monstr. 343, 347, 350.   [10] Turmair, v. 539.

[11] Venus in ipsis sic regnat quod inter affines et propinquos raro tuta sunt matrimoniorum fœdera, St Denys, v. 576; more Francigenarum, ibid. 380; Postel, 5.

[12] Riezler, Nachtselden, 540.

[13] i.e. May 2, 1447, H. Sauvage, 238; Allgem. deutsche Biogr. xix. 502; called July 3 in Odolant-Desnos, i. 454. See App. L.

entry of the Duke of Orleans into Paris, though it was hard to get him to lay aside the mourning that he wore for his murdered father[1]. Henceforth " Burgundian " and " Armagnac " were to be forbidden terms, peace was to reign sweetly between the rival dukes[2] and Gerson, who claimed that the University of Paris had the right to speak not only in the name of France but of the whole world[3], now protested that in supporting the Cabochians she had acted under terrorism and threats[4]. His house in the close on the north side of Notre Dame[5] had been pillaged by the mob, because he had abandoned it rather than submit to pay their demands[6], and he had to take sanctuary[7] in a garret[8] in one of the towers of the church for the last six weeks[9] of that perilous time. He now came down from his hiding-place and sketched the outlook in a lengthy sermon[10], which he preached before the University of Paris on

---

[1] Juv. 486; Sismondi, xii. 434; Coville, 377.

[2] St Denys, v. 136; Sismondi, xii. 432; Coville, 364.

[3] Gerson, iv. 583; Chéruel, Administr. i. 89.

[4] Propter minas et terrores, Denifle, Chartular. iv. 269, Nov. 15, 1413.

[5] In claustro Beatæ Mariæ, Launoi, 84, 483. For Jean Fusoris' house in claustro parisiensi, see Mirot, 245. For pictures see Zeiler, pt. i. p. 51 (1620); Hoffbauer, i. 1, 45, 46, 63; Bournon, 185; Masson, 116; called Hôtel de St Jean-en-Grève in Dufour, Chancelier, 195, who thinks that it was burnt by order of the Duke of Burgundy. For statement that Gerson lived in the Collège de Navarre as Chancellor of the University, see Launoi, 84, 98, 99, 489. Up till the end of the 14th century the Chancellor of Notre Dame had been head of the faculty of theology in the University; after that date they only recognised their dean as president, Feret, iv. 22.

[6] St Denys, v. 64; Perrens, ii. 238; Michelet, v. 125, who calls him cet homme de combat et de contradiction.

[7] Not comme dans une forteresse, as Geruzez, i. 223; Masson, 269, who heightens the picture by supposing that he was up amongst broken stones and cross-beams after having watched his clothes being torn up in the parvis below and his books pitched into the Seine. Cf. dans les combles de l'Eglise, Meindre, iii. 53; Ayroles, ii. 24; au dessus des voutes, ibid. i. 22; sous les combles, Faguet, 170 [137]. For sanctuary in the tower of the cathedral at Rouen, see Bibl. de l'École des Chartes, xv. 342. For une chambre pour ceux qui y seront en franchise (i.e. sanctuary) in the church of St Jacques de la Boucherie in Paris, see Le Villain, 45, where it is said to be sur les voutes; not "in the vaults" as Péchenard, 56; Alcock, 38; Ménorval, ii. 48; nor "in the crypt" as Haggard, 95; called "high vaults" in Coville (Lavisse), 348; Kitchin, i. 511, 513.

[8] Crevier, iii. 366; Michelet, v. 315; H. Martin, v. 538; Schwab, 450; Thomassy, Gerson, 211, 219; Lasale, 16; Fougère, 19; L'Etuy, ii. 68. It was called la Crastine (i.e. the Morrow) or the Holiday (vacatio, see Ducange, s.v. *Crastina*), Bibl. de l'Ec. des Chartes, xv. 161. For garite=a place of refuge see Athenæum 20/1/09, p. 107; or a watch tower, Halliwell, s.v. *Garett*; Murray, Dict., s.v.

[9] i.e. since June 27, 1413; propter malignitatem temporis currentis, Bibl. de l'Ec. des Chartes, xv. 161, from the Chapter Registers of Notre Dame; not 1411, as Dufour, Chancelier, 195.

[10] Gerson, iv. 657–677; Schwab, 449; St Denys, v. 136; Juv. 486; Boulay, v. 236–253; Crevier, iii. 368. He is called "le Bossuet du xive siècle" in Faguet, 170 [137]. For 60 of his sermons in French not yet edited in the original but translated into Latin by Jean Brisgoek and published in Wimpheling's edition (1502), see Petit de Julleville, ii. 246.

Sept. 4, 1413, in the church of St Martin-in-the-Fields[1]. What need for him, he said, to speak of the coming government of the Dauphin and the Queen? The great lords and ladies knew all about that and he himself had no illusions on the subject. The more the wealth the greater the licence. The University was stuck ten times more full of eyes than Argus and they knew already that the peace would soon be broken[2]. Still he called upon the dominant party to seek no vengeance for the past, but only to stand for truth in the future[3], reminding them that peradventure there were not only 10 but 1000 righteous in the city, who ought to be pardoned if they did not persist in evil[4]. True that for the last few months they had kept their king and queen in durance and rendered more obedience to a set of whoreson varlets[5] than to King or Dauphin, knighthood or clergy. But you cannot make a greyhound of a ban-dog[6] or a sparrow-hawk of a buzzard. Henceforward let them bundle out[7] all free-lances, make a good treaty with England and let no subject strike alliance with his country's enemies without the king's permission. Let the knights be paid and rest content with their wages. Then if they fall defending truth and justice, they will be God's martyrs, if otherwise they will be martyrs of Hell. Let the bishops be inquisitors to root out error from the Faith, even unto death[8]; and let the clergy stand for truth, not labouring with their hands[9]; while the citizens must know their place, not striving to be arms when Nature meant them to be legs[10]. Within the last few years 100,000 persons had been killed[11] and France was impoverished by more than 3,000,000 livres. But now the king must be above party, for a king who takes a side is lost[12]. And let there be one central court of justice with officers not sworn to either party and not so poor that they

---

[1] Feret, iv. 91.　　　　　　　　[2] Gerson, iv. 673.
[3] Ibid. iv. 658.
[4] Ibid. iv. 659.
[5] Varlet paillard, ibid. iv. 660; see Cotgr., s.v. For "horsson" see Brut, ii. 593.
[6] Mâtin, Gerson, iv. 661, see Cotgr., s.v. *Mastin.*
[7] Bottés hors, Gerson, iv. 661.
[8] Ibid. iv. 670.
[9] For clergy forbidden to trade see Vidal, Perpignan, 373.
[10] Gerson, iv. 675.
[11] Ibid. 666. For 200,000 killed through the schism see Fages, ii. 98; Wylie, iii. 5.
[12] Un roy se perd qui se partit, Schwab, 451.

must suck the people's blood and leave them like the wretched beggar, who cried out not to chase away the full flies that had gorged enough from his sores, lest hungrier ones should come and sting him worse[1]. Paris had just taken on the Armagnac device—*le droit chemin*[2]— yet each party still holds that those who are not with them are against them, and the man who keeps "the right way[3]," without turning aside to either, falls between two stools or drowns between two floods[4]. Henceforward, therefore, if any man should ask you who you are for, say: "I am just a Frenchman, for my king and no one else; that is my 'right way' and God grant I may never swerve from it[5]!" The one strong power must be the king[6]. Look at your schoolboys! If one hits another he must not hit back but complain to the master, otherwise he gets birched himself. But since the night of the Porte Barbette our teaching has been all the other way. The preacher names no names and calls for no punishment on any man, but he strikes at the speech of Jean Petit[7], which not so long ago the University of Paris had solemnly approved, when even he himself had been so far carried away by his indignation as to assert that force for force was Nature's law and that in the words of Seneca a murdered tyrant is the most welcome offering to God[8]. But now his conscience took

[1] Thes newly come me shal moche more smertre assayle, Secreta, 180.

[2] Gerson, iv. 657, 660; Masson, 271; cf. "la droicte voie," Blondel, i. 150. For "Regardez Roi la droyt voy" on a subtlety at the coronation feast of Henry V, see Cookry, 4. For payment for embroidering "le droit chemin" on 4 mantles of violet Brussels cloth for chamberlains and other officers of the Duke of Orleans see Add. Chart. 2424 (Sept. 5, 1413). The Duke wore this motto on his jacket at the reception of the Duke of Bourbon in Paris in 1413, Le Fèvre, i. 117; Coville (Lavisse), 350; Maulde La Clavière, i. 35. For jackets (*huques*) embroidered with this motto given to the Orleanists by the Dauphin see Odolant-Desnos, i. 485. Cf. Weiss, i. 119; also on a violet band, see Capefigue, iv. 32.

[3] Cf. I will keepe the right way, Stow, Chron. 349. For "the rizte way" see Lydg. Troy Bk. 224, 244, 251, 320, 383, 407, 468, 474, 484; ryzt as line, ibid. 419, 422, 430, 440; do. Nightingale, 27.   [4] Gerson, iv. 668.   [5] Schwab, 452, 456.

[6] For coins struck in Paris with the legend "Vive le Roi et ses Amis" see Affry de la Monnoye, xx. 3. Cf. l'autorité du roi était à la base, au centre, au sommet à tous les degrés de l'édifice de l'administration, Rivière, i. 216. For the king as "tout puissant," see Ménorval, II. pp. iv, viii.

[7] Wylie, iii. 94. See App. M.

[8] Nulla Deo gratior victima quam tyrannus, see Michelet, vi. 94; Thomassy, Gerson, 206; Schwab, 456;

> Quant tirant d'autruy sang rempli
> Puet on murtrir et acourer
> Ce qu'on luy doit est accomply
> Ne on ne doibt sa mort plourer.

Blondel, i. 125, who defends tyrannicide in his *Oratio Historialis*.

the larger view[1] that man must not do evil in order that good may come and when we defend perjury and lying, we destroy all possibility of human government and leave the state a helpless body without nerves or tendons. And this leads him to the stories of how the shepherds made a treaty with the wolves and the wolves broke it[2] and how the lion was sick and the fox prescribed a stag's heart for him as a cure, much like the courtiers now-a-days who recommend cutting-up so that they may get their share, and how the lion invited the stag to come to him in confidence and lifted his paw to rend him but the stag swerved and lost his horns; how when the lion called him a second time he went, like a fool, trusting to the fox's oath, and how the lion tore him open, while the fox watched his chance, stole the heart and ate it, and when the lion asked where it was, he laughed and said: "Do you suppose, my lord, that stag ever had a heart? If he had, he certainly would never have gone back to you a second time[3]." And then after this playful sally the preacher relapses into columns of the dullest of commonplace theology.

The sermon was followed by a royal banquet together with plentiful oaths and tears and a general request to disarm and turn hatred to goodwill, but within three days the vengeance began. All supporters of the Duke of Burgundy were removed from office[4]; Savoisi, Courcelles and many others took to flight[5], and the gallows was loaded again from the other point of view[6]. The Duke of Burgundy himself, when he found that the wind was all blowing in his face[7], had left Paris in disguise[8] on

---

[1] Not that he had opposed Jean Petit from the first as Jadart, 30; Henry, 149; Dufour, Chancelier, 194; Hoffbauer, ii. 34; Masson, 261; Alcock, 26; Steyert, ii. 590.
[2] For the fable see H. L. D. Ward, ii. 282, 289, 319, 338, 344, 349.
[3] Gerson, iv. 672. For the story cf. Quant tierce feiz i repaira sachiez qu'il naveit point de quer, Warnke, Fabeln, 227–231, from Marie de France (circa 1180); do. Quellen, 220; H. L. D. Ward, ii. 303.
[4] St Denys, v. 214, 220; Baye, ii. 154; Bourgeois, 617; Ménorval, ii. 52; e.g. Jean de Troyes, surgeon, one of the skevins of Paris, ceased to be concierge of the Palais, the post being given back to Antoine des Essars, whom he had displaced in the previous March, Aubert, Organisation, 320; cf. ou temps que Caboche et Maistre Jehan de Troyes regnèrent à Paris, Mirot, 194.
[5] St Denys, v. 144.
[6] Paradin, 568.
[7] Ibid. 570; Serres, 954.
[8] En abit dissimulé, Cagny, 85; Coville, 433.

Aug. 23, 1413[1], "with as much speed as if his deadliest enemies were on his track[2]," without saying good-bye to the Queen or the Dauphin[3], after an ineffectual attempt to spirit away the King with him to Flanders[4]. Accompanied by a very small band of followers[5] he made his way to Arras and arrived at Lille on Aug. 29[6], where he straightway opened negotiations with the English[7]. From Lille he moved by Audenarde and entered Bruges on Sept. 15, where he was presented with a cue of Beaune and another of red French wine[8]. Here he conferred with Chichele and the other English envoys[9], and on their departure for Calais he removed to St Omer, where he stayed from Sept. 25 till Oct. 10. On Oct. 19, as we have already seen[10], he had another interview with the English envoys at Lille, where he remained till Oct. 29[11]. After this he passed to Tournai which he entered on Nov. 5, 1413[12], together with his brother Anthony, Duke of Brabant, and his Chancellor, Jean de Thoisy[13], who had been appointed Bishop of Tournai in 1410[14] but had not

---

[1] Itin. 400; Le Laboureur, 899; Bourgeois, 616; Michelet, v. 319; H. Martin, v. 542; Schwab, 448; Barante, iii. 77; Lettenhove, Flandre, iii. 82; Coville, 374. It would appear from Plancher, III. ccxlvii, that he actually left on Aug. 22; not Aug. 31, as Cagny, 85; nor September, as Tyler, ii. 84. For a letter written in Paris on Aug. 23, 1413, announcing this news to the Duchess of Burgundy who sent a copy of it to Dijon from La Perrière near Dôle (Franche-Comté) on Aug. 29, 1413, see Gachard, 109.

[2] St Denys, v. 148; bien soudainement, Juv. 486; le plus hastivement que faire le peut, Cagny, 85; Coville, 433.

[3] St Denys, v. 166, 212, 262.

[4] A rege captâ licentiâ, Brando, 162; cf. Trahisons, 125; Cochon, 268; Le Fèvre, i. 108; Ordonnances, x. 453. De Florentin (i.e. Charles VI) a pris congiet
Et retourna avecques hastis
A poy gens dedens ses pastis. Pastoralet, 727.

[5] A bien petit estat, Cordeliers, 219.

[6] Monstr. ii. 401, 413; Itin. 400; St Denys, v. 220; Lettenhove, Flandre, iii. 83. He was still at Lille on Sept. 8, 1413, Gilliodts van Severen, Inventaire, iv. 254.

[7] Itin. 401, 402; Monstr. ii. 408.

[8] Eene queue rood wyns van Beane and eene queue roode vranx wyns, Gilliodts van Severen, iv. 254. He was still at Bruges on Sept. 22, 1413, ibid. 252.

[9] Page 152, note 1.

[10] Page 152, note 3.

[11] Itin. 402; Monstr. ii. 412; though from Coussemaker, 102, it would appear that he was at Bruges from Oct. 25 to 28, 1413, and at Ghent on Oct. 29.

[12] Itin. 403; or Nov. 6, Vandenbroeck, 102, 103.

[13] Valois, Conseil, 121, 123. He was also Chancellor to his father Duke Philippe le Hardi and his son Philippe le Bon, Feret, iv. 105, where he is wrongly called Choisy.

[14] He was translated from Auxerre on Sept. 17, 1410, Gams, 251; Eubel, i, 517. He died at Lille in 1433 and was buried in the cathedral at Tournai, Coussemaker, 136. For his seal Dec. 9, 1417, see Gilliodts van Severen, Invent. iv. 348. For his predecessor, Louis de la Tremouille, who was installed April 21, 1392 (Wylie, ii. 369, note 5), but did not make his public entry till Nov. 6, 1404, see Vandenbroeck, 59. He made his will on July 30, 1410, and died in the same year, Tuetey, Test. 261. He was a member of the Cours d'Amour in Paris, Piaget, 430.

yet made his public entry, for there had been some difficulty about his reception, and the Austin Canons had been preaching against him, possibly because he was a pronounced Burgundian partisan, the town being at that time loyalist[1]. At any rate the citizens now presented him with two fat oxen and two cues of Beaune and Rhenish, claiming in return, according to an ancient custom[2], the dapple-grey horse[3] on which he had ridden and the silver-gilt cup (*godet*) which he had used at the feast, the horse being subsequently sold and the money handed back to him in cash. The Duke afterwards visited Audenarde[4] and Ghent[5] and was back in Bruges on Nov. 21, 1413, this time accompanied by his future son-in-law the Count of Cleves, and there was much dancing and festivity[6]. From Dec. 7 to 13 he was at Antwerp[7], where he held a conference with his supporters to consider how best to recover his lost ascendency. Meanwhile the news of his preparations had reached Paris, where on Nov. 14, 1413[8], the Council issued letters requiring the northern towns to close their gates against him if he should again appear. The astronomers said that he was under the influence of Saturn[9]; his name was hissed in the streets of Paris and ribald songs were sung in the public squares deriding him and blackening him as a traitor[10].

Yet all this time the victorious Armagnacs were by no means a harmonious party and even the feasting was marred

---

[1] Vandenbroeck, 90, May 10, 1412. For picture of Tournai market-place and cathedral see De Witt, 65. For seal of Tournai, ibid. 441.

[2] Wylie, Constance, p. 45. For the jus dextrarii see Ducange, s.v. *Dextrare*; Cotgr. and Godefroy, s.v. *Adestrer*; or jus sescalcie (i.e. seneschalciæ), Ducange, s.v.; or la Vigaria, do. s.v. *Vigerius* (i.e. Vicarius).

[3] Qui estoit de pois gris lyart pomelé, Vandenbroeck, 104. Cf. Cotgrave, s.v. *Pommelé*; Halliwell, s.v. *Pomelee*.

[4] i.e. Nov. 7, 8, 1413, Itin. 403; Monstr. ii. 413. For view of Audenarde, see De Witt, 445, 593.

[5] From Nov. 12 to 20, 1413, Itin. 403.

[6] Daer daden dansen frauwen ende joncvrauwen van der stede, Gilliodts van Severen, Inventaire, iv. 258.

[7] Coville, 388; not Amiens, as Monstr. 307. Itin. 404–406 shows that he was not at Amiens at all during 1413 or 1414. He was at Arras from Feb. 26 to March 6, 1414, Itin. 406; also from March 23 to April 12, 1414, and again in May, 1414, ibid. 408.

[8] Bouchot, 273.

[9] Hemmerli, v. 3; Reber, 59, 460.

[10] Cochon, 270; Le Fèvre, i. 155; Barante, iii. 102. For children kicked and cuffed (*toucez et navrez*) for singing songs in favour of the Duke of Burgundy, see Leroux de Lincy, I. xli; cf. faulx traistre, murdrier et qu'il avoit faulsement tué le propre frère du roy (1411), Soc. de l'Histoire de Normandie, Mélanges, ii. 300 (1893).

by altercations, where the Dukes of Brittany and Orleans[1] "had words" over a question of precedence, and their followers nearly came to blows about it, in the course of which the Count of Alençon told the Duke of Brittany that if he really had a lion in his heart at all, it must be about the size of quite a little baby[2]. But if on some points they were divided, they were at least at one in their thirst for vengeance on the routed Cabochians. On Sept. 5, 1413[3], the ordinance was solemnly annulled at a *lit de justice*[4], a copy of it being officially torn up by the registrar, Nicholas de Baye, with his own hands[5]. On Sept. 18[6], the council[7] addressed a manifesto to the various courts of Europe repudiating all concessions made by the French king during the Terror[8] as extorted from him by violence[9]. Enclosed with this was a list of more than 60 names of the

---

[1] For documents of the Duke of Orleans signed in Paris Sept. 5, 30, 1413, and March 20, 1414, see Add. Chart. 2425, 2429, 2440.

[2] Monstr. ii. 409; Le Fèvre, i. 123; Paradin, 570; Barante, iii. 84; Odolant-Desnos, i. 486; Cosneau, Connétable, 29. For previous quarrels between the Count and the Duke see Dupleix, ii. 707; Villaret, xiii. 335; Roujoux, iv. 143, 166.

[3] Denifle, Chartularium, iv. 269; Aubert, Organisation, 199; called Sept. 3 in Finot, Paix, 11; or Sept. 8 in D. Sauvage, 200.

[4] i.e. a special meeting of the Parliament called with special solemnity to give publicity to edicts, Aubert, Organisation, 196. For picture of a lit de justice in 1331 see Bordier-Charton, i. 444. For un beau lict tout tendu et bien ordonné de tapisserie to represent a lict de justice see Juv. 366; Dreux du Radier, iii. 124; called trône du roi in Littré, s.v.

[5] Baye, ii. 306; Viollet, Textes, 168; Marle, 34; not by the king himself, as Laferrière, xx.

[6] Rym. ix. 51; St Denys, v. 170, 182; Finot, Paix, 49; not 14th, as Isambert, vii. 401; cf. Sismondi, iii. 435; Coville, 385. For the copy sent to King Sigismund see Finke, Acta, i. 219, from Vatican MS. Codex Palatinus, 594. For a copy in the Bibliothèque Communale at Chartres see Procès Verbaux de la Société archéologique d'Eure et Loir, i. 44 (1861); Viollet, 160–167; for copies at Dijon see Gouvenain, i. 4, and at Rodez see Affre, Aveyron, ix. 171, where the rising is called "la congrégation." For lists proclaimed in Paris Aug. 29, 31, 1413, see Boulé, Hélyon, 15, 24–26.

[7] For contrast between the composition of the Grand Council, i.e. mostly composed of soldiers under Burgundian rule, but including more clerics and civilians under the Orleanists, see Valois, Conseil, 136.

[8] St Denys, vi. 106, 152, 184, 192; Juv. 487; Le Laboureur, 909; Ordonnances, x. 170; Le Fèvre, i. 110–116, 143; Isambert, vii. 400; Brando, 164; Perrens, ii. 248, 253; Baye, ii. 140–143, 306; Mem. de la Soc. de l'Hist. de Paris, iv. 168; Sismondi, xii. 434; Barante, iii. 80; Thierry, i. lxix; do. Essai, 60; Coville, 380; Aubert, Comp. xxi; Beaucourt, i. 13; "durant les brouillés," Ordonnances, x. 140; Waurin, ii. 164; "durant les debaz et dissensions," ibid. 163; "les tribulations," Le Fèvre, i. 84; "les desroys," ibid. i. 119; "l'Émeute," Isambert, vii. 411; "les divisions," Mirot, 194.

[9] Subrepticement et obrepticement impétrée par grande impression de gens d'armes; cf. frauduleuses et subrepticement obtenues, i.e. the letters of proscription issued against the Dukes of Berry, Orleans, Bourbon, and Alençon, Charles d'Albret and others recalled Sept. 5, 1413, Huillard-Bréholles, ii. 193. For letter of Charles VI dated May 24, 1413, approving the arrests at the Hostel de St Pol, see Ordonnances, x. 68, 140, 141; Isambert, vi. 282. For a declaration by the Dauphin that his house had been broken into de son contentement et pour le bien de la chose publique, see Gouvenain, i. 4, from the archives at Dijon.

ringleaders who had escaped[1], including Simon Caboche, John of Troyes[2] and his son Henry[3], four of a family named Legoix[4], the butcher Garnot de St Yon[5], and Master Pierre Cauchon, a learned doctor of Rheims[6], whom Gerson dearly loved as a compatriot[7], and Clamenges as a tried and faithful friend[8], but whom the Frenchman of to-day feels it his duty to stigmatise as a vile, ambitious, murderous traitor[9]. In this manifesto the French Council called upon all kings, princes, lords and others to rally to the side of law and order, to have the document cried in their cities and fastened to the doors of their churches[10], and to punish any of the murderers whom they might find, or send them across to Paris where they would meet their well-merited doom.

There is no evidence that this early attempt at international extradition[11] was attended with any measure of

[1] Not that some of them were actually in England, as Lavallée, i. 375. In subsequent amnesties 500 *ignobiles* whose names were to be given were formally excluded from pardon, St Denys, v. 426; Monstr. 356; Juv. 502.

[2] He is called un quasi-littré in Ménorval, ii. 43; a "venerable surgeon," Haggard, 89.

[3] For 100 crowns taken by force in 1411 (*sic*) from William Cousinot, councillor of the King and chancellor to the Duke of Orleans, by Henricus de Trecis (i.e. Henri de Troyes), Simon Caboche, and Dionysius de Chaumont, see Moranvillé, 429, March 31, 1417.

[4] i.e. John (who was an échevin of Paris in 1412), William, and a father and son named Thomas Legouais, Rym. ix. 55. They were one of the four butcher families, Longnon, Paris, 39. In Nov. 1411 the Orleanists taunted the followers of the Duke of Burgundy as "Goys," as Legoix had headed the mob that demolished the château at Bicêtre, and the Burgundians retorted by calling them "Armagnagoys," Soc. de l'Hist. de Normandie, Mélanges, ii. 303, 314; cf. Gouays, bouchers et autres villains de Paris, Raoulet, 163.

[5] Not St Yno, as Juv. 511. He became pantler to the Duke of Burgundy, Longnon, Paris, 39 note, quoting La Barre, ii. 140. For a reference (Oct. 28, 1415) to butchers' stalls confiscated from Gernerius et Johannes de St Yon fratrum bannitorum, see Moranvillé, 423.

[6] Doctor theologus sed licentiatus in legibus, Gall. Christ. ix. 758; grand practicien et maître de droit, Quicherat, Aperçus, 99; un des plus savants de son temps, Cerf, 368.

[7] Gerson, ii. 328, who addresses him as compatriota carissime quem ego diligo, in veritate dilexi et diligam, though supposed to be his adversary in Hanotaux, 271.

[8] For letter of Clamenges written "apud Fontem" referring warmly to his fidelem et spectatam amicitiam, see Clamenges, Epist. p. 324; Beaurepaire, Juges, 29.

[9] Cerf, 363; cf. son odieuse personne, Sarrazin, Jeanne d'Arc, 19; le futur meurtrier, le nom exécrable, Ménorval, ii. 46, 54; "the miserable tool of Bishop Beaufort," Haggard, 187; Hanotaux, 272, regards him as a Fouquier-Tinville with an admixture of Talleyrand and Marat.

[10] As had been done in Paris, Ménorval, ii. 54.

[11] For an understanding between the rulers of Brabant and Liège to expel the remainder of the haterights and mootmakers who had been so badly beaten at Othée in 1408 (Wylie, iii. 180), see Dynter, iii. 307, 757, where they are called malefactores communiter heydrote et moytmakers appellat'. For "muytmackers" see Daris, iii. 42, 80; cf. Godefroy, s.v. *Muthemathe, meutemacre*, also s.v. *Siereshomme*. Cf. stershomme ou muetemakers, Mart. Anec. i. 1623. For "haidroits" see Moke, 278; "hedries," Henaux, i. 563, 567, 578. For "ryghtes and droytes" see Caxton, Curial, 14, translating Chartier, 395.

success, and indeed, even while the vengeance was in full cry, the Armagnacs were brought up sharply with the news that the enemy was again at their gates. For already the Dauphin had tired of the new control and had thrice sent letters[1] to his father-in-law, the Duke of Burgundy, begging him to come back and release him from this latest form of servitude. The summons was welcome and the Duke lost not a day in responding. On Jan. 23, 1414[2], he was at Lille, whence he moved with 2000 men-of-arms[3] by Arras, Noyon, Soissons and Compiègne[4], and entered St Denis[5] on Feb. 7[6]. On the following day he was before the St Honoré Gate[7] with his troops spread out between Montmartre[8] and Le Roule[9] outside the western wall of Paris, whence he sent a herald claiming entrance to the capital that he might lay his case before the King.

But the Armagnacs were forearmed. On Jan. 24, 1414[10], they had issued an order warning their enemy off and three days before his arrival there were solemn processions to the churches[11], and the Dauphin rode in full panoply to the

---

[1] i.e. on Dec. 4, 13 and 22, 1413. Cf. trois paires de lettres écrites et signées de sa main, Monstr. 399. For text see Plancher, III. p. ccxcviii; J. Meyer, 242 a; Paradin, 573; Barante, iii. 92.

[2] Monstr. ii. 424; Paradin, 575.

[3] For list of his principal followers see Plancher, III. 586. On March 5, 1414, a letter from the French king was read at Tournai stating that the Duke was approaching and that the goods of all the burgesses of Tournai who were with him must be confiscated, Vandenbroeck, 107.

[4] Ordonnances, x. 193.

[5] Pastoralet, 728.

[6] Itin. 407; St Denys, v. 242; Juv. 488; Fenin, 36; Bourgeois, 47; Baye, ii. 164, 167, 307; Monstr. ii. 431; Coville, 392; Barante, iii. 97; not Feb. 2, as Cochon, 271.

[7] For position of it in the enceinte of Charles V, now in the Rue St Nicaise (or Rue de l'Echelle) fronting the Hôtel de Normandie to the north of the Place du Carrousel, see Hoffbauer, ii (Tuileries), 3, 5, 29, Plate 1; do. (Palais Royal), 3; Lavallée, Paris, 327; Leroux de Lincy, i. 163; Truschet, III. v; Braun, vol. 1; Plan of Paris (1591) in Mem. de la Soc. de l'Hist. de Paris, ii. 402; Bonnardot, 96 (Plate VIII), 180 (Plate X), 262, 284; Berty, i. 164; do. ii. App. p. ix; Belloc, 269; Kitchin, i. 453. For picture of it see Bonnardot (Plate XII), 9, 10; Duruy, i. 295; Berty, ii. 317, 324; De Witt, 251; Wallon, 177 (restoration).

[8] For position of the Porte Montmartre, see Kausler, iv. Plate 14.

[9] Le Role, called Roole-lez-Paris in 1370, Berty, i. 283, 285, who locates the Chemin du Roule, now Rue St Honoré, cf. Tuetey, 434; Tollet, 39; Cosneau, Connétable, 32; entre Montmartre et Chaillot, Monlezun, iv. 166, i.e. a suburb on the south-west of Paris, the name of which is still preserved in the Rue de Chaillot near the Arc de Triomphe. For the Commanderie du Roule belonging to the Knights of St Lazarus of Jerusalem and Our Lady of Mount Carmel, see Vignat, 325. For their headquarters at Boigny near Orleans, see ibid. v–ix (with picture); also long list of their commanderies in France, ibid. 315–364.

[10] Plancher, III. ccxix.

[11] For officials of the Parliament accompanying the Chancellor to the church of St Magloire montez et compétement habillez on Feb. 5, 1414, see Delachenal, 131.

Place de Grève¹, where a notice was read out that the reasons given by the Duke for his intended return were all falsehoods and inventions. So, when he actually appeared, the gates were closed against him ; the walls were manned by trusty Armagnacs, and the workers of the Halles, on whose help he had relied², were kept disarmed at their daily toil³. Thus no answer followed the Duke's summons and for an hour and a half⁴ not a bow was drawn nor a shot fired. Neither side dared to begin and the aggressors drew off sullenly to bide their time again at St Denis⁵. On Feb. 10⁶ a royal ordinance was published in Paris, in which all the political crimes of the last six years from the assassination at the Porte Barbette to the drownings and hangings by the Cabochians were laid to the charge of the Duke of Burgundy, and after plentifully setting forth his "notorious lies" and "damnable designs" it declared his goods to be confiscated and himself a rebel and a traitor⁷. Finding himself thus checkmated he dared not fight, for though he had exhibited the Dauphin's very letters⁸ calling in his aid, yet the Dauphin now declared that he had never sent for him at all⁹. Accordingly he left St Denis at daybreak on Feb. 16¹⁰ and reached Arras on Feb. 26¹¹, where he summoned the Estates of Artois to meet him on March 2, 1414¹². On his departure the gates of Paris were reopened after having been closed for 14 or

¹ i.e. a sandy space on the north bank of the Seine with a cross for the prayers of condemned criminals executed there, see Zeiler, pt. 1. p. 51 (1660); Guilhermy, Itin. 321; Lavillegille, 12; H. Legrand, 59; Rittiez, Hôtel de Ville, 147-149; Leroux de Lincy, 197, from Missal of Jacques Juvenal des Ursins; Hoffbauer, i. 6, 10; Bournon, 45; MS. Reg. 20, vii. 189; Lavallée, Jean sans Peur, 200.
² Monstr. ii. 412, 413; Cordeliers, 219; Fenin, 36; Cousinot, 151; D. Sauvage, 226.
³ Monstr. ii. 457; Le Fèvre, i. 154.
⁴ Called 7 hours in Cordeliers, 220; or 3 hours in Cagny, 86; Coville, 43.
⁵ Vandenbroeck, 109.
⁶ St Denys, v. 268; Monstr. ii. 442-456; Isambert, vii. 412; Lettenhove, Flandre, iii. 84; Coville, 394, where the date of publication is Feb. 12, 1414, also Juv. 488; not Feb. 17, 1413, as Belleval, 6.
⁷ Ordonnances, x. 199; Bourgeois, 49; Le Fèvre, i. 153; Le Laboureur, 927; Isambert, vii. 412; J. Meyer, 242; Rapin, i. 507; Barante, iii. 100.
⁸ Cf. à la singulière requeste de Monsieur de Ghienne et par ses lettres, Vandenbroeck, 109, from the Duke of Burgundy's own statement on May 13, 1414. Cf. Le Fèvre, i. 140, 146, 151; Perrens, ii. 146.
⁹ Vandenbroeck, 107, Feb. 22, 1414. Cf. Celly te fuit que tu reclames, Pastoralet, 731; mais pour Florentin y delaie et se retrait de celle paie, ibid. 732.
¹⁰ Itin. 407; Coville, 393.
¹¹ Itin. 407.
¹² Monstr. ii. 440; Fenin, 38.

15 days[1], and the Armagnacs marked their triumph by publicly burning a copy of Jean Petit's apology for the murder of the Duke of Orleans. The author himself had been dead nearly three years[2], though his thesis had remained unrevoked since the day when it had been listened to without opposition by the Parliament and the University of Paris six years ago[3]. But now that his master was down, the moment seemed to have come to cast off the shame of it for ever. And so on Nov. 3, 1413[4], a gathering known as the Council of the Faith had met in Paris to reconsider the case, and on Dec. 27[5] the University condemned the propositions as erroneous in faith and morals. Further action in this direction would doubtless have ceased had the Duke of Burgundy recovered his ascendency, but now that he had fled a formal condemnation was pronounced on Feb. 23, 1414[6], by the Armagnac Bishop of Paris, Gerard Montaigu[7], whose masterful brother John had been beheaded by order of the Duke of Burgundy[8]. Two days later a copy of the odious disquisition was publicly burnt[9] on a scaffold in the parvis in front of Notre Dame[10], many persons clamouring that the author's bones should be dug up and burnt with it[11]. The condemnation was backed by a royal ordinance issued on March 16, 1414[12], and now

---

[1] Bourgeois, 48; Baye, ii. 169.

[2] See App. J.

[3] i.e. on March 8, 1408, Wylie, iii. 94.

[4] Mansi, xxvii. 712; Boulay, v. 257; not Nov. 30, as Bonnechose, Ref. ii. 109; Hefele, vii. 177.

[5] Lenfant, i. 360; Boulay, v. 258–264.

[6] St Denys, v. 276; Juv. 488; Hardt, iii. 9, 10, 12; Le Laboureur, 933; Baye, ii. 170; Monstr. ii. 419, 461; Isambert, vii. 411; J. Meyer, 241; Plancher, iii. 403; H. Martin, v. 545; Hefele, vii. 180. Not March, as Baye, ii. 307; nor 1411, as Thomassy, Gerson, 215. For condemnation by the theologians of Paris on Feb. 19, 1414, see Feret, iv. 97.

[7] He was appointed Bishop of Poitiers on Sept. 27, 1403, Eubel, i. 419 (called 1405 in Gall. Christ. ii. 1197; Gams, 602), whence he was translated to Paris on July 16 (or 26), 1409, Gall. Christ. vii. 143. He died on Sept. 25, 1420, and was buried in the chapel of the Celestines at Marcoussis, Gall. Christ. ii. 1198; Gams, 597; Eubel, i. 410.

[8] i.e. on Oct. 17, 1409, Gall. Christ. vi. 142; Merlet, 277. His body was hung on the gibbet of Montfaucon, Maillard, 69; Lavillegille, 66; Sellier, 30, 77, who calls him "un véritable maire du palais" (p. 33); Ménorval, ii. 36, 37.

[9] For similar treatment required at Tournai on May 26, 1414, see Vandenbroeck, 114.

[10] Maimbourg, ii. 356; Fleury, vi. 336; Crevier, iii. 376; Berault-Bercastel, xv. 103; Zürcher, 118. In Thouron (iii. 149), the sentence is pronounced and carried out on the same day, viz. Feb. 26, 1414; not 1411, as Masson, 261; nor Feb. 5, 1414, as Danvin, 117; nor Feb. 29, 1414, as ibid. 314. For picture of the Place du Parvis, see Tollet, 76; Kraus, II. i. 182.

[11] Bourgeois, 46, 49.

[12] Feret, iv. 98.

that their tide was at flood the victors further clinched their triumph by a great apotheosis of the murdered voluptuary and a big procession was organised to his grave in the church of the Celestines on June 10, 1414[1], when the students of the French nation of the university outdid themselves in the lavish sums they paid for wax[2].

But sterner preparations had already been advanced, for the Duke of Burgundy was not likely to be outfaced with paper resolutions and party processions, and on April 3, 1414[3], the King put himself at the head of a large army that had assembled at Senlis[4]. But he so far forgot the warning voice of Gerson that, instead of the white upright cross on the blue ground of France[5], he wore the white faction scarf or band of the house of Armagnac[6].

---

[1] Crevier, iii. 381, gives the year as 1415, because June 10 fell on a Monday in that year. For great obsequies at Notre Dame (at which Gerson preached), at the church of the Celestines (where the preacher was Jean Courtecuisse, the sublime doctor, Feret, iv. 144; Wylie, iii. 25), and at the Collège de Navarre on Jan. 5, 7, 1415, see Monstr. 353; Le Fèvre, i. 197; L'Ecuy, ii. 75; not that this was for the death of the Dauphin, as Boulliot, i. 448.

[2] Boulay, v. 270.

[3] Bouvier, 427; Paradin, 580.

[4] Isambert, vii. 412.

[5] De porter la croix droicte pareillement que noz diz ennemiz (i.e. the Dauphinists), Stevenson, i. 46; Longnon, Paris, 308.

      La droite crois ont au jupal

Florentinois (i.e. the French) pour leur enseigne. Pastoralet, 851.
For the white upright cross on French soldiers in 1484, see Wallon, 222; A. France, iii. 49, from MS. fr. 5054 in Bibl. Nat.; crucem albam rectam, St Denys, vi. 152; D. Lacroix, 26; Dusevel, i. 273; Paradin, 580. Charles VII adopted the white flag instead of the blue which was used by the English, Leroux, 95, though in St Denys, vi. 88 (1417), it is the badge of the Armagnacs. Cf. la croix droite blanche, Juv. 534, 535, 565; Beaucourt, i. 92; and in Monstr. 389, the Burgundians wear les droits croix devant. For Orleanists with white upright cross and Burgundians with the saltire or St Andrew's Cross at the bridge of St Cloud in 1411, see Zeller, Armagnacs, 77, from MS. fr. 5054.

[6] Monstr. ii. 466; Cordeliers, 221; Le Fèvre, i. 159; Barante, iii. 102; Coville, 395; Leroux, 82; Monlezun, iv. 137, 165, 168.

CHAPTER XIV

CONVERSION

THE belief in the wild days of Henry's youth before he ascended the throne has hitherto been bound up inextricably with the story of his altercation with the judge[1], as to which it must be acknowledged that, when all the evidence is sifted, nothing whatever remains but a 16th century tradition having no proved foundation in any known historical fact that comes within a hundred years of the reputed event. After having cut an indelible mark deep into the national mind through the Elizabethan drama the story slept for some 200 years, but interest revived when Alexandre Duval presented *La Jeunesse de Henri V* in Paris about a century ago[2]. Since then poetic treatment has ceased and the question has been more prosily, but not more profitably, debated from the standpoint of national and patriotic prejudice, with the unfortunate result that English writers have usually approached the story of the wild days with the prepossession that this slur ought to be removed from the character of their national hero, while the French still cast it up against the vaunted piety of their nation's ruthless conqueror.

As facts are wholly wanting[3] as to the episode of the judge, it is not surprising that under these conditions little progress has been made towards a settlement of the general

[1] See App. D.

[2] It was produced at the Théâtre Français on June 9, 1806, Duval-Pineu, x. p. 69. The author has himself given an interesting account (ibid. x. pp. 89, 92) of how he originally meant his royal libertine to be Charles II, but was forced to change the name lest he should be suspected of a reference to Napoleon Bonaparte who was the Cromwell of the hour. The piece was received in Paris by crowded houses for a period extending over 16 years (ibid. x. pp. 70, 91, 93), being twice translated, in Italy as *La Gioventà d'Enrico V* (Riccardo Castellani, Teatro Inedito, tom. 2, Leghorn, 1816), and in Spain as *Las Mocedades de Enrique Quinto*, Valencia, 1817.

[3] Kingsford, Chron. pp. xxxvi, 341.

question. Thus the Frenchman still delights in calling
Henry a hypocrite and a debauchee[1], while the Englishman,
if he gets so far as to admit that there is any basis[2] at
all for the stories of his "riotous fits of wine and harlotry[3],"
still palliates[4] them as "early petulance much exaggerated
by the vulgar minds of our chroniclers[5]" or "jollities and
practical jokes[6]," "the indiscretions and frolics of a high-
spirited young man[7]," or "boisterous amusements[8]," "noisy
pranks[9]," "tricks of youth[10]," "rampant hilarity[11]," "excess of
bubbling vivacity[12]," and so forth.

But just as the latest guesses appeared to be drifting us
into a non-committal admission that, after all, the tradition
of the wild days "may or may not be true[13]," we seem at
last to have come upon substantial evidence that even the
stories of the Prince's rifling the males[14] on the highroad

---

[1] Il se mit avec beaucoup d'affectation à se livrer aux pratiques de la religion et il
espérait se rendre populaire en agissant ainsi, Mazas, Vies, v. 554. De débauché il s'est
fait pieux et mystique, Lavisse-Rambaud, iii. 137. Sa jeunesse n'avait pas été aussi
turbulente et débauchée que lui-même voulait le dire par fausse humilité, Coville,
Valois, 364.

[2] "It seems very difficult to admit the possibility of there being any truth in these
stories," Sanford, 174, though he admits (p. 184) that they "may have been founded on
some unguarded actions." R. F. Williams (i. 193) finds "little historical evidence for
them." Aubrey (Rise, ii. 12) calls them "manifest exaggerations if not pure inventions."
Church (125) regards them as "dubious reports." Murray-Smith (60, 66) finds it
impossible to look upon the bust in the Jerusalem Chamber (which is of course a modern
production) and still believe in the legend. Oman (Hist. 219) considers the stories to be
"entirely worthless," and thinks that there "seems little room in his busy life for these
curious tales"; see also his Hundred Years' War, 104.

[3] Tennyson, 523. Tyrrell (i. 283) believes in "the riots of his youth"; do. Royal
Hist. 166.

[4] Purey-Cust (i. 215) thinks we may condone his unworthy conduct because his
mother died when he was only 8 years old. Cf. his "fast, disorderly, *somewhat*
scandalous life," Bearne, 261.

[5] Hallam, 574; Historians' Hist. xviii. 526; Rowlatt, p. iii; Aubrey, Rise, ii. 34,
who thinks that "Fabian seems to have led off the accusation."

[6] Cassell, i. 516, who thinks (i. 512) that he was "as dissipated as an heir-apparent
generally is" and "obliged to amuse his active mind with those youthful dissipations and
escapades" of "an intrinsically great mind temporarily occupied by the levities of youth,"
ibid. i. 516.

[7] Stubbs, iii. 83; cf. E. Hardy, i. 81, who thinks (p. 21) that his "follies" were
"heightened and exaggerated by selfish designers." Tout (Advanced Hist. p. 260)
thinks that he "caused some scandal by his wild and injudicious pursuit of amusement
during his scanty leisure."

[8] Gardiner, 299, who thinks that he may have developed these tastes after 1410, but
that there is no foundation for the stories of the judge, etc.

[9] Towle, England, 158.

[10] Famous Victories, 3, 3.

[11] Hudson, ii. 67.

[12] Ein Uebermass sprudelnder Lebenskraft, Pauli, Bilder, 270 (298).

[13] C. R. L. Fletcher, 313; who, however, "sees no reason to question the tradition
that he was a wild young man," Fletcher-Walker, 7.

[14] Wylie, iv. 92. Cf. in bagge nor male, Hazlitt, iv. 42.

are not merely "the fruits of Stow's imagination[1]," as has been previously supposed, but are genuinely vouched for by a prominent contemporary[2] who had excellent means of knowing what he reports, and the discovery must have far-reaching consequences in regard to other incidents of the reign which it has hitherto been the fashion to reject— including the dismissal of the "young lords and gentlemen that were followers of his young acts[3]."

However this may be, it is certain that from the very opening of his reign as King of England Henry had secured the goodwill of the clergy[4], who lavished flattery on him as the "Church's Champion[5]" and the "Christ of God[6]." Five days after the coronation, John Burghersh, the Prior of Lewes, wrote from London that the momentary gloom that had fallen upon England at the death of Henry IV had been dispelled by the glad consolation that he had left behind him a son of like name and equal virtue[7], without a hint of any apprehension for the future. Adam of Usk, whose eye was always on promotion, calls him a young man of the highest uprightness filled with wisdom and virtue[8], while Jean Waurin, a Frenchman who afterwards served

[1] Tyler, i. 307.

[2] i.e. James Butler, Earl of Ormond (see page 70); Wylie, iv. 90, note 1. "As I have learned of the credence before rehearsed," Kingsford, Biogr. 81; First Life, 17, where I expect that "the Translator" will turn out to be James Yonge (see page 81).

[3] Kingsford, Biogr. 74; do. First Life, xxix. 19. The story is in Stow, Chron. 557, followed by R. Brooke, p.p.p. 2. It appears also in Brut, ii. 594, where it is said that he "voyded al his housolde" (=charged them to avoyde his presence, Caxton, Polychron. 224), except three who had counselled him to forsake riot, to whom were added "12 gentylmen of sad governaunce" selected for him by "Dame Kateryn Swynfor, Countesse of Herforde," meaning apparently his grandmother, Joan de Bohun, for Catherine Swinford had died 10 years ago (i.e. in 1403, Wylie, ii. 283; iii. 259).

[4] Michelet (vi. 2, 11) calls him "l'homme de l'Église."

[5] Miles Dei, Gesta, 54; Goddis champioun, Pol. Songs, ii. 143; Christi militem, Rym. ix. 644; fortem pro fide pugilem christianissime zelantem, Usk, 121; sacrosanctæ Ecclesie pugilem atque protectorem, Clamenges, Epist. p. 348; Machabaeus, Gesta, 47, 86, where the words are the author's, not Henry's, as Nicolas, 242; see also Garter Black Book (temp. H. VIII), in Anstis, ii. 62.
            Of holy Churche he was chief defensour
            In all suche causes Christes chosen knyght.
                                Lydg. Fall of Princes, xxxiii.
        And thow (i.e. Henry VI) mayst be goddis champioun
        As that he was Judas the Machabee. Pol. Songs, ii. 143.
For his father's dying advice, ecclesiam orna et honora, see Strecche, f. 264 b.

[6] Gesta, 26; Chron. Giles, 24; nec solum te regem fecerit sed communione sui nominis te Christum et esse et dici voluerit, Clamenges, Epist. p. 350. For the king becoming by his consecration le Christ du Seigneur, see A. Gasquet, i. 42.

[7] Duckett, i. 256, April 14, 1413. Cf. Lyche his fader of maneris and of name, Lydg. Troy Book, p. 3.

[8] Usk, 120.

with him at Agincourt, pronounced him to be the most
virtuous and prudent of all the Christian princes then alive[1],
and shortly after his death his example was held up as
"stable in virtue without variance[2]." Onlookers at home
noted that he made a weekly shrift[3] and did no business
while hearing[4] or seeing[5] mass, as his custom was, three
times each day[6], but worshipped in rapt devotion[7], parked
in his pew[8] or oratory[9] and reverently crossing himself
when the service was done[10]; and the fact that these details
are put into such prominent notice would seem to indicate
a marked contrast to the outward demeanour of the ordinary
worshipper.

It was an age in which the writing of individual biographies was just beginning to bud[11] and we still possess
some highly interesting appreciations of Henry's character
sketched by friendly recorders who had means of first-hand
personal knowledge. One of these was a Benedictine monk
at Westminster[12], whose estimate was written during the first

[1] Waurin, i. 165; cf. la sua gran bontat, Jurade, ii. 257.

[2] Pol. Songs, ii. 144.

[3] Qualibet hebdomada culpas confessio mandat, Memorials, 66.

[4] In Caxton, Dial. 48, " oyr messe "= " here masse."

[5] Cf. goo *see* the sacrament is a good breakfast, Caxton, Dial. 48. Cf. Elle *vit* chascun jour messe, Deschamps, vii. 14.

[6] Il avoit coustume d'en oyr trois lune après lautre, Waurin, ii. 202. Que tous les jours il n'oye messe, Petit, 129, as a direction for the education of nobles. At his daily mass Henry gave the usual big penny (= 7d.) in alms and a gold noble (6/8, not 5/8 as Purey-Cust, i. 89) at the Maundy, at Easter and at Whitsuntide, with 40/- as a fee to the preacher on set occasions, Exch. Accts. 406/21, 19; Wylie, ii. 211, note 1; iv. 202, 306.

[7] Vita, 22.

[8] Dum missas audit illum clam cellula claudit, Memorials, 66. Cf. all thinge for his pewe bothe cosshyn, carpet and curteyn, bedes and boke, Manners and Meals, i. 179; Littlehales, II. xix; Hoskyns, xvii. For "yparroked in pews," see Neale, 7; Wylie, iv. 357; emparkez, Rot. Parl. iv. 78. For pewes or carrels (i.e. for books) at Durham, see Hurry, 125; also in the cloister at Westminster see Robinson and James, 2, where they are called studies. For 15th century instances of pews in churches, see Neale, 7–12, who believes that they were always benches. For payments charged for them, see Kerry, 77; Ch. Quart. Rev. li. 99. For ung petit parquet for the singers at Le Puy in 1416, see Medicis, i. 233; privy closett, Hodgson, 335.

[9] Cf. entre into an oratorie, Lydg. Temple, 29, 66. For an oratoire de cendail vermeil tiercelin with an altar and seat, see Mirot, Trousseau, 133, 150. For sendal (i.e. sarsenet, Cotgr. s.v.) de Tripe see Rot. Parl. iv. 228; cendal tiercaine, tercelaine noir, Godefroy, s.v.; or cindon de tripl', Wylie, iv. 197, i.e. three-ply, not of Tripoli as ibid. ii. 444.

[10] Walden, ii. 980.

[11] Cf. the biography of Filippo Maria Visconti, Duke of Milan (b. July 23, 1401; d. March 8, 1466), by Decembri, in Muratori, xx. pp. 986–1019; also of Francesco Sforza, finished in 1462 by John Simonetta, in Muratori, xxi. pp. 176–782; with another by Decembri in Muratori, xx. 1024–1045.

[12] Versus Rhythmici, in Memorials, 63, 75. Not by "the Chaplain of Henry V" (i.e. Elmham), as Bridgett, ii. 214.

year or two of the reign. This writer knows nothing about any marvellous conversion, but assumes that the new king had been a saint from his earliest years[1]. He pictures him as devout, abstemious, liberal to the poor, sparing of promises but true to his word once given[2], a quick, wide-awake man, though at times reserved and moody[3], intolerant of laxity in priests, chivalrous towards women, rigid in repressing riot and crime. His household was sound and sweet as spikenard, no Lollard or unholy thing could enter there; his stores were filled and his halls open and no loyal, well-conducted man need ever go empty away. He kept 24 beadsmen praying for him at a cost of 2*d.* each per day[4]; his chapel was stocked with singers and, when the service of praise swelled up to Heaven, all talk and jesting ceased[5] and every thought was chained intent upon the altar of prayer.

Another friendly estimate comes from the pen of John Strecche[6], who was a canon in the Augustinian Priory at Kenilworth, where Henry was as well known as he was at Westminster. It was at Kenilworth that he had been nursed after receiving his "shallow scratch" at Shrewsbury[7]; he stayed there for some time in the spring of 1408[8]; in 1414 he was there for building operations and boating on the pool and he spent some weeks there in the winter of

---

[1] In primo flore productus dogmate claro non traheris vitiis, Memorials, 64. Doctis consiliis seniorum teque dedisti, ibid.

[2] Raro promittit nec fit promissio ficta, Memorials, 67. Cf. rigide et dur mais fidèle à sa parole, Coville, Valois, 375.

[3] Nunc vivax nuncque morosus, Memorials, 67. Strickland (ii. 91) credits him with "a vindictive temper." Cf. tiiste et sombre, Bordier-Charton, i. 500.

[4] Oratores domini, Exch. Accts. 406/21, 19.

[5] Non fuit quispiam etiam de primoribus et optimatibus suis qui mediis interloquiis ea potuit aliquocies dissecare, Gesta, 91; Chron. Giles, 80.

[6] This highly interesting contemporary chronicle, now in the British Museum (Add. MS. 35295), was purchased from the Earl of Ashburnham's collection in 1897, and has not, so far as I know, been consulted by any writer who has hitherto dealt with the reign as a whole, though a short extract from it appears in Kingsford, First Life, p. xxviii. Though frequently very inaccurate in dates and figures it is to a large extent an independent account and certainly deserves to be published in full. The author is often a year wrong in his reckoning; e.g. he dates the marriage of Henry IV in 1402 (f. 263) instead of 1403, the meeting of the Coventry Parliament in 1405 (f. 263 b), instead of 1404, the execution of Archbishop Scrope on June 6, 1406 (f. 263 b), instead of June 8, 1405, and the landing at Touques in 1418 (f. 271 b), instead of 1417. He follows J. Page for the siege of Rouen and gives the number of the killed at Shrewsbury at 11,000 (see Wylie, i. 363), locating the battlefield as super ripa Sabrinae non longe a Salopia. Palmer, Shrewsbury, 10, gives the total of killed as 6000, of whom 4000 were on the side of the Percies.

[7] Hy IV, Pt I, v. iv. 11. Curatus per artem medicinae, Strecche, 263 b; Harpsfeld, Hist. 586; Wylie, i. 362.

[8] Wylie, iii. 118.

1416[1] before he made his second voyage to France, while near at hand was his manor of Cheylesmore[2], including the town of Coventry[3], where tradition says that he got into trouble with the mayor[4]. It is highly probable therefore that Strecche[5] must have known about him from personal observation. Yet he gives us no hint of any wild escapades or sudden conversion. On the contrary he describes him as a second Solomon, a Paris in looks, a Hector in valour, an Achilles in might, a Julius in talent, an Augustus in character[6], or dropping the comparisons he calls him circumspect, sagacious[7], wise in government, prudent and far-seeing in all his war plans with the added personal touch that he spoke in a low tone of voice[8].

In the next generation a biography of Henry V was written by an Italian humanist who was named Tito Livio[9],

[1] Wals, ii. 317.

[2] The manor (not a Priory, as Wylie, iv. 93) had belonged to the Earls of Chester, M. D. Harris, 130, 133, not to the Duchy of Cornwall, as Cassell, i. 156. It is called a royal manor in Dugd. Warwickshire, i. 139, 140. On Aug. 23, 1344, it was granted for life to Isabella, the mother of Edward III, Hist. MSS. 15th Report, App. Pt. x. 111, 112.

[3] For the Acct. Book of the Manor, 1542–1561, see ibid. 104. For the Chilesmore gate in the southern wall of Coventry, see Dugd. Warwickshire, i. 135.

[4] For the story of his arrest in St Mary's Priory at Coventry by the Mayor, John Hornesby (not Horne as First Life, xli), in 1412, see French, 78; Yonge, Cameos, 251; Dugd. Warw. 148; Wylie, iv. 93; from a list of the Mayors of Coventry ending in 1675, i.e. Coventry Corporation MS. B. 37, M. D. Harris, 140, quoting Harl. MS. 6388, f. 15; Athenaeum, 8/10/10, p. 420, from MS. 115915, in Birmingham Public Library; see also Reader, 26; Royal Visits, 8. In 1401 the Prince is known to have been at Chester in April, in London July 10, Barnet Aug. 9, St Albans in Aug., Coventry Aug. 12, and Shrewsbury, Sept. 5, 12, Add. MS. 24,513, f. 6.

[5] Strecche died after 1422. His family would seem to have been connected either with Norfolk or the West Country; e.g. John Strecche, esq. of Norfolk advances £16. 13s. 8d. to the king, in Rec. Roll 5 H. V, Pasch., April 23, 1417. For his seal, see Birch, 183, Plate xxv. For grants of land to John Strecche in Normandy, see Charma, 5. For John Strecche or Stretche, kt., of Sampford Arundel, near Wellington in Somersetshire, who was Sheriff of Somerset and Dorset in 1383, and died in 1390, see Collinson, I. p. xxxv; III. p. 26; Sheriffs Lists, 123; Inq. p. Mort. iii. 119, 127. For grants of property in Taunton, by John Strecche in 1415, to the Prioress of Whitehall or Blaunchesale at Ilchester, see Ad Quod Damn. 371; do. (List), ii. 741; Cal. Pat. P. R. O. H. V, i. 371; Collinson, iii. 300. For his property in Dorsetshire, near Sherborne, see Inq. p. Mort. iv. 34 (1418). For John Strecche "Chaundeller," of London, in 1415–16, see Cal. Pat. P. R. O. H. V, i. 415. For Katherine (d. 1422), widow of John Strecche, kt., who owned property in London which yielded 73s. 4d. p.a. in 1412, Archaeol. Journ. xliv. 81, see Inq. p. Mort. iv. 70. For William de la Wardrobe, otherwise called William de Stryche, see Waltham Rolls. For seal of Richard Strecche (i.e. a falcon), see Bloom, 179.

[6] Strecche, f. 279.

[7] Sagax et circumspectus, the same words as those with which he characterises Henry IV, ibid. f. 262.

[8] Voce pressâ verba parcens, ibid. f. 265 b; cf. Wylie, iii. 332; not that he was loquacious, as E. Hardy, i. 110.

[9] Called "Titus Livius Frulovisus," or "Forlivesi," Borsa, 68 (i.e. of Forli, Borsa, Corrdce, 509; Lyte, Oxford, 320, quoting Tiraboschi, vi. 1648; Pauli, v. 688;

in all probability on account of the elegance of his latinity[1]. He appears to have come from Forli near Ferrara[2], where he had often heard his father speak of the fame of the great English king, the conqueror of France. He studied the subject for months and years[3] and when his funds had run out[4], he made his way across to our country and obtained a position, like others of his fellow countrymen[5], in the household[6] of Humphrey, Duke of Gloucester, probably through his friend Pier Candido Decembri[7], himself a writer of biographies[8], who was preparing a Latin translation of Plato's Republic for the English Mæcenas[9], whose reputation for liberal largess[10] as a rich bibliophile[11] had

---

Kingsford, p. vii; Dict. Nat. Biogr. xxviii. 248), in his letter in the Biblioteca Riccardiana in Florence MS. 827, Borsa, 428, which has been kindly verified for me by Dr S. Morpurgo from the original; called "the *English* (!) Chronicler who ambitiously calls himself Titus Livius," Macfarlane, 34; Craik-Macfarlane, ii. 31; Macfarlane-Thomson, i. 569; "an unknown Italian who took the high-sounding title of Titus Livius," Creighton, Renaissance, 22. He has been usually called Forojuliensis (i.e. fr. Friuli), Tit. Liv. title-page; Warton, iii. 51; Kabel, 16; Kingsford, Biogr. 58; not from Cividale, as Niethe, 8.

[1] Certe fictitium, Hearne, Tit. Liv. iv; a pseudonym, Church, 45; a name obviously partially borrowed, Vickers, 379, though G. Voigt (ii. 255) thinks that Titus Livius was possibly his Christian name. For the practice of selecting great literary names for sons in the early days of the Italian Renaissance, see the case of Uberto Decembrio the father of Pier Candido.

[2] He is called "de Frulovisiis de Ferrara" in Rym. x. 661; Arundel MS. XII. in Black, 19; Kingsford, Biogr. 59; Emmerig, p. 5; or "Frulovisii Ferrariensis," M. Parker, Preface to Walsingham, § 2; not "Filonisiis," as Cotton, Cat. 198. Cf. aus Forli *oder* Ferrara, Caro 9. There is no evidence that he was a monk, as supposed by Mazas, Vies, v. 554.

[3] Multarum vigiliarum et lucubrationum causa fuerat, Tit. Liv. 2.

[4] Hinc amor itineris, hinc tanti laboris, hinc pecuniarum consumptio et in patria totius emolumenti mei exterminium, Tit. Liv. pp. vi, 2.

[5] e.g. Antonio de Beccaria of Verona, who was one of Duke Humphrey's secretaries; called "Antoine de Beccaria Verneys (or né de Verone) mon serviteur," the translator of the Periegesis of Dionysius Afer, *De Situ orbis*, Warton (Hazlitt), iii. 51; Epist. Acad. 767. For his translation of Athanasius' *De Humanitate Verbi*, with dedication to Duke Humphrey, now in the British Museum, Royal MS. 5, F. ii, see Macray, Ann. 10 (who calls him Antonio Beccara); Vickers, 377, 481, who calls it "one of the less known treatises of St Athanasius." For dedication of his translation of the Corbaccio, i.e. Corbacium adversus mulieres or "Laberinto d'Amore," of Boccaccio to Duke Humphrey, see Vickers, pp. viii, 377, 391.

[6] Qui me nutrivit et sustentavit, Tit. Liv. 2.

[7] See App. N.

[8] See p. 189, note 11.

[9] Mæcenas unicus, Bale, 583; Mæcenas, general of goodness and learning, Fuller, Worthies, i. 289; Pecock, Reule, 6; Pauli, v. 283; Borsa, 63; do. Corrdce, 509; Vickers, 417.

[10] Cf. "My lordes fredom and largesse," Lydgate, Tragedies, Bk. iii. f. lxiiii; "your liberal largesse," or "bountiful largesse," ibid. f. 67 d, translated for Duke Humphrey by Lydgate, circ. 1430–1439, see Lydg. Temple, pp. xcvi, xcviii, cv; Burlington Mag. vii. 198; G. G. Smith, 8; E. P. Hammond, 381.

[11] For books ordered by Duke Humphrey through Decembri in Italy, see Newman, 488, 492.

spread far and wide[1] among the humanists of the Italian Renaissance[2]. Duke Humphrey had a special interest in medical treatises, and as Tito Livio was himself a physician[3] as well as a poet and scholar[4], the road to advancement seemed open to him. In his new position he is officially referred to as Duke Humphrey's "poet and orator[5]" and on March 7, 1437, he received a writ of indigenation[6], whereby he was authorised to hold benefices and offices, just as if he had been an Englishman born. There is also a statement that he was made a member of the Privy Council[7], but this has so far eluded verification. Soon after this, having finished his Biography of Henry V[8] and being

[1] For his "name sprad thorough alle cristyn reaumes and in heathynesse," see Noblesse, 45.

[2] For his patronage of Italians, see Pauli, v. 688; Garnett, i. 242; qui studia humanitatis summo studio in regnum vestrum (i.e. England) recepit, Æn. Sylv. Op. 548. Ex Italiâ magistros asciverit poetarum et oratorum interpretes, Æn. Syl. Epist. (Basle), 105, i.e. to Sigismund of Austria, in Creighton, Corrdce, 99; Vickers, 376, who calls him "the typical Renaissance Prince" (p. 346), or "a son of the Renaissance" (p. 348), who was "unique in the history of his country and his age, in taking an interest in the classical authors of Greece and Rome" (p. xviii). He is called "this universal patron," in Warton, iii. 51; "the nearest approach in England to an Italian Prince," Creighton, Renaissance, 18.

[3] Cf. inter physicos et artistas doctor unus declaratus sum, i.e. at Toulouse in 1441, Borsa, 63, 428. For Livio's knowledge of and liking for medicine, see Borsa, 68; do. Corrdce, 509. In his letter to Decembri Duke Humphrey refers to copies of Celsus and Galen, which Decembri is sending to him, adding that he possesses several volumes of the latter (Galieni plura volumina possideo, Borsa, 428, 429). For Giovanni dei Signorelli, a native of Ferrara, physician in the household of Duke Humphrey, naturalised in 1433, see Rot. Parl. iv. 473; Vickers, 381.

[4] For some of his Latin hexameters, see Kingsford, Biogr. 59, from Cott. MS. Claudius, E. iii. f. 353vo, in which he speaks of himself as "solvite vatem," "favens vati," &c.

[5] Rym. x. 661. Cf. qui et poetas mirifice colit et oratores magnopere veneratur, Æn. Sylv. Op. 548, i.e. in a letter to Adam Moleyns, who was then a protonotary of the Apostolic See and afterwards became Bishop of Chichester, whom Æneas describes as dignitate parens, aetate frater; cf. Creighton, Renaissance, 20, who calls him Molyneux; Vickers, 348. Adam Moleyns was presented to the living of Winterbourne Earls, in Wiltshire, on Oct. 18, 1432 (Cal. Pat. Hy VI, ii. 223), also to Kempsey, in Worcestershire, Oct. 14, 1433 (ibid. ii. 322), and Gisleham, in Suffolk, June 18, 1435 (ibid. ii. 457). He was connected with the foundation of King's College, at Cambridge (ibid. iii. 516, 532, 557), and died Jan. 9, 1450 (Dict. Nat. Biogr. xxxviii. 131).

[6] Quod ipse sit indigena, Rym. x. 661. For Duke Humphrey's French secretary, Maufurny, naturalised in 1425, see Rot. Parl. iv. 314; Vickers, 377, i.e. Master Dreux Manfurny or Manfurni, Cal. Pat. Hy VI, i. 131, 283, where he receives the prebend of Coton in the collegiate church of Tamworth on July 16, 1423, also a prebend in St Stephen's Chapel at Westminster, May 21, 1425, and that of Brightling in the Free Chapel of Hastings, June 9, 1425 (ibid. 283), which latter he resigned on Feb. 18, 1438 (ibid. iii. 156), where he is still secretary to the Duke of Gloucester. His name does not occur as a graduate of Paris in Denifle, Chartularium, Vol. iv. For Vincent Clement of Valentia who had been naturalised on Oct. 7, 1439, and is described as Duke Humphrey's orator in 1440, see Papal Letters, viii. 274, 275; Kingsford, Biogr. 70.

[7] Hearne in Tit. Liv. p. vii, quoting from a MS. of Francis Thynne penes Cl. Anstisium (?=J. Anstis).

[8] Kingsford, Biogr. 60, 68; he began it after his naturalisation in 1437, Eng. Hist. Rev. xxiv. 84; called between 1437 and 1447, in Emmerig, p. 5.

entangled with debt, he discovered that Britain was not such a rich place as he had been led to expect[1]. So with the hope that he might live to serve the English king and some day sing our country's praises[2] he returned to his native land[3] and up till quite recently all further trace of him had disappeared.

But about 15 years ago an undated letter[4] of his was discovered written to Pier Decembri from Barcelona[5] and still preserved in the Palazzo Riccardi[6] at Florence. The letter[7] shows that by that time he had returned to Italy, where he had visited Decembri at the court of Duke Filippo Maria[8] at Milan, and had been staying at Toulouse where he had a copy of his book made[9] which he sent to his friend, who subsequently made an Italian translation of it which is still preserved in the Imperial Library at Vienna[10]. Nearly 300 years elapsed before Livio's book was printed in this country in the original Latin[11] but a manuscript translation of it into English was known to the historians of the Tudor age[12]

[1]
> In Britones habitat talis penuria rerum
> Ut si quippe meos nolui sufferre labores
> Insontemque meam morbo sine ducere vitam,
> Unus ego multis pauper multo ere ligatus
> Sum quod ego teneor persolvere; solvite vatem,
> Sic liber valeat fines remeare suorum
> Et liceat veniens quantus fuit ipse reverti
> Corpore vel studiis animum cum mente paratus.
>> Cott. MS. Claudius, E. iii. f. 353 b.

[2]
> Da pater hoc mihi da regi servire britann̄
> Alta canam clarissima gesta tuorum.
>> Ibid. f. 353; Kingsford, Biogr. 59.

[3] Cum mihi jam instaret in patriam meam reditus, Tit. Liv. 2.

[4] Supposed to have been written in 1441, Borsa, 63; or "about 1440," Kingsford, Biogr. 59.

[5] Baigusiam (or Bargusiam; for the Bargusii see Liv. xxi. 19, 23) quam Barzanonam vocant.

[6] i.e. the ancient palace of the Medici (Rothschild, 61), now the Biblioteca Riccardiana, the property of the State.

[7] It, together with Decembri's reply, is in a volume of Decembri's correspondence, Cod. Riccardiano, 827, ff. 83, 84; Borsa, 63, 428; do. Corrdce, 509; Vickers, 380.

[8] Decembri was made secretary to the Duke in 1419, Harl. MS. 1705; Borsa, 11; and wrote a detailed biography of him, see page 189; Borsa, 373 (quoting J. Burckhardt, ii. 79); also Borsa, Corrdce, 510. Decembri himself became President of the Republic of Milan on the fall of the Visconti in 1447, Geiger, 167. He died there in 1477 and lies buried in the church of St Ambrose. For his tomb, see Borsa, 419.

[9] Statim ut per librarios mihi licitum fuit historiam illam clarissimi regis Anglorum transcribi jussi.

[10] i.e. MS. 2610; Voigt, ii. 256; Eng. Hist. Rev. xxiv. 85; Kingsford, Biogr. 59.

[11] viz. by T. Hearne in 1716. Holinshed (ii. 435) says that "it is onelie now in the hands of one painfull antiquary" (i.e. John Stow, see ibid. iii. 585; Kingsford, Biogr. 58).

[12] Harpsfeld, Hist. 586; Holinshed, iii. 585; Speed, 765; First Life, pp. v, xlvi, xlvii; Stow, Chron. in Kingsford, Biogr. 72, 73. This is now satisfactorily proved to be

and was justly regarded by them as one of the most valuable authorities for the events of the reign of Henry V. As might have been expected from his nearness to Duke Humphrey, he had access to much first-hand information[1] and, as a consequence, he often shows minute and accurate knowledge as to details of episodes in which his patron was personally engaged[2]. He has thus put together a sober and dependable account of the reign of Henry V vouched at times by extracts from state documents[3] which give it a distinctly additional value. In regard to the question of the mad-cap days he testifies that before coming to the throne Henry had certainly given way to some indulgence like all young soldiers of his age[4], but that when his father lay dying he called a priest to him, confessed his past sins and so mended his life and conduct that no place for wantonness was found in him ever after.

But side by side with this undoubted work of Duke Humphrey's poet there exists another which is absolutely identical with it in thought, sequence and general treatment[5], though nearly its double in bulk, owing partly to the fact that here and there it gives far larger extracts from official documents[6], but chiefly because episodes that are set down by Livy in plain, short, terse sentences are here padded out beyond all measure in a cloud of bombastic rhetoric[7], which is quite the usual stock-in-trade of the Renaissance writers. The book is usually known as the *"Life* of Henry V"

embodied in Bodl. MS. 966, Kingsford, Biogr. 78–85, who calls it (p. 86) "a lost English life of Hy V written about the middle of the 15th century, i.e. after 1455 (pp. 83, 92), based in the main on Tito Livio or on that by the Pseudo-Elmham," i.e. Harl. MS. 530, though the evidence for the latter is purely negative.

[1] Harpsfeld (586), writing before his imprisonment in 1559, calls him homo exterus sed instructus potissimum ab Humfredo Gloucestriæ Duce.

[2] e.g. at Cherbourg, Tit. Liv. 72, 79.

[3] e.g. his summary of the treaties of Canterbury, Tit. Liv. 27; and of Troyes, ibid. 85; and the written order not to drink strong wine at Troyes, ibid. 83.

[4] Veneria et martialia mediocriter secutus et alia quae militaribus licentia praebere solet quoad rex illius pater vixit, Tit. Liv. 5; First Life, pp. xxx, 17.

[5] Sachlich stimmen sie fast ganz überein, Lenz, 9.

[6] e.g. from the treaty of Canterbury, Vita, pp. 84–87; Lenz, 10, who argues from this that the same author cannot have written both books; also the Treaty of Troyes, Vita, pp. 253–266. For supposition that it contains "little more than the details of our war with France," see Amundesham, 1. p. x.

[7] "A certaine poeticall kinde of writing," Holinsh. iii. 585; Kingsford, Biogr. 58; une phraséologie redondante, tourmentée et *barbare*, son langage *inculte*, Puiseux, Rouen, vi, viii, the last epithet being particularly unfortunate, for to the 15th century reader this style was the most advanced evidence of civilisation; eine höchst schwülstige Sprache, Niethe, 8, who thinks that the style is not classical like that of Titus Livius.

(*Vita Henrici Quinti*) but the author, who distinctly calls himself a foreigner[1], nowhere gives his name[2]. It has been supposed that he was with the English army during the second invasion of France[3] and that he was present when the Earl of Warwick escaped an ambush on his way from Vernon to Provins in April 1419[4], but the passage relied on seems really to prove the very opposite for in it he distinctly says that he was *not* there in person[5]. On the other hand the book itself contains evidence enough that it was certainly not written at that date, for in referring to the establishment of the Bridgettines at Syon, the writer says that actual experience reveals their methods "even to the present day[6]," a phrase which would have been quite out of place anywhere near the year 1419 when the Order was starting in its English home, while in describing the welcome given to Henry by Duke Philip of Burgundy at Troyes in 1420 he uses language[7] that can only be explained by the altered feeling of the English towards the Duke after he had renounced our alliance by the Peace of Arras in 1435[8].

And indeed we have clear proof of the date at which the book was actually issued, for the writer, whoever he was, presented it to Doctor John Somerset[9], who was a man of great influence holding the offices of Chancellor of the Exchequer and Warden of the Mint, and as physician and

---

[1] Peregrinus et advena, Vita, pp. xv, 3, where there seems no reason to take this in a metaphorical sense, as Elmham, Hist. Mon. Aug. xxii; Lenz, 9. Cf. per auctorem anonymum sed peregrinum, J. Tyrrell in Vita, p. xvii; Niethe, 8, 10, i.e. fr. MS. Arundel, 15; Kingsford, Biogr. 61; auctorem anonymum, Parker in Preface to Walsingham, §2; non Anglus sed transmarinus, Fabricius, vi. 252.

[2] Cott. MS. Julius E. iv. 2, has no heading and in Harl. 864, the front page is wanting and has been copied from Julius E. iv. in a 17th century hand, the titles in Catalogue, Cotton, 17, and Catalogue, Harl. i. 463, being in both cases modern descriptions taken from Hearne, see Lenz, 9, 14.

[3] Puiseux, Rouen, p. v.

[4] Kingsford, pp. vi, 282; Köhler, 750, who supposes that the book was written before the Liber Metricus, which ends in 1418.

[5] Hos conflictus *quibus nequaquam interfui* punctatim non presumam describere, Vita, 215, though no such words occur in Tit. Liv. 73. Cf. virorum nobilium gesta fortia, *quia non ipsis interfui* relinquo aliis qui viderant exponenda, Vita, 140, where Livio says, quia id exculpere nequivi, Tit. Liv. 50.

[6] Quia earum conditiones et modos vera experientia *usque hodie* manifestat, Vita, 25; the phrase is not in Tit. Liv.

[7] Si gestus exterior fidem promeruit, Vita, 250; falsidicus dux, frangendo fidem falsus undique miles, Pol. Songs, ii. 150. Cf. ducis Burgundiae cordi tremulo, ducis formidulosi, Vita, 281; Kingsford, Biogr. 63.

[8] Kingsford, pp. vi, 319; do. Hard. 474. Thow Phellippe foundour of new falsehede, capiteine of cowardise, &c., Pol. Songs, ii. 148; "prynce perjured," J. Coke, 77.

[9] See App. O.

formerly tutor to King Henry VI was in constant personal attendance at the Court. In addressing Somerset the author refers to his *recent* foundation of a chapel that we know him to have founded close to the bridge at Brentford in the year 1446[1], but he makes no reference whatever to the arrest (Feb. 18) and death of the Duke of Gloucester which took place on Feb. 23, 1447[2], though strong prominence is given to the great deeds of Duke Humphrey throughout the text of the book[3], thereby enabling us to take it as proved that it was not issued till about the end of 1446[4] in which year the writer was looking out for an influential critic for his book[5] to hide its rudeness and nakedness and save it from lurking about in unrecognised obscurity[6]. These facts are all so obviously on the surface that it might have been thought that no other inference as to the history of the book was possible, but unfortunately the editor who first issued it in printed form nearly 200 years ago[7] made up his mind that the author was Thomas Elmham, who, as we shall see, accompanied the army to Agincourt, and up till quite recently subsequent enquirers have never got away from this initial mistake. Under the belief that we have here the work of an author who was strictly contemporary and that he wrote before the year

---

[1] Quam *nuper* procuratio sua construxerat, Vita, 339, i.e. the chapel and guild of All Angels in the hamlet of Brentford End, in the parish of Isleworth, Cal. Rot. Pat. 289; Aungier, 215, 224; Dict. Nat. Biogr. liii. 245; Vita, 339, 358; Lysons, ii. 24; Newcourt, i. 753. For the nine orders of angels, see Aungier, 215. Called the new stone bridge leading from Braynford to Houndeslowe, in Cal. Pat. Hy VI, iv. 29, Oct. 12, 1446, i.e. the licence to found a guild in the chapel of "the Holy Angels by Syon."

[2] Lib. Nig. Scacc. I. xxxiv; Lenz, 11; Dict. Nat. Biogr. xxviii. 246; Vickers, 293; not Feb. 28, 1446, as Doyle, ii. 23.

[3] e.g. in the siege of Cherbourg, 1418, where the Duke is princeps illustrissimus, nobilissimus, serenissimus cujus innatae magnanimitatis industria, &c., Vita, 149, 153, 159, 160, 162, 190; duci magnanimo, Vita, 211, all which is only an amplification of such phrases as strenuissimus dux, strenuus princeps, &c., in Tit. Liv. 51, 55, 56, 64.

[4] Kingsford, Biogr. 70; called between 1435 and 1440, in Eng. Hist. Rev. xxii. 579; or circa 1440, Elmham, Hist. Mon. Aug. p. xxiv.

[5] In suum correctorem, Vita, 338; incultam polias, rejice mendas, si tergat maculas horrida limans, ibid. 342; Memorials, xli.

[6] Cf. in lustralibus latebris et abditis desertis latitare decrevisti, Vita, 338, where the author is addressing his book, which he calls vecors, pauper et pannosa pagina.

[7] i.e. Thomas Hearne in 1727, though the MS. (Arundel xv. in the Heralds College), which he edited, has no title or evidence of authorship. This MS. contains the line "Claudatur *muro* constat liber iste Rogero" (Black, p. 24; Kingsford, Biogr. 61); i.e. it belonged to Roger Wall, a canon of Lichfield in 1454, Kingsford, Biogr. 63, from Vitellius A. x. f. 163, and is probably in his handwriting. He held the prebend of Eccleshall (Lichfield) from 1443 till 1454 (Le Neve, i. 601), was Archdeacon of Stafford in 1442 (ibid. i. 572) and became Archdeacon of Coventry on May 30, 1442, which office he held until his death in 1488 (ibid. i. 569); Kingsford, Biogr. 63.

1417, or at any rate within the lifetime of Henry V, it has been customary to suppose that Tito Livio was a downright plagiarist, who had the *Vita* before him and merely planed down its turgidity to a sober level, or even that he deliberately cut out a quantity of it in order to escape detection[1]. Other writers have supposed that Tito Livio was first in the field and that the *Vita* is copied from him[2], though it is impossible to harmonise this with the view that the latter was written by Elmham during the lifetime of Henry V. Others again, while attributing the two works to two separate authors, are content with the remark that both are "largely derived from the same sources[3]," or that there must have been some communication between them, or that each treatise contains some particulars that are not recorded in the other[4], without actually deciding whether it is a case of the *Vita* expanding Livy or Livy reducing the *Vita*.

But if the question could be impartially approached without any prepossession in favour of a theory that the *Vita* was actually written by Thomas Elmham, which it certainly was not, the most probable solution would seem to be that both works are by the same hand[5], and that just as Elmham first wrote his *Gesta* in prose and afterwards re-wrote it in elegiac verse of which he was proud to show himself a master, so Livy transformed his first smaller book into a larger edition, improving it, as he supposed, with plenty of erudition and literary embellishment, though our

---

[1] Purus, puteus plagiarius vel abbreviator, Parker in Preface to his edition of Walsingham (1574), § 2; Wilkins in Preface to Tanner, Bibliotheca, xliii; Hearne in Tit. Liv. p. xii; Memorials, xlii; Gent. Mag. (1859), ii. 350; R. F. Williams, i. 202; called "another version of Elmham" (i.e. of the *Vita*), Church, 45, 102; "a compilation from Elmham," Köhler, ii. 750; "Elmham's copier," Aubrey, ii. 34; Baeske, 37; eine stark gekürzte Wiederholung der Vita, Kabel, 16.

[2] Pauli, v. 104, 689; Holinsh. iii. 585, who calls the author of the Vita "another writer who hath followed the said Livius in the order of his book as it were chapter for chapter"; Kingsford, Biogr. 58, 64.

[3] Dict. Nat. Biogr. xxvi. 55; Stubbs, iii. 80, 81, who regards them both as "professed panegyrists," "dasselbe Quellen- und Urkundenmaterial *teilweise* benutzt haben," Niethe, 9.

[4] Lenz, 10, who gives some examples of independent information in each; also Emmerig, p. 6; Kingsford, Biogr. 64, who compares the differences in much greater detail, one singular example being the determination in the *Vita* not to disclose the name of the knight who specially distinguished himself at the siege of Cherbourg, in order to protect him from the sting of jealousy (ne livoris exasperetur aculeus, Vita, 155), though Livio gives the name straight out as Lewis Robsart, Tit. Liv. 54.

[5] As supposed by Anstis in Vita, p. xi, and for a time by Kingsford, in Eng. Hist. Rev. xxii. 579 (1907), xxiii. 560 (1908); though now abandoned by him, Biogr. 67 (1910).

modern taste has generally preferred the first plainer fare, regarding all the later flowers of rhetoric as "more suited to the taste of Persia than of England[1]." Nevertheless the recent discovery of Livy's letter showing that he had certainly left this country by 1440, and the improbability that he ever returned, may well make us pause before adopting the above theory, in which case there seems nothing for it except to regard the question of the personality of the author of the *Vita* as an "unsolved problem[2]," at any rate for the present.

But whoever may have been the author, it is certain that in this expanded version great stress is laid on the suddenness[3] of the new king's conversion. No sooner, it is said, had the breath left his father's body[4] than Henry betook himself to silent and solitary prayer. Kneeling on his bare knees he smote his breast, while tears in copious floods streamed from his eyes all day until the evening. The funeral day was passed in groaning and lamentation and then in the darkness of the night he went in secret to a hermit[5] who lived within the precinct at Westminster, laid bare before him all the secrets of his life, washed in the laver of repentance, put off the cloak of vice and came back decently adorned in the garment of virtue. And so the barren willow[6] became the fruitful olive, Cocytus became Euphrates, the left became right, and so forth.

But in all this view the renewing of the old man is expressly said to consist in devotion to the Church and the destruction of Lollardry[7], and when the writer once

---

[1] S. Turner, ii. 377; Gesta, v. For a specimen of his bombastic style, see Henry, v. 568.

[2] Kingsford, Biogr. 71, who puts in a conjectural claim for Vincent Clement of Valentia (see p. 193, note 6).

[3] Vita, 12; cf. "anon and sodaynly," Fab. 577; "*sodaynly* he was chaunged into a new man," Caxton, 125; Brut, ii. 494; First Life, xxix, xxx, 17, where the conversion is compared with that of Thomas à Becket (quoting from his anonymous biographer, see Materials, iv. 19).

[4] Vita, 14, 15; Tit. Liv. 5; followed by Pauli, v. 75; Lingard, iii. 235; Adams, i. 205; Ramsay, i. 162; Hartwright, 135.

[5] Probably William Alnwick, who afterwards became General Confessor at Syon, Amundesham, i. 27. See App. P.

[6] Not "falix," as Kabel, 15.

[7] Cf. rex hominem veterem *sic* renovare studet, Elmham, Lib. Metr. 100, referring to Colossians iii. 9, 10; in maynteynyng of holy church, destroying of heretikes, keping justice and defending of his Reame and subjectes, Brut, ii. 494; cheryschynge the chyrche, the Lollers hadde a valle, &c., Greg. Chron. 170; to stroy Lollardes he het al his labour, Lydg. Fall of Princes, xxxiii; Wylie, iv. 92.

begins to paint, he loads his canvas with the crudest un-realities, so that although he was undoubtedly in a position to get his information at first hand, yet he was to such an extent a victim to his style that large deductions must be made from his encomium if we are to see his hero in the light of sober fact, while his only circumstantial item about the Westminster hermit cannot be altogether true, for the funeral day was taken up with a river-journey to Gravesend and thence to Canterbury by road in presence of a large number of courtly and ceremonial mourners. Moreover we know that even in the panegyrist's own estimate the change of heart did but instigate him to contrive tricky plots, sham friendships and lying compacts with the French[1], so that if this is to be the true Henry we shall have to do with a perjured pietist as well as a ferocious bigot[2], whom no candid man could now honestly respect.

Setting aside however all such literary exaggerations, there can be no reasonable doubt that the new king did really turn away from his former self[3] and the wild-headed[4] promise of his greener days[5]. Moreover the most recent research has demonstrated that even the story of his robbing his own retainers on the high road is no mere baseless legend[6] and the general fact of his reform of life is well attested by several of his contemporaries[7]. In 1415 his intimate friend Bishop Courtenay told a Frenchman that he did not believe that the king had once broken his continence since his accession to the throne[8], and the very same statement comes to us on the authority of the Earl of

---

[1] Perpendit igitur hostiles insidias, fallaces concordias, fictas amicitias secreto apud se cogitat et disponit *divinae gratiae mediante suffragio*, Vita, 27.

[2] For a defence of him against the charge of persecuting, see Tyler, ii. 8, 319; Stubbs, iii. 80, who thinks that he persecuted "merely as a religious or as a legal duty"; so also Sanford, 187.

[3] 2 Henry IV, v. v. 62.

[4] Famous Victories, 34.

[5] Henry V, II. iv. 136.

[6] Speed, 766; "As I have learned of the credence before rehearsed (i.e. from the Earl of Ormond) and also as the common fame is," Kingsford, Biogr. 74, 81, 87; do. First Life, xxix. 17, who thinks (p. xxxii) that "there must be some foundation for the story of his change into a new man." For the tavern scenes and riotous conduct, see Wylie, iv. 93; Kingsford, Chron. pp. xxxvi, 268, 341.

[7] Sanford, 184, thinks that any adverse reflections by contemporaries represent "the slanders spread abroad by the party which succeeded in removing him from the council" and can only be regarded as "distortions of the real facts."

[8] Non credebat quod cognovisset mulierem carnaliter *postquam ipse coronam susceperat*, Mirot, Fusoris, 243.

Ormond, who likewise knew him well[1]. Thomas Walsingham, writing within six years of his accession[2], says that at his coronation he was suddenly transformed into a new man in gravity, honesty and moderation[3], and the phrase was freely copied by subsequent writers[4], while on the very day of his accession Hoccleve plied him with much lofty advice that as God had given him substantial wit and kingly might, so he would put virtue in assay, be clean in heart, love charity, fear God and fix his trust in Him, be sober, sad and just, help truth, take good counsel and do after it, be meek[5] in spirit, temperate of tongue, prudent, pitiful and debonair, not over-spending nor a slave to gold, but in measure free, a shield and wall to his people, to govern them in equity, conquer their love and have them all in charity[6]. It is true that these strict precepts do not in themselves enable us to estimate the Prince's former life, but they are at least consistent with a covert hint that the time had come to turn his back upon a doubtful past, though they are a trifle disedged when we know that the writer's own life was of none too saintly a stamp, that he was then but 46 years old[7] and was always cadging for something to abate his indigence and save him from trotting to Newgate[8].

[1] From his father's death until the marriage of himself he never had knowledge carnally of women, Kingsford, Biogr. 72, 80; do. First Life, pp. xx, 5; Harpsfeld, Hist. 589.

[2] i.e. circ. 1419, Wals. Hypodig. pp. x, 5. For payment to Thomas Chaucer per manus Thomae Walsingham clerici, see Iss. Roll 1 H. V, Pasch., May 4, 1413.

[3] Repente mutatus est in virum alterum, Wals. ii. 290; Hypodig. 438; Wylie, iv. 92, which Kabel (12) considers as der erste Keim einer Mythenbildung.

[4] See page 199, note 3. A newe man made by all good regimence, Hard. 372; he was turned into another man, Capgr. Chron. 302; I am borne new again, Fam. Vict. 21; atque ita mutatus facit omnia principe digna, Ocland in Holinsh. iii. 546; Brougham, 369; S. Turner, ii. 383.

[5] For "meke" as the equivalent of humble, see Caxton, Dial. 50; cf. to meke hem to oure kyngys methe, J. Page, 2; in helle he may be meked tame, Kail, 99; for thy love I meked me lowe, ibid. 86, 87; also Wylie, iii. 299; thou mekyd us (=nos humiliasti), Misyn, 17; y meked me, Secreta, 48; that I scholde now me meke, Laud Troy Bk. 513; ourself lat us meke, Misyn, 20.

[6] Hoccleve, Min. Po. 40; cf. if thou keepe them thus in subjection mixed with love and feare...thou shalt have the most lovinge, faithfull and manly people of the world, First Life, 15; Tyler, i. 308.

[7] Of age I am fifty winter and thre (written in 1422), Hoccl., Min. Po. 119.

[8] Ibid. 62; cf. Wylie, ii. 22. For prisoners in "Bocardo," a part of Newgate Gaol, see Lett. Bk. I, 49.

CHAPTER XV

RELIGIOUS HOUSES

But whatever may have been the effect of this conversion on Henry's personal character, his new-born zeal for the Church had one result that has remained a national gain for England until this day. He loved the church of St Peter in the Abbey at Westminster[1], first doubtless as an adjunct to the royal palace[2] but equally so as England's head and crown[3], and many were the thank-offerings that he bestowed upon it. Here he was crowned and here he made his services at Ascension (June 1) and Whitsuntide (June 11)[4], while on Nov. 5, 1413[5], he freed the Abbot from the onerous duty of levying and collecting the tenths from the clergy. He sent the monks presents of game when he was away at the hunt[6], and on his first New Year's Day[7] he restored to them a ring valued at 1000 marks which had been given to the shrine of the Confessor by Richard II[8], subject to the condition that he should still

---

[1] For seal of Westminster Abbey with St Peter and Edward the Confessor, see Pedrick, 136, Plate XXXII.

[2] Lethaby, 61, who compares it to the connection of St Mark's with the Doge's Palace at Venice and the Cathedral at Aix-la-Chapelle with the palace of Charlemagne. F. Bond, 37, regards it as the royal chapel of the Court with St Stephen's as its rival (p. 111) in this respect.

[3] Regni summam quasi sedem, Memorials, 73; caput Angliae diademaque regni, Flete, 63, 76; F. Bond, p. vii. For his veneration for Canterbury as "the chief church of this royaume which he worshipped duely as ever did prince," see Stephenson, i. 441; Stanley, 127. In Manners and Meals, i. 192, 193 (written circ. 1450), Canterbury is "the cheff churche of dignitee" and the Abbot of Westminster is the "hiest of the lande," Tintern being the poorest of the Abbeys. F. Bond, 28, calls the building "one of the noblest works of humanity."

[4] Exch. Accts. 406/21, 19.

[5] Pat. 1 H. V, 516; Priv. Seal 659/144, Nov. 25, 1413.

[6] Page 50.

[7] Cum donante dati novus annus fit dator harum, Memorials, 72; in regno primo sic nobis contulit anno, ibid. 70.

[8] i.e. on Nov. 14, 1388, Hist. MSS. 4th Rept. 191; Stow, Ann. 362; Neale and Brayley, i. 89.

keep it in his own possession so long as he was not away
from England. At the same time he presented them with
a sceptre, a Psalter, a copy of the Great Chronicle known
as the "Flowers of Histories" and several rich vestments,
ornaments and vessels, all of which have long since disappeared with the exception of the Chronicle, which is still
preserved in Humphrey Chetham's Library at Manchester[1].

But the building in which Henry was crowned was
but a stunted fragment[2] of height without length, like the
splendid architectural abortions at Beauvais[3] and Cologne[4].
The choir, transepts and four bays[5] of the nave extending
to the present screen[6] had been built, as we see them now,
by Henry III[7] more than a century before, but the builders
had left the remainder of the nave of the earlier Norman
church[8] extending as far as the west side of the present
cloister[9]. What to do with this antiquated nave long
remained a puzzle. In 1258 an order had been given for
its demolition[10] but this was not carried out, and in 1342[11]

[1] i.e. Chetham MS. 6712, or D. 2. 2. 41587; Matt. Paris, Preface I. xv; Ramsay,
i. 308; J. A. Robinson, Langham, 346. It was presented to the Chetham Library by
Nicholas Higginbottam of Stockport in 1657, and its former habitat at Westminster is
proved by a note on the last leaf containing the names of two Westminster monks, viz.
R. Teddington (who entered the Monastery in 1428) and T. Gardener (who celebrated
his first mass there in 1501, and was still living in 1525), Robinson and James, 25, 83.
For another copy of the Flores Historiarum still at Westminster, see ibid. 82. For a
picture of Matthew Paris from Cotton MS. Nero D. I, see Cassell, i. 459, where it is said
to be "drawn by himself," i.e. MS. Reg. xiv. C. 7, Matt. Paris (Luard), i. frontispiece.

[2] Dulcken, 399.

[3] For the choir at Beauvais, see Bordier-Charton, i. 414; Loth, 78. Called "l'in-
concevable chœur" in Renan, L'Art, 216.

[4] For picture of Cologne Cathedral in 1497 with the crane on the stump of the south-
western tower, see Schedel, 100. For a sixteenth century view, see Lacroix, 425.

[5] Called 5 bays in Besant, Westminster, 111; i.e. 5 bays of the ground storey and
triforium, but only 4 bays of the clerestory, F. Bond, 117.

[6] Rackham, Plan; Bradley, Annals, 386. For evidence of thick stone wall at this
point, see ibid. 389. Benham-Welch (p. 6) supposes that it divided the choir which
belonged to the monks from the nave which was intended for the general congregation,
and says that it was removed in the reign of Henry VII, but I find no mention of this in
Neale.

[7] For objection to the usual assumption that Edward I continued the work, see F.
Bond, 24, 111, who finds it "quite at variance with the fabric rolls."

[8] Built in the twelfth century, Rackham, 6, showing that the roof of it was *ruinosa* in
1388. For a conjectural view, see E. T. Bradley, Popular Guide to Westminster Abbey,
p. 8; do. Annals, 388; Stanley, Westminster, 127; G. G. Scott, 54, 212; Feasey-
Micklethwaite, 77; Lethaby, 98.

[9] See plan in Archaeologia, lxii. 94, where Dean Robinson doubts Micklethwaite's
theory that it extended as far as the present west front, see Bradley, Annals, 384, 385.
For picture of the west front before Wren's additions, see Monast. i. 264; Rackham, 50.
For present day west front, see Feasey-Micklethwaite, 58; F. Bond, 28.

[10] F. Bond, 22.

[11] Bradley, Annals, 389; Feasey-Micklethwaite, 87.

a plan was worked out for lighting it with more modern windows, but in 1388 the whole of the old portion was demolished[1] except the western towers[2], and though King Richard II had intended to have it rebuilt in harmony with the choir and transepts, yet he was only able to make a beginning[3] by the erection of the Purbeck marble pillars[4] and the lower portion of the outer walls[5], the Abbot in the meantime giving his first attention to the completion of the cloisters[6] and the Place[7], now the Deanery, at the south-western corner of the church, containing the room which was destined soon to become famous as the death-chamber of King Henry IV. During that king's reign the "new work[8]" of the nave proceeded very slowly indeed, little being done beyond some temporary roofing[9] for the protection of the interrupted work, and when his son succeeded him the nave is described as having been "long in ruins and undone[10]," while the balance in hand at the Abbey

[1] The demolition began in 1376, F. Bond, 116; Feasey-Micklethwaite, 87, who thinks that it went on all through this reign.
[2] G. G. Scott, 255, 258; Lethaby, 204.
Cf.   E deux (turs) en frunt del occident
              E bons seinz (bells) et grantz i pent,
Luard, Lives of Edward the Confessor, 90; Feasey-Micklethwaite, 70; Hiatt, 6.
[3] Nova fabrica navis ecclesiae sancti Petri Westmonasteriensis per nos incepta, Wills of Kings, 195; Rym. viii. 76; Rackham, p. 8; not that he rebuilt the nave, as Jusserand, Lit. Hist. 353, or that "great progress was made during the time of Abbots Langham and Litlington," as Bradley, 389, their work being apparently limited to the preliminary demolition, Rackham, 7. For addition to the north entrance by Richard II see Hollar's view in Hiatt, p. 2; Carrick, 284.   [4] Rackham, 10, 51.
[5] i.e. up to the level of the triforium, Rackham, 11; F. Bond, 116, who supposes (p. 118) that in 1399 the south aisle was ready for glazing, the rest of the nave being represented by two rows of pillars and arches with unfinished aisle walls, a walled-off enclosure in its eastern bays and a low-roofed south aisle extending from the west cloister to Henry III's choir aisle. For picture of the junction of the thirteenth and fourteenth century work, see ibid. 121.
[6] Chiefly built by Abbot Simon Langham, though usually attributed to Abbot Litlington, F. Bond, 113. For Litlington's missal (costing £34. 17s. 7d. spread over 2 years) completed in 1384 and still preserved in the Abbey, see Lethaby, 281; Flete, 135; Legg, i. pp. v, x; E. M. Thompson, Notes, 226; Robinson and James, 7; Herbert, 231, who calls it "heavy and dull despite the plenteous use of gold." Also his initials in the cloisters, Lethaby, 201; Hugo, 111; Wylie, iv. 103, note 9. He died Nov. 29, 1386, Flete, 139.
[7] Rackham, 7. For picture, see Perkins, 22; Feasey-Micklethwaite, 88, 90; F. Bond, 114, 299, 300; Loftie, ii. 41, 53 (with plan). For a "place" of the Abbot of Westminster at Stratford-le-Bow (6 H. VI), see Ad Quod Damn. 353, though there is no mention of this in Lysons, Environs, Vol. III. For placeam illam cum gardino (1227), see G. F. Turner, 7, 25; in gardinis vel placeis ad eas pertinentibus, ibid. 27.
[8] For the "novum opus," see Rackham, p. 4.
[9] Supra muros et columpnas, Rackham, 12. The sum of £154. 9s. 10d. said to have been spent on the work in 1411-1412, in G. G. Scott, 260, looks like the £144. 9s. 10d. which was in hand on Nov. 22, 1411 (see Rackham, 13), nearly all of which was used for other purposes.
[10] Quae *a diu* ruinam passa fuit et infecta remanet, Rym. ix. 78.

available for the building fund amounted to just £3 in cash[1].

The new king at once contributed 100 marks for the new work[2], and on Aug. 24, 1413[3], sent an order to the Mayor of London to engage stone-cutters, carpenters and labourers for the operations which had already begun[4]. On Dec. 11, 1413, the grant was raised to 1000 marks per annum[5] to be continued during the king's pleasure for completing the nave, half of which amount was to come from the fees received in the chancery[6] and the other half was to be charged on the customs of the port of London. The work was to be carried out under the supervision of the Duke of York and Bishop Henry Beaufort, the disbursements being made through Richard Whitington[7], who was collector of the customs of London, and Richard Harowden[8], one of the monks, who afterwards became Abbot of Westminster. It is apparently on this account that it has become customary to speak of Whitington as "the great architect of that age[9]," but his connection with

[1] Rackham, 13.

[2] Iss. Roll 1 H. V, Pasch., July 17, 1413, records £66. 13s. 4d. paid to the Abbot and Convent of Westminster per manus Ricardi Haroughden monk super facturâ novi operis ecclesiae beati Petri infra Abbatiam; cf. Bradley, 98.

[3] Pat. 1 H. V, iii. 20d; Hist. MSS. 4th Rept. p. 177; Lethaby, 206, where the order is addressed to the mayor (William Waldern), the keeper of the wardrobe (Thomas Carnika, see p. 28), and Brother Richard Harweden (monk); also Pat. 1 H. V, iv. 19 d, Nov. 8, 1413; v. 18, March 8, 1414.

[4] The accounts now in the Abbey begin on July 7, 1413, Rackham, 14.

[5] Pat. 1 H. V, iv. 5; Memorials, 71; called Dec. 14, 1413, in For. Accts. 5 H. V.

[6] In For. Accts. 4 H. V, 14, it comes out of the fees received by the clerk of the Hanaper, i.e. Henry Kays or Keys. For order dated Jan. 18, 1418, that 500 marks per annum shall be charged upon the Hanaper for the building of our church of Westminster, see Chancery Warrants, Ser. 1. 1364/42. For £2264 received from that source during Henry V's reign, see Rackham, 14. See App. Q.

[7] See App. R.

[8] Called Harweden in For. Accts. 5–6 H. V, m. 21; or Haroughden, Harounden, Harouden, Devon, 329. In Neale and Brayley, i. 89; Rackham, 14, he is custos novi operis; not "Harnden," as Wylie, iii. 349, note 8. For £20 per annum granted to him, see Iss. Roll 6 H. V, Mich., Jan. 16, 1419. He is called Harowden in Iss. Roll 7 H. V, Pasch., July 10, 1419, where he receives £100 super facturâ nove (sic) op. ecclie. For William Harwedone (variously spelt Harewdone, Harwdone, or Haryngdone), Prior of the Trinity or Christ Church in Aldgate in 1407, 1408, 1412, 1413, 1414, and Rector of St Botolph-without-Aldgate, see Letter Book I, 60, 69, 108, 118, 128, 130. For plans of the Trinity Priory temp. Elizabeth, see Besant, Survey, ii. 244. It was called Crichirche, see Wylie, iv. 418; Archaeol. Journ. xliv. 58, where its annual rents from property in London = £31. 2s. 8d. in 1412.

[9] Stanley, Westminster, 127, who speaks of the prolongation of the nave by him, ibid. [35]; Hiatt, 128; Axon, 278, thinks that he "aided in building the nave"; Feasey-Micklethwaite, 59, that he "assisted in promoting the restoration of the nave." He is called "chief supervisor of the rebuilding of the nave" in Fox-Bourne, 61; Kingsford, 386; "keeper of the works," Lethaby, 206. For his previous connection with the same work in 1402, see Rackham, 14. The rebuilding of Newgate and of the Guildhall Chapel,

the work appears to have been purely administrative and financial.

The actual workmanship[1] was entrusted to the care of William Colchester[2], the master-mason, who was also employed at the same time on the works then proceeding at York[3]. His fee was £10 a year[4], and the workmen, though they brought their own tools, had all to be found in aprons, gloves, clogs, drink, meat, harbourage and other usual courtesies of masoncraft, besides their regular weekly wage, including a coat at Christmas time, the cost of which might be put down at a mark. The stone was quarried at Reigate[5] in Surrey, Bere in Dorset[6] and Stapleton in Yorkshire[7], with Caen[8] stone for the finer parts, and some of it was certainly brought by water, for we have a record[9] of a shout[10] laden with stone for the work being wrecked while passing through the middle arch of London Bridge, whereby three of the boatmen lost their lives. Thereupon, in accordance with the established custom[11], the hull was

his college in the Royal and his library at the Grey Friars (for picture see T. F. Smith; Knight, London, ii. 333, 338), were all really the work of his executors, Letter Book I, 50; Chron. Lond. 165.

[1] For "werkemanschippe," see Raine, Catterick, 8.

[2] Cf. "that hyght Colchester was our master-mason," Chancery Warrants, Ser. 1. 1364/58, June 2, 1418. He was chief mason in 1 H. IV, see Lethaby, 205, who refers to his position as master-mason at York in 1406. For grant to him (July 6, 1418) of officium dispositoris operationum nostrarum cementarie at Westminster and the Tower with an allowance of 12d. per day and a roba hyemalis at Christmas, see Pat. 6 H. V, 20. He was succeeded in 1421 by John of Thirsk, Rackham, 16.

[3] Wylie, ii. 354; Fabr. Rolls 39, 201.

[4] G. G. Scott, 214. In 1400 he received only £5 per annum, ibid. 260; Wylie, ii. 354, note 9.

[5] For pere de Reigate sciez used in repairing Westminster Hall, March 8, 1395, see Rym. vii. 794; called "bluish fire-stone," Archaeologia, l. p. 2. For a quarry rented at Chalfdon (? Chaldon) near Caterham, see Rackham, 11, 39.

[6] For stone from Bere, Caine (i.e. Caen) and Reigate called sherches (i.e. wrought stone) and nowels, rag (Rackham, 45) or ragstone (Wylie, iv. 215; Baildon, Star Chamber, 35) from Maidstone and stone called Urnell used in building the Bell Tower at Westminster in 1365, see Archaeologia, xxxvii. 24. For pierres nommées *serches* pour reserchier the well in the Hôtel Dieu in Paris in 1416, see Brièle, iii. 43; also pierre de liaiz (lias, see Godefroy, s.v. *Liois*) for the steps of the Petit Pont, ibid.

[7] G. G. Scott, 214; Wylie, ii. 207, note 9; Purey-Cust, i. 324, who adds Thievesdale (ibid. ii. 37) as a Yorkshire stone; also ibid. York Minster, 23.

[8] For stone de Came, see Rackham, 11, 42; Add. MS. 4603, f. 57, quoted in Ramsay, i. 318.

[9] Pat. 2 H. V, ii. 28, Sept. 18, 1414; Cal. Pat. H. V, i. 236; see Rym. ix. 447 (April 14, 1417), where in hiring boats (*batelli*) to bring stone for the repair of the king's highway at Holborn exemption is expressly reserved in the case of those actually employed for the building of the church at Westminster.

[10] For showtes, showtemen, shouthire, see Rackham, 11. For charges for shoutagium, carriagium, frectagium, cranagium of goods of Queen Joan, see Exch. Accts. 406/30. Cf. Wylie, iii. 67; for stowagium, see Lyte, Dunster, 116.

[11] Page 31.

declared forfeit to the king, who however at once restored it to its owners, William Atte Brook and John Dawe.

Meanwhile, expenditure on the nave went steadily on, and by Christmas, 1416, over £1400 had been received and accounted for[1], the numbers of righolts, wainscots and staybars used in the operations being all minutely scheduled. The new portion was carefully copied from the earlier thirteenth century design[2], though it is somewhat less ornate in detail and slight deviations may still be detected both within and without[3]. Up till quite recently it has been usual to assume that by the help of King Henry's liberality the nave was fully or nearly completed long before his reign came to an end[4]. Others on the other hand have either entirely ignored or much belittled the share that he undoubtedly had in the operations[5]. But a more complete search by a recent investigator makes it certain that the king contributed altogether £3861[6] to the work and that at his death the walls to the extent of six bays[7] had been carried through the triforium and well up to the clerestory[8], and that when the contributions ceased at his death, the unfinished structure remained practically at a standstill for the next 50 years[9].

But King Henry did not wait for the completion of the church before carrying out another project upon which his heart was set. He had always been a special favourite with King Richard II[10], who had told him as a lad that he believed he was destined to fulfil the prophecy of

---

[1] i.e. £1397. 6s. 8d. received and £1400. 11s. 5½d. paid out, G. G. Scott, 214, but this should be corrected by extracts from Fabric Rolls in Rackham, 14. For £88. 13s. 4d. paid in 3 H. V for lead *pro unâ costâ navis*, see Hiatt, 11.

[2] Lethaby, 27, who notes this as "one of very few instances in which the builders of a later time tried to make their work like that which they were completing"; Bradley, Guide, 29.

[3] For the junction, see Neale, ii. 24, Plate XXVII; Bradley, 386; F. Bond, 121.

[4] i.e. by the thanksgiving day after the king's return from Agincourt, Nov. 23, 1415, Stanley, 127; Feasey-Micklethwaite, 36, 87; G. G. Scott, 260.

[5] e.g. Christopher Wren writing in 1713, Widmore, 48, 58; also Neale, ii. 24, who ascribes the work to "the Abbots of subsequent ages"; also Besant, Westminster, 77, 111; Benham-Welch, 7.

[6] Rackham, 14, 58, 59. Called £4300 in Athenaeum, 27/3/09, p. 380.

[7] Ramsay, i. 318; the 7th being added in Tudor times, Neale, ii. 241, Plate XXVI.

[8] Rackham, 17, 23, who shows ground for believing that a beginning had been made with the west front; F. Bond, 119.

[9] Rackham, 17.

[10] Postea provexit te Richard rex et amavit, Memorials, 65; Chron. R. II to H. VI, 39; Rowlatt, 17, who calls him Earl of Hereford ; see Wylie, iii. 328.

Merlin[1] that a prince should be born in Wales[2], whose praise would one day sound throughout the world, while he on his side had been heard to say that he owed as much veneration to King Richard as he did to his own father[3]. When Richard II[4] made his will in 1399[5], he had made provision for all eventualities such as his possibly dying abroad or at sea in his passage across to Ireland. But in any case he had desired that his body should be brought to Westminster and buried by the side of his wife, the good Queen Anne, in the tomb that he had himself erected during his lifetime[6] in the choir of the Abbey church, and he had bequeathed his crowns, cups, ewery and jewels to his successor on the express condition that he should faithfully carry out the terms of the will. Conscience now pricked the newly awakened king to make a public reparation, for though his courtiers saw in it only the virtue of a kind and loving heart[7], yet he must have known that the world would take him to witness that his father had killed the prophet and that he himself was building the sepulchre[8].

His first Easter had been spent at Langley[9] where he arrived on April 15, 1413[10]. Here he gave 4*d.* apiece to

---

[1] Elmham, Mon. Aug. 257; Harpsfeld, Hist. 586.

[2] In which Monmouth was included, Tit. Liv. 3; Vita, 4. Cf. Patria Walligenis, Memorials, 64.

[3] Ott. 274; Wals. ii. 297; Carte, ii. 674.

[4] See App. S.

[5] i.e. April 16, 1399, Wills of Kings, 192, 193; Rym. viii. 75.

[6] Cf. en son sarcus qu'il avoit fait faire pour luy et la royne sa première femme en son vivant, Waurin, ii. 167.

[7]
    Eek hath our kynges benignitee
    And loving herte his vertu can bywreye
    Our Kyng Richard that was ye wel may see
    Is not fled from his remembrance aweye.
                      Hoccleve, Min. Po. 48.
Cf. for gret love and gedenesse, Brut, ii. 373. R. F. Williams (i. 194) finds in it "unquestionable evidence of his goodness of heart."

[8] Ad fin de acquiter et deschargier lame de son feu pere, Waurin, ii. 167; in remissionem paterni delicti, Croyl. Hist. 499; murder forgiven in his obsequies, G. Daniel, iv. 111; Hardyng (372) adds that he also let all men offer at Archbishop Scrope's grave in York Minster; Carte (ii. 674) thinks that "he looked upon all concerned in Richard's murder as the worst of traitors," but his reference to Otho B. xiii. p. 131, does not correspond with the Cottonian Catalogue. Tyler (ii. 12) argues against any "consciousness of guilt on the part of his father," but thinks that Henry "might have considered Richard as an injured man," &c., &c. Milman (Ann. 81) calls it a "solemn and wicked mockery." Strickland (ii. 110) thinks that it was "a deep laid measure of state policy" due to reports about the maumet in Scotland. Stubbs (iii. 84) takes it to symbolise the burial of all old causes of enmity.

[9] i.e. King's Langley (see Cussans, Dacorum, 197); not Abbot's Langley, as Buckley, 111; Murray-Smith, 56.

[10] Page 47.

3000 poor at the Maundy[1], and on Good Friday[2], April 21[3], besides giving £433. 6s. 8d. in alms[4] he offered 25s.[5] at the crawling of the cross[6] in the Priory[7] church of the Black Friars where King Richard's body lay buried[8]. It was probably at this visit that Henry announced his plans. At any rate, in the first winter of his reign after the Convocation broke up on Dec. 4, 1413[9], he had King Richard's body brought up from Langley where it had lain for the last

[1] For l'office du Mande, le jeudi absolu, absolutionis dies, Nicolas, Chron. of Hist. 110 (i.e. Maundy Thursday, Cotgr., s.v. *Jeudi*), see Brièle, iii. 32; Godefroy, s.v. *Mandé*. Called le Manday du grand jeudi, Renard, 212; jeudi sainct, ibid. 137. Cf. faire mande (i.e. to wash the disciples' feet), Coyecque, i. 93; A. Chevalier, 94; pro mandato, Walcott, Vestiges, 53. Rock (iv. 95) derives it from the mandatum novum in John xiii. 34, called die Paraseues or die caenae dominicae in Ròżmital, 45, where Edward IV invites 13 poor people and washes their feet, giving to each a new gown and a noble (numum qui nabel nuncupatur). For Dies Parasceves either on Maundy Thursday or Good Friday, see Rym. ix. 357; Wylie, ii. 160, note 1.

[2] Rot. Parl. iv. 56, 57; le jour de grand vendredy, Bourgeois, 137; le jour du vendredi, Brièle, Notes, 40, or du vendredi benoit, do. Doc. iii. 26; lo jour del vendres sainct, Medicis, i. 241; Holy Friday, Nicolas, Chron. of Hist. 121; "The Good Fryday," Pol.-Relig. Po. 122; J. Page, 29; Rym. ix. 30; Lydg. Min. Po. 99; le grand vendredi, Cousinot, 137; Dupleix, ii. 717; Delaborde, 311, 318; Renard, 37; le vendredi que nous appelons sainct, Coyecque, i. 131; A. Chevalier, 107, 110, 113; lo divendrés sant, Contemplacio, in Ferrer, i. p. 7; an vendredi benoist, Regnier, 138; an dem stillen vritage, Janicke, 340; le bon vendredi aorez, Priv. Seal 664/659, i.e. dies adoratus, Nicolas, Chron. of Hist. 123, or adourez, Coyecque, i. 75; Brièle, iii. 32; or aorez, Ord. Priv. Co. ii. 149; or "aouré," Deschamps, ix. 379; or "douré," Nicolas, Chron. of Hist. 112; cf. il fist aourer son image, Blondel, i. 133; pour aourer par mains matins, Pastoralet, 149; cf. Cotgr., s.v. *Oré, orez*. Not "a ovez," as Wylie, ii. 160, note 1; iii. 259.

[3] Called *praesentis* diei Paraseves, Pat. 1 H. V, i. 23, April 21, 1413.

[4] On this day the cost of the Royal Household was £333. 6s. 8d. besides £433. 6s. 8d. given to the poor in propriâ personâ Domini Regis, see Q. R. Accts. 406/21(1); Iss. Roll 1 H. V, Pasch., May 4, 1413. For £200 distributed to the poor through Stephen Payne the king's almoner (Rym. ix. 163, 292, 594, 595, Oct. 16, 1414; July 24, 1415; June 9, 1418), see Iss. Roll 4 H. V, Pasch., April 30, 1416. For his retinue of 3 archers at Southampton in July, 1415, see Exch. Accts. 47/26 (with names); Nicolas, Agincourt, 382; all were present with him at the battle, L. T. R. Misc. Enrolled Accts. 6/9, where he is defunctus early in H. VI. For 3 trotters granted to him on account of his old age and infirmity (i.e. between Mich. 1414 and Mich. 1416), see For. Accts. 6 H. V, 19, with their names in Exch. Accts. 106/24(1). On March 4, 1417, he is still almoner, Exch. Accts. 106/24(2). In Memoranda Roll K. R. 3–4 H. V, 19, June 12, 1415, Simon Stobey and Stephen Payn are "nos Alsmoigns."

[5] i.e. 3 gold nobles + 5s., Pat. 1 H. V, i. 19.

[6] Or creeping to the cross, Maskell, iii. 391; or kissing the cross, Rock, iv. 99.

[7] Not the *Abbey* of Langley, as Rowlatt, 28.

[8] Wylie, i. 117; cf. At Langle byryde fryste, Greg. Chron. 53; and to Langley was he bore, Petegrue, 593; N. Bell, 39, supposes that "where its resting place was is not known." Not "en une petite église assez près de Pomfret," as Waurin, i. 40, 167. Called "the Frerys of Langley," in Brut, ii. 373, 592, who gives a Yorkist story that Richard's life was prolonged for a day or two by a vision in which a fair woman fed him with a kercher full of white roses.

[9] Chron. Lond. 96; not "before harvest," as Fabyan, 577; or "soon after Easter," as Kennett, i. 309; or "before the funeral of Henry IV," as Larrey, 806. Hoccleve's poem "faite tost apres que les osses du roi Richard furent apportez à Westmoster," according to the French colophon (which dates soon after the death of Henry V, que Dieu pardoint, Hoccleve, Min. Po. p. 41), was evidently written before the Lollard outbreak, ibid. 47; Mason, 14; Anglia, v. 20.

14 years[1] and buried with a royal terment[2] in his own tomb at Westminster. A hearse was fixed up with lights for the service and the banners recently made for the funeral of Henry IV were borrowed for it from the cathedral at Canterbury[3]. The body was stripped of its leaden lap, laid in a new elm coffin and placed on a horse-bier[4] housed[5] with black velvet[6], 120 torches[7] being sent down from the royal chandry[8] to burn around it as it trundled along at a crawling pace, for even the exact rate of speed[9] had been minutely prescribed in the details of the unfortunate king's will. A crowd of bishops, abbots, lords, knights and squires[10] followed with it and 100 marks were distributed as largess

---

[1] Wals. ii. 297; Hypodig. 446; Worcester, ii. 453. For supposition that the body had never been removed from Pontefract based upon a wrong inference from dates of entries in the Issue Roll of 1 H. IV (Wylie, i. 115), see Traison, lxi; Kervyn de Lettenhove, Richard II, 335; Moberley, 289. For picture of King Richard's funeral in 1400 with the whole body shown on a car drawn by one horse, see Benham and Welch, 74 (from Froissart MS. Harl. 4380); Gee, 12; Knight, Shakespeare's Rich. II, p. 158.

[2] Caxton, i. 224; Brut, ii. 373; more regio, Wills of Kings, 192, 194; of royall greate araye, Hard. 372; don a dirige royally, Chron. Lond. 96. Cf.

> My wit souffysith nat to peyse and weye
> With what honour he broght is to this town
> And with his queene at Westmynstre in the abbeye
> Solempely in Toumbe leid adoun. Hoccleve, Min. Po. 48.

He was leyde at Westminster by Anne the Quene, Petegrue, 593; Weever, 471. For terment, see Wylie, iii. 208; Grey Friars Chron. xliii. 50; or enterment, Secreta, 151; or entierment, Brut, ii. 494.

[3] See page 48. For £10 paid for this to the Prior of Christ Church, Canterbury, see Devon, 325, Nov. 8, 1413; Hope, Effigies, 18. For £55. 6s. 8d. paid to the sacrist at Westminster for wax, torches, banners, guytons and barriers round the hearse p' annivers' Ricardi II lately buried within the Abbey at Westminster, see Iss. Roll 1 H. V, Mich., Feb. 19, 1414.

[4] Devon, 326, 332. For illustration showing two horses tandem, see Harl. MS. 4379; Humphreys, Frois. II. Plate xxxvi; Archaeologia, vi. 314; Macfarlane-Thomson, i. 553; Aubrey, ii. 9; Benham-Welch, 74; De Witt, 823. For a one-horse bier, see Dulcken, 372; Besant, Survey, i. 94. Cf. cary hym in a chare, Archaeologia, i. 349; Maskell, II. lxxvi; a ryal chare, Brut, ii. 373; Caxton, Chron. i. 224; chaire royale, Weever, 471; not that "the mouldering corpse was *seated*(!) in a rich chair of state," &c., as Strickland, ii. 116, or a "throne of cloth of gold," as Towle, 253.

[5] For house de Turkeie, see Boys, 138; horsehouses de rouge drap, Rot. Parl. iv. 228.

[6] Trapped yn black and bete with diuers armez, Brut, ii. 373; Caxton, i. 224.

[7] Waurin, ii. 167. For £43. 11s. 2d. paid for this item, see Devon, 327, Dec. 1, 1413. King Richard had specified 24 torches with an additional 100 as they passed through London, Wills of Kings, 193. Cf. "with taper and torche and gret rialte," Laud Troy Book, 350.

[8] For Giles Thornton serviens de la chaunderie, see Iss. Roll 1 H. V, Mich., Dec. 1, 1413; cf. Halliwell, 240; cerarii, Rym. ix. 291. The unused wax was removed when the service was over, see payment in Devon, 328.

[9] viz. from 14 to 16 miles per day, Rym. viii. 75; Wills of Kings, 193; Gough, i. ii. 164.

[10] Waurin, ii. 167. For £56. 0s. 22d. (*sic*) paid for expenses of divers lords and other officers at Langley and thence to Westminster, 4 days in December, for transfer of the body of Richard II, see Rym. ix. 189.

on the route[1]. At Westminster the service was attended by the king[2], who ordered that 4 large tapers were to burn continually at the tomb[3] and gave 4 pieces of gold racamas[4] to adorn it, arranging for a dirge and requiem mass to be sung and 6s. 8d.[5] to be given to the poor every week, together with £20[6] in pennies[7] at every yearly mind[8]. After receiving King Richard's body the tomb was closed down again, but not left airtight[9] as it had been when the remains of Queen Anne were laid in it 19 years before[10]. A wedge was inserted at the foot to level and steady it and the plumber who was employed to do the soldering left his iron pincers inside it, and there they lay for over 450 years till the tomb was opened again in 1871. But for at least a century before this, poor Richard's body had been poked at by antiquaries[11] and schoolboys through a hole in the stone-work and his jawbone found its way successively to country rectories in Kent[12] and Hampshire[13], whence it has been recently returned and replaced within the tomb at Westminster.

Queen Anne had died[14] in the royal manor-house at

---

[1] Devon, 328. For 40s. to be distributed circa corpus Ricardi II from Langley to Westminster tempore exequiarum and £20 paid fratribus de Langley, see Iss. Roll 1 H. V, Mich., Feb. 22, 1414. Waurin (i. 167) supposes that the body rested for a night at St Paul's before being interred at Westminster.

[2] Worcester, 453; Hume, iv. 35.

[3] Harpsfeld, 587.

[4] i.e. embroidered, see Godefroy, Cotgr., s.v. *Recamer.* Draps dor dragmas blank, Pat. 2 H. V, ii. 38; Cal. Pat. H. V, i. 228, Apr. 18, 1414; not raginas, as J. T. Smith, 171; Rackham, 9. For panno nuncupato racami, see Tuetey, Test. 350; cf. sa cote de racami, ibid. 416; or racamat, Wylie, ii. 444.

[5] First Life, 21; Stow, 343; Speed, 767; Weever, 471; more probable than 11s. 8d. as Brut, ii. 494; Caxton, i. 224; Fabyan, 577; Anstis, ii. 61; Goodwin, ii. 447; Lingard, iii. 236 note; Bradley, 98; Church, 49; Cassell, i. 517.

[6] Not £70, as Hartwright, 108.

[7] To be delyd penny mele, Brut, ii. 494.

[8] In Caxton, Dial. 25, "a yeresmynd" = "ung annyversaire."

[9] Archaeologia, xlv. 312.

[10] i.e. on Aug. 3, 1394, Strickland, i. 612.

[11] Neale, ii. 110; Archaeologia, xlv. 313. Cf. "in the holes of which (i.e. where the shields had been torn away) putting my hands I could turn the boards of his coffin," Dart, ii. 45.

[12] i.e. Wouldham near Rochester, Archaeologia, xlv. 314. Murray-Smith (58) says that it is still treasured by the grandchildren of the Westminster schoolboy to whom it was given by a schoolfellow who purloined it in 1766, see Wylie, iv. 147 note.

[13] i.e. Chilcomb near Winchester in the possession of Rev. G. T. Andrewes, who returned it to Westminster for burial on Feb. 26, 1906.

[14] i.e. on June 7, 1394, from her epitaph, Weever, 473; R. F. Williams, i. 163; Garnett, Richmond, 8; Hope, Effigies, 28; not June 10th, as Mirot, Trousseau, 125; do. Isabelle, xviii. 558. For picture of her death-bed, see Humphreys, Frois. II. Plate xxxi, where she wears a large night-cap.

Sheen[1] on the south bank of the Thames, and in his passionate grief King Richard had cursed the place and had the buildings demolished[2]. Though standing in a lovely spot[3], it had never been a place of royal dimensions[4] and during the whole of the reign of Henry IV the manse was left in ruins. But his son had other plans in view. On the site of the ruined house now occupied by the terrace[5] which George III built for his Maids of Honour on the western side of Richmond Green, he erected a "curious and costly" building[6], which after standing for 80 years was burnt down[7] in the reign of Henry VII, who rebuilt it[8] as Richmond Court on so magnificent a scale that men called it a second Paradise and claimed that it had no equal in all the world[9]. It was this king who changed the name of the place to that

[1] In manerio regio de Shene, Wals. ii. 186; Wylie, iv. 207. Cf.
And when this boke is made give hit the quene
On my behalfe at Eltham or at Shene.
                                        Chaucer (S.), IV. pp. xx, 101.
[2] Mansum de Shene quod fuit absque domo, Lib. Metr. 102; ad solum usque prostratum, Gesta, 7; Chron. Giles, 9; Dugd. Monast. vi. 31; Lambarde, Dict. 351; "overthrew the whole house," Weever, 473; E. T. Bradley, 65, 88, though this is doubted in R. F. Williams, i. 171, who thinks (p. 195) that Henry V only "restored the old structure probably with improvements." N. Bell, 7, thinks that the house was only partially destroyed; Hodgson (324) that "there may be some truth in the story."
[3] Delectabilem mansionem, Vita, 25. For position of it see the picture in Nichols, Progresses, ii. 412.
[4] Manning and Bray, i. 409. For evidences of a royal residence there temp. Ed. I, see Nichols, Progresses, ii. 404; Hodgson, 323.
[5] i.e. Maid of Honour Row, Chancellor, 84; do. Historic Richmond, 134. For picture, see N. Bell, 26.
[6] Tit. Liv. 5; Wals. ii. 300; Chron. Giles, 9; Monast. vi. 30, 542. For the "grete work" begun in 1414, see Chron. Lond. 99; Mon. Francisc. ii. 165; which as yet is knowne to manie men that have seene the same, First Life, 19 (written in 1513). For the waterbridge and the great quadrangle with the gatehouse to be rebuilt in 1445, see Ord. Priv. Co. vi. 32; Hodgson, 328.
[7] i.e. on Dec. 21, 1497, Kingsford, Chron. 222; Stow, Chron. 481; Excerpt. Hist. 97; not 1498, as ibid. p. 115; Nichols, Progresses, ii. 404; Manning and Bray, i. 410; Archaeologia, xlix. 246; nor 1499, as J. Evans, 18; N. Bell, 11.
[8] i.e. in 1501, Kingsford, Chron. 233; Nichols, Progresses, ii. 404, 412; Archaeologia, xlix. 247. Called "about 1500" in Aubrey, i. 58.
[9] This erthely and secounde paradise of our regioun of Engelond and as I credibly suppose of all the great parte and circuit of the world (written in 1502), Antiq. Repert. ii. 314*; Chancellor, Historic Richmond, 78. For pictures and description of Richmond Court, see Nichols, Progresses, ii. 404, 412; Roujoux-Mainguet, i. 743; Craik-Macfarlane, ii. 841, from Vetusta Monumenta, II; Lysons, Environs, i. 442; Cassell, ii. 252, 253; Garnett, 10, 11, 12, 24 (from Holler, Vinkenboom and Buck with a modern sketch of the existing gateway fronting towards the Green, ibid. 26); Macfarlane-Thomson, i. 139; S. Maurice, 58, and Frontispiece; Aubrey, i. 60 (who says (p. 58) writing in 1719 that "some umbrages of it is to be discovered in J. Speed's Map of Surrey"); Chancellor, 3, 13; do. Historic Richmond, Frontispiece; N. Bell, 10; Hodgson, 337. For view of the ruined frontage towards Richmond Green in 1737, see Buck, ii. 283; Chancellor, Historic Richmond, 6. For survey of the buildings in 1649, see Chancellor, App. p. vii; do. Historic Richmond, p. 91.

of the Yorkshire honour in Swaledale from which he took his title[1], but in Henry V's day it was still called the manor of Sheen. In the accounts of the opening years of his reign the names of John Strange[2] and John Hartshorne[3] occur as clerk of the works and controller respectively; orders were given for tin[4], glass[5], timber[6] and other necessary stuff[7]; barrels of lead and plaster[8] were sent up by sea from Lancaster; Yorkshire stone[9], Maidstone rag[10] and marble[11] were

[1] That then was called Shene but nowe Richmond, First Life, pp. x, 19.

[2] For John Strange (or Straunge), clerk of the works for the Palace at Westminster, the Tower, the castle at Berkhamsted and the manors of Kennington (i.e. Cold Kennington or Kempton, called "our manor of Colde Kenynton in Middlesex," in Claus. 1 H. V, 8, Dec. 18, 1413, cf. Wylie, ii. 292, note 5. For documents dated at Kempton manor, see Cal. Pat. H. VI, iii. 82, 91), Eltham, Clarendon, Shene, Byfleet, Chiltern Langley, Feckenham (near Droitwich, Cal. Pat. H. IV, i. 59), Hatheburgh Lodge in the New Forest (cf. Burrows, Brocas, 126; Chaucer (S.), I. xii), and the mews for the king's hawks at Charing, see Iss. Roll 1 H. V, Mich., Dec. 11, 1413, Feb. 16, 1414; ibid. 3 H. V, Pasch., Sept. 2, 1415; ibid. 6 H. V, Pasch., May 14, June 1, 20, 1418. For Strange's appointment on April 7, 1413, see Pat. 1 H. V, i. 29, when he succeeded Robert Rolleston, see Exch. Accts. 502/30, his deputy being John Skipton, in Claus. Pat. H. V, i. 59. In 1408-9 Strange had been controller of the wardrobe, see Wylie, iv. 210. For grant to him of the parkerwick of Henley-on-the-Heath on July 18, 1413, see Pat. 1 H. V, ii. 10. In Iss. Roll 6 H. V, Mich., Oct. 10, Dec. 6, 1418, 7 H. V, Pasch., July 10, 1419, 7 H. V, Mich., Oct. 27, Nov. 22, 1419, 8 H. V, Pasch., May 23, July 12, 1420, John Straunge is *late* clerk of the works for Shene and Eltham, also ibid. 8 H. V, Mich., Oct. 12, 15, Nov. 27, 29, 1420, where William Merssh is capitalis faber.

[3] For John Hertishorne (or Herteshorne, Wylie, iv. 243), sergeant-at-arms with allowance of 12d. per day (Pat. 1 H. V, iv. 32; Claus. 1 H. V, 11, Nov. 18, 1413), appointed controller of works at Byfleet and Shene Sept. 28, 1413, see Priv. Seal 658/93, 95; Pat. 1 H. V, iii. 14; iv. 23; extended to all works throughout the kingdom on Feb. 3, 1414, Priv. Seal 659/179; Pat. 1 H. V, v. 22. For 25s. paid to him as an esquire of the king's chamber, see Exch. Accts. 406/21, 27.

[4] For tin for works apud Shene, see Iss. Roll 8 H. V, Pasch., July 12, 1420, where Walter Brigg is clerk of the works, also in Iss. Roll 7 H. V, Mich., Nov. 30, 1419, Jan. 20, Feb. 19, 1420. In Iss. Roll 8 H. V, Mich., Feb. 27, 1421, he is *late* clerk of the works.

[5] For £12. 16s. 0d. paid to Richard Coventre mercer of London for glass for works at Shene, see Iss. Roll 5 H. V, Mich., March 5, 1418.

[6] Pat. 1 H. V, iii. 19d (Sept. 24, 1413); do. 2 H. V, i. 19d (June 14, 1414); do. 5 H. V, 11, 20 (Aug. 7, Nov. 17, 1417). For £233. 6s. 8d. paid for the new works at Shene, see Iss. Roll 3 H. V, Pasch., Sept. 2, 1415. For other payments, see Iss. Roll 7 H. V, May 1, 1419.

[7] For carriage of divers estuffamenta for Shene, see Iss. Roll 8 H. V, Mich., Nov. 7, 1420.

[8] For 60 barrels of plaster and 15 of lead sent by boat from Lancaster to Shene, see Iss. Roll 6 H. V, Mich., Oct. 27, 1418; also vessels and utensils costing £48. 0s. 2od., ibid. Dec. 7, 1418.

[9] For £33. 13s. 4d. paid pro petris de Stapelton, see Iss. Roll 8 H. V, Mich., Feb. 27, 1421. For Yorkshire stone for building our manor at Shene, see Pat. 1 H. V, v. 21 d, Feb. 12, 1414. For order to John Atte Welle and William King to provide stone for the same, see Pat. 3 H. V, ii. 35.

[10] See p. 206, note 6. For payments to William Catton, clerk of the king's ships, for carrying stone and divers things and harness from Maidstone to Shene and elsewhere, see Wardrobe Accts. 406/26 (1415).

[11] For payments for 300 doliat' petri de mar', see Iss. Roll 7 H. V, Pasch., May 1, 12, 1419; also for 25 dol' de plastre and 5 dol' petrar' de marr', see Iss. Roll 8 H. V, Mich., Oct. 2, 1420, i.e. marble (perre de marbre, Rym. vii. 796), not Caen stone, as Lethaby, 176.

brought round by boat[1], and there are plenty of payments for the wages of the masons and carpenters and other artificers who were employed[2]. Among these records two items are of special interest, one of which gives the payment for lifting fruit-trees and plants in the gardens[3], several of them being brought over from Normandy[4]; the other shows 52s. paid to Robert Brown for carving swans in the king's room at Sheen[5]. Some few years ago a gorged swan[6] carved in stone was unearthed in digging foundations in the grounds of Queensberry House between the riverside and Richmond Green[7], and if this be one of the swans of Robert Brown's workmanship it would appear to have been the only relic that remains of King Henry's building, and the fact that even this carved stone cannot now be traced is typical of the total annihilation that has overwhelmed his short-lived royal residence at Sheen.

But the rebuilding of this manse was only a portion of a far larger scheme upon which the zealous young king had set his heart. In making his peace with Pope Gregory XII in 1408[8] his father had been enjoined to build three religious houses in expiation for his share in the deaths of King Richard and Archbishop Scrope[9]. But more than five years had elapsed and nothing seemed likely to be done, now that Gregory had been himself deposed and had become a helpless laughing-stock to the mass of Englishmen[10], though the new king's tenderness for Richard's memory would have been incomplete without a further effort to carry out his father's expiation to the full. Accordingly he made a grant of land on the river-bank to the north of his

[1] For boats of 2 tons portage bringing stone to Shene, see Rym. ix. 447, April 14, 1417.
[2] e.g. £26. 13s. 4d., in Iss. Roll 5 H. V, Pasch., Aug. 3, 1417; also ibid. 6 H. V, Pasch., May 14, June 1, 20, 1418.
[3] i.e. to Jean du Pont gouverneur et sourveour de noz jardins de nostre manoir de Shene, Chancery Warrants, Ser. 1. 1364/31, July 27, 1417. For his appointment as governor and supervisor of the gardens at Shene, see Pat. 5 H. V, 1, July 17, 1417.
[4] For £4. 7s. 8d. paid for shipping of 3 pipes cum plant' diversarum arborum from Rouen to Southampton to be carted thence to Shene, see Iss. Roll 8 H. V, Pasch., May 9, 1420.
[5] Devon, 357, Oct. 3, 1418.
[6] For swans and harts on the screen of Henry V's Chapel in Westminster Abbey, see Le Keux, 40.
[7] Chancellor, Historic Richmond, 57, 73.
[8] Brut, ii. 494 ; Wylie, ii. 352.
[9] See App. T.
[10] Wylie, iii. 395.

new manse[1], on which to build a priory for 40 Carthusian monks[2], where prayers should be said for his soul and that of his grand-parents and other ancestors[3]. The monastery was to be called " Bethlehem[4]," or more fully "the House of Jesus of Bethlehem of Shene[5]" because Jesus had cast down the heretics, preserved the Catholics and given peace abroad and security at home[6]. With a view to making the necessary start Henry wrote to the Prior of the Grande Chartreuse[7], announcing that he was building a house to the honour of God and begging that the Prior would send him over with all speed seven monks of the Teutonic province[8] and of specially good conversation. The foundation charter was signed on April 1, 1415[9], and an Englishman, John Widrington[10], was appointed the first prior.

[1] Tit. Liv. 5; Vita, 25; Manning and Bray, i. 417; Monast. vi. 29, where the site extends from Hakelot by Divers-bush on the south to the cross called Cross-Ash on the north; not " on the site of Richard II's palace" as Tyler, ii. 28; Yonge, Cameos, 256.

[2] For the solitary life of the Carthusians, who quitted their cells only three times a day, i.e. for the office in the night, High Mass in the forenoon and vespers in the evening, see Monget, I. viii, who gives a picture of the interior of a cell (i. 106). For the dress of the Carthusians, made of white woollen serge, see ibid. i. 160. For the nine Carthusian houses in England see Monast. vi. 3; Harris, 15.

[3] "After he made religious at Shene then," Lydgate, in Gesta, 214; or "at the Shen," Petegrue, 594. Circumcinctus in his fragrans fert gesta notata. Dum rex probra piat alter et annus erat, Lib. Metr. 102; i.e. in fundacione monasteriorum et reparacione manerii de Shene, Bodl. MS. 496, fol. 224*b*.

[4] Domus Carthusiensium quae vocatur Bethleem, Rym. ix. 290; Tit. Liv. 5; Vita, 25; notre maison de Betleem, Cott. MS. Otho B. xiv; Sandford, 291; Gesta, 7.

[5] Monast. vi. 29, 31, from the foundation charter; French Roll 4 H. V, 4; Ewald, xliv. 588; Mart. Anec. i. 1746; domus Jhū de Bethleem de Shean, Q. R. Miscellaneous Books, no. 7, p. 93; Carte, Rolles, i. 260; or " de Bedleem de Shene," Pat. 3 H. V, ii. 30, July 12, 1415; Domus Jhū de Betheleme, Iss. Roll 3 H. V, Mich., Oct. 30, 1415; Cal. Pat. P. R. O. H. VI, ii. 250; "apud Schene," Wals. ii. 300; Hypodig. 450; "la meason de Chartuse de Shene," or "domus Carthusiensis de Shene," Rym. x. 317, Feb. 12, 1424; "the Charterhouse of Shene," Greg. Chron. xliv (1465); "meason de Jhū de Bethleem pres de Shene," Priv. Seal Writs 1423/114; "Jhū of Bethlehem of Shene," Statutes, iii. 406; not "St Jean" as Bréquigny, 266. In the survey of 1649 it is called "the monastery of West Shene," its wall forming the western boundary of Richmond Little Park, Chancellor, p. 111. For seal of the Priory, see Birch, 131.

[6] Pacificat aemulos exteriores et domat intrinsecos, Monast. vi. 31.

[7] Domus Cartusiensis in Sabaudiâ, Add. MS. 24,062, f. 145.

[8] De provinciâ teotonicorum, including among them dominum Wynemarm in regno nostro professum et presencialiter in domo Hollandie aut illorsum ut concepimus constitutum, ibid. f. 145.

[9] Monast. vi. 33.

[10] Cura et regimine *alicujus* prioris de regno nostro, Add. MS. 24,062, f. 145, showing that this letter was written before Widrington's actual appointment. Widrington is called Prior on March 7, 1416 (3 H. V), Manning and Bray, i. 420; not March 7, 1414, as Monast. vi. 29. For £20 granted to him pro certis operationibus in prioratu de novo faciendis, see Iss. Roll 3 H. V, Mich., Oct. 30, 1415. In Fr. Roll 4 H. V, 3, March 13, 15, 1417; Ewald, xliv. 588, he is going abroad, attorneys being appointed for him and John Maplestede, Prior of the House of the Salutation of the Mother of God (i.e. the Charterhouse) in London, though the name of the latter does not occur in the list of Priors in Monast. vi. 9. For the London Charterhouse founded by Walter

Masons, carpenters, tilers[1] and labourers were soon engaged
to get forward with the building[2], and as soon as King
Henry was master of Lower Normandy he did not forget
to have the monks supplied with the beautiful white stone
from the quarries at Caen[3] to build their church, their cells
and their cloisters[4]. Books and other valuable accessories
were supplied by the brethren at Mount Grace[5] in the
North Riding of Yorkshire, to whom large sums of money
were paid on this account from the Exchequer[6].

Within the priory was a cell for a hermit who was
always to be a priest[7]. This cell was separately endowed[8],
and it comes as somewhat of a shock to our preconceived
opinions as to the rigid austerity of the 15th century
hermit's rule of life to find that the first holder of the
post at Sheen, whose name was John Kingslow[9], had two
servants to wait on him and a personal allowance of
20 marks a year[10].

Manny, who died in 1361, see W. H. Hale, 312, who gives the text of his will. It was
built in 1371 on a space called "Nomansland" (Letter Book I, 82), or "The Spittle
Croft," or "the new Churchhaw" (i.e. churchyard, Halliwell, i. 249. For the Pardon
Chirchehawe, i.e. St Paul's Churchyard, see Sharpe, Wills, ii. 423), now Charterhouse
Square, where the bodies of 50,000 victims of the plague were buried in 1348, see
Knight, London, ii. 114, 117; Hale, 311; Loftie, i. 227; Hope, Charterhouse, 294,
306; Vict. Hist. London, ii. 209. For plan of the buildings see Hale, 328.
   [1] For order for tilers to make tiles for Bethlehem see Pat. 5 H. V, 28 d, March 22,
1417. For whityng and anelyng (i.e. tempering, Halliwell, 61), de Tewle appellez
pleintile, autrement nommez thaktile, roftile ou crestile, cornertile et guttertile, see
Stat. ii. 463.
   [2] In Pat. 4 H. V, 3 dors., Add. MS. 4601/93 (120) is a document dated Mortlake,
March 20, 1417, arranging for masons, carpenters, tilers, labourers and others for the
work, also for timber, stone, and other necessaries to be brought in a boat, showing that
the letters quoted in Gesta 7, from "Letters missive Hy V, in Tower of London,"
written at Mortlake, March 17, 20, probably refer to the year 1417; not 1414 as usually
supposed, see R. F. Williams, i. 198; Chancellor, 69.
   [3] For quarries of white stone at Vaucelles, Calix, Quilly, and Haute Allemagne, all
in the neighbourhood of Caen, see Vaultier, Recherches, 3, 26, 32, 45. For the church
of St Michael at Vaucelles see Britton, 19, and Plate.
   [4] Bréquigny, 260, May 1, 24, 1418; Carte, Rolles, i. 260; Ewald, xli. 686; Caumont,
Journal, 307.
   [5] Wylie, ii. 220. For seal of the Priory see Birch, 125.
   [6] For £100 paid to them as part of a larger amount ordered for their Abbey (*sic*) at
Shene, see Devon, 340, April 11, 1415; not for the Bridgettines at Syon, as Tyler, ii. 31.
   [7] Brut, ii. 496; Caxton, 234. It was situated infra precinctum, Priv. Seal 5 H. V
(857), Aug. 8, 1417, and is called reclusorium perpetuum for one recluse chaplain, or
the "Anchorites cell," in the survey of 1649. Not that it was built in 1616, as
N. Bell, 40.
   [8] i.e. with 20 marks p.a. charged on the revenues of the alien priories of Lewisham
and Greenwich, Manning and Bray, i. 420. For 6s. 8d. paid in 1415 by the Prior and
monks of Shene on goods and chattels in the Hundred of Blackheath, see Q. R.
Miscellaneous Books, no. 7, p. 93.
   [9] Manning and Bray, i. 420, quoting Bishop Wainflete's Register, 2, f. 37.
   [10] Pat. 5 H. V, 22; called "A servaunt" in Brut, ii. 496; Caxton, 234; or "another
priest to attend upon him," First Life, 20.

Besides their ample site the monks were endowed with lands belonging to the foreign abbeys of St Évroult[1], Ghent[2], Jumiéges[3], and Lyre[4], with a proviso that, if these lands should ever be resumed, a grant of 700 marks per annum should be secured to them from other sources as an equivalent instead. This confiscation was naturally resented by the foreign houses who suffered under it, and we have still extant a letter written by the Abbot of St Évroult to the Prior of the new Charterhouse at Sheen, urging him not to lay his foundations in plunder and thus help the Church to destroy the Church. But the Abbot might have known beforehand that his case was hopeless, for the popes themselves were recognising these confiscations as accomplished facts[5], and the protest was unheeded, even though it was afterwards solemnly brought up before the Great Council at Constance[6]. Besides these sources of income the monks were to have fishing rights and gifts of wine[7], to be exempt from taxation[8], and not to be bound to entertain the king or any of the great ones of the land, or

[1] In the forest of Ouche (pagus Uticensis), Freeman, ii. 215–228; known as Notre Dame du Bois, near Échauffour (Orne).

[2] Not Gaurot as Monstr. vi. 33; Goodwin, 341; i.e. the manor and priory of Lewisham and Greenwich, called Prioratus de Lewisham et Greenwich or Estgrenewiche, (Stat. iii. 406), which had belonged to the Abbey of St Pierre at Ghent since the time of King Alfred, Monast. vi. 34, 987, 1652; Cal. Pat. P. R. O. Henry VI, ii. 250; Hasted, i. 15; Lysons, iv. 428; L'Estrange, Greenwich, i. 18, 67. For another priory, said to have been founded at Greenwich by Edward III, see Hasted, i. 30, though this is denied by Lysons, Environs, iv. 464.

[3] i.e. Hayling, as a cell of Jumiéges, Manning and Bray, i. 418. It was appropriated to them, together with Carisbrooke, on April 6, 1417, Pat. 5 H. V, 35; cf. Goodwin, 341, who thinks that Hayling belonged to "the Abbey of Lesne in France."

[4] Including Carisbrooke, Monast. vi. 29, 1030, 1652; Pat. 3 H. V, ii. 30; Manning and Bray, i. 420. For account of the Abbey of Lyre, near Conches (Eure), see Gall. Christ. xi. 644, called Ste Marie de Lira in Carte, Rolles, i. 265; Memoranda Roll K. R. 3–4 H. V, m. 28.

[5] e.g. the alien priory of Stoke Clare in Suffolk, belonging to the Abbey of Bec which had been seized by Edward III, and granted to Westminster in 1391 (J. A. Robinson, 17), see Bull of John XXIII, dated at Constance, Jan. 17, 1415, in Papal Lett. vi. 456; Monast. viii. 1416, from Cotton MS. Vitellius D. xiii. f. 75 a.

[6] For fruitless appeal to the Council of Constance against Henry V, dated Oct. 27, 1416, by Michael Philippi, Abbot of St Évroult (i.e. from June 11, 1408, to March 23, 1439), for granting three of his priories to the Carthusians in England, news of which had been brought to him by Friar Richard Bussain, see Mart. Anec. i. 1746; Gall. Christ. xi. 827; L. Hommey, ii. 377. Two of these priories would be Ware in Hertfordshire (Wylie, iii. 143, note 1), and Middleton Cheney near Banbury (Monast. vi. 29, 133; Bridges, i. 184; Manning and Bray, i. 417); the third was probably one of the Abbot's cells in Normandy, called Noion and Newmarket in Monast. vi. 31; Goodwin, 341; Manning and Bray, i. 418, but de Nogione and de Novoforo in Gall. Christ. xi. 823; i.e. Noyon-sur-Andelle (Eure) and Neufmarché near Gournay (Seine Inf.), Cal. Pat. H. V, i. 501.   [7] N. Salmon, 201.

[8] For the Prior of Sheen to be "discharged of dimes and quinzimes" see Chancery Warrants, Ser. 1. 1364/55, May 20, 1418; cf. "neither quinzisme, disme nor taxe,"

to find pensions or corrodies[1] for their dependents. They were to have leets and lawdays and other manorial institutions, and both they and their tenants were to be free from the payment of pickage[2], stallage, carriage, and all other such seigniorial dues.

Before the king left England on his first voyage to France the monastery had been consecrated and sufficient endowment had been provided for the 40 inmates, but the buildings, which were known as his "great work[3]," were not yet completed[4], and in the will that he made on July 24, 1415, he left money for erecting their "larger house[5]." When the brethren were dispossessed at the Dissolution they retired to Nieuport in Flanders[6], and although the buildings at Sheen were still entire in Queen Elizabeth's days[7], yet all trace of them has now long since disappeared, though we know with some exactness the position and

---

Tit. Liv. 218 ; for "quinsimes and dessimes" see Fortescue, 139 ; Murray, Dict., s.v. *Dime*; "desmes and fifteens," Cotton, Abridg. 468.

[1] See Blount, s. v. *Conredium, Corody, Corredy*; called "a convenient method for rewarding officials," Fisher, 370.   For corrodies, pensions, fees, and annuities, see Rot. Parl. iv. 104.   For corrodies at accession, called "don ou droit de joyeux avènement," see L. Legrand, Maisons Dieu, 142.   For 40*s.* nomine corrodii at Croyland see Croyl. Cont. 513.   For corrodies at religious houses see Wylie, ii. 25, note 10.   Also at Coventry, Claus. 4 H. V, 7 d; Hist. MSS. 15th Rept. App. Pt. x. p. 137 ; at Bermondsey for a varlet of the King's kitchen, Claus. 4 H. V, 7 d ; Priv. Seal 665/757 ; at St Osyth for a serviens stabuli, Claus. 4 H. V, 14 d; Priv. Seal 664/666 ; at Winchester, Priv. Seal 659/156, 665/769 ; Vale-Royal, ibid. 665/786 ; Abbotsbury, Claus. 5 H. V, 4 d ; Priv. Seal 665/872 ; Abingdon, Excerpt. Hist. 145 ; St John's Hospital, Sandwich, Boys, 139, 140 ; Westminster, Hist. MSS. Rept. iv. 174 ; Worcester, Carte, Rolles, i. 270 ; Priv. Seal 659/162 ; at Whitby, Priv. Seal 659/125 ; at York, ibid. 659/153 ; at Reading, Hurry, 73.   For dispute (1364) as to a corrody at Plympton near Plymouth see Oliver, Mon. 129.   In 1391 the six monks at Hamble had a corrody from St Swithin's Priory at Winchester, consisting of six gowns (*pelliciae*), six pairs of boots and shoes, 21 loaves and 42 flagons (*justae*) of ale, giving in return 20,000 oysters at Mid-Lent every year, Kirby, Hamble, 253, 260.   For a corrody in the Hospital at Bury St Edmunds, granted (1445) to Robert Curteys, probably a relation of the Abbot, see Monast. iii. 130.   For corrodies sold at Tickford to free the house from debt, see Vict. Co. Hist. Bucks. i. 363, where a corrody consists of a loaf of bread and a gallon of beer per day and four dishes of meat per week.   For a corrody at Malmesbury obtained by a forged bull in 1412, see Letter Book I, 105.   In 1315 Edward II promised that appointments to corrodies should not be made unduly onerous, Stat. i. 173 ; Clay, 213.   For 100 marks left to two persons pour achatre à eulx une corrodie durant ses vies, see Wills of Kings, 228.   For the king's right to nominate a clerk to an annual pension in ecclesiâ vestrâ on the appointment of a bishop, see Claus. H. V, 1 d.

[2] i.e. payments for breaking the ground to erect stalls at a fair, Bateson, I. xxxvi ; II. xxii ; pikagium et stallagium, Boys, 518 ; Hist. MSS. 8th Rept. p. 414.   For pickage and stallage belonging to the manor of Ashton-under-Lyne see Baines, i. 424; also payable at the Lammas Fair at Exeter, see Exeter Deeds, 1449, 1498.

[3] Grey Friars Chron. 13.

[4] Quam domum per nostros fecimus pontifices conservari...quae domus nondum plenè constructa ad complementum celeritate possibili se festinat, Add. MS. 24,062, f. 145.

[5] Ad aedificationum majoris domus suae, Rym. ix. 290.

[6] Where they were finally suppressed in 1783, Hamilton, 111.   [7] Ibid. 103.

dimensions of the hall, quadrangle and cloisters[1].   Before
the destruction fell Dean Colet made his last home within
the monastery, and died there on Sept. 16, 1519[2], and as
late as 1650 the church with the Prior's lodgings, the
refectory and the hermitage were all still partly standing;
but a generation later even these had crumbled, and
amongst the ruins had been built some "pretty villas[3]," in
one of which lived Sir William Temple with his wife,
Dorothy Osborne.   Temple called it "my little corner
at Sheen[4]," and here he grew his vines and oranges and
wall-fruit trees[5], with young Jonathan Swift at hand as his
secretary, and little Hetty Johnson[6], then a dark-haired,
bright-eyed, delicate child, the daughter of a servant in the
household[7].

One by one, however, the ruined fragments of the
monastery have gradually vanished, the last to go being
the great gateway, which was removed together with the
hamlet of West Sheen to make way for the Observatory[8],
which was erected by George III in 1767[9], and still stands
in what was known as the Old Deer Park or Richmond
Gardens.   Thus has every trace of the Carthusian buildings been long since obliterated, and local indications of

[1] J. Aubrey, v. 340; B. Willis, Mitred Abbeys, ii. 337; Manning and Bray, i. 417.
[2] Manning and Bray, i. 420; Dict. Nat. Biogr. xi. 326; N. Bell, 42.   For his will
dated June 10, 1514, see Leach, St Paul's, 204.
[3] Evelyn, Diary, ii. 122, Aug. 27, 1678; Crisp, 111; Chancellor, 72; do. Historic
Richmond, 128; Home Counties Magazine, vii. 11 (1905); N. Bell, 44.
[4] Temple, Works, ii. 41; Crisp, 110; Lysons, i. 452; not to be confused with the
house since known as Temple Grove at East Sheen, J. Evans, 34.
[5] Evelyn, ii. 272, March 24, 1688 (not Feb. 24, as Home Counties Mag. vii. 12);
Garnett, 28, 29.
[6] Stella was born at Richmond on March 13, 1681, and baptised on March 20th
following, Home Counties Mag. vii. 11.   Swift himself says (ix. 281): "I knew her
from 6 years old," i.e. from 1687, showing that they must both have been at Sheen
(as Craik, i. 26, 27, 29; Hay, 9), though it is usually supposed that Swift was only with
Temple at Moor Park, Dict. Nat. Biogr. iv. 206; J. C. Collins, 26; cf. Taine, ii. 121,
122, who calls Stella "a charming, well-informed modest young girl."   "She was
sickly from childhood until the age of 15," but as she grew up she was "a little too fat,"
Swift, ix. 281; J. C. Collins, 73; Ainger, i. 199.   For Temple's removal to Moor Park,
near Farnham, in 1686, see Manning and Bray, i. 422.
[7] Her mother was waiting-woman to Temple's sister, Lady Giffard, and "indeed
she had little to boast of her birth," Swift, ix. 281; Hay, 11, 126, who resents Macaulay's
description of the "pretty waiting-maid," and the "flirtation in the servants' hall,"
Essays, ii. 43; Hist. vi. 382.
[8] Manning and Bray, i. 422; Monast. vi. 30; Chancellor, 74; do. Historic
Richmond, 121, 128.   For picture see Lysons, Environs, i. 444; Chancellor, 67, 75;
not that this was the site of the palace as Tyler, ii. 28; Towle, 284.
[9] N. Bell, 133; i.e. for observing the transit of Venus, which took place on June 3,
1769; not 1768 as J. Evans, 30; see also Manning and Bray, i. 414.

their exact position give no more definite guidance than a shadowy reference to "some old trees and a slight unevenness of ground[1]," while a still greater disappointment awaits the searcher when he finds that pictures still passing for authentic representations in local histories[2] are altogether untrustworthy, one of them being in reality a sketch of the Friary buildings erected for Observant Friars near the Palace by Henry VII in 1499, and another painted in the time of Charles I is really a picture of the palace built by Lord Burleigh at Theobalds near Cheshunt from 1560 to 1571.

On the opposite bank of the Thames King Henry also founded a monastery for Bridgettines, which he called Syon[3], or "Mount Syon of Shene[4]," or more fully "the Monastery of St Saviour and St Brigit of Syon[5]," in the park of Twickenham[6], which formed a portion of his manor of Isleworth[7], and he whose whole reign was one ceaseless

---

[1] Monast. vi. 30.   [2] e.g. Crisp, 104; Chancellor, 75; Hodgson, 340. See App. U.

[3] Tit. Liv. 5; Vita, 25; Gasc. 140, 170; Sandford, 291; Lambarde, Dict. 352; "Syon beside Braynford" (i.e. Brentford), Brut, ii. 496; Caxton, i. 233. The names Sion and Bethlehem may have been chosen on account of Henry's reverence for the Holy Land, as suggested in Pol. Verg. 440.

[4] "De monte Syon de Shene," Iss. Roll 8 H. V, Pasch., May 9, June 25, 1420; Cal. Pat. H. VI, i. 539.

[5] Dugd. Monast. vi. 542; Rym. ix. 290; Rot. Parl. iv. 395; Aungier, 28; Iss. Roll 8 H. V, Mich., Feb. 8, 1421; Baxter, p. 6. In 1421 it is called "St Saviour, SS. Mary the Virgin and Brigit of Syon," Rot. Parl. iv. 121, 243; Myroure, xv; and frequently afterwards, Aungier, 74, 79, 465; or "Monasterium sancti Salvatoris de Syon" in a bull of Pope Martin V, dated at Geneva, Aug. 8, 1418, Cotton MS. Tiberius B. vi. f. 47; Rym. ix. 617; Monast. vi. 543; Stevens, ii. 376; Aungier, 36. In June, 1415, it is called "Ordinis Sancti Salvatoris apud Shene," Rym. ix. 275, 617; cf. "the monastery of Shene which is Syon," Aungier, 422; "the house of nonnes of Syon" (1465), Greg. Chron. xliv; "yowre Hous of Sion" (1420), Orig. Lett. II. i. 91; "Syon juxta Shene," Memorials of St Edmund's Abbey, iii. 296; "Domus sancta Syon," Amundesham, i. 27; "Domus Sancti Salvatoris juxta Shene," Kal. and Inv. ii. 97; "La meason de Seint Saveour de Shene" (1426), Ord. Priv. Co. iii. 190; Cal. Pat. H. VI, i. 380; Aungier, 201. Called "Mount Sion" or "Sion House" in Tyler, ii. 28; Ramsay, i. 191; Flavigny, 557. For seal with figures of St Adrian and St Brigit see Archaeol. xvii. 329; also showing St Brigit and the arms of Henry V, Birch, 132, who calls it "an Austin Abbey," i.e. they followed the Augustinian rule, Rym. ix. 617; Lenfant (Whatley), i. 106; cf. de l'ordre de Seint Austyn Seint Saviour appellé, Rot. Parl. iv. 243; de ordine Salvatoris, Add. MS. 24,062, f. 150. Cf. the Augustinian house of Brigittines, Maidstone, Tracts, xxviii.

[6] So described in the foundation charter, Monast. vi. 542, 543; also Rot. Parl. iv. 243, 395; infra parcarium de Twykenham, Ad Quod Damn. 372 (4 H. V); called Isleworth Park, in Cobbett, 224; or meadows belonging to Lord Frederic Cavendish, in Lysons, Environs, iii. 83; or to the Marquis of Ailsa, in Aungier, 52. For grant of a pasture in the parish of Twickenham to Bishop Langley, Henry Fitzhugh, John Rodenall, and Thomas Fishburn (who afterwards became Confessor General at Sion, p. 223), see Pat. 4 H. V, 22; Cal. Pat. H. V, ii. 34, April 20, 1416.

[7] Dans son manoir de Istilworth, Rot. Parl. iv. 243; apud Tystelworth, Amundesham, i. 27; not "a portion of the royal manor of Richmond," as Baxter, p. 6. For appointment of Robert Martin to be custos of our park de Istilworth, see Pat. 5 H. V,

battle-storm dedicated his foundation as "a true son of the God of Peace, who gave peace and taught peace and chose St Brigit as a lover of peace and tranquillity[1]." For both of his religious houses he obtained ample indulgences from Rome, which brought them in a very handsome income every year at pardon-time[2].

The foundation charter of Syon was drawn up on March 3, 1415[3], one of the witnesses being Henry, Lord Fitzhugh, the King's Chamberlain[4], whose previous visit to Wadstena[5] had been the means of the first introduction of the new order into England[6]. Fitzhugh had great influence with the king, and had for several years maintained some of the brethren at his own cost in England[7], and it may have been at his instigation that a proposal had been made to convert the decayed hospital of St Nicholas without the Walmgate Bar at York into a monastery for Bridgettines in the North[8]. He now became one of the first trustees[9] for the new community on the Thames, to

27, May 1, 1417. For manor of Isleworth granted to the Abbess on Dec. 1, 1421, see Cal. Pat. H. VI, i. 539.

[1] Monast. vi. 542; Aungier, 26.

[2] Excerpt. Hist. 98; Lysons, Environs, iii. 86; Fordun (Hearne), v. 1399; Aungier, 422. See App. V.

[3] i.e. 2 H. V, Monast. vi. 542; Lel. Coll. i. 47; not 2 H. IV, as Wylie, ii. 458, note 8; nor 1413, as Stevens, ii. 223; nor 1414, as Lysons, Environs, iii. 83; Monast. vi. 540; Excerpt. Hist. 414; Goodwin, 340; Cobbett, 224. Called de novo aedificanda in Rym. ix. 289, July 24, 1415. For an extract from the charter with confirmation of privileges in 25 H. VI, 1446/47, see Aungier, 411; also by Henry VII, Aug. 17, 1486, which confirms a charter of March 24, 1465, see Exeter Municipal Records, no. 56; do. Miscellaneous Rolls, 80, and Transcripts, 2126.

[4] See page 15, note 2.   [5] Aungier, 25; Wylie, ii. 458.

[6] Tantae laudis praeconium de ordine Sancti Salvatoris per Sanctam Brigidam Suecie regionis de novo fundato quam plurium fidedignorum nobis facta relatione frequenter audivimus, Add. MS. 24,062, f. 150 (undated). In Amundesham, i. 27, Henry V is ejusdem religionis *inductor* et fundator.

[7] Myroure, xiv. For a charter of indigenation for Magnus Hemmingi (i.e. Hemmingson, cf. Wylie, ii. 458), chaplain in Sweden, see Pat. 1 H. V, v. 21, Feb. 10, 1414; Priv. Seal 659/185; Aungier, 525. Flavigny (p. 557) supposes that a colony of brethren *and sisters* was established at Hinton-Upperhall.

[8] For Henry's application to the Pope for sanction to this scheme, see Add. MS. 24,062, f. 150.

[9] Rot. Parl. iv. 243; Aungier, 32. In a deed dated July 3, 1424, in the parish chest at Twickenham, quoted in Cobbett, 226, Henry Fitzhugh appears with the Earl of Dorset, Robert Morton, esquire, and John Rodehale, knight (or Rothenhale, see p. 3, note 10), as trustee for the manors of Chilham, Molessh (i.e. Moldash or Molash) and Trewlegh (i.e. Throwley), between Faversham and Ashford, part of the confiscated property of Queen Joan (Wylie, ii. 285; they are in her keeping in Pat. 10 H. IV, i. 15, July 1, 1409) granted to Syon Abbey in 2 H. VI. For the churches of Chilham, Molesh and Throwelegh (cf. Ord. Priv. Co. i. 196), formerly belonging to the Abbot of St Bertin (in St Omer), together with the alien priory of Otterton (Devon) granted to the Earl of Dorset and others, see Pat. 3 H. V, ii. 21, April 1, 1415; Cal. Pat. H. V, i. 395; ii. 28; ibid. H. VI, i. 207 (Oct. 20, 1424).

whom he granted his manor of Hinton-Upperhall[1], near Cambridge, and when he died on Jan. 11, 1425[2], he left them £20 a year to celebrate his obit[3].

A messenger was sent over to the King's sister Philippa[4] in Sweden, and at her request four of the nuns[5] and two of the brothers sailed for England. They were escorted from Wadstena to the ship on May 20, 1415[6], by the Archbishop of Lund and a long train of Swedish knights, one of whom, together with a Swedish bishop[7], accompanied them to England. These were entrusted with a message from King Eric to King Henry, and each received a cup and a silver-gilt ewer out of the forfeited property of Henry, Lord Scrope, after his execution at Southampton. The foundation stone of the building was dedicated by Richard Clifford[8], Bishop of London, in presence of King Henry, on Feb. 22, 1415[9]. The first Abbess, Maud Newton[10], was a strict recluse from the Benedictine Abbey

---

[1] Wylie, ii. 458; Aungier, 59, 77; not Hintrim, as Flavigny, 557. It is called Hynton or Henton in Whitford, xxx; Uphale in Hinton, Monast. vi. 541; Lysons, Environs, iii. 85.

[2] Beltz, clix; Ashmole, App. ; Archaeologia, xxii. 387; Comp. Peer. iii. 364; Wylie, ii. 221, note 6.

[3] Aungier, 55, 528; Myroure, xiv. For his name in the Martiloge under December 31, see Whitford, xxx, from Add. MS. 22,285; Flavigny, 557; Hamilton, 3.

[4] For her tombstone at Wadstena see Andersen, 188; Marryat, i. 295, 300; Hamilton, 56; Baxter, 7; Higgins, i. 169, who thinks (p. 146) that her fondness for Wadstena was due to the fact that her mother Mary de Bohun was "educated in a Clarist convent," see Wylie, iv. 132. For Wadstena (called Wastein in Whitford, xxvii, now "the Bedlam of Sweden," Hammerich, 285) see Higgins, i. 96, 100; Hamilton, 1 (with picture of the Chapter-house); Wylie, ii. 453. For Margaret Abbissa Wastenae, who wrote a life of St Brigit, see Oudin, iii. 2316.

[5] Their names appear in a list of the inmates of Syon drawn up in 1428, Aungier, 51, but Dan Magnus Hemmingson and John of Calmar are not in it. Higgins (i. 148) adds three novices; also Bateson, Catalogue, xii; Baxter, 6. For "monastères doubles" and "la double communauté" in hospitals, see A. Chevalier, 1. pp. vi, xi, 53.

[6] Wazsten. Diar. 54; Myroure, xiv.

[7] Iss. Roll 3 H. V, Mich., Oct. 30, 1415, shows £4. 4s. 9½d. paid for their meals and other expenses, jam *raro* venient' (= "who lately arrived," Devon, 343), conducting certain ladies versus Shene infra quandam abbatiam pro illis constructam includend', &c.

[8] Not *Thomas* Clifford, as Hamilton, 95. For Bishop Clifford's gift to them (£10) see Whitford, p. 30. In Priv. Seal Writs 1423/114 the Prior of the Carthusians at Shene is to have the nomination of four out of the 24 scholars at "Clifford College," which the Bishop proposed to found at Oxford. For his pontifical now in the library of Corpus Christi College at Cambridge (MS. no. 79) with his arms see York Pontifical, p. xxxix. For office for the admission of nuns and friars to the order of St Brigit in Archbishop Chichele's pontifical, see ibid. pp. xli, xlii.

[9] Archaeologia, xvii. 327; Myroure, xv; Aungier, 31; Bateson, Catalogue, xii; not as a thanksgiving for Agincourt, as Flavigny, 557.

[10] Monast. vi. 542, where she is monialem professam ordinis predicti (i.e. Augustinian); Lysons, Environs, iii. 84; not Joan North, as Whitford, xxvii, who was not elected till 1420; Ellis, Orig. Lett. ii. i. 91, where Bishop Clifford states that he installed her on Sunday, May 5, proving the year to be 1420, not 1421 as Monast. vi. 541.

at Barking[1], and the first General Confessor was William Alnwick, the Westminster hermit, who had played so large a part in the king's opening conversion[2]. Syon has been called "the youngest child of monkery[3]," "the centre of the devotional life of the period, representing the very pink of pious orthodoxy[4]." It was founded in a time of religious alarm and, as might have been expected, the Bridgettine life was based upon an ideal of exceptional strictness and severity[5]. This is reflected not only in the well-known code of silence[6] planned out for the daily routine, but in the character of the appointment of its earliest administrators. But Alnwick was already getting old, and after a year of "looking after women[7]" he went back again to his Westminster cell[8]. He was succeeded in 1420[9] by Thomas Fishbourne, who had had a much more worldly training before accepting such responsibilities. He had

---

[1] In Pat. 5 H. V, 20, 29; Priv. Seal 5 H. V (822), Mathilda Newton is a recluse (*inclusa*) at Barking on May 12, 1417; also Claus. 6 H. V, 19, April 24, 1418; Chancery Warrants, Ser. 1. 1364/46. For payment to her (moniali incluse apud Berkyng) see Iss. Roll 6 H. V, Pasch., June 20, 1418. For 1000 marks p.a. granted to the Abbess on March 3, 1415, see Iss. Roll 8 H. V, Mich., Feb. 8, 1421. For £50 paid to the Abbess see Iss. Roll 8 H. V, Pasch., May 9, June 25, 1420. In the parish church chest at Twickenham is an inspeximus dated in the Chapter-house at Syon Nov. 29, 1444, referring to Johanna *nuper* abbatissa (i.e. Joan North, elected Sept. 30, 1428, Aungier, 108); also a deed dated Dec. 3, 1444, whereby Abbess Mathilda (i.e. Maud Muston, who was Abbess in 1448, elected on Oct. 5, 1433, Aungier, 56, 108, who dates her death on Jan. 8, 1447, when she was succeeded by Margaret Ashby; Monast. vi. 541) releases her tenants in Istelworthe (i.e. Isleworth) from payment of a tallage of £20 p.a., see Cobbett, 226. For seal of the Abbey at Barking see Pedrick, p. 30, Plate xvi. For pardon to Sybilla de Felton, Abbess of Barking, see Memoranda Rolls K. R. 3-4 H. V, m. 80, Nov. 8, 1415. For a book (MS. Wood, t. xxx), probably compiled by Sybil Felton in 1404 for use of future Abbesses of Barking, see Monast. i. 437. For confirmation of charters to Barking, May 8, 1424, see Cal. Pat. H. VI, i. 208.

[2] Page 199, note 5.

[3] N. Salmon, 201. Fisher, 370, notes that there were "only about 8 religious houses founded from 1399 to 1509."

[4] Gasquet, Bible, 125; Church Quart. Rev. li. 276.

[5] For the Bridgettine life see Higgins, i. 102, 104-106. For brass of a Bridgettine nun (1561) in Isleworth Church, see Lysons, Environs, iii. 104; Hamilton, 66.

[6] Wylie, ii. 455.

[7] In custodiam foeminarum praefectus, Amundesham, i. 27, where he is taedio et senio confectus.

[8] He is not to be confounded with Wm Alnwick, the plotter of 1407, or the Wm Alnwick who became Bishop of Norwich (1426-1436) and Lincoln (1436-1449), as Dict. Nat. Biogr. i. 343; Wylie, iii. 149, note 2; called William Alwyk in Stone, 20, who gives his consecration as Bishop of Norwich by Archbishop Chichele at Canterbury on Aug. 18, 1426. He had previously been a monk at St Albans, and was made Prior of Wymondham in 1420, Archdeacon of Salisbury in the same year, and confessor to Henry VI, Dict. Nat. Biogr. i. 343. For William Alnwick, decretorum doctor, commissioned to negotiate with representatives of the Duke of Brittany, July 7, 1420, see Rym. x. 1.

[9] Not 1421, as Wylie, ii. 360, note 6.

originally been a sewer or table-setter[1] in the monastery of St Albans in the days of Abbot Heyworth, whence he had travelled to Rome and obtained a special dispensation to be ordained. He afterwards lived a hermit's life at St Germains near Paris, where he was brought under King Henry's notice through his obsequiousness to some great ladies[2]. His personal influence with Henry is proved by the fact that Archbishop Chichele consulted him when asked to recommend a new confessor for the king in 1418[3], and he was present at the recantation of the Lollard priest, William Taylor, in the chapel at Lambeth, on Feb. 14, 1420[4]. He is known as the friend of Thomas Gascoigne[5], and his own bookish taste is shown in the collection of up-to-date volumes[6] that he bequeathed to the monastery at his death, which took place on Sept. 13, 1428[7]. Incidentally we know the name of the first Prior, James Cole[8], but as this is in connection with the acceptance of a prebend at St Paul's[9], it would seem that the literal Bridgettine ideals soon proved as unattainable in England as they did in Sweden[10]. The "rule of the Saviour" forbade individual

---

[1] Dapifer, Amundesham, i. 27.

[2] Inhaerendo et obsequendo, Amundesham, i. 11, 27, naming Eleanor Hulle, Elizabeth Beauchamp, and others. While at St Germains he had a cell built there for an anchoress (*reclusa*), and on Sept. 14, 1428, he obtained permission from the Pope to extend the buildings at Isleworth.

[3] Ellis, Orig. Lett. Ser. I. i. 3, where he is called "your priest and bedeman." He is called the King's confessor in Aungier, 55; Bateson, Catalogue, xxv; or "capellanus," in Claus. 1 H. V, 10, Dec. 5, 1413.

[4] Conc. iii. 405.

[5] For some books left by him to the monks at Syon, four of which appear in the catalogue drawn up circ. 1504–1526, see Bateson, v, xiii, xxv; Wylie, ii. 360. For Gascoigne's books left to Lincoln College, Oxford, see A. Clark, Lincoln, 8.

[6] Bateson, Catalogue, xxv.   [7] Amundesham, i. 28; Wylie, ii. 361, note.

[8] For Master James Cole, Prior unto our house of Syon at Shene, see Chancery Warrants, Ser. I. 1365/36, Apr. 30, 1422, where he is appointed to a prebend at St Paul's, vacant by the death of Master John Malvern.

[9] i.e. the prebend of Chamberlainwood, Hennessy, 20, where the appointment is dated June 12, 1422. It had been held by J. Malvern from Jan. 8, 1406, till his death on March 12, 1422. For his will dated March 12, 1422, proved March 14, 1422, see Challoner Smith, ii. 352. He had been parson of St Dunstan-in-the-East since March 8, 1412 (Hennessy, 135), and physician to Henry IV (Wylie, ii. 238). For Master John Malvern exchanging a prebend in St George's Chapel at Windsor with John Coryngham, keeper of the Free Chapel at Jesmond near Newcastle-on-Tyne, see Pat. 4 H. V, 25, June 11, 1416. For argument that the latter portion of the continuation of the Polychronicon (see Wylie, ii. 238) was not written by John Malvern, but by some unknown monk of Westminster, see J. A. Robinson, *passim*, who however offers no suggestion as to the author's actual name. For Higden (temp. Ed. III) see Gairdner, Chroniclers, 274, who calls him "a literary glutton who devoured all kinds of literature."

[10] Wylie, ii. 455, note 10. For dissensions at Wadstena with the increase of wealth and political influence, see Higgins, i. 115. For the brethren and sisters drinking wine and dancing in the orchard, see Andersen, 182.

members to have even a half-penny of their own[1], but no house could be opened which had not endowment enough to meet each year's expenses, so that the inmates might lead their secluded life with quiet minds apart from beggary and want. Accordingly, as each November came round, they figured out their estimated budget for the ensuing year and, if anything was over at the year's end, it was to be given to the poor.

Following the Wadstena pattern the members of this "holy company of men and women[2]" were to consist of 85 in all[3], i.e. 60 nuns and 25 men, including 15 professed brothers, but this number was evidently not reached all at once, for we know that on Feb. 5, 1420[4], there were only 24 nuns, five priests, two deacons, and four lay brothers[5]. From the first the king granted them 1000 marks per annum, to be paid half-yearly from the Exchequer, though shortly afterwards arrangements were made[6] for taking the money from the funds of the confiscated alien priories[7]. Further gifts and legacies came in from pious well-wishers[8],

[1] Wals. ii. 301; Hypodig. 450; Capgr. 300, 307; Wylie, ii. 457; cf. Ne kepe no jewels ne propre in store That nes no religeous ne but dedly synne, Kail, 83.

[2] Ellis, Orig. Lett. Ser. II. i. 91.

[3] i.e. to correspond with the 13 apostles (including St Paul) and 72 disciples, Otterbourne, 275; Fuller, iii. 287; Lysons, Environs, iii. 83; Higgins, i. 96; Bateson, xi; Flavigny, 148; Cobbett, 224; Hamilton, 99; Wylie, ii. 455.

[4] Archaeologia, xvii. 327; Aungier, 38; Myroure, xvi; Hamilton, 5; not 27 nuns, as Baxter, 6, who imagines that the king was present, though he was in France at the time.

[5] For picture of a lay brother serving with a pittance in a bowl see Vigne, ii. 17, Plate 41.

[6] Rot. Parl. iv. 243; Aungier, 39, 55, 528.

[7] See App. W.

[8] For £20 bequeathed to them by Archbishop Chichele, see Whitford, xxix, xxx, who adds: qui hic (i.e. at Syon) fecit primam professionem, which may mean that he took the first professions for admission after the convent was established. Henry, Lord Scrope of Masham, in his will dated June 23, 1415, gave them books and vestments to the value of £20. He appears to have been interested in the new settlement through Henry Lord Fitzhugh and the Fishbourne family, see Wylie, ii. 360; Rym. ix. 274, where he specially names Maud Fischeburn of Kilvington (i.e. South Kilvington near Thirsk, in which parish Upsall Castle is situated) and Scurneton (i.e. Scruton near Bedale, Inq. p. Mort. iv. 372). He possessed a copy of the Revelations of St Brigit, which he had bought at Beverley, and he was a friend of Sir Halneth (who cooperated with Fitzhugh in bringing the Bridgettines into England, Wylie, ii. 458) and Mary Maleverer, to whom he left a gold ring, a French book, a black box, and a white horn in his will, Rym. ix. 277. For Halnatheus Mawleverer, kt., see Papal Letters, v. 565, April 24, 1408, where a portable altar is granted to him and his wife Millicent. For Millicent wife of Halneth Mawleverer see Claus. 4 H. V, 22 d, March 23, 1416. On May 29, 1415, he is a commissioner for arraying the forces of the West Riding, Rym. ix. 253 [255]. He was M.P. for Yorkshire in 1419, Return Parl. i. 292, where he is Haulatheus Maulever miles et chivaler, but Alnatheus in Rec. Roll 8 H. V, Mich., Oct. 29, 1420. He has custody of the alien Priory of Allerton Mauleverer, near Knaresborough, in Rec. Roll 7 H. V, Mich., Jan. 19, 1420, do. 8 H. V, Pasch., June 17,

but in 1418 the monastery was returned as not yet endowed[1],
and the necessary funds could only be procured by recourse
to the old bad practice of appropriations[2] from the fruits
and profits[3] of parish churches[4], leaving only a meagre
allowance[5] to the local vicar just to enable him to live
decently after paying his episcopal dues and other burdens
that lay on every vicar's shoulders[6].

But, in spite of the fact that a large new ditch had been
expressly cut to drain their ground[7], the Twickenham site
proved unhealthy and too cramped for the intended numbers[8], even though permission was obtained to extend the
accommodation by adding an adjoining house[9].   Moreover
the king was soon taken to task for granting away the
manor of Isleworth, which could not be legally alienated
from the Duchy of Cornwall[10], while the exemptions from

1420.   For John Maulever of Co. Yorks. see Early Chan. Proc. i. 28.   For seal of
Maulevrier see Demay, Inventaire, i. 620.   For the Forêt de Maulevrier near Caudebec
see Labutte, 157; Delisle, Agric. 404; also Maulevrier (Maine et Loire) near Cholet in
Anjou.   For comitatus mali leporarii at Melay near Charolles (Saône et Loire) see
Bruchet, 24, 53.

[1] Quod nondum dotatum est, Monast. vi. 543; Rym. ix. 617; Aungier, 36; Stevens,
ii. 376.   For grant of the manor of Isleworth to the Abbess Dec. 1, 1421, see Cal. Pat.
H. VI, i. 380, 539.

[2] Wylie, iii. 240.   For Pope Martin V's approval of the foundation of Syon and of the
appropriation of the churches, see Tiberius B. VI. f. 46 b; Rym. ix. 617.   For protest
against appropriating parish churches in augmentum scienciae, virtutum et doctrinae, see
Gascoigne, 5, who holds that the founders of religious houses should build them out of
their own property.   In 1414 the University of Oxford objected to appropriations of
parish churches mensis episcopalibus ac etiam monasteriis in bonis temporalibus sufficienter
dotatis, whereby great desolation is caused to the parishioners, hospitality is withdrawn
and cure of souls neglected, as no perpetui vicarii are put in but merely sacerdotes ad
nutum remotivi qui curas vix annuales habeant, Conc. iii. 363.   For appropriations in
Scotland, see Dowden, lviii.   In 1289 the Abbey of Reading took £45. 6s. 8d. from the
parish of Eye in Herefordshire, the vicar on the spot receiving £4. 6s. 8d., Webb, ccxi.

[3] For "proffytes and frutes," see Melusine, 86.   For duties of those who received
these proceeds, see Othonis et Ottoboni, 119; Webb, cxxxvi.

[4] i.e. of Yeovil (Collinson, iii. 205, who says the manor also) and Croston near
Preston in Lancashire (Monast. vi. 543; not Crofton, as Lysons, Environs, iii. 85;
Aungier, 37, 77; Hamilton, 4, who supposes it to be in Somersetshire), the revenues
from which were estimated to yield 200 marks and 140 marks per annum respectively,
the latter through its connection with the alien Priory of St Mary at Lancaster being
dependent upon St Martin's Abbey at Séez, Baines, ii. 116.

[5] Exilis portio, Conc. iii. 363; modicam relinquent fructuum portionem, Othonis et
Ottoboni, 120.

[6] Cf. Rym. ix. 730; Conc. iii. 391, where the parish clergy should be competenter
dotati pro hospitalitate ibidem tenendâ et omnibus debitis supportandis.

[7] Fossati ibidem de novo propter religiosos constructi, Pat. 3 H. V, ii. 21, 33, 36,
April 1, July 29, Oct. 3, 1415, referring to ground in Twickenham within our coney-garth
(*cunicularium*) in our domain of Istilworth as well as to a "sewer" (Cal. Pat. H. V, i.
358) in the Thames called "Hamwere" near Kingston.

[8] Propter indispositionem et arctitudinem loci, Rot. Parl. iv. 395.   For its extent
see Lysons, Environs, iii. 83.

[9] i.e. on Sept. 14, 1428, Amundesham, i. 27.

[10] Rot. Parl. iv. 141; Lysons, Environs, iii. 84, 94; Aungier, 200.   For Isleworth

taxation[1] were opposed and rejected by Parliament as soon as the royal founder was dead[2]. Thus in 1432 it became necessary for the Bridgettines to remove and start afresh on another site a little lower down the river[3], where they remained for a hundred years and prospered greatly under the favour of legates, cardinals, bishops[4] and popes, who granted indulgences on a lavish scale to all who came and gave something towards the repair or building of their house. These benefits could be obtained by the faithful at varying rates according to the season of their visit. Thus Clean Lent[5], Shere Thursday[6], the Pask[7] and Mary Maudele were all honoured in their turn, but the big throng came at Lammas or " Peter's Chains " (i.e. Aug. 1st), when the "pardon of Syon[8]" became one of the great holidays of the Englishman's year, for on that day any contributor could secure 140 days of pardon for every penny he paid in[9], while persons at a distance could buy 500 days' worth for every creed and Lord's Prayer told off on their beads at their own homes without the cost and trouble of a personal journey[10], and over 1000 years of pardon could be had, if a man could pay for it, together with full remission for all cases reserved or unreserved, unless the applicant had broken a vow of chastity or of pilgrimage to Compostella or had smitten and killed a priest[11].

annexed to the Duchy of Cornwall by Edward III, see State Papers, Cal. Dom. (1603–1610), p. 532. A copy of this exists in the muniment room at Syon House, so I was informed by Mr C. H. How on July 10, 1905.

[1] On Oct. 20, 1424, a proviso is inserted: " except the clauses relating to exemption from taxation," Cal. Pat. H. VI, i. 207.

[2] For his obit at Syon in August, see Whitford, xxix; Aungier, 54, 528.

[3] i.e. on the site of the present Syon House, Lysons, Environs, iii. 83. On Dec. 17, 1436, the buildings are said to have not yet been brought to full perfection, Papal Lett. viii. 617.

[4] e.g. John Stafford, Archbishop of Canterbury (1446–1452); John Lettert, or Lettart, Bishop of Norwich (1446–1472), otherwise called Lyhert, Lyghard or Lyghert, Le Neve, ii. 467; Stubbs, Reg. 89; Aungier, 424, 425; Fordun, v. 1402; Vita, 25; Lysons, Environs, iii. 86.

[5] York Plays, xli.

[6] Wylie, iii. 326; Lydg. Min. Po. 36, 40, 92, 115; Worcester, Itin. 372. Called Schere Thursday, Mirk, 20; Schroffe Thursday, Pol.-Relig. Po. 28, 157. Cf. maken scheren hem honest and dode her heads and clyppen here berdes and so maken hem honest ageyn a Saturday, Gasquet, Rcl. Instr. 28.

      A tabull ther ys that men may se
      That Cryste made on his monde
      On Shere Thorsday when he breke brede
      Before the time that he was dede. Pol.-Relig. Po. 156.

[7] Cf. syth Pask, Rym. ix. 883; jour de la Paesques, Regnoult, 95; Paschalis Dies, Nicolas, Chron. of Hist. 121; la jorn de Pacas, Tardieu, Herment, 155; Wylie, ii. 419.

[8] Caxton, Dial. 28.   [9] Aungier, 424.   [10] See App. V.   [11] Aungier, 424.

With such productive resources it is not surprising that Syon grew immensely rich, and when the blow fell, the income of the house amounted to nearly £2000 a year[1]. Its wealth was then diverted and its inmates dispossessed, but for generations they carried on their direct succession in foreign lands[2] in spite of fire and earthquake. But wherever they went they called their house by the old name of Syon, ever treasuring the key of their "infinitely beloved and wished-for[3]" home on the Thames, though its doors and locks had long since perished in the general demolition[4]. In 1810 they found a refuge again in England[5], and after many changes here, they are now represented by a community living in a secluded house in Devonshire[6], where masses are still said once a year for the souls of their founder King Henry V, his sister Philippa, and their great benefactor Henry Lord Fitzhugh[7]. Yet Syon has left at least some tangible memorials, which still exist among us to remind us of her past, in the shape of a cope now shown in the Museum at South Kensington as a splendid specimen of twelfth century English needlework which the Bridgettines had acquired[8], and an English version of the New Testament which was presented to the brethren in 1517[9], and has been lately brought into prominence in a controversial

---

[1] i.e. £1944. 11s. 5¼d. or £1731. 8s. 4¾d., Aungier, 485; Wylie, ii. 458.

[2] e.g. in Zierickzee, Dendermonde (1539), Antwerp, Malines, Rouen (1584), and Lisbon (1594), Lysons, Environs, v. 202; Hamilton, 6, 102, 105, 110. In the latter city their convent was destroyed by fire in 1651 and a second time demolished by the earthquake in 1755, Monast. vi. 540; Bateson, xvii.

[3] Hamilton, 103.

[4] The keys appear to have been in their possession at Lisbon as well as the iron cross from the top of the church, Aungier, p. 111. The latter is still at Chudleigh but the Lady Abbess informs me (18/7/12) that the keys are no longer preserved.

[5] e.g. at Walworth (1811), Archaeologia, xvii. 327; in the Potteries (Staffordshire), 1825; at Spetisbury near Blandford in Dorsetshire (1861), Binder, 193; Hamilton, 6.

[6] i.e. at Chudleigh near Newton Abbot, Whitford, xxvi, where by a curious coincidence a gold noble of Henry V was found in a neighbouring field soon after their settlement in 1888, Hamilton, 6, with a view of Chudleigh (p. 81) and the capital of a column supposed to have been part of the original gateway at Syon on the Thames, now at Chudleigh (p. 85), who supposes it to have been "carried with the nuns in all their wanderings." It is figured also in Baxter (p. 12) together with a marble statue of St Brigit which is said to have once been at Syon on the Thames "and which the nuns managed to preserve through their wanderings *despite its weight*!" (p. 20).

[7] Hamilton, 3, 87; Baxter, 19.

[8] Barnard, 126, Plate lxxxvi; Burlington Magazine, vi. 278, where it is supposed to have come from the neighbourhood of Coventry; Clinch, 238, where it is dated late in the 13th century; Baxter, 19, who considers it to be "worth untold thousands." For opus anglicanum in needlework, see Dillon-Hope, 279.

[9] Now among Ashburnham MSS. App. xix, Forshall-Madden, 1. p. lxii, who dates it circ. 1400. It was published in facsimile by Lea Wilson in 1848.

attempt to prove that a complete translation of the Scriptures into English existed independently of the work of Wycliffe[1], while a copy of the Sarum Pye known as the Priest's Directory, giving information as to the services for every day of the calendar, together with a treatise called the "Defence of the Directory[2]," both written at Syon by Clement Maidstone[3], one of the brethren, takes a high place as the source of much of our knowledge in regard to the service-books of those days.

By means of his two religious houses King Henry provided a channel for incessant prayer for his soul, which was kept up for several generations day and night, the ceasing of the Carthusians being signalled by a tolling bell, at which the Bridgettines took up the service on the other bank and kept it going until they tolled it back across the river to the Charterhouse, which in its turn took up the prayers again[4]. But though both his pious schemes could only be floated by means of plunder and illegality, yet so keen was the royal convert that he actually had plans for founding a third monastery for Celestines[5] as part of his father's unfulfilled obligations, together with other Bridgettine houses[6] and a college for artisters and theologians in the castle at Oxford[7], to which the whole of the property of the aliens was meant to go. He intended also to found a chantry with two chaplains at Guy's Cliff[8] as a token of the great admiration that he had conceived for the memory of the hermit Guy the giant-killer[9], when he visited

---

[1] Gasquet, Bible, 144; do. (1908), pp. 86–155; J. M. Stone, 48. See App. X.

[2] For text of the *Defensorium Directorii*, see Maidstone, Tracts, pp. 5–24; Maskell, ii. 349.

[3] He died at Syon on Sept. 9, 1456, Maidstone, Tracts, xxix, xxx, where the editor calls him "a competent ritualist"; Maskell, ii. 347. For his obit, see Whitford, xxx.

[4] Brut, ii. 496; Caxton, i. 234; Antiq. Repert. ii. 317*; Hamilton, 99.

[5] Not "Augustines," as Brougham, 93. N. Bell, 49, refers to yet another at Sheen, which was removed to Oxford, but gives no reference.

[6] Monast. vi. 543; Rym. ix. 617; Aungier, 37.

[7] Gasc. 219; Rouse, 208, who had seen the order at Oxford as a boy; Harpsfeld, Hist. 586; Tyler, ii. 26; Vickers, 397.

[8] Called "Gibbeclyf" in Cal. Pat. H. VI, i. 136, i.e. Pat. 1 H. VI, v. 5, where licence is granted July 1, 1423, to the Earl of Warwick to found a chantry there; "Gyb Cliffe" in Rous, 208; Worcester, Itin. 352, where Richard Beauchamp Earl of Warwick founds two chantries for "presbiteros vocatos heremites," as well as a pulchra domus for them. For "Kybbeclive," see Dict. Nat. Biogr. xxiii. 387. For picture of Guy's Cliff, see Dugd. Warw. i. 274; Windle, 166.

[9] For story of Guy of Warwick, see J. Coke, 74; R. F. Williams, i. 165. For figure of him in the chantry or chapel erected circ. 1422, see Bibl. Top. Brit. IV. viii. 29.

Warwick[1], but he found that his piety had outrun his resources and none of these latter schemes ever went beyond the region of good intentions.

As to the Celestines, we know that quite early in his reign King Henry had written to the Duke of Berry in France, telling him that he wished to found a monastery for Celestines in England and asking him to arrange to have two members of the order sent over to him, one noted for his experience of the contemplative and the other of the practical side of their conventual life[2], and that the Duke had put himself into communication with Adam Cousinet, the Prior of their house in Paris; that the Prior talked over the proposal with the monks, but they could not agree as to the desirability of complying; that when the English envoys were in Paris in August 1414, two of them, viz. Bishops Courtenay and Langley, visited the church of the Celestines there and took some refreshment in the guest-chamber[3]; that while Langley was looking up the Benedictine rule and comparing it with the Constitutions of the Celestines which were based upon it[4], Courtenay strolled with the Prior in the garden, where he noticed the almonds that were still green on the trees and the grapes just turning ripe; that having tasted the almonds he asked if the Prior would give 1000 of them to King Henry as a present; that the Prior offered 2000 but that the Bishop only took 1000 away; that he also visited the Celestine convent at Mantes[5], after leaving Paris on his way home, and that, as a result, he was accompanied back to England[6] by the Prior of the Celestines at Marcoussis[7] and one of the brethren named Jean de Franford together with the sub-prior from Mantes; that these three stayed several months in England and that a beginning was actually made[8] with the new establishment.   But the

---

[1] Said to have been "on a time" in Dugd. Warw. i. 273; or in 1417, Windle, 63, who gives no reference; but more probably in 1415.

[2] Mirot, Fusoris, 221.

[3] Ibid. 149, 220.

[4] i.e. by their founder, circ. 1260, afterwards Pope Celestine V.

[5] Mirot, 252.   [6] Ibid. 150, 221.

[7] Who afterwards became prior of their house at Ambert near Orleans; called Jean le Brasseur in Champion, Vie, 163.

[8] *Cepit* fundare, Wals. ii. 300; Gesta, 7; Chron. Giles, 8; Ott. 275; Usk, 124, 305; "intended to have builded," First Life, 20; monasteria *tria* struxerat, Elmham, Lib. Metr. 102; but *duas* domus in Vita, 25; aedem *binam*, Tit. Liv. 3; ij houses of Religion,

visitors could not come to terms about the endowment, which Henry proposed to draw from the "revenues of certain monasteries in France," though he afterwards offered to charge it upon his own domains, and when Jean Fusoris crossed to England in June 1415, he offered to carry letters to them, but the Prior in Paris declined, knowing that he was a partisan of the Burgundians. The three monks returned to Paris empty-handed (*vacui*) in July 1415 with the French envoys who had failed in the negotiations at Winchester, two of them having received their *congé* from the king in the royal chapel after mass on the very morning of the final rupture[1].

Such is the French account, which seems well substantiated by facts. The English version represents that King Henry not only began the foundation and often went over to see how the services were kept, but that when the monks, being Frenchmen, proved too patriotic to pray for him as their country's enemy, he turned them out, let their house go to ruin and put the land to other uses[2], so that 150 years later its existence was altogether ignored[3] and no one now knows exactly where the buildings really stood, except that they were somewhere on the river-bank on the opposite side from Sheen[4].

Brut, ii. 496; Caxton, i. 224, 233; loca de Shene et Syon, Rouse, 207; Stow, Chron. 243. Rapin (i. 508) confuses the Celestines with the Bridgettine monks, and Pauli (v. 86) supposes Shene, Bethlehem and Syon to be three different places. Lydgate gives "Sion, Jerusalem and eke Bedelem," Harl. MS. 4205; Gesta, 214, quoting Julius E. iv. f. 7 b; Weever, 474; Petegrue, 594. An account written in 1502 mentions only two "houses of religion" called Syon and Sheen on opposite banks of the river, Antiq. Repert. ii. 316*; Chancellor, Historic Richmond, 86, though the Friary for Observants had been recently built in the immediate neighbourhood, Monast. vi. 1532; Chancellor, 76; do. Historic Richmond, 31; not that the Observants were introduced by Henry V, as Fabyan, 589 (from the "Register of the Mayors"); Kennett, i. 309, who makes Bethlehem different from Sheen. Fox (iii. 404) confuses everything and puts the Friars Observants on one side of the river and on the other a monastery "called Sheen and Zion dedicated to Charterhouse monks with certain Bridget nuns or recluses dwelling within the same precinct."

[1] Mirot, 241, 270, where Fusoris spoke with them quia erant de Franciâ et cognoscebat eos.

[2] Utterly empesshed and voyded, First Life, 20; Fabyan, 589; Goodwin, 341; Aungier, 21; Myroure, xii; R. F. Williams, i. 198.

[3] Hamilton, 98, where Father Parsons believed that Henry V had built two monasteries only, one for religious men (Sheen) and the other for religious women (Syon); also Ramsay, i. 191.

[4] "At Thestleworth" (i.e. Isleworth), Kingsford, Biogr. 81; First Life, xxxii. 20, on the authority of the Earl of Ormonde; see also Cal. Pat. H. VI, i. 207, 380, Oct. 26, 1426; "upon that other side of Thames," Fab. 589; "besides Sion," Stevens, ii. 233; "prope Schene," Usk, 174, 305 note, where it is supposed to be the same as the hermitage in the Charterhouse.

In London the king founded a brotherhood of St Giles, which he established for the relief of the poor in a house in Whitecross Street just outside the Cripplegate postern[1] at the expense of some French religious who had occupied it as a hospital since the days of Edward I, and in yet another case his piety stood out in striking contrast to his father's sacrilege. The monastery of the Grey Friars at Llanfaes[2] near Beaumaris had been abandoned and in ruins since Henry IV's troops had plundered it in 1400[3]. It had been founded many years before by Llewelyn, Prince of North Wales, as a burial place for his wife Joan, who was a natural daughter of King John of England, and many famous Englishmen, who had fallen fighting against the Welsh, had found their last resting place there[4]. The friars now laid their case before the new king and on July 3, 1414[5], he directed that a community of eight, two of whom were to be Welshmen, should be reinstated there to pray for the souls of his father and mother and for his own soul as soon as he was gone.

Very early in his reign he had paid £43 to a London coppersmith to make a figure of his mother to be placed on her grave at Leicester[6]. She had died at Peterborough[7], when he was only eight years old, and her body was buried in the unfinished church of St Mary in the Newarke at Leicester, towards the completion of which his father had from time to time contributed[8]. On Nov. 8, 1414, the new king ordered stone and timber to be supplied for the same purpose, 24 cementers, carpenters and other workmen being at once put on to get the fabric finished and the work out of hand, if possible, by the next Lady Day[9]. The church has long since been demolished[10] and with it the metal figure,

---

[1] Stow, London, iii. 88; Sandford, 291.
[2] Bradley, 127; Llanvaes, L. J. Roberts, 19; Llamaysi, Pat. 2 H. V, ii. 29; Monast. viii. 1545; Appleyard, iii. 60.
[3] Wylie, i. 147, where it is wrongly called " Llannas."
[4] Rym. ix. 147; Archaeol. Cambr. III. xv. 384; J. E. Morris, 19.
[5] Rym. ix. 148.
[6] Devon, 321, May 20, 1413; Towle, 170; Ewald, 23.
[7] In partu prolis, Strecche, 262; Higgins, i. 136, 481; Wylie, iii. 236, 327; not that she died at Leicester, as J. S. Hardy, 336, 355; Wylie, ii. 436.
[8] Ibid. iv. 190.
[9] i.e. March 25, 1415, Pat. 2 H. V, ii. 18 d, where it is said to have been begun by Henry Duke of Lancaster and his son (i.e. son-in-law) John of Gaunt.
[10] J. S. Hardy, 358, i.e. circ. 1690, T. F. Johnson, 105.

like so many of the evidences of King Henry's devotion, has
now altogether disappeared, though the tomb with her effigy
in alabaster is still preserved in the chapel of the Newarke
Hospital (now the Trinity almshouse[1]) on the adjoining
site[2]. But side by side with this pious reverence for the
memory of his dead mother may be set his grant of £20
per annum to Joan Waryn[3], the nurse[4], still living, who
had reared him in his infancy, and another pleasant item
in the rolls records provision for an old carter named
William Bruer[5], who had been in the service of his grandfather, John of Gaunt. Bruer had gone quite blind and
the king now secured for him a vacant corrody, whereby
he would have a room in the Maudlin Hospital at Reading
with a daily pittance from the neighbouring Abbey of a white
loaf and a copyn[6] with a gallon of ale and service from the
kitchen together with two cart-loads of fuel every year for
winter use. Henry likewise granted a corrody at Burton
Abbey to William Albertyn, one of his chamber-varlets[7],
while he secured a maintenance in the college at Windsor for
an old knight named Adam Toker[8] then disabled and in

---

[1] Not the King's College, as Lethaby, 291.
[2] The view that this is the tomb of Henry's mother was supposed to have been upset
(see Leicestershire and Rutland Notes and Queries, iii. 26) by the discovery of "the
original bill" for the monument proving it to have been made of metal. But this turns
out to be nothing but the extract from the Issue Roll printed in Devon, 321 (*ut sup.*),
see W. Kelly, Royal Progresses, p. 179, inserted by him in an annotated copy of Throsby's
Leicestershire now in the Reference Library at Leicester. For this information I am
indebted to the kindness of Rev. H. S. Biggs of the Wiggeston School. The evidence
for the identity comes from Leland, Itin. 363, who saw "a tumbe of marble in the body
of the quire" in the collegiate church, and "they told me that a countess of Darby lay
buried in it and they make her wife to John of Gaunt or Henry the 4." For a description and picture of the monument in the Trinity Hospital see J. S. Hardy, 369–372, who
argues that the tomb was removed to its present position when the church was demolished,
though for this there is no actual proof, see Wylie, iii. 236 n.
[3] Pat. 3 H. V, i. 13, June 5, 1415; Cal. Rot. Pat. 264; Ord. Priv. Co. iii. 190;
Aungier, 201. For previous allowances granted to her by Henry IV, see Wylie, iii. 326;
iv. 177, 179, 185.
[4] For sage femme, see Tremoille, 72, called mir aleresse (i.e. mère alerresse, see
Godefroy, s.v.) or ventrière in Vigne, ii. 30, Plate 77. Cf. et que ta nourrice alaitoies,
Pastoralet, 607; nourrice dont très bon lait puist yssir, Deschamps, in Collas, 95,
204.
[5] In succession to John Goderich deceased, Pat. 2 H. V, i. 16, April 20, 1414; Cal.
Pat. H. V, i. 202.
[6] Perhaps a coupe, i.e. slice, see Halliwell, i. 274; or a choppine (i.e. a measure),
ibid. i. 248.
[7] Vallettus noster, Priv. Seal 659/102; Claus. 1 H. V, 16 d, Oct. 15, 1413.
For 2s. 6d. and shoes given to him before Oct. 31, 1413, see Exch. Accts.
406/21, 27.
[8] Or Koker, Priv. Seal 658/21, May 13, 1413; Cal. Pat. H. V, i. 21.

poverty, who however did not live long to enjoy the benefit[1].

Workmen were also still busy[2] on another of the great foundations of that age, viz. the college of the Blessed Virgin and All Saints at Fotheringhay[3] in Northamptonshire, which the king officially called "our college[4]" though its origin was certainly due to the Duke of York[5]. The college had been already endowed[6] with some of the proceeds of the confiscation of the alien priories and King Henry now showed his continued favour by appropriating to it the parish church of Fotheringhay[7], while the Duke of York granted six acres of ground and the manors of Fotheringhay and Anstey[8] (in Hertfordshire). If to all the above evidence we add his maintenance for scholars

---

[1] In Pat. 2 H. V, iii. 9, Feb. 14, 1415, Cal. Pat. H. V, i. 286, William Lisle, kt. (see page 40, note 2; Wylie, ii. 231 n.; iii. 274) is to have maintenance in the college at Windsor in his old age *vice* Adam Toker, kt. defunctus.

[2] Pat. 1 H. V, v. 12 d, which contains an order dated Feb. 22, 1414, to collect carpenters, stone-cutters and labourers for the works.

[3] For seal of the college, see Bonney, 46.

[4] Pat. 2 H. V, iii. 12, Feb. 12, 1415; Champollion-Figeac, Lettres, ii. 331; cf. Wylie, iii. 238.

[5] Ibid. iii. 243. In the charter of Henry IV dated Dec. 18, 1411, the Duke of York is to be alter fundator perpetuus, Monast. vi. 1411; Bibl. Top. Brit. iv. 22, 62.

[6] Not *after* the death of the Duke of York (i.e. Oct. 25, 1415), as Leland, Itin. i. 6. For grants of £67. 6s. 8d. and £55. 6s. 8d. to it on Dec. 18, 1411, see Rot. Parl. iii. 655; Monast. vi. 1411; Bibl. Top. Brit. no. 40, iv. 82. The former sum was the money paid annually by John Cheyne (or Cheigne) *firmarius et occupator* for the custody of the manors of Kingston near Rudhall in the parish of Weston-under-Penyard in Herefordshire (Duncumb, Greytree Hundred, iii. 151, 218, 376; Atkyns, 299, where there is a reference to a church at Kingston temp. H. I) and Newent in Gloucestershire (Wylie, iii. 144, note 6), both belonging to the alien priory of Newent (called "Newet by Leghe Market on the borders of Wales," ? Lea near Micheldean, in Leland, Itin. i. 6) which had been granted by William the Conqueror to the Abbey of Cormeilles near Lisieux, Monast. vi. 1048. The second sum (£55. 6s. 8d.) was paid by John Rome, clerk, for the custody of Avebury (Wilts.) which was a cell to the Abbey of St George de Boscherville near Rouen. These possessions were specially reserved in the Leicester Parliament, Bridges, ii. 456, quoting Fin. 2 H. V, m. 4.

[7] Rym. ix. 203. It was then claimed by the nuns of Delapré Abbey on the Nene near Northampton as part of their original settlement dating from the reign of King Stephen, Lel. Itin. i. 5; Bridges, ii. 456; Bibl. Top. Brit. iv. 22; Bonney, 34. It was replaced by the present church (Bonney, 47, 48), the first stone of which, according to an inscription in Bridges, ii. 454, was laid on July 2 (SS. Processus and Martinianus), 1414 or 1415 (not November 11, as Bibl. Top. Brit. iv. 24), though the main part of the choir (now destroyed, Parker, 2,8) was not seriously undertaken till 1434, Wylie, ii. 193, note 2; Bibl. Top. Brit. iv. 88 (not 1435, as Bonney, 42; Parker, 5). For picture of the church see Bibl. Top. Brit. iv. 20. For figure of Archbishop Scrope in one of the windows temp. Ed. IV, see Bridges, ii. 453; Bibl. Top. Brit. iv. 31; Bonney, 47.

[8] Inq. p. Mort. iv. 14. It had been granted to his father Edmund temp. Rich. II, Chauncey, 107; Cussans, 1. B. 57; Devon, 338, Feb. 4, 1415, where there is a reference to Joan (i.e. Holland) widow of Edward (should be Edmund) Duke of York, wife of Henry Lord Scrope, see Wylie, iii. 284, note 5.

at the King's Hall at Cambridge[1] and his grants to hermits[2] and friars (black, white and grey[3]) in various parts of the country, it will be clear that the churchmen were likely to lose nothing by England's change of rulers.

[1] Priv. Seal 658/8, April 5, 1413. See App. Y.

[2] See App. P.

[3] For continuance of 25 marks per annum to the Grey Friars at Cambridge, Nov. 6, 1413, see Iss. Roll 1 H. V, Mich., Feb. 22, 1414; Wylie, iv. 144, note 9. Also 25 marks per annum to the Black Friars at Cambridge, Pat. 1 H. V, 5, 17, Nov. 28, 1413; Priv. Seal 659/142, Nov. 24, 1413, and 50 marks per annum to the Black Friars at Oxford, Priv. Seal 659/150, Nov. 28, 1413; Tyler, ii. 27. Also 20 marks per annum to the White Friars at Calais, French Roll 1 H. V, 36, June 5, 1413. For protection for three years granted to the White Friars at Aylesford (called Aysseford in Priv. Seal 658/17), see Pat. 1 H. V, i. 28, May 1, 1413, where none are to take from them stonecutters, carpenters, workpeople, carts, horses, timber or anything else.

CHAPTER XVI

OLDCASTLE'S TRIAL

It has been truly said that the dangerous side of the new king's character as a civil ruler lay in his piety[1], and it was certain that he would not limit his zeal to overspending himself in impossible gifts to religious houses. He had told the bishops that he was all a-glow to work with them[2] and hear what was acceptable to them before God, and the churchmen were not slow to keep him well informed.

In obedience to his father's dying voice[3] he chose his spiritual guides from the men of religion[4] and appointed a learned Carmelite[5], Doctor Stephen Patrington, as one of his confessors. Patrington was a Yorkshireman, who in

[1] Goldwin Smith, i. 256. Cf. his "fierce orthodoxy," Tout, 262; "a sincerely religious man after his lights, an honest fanatic, a sincere if narrow piety," Oman, 231, 271; "his mind was of a narrow fanatic type," C. R. L. Fletcher, 304; "the royal casuist," Cassell, i. 519. R. F. Williams (i. 200) thinks that "he left church matters to church government and was not aware of the extent to which his confidence was abused." Tyler (ii. 413) believes that "the sanguinary intentions of the priesthood were frustrated by Henry's known love of gentler means."

[2] In Wals. ii. 344, he is "Deo devotus." For the Lancastrian dynasty "in strict alliance with the clergy," see Wakeman, 162.

[3] Wylie, iv. 105. Kingsford, Hard. 479, thinks that "its contents were probably a matter of common report." For confirmation of grant of 40 marks per annum to Friar John Till, late confessor to Henry IV, see Pat. 1 H. V, ii. 30; Iss. Roll 1 H. V, Mich., Dec. 9, 1413; Memoranda Roll K.R. 3–4 H. V, 62, Dec. 1, 1415, where it was granted June 6, 1400; Wylie, iv. 100, note 5. Called "Parson Tille" in Belloc, 165. He took part in the trial of William Taylor for heresy in 1423, Conc. iii. 409; Palmer, Fasti, 26.

[4] Cf. Have in reverence folks of Relygioun, Secreta, 137.

[5] Fascic. lxxvii; Gibbons, 139; Le Neve, i. 296; vir eruditus in trivio et quadrivio, Wals. ii. 300; Carmelita pater regia vota pians, Elmham, Lib. Metr. 162; cf. Ens Carmeliticus Rector, Doctor, Prior Anglis, Confessor celebris Regis et ipse manens, Weever, 437, where it is stated that he was also confessor to Henry IV and his queen and that he went as a representative to the Council at Constance, but this is probably a mistake for Bishop Caterick, his predecessor at St David's, Dict. Nat. Biogr. xliv. 48. In Rym. ix. 384 (Aug. 25, 1416) Patrington is confessor noster; cf. Confessor domini regalis, Elmham, Lib. Metr. 132, 162. For 6s. 8d. paid to John Larke a Carmelite for hearing confessions during Lent 1413, see Q.R. Accts. 406/21, 19.

his early days had been a leading opponent of Wycliffe at Oxford[1] and had fiercely resented the ill-blood caused by his castigation of the friars[2]. He had been in the thick of the "naughty time of heresy[3]," when hot-headed partisans attended lectures in the schools with daggers under their gowns and each side charged the other with having caused the Peasants' Revolt. He had seen the old reformer banished from his university, and amongst his other works he wrote an account of those fiery Oxford days[4]. Afterwards he had removed to London, where he drew crowds by his forceful preaching[5]. In 1399 he became Provincial of his Order[6] and he had lived to see his old opponents, Nicholas Hereford[7], John Purvey[8] and Philip Repingdon[9] one by one recant their early Lollardry. As the king's confessor Patrington received the usual 3s. per day[10] for himself and one companion; he lived in the king's hostel, wore the king's livery[11], and kept four horses

---

[1] Fascic. 316. For account of him, see Fuller, Worthies, ii. 502. In the library at St John's College, Cambridge (Crashaw MS. D. 28), is a MS. written in a clear small hand entitled Repertorium magistri Stephani de Patrington quod collegit Oxon' et alibi antequam ad gradum assumptus fuerat doctoralem.

[2] Fascic. 295.

[3] Church Quart. Rev. li. 277.

[4] Fascic. lxxvii; Creighton, Essays, 197.

[5] Leland, Comment. 429; Fuller, Worthies, ii. 502; Weever, 437; Villiers, ii. 765.

[6] Dict. Nat. Biogr. xliv. 47, from Harl. MS. 3838, f. 31 [33], where he is called confessor to H. V and his queen Catherine (!) as well as to the Prince of Wales and the Duchess of Lancaster. In his epitaph dated 1417 he is said to have been Prior for 15 years, though Weever (p. 438) may have copied the figures wrongly.

[7] For Nicholas Hereford at Oxford opposed by the Carmelite Peter Stokes, see Gairdner, Lollardy, i. 21; Capes, 126. For his recantation, see Wylie, iii. 313 note. For his translation of the Old Testament from Genesis to Baruch iii. 20, see Brute, Thorpe, &c. p. 3; Westcott, 12; Kenyon, 200, with facsimile page from Bodl. MS. 959; Gasquet, Bible, 115, 165; J. M. Stone, 48; Pollard, xx; Church Quart. Rev. li. 268; Garnett, 213; Mombert, 44, where he is Vice-Chancellor of Oxford University, Chancellor of Hereford Cathedral 1394, and Treasurer of do. 1398. For his retirement to the Charterhouse at Coventry in 1417, where he died, see Workman, i. 235; Gasquet, Bible, 99. For Nicholas Hereford, Prior of Evesham (1350–1392), see Monast. ii. 7, with a list of his books, including Mort d'Arthur cum Sankreal, Beuffys de Hampton, &c. For receipt for 10 marks from revenues of the bishopric of Worcester signed by him at Worcester May 26, 1395, see Bund, 371.

[8] Gairdner, Lollardy, i. 54. For account of him, see Westcott, 13; Gasquet, Bible, 116; Workman, i. 237, 305; Garnett, 214, 216; Capes, 126, 146, 148, 181; Carrick, 209; L. Wilson, Pref., who calls him "Wycliffe's curate"; Church Quart. Rev. li. 269; Workman, i. 236; Cambridge Hist. Lit. ii. 61; Wylie, i. 179; iii. 312; Ollard-Crosse, 336; not Purney, as Seyer, ii. 164. Pollard, xxiv, states that the revised edition of Wycliffe's (i.e. Hereford's) Bible was not attributed to Purvey till 1729, i.e. in Waterland, x. 361.

[9] Wylie, i. 301. For his sermon at St Frideswide's at Oxford, June 5, 1382, see Fascic. 299; Gairdner, Lollardy, i. 21.

[10] Wylie, i. 482.

[11] For robes for him as confessor against the King's coronation, see Exch. Accts. 406/15.

and a hackney[1]. For each horse he had a groom who drew 1½*d*. a day, and his whole allowance to cover everything including extras amounted to £69. 10*s*. 6*d*. a year[2].

Under Patrington's hands it was soon apparent that the king's conversion was complete. If he had ever really sympathised with the novel beliefs of Lollard knights in his irresponsible days, the weight of office now made him a ready listener to the warning note of danger. In the proclamation issued on the first day of his reign he had given orders to stop all riots, insurrections and extraordinary meetings[3] under whatsoever pretext they were gathered together and, as a specimen of the great expectations that had been formed of a coming crusade against the ferment of heresy, we may point to an interesting exhortation addressed to him at his accession by Thomas Hoccleve[4], who called upon him to show himself Christ's knight and stand forth as the champion of His church, to chase away the error that the sons of iniquity were sowing broadcast in the land and, if he valued his security, not to suffer the faith to take a fall.

Very soon after the coronation a busy young Carmelite[5]

---

[1] For haquenées for women, see Joubert, Vie, 154. For 52 francs paid for a haquenee baye, see Roman, Inventaires, 9.

[2] Rym. ix. 72; Pat. 1 H. V, iv. 10, Nov. 24, 1413; Priv. Seal 659/139; Devon, 337, Dec. 5, 1414. For £34. 0*s*. 23*d*. (*sic*) paid to him, see Rec. Roll 3 H. V, Pasch., June 25, 1415. For a closet altar for his oratory with chalice, candlesticks and basins left to him by the king in his will in 1415, see Rym. ix. 291.

[3] Page 1. Conventicula excessiva, Rym. ix. 1.

[4]
> Be holy chirches champioun eek ay
> Susteene hir right suffre no thing doon be
> In prejudice of hir by no way.
> Strengthe your modir in chacyng away
> Therrour which sones of iniquitee
> Han sowe ageyn the feith it is no nay
> Yee therto bownde been of duetee
> Your office is it now for your suretee
> Souffreth nat Crystes feith to tak a fal
> Unto his peple and youres cheerly see
> In conservyng of your estate real. Hoccleve, Min. Po. 40.

[5] Other Carmelites who preached strongly against the Lollards include Robert Mascal, confessor to Henry IV (Wylie, iv. 492); Harl. MS. 3838, f. 32 [34], where it is said that he was buried at Ludlow Dec. 21, 1417, which is a mistake for Dec. 22, 1416, Le Neve, i. 463; Eubel, i. 285; Dict. Nat. Biogr. xxxvi. 406; Wylie, iv. 101 note. For his will dated Nov. 28, 1416, proved Jan. 17, 1417, see Gough, ii. 49*. Also Walter Diss, who had been confessor to John of Gaunt, Clemanges, iii. 30; Fascic. pp. xxvi, 286, 508; Feret, iv. 362; Tyler, ii. 55; Gaunt, Reg. i. 522, 523; ii. 283, 312. He died on Jan. 21, 1405, Dict. Nat. Biogr. xv. 120. For his Juvenalian verses on the schism, see Clemanges, iii. 31–34; Lenfant (Whatley), ii. 306, quoting Hardt, 1. ix. p. 500. For his preaching against schismatics in Castile, Leon, Aragon, Navarre, Grenada and Portugal, see Harl. MS. 3838, f. 31 [33], where he is patria Nordonolgius, which may possibly

preaching at Paul's Cross reproached him for his slackness in dealing with the Lollards[1]. The preacher, known as Friar Thomas Walden or Netter of Walden[2], was called "the swiftest fire that ever smote the trunks of heresy[3]." His father was a netter, or pantermaker[4], at Saffron Walden[5] in Essex, but we know nothing more of his parentage except that his mother's name was Maud[6]. He was thus, as he says, no noble eagle, but just a poor crow from an English brook sent to peck out the eye that despised its own mother's young[7]. He had long brooded over the shadow that was hiding the church's truth. In his student days he had come under the influence of William Woodford[8], the

mean an Englishman from the North. For Carmelites called "barrés" in France, see Hoffbauer, ii. 10, or "Carmes" or "White Frerys," Caxton, Dial. 42; Wylie, ii. 361. For the Carmelites in the royal manor of Beaumont, or Belmont, beyond the Northgate at Oxford, see Monast. vi. 1577. The house was originally built by Henry I and was the birthplace of Richard I, but was given to the Carmelites by Edward II, see Brodrick, Univ. 50; C. R. L. Fletcher, 123; Wylie, iii. 414. For the site called Belmont Fields in 1578 (now Beaumont Street), see map in Goldie, with picture of remains in 1800 in Ingram, iii. 14 (St Mary Magdalen). For seal, see Pedrick, p. 121, Plate xxxvii. For Carmelites as preachers, see Church Quart. Rev. li. 88.

[1] Principem ipsum idque publicè in suggestu socordiæ in tam periculoso malo admonuisset, Lel. Script. 439; Villiers, ii. 833; Tyler, ii. 9; Dict. Nat. Biogr. xl. 232; Stubbs, iii. 80, who disapproves of Henry's "impolitic delay," though on p. 83 he thinks that the removal of Archbishop Arundel from the Chancellorship (p. 7) "enabled him to renew his attack upon the Lollards and emboldened the Lollards to more hopeful resistance."

[2] He is called Frater, Magister, Dominus or Doctor Thomas Walden in Gascoigne, 2, 140, 186, or "Walden alias Nettar," ibid. 11; or "Waldensis," Cochlaeus, 89; "Netterus Waldensis," Oudin, iii, 2214.

[3] Lawrence Burrell, Provincial of the Carmelites of Narbonne, Harl. MS. 1819, f. 68 b, in Dict. Nat. Biogr. xl. 233. Cf. "Maillet des hérétiques," Thevet, i. 156, who calls him "Waldem" and refers to his portrait in the Carmelite library in Paris.

[4] For netter or netmaker, see Letter Bk. I, 13, 212, 213; Wylie, iv. 275. The "nattemakere" in Lydgate, Pilgrimage, 308, is probably a maker of mats or wattle-work. For pantermaker, see Wylie, iv. 275; Halliwell, s.v. *Panter*. For pantire or panter, see Lydg. Temple, 26, 102; Chaucer (S.), iii. 74, 295; Cent. Dict., s.v. *Painter*. Cf. Netter quod sonat Anglicè compositor retium, Walden (Blanciotti), i. xiii; Wood, i. 209; Tyler, ii. 9, who thinks that he was called Netter because he was "so able a disputant," or from the expertness with which he caught his antagonists in argument (p. 56). He supposes that his works are "either totally lost or buried in temporary oblivion." For a list of them, see Bale, 569; Wharton, Hist. Lit. 88; Oudin, iii. 2217. For abstract of contents of his Doctrinale, see Du Pin, iii. 61. For his death at Rouen Nov. 3, 1430 (called Nov. 2 in Holinsh. iii. 662), and burial there in the church of the White Friars, see Tritheim, Cat. 137; Oudin, iii. 2215.

[5] For account of Saffron Walden, see Essex Review, xiii. 193. For growth of saffron, see page 83.

[6] Walden, iii. 272; ab humilissimis parentibus originem habuit, Harl. MS. 3838, f. 33 [35], where his father is called John.

[7] Walden, i. 24, from Proverbs xxx. 17.

[8] Or Wydeford, Coxe, New Coll. MS. cxxiii. Called acerrimus haereticorum extirpator, Dict. Nat. Biogr. lxii. 397. He died circ. 1411. For his treatise against Wycliffe, see Graes, Fasciculus, ii. 191; called a reply to the Lollard manifesto of 1396, Brute, Thorpe, &c. p. 8. For a copy of it in the library at Syon, see Bateson, 139. For list of his works, see Little, Grey Friars, 246.

Franciscan friar, who had been at first the friend of Wycliffe and afterwards the keenest strier[1] of heretics, and it was the vision of Wycliffe that loomed ever before Walden's eyes, as the Philistine of Gath coming out to defy the armies of the living God. He heard the mocking challenge of the Lollards boasting that their Wycliffe was a giant of knowledge[2]. He felt the sting and braced himself for battle. He was but a poor religious, alone, unarmed, afoot, in rags and sorrow[3], but he cried aloud to the English king and people : " Let no man's heart fail him because of Wycliffe! *I* will go out against this Philistine[4]!" He would fight with that Bible to which Goliath had himself appealed, for, as he said, "the doctrine is not mine but His that sent me[5]." He called God to witness that he had no quarrel with the man himself, whom indeed he had never seen, for he was but an infant[6] when the earthquake council shook all England in 1382[7]. It was therefore no petty or personal malice that stirred him to the fight. Nought but the onslaught on the Faith provoked him. He boasted that England had always been a Christian land, that no English king had ever favoured heresy and he stood out against the frauds that were being practised on a guileless and deluded people. One of his dearest Oxford friends, John Luke, or Luck[8], had been swept into the lake of heresy and he had thereupon taken up a challenge from Peter Payne[9], the Lollard Principal of St Edmund's Hall, but when the day came Peter had run away[10].

---

[1] Cf. Wylie, iv. 92, note 11; to stroye hym and to schende, Lydg. Troy Bk. 130; he stroyed Lollardes, Harl. MS. 4205; Petegrue, 594; Gesta, 214, from Cotton MS. Julius E. iv. f. 7 b; Weever, 474, from Heralds' Office MS. lviii; W. H. Black, 109; MacCracken, xvi; not " seried" as R. F. Williams, i. 203; Chancellor, 123. Cf. "some lords liveré that the lawe stried," Pol. Songs, i. 381.

[2] Walden, i. 7; Lechler, ii. 331.

[3] Unum peditem inertem (? inermem) pannosum et lugubrem, Walden, i. 24. Cf. religiosus et infirmus Carmelita, ibid. 26.

[4] Walden, i. 7.

[5] Ibid. i. 6.

[6] Dum infans fueram, ipse (i.e. Wycliffe) fuit, Walden, I. xiii, II. 28; Fascic. lxx.

[7] Capes, 141.

[8] Dict. Nat. Biogr. xl. 232; Wylie, iii. 435. For Walden's letter to him, see Villiers, ii. 840.

[9] Called Petrus Payne sed apud nos Clerc, in Bekynton, i. 187; Master Pers, a clerk, Kingsford, Chron. 135; Mayster Perrys, clerke, Greg. Chron. 176; Peter Clearke, Holinsh. iii. 662; Petrus Crek, Scotichron. iv. 1299; Master Englis, Lützow, Prague, 67; Wylie, iii. 425, note 6.

[10] Venimus, affuimus, sed, ut sciunt et huiusque declarant qui intererant, prius quam conseruimus manus defecit Petrus clericus vecordiâ suffocatus, Walden, i. 8.

Walden was now about 33 years of age[1] and had lately
returned from Pisa[2], where he is said to have stood for the
rights of the council as higher than the authority of the
Pope[3].   In 1410 he had been present at John Badby's trial[4]
in St Paul's and had seen the spider cross his face[5], but his
memory was so clouded with his persecuting zeal that when
he wrote about twelve years later, he described it as a horrid
big creature that dropped from the roof and tried to get into
the heretic's mouth and that it took quite a lot of men[6] to
keep it off.   Such was the man who later in the reign was
called to be the guide of King Henry's conscience[7], who
kept him faithful to the Church's cause, and in whose arms
he died.

Very soon after his coronation[8] the new king expressed
his joy that he was the first to raise the standard of the
cause of Christ and the Church, not as the successor of
Duke William but as the heir of Duke Moses[9], who slew
the Egyptian that he might deliver Israel.   For already it
was reported that certain priests and chaplains were preaching—or rather, profaning—the word of God in London and
throughout the country, sowing discord amongst the people
and the pestilent seed of Lollardry[10], that crowds were
collecting to listen and that murmuring and sedition were

[1] He was born circ. 1380, Fascic. lxx ; H. Morley, vi. 142.   Called circ. 1375 in
Baeske, 36 ; or 1377, Walden, I. p. xiii.
[2] Leland, Script. 440 ; Villiers, ii. 833.
[3] Harl. MS. 3838, f. 36, where he is said to have been coram Cesare Sigismundo (!);
Dict. Nat. Biogr. xl. 232.
[4] He calls him quendam sartorem de partibus Wigorniae, Walden, ii. 387 ; called
a tailor in Tyler, ii. 339; Lechler, ii. 64 ; Capes, 181 ; Gairdner, Lollardy, i. 67; Besant,
Survey, i. 100, who calls him John Bradby of *Worcester.*   He was really of Evesham ;
not of Pershore, as Kingsford, 67 ; nor of Kemerton, as Workman, i. 260.   He is not to
be confounded (as in Dict. Nat. Biogr. xl. 232 ; lv. 474) with Magister Gulielmus cog-
nomine sartor (Walden, ii. 33) who is clearly Master William Taylor the priest who was
condemned for heresy in 1423, Conc. iii. 404; Tyler, ii. 405.
[5] Wylie, iii. 439.   For the spider as a venomous creature, see Herbert, 24.
[6] Multorum manibus vix potuit prohiberi, Walden, I. p. xv; ii. 387.   He notes the
presence of Bishop Tottington and of *Princeps* Thomas Exoniensis Dux, tunc Cancellarius
regis, i.e. Thomas Beaufort (made Chancellor Jan. 31, 1410, Wylie, iii. 301), who was
created Duke of Exeter Nov. 18, 1416, Dict. Nat. Biogr. iv. 50 ; Wills of Kings, 264.
Yonge (241), who calls the victim "Bradby," thinks that the bystanders *imagined* that
they saw a large spider running about his face.
[7] For Walden as confessor to Henry V, see Bale (Oldcastle), 251.   Exch. Accts.
407/3, Nov. 27, 1421, shows livery for Thomas Wavyn (? Walden), our confessor ; de
nove (*sic*) electo, Ord. Priv. Co. ii. 331 (1422).
[8] Non diu post primaevae unctionis et fastus regii sacramentum, Walden, i. 4, 486.
[9] Walden, ii. 4 ; James, 174; for duk Moyses, see Lydgate, Burgh, 12.   Cf. this noble
duk, this prudent Moyses, ibid. Min. Po. 96.
[10] Rym. ix. 46 ; Letter Book I, 116,

rising and would lead to mischief, if the meetings were not promptly stopped.   These preachers held no licence from their bishops and were acting in defiance of the Constitutions of Oxford[1], and the bishops were doing their best to put them down[2].

When the Parliament met, the Convocation of the Southern Province was still in session in the Chapter-house at St Paul's[3].   It had originally met on March 6, 1413[4], and its sittings had been continued from day to day till May 8[5] when there was an adjournment, but in the meantime certain books, whose titles are not now known, had been scheduled and solemnly burnt at the cross in the churchyard of St Paul's, Archbishop Arundel being present to explain to the public the nature of the poison that they contained. The Convocation re-assembled[6], and we have a record of its proceedings on June 26, 1413[7], and the following days.   The archbishop was not able to be there in person[8] and, in his absence, the deliberations were presided over by Richard Clifford, Bishop of London, whose previous moral record had not erred on the side of excessive strictness[9].

The first business was to consider a statement which had been prepared by certain of the clergy[10].   In a mixture of

---

[1] i.e. Nov. 28, 1407, Wylie, iii. 427 ; repeated in the Convocation that met at St Paul's Jan. 14, 1408, Conc. iii. 314; Wake, 347, whence they are usually dated in 1408, as Forshall and Madden, I. p. xxxiii; Kenyon, 205 ; Westcott, 17 ; Ch. Quart. Rev. li. 273, 279, 280, 282, 287; Gasquet, Rel. Instr. 10; do. Bible, 105, 147; Lechler, ii. 74 [456]. Not 1409, as Vict. Co. Hist. (Hants.), ii. 45; Gairdner, Lollardy, i. 61 (who regards them as "well-devised"); Workman, i. 242. Not after 1411, as Brodrick, Univ. 37.   Parker (275) seems to think they were passed in the Convocation of 1413.   For a copy of them in Bishop Beaufort's Register at Winchester, ff. 18–20, see Vict. Co. Hist. (Hants.) ii. 45.

[2] For order to stop preachers in the diocese of Hereford, see Pat. 1 H. V, i. 29 d, March 23, 1413; cf. Cal. Rot. Pat. 260; Pat. 1 H. V, i. 36 d.   Also in Exeter by Bp. Stafford, dated at Bishop's Clyst near Honiton, July 24, 1413, Conc. iii. 357; Staff. Reg. 245.

[3] Wals. ii. 290 ; Hypodig. 438.

[4] Conc. iii. 357.

[5] This is expressly stated in Pat. 2 H. V, iii. 8, Feb. 19, 1415, where the Abbot of Lavendon receives pardon for £20 which he was unable to get in as collector for the Archdeaconry of Buckingham because of the poverty of the district.   For account of the Praemonstratensian Abbey of Lavendon near Olney, with seal, see Lipscomb, iv. 214.

[6] Apparently on June 6 in Lambeth church, according to Waugh, 446.   Called June 7 in Gairdner, Lollardy, i. 7, who quotes Waugh for blank space left unfilled in Arundel's Register.

[7] i.e. Monday after Corpus Christi, which fell on June 22, Conc. iii. 351; Tyler, ii. 7; Vict. Co. Hist. London, ii. 220.

[8] He was at Ickham on July 13, 1413, Riley, Mem. 594.

[9] Wylie, i. 2, note 3.

[10] Gairdner (89) represents that the clergy were stirred into activity by the Lollards posting bills on London churches stating that 100,000 men were ready to rise, but this

metaphors they represented the English people as a tree withering in its leaves, which might revive if its root were restored—that if its stomach (that is to say, the clergy) were well ordered, its food (that is to say, their doctrine) would become nutritious and sweet and so stop the mouths of objectors, whose murmuring, however just, was not put in quite proper form[1]. And then came the nourishing food. Bishops and clergy should reside at their cures; the dress and bearing of their servants should be more ruly; penance should be imposed for notorious crimes; money should not be accepted for spiritual offices; there should be no traffic in the churches, no hair-cutting or shaving on Sundays[2], no bargaining with patrons of livings and no perjury in the courts. The Constitutions of Oxford must be made more stringent and whole parishes must be excommunicated, if there was any unauthorised preaching within them. But above all they urged that the rent in the seamless coat could never be repaired, unless they could sternly repress certain great men of the realm who were favourers and protectors of the Lollards[3]. They then granted a tenth which would be payable next Martinmas[4], and the session closed about the end of June[5].

was not till after Oldcastle's condemnation. Milman (viii. 217) also asserts that "the Lollards seem to have begun the strife."

[1] Justè, licet non ritè, murmurantium, Conc. iii. 351.

[2] For Archbishop Arundel's letter to the Mayor of London dated at Ickham July 13, 1413, threatening to excommunicate the London barbers, see Letter Bk. I, p. xviii, 115; Riley, Mem. 593; S. Young, 48; Vict. Co. Hist. London, ii. 225. But as people now think more of a punishment which touches the body or the purse than of one that kills the soul, he recommends a fine to be fixed for keeping open on Sunday and 6s. 8d. was decided on accordingly, 5s. of which would go to the new work at the Guildhall (Wylie, ii. 111) and the rest to the Warden or Masters of the Barbers' gild. For order issued by the Mayor and Aldermen to this effect on July 24, 1413, see Letter Bk. I, p. 116. Archbishop Chichele subsequently at Lambeth authorised these ordinances to be read out at Paul's Cross or in the London churches whenever the wardens of the craft required it, Conc. iii. 360, where Sunday is "Dies Dominicus videlicet dies septimus cui Dominus benedixit." The order was however evaded and in consequence a similar one was issued by Archbishop Stafford from Lambeth on April 19, 1445, see Lancet, 23/1/09. For order (1408) against exposing vegetables for sale on Sundays or eves of feast-days at Louvain, see Dieve, Op. 40. For protest of Oxford University in 1414 against the prevalent and growing practice of holding fairs and markets on Sundays and feast-days and *in locis secretis* whereby God is offended, devotion of contemplation is withdrawn and the Christian faith is injured, see Conc. iii. 365. For Bishop Braybrook's order against barbers shaving on Sundays (1392), see Milman, Ann. 82, with reference to Conc. iii. 218, which forbids cordwainers (*allutarios*) to make or mend shoes on Sunday instead of attending mass and threatens them with the greater excommunication.

[3] Lechler, ii. 79.

[4] Page 34; Pat. 2 H. V, iii. 8, Feb. 19, 1415. For a tenth granted by the clergy anno primo, see Rec. Roll 1 H. V, Pasch. and Mich., July 10, Dec. 11, 1413; Pat. 1 H. V, iv. 5, Nov. 30, 1413; ibid. v. 22, Jan. 27, 1414. For £7134. 6s. 8d. borrowed on the strength of this grant, see Rec. Roll 1 H. V, Pasch., July 17, 1413.

[5] Stubbs, iii. 84.

The Northern Convocation met subsequently in York Minster on July 27, 1413[1], and voted their tenth on the following day "after much altercation and various excuses[2]."

Of the books that had been seized by order of the Convocation one is known to have been a bound book from Coventry[3] and another had been seized at a limner's[4] in Paternoster Row in London. The latter was in unbound sheets, or quires, and contained several small tracts of a specially dangerous character. The limner was asked who it belonged to and he said "Sir John Oldcastle[5]." So in the month of June[6] Oldcastle was summoned to Kennington[7], where the worst passages from the book were read out to him in presence of the king and nearly all of the bishops and barons who were attending the sittings of the Parliament[8]. The king was greatly shocked[9] as he listened to these extracts. He said they were the worst attacks he had ever heard against the Faith and the Church and he asked Oldcastle whether he did not think that the tract ought to be condemned. Oldcastle said that he did, and when they asked him why he owned such a book, he said that he never used it and had not really read more than two leaves of it. But in a subsequent sitting of the Convocation it was urged that the accused had certainly held and defended heretical opinions, that he had denied the legality of the Constitutions of Oxford and that he was one of the leading men who had sheltered suspects and enabled them to sow their evil seed in various places, especially in the dioceses of Hereford,

---

[1] Conc. iii. 358. For summons dated June 9, 1413, to meet at York on next Peter ad vincula, i.e. Aug. 1, 1413, see Claus. 1 H. V, 27 d.

[2] Archbishop Bowet's certificate was sent up on Sept. 30, 1413, Conc. iii. 358. For 2nd half of tenth granted by clergy at York anno 1, see Rec. Roll 3 H. V, Pasch., June 4, 1415.

[3] Tyler, ii. 360; Workman, i. 264, who supposes that this was the volume found in Paternoster Row.

[4] Not "a certain Lynmore," as C. E. Maurice, ii. 254.

[5] Called "Eldrastellus" in J. Major, 126, or "Odecossez" in Varillas, i. 72. Not that he was "alleged to be the author," as Benham, Tower, 31.

[6] Pages 47, 49. Called June 6, 1413, in Waugh, 447. Kingsford (in Eng. Hist. Rev. xxii. 577) thinks that the proceedings against Oldcastle were begun in March, 1413, before the death of Henry IV.

[7] Not Kensington, as Towle, 264; Baeske, 7. For the manor house at Kennington, see Loftie, ii. 278. The site is now occupied by the tramway depôt at the junction of Upper Kennington Lane with Kennington Road, see Montgomery, 9, who supposes (p. 16) that the king is Henry IV.

[8] Called "nearly all the barons of England" in Gairdner, Lollardy, i. 71.

[9] Maxime abhorruit.

London and Rochester[1], and they prayed that he might be called before them to make answer on these points.

But Archbishop Arundel counselled caution, for he knew that Oldcastle had been one of Henry's intimate friends[2]. Accordingly he and some bishops approached the king at Kennington[3] and consulted him about the matter. The king thanked them, but partly on account of his previous comradeship and partly out of regard for the whole order of knights of which Oldcastle was an honoured member[4], he begged them to defer the question for a while and he would try what he could do to school him privately[5] and win him back by kindness from the maze of error to the straight path of truth. If he should fail he would then hand the offender over to them to be dealt with by church law[6], which he for his part would certainly support by the aid of the secular arm. In this view the archbishop and bishops acquiesced, but the rest of the clergy did not hide their dissatisfaction.

That the king was not yet personally incensed against his old friend is evident from the fact that a party of 26 wrestlers sent by Oldcastle and Sir William Bourchier came before him to give an exhibition of their skill in Windsor

[1] Conc. iii. 353; Rym. ix. 61; Hook, iv. 513.

[2] Eo quod familiaris ejus extiterat, Conc. iii. 352, 353; Rym. ix. 61; Fascic. 434; unum de praecarissimis et magnis domesticis suis, Chron. Giles, 4; Gesta, 2; regi propter probitatem carus et acceptus, Wals. ii. 291; Hypodig. 439; Baeske, 27; principi carissimum, Redman, 15. Not "the King's Domestick," as Rapin, i. 505; Gilpin, 12; or that he "belonged to the royal household," as Gairdner, 89. In Vita, 31 (followed by Pauli, v. 82; C. E. Maurice, ii. 254), it is represented that Henry dismissed Oldcastle a suo famulato (*sic*) domestico for Lollardry before he came to the throne, but this seems inconsistent with the writer's theory of the king's conversion. Not that Oldcastle was a friend of Henry IV, as Wetzer, viii. 136. Pol. Verg. 441, calls him "vir fortis sed impius" and thinks that a little before he had been turned out of the army.

[3] Wals. ii. 291; Hypodig. 440. Called Kennington near Lambeth in Lel. Coll. v. 355.

[4] Called "a lord of name" in Cotton MS. Julius B. II. f. 67[vo]. For representation that he was of lowly birth but knighted for his services against the Welsh, see Gesta, 5; Chron. Giles, 7.

[5] Drayton, Oldcastle, 322.

[6] For courte christiene devaunt juges espirituelx, see Rot. Parl. iv. 20; Stat. ii. 176; Ord. Priv. Co. i. 282. For subjects reserved for church courts in France in 13th and 14th centuries, see Aubert, Comp. 121–136. For writ "Circumspecte agatis" (1285) restricting the power of church courts, see Tout, 184; Wakeman, 147. For "criminal immunities" of the clergy, see Goldwin Smith, i. 247. Cf. feodo ecclesiae dumtaxat exempto, i.e. as to provisions and herbergage, Pat. 3 H. V, i. 18, April 26, 1415. For "his clergie," i.e. benefit of clergy, see Wycl. (A), iii. 297, 314; cf. privilége de clerc, Ableiges, 628; nonobstant sa couronne, ibid. xix. For statement that it was "only after conviction" (i.e. in the secular court) that a clerk could "plead his clergy," see Leach, Winchester, 155.

Park[1] at Lammas and were handsomely rewarded for their pains[2]. But when he himself came to try a fall with his heretic quarry, Behemoth's body proved like yoted shields[3] and his scales so stuck together that they could not be sundered[4]. The more the king poured in his oil and wine[5] the worse the wanderer got[6]. For Oldcastle's Lollardry was deadly earnest. This teaching had been to him the salvation of his life[7], and he had told the king that every friar's head that he struck off would mean a noble to his Treasury[8]. At length the king took him smartly to task for his obstinacy and threatened him seriously with the consequences[9]. Not liking this snib Oldcastle withdrew to Cooling[10] without asking the king's permission and barred himself in[11]. This would appear to have been his first act of insubordination towards the king, but to be fair we ought to note that the whole case is stated from the king's and the archbishop's side alone[12], that we have no counter-statement by the

[1] For a document dated at our manor of Henley le xi jour de... (possibly Aug. 1413), see Priv. Seal 660/210. Cf. page 50.

[2] For £12. 13s. 4d. paid to Richard Joskyn and 25 socii sent de Domino de Cobham et Willelmo Bowrser kt. p' luctac' faciend', see Exch. Accts. 406/21 (23). For a similar amount paid to John Chilley and his companions wrestling in the king's presence at Hertford on Aug. 1, 1414, see Rym. ix. 189.

[3] Cf. corpus illius quasi scuta fusilia, Job xli., in Elmham, Lib. Metr. 97=zoten sheeldes, Wycl., verse 6. For yoten, see Stratmann, 282; Halliwell, ii. 948; Century Dict., s.v. *yote*. Cf. joten bras, S. D. Scott, i. 186, from Romaunce of Richard Cœur de Lion; zotyng and castyng of metals, Paues, xlvi; al of zoten bras, Lydg. Troy Bk. 162.

[4] Cf. with skalys hard as any plate, Lydg. Troy Bk. 20.

[5] Chron. Giles, 4.

[6] Halle, 48; Holinsh. iii. 544; Trussel, 94. For fancy picture of the scene, see Holt, Lights, 59. Adams (i. 209) supposes that these conversations lasted from Sept. 23 to Oct. 10, 1413, and that they were held *after* the rising in Fickett's Field, but it is certain that they took place at Windsor in Aug. 1413, Conc. iii. 353. Baeske (53) regards the story of this interview as "höchst unwahrscheinlich" because Oldcastle's previous breach with the Church must necessarily have put a stop to all intercourse with the king.

[7] "O" audivi dicere Johannem Castri Veteris "nunquam ante hanc doctrinam cessavi peccare," Walden, i. 21; Goodwin, 22; Gilpin, 23; Pauli, v. 82; Lechler, ii. 80. Hook (v. 29) considers Oldcastle as "one who sought the pabulum for his vanity in the plaudits of Puritanism." Lingard (iii. 236) thinks that "hitherto he had made no great display of religious principle." Sanford (185) calls him "gallant religious Oldcastle— the Havelock of his day." Dixon (i. 59) pictures him as "a high, swift sort of man, full of fight and keen of tongue."

[8] Walden, i. 819; Goodwin, 29. For threat of the rioters in 1431 that they would have three priests' heads for a penny, see Kingsford, Chron. 97, 134.

[9] Capgr. De Illustr. Henr. 112.

[10] For plan of the castle, see Scott-Robertson, 132. For picture, see Thomson, Part II; Sparvel-Bayley, 28, with the inscription and licence to crenellate dated Feb. 10, 1380; see also T. H. Turner, iii. 303; Wylie, iii. 289.

[11] Se incastellat et fortificat, Conc. iii. 354; Rym. ix. 62; Berault-Bercastel, xv. 99.

[12] The king had communicated the facts to the archbishop both orally and in writing, Conc. iii. 354; Rym. ix. 61; Hook, iv. 514.

accused himself and that the particulars of the Cooling incident are merely vouched as "commonly reported in the neighbourhood[1]."

It was now the middle of August and the archbishop was down at Chichester for the Feast of the Assumption (Aug. 15). The king at once sent for him for an interview at his manor in Windsor Park[2], at which he told him to take immediate steps against Oldcastle according to the law of the Church, supplying him in the meantime with certain letters which were subsequently submitted to the Convocation when they met in the following year. By Aug. 21, 1413[3], a proclamation had been sent out calling upon the sheriffs in every county to arrest all priests and chaplains who were casting the evil seed of Lollardry, while the archbishop took instant steps to bring the knight to heel by sending a summons to him at Cooling citing him to appear and answer to a charge of heresy.

But now a difficulty arose. The gates of Cooling Castle were shut and the archbishop had no right to force them to get his summons served. His messenger however was accompanied by an usher of the king's chamber named John Butler[4] who could insist on admission in the king's name[5]. Butler was admitted and made his demand either that the archbishop's sumner[6] should be allowed to enter or that Oldcastle should himself come outside and accept service

---

[1] Prout haec omnia publicè dicebantur, Conc. iii. 353; juxta assertionem et prout communiter praedicatur in partibus ubi dictus dominus Johannes moratur, Conc. iii. 354; Rym. ix. 62; Fascic. 436.

[2] For a document dated a nr̃e manoir dans nr̃e parke de Windesore Aug. 26, 1413, see Chancery Warrants, Ser. I. 1364/1. For another dated at Windsor Sept. 20, 1413 (not Sept. 29 as in the heading), see Cotton MS. Calig. D. v. f. 1. For Norden's map of Windsor Park (circ. 1608), see Tighe and Davies, ii. 31 and Frontispiece showing "the Lodge" in the middle of the Little Park, i.e. nearest the castle, with four other lodges (i.e. Nories, Langland's, Grene's and Heyboth's) in the Great Park.

[3] Rym. ix. 46; Cleop. E. II. f. 297; Letter Book I, 116; Lechler, ii. 98. For proclamation in Lancashire, see Baines, i. 129, from Claus. 1 H. V.

[4] Rym. ix. 292, 813; Beamont, i. 252. He was the younger brother of William Butler, Lord of Warrington, from whom he received the manors of Eccleshall (i.e. Exhall near Coventry) and Crophill (now Cropwell-Butler near Nottingham) for life, Inq. p. Mort. iv. 12, 208; Thoroton, i. 191, 193; Dugd. Warw. i. 122, 124; Beamont, i. 255. He is called Master Butler of the Privy Chamber in Drayton, Oldcastle, 324.

[5] Not that Butler "had no business there," as Dixon, i. 60.

[6] Capgr. 304. Called "the Archbishop's creature" by Gaspey, i. 195. There seems no reason to charge the archbishop with "fraud" in this step, as Brougham, 65, neither was Oldcastle "besieged in his castle," as Green, 260; J. M. Stone, 51; Adams, i. 209 (who thinks that the king "sent an army to capture Cowling Castle" and that Oldcastle was "forced to surrender"). In Drayton, Oldcastle, 329, 340, the "paritor" is made to eat his process, parchment, seal and all.

there[1], to which he replied in the hearing of many that he would let no man summon him at all[2]. Failing in this the archbishop had the writ fastened to the cathedral door at Rochester on Sept. 6[3] calling upon the recusant to appear before him within five days at his castle at Leeds[4].

Oldcastle had now the chance of acting out in his own person the advice he had lately written to his friends in Prague—never to draw back from Truth, even unto death[5]. On the day appointed, i.e. Sept. 11, 1413[6], the archbishop's court opened in the large chapel at Leeds Castle, but the accused did not appear. He was called in a loud voice by the public crier, and when there was no reply the archbishop pronounced him contumacious and cursed him in his absence there and then[7]. Straightway he was declared to be under strong suspicion and warned to appear on Sept. 23 to show cause why he should not be pronounced a heretic and schismatic and an enemy of the Church and handed over to the secular arm for graver treatment. But in the meantime the king's officers had presented themselves at Cooling with a warrant for his arrest[8]. He offered no resistance but was quietly removed and imprisoned in the Tower[9].

---

[1] Seu saltem extra castrum suum faceret sui copiam, Conc. iii. 354; Rym. ix. 61.

[2] Called the "theoretical position that the Church had no jurisdiction over him" in Trevelyan, 336. Carrick (p. 215) thinks that he was "availing himself of the special privileges of an English noble."

[3] Foxe, iii. 323; State Trials, i. 228.

[4] Not at Canterbury, as Dixon, i. 60. For Archbishop Arundel at Leeds (in castro meo de Ledes) in 1413, see Somner, i. 136. For Leeds Castle granted to Joan Countess of Hereford on Feb. 9, 1414, see Escheators Inquisitions, Ser. I. 1008, Nov. 5, 1414.

[5] Wylie, iii. 462. Walden (i. 623) says that Hus had asked Oldcastle to have a copy of Wycliffe's Trialogus sent to Bohemia, cf. Harl. Miscell. ii. 254; Weever, Oldcastle, 214. It was copied by Jerome of Prague at Oxford, Wylie, iii. 468; i.e. in 1399, Waugh, 444; or about 1401, Wetzer, vi. 440.

[6] Wals. ii. 292; Hypodig. 440; Fascic. 436; Foxe, iii. 323; Weever, Oldcastle, 220; State Trials, i. 228; Kennett, i. 310; Hook, iv. 514; Gaspey, i. 187; Stubbs, iii. 85; Dict. Nat. Biogr. xlii. 88. Not Sept. 2, as Rym. ix. 62, followed by Carte, ii. 675; Collier, iii. 294 (edn. 1852); Pauli, v. 84; nor Sept. 6, as Goodwin, 17.

[7] Cursed him for contumacie, Capgr. 304; "On the payne of cursynge," Secreta, 185. For "the execucyon of the curse," see Greg. Chron. 230. For text of the ritual of excommunication, see Barnes, 287, i.e. a liminibus sacre ecclesie te excludimus et ab omni societate christianâ separamus, no priest was to dare to celebrate mass if the excommunicated person was present and all who consorted with him were to be smitten with anathema. Cf. cruce erectâ, campanis pulsatis, candelis accensis et in terram projectis, Conc. iii. 386, 388. Cf. book and belle and holy clothes, Laud Troy Book, 501, 518.

[8] Not in 1412, as Purey-Cust, ii. 71.

[9] Rym. ix. 62; Wals. ii. 293; Hypodig. 441, though not in Concilia. In Greg. Chron. 107; Brut, ii. 551, he is "arestyd at Wynsore." R. S. Gower (102) thinks that he was "taken by force at Cowling." In Cassell (i. 519) he goes back to Windsor. Waugh (449) thinks that "what happened is far from clear."

On Saturday, Sept. 23, 1413[1], the archbishop was present in the Chapter-house at St Paul's[2] with Bishops Clifford and Beaufort as assessors[3] and 12 learned legists and theologians[4], amongst whom were three future bishops. These were two Welshmen[5] (viz. Henry Ware[6], a diplomatist[7] who afterwards became Bishop of Chichester, and Philip Morgan, successively Bishop of Worcester[8] and Ely[9]), and John Kempe, a Kentish neighbour of Oldcastle's[10], who was now 33 years old[11] and in full practice as a lawyer[12]. He afterwards rose to be Keeper of the Privy Seal,

---

[1] Rym. ix. 62 ; Conc. iii. 354 ; Chron. Giles, 5 ; Gesta, 3. Not Sept. 28, as Rapin, i. 505.

[2] Called the Black Friars in Brut, ii. 551; Halle, 48; Redman, 16; Holinsh. iii. 544.

[3] Roujoux, ii. 239, adds Chichele but gives no authority; also Cassell, i. 520.

[4] Conc. iii. 355 ; Rym. ix. 63 ; For. Accts. 3 H. V.

[5] For permission for Henry Ware, Philip Morgan, and many other Welshmen to live in England on paying 6s. 8d. each to the hanaper, see Pat. 1 H. V, iv. 34; Cal. Pat. H. V, i. 124, Dec. 16, 20, 1413.

[6] Or Warr, Rot. Parl. iv. 110. Called De la Ware in Stubbs, Reg. 86.

[7] Called virum famosum et in ore populi Deo et hominibus non ignotum, Gesta, 95, where he is an official of the Court of Canterbury (called Chancellor in Harl. MS. 530), i.e. he was Dean of the Arches in 1415, Hennessy, 311. He had been Rector of St Mary Aldermary in Bow Lane, London, from June 3, 1401, Hennessy, 299. On Feb. 19, 1418, he was Vicar General for the Bishop of London, Test. Ebor. iii. 323, i.e. Richard Clifford who was absent at the Council of Constance. In 1414 he held a canonry at Llandaff, Rym. ix. 110, 118. On May 24, 1414, he is parson of Tring (Herts.), Cal. Pat. H. V, i. 185, and on Oct. 28, 1417, he received the prebend of Wilsford and Woodford (Salisbury), Cal. Pat. H. V, ii. 122. On Feb. 16, 1417, he was appointed to the prebend of Rugmere in St Paul's, Le Neve, ii. 433. For his will dated July 7, 1420, proved July 26, 1420, see Hennessy, xlv ; Geneal. vi. 225.

[8] Elected April 24, 1419, Le Neve, iii. 60.

[9] Appointed Feb. 27, 1426, ibid. i. 338.

[10] Cf. Johannes Kemp de Canciâ, Gasc. 36.

[11] When founding his college in connection with the parish church at Wye (Monast. viii. 1430 ; Hasted iii. 170–173), where he had been baptised as a child (Godwin, De Praesulibus, 128 ; Raine, Historians, iii. 328), he himself says that he was then 67 years of age (i.e. on Jan. 14, 1447) and that he was "boryn and bro3t forth withinne the said parisshe wher also the bodyes of his auncestrys restyn," Monast. iii. 254, i.e. he was born at Ollantigh near Ashford (not "Olantleigh," as Hennessy, p. viii). For his "gardyn at Olyntye in the said lordship of Wy," see Monast. iii. 254) in 1380, where his father Thomas was the owner of the estate, see Hasted, iii. 170 ; Foss, iv. 334 ; Hook, v. 193 ; Dict. Nat. Biogr. xxx. 384. Not that he was "a pore husbandman's sonne of Wye," as Lel. Itin. vi. 2 ; or "of parents in a very low condition of life," as Campbell, Chancellors, i. 341 ; or "of humble parents," as Brodrick, Merton, 221 ; Wheater, 213. In 1407 and 1408 he was Rector of St Michael's in Crooked Lane, London, Hennessy, 2, 276; Hook, v. 193. For account of his preferment, see Hennessy, viii, including the rectories of Southwick near Shoreham (Sussex), Dallaway, ii. 68, and Slapton near Leighton Buzzard (Bucks.). In 1414 he was Dean of the Peculiars (i.e. the private patronage of the Archbishop of Canterbury), Hennessy, 313. In Coram Rege Roll, 35, Easter 3 H. V, copied in Cleop. E. ii. 309, he is Dean of the Church of the Blessed Mary de Arcubus (i.e. St Mary-le-Bow in Cheapside), and is called Dean of the Arches in Hook, v. 193; Dict. Nat. Biogr. xxx. 384, though his name does not occur in the list of Deans in Hennessy, 311.

[12] For Master John Kempe, Doctor of Laws, appearing in appeal of John Saunders in the Admiralty Court, see Pat. 2 H. V, i. 14, July 1, 1414.

Archdeacon of Durham and successively Bishop of
Rochester, Chichester and London, Archbishop of York,
Archbishop of Canterbury, Chancellor of England, and a
Cardinal. With these also were Robert Wombewell, vicar
of St Laurence Jewry, in West Cheap[1], and Thomas Walden,
whose known virulence against all heretics should have
kept him away from the enquiry, had that age understood
anything even of the first rudiments of judicial impartiality
in legal questions where religion was concerned.

Before this court Oldcastle was brought up in the custody
of Sir Robert Morley, keeper of the Tower[2]. Archbishop
Arundel[3] opened the case in his suavest manner[4], announcing that he was ready even now to grant forgiveness and
withdraw the curse. But the accused heeded not. He
altogether declined to ask for pardon[5], but begged permission to make a profession of his faith[6]. To this the
court agreed and he then produced from his gown[7] a
schedule written in English[8], handed a copy to the archbishop and read aloud to the following effect.

He believed faithfully and fully all the sacraments that
ever God ordained to be done in His Holy Church and
summarised his belief under four heads:

(1) That the worshipful sacrament of the Altar was
Christ's body in the form of bread[9], the same that was born
of the Blessed Virgin and is now glorified in Heaven.

(2) As to the sacrament of Penance he believed it was
needful to every man that should be saved to forsake sin

---

[1] Gibbons, 126; Newcourt, i. 385.
[2] He was appointed on July 8, 1413, Pat. 1 H. V, iii. 41; cf. Claus. 1 H. V, 22, 24,
July 19, 28, 1413; Iss. Roll 1 H. V, Mich., Oct. 21, 1413, which shows £100 paid to
him. For other payments to him as Custos of the Tower, see Iss. Roll 1 H. V, Pasch.,
Mich., June 27, Oct. 2, 1413.
[3] Not Chichele, as Yonge, 243.
[4] Bonis et modestis terminis ac modo multum suavi, Conc. iii. 355; Rym. ix. 63.
[5] Petere absolutionem omnino distulit, Conc. iii. 354, though these words are not in
Rymer. Cf. wolde not aske, Capgr. 305.
[6] The ground of his belefe and the botome of his stomacke, Halle, 48.
[7] De sinu suo, Conc. iii. 354, 406; Rym. ix. 62. Called his "bosom" in Gairdner,
Lollardy, i. 76.
[8] Schedulam indentatam, Conc. iii. 354; Rym. ix. 62; see also Fascic. 438; Pollard,
180; un papier dentelé (i.e. an indenture), Fleury, vi. 335. Cassell (i. 519) is "at a loss
to discover in it what any true Catholic could object to." Waugh (452) thinks that "the
language is vague and the main questions at issue are evaded."
[9] Conc. iii. 354; sub panis specie, Rym. ix. 63; cf. Wylie, iii. 463, note 7. His body
in form of brede o whete, Kail, 40; Lydg. Min. Po. 67, 92, 99, 101; do. Nightingale, 24.

and do due penance for sins already committed with true confession[1], very contrition and rightful satisfaction. Such penance he desired every man to do.

(3) As to Images[2] he understood that these were not of faith, but ordained by the Church[3] to be calendars to lewd[4] men to bring to mind the passion of Christ and the martyrdom and good living of other saints, but that if a man did the worship to dead images[5] that is due to God or put such hope and trust in them as he should do towards God, he did in that the great sin of maumetry[6].

---

[1] For confession as tempus procationum scilicet wowing, see Ann. 179; Conc. iii. 222; ye beste time of wowing, Cronin, 309; Fasc. iii. 205; Wylie, iii. 432. For rule of the Observants 1451, quod nullus frater pro confessione audiendâ juxta mulierem stet vel sedeat, see Mon. Francisc. II, xxiv. 96.

[2] For attack on image worship by Matthew of Janov (d. Nov. 30, 1394), see Lützow, Hus, 52. For account of him, see Loserth, xxi ; Lützow, Hus, 4.

[3] Sythe beleve was ȝewe (i.e. given), Conc. iii. 355 ; not "sewe," as C. E. Maurice, ii. 260.

[4] Laicis ac ignaris, Rym. ix. 63. Cf. not for ye ymage but in worship of that seint that ye ymage bitokened, Krapp, 74. Pecock (i. 148) urged that "ydolatrie is nevere doon save whenne a man takith a creature for his God and so doith no man with eny ymage now in Cristendom after he is passid childhode and which is not a natural fool," Blackie, 483.

[5] Preyeris and offringis made to blynde rodys (certis crucibus sive *rodis*, Ann. 178) and deve (i.e. deaf) images of tre and ston ben nere of kyn to ydolatrie, Cronin, 300. Cf.

> He wer ful lewde that wolde byleve
> In figure mad of stock or ston
> Yet forme shude we none repreve
> Nether of Mary ne of Jon,
> Petre, Poule ne other none
> Canonised by clergie. Pol. Songs, ii. 246.

[6] Idolatria, Rym. ix. 63. Cf.

> Thes Lollardes that lothen ymages most
> With mannes handes made and wrouȝt
> And pilgrimages to be souȝt
> Thei seien hit is but mawmentrie. Pol. Songs, ii. 246.

For "mawmentrie," see Lydg. Troy Bk. 301, 302, 311. For protest against too many images in churches except the Virgin and the Crucifix, cf.

> Ne faites pas les dieux d'argent
> D'or, de fust, de pierre ou d'arain
> Qui font ydolatrer la gent.

> La beauté de l'or reluisant
> Font croire a maint peuple incertain
> Que ce soient Dieu pour certain.

> Ne croire en tant de marioles
> De babouins et de fyoles
> Ou trop de fois ydolatrons. Deschamps, viii. 201, 202.

Cf. On poet Dieu pryer sans ymages sensibles et corporelles pour eviter grans maulx corporelz et espirituelz qui adviennent souvent a ceulx qui s'arestent trop a faire meditation d'aulcunes choses corporelles ou semblables as corporelles. Gerson, in Jadart, 141.

(4) As to Pilgrimages[1] he supposed fully that every man on this earth is a pilgrim towards bliss or pain[2] and that he that will not keep God's commandments here shall be damned if he die so[3], albeit that he go on pilgrimage to all corners of the world, while he that keepeth them shall be saved, though he never in his life should go on pilgrimage to Rome[4] or Canterbury[5] or any other mind-place[6] of the saints whatever.

The archbishop consulted with his colleagues and announced that the statement contained much good Catholic truth[7], but that they wished to know a little further[8]. Did the accused believe

(*a*) That the material bread remained after consecration[9]?

(*b*) That confession to a priest was necessary in the sacrament of Penance?

To which Oldcastle replied that he would not say anything on these points except what he had read out from his bill[10].

The court felt sorry for him[11] and the archbishop gave him a kind and friendly caution[12] that if he did not answer within a fixed time they had power to declare him a heretic,

---

[1] Also yee holden ageyn pilgrimages, Hoccl. Min. Po. 20; Anglia, v. 34; James, 155. Cf. better to abide at home and beet the stools with their heels, Foxe, iii. 539.

[2] Every citizen of the heavenly country is a pilgrim of this world for all time of this present life, Brute, Thorpe, &c. 176.

[3] Not "lye."

[4] Cf. vezitar S.P. e S.P., Bonis, I. xix.

[5] "Neque Compostellam" added in Rym. ix. 63; also "Walsingham" in State Trials, i. 234. For vicarious pilgrimages to Rome and Santiago, see Vict. Co. Hist. London, ii. 208. For 50 pilgrims going to Galicia from Fowey and Falmouth June 8, 1413, see Rym. ix. 16. For 60 in the Cristiene de Dertemouth and 40 in the Andrewe de Valme (i.e. Salcombe, Wylie, i. 383), 50 in the Margaret of Plymouth, and 40 in the Elen de Lanant (i.e. Lelant on St Ives Bay; not "Levant," as Rym. ix. 8), see Fr. Roll 1 H. V, 36, 37; 40 in the Leonard of Weymouth (May 31, June 8, 1414); 50 in the Elena of Ipswich (John Joy, master), Rym. ix. 133, 139; 50 in the James of Fowey July 3, 1414, Rym. ix. 147; and 24 in La Marie of Pensans, Feb. 16, 1415, Rym. ix. 201. For Compostella and what they saw there in 1466, see Rożmital, 85.

[6] Cf. the memorialis or mynde placis of seintis, Pecock, 4.

[7] Wals. ii. 293; Hypodig. 441; "an orthodox confession," Stubbs, iii. 85; "an enlargement of the Apostles' Creed," Snow, 54.

[8] Not "a new demand for a layman," as C. E. Maurice, ii. 261. See the case of Badby in Wylie, iii. 438. Waugh (452) thinks that the archbishop "knew that no good could arise from argument."

[9] Called "the murderous question" in Aubrey, iii. 39.

[10] Capgr. 305. Dixon (i. 60) thinks that Oldcastle was "a learned clerk."

[11] Eidem nihilominus compatientes, Rot. Parl. iv. 109.

[12] Benigno et affabili modo. Carrick (219) thinks that "it was Arundel's practice to cover his malignity with a seraphic smile."

but he still refused to say anything more.   After further
consultation the court explained to him the Church's teaching on these points as expounded by Austin, Jerome, Ambrose and other sainted doctors[1].   He answered that he was
ready to believe it[2], but he could not admit that Popes,
Cardinals and Bishops had power to settle such things.
At this stage the court adjourned, it being understood that
Oldcastle should be supplied by the following day with a
written statement of the Church's views translated into
English so that he might the more easily understand
them[3], and that he would be expected to give his answers
by Monday next, and on the following day, Sept. 24, 1413,
processions were ordered for the "extirpation of the exe-
crable plague of Lollardry[4]."

The court reassembled at the Black Friars[5] on Monday,
Sept. 25, 1413[6], the Bishop of Bangor[7] (Benet Nicole[8])
having been added in the meantime to the archbishop's
two other assessors[9].   Oldcastle was again brought in and
asked to give his replies.   On the first point he said that
the bread remained veiling the body of Christ, as His
divinity was veiled beneath His visible humanity.   If the
Church taught that no material bread and wine remained,
this was not according to the Scripture, but a finding given
after she had become corrupted with endowments.

Secondly, confession, though expedient and good, was
not a necessity for salvation, for by contrition only could
sin be blotted out.

Thirdly, adoration must be reserved for Christ alone
and not given to the cross on which He hung.   And when
they asked what honour he would pay to a crucifix, he said

---

[1] For Austin, Ambrose, Jerome and Gregory as "the foure greete doctouris," see
Forshall-Madden, i. 59; Wylie, iii. 421.   They were the four stots that drew the harrow
after the Church's plough, P. Plo. i. 566; ii. 270; Morley, vi. 188.   For "seynte Aus-
tyne," see Secreta, 145, 153, 159, 161, 170, 173, 177, 191, 202, 206.

[2] Voluit eas determinationes credere.   For other readings, see Rym. ix. 63; Fascic.
441; Wals. ii. 294; Hypodig. 444.

[3] Pro leviori intellectu ejusdem, Rym. ix. 64; Conc. iii. 355.

[4] Pestis illa execrabilis Lollardriae, Hist. MSS. Var. Coll. iv. 40.

[5] Rot. Parl. iv. 109.   Called "an obscure Dominican convent on Ludgate Hill" in
Dixon, i. 61.

[6] Not 20th, as Conc. iii. 355.   In Bermondscy Annals, 484, the date of Oldcastle's
condemnation is given as 1 H. V, lunâ currente per ix, which would appear to mean
Oct. 4, the new moon falling on Sept. 25.

[7] Rot. Parl. iv. 109; Fascic. 414; not St David's, as Carte, ii. 675; Hume, iv. 38.

[8] Wylie, iii. 141.

[9] For costeers that is to say sitteres bysyde, see Secreta, 139.

he would wipe it and keep it clean[1].   What of the power
of the keys?   The Pope was very Antichrist, or rather he
was the head[2], the bishops were the limbs and the friars[3]
the tail[4].   No obedience was due to them, except in so far
as they followed Christ in life and conversation.   He and
no other is Peter's heir who is of better life and purer ways
than Peter, and with this he stretched out his hand and
shouted[5] to the bystanders in the court: "These men who
are bent on damning me mislead themselves and you and
will drag you down to Hell!   Therefore beware of them."
Again and again did the archbishop with tears in his eyes
exhort him to believe and hold what the Roman church[6]
believes and holds.   He only answered that he believed
and held no otherwise than he had told them before.   Then
seeing that they were making no way the archbishop "with
sorrow and bitterness of heart[7]" pronounced him a heretic
and left him to be dealt with by the secular judge, excommunicating all who should henceforth favour or support
him[8].   And so the court broke up.

[1] Capgr. 306.   For a crucifix spat upon by Jews compared to a mirror which a
woman cleans by spitting on it, see Petit de Julleville, ii. 245.   Bale (in Harl. Misc. ii.
269) adds: "and that He (i.e. Christ) should not be robbed of his goods as He is nowadays,"
followed by Foxe, iii. 335; State Trials, i. 244; C. E. Maurice, ii. 265.

[2] Cassell (i. 520) thinks that this statement is "exaggerated or distorted," but it seems
to have been taken from the Lantern of Light, where the friars are "the venomous tail,"
Brute, Thorpe, &c., 148; Foxe, iii. 533.

[3] Called the monks in Hefele, vii. 24.

[4] "Which couvereth his most filthy part," adds Bale in Harl. Misc. ii. 267; State
Trials, i. 241.   But this was too strong apparently for Foxe (iii. 333), who does not enter
it; cf. Gilpin, 27; Towle, 269; Brougham, 71; called "even a less dignified part of
the body" in Ainger, i. 124.   Idée assez noble pour avoir persévéré jusqu'à nos jours
depuis le temps grossier dont elle date, Berault-Bercastel, xv. 100; cf. Conc. iii. 374;
Foxe, iii. 532; Adams, i. 209, who thinks that Oldcastle said this to the king at Kennington.

[5] Propriâ confessione, immo violenti et obstinatâ assertione convictum, Chron. Giles, 5.
Guthrie (ii. 450) thinks that Oldcastle "behaved with an indecency and haughtiness that
neither became a gentleman nor a Christian."   Lingard (iii. 237) says that "his demeanour was as arrogant and insulting as that of his judge was mild and dignified"; followed
by Vattier, 307; Snow, 54.   Cf. "heretical arrogance," Tennyson, 521.   Gardiner (300)
thinks that the archbishop and Oldcastle both "played their parts with dignity."   Waugh
(453) thinks that Oldcastle became "at last simply abusive."   Called "insolently provocative" in Saturday Review, 17/4/09, p. 501.

[6] Ecclesia Romana, Conc. iii. 356, 405; Rym. ix. 65.   For the abbey at Evesham
as Romanae ecclesiae nullo medio pertinens, see Pat. 6 H. V, 11, Dec. 12, 1418.   This
phrase does not occur in the Evesham documents printed in Monast. ii. 13, which
however contain abundant evidence of the assertion of exemption from dependence on
the Bishops of Worcester.

[7] Cum dolore et amaritudine cordis, Rot. Parl. iv. 109.   Brougham (75) thinks this
was "a false show of compassion."   Pauli, Bilder, 278 (307), that the archbishop "längst
nach einem vornehmen Opfer der Inquisition gelechzt habe."   Cf. il est impossible de tuer
avec plus de sensibilité, Michelet, vi. 12.

[8] Rot. Parl. iv. 109.

It has long been, and still is, the fashion to regard Oldcastle as a mere pestilent demagogue, who led a rebel mob to pull down church and throne[1]. But it cannot be too clearly borne in mind that in the whole of the record of his trial no word is uttered about insubordination to the secular power[2]. His crime thus far was solely against the law of the Church and, like Badby, he stood firm by his conscience, when conscience as he knew meant death.

In putting together the above sketch of the proceedings at his trial I have thought it best to draw solely from the contemporary official record, neglecting altogether a later and highly coloured version which has been too long accepted as historical narration. It was published by Bale[3] more than a century after the events[4] under the stimulus of acute religious exasperation, but it appears to be nothing but a "bilious[5]" dramatic expansion of the original record, inflated to depict the typical Protestant martyr as a lamb, like Stephen, disputing in the midst of wolves[6], the other side being suitably tricked out as "beastly blockheads," "belly-gods," "spiteful murderers," "bloodthirsty raveners," "subtle sorcerers," "blusterers," "idolaters," and "blasphemous Sodomites[7]." Most writers in the past have followed it quite blindly[8], some thinking

---

[1] Hook (v. 30) thinks that he "put himself at the head of a discontented faction because he was looked down upon by the ancient aristocrats." See also Tyler, ii. 352; Jennings, 128; Wakeman, 162, who describes the Lollards as "political revolutionaries." Cf. "a mere revolutionary faction in the state," Purey-Cust, ii. 360; Vict. Co. Hist. (Hants.) ii. 45.

[2] *Postquam insultum regi fecerat apud Eltham*, says Otterbourne, 274, but it is difficult to reconcile this with the known particulars of the case.

[3] Harl. Misc. ii. 249–272; copied into Foxe, iii. 320–342, 541–543; Brute, Thorpe, &c., 110–137; State Trials, i. 226–251. Parts of it are printed in Pollard, pp. 175–189, as supposed specimens of 15th century prose.

[4] i.e. in June, 1544, when Bale was in exile at Marburg, Baeske, 47. In it he refers (p. 251) to an account of the trial written in the "Tyme of the said Lord's Trouble by a certein Frinde of his." Who this was is not known, though it may have been taken from Wm. Tyndale's "Book of Thorpe or of John Oldcastle," which was ordered to be destroyed as a heretical book Dec. 3, 1531, Letters and Papers of Henry VIII, v. 769; Waugh, 434; Baeske, 49. In any case Bale states that he had afterwards seen "the great process which Thomas Arundel made against him" which makes it certain that his chief evidence was the official record. For his quotations *ex vetusto exemplari Londincnsium*, see Bale, 257, 265, 272.

[5] Harl. Misc. i. 102; Fuller, Worthies, iii. 61.

[6] Harl. Misc. ii. 263, 267; Foxe, iii. 333; State Trials, i. 242; Baeske, 51, 55, 56, who regards his sources as "unzuverlässig," "unkontrollierbar," "ganz problematisch," &c. [7] Harl. Misc. ii. 251, 254, 255, 256, 278.

[8] e.g. Goodwin, 16; Weever, Oldcastle, 212; Gilpin, 11–28, 34; A. M. Brown, 20, 42, 46; Brougham, 64–74, 373–377; C. E. Maurice, ii. 257, 258, who has a great belief in the veracity of the "sturdy Protestant" (i.e. Bale); Milner, iii. 311–318; Towle, 266–

that it is "mainly based on the notaries' reports[1]," others regard it as "collected from ancient manuscripts[2]" or "derived from documents of uncontestable authority[3]" or as "a more detailed report[4]" of "the proceedings in full[5]," while the very latest pronouncements declare it either to be "in the main perhaps trustworthy," though its sources "cannot always be traced[6]," or that its facts are drawn from second-hand authorities and often, it is to be feared, from no authorities at all[7], though "in some of his details" Bale "really had some authority for his statements," and that it is hard to believe "that it is all fiction." But in its own time this version did not have it all quite so much its own way. For in 1573 Nicholas Harpsfeld published an argument against "Foxe's lies" and maintained his position well[8]. Whereupon the angry martyrologist, whose pen was too often "governed by his prejudices and passions[9]," crumpled him up with abuse about his "foul mouth" and "stinking breath," the "offals of his railing talk," and his "dunghill of dirty dialogues," calling him a "dirt-dauber's son," "a wild Irishman crept out of Patrick's Purgatory" with his "viperous wrangling[10]" and "cockish brags." He assumes that no one can deny any part of Bale's story, which he takes to be "true originals in ancient records[11]," and he then elaborates pages of monumental sophistry which proved too much for Fuller, who wrote: "Let Mr Fox be this Lord Cobham's compurgator. I dare not[12]."

270; Workman, i. 265; Carrick, 219; Milman, viii. 218; Pauli, v. 85; see also Hume, iv. 37; James, 187; Brief History of the British Reformation (Religious Tract Society), 26; The Lollards (Rel. Tract Soc.), 29; Gaspey, I. ix. 203; Mackintosh, i. 352; Halliwell, Letters, i. 75; Tyler, ii. 358, 369 n., 370 n.; Aubrey, ii. 39; R. S. Gower, 102, who still speaks of the "bloodthirsty prelates." Neither Collier (iii. 296) nor Stubbs (iii. 189) has drawn upon it, and Guthrie (ii. 450) seems to have been the first to throw doubt upon it.

[1] Gaspey, i. 189, 198, 204, 235.
[2] Milner, iii. 317.
[3] Wordsworth, i. 355–399; aus urkundlichen Quellen geschöpft, Lechler, ii. 88; "documents authentic and indisputable," Brute, Thorpe, &c., 109.
[4] Ramsay, i. 175, 178.
[5] Ainger, i. 125.
[6] Tait in Dict. Nat. Biogr. xlii. 89, 93. Gairdner, Lollardy, i. 75, supposes it to be based "on the authority of some old MS. now unknown."
[7] Waugh, 435–451, 454.
[8] Harpsfeld, Dialogi, 63.
[9] Collier, iii. 325.
[10] Foxe, iii. 349, 372, 376, 380, 383.
[11] Foxe, iii. 350.
[12] Fuller, Church Hist. ii. 416; Lingard, iii. 238; Tyler, ii. 387; Snow, 58. Speed (788) leaves Foxe to deal with "Copus" (i.e. Alan Cope, to whom Harpsfeld

Nevertheless the account continued to be regarded as
conclusive up till Guthrie's time and has not yet ceased
to be looked upon as authentic[1], one devotee going so far
as to call on us to believe that Bale's particulars must have
been before the officials who compiled the original records,
but that they were "designedly omitted[2]." For myself
I have little doubt that Bale's account is quite untrustworthy for any sound historical purpose, except as an
illustration of the treatment of Oldcastle's story under the
raging heat of 16th century religious passion[3].

entrusted his "Dialogi Sex" for publication at Antwerp, Dublin Rev. cxviii (1896), p. 11;
Baeske, 65 ; called "a certain Alanus Copus" in Waugh, 646) but has a strong reference
to the "slanderous report" of "N.D. author of the 3 conversions," which may mean
Nicholas Harpsfeld Dialogi.

[1] Cf. "may be read in Foxe," Ainger, i. 124.
[2] Milner, iii. 317.
[3] Eine flammende Parteischrift für die reformatorische Sache, Baeske, 61.

CHAPTER XVII

THE LOLLARD RISING

IMMEDIATELY after Oldcastle's condemnation Archbishop Arundel had a personal interview with the king and prayed that the carrying out of the death sentence should be put off for the usual 40 days[1]. He then went down to Maidstone, whence on Oct. 10, 1413[2], he sent out notices to the bishops of his province requiring them to have the sentence read out in English in the churches of their dioceses whenever the congregations were largest. The Bishops of London[3] and Winchester[4] gave orders to this effect on Oct. 23, and the dioceses of Exeter and Hereford were notified on Nov. 8 and 17 respectively[5].

Oldcastle's goods and belongings at Cooling and Cobham were all scheduled for confiscation and the list was put into a box and deposited in a green chest in the Exchequer at Westminster[6], and in the meanwhile the heretic himself was kept a prisoner in the Tower[7], the

---

[1] Wals. ii. 296; Hypodig. 445; Capgr. 306; Chron. Lond. 96. Not 50 days, as Lingard, iii. 237; Snow, 55; Cassell, i. 520; Pauli, Bilder, 278 [307] (who thinks that such a period was required by the statute though it does not appear in the text, Stat. ii. 128); Tyler, ii. 373, who thinks that 50 days would be required to forward his supposed appeal to the Pope; Vict. Co. Hist. (Hants.), ii. 46. For this appeal see Gesta, 5, note (quoting Hargreaves, State Trials, i. 38); Waugh, 450.

[2] Conc. iii. 357; Rym. ix. 66; Fascic. 449; Harl. Misc. ii. 271; Foxe, iii. 337, 348; State Trials, i. 247; Hook, iv. 524. Not Oct. 5, as Goodwin, 26; Gaspey, i. 245; nor before the trial, as C. E. Maurice, ii. 256. On the same day messengers received payment for carrying the king's proclamation to the like effect, Devon, 324.

[3] Dated from Much Hadham, Conc. iii. 357; Hist. MSS. Var. Coll. iv. 40.

[4] Vict. Co. Hist. (Hants.), ii. 46.

[5] Fascic. 450.

[6] Oct. 10, 1413, Kal. and Inv. ii. 89.

[7] For supposition that he was imprisoned in the Beauchamp Tower (built temp. Ed. III), see Knight, London, ii. 238; Dixon, i. 53; Lechler, ii. 80. For picture of it see Knight, London, ii. 246; Cassell, ii. 373; Dixon, i. 53, 60, 368; Dick, Frontispiece, Plate v. It was called the Cobham Tower, not from Oldcastle, as Dixon, i. 53, but from the fact that the three sons of Lord Cobham were imprisoned there in 1555, the youngest Thomas having carved his name in one of the recesses, Dick, 5, 26, Plate XXIX; do. Sketch, p. 39; Dixon, i. 126.

king being still hopeful of winning him back to the fold[1].
Accordingly he was plied with visitors who are said to
have extracted from him a promise that he would recant
his heresy and abide by the judgment of the Church,
remaining in prison[2] till the Convocation should meet again.
There is indeed a document extant which purports to contain his formal recantation[3], but it cannot be genuine or the
fact would have been certainly cast in his teeth, though it
may have been prepared beforehand in readiness for his
expected surrender.   Indeed a special synod of the clergy
appears to have assembled in St Paul's on Nov. 20 and to
have sat till Dec. 4[4], at which 12 inquisitors were present[5];
but the synod merely met to pronounce the great curse
against Oldcastle and his supporters and, as soon as the
meeting was over, the archbishop published it with due
solemnity at Paul's Cross[6].   But by this time there was no
question of reconciliation, for long before the synod met,
their victim was at large again and London was on the
brink of a revolution.

In the night of Oct. 19, 1413[7], Oldcastle broke the
Tower[8] by the help of some daring Lollard friends, the

[1] Wals. ii. 296; Hypodig. 446; Elmham, Lib. Metr. 97.

[2] He should tarry in holde till such time as it were of the Pope allowed and then,
would he nyld he, the Archbishop should be his judge, Foxe, iii. 326; Tyler, ii. 369;
Gesta, 5, note, from Hargreaves, State Trials, i. 38.

[3] Fascic. 414, with translation in Foxe, iii. 339, who heads it: "counterfeited by the
Bishops"; um die Bevölkerung irre zu führen, Lechler, ii. 95.   Cf. Milman, viii. 224
(who believes it to be a forgery); Ramsay, i. 178; Dict. Nat. Biogr. xlii. 90.   Waugh
(456) thinks that "it is just possible that he may in a moment of weakness have signed
the document and afterwards withdrawn from it."   Gairdner (Lollardy, i. 79) regards the
unsigned document as "only a draft of what he was expected to declare," but thinks that
"he had substantially agreed to its contents."   Baeske, 36, calls it a "Mährchen."

[4] Page 209, note 9; Tyler, ii. 357; Loftie, i. 263.

[5] Gesta, 3, from Bodl. MS. Digby, 235, i.e. Chron. Lond. 96; see Coxe-Macray,
ix. 247.

[6] Dec. 5, 1413, Chron. Lond. 97; Tyler, ii. 357.   Called Sunday, Dec. 10, in Vict.
Co. Hist. (London), ii. 220.

[7] The date is fixed in Letter Book I, 166 ; Riley, Mem. 641; Ramsay, i. 178; Waugh,
637; Oman, Pol. Hist. 236.   Called "about Mykelmesse" in Capgr. 306; "in September," C. R. L. Fletcher, 317; "in October," Baeske, 22; Radford, 37; "before Oct. 10,"
Baildon, 108; Workman, i. 265; "about Oct. 10," Holt, Lights, 113 (this date is
based on Devon, 324, which shows payment entered on Oct. 10, 1413, to messengers
carrying orders that none should harbour Oldcastle as he was a convicted heretic.
Waugh (640) rejects the date because of the looseness of the chronology of the roll);
"intra fines Octobrium," Chron. Giles, 5; Tyler, ii. 365; "about the Feast of Simon
and Jude" (i.e. Oct. 28), Stow, 344; Kennet, i. 311; Gaspey, i. 264; Dixon, i. 61;
Lechler, ii. 89; "about Nov. 1," Cleop. E. II. 303, from Coram Rege Roll 1 H. V;
"with Inne a ffewe dayes," Kingsford, Chron. 69; "almost immediately," Stubbs, iii.
85.   Not Nov. 20, as Weever, Oldcastle, 226; nor *after* the rising, as Pol. Verg. 441.

[8] Excerpt. Hist. 145; rupit carceres, Chron. Giles, 5; prisonam fregerit, Letter Book I,
120; Waugh, 638; brake prysonne, Caxton, i. 224; debruse prison, Conc. iii. 360;

names of two of whom are still known, viz. Richard
Wrothe, described as "one of the greatest supporters of
that bad sect[1]," and a London parchmener[2] named William
Fisher[3]. It has been suggested that Oldcastle's escape
may have been arranged with the connivance of the king[4],
and in any case it is evident that there was no excessive
strictness in guarding the prisoner, for we know that not
only were Wrothe and Fisher still at large six weeks after
the escape, but that Mistress Wrothe, wife of the former,
was allowed to visit other prisoners in the Tower, where
she would not hold her tongue but blabbed openly about
God's stout knight who had been falsely condemned by the
limbs and ministers of Antichrist[5]. It was not till Oct. 28,
1413[6], that a proclamation was put out forbidding all intercourse with Oldcastle, and this was followed up by another
on Nov. 5, requiring the enforcement of the statute against
liveries passed in the previous reign[7]. John Selby, a clerk
of the Counter prison[8], was falsely charged with having
harboured the fugitive[9], but he had really been hiding

Stat. ii. 183; "brake them," Lel. Coll. ii. 488, where it is dated 1417; "brake out of
the Toure," Brut, ii. 551. Not that William Fisher and others "broke into the Tower,"
as Letter Book I, p. xix.

[1] Une de les pluys grantz susteignours del malueys secte, Baildon, xlix. 109; Early
Chanc. Proc. i. 26, from Bundle 6/37, where he is sued by Thomas Okore, keeper of the
prisoners in the Tower under Sir John Daubrygecourt (sic) for his connection with the
escape. For John Wrothe, kt. in 1406, see Letter Book I, 48.

[2] Parchemyner, Letter Book I, p. 166, i.e. a parchment-maker. Not a tailor, as Baildon, xlix. 109, meaning a parmyter or parmenter, cf. Lib. Alb. iii. 345; Godefroy, s.v.
Parmentier, derived from *parement*, i.e. furs as adornments to a robe, see Murray, s.v.
Parament; Du Cange, s.v. *Permentarius* (i.e. qui vestes parat vel ornat), *Parator*, *Pelli-
parius*; Littré, s.v. *Pareur*. For parchment in the Middle Ages, see Hochart, Nouvelles,
104, 110.

[3] Letter Book I, 166; Riley, Mem. 643, showing that his goods, lands and tenements
were *nil* when he was drawn from the Tower through the city by Cornhill and Chepe
and hanged at Tyburn on Oct. 8, 1416, after an inquiry held in Newgate on Oct. 5, 1416,
for assisting in Oldcastle's escape, Sharpe, London, i. 254; see also Iss. Roll 1 H. V,
Mich., Feb. 19, 1414; Devon, 332; Tyler, ii. 377; Chron. R. II to H. VI, p. 185,
quoted in Gairdner, Lollardy, i. 93. For order dated Sept. 22, 1416, to transfer William
Parchemenmaker, alias dictus William Fisshere, from the Tower to the custody of the
Sheriffs of London, see Claus. 4 H. V, 14.

[4] Tyler, ii. 373; Tyrrell, i. 285; Cassell, i. 520. This theory is worked out in *The
Fair Witch of Glas-Llyn*. Benham (Winchester, 144) thinks that Bishop Beaufort might
have also helped, but this is merely based on the supposition that he was averse to the
condemnation of Oldcastle, for which there is no evidence at all.

[5] Le fort Bachiler de Dieux fauxement forjugez par les Ministres d'Anticrist et ses
membres, Baildon, 109; Vict. Co. Hist. London, i. 220.

[6] Letter Book I, pp. xix, 119.

[7] Ibid. 119; Wylie, i. 69, 169.

[8] i.e. in Bread Street or the Poultry. For picture of the Counter in Wood Street
built 1670, see S. Young, 213.

[9] Riley, Mem. 676, where the charge was made by a winedrawer named John Derby

for some weeks in Fisher's house in Turnmill Street[1] which stood on the Cobham estate near Clerkenwell. The keeper of the Tower (Robert Morley) had been relieved of his office[2] before the actual escape took place, and a temporary successor was not appointed till Oct. 28[3]. On Oct. 29, Morley was himself committed to the Tower as a prisoner, though, as he was released on Nov. 15[4] and two of his servants were put on to watch the house in which Oldcastle was suspected to be lying[5], it would appear that his responsibility for the evasion was never really established.

The condemnation of Oldcastle was a blow aimed at the head of the Lollards, and it was not to be expected that they would long sit still under it with folded hands. They saw that the new king had resolutely set his face to crush them out[6] and that, if their leader fell, no mercy would afterwards be extended to them, though almost all England[7] was now on their side. They posted bills upon the London church doors threatening that 100,000 men were ready to

who was imprisoned in the Counter for theft, though he confessed that it was false on Oct. 17, 1419.

[1] Called Trillmell or Tremill Street in Chron. Lond. 104; Stow, Chron. 352; but "Turnmylle Strete" in Copland (circ. 1540), see Hazlitt, iv. 35. It was named from the Tremill Brook (Turmylbroke, Kingsford, Chron. 258, 338; Trillemylle Brook (1429), Hall, 317), otherwise called the river of the Wells or the Fleet. For the course of the Hollbourn from its source at Hampstead, see Loftie, i. 9, who shows that it was called the Fleet in its lower course, i.e. from St Pancras to its outflow into the Thames at the Black Friars, Stow, Lond. i. 23, 58. For the Cobham estate, now Coldbath Fields, see Knight, London, iii. 139.

[2] i.e. before Oct. 10, 1413, Devon, 324; Cal. Doc. Scot. iv. 171; Tyler, ii. 373. Waugh (638) believes that the dates in this roll are far from trustworthy. For £6. 13s. 4d. paid to Robert Morley, knight, *late* custos of the Tower for arrears of his salary (£100 per annum) on the day of his *exoneratio*, see Iss. Roll 1 H. V, Mich., Feb. 24, 1414; Cal. Doc. Scot. iv. 171. In Iss. Roll 1 H. V, Mich., Feb. 22, 1414, he is *late* custos of the Tower. For Robert Morle, kt., in retinue of the Earl of Arundel at Southampton in July, 1415, see Exch. Accts. 47/1; W. D. Cooper, 128. For Petronilla widow of Robert Morle, kt., see Claus. 4 H. V, 24, March 24, 1416.

[3] i.e. Sir John Dabridgecourt, Pat. 1 H. V, iii. 12, see page 260, note 1. He is called Custos on Nov. 16, 1413, Claus. 1 H. V, 14; also Nov. 25, 1413, Baildon, 108; Topogr. and Geneal. i. 197. For £8. 13s. 4d. paid to him ordinat' custos of Tower pro temp' post exonerationem Roberti Morley, see Iss. Roll 1 H. V, Mich., Feb. 19, 1414. For £100 per annum paid to Edward Duke of York as Constable of the Tower for life (cf. Wylie, ii. 481, note 4), see Iss. Roll 1 H. V, Mich., Jan. 27, 1414. Also £50 p. turri London, Rec. Roll 3 H. V, Pasch., June 22, 1415. In Iss. Roll 1 H. V, Mich., Dec. 1, 4, 11, 1413, payments for the King of Scots in the Tower are made through John Hall, Esquire, from Oct. 30 to Dec. 2, 1413.

[4] Claus. 1 H. V, 13.

[5] For payments to them, see Devon, 330, Feb. 19, 1414.

[6] Pol. Verg. (441) thought that the rising was due to the burning of John Hus, which did not take place till 18 months afterwards.

[7] Paene totam patriam, Wals. ii. 299; Hypodig. 448; though C. R. L. Fletcher (317) thinks that the rising was organised by "his Kentish tenants."

rise[1], and they sent out messengers who carried with them money and letters to the Lollards throughout the country in which the new king was called "the Priests' Prince[2]," and their friends were summoned to collect quietly[3] near London, where 50,000 apprentices and servants[4] would be ready to join them on a certain date which would be disclosed before Epiphany[5], many who did not know what they were to meet for being told that it skilled[6] not, so they got good pay.

The king was arranging to spend his Christmas at Eltham[7], where the red Gascon and Portuguese wine[8] had been already laid down for the merry-making, and the plotters meant to assemble on the day after Twelfth Night[9].

---

[1] Wals. ii. 291; Hypodig. 439; Capgr. 303; doubted in Baeske, 27, 39; Gairdner (i. 75) thinks that "this number was of course preposterous" and regards 50,000 as "much exaggeration" (p. 81); called 25,000 in Tyrrell, i. 286; Lingard (iii. 239) supposes that this was done "during Henry's first parliament," i.e. before June 9, 1413; also Snow, 55; but there is no mention of it during Oldcastle's trial. Tyler (ii. 6) remarks upon the absence of any Lollardism in the first parliament of Henry V.

[2] Princeps presbyterorum, Wals. ii. 306; Hypodig. 457; Walden, i. 486; Foxe, iii. 358; James, 151, 174, 175, 176; Weever, Oldcastle, 217; Milner, iii. 330; Tyler, ii. 32; Gairdner, Loll. i. 84; Wylie, iii. 334; Prince of preestis our lige Lord yee calle In scorn, but it is a style of honour, Hoccleve, Min. Po. 17; Anglia, v. 31; Baeske, 18. For St Louis of France reproached as a king of priests, see G. W. Cox, 196. For the Emperor Frederic II as "Pfaffenkönig" and his edicts against heresy in 1220 and 1232, see Gregorovius, v. 98, 157; also King Rupert, Stacke, i. 652. For Charles IV as "Pfaffenkaiser," see Lodge, 110; Hollweg-Calthrop, 187, 190.

[3] Privatim insurgent', Rym. ix. 171; Cotton MS. Cleop. E. II. f. 304 b; privatè congregand', ibid. f. 303.

[4] Capgr. 307; not 25,000, as Snow, 55, which he considers to be half the population of London; nor 5000, as Sharpe, London, i. 254; called "many followers" in Vict. Co. Hist. London, ii. 220. Cf. "but our chief strength must be the Londoners," Drayton, Oldcastle, 333.

[5] Wals. ii. 297; Hypodig. 446. For Tiffanie, Tiphain, see Rot. Parl. iv. 18, 20; or "Twelfth Day," Pol. Relig. Po. 118; or "la feste des Roys," Toulgoët-Treanna, 105. For "la semaine de la Tiphanie," see Darne, 75; gasteaux de la Tiphanie at the Hôtel Dieu in Paris, Coyecque, i. 193; Champion, Vie, 427.

[6] Capgr. 306. Cf. Taming of the Shrew, III. ii. 134; Famous Victories, 4, 45.

[7] Not "im Schlosse zu Elmham," as Baeske, 22. For account of Eltham Palace with illustrations of the great Hall, see Hasted, i. 52 (with plan); Lysons, iv. 398; Archaeologia, vi. 366–371; T. H. Turner, iii. 303; Brit. Archaeol. Assoc. Transactions, ii. 329; Purey-Cust, ii. 105, 106. For John Wodcok appointed custos and janitor of Eltham for life Dec. 8, 1415, see Pat. 3 H. V, ii. 18. For payments for repairs to the manor at Eltham, see Iss. Roll 6 H. V, Pasch., Apr. 4, 1418; also in 1413, Exch. Accts. 502/29.

[8] For payments to Thomas Chaucer on this account, see Iss. Roll 1 H. V, Mich., Nov. 15, 1413. For 15 casks and 8 sesters of red Gascon and Rhenish wine at Westminster, the Tower, the Vintry, Eltham, Langley and Windsor, with payments for bermanage, cranage, guidage, ollage and cartage, see Exch. Accts. 406/21, 22, 22 d. For payment to winedrawer for removing 60 casks of Portuguese wine from London to Westminster, see Iss. Roll 1 H. V, Mich., Feb. 22, 1414.

[9] For "xij^te Day" and "xij^te Even," see Brut, ii. 546. For the day after Twelfth Night known as St Distaff's Day, see Nicolas, Chron. 135; Halliwell, 306; or Rock Day, rock being another name for a distaff, Halliwell, 689. For Rock Monday (i.e.

The rising however did not actually take place till the evening of Tuesday, Jan. 9, 1414[1]. The meeting-place was to be in Fickett's Field[2], an open space lying to the west of the Bishop of Chichester's Inn in the New Street, or Chancellor's Lane[3], near Temple Bar[4]. Its site is occupied by New Square[5], King's College Hospital and the burial ground of the church of St Clement Danes, now all built over near Clement's Lane, but in those days it formed a public recreation ground largely used by the clerks of the chancery[6], the law apprentices[7] who lived in the adjoining inns[8], and by the London citizens generally[9], and as it joined on its northern side with the Purse Field and the Cup Field, now known as Lincoln's Inn Fields[10], it formed part of a vast area of unbuilt ground that stretched from the Old Temple in Holborn to the dreary leperhouse[11] that stood in the field by St Giles' Church.

By the help of their friends within the walls the Lollards meant to occupy London, capture the king and his brothers at Eltham[12], destroy all the clergy[13], seize the relics and other valuables at St Paul's Cathedral and the Abbeys at Westminster and St Albans, slay and spoil all men of

Monday after Epiphany), see Cent. Dict., s.v., where it is supposed to refer to the resumption of work (spinning) like Plough Monday.

[1] As proved by Coram Rege Roll 1 H. V, roll 5 in Cotton MS. Cleopatra E. II. 303, where the conspirators are captured on Wednesday after Epiphany (i.e. Jan. 10) mane in aurorâ; Kingsford, Eng. Hist. Lit. 293.

[2] See App. Z.

[3] For Chancellor's Lane extra Templebarram (now Chancery Lane), see Lincoln's Inn Black Books I, ii. 90; Baildon, Site, 20, 21; Foss, iv. 257; G. J. Turner, 15, 22, 30. It was also called Convert's Lane from the neighbouring Domus Conversorum.

[4] Apud Fikeysfeld juxta le Templebarre (1339), G. J. Turner, 29, i.e. le barre de nouel Temple de Loundres, Baildon, 81, the old Temple being at Holborn Bars; not "near St Giles' Church," as Besant, Survey, i. 104.

[5] Foss, iv. 255.

[6]   Unto the Rolls I got me thence
                      Before the Clerks of the Chancery.
                                        London Lickpenny (Bell), p. 11.

[7] For apprenticii ad legem, see Maitland and Turner, IV. p. xxi; Pulling, 8.

[8] H. Hall, Studies, p. 20. For the Temple as the headquarters of the lawyers in 1381, see Oman, Revolt, 58.

[9] G. J. Turner, 22, 30.

[10] Parton, 27, 62, 78, 105, 110, 139, 141, 143, 160, 177, 178; Clinch, 86. Not the Cap Field, as Besant-Mitton, 32.

[11] Hospitalis Sancti Egidii extra Londoniam, Lel. Coll. ii. 418; Monast. vii. 635; G. J. Turner, 24; Letter Book I, 13, 14; extra barram veteris templi, Rot. Parl. iv. 108; Archaeol. Journ. xliv. 58, where its income from land in London=£29. 14s. 6d. in 1412; or "without Holbourne," Sharpe, Wills, ii. 428.

[12] Elmham, Lib. Metr. 98; Capgr. De Illustr. 113. Under the coloure of the mummyng, Brut, ii. 551.

[13] Claudius, A. VIII. 1; Brut, ii. 551; Pol. Verg. 441.

estate, thrift and worship[1], plunder the London friaries[2] and drive out their inmates, making the religious work with their hands[3] and rewarding their own friends out of the proceeds of the general spoliation[4]. Such at least was reported to be their purpose by their enemies, though we have no record of their intentions from their own point of view, and it is probable that they had formulated no definite plans beyond securing the person of the king and rescuing him, if possible, from the influence of the priests[5]. For London was in panic and the rumour ran that they were going to kill the king[6] and proclaim Oldcastle regent[7], behead the nobles, destroy St Paul's[8], put out the bishops' eyes and have no priests henceforward except from among themselves[9].

But there were traitors among them[10] and spies had long been keeping an eye on their movements[11]. Fisher's

---

[1] As yei p'posed to have do in oure fadres daies, Archaeologia, xxiii. 339 (1431).
[2]   Withdrawen wolde hir riche paramentes.
            O prudent prynce, thynke what her entente is
            Who falsely the hooly churche accuse
            For thai hemsilff the riches wolden use.
                                        Harl. MS. 1245, f. 182.
[3] Ad mundanas occupationes revocare, Rym. ix. 193; or provocare, Cleop. E. II. f. 304; Rym. ix. 171; Rot. Parl. iv. 108; Waugh, 649. Cf. "put a spade instead of a crozier into the bishops' hands," Collier, iii. 299 (edition 1853). One of the heresies current in Bohemia was quod sacerdotes debent manibus laborare et de labore vivere sicut fuit antiquitus, Hardt, iii. 668. Cf. For alle the wordely (*sic*) relygyous do nat the office of an hundred curates ne of a secular lord, ne of a trewe labourer, Amundesham, i. 456.   [4] Chron. Giles, 8; Gesta, 6.
[5] Trevelyan (337, 338) thinks that there was no other motive but religion in their action, which was "unwise and wrong because with small resources and few supporters they could never hope to establish a government," etc. Called "a wild undertaking," "a desperate plan" in Oman, Pol. Hist. 236.
[6] Pat. 1 H. V, v. 16; Rym. ix. 119, 193; Otterbourne, 274; Wals. ii. 297; Hypodig. 446; Julius B. I. 37; Lingard, iii. 238.
[7] For Oldcastle to be the head of a Republic, see Vattier, 306, who dates the second rising in 1416 instead of 1417.
[8] Cf. strages principum, neces nobilium, basilicae dirutae, civitates eversae, Conc. iii. 360.
[9] Memorials, 69; Holt (Lights, 114) thinks that the very extravagance of these accusations is almost sufficient to disprove them; Oman, Pol. Hist. 237, thinks that they "*may* be a calumny of the enemy."
[10] For proclamations dated at Westminster on Jan. 7, 1414, see Claus. 1 H. V, 6 d, where the king declares that some Lollards *jam tardé capti* had been brought before him and confessed that such meetings were going to be held.
[11] Speculatores, Devon, 333; cf. exploratores assiduo scrutineo de gubernatione Lollard', Iss. Roll 1 H. V, Mich., Feb. 22, 1414; Tyler, ii. 377. For 10 marks per annum granted to John de Burgh, carpenter (eo quod detegit certos Lollardos), and Thomas (called "William" in Waugh, 640) Kentford quia detexit et revelavit conjectamenta proditoria Lollardorum, see Pat. 1 H. V, v. 22, Jan. 5, 1414; Cal. Rot. Pat. 262; Cal. Pat. H. V, i. 157; Tyler, ii. 377; Waugh, 640; Snow, 55. For John Burgh, vintner in 1412, see Letter Book I, p. 99.

house was watched and many letters were seized and taken to the king[1]. No time was to be lost. Prowlers began to appear on the ground at Eltham, but they were captured, handcuffed[2], and thrown into prison, and in the night of Jan. 8 the king left suddenly[3] for Westminster accompanied by his three brothers, together with Archbishop Arundel, Bishop Courtenay and many lords and bachelors. Passing round to the Priory at Clerkenwell[4] he received conclusive evidence of the danger and immediately gave orders that the gates of London should be closed and all meetings broken up. The watch was set throughout the city, horsemen patrolled the roads and fields outside, and when the darkness fell[5] in the evening of Tuesday, Jan. 9, the king posted himself with a hastily collected force in St Giles' Field[6].

The night was still and, as he stood on the ground, a splendid meteor[7] shot across the wintry sky from west to north shedding a trail of light about two bowshots long. All sorts of explanations were at once started amongst the excited crowd, most of whom believed that it came as a sign to the orthodox to illuminate the faith and to the other side to smite them with the lightning of vengeance, but Prior Elmham, who was on the spot[8], declined to thrust his face into heaven[9], preferring to leave the solution to the God of Nature and the working of the elements.

All this time the unsuspecting Lollards were moving

---

[1] Devon, 330. For pictures of the king being secretly informed of the plot and the Earl of Warwick arming to subdue traitors and heretics, see Strutt, Manners, ii, Plates 29, 30; Rous, 365; Kingsford, 104.

[2] For 16s. 8d. paid to Sir Thomas Erpingham for fetters (4 pair), manacles (2 pair) and "cleralls" (6 pair) with locks, see Devon, 330, Feb. 16, 1414. For 35s. paid to Margaret Merssh for 18 pairs of fetters and 8 pairs of manacles made by her and delivered to the constable of the Tower, see ibid. 358 (Feb. 23, 1419).

[3] Claudius, A. VIII. 1; not Christmas, as Aubrey, ii. 40. Cassell, i. 521, supposes that the king had removed to Westminster before the Lollard threats of violence were published.

[4] Sent Johanes withoute Smethfeld, Claud. A. VIII. 1; Caxton, Chron. 144; Brut, ii. 373; the feld beside Saint Jones and Clerkyn-welle, Brut, ii. 551.

[5] Nocte illâ, Chron. Giles, 8; campum mane petens, Elmham, Lib. Metr. 98.

[6] Not that he "shut himself with an armed force within the capital," as Tout, 263.

[7] Fulsit stella Dei, Memorials, 68; Weever, Oldcastle, 209–211; fulgur amoenum, Elmham, Lib. Metr. 99. Gairdner, Lollardy, i. 81, thinks that Henry "was assisted by some flashes of lightning to discover the enemy."

[8] In occiduo *nostro* inter *nos* et Boream, Chron. Giles, 7; Gesta, 6; Elmham (Lib. Metr. 99) seems to place this on Jan. 10, but the passage is obscure.

[9] Reading "nolens" for "volens" in Chron. Giles, 7. Gesta, 6, reads "*omnia*' for "*os*."

up in groups and knots along the high roads to the *rendez-vous* in Fickett's Field, and the little knowledge that we have of these events may yield some scraps of detailed information as regards the movement in the Midlands, which are typical of what was happening in other parts of England. On Dec. 30, 1413[1], a party had assembled at Thurlaston near Leicester under the lead of William Ederic, a priest from Aston-on-Trent in Derbyshire, and rode up to Ware in Hertfordshire probably to join a large body who were to meet in the woods at Harringay. Another group turned out at Kibworth on Jan. 5 under William Upton of Smeeton-Westerby[2], others came armed with swords and bows from Leicester and Belton near Loughborough, where they assembled the day after Christmas under a substantial resident named William Ward[3]. New Year's Day saw another armed band set out from Woodstock and Bladon under a leader named William Brown[4], and we know of a man named Philip Turner who was arrested at Barnet on Jan. 5 on his way up from Daventry ostensibly for the purpose of buying some wine[5]. All through the day groups such as these had thronged the lanes and paths and roads that led to London, and when they were asked whither they were going in such haste they said "to Cobham[6]," and as they neared the capital they mingled with any party that was at hand.

When the king came up, the crowd was threateningly large[7] and he was advised to hold back till daylight and wait for reinforcement[8]. But the threads of the game were already in his hands and he wisely stood his ground. The

---

[1] Cotton MS. Cleopatra, E. ii. f. 305, i.e. extracts from Coram Rege Rolls, where Ederic is stated to have given 13s. 4d. to John Lake and others to support Oldcastle. The men came from Aston, Chaddesden and Thurlaston. For pardons July 3, 1414, to Thomas Mason and John Glede, both of Thurlaston, see Cal. Pat. H. V, i. 200.

[2] Cleop. E. ii. f. 302.

[3] Ibid. ff. 306, 322, where he is called the farmer of Muriell Park (possibly Merril Grange) near Belton. In Rym. ix. 194 he is called a "ploughman." In Cleop. E. ii. 306 he was sentenced to be hanged on the new gallows et usque ad cineres simul cum furcis praedictis ardeat, though he was afterwards pardoned (June 16, 1414), ibid. f. 307.

[4] He was pardoned on Dec. 10, 1414, ibid. f. 303.

[5] Fuit devillans causâ emptionis vini, ibid. f. 322.

[6] Capgr. 307; Stow, Chron. 344; Holinsh. iii. 544; S. Turner, ii. 472. Cf. "Say thou but Sir John and they will let thee pass," Drayton, Oldcastle, 335.

[7] Waugh's (647) estimate of 400 or 500 men seems altogether too low, though an official entry in the inquiry at Oxford gives the number as 200, Cleop. E. ii. 303 [271], which is also officially called 20,000, ibid. f. 304 b; Rym. ix. 171; Rot. Parl. iv. 108.   [8] Had not the king then made suppowelment, Hard. 371.

Londoners had been expected to rise and join the provincials in their thousands, but they made no sign and no one could get beyond the gates who did not know the pass-word. Thus, as each set came up in the darkness, they walked innocently into the midst of the king's guards, who forthwith disarmed them and marched them off to prison[1]. One of the leaders, William Morley or Murlee[2], a rich brewer, came in from Dunstable with high hopes. He had helped the movement that was to make lords of lurdens[3] and was ready for his reward. He had been promised knighthood if all went well, and he had travelled up with two destrers housed in gold trappings and a pair of gilt spurs in his bosom[4], in readiness for the ceremony which was to make him Earl of Hertford. He was to get the plunder of St Alban's Abbey to himself and he had a list of the inmates up his sleeve. When he heard that the king was on the ground, he turned back, but was captured in the park at Harringay[5] near Hornsey on the northern heights. Search was then made in London itself. Fisher's house was entered and many of Oldcastle's papers were seized, but the heretic himself had fled. Several suspects were dragged out from the house of John Burgate[6], a carpenter, bearing the sign of the Axe without Bishopsgate[7], and large numbers of accused persons were imprisoned in the Tower, in Newgate, in the Marshalsea and in the two London counters[8]. Jurors had been empanelled many weeks beforehand[9] when matters

---

[1] Elmham, Libr. Metr. 99.

[2] Capgr. 307; braciator, Wals. ii. 299; plain William Murley, Drayton, Oldcastle, 327, 333, where he is "meal-man, malt-man, miller, corn-master and all"; or "Murle" in Cassell, i. 521, where he is called a "silly fanatic." Cf. "the fatt Maultman," G. Daniel, iv. 113.

[3] Archaeologia, xxiii. 342; Froude, i. 503. For lurden (a lout), see Halliwell, ii. 534; Murray, Dict., s.v. *Lurdan.*

[4] Cf. Your bosom's no place for spurs, Drayton, Oldcastle, 333.

[5] Stow, Chron. 343; called Harensey in Strecche, 265 b; civitatem repetiit, says Wals. ii. 299; Hypodig. 448, who of course had a special interest in his case. Harringay was a frequent meeting-place of conspirators, e.g. in 1387, Wals. ii. 164; Dugd. Bar. ii. 185.

[6] Greg. Chron. 108; Stow, Chron. 344.

[7] Called "The Ax without Cripilgate" in Brut, ii. 551; "The Axe Inn near Bishopsgate" in Drayton, Oldcastle, 327; not the "Ark," as Cassell, i. 521. In Walpole, Catalogue, i. 189, this becomes: "Henry arrived at the sign of the Axe without Bishopsgate, took the man of the house and 7 other prisoners which closed his first campaign."

[8] Caxton, Chron. 144; Brut, ii. 373.

[9] For 66s. 8d. paid to Robert Warner, sub-sheriff, for riding daily in the county of Middlesex pro panel' fiend' et summonend' pro Lollardis jam sero insurgentibus against the king and his lords; also £7 paid to Richard Mayhewe and his fellow-jurors of

looked threatening after Oldcastle's escape, and on the next day, Jan. 10[1], a commission was appointed[2] consisting of the Earl of Arundel, Henry Lord Scrope, William Lord de Roos of Hamlake[3], Hugh Hals and William Cromer[4], the Mayor of London, to try the prisoners either at Westminster or in the Tower[5]. Many of the accused were priests[6]

Middlesex summoned and attending every day at Westminster for certain causes, see Iss. Roll 1 H. V, Mich., Dec. 11, 1413. For hatred to jurors (jurrours), cf.

> Nought loved but drad of high and low degree
> For whom one list by craft I could endite
> Hongen the true and the thief respite.
>   Lydgate, in Monast. (1773), iii. 373.

For a jury of 24 knights and of the view (*de visu*) of the town and parish of St Giles' at the trial of Lollards in Jan. 1414, see Cleop. E. II. f. 306.

[1] i.e. Wednesday after Epiphany, Rot. Parl. iv. 108; Pat. 1 H. V, v. 16; Cal. Rot. Pat. 7 H. VI, i. 19 d, p. 546; Cal. Pat. H. V, i. 175; Cleop. E. II. 294; Placita Coram Rege, Hil. 1 H. V, roll 7; or Jan. 10, Pat. 1 H. V, v. 30 d; Foxe, iii. 367, 369, 379.

[2] Not "eine *geistliche* Behörde," as Pauli, Bilder, 279 (308).

[3] Rym. ix. 170, 193. For confirmation to him of grant of 100 marks per annum for life (Wylie, ii. 179), see Iss. Roll 1 H. V, Mich., Oct. 10, 1413. In Pat. 2 H. V, ii. 28, Sept. 22, 1414, and Sloane MS. 4600, ff. 306, 311 (May 23, 1415), he is referred to as dead and the custody of his lands is granted to the Earl of Dorset during the minority of his heir. He died on Sept. 1, 1414, Wylie, ii. 180 note. He was succeeded as K.G. by Thomas Lord Camoys, Beltz, clvii.

[4] His father lived at Aldenham in Hertfordshire and the family probably derived its name from the hamlet of Cromer near Stevenage, Hasted, ii. 575; Clutterbuck, iii. 602; Cussans, Odsey, 86. He is called Crowmere in Pat. 2 H. V, i. 1, Aug. 24, 1414; Croumer, Letter Book I, 119; or Crowmer, Pat. 2 H. V, ii. 29, Aug. 17, 1414; Chron. Lond. 96; Fabyan, 578; Riley, Mem. 598, 599, 601; Rym. ix. 131. He was a draper (Letter Book I, 68) and had been sheriff in 1406, Riley, Mem. 562. He was mayor again in 1423, Chron. Lond. 111; Greg. Chron. 157; Kingsford, Chron. 75; Three Fifteenth Cent. Chron. 58. For his will dated May 9, 1431, in which he left lands and tenements in St Swithin's Lane (not Sweeting Lane, as Newcourt, i. 417), see Sharpe, ii. 551, who gives an earlier will dated June 10, 1421, in which he leaves houses and gardens in Crutched Friars, Aldgate, and gives £30 to repair the church and roads at Tunstall near Sittingbourne, a manor which he had bought. He died in 1433 and was buried beside his first wife Catherine in the church of St Martin Orgar, off Candlewick Street, where he had built a chapel to St Mary, for the repair of which he left quit-rents in Hardeles Lane (for Hardel as a family name in London, temp. Ed. I, see Sharpe, Letter Books A, B *passim*) in the parish of St Martin in the Vintry, Stow, Lond. Book II. p. 187. His second wife Margery, to whom he left lands in the parish of St Olave near the Tower (Sharpe, ii. 551), was the daughter of Thomas Squerie of Westerham near Sevenoaks (Hasted, i. 384). She survived him and afterwards married Robert Lord Poynings. For her will, dated at St Martin Orgar and proved at Lambeth in 1448, see Genealogist, v. 328; vi. 134, from Stafford Reg. 167 a, where she is called Margaret Lady Ponyngges. She died on Nov. 3, 1448, Inq. p. Mort. iv. 238, and was buried in the church of St Martin Orgar, Comp. Peer. vi. 300. For Robert Lord Poynings as a commissioner to array the forces of Sussex May 29, 1415, see Rym. ix. 253. For William Crowmer, sheriff of Kent, son-in-law of Lord Say, beheaded at Mile End in Jack Cade's rebellion of 1450, see Greg. Chron. 192; Three Fifteenth Cent. Chron. 67, 98; Kingsford, Chron. 160, 161, 276.

[5] For £2. 16s. 8d. paid for their breakfast, see Devon, 331, Feb. 16, 19, 1414. For order dated Jan. 16, 1414, to the Constable of the Tower to allow them to hold their inquiry in the Tower if they like, see Claus. 1 H. V, 6; cf. Milman, viii. 223; Ramsay, i. 179.

[6] Preestes, clerkys and othir lewd men, Caxton, i. 224. Called "lowe men" in Kingsford, Chron. 69.

and most of them, says the chronicler, did not even take the trouble to repent[1]. The process was therefore sharp and summary. Four pairs of new gallows known as the Lollers' gallows[2] were fixed up on the high road adjoining St Giles' Field. The condemned men were drawn from their prisons through the streets on hurdles[3] and hanged in batches, seven who were known as pronounced Lollards[4] having fires lighted under them, so that they might burn as they hung —a two-edged weapon[5] forged expressly by the Priests' Prince to smite their double guilt, the halter for the king[6] and the fire for God[7]—and on Jan. 11, 1414[8], commissioners were appointed to try suspected Lollards in London[9], Bristol[10] and 20 Eastern, Western and Midland counties[11],

[1] Quorum plurimi nec quidem paenitere curabant, Wals. ii. 299; Hypodig. 449.
[2] Brut, ii. 551. See App. Z.
[3] Tracti prius, Elmham, Lib. Metr. 100; non solum tractioni, Wals. ii. 299; Hypodig. 448. For picture of a criminal drawn by two horses with ropes fastened from his arms to the saddles, see Royal MS. 20 C. vii. 60. See also Marks, 90, 166; Lib. Alb. iii. Frontispiece; Infessura, 38.
[4] Kingsford, Chron. 69.
[5] Ancipiti mucrone, Elmham, Lib. Metr. 97; utriusque gladii penam, Usk, 131; double dethe, Pol. Songs, ii. 247.
[6] Cf. "arrysers against the kynge," Harl. MS. 565, 72.
    That rereth riot for to ride
    Agayns the kynge and his clergie. Pol. Songs, ii. 244.
[7] Duplici paenae dandi, incendio propter Deum suspendio propter regem, Walden, i. 4; ii. 4; suspendi jussit et cremari, Otterbourne, 274; post infelicia fata cremati, Wals. ii. 299; post crucis exitium igni traditos, Vita, 32; ultra ignem haeresi condignam etiam tractus et surpassus ad furcas adderentur paenae, Usk, 122, who attributes this to Archbishop Arundel; suspendii ob laesam majestatem, incendii ob haeresim, Harpsfeld, Dialogi, 611, 613, 690; Foxe, iii. 353; Holinsh. iii. 544; Vignier, Recueil, 576; juxta reperti unius vel utriusque laesae majestatis et blasphemiae criminis qualitatem, Chron. Giles, 7; Gesta, 5; "brent hanging," Caxton, i. 225. "He should be hanged for treason, burnt for heresie," Weever, Oldcastle, 223; yet Church (102) thinks that "the punishment was for heresy, *not for treason.*"
[8] Pat. 1 H. V, v. 23 d; Letter Book I, pp. xx, 123; Cal. Pat. H. V, i. 175.
[9] i.e. the Mayor (William Cromer), Richard Whitington, Robert Chichele, Richard Merlawe, Thomas Knolles, J. Preston and William Waldern. For William (not Walter, as Pat. 1 H. V, i. 23 d) Waldern, mayor of London in 1413, see Letter Book I, 109; Rec. Roll 1 H. V, Pasch., May 16, June 9, 1413; Wylie, iv. 26 note. Also M.P. for the city in the Parliaments of 1414 (Nov.), 1415 and 1421, Letter Book I, 129, 251; Return Parl. i. 284, 286, 297.
[10] Including J. Stevens, senior. In Iss. Roll 1 H. V, Mich., Feb. 12, 16, 1414, he and Thomas Saunders are *late* collectors of the subsidy at Bristol, see Wylie, ii. 305, note 6. On May 29, 1415, John Stevens, sen., and John Droys are on a commission for arraying the forces of Bristol, Rym. ix. 253.
[11] Ubique per regnum, Usk, 121, viz. Beds., Berks., Bucks., Derby, Devon, Dorset, Essex, Gloucester (for fines at a session of the peace at Cheltenham 1 H. V, see Accts. Excheq. Q.R. 111/36), Hants. (including Bernard Brocas), Hereford, Kent, Leicester, Northants., Notts., Oxford, Rutland, Salop, Somerset, Warwick and Worcester. The conjectural map in Trevelyan, 352, omits Beds., Devon, Notts., Oxford, Rutland, Salop and Warwick. The commission for Salop includes Thomas Earl of Arundel, J. Talbot of Hallamshire, Edward de Powys, David Holbache, etc.; and that for Hereford Gilbert Talbot of Irchenfield, John Skydemore, John Merbury, John Bodenham, John Brugge, Thomas de la Hay, Thomas Holgate, John Russel and Roland Leynthall. Waugh (649)

and on the same day a proclamation was issued that no unauthorised rush was to be made upon the goods of the suspects[1].

On Jan. 13, 1414[2], the London victims were hanged at the cross roads opposite to the gate of St Giles' leperhouse just where the throng of modern traffic is at its thickest[3]. Their numbers vary from 29 to 69 in different accounts[4]. The list includes a London priest named John Beverley[5], a squire of Oldcastle's named John Brown[6], William Murlee the brewer, John Burgate the carpenter, a dyer, a glover and other craftsmen[7] of smaller repute. The following also are known to have fallen into the king's hands, but though the death sentence was passed upon them, their lives were spared for the moment and they remained for a time prisoners in the Tower[8]. Five of them were knights[9], viz.

thinks that Surrey was "unimpeachably orthodox." Snow (58) finds "scarcely any trace of Lollards north of the Humber." C. R. L. Fletcher (304) thinks that "not till 1415 did the movement take hold of the Eastern counties."

[1] Claus. 1 H. V, 9 d ; Letter Book I, 122.

[2] Elmham, Lib. Metr. 100. Not 1413, as Bale in Harl. Misc. ii. 253. Called Jan. 19, Stow, 34; Dict. Nat. Biogr. iv. 449; or Jan. 24 in Pauli, v. 88. Halle (49) thinks that they were condemned in the Guildhall on Dec. 12, 1413 (see page 268), but he was puzzled by the contradictions that had crept into the story and came to the conclusion that "all writings are not the gospel"; cf. Foxe, iii. 373. Holinsh. (iii. 544) adopts the Guildhall but avoids the date, see also Foxe, iii. 371, 375, 379. For the story of how Halle altered his account after reading Bale, see Foxe, iii. 378. Fuller (Church History, Bk. iv. 167) was "so lost in the intricacy of these Relations" that he knew not what to assent to. [3] Dobie, 8.

[4] e.g. 29 in Besant, Survey, i. 105; 30 in Tyrrell, i. 286 [167]; 35 in Ling. iii. 238; Snow, 55; 36 in Kingsford, Chron. 69; 37 in Chron. Lond. 97; Grey Friars Chron. 12; 38 in Greg. Chron. 108; Brut, ii. 551; Waugh, 644 (quoting Claus. 1 H. V, 1); 39 in Caxton, i. 225; Fabyan, 578; Pauli, Bilder, 279 (308); Green, 260; Carrick, 221; Bright, i. 289; Tennyson, 522; Lechler, ii. 90 [458], who thinks that only the names of four of them are known; R. S. Gower, i. 102, who calls it "a wholesale butchery"; J. M. Stone, 51; 40 in Oman, Hist. 221; 42 in Short Chron. 54; 44 in Strang, 17, though called 37, ibid. p. 151; "nearly 60" in Oman, Hundred Years, 106; Hassel, 223; 69 in Stow, 344; Trussel, 94; Oman, Pol. Hist. 238, who thinks that 69 were convicted of whom 37 were hanged; "about 70," Cassell, i. 521. For picture showing two gallows with 39 Lollards hanging fully dressed and a fire burning beneath, see Dobie, 28.

[5] Greg. Chron. 108; Inq. p. Mort. iii. 29, 299; iv. 23, 184; Harl. Misc. ii. 255. Not Burnley, as Milman, viii. 222; called Jean Beverlaw ministre de la Parole in Crespin, 25; or Breuerlan in Vignier, Rec. 576. It is hardly likely that he is identical with John of Beverley, a learned Carmelite, whose Quæstiones in magistrum sententiarum and Disputationes ordinariæ are still preserved in MS. at Queen's College, Oxford, as Dict. Nat. Biogr. iv. 449.

[6] Brut, ii. 551; Blakeway, Sheriffs, 60; called "Brown, a knight," in Carrick, 221. For order for his arrest, Jan. 23, 1414, see Waugh, 644, quoting Pat. 1 H. V, v. 25 d, though not in Cal. Pat. H. V, vol. i.

[7] Cf. "man of craft," Hoccleve, Min. Po. 13; Anglia, 27; James, 145.

[8] They were there on March 18, 1414, Rym. ix. 120.

[9] Trevelyan (338) thinks that "only one knight (i.e. Acton) besides Oldcastle was implicated." For the spread of Lollardry among "persons of the best rank and quality," see Goodwin, 168, quoting Vignier, Rec. 580.

Roger Acton[1], Thomas Talbot of Davington near Faversham[2], Thomas Beauchamp[3] from Somersetshire, Thomas Maureward, ex-Sheriff of Warwickshire and Leicestershire[4], and Thomas Chaworth, who had been arrested and released two years before[5]. Besides these there were six clerks (viz. Robert Shene, William White[6], Walter Blake, a chaplain from Bristol[7], William Ederic[8], William, chaplain of the parish of Thaxted in Essex[9], and Thomas Drayton[10], rector of Drayton Beauchamp near Tring[11]), five squires (viz. Thomas Brook of Olditch in Devonshire who had had intimate personal relations with Oldcastle[12], Henry del

---

[1] Caxton, i. 225; not John, as Tit. Liv. 6. Not Arcton, as Major, cxxvi; nor Areton, as Vignier, Rec. 576; nor Aston, as Aubrey, Rise, ii. 10; nor Sir George Acton, as Carrick, 221. He had lands at Sutton Park near Tenbury (Nash, ii. 418) and at Acton Scott near Church Stretton in Shropshire (Inq. p. Mort. iii. 222); he had been Constable of Criccieth circ. 1401-1403 (Ord. Priv. Co. ii. 64), Governor of Ludlow (1403), and Sheriff of Shropshire (1410), Blakeway, Sheriffs, 60; see also Wylie, iii. 296, note 4. For the blazon of "Actoun" (*sic*), see Harl. MS. 4205/23. For Andrew Ekton, Ecton, or Acton, knight, who was with Oldcastle in Gascony on June 28, 1413, see Priv. Seal Bills 1114/48; Rot. Vasc. 1 H. V, 10; cf. Wylie, iv. 252.

[2] Waugh, 642. He is so called in a writ directed on Jan. 24, 1414, to John Darell Escheator of Kent, showing that he and Oldcastle were both positi in exigend' ad utlagand' at Westminster on that same day, Escheators' Inquisitions, Ser. I. file 1008, m. 24, where at an inquisition held at Ospringe on Feb. 6, 1414, he is returned as owning the manor of Babington in Kent. In Claus. 5 H. V, 1, Oct. 12, Dec. 17, 1417, he is summoned to appear in the Chancery on Nov. 5, 1417, *re* forfeited manors, including Rishton near Great Harwood in Lancashire.

[3] For order for his committal dated Jan. 23, 1414, see Claus. 1 H. V, 6; Sloane MS. 4600, f. 115; Waugh (644) who calls him "William." For his release pour aler en son large Sept. 13 [1414], see Chancery Warrants, Ser. I. 1364/18.

[4] i.e. Nov. 3, 1412, Sheriffs' List, 145. In Rec. Roll 1 H. V, Mich., Oct. 30, 1413, he is still Sheriff of Warwickshire and Leicestershire, but *late* Sheriff, ibid. Feb. 12, 1414, cf. Wylie, iv. 227. He appears also as Sheriff of Warwick and Leicestershire on Nov. 8, 1401, and May 1, 1422, Sheriffs' List, 145. On March 21, 1413, he was appointed a Justice of the Peace for Leicestershire, see Pat. 1 H. V, i. 36 d; also July 28, 1414, Pat. 2 H. V, ii. 32 d, expressly to enforce the Leicester Statute against the Lollards. He is called Mawereward in Pat. 8 H. V, July 3, 1420.

[5] Wylie, iv. 40, note 4. For order to Richard Grey, Lord of Codnor, to arrest him Jan. 8, 1414, see Cal. Pat. H. V, i. 148. On March 21, 1413, he was a J.P. for Nottinghamshire, ibid. 422.

[6] Walden, ii. 4. For his trial for heresy Sept. 13, 1428, see Fascic. 417.

[7] He was condemned to be hanged on Jan. 25, 1414, but his life was spared, Cotton MS. Cleop. E. II. 294.

[8] See page 266, note 1. He was imprisoned at Kenilworth and afterwards "remitted to his ordinary" on Feb. 6, 1414, Cleop. E. II. 305. He had been repeatedly in trouble for the last three years, and as late as Nov. 6, 1413, he was charged with having said at Derby, Tutbury and elsewhere that Lollard opinions were sound and healthy doctrine.

[9] Cleop. E. II. 323. The name does not occur either in Newcourt, ii. 581, or Morant, ii. 445.

[10] Rym. ix. 119; Tyler, ii. 383. For Thomas Drayton, appointed Assayer of the Mint in 1412, see Wylie, iv. 47. For order for the arrest of John Drayton, kt. (Oxon and Berks.), see Pat. 2 H. V, i. 35 d, May 7, 1414.

[11] Not in Lincolnshire, as Goodwin, 32. He exchanged from Dadcote (probably Didcot formerly called Dudcot, Lysons, Magn. Brit. Berkshire, p. 272) on Oct. 4, 1410, and again on Jan. 6, 1415, Lipscomb, iii. 334.

[12] Wylie, iii. 293.

Bothe from Lancashire[1], John Wickham[2] of Swalcliffe near Banbury, Thomas Tickhill[3] from Derby, and Richard Colfox[4], who had been a co-executor with Oldcastle under the will of the ex-Lollard knight Lewis Clifford[5]), and other names such as William Parchemener[6], John Hooper, Thomas Sernes[7], Roger Cheyne[8] of Drayton Beauchamp[9] and his sons Thomas and John[10], John Bryan, Thomas Eston a London mercer, and one Elys[11] (or Elias) who had already taken sanctuary. On Feb. 8, 1414, Sir Roger

---

[1] Though Waugh (643) supposes that "no county north of Notts and Derby seems to have required the attention of the authorities."

[2] For his pardon dated Nov. 6, 1414, see Rym. ix. 170; Cal. Pat. H. V, i. 250.

[3] On March 21, 1413, he had been appointed to act as the king's general attorney in any of the courts, see Cal. Rot. Pat. 260; Cal. Pat. H. V, i. 9. On March 21, 1413, Feb. 14, 1415, he is on a commission of the Peace for Derbyshire, ibid. pp. 9, 418.

[4] For pardon to him and restoration of his forfeited lands dated May 23, 1415, see Sloane MS. 4600, ff. 306, 311. For his examination at Westminster together with Ralph Barton of Coventry and others on Jan. 8, 1414, and his subsequent appearance in court at Westminster on Jan. 31, 1414, see Cleop. E. II. f. 304.

[5] Wylie, iii. 296; Lechler, ii. 79; Gairdner, Lollardy, i. 40, 48. The other executors were Thomas Berlowe, Walter Gayton and John Andrew. In this capacity they had sold to the king a gold morse or clasp (quoddam firmaculum quod vulgariter morsus dicitur, cf. Du Cange, iv. 506; Rock, ii. 37; Lee, 228, 279, s.v. *Pectoral*), set with precious stones, for £800, half of which sum was to go to the king's grandmother, Joan Countess of Hereford (Devon, 323), but 400 marks of this were still unpaid by the king on July 20, 1413, who however was under a promise to pay it before Michaelmas 1414, Pat. 1 H. V, iii. 34; Rym. ix. 41, July 20, 1413.

[6] He may be the same as William Fisher, see page 260, note 3.

[7] Or possibly Serves, see Wylie, iv. 48. In Beaven, 216, Serves Tower is named from William Servat, who was Alderman of Walbrook Ward, 1309–1368, Stow, Kingsford, ii. 329; called Cernettes Tower, ibid. i. 266. Not Seute's Tower, as Walcott, Westminster, 227, where it is granted to St Stephen's Chapel by Edward III; Topham, 6.

[8] Bridges, i. 348; Lipscomb, iii. 270. He died in 2 H. V (1414–1415), Inq. p. Mort. iv. 7. Waugh (644) calls his "a name of ill omen to the orthodox." For John Cheyne de Isnamstede Cheyne (i.e. Chenies or Isenhampstead Cheynes near Amersham, M.P. for Bucks. in May, 1413) see Return Parl. i. 278; or Isenhamsted Latimer in Inq. p. Mort. iii. 102, 296; iv. 232; cf. Dugd. Baronage, i. 297; ii. 33; Lipscomb, iii. 269. Called Islamstede Cheyne in Rec. Roll 4 H. V, Mich., Jan. 18, 1417, where he received 40s. 3d. from the goods of John Angret, parson of Islamstede Latimer, convicted de proditione. In Claus. 6 H. V, 17 (1418) John Cheyne is lord of the manor of Isnamstede Cheyne. For John Cheyne of Isnamstede, Sheriff of Beds. and Bucks. in 1430, see Sheriffs' List, 2. For John Cheyne of Pinhoe near Exeter, 1402, see Cotton and Dallas, iv. 169.

[9] The manor had been granted to Thomas Cheyne, banneror to Edward III in 1364, Lipscomb, iii. 332. For his brass there (1368), see Hewitt, ii. 125 (vii); Macklin, 53. Also brass of William Cheyne (d. 1375) in Waller; Lipscomb, iii. 332.

[10] For order dated Jan. 18, 1414, committing Roger Cheyne to the Tower, together with his son John and John Bryan, see Claus. 1 H. V, 2; Sloane MS. 4600, f. 112. For pardon dated Nov. 2, 1414, to John Cheyne, esquire, son and heir of Roger Cheyne of Drayton Beauchamp (Bucks.), see Pat. 2 H. V, ii. 20; Claus. 4 H. V, 10 (Nov. 15, 1416); Priv. Seal 665/703, Nov. 15, 1416.

[11] It may have been his son (William Elys' son) who was put in irons in the Tower in 1415 for "tales that he had told about the king." It was popularly believed that no irons or fetters or locks would hold him, so he was brought out and chained to an iron post at the gate of the sheriff's counter in Chepe (i.e. the Poultry counter, Stow, London, iii. 50) close to the standard where everybody came to draw water, Chron. Lond. 99. For John Elys, mercer of London in 1405 and 1409, see Letter Book I, 44, 81; also John Elys "yoman taillour" in 1417, ibid. p. 187.

Acton was committed to the Tower[1], and a few days after-wards he was hanged at St Giles[2], and his body, after hanging for more than a month[3], was buried beneath the gallows[4].

When their work was done in London[5], Lord Roos and some of his fellow-commissioners started to hold inquiries in various disaffected parts of the country. They sat at Leicester on Feb. 5, at Loughborough on Feb. 6, at Oxford on Feb. 20, at Daventry on Feb. 25, at Derby on March 8, and at Shrewsbury on June 20[6], but of the results of these inquiries very scanty records remain. We know moreover that Chief Justice Norton was despatched to try cases in Devonshire[7], though nothing is known of the outcome. In Buckinghamshire four Lollards from Amer-sham and one from Little Missenden were condemned to death on Jan. 26, 1414[8]. In each case the goods of the delinquents were confiscated, though small sums varying from six to thirteen marks were allowed for maintenance to their widows. Somewhat fuller particulars relate to the Leicestershire quests. At Loughborough it was proved that Thomas Iles of Braybrooke near Market Harborough had written and distributed bills in favour of Oldcastle[9], and that he had passed some of them on to John Belgrave of Leicester, who used his ready tongue against popes,

---

[1] Claus. 1 H. V, 3 d; Sloane MS. 4600, f. 119; not Jan. 8, as Ramsay, i. 180. Called Claus. 1 H. V, m. 2, in Waugh, 644.

[2] In Cleop. E. 11. f. 294, Roger Acton de Salop. (i.e. Shrewsbury) in Comit. Salop. is brought up from the Tower on Feb. 9, 11, 1414, and condemned to be drawn through the city usque novas furcas in campis S. Egidii factas and there hanged, but as he is not called *miles* and it is expressly stated that he owned neither goods, chattels, lands nor tenements, it is possible that this is a different man from the knight.

[3] Adhuc stat suspensus, Usk, 121 [301], who says that he was the son of a tiler (not a weaver, as Waugh, 641) in Shropshire, who had grown rich by plunder during the Welsh wars.

[4] Stow, Chron. 344. Called Rogier Acton, Chevalier de l'ordre, in Crespin, 25, where he is said to have been burnt under an order of the Leicester Parliament. For pardon dated Oct. 24, 1414, to John Hertwell, mercer of London, for keeping a cloak of cloth of gold belonging to Roger de Acton, kt., attainted and convicted of high treason, see Pat. 2 H. V, ii. 19. For a statement that he was hanged naked and that his body was taken down for burial by Thomas Cliff, trumpeter to the king, see Dobie, 28. For *John* Cliff, one of the king's minstrels in 1415, see Nicolas, Agincourt, 389.

[5] For Lollards brought coram Rege at Westminster on Jan. 21 and Feb. 6, 1414, see Cleop. E. 11. ff. 300, 305.

[6] Ibid. ff. 301, 302, 303, 305, 306, 322; Ad Quod Damn. 370.

[7] Iss. Roll 1 H. V, Mich., Jan. 25, 1414.

[8] viz. Richard Turnour, Walter Yong, John Horewode and John Fynche, Pat. 1 H. V, v. 24; Cal. Pat. H. V, i. 156; Waugh, 645.

[9] Compositor et asportator billarum Johannis Oldcastle, Cleop. E. 11. f. 301.

prelates and clergy, asserting that there had been no proper pope since the end of the first century[1] to the present day. Such documents as remain are usually records of pardons at a later date, but there is every reason to believe in the accuracy of the reports that were everywhere current throughout Europe to the effect that many of the accused paid the penalty with their lives[2].

But it was no part of King Henry's policy to fret a rankling sore, and as soon as the day of danger was over the day of clemency was allowed to begin. On Jan. 23, 1414, a London fuller named Henry Dene was pardoned[3]. On Jan. 30 a pardon was granted to John Ludbrooke an ironmonger from Mountsorrel[4] in Leicestershire, who had been brought before Lord Roos and condemned to death. On Feb. 8 Thomas Chaworth was released from prison by order of the Chancellor, while other leading prisoners, viz. Beauchamp, Brook, Bothe, Maureward and Tickhill, were henceforward relieved from the indignity of being chained in cells[5] and were allowed to occupy better rooms within the Tower precincts, on finding bail to the amount of 4000 marks each[6] that they would not attempt to escape, and within three months[7] all of them seem to have recovered their liberty. On Feb. 15 no less than 106 accused persons were pardoned at Chichester[8] and, seeing that accusations were multiplying, the king issued a proclamation on March 28, 1414[9], offering a general pardon to all who

---

[1] i.e. Clemens Romanus (A.D. 91–100), the third pope on the list after St Peter.

[2] Multos esse interfectos, Vrie (writing at Constance in 1418) in Hardt, i. 127.

[3] Cal. Pat. H. V, i. 162. He had been condemned on Thursday, Jan. 11, 1414, Pat. 1 H. V, v. 16; Cal. Pat. H. V, i. 160; Waugh, 644. His goods and chattels to the value of 50s. were restored to him on Feb. 10, 1414, Pat. 1 H. V, v. 17.

[4] Called Mounstrell in Pat. 1 H. V, v. 28.

[5] Waugh (645) thinks that their life in the Tower was "not surrounded with hardships."

[6] Richard Whitington was one of the sureties for Beauchamp and William Pelton and three other westcountrymen went bail in 1000 marks each for Brook, Claus. 1 H. V, 1 d, 5 d.

[7] For order dated May 12, 1414, to release Thomas Chaworth, kt., Thomas Tykell, William (*sic*) Cheyne sen., and Henry del Bothe from the Tower, see Sloane MS. 4600, f. 287. For William Cheyne, present at Salisbury Sept. 21, 1420, see Claus. 8 H. V, 5. For possessions in Lincs. and Yorks. of Margaret widow of William Cheyne, formerly wife of William Mowbray, see Inq. p. Mort. iv. 45 (7 H. V, i.e. 1419). For John Cheyne, kt., of Bucks., as manucaptor of lands of William Cheyne, kt., see Pat. 8 H. V, 6, Oct. 27, 1420, where his widow is Cecily and the lands are in the custody of Bishop Beaufort. In Rec. Roll 8 H. V, Mich., Nov. 29, Dec. 14, 1420, Bishop Beaufort and others have custody of the lands in Wiltshire belonging to the heir of William Cheyne, kt., defunctus. [8] Pat. 1 H. V, v. 9.

[9] Rym. ix. 119; Tyler, ii. 383; Letter Book I, p. xxi; Baines, i. 129. For payments

should sue for it before Midsummer Day (June 24), excepting those who were already in prison.   On May 20[1] pardons were granted to 25 Lollards chiefly from the Midland counties, the lists including John Angret, parson of Iselhampstead Latimers near Chenies in Buckinghamshire[2], six clerks and chaplains[3], two goldsmiths from Coventry and London, a plumber from York, a travelling-man, a fletcher from Little Missenden or Wycombe Heath, a cooper from Wycombe, a weaver from Cousin Lane in London, a scrivener from Shangton in Leicestershire, a Coventry glover, a Northampton hosier and other accused persons[4] from Blakesley[5], Daventry, Mildenhall (in Suffolk), Bladon near Woodstock, Stanbridge in Bedfordshire and Whittington[6] in Leicestershire, and before the end of the year many incriminated clerks had been "remitted to their ordinaries" and large numbers of obscure persons, who had anything that they could call their own, had made their peace and saved their necks by payment of a fine.   Lists still remaining[7] include the names of bakers, brasiers, carpenters,

to messengers carrying proclamations of pardon for Lollards, see Iss. Roll 1 H. V, Mich., Feb. 22, 1414.

[1] Rym. ix. 129. For other pardons, see Cal. Pat. H. V, i. 261; Waugh, 652, quoting Pat. 2 H. V, i. 17; ii. 13, 27.

[2] For an account of Latimers or Iselhampstead Latimers, see Lipscomb, iii. 247, 268. See also page 272, note 8.

[3] viz. John Frank, Thomas Joye, Thomas Spencer of Pitsford (Northants.), John Walkelyn, John Parlibien of Mountsorrel (Leic.), and John Coulson of Goudeby (? either Goadby near Market Harborough, Lewis, ii. 309; or Goadby Marwood near Melton Mowbray, spelt Gawdeby, Gauteby, Gouteby in Nichols, Leicestershire, ii. 1194).

[4] Hook (v. 34) adds "honeymongers."

[5] Called Blacolvesley, Blacolvesle, Blaconsle, Blaculveslee, Blacheslewe, Blakcolsle in Inq. p. Mort. i. 254; ii. 300, 307; iii. 80, 192, 193, 262, 310; iv. 15; Bridges, i. 164, 231, 234.

[6] e.g. John Wytheryn of Wydyngton, Rym. ix. 129; cf. Inq. p. Mort. ii. 93, probably Whittington Grange near Markfield. It was part of the manor of Ratby or Whitwick and is spelt Wydington, Wyrdington, or Whytington in Nichols, iii. 1112, 1113; iv. 877, 899.

[7] For pardon dated Sept. 18, 1414, to John Goddeshull of London, parchmynmaker, who had been sentenced to be hanged by Wm. Lord de Roos but had been kept in Newgate, see Pat. 2 H. V, ii. 27; Cal. Pat. H. V, i. 237.   Also to Richard Bregg (labourer) of Barwell, Thomas Mason of Thurlaston near Hinckley, and John Bryan of Wycombe, ibid. i. 2, May 18, June 26, 1414.   For pardons dated Dec. 6, 1414, see Rym. ix. 194; Tyler, ii. 384; C. E. Maurice, ii. 267.   These include John Langacre (mercer) of Wycombe, formerly of London, John Parchemyncr of Handborough near Woodstock, Nicholas Selby (ironmonger) of Leicestershire, Richard Sprotford (carpenter) of Amersham, Thomas Grey (clerk of Oxford), a Northamptonshire man, John Green (webbe) of Chaddesden (near Derby, cf. Inq. p. Mort. i. 49, 116, 142, 296, 309, 332), John Donne from Frome in Selwood Forest (Somerset), Robert Hierne of Gnosall (Staffs.), Thomas Pelle (cordener) of Colchester, John Garthorpe (scholar) of Oxford, Thomas Blake (weaver) of Chester, William Ward (ploughman) of Belton (Leicestershire), and Thomas Ydeoz or Idyoz (carpenter) of London.

cordeners, curriers, drapers, dyers, fullers[1], glovers, hosiers[2], ironmongers, labourers, mercers, parchmeners[3], tailors, saddlers, spurriers, smiths, webs[4], ploughmen and others chiefly from Buckinghamshire, Derby, Leicester, Northampton, Oxford and other Midland districts.

On Jan. 15, 1414[5], the king attended a solemn service in London, where Archbishop Arundel sang a litany and recited the prayer for heretics, and processions and thanksgivings were ordered to be held three times a week[6], at which the people joined heartily in the hymns of praise with three *vivas* for their conquering king, who had gone out against Leviathan[7] and foiled the damned lying counsel of Achitophel[8], and no wonder, says the eulogist, for they saw the change that had come over him and they had hope that the bad old times had been quite reformed away[9].

But Oldcastle himself was still far to seek. It was known that he had fled westward[10] and in the thick of the panic, viz. on Jan. 11, 1414[11], the king issued a proclamation[12] offering 1000 marks out of his privy purse[13] to whoever should effect his capture, while the town or village that should arrest him and give him up should be free of taxes, tallages, tenths, fifteenths, and all public imposts for ever.

At first it was confidently believed in London that the

---

[1] Cal. Rot. Pat. 262.

[2] For "hosyer" as a designation, see Pat. 3 H. V, ii. 34 d; Cal. Pat. H. VI, i. 303; Maldon Rolls 8/3; Wylie, iv. 273.

[3] For John Warwick of Saddington near Market Harborough, William Mabley (parchemener) and other persons of Leicester, see Cleop. E. II. 301.

[4] For webbe (i.e. webster), see Rot. Parl. iii. 112; Pat. 4 H. V, ii. 25; Letter Book I, p. 7; Cotton and Dallas, v. 136; Waltham Rolls, Feb. 28, 1393; Wylie, iv. 279. For webber (tistour, i.e. weaver), see Black Book of Admiralty, ii. 133; cf. tixerant, Piton, 162; Brièle, Doc. iii. 27. For tisseranderie (weaving) at Troyes, see Aufauvre, 51.

[5] Vict. Co. Hist. London, ii. 112, from St Paul's Chapter MSS.; for this reference I am indebted to the kindness of Miss E. J. Davis.

[6] Hist. MSS. Rept. ix. 57; Capgr. De Illustr. 113.

[7] For Leviathan or Behemoth as the crooked serpent, i.e. the Devil, see Isaiah xxvii. 1; cf. ipsius leviathan filii perversissimi, Conc. iii. 385; Elmham, Lib. Metr. 158, 159.

[8] Defecit Achitophel cum damnato consilio suo falsitatis, Add. MS. 4601/146 (186), from Bishop Clifford's Register.

[9] Prisca reformari tempora spes fit eis, Elmham, Lib. Metr. 100.

[10] Hardyng, 372. Not to the border of Scotland, as Roujoux, ii. 239. For messenger with letters to Sir Hugh Luttrell touching his escape, see Devon, 331. Hook (v. 31) seems to think that he had come up from Wales for the rising; Holt (Lights, 111) that he was at St Albans.

[11] Letter Book I, 121; Rym. ix. 90; Cleop. E. II. f. 297; Tyler, ii. 382; with English translation in Halliwell, Letters, i. 74; Towle, 272. Not Jan. 9, as Cassell, i. 521.

[12] For £7. 1s. 8d. paid to messengers for carrying it, see Devon, 330, Feb. 16, 1414.

[13] Wals. ii. 299; Hypodig. 448; Halliwell, Letters, i. 74; Gaspey, i. 266, 294, 295; Tit. Liv., 218. Called mille marcæ *auri* in Redman, 17.

law would very soon make him lout[1], lolle he never so long; but though there was plenty of the usual lawlessness and private feuds enough along the Welsh border[2], yet all western England was proof against this bribe and, though pardons were afterwards offered[3] to the fugitive, yet he would not come in to claim them, but remained in safe hiding[4] for four years amongst the fens and forests of his native Herefordshire. On Jan. 22, 1414, the sheriffs[5] reported that Oldcastle was not to be found, but were told to bring him up by the 1st of July. On Jan. 24[6] he was put in exigent[7] on a charge of treason, his goods were declared to be forfeited and inquiries were ordered to be held as to the extent of his possessions[8]. On June 7[9] the coroners sat at Brentford[10], but Oldcastle did not appear. He was then declared an outlaw; and his lands and tenements were

---

[1] Pol. Songs, ii. 245; for "lought" or "loute," see Laud Troy Bk. 22, 68, 175, 183, 263; Lydg. Troy Bk. 79, 243; Krapp, 74.

[2] e.g. inquiry held Feb. 12, 1414, Pat. 1 H. V, v. 25 d, on complaint of John Baskerville, kt., that Richard de la Beere, esquire, collected 100 Welshmen and Englishmen on Dec. 23, 1413, armed with lances, basnets, plates and other armour at Over Walshton (now Upper Welson) within the domain of Eardisley, broke into Baskerville's house, carried off two of his servants and 80 of his beasts to places unknown, threatening never to stop till grass grew where the house then stood. For pardon (July 24, 1414) to Thomas fflynteshemde (or Flyntesheinde, Cal. Pat. H. V, i. 236), bailiff of Shobdon, for death of Richard Greene of Ledycote (now Ladicot) at Shobdon, see Pat. 2 H. V, 227.

[3] i.e. March 4, 1415, Chron. Lond. 99; Waugh, 652.

[4] Gesta, 5.

[5] i.e. of London and Middlesex, viz. John Sutton and John Mitchell, Letter Book I, 119, 278; Sheriffs' List, 203. Not Nicholl, as Kingsford, Chron. 69; Greg. Chron. 107.

[6] Rot. Parl. v. 401, 402; Pat. 5 H. V, 26, Apr. 27, 1417; Claus. 6 H. V, 8, Nov. 22, 1418; Pat. 8 H. V, 18 d, March 4, 1421, where he is John Oldecastell de Couling miles. Called Coolynge or Cowlynge in Escheators' Inquisitions, Ser. 1. 1008; also Inq. p. Mort. iv. 47, 115, 134; Letter Book I, pp. xxi, 133. In Wals. ii. 327 he is *quondam* dictus dominus de Cobham; per uxorem, Usk, 121. In Pat. 2 H. V, i. 17, July 3, 1414, he is John Oldcastel *Bachiler*, though still called a knight in Pat. 2 H. V, ii. 16, Oct. 18, 1414. He is called "John Oldcastle" in the will of Margery Norford dated Oct. 31, 1417, who leaves to his wife Joan dominae de Cobham librum meum quondam domini de Cobham (i.e. probably her grandfather who died in 1408, Wylie, iii. 288), Freshfield, 1, 8.

[7] Page 271, note 2; Cal. Pat. H. VI, i. 90; in exigendis positus et postmodum utlagatus, Pat. 8 H. V, 18 d, March 9, 1421. Cf. exigend', Stat. ii. 202; Murray, Dict., s.v. *Exigent*.

[8] For inquisitions held before the escheator of Norfolk at Burnham near Lynn on March 1, 1414, and at Loddon near Reedham on July 26, see Cal. Pat. H. VI, i. 90; Rot. Parl. v. 401; Pat. 8 H. V, 18 d; also at Canterbury Feb. 5, 1414, and Cooling Feb. 8, 1414, as to his property in Kent, see Escheators' Inquisitions, Ser. 1. 1008. For writ to the escheator of Northamptonshire July 1, 1414, see ibid. 1278, i.e. to Ralph Green, who was sheriff of Northants. in the year beginning Nov. 10, 1414, Sheriffs' List, 93. He was succeeded as escheator by Roger Flore on Nov. 12, 1414, Escheators' Inquisitions, 1278.

[9] i.e. Thursday before St Barnabas' Day, Cal. Pat. H. VI, i. 90, 546; Rot. Parl. v. 401; Pat. 8 H. V, 18 dors. Not June 14, as Waugh, 651.

[10] Apud Braynford, Cleop. E. ii. f. 294; Rot. Parl. iv. 108.

placed in the hands of his sons-in-law Richard Clitherow[1] of Kent and Thomas Brook of Somerset[2], but it was found that he had made over all his goods, chattels and other moveables to John Prophet[3], Keeper of the Privy Seal, who was a relative of his wife Joan. She was at first arrested and thrown into the Tower though subsequently released[4], but although she had an allowance of £40 per annum[5], it is evident that she was brought to poverty and forced to do without the cups and dishes which had dressed her board

---

[1] For his seal, see Boys, 155, where he is said to be of Golstone, see Wylie, ii. 422; iii. 293. He was sheriff of Kent in 1403, 1418, Sheriffs' List, 68. Not Cliderson, as Bree, 4, 82, from Cotton MSS. Faustina, C. IX; Otho, E. IX (Cliderhou). His name appears among the conspirators against H. IV in 1399–1400, Letter Book I, 2; he afterwards became alnager of woollen cloth and canvas in the city of London, ibid. p. 84. For his property in London yielding 100*s.* per annum in 1412, see Archaeol. Journ. xliv. p. 81. On May 29, 1415, he was on a commission for the array of forces in Kent, Rym. ix. 253 [255]. He was on a commission for gaol delivery at Maidstone July 1, 1416, Pat. 4 H. V, 26 d. For silver vessels bought from his executors, see Iss. Roll 8 H. V, Mich., Nov. 8, 1420. For bailiwick (*balliva*) of Gartree (Leicestershire) granted to Robert (*sic*) Cliderowe, esquire, see Pat. 2 H. V, iii. 7, Feb. 17, 1415. For grant of £20 to Robert Cliderowe, a varlet of our chamber, from confiscated estate of Thomas Gardyner of Brantingthorpe (Leic.) who had killed Alfred Jacob of Brantingthorpe and fled, see Pat. 2 H. V, i. 28, May 27, 1414.

[2] Waugh, 651, quoting Escheators' Inquisitions, Ser. I. file 1008, mm. 1–17, 18, 29; do. file 1278, m. 10. For £100 received from them on this account and paid over to Humphrey, Duke of Gloucester, see Rec. Roll 3 H. V, Mich., Oct. 23, 1415. See also Waugh, 652, from Escheators' Inquisitions, Ser. I. file 959, m. 3; Rym. viii. 331; Claus. 5 H. V, m. 15 d, for statement that till March, 1416, the revenues were drawn by John ap Harry (for his account as late escheator of Hertfordshire 1402, see Wylie, iv. 252). In Rec. Roll 4 H. V, Mich., Dec. 19, 1416, March 3, 1417, Thomas Broke has custody of Oldcastle's lands in Kent. For the town of Lyme (i.e. Lyme Regis in Dorsetshire, not Lynn, as Cal. Rot. Pat. 264) belonging to Thomas Brook and Joan his wife (heiress to the Cobham estates, Wylie, iii. 291, 294), see Pat. 3 H. V, i. 18, May 12, 1415. In Pat. 6 H. V, i. 4 d, July 12, 1418, he is called Thomas Broke of Somerset, junr. He was 26 years of age at the time of his father's death in 5 H. V, Collinson, ii. 128. For inquisition held at Bristol as to property of his father Thomas Brook, kt., see Claus. 6 H. V, 11, Dec. 5, 1418, where the wife's name is Joan. He was patron of the livings of Bagborough near Taunton (1402) and Kingston (i.e. Kingston-Pitney) near Yeovil (1404), see Holmes, Reg. 35, 53. For John Broke, collector of the subsidy in Kent, see Rec. Roll 4 H. V, Mich., Feb. 25, 1417.

[3] See App. A[1].

[4] Bayley, 307, quoting Claus. 5 H. V, m. 7, also m. 18, for "a great many other persons." Cf. Britton and Brayley, 31.

[5] From the revenues of her manors of Ashby David (i.e. Castle Ashby near Northampton, which came to her through her second husband Reginald Braybrooke, Bridges, i. 342), Chesbury (or Chisebury, Inq. p. Mort. iv. 38, probably Chisenbury in the parish of Enford near Pewsey, Hoare, Everley, 16, where it is supposed to belong to Lord Cobham of Starborough), and Bynknall (Wilts.) and Burnham (Norfolk), Escheators' Inquisitions, Ser. I. 1278. For the manor of Polsted Hall in the parishes of Burnham Norton and Burnham Westgate (or Burnham Market), near Wells at the entrance of the Wash in Norfolk, held by Reginald Braybrook in 1401 in right of his wife Joan, see Blomefield, vii. 16, 33, 34. It must have originally come to her with the manor of Burnham from her first husband, Robert Hemenhall, who was then water-bailiff of Wiggenhall and gauger of Lynn, see Wylie, iii. 290. For Robert Hemnale, one of the men-of-arms in the retinue of Sir William Phelip at Southampton in July, 1415, see Exch. Accts. 44/30 (4).

in happier days[1]. On Oct. 18, 1414[2], she was allowed
the use of a hostel in London that had been part of her
original dower[3] and some of her husband's goods to
the value of 10 marks per annum, for which favour she
had herself petitioned. But for all this there was no
sign from Oldcastle himself nor any hint of any coming
submission.

The suddenness with which the movement had burst
and blown itself away was noted by contemporaries[4], but
Protestants writing in the sixteenth century made use of
this very fact to minimise the gravity of the whole occur-
rence, as a groundless panic cunningly worked up to crush
out a handful of innocent, though troublesome, sectaries.
Some attempted to exonerate Oldcastle by laying all the
blame on Acton[5], while others represented that it was only a
matter of 20 or 30[6] simple unoffending religionists, who had
merely met quietly in the ordinary way in St Giles' Field
to hear Beverley preach, and this view continued for a long
time to be the popular one with writers of a much later
date[7].

[1] Dum agebat in prosperis, Wylie, iii. 295, note 4. Cf. our substance seized unto his
highness' use even to the garments hanging to our backs, Drayton, Oldcastle, 340.

[2] Pat. 2 H. V, ii. 16.

[3] Probably Cobham's Inn in the parish of St Dunstan-in-the-East (called now East
Cheap in Kingsford, First Life, p. xlii), Inq. p. Mort. iv. 38. In the Subsidy Roll of
1412 dominus de Cobbeham owns property in London yielding £9. 15s. 4d. per annum,
Archaeol. Journ. xliv. 59.

[4] Qui nobis de pluribus inimicorum praedictorum *repente* tutelam concessit et vic-
toriam, Rym. ix. 119; *confestim* absque tumultu hujus rumoris patefacto, Vita, 31; to
shape *sodeyn* surreccioun, Pol. Songs, ii. 247.

[5] Redman, 23; Fabyan, 578; Rastell, 247; Halle, 48; see also Trussel, 94; Weever,
Oldcastle, 232; C. E. Maurice, ii. 268.

[6] Cf. "20 men," Cotton, Abridg. 554; State Trials, i. 255; only 80, of whom 20 were
killed, Tyrrell, i. 286; "about 80 persons," Historians' Hist. xviii. 528; "about 100,"
Pennant, London, 180.

[7] Holinsh. iii. 544; Foxe, iii. 351, 359; Speed, 769; Echard, 182; Rapin, i. 507 (who
adds : "unhappily they had brought arms, &c."); Gilpin, 31–34; Lewis, 251; Pauli, v. 88;
"a religious assembly for the worship of God," Kennett, i. 311; "met for religious purposes," Tyrrell, i. 286 [167]; "made a practice of assembling in St Giles' Fields, the scene
of their devotion," Guthrie, ii. 449 (who however is far more critical than his predecessors
in his general estimate of the movement) ; "a few poor Lollards assembled probably for
praise and prayer," Carrick, 221. Goodwin, 32, thinks that "it is not the work of a
historian to dispute" and so he refers his readers to Foxe. See also Milner, iii. 323;
Tyler, ii. 381. Church (150) thinks that "the insurrection *which is said to have been made*
by some of Oldcastle's friends is a matter involved in great mystery." Cf. "whether
Oldcastle were concerned with these men or not—which is doubtful," Anglia, v. 11;
"And meet in fields and solitary groves," Drayton, Oldcastle, 321; "an insignificant rout,"
Andrews, ii. 16; "only a few persons," Aubrey, ii. 40; "a series of supposition, rumour,
private information, apprehension and anticipation, but that the plots were really formed
there is no evidence," S. Turner, ii. 451, 453, 472; H. Noel, 25; "the outbreak, or
suspected outbreak," Milman, Annals, 89; "a pretended conspiracy," Dobie, 26;

But though the official statement that 20,000 Lollards assembled under arms in St Giles' Field[1] may possibly be exaggerated and the belief current abroad that the whole kingdom was betrayed outright[2] will not stand the test of close examination, yet there can be no doubt that at the time the peril was extremely urgent and that the conservative forces in England had reason to thank the new king's promptness and decision for rescuing the country from a very real and active form of danger.

As to the king no words were strong enough for the churchmen to express their gratitude. He was the lock and key of Albion's health[3], the very pillar of her faith[4]. To him they looked as to Christ's champion and God's holy knight, the worthy bearer of the sword of the Lord[5] preserved by God to be the mighty wall of Holy Church, her guardian and defence against her mortal foes[6]. The University of Oxford belauded him as a Constantine, a Marcian, a Theodosius, a Maccabæus come back to life

Clinch, 40; "a *sort* of insurrection," Tyrrell, Hist. 166; die *angebliche* Verschwörung, Lechler, ii. 91. Knight (ii. 54) thinks that the "rumoured plot" was "a gross exaggeration of some indiscreet assemblies for the purpose of petition"; Historians' History, xviii. 527; Bright (i. 289) that Oldcastle's connection with the rising is "very slightly supported by evidence"; Tyrrell, i. 286 [167], that it seems most likely that he had nothing to do with it; "the so-called rising," Besant, Survey (i. 105), who thinks (p. 104) that it was "no more a plot than any fabricated by Titus Oates." Cf. "the conspiracy, *if conspiracy there were*, had for its sole object the mitigation of the penal laws against the preachers and receivers of Wycliffe's doctrine," Historians' Hist. xviii. 528. Cassell (i. 520) thinks that "over the whole of these transactions there hangs a veil of impenetrable mystery," and finds that "this unaccountable affair" (ibid. i. 521) wears "so wild, so misty and so inconsistent an aspect" that he can only conclude that "the bishops concerted the plan and probably themselves disseminated the summonses to the meeting," but that "there is not the slightest evidence of the complicity of Lord Cobham"; also Lechler, ii. 94 [459]; Workman, i. 265.

1 Rot. Parl. iv. 108, 109; Rym. ix. 170, 193; Cleopatr. E. II. 294; Foxe, iii. 368, who argues (iii. 351, 352, 362, 370) that there cannot have been so many because the names of only three (!) are known; so also Fuller, Hist. ii. 416, who calls it a "story clogged with much improbability," which appears to have had no foundation whatever; see Dobie, 27; Aubrey, ii. 40. Prynne actually altered the figures on the Roll to 20 (!), Cotton, Abridg. 554; cf. Waugh, 646. Collier (iii. 324) replies to Foxe and thinks that he "does but discover the strength of his wishes and the bias of his inclination."

2 Einmal war das Königreich ganz verrathen, das bracht ein Lollhard zu wege, Reiser, 40. In H. Martin, v. 552, it is "une grande insurrection politique et religieuse"; cf. "a vast rebellion," Grey, 14, who thinks that "the object of it is not very clear."

3 Hoccl. Min. Po. 48; Anglia, v. 20.

4 Hoccl. Min. Po. 41; Chaucer (S.), vii. 233.

5 Qui dignè portat gladium Domini, from *Confutatio Lollardorum* addressed to Henry V by John Barton medicus, in All Souls MS. xlii. f. 308; Coxe, ii. 13; Dict. Nat. Biogr. iii. 346.

6 Lydgate, Min. Po. 34. It is clear that the prince addressed is Henry V, and I incline to think that Hoccleve may be the author, though MacCracken (Lydgate Canon, p. xii) prefers Lydgate.

again in whom God had raised up the horn of his Christ[1], and they prayed that every bishop should be deposed who showed any slackness in hunting the heretics down[2]. Men cried to him to go forth and hold up Christ's banner. They shrank from the mere thought of what might have happened to the folk of good belief had his affection bent to the wrong part[3]. Let no false pity make him spare his sword[4] but kill the buzzard that had marked his people for its prey[5]. God bade him smite, as Samuel did with Agag and Elijah with the priests of Baal. Let vigour hold the scales and let his lode-star be Christ's cause first and death to the enemies of God. Destroy them in spite of any feigned repentance, for they war on their own mother whom they should obey[6]. Then would they pray that he might reign for many a million years[7], and in such a fervour of blood-thirstiness they pressed for a law to be passed forbidding all public discussion of the faith[8] where heaps of men were blind and halt[9], lest the fickle fiend, if left unchecked, should catch his hour and plunge this island back in heathen-ness[10].

So when the Parliament met at Leicester three months after the rising had been crushed[11], a drastic statute was

---

[1] Conc. iii. 360.

[2] Cf.   Qui pugiles estis fidei populisque præestis
            Non horum gestis ignes prohibere potestis. Pol. Songs, ii. 128.

[3]   A Kyng set in that wrong opinioun
                    Might of our feith be the subversioun.
                            Hoccl. Min. Po. 48; Anglia, v. 20.

[4] Feyned fals pitee, Lydg. Min. Po. 34.

[5] Ibid. 32.

[6]   And althirnexte thi knyghtly state preserve. Ibid. 34.

[7]   Regne on us yeares many a millioune. Hoccl. Min. Po. 48.

[8]   Commandith that no wight have hardiness
            Of the feith to despute more or lesse
            Openly among peple where errour
            Springith al day and engendrith rumour
            Makith swiche lawe and for aght may befalle
            Observe it wel. Ibid. 42; Chaucer (S.), vii. 234.

Cf.   Despute no more of the sacrament
            And of our feith noon argumentis meene.
                    Hoccl. Min. Po. 42; Anglia, v. 27; James, 144.
In this respect he is hailed as the "heir and successor of Justinian," see Chaucer (S.), vii. pp. xli, 233, 502.

[9] Lydg. Min. Po. 33.

[10]   This yle or this had been but hethenesse
            Nad been of your feith the force and vigour.
                    Hoccl. Min. Po. 42; Chaucer (S.), vii. 234.

[11] Not that the rising was the *result* of the passing of the Leicester statute, as Goldwin Smith, i. 256.

passed which placed all the civil power of the country at the disposal of the Church for the detection and uprooting of Lollardry[1]. By this it was enacted[2] that every secular official from the Chancellor downward, including mayors, baillies and all other officers "having governance of the people" should take an oath on entering upon his term of office[3] that he would put his whole pain and diligence to destroy every kind of heresy and error in the district over which he exercised control, the bishops paying for his services[4]. The secular officers were henceforward empowered to question any Lollard as to who had supported him or favoured him, or written out his books or sermons, or attended his schools or conventicles, and to have such persons at once arrested and examined within ten days, either in the secular or Christian courts according to the nature of the charges brought against them[5], and any such accused person who should break bail or escape from prison should forfeit everything that he possessed.

At Cambridge there was much heated discussion as to the new statute, but on Sept. 17, 1414, the Chancellor, Stephen Scrope[6], was summoned to appear before the Convocation which was to meet at St Paul's on Oct. 1, and we hear no more of any difficulty in that quarter. On July 28, 1414[7], commissions were issued to all the

---

[1] See App. B[1].

[2] Rot. Parl. iv. 24; Stat. ii. 181; Conc. iii. 359; Stafford Reg. p. xi; Foxe, iii. 353; Hale, i. 399; Collier, iii. 309; Guthrie, ii. 453 (who calls it "an infamous Act driven on by Henry's bloody jealousy of the Lollards' civil principles"); Hume, iv. 40; Lingard, iii. 238; Tyler, ii. 7; Sharpe, London, i. 235; Letter Book I, pp. xxi, 130. Not that it applied only to judges and justices, as Ollard-Crosse, 337. It is officially referred to as the Statute of Leicester contra Lollardos in Pat. 8 H. V, 20 d, July 3, 1420.

[3] For a suggestion in this sense made by the University of Oxford in this year (1414) which seems to fix the date of the document as prior to May 29, 1414, see Conc. iii. 365.

[4] Les princes doivent mettre leurs officiers à son service (i.e. l'Inquisition) et permettre la violation perpétuelle des lois civiles dont ils ont la garde afin d'assurer le triomphe de sa législation particulière, Molinier, 458. This was the essential provision of the statute of Leicester, Stephen, ii. 450, corresponding with the edict of the Emperor Frederic II at his coronation at Rome, Nov. 22, 1220, Gregorovius, v. 122; Zeller, v. 195; Ollard-Crosse, 271. For the irregular statute of 1382 which empowered the sheriffs to arrest preachers of heresy, but which never received the assent of the Commons, see Stat. ii. 25; Hallam, 509; Creighton, Essays, 197.

[5] Not that "whoever read the scriptures should be condemned as a heretic," as Bale, 275; Goodwin, 39; H. Morley, vi. 139; Brougham, 92, 381 (who thinks that such proposals were presented but defeated); also Towle, 284; disproved in Gasquet, Bible, 140.

[6] Cal. Pat. H. V, i. 417; Wylie, ii. 195.

[7] Pat. 2 H. V, ii. 32 d, &c. The names include the Earl of Westmoreland and his son John Nevil for Cumberland, the Earl of Dorset and Thomas Waterden for Lynn, William Ferrers of Groby, Lord Grey of Codnor, John Cokayne, Thomas Maureward

influential men in every county throughout England to
act as Justices of the Peace for carrying out the provisions
of this new statute and the fact that the names of ex-
Lollards, such as Thomas Erpingham and Thomas Maureward, should be found in the list shows clearly that all
chance of support from the landed classes was closed to
the heretics at least for the present generation.   Indeed
a Franciscan, Thomas Brampton, writing in this very year
is clear that the king will now destroy all heretics, and
prays to God that England's knighthood may never be
lost in treason and subtlety[1].

A modern writer has denounced the Leicester statute
as "legislation of iron[2]," but in its own day it was officially
described as "good and necessary[3]."   It certainly served
its purpose quite effectually, and in the opening years of
the following reign it was an Englishman's favourite boast
that their great King Henry had "voided all cockle far
out of Sion[4]" and that "in this lande no lollard dare
abide[5]."   It may be well therefore to look for a moment
at the means whereby these notable results were obtained.

The earliest known heresy case undertaken after the
passing of the statute is preserved in a record[6] of the trial
of a batch of Lollards at Bristol.   One of the accused was
a woman named Christina More of Bristol, and the others
include a dauber, a mustard-maker, a barber, a dyer and a
web.   The proceedings are instructive.   All of the suspects
had been imprisoned for their Lollardry, but they were all
released on June 29, 1414, only to be brought before Bishop
Bubwith on July 5 following, in the parish church of his

(page 271, n. 4) and Henry Nevil for Leicestershire, William Gascogne (page 17), Robert
Mauleverer, Henry Fitzhugh, and Robert Tyrwhit for Ripon and Beverley; the Earl of
Arundel, Robert Poynings, and John Pelham for Surrey; John Talbot (page 64), Roger
Leche, and William Curson for Derbyshire; Richard Norton and John Hals for Yar-
mouth; the Duke of York, the Earls of Dorset and Suffolk, Thomas Morley, Thomas
Erpingham, and Simon Felbrigge for Norfolk.

[1] Brampton, pp. vii, 33, 34.   Cf.
                All day we se in trust is tresoun
                And preysing prevyd sotylté.   Ibid. 31.

[2] Une législation de fer, H. Martin, vi. 3.   For its repeal in 1547, see Stat. iv.
pt. I. 19.

[3] Bones et necessaries leies, Rot. Parl. iv. 94.

[4] Pol. Songs, ii. 143.

[5] Lydgate, Tragedies, Prologue; Vickers, 392.

[6] Cotton MS. Cleop. E. II. 324.

manor at Banwell[1] near Weston in Somerset. Here the Bishop explained to them in English all about the articles of the Faith, the Ten Commandments, the seven Sacraments, the seven Works of Pity and the seven Cardinal Virtues, and asked them what they thought; and they said that they thought well and catholicly[2] on all these great subjects and had never thought anything else. He next took them on the seven Deadly Sins and they said that they ought to be avoided by every Christian man and their answers were considered to be sound[3]. They were then asked on their oath whether they had ever been Lollards or had ever read any Lollard books or heard them read, or given any counsel, help, consent, or favour to anyone who had read them and whether the rumours about their being Lollards were true or not, and they all said that the rumours were not true and offered to purge themselves at the hands of a jury at any time or place that the Bishop chose to select. So the Bishop appointed July 23 as the day, and the church of St Thomas the Martyr[4] on the south side of the Avon at Bristol as the place, for the compurgation, and notices were given out in that church and the neighbouring churches of Redcliffe[5] and the Temple[6] at Bristol that any man who would like to inform against them should attend for the purpose there and then. The day arrived and the accused were ready in the church. The Bishop was there and the Mayor and Sheriffs and a great multitude of others. Twelve Bristol citizens were sworn in as a jury but no informer appeared, so the accused all took an oath on the Gospels that they would abstain from heresy in future and that if any of them should ever know of any Lollard afterwards, he would instantly inform against him and then they were, somewhat illogically, put back into prison for another six months and not actually set at liberty till Feb. 6, 1415.

---

[1] For letters dated from Banwell by Bishop Bowet in 1405, 1406, see Holmes, Reg. pp. xxii, 58.   For palace built at Banwell by Bishop Beckington now in ruins, see Collinson, iii. 567.

[2] Bene et catholicé. Cf. First Life, 18.

[3] Cum congruis et catholicis responsionibus.

[4] For account of the church, see Barrett, 557.

[5] For St Mary Redcliffe church, built by William Canynges in 1376, see Ricart, 36; Barrett, 566. For commission Aug. 2, 1408, from the Chancellor of Wells to the Dean and the Chaplain of Redcliff to forbid unlicensed preachers in Bristol, see Holmes, Reg. 75.

[6] For the Temple Church, otherwise Holy Cross (Sanctae Crucis Templi), see Barrett, 541; Seyer, ii. 44.

On Feb. 25, 1415, their purgation was declared to be sufficient and they were restored to their good reputation, so far as that was possible. But it is evident that they were all kept under observation, for when special vigilance was being exercised two or three years afterwards, certificates of these proceedings were called for by the king's officers[1] and extracts were made from the bishop's registers accordingly, but whether the necessary informers came forward against them then, we do not now know. The whole process looks as if no shadow of evidence could be produced against any one of them, unless indeed we are to assume that the whole population of Bristol was so infected with the taint of heresy that not a man could be found to offer a word of information. Certainly, if such had been forthcoming, it would have gone hard indeed with them, as the following authentic narrative will abundantly show.

In St Martin's Lane, in the parish of St Anne's near Aldersgate, lived a well-to-do pelterer[2] named John Claydon[3], who furred gowns[4] in the City of London. He had been known as a sympathiser with Lollardry for the last 20 years[5]. In the time of Bishop Braybrooke[6] he had undergone two years imprisonment on this account in Conway castle and a subsequent term of three years in the Fleet prison in London, but early in the reign of Henry IV, when Sawtre had been burned[7], Claydon recanted before

---

[1] Cleop. E. II. 323, from Coram Rege Roll 23 (5 H. V), contains the king's letter to the Vicar of Bishop Bubwith dated June 23, 1417, asking for the certificate within 20 days after Michaelmas. This was forwarded on Oct. 4, 1417, but as it said nothing about Christina More, a further request was made for information on the decision in her case, to be sent in by Jan. 20, 1418.

[2] Chron. Lond. 99; Short Chron. 55; Cal. Rot. Pat. Richard II, iii. 159, where he appears as a surety on June 3, 1386; Foxe, iii. 375. Cf. Pelletiers qui doivent fourrer les vêtements, Cuissard, 63. Called a currier in Foxe, iii. 530; Riley, Mem. 618; Sharpe, London, i. 256; Letter Book I, xxi. 139; Besant, Survey, i. 105; or a skinner in Kingsford, Chron. 69; Greg. Chron. 108; Tyler, ii. 396; a fellmonger, Aubrey, ii. 41; a furrier, Tyrrell, i. 287 [168]; Lechler, ii. 96; Carrick, 222.

[3] Conc. iii. 371; Milman, Ann. 89; or Cleydone, Letter Book I, 139, 140.

[4] For a "hoppelande chevronnée d'or fourrée de gris à dix tires" (1415), see Garnier, Invent. 617.

[5] Inveteratus Lollardus, Wals. ii. 307, who calls him *William* Claydon; also Collier, iii. 312; Brougham, 80; Victoria Co. Hist. London, ii. 218, 220. Called William Cleydon in Gairdner, Lollardy, i. 88.

[6] He was Bishop of London from 1381 to 1404, Le Neve, ii. 293.

[7] For supposition that the Statute of 1401 was passed "without the consent of the Commons" and was therefore not legally enacted, see Brute, Thorpe, &c. p. 9; Aubrey, Rise, ii. 7; Pauli, Bilder, 275 [303]. But there is no foundation for this view, see Hallam, 510; Hale, i. 397; Wylie, i. 190; the real fact is that Sawtre was burned before the statute was passed, see Hale, i. 396; Gardiner, 292; Stephen, ii. 447; Wakeman, 153;

the chancellor, John Scarle[1], and two years later he abjured again before Archbishop Arundel and the Southern Convocation, though he never really turned his heart away from the doctrines that his conscience told him were true. He absented himself from his parish church[2], and when his wife recovered from her lying-in, he did the churching for her in his own house[3]. He had lately heard a sermon preached in the fields at Horsleydown[4] on the other side of London bridge, in which the Pope was called the worst Antichrist[5], sowing his rotten laws on the top of the laws of Christ. The preacher called the bishops the seats on which the beast sat in the foul darkness of error and said they should only be obeyed when they watched over the souls of their flocks in holy conversation. Their licence to preach was but the mark of the beast, while simple faithful priests did not need it and were bound to preach in spite of it.

John Claydon's heart was stirred as he listened to the true Wycliffe ring[6], that told that those alone were predestined members of the Church who kept faith and charity in word and deed; that followers of Jesus Christ would humbly worship God in a plain simple house[7] and not in gaudy churches decked with gold and silver and precious stones[8] and grounded in poor men's blood; that all the evils from which Christendom was suffering were caused by the priests

Gee-Hardy, 138; Workman, i. 259, 306; Capes, 180; Maitland, 176, 177; Ollard-Crosse, 271; Wylie, i. 186. Not "in accordance with it," as Tyrrell, p. xi; Adams, i. 207; Towle, England, 154; Tout, 256; Oman, Hist. 215; do. R. II–R. III, 171; Historians' Hist. xviii. 521; Snow, 51 (who dates the statute in 1400, also Knöpfler, 462; Stephen, ii. 447); Loserth, Gesch. 540; J. M. Stone, 51; Durham, 3. Besant, Survey, i. 100, thinks that Sawtre was "chosen as the first victim on account of his personal popularity."

[1] Not Searle, as Conc. iii. 371; Malden, 72; Foxe, iii. 531; Tyler, ii. 396, 398; Lechler, ii. 96. See Wylie, i. 28.

[2] For major excommunication threatened against cobblers for staying away from mass on Sundays, see Conc. iii. 218; Milman, Ann. 82. In 1409 the Bishop of Orleans excommunicated and put en la compagnie du diable all citizens who shot rubbish (*ordures, gravois ou autre immondices*) outside the Paris gate at Orleans, but the Duke's officers interfered and prevented it, Lottin, i. 178.

[3] Wals. ii. 307, who says that he made his son the priest, which can scarcely mean "giving Holy Orders to his son," as Brougham, 80; cf. Gairdner, Loll. i. 88.

[4] Then known as Horsedown or Horsefaldown, Riley, Mem. 474. Not Hothfield near Ashford, as Lechler, ii. 99.

[5] See Church Quart. Rev. xlviii. 414; Camb. Hist. Lit. ii. 56; Wylie, iii. 431.

[6] See App. X; Wylie, iii. 431–433.

[7] Christ our poor lord hath hallowed the house of our poverty, Brute, Thorpe, &c. 156.

[8] Many deceive men's eyes with envious churches and many vain staring sights in their churches; many build arches and pillars they pave with marble stones, the beams glister all with gold, the altars are diversely arrayed with precious stones, Brute, Thorpe, &c. 156; Conc. iii. 374; Foxe, iii. 533.

possessing worldly goods and the friars' illegal beggary; that alms must only be given out of honest winnings and to persons who were really and genuinely in need[1]; that instead of all this unscriptural singing in church the priests ought to be busy studying how to preach Christ's law[2]; that indulgences and pilgrimages were useless, and that no Christian should bow to any image or worship it in any way[3].

The sermon was in English and formed part of a book called "The Lantern of Light[4]," a copy of which was printed a hundred years later[5] by Robert Redman in the days of the struggle between Henry VIII and the Pope, and although this copy is now very scarce, the text was re-issued in a cheap form some 80 years ago[6], so that we are now able to estimate the real contents upon which the condemnation of Claydon was based. The book had evidently been quite recently composed and soon attained a wide popularity[7]. Its very words were used by Oldcastle before his judges, and the crowds of Bible texts quoted in the English tongue prove that we have here a living specimen of the straight blunt talk of one of Wycliffe's "poor priests[8]." The book contains a distinct reference to the new constitutions which had been promulgated in 1407[9], whereby churches were interdicted and preachers examined unless they bore the mark of the beast[10], who "busily spies and hearkens where he may find any man or woman that writes, reads, learns or studies God's law in their mother tongue[11]," constraining them to swear and lay their hands on books

[1] Feed many wretches as strong stiff beggars and strikers over the land and groaners without cause that need not their goods, yea to minstrels and jugglers and other vain japers they deal largely their goods and call it alms, Brute, Thorpe, &c. 164.

[2] They preach chronicles with dreamings and many helpless tales that are of no avail, ibid. 164.

[3] Ibid. 179.

[4] Qui erat scriptus in libro illo, Conc. iii. 372. Not "one of Wycliffe's writings," as Aubrey, ii. 41.

[5] i.e. between 1523 and 1540.

[6] Brute, Thorpe, &c. pp. 141–188.

[7]   The lanterne of lyghte
                Non fulget luce serenâ.   Pol. Songs, i. 278.

[8] Called "illiterate and crude fanatics," in J. M. Stone, 43; but "a new order as distinctly a creation as the Dominicans and Franciscans" in Church Quart. Rev. xlviii. 425, where they are supposed to have been "suppressed without any sign of popular regret." In Camb. Hist. Lit. ii. 57, their only qualifications are "simple piety, a love of the Scriptures and a readiness to preach."

[9] Page 242, note 1.

[10] Brute, Thorpe, &c. 149; Conc. iii. 379; Foxe, iii. 532.

[11] Brute, Thorpe, &c. 149, 177.

and then putting them to open shame, and if they leave his bidding, he saith by law they are relapsed[1] and afterward the knights of Herod's house are full ready to make an end[2]. "Whereto," exclaims the writer[3], "make ye shrines for saints and yet ye draw, hang and burn those that hold the way of Christ and follow after them[4]?" But "tribulations that bruise us down in this wretched world" do but "constrain us to go to God. If we would have the kernel, we must needs break the nut. We must needs suffer travail, if we will come to rest, and pain, if we will come to bliss. He is a false coward knight that fleeth and hideth his head when his Master is in the field beaten among his enemies, and if we become not renegades for pain that may befall, but think on Christ's passion that assuages all heaviness, then are we most clear-worthy and worthy highest merit. Join we then the cross of Christ to our bare flesh, that our part may be found among those holy saints who willingly forsook themselves and joyed in tribulation." From end to end the book contains not one word of political sedition, the whole being one torrent of protest against the enemy that clouts his laws as rotten rags to the clean cloth of the gospel of Christ[5].

Hundreds of uneasy Englishmen must have been lulling their souls with the common cry that it was enough for them to live as their fathers did[6], and that it was much

---

[1] Brute, Thorpe, &c. 176.

[2] Ibid. 160. Cf. Wylie, Constance, p. 168.

[3] For William Hardy, curate of Barling near Southend, as its possible author, see Brute, Thorpe, &c. p. 159. Nothing is known of him in Newcourt, ii. 36; Morant, i. 308, but he may be the same as William Hardy, who had been vicar of Skidbrook near Louth in Lincolnshire, also of St Mary, Islington, from Sept. 21, 1395, to Jan. 1397, and of Measden near Buntingford, from Jan. 17, 1397, to March 21, 1398, Cussans, Edwinstree, 133. He afterwards became rector of Ash in Kent, where he is said to have been reported a Lollard in 1407, Hennessy, 230, cvii.

[4] Brute, Thorpe, &c. 159.

[5] Ibid. 144, 164; Conc. iii. 374; Foxe, iii. 532.

[6] Brute, Thorpe, &c. 177. Cf. Stand therefore in thy degre and hye thingis desire thou not, Misyn, 15; Wylie, iii. 204. Cf.
For holy saints and old clerkys wise
Written contrary her falseness to defame.
Lydgate in Monast. (1773), iii. 374.

Translating: Les livres que firent jadis
Les sains le monstrent en beaux dis. Dufour (le Cordelier).

Cf. Let us therfore beleve as we are bounde.
Lydg. Min. Po. 99.

Muse not hereon
To hys doctryne all crystyn men must obeye. Ibid. 104.

For argument that the Feast of Fools came to us from our fathers and that il nous

folly to be burnt for false belief[1], but to Claydon the fear-less rhetoric of the "Lantern" came deeply home. He was so carried away by it that he got a scrivener[2] named John Grime[3] to write him out a copy on calfskin membranes, which he had nicely bound in red leather. He was no scholar and could not read himself, but he had a servant named John Fuller, who would often read aloud parts of the book for him on holidays when nothing was doing in the shop; and when Grime brought in the last quires and sat with Fuller reading and correcting them from eight in the morning till dusk on mid-Lent Sunday, 1415, Claydon sat by and asked questions and said that he would gladly have paid three times as much for the book rather than miss the chance of having such a treasure in his own possession.

He was often visited by two Lollard friends, Richard Gurmyn[4] a frenchbaker[5] from Lombard Street, and a man named Montford, who came and talked over the book and discussed the "articles of the faith." But besides this he had two apprentices named Saunder (i.e. Alexander) Philip and David Berde, aged 15 and 23 years respectively, who lived in his house and took their meals at his table[6], and two other servants who did the menial work. None of these could read, but they listened to Fuller, and in the spring of 1415 Philip, the younger of the two apprentices, after $2\frac{3}{4}$ years spent with Claydon passed over to finish his time with a mercer named Thomas Fauconer[7], who became Mayor of London in October, 1414[8], so that he was the

suffit de vivre comme eux, see Feret, iv. 115, where it is condemned as un argument diabolique et une infernale suggestion.

[1] Pol. Songs, ii. 243.   [2] See App. C[1].

[3] Not that Grime was the author of the book, as Goodwin, 164, which is still entered under his name in the catalogue of the British Museum.

[4] Letter Book I, 180. Not Surmyn, as Riley, Mem. 630; Chron. Lond. 99; Tyrrell, i. 287 [168]; called Turmyn in Gregory, Chron. 108; or Turmyne, Ramsay, i. 227 (who says that he was condemned but afterwards pardoned); Waugh, 653, who calls him *William* Turmyne; or Turming, Foxe, iii. 530; Brute, Thorpe, &c. 139; or George Gurmyn, Cleop. E. ii. 322 b; Tyler, ii. 394, 401; Letter Book I, 180, quoting Pipe Roll 3 H. V; or Richard Gurnion, Mon. Francisc. ii. 165; or Gurmon, Grey Friars Chron. 13; or Gutmyn, Short Chron. 55; or Turning, Carrick, 222.

[5] Hence called Richard Baker in Kingsford, Chron. 69; Caxton, 225.

[6] See App. D[1].

[7] For his trade mark, see Wylie, iv. 305, note 2. For merchants' marks at Leicester, see Bateson, ii. lxxx; at Coventry, Bloom, 184; at Ypres, Claus. 8 H. V, 12; in London (coopers), Besant, Survey, ii. 178/14; Hazlitt, Companies, 436; also on brasses, Macklin, 162.

[8] Letter Book I, 130; Rec. Roll 3 H. V, Pasch., May 2, Sept. 3, 1415. For permission granted to him Sept. 1, 1415, to ship 1000 quarters of corn to Bayonne or Bordeaux, see Gasc. Roll 3 H. V, 2; not to Bruges, as Carte, Rolles, i. 199.

first mayor elected after the passing of the Leicester Statute and had accordingly bound himself under the new oath to put his services at the disposal of the bishops. Being a keenly orthodox tradesman and knowing what he did from his new apprentice, he had Claydon arrested and his books seized, pronouncing them to be the worst and most perverse books that he had ever read or seen— especially the "Lantern." Grime and Montford were nowhere to be found, but Gurmyn was soon clapped into the sheriff's counter, while the other apprentice and one of the servants, named Balthasar Mero, were available as witnesses and were able to prove that they had never heard their master say anything against the book as contrary to Catholic doctrine.

It was on the strength of such evidence that Claydon was brought before a large gathering of theologians and lawyers in the chapter-house at St Paul's on Aug. 17, 1415[1]. Archbishop Chichele presided, being supported by Bishops Clifford and Caterick and Mayor Fauconer, with William Lyndwood and John Hovingham among the assessors. After the usual interrogatories by the ordinary[2], in which Claydon was asked if he thought the "Lantern" was a good, true and useful Catholic work and had replied that he thought it was, for it had proved very useful to him, the court adjourned till Monday, Aug. 19, the books being handed over in the meantime to four experts selected from the Black, Grey and Austin Friars and the three witnesses being taken in hand by the examiner-general of the Court of Canterbury.

When the court re-assembled it was strengthened by the presence of Bishop Patrington, but the interval had not made the prospect brighter for the accused, for in addition to all the other Wycliffry in the "Lantern" the examiners had found in it a statement that Judas received the body of Christ in bread and the blood in wine, which language they interpreted as a denial of Transubstantiation, whereupon the archbishop ordered the books to be burned and Claydon to be handed to

---

[1] Conc. iii. 371; Foxe, iii. 375, 531; Goodwin, 163; Milman, Annals, 89.
[2] Stat. iii. 454 (1533).

the mayor to be dealt with as a relapsed heretic[1]. On
Aug. 22, 1415, the mayor notified the king[2], who had
already started for France[3], that he was preparing to assist
at the execution, and on Sept. 10[4] Claydon was burnt alive
in West Smithfield[5] in accordance with the requirements of
the law[6].

Of the execution itself nothing but the bare fact is recorded[7]. There is no evidence that any of the bystanders
were shocked, and it is probable that few of them really were.
It is the custom nowadays to suppose that the Lollards at
that time were hypocritical and cowardly conspirators who
richly deserved their fate[8]; but that Claydon was merely a
sober, serious, convinced Puritan, is proved from the fact
that there is no hint of treason in any of the charges made
against him, even though he had been in London all
through the panic of Fickett's Field. But though the
Leicester Statute was long regarded by most Englishmen
as "fruitful and profitable[9]," yet there were not wanting
some who saw that under it "a hideous cloud had come
upon the shining day[10]," and with it England had started
on a new career which placed the privacy of her worthiest

---

[1] For the archbishop's warrant (undated) to the Mayor of London, see Letter Book I,
139. Foxe, iii. 534, wrongly says "unlawfully for that the temporal magistrates had no
such law sufficient for them to burn any such man for religion condemned of the prelates."
See page 285, note 7.
[2] Letter Book I, pp. xxii, 140; Riley, Mem. 617; Besant, Survey, i. 105. Tyler
(ii. 403) argues that he knew "that the execution of this man would have given the king
displeasure." Michelet (vi. 16) thinks that "le roi prit part à tout dévotement."
[3] He sailed from Southampton on the Sunday preceding Claydon's arrest, Tyler, ii.
397, 404.
[4] Grey Friars Chron. 13. Not in August, as Engl. Hist. Rev. xxii. 578.
[5] For picture of Smithfield, see Aubrey, ii. 517; Knight, London, ii. 313; Cassell,
ii. 384.
[6] Riley, Mem. 617.
[7] Greg. Chron. 108; Kingsford, Chron. 69.
[8] Profane, aller Religiosität baare Menschen, oder schlaue Heuchler die wohl selten
den Muth hatten für ihre Ueberzeugung einzutreten, Zimmermann (in Wetzer, viii. 134).
In Ollard-Crosse, 337, Oldcastle "played with rebellion and heresy as more a political
than a religious matter." Lechler (ii. 104) draws a distinction between the character of
the movement before and after the death of Oldcastle in 1417, after which date he thinks
it was based upon "eine gediegene Gottesfurcht welche durch religiöse Innerlichkeit
und sittlichen Ernst sich auszeichnet." Wakeman (153), believing that the object of
the Leicester Statute was "plainly in defence of the government," claims that the executions of Sawtre and Badby were the only ones "carried out on the initiation of the
ecclesiastical authorities," crediting the deaths of 50 Lollards ("and there may have
been many more") to the secular authorities alone. R. L. Poole (116) thinks that
"only two heretics are known to have suffered death," and that after 1417 "no further
action was deemed necessary against the Lollards" (p. 118), followed by J. M. Stone, 51.
[9] First Life, 27.
[10] Brute, Thorpe, &c. 176.

and steadiest homes at the mercy of trade rivals and domestic spies[1].

Three days before Claydon suffered, his friend Richard Gurmyn had been tried at St Paul's, convicted and burnt for the same offence[2], though in his case there was evidently some excess of zeal on the part of the authorities, for it was rumoured that the mayor had burnt him in spite of some letters of pardon that had been granted to him by the king. No record of his trial or condemnation has been found[3], though it was stated that he had been declared a manifest heretic "according to canonical sanctions[4]." It is possible that he had paid his fine and taken out his pardon, like many others, through the commissioners appointed after the Epiphany rising, and that the mayor who was pledged under the new statute to effect the "entire destruction of all such enemies of the king," allowed his zeal to run away with him and when Claydon's burning was in hand, burnt Gurmyn also without more ado. At any rate we know that the sheriff's charges for burning the two amounted to 20s. in one lump sum[5], while many people believed that the mayor was ordered to the Tower and fined £1000 for this illegality. This latter fact comes out in the case of a woolpacker[6] named John Russell[7], who was afterwards charged with circulating this rumour on three separate market-days. Several respectable citizens went bail for him, but he was put in the pillory as a liar with a whetstone round his neck and made to withdraw his statement and to say that he had been repeating words that he had heard from "untrue men."

---

[1] Every bond of relative and social life was destroyed by these measures, Brute, Thorpe, &c. 12.

[2] Cleop. E. II. 322 b.

[3] Tyler, ii. 394, who had searched "the records in St Paul's Cathedral," but without success.

[4] Riley, Mem. 618.

[5] Tyler, ii. 394, 401, from Pipe Rolls 3 H. V. For 70 sols paid to the executioner (*bourrel*) for executing a criminal at Auffay near Dieppe in 1388, together with 2 sols for his expenses and 9d. for a noose (*gans*), see C. Beaurepaire, Notes, ii. 95. For 55 sols paid in 1412 for execution of Olivier Bourgaut, one of the assassins of the Duke of Orleans, see Lottin, i. 181; Sellier, 51; viz. for cutting off his hand in the pillory (5s.), for cutting off his head (5s.), do. his arms and legs (20s.), for hanging them up in different places (20s.), for burning his body (5s.).

[6] For "wolpakker," see Letter Book I, 26, 44, 82; Wylie, iv. 279.

[7] Letter Book I, pp. xxii, 180; Riley, Mem. 618.

CHAPTER XVIII

ARCHBISHOPS AND BISHOPS

WITHIN a year after the passing of the Leicester Statute one of the English representatives at Constance was able to assure the Council there that every suspected master in England had abjured his Wycliffry at the bidding of the Archbishop of Canterbury[1], but Archbishop Arundel himself had not lived to see this great triumph of his Church[2]. Soon after Oldcastle's condemnation[3] he had been seized with a quinsy[4] or stricture in the throat[5], so that for some days he could neither speak nor swallow[6]. He made his will on Feb. 16, 1414[7], and about midnight[8] on Feb. 19[9] he died at the age of 62 in the rectory house of his

[1] Palacky, Doc. 136; Hardt, iv. 346; Lechler, ii. 303; J. M. Stone, 63.
[2] Not that the statute was passed before his death, as Usk, 123.
[3] Not before the death of Henry IV, as Fuller, Church Hist. ii. 413.
[4] For squinancy, see Halliwell, ii. 792. Cf. "in the sqwynancy and in all the swellynges of the throte and the nekke and in all the lettynges of swolowynge," Arderne MS. at Emmanuel College, Cambridge, f. xxvi.
[5] Gasc. 35, 61; per os descendens in guttur suum, ibid. 180, 181.
[6] For "tortura oris that is to seye the crokydnesse of the mowth that turneth the mowth downe to the ere in the manere of a ffyssche that is called a ffloundre," see Arderne, f. xii, who records a cure effected by the "kyngis leche of Spayne" of a knight who was with "Duke Harry of Lancaster" at "Algezire in Spayne" (f. xiii).
[7] He left his portos to William Milton, Archdeacon of Buckingham, who afterwards became Dean of Chichester and died in 1424, Le Neve, i. 256; ii. 69. For Arundel's seal showing the martyrdom of Becket, see Birch, 75; Bloom, 128. His executors were Gilbert Humfrevill (sic), kt., the Prior of Canterbury, Master Philip Morgan, William Milton, John Wotton Master of the College at Maidstone, Bartholomew Brokesby and Wm. Maydestone, Memoranda Roll K.R. 3-4 H. V, 24, July 9, 1415.
[8] i.e. between 3 and 4 o'clock in the morning, Goodwin, i. 125.
[9] Chron. Lond. 98; Usk, 121; Duck, 23; Le Neve, i. 22; Arundel MS. 68/57, Catalogue, p. 15; De Gestis Thomae Arondelle archiepiscopi, in Register of Priory of Christ Church, Canterbury; Ramsay, i. 180; Hartwright, 133; or Feb. 20, as Wals. ii. 303; Foxe, iii. 403; Stow, Chron. 344; Fleury, vi. 337; Pauli, v. 88; Lechler, ii. 92. Not January, as Campbell, Chancellors, i. 320; nor March 23, as Goodwin, 32; Gaspey, i. 125; nor 1413, as Somner, i. 136; Woolnoth, 162; nor 1415, as Bale, 276; Pits, 595; State Trials, i. 254.
        Cancia flere potest quia Thomas cessit Arundel
        Mil C quater plena annis tribus et duodenis. Stone, 19.

Archdeacon, John Wakering[1], at Hackington[2], just outside the city of Canterbury. On the day following his death his body was buried in the new nave of the cathedral[3].

What chiefly struck his contemporaries about him was that he was the son of one earl and the brother of another[4], and we know that he left over £6000, all of which was absorbed with legacies even to the uttermost three-farthings[5]. Later writers say that to the distinction of high birth he added the distinction of great learning[6], but at Oxford his attainments are said to have been treated with ridicule[7]. On the other hand we have incontestible evidence of his literary tastes from an unexpected light thrown on his life, when he was banished from England by Richard II[8] and wandered through Europe as the sport of fortune[9]. During this time of trial he visited Florence and was received by Pope Boniface IX at Rome[10], and it was while at Florence that he became acquainted with the venerable humanist, Coluccio Salutati[11], who afterwards cherished a courtly feeling

---

[1] Hasted, iv. 778, 783. For his appointment March 10, 1409, see Wylie, iii. 301, note 2; not July, 1408, as Archaeologia Cantiana, xiii. 382.

[2] Stone, 10; Somner, ii. App. 33; Hasted, iv. 727; Foss, 74. Not that he died at Lambeth, as Holt, Lights, 115. The living of Hackington was attached to the Archdeaconry in 1227, Antiq. Repert. iii. 120.

[3] Angl. Sacr. i. 123; in boriali parte navis ecclesiae, Parker, 276; Somner, i. 136.

[4] Walden, ii. 386; Usk, 38, 122; altae prosapiae, Gesta, 3; Chron. Giles, 5; rarum dignitate, rarissimum sanguine, Salutati, iii. 619. In Lit. Cantuar. iii. 123, he calls Thomas Earl of Arundel (d. 1415) his nephew (*nepos*), i.e. son of Richard E. of Arundel (d. 1397), who was the archbishop's brother. In the same document he calls Joan Countess of Hereford and Alice Countess of Kent his sisters, both of them being daughters of Richard FitzAlan Earl of Arundel, who died in 1376. Hook (iv. 424) calls him "a perfect gentleman except when his passions were roused."

[5] viz. £6008. 17s. 7¾d., Angl. Sacr. i. 795. See the inventory in Somner, ii. App. 34; not £5008, as Hook, iv. 528. On Jan. 27, 1414, he was excused from payment of the tenth lately granted by the clergy, because of the great expenses he had undergone for the king, Pat. 1 H. V, v. 22. For a gown of scarlet velvet bought by the king from his executors and presented to Bishop Beaufort in 1415, see Rym. ix. 291. For £29. 7s. 8d. received at the Exchequer from his executors de diversis debitis suis, see Rec. Roll 8 H. V, Mich., Nov. 18, 1420.

[6] Eximiae scientiae, Angl. Sacr. i. 62; Pits, 595, who adds a list of his writings. Capes (157) calls him "a capable and resolute statesman with no pretensions as a theologian or a scholar." Woolnoth (162) thinks that "his mind was of a superior cast."

[7] Wylie, iii. 443. For statement that he was a student of Oriel College, Oxford, and that he completed the chapel there which had been begun by his father, see Bekynton, ii. 405; Purey-Cust, ii. 358.

[8] For an undated petition to Parliament that his sentence might be reversed and his goods and possessions restored, see Hist. MSS. Rept. iv. 194.

[9] Fortunae singularem (*sic*) ludibrium, Salutati, iii. 619, who praises his fortitude and patience under the trial.

[10] Wylie, i. 20, 70; iii. 444. For Pierre Salmon's interview with him in Easter week at "Utrecq" before his visit to Rome, see Salmon, 65.

[11] G. Voigt, ii. 251.

towards him[1] and letters passed between them, though it is only recently that the contents of these letters have become known[2]. Salutati, the grand old man, was then 68 years of age[3] but still wonderfully vigorous, and when Arundel had effected his adventurous return to England[4] he wrote to him hoping that God would help him to stand against the malice of his enemies[5]. Eighteen months after Arundel's return Salutati sent him another letter[6] congratulating him on the ease with which he had recovered his old position and recommending to him a young[7] Florentine named Antonio Mannini, who had previously been employed by King Richard to discredit him with the Pope and secure the recognition of Roger Walden, who had supplanted him in the archbishopric[8]. He urges that the past should be forgotten and that Mannini should not be made to suffer, as he only acted under orders[9]. As far as Walden was concerned this prudent advice had been already followed[10]. Mannini was back in Florence in 1403, but was certainly amongst us again a few years later[11]. Yet one more letter was addressed by Salutati to the restored archbishop in

---

[1] Nullis temporibus de memoriâ te deponam, Tu mihi semper ades, &c., Salutati, iii. 101; cum te licet senex viderim possumne non continuè reminisci, ibid. iii. 619.

[2] Salutati, iii. 360; iv. 255, quoting S. Meerkle, Acht unbekannte Briefe von Coluccio Salutato, in Rivista Abruzzese di Scienze, Lettere ed Arti, 1895, p. 564.

[3] Writing on Aug. 30, 1397, he says that he has reached his 66th year (Salutati, iii. 197), and in a letter to Archbishop Arundel written on Jan. 29, 1403, he tells him that he will be 72 on Feb. 16 next, showing that he was born on Feb. 16, 1331, ibid. iii. 619. His wonderful collection of letters to popes, princes and savants runs from 1360 to 1406. For account of him, see G. Voigt, i. 190. For portraits of him, see Salutati, i. iii. (Frontispiece); iv. 160 (medal). For his mark with complicated flourish, see ibid. iv. 241.

[4] For his visit to Henry IV at Bicêtre near Paris, see Bouchart, 165a.

[5] Audio te in patriam rediisse super quo timeo et spero, Salutati, iii. 363, addressed Thomae de Rondello from Florence Aug. 30, 1399.

[6] Salutati, iii. 497, April 4, 1401. In this he offered to send him a tract that he had just written called *De Nobilitate Legum et Medicinae*. It was only a trifle (nugas meas, ibid. iii. 501) that he had put together as the result of a discussion he had recently had with a doctor, but as Arundel had promised to let him have a copy of Augustine's treatise on Music (de musicâ ratione, ibid. iii. 620) if ever he got back his books at home, he thought this might be a little acknowledgment of his kindness, moreover he thought that servus tuus Nicolaus Lucefri might like to see it.

[7] He was born in 1371.

[8] For the pall presented to him by Bishop Wickham at Highclere near Newbury on Feb. 17, 1398, see Stubbs, Reg. 193.

[9] Urgebat enim regis jussio et emulorum factio.

[10] Wylie, iii. 125, where the reference to any "General History" written by Walden needs correction, Julius B. xiii. 1, being a 13th century set of Chronological Tables of patriarchs, popes, kings and emperors, where a much later hand (circa 1600) has called it "Epitome Historiae Rogeri Waldon," but apparently without any reason. Giraldus, VIII. p. viii, where his death is wrongly dated 1405; Dict. Nat. Biogr. lix. 25.

[11] For his visit to St Patrick's Purgatory in 1411, see p. 77.

England. Writing on Jan. 29, 1403, he expressed his pleasure that he had got back not only his old position but his books[1], and after reminding him of a pleasant visit he had paid to the Convent of Santa Maria de Angelis when he was in Florence, he asked him for a contribution for the monks, who had had some heavy expenses in connection with an adjoining property. What answer the archbishop made we do not know, but not long afterwards, viz. on March 26, 1406, his aged friend wrote the last of his surviving letters, in which he longed to be released and be with Christ[2]. He had not long to wait, for on May 4 following he passed away[3].

Adam of Usk, to whom Archbishop Arundel had proved a good friend[4], belauds him as a staunch pillar of the Christian faith[5], a lamp of virtue, the wisdom of the people, the joy and torch of the clergy, and so full was he of the light simile that, on the day on which his patron died, he dreamed that he saw him running hard with his skirts tucked up and a lighted candle in his hand, and when he tried to catch him up, the archbishop told him to cut the candle in two and keep half of it himself, and so he vanished from his sight[6].

The tears that Arundel shed at Oldcastle's trial prove him to have had a tender heart, but his memory has long been execrated as the initiator in England of the hateful policy of burning for misbelief[7]. Even orthodox contemporaries resented the strictness of his constitutions and believed that God tied his tongue[8], because he tied up God's

[1] Recuperasti sedem et gradum et libros tuos, Salutati, iii. 618.
[2] Salutati, iv. 158.   [3] Kopp, 280; G. Voigt, i. 203.
[4] He had found employment for him in the Chancery at Canterbury in 1411 when he had lost all his previous preferment and gave him the living of Merstham near Reigate (see page 113), Usk, 119, 122; see Wylie, i. 153. For permission granted to Adam of Usk (Dec. 6, 1413) to live in England, for which he paid 6s. 8d., see Cal. Pat. H. V, i. 125. For his previous tenure of the livings of Mitchel-Troy (Monmouthshire) in 1383, Babcary (Somersetshire) in 1385, and Castle-Combe (Wilts.) in 1396, see Wylie, i. 153, where his tithe had been forfeited owing to his adherence to the French and the rebels in Wales, Cal. Pat. H. IV, iv. 159, Jan. 24, 1410; also of a prebend in the church of Bangor, see Usk, pp. xv, xvii.
[5] Holinsh. iii. 545, calls him a "stoute prelate."   [6] Usk, 122, 302.
[7] He is called "the great originator of church persecution in this country" in Cassell, i. 521. Purey-Cust (ii. 360) defends him on the ground that the statute of 1401 was "a national Act" and he "had no choice in the matter."
[8] Gasc. 35, 61, 180, 181, for whom this particular form of gloating seems to have had a peculiar fascination; e.g. he says (p. 155) that Martin V was percussus in linguâ quae in quantitate intumescuit pendens extra os ejus. For similar stories of Wycliffe and

word and let no parson preach outside his parish church except by paying for a licence. He had been five times Chancellor of England[1] and 40 years a bishop either at Ely, York or Canterbury. To the two former cathedrals he had made handsome presents[2], and at Canterbury, besides giving £5 for the new cloister and £2 for the new chapter-house[3], he gave 1000 marks to the fund for rebuilding the nave, which had been taken down by Archbishop Sudbury 30 years before[4]. In this new nave he endowed a chantry to be called after his name[5]. He also built a lofty spire or cap to the old tower at the north-western corner of the church, and in this "Arundel steeple[6]" he placed five bells christened respectively The Trinity, Mary, Gabriel, Blase[7] and John, which were long known as the "Arundel Ring[8]." He likewise gave a mitre, a pastoral staff and two costly chalices to the cathedral, besides many valuable copes and ornaments, two missals and other

Innocent VII, see Wylie, iii. 14. For "paleseye of the tunge," see Arderne MS. (Emm. Coll., Camb.), f. cvii. For the Protestant view, see Foxe, iii. 403; Speed, 769 (ut scribitur); Parker, 276; Echard, 182; Kennet, i. 311 (who believes that his sore throat began when he was in the act of excommunicating Oldcastle); Gaspey, i. 295. "To the great destruction of Chrysten belieue," State Trials, i. 254. For picture of Archbishop Arundel preaching, from Harl. MS. 1319, see Strutt, Antiq. 45; Archaeologia, xx. 53; see Neale, 18, who dates it 1309 (*sic*), quoting British Critic, lxiv. 499.

[1] Gesta, 3; Wylie, i. 27. For dates, see Early Chanc. Proc. I. p. v.

[2] Bentham, 167; Fabr. Rolls, 309; Angl. Sacr. i. 665; Weever, 225; Purey-Cust, ii. 363. For his gift to Ely of a gold tabula with precious stones valued at 300 marks formerly belonging to Pedro, King of Castile, which he had bought from the Black Prince, see Lel. Coll. ii. 608.

[3] i.e. in Prior Chillenden's time, who died Aug. 15, 1411, Angl. Sacr. i. 142; Stone, 12, 18; Wylie, iii. 127. On Dec. 12, 1411, the Prior is John Wodnesburgh, Chillenden being *late* Prior, Lit. Cantuar. iii. 123. For his buildings, including the Checkers Inn, at the corner of Mercery Lane, and the Crown, see Angl. Sacr. i. 142; Walcott, Cant. 7; Wylie, iii. 127. For plan of the monastic buildings at Canterbury, see R. Willis, p. 48.

[4] He was beheaded by the mob on June 14, 1381, before he could begin the rebuilding. For picture of the murder, see Humphreys, Froiss. i. Plate xxv. The chief builder of the nave was Prior Thomas Chillenden, Stone, 19, 161, qui navem istius ecclesiae de novo fecit, from his epitaph in Weever, 230; Somner, i. App. 62; Woolnoth, 33; Walcott, Canterbury, 10, 11, 18, 19, 25, 27.

[5] "Arundell Chauntereye," Lit. Cantuar. iii. 123, where it is called oratorium seu canteria; Gibbons, 136; Somner, ii. App. 33; Woolnoth, 116.

[6] It was 100 feet high and was wrecked by a storm in Nov. 1703, Lel. Coll. vi. 88; do. Itin. vi. f. 3, p. 5; Angl. Sacr. i. 62; Gostling, 147, 148; Godwin, i. 125; Goodwin, 33; Parker, 276; Somner, ii. 23; Hook, iv. 409, 429, 526.

[7] For "Bysshop Blasy" that "haddist thy body with Iren kombes rent," see Lydg. Min. Po. 120. For "La Vie Seint Blese" among the books of Charles V see Delisle, Recherches, ii. 150.

[8] For a bell called Dunstan given by Prior Molash to the south-western tower called "Dunstan Steeple," see Woolnoth, 34. On Dec. 29, 1425, a priest named John Grove, who had been admitted as one of the monks of Christ Church, Canterbury, nine years before, was walking super valtas ecclesiae (i.e. the cathedral) *in novo opere campanilis australis*, when he missed his footing and was dashed to the ground breaking his neck and fracturing his skull. He died the same night, Stone, 12.

books, including a volume containing all the works of Gregory the Great[1], which was never to be taken out of the building[2] on pain of being forfeited to the king[3]. His executors sent to York for a copy to be made in wood of an effigy[4] of him which was in the minster there; but this, together with his monument, tomb and chantry, has long since disappeared[5], though the manse that he built for his two chantry priests[6] still stands on the south side of the cathedral close at Canterbury to this day[7].

On Feb. 27, 1414[8], the temporalities of the see of Canterbury were committed to the charge of John Wotton[9], master of the college at Maidstone, who was one of the archbishop's executors, and Richard Clitherow, who had been one of the merchants' Admirals in 1406[10], and on March 9, 1414[11], the castle and manor of Leeds in Kent,

---

[1] Seynt Gregour-le-pape, i.e. Gregory I (590–604). For "moral Gregore" as one of "the foure doctoris," see Lydg. Min. Po. 41, 56, the others being "hooly Geronimus," "blessed Austyn," and Ambrosius with "sugred eloquence"; see page 253.

[2] For devotional books to be chained in the choir of the cathedral at Troyes Aug. 27, 1421, see Arbois de Jubainville (1873), p. 243. In 1422 a hutcher supplies pourpitres et formes a seoir for the cathedral library at Troyes, also 8 verges de fer ès popitres esquelles sont encheinnés les livres, also 80 mors a ataicher les and 40 anneaux avec les toirez mit ès cheinnez des dis livres, ibid. 310. For a Psalter and a Dominical (see Du Cange, *s.v.*) chained in a caisse in the parish church at Marillac near Rodez in 1400, see Affre, Aveyron, ii. 394. Cf. un livre grant comme un missel qui de ij chaines d'or tenoit, Romania, xxxi. 345.

[3] Gilbert Umfraville as one of the executors lent this volume to Henry V, pour inspection avoir, who kept it at the Charterhouse at Sheen, but in his will ordered it to be returned to the monks at Canterbury, Rym. x. 317 (Feb. 6, 1424); Somner, ii. 33; Brayley and Britton, Houses of Parlt. 311; Antiquary, x. 226; Lannoy, Survey, 296; R. F. Williams, i. 225; Wylie, iii. 332. Not that he left it to the Charterhouse at his death, as Gasquet, Libraries, 5; do. Bible, 7.

[4] For carriage of it from York to London (3*s*. 4*d*.), see Fabric Rolls, 39; Purey-Cust, ii. 362, who thinks that this shows that preparations were being made for his burial in the minster at York. For a portrait of him in the possession of Lord de L'Isle and Dudley, see Catalogue, New Gallery Winter Exhibition, 1901–2, p. 3, where it is described as half-length with black cap, episcopal robes, furred tippet and cuffs with open book before him and gilt cushion, rose in right hand, with mitre and crosier in background. On panel 44′ × 36′. It was one of the portraits of the constables of Queenborough Castle (see Wylie, iv. 101) collected by Sir Edward Hoby, who was himself Constable from 1597 to 1617, see Gent. Mag. lvi. Pt. I. pp. 5, 6. These pictures were afterwards removed to Penshurst, cf. Wylie, iv. 122, note 7.

[5] Somner, i. 136; Walcott, Canterbury, 27.

[6] They were not to be beneficiati aliunde, but their stipends were fixed at £10 per annum each, to be drawn from the revenues of the church of Northfleet near Gravesend, the vicar of which was to have an income of 40 marks per annum, Lit. Cant. iii. 131.

[7] Somner, i. 136; Hasted, iv. 727; Walcott, 73.

[8] Rym. ix. 117.

[9] See page 293, note 7. He had been an executor under the will of Archbishop Courtenay (d. 1396), rector of Staplehurst and a canon of Chichester. He died on Oct. 31, 1417, and is buried in the collegiate church at Maidstone, Hasted, ii. 114, 565.

[10] See page 278, note 1.

[11] Pat. 1 H. V, vi. 9; 2 H. V, ii. 4; Priv. Seal 659/195, 196; Wylie, iv. 102. For grant of Leeds Castle by word of mouth to John Stiward, see Cal. Doc. Scot. iv. 171,

vacated by the archbishop's death, were granted to the king's grandmother, Joan Countess of Hereford[1], for the remainder of her life. But King Henry had already settled how the vacant see of Canterbury was to be filled[2], and he now promptly notified[3] the Prior and Convent that he recommended one of his confessors[4], Master Henry Chichele[5], for their choice.

That age was peculiarly full of instances of men of poor parentage who rose to positions of the highest eminence through the channels of the Church[6], and Chichele was too prominent a figure to escape the distinction of a legend, according to which he was picked up by Bishop Wickham of Winchester, as a poor boy herding sheep[7]. But though this fable must be abandoned, it is certain that Bishop Wickham meant his foundation at Winchester[8] to be a school for the "poor and needy," and that Henry Chichele

from Pat. 1 H. V, v. 8, March 10, 1414, where he receives £40 per annum as compensation in lieu of it.

[1] On Jan. 9, 1414, she had been allowed all the game (savagina, savagyne) in Hatfield Forest (Essex), Pat. 1 H. V, v. 29; Priv. Seal 659/176. See also Pat. 2 H. V, ii. 4.

[2] Hook (v. 26) speaks of Chichele's "mortification and surprise" on hearing of his election.

[3] For the *congé d'élire* dated Feb. 27, 1414, see Pat. 1 H. V, iv. 2. Not 1413, as Godwin, 125.

[4] Wals. ii. 300; Hypodig. 449.

[5] Magister Henricus Chichele, Wals. ii. 300; called "Sir Herry Chicheley" in Chron. Lond. 98; see Fuller, Worthies, ii. 163, 172; Godwin, 125 note. For his seal with representation of himself adoring the Trinity, see Birch, 75. In Halle (49) he is said to have been "a monk of the Carthusians," which is probably a mistake in copying from Pol. Verg. 440, where he is "ordine *cantuariensium* archiepiscoporum sexagesimus"; but the mistake has been perpetuated, e.g. "a Chertosin monke," Biondi, 105; "a monk of the cankered Carthusian sect," Watson, 111; also French, 102. Oman (Pol. Hist. 239) calls him "a far weaker and milder man" than Arundel, and refers to his "comparative insignificance and lack of truculent energy." Radford (62) calls him "a churchman in whom the lawyer and diplomatist gave place more and more to the bishop."

[6] e.g. Cardinal Nicholas Chrypffs or Krebs (b. 1401, d. 1464) known as de Cusa, i.e. of Cues near Berncastel on the Moselle, where he is buried. For his brass, see Creeny, 33. For other examples, see Pey Berland (Wylie, iii. 365), Gerson (Jadart, 46), D'Ailli, Netter of Walden (page 239). For J. A. Compagni, successively Bishop of Cotrone and Teramo (d. 1477, Gams, 879, 932, Eubel, ii. 101, 154), author of the Life of Andrea Braccio, quem rustica in agro mulier fessa opere suo sub lauro peperit, see Campanus, 433. For the legend of Cardinal Brogny, see Wylie, iii. 343. Lodge (517) thinks that "the only way in which an able and ambitious man could hope to rise from obscurity to eminence was by entering the church"; called "their one great chance of rising in the world," Duchesne, 259.

[7] Hook, v. 3; L'Estrange, 20; Clay, 81; J. Cole, 172, who supposes that his father was "an agriculturist," and that the sheep were on "Cheling's Leys" near Higham Ferrers on the strength of "an oral report." Cf. "of good yeoman stock," Fletcher-Walker, 176; Ollard-Crosse, 109. Not that his father was twice "Lord Mayor of London" and built the church of St Stephen's, Walbrook, as Leach, 198, who calls him "Sir Robert" and confuses him with his son Robert the rich London grocer; also Rashdall, New College, 91. See Wylie, iii. 137.

[8] App. E[1].

as a boy was one of the earliest of the scholars[1], but on
the other hand we know that his father was a substantial
clothier[2] at Higham Ferrers[3], and that his brothers,
William and Robert, attained to positions of great wealth
and high dignity in the City of London[4]. Long after the
archbishop's death there was a story[5] current that King
Henry VI once sent him a rag pie to remind him of his
lowly origin, to which insult he made a dignified reply, hoping
that the king would as far outdo the fame of his great
father as he himself had outshone his in honour and preferment. This pretty legend does not appear till the days of
the Commonwealth, when it was given by an anecdote-
monger[6], who had it apparently from one of the numerous
descendants of the Chichele family[7] who took care to tell
him that while on the father's side his famous ancestor
was the son of a "broker or draper" who rose to be a
cardinal (which of course is quite wrong), his mother was
descended from an archbishop and a cardinal also[8]. The
story has its interest not as yielding any solid historical
evidence as to the archbishop's family, but as pointing
to the inevitable break up of the landed class distinctions

---

[1] Wylie, iii. 138.
[2] Some called him a tailor, Buckler, Stemmata, vii; or a "yeoman," Ollard-Crosse, 109.
[3] For his brass with his wife Agnes placed in the church by Archbishop Chichele, see Cole, 51; F. Hudson; Druitt, 22; Wylie, iii. 135, note 6.
[4] Wylie, iii. 135–138. For Robert Chichele, Mayor of London 1411 and 1421, see Letter Book I, 97, 262; Wylie, iii. 137. For will of William Chichele (sheriff of London 1409–10, Letter Book I, 75, 88), dated at Stanwell May 9, 1425, see Cole, 45, 174. It was proved (not dated, as Wylie, iii. 136, note 7) in London on July 20, 1425. For his burial at Higham Ferrers, see Hardy and Page, i. 174. For his son William Chichele (Wylie, iii. 136, note 6) "serving in the Conclave" of Bishop Caterick at Con-stance on Nov. 11, 1417, see Papal Lett. vii. 146. For John Chichele [in addition to Wylie, iii. 136, note 1] see Claus. 1 H. V, 11 d; Fr. Roll 1 H. V, 21, July 15, 1413. For custody of the alien priory of St Clears in Carmarthenshire, a cell of the Cluniac Priory of St Martin des Champs in Paris (Monast. vii. 1056), granted to John Chicheley of London from Michaelmas, 1414, on payment of £15 per annum, see Pat. 3 H. V, ii. 33, Aug. 9, 1415; also a house in Harfleur in Jan. 1421, Ewald, xlii. 401; Carte, Rolles, i. 355. For John Chichele, Chamberlain of London in 1435, see Letter Book I, pp. 247, 266.   [5] Hook, v. 4.
[6] i.e. Richard Symonds (b. 1617, d. 1692), Harl. MS. 991, f. 72; Cat. p. 500, no. 27. For extracts from the volume, see Gent. Mag. lxvi. Pt. 1. 466 (1796); lxxxvi. Pt. 11. 498 (1816); Notes and Queries, Ser. 11. vii. p. 141, adding: "the mother of Mr Tho. Ch. was descended from Kemp, Bishop of London and Cardinal."
[7] For 120 English and 60 or 70 Scotch and Irish families claiming relationship with him on account of the next-of-kin fellowships at All Souls' College at Oxford, see Musgrave, 266.
[8] This may possibly refer to Emmeline Chiche, a grand-daughter of Robert Chichele, who married Thomas Kemp (d. 1520) of Ollantigh, Hasted, iii. 170; Buckler, Stemmata, p. 1.

through the progress of the intrusive traders of the towns[1].

After passing from the school at Winchester to Wickham's New College[2] at Oxford, Henry Chichele took subdeacon's orders in 1392[3]. He was ordained deacon on May 26, 1396[4], and at once became rector of the church of St Stephen on the Wallbrook in London, to which his elder brother Robert was afterwards a great benefactor[5]. He was fully priested on Sept. 23, 1396, and on Sept. 10 in the following year he exchanged his London living for that of East Hendred[6] near Wantage on becoming Archdeacon of Dorset[7]. I have already traced his prosperous progress on the ladder of ecclesiastical promotion[8] right up to his appointment as Bishop of St David's in 1408[9]. His subsequent career was mainly legal and diplomatic[10],

[1] Cf.

> Marchaundes in perile ride and gon
> Bryngen wynnyng, gold and fee
> Make high houses of lym and stone
> Mayntene burgh town and cite
> Welthe and worschip in here won
> And good houshold of gret plente. Kail, 66.

For town families ennobled at Rouen in the 14th and 15th centuries, see Chéruel, 11; also at Troyes, Batiffol, 21.

[2] For his name on the first page of the Hall Steward's book at New College, Oxford, which begins in 1387, see Hist. MSS. Rept. ii. 133; Rashdall, 91; Leach, 198, where it is spelt "Chechely."

[3] i.e. at the hands of John Dongan (Wylie, ii. 160; iii. 166), Bishop of Derry, who was then acting for the Bishop of London, Hennessy, cliv; Stubbs, Reg. 205; called a Cistercian named John who died in 1417, Cotton, Fasti, iii. 313. For statement that he held the living of Llanvarchall (i.e. Llanfarchell near Denbigh) in the diocese of St Asaph in 1391, see Tanner, 176; Hennessy, cliv; Dict. Nat. Biogr. x. 227.

[4] Oliver, Bishops, 95; do. Mon. 334; Wylie, iii. 138.

[5] Wylie, iii. 137; Lethaby, 206.

[6] Called Estherith in Harl. MS. 6955, f. 17, extracted by Matthew Hutton from Bishop Braybrook's Register, f. 153; called Estenrith or Eastentrath in Hennessy, cliv, or Estanrede, Estenreth, Inq. p. Mort. i. 54, 173; iv. 171, 242; Cal. Pat. H. VI, ii. 64. The manor of East Hendred was given to Reading Abbey by Mathilda the daughter of Henry I, Monast. iv. 29. On Nov. 14, 1403, Sir John Robtot became rector of Estenreth by exchange with Sir William Mey, Holmes, 43.

[7] Wylie, iii. 139.

[8] Ibid., to which should be added the prebend of Wellington (Lichfield) to which he was appointed on Oct. 2, 1400, Le Neve, i. 637; see also Hennessy, cliv; Le Neve, i. 296; Bund, 378, where he is patron and rector of Sherston Magna near Malmesbury. For a letter from the Bishop of Salisbury (dated at Sherborne Castle, July 20, 1402) notifying appointment of Master Henry Chichele, Doctor of Laws, to the prebend of Bedminster and Redcliffe, see Holmes, Reg. 34.

[9] He was consecrated at Siena, Wylie, iii. 139; not Vienna, as Fuller, Worthies, ii. 172. He was enthroned at St David's on May 11, 1411, Dict. Nat. Biogr. x. 227.

[10] On May 22, 1413, he and Bishop Stafford had been appointed on behalf of the king to hear an appeal from the Constable's military court in the cause of arms between Reginald Lord Grey of Ruthin and Sir Edward Hastings, Pat. 1 H. V, i. 30; Cal. Rot. Pat. 260; Wylie, ii. 236; Purey-Cust, i. 132, who gives the arms of Hastings in York Minster (p. 130). For order committing Edward Hastings, kt., to the Tower, see Claus. 1 H. V, 13, Nov. 20, 1413. On July 5, 1413, Bishop Chichele and William Hankford

and when at the age of 52[1] he entered on his 30 years tenure[2] of the see of Canterbury, he stands out as a trained and experienced politician[3] fully equipped to face the thousand troubles of one of the most troublous generations in his country's history.

After some technical fencing as to the respective rights of the King and the Pope the Chapter of Canterbury unanimously elected him as the king's nominee to succeed Archbishop Arundel on March 4, 1414[4]. Two of their number[5] announced the result to him on March 15, when he asked for a little time for consideration, but on the following day he informed them of his acceptance at the Bishop of Norwich's hostel in presence of the Duke of York and other notables. The king gave his assent on March 23[6] and the next day[7] notification of the election

were commissioned to inquire as to owners of goods captured on the high sea, Pat. 1 H. V, ii. 14 d.

[1] For his birth circ. 1362, see Wylie, iii. 138; Hoccleve, Min. Po. xxxiv; Courtenay, i. 161. For portrait of him at Lambeth Palace, see Duck, Frontispiece; Fletcher-Walker, 174; J. Cole, 172, who says that it is "probably taken from stained glass"; not "a window in the Great Hall," as Dict. Nat. Biogr. x. 230. In this he wears the pall and is giving the benediction, holding a cross in his left hand, Catalogue New Gallery, Winter, 1901–2. For a carving of him in a miserere at Higham Ferrers, see Cole, 43. For representation of him in Thomas Chandler's MS. at New College, Oxford, see Archaeologia, liii. 233; Vict. Co. Hist. (Hants.), ii. 292; Wylie, iii. 138, note 4; App. F[1]. For a picture of him in a window at All Souls' College, Oxford, see Vict. Co. Hist. (Hants.), ii. 262. For his arms on the seal of All Souls' College at Oxford, see Bloom, 240. For the library built by him over the Prior's chapel at Canterbury, demolished at the end of the 16th century, see R. Willis, 67; J. W. Clark, Libr. 25, 28; do. Care of Books, 100, 184; Godwin, i. 126. He died April 12, 1443, Fuller, Worthies, ii. 172; Monast. i. 86.

[2] Called 29 years, 4 months and 11 days in Stone, 30, who records his death at Lambeth April 12, 1443; see also Le Neve, i. 22; Stubbs, Reg. 84; Hennessy, cliv.

[3] He is called "the Politick Elect" in Echard, i. 182.

[4] Le Neve, i. 22. Not May 4, as Duck, 37; nor 1413, as Cole, 165.

[5] viz. William Molash and John Moland, Duck, 24. The former was almoner to the monks at Canterbury, Rym. x. 317, where he is *Friar* William Molash, monk (*moyne*). On July 12, 1415, he is warden and chaplain to the Prior, Somner, i. App. 64; called "discipulus" in Walcott, Cant. 11, who supposes him to have been clerk of the works during the building of St Michael's Chapel in the Cathedral. He became Prior on March 30, 1428, and died Feb. 19, 1438, Stone, 12, 21; Angl. Sacr. i. 144, 161, 184. His register was given to the Bodleian Library by Archbishop Sancroft, i.e. MS. Tanner, 165. It begins: Incipit registrum Willelmi Prioris quem dominus Henricus Chychele ultimo die Marcii 1428 prefecit in Canonem. It contains the obit of his predecessor John Wodenysborugh or Woodnesburgh, who was Prior from Sept. 3, 1411, till his death on Feb. 27, 1428, Angl. Sacr. i. 143 (f. 7), the creatio Willelmi Molassh Prioris (f. 9), a letter of William Pole Earl of Suffolk (f. 119), proceedings against Cardinal Beaufort pro legacione ejus contra consuetudines Regum Angliae (f. 136), several documents relating to the Hussites and a list of books in the library of St Augustine's, Canterbury (f. 162). For abstract of contents I am indebted to my friend Mr R. J. Whitwell. John Moland (or Molond, Goodwin, 36) was sacrist at the time of his death, which happened on Apr. 18, 1428, Stone, 14.

[6] Le Neve, i. 22.

[7] Pat. 2 H. V, i. 41; Rym. ix. 119; Godwin, 125; Papal Lett. vi. 454.

was despatched to Pope John XXIII, who issued a bull from Bologna conferring the archbishopric upon him on April 27, 1414[1]. The temporalities were granted to him on May 30[2], and his new title first occurs in connection with the probate of wills in the Prerogative Court of Canterbury on June 8, 1414[3]. The pall[4] or pallium, i.e. the scarf woven from white lamb's wool which had lain all night before the shrine of Saint Peter and St Paul at Rome, was brought across from the Pope by Richard Appleton a canon of York[5], and was conferred on him by Bishops Beaufort and Courtenay[6] at Sutton on July 24, 1416[7], in presence of the king, his brother Humphrey, the Earl of Warwick, and the Earl of March[8]. On receiving the pall the new archbishop took an oath of canonical obedience to the Pope[9] from whom he had received this

[1] Godwin, 125; Duck, 40; Le Neve, i. 22; Papal Lett. vi. 454; Lacy, xi.

[2] Rym. ix. 131; Godwin, 125; Le Neve, i. 22; Duck, 43; Hook, v. 27. Not May 13, as Spencer, 32. Goodwin (38) says that he swore allegiance at Leicester. Parker (276) that he paid 600 marks for half a year's rents that had fallen to the Exchequer during the vacancy of the see.

[3] J. Challoner Smith, I. p. xiii.

[4] See App. F[1].

[5] Duck, 44, i.e. he held the prebend of Bilton (York) from March 12, 1409, to April, 1423, Le Neve, iii. 173, and was one of the proctors who represented the northern clergy at the Council of Constance, Rym. ix. 342 (April 29, 1416), where he is to stay at Constance till the Council ends, though he had been ordered to return to England on Jan. 28, 1416; see also Goodwin, 3; Dacher, 31, where he is called Rupert Appulton, licentiate in canon law. For Richard and Roger Appleton (or Appulton), both auditors of accounts in the Exchequer, see Iss. Roll 4 H. V, Mich., Dec. 14, 1416, March 13, 19, 1417; do. 5 H. V, Pasch., July 15, 1417; Pat. 4 H. V, 27, Feb. 10, 1417; Exch. Accts. 48/16; Iss. Roll 6 H. V, Pasch., May 6, July 11, 15, 1418; Rec. Roll 6 H. V, Mich., March 11, 1419; Iss. Roll 7 H. V, Pasch., July 10, 1419; Pat. 8 H. V, 24, May 22, 1420. They are both auditors of the Duchy of Cornwall in Pat. 5 H. V, 19, July 10, 1417; Iss. Roll 6 H. V, Mich., Dec. 10, 1418. For Master Richard Appilton, clerk, see Claus. 4 H. V, 23, April 29, 1416. For Roger Appleton, buried in the church at Crayford near Dartford in Kent, together with his wife Agnes and their daughter Elizabeth, who married Henry Elham of Elham in the same parish, who also became an auditor in the Exchequer, see Hasted, i. 206, 209. For John Appleton, Master of the Mickle Hall at Oxford in 1404, see Le Neve, iii. 536; Wylie, ii. 482, note 7. In Rec. Roll 5 H. V, Pasch., Apr. 23, 1417, John Appulton, vicar of Grantham, lends 66s. 8d. to the king. For 20 marks per annum, granted July 6, 1416, to Thomas Appulton, Esq., see Claus. 4 H. V, 4, Nov. 29, 1416.

[6] Duck, 41. For mandate issued at Bologna May 9, 1414, from Pope John XXIII to the Bishops of Winchester and Norwich to assign the pallium to the new archbishop, see Papal Lett. vi. 443. For office of enthronization of an archbishop with the pallium, see Maskell, ii. 310–320; York Pontifical, 232; Barnes, 281. For pontifical used at Canterbury in Chichele's time now in the library at Trinity College, Cambridge, see York Pontifical, xli, with musical notes. A portion of it is in Add. MS. 6157, ibid. xlii.

[7] Le Neve, i. 22; Hook, v. 27; called July 29 in Parker, 276; Collier, iii. 302; Godwin, i. 126; Stubbs, Reg. 193.

[8] Called George in Duck, 41; Goodwin, 37.

[9] Duck, 42; Collier, iii. 302. For oath taken by Archbishop Courtenay on receiving the pall in 1382, see Conc. iii. 154.

emblem of authority, without which he could neither dedicate churches, consecrate bishops, ordain priests nor use the title of archbishop[1]. It was bestowed on him by the Pope at his installation and was to be buried with him at his death[2] and a fresh one must be issued to his successor, thereby ensuring a constantly recurring reminder of the dependence of "the Church of England[3]" on the central authority at Rome.

One of Archbishop Chichele's first public acts was the appointment on Aug. 1, 1414[4], of the learned canonist, William Lyndwood[5], as his official or vicar in the Court of Arches, which sat in the church of St Mary in West Cheap as the court of appeal for the province of Canterbury[6]. He was the son of a Lincolnshire woolman and was born at Linwood[7] near Market Rasen about 1375.

[1] In quo est plenitudo pontificalis officii cum patriarchalis vel archiepiscopalis nominis appellacione, Maskell, II. cliii; a sign of the plenitude of metropolitan power, Gent. Mag. ccix (1860), pp. 522, 524; called "apostolic power" in Hook, Dict. 556, i.e. since the Fourth Lateran Council (1215); "a sign or token of his jurisdiction," Gasquet, Pall, pp. 8, 11; "a token of union with Rome," ibid. 17.

[2] Debeat cum eo sepeliri, Maskell, II. cxlviii, who takes this as a proof of "the personal character of the ornament"; Legg, 128.

[3] For Ecclesia Anglicana, Ecclesia Angliae, l'Eglise d'Engleterre, see Rym. ix. 253, 429, 730; Conc. iii. 364, 391; Ann. 174; Dugd. Summons, 403; Stat. i. 316; ii. 70; iii. 493; Riley, Mem. 613; Gesta, 51; Kal. and Inv. ii. 106. "The holi Chirche of Yngelond," Cronin, 295, 296; Purvey in Forshall-Madden, i. 58; Gairdner, Lollardy, i. 44; Wylie, ii. 133, note 3, which is no evidence that it had any independent position, see Maitland, 44, who calls it "a dependent fragment whose laws had been imposed upon it from without." Cf. nedum Anglicanam sed et universalem ecclesiam, Add. MS. 24062, f. 143b, written in 1418. For "Ecclesia Scoticana," see Scotichron. iv. 1189, 1191. For "Ecclesia Romana," see page 254, note 6; Wylie, ii. 216, note 2.

[4] Godwin, 583; Fuller, Worthies, ii. 10; Dict. Nat. Biogr. xxxiv. 340.

[5] Called Lyndwode in Exch. Accts. 48/9; or Lynwode, Mirot-Déprez, lxi. 30, from Exch. Accts. 322/1, 2.

[6] Officialis curiae nostrae Cantuariensis de Arcubus London, Conc. iii. 389, 406 (Dec. 10, 1417, Feb. 11, 1423); Tanner, Bibl. 493 (1426); Hennessy, 311; also 1419, Bund, 391, 404; Amundesham, I. 250; II. p. xl; supremum in Angliâ fori ecclesiastici judicem ordinarium, Pits, 609; Bale, 561; auditor causarum, Tanner, Bibl. 494. Called the Archbishop's vicar-general in Dict. Nat. Biogr. x. 208; not that he was appointed Dean in 1426, as ibid. xxxiv. 340; Ollard-Crosse, 343. For decanatus de Arcubus jurisdictionis immediatae ipsius reverendi patris, see Conc. iii. 386. It was a probate court for wills where the property concerned lay in different dioceses, Bloom, 123. For Register "Marche" containing wills from 1401 to 1423 now in Somerset House, see J. Challoner Smith, I. pp. xii, xxxii.

[7] Where his father John (who died in 1419), his mother Alice Lynwode, and his brother John Lynwode, who was also a woolmonger (d. 1421), are buried. For their epitaphs, see Gough, ii. 52, 53 (showing that there were four sons altogether and three daughters); Archaeologia, xxxiv. 411; Brabner, iv. 28. For their brasses with inscriptions, see Lincolnshire Notes and Queries, ii (1891), Supplement, p. 42; Haines, i. 172, 202; ii. 119, 262; Macklin, 167, 170, who gives the brasses of other woolmen, several of them in Lincolnshire. For the brasses at Northleach near Cheltenham, see Cutts, Middle Ages, 522; Wylie, iv. 119; also at Dartford, Clinch, 52; Macklin, 158. For John Lyndewoode of the wapentake of Walscrop (Lincs.) (i.e. the Hundred of Walshcroft about Market Rasen) who lent money to the king on April 23, 1417, repaid on the same day,

He studied at both the universities of Oxford and Cambridge, at the latter of which his name occurs in connection with Pembroke Hall and Gonvile Hall[1], and he had secured a great reputation for learning[2]. From time to time he appears as the accredited spokesman for the clergy in the meetings of the Southern Convocation[3]. In 1417 he went to Normandy in the retinue of the Earl of Huntingdon[4], but he must have soon returned, for in the winter of the same year[5] he received a licence to preach anywhere within the Province of Canterbury, which has been supposed to be a counter-move on the part of the archbishop to check the activity of the itinerating Lollards. Amongst other preferment he held the living of Walton-on-the-Wolds near Loughborough and prebends in connection with the cathedrals of Hereford, Salisbury and Wells[6], and on Oct. 9, 1418, he became rector of the church of All Hallows in Bread Street, London, and retained that living till 1433[7]. In 1422 he spent eight months abroad on an embassy to the King of Portugal[8], and he was frequently employed on diplomatic missions[9] to Castile, Holland, Brittany and elsewhere. About the year 1430 he completed his great collection of glosses on the Constitutions of the Archbishops of Canterbury[10] which he dedicated to Archbishop Chichele, and by this learned work he established a lasting European fame. In Aug. 1442, he was

see Iss. Roll 5 H. V, Pasch. For Master John Lynwode (*sic*), Doctor of Laws, employed in appeal of John Saunders in the Admiralty Court, see Pat. 2 H. V, i. 14, July 1, 1414. In Pat. 2 H. V, i. 8, Oct. 3, 1414, William Lyndewod sues Joan widow of Thomas Wilton for a debt of £18.

[1] Lel. Coll. v. 402; Oudin, iii. 2334; Tanner, Bibliotheca, 493, 494; Archaeologia, xxxiv. 411; Fuller, Worthies, ii. 10; Venn, i. 8; Wylie, ii. 157.

[2] Literarum scientiâ morumque laudabilis vitae sufficienter insignitum, Conc. iii. 389.

[3] Organum procuratorum cleri gerens, Conc. iii. 395 (i.e. in 1419); Wake, 354.

[4] French Roll 4 H. V, 3, March 10, 1417; Ewald, xliv. 589.

[5] Conc. iii. 389; Lechler, ii. 306 [457].

[6] Tanner, Bibliotheca, 494; Le Neve, i. 509; W. A. Jones, 364, 414.

[7] Hennessy, 75. For list of his preferments, see ibid. lv; Vict. Co. Hist. London, i. 228.

[8] Exch. Accts. 48/9, where he is absent with Thomas Carew on an embassy in secretis negociis to the King of Portugal from Feb. 23 to Sept. 8, 1422; called March 3, 1422, to Sept. 14, 1422, in Mirot-Déprez, lxi. 30, from Exch. Accts. 322/1, 2. See also Carte, Rolles, ii. 246, Jan. 14, 1422; Archaeologia, xxxiv. 404.

[9] Carte, Rolles, ii. 260, 271 and *passim*; i.e. from Feb. 24, 1422, For. Accts. 1 H. VI, E.

[10] It was written between 1423 and 1429, Gough, ii. 53, i.e. finished in 1430, Maitland, Lyndwood, 447, who calls it "a text-book for beginners" (p. 455); do. Canon Law, 5, 33, who refers to his opinions as "stark exuberant papalism" (pp. 47, 99); do. Lyndwood, 477.

appointed Bishop of St David's[1]; he made his will on Oct. 21, 1446[2], and dying soon afterwards was buried in the chapel of St Mary[3] in the crypt[4] under St Stephen's Chapel[5] in the Palace at Westminster, where his body was accidentally discovered in 1852[6].

Some modern writers have discovered that there is a complicated constitutional question as to whether Archbishop Chichele owed his elevation to the choice of the Chapter or the King by provision of the Pope[7]. On his tomb[8] in Canterbury Cathedral it is recorded that he was "postulated[9]" to the archbishopric, and when Lyndwood dedicated his *Provinciale* to him he styled him Archbishop "by the grace of God," a courtesy which is supposed to have survived in the title of "Your Grace" to the present day[10]; though it is quite well established that the phrase "Dei Gratiâ" was common enough as an official appendage to a bishop's title[11], and "your Grace" was even a mere everyday conventional civility amongst strangers meeting accidentally on the high road[12].

---

[1] Le Neve, i. 297.

[2] It was proved Nov. 28, 1446, Hennessy, lv; J. T. Smith, 113; Archaeol. Journ. ix. 120.

[3] Called the under-chapel in J. T. Smith, 113; the undercroft or St Mary in the Vaults, Lethaby, Palace, 181.

[4] For picture of the crypt taken in 1842, see Benham-Welch, Plate 16; also Wright and Smith, 7.

[5] See App. G[1].

[6] Archaeological Journ. ix. 120 (1852); Journ. of Archaeol. Assoc. viii. 62, 63, 70–72 (1853); W. H. Jones, Fasti, 364; Wylie, iv. 111, note 3.

[7] Parker, 276; Spencer, 32; Goodwin (37) thinks that "slighting the power of the king he (Chichele) would refer the whole business to the Pope."

[8] For the tomb with effigy and skeleton (called "a disagreeable practice" in Druitt, 23), see M. Parker, 427 (edn. 1729); Gough, ii. 129; Somner, ii. 34; Woolnoth, 91; Musgrave, 266; Kingsford, 274.

[9] In archiep'm postulat', Godwin, 126; Gough, ii. 30; Le Neve, i. 22. In Elmham, Lib. Metr. 132, the word "postulatus" is given in an explanatory note as the equivalent of "datus"; cf. "demanded to his see," Le Neve, i. 22. Godwin (136) thinks that this term was used because by the Canon Law a bishop when once consecrated could not undo his bond and be consecrated over again, but see Murray, Dict., s.v. *Postulation*, also the letter of the University of Paris in Aug. 1420, recommending Pierre Cauchon to the Chapter at Beauvais for their choice as bishop, quem tantâ tantorum principum (i.e. Charles VI, Henry V and the Duke of Burgundy) concordiâ peti et a domino nostro sanctissimo (i.e. Martin V) *postulari* videtis. For the "postulation" of Caterick when translated to be Bishop of Exeter, see Hist. MSS. Rept. Var. Coll. iv. 41. Pat. 8 H. V, 25, May 1, 1420, shows that at the translation of Edmund Lacy to the bishopric of Exeter, the Dean and Chapter *postularunt*, the words of the royal assent being postulacioni assensum adhibemus.

[10] Hook, v. 27.

[11] Selden, 124; Spelman, Gloss. 166; Somner, i. 136.

[12] Cf. sauve vostre grace, Stengel, 7; sauf your grace, Caxton, Dial. 28; sauf la reverence du roi, Monstr. 409; Le Fèvre, i. 304; sauve vostre très noble discretion,

The vacancy caused at St David's by Chichele's elevation was filled by the appointment of John Caterick[1], Archdeacon of Surrey[2], who was then absent in Italy, where he had been appointed a papal notary on July 7, 1409[3]. He was consecrated Bishop of St David's[4] by Pope John XXIII at Bologna on April 27, 1414[5], on the understanding that he should retain all his existing benefices till he should be promoted to a fatter see[6]. He received the temporalities on June 2 following[7] and made his profession of obedience on July 18. But just as he had accepted the poor bishopric of St David's the fatter see of Lichfield fell vacant by the death of John Burghill[8] in

Gilliodts van Severen, 348; saving his worship, conscience and title, Ord. Priv. Co. ii. 354.

[1] Called "Keteryk," Lacy, xix ; or "Kedryk," Usk, 123; or "Catrik" in Rec. Roll 6 H. V, Pasch., April 8, 1418 (where he is *late* Bishop of St David's), also in official documents, see Gilliodts van Severen, 251, 288, 289, 301, 321; and on his seal, Add. Chart. no. 12,508 (Aug. 21, 1411); Lacy, p. ix; and in his will, ibid., and Wylie, ii. 345. Called "Catherike" or "Caric" in Vowell, G. ii; expanded in Izacke, 71, into two bishops, whom he calls "John Catherick" and "James Carey." Not "Keterich," as Speed, 775; Goodwin, 38; or "Ketterich," as Le Neve, i. 296; Tyler, ii. 49; Dict. Nat. Biogr. xxxi. 78. For account of him, see Wylie, ii. 344; iii. 44, note 1; Lacy, pp. ix–xix, where full information is given as to his ecclesiastical benefices, though the details of his diplomatic career are incomplete. For John Catrick of Leeming near Bedale, see Pat. 2 H. V, iii. 9 d, Feb. 17, 1415.

[2] Conferred upon him by his friend Bishop Beaufort on Nov. 12, 1410, see document dated in manerio nostro de Suthwerke in Lacy, p. x. When Bishop Beaufort was translated to Winchester in March, 1405 (Wylie, iii. 264), Catrick was made Chancellor of that diocese, and it was through Bishop Beaufort that he had been made Treasurer of Lincoln Cathedral, which office he evidently held before March 25, 1406 (Wylie, iii. 44), see Papal Letters, vi. 14, 39, Nov. 11, 1404, Jan. 18, 1406, where a portable altar is granted to him. He also received the Lincoln prebends of Brampton in 1401, Cropredy in 1402 called Cropri in Papal Letters, vi. 39, Nov. 11, 1404), and Stow Longa in 1406, Le Neve, ii. 117, 140, 214; Dict. Nat. Biogr. xxxi. 78; Lacy, p. ix. At the time that he was priested by Bishop Beaufort in the Abbey at Peterborough on Sept. 21, 1398, he held the vicarage of Norham on the Tweed. He subsequently obtained the prebends of Highworth near Swindon (Sarum) in 1406 (Wylie, iii. 44) and Oswaldwick (York) in 1407. On Nov. 6, 1406, he was made Master of the Sandon Hospital (Manning and Bray, ii. 751; Monast. vii. 676; not Sandown, as Dict. Nat. Biogr. xxxi. 78; Lacy, p. ix) at Esher in Surrey, which he is said to have exchanged for the rectory of Crick near Rugby, though it is clear that he held this rectory as early as Nov. 11, 1404, Papal Letters, vi. 39, where it is called "Crek." One of the executors of his will was Walter Peres, rector of Crick, Lacy, p. xv.

[3] Papal Letters, vi. 155.

[4] Not of Hereford, as Wakeman, 153; nor of Worcester, as Towle, 278.

[5] Papal Letters, vi. 454; Le Neve, i. 296; Lacy, p. xi; Stubbs, Reg. 85; Oliver, Bishops, 99.

[6] Pinguiorem, Papal Letters, vi. 443, 473; Lacy, xi.

[7] Rym. ix. 135.

[8] Presul Cestrensis obiit frater Jacobita, John Catric sequitur a Menevense vacans, Elmham, Lib. Metr. 103. In Rym. ix. 161, he is referred to as dead on Oct. 13, 1414. Usk (123) calls him vir avarissimus and tells a story of how he kept a lot of money in a hole in his room and how two magpies wanted to build there and pitched it all out among the trees in the garden.

May, 1414[1]. The *congé d'élire* was issued on June 20, 1414[2], and as Caterick was one of the English representatives appointed to attend the coming Council at Constance[3] it was thought to be a suitable arrangement that he should have the richer table[4]. Accordingly on Oct. 13, 1414, the king granted him the custody of the temporalities of the see of Lichfield to enable him to keep up his position[5], and he was formally translated from St David's by a document issued from the papal court on Feb. 1, 1415[6]. On April 9[7], the Cardinals at Constance remitted the dues that he should have paid at his translation, and the temporalities were definitely granted to him as Bishop of Lichfield on May 15[8]. Thereupon he at once returned to England and received the spiritualities for Lichfield on professing obedience to the Archbishop of Canterbury on June 21, 1415[9], but, as much of his subsequent life was spent abroad, the duties at Lichfield were mostly performed by his vicar Robert Mulfield[10], Bishop of Killaloe[11].

[1] Angl. Sacr. i. 451; Stubbs, Reg. 82, 226.
[2] Pat. 2 H. V, i. 16.
[3] Finke, Forsch. 256. Called orator pro rege specialiter deputatus, Baumgarten, cxviii. For letters of attorney issued for him Oct. 16, 1414, see Rym. ix. 163; not that the Bishops of Lichfield and St David's at Constance were two separate persons, as Monast. i. 107.
[4] Lacy, xi. For mensa (i.e. personal allowance) for the scribe who wrote out Abbot Litlington's missal at Westminster in 1383, see Robinson-James, p. 7. Cf. pro tabulâ pueri sui, Oliver, Mon. 125, 126.
[5] In relevamen status sui, Rym. ix. 161; Le Neve, i. 552.
[6] In curiâ Romanâ, For. Accts. 5 H. V; Le Neve, i. 396, 552; Hardt, v. 15; Lacy, p. xii; Papal Letters, vi. 350. He is called Bishop of Lichfield in Mansi, xxvii. 637, or "Johannes de Lichfeldia" in Glassberger, 250; Add. MS. 24062, ff. 195, 196, Aug. 8, 1419; also Bishop of Lichfield and Chester in a document among the Chapter Records at Exeter, Hist. MSS. Rept. Var. Coll. iv. 41, where his name is spelt "Catteryk." On May 28, 1415, the see of Lichfield is still vacant and under a custos spiritualitatis, Rym. ix. 256 [254], but on June 16, 1414, Caterick is said to have been translated to it, ibid. ix. 268.
[7] De communi et minuto servitiis, Baumgarten, cxviii.
[8] Rym. ix. 248, where he is stated to have been long at Constance and at great expense.
[9] Angl. Sacr. i. 452; Lacy, p. xii, quoting Reg. Chichele, Vol. i. f. 8; Le Neve, i. 552; Hardt, v. 16; Lenz, 71. He was present at Claydon's trial in St Paul's on Aug. 17, 1415 (page 290). For his assent to a document at Westminster Palace dated Nov. 8 [1415], see Gilliodts van Severen, 361. He attended a council at Westminster on Jan. 30, 1416, Ord. Priv. Co. ii. 187, and took part in the consecration of Bishop Wakering at St Paul's on May 31, 1416, Stubbs, Reg. 85.
[10] He was a Cistercian from Meaux in Holderness, Cotton, Fasti, i. 399. For the library at Meaux, see J. W. Clark, 24.
[11] Papal Letters, vii. 8, Dec. 1, 1418, i.e. from Sept. 9 or 11, 1409, to July 6, 1418, Eubel, i. 305. For Walter Bullock as custos spiritualitatis for the see of Lichfield on Sept. 13, 25, 1414, see Rym. ix. 158; Pat. 2 H. V, ii. 28. He received the prebend of Eccleshall on Oct. 19, 1405, which he exchanged for that of Dernford on Apr. 21, 1431, Le Neve, i. 596, 601. He also held the prebend of Scamblesby (Lincoln) from 1405

In Aug. 1416, Bishop Caterick set out again for Constance[1], and as he rested for the night at the George Inn at Dartford on Aug. 6, he took the precaution to make his will[2]. In this he left to Bishop Beaufort 12 silver-gilt tasses[3] which he had received from the King of France and the Duke of Berry in one of his numerous embassies to France[4], with many gifts to his two sisters Maud and Margaret, to the wife and daughter of John Hyrnmonger, and all his law-books and service-books to his nephew Robert[5]. The residue, after providing for masses for his soul and presents to his servants, was to be given to poor farmers, whose beasts had died in murrain or who had suffered similar losses from other causes. He remained at Constance till the death of Bishop Hallum, which took place there on Sept. 4, 1417[6], and on the following

till 1431, Le Neve, ii. 203. In Ancient Corrdce, Vol. lvii. no. 43, he is acting as vicar in spirituals for the diocese of Lichfield on Aug. 30, 1418. He was Archdeacon of Derby in 1417 and 1428, Le Neve, i. 576; ii. 203; and was one of the executors of Caterick's will, Lacy, p. xv.

[1] Rym. ix. 374. He was at Constance on Oct. 31, 1417, Wals. ii. 319. He was still at the Papal Court on Dec. 30, 1417, and May 21, 1418, Papal Letters, vii. 41, 48.

[2] For text, see Lacy, p. xiv, from Reg. Chichele, i. 328. He subsequently confirmed this will at Florence on Dec. 21, 1419 (Lacy, p. xv), in the presence of three esquires, viz. William Burley (see Wylie, iv. 145), who appears to have been back in England by March 28, 1420 (Lacy, p. xviii), Thomas Gretham, and Giles Swinton of the dioceses of York, Lincoln and Lichfield respectively, besides other Englishmen. The will was proved at Lambeth on Feb. 10, 1420, Lacy, p. xv.

[3] Cf. duas pecias (i.e. cups, Baildon, Inv. 171; Halliwell, ii. 853) sive tassas, Lacy, p. xvii; Cent. Dict., s. v.

[4] For six such cups presented to him by the Duke of *Burgundy* in 1411, see Wylie, iv. 57.

[5] i.e. Robert Catrik or Keteryk of Redehall (Yorks.), who was born in 1397, was admitted as one of Bishop Wickham's scholars at Winchester in 1409, studied law at Geneva in 1418 (Lacy, p. xviii), received the prebend of Weeford (Lichfield) on May 1, 1416 (Le Neve, i. 635), and was presented by Bishop Beaufort to the living of Witney in Oxfordshire.

[6] i.e. the Translation of St Cuthbert, as proved from the inscription on his brass in the cathedral at Constance:

> Festum Cuthberti Septembris mense vigebat
> In quo Roberti mortem Constantia flebat.
> Archaeol. xxx. 432; li. 364.

Not fiebat, as Le Neve, ii. 602. See also Wals. ii. 326; Ciac. ii. 813 (who calls him "Alun" and gives the arms of England as his arms); Gams, 197; Eubel, i. 32, 458; Ord. Priv. Co. ii. 237; Ramsay, i. 256, though the same inscription wrongly gives the year as 1416, i.e.

> Anno milleno tricent' octuageno
> Sex cum ter deno,

but this is unquestionably a mistake. He was buried on Sept. 13, 1417. For his will dated Aug. 23, 1417, proved Sept. 10, 1417, see Le Neve, ii. 602, from Reg. Chichele, f. 21, also Wylie, ii. 345, note 2. For the *congé d'élire* dated Oct. 11, 1417, see Le Neve, ii. 602. The brass appears to have been worked in England subsequently, see Tyler, ii. 49; Waller, p. iii; Druitt, 57; Baxter, 33. Richental, quoted in Archaeologia, xxx. 434, dates his death an dem vierten tag des ersten Herbstmonats (i.e. Sept. 4) but calls the day Zinstag (i.e. Tuesday) which fell on Sept. 7 in 1417. He states that he died at

day[1] Cardinal Giordano Orsini, on behalf of the College of Cardinals, sent an autograph letter to the King of England recommending Caterick as Hallum's successor in the see of Salisbury. But in spite of this high testimonial, in which he is described as the best and most upright of men working night and day for the union of the Church and that no tongue could rightly tell his worth, he failed to secure the appointment, which fell to John Chandler[2], Dean of Salisbury, who was chosen Bishop of that diocese on Nov. 15, 1417[3]. But shortly afterwards, on the death of Bishop Stafford, Caterick was made Bishop of Exeter by Pope Martin V at Florence on March 20, 1419[4]. He never again, however, returned to England but died at Florence on Dec. 28, 1419[5], and was buried there under a white marble slab[6] in the church of Santa Croce[7].

8 stund nach mittag (i.e. 8 p.m.) in d' festin Gotliebe (in castro Gotlieben, Le Neve, ii. 602; Janicke, 341) and that Sigismund (unser herr d'Künig) was present at his funeral. In a letter written at Constance soon after Oct. 22, 1417, is a reference to "my lord of Salisbury that *was*," quoted in Scottish Hist. Rev. VII (1910), p. 21; Ord. Priv. Co. ii. 236. For the funeral oration, see J. M. Vidal. Capes (161) thinks that Hallum was one of the few men of his time who opposed religious persecution. For his sermon at Pisa Apr. 30, 1409, see Serravalla, xlv, from Arch. Vat. Manual Concil. Pis. domini Thomae Troteti, Vol. 85, Arm. 63, fol. 67; Wylie, iii. 377.

[1] Rym. ix. 487, from MS. Cleop. E. 2; Tyler, ii. 49.

[2] Called "Jon Chaundler," in Elmham, Lib. Metr. 163. On Aug. 7, 1401, he was rector of Hampstead-Marshall near Newbury, which living he exchanged for Quennington near Fairford in Gloucestershire.

[3] The *congé d'élire* was issued on Oct. 11, 1417, Le Neve, ii. 602. In Pat. 5 H. V, 12, Oct. 28, 1417, the see of Salisbury is vacant. The royal assent was given to Chandler's appointment on Nov. 22, 1417, ibid. 5 H. V, 11, where he is dean, canon and frater of Salisbury. This choice was confirmed on Dec. 7, 1417, Le Neve, ii. 602; called Dec. 17 in Chancery Warrants, Ser. I. 1364/41, formerly called Letters Missive. He was consecrated at Lambeth by Archbishop Chichele, assisted by Bishops Langley, Zouche, Nicole and Lacy on Dec. 12, 1417, Stubbs, Reg. 86; Eubel, i. 458 (not Sept. 16, as Gesta, 117 note), and on Dec. 17, 1417, King Henry wrote from Falaise to the Duke of Bedford to deliver the temporalities to him, which was done on Jan. 8, 1418, Rym. ix. 539. He was installed on Apr. 17, 1418, Le Neve, ii. 603, when the citizens presented him with 10 marks, Hist. MSS. (Var. Coll.) Rept. iv. 194. For menu at his inauguration feast in three courses, see Two Cookery Books, 60.

[4] Papal Letters, vii. 134; Lacy, p. xiii. Cf. J. Bishop of Exeter *nuper* racione nove creationis vestre, Claus. 8 H. V, Nov. 5, 1420.

[5] From his epitaph, Lacy, p. xiii. Not Dec. 26, as Oliver, Bishops, 99; nor Jan. 11, 1419 (i.e. 1420), as Izacke, Catalogue. He is called nominis umbra, Reynolds, 125.

[6] A small copy of this may be seen in the Cathedral Library at Exeter. On this he is described as ambassiator serenissimi domini regis Anglie, Oliver, Bishops, 100; Freeman, 194; Lacy, p. xiii.

[7] Lassells, i. 132; Le Neve, i. 374. Not San Lorenzo as Monumental Brass Society Transactions, iii. 114, Druitt, 57; nor at Avignon, as Izacke, Catalogue, with his arms and motto ("Fato Prudentia major") and his arms 3 cats argent on a sable shield, though called fleurs de lis in Izacke. For his seal with a shield charged with 3 cats, see Add. Charter 12508 (where they are distinctly animals though quite unlike the arms in Izacke); Lacy, p. xi. This is attached to a document dated at Calais Aug. 21, 1411, see Wylie, iv. 26 note.

Bishop Caterick was succeeded at St David's by Stephen Patrington, the king's confessor[1], who was consecrated in All Saints' Church at Maidstone by Archbishop Chichele and Bishops Courtenay and Clifford on June 19, 1415[2]. Two years later he was called[3] to the see of Chichester, which had been vacant since the death of Robert Reade on June 23, 1415[4]. Keepers of spiritualities and temporalities were appointed on June 29 and July 1, 1415[5], and the *congé d'élire* was issued on July 2[6], but no appointment followed on account of the recent deposition of the Pope by the Council at Constance[7], and for a long time afterwards the see is always spoken of as vacant[8]. Thus, although Patrington was "called" to be Bishop of Chichester and was actually in possession of the temporalities from

---

[1] Page 236.   Meneviae Stephanus Patryngton praesul habetur, Elmham, Lib. Metr. 163.

[2] Stubbs, Reg. 85; Le Neve, i. 296; Fascic. lxxvii; Fleury, vi. 337.   He had been provided to the see of St David's on Feb. 1, 1415 (Papal Letters, vi. 350), and received custody of the temporalities on April 6, 1415 (Rym. ix. 217), which were finally granted to him on June 16, 1415 (Rym. ix. 268).

[3] Hic fuerat sedi Cicestrensi vocitatus, Elmham, Lib. Metr. 162; praesul successor fit Menevensis ei, ibid.

[4] Stubbs, Reg. 82.   For account rendered by the keeper of the temporalities of Chichester from the death of Bishop Reade June 23, 1415, see For. Accts. 5 H. V; G. J. Turner, Lincoln's Inn, p. 31.   Reade appears to have been incapacitated on account of his health for some time before his death.   His register ends on April 14, 1414 (Sussex Archaeological Collections, xvii. 199), and he made his will on Aug. 10, 1414, but it was not proved till July 6, 1415, Dict. Nat. Biogr. xlvii. 361; not 1414, as Genealogist, vi. 217.   He was a Dominican, and had been confessor to Richard II.   For a letter from him to Henry IV written in his hostel in London March 5, 1406, see Roy. Lett. ii. 24, where it is wrongly dated 1405.   In this he is attending the Parliament that met at Westminster on March 1, 1406, and explains that it has been impossible to bring with him the episcopal registers as required propter locorum distantiam quibus praedecessorum nostrorum registra separatim in nostrâ dioecesi fuerunt et sunt reposita.   For pardon dated July 16, 1414, for the escape of William Fretton from his prison at Amberley, see Pat. 2 H. V, ii. 34.   Fretton is called late clerk of Combs near Stowmarket who became a travelling-man (see Wylie, iv. 365) and was convicted of felony in Sussex, Pat. 2 H. V, i. mm. 1, 19, July 26, 1414.   For aliis hominibus mendicantibus qui se nominant "travelyngmen," see Pat. 5 H. V, 26 d, May 23, 1417.   Also travaillyngman, Exch. Accts. 215/2; Pat. 6 H. V, 28, June 1, 1418 (i.e. in comitiva of John Talbot going to Ireland).   See page 275.

[5] Pat. 3 H. V, i. 3; Le Neve, i. 244.

[6] Pat. 3 H. V, i. 4; also Pat. 3 H. V, ii. 39, June 21, 1415, in Le Neve, i. 244; also on Oct. 11, 1415, Pat. 5 H. V, 15.

[7] Tardantur bullae schismate stante diu, Elmham, Lib. Metr. 132.

[8] e.g. Feb. 24, Sept. 30, Oct. 15 and 22, 1417, Pat. 5 H. V, 15; Privy Signet Bills, temp. H. V, quoted in Le Neve, i. 244; Rym. ix. 505.   For custos spiritualitatis at Chichester Nov. 4, 1415; Nov. 8, 1416; Jan. 6, Oct. 29, 1417, see Pat. 3 H. V, ii. 30; do. 4 H. V, 7, 8; do. 5 H. V, 11.   For temporalities still in the king's hands June 3, 1416, see Rec. Roll 4 H. V, Pasch.; also Sept. 30, Nov. 2, 1417, Chancery Warrants, Ser. I. 1364 (39, 40).   For Archbishop Chichele as custos of Chichester on May 10, 1417, see Rec. Roll 5 H. V, Pasch.   For his official progress through the diocese in September of that year, see Cleop. E. II. f. 334.

Michaelmas, 1416[1], yet he never formally took over the
spiritual duties[2], and up to the day of his death, and even
after his death, he is always spoken of as Bishop of St
David's[3], while Chichester still continued to be a vacant
see for some time after he was dead[4]. Just as he was
preparing to join the king in Normandy[5] he died in the
White Friars Priory[6] on the south side of Fleet Street
in London on Dec. 22, 1417[7], and was buried in the choir
of their church[8]. He was succeeded at St David's by Benet
Nicole, Bishop of Bangor[9], who received the temporalities
on Jan. 1, 1418[10].

Another episcopal vacancy had occurred through the
death of Alexander Totington, Bishop of Norwich, which

[1] By writ dated Aug. 25, 1416, For. Accts. 5 H. V; Le Neve, i. 296; Rym. ix. 384;
Elmham, Lib. Metr. 162. For *late* keepers of temporalities of the see of Chichester,
see Ord. Priv. Co. ii. 207, Feb. 1417, i.e. John Blownham, John Stras (or Scrace, For.
Accts. 5 H. V), John Lylye and Walter Bolne (or Belney). The first of these, John
Blownham, was Precentor of Chichester (Le Neve, i. 265), and had been Treasurer of
the Cathedral in 1410, 1411 (ibid. 268). In Rec. Roll 4 H. V, Mich., Dec. 14, 1416,
he is *late* keeper of the temporalities of Chichester with others. Their account contains
payments in connection with the cathedral and a hospital adjoining the city (probably
St Mary's, see Monast. vi. 776), also for wages of bailiffs, parkers, warners, foresters,
haywards and reapers of various manors, the total receipt from June 23, 1415 (cf. page
311, note 4), to Sept. 29, 1416, being £530. 6s. 8½d., see For. Accts. 5 H. V.
[2] Idem postulatus vester (he is so called in his epitaph in Weever, 438) decessit ante
ipsius ecclesiae Cicestren. assecutionem, Pat. 5 H. V, 5, Feb. 3, 1418; Rym. ix. 537.
Quâ dignitate nunquam gavisus est, Leland, Comment. 430, who adds causa licet mihi
incerta est; though in Monast. vi. 1159 he is said to have been appointed Bishop of
Chichester in December, 1417; called September, 1417, in Leland, Script. 430; Weever,
438; Villiers, ii. 765.
[3] e.g. on May 31, 1416, Stubbs, Reg. 85; also Nov. 10, 1417, Devon, 353. In Ellis,
Orig. Lett. Ser. 1. i. 3, Archbishop Chichele writing on Feb. 16, 1418, calls him "my
brother of Seint David"; though in a letter written to the Pope urging the appointment
of Henry Ware as his successor Patrington is referred to as ultimus ejusdem ecclesiae
(i.e. Chichester) episcopus, Add. MS. 24062, f. 143 b. Ware was appointed Bishop of
Chichester on July 17, 1418, Stubbs, Reg. 86.
[4] e.g. March 28; May 19, 30; June 1, 1418, Chancery Warrants, Ser. 1. 1364 (47,
53); Pat. 6 H. V, 21, 28, 31.
[5] For money paid for hire of ships and boats for passage of himself and his familia to
Normandy, see Devon, 353 (Nov. 10, 1417).
[6] For the choir, steeple and presbytery built by Robert Mascal (not Marshall) Bishop
of Hereford, who was buried there in 1420, see Stow, 148; Monasticon, viii. 1572. For
previous benefactions of Robert Knolles, see Wylie, iii. 238; called "the ffreres Karmes,"
Kingsford, Chron. 65.
[7] Le Neve, i. 244; not Sept. 22, as Harl. MS. 3838, f. 31 [33]; Leland, Comment.
429; Pits, 597, who gives a list of his works; Weever, 438, from his epitaph; nor Nov. 22,
as Stubbs, Reg. 85; Gams, 185; Eubel, i. 194. For his will dated Nov. 16, 1417, proved
Dec. 29, 1417, see Genealogist, vi. 133; Le Neve, i. 244, 296.
[8] For his epitaph, see Weever, 437.
[9] Hinc Bangorensis Praesul datus est Menevensi, Elmham, Lib. Metr. 132; called
Benedictus, ibid. 162. Called Nicolls in Le Neve, i. 101, 296 (who says that he was
appointed to St David's on Dec. 15, 1417); Gams, 181; Eubel, i. 130.
[10] Le Neve, i. 101, 296, finally granted by the king in a letter written at Bayeux to
the Chancellor on March 16, 1418, Ancient Corrdce, xliii. 158.

took place on April 28, 1413[1]. His body was buried in
the Lady Chapel of Norwich Cathedral[2]; the custody of
the temporalities was entrusted to Sir Thomas Erpingham[3]; the *congé d'élire* was issued on May 3, 1413[4], and
the vacancy was filled by the appointment of one of the
king's most trusted friends and comrades[5], Richard
Courtenay[6], who was then Dean of Wells[7] and Receiver or
Treasurer of the King's Chamber[8]; the temporalities were
granted to him on Sept. 11, 1413[9], and he was consecrated
by Archbishop Arundel on Sept. 17[10] in a chapel belonging
to the king in Windsor Park[11]. He was the second son of
Philip Lord Courtenay, and grandson of Hugh Courtenay,
Earl of Devon[12], and had been carefully trained by his late
kinsman, Archbishop William Courtenay[13], who in 1396 left
him 100 marks in his will besides several books, in case
he should become a clerk, and his best mitre for use if he
should ever rise to be a bishop. Time had now fulfilled
the forecast, though during his short tenure of the bishopric
he was too constantly about the king's person or too busy
with public affairs[14] both at home and abroad to be able to

[1] Stubbs, Reg. 84; Monast. vi. 2; Le Neve, ii. 465; Gams, 195; Eubel, i. 389. For
his will dated April 20, 1413, proved May 4, 1413, see Reg. Arundel, ii. 166; Genealogist,
v. 212; Godwin, 438. For his executors, Thomas Dalling, William Bernham, John
Thornham (clerks), Edmund Oldhall (esquire), and William Paston, see Pat. 5 H. V, 31,
Feb. 7, 1418.   [2] Angl. Sacr. i. 416; Blomefield, iii. 526; Godwin, 438.
[3] Rec. Roll 1 H. V, Pasch., July 24, 1413.
[4] Priv. Seal 658/18; Pat. 1 H. V, i. 37.
[5] Regi fidissimus, Wals. ii. 309; unius de amantissimis et praecarissimis suis, Gesta,
26; regiis continue et consiliis putabatur prae omnibus gratiosus...ex amore tenerrimo,
ibid. 27; Chron. Giles, 24; Godwin, 438; Wylie, iii. 112. Tout (Dict. Nat. Biogr. xi.
341) thinks that he "could never have been of doubtful orthodoxy, because he was a
friend of the Prince of Wales."
[6] Wals. ii. 291; Hypodig. 438; Capgr. 303. Not *John*, as Angl. Sacr. i. 589.
[7] Wylie, iii. 112, note 8. He held the prebend of Hayes (Exeter) from July 3, 1403,
till Sept. 1413, Oliver, 199.
[8] Iss. Roll 1 H. V, Pasch., Mich., July 17, 1413; Feb. 22, 1414. Called "Treasurer
of the King's Household" in Hunter, 6. On June 16, 1415, he is Treasurer of the King's
Chamber and Keeper of the King's Jewels, Riley, Mem. 613; also Rym. ix. 3, 257, 284;
Nicolas, App. p. 52, March 26, May 30, July 12, 1415.
[9] Pat. 1 H. V, iii. 16; Rym. ix. 50; Monast. iv. 2; Godwin, 438.
[10] Not 27, as Godwin, 438; Monast. iv. 2. He appears as Bishop of Norwich in Iss.
Roll 1 H. V, Mich., Oct. 2, 1413. The see is referred to as vacant on Aug. 3, 18, 1413,
in Pat. 1 H. V, iii. 17, 21.
[11] Page 50, note 9. Not at Canterbury, as Angl. Sacr. i. 416.
[12] Prince, 162; Le Neve, ii. 466. For arrangements made by Bishop Courtenay for
daily mass for the good estate of himself and the king at "Courteney's Auter" in the
Church of Ottery St Mary, see Pat. 3 H. V, i. 4, June 25, 1415.
[13] Angl. Sacr. i. 416; Fuller, Worthies, i. 278; Prince, 162.
[14] For grant to him (dated Oct. 16, 1414) of the towns of Plaistow and West Ham for
harbourage of his horses during his stay in London or thereabouts, see Pat. 2 H. V, ii. 20.
For his expectatives (*gratias expectativas*), see Pat. 1 H. V, iii. 21, May 28, 1413.

attend to his spiritual duties.   And so it came about that he never even found time to visit Norwich for his installation[1], but left the care of his great and wealthy diocese to a suffragan, John Leicester, a Carmelite Friar, who as titular Archbishop of Smyrna[2] had performed the same duties for his two predecessors for the last 15 years[3].

[1] Angl. Sacr. i. 416; Prince, 163.
[2] Stubbs, Reg. 198; Gams, 444.
[3] i.e. since 1398, Gams, 444; Eubel, i. 480.

CHAPTER XIX

THE LEICESTER PARLIAMENT

WHILE the Lollard tumult was being crushed, the king had taken up his quarters in St John's Priory at Clerkenwell[1], where he was near the centre of disaffection, but when quiet was restored, he moved by St Albans[2] to Kenilworth, where he arrived on Jan. 27, 1414[3]. He would then appear to have journeyed on to Leicester, Ravendale and Fotheringhay[4], and to have returned to Kenilworth[5] during Lent[6]. Here he had a row-barge[7] sent down to him from London with oars, cables, anchors and an iron chain[8] to be used on the large pool[9] that lay

[1] Sent Johanes withoute Smithfeld, Claud. A. VIII; Grey Friars Chron. 13; Greg. Chron. 108. Cf. Benham and Welch, 13; Wylie, iv. 224, 225. For its position on the west side of St John's Street, see Hale, 310. For picture of the hospital buildings as rebuilt after their destruction in 1381, see Monast. vii. 799; Knight, London, ii. 147; Bedford-Holbeche, 56, with the Tudor gateway still existing, ibid. Frontispiece; Knight, London, ii. 133, 148; Besant, Survey, ii. 271, from R. Wilkinson, Londina Illustrata, Vol. i.

[2] For 5600 marks (£3733. 6s. 8d.) delivered to the king at St Albans, see Iss. Roll 1 H. V, Mich., Feb. 20, 1414. For documents dated at St Albans Jan. 26, 27, 1414, see Pat. 1 H. V, v. 22, 24; Cal. Pat. H. V, i. 156; Waugh, 645.

[3] Elmham, Lib. Metr. 100; Rym. ix. 117; Iss. Roll 1 H. V, Mich., Jan. 27, 1414, shows that Bishop Courtenay had delivered to the king £1333. 6s. 8d. at St John of Jerusalem near Smithfield, £3666. 13s. 4d. at St Albans, and £3000 at "Killingworth."

[4] For one large coffer, two small ones and other harness for carrying money to St Albans, Killingworth, Leicester, Ravendale and Fotheringhay, also £4. 13s. 4d. paid for a horse to carry money to the king at Kenilworth, see Iss. Roll 1 H. V, Mich., Feb. 19, 1414.

[5] See page 165. For documents dated at Kenilworth Castle on Feb. 27, 28, March 2, 7, 16, 1414, see Pat. 1 H. V, v. mm. 4, 6; Cal. Rot. Hib. i. 205; Chancery Warrants, Ser. I. 1364/2, 3, 4, 5, 6, 7. For picture of the ruins of Kenilworth, see Macfarlane-Thomson, i. 398; also Great Hall (ibid. 448); Historians' Hist. xviii. 221. For John Ashford, Constable of Kenilworth on Feb. 6, 1414, see Cleop. E. II. 305; also Nov. 18, 1405, Wylie, ii. 49, 246.

[6] Elmham, Lib. Metr. 100. Ash Wednesday fell on Feb. 21 in 1414.

[7] For repair of a "row barge" called "Esmond del Toure" sent to the Seine, see Devon, 367, June 18, 1421.

[8] For £10 paid for a barge bought and carried to Killingworth Castle + 6s. 8d. to a bargeman accompanying it, see Iss. Roll 1 H. V, Mich., Jan. 25, Feb. 22, 1414. Also £5. 8s. 8d. paid to a "botman" (cf. boteman, Pat. 1 H. V, ii. 11) for a new boat (batella), including carriage from London to Killingworth, see ibid. Feb. 19, 1414.

[9] For plans and pictures of Kenilworth showing the Pool, see Dugd. Warwickshire, i. 243, 249; S. E. Harding; Nichols, Progresses, i. 422 (dated 1620); Scott, Kenilworth,

outside the western wall, and he amused his leisure time by clearing a swampy place near the tail of the pool[1], which was overgrown with briars and formed a cover for foxes. This he now laid out as a garden, on which he built a pretty timber banqueting-house[2], which was known as the Pleasaunce-in-the-Marsh[3] and remained till it was removed to make way for alterations in the reign of Henry VIII[4]. The courtiers, of course, turned the incident into a parable in which the briars were the Lollards and the foxes the French. But if the sequel be closely scanned, the balance of foxiness will mostly be found on the English side of the account[5].

On April 2 the king was at Tewkesbury, where he gave £200[6] at the Maundy on April 5 to be distributed amongst 12,000 poor persons, who had suffered from the recent disastrous fire[7]. Easter Day fell on April 8[8], and he kept St George's Feast at Windsor on April 23 with great solemnity[9]. His elevation to take his father's place as Sovereign of England and Superior of the Order of the Garter had caused a vacancy among the knights companions

Vol. ii; Aubrey, ii. 650; Craik-Macfarlane, ii. 874; Thomson, Pt. VI; Windle, 45, 47. Cf. " Hard on the west still nourished with lively springs a goodly Pool of rare beauty, bredth, length, deepth and store of all kind freshwater fish delicate, great and fat and also of wild fooul byside, a flightshot broad on the west," from letter of Robert Laneham written in 1575, in Nichols, Progresses, i. 422 (1629). Cf. "a faire Poole contayning 111 acres well stored with fish and fowle which at pleasure is to be lett round about the Castle," Survey of Henry VIII, in Furnivall, 63; Kenilworth Illustrated, 37, where it is spelt Killingworth or Kenelworth or Kenelmworth, Furnivall, 2, 4, 5, 63; also Kelyngworth, Pat. 8 H. V, 19 d; Kyllyngworth, Kingsford, Chron. 66. See also Wylie, ii. 49, note.

    [1] Kenilworth Illustrated, 27, 54.
    [2] Lel. Itin. iv. 120. For 33s. 4d. paid for carrying timber to Kenilworth, see Iss. Roll 1 H. V, Mich., Feb. 22, 1414. For £6. 13s. 4d. paid for carriage of wainscots and "regals" (i.e. rygolbords, Baildon, 27, or righolts, Wylie, iv. 360; Halliwell, s.v. *Regal*). For doors, windows, &c. for a chamber in the water under Killingworth Castle, see Devon, 339, Feb. 26, 1415. For order to Robert Babthorpe, kt. to provide workmen pro operationibus novi operis de Kyllyngworth, see Pat. 5 H. V, 28, Apr. 2, 1417.
    [3] " Plesant Mareys," Elmham, Lib. Metr. 100; Stow, 345; "Plesans in Marys," Rouse, 209; Dugdale, Warwickshire, i. 249.
    [4] No trace of Henry V's building now remains, Kenilworth Illustrated, 61, though Rowlatt (8) supposes that it is the same as " King Henry's lodgings" (i.e. Henry VIII, Dugdale, Warwickshire, i. 249) on the eastern side of the inner court.
    [5] Page 200, note 1.
    [6] Rym. ix. 188, where it is called le bon Vendredi; allotted Feb. 16, 1414, for die Passeves (sic) next, Iss. Roll 1 H. V, Mich. Cf. Wylie, ii. 211, note 1; iv. 202; also page 209, notes 1, 2. Cf. "at his mawnde," Lydg. Nightingale, 24; ibid. Min. Po. 66. For Good Frydaye, see ibid. 39, 93, 98.
    [7] Page 9.
    [8] Itin. 408.
    [9] For messengers to Knights of the Garter to be at Windsor next St George's Feast, see Iss. Roll 1 H. V, Mich., Feb. 22, 1414.

of the Order, which had already been filled by the appointment of Sir John Dabridgecourt[1], whose grandfather[2], the
Henower Sanchet Dabrichecourt, had been one of Edward III's original 25 knights[3] at the founding of the
Order 68 years before. Sir John however did not live
long to enjoy his new honour, but died within 18 months
afterwards[4]. Another gap had been caused in the ranks

---

[1] Burwell, 81; Ashmole, 508; Nicolas, Knighthood, i. 58; Beltz, lv, clvii; Wylie,
iii. 167, note 5. For his arms, see Ashmole, 710 (edn. 1672). For confirmation of grant
of 100 marks per annum to him, see Iss. Roll 1 H. V, Mich., Jan. 27, 1414, and of the
Kentish manors of Merdale Chapel (in Boughton Aluph near Wye) and Maplehurst (near
Staplehurst), see Cal. Pat. H. IV, i. 430, Feb. 8, 1401; repeated except as to Maplehurst
in Pat. 1 H. V, ii. 3, June 12, 1413; Cal. Pat. H. V, i. 55. Also 100 marks per annum
from revenues of the manor of Duffield near Derby, see Duc. Lanc. Accts. Various, 27/6.
On March 21, 1413, John Dabridgecourt was appointed a Justice of the Peace for Derbyshire, Pat. 1 H. V, i. 35 d. For scutage return dated Jan. 2, 1412, of names of holders
of land worth £20 per annum in Derbyshire certified by John Dabridgecourt, kt. and
others, see Yeatman, i. 483, where Dabridgecourt has £40 per annum and an annuity
(£75. 13s. 4d.) from Tutbury and Duffield. In the subsidy roll of 1412 he has property
in London yielding £8. 16s. 8d. per annum, Archaeol. Journ. xliv. 60.
[2] Or uncle (called "father" in Topographer and Genealogist, v. 197), from Auberchicourt, Abrichecourt, Abricicourt or Aubercicourt near Bouchain in Ostervant, Ashmole,
50; Nicolas, II. pp. x, lv*; Beltz, 90; Harl. Soc. (Notts.), iv. 37; Wylie, iv. 420. For
his stall-plate executed circ. 1421, see Hope, 15, Plate v, where he is called Aubricicourt.
It was stolen circ. 1844, but a copy made in 1758 still exists at the College of Heralds.
For Daubriggecourt in the retinue of the Duke of Clarence at Southampton July, 1415,
see Exch. Accts. 45/3. For François son of Eustache d'Auberchicourt (al. Aubischecourt,
Aubiscourt, Aucrecicourt) Lord of Ville-oiseau, Chamberlain to the Duke of Bourbon,
see Anselme, vi. 277; Cent Ballades, 241. For his réponse on behalf of constancy in love,
see ibid. 223. For the Hainaulter Eustache d'Auberchicourt as a captain of mercenaries
in 1358, see Delachenal, ii. 40; Duruy, i. 372, where he is called "d'Aubrecicourt."
[3] Foure and twenty cladde in oo lyveree, Lydg. Min. Po. 145.
[4] i.e. between July 26 and Oct. 1, 1415, Beltz, clvii, though his inquisition is not
entered till 1417, Inq. p. Mort. iv. 28. In Cal. Rot. Hib. i. 206, Feb. 6, 1415, he is
referred to as in England. For his will dated at Wimborne April 20, 1415 (called Friday
after the Feast of St James, i.e. July 26, 1415, in Anstis, i. 17, or July 20, 1415, with a
codicil dated Aug. 6, 1415, see Topographer and Genealogist, i. 197, 202, where he is
of Strathfieldsaye, Hants.), see Wylie, iii. 167, note 6. For John Blount and Roger
Trumpington as supervisors of his will and John Appleby one of his executors, see Exch.
Accts. 187/6; Hardy and Page, i. 174 (8 H. IV). In this will, in which he is called
Daubriggecourt, he leaves £20 to liberate prisoners for debt from Newgate and 5s. to
a hermit in the gate at Bishopsgate within the wall towards Cripplegate. He owned
manors at Aylwarton (in Derbyshire, Inq. p. Mort. iv. 203, 239), Bodemthwayte, Coges-
more, Mapyrlegh (i.e. Mapperley near Derby), Wofaton and Chirche. The will was
proved on Nov. 8, 1415, Topographer and Genealogist, i. 197; also at the Old Temple
in London Nov. 30, 1415, Gibbons, Linc. 117; Genealogist, v. 329. In Dec. 1415, he
is referred to as dead in Pat. 3 H. V, ii. 28, where the manor of Maplehurst is granted
to Lewis Robsart; see also Pat. 8 H. V, 2, Feb. 18, 1421; page 60, note 2. For possessions in Hants. and Wilts. belonging to his wife Joan, who died in 1419, see Inq. p.
Mort. iv. 47. His daughter Joan married Sir John Cokayne of Pooley near Tamworth,
see Dugd. Warw. ii. 1118, 1120; Nichols, Top. and Gen. i. 197, though called Hugh
Wiloughby, ibid. 202. John Cokayne's will is dated at Pooley, June, 1412 (probably
1435, i.e. 13 H. VI, not H. IV, as Dugd. Warw. ii. 1120), and his wife Joan is buried
in Westminster Abbey (Stow, Kingsford, ii. 110, 377). It was through this connection
that he acquired the neighbouring manor of Baddesley-Ensor, showing apparently that
"J. Cockayne Chlr del Countee de Derby" is not the same as the Judge, see Wylie, ii.
189. Cokayne afterwards married Isabel daughter of Sir Hugh Shirley, and dying in

of the knights by the death of Sir John Stanley[1] in Ireland
and his garter was now bestowed on Thomas Montague,
Earl of Salisbury[2]. Liveries of cloth, both black and
blanket[3], together with furs and garters, were supplied to
Queen Joan, Margaret the newly married Duchess of
Clarence[4], the Duchesses of York (i.e. the Duke of York's
wife and his mother), the Countesses of Huntingdon,
Westmoreland, Arundel and Salisbury (both dowager and
junior), and the Ladies Beauchamp, Roos and Waterton,
all of them wives of past or present knights[5], together
with the usual mantle and miniver cape to the Bishop of
Winchester as Prelate of the Order[6].

The feast was made the occasion for a stirring call by
Thomas Hoccleve[7] to all who were of St George's livery,
who by their style were foes to shame[8], to shove on and

1438 (Inq. p. Mort. iv. 182), was buried in the church at Polesworth, where his monument may still be seen, figured in Cockayne, i. 19.   See page 15, note 6.

[1] i.e. on Jan. 18, 1414, see page 59.   For his appointment as a Knight of the Garter April 23, 1405, see Wylie, ii. 292.   For a letter from him to Henry IV, written at Vale Royal Abbey, July 30, 1405, in which he refers to "mon meison à Lathum," see Roy. Lett. ii. 76–79; Wylie, ii. 290.

[2] For his portrait from Harl. MS. 4826, see Doyle, iii. 241; Strutt, Reg. Antiq. 89; Kingsford, 352; Planché, i. 104; Lydgate, Burgh, xiv; Dillon, Besague, 15; Wylie, iv. 531.   For picture of his death at the siege of Orleans in 1428, see Wallon, 19, from Bibl. Nat. MS. 5054 (dated 1484).   For grants to him (June 1, 1418) of Neufboro (i.e. le Neubourg), Coubon (i.e. Combon) and La Rivière Thibouville, see Rot. Norm. 6 H. V, i. 13; Carte, Rolles, i. 267.   Arundel MS. xlviii. f. 295, in Heralds' College (Black, p. 82), has household expenses of Jeoffrey à Loundres en hostiel mons. Thomas Mountagu Conte de Sarisberi remowez a Saint Elene, Apr. 1, 1421.   Called vir strenuus et bellicosus in Amundesham, i. 32, who records his burial at St Paul's, adding nullus eo felicior dum vitam vixit in bellis et post mortem istius viri stirpis Montis Acuti in hoc regno cessavit finaliter.   He died Nov. 3, 1428, Beltz, clix; Anstis, i. 39; Calig. D. v; Wylie, iii. 287, note 3.   For his arms, see Ashmole, 710, edn. 1672.   For his seal, Jan. 18, Oct. 4, 1424, see Demay, ii. 183; Doyle, iii. 242; A. France, i. 133.

[3] Cf. Anstis, i. 174.   For drap blanchet de Malines (1396), see Collas, 241.   For 12 virgat' of blanket (5s.), see Maldon Rolls, Jan. 15, 1420; called "a coarse pale cloth" in Duchange, 250; cf. pannorum de blankecta (1401), Beccario, 83; a russet goune lynyt with whythe blanket (1425), Fifty Wills, 49; Clinch, 57.   Cf. le blanquet, Bonis, 1. liv; chausses de blanquet for a labourer, ibid. lxx.   For a corset (i.e. jacket) de drap blanquet for an apprentice, see Affre, Aveyron, 367.   For six aulnes de brunette et six de blanchet pour faire un habit, see Blanchard, ii. 249.   For doublette de Baudekyn nigro et Blunket (sic), see Letter Book I, 113.

[4] For robes with 4300 garters for Duke and Duchess of Clarence for the feast of St George possibly in 1413, see Q.R. Accts. 406/15; also Claus. 1 H. V, 14, 17, Oct. 1, 1413.

[5] Anstis, i. 14; Beltz, lv, ccxxii; Nicolas, II. xxxii.   [6] Nicolas, II. lxxv.

[7] He is called "a poetical journeyman executing commissions for patrons," Garnett, i. 190, 192.   For his "jolting verse," see G. G. Smith, 18, who regards his "bad-boy confessions" (p. 16) as "rather priggish memorabilia" (p. 109), probably more those of "a literary than an actual rake" (p. 19), and that he "could never have dreamt himself out of a respectable mediocrity" (p. 17).

[8] For "Hony soit q imal pense," embroidered on a cope (1397), see Dillon-Hope, 279; or "Honny, &c." Taillepied, 139; Chauc. (S.), vii. 502; see Wylie, i. 41; iv. 28, 207, 221.

put Christ's foes to the utterance, to tame the wild wodeness[1] of the Lollards, quench all this nuisance and rip it right to the root and turn what now was earnest into game[2]. And with these words ringing in his ears the king left Windsor to be present at the opening of the Parliament that had been called to meet at Leicester at the end of April, 1414.

In the original writs issued from Westminster on Dec. 1, 1413[3], it had been proposed that the sittings should begin on Jan. 29, 1414[4]. The collectors of the subsidy had been summoned to be at Westminster at Martinmas (Nov. 11, 1413[5]) and tellers attended for eight weeks at the Exchequer to receive and check the tenths and fifteenths as they came in[6]. But three days after the first writs had been issued messengers were despatched all over the country to alter the day, and under the stress of the Lollard panic fresh writs were issued on Christmas Eve[7] fixing the meeting for April 30, 1414[8], the Southern Convocation of the

---

[1] i.e. madness, Bosworth, 473; Ogilvie, iv. 652; Jamieson, iv. 820; Hunter, vii. 586.

[2] Hoccleve, Min. Po. 92; Bell, Chaucer, iv. 424; Chaucer (S.), vii. 234. The circumstances seem to fit in better with 1414 than with 1416, as suggested by Skeat in Academy, xxxiii. 325; or Aug. 1415, in Chaucer (S.), vii. p. xli.

[3] Dugd. Summons, 390; Cotton, Abridgment, 533; Claus. 1 H. V, 9 d; Letter Book I, 121. For order for carts, horses and carters to take the rolls, records, &c. from London to Leicester, see Pat. 1 H. V, iv. 12 d, Dec. 1, 1413. For subsequent order dated April 17, 1414, see Pat. 2 H. V, i. 39 d.

[4] Not Feb. 29, as Tyler, ii. 21.

[5] For payment to messengers, see Iss. Roll 1 H. V, Mich., Oct. 2, 1413, Feb. 22, 1414.

[6] For six ells of green woollen cloth to cover a table for *numeratores* for fifteenths and tenths at the Exchequer of Receipt, also £10 paid to Simon Gaunstede, clerk in the King's Chancery, for writing original writs of Exchequer, see Iss. Roll 1 H. V, Mich., Oct. 10, 1413. For writs signed "Gaunstede," May 30, June 11, Aug. 24, Nov. 12, 1414, see Escheators' Inquisitions, Ser. 1. files 1008, 1278. For 40s. paid for a horse to ride to Lynn, Boston, Hull and Ipswich to receive moneys and securities and bring them back on the same horse, see Iss. Roll 1 H. V, Mich., Feb. 19, 1414. For £8. 6s. 8d. paid to *computatores*, attending at Westminster every day for eight weeks to receive tenths and fifteenths, also 3d. per day each to *numeratores* and ushers, all the staff remaining during the whole vacation; also payments for carrying divers rolls, memoranda, &c. from the Treasurer's hostel to Westminster and from the Earl Marshal's hostel to that of the Bishop of Worcester and back, and 12d. paid *pro tribus Cathatis* (? cases) to carry divers of the king's vessels secretly to Westminster and for messengers to hurry collectors, the moneys to be paid in crastino clausi Paschae (cf. Wylie, iv. 42, note 9) and to merchants to hasten payments due XV Pasch. prox. futur. (= April 22, 1414), see ibid. Feb. 22, 1414. For 15s. 10d. paid for breakfast for the Chancellor, Treasurer and others of the Council at Westminster for one day, see ibid. Jan. 27, 1414.

[7] Claus. 1 H. V, 8 d, Dugdale, Summons, 392; Letter Book I, 121; Return Parl. i. 281; Prynne, 502; not Jan. 29, as Hook, v. 35. For payment of messengers to sheriffs, see Devon, 330, Feb. 16, 1414.

[8] Iss. Roll 1 H. V, Mich., Dec. 4, 1413, has payments to messengers for election of knights and burgesses for a Parliament at Leicester on April 30, 1414.

clergy being summoned to assemble in the same town on the same day[1].

Comparing the summons to Barons with those of the last Parliament at Westminster the following changes may be noted. Writs are now sent to the Dukes of Clarence and York, both of whom in the previous year had been abroad[2], also to Michael de la Pole, Earl of Suffolk, and Richard de Vere, Earl of Oxford, who had received no summons since 1411[3] apparently for the same reason[4]. Oldcastle's name of course drops out together with those of Hugh Stafford and Henry Beaumont[5], the latter of whom had died on June 15, 1413[6], leaving a little son John then only three years old[7], under the charge of his widow Elizabeth[8] burdened with 3000 marks of debt[9]. No new name of any note appears, except that now for the first time young Edmund[10], Earl of March, received his summons to attend. He had come of age before the close of the last Parliament, had done his homage "with a glad heart[11]" and had entered into the full possession of his property. He had been made a Knight of the Bath[12] at Henry V's coronation and in this Parliament he was appointed a Trier of Petitions[13], and the fact that it was considered safe that he should be thus generously treated, though he certainly had a formidable following in the country, is another evidence of the strong position that the new dynasty had already taken up in the hearts of the majority of Englishmen.

---

[1] Crespin (25) thinks that Leicester was chosen because many in London favoured Oldcastle, but it is certain that Leicester was deeply disaffected likewise.

[2] Rot. Parl. iv. 17.

[3] i.e. at Westminster Nov. 3, 1411. His name is omitted in writs for Feb. 3, 1413, and May 14, 1413, Dugdale, Summons, 386, 389.

[4] Dugdale, Baronage (ii. 186) says that he was employed beyond the sea in 9 and 11 H. IV, quoting Rot. France; see Carte, Rolles, ii. 196, 198; Wylie, iv. 73.

[5] Wylie, ii. 411.

[6] Thursday after St Barnabas, Dugdale, Baronage, ii. 53; Inq. p. Mort. iv. 3; Test. Vet. 259; Doyle, i. 145.

[7] He proved his age in 9 H. VI, Dugdale, Baronage, ii. 53. In Doyle, i. 145, he is said to have been born in 1409.

[8] She was the daughter of William fifth Lord Willoughby of Eresby, ibid.

[9] Pat. 2 H. V, i. 26, June 8, 1414.

[10] Not Edward, as Cotton, Abridgment, 533; Complete Peerage, ii. 120.

[11] Laeto corde, Claus. 1 H. V, 28, June 9, 1413; Tyler, ii. 18, quoting MS. Donat., i.e. Add. MS. 4600; Wylie, ii. 42, note 10.

[12] Page 3; Dict. Nat. Biogr. xxxix. 124.

[13] Rot. Parl. iv. 16.

In the Commons all the 37 counties[1] were represented, each sending up two members except Yorkshire, for which only one name appears, making a total of 73 knights of the shire[2]. But only 33 boroughs[3] were represented compared with 89 in the previous year[4], yielding 66 borough members, though it is obvious that the list is incomplete[5]. Thomas Chaucer no longer appears in it, but of familiar names there are still John Doreward[6] (Essex), Robert Whitington[7] (Gloucestershire), John Skidmore[8] (Herefordshire), David Holbache[9] (Salop), and Nicholas Merbury[10] (Northants.), while Thomas Cumberworth[11], the

---

[1] Page 21.

[2] One of the members for Dorset was Humphrey Stafford, knight, Return Parl. i. 281. He also represented Dorsetshire in 1417, 1419, 1420, 1422 and 1426, ibid. i. 289, 291, 294, 302, 310. On May 29, 1417, he was on a commission of array for Somerset, Rym. ix. 253 [255]. For pardon to Humphrey de Stafford, kt., see Memoranda Roll, K.R. 3–4 H. V, 79, Oct. 11, 1415. His father Humphrey Stafford, senior, had represented Dorset in 1410, Return Parl. i. 27, but he had died at Abbotsbury, Wylie, ii. 285, note 5. For lands in Cornwall and Devon belonging to Catherine widow of Humphrey Stafford, esq., see Inq. p. Mort. iv. 33; Ad Quod Damn. 373, where she is *defuncta* in 1417.

[3] Including 10 in Return Parl. App. xix.

[4] Return Parl. i. 281.   [5] See page 21, note 9.

[6] On March 21, 1413, he and John Leventhorpe (see page 22, note 6) were appointed Justices of the Peace for Essex, Pat. 1 H. V, i. 34 d.

[7] See App. R.

[8] He represented Herefordshire again in the Westminster Parliament in November, 1414 (Return Parl. i. 283), and was present at Agincourt, Nicolas, App. 17.

[9] Wylie, ii. 413. He was appointed a Justice of the Peace for Shropshire on March 21, 1413, Pat. 1 H. V, i. 35 d. For confirmation of grants to him, see ibid. iv. 29, Nov. 25, 1413. He again represented Salop in the Westminster Parliament in Nov. 1414, Return Parl. i. 283. In Rec. Roll 3 H. V, Mich., Oct. 26, 1415, he is escheator of Salop. For his appointment as a Justice ad Assisam for Shropshire March 1, 1417, see Pat. 4 H. V, 3 dors.

[10] Wylie, i. 293, note 9; iv. 144, note 3. He was appointed a Justice of the Peace for Northants. on March 21, 1413, Pat. 1 H. V, i. 35 d. In 1415 King Henry left him £100 in his will, Rym. ix. 292, where he is an usher of the king's chamber. He was present at Caen in May, 1418, as magistr. ordinacion', For. Accts. 1 H. VI, c, and was at the siege of Rouen in 1418, Rym. ix. 595. For Richard (*sic*) Marbury, écuyer tranchant to the Duke of Bedford in France in 1424, see Beaurepaire, Administration, 171. For his seal "Richard de Merbury" as Captain of Meulan, Apr. 15, 1432, also of Vernon, Nov. 27, 1440, see Demay, Inventaire, i. 632. On Oct. 1, 1418, Robt. Morton is Master of the Ordnance but *late* Master on Dec. 15, 1423, For. Accts. 1 H. VI, c. For custody of the park and warren at Moulton near Northampton granted to Nicholas Merbury March 7, 1417, see Pat. 4 H. V, 3, but cancelled quia aliter inferius, see Priv. Seal 665/790, March 8, 1417. On Aug. 12, 1416, he was commissioned for gaol-delivery at Leicester, Pat. 4 H. V, 18 d. He had married Margaret widow of Edward Latimer (d. 1410) of Braybrook near Market Harborough (Bridges, ii. 12, i.e. brother of Thomas Latimer the Lollard who died in 1401, Wylie, iii. 296, note 2), and he represented Northamptonshire in the Parliaments of 1413 and 1414, Return Parl. 279, 282. He was present at the battle of Homildon Hill on Sept. 14, 1402, as a squire of the Earl of Northumberland, Cal. Doc. Scot. iv. 402, and received a grant of £40 per annum for bringing news of the victory to the king, Iss. Roll 1 H. V, Mich., Dec. 9, 1413; Pat. 1 H. V, ii. 3, June 12, 1414.

[11] Page 18.

friend of Judge Gascoigne, sat for the first time for Lincolnshire. Trade was scarcely represented at all, except in so far as we may judge from the presence of a John Boteller[1], who was one of the members for the county of Huntingdon, and a Thomas Armourer[2] who sat for the borough of Southampton.

The session opened on Monday, April 30, 1414[3], in a large hall which had been built expressly for the purpose[4] in the centre of the town near the mansion of the Grey Friars which stood on the south side of St Martin's churchyard[5]. The king stayed at the castle[6] and was present at the opening[7], when the Chancellor (Bishop Beaufort) preached from the text: "He set his heart to search the laws[8]," showing how the "Church of England[9]" had been long and grievously troubled by certain men infected with heresy called Lollards, who had just now traitorously purposed to destroy the Christian Faith, the Church and its ministers, and all the temporal estates of the realm, and stating that in view of this the Parliament should pass such ordinances as would be pleasing to the Almighty. Secondly, that proper steps should be taken to secure respect for treaties and the safety of the sea, and thirdly, to put down rioters and evil-doers generally.

---

[1] Cf. Wylie, iv. 269. For Botelmaker, see Letter Book I, pp. 14, 100; Botilmaker, Iss. Roll 8 H. V, Pasch., May 11, 1420. Cf. Botellis of tyn, of wode, of leather men fynd in al maneres, Caxton, Dial. 7; a pere of botell of silver and of gilt, Fifty Wills, 108; Baildon, Inv. 172, where one of them has an entreclos or division (Halliwell, i. 336) of gold leaf (*foille d'or*); Bouteille de jaspre noir, or pourfire (porphyry) de Romme, Guiffrey, i. 193. Cf. grete and huge botellis, Amyot, 236; 2 petites bouteilles d'argent doré, Mirot, Trousseau, 149.

[2] For the armourer, armurer or armurrer, see Caxton, Dial. 33; Letter Book I, 7, 94, 144, 207, 215; Wylie, iv. 268. For armourer's marks (16–17th cent.), see Brett, Plates cxxxi, cxxxii; cf. "armarius," Claus. 8 H. V, 16 dors.

[3] Rot. Parl. iv. 17, 30; Stat. ii. 175; Staff. Reg. p. xi. Not Jan. 29, as Manning, 55; Dict. Nat. Biogr. xxviii. 258; nor May 31, 1415, as Mazas, Vies, vi. 558, who places it after a meeting of high barons whom he supposes to have assembled in London on May 1, 1415.

[4] De novell ordeignée par le Roi par celle cause, Rot. Parl. iv. 15; Strecche, 265 b, who says that it measured 120 ft. by 40 ft. and was completed in 24 days. For a house recently demolished in Red Cross Street, Leicester, traditionally known as the Parliament House, see T. F. Johnson, 142.

[5] Monast. viii. 1513.

[6] Rym. ix. 137, 138.

[7] For documents dated at Leicester April 30, 1414, see Pat. 2 H. V, i. 39; also May 26, 1414, Letter Book I, 126.

[8] Rot. Parl. iv. 15, possibly from Ezra vii. 10, where the Vulgate has: Paravit cor suum ut investigaret legem. Not "he hath applied his heart to observe the laws," as Radford, 37.

[9] See page 304, note 3.

After planting down these hardy annuals[1] the Chancellor
made an announcement that the king would not raise any
tenths or fifteenths from his faithful people[2] during this
Parliament, in the hope that he would find them all the
more ready and willing to provide for his necessities in
the time to come.   Receivers and Triers of Petitions were
then appointed to transact their business in the Refectory
and Chapter-house and the Commons were told to assemble
in the Infirmary[3] and choose their Speaker, who was to be
presented for the king's approval before breakfast on the
following morning.   The next day, accordingly, they nominated Sir Walter Hungerford[4], one of the Wiltshire[5] members, as their Speaker and the king was graciously pleased
to signify his assent.

The new Speaker was a Wiltshire man, though his
family sprang originally from Hungerford in Berkshire.
His father, Sir Thomas Hungerford[6], had been Sheriff of
Wiltshire[7] and Speaker of the House of Commons in
1377[8], and after trading with success at Salisbury had
bought the manors of Farleigh-Montford[9] near Bradford,
which he crenellated in 1383[10], changing the name to
Farleigh-Hungerford[11], and Heytesbury[12] on the western
fringe of Salisbury Plain.   He had been Chief Steward

---

[1] Called "the usual petulant petitions" in Oman, Pol. Hist. 261.

[2] Non decimae clero populis exactio nulla Imponuntur ibi, Elmham, Lib. Metr. 102;
so also Capgr. De Illustr. 114; Brougham, 89.

[3] "Fermerie," Rot. Parl. ii. 10.   Cf. Infirmaria, Infirmitorium, Prompt. Parv. 157,
though "Firmari"=refectorium in Stratmann, 220.   For the "firmaress," see Wylie,
ii. 456.

[4] Rot. Parl. iv. 16; Manning (55) still thought that the roll was lost and the name
of the Speaker not officially recorded, though this mistake had been corrected in Nichols'
Leicestershire, i. 369.   See App. H[1].

[5] Prynne, 504; Return Parl. i. 282.

[6] For picture of him in a window at Farleigh, see Dasent, Frontispiece, with a later
portrait from a drawing in an album in the library of the Nat. Portr. Gall., ibid.
pp. xxiv, 52.

[7] Sheriffs' List, 153.

[8] Test. Vet. 257; Hoare, Hungerfordiana, 6; Stubbs, ii. 475; Manning, pp. 1–3,
where he is called "the first Speaker of the House of Commons on record" from Rot.
Parl. ii. 374 ; but there is an earlier case, viz. Wm. Trussell in 1343, ibid. ii. 136.

[9] i.e. in 1369, J. E. Jackson, Guide, 4.   For documents relating to this purchase,
together with the Hundred of Wellow, from Bartholomew de Burghersh, see Jackson,
98–106; T. Taylor, 16.

[10] Collinson, iii. 353; T. H. Turner, iii. 339; J. E. Jackson, 9, 103.

[11] The name which it still bears, Hoare, Hungerfordiana, 35, 98–102, 133; J. E.
Jackson, Guide, 5.

[12] Hoare (Heytesbury), i. 90; do. Hungerfordiana, 112, 113.   On his wife's epitaph
he is called Lord of Farleigh, Wellow (not Belawe, as Gough, i. 158) and Heytesbury,
see Lel. Itin. iii. 99; Dugd. ii. 204; Nicolas, Navy, ii. 469.

of the lands belonging to the Duchy of Lancaster south of the Trent in the days of John of Gaunt[1], and reverently preserved a silver hanap out of which his master used to drink[2]. Walter was his fourth son, but the three elder ones had died young and he thus became his father's heir, adding to his inheritance by good wiving[3]. When young he studied at the Mickle Hall at Oxford[4]; he was made a knight on the accession of Henry IV[5], and at the abortive rising soon afterwards the conspirators seized him as a preliminary precaution, when planning the death of his usurping master[6]. In 1406 he became Sheriff of Wiltshire[7] and in the same year he escorted the Princess Philippa to Denmark as her chamberlain[8] on the occasion of her marriage with King Eric. In 1413 he was Sheriff of Somerset and Dorset[9]; soon after this Parliament dissolved he was sent as an envoy to King Sigismund at the diet that met at Coblenz in Aug. 1414, and when King Henry made his will at Southampton in 1415 he made him one of his executors and left him a gold cup as a memento, together with £100 in cash[10].

The record of this Leicester Parliament is very short and the sittings lasted less than a month, but the subjects with which it dealt are of unusual interest. Its chief fruit was the famous Lollard Statute, the provisions of which I have already described in a previous chapter[11], a measure which earned for the king unstinted praise from the clergy, while the announcement of the exemption from direct taxation helped to keep the country generally in a good temper for the coming attack on France. On May 16,

---

[1] Gaunt, Reg. I. pp. xiii, 65, 66, 114, 154, 287, 288; II. pp. 181, 213, 216, 220, 262, 268, 282, 287, 288, 315; also in Wales, ibid. II. 105, 200, 219, 222, 238, 251, 255, 265, 273, 311, 325. See App. I[1]. For "henap" see Douet d'Areq, Comptes, 274.

[2] Test. Vet. 259; Manning, 57; Hoare, Hungerfordiana, 113.

[3] Cf. by wyfing ne by marriage, Coudrette, 218.

[4] Carr, 72.

[5] Kingsford, Chron. 48; Archaeologia, xx. 275.

[6] Rym. viii. 165; Letter Book I, p. 3, where they strip him of his collar (liberata nostra vocata colere) valued at £20.

[7] Sheriffs' List, 153; Collinson, iii. 353; Wylie, iv. 241.

[8] Ibid., ii. 447.

[9] Sheriffs' List, 123; Collinson, I. xxxv. In For. Accts. 3 H. V, he is *late* sheriff.

[10] Rym. ix. 291, where he is senescallus noster. Cf. senescallus hospitii nostri et graunt maistre d'ostiel du roy.

[11] Page 282.

1414[1], the king created his brother John Earl of Kendal and Duke of Bedford, and his younger brother Humphrey Earl of Pembroke[2] and Duke of Gloucester[3], a possible claimant for the latter title having just been removed by the recent death of young Richard le Despenser[4], whose father Thomas had forfeited the earldom of Gloucester by his rebellion against Henry IV[5]. Six months later[6] the new Duke of Bedford was made Earl of Richmond[7] with the reversion of the castle and honor on the death of the Earl of Westmoreland, the existing life tenant. Both the titles of Bedford and Richmond were granted for the new duke's lifetime only[8], and the latter was accompanied by an allowance of £60 a year, though the prospective value of the honor of Richmond was fixed at £2000 per annum[9]. He still retained the office of master of the king's falcons

[1] Pat. 2 H. V, i. 36; Rym. ix. 129; Rot. Parl. iv. 17; Sandford, 313; Comp. Peer. i. 293; Doyle, i. 150; iii. 13; Vita, 33. Not May 6, as Dugdale, Bar. ii. 200; nor 1415, as Chaucer (S.), i. 83; vii· p. xlii.

[2] For seal of the Chancery of Pembrokeshire (1424) representing him riding in armour, see Birch, 158. For grants to him of the castles of Pembroke, Tenby and Kilgerran, and the commotes of Ostrelawe (i.e. Oysterlowe), Treyne and St Clears, see Pat. 1 H. V, v. 8, July 20, 1413, together with 500 marks per annum, Nov. 30, 1413, ibid. iv. 4; Iss. Roll 6 H. V, Pasch., July 16, 1418; do. 7 H. V, Pasch., May 18, 1419; Vickers, 9. For his gift of the alien priory of Pembroke to the Abbot of St Albans to pay for masses and other expenses in connection with his tomb, see Monast. ii. 244, 245; Whethamstede, i. 94; Vickers, 439. As Earl of Pembroke he received £20 per annum, and £40 per annum as Duke of Gloucester, Rot. Parl. iv. 443; not £60, as Vickers, 10.

[3] Comp. Peer. iv. 84; Hard. 373.

[4] In Pat. 2 H. V, i. 28, ii. 16, he is referred to as dead on April 16, 1414, showing that the reputed dates of his death, viz. Oct. 7 or 14, 1414 (Comp. Peer. ii. 78, iii. 93; Wylie, ii. 38, note 5), or "end of 1415" (Fonblanque, i. 246), are certainly wrong. For order dated Feb. 1, 1415, that his widow Alianore, 12th daughter of Ralph Earl of Westmoreland, should have her dower, see Pat. 2 H. V, iii. 8. His heiress was his sister Isabel, wife of Richard Beauchamp, kt., Lord of Abergavenny, Pat. 2 H. V, iii. 9, Feb. 17, 1415; Wylie, ii. 39.

[5] Doyle, ii. 21; Kingsford, Chron. 59; Harcourt, 371; Wylie, i. 74.

[6] viz. Nov. 24, 1414, Pat. 2 H. V, ii. 2; do. 3 H. V, ii. 37; Rot. Parl. iv. 40; Gale, xxix, 207; Comp. Peer. ii. 294, vi. 356; Doyle, i. 150, iii. 117. On Nov. 27, 1415, he is Lord of the Channel Islands, Doyle, i. 150; also Apr. 27, 1418, Rym. ix. 580.

[7] C. Barthélemy (171) supposes that the Duke of Brittany did homage to Henry IV and received the Earldom of Richmond from him in 1404; also Trébuchet, 28, who adds that it was ratified by Henry IV at Northampton on Aug. 2, 1410 (p. 29). But this view is quite given up by more modern inquirers, e.g. Cosneau, p. 4; Trévédy, 12, 330. According to Mazas (vi. 12) Henry IV had allowed his stepson, Arthur of Brittany, to bear the title Earl of Richmond on condition that a treaty should be made between England and the Duke of Brittany. But this is quite improbable, and when Arthur was captured at Agincourt he is always referred to as "Arthur brother to the Duke of Brittany," Carte, Rolles, ii. 226, 233 and *passim*; Rym. ix. 326 (though called *Duke* of Brittany apparently by a mistake, ibid. ix. 432); Wals. ii. 313 (who adds qui se dicit comitem Richemundiae); do. Hypodig. 367; Barante, iv. 94. Yonge (283) supposes that he came to England to receive the investiture in 1403.

[8] Rym. ix. 128.

[9] Rot. Parl. iv. 41.

which he had held during part of his father's reign[1], and one of his accounts[2] rendered in this capacity still extant supplies many interesting details as to dress, drugs and other necessary equipments of the king's mews[3].

Likewise, at this general time of reconciliation, the Duke of York[4] was cleared of all consequences of the judgment passed upon him in October, 1399[5], and his brother Richard of York[6] was now made Earl of Cambridge[7].

[1] Wylie, iv. 209, 210, 222.

[2] Exch. Accts. 407/9, where he receives a livery of russet and blanket together with liveries for three squires, 12 varlets and 12 boys, all falconers. This account also refers to four dozen carde bags, six dozen leathern hoods and 120 pairs of laton bells, also leathern gloves and skins, pairs of vertmell (for vetmell, see Wylie, ii. 474, note 7, but probably vervels, see Halliwell, ii. p. 909), 12 lbs. of orpiment (auripigmentum, Arderne (Read), 99), 1 lb. of sugar candy (sugō candi) and 6 lbs. of dragon's blood (sangdḡon), cf. sangdragone, Arderne MS. (Emm. Coll., Cambr. ff. lxii, clix^b), sanguis draconis, Arderne (Read), 106; sang du dragon, Margry, 192; Wylie, iv. 343. For sang de dragno pour les faucons, see Bonis, I. p. cxxix. It was transplanted to Madeira by Prince Henry the Navigator circ. 1450, Azurara, II. p. c.

[3] For accounts for works at the Mute juxta Charring Crouche in 1413, see Exch. Accts. 502/30, including 800 green turves dug at Tybourn pro falconibus desuper sedendis, 13 wooden stocks (stipid' maerem') for the same, and 25 iron terrets (turettys ferri, i.e. rings) firmat' in stipite. For terra nostra de mewes, see Rym. xi. 29. This was where the king's hawks were shut up while muting (i.e. moulting), Stow, vi. 2; J. T. Smith, 12; Barnard, 237. Cf. l'espervier au mue, Menagier, ii. 311; ung oyseau qui est en mue, Champollion-Figeac, 136; skulk like moulting birds together, E. Taylor, 288; as hauke on perche that sittes in mewe, Laud Troy Book, 190; Kempe, 25; shet in mewe, Lydg. Troy Book, 873; close in mewe, ibid. 68, 77; keep tounge in mewe, Lydg. Burgh, 66. For nid' d'oiseaux of Duke of Orleans, see L'Intermédiaire, xxiii. 100, from Jean Chusat's account in 1406.

[4] Rot. Parl. iii. 452; Comp. Peer. i. 57. For confirmation to him of the Channel Islands and the Isle of Wight with Carisbrooke, see Pat. 1 H. V, iii. 17, Sept. 12, 1413. For £1000 per annum granted to him from confiscated estates of the Earl of Gloucester after the death of his son Richard le Despenser to meet his unpaid claims as Lieutenant of Aquitaine, see Pat. 2 H. V, i. 28; ii. 16, April 16, 1414; cf. Wylie, ii. 38. His allowance as Constable of the Tower (see page 1, note 11) was still unpaid as well as an annuity of 100 marks, but he retained the custody of the estates of the late Lord Despenser in Gloucestershire and on the Marches of Wales, a knight being appointed sheriff of Glamorgan to save his rights and those of the king on the understanding that the lands should not be granted away till the Duke of York's return. On March 14, 1415, he is called Earl of Rutland and Cork, Riley, Mem. 603, who supposes that these titles were only held by him during his father's lifetime but this is a mistake, see Comp. Peer. viii. 213, quoting Sandford, 381. Stow (347) calls him uncle to the king (cf. "my uncke ye Duke of York," Famous Victories, 36) and (348) High Constable of England, an office which he only held from July 12, 1398, to Sept. 30, 1399, Doyle, iii. 744. In 1415 the wages of "menials" in his household for a "term" are for a squire 50s., a varlet 20s., a garçon 10s., a page 6s. 8d., see Rym. ix. 308; Wills of Kings, 218.

[5] Wylie, i. 74.

[6] He calls himself "Richard York," Rym. ix. 301; see also Orig. Lett. II. i. 48; Elmham, Lib. Metr. 105. Contemporary writers call him "Sir Richard of York," Chron. Lond. 100; or "Sir Ricardus de Yhorke," Otterbourne, 276; Hunter, 17; or "Ricardus Langley," Croyland, 500; or "Ricardus de Connesburgh," Monast. vi. 355, from his birthplace, i.e. Conisborough Castle near Doncaster, Hunter, South Yorkshire, 112. He was born circ. 1374, Comp. Peer. ii. 120. For a representation of him in a window in Canterbury Cathedral circ. 1414, see Doyle, i. 294, from Harl. MS. 5805, fol. 323; cf. Orig. Lett. II. i. 49. For his arms in a window in the college at Fotheringhay, see Bonney, 46; also Monast. viii. 1601; Doyle, i. 294, from Cotton MS. Julius C. vii.

[7] Chron. Lond. 98; Comp. Peer. ii. 120, viii. 212, where the creation is dated

As Warden of the East March of Scotland[1] the newly created Duke of Bedford took occasion immediately to call attention to the desperate condition of the defences of Berwick[2]. The town walls were in ruins and the gates and drawbridges all weakened. No guns, powder, artillery or stones had been supplied since the place was plundered by the Scots in 1405[3]. His own allowance as Warden was in arrears to the amount of £13,099. 9s. 6d., to cover which he had coined his plate and pledged his jewels and was practically a ruined man. In spite of recent instalments of pay[4], his troops were sending round "ragmans[5]" threatening to abandon the place, and the burgesses had drawn up a resolution under their common seal that they would have to do the same. The Duke had now been Warden for nearly 11 years[6], during which time he had received 11,500 marks less than Hotspur had received before him, without a penny to meet the extra cost of march-days, for which his predecessors had been allowed an additional £1000 a year. If nothing could be done to secure payment for his men, he now declared that he must resign his charge, though with great regret, for his full desire was to serve his sovereign with all the loyalty that lay in his power. Within a short time he actually carried out his threat, and on Sept. 29, 1414[7], the Duke of York was appointed Warden of Berwick and the East March of Scotland in his stead, on the understanding that the allowance for himself and his troops should be punctually paid every quarter, and on Dec. 27, 1414[8],

---

May 1, 1414, his brother the Duke of York having previously resigned the title. Called "Cambrai" or "Cantbrie" in Monstr. 366, or "Cambéri" in Le Fèvre, i. 222. For payments to him as Earl of Cambridge May 16, 1415, see Rym. ix. 248. For £40 paid to him out of £133. 6s. 8d. per annum granted to him by Richard II and confirmed by Henry V, see Iss. Roll 3 H. V, Pasch., May 15, 1415. Cf. multis bonis ditaverat et prae caeteris honoraverat ratione generis et parentelae, Wals. ii. 306; Hypodig. 457.

[1] Page 1, note 9.
[2] Ord. Priv. Co. ii. 136–139.
[3] Wylie, ii. 264.
[4] Page 53.
[5] p' lor sev'alx lres ragmans, Ord. Priv. Co. ii. 138. For Rageman (1296), see Stat. i. 44; Robinson and James, 36; Marks, 14; Cent. Dict., s.v. *Ragman's Roll*; called Ragman's Bonds in Rankin, 238; Jamieson, iii. 603; Pollard, 122, 212; Skeat, s.v. *Rigmarole*; Wylie, iv. 359. For the game of "Ragman Roll," see Hazlitt, i. 69, where "Kinge Ragman" is supposed to mean the Devil.
[6] i.e. since Aug. 1403, Wylie, i. 368, iv. 252; Doyle, i. 150.
[7] Rot. Scot. ii. 211; Ord. Priv. Co. ii. 143; Doyle, iii. 744; Dict. Nat. Biogr. xlv. 403. Called Aug. 19, 1414, in Goodwin, 46, quoting "Arch. Reg." On May 9, 1415, he still appears as Warden of the East March, Rym. ix. 241; Rot. Scot. ii. 213.
[8] Rym. ix. 194; Rot. Scot. ii. 212.

he was authorised to meet the Earl of Douglas on the border and conclude a further short truce for a period not exceeding three months.   Negotiations for the reparation of breaches of the truce with Scotland were then resumed, some of the Duke of Bedford's officers being present to supply information as to details when required[1].   On May 9, 1415[2], Robert Umfraville and James Harington[3], who was the Duke of York's lieutenant at Berwick, were authorised to negotiate a fresh treaty or prolong the old one, but on May 16, 1415[4], a new Warden of the East March was appointed in the person of Richard Lord Grey of Codnor[5], who was empowered together with Robert Ogle and Master Richard Holme[6] to meet commissioners from the Duke of Albany to discuss the subject on August 6, 1415[7].

Since the opening of the new reign some stronger efforts had been made to put a stop to piracy on the high seas, which was rapidly getting out of all control and involving the country in constant broils with its foreign neighbours. Owing to the war between Denmark and the Hansers[8], no English ships could pass the Sound and the whole of the Baltic trade was paralysed.   Nearer home the seas were still unsafe[9].   English vessels lay off Queenborough[10] and

---

[1] Ord. Priv. Co. ii. 142.   For £490 paid to the Earl of Douglas for expenses in diebus treugarum et equitationibus tempore guerrae super marchias, see Exch. Rolls Scot. iv. 353, which also contains payments to the Abbot of Kelso for expenses of commissioners holding march-days for truce between June 21, 1415, and June 26, 1416.

[2] Rym. ix. 241; Rot. Parl. ii. 213; Ridpath, 382.

[3] Cf. Cal. Doc. Scot. iv. 172.   He was the captor of the Earl of Douglas at Shrewsbury, Wylie, ii. 59.   For William Harington, knight, "our Banyour," who had £100 per annum granted to him on Dec. 16, 1413, see Priv. Seal 659/166.   He was sheriff of Yorkshire in 1415, Rym. ix. 248.

[4] Or May 12, in Sloane MS. 4600, f. 266, where he is to receive £2100 per annum in time of peace or £5000 in time of war.   Cf. Rot. Scot. ii. 214; Dugd. Bar. i. 711; he is called "le sire de Grey" in Ord. Priv. Co. ii. 165, May 25, 1415.

[5] For £775. 13s. 7½d. paid to Richard Lord de Grey as custos of Berwick and the East March for wages, see Iss. Roll 3 H. V, Mich., Jan. 23, 1416; also ibid. 4 H. V, Pasch., June 27, July 4, 1416; do. 4 H. V, Mich., March 9, 1417, which shows £1332 paid to him as Warden of the East March till Easter, 1417.

[6] See App. J[1].

[7] Rym. ix. 302, 303; Rot. Scot. ii. 214.   The documents in Rym. ix. 307, 310, dated at Southampton Aug. 14 and Westminster Aug. 24, 1415 (3 H. V), referring to an expected attack on Berwick by the Duke of Albany, though followed by Tytler, i. 380, and Menteith, i. 222, evidently belong to the year 1417 (5 H. V).   The former contains a reference to a letter written at Warkworth on July 21 last by the Earl of Northumberland as Warden of the East March, but he was not appointed to this office till April 11, 1417, Doyle, ii. 647.

[8] Hirsch, iv. 381.

[9] Ord. Priv. Co. ii. 131; St Denys, v. 280.

[10] Claus. 1 H. V, 34, April 28, 1413.

captured shipping with provisions from Holland and Zeeland at the mouth of the Thames. Corn-ships were plundered in transit between the Dutch ports and the southern and eastern coasts of England[1], while the traders of the injured countries were not slow to retaliate upon our shipping wherever they saw their opportunity[2]. To meet this the English stationed two armed balingers in the narrow seas to protect the fishing boats and the merchants taking wool over to the Staple at Calais[3]. Letters of marque were issued as in the preceding reign, and on Aug. 26, 1413[4], the wine-ships were warned that they must not attempt the voyage singly, but always in company, so as to protect one another when at sea[5]. But in view of his coming plans it was obviously to the new king's advantage that some effort should be made to arrive at a better understanding. Accordingly, when the first Parliament closed in the summer of 1413, a squire named Nicholas Soterley[6] had been despatched to Flanders on secret service, and inquiries were ordered as to the restoration of Flemish goods that had been captured at sea[7]

---

[1] For 23 (or 24) ships of Holland and Zeeland loaded with corn from the Somme and proceeding to Holland captured by Peter Brant, captain of a balinger "le Margaret de Cales," partly owned by Thomas Pickworth, knight, the lieutenant-governor of Calais (Wylie, iii. 63, 306), and taken to Sandwich, see Claus. 1 H. V, 30, April 12, 26, 1413, where satisfaction is to be made. For £306. 6s. 8d. paid to merchants of Holland for certain quarters of corn captured at sea, see Iss. Roll 1 H. V, Mich., Jan. 27, 1414; Pat. 1 H. V, iii. 5, Oct. 21, 1413. For the Maryknight of Holland with a cargo of Hamburg beer captured on June 20, 1413, off the coast of Zeeland and taken to Winchelsea, see Claus. 1 H. V, 18, July 27, 1413. For the Christopher of Danzig (in Iss. Roll 4 H. V, Mich., March 19, 1417, her master is Henry Mingterburg) detained at Southampton, see Pat. 1 H. V, ii. 13 d, July 13, 1413. For 1000 quarters of barley and oats from Yarmouth to Holland and Zeeland, see French Roll 1 H. V, 37, Apr. 12, 1413; Carte, Rolles, ii. 207; Ewald, xliv. 545.

[2] For men of Devon and Cornwall lately captured on the sea and held to excessive ransom, see Pat. 1 H. V, iii. 17 d, Sept. 12, 1413.

[3] i.e. between Sept. 8 and Nov. 1, 1413. Iss. Roll 1 H. V, Pasch., Aug. 14, 1413, has payment to John Bohoun a Sussex knight for this purpose, also £100 paid to Richard Whitington for convoying merchants to Calais, Iss. Roll 1 H. V, Mich., Oct. 10, 1413, and £25 to London merchants for a similar service, ibid. Feb. 22, 1414. In Rot. Parl. iv. 115 foreign merchants have wool weighed at the port at which they have purchased it in England. They are then provided with billas appelez cokets certifying that the customs duty has been paid, but the wool itself is only to be delivered to them à la troone de Calais. This is called "forcing export trade into certain channels" in Malden, viii. For the wool staple at Calais, see Higden, ix. 262; for do. at Middelburg, ibid. ix. 90; at Westminster, J. A. Robinson, 10; see also Sandeman, 66, quoting Rot. Parl. ii. 246. For arms of the Staple of Calais in the church of St Olave's, Hart Street (1516), see Macklin, 170. For gateway of the Staple at Calais temp. Edw. III, see Thomson, Pt. vi.

[4] Rym. ix. 47.   [5] Cf. page 118, note 7.

[6] For order for payment to him, see Iss. Roll 1 H. V, Pasch., July 17, 1413.

[7] i.e. July 10, 1413, Pat. 1 H. V, iii. 43 d. For inquiry as to breaches of truce with

with the result that the usual adjustments of compensation
were allowed in due course[1].   On Aug. 10, 1413[2], an order
was issued for the arrest of John Hawley[3], son of the respectable and powerful Dartmouth rover[4], even though he
had been himself commissioned earlier in the same year to
hold inquiries as to the detention of Spanish shipping captured under letters of marque issued in the previous reign.

It was now enacted[5] that an officer should be appointed
in every port, who was to be a substantial man owning land
that yielded at least £40 a year.   As a royal official he
would receive an annual stipend of £40 and be assisted,
if need be, by two lawyers, and he would hold a court
entrusted with large powers corresponding in all respects
with those of the Admiral, except as regards questions of
life and death.   Every vessel proposing to clear from his
port must be scheduled on a list together with the name
of her owner, the numbers of her crew, the nature of her
cargo and other such particulars[6], and all prizes taken at
sea must be forthwith notified to him as the "Conservator
of Truces and Safe-conducts."   Henceforward any breach

Flanders and Brittany, see page 102, note 9, Pat. 1 H. V, v. 21 d, Feb. 12, 1414.   For
a Flemish ship seized by men of Sandwich, see Pat. 1 H. V, v. 29 d, Jan. 14, 1414.

[1] For £140. 19s. 10d. and £138. 17s. 6d. paid as compensation to Geoffrey, or Godfrey Savage (or Sabage) of Flanders for losses at sea tempore treugarum, see Iss. Roll 1
H. V, Mich., Feb. 19, 22, 1414.

[2] Pat. 1 H. V, iii. 21 d; Cal. Pat. H. V, i. 116.

[3] For order dated April 13, 1413, to John Hawley to release a Spanish balinger called
Seint Croice now at Dartmouth, see Claus. 1 H. V, 34.   For a suit brought against him
by Peter Gunsales the master of this ship, which was captured under letters of marque
granted to Margery de Coventry against the men of Santander, see Early Chanc.
Proc. i. 29.   For commission dated April 14, 1413, to Thomas Carreu, knight, and John
Hawley, esquire, to inquire as to a balinger of Spain captured under letters of marque
temp. Henry IV and detained at Dartmouth, see Pat. 1 H. V, i. 28 d, in which they are
to distinguish between Frenchmen and Spaniards on board of her; see also Claus. 1 H. V,
27, June 2, 1413.   For rule that a quarter of the goods taken at sea should go to the king,
a quarter to the owner of the capturing ship, and half to her crew, see Black Book of the
Admiralty, i. 21; Nicolas, Navy, ii. 488.   For John Haule of Trematon (Cornwall)
alias John Hauele of Dartmouth, see Dep. Keep. Rep. xliv. 616, Feb. 25, 1420, where
he is in the king's retinue.   In Baildon, 91, the Baron of Carew and John Hawley explain in 1412 that having ships on the sea to destroy the king's enemies they captured a
balinger with French merchandise called the George of Paignton, took her first into Tor-
quay (le getee de Torrebaie) and thence into Dartmouth.

[4] See Wylie, iv. 454.   For suit brought against him and his son by John Dizco,
merchant of Pampeluna, for oil captured at sea by men of Bristol and Dartmouth, see
Early Chanc. Proc. i. 15; also by Robert Russell, merchant of Bristol, for the seizure of
the Grace Dieu of Brittany, ibid. i. 29.

[5] Rot. Parl. iv. 22, 105; Stat. ii. 178; Statutes at Large, iii. 16; Southey, ii. 52;
Nicolas, Navy, ii. 405; Black Book of Admiralty, i. 414–419.

[6] For "minuments (i.e. ship's papers), endentures, writyngs and coketts," see Black
Book of Admiralty, i. 29; Rym. xiii. 331.

of a truce or any attack upon holders of safe-conducts[1] would be considered as an act of treason against the king and punished accordingly. This Statute of Truces appears to have been based upon an ordinance issued in France by King Charles V under somewhat similar circumstances some 40 years before[2], but it differs from the French precedent in that it established a new local authority with a regular permanent court and fixed statutory powers.

Various opinions have been held in regard to its purport and intention. One modern writer considers its institution as "one of the most honourable acts of Henry's life, because he was satisfied with setting an example of humanity without stipulating that other governments should do the same[3]." But this is certainly too quixotic a view. Others have thought that the statute was passed "with the object of regulating the conduct of maritime warfare[4]." Its immediate purpose must probably be sought for in a desire to secure more friendly relations with Brittany[5], Portugal[6], Castile and Flanders, and to bring the operations of English pirates more effectually under systematic control[7]. But whatever eulogies are bestowed by modern writers upon this interesting experiment, it is certain that it did not work and two years later it was admitted to have failed[8]. Subsequent protests in Parliament[9] led to its periodical suspension[10], and henceforward recourse was regularly allowed to the old rough method of reprisals by letters of marque[11] which

---

[1] Every vessel having a safe-conduct paid 1s. a year per "tonne lode" certified, besides 3s. 4d. for every trader or sailor on board (two boys being reckoned as equivalent to one man), with lower rates for shorter times, Black Book, i. 400. For Breton ships loading at Bristol contra formam literarum nostrarum de salvo conductu, see Pat. 4 H. V, 16 d, Aug. 18, 1416, where the Mayor and Sheriff are to inquire into the case.

[2] viz. on Dec. 7, 1373, Black Book of Admiralty, I. pp. lxxxv, lxxxvi, 430–442.

[3] Nicolas, Navy, ii. 405; Simon, ii. 11; cf. Plummer, in Fortescue, 233.

[4] Black Book of Admiralty, i. 419.

[5] Page 103.

[6] For suit by Fernan Lopez for seizure of a Portuguese ship, see Early Chanc. Proc. i. 41.

[7] C. R. L. Fletcher, 317.

[8] For modification of it to suit particular cases in 1415, see Rot. Parl. iv. 68. Simon, ii. 11, thinks that "it was to bear fruit in the near future."

[9] e.g. in 1429 and 1433, Rot. Parl. iv. 351, 452.

[10] e.g. for seven years in 1435, ibid. iv. 493. For its revival in 1451 and renewal temp. Ed. IV, see Vict. Co. Hist. Cornwall, 482; do. Essex, 266; do. Sussex, 141, but subject to the same nugatory conditions that prevailed in 1416, Rot. Parl. iv. 351, v. 224; Stat. ii. 358. It is said not to have been formally repealed till 1863, Black Book, i. 419, though repealed by implication in 1547, Stat. IV. Pt. I. p. 19.

[11] Rot. Parl. iv. 105; Stat. ii. 198. Not "mart," as Cotton, Abridg. 552. Cf. Rot. Scot. ii. 218, 219; Guthrie, ii. 471.

had in fact never been really discontinued. For at this very time King Henry issued such letters[1] to John Waghen (or Wawne) of Beverley, who had long had a claim[2] against two merchants of Delft and Leyden for losses inflicted at sea, and he sanctioned the continuance of existing arrangements whereby the Londoners were allowed to exact reprisals from the Genoese[3]. Remonstrances against piracy had been made in vain by the Count of Holland[4] and letters of marque against Dutch shipping were now issued which were to hold good until the amount in dispute[5] had been recovered. But it was found that this policy had a tendency to cut both ways, for stores of various kinds were freely carried in Dutch bottoms for the garrison at Calais, and if these were to be seized, a steady and valuable source of supply would be inconveniently stopped. So that before many weeks had elapsed and in view of the projected invasion of France, it was found necessary to make exceptions, and on July 24, 1414[6], an order was put out that the above letters of marque were not to apply to the Calais trade.

On May 28, 1414, the Commons made a grant of 3*s.* on every tun of wine and a poundage of 1*s.* on all goods imported or exported, with the usual exceptions, including beer[7] from Bawdsey, Falkenham, and Alderton for the garrison at Calais[8]. The grant was made for three years from Michaelmas, 1414, the proceeds being used for safeguarding the sea, and the sittings closed on the following day, May 29, 1414[9].

The legislative work of this Leicester Parliament had been, as we have seen, of the utmost importance and many of the petitions presented touch upon matters of special interest. In one of these the Commons prayed that no

---

[1] Dated May 14, 1414, Rym. ix. 125; repeated Dec. 5, 1414, ibid. 188.
[2] Rym. viii. 96, 733.
[3] Rot. Parl. iv. 51. See page 105.
[4] i.e. William VI, Duke of Bavaria (1404–1417), Mas Latrie, 1749; Grande Encycl. xx. 104; Wylie, i. 90.
[5] viz. 851½ nobles and 22*d*.
[6] Rym. ix. 156.
[7] Cervoise; not corn, as Nichols, Leicestershire, i. 369.
[8] Wylie, iii. 58, note 7. On April 25, 1415, Sandwich, Faversham, Dover, Deal and Mongeham are appointed to supply beer and victuals to Calais for a year in place of the "town of Gosseford in Suffolk" which is returned as no longer able for the work, Rym. ix. 224. For Gosford haven aliter dict' Bawdsey haven, see Marsden, 96.
[9] Rot. Parl. iv. 17; Prynne, 507; "about the end of May," Wake, 350.

law should be engrossed as a statute which would change its meaning and intent as asked for in their petitions; to which the king assented, with the proviso that he should still retain his prerogative right to grant so much as he liked of the petition and refuse the rest[1]. It seems however to be going too far to call this "a great constitutional boon[2]" or "a landmark in political history[3]," merely because in the petition itself the Commons assert that "it hath ever been their liberty and freedom that there should no statute be made, oflasse they gaf thereto their assent[4]," and it has been rightly noted by historians that in spite of the king's assent we find no vestige of the incident on the statute-book[5].

By the Statute of Labourers passed at Cambridge in 1388[6] any labourer or servant found away from his own neighbourhood without a sealed permit was to be put in the stocks until he undertook to go back to his own place. But labourers still strayed away and took their chance of being caught; so it was now ordered[7] that copies of all statutes[8] relating to them should be forwarded to the sheriff in each county with instructions to call the attention of the Justices of the Peace to their duties and get the penalties enforced.

In the north the franchises of Tynedale, Ribblesdale and Hexhamshire[9], where the king's writ did not run[10], had become nests of murderers and robbers, who were in league with the Scots and defied both the sheriff and the law. An effort was now made to get at these offenders by making the Lords of the Franchises submit to fines for their evil deeds. An Act was also passed dealing more sharply with cases where justices, sheriffs and coroners failed to enforce

---

[1] To graunte which of thoo that you luste and to wernne (i.e. refuse, Halliwell, ii. 923) the remanent, Rot. Parl. iv. 22; Stubbs, iii. 88; Anson, i. 248; Kail, xviii; Dasent, 74.

[2] Stubbs, iii. 87.

[3] Goldwin Smith, i. 255.

[4] Kingsford, 107, thinks that they were now recognised as assenters and not merely petitioners.

[5] Hallam, 511. Guthrie, ii. 456, thinks that "had this petition been ever examined (i.e. accepted) it would have given an irrecoverable blow to the arguments advanced by the enemies of the Commons in Parliament."

[6] Stat. ii. 56; Stubbs, ii. 525; Wylie, ii. 465.

[7] Stat. ii. 177.

[8] e.g. 1349, 1351, Stat. i. 307, 311; Tout, 223; Green, 242.

[9] Not "Erehamshire," as Kail, xviii.

[10] Rot. Parl. iv. 21; Stat. ii. 177; ou les briefs du roy ne current, Conc. iii. 360; Goodwin, 40; Wylie, ii. 257.

the existing law against rioting, and as the preamble refers to felons who fly to woods and inaccessible places[1], it would seem to have been levelled against the fugitive Oldcastle whom proclamations and promises of abundant rewards had so far failed to dislodge.   But apart from the Lollard rising there is plenty of evidence of the existence of disorder in every part of the land.   Rioting was reported to be rampant in the Midlands[2], in the Universities of Oxford and Cambridge[3] and indeed all over the country, the clerics being often very bad offenders[4], especially the Cluniacs and Cistercians who took advantage of their exemption from episcopal control to carry their "detestable brawls[5]" to all lengths.

On July 30, 1410, Roger Frank had been elected Abbot of Fountains in succession to Robert Burley[6], but his claim had been disputed by John Ripon[7], Abbot of Meaux[8] near Hull.   But Ripon, who was a man of the world and had spent much time at the papal court, had taken the law into his own hands before[9], and after much expense Frank was driven out[10].   Both sides appealed to Pope John XXIII, and Cardinal Uguccione the Archbishop of Bordeaux[11], who held the archdeaconry of York[12], was commissioned to adjudicate.   He gave his decision in favour

---

[1] Goodwin, 40.

[2] For appointment of Henry Fitzhugh, John Rothenale, John Hals and John Barton, junr. to inquire into rioting in Lincolnshire, Notts. and Derbyshire, see Pat. 2 H. V, i. 9 d, May 22, 1414.

[3] Rot. Parl. iv. 31.

[4] For three canons and other monks from Barnwell who lay in wait for Thomas Paunfeld on Sept. 10, 1405, on the king's highway between "Sterisbrigge Chapel" and Cambridge with force and arms, beat him and wounded him and took his books and bills, see Rot. Parl. iv. 60.   After seven years' imprisonment Paunfeld now brought his case before the Parliament.

[5] Brigae detestabiles, Conc. iii. 363; grande debate, Rot. Parl. iv. 101.

[6] Who died May 13, 1410.   In T. Burton (Melsa, iii. 277) he is immediatus visitator of Meaux.

[7] He was appointed a papal chaplain on Sept. 3, 1397, Papal Letters, v. 27.   For a portable altar granted to him with permission to celebrate mass before daybreak, see ibid. v. 29, 60, 565.   He was Forester of Nidderdale, ibid. v. 355, 552.

[8] He is so called in Cleop. E. II. 298; Papal Letters, vi. 380, but his name is not in the list of abbots in T. Burton or Monast. v. 388.

[9] For rehabilitation for him dated April 18, 1403, for pursuing robbers who plundered some of the Fountains property and beheading one of them, see Papal Letters, v. 551.

[10] J. Burton, 211.

[11] For his visit to England in 1408, see Wylie, iii. 363; Souchon, i. 75, ii. 278, 311; Earle, Perpignan, pp. vii, 641.   Called Hugocinio or Uguccioni, Eubel, i. 25.

[12] i.e. since 1384, Le Neve, iii. 133; also the prebend of Hansacre (Lichfield) since Nov. 10, 1410, Papal Letters, vi. 197, though not mentioned in Le Neve, i. 611.   He died before Aug. 4, 1412, Gouget, 131, 239, who gives the account of the receiver who left the palace at Bordeaux on the arrival of the Duke of Clarence on Dec. 11, 1412.

of Frank and excommunicated Ripon[1]. The two claimants however still carried on their animosities and a disgraceful *fracas* ensued between their respective partisans on the high road between a large pool[2] and the entrance to the park at Welbeck in Nottinghamshire. On the accession of Henry V the tide turned in favour of Ripon. On March 24, 1413[3], the Pope reversed his decision; the new king took over the custody of the Abbey on Dec. 14[4] and on May 7, 1414[5], issued a writ putting John Ripon in possession, who henceforward appears as the recognised Abbot of Fountains, though as late as December, 1416[6], the matter was still under the consideration of the Council at Constance, to which Ripon had been appointed a delegate[7]. But his actual possession was not yet quite secure. On April 7, 1418[8], he received a pardon for all past offences and retained his post[9] till his death, which happened on March 12, 1434[10], at Thorpe-Underwoods near Boroughbridge, a Yorkshire manor belonging to the Abbey. He was buried in the chancel of the adjoining church at Little Ouseburn.

As illustrations of the prevailing lawlessness we have a record of a love-day[11] being broken up with violence in Staffordshire[12], while the Duke of York[13] was specially

---

[1] Papal Letters, vi. 380.
[2] Estank, Rot. Parl. iv. 27. Cf. stanks and laies, York, 20, 198; ponds and stangkes, ibid. 40; stankis and louchis (i.e. loughs), J. Stevenson (James I), 18; Wylie, ii. 64, note 7; estans, Bouvier, Descr. 40.
[3] Papal Letters, vi. 380.
[4] Monast. v. 288, from Pat. 1 H. V, 4, in Harl. MS. 6972, p. 12.
[5] Chancery Warrants, Ser. I. 1364/6; Cal. Pat. H. V, i. 180.
[6] Rot. Parl. iv. 101; Cotton, Abridg. 551.
[7] Rym. ix. 162, Dec. 5, 1414; Richental, 173; Mansi, xxviii. 626.
[8] Carte, Rolles, i. 257; Ewald, xli. 683; Bréquigny, 206, where the editor wrongly supposes him to be Abbot of Fontaine-Guérard (Eure) on the Andelle near Pont de l'Arche, which was really a Cistercian nunnery under an Abbess, Gall. Christ. xi. 320. For protection granted by Henry V to the Abbey of Fontaine-Guérard on July 8, 1418, see Bréquigny, 208; Ewald, xli. 693; Carte, Rolles, i. 264.
[9] He is still Abbot of Fountains on May 5, 1420, Papal Letters, vii. 144, where certain of his privileges are annulled. In Early Chanc. Proc. i. 36 (circa 1421) John Rypon, Abbot of Fountains, sues Nicholas Tempest in regard to a grange at Sutton, i.e. Sutton-Howgrave, Monast. v. 291, 313, in the parish of Kirklington. For suit by the Abbot of St Mary Fountains v. William Bolton, chaplain, see Early Chanc. Proc. i. 43.
[10] J. Burton, 211; Monast. v. 314.
[11] Cf. Laud Troy Book, 217, 531; Pol. Songs, ii. 255; men that make love days, Brute, Thorpe, &c. 161; Wylie, ii. 189; P. Plo. ii. 47. Cf. make hem kyssen and be frende, Kail, 69. For 6d. for beer and 6d. for a gallon (*lagena*) of wine in die amoris with Lord Boucher at Maldon apud domum frumenti in 1408, see Maldon Rolls 4/2.
[12] Rot. Parl. iv. 32, 33.
[13] Godwin, 41, from Trin. Term Rot. xxxvi, Salop.

despatched to see that a grand jury was empanelled to deal with and punish cases of murder and robbery in Shropshire[1]. In that county Sir John Cornwall[2], the sheriff, had been recently fined 60s. for failing to furnish a sufficient retinue, and the tenths and fifteenths could not be got in because Robert Corbet[3] and Richard Leighton[4], the two knights who had represented the county in the last Parliament, set upon and maimed the tax-gatherers and killed their horses[5]. For when the collectors presented themselves at Eaton and Moreton-Corbet to levy a distress for non-payment of the tax, the servants of the aforesaid knights assaulted them with swords and they had much ado to get away. They lodged for a night at Oldbury with some money that they had succeeded in getting in. But a band of from 120 to 140 armed men came out from the adjoining town of Bridgnorth[6] intending to rob them and kill them in their beds. They were already early up, however, when the mob rushed on them shouting: "Slay! Slay!" and though they themselves escaped, yet some of

[1] For order dated June 4, 1414, that judges in Shropshire and elsewhere shall redress riots against the law, see Chancery Warrants, Ser. I. 1364/9. For £15 paid to the sheriff of Shropshire for his expenses when the King's Justices were in Salop for sessions, see Iss. Roll 3 H. V, Pasch., April 12, 1415.

[2] Called "Cornewayle," Rec. Roll 1 H. V, Pasch., May 4, 1413, or "Cornewaille," ibid. Mich., Oct. 2, 1413, where he is *late* sheriff of Salop, and John Cornewale is *late* sheriff of Oxfordshire, though his name does not occur among the sheriffs of Oxfordshire in Sheriffs' List, 108. John Cornwall is sheriff of Salop in 1399, 1403, 1405, but no name appears as sheriff in 1414, ibid. 118. For 20s. paid to a messenger for carrying a letter with all speed to the escheator of Salop, see Iss. Roll 1 H. V, Mich., Feb. 16, 1414. For £20 pardoned to Edward Sprenchouse, late sheriff of Salop (i.e. in 1410, Sheriffs' List, 118, where he is called Sprengeaux), from his account because of his losses, see Pat. 2 H. V, i. 28, Feb. 26, 1415.

[3] For Robert Corbet *late* sheriff of Shropshire, see Pat. 3 H. V, i. 34, April 16, 1415; Rec. Roll 3 H. V, Pasch., April 27, 30, 1415; Iss. Roll 3 H. V, Pasch., April 12, 1415, i.e. he was sheriff in 1413, Sheriffs' List, 118. In Priv. Seal 5 H. V, 840 (July 13, 1417), Robert Corbet is referred to as dead; also Claus. 5 H. V, 13, Sept. 25, 1417, which refers to inquiry at Shrewsbury as to his estate where his wife Joan is to have her dower, ibid. Oct. 9, 1417, though in Sheriffs' List, 118, he appears as sheriff of Salop in 1419, and is said to have died Aug. 12, 1420. For Sibilla daughter of Robert Corbett, esquire, wife of John Grenell, esquire, see Pat. 8 H. V, 14, July 5, 1420.

[4] Called Lacum, Lacon (Wylie, iii. 267), Laken or Lakan (Claus. 4 H. V, 13 d). He was M.P. for Salop in Nov. 1414, Return Parl. i. 283; also in 1413, 1421, 1423, 1431, 1433, ibid. i. 279, 300, 306, 319, 325. In Sheriffs' List, 118, he is sheriff of Salop in 1415.

[5] Rot. Parl. iv. 30, 80.

[6] On June 8, 1413, David Holbache and three others had been commissioned to hold an inquiry as to Bridgnorth tenants in Claverley and Morf Forest, Pat. 1 H. V, i. 12 d; also ibid. iv. 29 d, Nov. 18, 1413. For order to arrest John Bruyn of Bridgnorth and bring him to the king's presence, see Iss. Roll 1 H. V, Pasch., Aug. 14, 1413. For order to the escheators of Staffordshire and Salop to seize his land for debts due to the king, see ibid. Feb. 19, 1414. He was himself sheriff of Salop in 1420, Sheriffs' List, 118.

their horses were shot[1] and several of their followers were
left for dead. Afterwards they found themselves again
attacked in the square at Shrewsbury, and when they were
on their way to London to render their accounts at the
Exchequer before Martinmas 1413 as required[2], one of
them was confronted in an inn at Dunstable by Sir Robert
Corbet himself, who cried out : " Who made thee so hardy
to put any bill to the king to undo me withal ? " at the
same time cutting him about the legs and inflicting " hor-
rible wounds."

This insecurity in the country, together with the frequent
and prolonged visitations of floods[3], plague and murrain,
had greatly reduced the value of property, and a case is
recorded in the previous year, where a manor that had
before been worth £20 per annum could not now fetch
half that sum[4].

Already the Commons appear to have been looking
with some alarm at the king's overmastering devotion to
the Church and fearing lest he should undo his father's
secularising work in the matter of the alien priories[5].
The previous Parliament had protested against these
Frenchmen securing themselves by becoming denizens[6]
and pressed for the strict enforcement of the statute against
Provisors[7], so that no foreigner should be allowed to hold
an English benefice[8]. They petitioned that all foreign

For confirmation of Roger (not Robert, as Wylie, ii. 280, note 8) Wyleley as custos of
the forest of Morff and Shirlet, see Pat. 1 H. V, i. 20, June 12, 1413.

[1] With seetes, i.e. settes (sagittae), see page 160, note 1.

[2] Page 319.

[3] For Peter de la Haye on commission for floods in Yorkshire, John Waterton (in
Lincs.), John Derehurst (in Gloucestershire) and others elsewhere, see Pat. 1 H. V, i. 21 d,
June 1, 1413. For pontage allowed at Aylesbury for repairing bridge over the Thame
at Walton, see Pat. 1 H. V, i. 24, May 15, 1413; also for Ayleswaterbrigg near St Nicholas
Hospital at New Sarum, ibid. v. 17, Dec. 31, 1413; at Kingston-on-Thames, where
causeways are destroyed by the recent flood, ibid. v. 25, Feb. 9, 1414; Priv. Seal 659/182;
at Maidenhead (five years) for repair of portus (*sic*), Pat. 2 H. V, ii. 8, Nov. 27, 1414.
For the great bridge at Cambridge confractus et dirutus, see Pat. 1 H. V, iii. 37 d, July
14, 1413.

[4] Comme pur la graunde trouble qeux ont esté en le dit royaulme pluisors ans en-
durantz avant cestes heures, Duckett, i. 259 (written April 16, 1413).

[5] Called "restes des dotations de la conquête," Puiseux, Insurrections, 143; Wylie,
i. 79, iii. 144. See App. K[1].

[6] Rot. Parl. iv. 13; Stat. ii. 172.

[7] Stat. i. 316, ii. 70; Rot. Parl. iii. 266.

[8] Rot. Parl. iv. 11; cf. Redman, 32; Halle, 57; Grafton, i. 509 (borrowing from
Pol. Verg. 440); Holinsh. iii. 547, where this is said to have been decided at a council
held in London at Michaelmas, 1414; Rosières, 430.

inmates should be expelled from religious houses and be replaced by fit and honest Englishmen[1], and that all their belongings, which had been, or ought to have been, confiscated for the relief and support of the whole community[2] during the previous reigns, should be kept in the king's hands after Michaelmas 1413, the right of pre-emption being reserved to those farmers who were already in actual possession[3]. But the University of Oxford had just protested against this religious property and these consecrated buildings passing into the hands of secular owners[4], and as a counter-stroke the Commons now prayed that the king would not return the confiscated property of the foreigners[5] under any circumstances, but keep it in his own hands and those of his successors for ever[6]. His piety saw no obstacle in this, as the French had already snapped up any English church possessions that lay within their grasp[7], so he readily gave his consent and, as a consequence, he has been generally credited with the great suppression of the alien priories[8], though his father had been the real confiscator and the blow had actually fallen long before he had succeeded to the throne[9].

[1] Idonei et honesti, Pat. 1 H. V, v. 10, Jan. 27, 1414; Claus. 1 H. V, 21, Aug. 26, 1413; honestes persones englois, Rot. Parl. iv. 11.

[2] En reliefment et supportation des communs, Rot. Parl. iv. 13.

[3] See Wylie, iii. 144, note 6. For Nicholas Blackburn as farmer of Beggar near Richmond in Yorkshire (not Surrey, as Wylie, iv. 383), see Rec. Roll 1 H. V, Mich., Nov. 15, 1413. For receipt from William Warde and others for custody of lands belonging to the Abbey of Conches near Evreux, see Rec. Roll 2 H. V, Pasch., May 4, 1414.

[4] Conc. iii. 361; Oudin, iii. 2213; H. O. Coxe, Catalogue Corpus Christi Coll. 73.

[5] Champollion-Figeac, Lettres, ii. 334, 588. Not that "they entreated him to seize *all* the ecclesiastical revenues and convert them to the use of the crown," as Hume, iv. 40; Cassell, i. 521.

[6] Rym. ix. 280, June 25, 1415; oustez et desheritez pour toutz jours, Rot. Parl. iv. 22; Monast. vii. 986; in perpetuum, Rym. ix. 281, x. 19; a dit roi et sez heires a remeyndrez, Rot. Parl. v. 412; Hasted, ii. 773; in perpetuum debent remanere, Pat. 8 H. V, 15.   [7] Duckett, ii. 13.

[8] Fuller (Church Hist. 304) places the suppression in 1415, and supposes that the alien priories were bestowed on the king. Stow (345) thinks that Henry V suppressed more than 100 alien priories; called 142 in Hasted, i. 15 (for a list of 141, see Monast. viii. 1652, but they are mostly the confiscations of 1407). Others say 122, as Brougham, 98; Pauli, v. 96; Bright, i. 291; or 110, as Reyner, ii. 71; Wade, 80; Drayton, Bataille, 104; Echard, i. 182; Larrey, 810; Rapin, iii. 436; Tindal, i. 509 (who supposes that there was an Act of Parliament, while admitting that he cannot find one except in Rym. ix. 281, which proves nothing); Horsfield, i. 235; Morant, ii. 407; Ruding, i. 257; Henry, v. 34; Lingard, iii. 486; Duckett, i. 31, 225, ii. 5, 7; Aubrey, ii. 46; Malden, 76; Low-Pulling, 552; do. Rise, ii. 13; Oman, Hist. 222; Scotière, 283 (who dates the Leicester Parliament in 1424); Church Quart. Rev. xlviii. 415.

[9] For previous confiscations, see Wylie, iii. 142, note 7; Speed (773) quoting Stat. 13 Richard II, which recites the Statute of Provisors 1351 (see Stat. i. 316, ii. 70, 172;

Wherever the majority of the inmates of these priories were of English birth, the houses had usually paid large sums to purchase charters of indigenation[1], promising henceforward to be good and loyal Englishmen[2], and undertaking that their Priors should never cross the sea[3]. Subject to these conditions, they were allowed to elect their own Prior and were declared to be denizens[4], being thereby enabled to pull at least a portion of their property out of the fire, besides escaping from their previous obligations to contribute money for the support of their parent houses abroad[5].

As illustrations we may take the case of the Priory of St Neots[6] in Huntingdonshire. After varying fortunes in Danish times it had been settled as a cell of the great Benedictine monastery of Bec-Hellouin near Bernay in the days of William the Conqueror[7]. During times of war with France it had been repeatedly seized by Henry III

Froude, i. 93; Tout, 223; Wakeman, 147). For confiscations temp. Ed. I, II, see Monast. iii. 208. In 1346 the possessions of the alien priories were in the hands of the king (i.e. Edward III) who resisted the petition of the Commons that the inmates should be personally expelled, Rot. Parl. ii. 162. For the great confiscation of the lands of alien priories by Edward III in 1369, see Rot. Parl. ii. 302. Napier (11) thinks that the alien priories were *all* dissolved in 1414; also Ransom, 144. Called 1338 in Ruskin, Val d'Arno, 129, quoting Henry, Book IV, Chap. I, 1721. Called a "general dissolution" in Kirby, Annals, 22 (who regards the confiscations by Edward III in 1346 as a "constitutional step"); "finally dissolved," do. Hamble, 256. Lestrange (Greenwich, i. 67) thinks that the *bishops* agreed to the surrender of all priories held by foreigners in order to escape from greater spoliation. C. R. L. Fletcher (316) thinks that "the church was obliged to lighten her ship by throwing over the alien priories." Tout (263) calls this "the first occasion on which Parliament ventured to suppress religious houses." Benham (Winchester, 144) regards it as "a sop thrown to the Cerberus of Anti-clericalism." Cf. Fisher, 369; Hassall, 223, who thinks that Henry V in 1414 "fully recognised the strength of the national movement which had led to the revolutionary *proposals* of Henry IV's reign." Clay, 228, says that Henry V followed the policy of Henry IV.

[1] Monast. v. 101; Rym. xv. 37; Du Cange, iv. 343; cf. "indigenavit," Monast. v. 78; "jam indigenantur," Usk, 124; not "are now in poverty," as ibid. 305. For payments to the clerk of the hanaper for charters of indigenation, see Exch. Accts. 215/2. For 200 marks paid by Bermondsey in 1380, see Monast. v. 92, 99, 101; Wylie, iii. 144. For Wenlock in 1395, see Monast. v. 72, 78, which was a cell of the Cluniac Priory of La Charité on the Loire, Lespinasse, 157, 363, where it is called "Venelot" or St Milburga, from its foundress. See also Marrier, 1711.

[2] For Thetford in 1377, see Reyner, ii. 72, App. 208; Monast. v. 145, 153 (or 1375 in Blomefield, ii. 106); Duckett, ii. 190, where the Prior and all the monks are legales et veri Angli nati et nutriti infra regnum et nihil apportant extra (loyalx et vrays Anglois neez et rien ne apportent par dela). For Lewes (1372) with the smaller Cluniac Priories of Castle-Acre (near Lynn), Prittlewell, Monkton-Farleigh (Wilts.), Horton (i.e. Monks-Horton near Hythe in Kent), Clifford (near Hay in Herefordshire), see Horsfield, i. 237.

[3] Monast. v. 153.

[4] For marchaunts densyns v. straungers, see Ord. Priv. Co. ii. 259.

[5] e.g. at Spalding, where the Abbot had previously paid £40 per annum to the Abbey of St Nicholas at Angers, Monast. iii. 220, 221; Reyner, App. 209.

[6] Monast. iii. 463, 476.

[7] i.e. in 1078.

and the three Edwards, but periodically restored to its French superiors. In 1409 the Prior, Edward Salisbury, was an Englishman and all the monks were English born. In that year accordingly they paid over 300 marks to the Exchequer to secure denization and thereby escape the risks and burdens likely to attach to aliens in the future, and their new position was confirmed in November, 1414[1].

At the Cluniac Priory of Montacute[2], near Yeovil in Somersetshire, 300 marks had been paid to the king on the election of their Prior (an Englishman named William Cryche) on June 18, 1403[3], in place of a foreigner, François de Baugé[4]. In 1407 the house recognised the English secular grantee as its patron and remained essentially English till the dissolution[5]. There is moreover a case in which an Englishman, John Rogger[6], Prior of the alien priory of Tywardreath[7] near Fowey in Cornwall, which had survived the confiscations, became the farmer of another alien priory at Modbury[8] near Ivybridge, of which he had before been Prior[9] but which had gone under in the storm. Other priories, such as that of St Andrew's at Northampton[10], paid over their annual pensions to the English king[11] instead of sending them across the water; in others such as Carisbrooke[12], the dispossessed Prior Odo

---

[1] Rot. Parl. iv. 42; Monast. iii. 480.

[2] For picture, see Cassell, ii. 54.

[3] Rot. Parl. iv. 27; Reyner, ii. 72. In 1411 it was reported quod ipse jam pene deficit per gravitudinem senectutis, Duckett, i. 232, though he lived on till 1415 (not 1419, as Monast. vi. 164, 175). For *congé d'élire* on his death dated May 17, 1415, see Pat. 3 H. V, i. 14.

[4] De Baugiaco or Balgiaco, Pat. 2 H. V, 17, June 25, 1414; do. 3 H. V, i. 26, April 25, 1415.

[5] Together with its dependent cells at East Holme near Wareham in Dorsetshire (Hutchins, i. 551), St Karrol (in the parish of St Veep near Lostwithiel in Cornwall), and Malpas (near Newport in Monmouthshire), Lyte, Chartularies, lxi.

[6] He was instituted on Dec. 14, 1406, Staff. Reg. 216, 307; Monast. iv. 655.

[7] Called Trewardrayth in Priv. Seal 664/639, April 10, 1416, where John Meschin is named as Prior in 1399 (or Maslyn, Staff. Reg. 216, 252) and one of the monks is a Benedictine from Dives. For seal of the Priory, see Oliver, Monast. 408. For list of the Priors, see Devonsh. Assocn. xvii. 273; Coll. Top. and Gen. iii. 106–111. It belonged to the Benedictine Abbey of SS. Sergius and Bacchus at Angers, Monast. iv. 656; Gall. Christ. xiv. 641; Oliver, Monast. 33, and was granted on Oct. 20, 1413, to Sir John Cornwall and his wife Elizabeth (see Wylie, i. 105; Lacy, 59), but the grant was cancelled in 1418, Oliver, Monast. 34.

[8] Pat. 4 H. V, 4 d, Feb. 26, 1417.

[9] Staff. Reg. 188, 307.

[10] Monast. v. 186.

[11] Ramsay (i. 311) gives the total receipts from alien priories in the English Exchequer in 1414 as £126.

[12] Pat. 4 H. V, 3, Nov. 11, 1416; Priv. Seal 665/794, March 9, 1417.

des Ormes (*de Ulmis*), who was a native of Normandy, obtained special permission to spend the rest of his days in England instead of returning to his own devastated country; while even a great religious foundation such as the Abbey at Burton-on-Trent, which had never been attached to any foreign house but was heavily in debt, with its tenants in revolt[1], its abbot living in immorality[2], and its buildings dilapidated almost beyond the possibility of repair, was driven to accept the secular solution and put itself into the king's hands[3], who appointed a knight (John Dabridgecourt[4]), a squire (Peter Melbourne[5]), and John Bluet, Dean of the collegiate church at Leicester[6], to manage the estates and, if possible, rescue them from utter ruin.

As to the property of the alien priories there was a haunting fear among the farmers[7] lest the confiscations should be annulled, if peace were ever patched up with France. This was the motive that prompted the Leicester ordinance, by which the king pledged his word that there should be no return to the old practice of sending "apports" of money[8] out of the country, but in the grants to the farmers a proviso was usually inserted that it was merely a custody vested in them so long as the property was in the king's hands on account of the war with France[9]; and that there was real ground for uneasiness became apparent, when a final peace was established between the two countries six years later[10], after which a proclamation was issued[11] requiring all holders of lands or

---

[1] Wylie, ii. 120, note 6. For proceedings taken by Abbot Sudbury for assault, see Early Chanc. Proc. i. 33. He is named as abbot in Memoranda Roll K. R. 3-4 H. V, 7, Sept. 24, 1415.

[2] i.e. John Sudbury, Monast. iii. 35. For licence (Aug. 19, 1424) to elect another abbot in place of him, see Cal. Pat. H. VI, i. 211. For royal assent to the election of William Mathew as abbot Sept. 10, 1424, see ibid. 231. Mathew in turn resigned on Sept. 16, 1430, Cal. Pat. H. VI, ii. 83; called Sept. 6 in Monast. iii. 35.

[3] Pat. 2 H. V, i. 13, June 31 (*sic*), 1414, where William Matthew is Prior and William Bromley is cellarer. For pardon dated Oct. 2, 1414, to them and to the Abbot John Sudbury, see Pat. 2 H. V, ii. 27. For indult granted (June 7, 1423) to William Matheu to choose his own confessor, see Papal Letters, vii. 7.

[4] See page 317.   [5] Wylie, iii. 322, note 1.

[6] i.e. St Mary in the Newarke, see page 232.

[7] For farmers of alien priories in 1419, see Rot. Parl. iv. 122; les queux annuitees les suisditz fermours bien et loialment ount paiez a ceux as queux mesmes Annuitees feurent grauntez.

[8] Rot. Parl. ii. 162; iv. 22; Rym. ix. 280.

[9] e.g. Cal. Pat. H. V, i. 24, 161, 235.

[10] i.e. by the Treaty of Troyes in 1420.

[11] Claus. 8 H. V, 5 d; Rym. x. 26, Oct. 21, 1420. The proviso according to which

other possessions of the alien priories to appear in the chancery and prove their titles. Pope Martin V subsequently arranged with Henry that this property should be converted into endowments for churches and religious houses, it being understood that compensation either had been, or would be, made to the parent houses in the form of lands in Normandy[1], but the king's death appears to have checked any further yielding to what looks like a policy of restitution and remorse. In 1414, however, the position was far different, and it was afterwards officially stated that all parties concerned, including the alien priories themselves, concurred in the decision of the Parliament[2], and the general hopelessness of the outlook for the aliens who did not resort to denization can be well illustrated by the perusal of a recently published collection of documents relating to the settlements in England, which still maintained connection with their powerful parent Abbey of St Peter at Cluny[3], near Macòn in Burgundy, or its sister houses at La Charité on the Loire, near Nevers, and St Martin's-in-the-Fields in Paris.

About three years before the meeting of the Leicester Parliament John Burghersh[4], Prior of Lewes[5], as vicar-general in spirituals[6] for the Abbot of Cluny[7], had proposed to make a visitation of the 42 Cluniac priories or cells then existing in England and Scotland[8] for the preservation and

---

the possessions of the aliens were only taken into the king's hands *durante guerrâ, durauntz les guerres,* appears to have been inserted in 1390, Stat. ii. 172.

[1] This statement was made at the Council of Basle in 1434 (Bekynton, I. p. xc; II. 265), but there is no reference to any such transaction in the Papal Letters.

[2] Bekynton, ii. 264 (1434).

[3] Monast. v. 105. It was founded in 910 by William the Pious, Duke of Aquitaine, and is called "the most important monastery in the whole world," J. M. Stone, 19, quoting S. R. Maitland, Dark Ages, 350, 405.

[4] His name is not in the list of Priors in Monast. v. 6; Horsfield, i. 238.

[5] Called "a very fayre *Abbaye*" in Neale, 138; but "ye Priorye," ibid. p. 130, where "hit lyeth plesantly amongst plesant medowes," from a letter of Peter Nelond dated Lewes March 26, 1433, describing the death of his brother Prior Thomas Nelond who had just died (not April 18, 1429, as Monast. v. 6). For his brass at Cowfold near Horsham, see Waller; Ogilvie, Imperial Dict. ii. 925.

[6] Camerarius et vicarius generalis ordinis Cluniacensis, Pat. 2 H. V, i. 19, June 11, 1414; Escheators' Inquisitions, 1278.

[7] i.e. Raymond de Cadoena (i.e. Cadouin on the Dordogne above Bergerac), elected abbot Sept. 10, 1400; d. Sept. 12, 1416, Gall. Christ. iv. 1157; Marrier, 1674 (not 1446, as Duckett, i. 2, 26); called Raimundus in Pat. 4 H. V, 16; Rym. ix. 283, Aug. 18, 1416. For a letter written by him on Aug. 10, 1416, excusing himself from attendance at the Council of Constance as he is now over 70 years of age, see Mart. Coll. vii. 1217.

[8] Monast. v. p. iv.

reform of the Order.   In the course of his travels for this
purpose he had passed through a district famed for its
breed of English palfreys[1], whose value the Abbot well
knew from experience.   He tells how he had exposed
himself to perils on the sea, to perils on the road and
to perils of robbers, when the pains of death had come
about him.   But his greatest grief arose from the opposition of his own brethren, who could bite though they
could not wound.   They would not recognise his authority, but poisoned the mind of his sovereign[2] against him,
tore off the seal from his commission, made him a scorn
and a hissing and sent him baulked and empty away,
and as a sample of these false brethren he singles out
Geoffrey Graner, a monk of the Cluniac Priory at Lenton
near Nottingham, who had expectations of one day becoming Prior of that house himself.

Amongst the property of the Cluniacs in England were
the four manors of Letcombe-Regis in Berkshire, Offord-
Cluny in Huntingdonshire, and Manton and Tixover in
Rutlandshire[3].   These four properties had been granted
away[4] by Richard II and Henry IV[5] for life to Simon
Felbrigge[6], a Norfolk knight.   Felbrigge had been bannerer[7]
to King Richard, who made him a knight of the Garter
in 1397[8], and, as he was now only 40 years of age, he was
reported as cut[9] to live for 40 years more, a prediction
which turned out to be very near the truth, for he lived
to be the senior knight of the Order[10], and did not die

---

[1] Duckett, i. 257; Wylie, ii. 237, note 4.

[2] i.e. Henry IV, Duckett, i. 233–238.

[3] Ibid. i. 244, 246; ii. 3; Wylie, iii. 143, note 4.

[4] Duckett, i. 137, 192, 219, 220, 249; ii. 6, 9.   They had been held by Gilbert Talbot
of Richard's Castle who was living in 1397, but had died before 1399, ibid. i. 137
(dated Jan. 9, 1393).

[5] Pat. 2 H. V, ii. 29; do. 3 H. V, ii. 40.

[6] Duckett, i. 219; ii. 6.   For Thomas Felbrigge at the siege of Rouen in 1418, see
Rym. ix. 595.

[7] Appointed April 7, 1395, Beltz, 309, 371; Anstis, i. 170; Duckett, i. 195.   For
a hunting-gown given to him by Richard II in 1393, see Baildon, Wardrobe, 498, 506.

[8] Anstis, i. 167; Beltz, vii, xvii, clv, 254, 316, 369; not temp. H. V, as Ashmole,
508.   For his arms, see ibid. 701 (edn. 1672).

[9] Taillé de vivre, Duckett, i. 249; cf. Cotgrave, s.v.; tailliez et enclin à assez de
maulx, Bulletin Hist. Soc. Archéol. de Tarn et Garonne (1883), xi. 134.

[10] Ordinis maximé senex, Anstis, i. 168; Beltz, 372.   For his retinue (12 + 36) at
Southampton July 8, 1415, see Nicolas, Agincourt, 379; Wylie, Notes, 136; with their
names in full, Exch. Accts. 45/3, 45/5, which gives indenture dated April 29, 1415, receipt
for first quarter's wages dated June 6, 1415, and indenture of jewels June 18, 1415 (ibid.

till December 3, 1442[1]. Prior Burghersh now reported that these manors were in bad condition and not likely to be recovered for the Abbot so long as war continued between England and France, as to which he saw no prospect of a termination yet.

Near to the villages of Tixover and Manton lived a wealthy landowner named William Porter[2]. He had been a squire to King Henry IV[3] and remained high in the favour of his son[4], who granted him the manor of Shotwick[5] near Chester, retained him as one of his carvers[6] with a livery of gilt velvet trimmed with marten and a scarlet hood furred with ermine and miniver and garnished with gold ribbon[7], employed him as an envoy on foreign missions[8], and made him one of the executors of his will[9].

45/21 (65)). Of the total of his men all the archers and six of the men-of-arms were present at Agincourt, two died at Harfleur, and six were invalided home *causâ infirmitatis*, so that two more must have joined beyond the stipulated 12.

[1] Inq. p. Mort. iv. 211; Beltz, clx, 372; Nicolas, II. liv. For his will dated Sept. 21, 1442 (not 1416, as Foster, Feudal Arms, 84), proved Feb. 20, 1443, see Test. Vet. 245. He was buried in the church of the Black Friars at Norwich, Weever, 805 (not at Cromer, as Burwell, 81). For his brass at Felbrigge (not at Cromer, as Weever, 856) bearing the date of the death of his wife Margaret, viz. June 27, 1413, with blanks left for his own death, see Anstis, i. 174, 391, 722; Gough, II. ii. 133; Cotman, xxvii; Blomefield, viii. 116; Beltz, 372; Foster, Feudal Arms, 84; Enguilly d'Haridon, 151, who takes it as an illustration of all-plate armour; Macklin, 147, 152, 153, who dates the brass circ. 1416.

[2] Duckett (i. 246; ii. 8) supposes him to be the ancestor of the Porters of Alfarthing in Surrey. He was appointed on Commissions of the Peace for Cambridgeshire Mar. 21, 1413, Jan. 16, 1414, Cal. Pat. H. V, i. 417. For a dispute between him and John Trussell, knight, as to the manor and advowson of Collyweston near Stamford, see Pat. 2 H. V, i. 7 d, Dec. 1, 1414; Cal. Pat. H. V, i. 223, where two persons are to be chosen on each side to arbitrate, and William le Zouche, knight, is to collect the proceeds in the meantime; see also Pat. 5 H. V, 24, June 4, 1417, where he is called William Porter, *knight*, and the manor is called Colyn Weston. "Tykesover" was in his possession at his death in 1434, Inq. p. Mort. iv. 163, 173. For William Porter, knight, farmer of the forest of Rockingham and the parks (*parcorum*) of Brigstock, see Rec. Roll 7 H. V, Mich., Jan. 17, 1420; ibid. 8 H. V, Mich., Feb. 8, 1421.

[3] Not to the Prince of Wales, as Duckett, i. 248.

[4] Astans a latere Principis in conciliis et agendis, Duckett, i. 223, 225, where he is carissimus to Henry IV and acceptable omnibus magnatibus.

[5] i.e. to him and his wife Agnes, together with 50 marks per annum, Pat. 2 H. V, ii. 29, Sept. 1, 1414; do. 3 H. V, ii. 40, July 7, 1415; Duckett, ii. 12; Cal. Pat. H. V, i. p. 161. She was aunt to the Earl of Salisbury, being the daughter of Adam Francis, knight (see Wylie, iii. 286), and his wife Margaret. Agnes owned valuable property in London and Southwark, Claus. 5 H. V, 16, 17, May 24, 1417; Inq. p. Mort. iv. 312, where her death occurs in 1461. For pardon granted July 12, 1417, to Conand Aske, esquire, for marrying Margaret, widow of Adam Fraunceys, kt. defunctus, see Claus. 8 H. V, 18, May 6, 1420. For Conand Aske in the retinue of the Duke of Gloucester in 1415, see Nicolas, 333; Belleval, 337.

[6] For the "kerver," see Mann. and Meals, i. 324.   [7] Exch. Accts. 406/26.

[8] Page 98. For his account for expenses from Dec. 14, 1414, to March 10, 1415, with Bishop Courteney's mission to Paris, see Mirot-Déprez, lxi, 28, from Exch. Accts. 321/24.

[9] Rym. x. 506; Rot. Parl. iv. 206, 213. In his first will dated July 24, 1415, the king left him a gold cup, a horse and £6 in money, Rym. ix. 291.

In Aug. 1415, he embarked for France with a retinue of eight men-of-arms and 24 archers[1] in the service of the Earl of Suffolk[2] and was knighted for his bravery at the siege of Harfleur, where he fell ill and was invalided home with 14 of his men[3]. Two years later he landed with the second expedition in Normandy on Aug. 1, 1417[4], and he served through the siege of Rouen in the winter of 1418[5], having previously received grants of some of Lord Scrope's forfeited lands[6] after the discovery of the plot at Southampton in the summer of 1415.

Porter saw that the four above-named Cluniac manors were going to ruin in their present hands, and being well-disposed towards the Church, he desired to get the property into his own possession, thereby not only relieving his conscience[7], but at the same time doing a business-like bargain in the interest of his family. He had already shown himself a good friend to the Cluniacs at Lewes[8], so that he had no difficulty in enlisting the sympathy of Prior Burghersh in furtherance of his views. Having ascertained that the four manors yielded an income of 200 crowns per annum, he approached Burghersh with an offer of a lump sum of 500 or 600 crowns for the lot. The Prior demurred and Porter went up to 700 crowns, and it was at this stage that Burghersh addressed a letter to the Abbot at Cluny on Aug. 9, 1411[9]. Looking to the

---

[1] Hunter, 39; Wylie, Notes, 122. For their names, see Exch. Accts. 44/30 (4), where one of the men-of-arms is called John Oudeby; another John Coton is invalided home in L.T.R. Misc. Enrolled Accts. 6/11.

[2] Nicolas, Agincourt, 340; Belleval, 342. For his indenture of jewels June 13, 1415, see Exch. Accts. 45/20 (105). For a gold cup weighing 31½ ozs. valued at 26s. 8d. per oz. pledged to him by Henry V for payment of his men but not redeemed till 1430, see Nicolas, App. 17.

[3] i.e. 3+11, Exch. Accts. Q.R. 44/30 (5), where he is called a knight but only esquire in the first retinue roll, though he is said to have been knighted at Windsor on Aug. 4, 1409, Chron. Giles (H. IV), 57, i.e. Cotton MS. Julius E. IV; Shaw, ii. 11. In Misc. Enrolled Accts. 6/11 (i.e. temp. H. VI) he is *nuper armig. nunc* miles and he claims to have reshipped from Calais to Dover on Nov. 16, 1415, with 7+24; see also Rym. xi. 89.

[4] Rym. ix. 479; Rot. Norm. 284, where he is Monsieur Guillaume Porter, *chivaler*.

[5] J. Page, 8; Archaeologia, xxi. 54; xxii. 388; Rym. ix. 595. In July, 1422, he was made captain of Vernon, Exch. Accts. 49/30, where his indenture of service is dated at Rouen July 20, 1422, and the garrison numbers 14+49.

[6] Rot. Parl. iv. 218, including Market-Harborough and Bowden in Leicestershire, Pat. 3 H. V, ii. 17, 35, Aug. 8, 1415, Jan. 16, 1416, with side note: "vacat quia aliter in hoc anno"; also Cal. Pat. H. V, i. 359, 385.

[7] Conscience par plusieurs foiz m'a donné de traittier avecques vous, Duckett, i. 246.

[8] Indefessus co-operator et benevolus coadjutor, ibid. i. 231, 241, 243, 254.

[9] Ibid. i. 225–233, endorsed as anno xii. of Abbot Raymond, i.e. 1411; not 1412 as given by the editor.

hopelessness of the prospect for aliens in England, he advised his superior that it would be better to sell the manors for a little, rather than lose them altogether, so that they might at any rate bring in "something useful[1]." He reminded him that the Order had not received anything from them for the last 42 years and, in all probability, never would again, and he then told him of Porter's offer, adding that he was sure he would make it 800, or even 1000, crowns rather than lose the present opportunity. He therefore strongly advised the abbot to consider the proposal, and for this purpose he sent on a written covenant for his signature to be used in future negotiations, promising not to let it out of his hands till he had secured the top price. The abbot need not be afraid of blemishing his conscience[2], or suppose that he would be setting a pernicious example[3] in thus alienating the property, for plenty of French religious houses had already done the same[4]; or let him look at Bishop Wickham[5], who built two big colleges out of this kind of property which he bought from foreigners. Indeed, from what he had heard, most of the possessions of the aliens in England had been sold to Englishmen already, and he believed that the rest would follow soon.

For it had lately come out that the French council had decided that no Englishman should derive any benefit from any possessions that he might own in France, and the English king (i.e. Henry IV) had been urged to retaliate by a recent Parliament[6], and it was generally expected that he would take prompt action in the next, which would meet before All Saints in 1411[7], so that the abbot had better make haste and decide, and he could not really do better than come to terms with Porter, who had promised to use his influence on behalf of the Cluniac Order, if he could once get this matter settled. But, above all, do not let him listen to Geoffrey Graner, who was a nice enough

---

[1] Aliqua utilia in vestris partibus, Duckett, i. 237.
[2] M. D. Harris, 41.
[3] Duckett, i. 230.
[4] For eight churches in England sold by the Abbess of Montivilliers (Catherine Hardouville) in accordance with a bull of Pope John XXIII in 1410 because she had received nothing from them for the last 30 years, see Dumont, Montivilliers, 19.
[5] See App. E[1], page 299.
[6] Probably Jan. 27, 1410, Wylie, iii. 300.
[7] For writs issued Sept. 21, 1411, see Letter Book I, pp. xv, 95; Wylie, iv. 41.

man and clever in some ways[1], but far too ambitious and
never still. Even now he was roaming the earth like a
vagabond and a fugitive[2], with no place to lay his head.
England was too small for him, but he must needs go to
Rome and presently the whole world would not be large
enough. So when he came to Cluny, the abbot would
do well to keep him there " to serve the Almighty in some
other way."

The abbot was in no hurry to reply to this letter,
and Burghersh had to write again on Oct. 9, 1411[3], to
press his point about the sale of the four manors, but in
the meantime Porter himself had crossed to France and
"bargainized[4]" his own case directly in person. He went
over with the English force that was called in to Paris
by the Duke of Burgundy in 1411, and he won the admiration of the French by his distinguished bravery at the
capture of the bridge at St Cloud[5]. He had already
written to the abbot from London[6] stating that the whole
property was not worth more than 40 marks and 40 florins
per annum. He received a reply on May 2, 1411, and
wrote again on Oct. 13[7] offering "a reasonable sum." On
Nov. 9[8] he wrote to the abbot from Paris suggesting that
he should buy the manors outright or lease them for a term
of 80 years. He pressed the argument that they had yielded

---

[1] Formosus aliquantulum et in multis abilis, Duckett, i. 232.

[2] Ibid. i. 232, 236. The Prior of Lenton had just resigned and Burghersh advises
that Graner should not be appointed, and eventually Thomas Elmham got the post.
Rayner (ii. 78) calls the Cluniacs "gyrovagi" (i.e. semper vagi et nunquam stabiles, Du
Cange, s.v., quoting the rule of St Benedict, cap. 1). For their changing habits and taking
duty in parish churches pro certo stipendio, see Duckett, ii. 23.

[3] Duckett, i. 254, 256.

[4] For permission to him to cross ad tractandum et barganizandum, Cal. Pat. H. IV,
iv. 369, Feb. 18, 1412; confirmed April 27, 1413, see Pat. 2 H. V, ii. 29; do. 3 H. V,
ii. 40.

[5] i.e. on Nov. 9, 1411, Wylie, iv. 61; Vandenbroeck, 87; Denifle, Chart. iv. 22;
not Nov. 19, as Brioc. Chron. 881. Burghersh describes him as valens et potens in opere
et sermone, Duckett, i. 225-233. For order dated Sept. 15, 1413, to take down from
the gallows the body of Colinet de Pisieux qui devant avoit vendu le pont de St Cloud,
see Bourgeois, 44; called "the bataylle of Seint Clow," Noblesse, 8; la prinse du pont
de St Cloud, Soc. de l'Hist. de Normandie, Mélanges, ii. 314 (1893). For picture of
the fight on the bridge, see Zeller, Armagnacs, 76, from MS. fr. 5054 in Bibl. Nat. For
payment to messenger who announced the news at Dijon, see Gouvenain, i. 27. Vatout
(v. 15) thinks that it was carried by la furie parisienne. Cf. Cagny, 66; Raoulet, 150.

[6] See his letter in Duckett, i. 247, dated London March 14. No year is specified,
but it is probably 1411, as he refers to what *will be* decided in the next Parliament, i.e.
Nov. 3, 1411, Wylie, iv. 41.

[7] Duckett, i. 245, though the year is conjectural.

[8] Ibid. i. 245 (s.a.).

no profit to the Abbey at Cluny for a long time past, and that the Parliament in England[1] had decided that they should not be given back till the war was ended, and he begged that an answer might be sent for him with as little delay as possible to the Cluniac Prior of St Martin-des-Champs[2], which was then the headquarters of the force with which Porter was serving in Paris[3]. The abbot replied from Tain on the Rhone[4], whither he had fled to escape the sickness that was raging at Cluny. In this letter he reminded Porter that within the last 20 years these manors had been let for 700 marks, and he pointed to other transactions relating to values of from 3000 up to 14,000 francs. These were for life tenures, and if he liked they might perhaps come to terms on some such grounds; but as to alienation for ever!—he would not hear of such a thing[5]. The threats of the English Parliament disturbed him not, for he had faith in God, who had always watched over Cluny. On Nov. 14[6] the Prior of St Martin's told Porter that he had been informed that King Henry had granted the manors to Sir John Cornwall[7],

---

[1] Selon les ordonnances des parlements d'Engleterre, Duckett, i. 246.

[2] i.e. Jean Alvernas (1401–1417), Marrier, 239, or l'Auvernac, i.e. from Auvernaux near Corbeil (Seine et Oise). For Guy de Norry (or Nourry), Prior of St Martin-des-Champs, see Gall. Christ. vii. 535, where his death is dated 1421, and his successor is appointed in October, 1421. On Dec. 10, 1416, he was Prior of the Cluniac Priory of Souvigny in the Bourbonnais (Houillard-Bréholles, ii. 207; Gall. Christ. ii. 380), and on Jan. 18, 1421, he was a member of the Council of the Duke of Bourbon, Houillard-Bréholles, ii. 220. For the Priory of St Martin-des-Champs, see Gall. Christ. vii. 515; Marrier, Bibliotheca, 1711. For view of it, see A. Lenoir, Statistique, 1211; Zeiller, Pt. I. p. 51 (in 1660); H. Legrand, 54; Guilhermy, Itin. 240; Bournon, 19. For the Great Hall or Refectory, see Lethaby, 170, 251. It was founded A.D. 1060 and given to the Cluniacs by Philippe I in 1079, Guilhermy, i. 385. It stood outside the Porte St Martin on the site of the present Conservatoire des Arts et Métiers.

[3] Wylie, iv. 59.

[4] Dated Nov. 11 (s.a.) in Duckett, i. 239, but the dates are exceedingly puzzling throughout this series of letters. This may possibly be explained by dating them in the latter part of the reign of Henry IV, see Duckett, ii. 21. Cf. sicut Gulielmus Porter miles dum armiger fuit (i.e. before the siege of Harfleur in Aug. 1415, see page 345, note 3) ea (i.e. Offord-Cluny and Letcombe-Regis) habuit de dono Henrici V, Rym. xi. 89.

[5] Duckett, i. 240.

[6] Ibid. i. 250.

[7] Not the king's son John, as supposed by Duckett, i. 250, who calls Cornwall the king's constable, possibly as Constable of Queenborough, Wylie, ii. 280; iv. 122, note 7. For a horse called Lyard Westmoreland, given to him by Henry IV at Eltham Jan. 2, 1401, see Add. MS. 24,513, f. 3; also Grysell Cornwall, given by him to Henry IV, ibid. Shortly before his death he gave up to the abbot of St Albans a rich chasuble with a red orphrey of cloth of gold, two tunicles and three copes, all of which he described as de mammonâ praedae quam rapuimus violenter ab inimicis nostris (i.e. the French), Amundesham, ii. 193, dated Ampthill Sept. 4, 1443, where he is Lord Vanehope, i.e. Fanhope.

who had paid 4000 crowns for the tenure of them during his own lifetime and that of his son, so that although the Duke of Burgundy, who was greatly indebted to him for his recent services[1], was doing all he could for him, there was no use now going further into the matter. The manors were originally given to the Order for perpetual alms, and goods accepted on behalf of the dead must not be eaten up or unjustly detained. God is their everlasting Judge, and in purgatory their souls cry aloud to Him against all who wrongly hinder the prayers that are their due[2].

Whether Porter ever paid anything to the abbot does not appear. We only know that as late as April 16, 1413, he was still haggling for his first offer of 40 marks and 40 florins, on the plea that times had changed and values had dropped one half because of the pestilence in the country[3]. Notwithstanding the alleged grant to Sir John Cornwall the four manors were certainly in King Henry V's hands soon after his accession[4], at which time their total annual value was declared to be 200 marks. On June 14, 1413[5], the custody of them was granted to Porter in return for a quit-rent of a rose, to be presented by him to the king and his successors every Midsummer Day. This being the case, Prior Burghersh's successor made no serious effort to get the manors back, but accepted Porter's assurance that he had come to an understanding with the abbot's representative in Paris, and that there the matter must end[6]. Tixover is the only one of the four manors recorded as

---

[1] En ceste presente année, Duckett, i. 252, which seems to fix it as 1411. In a letter written by the Prior in the same year it is stated that the French king, Charles VI, had been *en bonne santé et entendement* for three days, but that it was now doubtful whether he was not relapsing *comme devant*. He had given orders that he would go himself against his enemies and rebels (i.e. the Armagnacs, Wylie, iv. 62), but Monseigneur de Guyenne and the Duke of Burgundy would now go without him, Duckett, i. 252.

[2] Duckett, i. 251. Cf. whyche by the masse byn delyveryd blyve out of torment, Lydg. Min. Po. 100.

[3] Lez graundes pestilence (*sic*) de people et la mortalité dez bestes, Duckett, i. 258.

[4] In Pat. 1 H. V, i. 19; v. 17, June 14, Dec. 22, 1413, they are said to have been "resumed into our hands in the last Parliament at Westminster" (i.e. May, 1413), page 20.

[5] Pat. 1 H. V, i. 19; Cal. Pat. H. V, i. pp. 24, 144, 161, 354; Pat. 2 H. V, ii. 29 (Sept. 1, 1414) refers to the custody of the four manors confirmed to Porter on Oct. 22, 1413 (not Sept. 1, 1414, as Duckett, ii. 15); also Pat. 3 H. V, ii. 40, July 7, 1415. They had been previously granted to. him by Henry IV, but this grant had not taken effect, Cal. Pat. H. IV, iv. 369.

[6] Duckett, ii. 21.

belonging to Porter at his death in 1434[1], and it afterwards
passed into the possession of the collegiate church at
Tattershall[2] in Lincolnshire.   The manors of Letcombe-
Regis and Offord-Cluny were granted to the Abbot of
Westminster in 1445[3], as a substitute for money that
Henry V had meant him to have, when he made his will
in 1421, of which Porter was one of the executors[4].

A special interest attaches also to the fortunes of the alien
priory of Stoke-by-Clare near Sudbury in Suffolk.   It had
belonged to the Abbey of Bec-Hellouin in Normandy, and
when the long war began with France, it had been seized
by Edward III and for some time its revenues yielded 250
marks per annum to the Exchequer.   Then followed evil
days.   The services were neglected, the church and the
priory buildings were burnt and ruinous[5], and on July 29,
1396[6], the Prior (Richard Cotsford) and the few monks
that remained, being all Englishmen by birth, took out the
usual charter of indigenation, for which they paid 1000
marks[7], and all connection with their foreign home was
thus for ever at an end.   Nearly 20 years of poverty had
now elapsed when the young Earl of March, who was lord
of the neighbouring honor of Clare, came to the rescue
with a great scheme for rehabilitation.   He sought and obtained from Pope John XXIII at Constance a recognition
of the severance from the parent house[8], and then proceeded to re-establish the foundation as a college.   The
charter for the new establishment was signed on May 19,
1415[9], and when all was forward, a set of statutes was
promulgated by the first Dean (Master Thomas Barnesley)

[1] Inq. p. Mort. iv. 173.
[2] J. Wright, 126.
[3] Rym. xi. 89.
[4] See page 344, note 9.
[5] For commission dated Bologna Aug. 21, 1410, to the Abbot of Bury St Edmunds
to inquire into dilapidations at Stoke in the diocese of Norwich with authority to dis-
miss the Prior if he were found to be responsible for them, see Papal Letters, vi. 201,
where the house is a Cluniac Priory and the Prior is called William, though John Ford-
ham was appointed Prior on Apr. 1, 1410, Cal. Pat. H. IV, iv. 215.   For indulgence
granted Nov. 28, 1429, by Pope Martin V to all who contribute to the repair of the ruined
chapel of St Mary the Virgin at "Stok by Clar," to which multitudes resort every year
because of the miracles wrought there, see Papal Letters, viii. 90.
[6] Monast. viii. 1415.
[7] Rackham, 9.
[8] See page 217, note 5.
[9] Monast. viii. 1417.   It was confirmed by Pope Martin V at Florence on April 26,
1420, Papal Letters, vii. 156.

on Jan. 28, 1422[1], which yield much instructive information as to the internal economy of this form of religious institution, which still attracted the generosity of pious founders in an age[2] when the old monastic foundations were on all hands being discredited and decried.

By these statutes it appears that the inmates of the college consisted of the Dean, who was the head of the whole establishment, eight canons[3] or prebendaries (for the name is used indifferently[4]), eight vicars, four clerks, six choristers and several subordinate officials, whose duties are exactly defined. The canons were to be seculars, not regulars, and each was to be allowed three weeks' absence every year to recruit himself[5] or to visit his friends. On the other hand he was bound to reside for at least 32 weeks in the year, when his duties consisted in being present at the daily services[6]. On what were known as "double feasts[7]," i.e. the feast-day itself and the octave, he must be there at least four times in the day, viz. at matins, high mass[8], vespers and compline. On other feast days he might choose one or other of these functions or, if the service was non-choral[9], his duty could be satisfied by attendance at any one of the little[10] canonical Hours,

---

[1] Monast. viii. 1417, from Cotton MS. Vitellius D. XIII.

[2] Called "the college-founding epoch par excellence," Rashdall, New Coll. 20; Wakeman, 165, 166, defines a college as "a body living under a common rule without vows"; cf. Wylie, iii. 242, note 1. For the college at Cobham founded in 1362, see Monast. viii. 1454. For Higham Ferrers founded by Archbishop Chichele May 2, 1422, see ibid. viii. 1425. For supposition that "probably only *one* new monastic house was founded in the 15th century," see Ch. Quart. Rev. xlviii. 424, or "hardly a single one from 1350 onwards," Leach, Visitations, p. xii. See p. 223, note 3.

[3] A century later these had been reduced to six, Lel. Coll. i. 74.

[4] Vocabitur canonicus sive prebendarius, Monast. viii. 1417; Gough, Pleshy, App. 70; cf. Sir Canon with many gret prebend, Lydg. 371.

[5] Ad solaciandum se, Monast. viii. 1421. In the Godshouse at Exeter (1436) the chaplain might be absent three weeks and three days in the year to visit his friends and relations vel ex causâ salubris peregrinacionis et necessarie recreationis, Gidley, 80, 113.

[6] For duties of canons, see Benham, 59. For their costumes at St Paul's, see ibid. 62, from Harl. MS. 2278; horas suo tempore psallere canonicas et ecclesiasticis insistere obsequiis, Montreuil, Ep. xlvii; A. Thomas, 85. For canons at Bar-le-Duc in their stalls for matins at five, mass at nine, and vespers at two, clad in copes in winter or "surpelis" in summer, with other duties at obits and processions, see Meuse, Inventaire, 211, 212, 215.

[7] In duplici festo, Monast. viii. 1417.

[8] For missa cum notis au grant autel, see Tuetey, Test. 307, 324.

[9] Called cum (or sine) regimine chori. In the latter group he might substitute prime or terce or sext or nones instead, Monast. viii. 1418.

[10] For Prime, Tierce, Sext and None called the four "petites heures," see Laffelay, 198. In 1395 Gerson recommends his sisters to say their heures au matin, à tierce, à vespres, au couchier, Jadart, 134.

i.e. prime, terce, sext or nones. In return for these easy conditions he received an allowance of 40s. a year[1] as his prebend[2] and the proceeds of certain parsonages[3] attached to his stall, besides a very liberal allowance for house room amounting to £26. 13s. 4d. every year, with a possibility that he might some day himself become the Dean. The canons dined together in hall at their own separate table, at which no places were reserved, the first to arrive having the first choice of seats. A special provision was made that none of them should be allowed to keep hounds or hunting dogs[4] in the college, or indeed hunt at all, unless he was able to spend £40 a year[5], though the Dean might keep two brace[6] in college if he liked.

Below the canons in dignity were the clerks and vicars, to whom hunting was absolutely forbidden, as tending to neglect of duty[7] and leading to insolence and vice[8]. These did not sit at the canons' table at meals, and had to sing, psalmodise, and officiate in the chapel[9] nearly all day long[10], where they wore black capes in distinction to the canons' grey[11], one of them being deputed to write down the names of

[1] See App. L[1].

[2] Pro corpore prebendae suae, Monast. viii. 1417; cf. Wylie, iv. 358. For canonicus prebendatus, see Rym. x. 66, 69; canonicatus cum prebendâ, Rym. x. 60; Prebendez suis en mainte eglise, i.e. the Canon in Dufour. For prebends = £2. 13s. 4d. per annum in Exeter cathedral, see Freeman, 71. For fall in the value of prebends at Paderborn from 70 Rhenish florins to below 30, see Engelsheim, 31. For a canonry at Rheims (1390) valued at 30 fr. per annum (or 100 fr. if with residence), see Humphreys, Froiss. II. Plate xxxv; Wylie, iii. 124, note 7.

[3] My benefice with many personages, Lydg. 371.

[4] In Wynard's Godshouse at Exeter (1436) the chaplains are not to be aucipes, venatores, fornicatores, adulteri nec loca suspecta aliqua accedentes, Oliver, Mon. 405; Gidley, 76, 108. For the hunting parson, see Ch. Quart. Rev. li. 98.

[5] Monast. viii. 1419.

[6] Ad numerum quaternarium.

[7] Cf. obmissiones suppleat utinam indulgeatque Deus qui si severius mecum agat scio confiteorque quod pessime michi esset, Montreuil, Ep. xlvii; A. Thomas, 85.

[8] Viciis incentivum. Cf. quos videtis ludos et spectacula aut ad capiendos lepores vel aves aut alia similia potius quam contemplationes frequentare, mulieres quam angelicas collationes perquirere, Mart. Anec. i. 1741 (written in 1418); hund und ross gon uf licht frowen, mulesel und ander unseylich wollust, Watt, i. 530; hakyng or huntyng or other synnes and vanities, Krapp, 69. For the hunting parson in Gower, Vox Clamantis, see Jusserand, 368.

And pricked aboute on palfrais fro places to maners
A hep of houndes at hus ers as he a lord were.
P. Plo. C. vi. 160; Garnett, Lit. i. 97.
Cf. nolebat equos quia volebat vivere scholasticè, Mirot, 255.

[9] Cantando, psalmodizando et officiando in choro, Monast. viii. 1419.

[10] i.e. matins, vespers et aliae horae canonicae cum missâ cum notâ, all according to the Salisbury use (ad usum Sarum), ibid.

[11] Almuciis griseis, ibid.; cf. almuciis de variis sive griseis pellibus, Conc. iii. 615. For almutium or amice, see Weiss, i. 194; Wylie, iv. 333.

absentees with a view to subsequent fines[1].   The choristers received £3. 6s. 8d. per annum besides their bed, food and clothing[2], and were under a master who was paid £2 a year to instruct them in reading, singing (i.e. plain-song and descant or part-singing) and good behaviour[3].   Besides these, there were two vestry-clerks[4], whose duty it was to ring the bell, light the lamps, dress the altar, take charge of the vestry, shut the doors, and attend to the clock.   There was also a precentor who drew £1 a year, and a verger[5] who touched his 2d. a day and a gown worth 6s. 8d. every Christmas.

Every morning the bell rang at five and no one was to lie in bed later than six or half-past.   High Mass was usually over by 11 o'clock[6], after which all dined together, with Bible reading in the hall.   Vespers were sung before five[7] and the curfew[8] tolled at eight so that it could be heard half a mile away, after which the gates were closed, and no one was allowed out without express permission of the Dean.   Outside the college no canon might frequent the common taverns at Esse or Stoke, or roam about without a servant or other reputable companion, or enter the house of any woman where his presence might give rise to scandal, though strangely enough the Dean might authorise private wines[9] in their own rooms at which *mulierculae* might be present, provided they were accompanied by respectable associates[10].   No quarrelling, giggling or laughing was allowed in church, where black caps only were to be worn and no extravagant copes or hoods[11].   No one might run into debt and most offences were punishable by fines, but

---

[1] i.e. 1d. for every non-attendance at matins, high mass and vespers, and ¼d. for the other hours, unless they had an exemption from the Dean.

[2] They were to be honeste vestiti pannis lineis et laneis, Monast. viii. 1419.

[3] Aliis bonis moribus et honestis.   See App. M[1].

[4] Clerici inferiores, custodes vestiarii; cf. Cotgr., s.v. *Chevecier*.   For capicerius, see Du Cange, s.v. *Capitium*.

[5] Virgarius seu virgam gerens, Monast. viii. 1420.

[6] Ibid. viii. 1419.   Cf. lye in bed tylle all masses be done, Hazlitt, iv. 62; syt in the chyrche tyll it be noone, ibid. iv. 67.

[7] For vespers about two o'clock in the afternoon in the godshouse at Exeter (1436), see Gidley, 77, 110.

[8] Pulsatur ad ignitegium, Monast. viii. 1419; comme queuvrefeu sonnera, C. Beaurepaire, Notes, 307; couvrefeu sonnant, ibid. 231; depuis l'eure de cevrefeu, ibid. 305; l'heure de coieffeu, ibid. 36.

[9] Privatas potationes.

[10] Cum honestâ comitivâ, Monast. viii 1420.

[11] Nigris pileis ancehuris et nullo modo capiciis sive cappis monstruosis, ibid. 1419.

for any one convicted of heresy, magic, sodomy or fondness for women[1], the penalty was immediate expulsion.

The whole *régime* is in singular contrast to the strictness of the earlier monastic rules[2], and under a weak or lascivious head it is clear that such a house might in a very short time degenerate to the level with which all students of the later Middle Ages have long been only too familiar[3], especially as in this case no effort at abstemiousness was encouraged, for besides giving to the college half a dozen silver spoons or a mark (13s. 4d.) to buy them with, every canon was required to give a dinner[4] to the other members which cost him 20s. on his appointment, and the Dean's feast was to be on double the scale for sumptuousness[5]. Free fishing was allowed in the Stour for three days every week between Sturmer and Clare; a dove-cot on the premises supplied the house with pigeons, and a garden divided into four portions, each being the property of two of the canons, yielded an abundance of the necessary worts[6].

[1] Sint soluti et nullo modo uxorati nec mulieribus affectati.

[2] Wakeman, 165, calls it "very much more pliant and elastic" than a "religious" foundation.

[3] Clamenges (i. 18) describes canons as indoctos, cupidos, ambitiosos, ebrios, incontinentissimos, utpote qui passim et inverecundè prolem ex meretrice susceptam et scorta vice conjugum domi teneant; in curâ ventris et gulae, in carnis voluptatibus hauriendis suae vitae felicitatem constituunt. For monks as lubricos, indisciplinatos, dissolutos, magis per loca publica et inhonesta (si modo frena laxentur) discursantes, ita ut nihil illis aeque odiosum sit quam cella et claustrum, lectio et oratio, regula et religio, &c., see ibid. i. 19; cf.

> Cenobita quilibet vivit dissolutus
> Effrons nec jam loquitur signis aut per nutus,
> Nam in claustris ubi grex debet esse mutus
> Vivitur ex rapto, non hospes ab hospite tutus.   Diss, 32.
> Nulle part n'a plus sureté
> Ne en cloistre n'en abbaye.   Champion, Prisonnier, 30.

For names of 44 priests in London convicted of immorality between 1401 and 1439, see Letter Book I, pp. xliii, 273–287; Besant, Survey, i. 95, ii. 137; though it is claimed that "in the towns there was a high moral standard" amongst the clergy at this time, Ch. Quart. Rev. li. 99. For story of a man who found his wife with a priest and tonsured her in Jacques de Vitry, see Herbert, iii. 17. For a 15th century Chapter Act Book of St Paul's referring *inter alia* to correction of vicars choral for devotion to forbidden sex, see Leach, St Paul's, 197; for fratres evidenter notati de suspectis consortiis et colloquiis mulierum, see Mon. Francisc. II. 101. For fines (1 franc each) for a monk and a priest found with two women after curfew in a hostel at Dijon in 1410, see Vallée, 204. For Southwell where the canons or their vicars "crawled through their lives, huddling through their duties, catching moles, dicing, flirting or worse," see Leach, Visitations, pp. lii, lxx, lxxvi, lxxviii, lxxix and *passim*; with similar facts at Beverley, Chichester, Lincoln, Norwich and Wells, do. Memorials, lxxii, xc, xciii.

[4] Cf. Wylie, iii. 124, note 7; à prendre leurs pasts, Godefroy, s.v. *Past*, i.e. Feast. At Bordeaux every canon of the Cathedral had to give a dinner to the porters of the Chapter, or 2s. 6d. instead, Brutails, Bordeaux, 165.

[5] Monast. vi. 1422.

[6] Ibid. 1420.   See App. N[1].

CHAPTER XX

GODSHOUSES

ANOTHER of the measures passed in the Leicester Parliament had reference to the Hospitals or Spitalhouses[1], which were established in every centre of population in England. By the intentions of their founders they had been meant to help poor blind folk[2], madmen, lepers, women with child[3], men of broken fortunes and other indigent faint souls past corporal toil[4]. But some 200 years before, many of them had been indignantly described as dens of thieves, where the funds were being spent in revelling and drunkenness[5]; and by the time we are now dealing with, most of those in England[6] had been robbed of their endowments and were falling into decay[7].

In 1410 the Commons had petitioned for the supervision of such charities by good and true seculars[8], because the priests and clerks who then controlled them had "full nigh

---

[1] For Robert Copland's "Hye Way to the Spyttel Hous" (circ. 1540), see Hazlitt, Remains, iv. 17–72.

[2] Cf.
A les Quinze Vins estoré
Povres gens qui ne voit gente. Deschamps, ix. 310.

[3] Veigles, lasers, hors de lour sennes et memoires, femmes ensintez, Rot. Parl. iv. 19, 80.

They that be at suche myschefe
That for theyr lyvyng can do no labour,
As old people seke and impotent
Poore women in chyldebed have here easement
Wayfaring men and maymed souldyers. Hazlitt, iv. 31.

[4] H. V, i. 1, 16. Cf. pauperum debilium qui sibi ipsis nequiunt subvenire (1436), Gidley, 75, 107.

[5] Vitry, Historia Occidentalis, p. 340 (written between 1223 and 1226); L. Legrand, Statuts, pp. v, 1, 4.

[6] La greindre partie, Rot. Parl. iv. 19; Stat. ii. 175.

[7] Les malveis et insolentz governances en ycelle eus, Rot. Parl. iv. 80; Clay, 212, who thinks that "upright, thrifty and faithful wardens were far from common."

[8] Fabyan, 576.

destroyed all the houses-of-alms within the realm[1]," and among the projects suggested for the better use of Church property was the establishment of 100 more alms-houses each with a maintenance endowment of 100 marks a year[2]. In this very year (1414)[3] the University of Oxford had protested that in many of the existing spitals the masters and wardens had turned out the poor inmates and put the funds to their own uses[4]. Abundant complaints of glaring misappropriation were everywhere to be heard, and it was probably with an apprehension of the coming changes that new arrangements were in contemplation at Harbledown[5] near Canterbury, under the belief that it would "probably be difficult in future to find suitable paid priests who will be willing to have intercourse with the poor inmates especially as some of them are infected with leprosy."

I have already noticed the fortunes of the leper-house at Ripon[6] and the hospital at Colchester[7] and to these may be added the case of the hospital of St Nicholas at York, which had been originally intended as an almshouse for poor men and women, but at a visitation by the Chancellor[8] in the reign of Edward I the endowment had been found to have been much diverted from its original purpose[9] and an attempt had been made at reform. An inquiry held in 1397[10] however showed that the old abuses still prevailed; the master was still there, but the inmates consisted of only

---

[1] Amundesham, i. 453, from Jack Sharpe's petition in 1431. For Bishop Wickham's experience of the craft and fraud perpetrated in ordinances and statutes "as I have seen happen in so many cases," i.e. of colleges and hospitals, see Leach, 75, who refers to the case of the Hospital of St Cross near Winchester. Cf. alimoniae pauperibus infirmis et debilibus subtrahuntur (1307), Stat. i. 150. For decay of hospitals in the 14th century, see L. Legrand, xxv. 48; Clay, 39–41, 212–225. For Gerson's proposals for reform in a synod at Rheims in 1408, see Jadart, 183. For a call to "amenden mesondieux," see P. Plo. i. 228, where another version has: "make mesondieux meseyse to helpe," Clay, 228.   [2] See App. O[1].

[3] Conc. iii. 365; Clay, 222, where many abbeys, priories and collegiate churches are charged with misappropriation of funds left to them on condition that part should go to the poor.

[4] e.g. the Maladrie or Hospital of the Holy Innocents at Lincoln, Pat. 3 H. V, i. 19, May 8, 1415; also the Hospital of St Mary at Ospringe, ibid. ii. 32, Aug. 1, 1415.

[5] Clay, 144, though there is no mention of this in Monast. vii. 653; Hasted, iii. 578.

[6] Wylie, iii. 334; Clay, 41; Shapter, 16–18, who states that the buildings were repaired in 1674.

[7] Wylie, iii. 202; Clay, 18.

[8] i.e. William Grenefelde, Dean of Chichester, Le Neve, i. 256.

[9] i.e. July 4, 1303, Drake, 250; Monast. vii. 709, where it is called a leper-hospital as it was required to entertain lepers during a certain part of the year.

[10] Monast. vii. 710. For a further inquiry to be held, see Cal. Pat. H. IV, iv. 65 (Nov. 18, 1408).

a few women and the funds had been put to other uses[1]. It was now proposed, as we have seen[2], to re-establish it as a religious house for Bridgettines who ultimately settled at Syon. Similarly at St Giles' Hospital at Maldon in Essex an official report had been issued in 1402[3] showing that for the last three years the master had neglected to maintain the leper inmates or their chaplain, while at Reading the spital or leperhouse within the Abbey precinct had lately been closed altogether because there were no lepers thereabouts[4]. At Oxford the property of the hospital of St Bartholomew had been "miserably eaten up for other uses[5]," while at Windsor there was a leper-house dedicated to St Peter[6] whose revenues had been wasted and whose property had been given away by Henry IV to his Clerk of the Poultry in 1411[7]. A few months later however a commission was appointed[8] to inquire into the wastage of the revenues, but nothing further seems to have resulted and in 1445 the property was granted with many others to form part of the endowment of the newly-founded college at Eton[9]. So when the Leicester Parliament petitioned for reform of the abuse of hospitals, the king, after referring the matter to the Convocation[10], agreed that all such charities should henceforward be officially certified by the bishops in order to check further strepments[11].

Orders and commissions were issued by some of the bishops[12] and we have evidence that an investigation was to have been held as to the revenues of the wealthy hospital of St Leonard at York[13], while at Canterbury an

---

[1] Pat. 3 H. V, ii. 29 d, Jan. 8, 1416; Cal. Pat. H. V, i. 410; Add. MS. 24062, f. 150, where numerus infirmorum non fuerat sustentatus sed unus magister (i.e. Robert Wolverton in 1409, Monast. vii. 709) et pauce mulieres reperiuntur ibidem et facultates ejusdem hospitalis non secundum intencionem fundatorum frequencius in usus extraneos sunt converse.

[2] Page 221. The buildings were destroyed in the siege of 1644, Drake, 250.

[3] Nov. 9, 1402, i.e. by Elming Leget, Monast. vii. 736.

[4] i.e. in 1413, Hurry, 39; Monast. iv. 31, vii. 754; G. Newman, 126.

[5] Monast. vii. 642, May 7, 1361; Clay, 145.   [6] Tighe and Davis, i. 76, 101.

[7] i.e. John Hannam, April 20, 1411, Cal. Pat. H. IV, iv. 285.

[8] i.e. Oct. 15, 1411, ibid. p. 372.

[9] Tighe and Davis, i. 341.   [10] Usk, 123, 304.

[11] For great estreppamenta et dilapidationes at St Mary's Hospital at Ospringe, see Pat. 2 H. V, ii. 16, 28 d, Sept. 28, 1414. Cf. vastum seu estrepamentum, Statham, 152.

[12] e.g. the Bishops of London, Chester and Carlisle, Pat. 2 H. V, ii. 27 d, iii. 9 d, Oct. 3, 1414, Jan. 8, 1415.

[13] i.e. by Robert Mauleverer, Pat. 1 H. V, iii. 41 d, July 16, 1413. For the Petercorn

inquiry was undertaken in 1414 by the Prior of Christ Church as to irregularities in St James' leperhouse in Wincheap[1], as a consequence of which the prioress was required to render a regular account of the revenues for the future and to correct certain inequalities in the distribution of bread and beer by the cellaress, and on Feb. 8, 1415, new statutes were promulgated, according to which the yearly allowance to the inmates was to be raised from 10s. to 13s. 4d. each and a male clerk was to be appointed to assist the chaplain at mass, so that henceforward no woman should minister at the altar nor touch the sacred vessels[2]. Taken as a whole, however, it is clear that nothing really effectual was accomplished in the direction of large reforms throughout the country and two years later the Commons again petitioned that every hospital should be reported and certified within 12 months, under pain of a fine of £50 to be paid by the bishop[3].

It may have been due to this stir that new life was infused into some old foundations, and in 1419 a substantial legacy was left[4] for the purpose of transforming a hospital at Brackley in Northamptonshire into a convent for Dominicans, but the scheme was not carried out and the disused hospital was restored to its original purpose under new statutes in 1425[5]. At Flixton, at the foot of the York Wolds near Filey, there was a very ancient hospital originally founded to provide a shelter for travellers in those remote wastes, who might otherwise have been attacked by wolves[6]

at St Leonard's Hospital, see Pat. 4 H. V, 12; Wylie, iii. 310, note 4; Clay, 155, 185, who gives the number of sick and poor in the infirmary in 1370 as 224, with 23 children in the orphanage.

[1] Or Winecheap, Hasted, iv. 394. It was in Thanington, Clay, 154; in suburbio civitatis Cantuar., Cal. Rot. Pat. 244.

[2] Hasted, iii. 585, iv. 456; Litt. Cantuar. iii. 132–135, where it is called St Jacob's.

[3] Rot. Parl. iv. 80.

[4] i.e. by Maud, widow of John Lord Lovel of Titchmarsh near Thrapston, Monast. vii. 617; Clay, 8. She was the daughter of Robert Lord Holand and died May 7, 1423, Baker, i. 563; Inq. p. Mort. iv. 73; Comp. Peer. iv. 236, v. 164. She was buried in the chapel of the hospital at Brackley (Baker, i. 582) by the side of her husband, who died Sept. 10, 1408 (ibid. i. 563; Inq. p. Mort. iii. 316). For his will dated July 26, 1408, proved Sept. 12, 1408, see Comp. Peer. iv. 236. For the lectionary (Harl. MS. 7026) executed for him containing his portrait and that of the artist John Siferwas, a Dominican Friar, see G. F. Warner, Reproductions, ii. Plate xvi; Herbert, 233; see also Appendix S.

[5] Hist. MSS. Rept. iv. 459; Baker, i. 581.

[6] Ne populus ille per lupos et alias bestias voraces et sylvestres devoretur, Monast. vii. 614.

and wild beasts of the forest. It had been placed under the charge of an alderman assisted by 13 brothers and sisters, but the site was marshy and with the disappearance of the beasts of prey[1], the inmates had also vanished and the building was abandoned, but it was re-established in 1447 under the name of Carman's Spital for the benefit of travellers who might otherwise be in danger from the floods, when the water was out[2].

Within a century from the date of the Leicester Parliament it is recorded that "there be but fewe or noon such commune Hospitalls in the Realm[3]," but it is evident that Henry's effort at increased strictness of legislative control did not at the time check the flow of individual charity, whether on the death-bed or otherwise, and some notable new foundations certainly date their origin from this very time. In 1422 Archbishop Chichele founded his beadhouse at Higham Ferrers[4]; in 1424, Bishop Bubwith[5] left money to build an almshouse at Wells[6]; and in 1442[7] the Papey or Pappy[8] was started near the Bishop's gate[9] in

---

[1] In Débat, 6, 157 (circ. 1456) the French herald says that the English have no boars or wolves or lynxes (loupxerviers, called foxes, Pyne, 12), see also Pyne, 97; Strutt, Sports, 12, 13. The Bohemians who visited England in 1466 noted the absence of wolves, and when they crossed to Brittany they observed how few there were there and that if they were caught they were hung up in their skins by the side of the high roads *tanquam fu:es*, Rożmital, 45, 49; also in Normandy, Delisle, St Sauveur, 247; G. Dupont, 502 (in the Cotentin); Coville, Recherches, 393 (near Rouen).

[2] In aquis labinis et mariscis saepissime periclitarentur, Monast. vii. 614; Clay, 2; Du Cange, s.v. *Lavinia*.

[3] i.e. in the will of Henry VII in 1509, Loftie, Savoy, 87; Clay, 12.

[4] Monast. viii. 1425; Clay, 27, 81, 157, 169, 173, 186.

[5] For his chantry in the Cathedral at Wells, see Holmes, Reg. 25. For his letter dated London, Jan. 31, 1408, stating that he is prevented from visiting Wells by various and arduous matters of our Church and our Lord the King, see ibid. 72. On Feb. 6, 1408, the temporalities of Bath and Wells had been committed to Archbishop Arundel, Bishops Beaufort and Langley, and two canons of Wells, ibid. 73. On April 5, 1408, Bubwith writes from his house at St Clement Danes, London, appointing Richard Bruton Chancellor of Wells as his vicar-general, ibid. 74. For a letter written by Bishop Bubwith at our manor of Wookey Jan. 12, 1409, see ibid. 80. For 15th century pictures of Wells with the Cathedral and Bishop's Palace, see Archaeologia, liii. 230.

[6] For picture of it, see Holmes, Wells, 147, where the foundation is dated Sept. 29, 1436; called circ. 1420 in Warton, i. 185; Collinson, iii. 384; or 1424, Holmes, 34; i.e. with money bequeathed by him, J. W. Clark, 117; Monast. ii. 279; Clay, 17, 81; Wylie, iii. 132. For his executors, John Shelford and others, see Early Chanc. Proc. i. 30.

[7] Hugo, 186; Besant, Survey, ii. 411; Stow (Kingsford), ii. 293; Clay, 25. Not 1430, as Stow, i. 146.

[8] So called from the neighbouring church of St Augustine de Papey, i.e. of Pavia, where his remains are preserved, Stow (Kingsford), ii. 293. For supposed derivation from papes (i.e. priests), see Stow, i. 146, though on page 161 he takes it to mean "poor."

[9] "Be twyne Algate and Bevysse Markes," Greg. Chron. p. viii. For its exact position at the north end of St Mary Axe Street, see Hugo, 184, 196, from Agas' map, 1560.

London, where a fraternity of blind and lame and impotent priests received each his allowance of 2*d*. a day with the services of a barber, a launder and others to provide and dress their meat and drink[1]. It was this age also that saw the opening of the famous godshouse or almshouse[2] founded in 1424[3] by the executors of the will of Richard Whitington[4], in conformity with his dying wish, in his house in the street called the Royal[5] in the city of London on the north side of the Paternoster church[6], which he rebuilt[7] and where he and his wife Alice[8] were buried. This almshouse he meant to be used by "such poor persons which grievous penury and cruel fortune hath oppressed and be not of power to get their living either by craft or by any other bodily labour[9]." Thirteen poor men were to live in it, one of whom was to be the "tutor" and to have a little house with a chimney[10], an easement[11] and other essentials to himself in which he could lie and rest. Each inmate was to have 14*d*. a week with two meals daily and over-clothing of dark brown colour, not staring or blazing[12] and of easy price according to their degree, and every day they were to come together

---

[1] Greg. Chron. viii; Monast. vii. 767; Clay, 25.

[2] Domus Dei sive Domus Elemosyne, Monast. vii. 738, 745; Stow, iii. 5. Not " an almshouse called God's House," as Besant, Survey, i. 97. Its position in the Vintry Ward is well shown in Stow, iii. 1; and on the map dated 1563 in Pennant, London, Frontispiece, in the lane leading to the Three Cranes on the water side, Pecock, I. xii; Dict. Nat. Biogr. xliv. 199.

[3] For the foundation charter dated Dec. 21, 1424, see Monast. vi. 738; not 1409, as Wylie, iii. 65, note 4. See also Report on London Livery Companies (1884), iv. 40.

[4] See App. R.

[5] Le Riole, Letter Book I, p. 77; or the Ryole, Sharpe, Wills, ii. 432, quoting Report of Charity Commissioners (1861) and Report of Livery Companies' Commission (1884), iv. pp. 39–41. It was named from La Réole on the Garonne, P. Cunningham, 333; Wheatley, iii. 402; Besant, Survey, viii. 223; Stow (Kingsford), ii. 324. Not from Tower Royal, as Stow, iii. 5; do. Kingsford, i. 243; Besant, Survey, i. 98, which was granted to the Canons of St Stephen's at Westminster by Edward III, Topham, 6.

[6] Or "St Michael de Paternoster church in le Riole," Letter Book I, 77; Litt. Cantuar. iii. 143, Dec. 8, 1424, where the Prior of Christ Church, Canterbury, is the patron, and William Brooke capellanus is the first master. It is now called St Michael Paternoster Royal, Hennessy, cxxxviii. 333; Loftie, i. 265; or St Michael, College Hill, Wheatley, ii. 535.

[7] Condidit hoc templum Michaelis quam speciosum, Stow, iii. 5. For gift by him of land for the rebuilding April 13, 1411, see Letter Book I, p. 78.

[8] See App. R.

[9] From statutes dated Dec. 21, 1424, in possession of the Mercers' Company, Stow, iii. 4, 5; do. Kingsford, i. 242.

[10] Domunculam cum camino, latrinâ et aliis necessariis, Monast. vii. 745; Stow, iii. 5. See App. P[1].

[11] For a house with cheminées et aesements, see C. Beaurepaire, Notes, 114, 116.

[12] For a similar regulation at Croydon, see Clay, 175, quoting Ellis-Davy.

about their founder's tomb in the adjoining church[1].
Besides this godshouse the executors founded also a
college for priests in connection with the Paternoster
church, long known as Whitington's college[2] or the college
of St Spirit and St Mary[3], for which generosity he was
described in his epitaph, not only as the "Flower of
Merchants," but the "Founder of Priests and Poor[4]."

All signs of Whitington's charitable foundations have
now disappeared from their original site[5], but interesting
remains of others are still to be seen in various centres of
busy life in modern England.   At Dover the refectory[6] of
the godshouse or St Mary's Hospital is now the Town
Hall and the chapel is the Sessions House[7]; a godshouse
still exists at Exeter[8], which was founded for 12 poor men
in 1436 by William Wynard, who placed the control of it
in the hands of the Mayor and 12 of the leading citizens
as his trustees; and at Ewelme[9] near Wallingford may still
be seen the "house of alms[10]" built in 1437 by William de
la Pole, Earl of Suffolk, and his wife Alice, daughter of
Thomas Chaucer, in which were lodged 13 almsmen[11] "that

[1] For a similar requirement at Ewelme, see Whethamstede, 552.
[2] Called "the college of Whitington," by Pecock (i. 112), who was master from 1431
to 1444.   [3] Benham-Welch, 15; Besant, Survey, viii. 234.
[4] Flos Mercatorum, Fundator Presbyterorum sic et Egenorum, Stow, iii. 5; Weever,
408; Gough, iii. 74; Price, 353; Fox-Bourne, 52; cf. "the sonne of all marchandy,
that lode-starre and chefe chosen floure," Pol. Songs, ii. 178; Pauli-Hertzberg, 41;
Wylie, iii. 65, note 4.
[5] The almshouse was removed to Highgate in 1822, Knight, London, vi. 344; called
1808 in Wheatley, i. 445; Besant, Survey, viii. 235; others say 1835.   College Hill is
between Cannon St. Station and Queen St., where the existing gateway is of much more
recent date.
[6] Called the Hostry or Great Chamber, Archaeol. Cant. vii. 273, 277, with inventory
of furniture and other contents taken in 1535, including tables, trestells, settles, forms,
turned chairs, a cubbord, a pair of andyrons and a fyre-forke.   In Caxton, Dial. 8, andyrons
of yron=brandeurs de fer; cf. brandernes of erne, Fifty Wills, 56, 57, 173; andyres,
fourches de fere pour le feu, Romania, xxxii. 58; andiers (=chenets), A. Lacroix, 19,
St Germain, 454; cf. duos chenetos pro ponendo ligna in camino, Tuetey, Test. 326;
andyrenes, Raine, Durham, 102.
[7] For many years it was used as an office for victualling the navy, i.e. since 1555;
not that it is still so used, as Monast. vii. 656.   For seal see Pedrick, p. 66, Plate XXII.
For 18th century picture of it by Buck, see Clay, Frontispiece, where it is at the south-
eastern corner of the town, near the quay, Clay, 4.   For a writ addressed magistro et
fratribus hospitalis domus dei de Dovorr, see Memoranda Rolls K. R. 3–4 H. V, m. 74,
Jan. 20, 1416.
[8] Oliver, Mon. 404; Gidley, 75–106; Exeter Deeds, 573–589.
[9] Whethamstede, 542, 546; Clay, 151.
[10] Amundesham, i. 453; Kingsford, Chron. 65.
[11] For 13 as a frequent number for inmates, see the hospital of the Annunciation, founded
in 1392 by John Plumptre near the bridge over the Trent at Nottingham, Monast. vii.
680; Nott. Rec. ii. 96; also at Hull, Clay, 13; at Oxford (St Bartholomew's), ibid. 145,
and St Giles' Hospital at Kepier near Durham, Monast. vii. 731.   For le mande de xiii.
povres,. see L. Legrand, 15.

ben letyn with grete penury of poverte" or "broke with
age," who must not own more than six marks yearly by
title of heritage or otherwise and were bound to leave to
the hospital such goods as they were possessed of at their
death.   They wore a tabard with a red cross on the breast
and a hood according to the same[1].   Each received an
exhibition[2] of 2*d.* a day and every morning they gathered
for prayer at the tomb of Dame Alice's "father and mother
Thomas Chaucer[3] and Mawte his wife" in the neighbouring
parish church.   Besides the 13 beadsmen there was a
school held in the building where "childer that actually
lernes gramer, besides petelles and readers" were to be
taught "freely without exaccion of any scole hire[4]."

The godshouses or hospitals were usually erected as
"hostries[5] or places of gistes and loggynges[6]" on the main
routes of traffic[7] and were specially frequent near to
bridges[8] and on great pilgrim roads[9], at sea-ports[10],
and even on mountain passes[11].   At Canterbury a night's
lodging and refreshment could be had free by any
needy pilgrim at the Eastbridge Spital[12] in the main
street, provided he were sound in health and not a leper.

---

[1] From a copy of the statutes in Hist. MSS. Rept. ix. pp. 217-222.
[2] Exibycion, ibid. 221. Cf. "Exhybycion," Hazlitt, iv. 45; Wylie, iii. 405.
[3] For his brass, see Dasent, xxiv, 71.
[4] See App. M[1].
[5] Halliwell, i. 461. For the hostry at the Black Friars in London see Conc. iii. 407;
also at Dover, see p. 361, note 6.
[6] Ord. Priv. Co. v. 106; i.e. guests, not "giftes" as Excerpt. Hist. 146; cf. "asile
de nuit," Tollet, 50; "places of hospytalite" where "moche people resort and have
lodgyng," Hazlitt, iv. 30.   For Repton see Morris-Jordan, 259.
[7] L. Legrand, xxv, 86; e.g. at Portsmouth, Dover, Arundel, as diversoria for pilgrims
to Canterbury, Winchester and Chichester, see Wordsworth, xlvii; also on the high road
from Windsor to Edinburgh, Ord. Priv. Co. v. 106.   For hostelries for Rome-bound pilgrims
in the Jewry at Troyes, see Corrard de Breban, 131, where a free lodging for one night
was provided for those carrying le baton et la gourde in vico qui dicitur vetus Roma in
Jueriâ.   For Hospitale Romipetarum, see Vidal, Perpignan, 391; Clay, 8.
[8] Rivière, i. 356. For masyndew super Pontem Usae (i.e. Ousebridge) at York, see
Auden, 200, with account of 21 hospitals and 17 godshouses in York, pp. 179-200.
For St Nicholas Hospital by the Fishergate Bridge at Salisbury, see Hoare, v. 43;
Jackson, Leland, 41; Wordsworth, xxxiv; Leach, Winchester, 86; Clay, 5.
[9] e.g. on the pilgrim roads to Canterbury and Walsingham, Clay, 4, 5.   For gifts by
King John of France in 1360 to les malades de 4 maladeries depuis Rocestre jusques à
Cantorbérie pour aumosne, also the communities of St James, St John without the Northgate at Canterbury, St Mary's, Harbledown and Ospringe, see Douet d'Arcq, Comptes,
272; Clay, 192.
[10] Clay, 19.
[11] Rivière, 356.   For maisons de refuge on the route de Rome by the valley of the
Durance over Mont Genèvre in Dauphiny, see P. Guillaume, Guillestre, xxv.
[12] Monast. vii. 691; Hasted, iv. 624; Bibl. Top. Brit. i. 297, 299; Clay, 1, 7, 8,
266; called "Estbruge" in Papal Letters, iv. 36, where indulgences for 1 year and
40 days are granted to contributors.

At Ospringe near Faversham there was a hostel for travellers as well as a leperhouse, the latter being a detached building, some walls of which still remain[1], while Dover had its hostel for poor travellers departing on a voyage[2].

St John, whether Baptist or Evangelist, was frequently the patron saint[3] of a hospital, as at Berkhampstead[4], Bury St Edmunds[5], Canterbury[6], Coventry[7] (where to this day the grammar school is held in what was formerly the chapel), Northampton[8] (near the south gate), Oxford[9], Stamford[10], Warwick[11] (where the old building is still preserved), Wells[12] and Winchester[13]. Other favourite patrons were St Giles, the poor folk's friend[14], St Nicholas[15] and St Catherine[16], examples of the second

[1] Monast. vii. 764; enclosing an alehouse, Hasted, ii. 802; Baildon, Inv. 165; l'ostel Dieu de Hospringe, Douet d'Arcq, Comptes, 272.

[2] Monast. vii. 655.

[3] Clay, 254. St John was the patron saint of the Maison Dieu in Paris, Coyecque, i. 95, also of the order of the Hospitallers at Clerkenwell.

[4] Priv. Seal 665/795; Monast. vii. 762.

[5] Monast. vii. 775.

[6] Called the Northgate Hospital, Monast. vii. 763; Hasted, iv. 366. For pictures, see Clay, 16, 240.

[7] Monast. vii. 658; Dugd. Warwickshire, i. 179.

[8] Pedrick, 113, with seal (Plate L).

[9] Clay, 1, 5.

[10] Monast. vii. 638; Clay, 29, 83.

[11] Dugdale, Warwickshire, i. 459.

[12] Holmes, 142.   [13] Monast. vii. 762; Clay, 8.

[14] Of pore folk chef patroun, Lydg. Min. Po. 171, where he is also "unto shipmen sauacyoun and gyde," ibid. 163.

[15] Clay, 254. For le manuel de l'ostel Dieu St Nicolas at Troyes, 1412, see Arbois de Jubainville, 425 (1873). For figure of St Nicholas (1236) with two boys and a tub in the church at Coursan near Ervy (Aube), see Fichot, ii. 53; also with a child in a kettle in Henry VII's chapel at Westminster, Bond, 214. For picture of his enthronisation as Bishop of Myra, see Gruyer, 155. For St Nicholas as the patron saint of sailors see Roncière, i. 296; F. Bond, 56, who calls him "a most kind-hearted, cheery old man." For sculptures in St Nicholas' Church at Burgos showing devils wrecking ships and Bishop Nicholas in the poop saving them, see Duro, 298. Causyd Seynt Nicholas to geve good counsayle, Lydg. Min. Po. 111. For a devil pulling a ship down by the prow, see Vallet de Viriville, Instruction, 132 (from a 14th century seal). For account of the church at Burgos, see Los Rios, 624. It was built in 1408 and dedicated to St Nicholas of Bari, whither his body was supposed to have been translated from Myra in the 11th century, A. Butler, ii. 989; Marest, 3. For miracles of St Nicholas in a 13th century window of the cathedral at Bourges, see Martin-Cahier, p. 263, Plate XIII; Barreau, 46, where he brings back the three scholars to life and throws money to the three young girls just as their father was going to put them on the street, cf. Wylie, iii. 221. For a 13th century jeu de St Nicolas by Jean Bodel of Arras, see Tivier, Dram. 105; Demogeot, 221. Among the Duke of Berry's relics was a phial containing oil distilled from the body of St Nicolas, Guiffrey, ii. 115. For miracles of St Nicholas on the font in the cathedral at Winchester, see Vict. Co. Hist. Hants. ii. 240, 242.

[16] For the Catherine Hospital in the Rue St Denis in Paris, see L. Legrand, xxiv. 270-278; quoting L. Brièle, Comptes de l'Hôtel Dieu, 1363-1599, published in 1884, see A. Chevalier, p. viii.

being abundant[1], as at Canterbury[2], Harbledown[3], Salisbury[4], Scarborough[5] and York[6], while the last is associated with Thornton's godshouse at Newcastle-on-Tyne[7], and the great foundation by the Tower of London[8], the site of which is now occupied with docks and shipping.

London has also preserved the memory of St Mary Spital that kept hospitality for poor men[9] just outside the Bishop's gate, whose name still survives in the quiet purlieus of Spital Square and the busy grime of Spitalfields. Her great Spital of St Bartholomew, which gave a shelter to poor men and to young women that had mis-done[10], still keeps on its beneficent work on other lines in Smithfield, and of the Elsing Spital[11] next Cripplegate, that was once a

[1] For St Nicholas' Hospital at Nancy, see Pfister, i. 290; at Troyes, Arbois de Jubainville, ii. 122; at Pontoise, Rym. ix. 892. For St Nicholas joust la cité de Caudville, see Priv. Seal 665/791. For the leper-house of St Nicholas at Bayeux, see Rym. ix. 559.

[2] e.g. Cokyn's or the Eastbridge Spital, see p. 362.

[3] Called Ospitalis S. Nicholai de Hebeldon, Duncombe, 207; Archaeologia, v. 349 (from seal); or Herbeldoune, Monast. vii. 653; Hasted, iii. 578; or Herbal, Oliver, Monast. 401; Helbedonne, Douet d'Arcq, Comptes, 272. It was rebuilt circ. 1685, Duncombe, 176 (with picture); Hasted, iii. 579; Clay, 35, 192, with picture. For the church of Reculver appropriated to it, see Hasted, iii. 578. For £31 pro decimis cariandis et intrandis from Reculver, Herne and St Nicholas in Thanet (or St Nicholas-at-Wade), see Stone, 18; Wylie, iii. 323. For writ fratribus et sororibus hospitalium de Northgate et Herbaldon, see Memoranda Rolls K. R. 3–4 H. V, 78, Oct. 28, 1415.

[4] See p. 362, note 8. For pictures of it see Wordsworth, xix, xxxviii, xliii; Clay, 129. For its seal with figure of the saint, see Wordsworth, 253. For plans, see Hoare, v. 49; Wordsworth, p. l.

[5] Priv. Seal 655/798; Monast. vii. 639, which shows that in 1297 the bailiffs and four townsmen audiunt compotum dictae domus singulis annis.

[6] For St Nicholas' Hospital or lazarhouse outside Walmgate Bar at York just beyond Milton St. on the Hull Road, now destroyed, see Auden, 184, 185. The porches were removed to the churches of St Margaret and St Lawrence.

[7] Built by Roger Thornton, Ad Quod Damn. 371; Wylie, ii. 255, note 7; Clay, 83.

[8] For St Catherine's Hospital by the Tower (juxta Turrim London, Archaeol. Journ. xliv. 58), see Monast. vii. 694; Benham-Welch, 15; Clay, 25, 72. It was removed in 1828. For pictures of the chapel and buildings, see Ducarel, 32, 34, 38; Benham, Tower, Plates 23, 24, from J. Carter (1780); also Reliquary, N. S. IV. 150 (1890); B. T. Pouncy (1779); Knight, London, vi. 341; Besant, Survey, i. 161. For documents relating to it, see Exch. Accts. 215/3. For 73s. 6d. paid to the master, brethren and sisters in compensation for damage to their property through elargac' fossati circa Turrim, see Iss. Roll 8 H. V, Pasch., July 12, 1420.

[9] Greg. Chron. ix, xliii, who notes that there are "sum susters yn the same place to kepe the beddys for pore men"; called Domus Dei in Monast. vi. 625; cf. Sharpe, Wills, ii. 409; Knight, London, ii. 387; Besant, Survey, ii. 322.

[10] For Bartholomew ys Spetylle as "a place of grete comforte to pore men as for hyr loggyng and yn specyalle unto yong wymmen that have mysse don that ben whythe chylde. There they ben delyveryde and unto the tyme of puryfycacyon they have mete and drynke of the placys coste." Greg. Chron. viii; Besant, Survey, ii. 257; Clay, 9. For St Bartholomew's Hospital (1341) receiving mulieres pregnantes quousque de puerperio surrexerint and taking charge of the babies up to seven years of age if the mother died, see N. Moore, 24.

[11] It was founded by William Elsing, a London mercer, in 1329, for paralysed or blind priests, Clay, 24, 81. The site was afterwards occupied by Sion College, Monast.

home for 100 blind and palsied poor[1], the only trace
remaining consists of an archway of the chapel now
forming the porch of the parish church of St Alphage by
London Wall[2]. Thomas Spital has moved from its old
site in Southwark[3], where Whitington made a new chamber
with eight beds for young women that had done amiss,
keeping secret all particulars in hope of good amendment,
for "he would not shame no young woman in no wise for
it might be cause of letting of her marriage[4]"; while the
Spital of Our Lady of Bedlem[5] still finds a home, though
on another site, for those that have fallen out of their wits[6].

But an even more striking survival of the spirit of
mediaeval charity is furnished by the Hospital of St Cross[7]
near Winchester. It was founded by a Bishop of Winchester in the 12th century and provided every day a
manchet[8] or a cast of bread[9] and $1\frac{1}{2}$ to 2 gallons of

---

vii. 703; Benham-Welch, 15. Called Elsinspetill in Archaeol. Journ. xliv. 58, where its
property in London yielded £113. 4s. 8d. per annum in 1412.

[1] Called caecos pauperes et miserabiles personas, Monast. vii. 706; Clay, 24; a
preference being given to priests.

[2] Besant, Survey, ii. 249. For picture see R. Wilkinson, I. pt. i; Knight, London,
iv. 224; Besant, Survey, i. 99; ii. 248.

[3] Ibid. ii. 309.

[4] Greg. Chron. ix.

[5] Domus de Bedlem, Archaeol. Journ. xliv. 58 (1412); i.e. Bethlehem, called
"Bedleem," Lydg. Min. Po. 50, 51, 55, 57, 59; not "Redelem" as Holmes, 19. For
account of it, see Besant, Survey, ii. 325; do. Tudors, 185. It was formerly on the site
of what is now Liverpool Street, Monast. vii. 621; alias "Old Bethlem," Bowen, p. 2;
or "Without Bishopsgate," Stow, i. 322; ii. 98, 144, 155. It was afterwards removed to
Little Moorfields by London Wall and to its present position in Lambeth in 1815,
Knight, London, v. 382; Wheatley, ii. 407. For a labourer put in the pillory in London
in 1412 for pretending to be a collector of alms for it, see Letter Book I, 105; Clay, 185.
Cf. we have chambers purposely for them (i.e. the man who is married to a shrewd wife
and is never quiet), or els they should be lodged in Bedlem, Hazlitt, iv. 57. For visitation
in 1403, see Char. Comm. Rept. xxxii. vi. 472, when there were 12 inmates, 6 of them
being "mente capti" with only the master to look after them, with the aid of 6 cheynes
de fer, 6 lokkes, 3 pair manycles de iren, and 2 paire stokkys, Clay, 32; cf. ystreyned
she was yn streyghte bondys, N. Moore, Foundation, ciii, of a mad woman at St
Bartholomew's Hospital.

[6] Greg. Chron. ix, who notes that "sum ben a-bydyng there yn for ever, for
they ben falle soo moche owte of hem selfe that hyt ys uncurerabylle unto man";
Clay, 33.

[7] For pictures of the church and hospital of St Cross, see Monast. vii. 721; Grose,
Antiq. Vol. II; Woodward, i. 230, 234; Lestrange, 244, 248; Sergeant, 124, 125, where
it is called "the oldest almshouse in England"; Clay, 81; Vict. Co. Hist. Hants. v.
59–68; Leach, Winchester, 35, who gives an account of the hospital, which was founded
by Henry de Blois, Bishop of Winchester, in 1136.

[8] "A chet lofe," Manners and Meals, i. 322; "manchet and chet," ibid. i. 320;
Halliwell, ii. 539; Cotgr., s.v. *Miche.*

[9] Called "a coarse loaf weighing 5 marks, 3 quarts of weak beer, pottage enough, a
herring and 2 pilchards (or 2 eggs) and a farthing's worth of cheese" in Vict. Co. Hist.
Hants. ii. 196. For charity loaves (lopa de la caritat) distributed at Agen every Whitsuntide, see Magen, 320.

ale[1] each for 100 of the poorest men in the town[2]. Bishop Wickham found it overrun with abuses which he did his best to reform[3], and when Bishop Beaufort remodelled it in 1440 as an almshouse for noble poverty[4], he nevertheless rebuilt the Hundred Men's Hall[5], where the mortrel[6] or pottage was prepared by the Hundred Men Cook in the Hundred Men Pot[7] and served with the Hundred Men Ladle[8]; and here the casual passer-by may still see the rude wooden salts and candlesticks and black leathern jacks[9] preserved with pious care, and claim his share, if he chooses, in the wayfarer's dole[10]—"the only remaining vestige left in the kingdom of the simplicity and hospitality of the old times[11]."

Taking the word in its widest sense a list has recently been compiled[12] showing that there were nearly 800 hospitals in England, while in Paris alone there were 26[13] and in the city of Florence no less than 35 have been counted as existing at the time with which we are now dealing[14]. But whether almshouse[15], beadhouse, blindhouse, guesthouse, leperhouse[16], madhouse, plaguehouse, rescuehouse, poor-

[1] Cf. if he have nothing than brede and good ale it should suffice me, Caxton, Dial. 30.

[2] Monast. vii. 721; Milner, i. 224, ii. 143, 146; Warren, 3, 77; Lestrange, 251; Wordsworth, xlviii.

[3] Lowth, 73–87; Milner, ii. 143. He put in John Campden as Master who died in 1410 (not 1384 as Boutell, p. 4). For his brass still existing in the church, see Waller, p. ii; Duthy, 268, 288; Leach, 78; Woodward, i. 227, 234, 241; Vict. Co. Hist. Hants. ii. 196; Clay, 151.

[4] Nova domus eleemosynaria nobilis paupertatis, Monast. vii. 722; Clay, 25; called 1445 in Woodward, i. 234; Dict. Nat. Biogr. iv. 47. For pauperes generosos at Staindrop, see Wylie, iii. 243.

[5] For picture, see Woodward, i. 230; Clay, 110; Vict. Co. Hist. Hants. v. 67.

[6] Monast. vii. 721; Lowth, 68; Milner, ii. 142; Duthy, 250; Lestrange, 257; Woodward, i. 234 (who derives it from a mortar or bowl); also Form of Cury, xix; R. F. Williams, i. 189; Warren, ii. 58; but cf. "mortrows," Manners and Meals, i. 151, 170, 172; mortrews, Wylie, iii. 213; mortress, Murray, Dict., s.v.

[7] For podyngers, or podegares (i.e. porringers), see Archaeol. Cant. vii. 279.

[8] Vict. Co. Hist. Hants. ii. 194; Leach, 35.

[9] Woodward, i. 235; Warren, ii. 70; do. Winchester, 84; Lestrange, 256.

[10] R. Warner, i. 205; Woodward, i. 238; Warren, 111; do. Winchester, 80.

[11] Milner, ii. 144; Monast. vii. 722; Clay, 170, 240.

[12] Clay, xviii. 276–337. For a list of hospitals in Normandy including Arques, Caudebec, Gournay, Aumale, etc. see C. Beaurepaire, Notes, ii. 32; also Bayeux, Torigni and Vire, Postel, 76.

[13] Guilhermy, Itin. 365.

[14] P. Monnier, ii. 170; one of which (Santa Maria Novella) was built by the citizens in 1285, ibid. i. 6.

[15] Cf. "howys of almes," Monast. iv. 47, e.g. at Hereford, Winchester and York; Leach, Winchester, 27.

[16] Domus leprosorum, Rym. x. 36.

house[1] or infirmary, all these Spitals or Houses of Hospitality[2] were fitly known as God's Hostels[3], Godshouses[4], or Maisondewes[5]; for in the language of our forefathers the want-wits were "God's minstrels[6]," the "daughters of sin[7]" were "God's daughters[8]," the lepers were "Christ's martyrs[9]" and the poor His "members[10]." At the opening of their feasts they "served God first[11]" by setting aside a loaf for the poor; they left some gravy in the dish "for Christ[12]"; and when they turned Bridewell Palace[13] into a workhouse for floisterers[14] and vagabonds, they said it was "to lodge Christ in[15]."

In large towns the chief godshouse was usually in the stricter sense an infirmary[16] (*nosocomium*) mainly for the care

---

[1] For the Hôpital des Pauvres at Clermont-Ferrand, see Tardieu, i. 439; hospitale pauperum at Riom (Auvergne), Rivière, i. 356; for l'Hôpital des Pauvres or Maisondieu at Bourbon-l'Archambault, see Annales Bourbonnaises, ii. 243.

[2] For hostel=hospitalitas, see L. Legrand, xxv. 88, 168; or domus hospitalitatis, do. Quinzevingts, 125.

[3] For l'Hostel Dieu in Paris, see Ordonnances, xi. 17; also at Pontoise, Fauquembourg, ii. 3; the Hôtel-Dieu or Maison Dieu or Domus Dei at Gonesse, Delisle, 14; L. Legrand, xxiv. 65, 237-250; xxv. 87; Coyecque, ii. 49; the Hostiel Dié at Cherbourg, Voisin La Hougue, 3, 58; Amiot, 277.

[4] Clay, 244. For Hospitalis sive Domus Dei at Alençon, see Rym. x. 87; at Pont de l'Arche, ibid. x. 59; Hospitalis de Hampton quod vocatur Domus Dei, Monast. vii. 674. Called "the Hospital of God's House" temp. Ed. VI, ibid. 675. "An hospitale caulyd Goddeshouse," Lel. Itin. iii. 92; "domum dei et pauperum hospitalis," Rym. ix. 892; Goddis House or ellys the House of Almesse at Ewelme, Hist. MSS. Rept. ix. 218; Clay, 151; in domo dei seu hospitali Parisiensi, Coyecque, ii. 48; called also Hostel Dieu, Maison Dieu, L. Legrand, xxv. 50; Hostel Dieu des Pestifères at Poitiers, Braun, Vol. 1 (with picture); pauperum caecorum hospitalis sive Domus Dei Quindecim Viginti caecorum nuncupati (i.e. the Quinzevingts in Paris), Felibien, iii. 272. For William Wynard's Godshouse at Exeter, see Gidley, 4, 75, 107; Clay, 27; a tenement called "Goddyshous" at Exeter in 1444, Cotton and Dallas, iii. 143. For the Domus Dei at Tours, see Bulletin Soc. Archéol. de Touraine, ii. 90-156. For pictures of Maisons Dieu at Compiègne, Brie-Comte-Robert and Vernon, see Tollet, 39, 40.

[5] Halliwell, ii. 537; for Mesondieu vocat' Thorntonishospitall at Newcastle-on-Tyne, see Ad Quod Damn. 371; do. Lists, ii. 743; p. 364, note 7. Cf. "mesyndew," Hasted, ii. 801; "mussendeue or spittel," Clay, 11.   [6] Wylie, ii. 290.

[7] Filles de péché, Collas, 99, 194; filles de joie, Couderc, Album, 25, Pl. LIX; H. Martin, v. 427; Michelet, v. 427; filles de vie, Collas, 194; fillettes, Gouvenain, i. 25.

[8] For l'Hôpital des Filles Dieu just within the Porte St Denis in Paris, see Bourgeois, 631; Sauval, iii. 587; H. Legrand, 60; Jaillot, ix. 22; Maillard, 20. It was originally a hostel for loose women (*communes mulierculas*, Sabatier, 92), who were being reformed through the preaching of William of Auvergne in 1225 to help them to observe chastity till they found husbands, L. Legrand, xxiv. 65, 250, 251, 253.   [9] Clay, 66.

[10] Ordonnances, xi. 17; Bowen, Bridewell, 10.   [11] Mann. and Meals, i. 324.

[12] Aliquid de potagio Christo pauperi semper in scultellâ dimittere, Ferrer, i. 27.

[13] For picture of it on the bank of the Thames at the outfall of the Fleet River near the Black Friars, see R. Wilkinson, I. pt. i. 11; Besant, Survey, i. 184; do. (Tudors) 186. For picture of Edward VI granting the charter, see ibid. 48.

[14] Trans. Devon Assoc. xliv. p. 225.

[15] Besant, Story, 106, from letter of Bishop Ridley, temp. Ed. VI.

[16] nosocomium or "firmerye," Archaeol. Cant. vii. 277; "enfermerie," Brièle, Doc. iii. 26; "enfermière," Legrand, Maisons Dieu, 135, from *L'Hôpital d'Amours*. For the Infirmary in the Abbey at Ourscamp, near Compiègne, see Tollet, 46.

of the sick; but where arrangements were on a smaller scale, it was a hostry[1] or guesthouse (*xenodocium*) for needy strangers also[2]. It was served by brethren and sisters[3] who were bound by strict rule[4]. They might not leave the building without first obtaining permission from the master[5] and they took the usual vows of poverty, obedience and chastity[6], though scandals were certainly far from unknown[7]. But they nobly took up burdens from which the prosperous world recoiled[8]. They reared the foundling[9], nursed the sick

[1] Cf. "ostries clepid innes for to logge gistis," Pecock, ii. 521.

[2] L. Legrand, Maisons Dieu, 134. For endowment provided for day inmates (*jurnelli*) at Winchester, see Leach, 140. Cf.

　　Wayfaring men and maymed souldyours
　　Have theyr relyef in this poore hous of ours. Clay, 1.

[3] For le maistre, frères et sœurs et familiers de l'Hostel Dieu de Paris, see Ordonnances, xi. 17. For fratres et sorores, see J. Garnier, 27. For the Prioress Fratrum et Sororum at the Hospital of St James at Canterbury, see Pat. 8 H. V, 2 d. For the Sustren Spital at Winchester, where the headmaster's house (built in 1748) now stands, see Leach, 27, 72, 109, 142, 377, where two women from the Spital dine with the fellows in the adjoining College in 1416. For the sisters professed at St Thomas' Hospital in Southwark mentioned in John Gower's will in 1408, see Clay, 154.

[4] Vivunt secundum sancti Augustini regulam, Vitry, 337; L. Legrand, Statuts, pp. v, vii, x, 2, 69, 129.

[5] L. Legrand, Maisons Dieu, 123; do. Statuts, 48. One of the questions asked by the Commissioners in 1532 at the Savoy Hospital was "whether any of the susters be commonly drunkards, sedicious, irefull or walking foorth to the Towne or elswhere without good cause," Loftie, Savoy, 105.

[6] For six sisters at the Hôtel-Dieu in 1416 specially described as "religieuses de cest hostel," see Brièle, Doc. iii. 28, 46, which seems to show that the sisters were not all religious. Another one is called "seur Perrenelle la louvette," ibid. In L. Legrand, Statuts, 102, La Meson Dieu le Comte (at Troyes) est meson de religion. Cf. velata fuit…fecit vota, Coyecque, ii. 40, and *passim*; Boullé, 155; L. Legrand, Statuts, 8, 44, 54. Called "some monastic vows and discipline," Wordsworth, xxxv, of St Nicholas' Hospital at Salisbury, where they are called "ministri" and "benefactores hospitalis fratres et sorores" (p. xlvi), which the editor interprets as "some nursed and some were nursed" (p. xlviii). At the Elsing Spital in London, where many of the inmates were infirmos jacentes et languentes, the ministri sunt et erunt seculares, Monast. vii. 706.

[7] e.g. in the Maison Dieu in Paris in 1354 an erring sister was locked up for 14 years for killing her baby and burying it under a tree, see Coyecque, i. 173, 175, who fancies that the state of things disclosed in the report of 1482 did not begin till circa 1450. Yet on Feb. 8, 1409, a sister and a brother reperti fuerunt in delicto horâ suspectâ videlicet medie noctis, ibid. ii. 43. The sister was required to withdraw from the house and enter another, but the brother was locked up in the chapter prison for a year, two months of which were to be spent in absolute silence, with a bread and water diet every Friday throughout the year. For a brother expelled in 1418 propter sua demerita with permission to be readmitted if repentant after four years, see ibid. ii. 58. For a scandal between the master and one of the sisters, see Luce, i. 90. A. Chevalier (p. 118), while admitting quelques fautes échappées à la fragilité humaine (p. 129), claims that the number of cases of immorality was very few up till the middle of the 15th century, when disorder had certainly been introduced, temp. Louis XI (pp. ix, 134). For a clerk and a sister in the leperhouse at Fontenay near Vincennes in 1351, sese ad invicem pluries carnaliter cognovisse, see L. Legrand, xxiv. 82; do. Maisons Dieu, 109.

[8] Tantas sustinent infirmorum immunditias et fetorum molestias pene intolerabiles, Vitry, 338; L. Legrand, Statuts, 3.

　　Ils ont toujours les coleurs fades
　　Et ne les fait pas bon sentir. Champion, Prisonnier, 32.

[9] For a foundling named Jehannete, 4½ years old, picked up in the street in Paris in

and the halt[1], ministered to the aged[2], and tended the blind[3] and the leprous[4], being often lepers themselves[5]; they did gracious service by offering the last bite of bread and the last cup of wine[6] to the criminal on his way to the gallows and they found Christian burial for outcast corpses thrown up by the river or abandoned in the street, the suicide alone being reckoned as beyond their care.

We may therefore take the godshouse as a common name for a house devoted to deeds of mercy[7] of every kind. It might be merely a guesthouse, where outcasts[8] and travelling-men, such as pedlars, rabbit-skin gatherers and

1403, and taken care of pour l'amour de Dieu, see Fagniez, Jurisprudence, 13, where the family who are bringing her up fear that by law this will give her a right to a share in their property. At Troyes no foundlings (pueri inventi, enfans getez) were admitted to the Meson Dieu le Comte, otherwise tanta affluerit copia puerorum, that the house would not be large enough. They also refused demembrati, contracti, manci et caeci, L. Legrand, Statuts, 115.

[1] For a hospital in a house still existing near the Church of St Vivien at Rouen, established in the 14th century, with 13 beds for pauperes claudi et debiles recipi cubari et recolligi, see C. Beaurepaire, Notes, ii. 25.   [2] Sains et malades, Boullé, 155, 159.

[3] For aveugleries, see L. Legrand, Maisons Dieu, 133. For the Meson des Aveugles, i.e. the Quinzevingts near the Louvre in Paris, see ibid. 114. Called also domus caecorum, la meson des tras cens aveugles, Berty, i. 68 (on their seal). It was founded by St Louis circ. 1260 for 300 poor blind, L. Legrand, xxiv. 261; xxv. 61, 64; Berty, i. 61, 62; Chauliac, xii; Guilhermy, i. 668; Tollet, 39. For legacies to it, see Le Villain, Flamel, 203, 377. For a plan of the buildings with picture of the Chapel of St Nicaise, see Berty, i. 67, 68, 286. The site (now the Place du Carrousel) was known as the Champ-pourri, but the charity is now in the Hôtel des Mousquetaires Noirs in the Rue de Charenton near the Gare de Lyon, ibid. i. 70.

[4] For la femme qui sert les ladres in the maladrerie at Clermont-Ferrand, see Tardieu, i. 447.

[5] For donats ladres at Brives-Charensac on the upper Loire near Le Puy, see Mandet, 284. For le Sovereyn meseal (i.e. a leprous prior), see Clay, 196. For similar cases at Dover, Lancaster and Rochester, see ibid. 144. At St Julian's Hospital near St Albans all the fratres were lepers, Monast. vii. 618. For the non-leprous called "haitiés" (i.e. sound), see L. Legrand, xxvi; Cotgr., s.v. *Haité*.

[6] For l'Hôpital des Filles Dieu (which had become a béguinage since 1346, L. Legrand, xxiv. 255) où il y a des religieuses qui donnent aux malfaicteurs la croix à baiser, l'eaue béniste, pain et vin bénis dont ils mengent trois morceaux quand on les manie pendre ou ardoir à la justice, see Bonnardot, Rues, 31; Lavillegille, 46; also page 367, note 8. For order, Feb. 11, 1397, allowing a confessor to criminals before execution, see Lavillegille, 17, 34. For 1s. 6d. charged for 1 chopin of wine and a glass for a criminal on his way to execution at Auffay near Dieppe on Jan. 25, 1388, see C. Beaurepaire, Notes, ii. 95. For "St Giles's Bowl" of ale offered to criminals on their way to Tyburn, see Knight, London, iii. 258; Grey, 13; Marks, 4; Loftie, ii. 206. The spot was afterwards named Bowl Yard, where Meux' Brewery now stands, Dobie, 71, though said to run into Broad Street where Endell Street now is, Besant-Mitton, 19, who refers to a public house called the Bowl, set up there in 1623 (pp. 8, 18). It was still called St Giles' Bowl even when the custom was transferred to the Bow Inn at Tyburn, where Jack Shephard left some ale for Jonathan Wild, see Cruikshank's picture in Dobie, 8; also see Stow, iv. 74; Maitland, ii. 1363; Newcourt, i. 611; Dobie, 82; Clinch, 9. For a similar custom at York, see Pennant, London, 179.

[7] Ou en soulloit faire les oeuvres de miséricorde, Bourgeois, 133.

[8] Cf.   They that do borow on theyr garments and napery
               They that borow and purpose not to pay
               Till in pryson they spend all away.   Hazlitt, iv. 59;

all the fraternity of unthrift and the sisterhood of drabs, sluts and callets could obtain a meal and a night's shake-down on the straw[1]; or a permanent home for the aged or the leper, who was a public danger and whose case was then regarded as incapable of cure ; or a house chiefly reserved for the treatment of the sick[2], where they would be tended until they were sufficiently restored to health[3], though even these admitted many inmates who were merely aged and infirm among them, besides a certain number of paying guests known as familiars or pensioners, who received a maintenance during their old age on the understanding that they bestowed their wordly goods on the house, either actually on admission or prospectively by legacy to be realised after they were dead[4]. Houses of this latter type were usually situated in the centre of the busiest cities, often under the shadow of some great church or cathedral[5], as a

with many other types of persons "that come .o end their days in the spittels." Also

> They that forget that to them is ough,
> And they that lend and set no tyme to pay,
> Old folks that all theyr goodes do gyve
> Kepyng nothyng whereon to lyve,
> Lechours, fornycatours and advouterers,
> Incestes, harlots, bawdes and bolsterers,
> Applesquyers, entycers and ravyshers. Hazlitt, iv. 59;

i.e. apronsquires (Murray, Dict., s.v.) ; but see Halliwell, i. 73.

> Drunkards who spend up all theyr thryft. Hazlitt, iv. 64.

> Pedlers ragged and jagg with broken hose and breche. Ibid. 69.

> Gaderers of cony skynnes
> That chop with laces, poyntes, nedles and pyns. Ibid. 69.

> Sailors and the fraternyte of unthrifte. Ibid. 70.

> The systerhood of drabbes, sluttes and callets
> With their bagges and wallets. Ibid. 71.

[1] Que els espitals meta hom palha (paille) per les paubres, Magen, 97; "asile de nuit," Tollet, 50; here have no beddyng but lye on the strawe, Hazlitt, iv. 54; a straw bed with a covering of bys or deerskin, Clay, 172; straturam et apparatum lectorum, Monast. vii. 706; cf.

> And all other which we seem good and playne
> Have here lodging for a nyght or twayne. Clay, 1, 224.

[2] Eleemosinarias pro decumbentibus, Fascic. 393.

[3] De jour en jour soient receuz, soustenuz et alimentez les povres malades qui de jour en jour y viennent et affluent de toutes pars en grande habondance, Ordonnances, xi. 17 (of the Hôtel-Dieu in Paris).

[4] e.g. the Hôtel-Dieu in Paris, Coyecque, i. 54, 60; though supposed to be jamais que des hôtes de passage in L. Legrand, Statuts, xxv.

[5] Tollet, 47 ; Coyecque, i. 20; Clay, 16. For the Hôtel-Dieu near the cathedral at Orleans, demolished circa 1847, see Didron, Vandalisme, 122. For the Hospital of Santa Maria de La Scala beside the cathedral at Siena, see Thureau-Dangin, 12. For l'Ostiel Dieu lez Notre Dame in Paris, G. Metz, 86. For Angers and Chartres, see Viollet-le-Duc, Architecture, vi. 103, 104. For almonries attached to cathedrals, see Leach, St Paul's, 197.

reminder that divine service was inseparable from the doing
of the deeds of mercy[1].

Life in an almshouse, which has been described as an
"essentially religious life[2]," may be pictured from the routine
laid down in several still existing sets of statutes, which
describe minutely the hours for rising, the fines for non-
attendance at the frequent chapel services, the light labour
implied in weeding the quadrate or removing any filth or
harlotry that caused stench or horror from the neighbourhood of the well, the prohibition against absence from
the house for more than an hour at a time, the forbidden
games and visits to taverns which must have resulted in
the low-grade type of tame, caged, dissatisfied, mechanical
life, which may be found in any corresponding institution
to-day, in spite of orders that the inmate must in no wise
be "a faitour or a chider or brigous among his fellows or a
smatterer of strange quarrels[3]" and other such well-inten-
tioned efforts to keep human nature out. But the life of an
infirmary has hitherto proved difficult to sketch[4]. It may
however now be studied in the abundant records of the
great Hôtel-Dieu[5] that stands on the river bank close to
the Petit Pont on the north side of the Parvis of Notre
Dame in Paris, the particulars of which have been recently
examined with the utmost care. For the year ending at
Christmas 1414 the expenditure amounted to nearly 7000
livres[6] of which the details are minutely worked out even
to the third of a pite[7].

---

[1] Ouquel les oeuvres de miséricorde et le service divin sont faites et accomplies chacun
jour, Ordonnances, xi. 17.   [2] Clay, 158.
[3] Hist. MSS. Rept. ix. 219.   [4] Archaeol. Cant. vii. 273.
[5] For pictures of it with the Chapel of St Agnes before the fire of 1772, see Husson,
480, 482, with plans (Plate 1); also Tollet, 76, 82; A. Chevalier, 113 (circ. 1524);
Meindre, ii. 99; Guilhermy, Itin. 366. For riverside view, see Hamerton, 5. For
account of the Chapel of St Julien le Pauvre, see Guilhermy, i. 641, 645. For seal of
the Hôtel-Dieu, March, 1375, see Demay, Inventaire, ii. 40. For its statutes (1217),
see A. Chevalier, I. pp. vii, 31, 40-50; L. Legrand, 43-50.
[6] viz. 6913*l*. 7*s*. 9*d*. pitte et le tiers d'une pitte from Christmas, 1413, to Christmas,
1414, Coyecque, ii. 51. In 1416 the receipts amounted to 6346*l*. 6*s*. 6*d*. and the
expenditure to 6666*l*. 6*s*. 5*d*. (poitevine), Brièle, iii. 47. For 50*l*. 19*s*. left to the Hôtel-
Dieu in 1416 by the patients who died there, see Brièle, iii. 26. In Sept. 1415, one of
the sisters found 80 crowns sewed up in the dress of one of them, ibid. One of their farms,
viz. at Mondeville, supplied them with 1634 sheep in 1416, which were killed and eaten
in the hospital, the pelts being sold to a meggacer (*mesgisier*) for 142*l*. 9*s*. 2*d*., ibid. In
1416 the cellarer's account shows 109*s*. 8*d*. realised from the sale of the lees of 311 cues
and 96 puncheons of wine, and they sold fat (*suif*) to a fishmonger at the Halles and
2 casks of grease to the tilers, ibid. p. 27. For an annual deficit of 2500*l*. see Gerson, iv. 683.
[7] Called a mite or a French farthing in Cotgr., s.v.

These accounts show the amounts spent on meat, poultry, fish, eggs, fruit, pottage, onions, spice, fuel, faggots and other necessaries[1], among which it is striking that only 1½ gallons of milk are used in the day, half of which is consumed in the sisters' refectory and only 3 quarts by the patients[2]. There are repairs to the chimney in the chapter-house[3] and the well in the court, with detailed particulars of the nails, bolts, bricks, lime, plaster and cement used in the process. There are payments for sacks and boulters for the flour, special payments for the brothers on five feast-days in the year, payments for green herbs for their refectory in the summer, with orpine and nut-boughs for Midsummer Day, 7 dozen common glasses with a large one each for the master, the prioress, the brethren, sisters and officers, 203 lbs. of almonds costing 41*l*. 7*s*. 3*d*., also 24*s*. for a cask of beer for the brethren to drink on Good Friday. White lambskins are bought to fur the brothers' amices, also trenchers for their refectory and for the chapter-house, bundles of parchment and reams of paper, and jetters for casting up the accounts[4]; New Year's gifts (*estraines*) are given to the varlets and servants as well as to messengers calling from outside ; and horses have to be bought for the master and bursar when they go out to visit the granges[5], on which occasions they require their supply of spices, comfits, Hippocras, obleys and "supplications." Ropes are wanted for the well and there are expenses for repairing the clock, castrating the pigs at the wine-press, and scouring the vat (16*s*.)[6]. The sum of 9*l*. 12*s*. was paid for a new dead-cart[7]; there is a special payment for a trench to bury their dead in the Trinity churchyard[8]; and in this year are included the costs of an action brought by them against

---

[1] Brièle, iii. 43.
[2] Ibid. iii. 45.
[3] Brique pour faire le contrecueur (back) de la cheminée, ibid. iii. 43.
[4] Ibid. iii. 92.
[5] Pour porter hors quant on chevauche vers les granches.
[6] p. curer le puys du traitouer, ibid. iii. 46.
[7] Chariot a mener les corps au cimitière de la Trinité, ibid. iii. 45. In 1416 there were 2077 deaths at the Hôtel-Dieu, the total cost for burying the bodies being 24*l*. 17*s*., i.e. at the rate of 3*d*. each, or 25*s*. per 100, or 12*l*. per 1000. The number of burials is recorded month by month, viz. in Jan. 150, Feb. 124, March 136, April 124, May 120, June 141, July 163, Aug. 170, Sept. 228, Oct. 274, Nov. 256, Dec. 171, which totals to 2057 only, or a score too few. In 1417 the total was 1730, ibid. iii. 51, which gives also the numbers for each month.
[8] 63 toise de fosse, ibid. iii. 51.

their tenant Nicholas Flamel[1], the famous bookseller in the Rue de la Tonnelerie near the Halles, to compel him to renovate his premises or else turn out[2]. There were 8 draught-horses in the stable, and the account supplies items of cost for their harness, such as ropes, collars for the shafts, saddles, dossers, breeching (*avalouers*), 6 pair of holsters (*fourreaux*), bridles, girths (*chevestres*) and other burlery[3], while 47*s*. was spent on physicking them with honey, verdigris[4], copperas, splints (*fust*), plaisters, arrement, bol-armenie[5], turpentine and other remedies[6], and the sheep on the premises had to be treated with an ointment made of quick-silver (*vif argent*), copperas, verdigris and rock-alum[7].

As to the patients the items of expenditure do not indicate any extravagance on the side of generosity[8], if we may judge from the supply of milk quoted above. 23 sols worth of groats[9] was entered for their porridge[10], and the expenses show that 1725 wooden platters[11] were bought for them together with 960 earthenware pots to hold their wine, 800 delf saucers (*godez de terre*), 3½ doz. of felt boots and 400 earthenware pails for their necessities[12],

---

[1] For a legacy of 16*s*. (du laiz Nicolas Flamel) left by him to the Hôtel-Dieu in Paris in 1418, see Brièle, iii. 53. See App. Q[1].

[2] Garnir ou quitter, Brièle, iii. 46.

[3] Ouvrage de bourrelier. For bourreliers=feseres de coliers à cheval et de dossières, de sèle et de toute autre manière de bourrelerie, see Boileau, 220; cf. cordouanier et bourrelier, Barbazan, ii. 303; Cotgrave, s.v.; Littré, s.v. For banner of the bourreliers of Paris, see La Croix, 313. For gantiers, bourliers, esguilletiers (i.e. point-makers or aglet-makers) et tanneurs forbidden to put skins of sheep, calf or kid into mesgismes (i.e. tanned hides), see Godefroy, s.v. *Megime*.

[4] Called vertegrece, vertegres, York, 50; vertgrez, Arderne, xxxii. For vertegres, coperose with argoil (i.e. cream of tartar used for dyeing), see Halliwell, i. 82; and in alchemy, Chaucer (16281).

[5] Bolearmine or sinople, Halliwell, i. 193; bole-armoniak, Chauc. 16258; do. (S.) v. 423=Sinopian red earth, Cotgr., s.v. *Bolearmenie*; or Armenian bole, Murray, s.v. *Armeniac*; bol d'Armenic, Cennini, 71.

[6] Brièle, iii. 45.

[7] Alum de glace, see Cotgr., s.v. *Glace*.

[8] For the infirmarer's account in Reading Abbey, see Add. Ch. 19649; Hurry, 184. In this the total expenditure for the year ending Michaelmas, 1413, amounts to £15. 18*s*. 6*d*., the items including spices, such as cloves, canell, ginger (22*d*. per lb.), saffron greyn and capons, but all these are for the Prior; also liveries for the garciones infirmorum, coal, talwood (Wylie, iv. 364) and fuel, barley for feeding the hens and torches for the chapel, with expenses for parchment (2*d*.), for mending spades (2*d*.) and weeding the garden, but the only item relating to the sick consists of 2*d*. paid for their beds.

[9] Gruyau, see Cotgr., s.v. *Gruau*.

[10] For "porage," see Clay, 168.

[11] Escueles de fust, Brièle, iii. 46.

[12] Paelles de terre pour faire leurs necessiteez, A. Chevalier, 82. For 2*s*. 7*d*. paid at Dunster pro 2 pellubriis de laton ad mingendum, see Lyte, 118; Ducange, s.v. *Pellubrium*, al. *Pelluvium*.

while 4*d.* apiece was paid for killing 36 stray dogs that got inside on to their beds[1]. We know also that the neighbouring canons of Notre Dame sent across to them any bread that was not found to be to their own taste[2], but the articles purchased on their behalf are limited to the barest necessaries of food and fuel, so that they must have welcomed any little additions to their pittance[3] that came in from charitable legacies[4] or the benevolence of sympathisers[5] from without. The year's receipts are derived from rents of lands and houses, sales of skins, wine-lees and other by-products, with occasional windfalls such as fines or market-forfeits[6], but a large section comes from alms, often from anonymous donors[7]; several are gifts in kind, the most usual being a bed with the necessary accompaniments such as a tick, mattress, featherbed, blankets, sheets, pillows, bolster, cushions, quilt and coverlet[8], and in some cases a contribution is given subject to the understanding that, should poverty overtake the donor, the brethren in their turn would minister to him and his all necessary things, just as if he himself were a brother of the house[9].

In the Hôtel-Dieu in Paris with its 400 or 500 inmates[10]

---

[1] p. tuer 36 chiens truans alans par ceans sur les lis des malades, Brièle, iii. 47. For 7 lbs. of lead bought at Dijon in 1437 to make a club for killing dogs and a bruiole to carry them to the fields, see Vallée, 27.

[2] Coyecque, i. 83. For food condemned in the markets given to the sick in hospitals at Oxford, Cambridge, Sandwich, Maldon, etc., see Clay, 168.

[3] Pour la pictance des pauvres malades, Brièle, iii. 24, 54.

[4] For a legacy to the poor of the godshouse at Chauny near Noyon, Jan. 31, 1376, see Matton, 29. On Oct. 11, 1419, Colart le Miroirier leaves property adfin que les povres qui y sont et seront receuz et herbergiez soient mieulz et plus largement gouvernez et alimentez, ibid. 5; also un livre en parchemin là u il a pluseurs livres escrips comenchans "Aemus(?) meurt qui à présens ne l'a," to be placed in the Hôtel-Dieu à la veue d'un chascun qui y volra lire. For legacies aux povres de l'Ostel-Dieu in Paris (1413), see Tuetey, Test. 557, 576.

[5] e.g. in 1417 Queen Isabel sent them 2 sous each for Good Friday, Brièle, iii. 49. For visits paid to les povres malades le vendredi bénoit by Louis, Duke of Orleans, see Champion, Vie, 9; Collas, 16, 120, 304, quoting Christine, ch. xv or xvi.

[6] For fines balliez a l'ostel Dieu pour la soustentation des povres, see Fauquembergue, ii. 11; also bread forfeited for light-weight, ibid. ii. 15.

[7] Aumosnes secrettes, Brièle, iii. 49, 52, 53 and *passim.*

[8] Ung lit fourni, i.e. with coulte (i.e. bed-tick, Godefroy, s.v.; or quilts, Cotgr., s.v. *Coitte pointe*; or coulte pour point, Littré, s.v. *Coitte*), coissin, ung serge perse et 2 draps de lin, Brièle, iii. 53; also with ciel d'osier (? dossier), iii courtines, iii coults pointes, ibid. 24. See App. R[1].

[9] For an example of a gift to St Bartholomew's Hospital in London (temp. John), see N. Moore, 23, where the necessaries are to be supplied to the donor in his own house.

[10] Absque illis qui sunt extra, Gerson, iv. 681.

the staff consisted of 30 brothers and 70 sisters[1], the latter of whom fed and tended the patients[2], washed and mended the linen[3], swept the floors, cleaned the bedding and undertook all the ordinary housework[4], though no woman must wash a man's head or make a man's bed[5], and much of the drudgery was actually done by the paid varlets, servitors[6], girls[7] (*puellae*) and maids (*ancillae*), of whom there were a large number resident in the building and employed in the kitchen[8], the bedrooms[9], the bakehouse, the new hall, the cellar, the carthouse (*chariot*), the gate or the brethren's dortour[10], while others were attached to the master, the prioress, the sisters, the laundresses[11], the sempstress, the peltier (*pelletier*), the shoemaker, the vine-dresser[12] and so on. Two of the sisters acted as *tronchières* and looked after the alms-box[13] at the entrance gate, while another had charge of the *pouillerie*, where the quilts and the patients' clothing were kept from the day of their admission, to be sold if they should never come out alive[14]. Eighteen clerks were attached to the hostel

[1] In A. Chevalier, vii, there are 25 sisters and the brothers never exceed 30; cf. L. Legrand, Statuts, 44, where the brethren are to be 30 (including 4 priests and 4 clerks) and the sisters 20.

[2] At St Pol they were to be fortes et habiles quae sciant et possint pauperis cubare et levare, L. Legrand, Statuts, 120; in cubando et levando et omnibus necessitatibus curiosé subveniant, ibid. 122; et les sereurs gardes des malades, ibid. 160. They were to put on and take off their shoes honestement, ibid. 163.

[3] For 3500 pièces de toile used every day in 1368, see Luce, i. 88; A. Chevalier, 97; quae erunt in aquâ Sequanae congelatae usque ad genua lavando panniculos pauperum, Gerson, iv. 682; A. Chevalier, 99; les draps laver en Seine, ibid. 129. For payments for cendres pour faire les lesives de cest hostel, see Brièle, iii. 45.

[4] The systers shall do their observaunce, Hazlitt, iv. 28. For the "sister huswyf" at Heytesbury, see Clay, 155.

[5] This was to be done par clers ou par vallez, L. Legrand, Statuts, 161.

[6] For salaries and wages (*louyers*) paid to "varles et serviteurs de cest hostel," see Brièle, iii. 32, 51, 56 in 1416, 1417, 1418. For ancillae to help in washing the sick, making the beds and sweeping the floors, see L. Legrand, Statuts, 48, 49; for les servans, ibid. 72. For gifts from Louis Duke of Orleans aux filles et serviteurs servans les povres de l'ostel Dieu de Paris, see Collas, 303.

[7] For 2 sisters *vel puellae* to sit up with patients at night, see L. Legrand, Statuts, 116, 163; Coyecque, ii. 42.

[8] Of whom one was a mute, Brièle, iii. 43.

[9] Chambrière ne autre feme, L. Legrand, Statuts, 161.

[10] Du dortouer (not doctouer) aux frères, Brièle, iii. 44; L. Legrand, Statuts, 75; cf. Wylie, iv. 343.

[11] For 24s. paid aux grans lavendieres, see Brièle, iii. 46; cf. Menagier, ii. 118; Leroux de Lincy, Femmes, 417; Walcott, Osyth, 17; lavendière de la Reine, Roman, 21; Beatrice the lauendre, Caxton, Dial. 31; chief lauendere, Lydg. Nightingale, 24.

[12] For the pressoir (or wine-press) of the Maison Dieu near the Porte St Michel, now the site of the Palais du Luxembourg, see H. Legrand, 72; Berty, iii. 83.

[13] Brièle, iii. 51, 56. For communem pixidem juxta portam at the godshouse at Exeter in 1436, see Gidley, 85, 118. For le tronc des aumosnes des pauvres, see Belfort-Mirot, p. xxv.

[14] For la chambre aux coultes et poullerie (*sic*), see Brièle, iii. 26, where the sale of

and were responsible for the chapel services[1], but they lived in a house outside. Besides the master, the bursar and two house-priests (*prestres maisonniers*), who were all brothers[2], there were three secular chaplains[3] in residence to confess and administer the sacraments to the sick. The professional staff consisted of two sworn surgeons[4], who received 12*d.* a day each for their services[5], a clerk of the counter[6], a cellarer, a master seamster, a furrier, a cordwainer (with a *frère familier* to assist him), a mason, a cartwright, a pantler, a baker, a shepherd[7], a butcher[8], a vine-dresser, a page for the saddle horses, a swineherd, a tripe-woman, a porter[9], a barber to shave the brethren, the chaplains and the clerks[10], and a master of the rougher class of work such as flushing the drains and sewers and cleaning the easements on the water-side[11], all of whom had paid varlets working under them[12]. The whole community was described as consisting of a master, a prioress[13], brothers, sisters, clerks and officers[14], the latter group being known as menials[15], though many of them were included amongst the brethren.

The brothers were often drawn from the chorister boys[16] after their voices had cracked and they were prepared for

---

vestments et robes de gens trespassez ou dit hostel realised 465*l.* 10*s.* in 1416, and 74*l.* 16*s.* for several vielles et petites coultes.

[1] In 1416 three extra priests had to be paid to take the daily mass parce qu'il y avoit trop peu de frères prestes en cest hostiel, ibid. iii. 95.

[2] Ibid. iii. 48.

[3] Ibid. iii. 44, where they vont à l'église comme les frères.

[4] A. Chevalier, 74. See App. S[1].

[5] Coyecque, i. 97. For other fees see page 139, note 7. In 1418 Jean le Conte cirurgien du roy left 400*l.* to the Hôtel-Dieu in return for boire, mengier, feu, lit, chambre et demourance en cest hostel with a varlet for the past three years, Brièle, iii. 46.

[6] Ibid. iii. 44.

[7] Ung berchier qui garde les brebis, ibid. iii. 43, which records a total consumption of 1708 sheep and 23 calves for the year 1416. At Christmas, 1415, there were 35 sheep in the building; bercher et frère familier, ibid. 50.

[8] Ibid. iii. 32.

[9] For the porter at Angers as a brother in 1176, see N. Moore, 22.

[10] Barbière (*sic*) pour reres les frères, chappelains et les clercs de cest hostel, Brièle, iii. Cf. fratres sint tonsurati, L. Legrand, Statuts, 44; la tonsure des frères soit faitte au dessus des oreilles, ibid. 133 (at Pontoise).

[11] Maistre des basses oeuvres pour curer les conduiz des eaux, des agoux, de la court et des aisemens des malades sur la rivière de Seine, Brièle, iii. 45. For aisances placed over the Seine at the Palais in Paris, see Aubert, Orig. 393.

[12] e.g. valet courdouonnier, varlet boulengier, do. portier, Brièle, iii. 53, 56.

[13] Prieuse et religieuse, ibid. 56.

[14] Frères, suers, filles, clers et autres serviteurs, ibid. 45.

[15] Frères familiers, ibid. 28.

[16] Coyecque, i. 283.

Holy Orders after their admission.   The sisters included many high-born ladies[1], about half of them being young women of from 18 to 25 years of age, who were as yet only novices or *filles blanches*[2], and the remainder professed sisters who after wearing the black veil for a year of probation, took the full vows of obedience to the Prioress as their religious head[3], though all final responsibility for the discipline and administration of the house rested ultimately with the Chapter of Notre Dame[4] who deputed some of their members to audit the accounts[5] and act as viewers[6], to hold a visitation every half-year and punish any grave breaches that came under their notice.   It has been urged that the hospital nurses were really lay-sisters, and it is quite true that they were not cloistered.   But their rule of life differed in no way from that of professed nuns.   Like the brothers, they took their meals in silence[7] and boisterous laughter was altogether disallowed[8]; they might not leave the precincts without express permission; their status was officially described as a "religion[9]," and their house as a "convent[10]."   They wore a distinctive dress consisting of a soutane[11] reaching to the feet, a woollen pellice, a jacket of black or russet serge (*sagio*), a woollen surcoat or super-tunicle, a walebrown[12] cloak, and linen or woollen capes, being shod with black or white shoes, rounded boots[13] or

[1] Coyecque, i. 55, where on Feb. 8, 1417, the authorities of the Maison Dieu at Blois who have only one sister ask for one of the Paris ladies to come and thus raise the status of the place; cf. A. Chevalier, 120.

[2] Filiae albae hoc est non velatae, Coyecque, i. 31; see page 368, note 6; cf. fille servant de l'abbit blanc (1416), Brièle, iii. 28.   For les novisses, see L. Legrand, Statuts, 80, 141.   [3] Coyecque, ii. 51.

[4] Ibid. i. 25; ii. 55; Luce, i. 87; A. Chevalier, p. vi.   [5] Brièle, iii. 46.

[6] Provisores, rectores, magistri, visitatores, Coyecque, i. 26; A. Chevalier, pp. vii, 52.

[7] L. Legrand, Statuts, 10, 49, 55, 68, 123, 134.

[8] Rire baudement (see Cotgr., s.v.; Godefroy, s.v. *Baldement*); L. Legrand, Maisons Dieu, 122.

[9] e.g. on Feb. 9, 1403, Agnes of London, who was a sister at the Hôtel-Dieu, asks permission to enter *aliam religionem*, Coyecque, ii. 39; Luce, i. 85, 86, calls them les religieuses, les sœurs de charité.   On Feb. 23, 1410, the patients of the Mont-aux-Malades at Rouen complain to the town authorities against les religieux du dit lieux leurs administrateurs who put off giving them leurs vivres, C. Beaurepaire, Invent. Rouen, 34.

[10] For the couvent des frères in the Hôtel-Dieu, see Brièle, iii. 45.   For 1 frère religieux in 1416, see ibid. iii. 46; deditae post vitam activam vitae contemplationis, Gerson, iv. 683.

[11] Chemise à soutane (suttania talaris), see Ducange, s.v. *Subtaneum*.

[12] Pannos ysambrunos, galambrunos, L. Legrand, Statuts, 9; cappas de ysambruno, ibid. 45; galebrunno.   Called étoffe de couleur fouche, Godefroy, s.v. *Galebrun*; cf. Walebroun de Maence (not a whalebone as Lib. Cust. 61, 774); i.e. the Augustinian dress, Vitry, 319; Clay, 174, 205; Moore, 21.

[13] Bottas rotundas.

blanket slippers[1]. The brothers are described by a modern inquirer as not members of any religious order, but as forming a community half-secular, half-religious[2], as typified by their bearded chins[3] and shaven crowns[4]. They also wore a uniform habit[5] comprising shirt and breeches[6], the stuff for which was not to cost more than 1s. an ell, a lambskin pellice, a black or russet jacket[7], fastened well up, the cost of the stuff to be limited to 5s. an ell at the most, a closed overcoat (supertunicle), white shoes with latchets[8] and a black cloak with the hood furred with white budge[9] and no purfling[10]. In church they wore a burnet[11] cope open and reaching to the ankles, with surplice[12], woollen pellice and boots.

It would probably be going too far to regard a mediaeval

---

[1] Coyecque, i. 35. In the Praemonstratensian Abbey of Ardennes near Caen in 1462 each priest costs 7½ liv. tourn. per annum, super administracione vestiarii, et calciamentorum, almuciorum, pelliciorum, candellarum pro studio, pinguedinum unguendo calciamenta, Bénet, Ardennes, 9.

[2] Une communauté particulière, Coyecque, ii. 54; L. Legrand, Statuts, xxiv, where they are often married men. Chevalier (p. vi) thinks that the brethren at the Maison Dieu in Paris were Augustinians, all of them being lay brothers except the master who was a priest (p. 52). For the disciplinati confraternitatis de Mariâ, laymen of all ranks who served the hospital of La Scala at Siena, see Thureau-Dangin, 13; Stanislaus, 5; Allies, 81, who supposes that they were "a sort of 3rd order." For "frères donnés," who served the hospital of St Barthélemy at Clermont-Ferrand, see Tardieu, i. 439, 445. Clay, 152, thinks that the brothers might be priests, monks or lay brethren holding honorary posts but supplied with food and clothing.

[3] Barbatos fratres, L. Legrand, Statuts, 4.

[4] Li rasure des frères sont grande et large ensi com il affiert a religieus, ibid. 77.

[5] Habitum domus dei, Coyecque, i. 31, 52.

[6] For a man's dress (1411), i.e. cotte, chaperon, chausses, solers, bray et chemise, see Tuetey, 536. For chertes, briches (*chemise, brayes*) with the pauntcher (*braieul*, i.e. ceinture au dessus des braies, Godefroy, s.v.), see Caxton, Dial. 8; for breches, see ibid. 42, where they are made of linen. For 10 chemyses et 12 br...kkes, see Add. MS. 4601/99 (122). For bragas et camisa (*brais et chemise*), see Bonis, I. pp. xlv, lxx, where the former are made of *toile*; cf. toile de fin lin for doublets, coiffes, chausses et braies, ibid. I. lvi; interulis et femoralibus, Duck, 48[72]. For linen shirts, linen drawers, hose of strong cloth and leather shoes for men, see Duclaux, 249. Dunster Accounts (Lyte, 117) show 20d. pro sotularibus (souliers), caligis, camisiis et braccis for a henxman in 1405; also 2s. 6d. for two doublets una cum braccis et calcaribus, ibid. 117. For picture showing unterhosen, see Schultz, 370.

[7] Nigri seu subrufi coloris, L. Legrand, Statuts, 45.

[8] Sotulares (i.e. souliers, see Ducange, s.v. *Subtalares*) cum corrigiis.

[9] For 7 doz. de peaulx d'aigneaux blanches pour fourrer les aumusses des frères, see Brièle, iii. 46. For houppelande de drap marbre fourrée d'aigneaux noirs, see Tuetey, Test. 483. For "blac bogge," see Legg, Coronation Rec. 200; "boge," Malden, xl; Wylie, ii. 183.

[10] Cf. perfold of martyrs (i.e. marten), Amyot, 252. For pourfileure, see Pannier, 219; cf. Wylie, iv. 359.

[11] Ysambrun, cf. Godefroy, s.v. *Isembrun*; or brunette, Romania, x. 229; Toulgoët-Treanna, 102. For drap de brunette for chaperons, mantel et côte-hardie for ladies in mourning, see Douet d'Arcq, Enterrement, i. 34.

[12] Induti superlicio et cappâ, Coyecque, ii. 42.

hospital, as is done by recent writers[1], as "an ecclesiastical, not a medical, institution for care rather than cure," where "faith and love were more prominent than skill and science[2]." This ideal description may be theoretically true of the beadhouses[3], where we know that a knowledge of the Psalter[4], the Lord's Prayer, the Ave Maria, and the Creed[5] was required before admission, as at Heytesbury[6] and Ewelme[7]. In the hospitals for the sick every applicant was required to make his confession when admitted[8], after which his clothing was taken off and removed for cleansing in the *pouillerie*[9]. In Paris the patients were housed in four "halls[10]," known as St Thomas, St Denis, the Infirmary and the *Salle Neuve*, a portion of the last being screened off to hide the bodies of the dead[11] before they were removed for burial. The sick were frequently washed[12]; their beds were curtained with keepers[13] and the

[1] G. Newman, 66.

[2] Clay, xvii.

[3] For picture of the beadhouse at Stamford, see Clay, 29.

[4] Our ladie Sawter, Clay, 160; called "a psawter conteyning thryes 1 Aves with xv. Paternosters and iij. Credes," Hist. MSS. Rept. ix. 219; cf. when he seith our lady sawter on hem (i.e. the beads), see Fifty Wills, 49 (1425); Church, 57. For the sauter see Purvey in Forshall and Madden, i. 34, 59; Lydg. Troy Book, 312; do. Min. Po. 72, 78, 90 (= Sawtyer); for a "salter glosed" valued at £8 in 1414, see Cotton MS. Cleop. É. II. f. 307. For Richard of Hampole's English translation see Garnett, Lit. i. 92. For saultier glosé and "Postilla super salterium" at Troyes in 1419 see Arbois de Jubainville (1873), p 397. Cf. "as to lernyd men by saying of sawters, vii salmes and the xv psalmes &c. by lewd men with the Pater Noster the Ave Maria and the Crede," H. D. Ward, 486; Krapp, 73; the youth are taught the Paternoster, Ave Maria, Creed and Ten Commandments all in Latin, Hoskins, xix, from the Primer of 1545; the Comaundements and the Crede, Kail, 76, 88; I knew it well as I did my Crede, London Lickpenny (Bell), 13; Hoccleve in Garnett, i. 190. For English version of the Creed temp. Ed. III, see Halliwell, ii. 958.

[5] For the Lord's Prayer, Angel's Salutation, Creed, Mattins and Hours of B.V.M. see Leach, 164 (1357); Wylie, ii. 490; cf. your Paternostre, your Ave and your Crede, Lydg. Min. Po. 105.

[6] Founded circ. 1472, Monast. vii. 724; Hoare, Heytesbury, 225.

[7] Thoo the which shall not conne say the De Profundis shall say iij Paternosters iij Aves and a Crede, Hist. MSS. Rept. ix. 219. For pictures of Ewelme Church see Napier, 54. Not that it was "old Chaucer's (i.e. the poet's) late inheritance," as G. Daniel, iv. 173.

[8] N. Moore, 22. Communié religieusement, L. Legrand, Statuts, pp. x. 11, 24, 40, 46, 113, 137 (se mestier est), 159.

[9] A. Chevalier, 76.

[10] Quatres salles des malades, Brièle, iii. 32. For "ffermary Hall," see Walcott, St Osythe, 7.

[11] For 16d. paid for 2 grans gons (hinges) à mettre une verge de fer qui est au bout de la salle neuve et soustient la custode (i.e. curtain) devant les trespassez, see Brièle, iii. 43. For 8s. paid pour un tableau de bois pour mettre et asseoir une ystoire sur le chaslit (bier) aux corps trespassez au bout de la sale, ibid. 51.

[12] L. Legrand, Maisons Dieu, 104.

[13] Custodes de toile noir, St Germain, 454. For custodes palées de blanc et de vermeil en la chambre de retraict, see A. Lacroix, 16. For 3 custodes for oratory of

sheets were changed every week or even every day[1], thereby necessitating a very great amount of laundering, while the extraordinarily large number of brooms used up is another indication of the thoroughness bestowed on the house work. The dormitories for the brethren and sisters and the halls for the patients were lit with oil lamps[2], but the sanitary arrangements were certainly very dark and primitive[3], for domestic sanitation is altogether a modern plant[4]. The bedridden however were provided with *bassins de nécessité*[5], and iron stoves or "chimneys[6]" were wheeled up to their bedsides to keep them warm in winter; but, in strange contrast to these comforts, it is remarkable that no precautions were taken to isolate infectious cases, except that supposed incurables were kept apart from the day of their admission. All the rest, whether they were suffering from a botch[7] or a carbuncle in the

Valentine Duchess of Touraine (Orleans) brought from Lombardy in 1389, see Roman, Inventaires, 13.

> Et si estoient encourtiné
> Les lictz du draps de bien celer.

L'Hospital d'Amours, quoted in L. Legrand, Maisons Dieu, 137.

[1] e.g. at Troyes, ibid. 137; do. Statuts, 116. In 1535 the Commissioners at the Savoy Hospital were to inquire "whether any poore man do lie in any sheetes unwasshed that any other lay in byfore," and "whether the suster were slack or lothsome to wasshe their geare," Loftie, 103.

[2] Lampes et fiolles de voires, Brièle, iii. 44. At St Pol two or three lamps were always to be burning at night, L. Legrand, 122.

[3] At Troyes there was a rule that in privatis pauperum lumen sit semper de nocte, L. Legrand, Statuts, 116. For retrait et fosse d'aisance, see H. Legrand, 18; chambres aisées et retraictz, Coyecque, 192; A. Chevalier, 92; aisemens, ibid. 82; chambres nécessaires, L. Legrand, Maisons Dieu, 141; chambres aesées Toulgoët-Treanna, 151. For aisements in the leperhouse at Brie-Comte-Robert, see L. Legrand, xxiv. 189, 191; xxv. 169; also in hospitals, Coyecque, i. 85; L. Legrand, Maisons Dieu, 131. For pelices et botes supplied for the sick à aler à lor besoigne, see L. Legrand, Statuts, pp. xvii, 13, i.e. one sheepskin pellice between two patients, quand ils aloient à chambres, ibid. 14; surgere ad privatas, ibid. 47.

[4] For the "bouteille" on board ship, see Roncières, i. 294; and the "skutvat," Wylie, iv. 267. Cf.

> And when that we shall go to bed,
> The pump was nygh our bedde hedde;
> A man were as good as to be dede
> As smell thereof the stynk.

Halliwell, Naval Ballads, 4; Clowes, i. 243, from Reliq. Antiq. 2.

[5] L. Legrand, Maisons Dieu, 137.

[6] See page 360, note 10; Oppenheim, Accts. 102. For Keminée de fer at Hesdin in 1333, see L. Legrand, Maisons Dieu, 139. For chariots de fer at the Hôtel-Dieu in Paris, see Coyecque, i. 51, 71; also at the Hostel Barbette, Sellier, 36. For a specimen with four wheels from the Archbishop's Palace at Narbonne, see Bordier-Charton, i. 421. For a "chymeney" to warm a dog's kennel, see York, 70.

[7] For mortalité de boce, see Bourgeois, 634; bocche, Arderne MS. Emmanuel Coll. Camb. f. xxi; a bots light upon ye, Fam. Vict. 8, 17; booches, York, 35, 55; bocches, Laud Troy Book, 380, 400, 410; boces, apostemes, papules, charbons, Boudet-Grand, 4, 5; cf. Wylie, iii. 430.

leg[1] or were eaten with pocks and pestilence[2], were massed together in one common hall[3] with the frenzied[4], the infect, and the injured, lying naked[5] two, three, or even four together in one bed[6], amidst the cries of newborn babies[7], whose mothers had died in gesine, leaving them to be wet-nursed sometimes at the rate of half-a-dozen to each foster-mother.

No charge was made for services rendered to the patients, except in so far as the expenses might be covered by legacies bargained for on admission, if the inmate should die and have anything to leave[8]. Two meals a day were served to them, with a special feast at Easter[9], on which day they were regaled with a loaf, a pottage, a measure of wine, a cracknel[10], two eggs and a portion of roast veal,

[1] Bosses et entraetz (i.e. bandage, Godefroy, s.v. *Entrait*; or salve, Cotgr. s.v. *Entract*) escharboucle, charbon en la jambe, Coyecque, i. 101.   [2] Hazlitt, iv. 31.
[3] As at Angers, Chartres, Ourscamp, Tonnerre, Canterbury and Chichester, Viollet-le-Duc, Architecture, vi. 104, 105, 107. See also Morris-Jordan, 259, 282.
[4] Cf. pour lier une religieuse qui estoit de frenaysie, Coyecque, i. 109. For a 13th century picture in a window in the Trinity Chapel at Canterbury showing a maniac tied and flogged, see Clay, 31.
[5] Coyecque, i. 76; Halliwell, ii. 569, s.v. *Naked-bed*. Though the brethren were required to sleep in their shirt and drawers, Coyecque, i. 92; L. Legrand, Maisons Dieu, 125; do. Statuts, 51, 75; according to the Augustinian rule (Vitry, 319), cf. nulle sereur ne se gise nue sanz chemise, ibid. 164. For pictures of naked men in bed, see Deguileville, Ame, Frontispiece; MS. Reg. 20 C. vii. ff. 8, 21, 37, 53, 68, 78, 201, 214, 215; Humphries, Froiss. II. Pl. XXVIII (death of Clement VII at Avignon); ibid. II. Pl. XXXI; Antiquary, x. 188; MS. Reg. I E. ix. 101, 120, 126; H. Martin, Boccace, Pl. lxxxviii, cxi, cxviii; Couderc, Album 13, Plate XXXIII.
[6] Though not as a rule, says L. Legrand, Maisons Dieu, 133, who gives instances of four in a bed at Noyon in 1384 and three in a bed from a window in the Hospice St Jacques at Vendôme; cf. Coyecque, i. 74; called two, four, or even eight in a bed in Besant, Survey, ii. 251, who gives no references, but supposes that " the physician was always in readiness" (p. 252). For three travellers in one bed in an inn (from a window at Triel near Poissy), see A. Chevalier, 78, circ. 1554. One of the questions asked in regard to the Savoy Hospital under the commission of 1535 was " whether any poore men laye moo than one in a bedde," Loftie, Savoy, 103. In Wardrobe Accts. 406/26 there are four beds for nine parsons of the King's Chapel in 1415. For father, mother and whole family including guest all in one bed, see Duclaux, 243.
[7] At Troyes no mulieres parturientes were admitted propter clamores et gemitus quos emittunt dolore partus, L. Legrand, Statuts, 115; but this was not usual, cradles (*petiz bers*) being provided for the infants si qu'il gisent à une part soul, ibid. 13. At St Pol they took in pauperes mulieres praegnantes ad gezinandum proximas, and allowed them to stay three weeks after the birth for recovery, ibid. 122, 162; cf. hae hic sunt in magno numero, i.e. in the Hôtel-Dieu, Gerson, iv. 682.
[8] Coyecque, i. 121.
[9] A. Chevalier, 76. For five pints of verjuice used at the dinner given by the goldsmiths of Paris to the malades at the Hôtel-Dieu in 1416, see Brièle, Doc. iii. 28. For verjus (1315), see Chéruel, Commune, i. 320; verjus de pommes, Gouvenain, i. 26; vertjus, Ménagier, ii. 162, 167; Lyte, Dunster, 115, where 2s. is paid for barrels to hold it. For three caques de verjus at 17s. 6d. per caque, see Tremoille, 7, 48, 97, called verdius, verdjus, virgeus, Mann. and Meals, i. 152, 158, 174; see also Wylie, iii. 214.
[10] Cf. Littré, s.v. *Craquelin*; 1 Kings xiv. 3, translating " crustulum." For panis crakenell, see Maldon Rolls, 9, 14.

and for their supper four pieces of pastry[1] and six florins[2].

But the largest section of the endowed hospitals had been concerned with the care of lepers who were secluded in separate houses or measlecotes[3], which had come into existence with startling rapidity to meet the enormous spread of leprosy or St Lazarus' Evil[4] in the 12th and 13th centuries, at which time it is estimated that there were 19,000 leperhouses in Europe, of which 2000 were in France[5], and a recent investigator has listed nearly 200 in England[6]. Their decline was equally abrupt, as the disease rapidly abated during the period with which this history is more immediately concerned[7]. But when the scourge was at its height and lepers were objects of public abhorrence, it was no uncommon thing to burn them[8]. Even boys and girls over 14 years of age and pregnant women were so dealt with in times of panic, though in the latter case it was thought to be merciful to let the child be born before burning the mother. But these periodical outbursts of savagery were only intermittent, and as the existing charitable foundations were altogether insufficient, in France, at any rate[9], it was quite usual for the inhabitants of a village or parish to erect some shelter for lepers, if it were only a

---

[1] Mestier, see Godefroy, s.v.

[2] A. Chevalier, 110. It may be some kind of fish, see Godefroy, s.v. *Florin*, or possibly flawns, see page 5, note 7.

[3] Wylie, ii. 251; ung ladre ou ung meseau, Schwab, 86.

[4] Mal St Ladre, L. Legrand, xxv. 126; Rochas, 20; Vignat, 39; Le Verdier, Documents, 340, leprosi qui vulgo lazari nominantur, L. Legrand, xxv. 107. For St Lazarus as the guardian of lepers, see Clay, 249.

[5] Tollet, 39; A. Lambert, 474; Tardieu, i. 447; Labourt, 2; Revue de l'Art Chrétien, année 7, p. 292; Rochas, 20; Vignat, 9, 10, quoting Matthew Paris (1244). See App. T[1].

[6] Clay, 35, 37. For legacies to 39 leperhouses in the diocese of Exeter in 1307, see Ellacombe, ix. For 130 in Great Britain at the end of the 13th century, see A. Lambert, 474, and for a list of 183 in England and Wales, 18 in Scotland and 20 in Ireland, see G. Newman, 108.

[7] For the disappearance of leprosy in the 14th and 15th centuries, see L. Legrand, xxv. 49; Garnier, 50, who says that almost all the rural maladreries in France were abandoned by the end of the 14th century. For the "Mallardri" (i.e. the Holy Innocents), at Lincoln, see Rot. Parl. v. 472; Cal. Pat. H. V, i. 323; Clay, 100, 180; now called "Malandry Close," G. Newman, 8.

[8] Wylie, ii. 251, note 3. For combustio leprosorum during the commotion of 1321, see Revue Lyonnaise, iii. 296 (1882); G. Garnier, 28; Mandet, 284, where they were charged with poisoning the wells in Le Velay; Chrétien, 7; L. Legrand, xxv. 141; Lambert, 486; Clay, 56; called "cet infernal complot" in Ledain, 160, 162, who believes it all.

[9] L. Legrand, xxiv. 225; xxv. 108.

board[1] or shed[2] for their own self-protection[3]. In such cases the control was vested in the skevins or jurats[4] or marglers[5], and everyone who was suspected of the taint[6] was reported to the bishop of his diocese, who forced him to go to some leperhouse and submit to a purge[7] or examination[8] conducted by the lepers themselves, during which he was stripped and subjected to an intricate variety of tests of sight, touch and feel[9], and there is a story of a wealthy suspect in Paris, who

[1] See Cotgr., s.v. *Borde*; cf. le curé doibt mener à sa borde, Grosley, i. 154. For calculation that at least 300 villages in the diocese of Paris subscribed to erect and maintain them, see L. Legrand, xxv. 113, 115. For bordellum leprosorum, see L. Legrand, xxv. 91.

[2] Hutte solitaire, Rochas, 11; los magistratz seran tengutz los accomoda de cabane por le retira aux depens deus habitans, ibid. 21; Wylie, ii. 251.

[3] e.g. the leproserie commune at St Cloud, Delisle, Gonesse, 16; L. Legrand, xxiv. 196, 269, 282.

[4] Tollet, 41. For Agen, see Lauzun, ii. 398, where the consuls are patrons des biens des lepreux. For the leperhouse at Beaulieu near Caen and the domus dei at Caen under the control of the jurats tanquam fundatores, see Rym. x. 48, Jan. 17, 1421; Labourt, 22.

[5] Wylie, iv. 353. For marregliers de la ville at Bar-sur-Aube, see Prost, i. 561. For marregliers et gouverneurs des églises, see Ordonnances, x. 244. For six marguilliers (i.e. matricularius or sacristan) of St Eustache in Paris in 1395, see Calliat, 3, 17, 35. In Tuetey, 523, they have power to refuse burial. For marriliers at Bar-le-Duc, see Renard, 194, 217. For payments to maregliers lays pour la sonnerie, see Douet d'Arcq, Enterrement, 131, 137. For clers marregliers at Notre Dame in Paris in 1380, ibid. 135, also at the Sainte Chapelle, Vidier, 347; marguillier prêtre in 1450, Arbois de Jubainville, ii. 28; marreliers, marilliers, Mem. Soc. Archéol. de Touraine, xi. 237, 239, 241. For marregliers of the church of St Séverin in Paris named in inscription on the bell (1402), see Guilhermy, i. 82. For 4 sols paid to marrigliers pour sonner et ordonner à chascun anniversaire, see Tuetey, Testaments, 306. They were usually trustees for charities, e.g. not to pay curé for obit unless he had announced it at the sermon (*prosne*), ibid. 570, cf. qu'ilz y facent offrir une quarte de vin, un pain de quatre Parisis et un tortis de cire, ibid. 531.

[6] For malades suspects de ladrerie at Thérouanne, see Bled, Reg. i. 403, Dec. 4, 1413.

[7] Tardieu, Montferrand, 69, where the consuls have jurisdiction called "la Purge," with power to search out lepers and shut them up in the Maladrerie d'Herbet. For seal of la Purge called le sea derbers, see ibid. 70. For "leprosi de Erbers," "l'infirmerie Derbers," at Montferrand, see ibid. 69.

[8] For picture of a doctor examining a leper, see Clay, 59. For a medical examination of a suspected leper in 1468, see Rym. xi. 635; Shapter, 62; A. Lambert, 483; G. Newman, 46, 146, where more than 40 tests are applied, including 25 juxta quod antiquiores et sapientissimi medicinae auctores in hujusmodi casibus docuerunt, the four varieties of leprosy being named as in Wylie, ii. 251, note 10. For decision as to which kind, left to a priest, see Clay, 60. For Alopesie qui est ladrerie au cueur et à la teste, see La Marche, i. 180, 346. For elephantiasis, where the lobes of the ear rot away, see Shapter, 52 (with picture); G. Newman, 59; Vignat, 12. For elephantiasis graecorum as the true leprosy, see Clay, 49, 62; elefantina, St Denys, iv. 770; cf. Camden, Brit. (Gough), ii. 195. For an order of the mayor of Dijon to examine a case together with two barbers selected from the jurats, see J. Garnier, 31.

[9] Super visitatione tactu et palpatione, C. Beaurepaire, Notes, ii. 21; cf. nudum, discalciatum, palpatum tractaretur, palparetur et examinaretur, L. Legrand, xxiv. 318; xxv. 131. For picture of a leper showing spots on his body, see Durrieu, Turin, Plates, xxviii. For symptoms of leprosy, see Garnier, 24, from Bernard Gordon and Guy de Chauliac. The former was Rector of Montpellier University in 1305; for his *Lilium Medicinae* (Lyons, 1754), see Rochas, 24; Paré, I. liv. For the latter, see App. S[1]. For treatment of leprosy, see Chauliac, 402; Wylie, ii. 250.

was advised by a Lombard to charm the taint away by boiling snakes in a kettle and giving the broth to his hens; but the snakes escaped[1] into the street and so alarmed the neighbourhood that the bishop had to make the man go to a leperhouse, whether he would or no.

It is too often assumed that the disease had quite disappeared in England before the 15th century began, but this is far from being the case, and the really important change that had taken place was that the one-man control of the leperhouses had broken down and the administration, which had originally been vested in the hands of some bishop or abbot or feudal lord[2], had been largely transferred to the mayors and jurats or other secular authorities[3]. In France this change is marked by a royal ordinance issued in 1321[4], directing that such houses should henceforward be maintained by the localities. At Dijon[5] the authority of the mayor over the leperhouse became superior to that of the Abbot of St Stephen's, who had formerly been supreme, and in England an instructive change had taken place a century earlier at Exeter, where the bishop, being unable to maintain an effective control over the Maudlin[6] or lazar-house without the south gate, had transferred it in 1244[7] to the city authorities, who at once drew up a set of disciplinary rules[8] preventing the inmates from entering the city and punishing offences committed within the house with bread and water and the stocks. At Sandwich[9] the Hospital of St Bartholomew was under the control of the town authorities. At Maldon in Essex orders

---

[1] Par un ayvier, L. Legrand, xxv. 125; the word is not in Ducange or Cotgrave.

[2] Postel, Aieux, 99; Clay, 211, regards a hospital as "a semi-independent institution, subject to royal or episcopal control."

[3] For municipal control, see Clay, 16, where it is called "an ancient custom." At Chauny near Noyon, on Apr. 28, 1363, an agreement was made between the Abbot of St Eloi-Fontaine and the mayor as to the nomination of frères et soeurs at the godshouse. On Sept. 29, 1404, the mayor admits two widows as sisters, and on Oct. 11, 1419, the mayor and jurats of the town are souverains gouverneurs des biens d'icellui hostel, Matton, 5, 27. On May 4, 1404, the administration of the leperhouse in the same town is confirmed to the mayor and jurats, ibid. 12. For order June 3, 1404, to the Provost of Paris to report on the leperhouses in the city, see Labourt, p. 5.

[4] Ordonnances, xi. 483.   [5] J. Garnier, 28, 30.

[6] For "Maudlin House" as synonymous with leper-hospital, see Clay, 252.

[7] Izack, 10; Shapter, 22–29; A. Lambert, 479; G. Newman, 19; Clay, 54, 151.

[8] Oliver, Monast. 402, where the date should be 30 H. III (i.e. 1245) not 30 H. IV; nor 1425, as Shapter, 29; nor 1428, as Cotton and Dallas, iii. 142; see also Clay, 139. For lepers specially tempted to loose living, see ibid. 148.

[9] i.e. circ. 1350, Boys, i. 2, who refers to a decree of the Council of Vienne (1311) that hospitals should be administered by laymen, quoting Mansi, xxv.

for the segregation of lepers were given by the wardmen[1]
and at Peterborough by the Court Leet[2].

I have already given a rough sketch[3] of the rules laid
down for the inmates of these "piteous places[4]," but
am able here to add a few extra touches from works
recently written on the subject by French investigators
drawn either from an examination of mediaeval records or
from personal study among the still existing leper-stricken
districts on both sides of the Pyrenees[5].   The sad lives
of these poor victims of the death-in-life treatment of the
Middle Ages can only be pictured in imagination, but long
habit had adjusted the burden to the back, and with the
frequent sight of the incurable leper in the streets and
public squares the horror at his loathsomeness was somewhat tempered by familiarity.   It has been doubted whether
he actually wore a distinctive dress[6], but we have clear
contemporary evidence that he did[7], and he certainly was
required to have a yellow badge on the left side of his
gown[8]; and though doubt has been thrown[9] upon the belief
that he was treated as symbolically dead, the fact seems
really past denial, for the ritual service remains as evidence
of the actual existence of the practice[10].   Equally well

---

[1] At a general court held at Maldon on May 4, 1414, the wardmen volunt quod
quaedam mulier lazara in Rabalstrete amoveatur propter contagiositates futuras, Maldon
Rolls, 9/14.
[2] Bateson, 528, giving an order in 1461 that a leper shall be removed by his friends
ad alium locum solitarium quocunque.
[3] Wylie, ii. 250.
[4] Lieux piteables, L. Legrand, xxiv. 64, 250; xxv. 49, 107; Belfort-Mirot, xxiv.
[5] Rochas, *passim*.
[6] L. Legrand, xxv. 143.
[7] Cf. indutus tunicâ seu chlamyde lazareâ (1414), Carlier, iii. p. cv.
[8] For badge enjoined at the Council held at Nogaro in Armagnac in 1290, see
A. Lambert, 470. For signet de drap rouge on the left side of the gown at Marmande
in 1396, see Rochas, 36; Geslin de Bourgoyne, III. cix (1475); Godefroy, s. v. *Caqueuse*.
For the brethren of Grand Beaulieu in the diocese of Chartres who wore an " L " in red
cloth six inches long on their gowns, see Robert, 153; cf. oripaux rouges, Rochas, 111.
For orpine, see Halliwell, ii. 591; i.e. orpiment, king's yellow or "base gold" (Cotgr.,
s.v.); called cuivre doré in Godefroy, s.v. *Oripal*; cf. sine habitu leprosali, at St Flour,
1490, see Du Cange, s.v. *Leprosi*. For a yellow duck-foot worn by lepers, see Robert,
170; Bascle de Lagrèze, i. 54.   For order (March 7, 1407) that lepers in Paris should
wear a distinctive mark, see Tarbé, xi.   For the "clapped pouch," so called from its
resemblance to the badge of leprosy, see A. Lambert, 483.
[9] L. Legrand, xxv. 134.
[10] Chéruel, Dict. 651, s. v. *Leproserie*; Rochas, 12; Courtalon-Delaistre, iii. 39, 41;
A. Lambert, 483; G. Newman, 35; Clay, 273; Grosley, i. 154, where the mass ne
doibt point estre des morts si comme curés sont accoustumez de faire, quoting ritual
of Odard Hennequin, Bishop of Troyes, 1541; Trou, 75. For order issued in 1414 by
Renaud de Chartres, Archbishop of Rheims (1414–1444), forbidding the use of the mass

established is the shocking and insanitary custom of feeding lepers on the mouldy bread, sour perry and cider[1], rancid pork, slimy veal, flat beer and stale fish[2] that had been seized in the markets by the town authorities as unfit for human food[3], in spite of protests raised by the best educated medical opinion[4]. But besides this tainted source their food and living was also procured by a system of organised begging[5]. This was originally done by outside collectors, who were authorised to enter the parish churches on Sundays and gather alms on

for the dead for lepers at Rheims, see Carlier, iii. p. cv; Tarbé, xviii, where they were to have no cerements nec debeat habere *cereos* circa se quod non est mortuus corpore or winding-sheets (*nec induitur pannis mortuorum*, ibid. 2, 4), to keep their special places in church, not to touch children, to stand the proper way of the wind, &c., ibid. 8–12; Wylie, ii. 251. Cf. "under the wind," York, 83, 92; "in the wind," ibid. 86; audessoubz du vent, Grosley, i. 155; au milieu de la charrière, au-dessus du vent et des gens sains, J. Garnier, 33 (i.e. while begging); cf. et si sera le dit varlet tenu crier par les carfours comme pour ung trespassé (at Fécamp in 1468), C. Beaurepaire, Notes, ii. 23; Vignat, 16; J. Garnier, 30; Bouchot, 239; G. Newman, 35; Wylie, ii. 251.

[1] Moulid bred, pirete and sider sour, A. Lambert, 481.

[2] Cf. ffysch medlyd with mylk causeth boody and fas with lepre to be smet, Lydg. Burgh, 53.

[3] e.g. at Sandwich the hospital of St John received omnes forisfacturas piscium et carnium contra ordinationes villae venditorum, Boys, 128; carnes immunde vel incommode usui humano, ibid. 499; pisces viles, ibid. 502; forisfacturas panis, cervisiæ, carnis et piscium non sanorum, Monast. vii. 937. In London, temp. Ed. I, meat killed by Jews and illegally bought by Christians was to be seized and given to dogs and lepers, Letter Book A, p. vii. For stynkyng fysche, roten shep, sussemy flesche and swyn of brym (i.e. in heat, going to boar, Murray, Dict., s.v. *Brim*; Halliwell, s.v. *Breme*; Wright, Dict., s.v. *Brimming*), see Coventry Leet, i. 25. At the leper hospital at Sherburn near Durham diseased flesh was forbidden, Clay, 168. For the body of a roe snared by a poacher in Rockingham Forest, first sent to the leperhouse at Thrapston in accordance with the Forest Laws, see G. J. Turner, 84; J. C. Cox, 243; Clay, 168, who adds the leperhouse at Cotes, nr. Rockingham (Monast. vii. 770). For a similar case, see Cox, 101, where the dead body of a buck found in Claughton Forest is given to the lepers at Lancaster as required by the Forest Charter. Cf. del dever dels meselers com es acostumat at Agen in 1348, Magen, 154. For viandes corrompues at Condom in Gascony, see Rochas, 64; ox tongues and sheeps' tongues at Sens, Vignat, 18; also at Dijon (1403), Gouvenain, i. 26; ii. E. 4; also pigs' "fillots," i.e. the liver and the spleen wrapped in the caul (ratelle, called the spleen or milt, Cotgr., s.v. *Rate*) or la toilette, J. Garnier, 28 (called a toylet or peau fine in Godefroy, s. v.). For "poissons forfets," strayed pigs, badly made candles, boots, cloth and other confiscated articles, see Coyecque, i. 129; A. Chevalier, 107, who thinks (p. 86) that this food was good of its kind, though insufficient in quantity. For flesh corrupte with eny maner of sekenes, see Bateson, xxxvi. 289; Wylie, ii. 251. For jurez (i.e. of the butchers' gild) qui aient esgart et visitation sur les chars qui seront exposés en vente, see Ordonnances, x. 384. For fines for selling "un porc puant," des triphes puans, poissons pourris and an eel de mauvaise mort, molvaises grevisses (i.e. écrevisses), un veau tout gléreux (= slimy, Cotgr., s. v. *Glaireux*) at Dijon in 1410, see Vallée, 21, 204, 205.

[4] For putrid food to be avoided by lepers, see John Mirfield in N. Moore, 39, who gives an account of his Breviarium Bartholomai (written circ. 1387, pp. 31–36; Dict. Nat. Biogr. xxxviii. 50; or 1380, N. Moore, Progress, 8–21) and Floriarium Bartholomaei (written circ. 1362, pp. 44–47; Wylie, i. 483).

[5] Querant d'aumosne comme ladres, Martial de Paris, i. 31.

their behalf[1], but as the public became less frightened, permission was often officially obtained for one or more of the inmates to sit by a bridge[2] or some other thoroughfare of traffic on market-days or great festivals[3] holding a clap-dish[4] for alms or a basket at the end of a pole for food[5], and ringing a bell[6] to draw the compassion of the charitable among the passers by.

Food obtained from such untempting sources can only have been for the support of the poor non-paying patients, but there were many inmates whose means allowed them to pay a fee[7] and to provide their own furniture and bedding[8]. An example of this occurs in the case of a patient admitted to the leperhouse of St Lazare in Paris on Dec. 3, 1418[9], who had to pay 72s. 8d. for his food (*pro pastu*) besides bringing a cloth (*mappa*) 10 ells in length as a gift for the Prior, and for his own personal use napery, towels, six dishes, six saucers, one saler or salt cellar, a quart pot, a pint pot and a tin chopin[10], a box, a table with a pair of trestles,

---

[1] Un homme attourné pour eux d'aler chescun dymenge es les Esglises parochians à coiller almoignes pur lour sustenaunces, Lib. Alb. 273. For officer appointed to beg for the lepers at Berwick, see Rochas, 21. For Sandwich, see Clay, 185. At Exeter this collecting was originally done by aliquis de civitate, Oliver, Monast. 402, but it is evident that the lepers themselves used to come into the city for the purpose at least as late as 1408, Izacke, 10, 68, an ancient right confirmed to them by the Bishop of Exeter in 1163, Clay, 54, 184.

[2] e.g. the Grand Pont in Paris, also the Petit Pont, where the amount collected for the Hôtel-Dieu in 1416 on Good Friday, Easter and Christmas amounted to 116s., Brièle, iii. 26.

[3] e.g. at Dijon, Garnier, 45.

[4] A. Lambert, 481, 486; Wylie, ii. 251. For picture of a leper with clapper and dish, see Clay, 48, 177. For un pot à aumosne d'argent doré, see Mirot, Trousseau, 149.

[5] Vignat, 43; Chrétien, 7. For bag, dish and staff of beggars, see Hazlitt, iv. 25, 28, 36, 40, 54.

[6] For picture of a leper with a bell, see Clay, 68. Unam campanam quae portatur per villas pro querendo panem infirmorum at the leperhouse of St Yon at Dourdan, Legrand, xxiv. 153. By the Cabochian ordinance of 1413 lepers were to be forbidden to come within the four gates of Paris pour quester ou autrement on pain of a month's imprisonment with bread and water, Ordonnances, x. 139; Chrétien, 21. For orders (Sept. 16, 1399, Jan. 5, 1412) for lepers to withdraw from Grenoble within 6 (or 3) days, see Prudhomme, 209, 211.

[7] For payments and gratuities required from inmates at Dover, see Clay, 139. For Richard Orenge who was mayor of Exeter in 1454 who is said to have died a leper, see Izacke, 83; Clay, 102, though this may be merely an inference from the fact that he was Warden of the Maudlin Hospital in 1461, 1463, 1465, and was buried in the chapel, Oliver, Mon. 401; Shapter, 34; G. Newman, 20. For his gifts to it, see Exeter Municipal Deeds, 80, 86, 89.

[8] e.g. Beauville, iii. 85, at Montdidier; L. Legrand, Statuts, 188. For furniture of leperhouses, see L. Legrand, xxv, *passim*.

[9] Ibid. xxiv. 316. For a corresponding list at Rouen in 1478 where the incoming leper pays 62s. 1d. to the prior and 5s. to the porter and varlets, see C. Beaurepaire, Notes, ii. 18.

[10] Copina stangni, see Murray, Dict., s.v. *Chopin*.

two ewers (*hydrias*), a maser[1], a copper candlestick, a brass dish[2], a tripod, a gridiron (*craticula*), a pestle (*pilum*) and mortar, a pair of bellows (*follis*)[3], a crock, two napkins (*mappas*) and a bed with two pairs of sheets, a kercher, a coverlet and the usual bed furniture[4]. But where, as in most cases, the leper was too poor to pay for these things himself, all necessary hustlements[5] were provided for him at the expense of the community[6].

From the leper's life, when once he had become interned, no record that I know of has yet lifted the veil, for the recently published statutes tell us little except the amounts of his regulation allowance of bread, salt, verjuice or peas[7]. If he happened to be a member of a gild, his fellows attended him at the mass for the dead[8] and escorted him with cross, bell and banner to the outskirts of the town[9], where he entered on his civil death[10]. Henceforward he must live apart from his wife, though in some institutions he might be visited by his mother or sister or "other honest matron[11]," and he might, as we have seen, roam into the town on certain days[12], provided that he clicked[13]

---

[1] See App. U[1].   [2] Platella (*sic*) (i.e. patella), L. Legrand, 123.
[3] Called a kind of vase, ibid.   [4] See App. R[1].
[5] Sharpe, Wills, ii. 413, 416, 422; Du Cange, s. v. *Hustillamentum*; Halliwell, i. 471, ii. 906; Wright, Dict., s.v.; Murray, s.v., where it is derived from hostel, but more probably from houstis (outils), see Richard, 292.
[6] e.g. at Luzarches, near Creil, where the leper was to have a bed (*culcitra*), a trunk (*arca*), pitancia et omnia necessaria, Boullé, 163.
[7] e.g. one flamiche pain (Cotgr., s.v.), one aimon de poys (Godefroy, s.v. *Émine*), L. Legrand, Statuts, 186, 187, 249.
[8] Le Verdier, Documents, 305, 340, where the mass is sung in the church of St Patrice at Rouen.
[9] For leperhouses usually beyond the gates of large towns, see L. Legrand, xxv. 48. For St Giles' Hospital, see page 263; Clay, 179, founded for infirmi de London in 1158. For the Lock Spital just outside St George's Bar in Southwark at the corner of the Kent Road, see Stow (Kingsford), ii. 146; Noorthouck, 685; Benham-Welch, 15 (where the name—"le loke," Clay, 54, 148—is derived from loques, i.e. rags); Wylie, iv. 29 n. For another leperhouse at Hackney, see Clay, 148. For St James' in Wincheap without the south-west wall at Canterbury, see page 358. For the bourg méséal outside the town at Dijon, see J. Garnier, 25. For the hôpital des ladres "hors la ville" at Agen, i.e. at the Porte du Puis, see Lauzun, ii. 398; cf. Wylie, ii. 251. For capella pauperum leprosorum *in campo* an dem Snelling (an Schnelling) in the parish of St Aurelius at Strasbourg, see Chrétien, 5; Schmidt, 420. For mettre aux champs, i.e. sequester (rusticate), see Vignat, 17.
[10] For leprosy as *mort civile*, see Viollet, Droit, 375, with bibliography, p. 377.
[11] e.g. at St Julian's Hospital near St Albans, Monast. vii. 619; A. Lambert, 478; G. Newman, 17, who points out that there was no efficient segregation.
[12] At Grenoble (May 19, 1435) no lepers were to enter the town except on Fridays, when two of *les moins malades* might circulate in the streets, sollicitant à haulte voix les aumônes; also on Sundays when they might go into the churchyard. Prudhomme, 214.
[13] For the vixen in heat (*à saute*) going a-cliqueting for the dog-fox, see York, 36; Halliwell, i. 255; Murray, Dict., s.v. *Clicket*.

his clapper[1] to give warning of his approach. But as a rule all access to the town was closed against him[2], and once "surrendered[3]" in his measlery[4] we lose sight of him completely, except for one solitary picture, in which he sits at table with his fellow-sufferers[5]; and there are some highly interesting representations of lepers still remaining carved on their tombstones in the chapel of a disused leperhouse at Dijon[6].

[1] Sonoran las tiquetas afin que tous passans se contregards d'elxs et de lour halena, Affre, Lettres, 314. Je vous baudrey (= baillerai) cloquette de frarie pour vous conduire jusqu'au mont de Rouen, Beaurepaire, Notes, ii. 19. For order of the Archbishop of Sens (1550) to use the rattle (crécelle), see Rochas, 13. For the tarterelle, see Grosley, i. 155; Du Cange, s. v.; Godefroy, s. v. *Tartarie*; L. Legrand, xxv. 127, 143. For cliquettes, crécelles et barillettes forbidden in Paris (1388), see Vignat, 40. For representation of the cliquette, see Tollet, 38; J. Garnier, 21, 50, from tombstones of lepers at Dijon, where it hangs at the girdle. For picture of lepers with wallet, cup and clapper from Moingt (Forez) near Montbrison, see Steyert, ii. 667; Grande Encycl. xi, s. v. *Cliquette*; Robert, 147, 152, 153, 156, 157, 158, 164; Plates II, VI.

[2] For orders that no lepers shall be at large in the City of London by night or day, see Lib. Alb. 250, 273, 590, 591; Riley, Mem. 230; Letter Book F, p. 138 (1346); Clay, 53. For barbers required to keep them out in 1373, see S. Young, 25. They were not allowed to shave or bleed them at Rouen in 1407, see E. H. Langlois, 150; also Boullé, 165 (1371); cf. extra villam fierent solitusque ad caeteros homines inhiberetur accessus (temp. Louis VI), L. Legrand, xxv. 107.

[3] "Qui fut randu" from inscriptions at Dijon, J. Garnier, 60; en rendre en sa borde, Courtalon-Delaistre, iii. 41.

[4] For le (*sic*) grande mesellerie, see Vignat, 10 (from Deguileville); meselrie, Wassebourg, 461, 465. For mesel, mesiac, misellus, see L. Legrand, xxv. 91, 108. For "sanglant meseaue" as a term of abuse in 1387, see J. Garnier, 47; cf. Wylie, ii. 249.

[5] Tollet, 36 (1493).

[6] J. Garnier, 21, 50. For the maladrière (*sic*) at Dijon, see Gouvenain, i. 26; ii. E. 4. For decree of the Lateran Council in 1179 ut leprosi, si excluduntur a cohabitatione hominum, oratorium habe aut et sacerdotem, see Matt. Paris, Hist. Angl. i. 411; Oliver, Mon. 401.

CHAPTER XXI

ARMAGNACS

It has been usual to associate the discussions in the Leicester Parliament with the famous story of the advice, which is supposed to have been given by Archbishop Chichele to the king, to busy his people's minds with foreign quarrels in order to divert their itching hands from plundering the property of the Church[1] by a revival of the scheme for secularisation that had been put forward in the Parliament of 1410[2]. But no mention of such a tradition appears in any contemporary account, and it was not till a generation later that a cautious entry in an English chronicle records that: "*It is said* that the spiritualty feared sore that, if he had not had to do without the land, he would have laboured for to have taken from the Church the temporal possessions[3]." But in the absence of any corroboration by contemporary writers it is safe to say that such a view completely misapprehends the real position. The Leicester Parliament was called together when the reaction against Lollardry was at its whitest heat; when the king and his brothers were belauded as the protectors of the Church[4], and so far

---

[1] Thei doubted sore that he wold have had ye Temporalties out of ther handes, Brut, ii. 495; Fab. 578; Goodwin, 41. Low-Pulling (552) thinks that the spoliation of the Church was warmly advocated by "the majority of lay-peers." See also H. Morley, vi. 140.
> He found a war with France must be the way
> To dash this bill else threatening their decay. Drayton, Bat. 15.

[2] Fab. 576. See p. 356.

[3] Caxton, 225; "as testyfye some wryters," Fab. 578; Church, 50; Kingsford, 109; Dict. Nat. Biogr. xxvi. 46.

[4]
> He maintenyth oure cherche graciouslye
> And kepyth it as ze may se.

Brampton, pp. vii, 34 (written in this very year). For Thomas Brampton, a Franciscan, see H. Morley, vi. 160. As hem that ben in degree of holy order in the service of God, Cotton MS. Julius B. i. 37; Harl. 565, 73, though the passage is omitted in Chron. Lond. Cf. pius cultor religionis, Pol. Verg. 441.

were the bishops and abbots from being almost broken in fear for their possessions[1], that the fear, as we have seen[2], was on the side of the laymen and was altogether the other way[3].

Such considerations as these however had no weight with the learned antipapal Yorkshireman Robert Redman, who wrote a life of Henry V in the first half of the 16th century[4], when the fame of the great hero of Agincourt was in danger of suffering eclipse[5]. Writing with a blazing disregard for accuracy as to his facts and a strong determination to work in his knowledge of the classics at any cost, he asserts that when all other defenders of the Church's goods had given up the game as hopeless, the position was saved by the skill of Archbishop Chichele, who recommended war with France in what our forefathers delighted to call "an elegant oration," just suited to show off his pretty Latin style. In reply to it there follow suitable speeches by the Earls of Dorset and Westmoreland, *pro* and *con*, the latter inveighing against the savage, inconsistent, wavering Scots[6] who would play the mouse in absence of the cat, and urging the king, as "superior lord and high Emperor over the under-kings of Scotland," to bring that runagate[7] region into its ancient course and former line; for Scotland must be tamed ere France can be framed, and he that will France win must with Scotland

---

[1] Desperatione pene fracti, Redman, 25. Expanded into "The fat abbots swet, the proud Priors frouned, the poor Friers curssed, the sely nonnes wept," in Halle, 49; Grafton, i. 508; Watson, 111 (who adds: "Bloudy bishoppes broyled, cullionly cardinals coured, white chanons chafed, poor nunes paled like Puttockes and all the sectarie Satanists were sore displeased); Speed, 769; Martyn, 178; Duck, 50; Collier, iii. 303; Rapin, iii. 436; Tindal, i. 509; Pauli, v. 96.

[2] Page 337.

[3] Rapin (iii. 434) though believing in the story is puzzled to explain this knock-down blow (*coup terrassant*) at the Church, seeing that il n'y avoit pas le moindre couleur à representer la Chambre Basse comme favorisant l'Hérésie; also Tindal, i. 509.

[4] Probably after 1536, Kingsford, 90; about 1540, Gardiner and Mullinger, 90; 1536 to 1544, Kabel, 39. He died in 1540, his will being proved Nov. 4, 1540. On Jan. 3, 1541, he is referred to as dead, Letters and Papers, H. VIII, xvi. 212; also 1545, do. xx. I. 311; Dict. Nat. Biogr. xlvii. 383; not that he was "un écrivain contemporain" as Puiseux, Rouen, 147.

[5] Senescentem prope Henrici Quinti laudem ab oblivione hominum et a silentio vindicare, Redman, pp. xvi, 6; Gent. Mag. 1859, N. S. vii. 344.

[6] Cf.   So may ye wele and saufly with baner
        Ryde into Fraunce or Scotlonde for your right,
        Whils your rereward in Englond stondyth clere.
                                        Kingsford, Hard. 751, written circ. 1440.
For "the falce Scottes"; "the vyle nacion Scottysshe," see Coke, 120, 124, writing in 1550. Cf. false, fraudulent, snatching Scots, Watson, 21. Redman, 29, merely calls them genus incautum, improvidum et rerum quae in vitâ communi geruntur ignarum. In Pluscard, 350, Henry asks his council (ut fertur) whether he had a better cause of quarrel with Scotland or with France, and is advised that he had no case against Scotland.

[7] Cf. Skeat, s.v. *Renegade*.

first begin[1], the reference being in itself a proof that the
speech was written to suit the events of the middle 16th
century with a reminiscence of the proceedings recorded
in the recalcitrant parliament when both French and Scots
had to be reckoned with in 1523; and so, says the story, the
confiscation bill was lulled asleep[2] and disaster was averted
from the Church by Chichele's wit and policy[3].   The speech
was taken up by Halle who inserted it in his history in 1542[4],
and on the strength of this it has been usual to assume that
Halle is the sole authority for the whole episode[5]. From him
the "pithy oration[6]" passed on to Grafton[7] and Holinshed[8]
and so into Shakespeare[9], thereby becoming a fixed item
in the historical faith of all English-speaking people throughout the world.   John Stow with an awakening critical
faculty omitted the story altogether, but it took no long
time to revive[10] it and from some present indications it seems
still destined to a fresh lease of life[11].

But in contrast to these imaginary debates we must now
turn our eyes to what was actually taking place in France,
if we are to find the real cause of the great aggressive campaign, which henceforward overmasters all other happenings
in King Henry's lifetime.   For while he was deliberately
completing his preparations for invasion, the canker of
internal discord had been eating viciously into the very
life of France and it becomes necessary to look back for a
brief survey of events in that country, if we are rightly to
estimate her chances in the coming struggle.

In spite of Gerson's sound advice after the fall of Caboche

---

[1] Merriman, i. 43, from the speech of Thomas Cromwell; Letters and Papers,
H. VIII, iii. Pt. I. cclxii, Pt. II. 1249; Fisher, 245.
[2] Grafton, i. 509.   [3] Goodwin, 41.   [4] Halle, 50. See App. V[1].
[5] Stone, p. viii, though thinking that he "may have followed Redmann" (p. v).
[6] Holinsh. iii. 545.   [7] Grafton, i. 508.
[8] Holinsh. iii. 547.   [9] Henry V, i. 2, 33.
[10] e.g. in Trussell, 97; Speed, 770; Biondi, 105 (who laboriously examines the
Archbishop's speech); Duck, 50–64; Goodwin, 43–45.
[11] It is accepted by Coville (Lavisse), 365; Beaucourt, i. 257; Oman, Warwick, 16;
H. N. Hudson, ii. 108; B. E. Warner, 139; Musgrave, 265; Boulé, i. 411; Gent.
Mag. (1859), N.S. vii. 344, where the king is "a puppet in the hands of an unscrupulous
priesthood"; Larrey, 807, who accepts the Scotch portion only. Oman (Hist. 222) accepts
the story and believes that "in his old age the Archbishop bitterly regretted the advice,"
and therefore founded All Souls' College at Oxford. Also Kail (p. xix), who confuses
Chichele with Beaufort. Brougham (87) believes that the advice was given by Henry IV
on his death-bed, to which Belleval (p. 15) thinks that Hume (iv. 41) "prête une certaine
consistance." The story is rejected by Pauli, v. 96; Courtenay, i. 169; Belleval, 5; Hook,
v. 37; Kabel, 31.

the king of France had avowed himself an Armagnac[1], and what had been at first a routine Parisian *émeute* had blazed up into the fury of a civil war. On April 2, 1414, the scarlet pennon, or oriflamme[2], was taken from its place above the martyr's altar in the church of St Denis[3] by Charles VI as Count of the Vexin[4]. The king, who seems to have had a special belief in its protecting efficacy[5], now solemnly committed it to the charge of Guillaume Martel, 8th Lord of Bacqueville, who, being an old man over 60 years of age[6], appointed younger deputies to relieve his feeble arm in carrying it to victory. On April 3, 1414, as we have seen[7], King Charles started from Paris accompanied by the Queen, the Dauphin and the Princess Catherine. Easter was spent at Senlis[8], where a great army had been collected[9] under the lead of the Dukes of Orleans[10], Bourbon[11] and Bar, to go forth and crush the Duke of Burgundy. Moving on through Verberie[12] the king reached Noyon[13] on April 18th, where the citizens presented him with a supply of oats and two fat oxen, and offered wine in pots and beakers[14] to many of the lords in his suite. Compiègne surrendered without a blow[15],

[1] Page 185.   [2] See App. W[1].
[3] Called l'enseigne St Denys, Galland, 32.
[4] For the Kings of France, standard-bearers of St Denis as Counts of the Vexin, see Conbrouse, Pt. II. p. 87. For connection of the oriflamme with the Vexin, the Count of which was the premier vassal of the Abbey, until the county was annexed to the crown of France by Louis VI in 1124, see Galland, 32 ; Lacroix, 20.
[5] Vallet de Viriville, Isabeau, 43. Cf.
      T'envoya sa Haultesse
      L'auriflamme qui t'a fait seigneurer
      Tes Ennemis. Champollion-Figeac, 173.
Pyne, 132, 133. The cornette blanche was mostly used instead of it by Charles VII and his successors.
[6] Anselme, viii. 208 ; Hellot, 96.
[7] Page 185 ; called April 15th in Cagny, 87 ; or "soon after April" in Pays-Bas, 345.
[8] Flammermont, 195, who shows that the town raised 300 liv. tourn. to give them as presents. For picture of the cathedral at Senlis see A. France, iv. 1.
[9] Flammermont, Positions, 22 ; reckoned as 80,000 men in Fenin, 582 ; Leroux, 851 ; reported in Venice as 140,000, Morosini, ii. 6.
[10] For a document signed by the Duke of Orleans at St Denis on Feb. 10, 1414, see Roman, 180.
[11] Though a truce with the Duke of Burgundy was arranged for the county of Le Forez by Anne, mother of the Duke of Bourbon in July, 1414, La Mure, ii. 113.
[12] Carlier, ii. 423.
[13] For cross-bowmen from Noyon with the royal army before Soissons, see La Fons Melicocq, Noyon, 12. For excuses sent from Noyon on May 6, 1414, to the king at Compiègne, see ibid. 63.
[14] Par pos et par buyrettes, ibid. 62.
[15] i.e. before May 7th, 1414, St Denys, v. 311 ; Barante, iii. 103 ; or May 8th, as Monstr. 334 ; Cochon, 271. For English among the garrison see Finot, Paix, 14. For picture of the siege from Bibl. Nat. MS. fr. 2678, see Zeller, 12. For fortifications of Compiègne see Bulletin de la Soc. hist. de Compiègne, i. 281–289; Zeiller, Pt. I. For

and by May 5th, 1414[1], the army was before Soissons[2], where an entrance was effected between three and four o'clock in the afternoon of May 21[3], through the treachery of some English archers in the pay of the Duke of Burgundy[4], who opened one of the riverside gates[5] to the attacking force, and 40 of whom were afterwards hung on gibbets for their pains[6]. On the next day a great procession[7] in Paris passed from Notre Dame across the bridge to offer thanks in the church of St Magloire[8], and pray for the recovery of their brain-sick king. But the sack of Soissons left a blot of shame upon him that no processioning could ever wash away, for the capture had been marked by scenes of horror that would have shocked a Saracen[9]. Houses were plundered, churches sacked[10], prisoners slaughtered or

plan of Compiègne (1509) with bridge see Wallon, 212; A. France, iii. 136; Hanotaux, 229. For account of modern Compiègne see Duclaux, 166–169. For supposition that guns were first used at this siege, see Lambert de Ballyhier, i. 121.

[1] Carlier, ii. 424, quoting Chronique de Longpont, 121, i.e. the Cistercian Abbey of Longpont near Villers-Cotterets, Gall. Christ. ix. 473.

[2]   Soissons qui siet en valée
    Moult bonne et de grant renommée. Pastoralet, 849.
For view of Soissons (1660), see Zeiller, Pt. II. 30. For plan showing the position of the Abbeys of St Jean-des-Vignes and St Crépin-en-Chaye (not St Quentin, as Champion, Vie, 125), where the King and the Dauphin had their headquarters respectively, see Leroux, i. 364; ii. 86; Bigot, 40, 52. For account of Soissons (et hanc placidus mediam perlabitur amnis) see Astesan, 574; Berriat-St-Prix, 211; Desrues, 108. For ruins of the Abbey of St Jean-des-Vignes with towers built in 1520 see Joanne, vii. 4677; Larousse, xiv. 819; Grande Encycl. xxx. 208; Didron, Vandalisme, 125. For crypt of the Abbey of St Médard at Soissons see Levallois, France, Frontispiece. For the Abbey of St Mary or Notre Dame at Soissons, now a barrack, see Lethaby, 152.

[3] St Denys, v. 322; Monstr. 335; Baye, ii. 186; Bourgeois de Paris, 642. For a letter of Charles VI dated near Soissons May 26, 1414, see Dognon, 437.

[4] Monstrelet, 335; Paradin, 581, who adds: avec lesquels le commun de la ville s'accordait fort mal; Gollut, 995; Duchesne, 821, who thinks that both Compiègne and Soissons were surrendered par les *garnisons* angloises. For English archers at Arras on May 5, 1414, see Itin. 409.

[5] i.e. the Porte St Quentin, J. Meyer, 242 a; Leroux, 94; Bigot, 53, 54, 61; Monlezun, 169.

[6] For 200 English archers "shamefully maltreated at Soissons" see Adams, Battle-stories, 107.

[7] Aubert, Organisation, 170.

[8] i.e. Maelor, R. Merlet in Bibl. de l'Ec. des Chartes, lvi. pp. 237–273. It stood on the south side of the Rue Salle-au-Compte between the Rue St Denis and Rue Quincampoix, near the junction of the Rue Rambuteau and the Boulevard de Sebastopol, Leroux de Lincy, 111. The remains of the Saint were removed to the church of St Jacques du Haut Pas in 1797, Baring-Gould, xii. 618; Alban Butler, ii. 742. For la cour de St Magloire, see Marle, 36.

[9] For rabies Saracenica, see St Denys, vi. 322.

[10] Fut lors toute la ville fustée et gastez de tous lez, Cordeliers, 222; dont ce fut grand dommage, Bouvier, 427.
    O le desroy incomparable
    Et le dommage irréparable. Pastoralet, 736.
Toute la ville fut pillée et les notables églises en tant qu'il n'y demoura que pou ou nyent, Cagny, 89; le surplus mis a saquement et desconfis, Raoulet, 152. Clamenges (Épist.

spared only to be subsequently executed in Paris prisons[1]; victorious captains outraged nuns, matrons and maids[2], and then handed them over again to the passions of their brutal soldiery[3], and it was long ere the atrocities of "the poor city[4]" faded from men's minds, even in those days of shameful savagery[5].

Meanwhile the Duke of Burgundy was passing about between Ghent[6] and Douai and Bruges helplessly pressing

287), writing to Nicholas de Baye (who had once lived at Soissons as a canon) soon after the sack of the town, has no word of reprobation against the atrocities, because he believed that God had sent them as a punishment, but he would have liked a little less sacrilege in the churches (*utinam in ecclesiis remissius saevitum esset*), which he regards as the worst of sins. In a letter to Reginald les Fontaines, Bishop of Soissons from 1423 to 1442 (Eubel, i. 493), he attributes the calamity to the anger of God at the general wickedness of the whole nation, Clamenges, Ep. 335-338. In three subsequent letters he urges the Bishop not to mind poverty and not to engage in worldly quarrels, for God will find him and make him rich, ibid. Ep. 339-345.

[1] e.g. in the Châtelet, Douet d'Arcq, i. 375.

[2] Et les bergières violer, Pastoralet, 736; Monstr. 336; femmes de religion et autres prudes femmes et bonnes pucelles efforcées, Bourgeois, 642; tant gentis femmes comme aultres, Fenin, 583; Le Fèvre, i. 165; les femmes violées, aulcunes present leurs maris dont plusieurs qui en parloient furent occis, Pays-Bas, 346; abusus matronarum et virginum, Basin, i. 14, who says that Paris and the towns near Soissons swarmed with prostitutes after these events; violant pucelles, femmes mariées et aultres et ossi desreubant le plat pays et toutes les églises, Ruisseauville, 142.

[3] The worst offenders were the Bretons, Gascons, Brabanters and Germans, quos innatus furor exagitare, rapacitas stimulare et libido praecipitare consuevit, St Denys, v. 325, 364, 378, vi. 152; Juv. 546; cf. Cosneau, Connétable, 34; Duclaux, 267; Wylie, iv. 54; qui de touz temps plus désirent et plaisance ont en pillerie que en leur honneur, Cousinot, 171 (of the Bretons). For Gascon brigands see Flourac, 48; Guessard, 457. For la procacité et paillardise militaire see Paradin, 542. Cf. Gens Gallica talibus in rebus omnium longè foedissima, J. Meyer, 242 a, who gives this as a reason why the French were castrated by the Turks when captured. For the Frenchmen's "shameless profligacy" before Nicopolis, see Brougham, 435, from Boucicaut, chap. xxvi. For French enormities against women see Ebendorfer, 106; cf. adulterii peccatum per Franciam nimis impunè, nimis licenterque publicum, Mart. Anec. i. 1730. Cf.

Preneurs de femmes en forche
Et rompent huis, fenestre, porche
Pour les jounes femmes forchier
Et les biens de l'hostel pillier.

Petit, 113; do. (Hellot) Nobles, 32. Written in 1389 of the French squires.

[4] La pauvre cité, Juv. 547.

[5] Comme en avoit fait à Soissons, Juv. 521; Bourgeois, 626 (1417). For description of the siege and sack of Soissons see Le Baud, 449; Leroux, ii. 83-99; Bigot, 55-63, who makes Charles VI run through the town pour respirer l'odeur de sang en riant de démence; Monlezun (iv. 171) thinks that he tried to stop the carnage ne pouvant oublier sa clémence naturelle; also Barante, iii. 110. For supposition that he gave large sums of money to rebuild Soissons, see Dupleix, ii. 708; Mézeray, ii. 565; others suppose that this story is legendary, Morosini, ii. 148, note 10; Serres, i. 957 (280) (anti-Burgundian), says that he "left the town in peace." Gollut (996) (Burgundian) regards the sack of Soissons as God's just chastisement for its bombance, paillardise, oisiveté et festins, relating a story that it had been predicted 40 years before, when a counter was found by a boy while fishing in a brook with the inscription: Vae tibi Suessio, peribus ut Sodoma, see Clamenges, Ep. p. 288.

[6] He was at Ghent on March 17, 1414, and Bruges on May 5, 1414, Gilliodts van Severen, Invent. iv. 320.

the Flemings for funds[1] or sending envoys to England to beg for men to help him in his need[2]. But as King Henry knew that he promised more than he could perform[3], he could only express regret that he found himself unable to comply. The Duke sent to Rouen calling upon the Normans not to pay the tallage that had just been levied[4] in the king's name, but his messenger was seized and sent to Paris, where he was beheaded, and in the hour of his black despair the Duke sent his brother, Anthony Duke of Brabant, and his sister Margaret Countess of Hainault across to Péronne[5], where they fell on their knees before King Charles and prayed that he would graciously spare their brother and his lands[6].

Still the victorious army swept on to finish its work. When the news of its approach reached Bapaume[7], many of the citizens fled to Arras and Douai. On July 12, 1414[8], the king arrived before the place and took up his headquarters in the Abbey at Avesnes[9]. The first difficulty of the besiegers arose from a lack of water, but wells were sunk to a depth of 150 feet and a good supply was thereby secured in face of the prevailing drought[10]. But Bapaume, though called the first fortress in Artois[11], was a busy trading

---

[1] Multo labore nitebatur subsidium a Flandrensibus impetrare, Brando, 168. For particulars see résumé by Paul Thomas (a Lille dissertation) "La Campagne de 1414" in Revue Internationale de l'Enseignement, xxxiv (1897), p. 227.

[2] Bien entendre a luy bailler gens, Juv. 497. See page 152.

[3] Wals. ii. 300; Hypodig. 452.

[4] Cochon, 272.

[5] i.e. on June 29, 1414, St Denys, v. 347; D. Sauvage, 230; Dieve, 218; Verhaer, i. 380; not before Arras on Aug. 31, 1415, as Plancher, iii. ccc. For account of Péronne see Dusevel, i. 19, where the citizens present three cues (i.e. queues, not kenes) of wine to the king at St Quentin. For documents dated by the Duke of Orleans at Péronne on July 8, 1414, see Add. Ch. 65, 66. For 20,000 crowns to pay expenses of deputies of the Three Estates of Flanders who went to the French King at Péronne and accompanied him to the siege of Arras see Delepierre, i. 63; Gilliodts van Severen, Invent. iv. 328, 330, 334; Cartellieri, Beiträge, iii. 20, 32. For statement that the Flemings here agreed not to serve against the king, provided that he did not attack Flanders, see Pays-Bas, 346.

[6] En très grant révérence et humilité, Finot, Paix, 54, 107. For the text of their petition see ibid. 20, 57–64; cf.

Leon (i.e. Burgundy) pourquoy attens tout
Que bien faitice bergierette (Countess of Hainault)
Vers Florentin (Charles VI) envoiera
Qui le moyen y trouvera.   Pastoralet, 743.

[7] Bédu, 61; Finot, Etude, 11.

[8] Bédu, 59.

[9] Devienne, Artois, iii. 36.

[10] Hennebert, iii. 280.

[11] Bédu, 55.

centre[1] and soon came to terms[2], and just as the English
envoys were feasting with the Duke of Burgundy at Ypres[3]
the royal army was settling down to a regular siege of his
great city of Arras[4]. Reinforcements had been steadily
pressed forward since the start from Paris, and a month
before the siege began a force of crossbowmen with their
pavisers had been despatched from Tournai[5] together with
tents, carts and other harness of war, so that it was reckoned
that the total number of the French host was little short
of 200,000 men[6].

But if the Armagnacs had started out to make a speedy
end of the Duke of Burgundy, they were not long in finding
out that this was no easy thing to do[7]. His lowest fall had
hitherto been followed by his biggest rebound, and fortune
did not fail him now. Arras was known as the shield, the
wall and the defence of Western Flanders[8], and its fortifications had been recently strengthened[9]. The defence was
entrusted to Philippe de Beaffort, known as the Fine-Beard
(*Belle-Barbe*)[10], who had given the usual order for the
destruction of all buildings in the suburbs[11] that might in
any way shelter or assist the attack, whereby large numbers
of religious houses were ruthlessly demolished[12]. At first

[1] See App. X[1].
[2] i.e. after July 12, 1414, St Denys, v. 361, 365. Vies et bagues sauvées, D. Sauvage,
230. For the garrison at Bapaume see Finot, Paix, 14. The king left Bapaume on
July 19, 1414, Bédu, 61.
[3] Itin. 409, 410, 411; J. Meyer, 245; not that the Duke was shut up in Arras, as
Lavallée, i. 375.
[4] i.e. July 20, 1414, J. Meyer, 243; called July 28th in St Denys, v. 370; Baye, ii.
191. For a letter written by the Duke of Orleans "en l'ost de Monseigneur le Roy
devant Arraz," July 24, 1414, see Roman, 179. For a letter of the Dauphin dated ante
Arras, Aug. 12, 1414, see Bruchet, 175; also a document of Charles VI au siége devant
Arras, Aug. 28, 1414, Huillard-Bréholles, ii. 197.
[5] i.e. June 13, 1414, Vandenbroeck, 115.
[6] Monstr. 341; Trahisons de France, 126; Le Fèvre, i. 173, 174; Gollut, 998;
called 100,000 in Fenin, 583; Basin, i. 12.
[7] Qui n'estoit pas toutefois chose aisée à faire, Juv. 498.
[8] Scutum, vallum et muri, J. Meyer, 244. For account of Arras see Hennebert, iii.
280–286. For plan and picture (1574) see Braun-Hogenberg, iii. 27; do. Théâtre, i. 14.
For seal of Arras, see A. France, i. 34. For clothe of Arras, see Amyot, 258 (1460);
travail d'Arras, Arbois de Jubainville, ii. 24; pannus qui vocatur Rasses, Finot, Etude, 382.
[9] i.e. in 1412, Locre, 496; Lecesne, 244.
[10] For the garrison at Arras including some English see Finot, Paix, 13, 14.
[11] For map of Arras and its surroundings, showing Blangy, Ronville, St Laurent, etc.
see Ardouin-Dumazet, xix. 89.
[12] Cagny, 91; Héricourt, 45; Lecesne, 245, from municipal archives. For damage
estimated at over 15,000 francs d'or to the Abbey of Mont St Eloi, where the church was
unroofed (*descouvert*), the buildings stripped of lead and the houses and granges all
destroyed during the siege, see Finot, Paix, 56. For destruction of the houses of the

the king took up his quarters at Wailli[1] and afterwards at the Maison du Temple in the suburb of Ronville[2]. Guns, engines, pavises, gunstones, caltraps[3], viretons and other war material were collected in full abundance[4], and the stern business of the siege[5] was diversified by jousts and challenges to feats of arms[6]. But before long the French king again fell grievously ill[7]; wages ran short, the plundered country yielded no supplies for forage[8], 11,000 men died of the flux[9], and towards midnight on Sept. 4, 1414[10], the siege was given up[11], amid shouts of " Noël!" the clanging of church bells and unfeigned delight on both sides[12]. On the next day an understanding known as the Peace of Arras[13] was patched

Black, White, and Grey Friars, Augustinians and Trinitarians, the Temple, the nunnery of La Thieuloye, and the churches of St Vincent and St Saviour, see Lecesne, 245; Hennebert, iii. 282; Pas-de-Calais (Arras), i. 113. For demolition of convents in the suburbs of Millau (Rouergue) in 1356, see Rouquette, 9, 101. For order to destroy suburbs of Troyes in 1417, see Boutiot, ii. 378; also at Senlis at the siege of 1418, Flammermont, 208.

   [1] Devienne, Artois, iii. 30; Hennebert, iii. 282; Pays-Bas, 346.
   [2] Locre, 498; Héricourt, 47; Lecesne, 246; do. Notice, 14.
   [3] For caudetrappes costing seven francs per 1000 stored at Lille during the siege of Arras, also gunstones from the quarries at Béthune and Escossine, see La Fons-Mélicocq, Artillerie, 15, 24.
   [4] For letter dated Aug. 22, 1414, to the authorities at Tournai countermanding previous order of Aug. 9th on the ground that the army was sufficiently supplied, see Vandenbroeck, 118.
   [5] For the siege of Arras see Locre, 498; Héricourt, 42–57; Lecesne, 245.
   [6] For champ-clos at Arras during the siege see Allier, Ancien Bourbonnais, ii. 15; Héricourt, 52; Lecesne, 248.
   [7] Griefment malade, Cousinot, 130; pas ne feust bien à luy par malladie, Pays-Bas, 345.
   [8] Juv. 499.　　　　　　[9] Bourgeois, 643; St Denys, v. 380.
   [10] Not Sept. 8th, as Trahisons de France, 127; nor Sept. 13th, as Stavelot, 149; nor Sept. 14th, as Vinchant, iv. 48.
   [11] N'y purent rien, mais y furent bien batus, Cochon, 273. There is no need to suppose (as Devienne, Artois, iii. 34) that this was caused by the treaty that Charles VI had recently entered into with Sigismund against the Duke of Burgundy, i.e. June 25, 1414, Altmann, i. 57; Pray, ii. 254; Aschbach, ii. 169; not Sept. 1414, as Lion, 88, who supposes that the siege came afterwards and lasted till August, 1415; also Danvin, 118.
   [12] See the letter of Thierry Gherbode, who signed the agreement on behalf of the Duke of Burgundy, in Finot, Paix, 17, 64–66, describing how he went with the Duke of Brabant and the Countess of Hainault to one of the gates of Arras and announced the result, whereat the church bells rang at midnight. See also Cartellieri, Beiträge, iii. 5; Coussemaker, 103, who refers to a commission issued by the Duke of Burgundy at Le Quesnoy on Oct. 16, 1414, ratifying the terms draughted at the above interview. For the Duke at Cambrai Oct. 5, 9, and at Le Quesnoy Oct. 16, 1414, see Finot, Paix, 24, 26, 56, 71, and at Pouilly near Auxerre circ. Nov. 20, 1414, Vallée, 22; Itin. 413.
   [13] Called officially "le traictié fait par devant ma ville d'Arras," Finot, Paix, 42, 45, 97, 100; ghemaect voor Atrect, Gilliodts van Severen, Invent. iv. 331; see Brando, 165; Monstr. 343; Le Fèvre, i. 182; Bibl. de l'Ecole des Chartes, xlvii. 533; Bourgeois, 646. The news of the peace reached Amiens on Sept. 6, 1414, and 11 pots of wine were drunk in honour of the event, the cost appearing at 20d. per pot in the municipal accounts, Héricourt, 330. For promulgation on Sept. 29, 1414, see Caillet, Traité, 225. For reception of the news in Venice on Oct. 1, 1414, see Morosini, ii. 6. For text of the treaty see Héricourt, 57, 323; Caillet, Traité, 226–234, from a copy dated Feb. 2, 1415, in the municipal archives at Lyons; also in Italian, Morosini, ii. 10, with summary in Barante, iii. 120; Caillet, Traité, 223. It is called the Treaty of Senlis in Lettenhove,

up between the two contending factions. The royal banner with the golden lilies was allowed to float over the gates of Arras[1], though the besiegers did not actually enter the town[2]. The Duke of Burgundy's treason was to be condoned[3], and henceforward all were to be friends together. No party-songs were to be sung, and any man would be hanged who wore the *bande* or saltire or spoke of Armagnac[4] or Burgundian or other such words of insult[5]—but what could be the chances for the peace, seeing that the Duke of Orleans put his hand to the bond with muttered reluctance[6] and the Count of Armagnac refused to be included in it at all[7]? The army set out on their return to Paris "quite powerless and beaten." The king was at Péronne on Sept. 8 and passed on through Noyon[8], where the burgesses presented two cues of wine and three jars[9] of oats. He was at Senlis on Sept. 26[10], and arrived in Paris by Oct. 1, 1414[11]. The troops set fire to several places in

Hist. 87, 88, 89, apparently because it was confirmed at Senlis. It was also confirmed at St Denis, Fenin, 266, seemingly on Oct. 16, 1414, Choisy, 314; Vatout, 137; Ménorval, ii. 51; and again on Jan. 29, 1415, Finot, Paix, 5.

[1] Finot, Paix, 32, 77; St Denys, v. 422, 442; Monstr. 355; Cagny, 92.

[2] Cordeliers, 227; except a very few, and these were not to stay more than six days, Cartellieri, Beiträge, iii. 16. For medal with emblematic representation of the surrender, see Mézeray, ii. 597. For the castle of Bellemotte (arx Bellae Motae, J. Meyer, 244) on an artificial mound on the Scarpe at Blangy on the south-eastern side of Arras, see Héricourt, 50; Pas-de-Calais, Dict. Arras, i. 141; Lecesne, 239; do. Notice, 14. It was here that Margaret Duchess of Burgundy died on March 21, 1405, Coussemaker, 125; Wylie, ii. 81 (not May 16th, as Namèche, ii. 145; iii. 32; nor April 13, 1402, as Lecesne, Notice, 14). She was born in 1350, Mas-Latrie, 1602, and was therefore 54 years old at her death; called 55 in Anselme, i. 238; Monget, ii. 8, who gives the number of foxes caught to provide remedies for her gout. For her Book of Hours in the British Museum see Prost I. Plate v.

[3] St Denys, v. 400, 402; Cartellieri, Beiträge, iii. 6. For fines inflicted at Dijon in 1413 for saying "Vous estes des Armiacs," see Vallée, 22.

[4] Variously called ''Hermignagues,'' Marest, pp. xxxix, 152; "Hermignas," ibid. 64; "Arminals," Cochon, 341; "Arminez," Brièle, Doc. III. p. ii; "Ermaingnacs," Trahisons, 159; "Armynacks," Pol. Songs, ii. 149; "Arminaz," Rym. x. 3; "Armagnacz," J. Chartier, iii. 244; "Armeniacos," Basin, i. 25, 35; "Armignas," Champion, Document, 37.

[5] Parolles injurieuses ou blamables, Finot, Paix, 19. E.g. the Burgundians called themselves "les bons" and the Armagnacs "les tristes," Champion, Document, 36.

[6] Attargation de paroles, Monstr. 346; Fenin, 585. For atargier (=retarder) see Godefroy, i. 465. [7] Trahisons de France, 127.

[8] For the Dauphin and the Duke of Orleans at Chauny near Noyon on Sept. 12, 1414, see Champion, Vie, 130.

[9] Aysains, see Godefroy, s.v. *Aise, Aisement.*

[10] Huillard-Bréholles, ii. 197; Flammermont, 196.

[11] St Denys, v. 446; Juv. 499; not Sept. 14th, as Monstr. 350; nor Oct. 13th, as Bourgeois, 643; Champion, Vie, 130; nor Oct. 14th, as D. Sauvage, 232. For a royal letter dated Paris, Oct. 2, 1414, see Ordonnances, x. 224. For a letter of the Dauphin dated at Gonesse near St Denis circ. Oct. 3, 1414, see Vaissète, iv. 436. He was in Paris on Oct. 7th, Huillard-Bréholles, ii. 197, and at St Denis on Oct. 8th, Finot, Paix, 23, 66. For the manor of Gonesse belonging to Pierre d'Orgemont destroyed in the Jacquerie of 1358, see Delachenal, i. 407. For Charles VI, called Charles de Gonnes or Gonness, see

Artois[1] as they hurried back at four times the speed they had taken to set out[2], and when they entered the capital in haggard groups they looked like bread-and-water men let out of gaol.

And well might the scribe who entered up the peace in his official register append his side-note of despair : " God of his pity watch over it[3] !" For the cries of "Noël[4] !" that greeted the poor disabled king had scarcely died away amidst the bonfires and the minstrelsy than the old feuds were all again ablaze. Scarves and badges, it is true, were taken off by order, but the rival Dukes had " little love " for one another[5]. Heavy rains drenched the country and great dearth and scarcity prevailed[6]. In Paris rain fell steadily from All Hallows till Easter, and in March, 1415, the city was flooded for seven or eight days[7]. Gascons, Bretons and other disbanded mercenaries swept over France like a devouring hurricane[8]. Her labourers were eaten up like pigs[9]; her finance was in the hands of the young and reckless Dauphin[10]; taxes were laid to fatten private purses[11], and men were cut into as it were for the stone[12]. At the

Leyden, 345, 346. For the leperhouse at Gonesse see L. Legrand, xxv. 96. For account of Gonesse in 1785 see Dulaure, 238, where it is famed for its cakes and bakers; for picture of it in 1660 see Zeiller, i. 69; also of the church, Grande Encycl. xviii. 1196.

[1] Including Pas, which belonged to the Lord of Heilly, Finot, Paix, 28, 73.

[2] Fenin, 585 ; si estraignement comme chascun scet, Finot, Paix, 73.

[3] Baye, ii. 211.

[4] For Noel see Pollard, 93 ; Wylie, iii. 93, note 10; Christmas pour quere Noel, Leroux de Lincy, Chants I. xxxvi; "Vespra de Nadal," Mager, 192; "Nowelle," Archaeologia, xxii. 383, 398; "Nowell, myssus est ad virginem angelus Gabriell," T. Wright, Songs and Carols, 79, 88; "Nowe Welle," J. Page, 45; Noel que bien peut-il estre venu, Deschamps, vi. 41, quoted in Thibault, 97. For "Noel" to the Duke of Brittany in 1413, see Le Baud, 449.
　　　　　Crier Noel très bien il appartient
　　　　　Quant en ce monde ung tel prince si vient
　　　　　A son peuple donner sa charité. Regnier, 113.

[5] Peu d'amour...grant envie, Fenin, 585, 586; quelque traité qu'il y eût n'avoient-ils pas grand fiance en eux, Monstr. 344; peu de sureté et d'amour, ibid. 354.

[6] Bourgeois, 643; St Denys, v. 448.

[7] Bourgeois, 644.

[8] Velut tempestas valida, St Denys, v. 448.

[9] Les assomans come pourceaulx, Martial, 11, 12.

[10] Cui commiseramus vices nostras, Ordonnances, x. 219, Sept. 22, 1414; Cousinot, 133; St Denys, v. 424.

[11] Juv. 500.

[12] Tous sont taillés comme s'ils avaient la gravelle, Roncière, ii. 211, quoting Mézières, Songe du Vieil Pèlerin MS. fr. 9200, ff. 217, 223, 307, 308, 309. For abstract of the poem see Brants, 6. For liber qui dicitur Somnium Viridarii qui est dialogus inter clericum et militem, i.e. *Le Songe du Vergier*, see Traitez des droits et Libertez de l'Eglise, Gallicune (1731), ii. pp. 1–152; Débat, 13; Pyne, 25; Geruzez, i. 214; Way, 221; Aubert, Comp. 135. It was attributed to Philippe de Mézières, Meunier, 134; Tivier,

tax-gatherer's approach the churchmen hid their treasures; peasants fled into the towns and townsmen put themselves into the hands of the devil[1] and lived like wild beasts with their wives and children in the woods[2]. The Duke of Berry withdrew from a government[3] that was "somehow always going wrong[4]." On Dec. 27, 1414[5], an ordinance was issued again declaring the Duke of Burgundy to be an enemy to his king, and all who favoured him were ordered to clear out of Paris[6] with their wives and families. Then any man that was known for a Burgundian ran the risk of having his tongue bored or his hand cut off or standing in the pillory[7], but a month later[8] the Dukes of Berry and Orleans were declared guilty of high treason, and the scales dropped the other way. Two constables[9] contended for the headship of the army and two admirals[10] for the headship of the fleet, while two provosts of the merchants[11] ousted each

45; Herbert, 253; Faguet, 164 [131], who calls it "ouvrage dogmatique par allégorie"; Luce, ii. 72; Jorga, p. vii; though the authorship is doubted, see Brants, 5; G. Paris, Esquisse, 218.

[1] Se mettent en la main du diable, Rambaut, i. 266; Labroue, Livre, 13.

[2] St Denys, v. 536.　　　　　　　　　　[3] Monstr. 349.

[4] Alloit tous jours aucunement mal, Juv. 502.　　[5] Juv. 505.

[6] Vuydassent Paris, Finot, Paix, 30, 75.　　[7] Ou pellory, ibid. 28, 73.

[8] i.e. Jan. 22, 1415, Pannier, 222.

[9] i.e. Waleran Count of St Pol (Burgundian) and Charles d'Albret (Armagnac), page 155, note 10; H. D. Sauvage, 221; Paradin, 569.

[10] i.e. Jacques de Châtillon (Burgundian), Fenin, 558, 586; Baye, ii. 188, 207; Monstr. 373; Aubert, Comp. 65; Roncière, ii. 212; Collas, 385; Wylie, iv. 32; and Pierre de Brébant (Armagnac). For his seal with "pierre de breba..." Feb. 28, 1406, see Demay, Inventaire, i. 159. He is called Clignet de Breban in Baye, ii. 253, see Wylie, iii. 82; or Clunetum cognomento Brabantum, Dieste, 215; Verhaer, i. 379; Clugnet de Brabant, Goodwin, 68, 87; not Huguet as La Fons-Mélicocq, Noyon, 17, 22, 103, where he is refused admission into Noyon on Feb. 13, 1414. He was probably named from Brébant near Vitry (Marne), though called Brabant in St Denys, vi. 585; Plancher, III. ccxcix; Lavallée, Jean sans Peur, 25, 34, 38; Bordier-Charton, i. 50, where he is one of the commanders at Agincourt, though "Breban" is certainly at times the equivalent of Brabant, e.g. Pol. Songs, ii. 152. He was known as Clignet or Clugnet (i.e. goggle-eyed), Christine de Pisan, i. 240; Clouet, iii. 530, 537; Grande Encycl. vii. 924, where he is Lord of Macon and Landreville (? near Bar-sur-Seine), called Landeville in Leroux de Lincy, Chants Historiques, i. 286; not Cluet, as Drayton, 69; nor "Cliquet de Brabant," as Adams, i. 226, 228; nor "Aliquot," as do. Battle Stories, 107, 110. He was one of the seven French champions in the combat against seven English at Montendre in Saintonge on May 19, 1402, Monlezun, iv. 86; Barante, ii. 120; Wylie, i. 324; ii. 325, note 5. For these jousts see Massiou, iii. 239–241; Moreau in Revue Anglo-Française, iii. 271–286 (1835); Aussy, Saintonge, 21. Cf.

En peust Montendre tesmoigner
Chasteau congncu ou fut l'emprise faicte
Et des Angloys honteux la deffaicte. St Gelais, 221.

Jacques de Châtillon was Lord of Dampierre, in Champagne-Pouilleuse, Anselme, vii. 817 (not Ampierre, as Voisin La Hougue, 74). He was a member of the Burgundian Cour d'Amours (Piaget, 423; E. Ritter, 467) and was killed at Agincourt, Waurin, ii. 224.

[11] i.e. André Marchant (Burgundian) and Tanguy du Châtel (Armagnac), Bourgeois, 644; Baye, ii. 194. On Aug. 31, 1415, Tanguy du Chastel is a councillor, chamberlain

other from office at alternate shifts of power. The pulpits[1]
rang with Armagnac laments for the past good days of the
murdered Duke of Orleans, and passionate denunciations
that the Duke of Burgundy should be humbled for the good
of his soul[2].

And surely his soul needed purging, for when the peace
was patched at Arras he had solemnly declared on his
honour that he had made no compact with the English,
or if he had, that it had been annulled, and he had sworn
that he would contract no marriage or alliance with them
for the future[3]. But if this extraordinary declaration tended
to serve a momentary purpose in cloaking another skin-
deep reconciliation between the lords of the blood[4], it is not
possible to force it into line with the real diplomatic facts
of that eventful year, the outline of which can be traced
with sufficient certainty to warrant a more detailed examination here.

to the King and Garde de la Prévosté de Paris, Ordonnances, x. 241. In Oct. 1414, he
was governor of La Rochelle, and on Feb. 19, 1415, he was made Provost of Paris for
the second or third time, Bourgeois, 644.
  [1] Firent faire prédications et escriptures diffamatoires, Finot, Paix, 28, 73.
  [2] See Gerson's sermon preached before the king at Notre Dame Jan. 5, 1415, Monstr.
352; Le Fèvre, i. 197; J. Meyer, 244; Boulliot, i. 448; Villaret, xiii. 326; Barante, iii.
128; Michelet, v. 322; Dufour, Chancelier, 196.
  [3] St Denys, v. 384, 388; Monstr. 345; Barante, iii. 121.
  [4] Ord. Priv. Co. iv. 259.

CHAPTER XXII

RESTITUTION OF RIGHTS

THE Leicester Parliament had broken up on May 29, 1414[1], and the king, who had stayed at the castle[2] during the whole of the session, remained there till May 31[3]. On that day he went to Market-Harborough[4], but he was back at Leicester on June 3 and 4[5]. On June 5 he was at Lichfield[6] and on June 8 at Burton-on-Trent[7]. On June 22[8] he was at the Palace at Westminster, whence he started soon after for a further round of journeying. July 5[9] found him at Blyth castle near Worksop. He was at Peterborough on July 10[10], at York on July 12[11], at Hertford castle on August 1, 16 and 17[12], and at St Neots in Huntingdonshire on August 18[13]. On Sept. 13 he was at

---

[1] Page 332.
[2] For plan of Leicester in the 14th century with the Newark and the castle on the bank of the Soar, see Bateson, vol. I. For plan (1722), see T. F. Johnson, 4. For the hall of the castle, now the Assize Courts, see ibid. 48, 80, 134, 268.
[3] For documents dated at Leicester on April 30, May 1–12, 14–31, 1414, see Pat. 2 H. V, i. mm. 9, 16, 19, 19 d, 20, 21, 25, 27, 28, 29, 31, 33, 34, 35, 35 d, 36, 37, 37 d, 39, 39 d, 41; ii. mm. 24, 25, 26, 29, 30, 34, 35, 36, 39; iii. mm. 7, 8; Rym. ix. 124–129, 131; Rot. Scot. ii. 210, 211; Prynne, 502, 505; Ewald, xliv. 552, 553, 554; Cal. Rot. Hib. i. 206; Nott. Rec. ii. 94; Cal. Doc. Scot. iv. 172; Sloane MS. 4600 ff., 287, 288, 289, 291, 292, 293; Escheators' Inquisitions, 1278. In Pat. 1 H. V, iii. 1 there is a document dated at Leicester, May 15, but the year must be 1414 (not 1413) as Archbishop Arundel is referred to as dead; cf. Cal. Pat. H. V, i. 109.
[4] Rym. ix. 133; Ewald, xliv. 553.
[5] Rym. ix. 137, 138; Gesta, xxviii; Chancery Warrants, Ser. 1. 1364/9. Ramsay (i. 185) supposes that he was at Westminster on May 31 and back at Leicester by June 4.
[6] Ad Quod Damn. 370.
[7] Chancery Warrants, Ser. 1. 1364/10, 11, 12.
[8] Rym. ix. 143; see page 106, note 6. For a document "teste me ipso" at Westminster, July 28, 1414, see Riley, Mem. 600.
[9] Rym. ix. 149; Chancery Warrants, Ser. 1. 1364/13; Ewald, xliv. 555.
[10] Chancery Warrants, Ser. 1. 1364/14.
[11] Gironde, iii. 63.
[12] Rym. ix. 188; Pat. 2 H. V, ii. 32 d; Jurade, 88; Chancery Warrants, Ser. 1. 1364/15, 16.
[13] Ibid. 1364/17.

Sutton[1], and on Sept. 23 at Westminster[2], where he remained till after Michaelmas[3]. On Oct. 3 he was at Sheen[4], but he was at Westminster again on Oct. 15, 18 and 19[5]. We find him at Hertford on Oct. 27[6], but on the following day he was back at Westminster[7] ready for attendance at his third Parliament which opened in the Palace on Nov. 19[8], where we also find him on Dec. 4, 5 and 12, 1414[9], and Jan. 23, 1415[10].

While the Parliament was sitting at Leicester he had been visited there by envoys from the King of France[11], and on June 1, 1414[12], a commission was issued appointing Bishops Langley and Courtenay[13], Thomas Montagu, Earl of Salisbury[14], Richard Lord Grey of Codnor[15], John Pelham[16], Robert Waterton[17] and Master Henry Ware[18] to cross to France

---

[1] Chancery Warrants, Ser. I. 1364/18.   [2] Chron. Lond. 98.
[3] Otterbourne, 275; Wals. ii. 302; Hypodig. 452.
[4] Rym. ix. 204.   [5] Rym. ix. 162, 167; Jurade, 171, 187.
[6] Pat. 2 H. V, ii. 18.   [7] Rym. ix. 170.
[8] Rot. Parl. iv. 34.   [9] Rym. ix. 182; Jurade, 132.
[10] Jurade, 138.
[11] Elmham, Lib. Metr. 102. For £24. 14s. 3d. paid for their expenses while at Leicester and elsewhere from May 17 to June 2, 1414, see Rym. ix. 188; not that they remained in London, as Kingsford, 114.
[12] Rym. ix. 131, 133; Lenz, 45; For. Accts. P. R. O. List, 86; Waurin, ii. 164, not instructions, as Ramsay, i. 185, who thinks that the document suggests that the way of marriage involved some sacrifice on Henry's part. Ou moys de Juign, Norm. Chron. 167.
[13] Called 1 bishop and 2 doctors in Strecche, 266ᵃ. For supposition that Sir Thomas Erpingham was one of the envoys, see Hope, Plate XLII.
[14] Called Richard in Rym. ix. 132, but his name was certainly Thomas; see Rym. ix. 141, 150, 151, 154, 204; Wylie, iii. 286. For his appearance in Parliament in November 1414, claiming that a mistake had been made in reference to his father's forfeiture, see Rot. Parl. iv. 35; Cotton, Abr. 539. For £33. 6s. 8d. received from him de fine p. velario suo, see Rec. Roll 3 H. V, Mich., Feb. 12, 1416.
[15] Chron. Lond. 98. For his expenses from July 10 to Oct. 3, 1414, see Exch. Accts. 321/21 (called Oct. 20 in Mirot-Déprez, lxi. 26, who refers to another acct. from July 10 to Oct. 3, 1414, in Exch. Accts. 321/19 as absolument illisible), showing that he crossed from Winchelsea to Dieppe, hiring the "Farescost de Redyng," three barges, i.e. the "Barge of Rye," the "Julian de Conquete" (i.e. Le Conquet near Brest) and the "Dame de Geronde" (called "Gerand" in Rot. Scot. ii. 218; i.e. Guérande, Wylie, iv. 26), also a passager of Dover called the "Catherine," a cogship and craier of "Smaly" (i.e. Smallhythe, called Smallhyde in Inq. p. Mort. iii. 93, or "Smallit" at the present day, Hasted, iii. 98). He returned from Harfleur to Southampton with the barge of Spain, the barge of Brittany, two cogships, one of them being from Goo (i.e. Gouda) and a ship called "le Busse of Winchelsea." His total expenses amount to £225. 6s. 8d., including £5 paid to le lieutenant et autres persones in the port of Harfleur.
[16] Called Messire Jehan Pheletin in Juv. 497. For writ dated Oct. 15, 1414, for payment to John Pelham for journey to France, see Exch. Accts. 321/18, showing that he took English vessels for Harfleur à cause que les niefs et vessaux d'Engleterre viendrent plustot au dit port.
[17] On March 21, 1413, he was appointed a Justice of the Peace for the West Riding of Yorkshire, Pat. 1 H. V, i. 36 d. He is called Vastreton in Chastellain, 167. On July 7, 1414, he is about to cross to France, Rym. ix. 141.
[18] For his account in the company of Bishop Langley and others going to Paris from July 11 to Oct. 2, 1414, see Exch. Accts. 321/15, showing that he crossed from Winchelsea

and continue negotiations for peace. Those English envoys who had just returned from Paris[1] had discussed the question of a marriage with the Princess Catherine, but to this had now to be added a new demand as a preliminary to peace[2], viz. that the French king should restore to Henry all the rights and other heritages that duly belonged to him. The French Council had expressed their willingness to discuss the question and the present embassy was charged to go into the matter in King Henry's name. And in order that there might be no lack of seriousness attaching to the demand, a Great Council[3] met at Westminster, at which the assembled lords and knights advised that the envoys who were about to cross to France should give formal notice that the King of England in his chivalrous heart and desire had determined to stir and labour for the recovery of the old rights of his crown[4], and promised their hearty support to the project. With regard to the proposed marriage with a daughter of the King of France an understanding had been already given[5] that King Henry would wed no other woman[6] before May 1, 1414, and this time had been subsequently prolonged to June 24[7]. It is said that the marriage question had been broached in the

---

to Dieppe in a cogship de Goue, returning from Harfleur to Seaford ; also Mirot-Déprez, lxi. 27.
    [1] Page 158.
    [2]
                Pax et amicitia queruntur et unio gratis,
                Dixerat hic ante quam mihi sponsa foret.
                                        Elmham, Lib. Metr. 103.
    [3] Caxton, 144; Brut, ii. 552; called "the representatives of the nation" in Goldwin Smith, i. 257, who thinks that the response to this appeal was at first guarded.
    [4] Ord. Priv. Co. ii. 140–142, undated, but endorsed "anno 2"; cf. Tyler, ii. 72; Nicolas, App. 64, where it is dated April 1415. This Council is generally supposed to have met in September 1414, e.g. Sept. 23, Chron. Lond. 98; or Sept. 24, Harl. MS. 565, 74; or Sept. 29, Otterbourne, 275; Wals. ii. 302; Kingsford, 115; Holinsh. iii. 547, where it is called "a Convocation," possibly a confusion with the convocation that met on Oct. 1, 1414 (p. 434) ; or Sept. 30, Ramsay, i. 186. But the mention of the coming departure of the envoys seems to show that it must have been somewhat earlier. In Brut, ii. 552; Caxton, 225, it is dated before the meeting of the Parliament at Leicester, or after the receipt of the tennis-balls; Chron. R. II–H. VI, 39, where it is called "a parlement at Westminstre," "all the lordis of the reme."
    [5] Page 159.
    [6] Mulier, cf. "mulire," Wylie, iv. 354: cf. "moglie," Supino, Medagliere, 50; Cibrario, Cronologia, 386, 387; "mogle," Sercambi, iii. 120; madona sa molher=sa femme, Magen, 251.
    [7] Rym. ix. 141 ; Harl. MS. 431, f. 104 b; Harl. Cat. i. 255; this undated document was copied by Bréquigny and is printed in Champollion-Figeac, Lettres des Rois, ii. 346, 589, who dated it as June 23, 1419, the first portion of the date being evidently a mere inference from the mention of June 24 in the document as being near at hand. The year is certainly altogether wrong.

Leicester Parliament[1], though there is no mention of it on the official rolls, and the envoys were now authorised to prolong the time till Aug. 6, 1414[2], or indeed indefinitely, if the French so desired[3].

They were accordingly now fully equipped for their departure. Passagers[4] and other vessels had been collected on the south coast and on July 4, 1414[5], orders were issued to assemble without delay at Winchelsea for an approaching start, 500 horses having to be shipped across the strait. On July 7[6] Bishop Langley and Robert Waterton were about to start. Their expenses actually began on July 11, showing that they crossed from Winchelsea to Dieppe[7], and on July 10[8] the Earl of Salisbury left London for Dover, whence he sailed with Bishop Courtenay[9], the bulk of whose party had already crossed to Dieppe by way of Winchelsea. On their arrival at Calais they saw the body of an Englishman, William Cole of Winchester, who had been hanged for murder and left according to Calais law to hang till the rope should rot[10], but at their request the body was cut down and buried by way of charity, though the man who actually cut it down was himself imprisoned

---

[1] Capgr. De Illustr. 114. Called the Parliament at Westminster in Chron. R. II–H. VI, 39.

[2] Rym. ix. 140, June 18, 1414.

[3] Rym. ix. 141, June 22, 1414. For extension to Nov. 1, 1414, see Harl. MS. 430, f. 104 b, in Champollion-Figeac, Lettres, ii. 346.

[4] Navigia vocata passagers, Rym. x. 148; in quâdam navi vocat' passag', Exch. Accts. 187/6. For a passagier of Dover, see ibid. 321/21; called barque de passage, Jal, 1138. Not a French name for a ship's pinnace, as Gesta, pp. vii, 96. Cf. Ord. Priv. Co. v. cxxxiv; Wylie, iv. 356. For passager called the George of Calais, see Iss. Roll 6 H. V, Mich., Dec. 7, 1418. For one crown charged for crossing from Calais to Dover, temp. Richard II, see Mirot, 186.

[5] Rym. ix. 148.

[6] Rym. ix. 141, 152; Chron. Lond. 98.

[7] Rym. ix. 190; page 404, note 18.

[8] See page 404, note 15.

[9] Rym. ix. 151, 154. For Courtenay's claim for expenses for his suite and horses from July 10 to Oct. 3, 1414, not Oct. 30 as Mirot-Déprez, lxi. 26, though he himself returned somewhat earlier, see Rym. ix. 189. For £17. 8s. 8d. and £28. 7s. 10d. paid for the crossing from Winchelsea to Dieppe, see Rym. ix. 204. For £387. 6s. 10d., expenses of Richard, Bishop of Norwich, from July 9, 1414, to Oct. 3, 1414 (i.e. 80 men and 74 horses), returning to Portsmouth from Harfleur, see Exch. Accts. 321/26, i.e. 18 horses in the Trinity, eight in navi de Smalhide, 16 in the Trinity of Smallhythe, seven in the John of Reding (i.e. Reading Street near Smallhythe), others in three cogships of Gou (Gouda), Dansk (Danzig) and Sketham (? Schiedam), and one in a balinger of Rye. There are also payments for boats and a shout to convey the horses to the ships and four lodemayns (sic) for piloting (salvus conductus) them in the harbour at Dieppe.

[10] Thei (i.e. wolves) ete men that have ben hangyd when thei fal from the galows, York, 34.

and sentenced to death for doing so, not being actually pardoned till six months later[1].

As the English envoys were prepared to open up the monstrous claim for restitution of King Henry's rights[2] picked from the worm-holes of long vanished days[3], it may be well to inquire on what legal basis these rights could be made to rest. Nearly two generations had passed away since the "Great Peace[4]" had been signed at Brétigny[5] near Chartres, according to which the French agreed that 3,000,000 gold crowns[6] should be paid as ransom for their captive King John[7] who had been taken prisoner at Poitiers[8]. The value of the crown was specified as equal to the English half-noble[9], so that the total amounted to £500,000

[1] Rym. ix. 195, Jan. 21, 1415.

[2] Pour le recouvrir de noz droiz, Ord. Priv. Co. ii. 264. Called "unwise claims," H. Morley, vi. 140; "the absurd and wicked claim," Fletcher-Walker, 7, who thinks (p. 8) that "it seems to be impossible that Henry really believed his claim to be founded in justice," but that "it suited him to say that he believed it." Freeman (Essays, i. 117) thinks that "before the tribunal of abstract right it must be admitted that Henry cuts but a poor figure, but that we must make allowance," etc. etc. "No claim could be less legal," Lang, Maid, 17; called "a low-minded invasion," H. Morley, vi. 151; "a jingo war," Baxter, Cardinals, 33.

[3] Henry V, 2, 4, 86.

[4] "The Grete Pees," Rym. ix. 428, 628, 629; Ord. Priv. Co. ii. 352, 357; "the gret peas," Noblesse, 40; "la grande paix," Rym. ix. 640, 641; "pax magna," Kal. and Inv. ii. 98; Rym. ix. 637, 638, 640; Black, Arundel MSS. p. 80; Tit. Liv. 24; Vita, 77; Noblesse, 37.

[5] i.e. May 8, 1360, Rym. vi. 219; Cosneau, 33; Delachenal, Chron. i. 267–296; Rouquette, 20; Monlezun, iii. 362; Villaret, xiii. 340; Lingard, iii. 91; Kitchin, i. 464; Lodge, 89; Aumale, 52; Ménorval, i. 423. Called May 4 in Douet d'Arcq, Argenterie, 201; or May 7 in Add. MS. 24,062, f. 152 b. For May 10, 15, 16, June 14, and final ratification, Oct. 24, 1360, see Denifle, Désolation, ii. 361, 362; called "after Cressy," in B. E. Warner, 136. For text, see Zeller, Invasion, pp. 92–110; Cott. MS. Tiberius, B. 12, ff. 42–51; for abstract, see Delachenal, ii. 201; Hume, iii. 308; Duruy, i. 378; Tyler, ii. 74; Harl. MS. 4763, ff. 41–50. Not "of Brittany," as Dumas, 132; nor "Bretigne," as Adams, Battle Stories, 99.

[6] Delachenal, ii. 204. For 600,000 crowns paid Oct. 25, 1360, see Aumale, 53. For "scutes of gold," see Fabyan, 583; "scutes of the kyng," Caxton, Dial. 17. For picture of an écu d'or of Charles VI, circ. 1389, value = 1l. 2s. 6d., see Wallon, 192; A. France, i. 214. For demi écu d'or of Charles VII, see ibid. ii. 107; iii. 144; iv. 147; also one of Charles VIII, Wallon, 192. In 1420, 1424, 1430, 1433 from 64 to 68 crowns are coined from one mark (weight) of gold, Broussillon, iii. 54; Huillard-Bréholles, ii. 218, 244, 250.

[7] See App. Y[1].

[8] Or Maupertuis, Sept. 19, 1356, Traill, ii. 177; Rym. v. 222, 255; Cosneau, 46; Oman, 6, 8; Aumale, 9; Douet d'Arcq, Argenterie, 193, 278; Delachenal, i. 227–244. For 12th eclogue of Petrarch on his capture, see Cott. MS. Tiberius, B. 12, ff. 58–59 b; Harl. MS. 4763, ff. 55 b–57 b.

[9] Of the whiche scutes tweyne algates shall be worth a noble Englyssh, Rym. ix. 916; Tillet, Guerres, 111; Rept. on Foedera, App. D, 307; W. Worcester, 351 (1419); Rym. ix. 424, 442; Kunze, 92 (1347); not "about 5s." as T. F. Kirby, Annals, 23. For six French crowns to the £ English, see Exch. Accts. 47/13. On June 13, 1374, the franc d'or = half a noble, Delpit, ccxli, 192, showing that the crown is of the same value as the franc d'or. For the franc d'or = 16 sols, see Schoetl, 9; Tuetey, Test. 322 (1402); Wylie, iv. 307. For picture of a good noble of Edward III, see J. R. Green (illustrated),

in English money. Of this sum one-third was to be paid within a year of the French king's release and the rest in five yearly instalments of 400,000 crowns each[1]. King John recovered his freedom temporarily on Oct. 25, 1360[2], and on the following day[3] he put his seal to a special bond, in which he undertook either by himself or his successors to fulfil the obligations to the letter, and his son, who afterwards became King Charles V[4], assented to it at the same time and place.

According to the Treaty of Brétigny[5] the King of France was to give up his claim to sovereignty over

i. 434; Nicolas, Navy, ii. 223; Clowes, i. 145; Ducarel, Anglo-Gallic, Plates 5, 14, 15; Wylie, iv. 45; also of Henry VI, A. France, iii. 127; cf.

> With this rownde see,
> Under the shyppe shewed ther the sayle,
> And oure kynge of royalle apparayle,
> With swerde drawe bryght and extente,
> King, shype and swerde and power of the see.
> Rex, navis et gladius.   Pol. Songs, ii. 193.

Pauli-Hertzberg, 55; Wylie, iv. 45; Venuti, Plate F, vii; Knight, Shakespeare, Richard II, p. 99; called "nobles of England," in Caxton, Dial. 17. Oppenheim, 7, thinks that they were struck in combination with the people of Flanders for political and trading purposes; see Archaeologia, iii. 316–324, where the superscription, transiens per medium illorum (Luke iv. 30), is interpreted as passing between England and France (i.e. illorum regnorum). For the half-noble or maille, see Archaeologia, iii. 317; Wylie, iv. 45, note 5; Maldon Rolls, Oct. 23, 1413, where the obolus aureus=40*d*. For "florenum de noble," see Rym. vi. 307 (1361), where it equals two florins de scuto; cf. Wylie, iii. 130, note 11. For florin as identical with the Venetian ducat or French franc, see Robinson, 117, where it equals about 9*s*. 8*d*. English. For franc d'or (=20 sols), or denier d'or (63 to the mark weight), first coined by King John of France, Dec. 5, 1360, see Hawkins, Anglo-Gall. 34; Grande Encycl. xviii. 957; also called denier d'or aux fleurs de lis of Charles V, May 5, 1365, ibid. 958. It ceased as an actual coin after Charles VI. Called also royal, with inscription, Christus vincit, etc., Conbrouse, Pt. I. Ser. 3 (2), pp. 16, 90, 92. For "escus d'or appelé couronnes," each=two liv. par. in 1407, see Gilliodts van Severen, Cartulaire, i. 452.

[1] Rym. vi. 222, 268; Cosneau, 47.

[2] Douet d'Arcq, Comptes, 278, 283; Cosneau, 35; Denifle, Désolation, ii. 367. Called Oct. 14 in Rouquette, 23; or Dec. 28 in Monlezun, iii. 363.

[3] The bond was signed at Boulogne, Oct. 24, 1360 (Rym. vi. 268; ix. 149; Kal. and Inv. ii. 98), and was ratified in the church of St Nicholas at Calais (Lennell, 10), hence it is called Tractatus Calesii, le traictié de Calais, by Jean de Montreuil in 1415, A. Thomas, 18, 22, 23, 24; or Calesie, Cott. MS. Tib. B. 12, ff. 64–76; Harl. MS. 4763, ff. 61–104; the "peace of Calais," Tout, 219; do. Pol. Hist. 396, 397; Oman, Pol. Hist. 172. For documents signed by King John at Boulogne, Oct. 25, 29, 1360, see Aumale, 55; Ledos, 91. He left London for Dover on June 30, 1360, arrived there on July 6, 1360 (Aumale, 52); landed at Calais on July 8, 1360 (ibid. p. 4; Douet d'Arcq, Argenterie, 282); spent three months at Calais and was at Boulogne on Oct. 25, 1360, and after more than three years spent chiefly in Paris (he was at Dijon on Dec. 22, 1361), he re-embarked at Boulogne for England on Jan. 3, 1364.

[4] See App. Z[1].

[5] For boundaries shown on a map, see Spruner, 52; Gairdner, Map I; Longnon, Pt. I. Plate XIV; Thatcher-Schwill, 532; Ramsay, i. 196; Tout, 220; Jervis, 112; Freeman, Geog. 340; do. Atlas, Pl. XXIV; Delachenal, ii. 201. In Wassebourg, 461, 465, they stretch "jusqu'à la rivière de Loire"; in Oman, Hist. 222, "from Normandy to the Pyrenees," though "Poitou and Saintonge were to remain French"; do. Hundred Years' War, 107.

Aquitaine, Gascony, Ponthieu and Montreuil (with the mouth of the Somme), and Calais, while the King of England was to abandon his pretensions to the crown of France. But these renunciations were never actually interchanged[1]. Edward III indeed went so far as to drop out the words "*Rex Francie*" in the new seal[2] which he had engraved after the treaty was signed; but in April 1369[3] Charles V formally repudiated the treaty and renewed the war, whereupon Edward III re-inserted the word "*Francie*" on his great seal[4] in 1372, and both he and his successors continued to use the title "King of France" on all official occasions.

When Richard II married Isabel, the daughter of Charles VI, in 1396[5], a truce was made between the two countries to last for 28 years from Michaelmas 1398[6]. But this truce was merely a *modus vivendi* and left the renunciations as they were. It was several times affirmed during the reign of Henry IV[7] and had quite recently been renewed by Henry V to last for one year from Feb. 2nd, 1414[8]. King John died at the hostel of the Savoy in London at midnight on April 8, 1364[9], and his ransom money had never been even half paid up. Thirty years after his death 1,600,000 crowns of it were still due, but the claim for this remainder seemed to have been tacitly dropped[10]. It was revived however by Henry IV when the French pressed him for the repayment of Isabel's dower,

[1] Cosneau, 38, 69; rex Francie nunquam renonciavit superioritati terrarum, Montreuil, in A. Thomas, 18; ne renonça onques à la souveraineté des terres, ibid. 23.
[2] Known as the Brétigny seal, described and figured in Wyon, 37, Plate 64, though the arms of France were still retained in it, ibid. 40.
[3] Manu forti viâque facti, Montreuil, in A. Thomas, 18. Cosneau, 69; Tyler, ii. 75; called 1370 in Rouquette, 228; not that the treaty was abrogated, as Adams, i. 210; cf. le traité fust trouvé nul, Juv. 551. Freeman, Essays, i. 120, claims that Henry's "formal justification" lay in this.
[4]
         Liche as the seale the grettest of this londe,
         On the one syde hathe as I understonde,
         A prince riding with his swerde idrawe,
         In the other side sittynge sothe it is in sawe.
                              Pol. Songs, ii. 182.
Pauli-Hertzberg, 45.
[5] Page 71.
[6] Cosneau, 71; not 25 years from 1396, as Strang, 39; Green (261) regards Henry V's attack on France in 1415 as "a renewal of the earlier struggle on the expiration of the truce made by Richard II," but this would not expire till 1426, see Wylie, i. 84.
[7] Cosneau, 100; Wylie, iv. 438.   [8] Page 156.
[9] Bapst. 6; Delachenal, Chroniques, i. 341; do. Hist. ii. 361. See App. A².
[10] For summary of the negotiations, see Cosneau, 70.

and these claims and counter-claims had been constantly bandied about[1] whenever negotiations were afoot, though neither side was determined enough to stand to them and resolutely drive them home.

But now that France was weak and divided[2] and England was united and strong, the new king saw his opportunity and resolved to reopen the antiquated claim. Two years before, both Armagnacs and Burgundians had called his father in[3] and had put him off by making up their quarrel at Bourges, but now they were both at each other's throats again and bidding for English help, and knowing well that divided sway soon gives way[4], King Henry saw that the time had come to help whichever side came nearest to his terms before they closed up their ranks against him again. Accordingly a copy of King John's admission of liability was officially authenticated at Westminster on July 5, 1414[5], which the English envoys were to make use of as occasion should require. As to the marriage scheme they were formally empowered to pledge their king's word that he was willing either to enter into an engagement for the future or to agree to an immediate betrothal with the French king's daughter Catherine, provided that satisfactory terms could be arranged about her dower[6]. In previous negotiations[7] he had promised that within certain dates he would keep himself free from all other matrimonial plans till the question of the engagement with the Princess Catherine should be decided. But we now know that all this time he was busy concocting a counter-scheme that was not merely steeped in prevarication

---

[1] Wylie, i. 152; iii. 54.

[2]
> Puisque les bergiers divisés,
> Sont ou pourpris alens conquerre,
> Ce qui fu nostre *et plus* par gherra
> Si ne le faisons maintenant
> Jamais n'y serons revenant. Pastoralet, 758.

Cognoissant le pais estre dégarny de gens d'armes et aussi les dissensions de France, Raoulet, 154. Pluscard. (352) thinks that Henry waited for this opportunity quod tirannidis naturae est quam boni ducis.

[3] Petit de Julleville (ii. 376) thinks that Henry IV "avec une habileté infernale *les soudoya toutes les deux*," which is just the opposite of the facts, see Wylie, iv. 35, 64, 69, 81.

[4] Divisa virtus cito dilabitur, St Denys, vi. 48. Cf. A realme stryvyng in itself gooth to desolacioun, Hazlitt, iv. 58.   [5] Rym. ix. 150.

[6] Rym. ix. 151. For a statement that Charles VI offered 450,000 crowns as Catherine's dower, see Strickland, ii. 116.

[7] Pages 158, 405.

and duplicity[1], but charged with downright, hard, official lies.

We have seen[2] that after the Duke of Burgundy fled from Paris before the triumphant Armagnacs in the autumn of 1413, he had had frequent communications with envoys from England, and these negotiations were continued through the medium of his representatives, who came to London during the ensuing winter and the spring of 1414. Their presence in London was certainly prolonged until the middle of June 1414[3], and must therefore have been perfectly well known to the French[4], for the envoys of both parties had openly visited King Henry at Leicester[5] in May, and King Charles' secretary, Gaultier Col, was certainly in London at the same time as the Duke's envoys in the following month[6]. Indeed, when the Flemish deputies were at Péronne at the end of June 1414, they were told that the King of France knew all about the transaction[7]. It is no wonder therefore that it was commonly reported[8] in Paris that the Duke of Burgundy was asking for English help in his distress. The purpose of his embassy[9], as we now know, was to arrange for an alliance with the English king to be cemented by a marriage between Henry and the Duke's fifth daughter Catherine[10], who was still under

---

[1] Called Doppelzüngigkeit, Lenz, 47; "a duplicity not creditable to his memory," Hallam, Europe, 54; une duplicité peu compatible avec les idées généralement reçues sur son caractère ouvert et généreux, Beaucourt, i. 256; Brougham, 96.   [2] Page 152.

[3] Rym. ix. 136. For £644. 12s. 10½d. paid for their expenses from April 19 to June 17, 1414, also 62s. expenses of "le chivaler de Duk de Bourgogne at Leicester for four days in June, 1414," see Rym. ix. 188. For writ (March 16, 1414) to the Chancellor to renew safe-conducts for ambassadors of the Duke of Burgundy till June 24, 1414, see Chancery Warrants, Ser. i. 1364/7.

[4] Schmidt, ii. 248; Daniel (iii. 857) even suggests that it was the knowledge of these counter-negotiations that caused the Duke of York to be so graciously received when he came to Paris with proposals for the hand of the Princess Catherine in the autumn of 1413 (see page 158); though elsewhere (iii. 870) he speaks of them as "des liaisons secrètes," which were only discovered by the French envoys on their visit to Winchester in 1415.   [5] Otterbourne, 275; Wals. ii. 300; do. Hypodig. 450.

[6] viz. June 11, 1414. For safe-conduct for him and John Launart domicellus, see Rym. ix. 139.   [7] Lettenhove, Hist. iii. 86.   [8] Disoit on communement, Juv. 497.

[9] For ambassiat, embassiat, embassatrye, see Lydg. Troy Book, 182, 187, 194, 298; or "sond," ibid. 181, 184, 187.

[10] Called Mademoiselle Katherine de Nevers in October 1400, March, April 1401, Itin. 304, 309, 310, 311; not a daughter of the King of France, as Hardy, Syllabus, 579; Coussemaker, 177; Rapin, iii. 433; Tindal, i. 509, who assumes that it was an arrangement to get the Duke of Burgundy to use his influence to bring about a marriage with the Princess Catherine. Brougham (385) has a long disquisition upon the possibility of Catherine having been mis-described as the Duke's daughter instead of the King's daughter, because "no historian in common vogue makes any specific mention of this offer," etc.

age[1]. At the hollow reconciliation at Chartres on March 9, 1409[2], a marriage had been arranged for her with Philip, the second son of Louis, Duke of Orleans[3]. But this connection was frustrated by a subsequent outbreak of family hatred, and on March 25, 1410[4], she was espoused[5] to Louis, Count of Guise, the eldest son of Louis II, Duke of Anjou, titular King of Naples, Jerusalem and Sicily[6]; but as the boy was then only six years old, it was of course necessary that the little couple should wait for each other for the present, and in order to make certain of the match, it had been agreed that the two children should be brought up together till they were of marriageable age[7]. But when passions were running high after the downfall of the Cabochians, the Duke of Anjou sent Catherine back to her father at Lille[8]. She was met with great ceremony at Beauvais[9], and was at Ghent on Nov. 29, 1413[10], whence she made a public entry into Bruges on Dec. 29[11], accompanied by her brother Philip and his wife, returning later

---

[1] For 7 *fr.* 17*s.* 6*d.* paid by her father in 1408, to his confessor, the Bishop of Arras (Martin Porée), for two ABC books and two books of the Seven Psalms (*sepse-aulmes*) for her and her sister Jehanne, see Prost, Acquisitions, 351.

[2] Wylie, iv. 31; Cartellieri, Beiträge, i. 10–19; cette triste comédie, Batiffol, 181; "shameful and useless," R. L. Stevenson, 174. For paix fourrée, see page 172, note 10; Champion, Vie, 64; Godefroy, ix. 652; cf. médaille fourrée in Littré, s.v. *Fourré.*

[3] Morosini, ii. 164, note, where she is wrongly called the second daughter; Finot, 3; Gachard, 42; Champion, Vie, 64, seems to think the marriage actually took place. See also ibid. 104, where Philip renews his engagement at Auxerre in Aug. 1412, from Arch. Nat. K. 57, no. 26; Cartellieri, Beiträge, i. 16. He really died unmarried, Anselme, i. 207.

[4] Boysset, 387; Wylie, iv. 36, note 4. For previous contract of marriage, Oct. 22, 1407, see Lecoy de la Marche, i. 23. On March 16, 1410, she is going to Gien on the Loire above Orleans for the marriage, Itin. 595; Barante, ii. 344. She actually left Rouvres on March 19, 1410, Bissey, 38. For 10,000 livr. tourn. spent on this account in 1410, see Coville, in Lavisse, Etudes, 412. For receipt for portion of her dower dated April 1, 1410, see Gachard, 30.

[5] Faire le mariage, Itin. 595; not that they were actually married, as Maulde la Clavière, i. 36; Wylie, iv. 36, note 4.

[6] Juv. 512; Mas-Latrie, 1569; Anselme, i. 240; Gachard, 30. For portrait of him, see Montfaucon, iii. 180, Pl. xxvii; Bouchot, Portrait, 64, 128; Couderc, Album, Plates xxxiv, lxviii, lxix. [7] St Denys, iv. 314; D. Sauvage, 225.

[8] i.e. on Nov. 20, 1413, St Denys, v. 160; Juv. 512; J. Meyer, 244; not Nov. 15, as Lecoy de la Marche, i. 23. This had been arranged at the conferences at Pontoise in July 1413, when the young Louis was to marry a daughter of the Duke of Brittany instead, Champion, Doc. 38; do. Vie, 114. He really married Margaret, daughter of Amédée VIII, Duke of Savoy, in 1431, Mas-Latrie, 1539.

[9] Monstr. 302. On Oct. 29, 1413, Thierry Gherbode was sent to Beauvais "querer Mademoiselle Catherine," empowered to receive her jewels from the King of Sicily, Coussemaker, 101, 102, showing that the jewels were handed over to Gherbode at Beauvais on Nov. 15, 1413, and that his journey took place Nov. 1–26, 1413.

[10] Itin. 404, 406, 408, 409 (not Oct. 29, as Coussemaker), showing that she was often there up to May 12, 1414.

[11] Gilliodts van Severen, Inventaire, iv. 259, where 12 silver-gilt scalen are presented to jonevrawin Katelines on that day.

to Ghent, where she remained till May 12, 1414, and it was
here probably that she was seen by the English envoys[1],
who extolled her as strong in the nobility of her birth,
sparkling in the dignity of her form[2] and bright in the honesty
of her manners, though the second of these items must
have been somewhat overdone, for in her own country she
was said to be like an owlet except for the feathers[3], and in
any case she soon ceased to be a factor in the game, for
she died at Ghent soon afterwards[4] of grief and despair.

Yet, notwithstanding his marriage pledge to the Court
of France, King Henry received envoys[5] from the Duke
of Burgundy at Leicester, where proposals were made for
the conclusion of a perpetual alliance between the Duke
and the King of England and for a marriage between the
latter and one of the Duke's daughters[6], either Catherine
or Anne, as should be afterwards determined, and a
document was signed at Leicester on May 23, 1414[7], the
terms of which are so startling that modern writers have
regarded it merely as a "draught of a treaty[8]" or a
"preliminary convention[9]," though there can be no doubt
that it represents a fully signed and completed deed, for
the original is still preserved in the archives at Dijon[10].
According to this the English king was to send 500 men-
of-arms and 2000 archers to help the Duke to conquer the
possessions of the Dukes of Orleans and Bourbon and all

[1] See page 414.
[2] For 6 *fr.* 15*s.* paid to Master Oranque, painter of Malines, pur paindre et faire la
figure de Mademoiselle Katherine de Bourgogne, see Laborde, i. 99 (i.e. between 1413
and 1417). For portrait of Isabel sent to Richard II see Mirot, Isabelle, xix. 73.
[3] For a man punished for describing her and her sister Isabel as vraies chouettes sauf
les plumes, see Maillard de Chambure, 112; Découverte des Corps, 403.
[4] Called June 11, 1414, in J. Meyer, 244. Cf. qui d'annuy et de despit en mourut a
Gand et la fut enterée, Chastellain, v. 2; also Paradin, 572; J. Bucelin, 377; Sismondi,
xii. 436; Brougham, 384 (who says that she died at the age of 32), following Anselme,
i. 240; also Coussemaker, 102, who adds that she was buried in the church of St Pharailde
at Ghent; Beaucourt, i. 15; Hookham, i. 92.
[5] The envoys were the Provost of St Donats at Ghent, Pierre de Vieuxville (*sic*),
Jean Lord of Roubaix and Roland d'Uytkerke, Rym. ix. 188.
[6] See App. B².
[7] Plancher, iii. 409; not May 24, as Barante, iii. 106; nor June 4, as Niethe, 11.
[8] Brougham, 387.
[9] Beaucourt, i. 132; Coville-Lavisse, 365; Cosneau, Connétable, 34.
[10] Gachard, 84, 85; also two MSS. in the Bibliothèque Nationale in Paris, i.e. V. C.
Colbert, 64, p. 529, and Moreau, 802, f. 29; cf. Brougham, 388; Ramsay, i. 184;
Vickers, 12. Called "geheimer Vertrag" in Pauli, v. 91, who (p. 93) sets Brougham
right as to his confusion of dates 1414, 1415, 1416, and the Marquis of Dorset's embassy
to Paris in Feb. 1415. Loserth (Gesch. 549) rightly calls it "ein Schutz- u. Truzbündniss."
Hallam (Europe, 54) thinks that the Duke of Burgundy made no alliance with Henry V
before 1416.

his enemies[1], and the spoil was to be divided between the Duke of Burgundy and King Henry "like brothers and allies," according to the proportion of their respective forces employed. English envoys were to be sent to see Catherine in view of the projected marriage, and on June 4, 1414[2], Henry Lord Scrope of Masham[3], Hugh Mortimer[4], Thomas Chaucer[5], Master Philip Morgan[6], and Doctor John Hovingham[7] were commissioned to act as Henry's proctors in accepting one of the Duke's daughters, either as his spouse for the future or as his wife in the immediate present, and to arrange about a dower and a deposit as earnest money[8]. Besides this they were to conclude a league, confederation and friendship with the Duke and to receive his formal homage as a vassal of the English King[9].

The truce with Flanders which had been prolonged for five years from June 15, 1411[10], had yet two years to run and Scrope and his colleagues were now authorised[11] to arrange for a further prolongation of indefinite length[12]. They left England on June 26, 1414[13], crossed the channel

---

[1] Beaucourt, i. 132.

[2] Rym. ix. 136; not during the Parliament at Leicester, as Pauli, v. 91; Lenz, 46, 47; nor at Lancaster Castle, as Plancher, iii. 409. Called June 5 and 14 in Gachard, 44, 85, or the end of May in Letter Book I, p. xxiii.

[3] On June 20, 1414, Scrope and Mortimer are empowered to issue safe-conducts till Michaelmas, 1414, Rym. ix. 142. Scrope was absent from England from June 25 to Oct. 28, 1414, For. Accts. P. R. O. p. 80; Ramsay, i. 185. He was present at a Council in the Blackfriars, London, in Feb. 1415, Ord. Priv. Co. ii. 145.

[4] His name is decipherable in Chancery Warrants, Ser. I. 1364/12, dated June 8, 1414, but much damaged.   [5] Dict. Nat. Biogr. x. 168.

[6] On June 18, 1414, he had letters of protection as going to Holland on an embassy from the king, see For. Accts. P. R. O. p. 80; Ewald, xliv. 553; Carte, Rolles, ii. 214. For his expenses from June 26 to Oct. 4, 1414, going successively to Duces Burgundie et Holandie, see Exch. Accts. 321/16; Mirot-Déprez, lxi. 26.

[7] See page 91, note 7.

[8] Pro arris (or arrhis) in hâc parte constituendis, Rym. ix. 136. For arrhes, l'erre, as the earnest of a ship (*les overes de la nef*), see Black Book of the Admiralty, i. 117; ii. 455. For arrhes, dots et obligations, see Gamez, 457, 536; cf. arrba et pignus, Clamenges, Ep. p. 137. See also Murray, Dict., s.v. *Arles*.

[9] Dupleix (ii. 706) fancies that the Duke of Burgundy would not submit "aux dures conditions d'une nation orgueilleuse."

[10] Wylie, iv. 25; Lünig, Germ. ii. 2153, 2157, 2161, 2163. For order to proclaim this extension in the city of London, see Letter Book I, pp. xvii, 104 (dated July 27, 1412). For proclamations at Hesdin of the trève marchande between England and Flanders in 1409, 1410, 1411, see Fromentin, 120.

[11] i.e. June 22, 1414; Rym. ix. 142.

[12] For truce with Flanders still pending on March 15, 1415, see Pat. 4 H. V, 4 d, March 13, 1417; Cal. Pat. H. V, ii. 86.

[13] Exch. Accts. 321/13 (in a bag), where Hovingham left London on June 25, 1414 (not 1413, as Mirot-Déprez, lxi. 25, 26), with Master Richard Holme (see p. 150, note 1), with nine men and ten horses, having an allowance of 20s. per day, crossed from Dover

to Calais and journeyed on to Ypres[1], where they were lodged at the Duke's expense till Aug. 9. Here they had an interview with him on July 16; they dined and supped with him personally on July 21 and 22, and as a result, a more detailed and precise engagement was signed on Aug. 7, 1414[2], according to which the Duke not only engaged to offer no opposition to Henry's attempt to seize the crown of France, but would even be ready to fight actively with him against his own sovereign, who was now openly attacking him at Arras. But if we are to estimate the relative sincerity of the diplomacy on both sides, we ought to bear in mind that at that very time the Duke of Burgundy had just solemnly sworn that he had made no compact with any foreigners, or if he ever had, he had now utterly annulled it[3], while at the very same moment King Henry was actually engaged in separate negotiations with the Duke of Orleans[4], who was bent on beating the Duke of Burgundy to his knees, and was despatching envoys to Coblenz to cajole King Sigismund[5] into the belief that he would join him and the French king in thwarting all the plans on which the Duke of Burgundy had set his heart[6]. Further personal interviews were held with the Duke on Sept. 22 and 24 at St Omer, where a supplementary convention was signed on Sept. 29, 1414[7],

to Calais and was back on Aug. 18, 1414. He left London a second time on Sept. 3, 1414, and returned on Oct. 27, 1414. There is some confusion in the dates in the document, which in one place refers to these two journeys of Hovingham as made in comitivâ of Henry le Scrope and other ambassadors in 2 H. V (i.e. 1414), while stating that he received £50 on June 21, *anno primo* (sic), i.e. 1413. For order (undated) from Henry V to the Barons of the Exchequer to pay expenses of Maistre Johan Hovingham, doctour des loys for going lately (jatard aland) on two journeys to Flanders in company with our other ambassadors, see Gilliodts van Severen, Galba, 374, who supposes the date to be 1416.

[1] Page 397, note 3; Gollut, 1002, where the English envoys spend four days "à Hypre."

[2] Beaucourt, i. 133; Coville-Lavisse, 365; Cosneau, Connétable, 34.

[3] St Denys, v. 384.

[4] For safe-conducts issued by him at Péronne on July 7, 8, 1414, for Richard de Œteville du pays d'Angleterre (which looks like Otwell or Atwell, though I cannot identify him), and 15 others from England, see Cagny, 90, note, from Bibl. Nat. Cat. des Titres, Pièces Originales, vol. 2157, pièce 489; also Champollion-Figeac, Louis et Charles, p. 290, who infers this from Rym. ix. 394, which seems to contain nothing on the point. See page 396, note 5.

[5] For letter of Sigismund to Henry, written in July, 1414, see Finke, Acta, i. 228, 373; Wylie, Constance, 14.

[6] Minimé habebit intentum ad que molitur, Finke, Acta, i. 1382.

[7] Beaucourt, i. 134, from Archives de Dijon, Layette, 81, liasse 2, no. 28; called Sept. 30 in Gachard, 45. Cf. Rapin, Acta Regia, ii. 127; Saint Foix, iii. 184. On Sept. 30, 1414, the Duke of Burgundy was at Bruges, Gilliodts van Severen, iv. 320.

and the English envoys were back in London by Oct. 28[1], bringing with them two horses (a sorrel and a white[2]) as presents from the Duchess of Burgundy to King Henry as her prospective son-in-law. On Sept. 1[3] and again on Nov. 16[4] safe-conducts were issued for the Duke of Burgundy's chamberlain, Copin de Viéville[5], who was coming to England to have audience with the king, and this was certainly granted to him more than once during the months of October and November 1414[6].

But from the midst of all this astounding duplicity stands out the cardinal fact in which all motives for the forward policy of Henry V will find their ultimate solution. He knew that he could play off Burgundian against Armagnac and Armagnac against Burgundian, and that when it suited him to enter France he would certainly find there plenty of friends[7], and it is significant that during the week which he devoted to receiving the Armagnac envoys at Winchester, which resulted in the final breach, eye-witnesses report[8] that among the crowds assembled in the city they saw a herald wearing the livery of the Duke of Burgundy. Such was the position when the great English embassy set out for France to press the famous claim for "justice."

---

[1] Page 414, note 3.
[2] These appear as Sorell Burgoyne and Blaunce Burgoyne in J. Waterton's account, 1414–1416, Exch. Accts. 106/24.
[3] Rym. ix. 158.   [4] Rym. ix. 179; Carte, Rolles, ii. 214.
[5] Viefville, as Dep. Keep. Rept. xliv. 554; or La Viefville, in Lettenhove, Hist. iii. 89; Vallet de Viriville, Assassinat, 260, 265, 267; or de Veteri Villâ, St Denys, v. 60, 80, 145, 396, where he acts for the Duke of Burgundy on Oct. 16, 1414, in ratifying the Treaty of Arras. See also Paradin, 566, 595, where he is one of the Governors of the Count of Charolais. He is called le Seigneur de Vièvile in D. Sauvage, 220; "Vyvyle" in Exch. Accts. 406/29; "Viezville" in Add. Chart. 13344; "Monseigneur de le (*sic*) Viesville" in Regnoult, 64; Deseille, 424; le Sire de la Viesville, Coussemaker, 132, 139, where he is called Pierre on Sept. 24, 1406. For a soldier of Calais in comitivâ de Copin de Vivill (? 1417), see Exch. Accts. 187/6; for Sire Jacques de la Viesville in Paris, Oct. 22, 1418, see Félibien, iv. 573. Called Viéville en Artois in Anselme, i. 255, i.e. La Viéville near Albert (Somme), Monstr. iv. 118, who calls him "natifve d'Alemaigne." In Piaget, Cour, 427, he is Lord of Norren (i.e. Norrent-Fontes near Lillers), and esquier tranchant to the Dauphin. For seal of Jean de la Vieuville, May 12, 1412, for service under the Duke of Burgundy, see Demay, ii. 300.
[6] He was in London on Oct. 30, 1414, Devon, 336, which shows £40 paid to him in two separate sums. For £20. 16s. 8d. paid for expenses of the Duke of Burgundy's ambassadors from Nov. 8 to Dec. 1, 1414, see Rym. ix. 189.
[7] Y trouvera foison de ses amis, Cochon, 273.
[8] Mirot, 241, 270.

CHAPTER XXIII

THE FIRST EMBASSY

THE English envoys[1], with Bishops Courtenay and Langley at their head, journeyed with a brilliant retinue of 500 mounted men[2] and reached Paris on Aug. 8, 1414[3], where they were received with the utmost distinction and respect[4]. Sixteen lords and several bishops rode out to meet them at La Chapelle[5] and conducted them to the Palace[6] on the Island, where they were received by the Duke of Berry in the Great Hall overlooking the Seine[7]

[1] For picture of the envoys, six in number, riding on asses, see Monstr. (edit. 1500).

[2] Bien pompeusement habillés et ordonnés, Juv. 497; sumptus maximi, Wals. ii. 300; Hypodig. 452.

[3] Rym. ix. 208–215; Juv. 497; Goodwin, 49; Brougham, 387; Tillet, Guerres, 110 a; not June, as Chastellain, 167, who supposes that Archbishop Chichele was at the head of the mission. Called "August last," i.e. 1414 (not 1413, as Brougham, 379), in Rym. ix. 208 (dated Jan. 12, 1415). In Mirot, Fusoris, 187; Champeaux-Gauchery, 126, Bishop Courtenay is in Paris environ le retour du voyage d'Arras (i.e. Oct. 1, 1414, see page 399) pou avant ou pou après.

[4] Magnificè, honestissimè, dapsiliter, St Denys, vi. 376.

[5] Baye, ii. 190. For capella Sancti Dionysii, see St Denys, iv. 512; Batiffol, Châtelet, lxii. 227.

[6] For regalis palacii, see Ordonnances, x. 229; for the conciergerie, Baye, ii. 191; i.e. the house of the Concierge du Palais, Aubert, Org. 391. For pictures of the Palais showing the Sainte Chapelle, the Tour de l'Horloge and the Grande Salle, see Durrieu, Très riches Heures, Plate VI; Guilhermy, Frontispiece; Rittiez, p. ii; Viollet-le-Duc, Architecture, vii. 8. For account of it (rebuilt 1299–1303), see Aubert, Org. 387.

[7] En la sale dessus Seine en ce Palacz, Baye, ii. 190; Wylie, iii. 20. For description of the Grande Salle with its black and white marble floor, its double-gabled roof and central pillars at which the booksellers and traders had their stalls, proctors their benches, and advocates conferred with their clients, see Delachenal, 112; Duchesne, Antiquités, 137, who pronounced it to be une des plus belles besognes qui soit au monde. See also Viollet-le-Duc, Architecture, viii. 82, 83, quoting Corrozet, Antiquités de Paris, 172, and based upon a drawing in Du Cerceau. It is called the Salle du Palais in G. Metz, 53; Salle St Louis in Batiffol, 165; Sale de Ceans (i.e. of the Parliament), Delachenal, 40, 41; Salles des Pas Perdus, Rittiez, Palais, 71, 89, who refers (p. 92) to a statue of Henry V, placed there among the French kings, the face of which was hacked about by order of Charles VII and was thereby recognised after the fire of 1618. Called "sa représentation" (i.e. his funeral effigy, Hope, Effigies, 37), in Prost, Quelques Documents, 241; Marcou, 11. It formed one of a series of stone figures from Philippe le Bel (d. 1314) downwards and was placed "ez grands sales du Palais royal," Prost, 241. The Hall was destroyed by fire on March 6, 1618, and rebuilt as the present Salle des Pas Perdus in 1622, Rittiez, 321, 323.

and afterwards handsomely lodged in the Hostel de Bourbon[1] at the French king's expense[2]. For the last four months King Charles VI and the Dauphin had been absent from the capital attacking the Duke of Burgundy in the north[3], but the envoys were fêted[4] and entertained at splendid banquets by the Duke of Berry in his newly acquired Hostel de Nesle[5] and presented with abundance of costly gifts[6], and then after several days of these festivities, they made their first official approach on Aug. 16[7] before the Duke of Berry in the Green Chamber[8] of the Palace to submit their preposterous demands[9].

Bishop Courtenay was the spokesman and he took for his text the words of the Gibeonites when they deceived Joshua: "We be come from a far country to make a league with you[10]," but neither the speaker nor his hearers appear to have noted the drift of the immediate context that those who used these words "did work wilily." After developing his theme at some length the bishop next proceeded to state the English king's case, which he had written out and delivered in Latin like his sermon. At the opening he solemnly asked for the hand of the Princess Catherine, subject to the condition that the crown and kingdom of France with all its rights and belongings should be given up to the King of England. But this was obviously a mere formal preface delivered under protest, and knowing, as he afterwards said, that no attention would be paid to this uncivil request[11], he at once "came down to other things[12]"—under protest also—announcing that

---

[1] Mirot, 173, 179, 187. Not in the Hostel du Temple, as Goodwin, 50.

[2] Add. Chart. 67, Sept. 11, 1414, which refers to commissioners for expenses of certain English ambassadors now in France at the king's charge.

[3] Barante, iii. 135.   [4] Grandement festoyez, Bouvier, 428.

[5] He bought it in 1380 and soon afterwards added the Séjour de Nesle. For position of it at the corner of the city wall on the south bank of the river, now occupied by the Hôtel des Monnaies on the Quai Conti, see Berty, 6, 45; Grande Encycl. xxiv. 970; Hoffbauer, ii. 1, 4, 6, Plates I, VI.

[6] Non sine fluxu munerum, St Denys, vi. 376. For 500 francs still due to a changer on this acct. on June 3, 1416, see Mirot, 273.

[7] Baye, ii. 191.   [8] Aubert, Org. 388, 391.

[9] Propositions d'une insolence sans égale, Belleval, 13.

[10] Juv. 497, who identifies the text with Josh. xx, though it would appear to be really Joshua ix. 6; quoted as venimus vobiscum facere pacem *magnam* in Mirot, 150.

[11] Jugeans leur demande incivile, Rept. on Foedera, App. D. 77.

[12] Ad alia conscendimus, Rym. ix. 208; ad alias petitiones sub certis protestationibus descenderunt, Transcr. For. Rec. 135/12.

without prejudice to his larger claim[1], the king of England might perhaps accept something less, that is to say absolute suzerainty and lordship[2] for ever over Normandy[3], Touraine, Anjou, Maine, Brittany, Flanders[4] and all the old Duchy of Aquitaine[5], in short all the portions of the land of France that were specified in the Treaty of Brétigny[6] together with the debateable ground between Gravelines and the Somme. Thereupon ensued various lengthy discussions and proposals on the part of the French[7], who preferred to take the marriage question first and hold everything else in abeyance for the present; but the English would abate nothing of their pretensions and ended by reasserting all the demands of Edward III together with an additional claim to a moiety of the county of Provence[8], with the

[1] Parte jurium suorum satis modicâ, Rym. ix. 786, 787; parte modicâ in respectu totalis et integri juris nostri contentari decrevimus, Add. MS. 24,062, ff. 192 b, 193.

[2] Homagium, superioritas et dominium, Rym. ix. 208; hommage, souveraineté et domaine, Rept. on Foedera, App. D. 77; sibi dari in perpetuum, St Denys, v. 408; à enjouir héritablement pur toujours, Monstr. 359; sans foi, hommage ne ressort (i.e. appeal), Juv. 497, 547; salvo directo dominio, ressorto et superioritate, Plancher, III. cclxxi; resortum et homagium, Rym. ix. 641. For ressort, souveraineté et parrie, see Stephenson, i. 60; Rouquette, 68, 139, 153, 215. For jus superioritatis et ressorti, see Ordonnances, x. 227; superioritate et ressorto salvis, Chabrol, in A. Michel, ii. 327; not "resson," as Mirot, Fusoris, 150.

[3]
> And that is all for Engelond ryght
> To geten agen that scholde it ben his,
> That is al Normandie forsothe y wys
> Be ryght óf eritage he scholde hit have. Harflet, 303.

For statement that France offered the Limousin instead of Normandy, see Haggard, 108.

[4] Rym. ix. 210; Nicolas, Agin. p. 2; Gesta, 215; Rapin, iii. 430; Tindal, i. 508.

[5] For Gallia Aquitania, i.e. Guienne, Gascony, Poitou, Angoulême, Périgord and Agenais, see J. Coke, 79. Redman (31) supposes that Normandy and Aquitaine might go to Catherine as part of her dower; also Halle, 57; Grafton, i. 509; Holins. iii. 546; Trussel, 98.

> That is Gyan and Normandie [Bodl. MS. 69 adds "Gascoyne"]
> He bad delyvere that this schulde be
> All that oughte Kyng Edward. Harflet, 302.

Normandie, Gascoyne and Guyhenne, Claudius, A. viii. 1. For the "noble duchie of Gascoigne and Guen," see Noblesse, 46; "Limoges and Tulle," Stone, xiii. At the time of the Treaty of Brétigny, Guienne comprised the Bordelais, the Landes, le Labourd, le Pays de Soule, and the Châtellenie of Lourdes, and at the beginning of the 15th century some places in Saintonge, Périgord and the Limousin, Longnon, Limites, 497.

[6] Illa videlicet que inclite memorie Edwardo regi proavo suo per tractum pacis finalis inter eum et Johannem, Add. MS. 24,062, f. 193; the hoole landys due to hym within the realme of France, Fabyan, 563.

[7] Post aliqua argumentiva verba, St Denys, v. 376; post varias tractatus, variasque dimissiones successive et variis diebus et temporibus, Rym. ix. 209.

[8] Not Provins, as Kingsford, 116, which was never a county. It is called e.g. vicecomitatum Pruvinensem in 1248, Bourquelot, ii. 204; or Pagus Provinisus (*sic*), or Pruvinensis, do. Notice, 219; the town being Villa Pruvini or Pruvinensis, Bourquelot, ii. 441, though certainly called "Provincia" in Worcester, Itin. 367. Medietatem comitatus Provinciae cum castris et dominiis de Beaufort et Nogent, Rym. ix. 210, 212, from

castles and domains[1] of Beaufort[2] and Nogent[3], as his by
"hereditary right[4]." In the case of the two castles we can
discern some shadow of his meaning, for about 150 years
before, they had belonged to the Duchy of Lancaster through
the marriage[5] of Henry's great-great-great-grandfather,
Edmund Crouchback[6], Earl of Lancaster, with the widow[7]
of a Count of Champagne who was thereafter styled
Earl of Champagne and Brie[8], though merely lieutenant
for his wife[9]; while the name of Beaufort was peculiarly
prominent at the moment from its having been adopted as
a territorial title[10] for the left-hand offspring of Edward III
by Catherine Swinford[11].

Calig. D. v. ff. 135–140, of which only some charred fragments now remain, though there
is no reason to doubt the accuracy of Rymer's copy.

[1] Goodwin, 50; Guthrie, ii. 456; Villaret, xiii. 340; Nicolas, Agincourt, 3; Beaucourt,
i. 258; Ramsay, i. 192; Kingsford, 116; Emmerig, 12, 13; Oman, Pol. Hist. 242;
Radford, 42. Called "dominia" in Gaunt Reg. ii. 349; not "counties" as Rapin, iii.
431, i.e. including the county of Forcalquier; nor "earldoms" as Tindal, i. 508.

[2] i.e. Beaufort near Chavanges (Aube); now Montmorency, the name having been
changed in 1689, Anselme, v. 709. Nothing now remains of the castle except the moat,
though in the 18th century the ruined walls were 40 feet high, Arbois de Jubainville,
Répertoire, 13; Pigeotte, 31. It is described as "entre Troies et Chaalons" in Froissart,
vii. 324, where it passes into the hands of the French in 1369; or "sises en Champagne,"
Tillet, Guerres, 111; Daniel, iii. 868; Rept. on Foedera, App. D. 7; "siz en la
province de Champagne," Pigeotte, 23; or "Beaufort en Champagne," Anselme, iii. 249,
where it is given by the King of France to Charles III, King of Navarre, as part of the
Duchy of Nemours on June 9, 1404; not to be identified with Beaufort-en-Vallée near
Angers, as Dict. Nat. Biogr. iv. 41; Radford, Cardinal, 102; Wylie, iii. 260. For
picture of Beaufort-en-Vallée, see Godard-Faultrier, ii. 342.

[3] i.e. Nogent l'Artaud near Château-Thierry, Arbois de Jubainville, iv. 454.

[4] Jure hereditario pertinentia, Rym. ix. 210.

[5] i.e. circ. 1275, Loftie, Savoy, 21. He died June 5, 1296.

[6] For representations of him, see Roujoux-Mainguet, i. 307; Doyle, ii. 309. For his
supposed deformity, see Loftie, Savoy, 19.

[7] i.e. Blanche of Artois, widow of Henry, Count of Champagne and King of
Navarre, Dugd. i. 779; Bourquelot, i. 258; Pigeotte, 10; Loftie, Savoy, 21; Armitage
Smith, 196; not that the castles were in Artois, as Radford, pp. 1, 42.

[8] Doyle, ii. 309; Comp. Peer. v. 5.

[9] Bourquelot, Notice, 268; do. Provins, i. 258; Tout, Pol. Hist. 144, 146.

[10] Armitage Smith, 198, who shows that there is no foundation for the supposition
that her children were born in the castle, though this belief is not yet given up by
Pigeotte, 16.

[11] For representation of her in the tower built by her son, Cardinal Beaufort, at
St Cross' Hospital at Winchester, see Milner, ii. 146. Her husband's name was Hugh,
Wylie, iii. 258, note 13, though called "Otto" in Pigeotte, 16; or "Ottes" in Purey-
Cust, i. 400. He fell fighting in Aquitaine in 1372, Radford, p. 1. For legitimation of
her marriage by Pope Boniface IX on Sept. 1, 1396, see Armitage Smith, 392; Papal
Letters, iv. 545, where she is styled "an unmarried woman," "damsel, of the diocese of
Lincoln," and it is stated that Edward III had been godfather to her daughter by
another husband. For a horse valued at £3. 6s. 8d. given to her by the people of
Leicester in 1379, see Bateson, II. pp. xxxii, 171. For four casks of wine granted to her
on Nov. 9, 1399, see Cal. Pat. H. IV, i. 218, April 12, 1403, where she is "*late* wife of
the King's father." For account of her, see Wylie, iii. 258; Armitage Smith, 462, who
refers (p. 392) to the "offensive terms" employed in reference to her in the "Scandalous
Chronicle." Cf. "Unde vocabantur (*sic*) Bowfurthes et Faerborne" in Percy MS. 78

As to the moiety of the county of Provence the claim can be traced back to Eleanor[1], second daughter of Raymond Berengar, Count of Provence[2], who became the wife of Henry's great-great-great-great-grandfather Henry III. It was believed that Raymond had died intestate[3], and that each of his four[4] daughters claimed a share of his estate. What is certain is that Louis IX, King of France, who was married to Margaret, the eldest of the daughters, granted the whole county to his brother Charles of Anjou, titular King of Sicily[5], who was married to Beatrice, the youngest of the four, and whose descendants still held it *de facto* as Counts of Provence. It is equally certain, however, that in 1286 Eleanor left her supposed portion[6] to her grandsons Thomas and Henry, the sons of Edmund Crouchback, Earl of Lancaster, and failing their male issue, to the reigning king of England. When Thomas was beheaded for treason in 1322, King Edward II claimed the county of Provence, but found it in the possession of Robert, King of Naples[7], and was altogether powerless to establish the claim. Twelve years later, Edward III confirmed[8] the pretensions of Henry, Earl of Lancaster, but it remained, as it always had been, nothing but a paper possession. Still the claim did not cease to be maintained, and when John Hawkwood took his mercenaries into Provence in 1388, he went with the sanction of Richard II, who appointed him his lieutenant under the pretence that the kings of England were the immediate lords of the county of Provence[9]. But the boundaries of Queen Eleanor's

---

at Alnwick, see Armitage Smith, 467, who supposes that this was "by the jesting wits of Richard II's court" (p. 391); Radford, 2.

[1] i.e. Henry III mar. in 1236 Eleanor, daughter of Raymond Berengar, Lingard, iii. 239; Cassell, i. 525; Tout, 163; do. Pol. Hist. 54. She died at Amesbury, June 25, 1291, Grande Encycl. xv. 806. Not Eleanor of Aquitaine, the wife of Henry II, as Strickland, ii. 116.

[2] Mas-Latrie, 1666.   [3] Ab intestato, ut refertur, Rym. iii. 995.

[4] Called five in Strickland, i. 357.

[5] i.e. in 1246, Anselme, i. 396, iii. 1; Lodge, 24, 47; which "removed Provence from the sphere of English influence," Tout, Pol. Hist. 64. The grant was confirmed by the Emperor Rupert of Hapsburg on March 28, 1280, Leibnitz, i. 20. For Beatrice's will dated June 30, 1266, in which she left the counties of Provence and Forcalquier to her son, Charles II of Anjou, see Anselme, i. 396, quoting d'Achery, Spicileg. vi. 422.

[6] Portionem terrae seu comitatus Provinciae, Rym. iv. 649; or comitatuum Provinciae et Forcalquerii, Rym. iii. 999; iv. 916; v. 148; vii. 570.

[7] Rym. iii. 995, Feb. 12, 1323. He was the grandson of Charles of Anjou, King of Sicily, Lodge, 26, 542.

[8] Rym. iv. 649, June 16, 1335.   [9] Rym. vii. 570, March 4, 1388.

"moiety" had never really been defined; the lands in question had never as a fact been occupied by the English, and Henry V's claim never really materialised as the negotiations proceeded, though the mention of it at this stage is significant as a forecast of his subsequent ambitious policy of hemming in his adversary on every side and securing a foothold for himself on the shores of the Mediterranean. In any case the English envoys in Paris now held that it would be premature to discuss the marriage question seriously until these larger issues, including the payment of 1,600,000 crowns still due on account of King John's ransom[1], were disposed of. But in the hope that better prospects might arise, they suggested that when the proposal did take shape the dower to be settled with the Princess Catherine should not be less than 2,000,000 crowns[2].

All these demands were handed in in writing, and the Duke of Berry straightway gave his reply to the effect that for the sake of peace the French king was willing to give up Agen[3] (with the two neighbouring towns of Condom[4] and Lectoure), Auch, Périgueux[5], Sarlat, Oloron, Lescar[6] (near Pau), Tarbes (in Bigorre), Saintes and the district of Saintonge south of the Charente[7], Cahors and the district

---

[1] Page 409.

[2] Church, 54, puts the total amount including the ransom at 3,200,000 crowns, which he calculates at "more than £1,000,000 in the currency of the time," but this is far too high, the value of the crown being 3s. 4d. (page 407, note 9), so that the amount would be a little over half-a-million.

[3] For special exemptions from taxation granted to Agen, Condom and Villeneuve, see Ordonnances, x. 226. Cf. Agen quae est de obedientiâ ffranciae, Exch. Accts. 187/12, i.e. between March 27, 1418, and Aug. 14, 1419. For extent of the seneschaussée of Agen, with list of 29 parishes, see Bellecombe, pp. ii, v, 50, 112-127, 160-185. For map of it, see Tholin, 154. For account of the diocese of Agen with details of archdeaconries and parishes, see Bellecombe, 93-100. For account of the city of Agen, see Desrues, 300, with plan and pictures in Joanne, i. 9, 10. For the fortifications, see Ducom, 203, who calls it (pp. viii, ix) cité indépendante et commune entièrement autonome. In Tholin, Ville, p. vi, it is la plus grande ville de Guyenne après Bordeaux. For view of it in 1648 with the cathedral of St Etienne, see Lauzun, i. Frontispiece; with plan before 1789, ibid. ii. Frontispiece. For picture of the cathedral, see A. Loth, p. 12. Cf. delectabilis, spaciosa, pluribus et diversis edeficiis constructa pluriumque personarum quasi innumerabilium receptiva, Bulletin Hist. du Comité des Travaux historiques (1899), p. 429. For plans of the castle of Bonaguil near Agen, see Viollet-le-Duc, Architect. iii. 165-167.

[4] Not Condoure, as Guthrie, ii. 456.   [5] Wylie, ii. 316.

[6] Not Lestarensem et Olerensem, as Rym. ix. 211; nor "Lescaire," as Goodwin, 51; nor "Escaire," as Rapin, iii. 431; nor "Escaire," as Rapin, iii. 431; Tindal, i. 508.

[7] Not "the river de la Charance," as Goodwin, 51; Guthrie, ii. 456; nor "le pays qui est entre la Tarantte pardevers Gascogne," as Normandie, 167, where it is represented that the English held out for all the country south of the Loire, and that they departed without peace or argument; cf. Nagerel, 166.

of Le Quercy as far as the Aveyron[1], Angoulême and Rouergue[2] with the towns of Rodez and Vabres. In other words they were willing to restore the old limits of Aquitaine[3] from the Charente to the Pyrenees, just as the rebel lords had promised to do in 1412[4]. As Provence did not come within the French king's domain[5], the claim to any part of it must be arranged with the Duke of Anjou[6] as Count of Provence, and the French must be regarded as neutral in the quarrel[7]. As to the unpaid ransom money the English would do well to wait a little longer as the French king was at the present time greatly extending his territory and dominions[8]; while in the matter of the dower the present was scarcely the occasion for considering it[9], though it was hinted that he might even go as high as 600,000 crowns, which would be more than was usually given in similar cases[10].

Such amazing docility[11] on the part of a great and

[1] Called "Veron" in Rept. on Foedera, App. D. 77.

[2] Not "Rovergne" as Goodwin, 51; nor "Rouvergne" as Guthrie, ii. 456. For evacuation of Rouergue by the English in 1370, see Rouquette, 233.

[3] Page 409; Green, 261; Norgate, i. 454, 463; Wylie, iii. 71. For map showing the concessions, see Ramsay, i. 196. The whole is summed up as "aliquas civitates comitatus et dominia" in St Denys, v. 376; Goodwin, 51; called "Bayonne (!)" and Angoulême in Towle, 285. For the Charente fixed as the boundary of Aquitaine in 1259, see C. R. L. Fletcher, 191. When Aquitaine was granted to the Black Prince in 1362 it included six dioceses and 14 seneschalcies, Rouquette, 61. It was otherwise known as Aidaigne or Daigne, a word represented by the later name "Guienne," see Grande Encycl. xix. 641. In 1452 the Duchy of Guienne includes Saintonge, Angoulême, Périgord, La Marche, Limousin, Cressy (i.e. Le Quercy), Agenais, Rouergue, Armagnac, Béarn and all the mountains to Aragon and Navarre, Bouvier, Descript. 41.

[4] Wylie, iv. 69.

[5] Terrae Provinciae non sunt de dominio domini nostri, Rym. ix. 211. It was not united with France till 1486. In 1452 the boundary between France and the Empire was given as the Rhone, from Aigues-Mortes to Lyons, thence following the Saône to Lorraine, thence down the Meuse and the Scheldt, Bouvier, Descript. 31, 32, 38, 45, 47.

[6] Provence had come *de facto* to Louis I, Duke of Anjou (who died Sept. 25, 1384, Mas-Latrie, 1539, 1666; not 1385 as Lodge, 154), in 1384 (Anselme, i. 228; Bouchot, Portrait, 64; not 1378, as Hallam, 235), on his adoption by Queen Joan I of Naples, who died May 22, 1382, Mas-Latrie, 1711; Grande Encycl. xxi. 102; Morosini, i. 210. He was a brother (not son, as Wylie, iv. 373) of Charles V, King of France, and the father of Louis II (d. 1417), see p. 412. For tables of succession of Anjou, Sicily and Hungary, see Lodge, 542, 543.

[7] Nec per ipsum (i.e. the French king) parti Angliae occupatae neque impeditae, Rym. ix. 211.

[8] Valde extendit in terris, dominiis et nobilitatibus, Rym. ix. 211 (i.e. at the expense of the Duke of Burgundy).

[9] On ne pouvait entendre a cette matière pour le présent, Bouvier, 428. Gaguin represents that the French king navoit loysir a cest chose, Mer des Chroniques, 140; Rosières, 430. Serres, i. 958 (281), thinks that the proposal was made by Henry *after* he had landed at Harfleur.

[10] Lingard, iii. 239; Tyler, ii. 86.

[11] Called "terms liberal beyond measure," Oman, Pol. Hist. 242; "too preposterous to be taken seriously as an overture of peace," Vickers, 13.

high-spirited nation can only be explained by the fact that the Armagnacs, who were then the dominant power in France, had already played off these very offers on England before[1]; that the English king actually held their hostages in his hand, and that they feared to lose their hold on their own country if the tide should again turn in favour of the Duke of Burgundy. But above all it is clear that the demand for the crown of France was treated on both sides as a mere diplomatic opening, not meant to be taken seriously, while the French Court regarded the marriage question as the main, if not the only, purpose of the embassy[2], through which they would be able permanently to upset the Burgundian schemes. At any rate the English demands were not treated with the derision that might have been expected; the envoys received costly presents of gold vessels and tapestry from the Duke of Berry's priceless stores[3], and made their way back to England promising that they would return shortly to notify further progress.

Bishop Courtenay and the Earl of Salisbury departed somewhat before the rest. They crossed from Harfleur[4] to Portsmouth, but I can find no confirmation for the story that was afterwards current, to the effect that they seized the opportunity to spy out the secrets of Harfleur and to take such notes of its resources as decided King Henry to make it his first point of attack[5]. Arrived in England they had an interview with the king at Sheen, bringing with them some jewels that they had bought for him in

---

[1] Wylie, iv. 64; Letter Book I, pp. xvii, 101; Goodwin, 61.

[2] Baye, ii. 190.

[3] For a gold ring with an emerald fly given to the King of England by the Duke of Berry, also another ring with a bear carved in serpentine stone, see Guiffrey, i. 123, 160. The latter had been previously given to the Duke of Berry by the King of Navarre on Dec. 16, 1405. It is uncertain whether these presents were made to Henry IV or Henry V. The former had been bought by the Duke of Berry at Mehun-sur-Yèvre on Feb. 13, 1403.

[4] Bouvier, 428; Gilles, ii. 61; not Honfleur, as Choisy, 315, from MSS. de Rousseau, Reg. 59.

[5] Gaguin, Mer des Chroniques, 140; Mazas, Vies, v. 576, who makes them cross that way seven or eight times, when des officiers de leur suite levèrent le plan de la baie des fortifications et de l'intérieur; Belleval, 45, who thinks that this was une odieuse perfidie *si ce détail est fondé*; Tillet, Guerres, 111 a, thinks that ceste ambassade servoit d'amusement et d'espie; Carte, ii. 679, that the king ordered them to do so; also Morlent, Arrondissement, ii. 25, who calls them the Duke of York, the Archbishop of Winchester (*sic*), the Lord of Cornwall and the Earl of Dorset.

Paris[1]. The rest of the party returned with the horses and harness to Southampton, reaching London by Oct. 3, 1414[2], and before the English representatives left for Constance soon after that date, it had become a matter of common knowledge that the king had certainly "demanded his rights" in France[3].

It is noteworthy in connection with this embassy to Paris that a well-informed French contemporary writer expressly says that the English envoys were "very pleased with the good cheer they had received[4]." Yet no sooner had they returned to England than a rumour[5] was in circulation that the Dauphin had sent an "ungoodly answer[6]" in the form of a tun[7] of tennis-balls to Henry, telling him to spend his time with these like a good lad and not presume to start a quarrel with so noble a nation[8]. To this it was said that King Henry had replied by letter that he would soon bandy[9] him some London-made

---

[1] For Bishop Courtenay's purchases in Paris, see Mirot, Fusoris, 147. One bookseller asked him six crowns for a copy of Boece, but he would only give four, so no sale was effected, ibid. 187; but he bought some romances, including a *Tristan*, for which he paid 157 crowns, "les fais d'un nommé Froissart," and an *Ovid* for 80 crowns, a copy of Nicolas de Lira for 80 frs., a small Bible for 12 crowns and a copy of the Book of Job for one crown, ibid. 190. He also looked at "un livre appelé Mappemonde," ibid. 194.

[2] Rym. ix. 189 (Dec. 10, 1414) shows £30 paid for passage in two ships to Portsmouth and £36. 6s. 8d. to Southampton, with an additional £4. 6s. 8d. on account of five men and six horses that were driven out of their course by a storm and crossed from Calais to Dover. Called 12 horses in Exch. Accts. 321/26, where they sail from Calais in a coggeship de Sketham (i.e. Schiedam). This document gives the account of Bishop Courtenay and the Earl of Salisbury from Harfleur to Southampton, in ships belonging to Gouda, Winchelsea and Dover, including hire of a boat (*navicula*) to take them on board at Harfleur; see p. 406, note 9.

[3] The English representatives at the Council told Sigismund so on their arrival at Constance, Jan. 21, 1415, and he wrote to Henry urging peace and offering mediation, Finke, Acta, i. 388–391.

[4] Bien contents de la chère qu'on leur faisoit, Juv. 497.

[5] "Fertur," Capgr. de Illustr. 114.

[6] Claud. A. viii; Emmerig, 15.

[7] A tonne of tenys ballys, Harflet, 302; a tonne full of Tenyse ballis, Caxton, 225; First Life, 25; "a Tunne of Paris tennis balles," Drayton, Battaile, 20; called a "barrel" in Holins. iii. 545; "a pipe" in Foxe, iii. 405; a "chest," Biondi, 111; a "box," Hume, ii. 354; a "basket," C. R. L. Fletcher, 319; *vasa plena pilis*, Leyden, 342; refertum pilis manualibus *dolium*, Croyland, 510; a cask or tun being the usual way of packing stuff of every kind, Wylie, iv. 380; e.g. 2 tonnel de lancees cum capitibus, Add. MS. 24,513, f. 2; 2 barilles de bosc ferres 5s., St Germain, 447; 1 tonel plain de caudestreppes (1365), La Fons-Mélicocq, Artillerie, p. 5; une queue pleine de chausse-trappes, Bourgeois, 633; cf. pipis fulle of arowes, Brut, ii. 382; les tonneaux ou pippes, Lhomel, Edits, 19. See pp. 136, 216. Mazas (Vies, v. 556) makes him send not only balls but racquets (also Drayton, quoted in Emmerig, 19) and nets, adding by way of gloss that "on savait que Lancastre aimait beaucoup de jeu de paume."

[8] For a similar story of Darius sending toys to Alexander, see Child, iii. 323; Emmerig, 43; do. Dariusbrief, 362.

[9] Speed, 786.

balls[1] that would rip the roof off his hall[2] and batter his towers and cities to the ground.

If this famous *mot* is to be submitted to serious examination, it must at the outset be remembered that, apart from the clear evidence that the English envoys were received in Paris with an exuberance of friendliness, such a flagrant affront must have at once put a stop to all further intercourse[3], whereas as a matter of fact they were really regarded by the French as visitors who had come with friendly proposals for the hand of their king's daughter and their progress was a round of pre-nuptial festivities rather than a defiant prelude to a bloody and disastrous war. Moreover the Dauphin, who is said to have given to the envoys the exasperating message, was about 150 miles from Paris when they arrived and never saw them personally at all. And though according to all mediaeval sentiment so deadly a public insult could only have been answered by a furious outburst of international rage, yet for months afterwards diplomatic communications between the two capitals were continued without interruption, as though nothing at all untoward had happened. It should be added that the French chroniclers know nothing whatever of the incident[4], but represent that King Henry did not decide on his attack till March 1415[5], after finding that he was unable to get his way about the marriage because of the refusal of his extortionate demands[6].

That a story based on such questionable foundations

---

[1] Pilas Londoniarun, Elmham, Lib. Metr. 101; Kabel, 10.
    Some hard tennys balles I have hither brought
    Of marble and yren made full rounde.   Harflet (Bodl.), 72.
[2] Queis sua tecta terat, Elmham, Lib. Metr. 101.
    Swyche tenys ballys I schal hym sende
    As schalle tere the roof all of hys all.   Harflet, 303.
do. Bodl. 70; Nicolas, 12; Emmerig, 14; Kabel, 6; Durham, 42.
    They shall youre wall have to ground,
or   Bet youre walles oute the ground.   Harflet, 309.
[3] This reasoning induced Nicolas (p. 12) to doubt the story, though he was impressed with finding it mentioned in Claudius A. viii, which he considered to have been "apparently written about the time" (pp. 10, 43). So also Tyler, ii. 136; called "a contemporary chronicler," Adams, i. 212; or "almost a contemporary," Lethaby, 207; Flete, 3; "a writer of the following generation," Kingsford, 109; i.e. "the Brut," do. pp. ix, xxix; "a form of the Brut," Dict. Nat. Biogr. xxvi. 55. It is really only an extract from the Brut continued to 1461, Brie, 110; Emmerig, 29-37.
[4] Emmerig (25) considers this to be the most important ground for rejecting the story.
[5] Monstr. 362.
[6] Puisc'on m'a m'amie escondit, Pastoralet, 757; Monstr. 359.

should have been rejected by many critical historians[1] is
in no way surprising, yet it is certain that it was soon
afloat in England and served the purpose of inflaming
passions and widening the breach. Yet none have been
able accurately to locate the particulars. Otterbourne, the
best authority for the story, said that the balls were sent to
Henry when he was at Kenilworth[2] before the meeting of
the Leicester Parliament, but the difficulty of harmonising
details is so great that modern writers who accept the story
differ widely when they endeavour to assign to it a suitable
date. Some for instance date it at the king's accession[3],
while others postpone it till two and a half years later when
he was just about to start for his first invasion of Normandy[4];
but most are agreed that it should be connected with Bishop
Courtenay's mission in the autumn of 1414[5], though whether
before it[6], or in consequence of it, is left an unsettled question.
What is certain is—that King Henry's contemporaries
believed that he had been made a laughing-stock[7] through
the rejection of his pretensions by the French and that
he himself afterwards officially repeated that charge[8], though
the ground for it can alone be based upon the open breach
with the French envoys at Winchester in the summer of
1415. Henceforward the English were convinced that the
French had from the first delayed their envoys with scornful
jibes and biting sneers[9] until their king, seeing that all

---

[1] See App. C[2].
[2] i.e. in Lent 1414 (page 315); see Otterbourne, 274 (where the Dauphin is called
Charles); Brut, ii. 552; Redman, 24; Holinshed, iii. 545; Stow, 345; Emmerig, 19, 41;
do. Dariusbrief, 362. Kingsford in Dict. Nat. Biogr. xxvi. 47 thinks that "the occasion
is uncertain," though inclining to Kenilworth in Feb. 1414, which he adopts definitely in
his Henry V, p. 113; or as "a probable enough date" in First Life, xliii; also
Vickers, 14.
[3] George, 81.
[4] Cassell, i. 526; i.e. after the receipt of his letter to the King of France, written
at Southampton on July 28, 1415.
[5] As Brut, ii. 374; First Life, 25.
[6] As Wade, 80, who thinks the Dauphin sent the balls on July 10, 1414.
[7]   Protrahitur truffis legatis tempus inane
                 Ridiculum praebent in regione duces.
                                   Elmham, Lib. Metr. 103.
Quasi derisi, Usk, 125, 306; turphis (i.e. trufis) et irrisionibus, Capgr. De Illustr. 114;
Tit. Liv. 6; Vita, 30; cachinnos eorum temporare et in derisores animadvertere, Wals. ii.
302; Hypodig. 452; probroso exennio, Croyl. 500; after many tretis and nothing that
they proposed was according to reson, Capgr. Chron. 308; Peter Chron. 487;
dysdeynously answered, Fabyan, 563.
[8] e.g. in his letter to the Duke of Lorraine in 1419, in which he refers to eorum
frequens irrisio, Add. MS. 24,062, f. 192.
[9] Mordaces irrisiones, Vita, 27.

hope of peace was gone[1] except by causing immense
damage to his crown and the loss of some of the noblest
portions of his inheritance[2], vowed that he would show
them what fools they were to wake a sleeping dog[3] and
forthwith resolved to commit his cause to God and all
the saints and fight for his right with the help of Jesus
Christ[4].

In such a heated atmosphere sprang up, as I believe,
the story that the Dauphin sent him not only some tennis-
balls to play with as long as he was gentle and small[5], but
some soft pillows to sleep on till he grew up to be a man[6],
to which he is said to have answered that, if the French
slept too long, he would knock at their door some morning
to wake them up earlier than they liked and turn their
mock into moan[7].   This latter side of the story does not
seem to have taken any permanent hold, but after the
victory at Agincourt the "bitter mock[8]" got well established
as an item in every good Englishman's patriotic creed and
the ballads ran riot with raillery about how he taught the
Frenchmen to play at ball[9] and how his big guns tossed
the balls[10] and played a set on the green[11] at Harfleur[12],

---

[1] Spe pacis omnino sopitâ, Wals. ii. 300; Hypodig. 450.
[2] Gesta, 8; Chron. Giles, 9.   [3] Wals. ii. 302; Hypodig. 452.
[4] Chron. Rich. II—H. VI, 39.   [5] Harflet, 302.
[6] Quousque in virile robur creverit in futuro, Strecche, 266 b, who dates the incident
in 1414 (2 H. V).   His account is of special interest as he wrote at Kenilworth, whither
the balls are supposed to have been sent, though he does not say so.   See also Emmerig,
Dariusbrief, 400; Kingsford, First Life, xliii.
[7] Jocum perdent in eventu et pro ludo luctum habebunt, Strecche, 266 b.   Not
lucrabuntur, as Emmerig, Dariusbrief, 400.
[8] Henry V, 2. 2. 122.   Your mock shall turn you to shame, Halliwell, Letters, i. 97;
cf. murionit him with mokkes, J. H. Millar, 29; Murray, Dict. and Jamieson, s.v.
Murgeon.   In Melusine, 79, "the mocke"="gaber" in Arras, 90; cf. Godefroy, s.v.
Gabet.   Called the "scornfull ansuare" in Brut, ii. 374, 552.
[9]   And send him ballis him with to play
               And tazt Frenchmen to play at the ball.
Emmerig, Dariusbrief, 397, from J. Awdelay the blind Canon of Haughmond, *De Rege
nostro Henrico Sexto*, written in 1426, see J. O. Halliwell, Percy Soc. XIV. p. viii;
Emmerig, Dariusbrief, 398, who quotes Speed, 772 (from Caxton); Rastell, 247.
[10]   At Harflete a sege he laid anon
               And cast a ball unto the towne.
               Awdelay, in Emmerig, Dariusbrief, 399.
And we will tosse him balles of brass and yren, Famous Victories, 30, 34, 37, 41; toss as
many balls of yron that the best racket he had should not be able to resist or return,
Grafton, i. 509.
[11]   My gonnes shall lyn upon this grene
               For they shall play with Harflete
               A game at tynes (i.e. tennis) as I wene. Harflet, 308.
Cf. quasi ludendo ut vulgo dicitur ad Tenisias, Croyland, 500.
[12] And there he plaied at tenys with his hard gunne-stoures, and they that were within
the towne when they should play, her song was welle-away and allas that ever any such

singing out: "15 before" and "30's mine[1]," with plenty
more as to racquets[2], courts[3], chaces[4], sets[5], hazards, bandies[6],
rebounds[7], and all the other terminology of the palm-play[8].
Then imaginary letters were concocted, in which the English
king was made to thank the French king for the present
he had sent him which was just what he wanted for war.
He was quite master of the game and he would bring his
sow over with him to werry and overturn and make plain
field; the boar would show the beasts the way to France,
and by the beasts he meant the white lion of Ireland
(possibly the Earl of March), the black bull with the gilt
horns, the wolf, the dragon, the white greyhound and many
more, and then he would blow his horn and let loose[9] his
band and the beasts would hunt through every corner of
France.   And so the story rolled along till in the spacious
days, 150 years later, the poets worked it up with their
"painful quills" to kindle the patriotism of those "declining

tenys ballis were made, Claudius A. viii. f. 23 in Nicolas, 213; Emmerig, 34; Brut, ii.
376; cf. women cryed alas that they were bore, Harflet, 310.   For "weylaway," see
Lydg. Troy Book, 237, 256, 266, 268, 459; Laud Troy Book, 50, 188, 534; "wallyway,"
Dep. Keep. 43rd Rept. 582; well-y-wey, Pol. Relig. Po. 125; alas and welaway, Pol.
Songs, i. 277; Hazlitt, iv. 48; Wylie, iii. 226, note 10.
    [1] Cf. j'ay quarante cinq sur bon gage, Chalvet, 347; Champollion-Figeac, Poésies,
187.
    [2] But canstow playen raket to and fro, Chaucer, Troilus and Cres. iv. 460; joueurs de
paulme et de rachas (raquette), Deschamps, viii. 93; en la main une raquette, Cuissard,
46, quoting Pantagruel in Rabelais.
    [3] Supposed to be derived from courte paume, J. Marshall, 4.
    [4] Of the tennis to winne or lose a chace, Gower, in Urry, Chaucer, 542.   As if
Fortune had made chases inow of the one side of that bloody Tenis Court went to the
other side of the line, Sidney, Arcadia, Bk III. ch. 8, p. 269; chases marked, hazards
invented, J. Marshall, 56.
    [5]   When we have matched our rackets to these balls
                    We will in France by God's grace play a set
                    Shall strike his father's crown into the hazard.
                                                    Henry V, i. 2. 261.
Emmerig, 18; cf. Daniel, Trinarch. iv. 119.
    [6] When over line with Bandies I shall drive, Drayton, Batt. 20; Emmerig, 19.
    [7] Racketts sufficient to bandy the rebound, Speed, 772.
    [8] Of pamplys schall ye here, Harflet, 309, 310.   Cf. "palmplay" or "palmball,"
jeu de paume, Strutt, quoted in J. Marshall, v. 55; "la paulme," Chartier, 617; for jeu
de paume at Orleans, see Cuissard, 246; also at Gaillon, built 1509, Deville, p. lxxxiv.
For joueurs de paume in the courtyard, see Duclaux, 277; or in the moat, Jusserand,
Roman, 59 [77].
    [9] Reading "reles" (i.e. release) for "relef" in Halliwell, Letters, i. 77, from
Lansdowne MS. 762, a common place buuk of the time of Henry VIII, though the
opening pages, viz. to p. 24, seem to be earlier.   These are written on parchment, on the
blank pages of which somebody has been practising the old script.   The rest of the
leaves are paper, fol. 26, Art. 3 containing the length measurement of England dated
4 H. V (i.e. 1416).   Towle (288) takes the above "racy epistle" quite seriously and
supposes that Charles VI had sent Henry V "a present of some animals"; Kingsford,
First Life, xlv, thinks that the letter "may well be an invention."

times[1]," the school boys sucked it in with their official state-prescribed hexameters[2], and the public looked for it as one of the stock situations of the transpontine stage[3], its endless popularity breaking out in doggerel folk-songs in the Midlands and the North well into Hanoverian times[4].

[1] I. Vaughan, in Drayton, Battaile. Cf. "our sinful times," ibid. p. 7.

[2] Ocland, H. ii; called "our English Poet" in Holinsh. iii. 546. See Queen Elizabeth's writ prefixed to the edition of 1582 of *Praelia Anglorum*, requiring the book to be used in all grammar schools, though the author eventually came to poverty in spite of this royal preference.

[3] Harflet (Bodl.), 70; Caxton, 225; Famous Vict. 29.

[4] For the ballad beginning: "A Council brave our King did hold," see R. H. Evans, ii. 351; Hales and Furnivall, ii. 166–173; Emmerig, 15; Kabel, 7. For the ballad: "As our king lay musing on his bed," see Nicolas, App. 78, 81; Tyler, ii. 197; Drayton, Battaile (Garnett), 118; R. Bell, 151; Hales and Furnivall, ii. 598; Child, iii. 321; Jewitt, Ballads, 4–6; Emmerig, 16; Roxburgh Ballads, iii. 358, in Brit. Mus., where it is "printed and sold in Aldermary Churchyard, Bow Lane, London," but bears no date, though the two soldiers that appear on it have "G. R." on their uniform. On the title-page to the volume (dated 1774) in which it appears it is supposed to have been written between 1660 and 1700, though Michelet (vi. 50) regards it as contemporary with the battle. In Tyler, ii. 197, it is called "that ancient and, as it is believed, contemporary ballad."

CHAPTER XXIV

THE SECOND EMBASSY

But in spite of the story of the tennis-balls there was absolutely no break in the friendly negotiations carried on between the Courts of Westminster and Paris. Within a very short time after the return of Bishop Courtenay and his colleagues two messengers[1] in succession arrived in London bringing letters from the French king containing a request that negotiations might be resumed, and on Oct. 18, 1414[2], John Prophet was authorised to act as King Henry's proxy in the marriage question, who on the next day gave an undertaking in London that his master would wait till Candlemas next (i.e. Feb. 1, 1415) before arranging to marry anyone else except Catherine, the French king's daughter. This promise was confirmed by Henry himself in the Palace at Westminster on Dec. 4, 1414[3], and on the following day another weighty embassy was appointed to cross to France and negotiate for a final peace.

But in the meantime another Parliament had been summoned to meet at Westminster and hear the king's latest views on the subject of his claim to the crown of France. The writs were issued on Sept. 26, 1414[4], and the king met the assembled members in the Painted

---

[1] viz. Master Jean André and Dorset herald, Rym. ix. 183. Called Maistre Jehan Andry, or Andrée, Mirot, 176. For his deposition in the Fusoris case, Feb. 25, 1416, see ibid. 218, where he is a councillor in the court of Parliament. For £4. 10s. 0d. expenses in England of one knight of France and one secretary from Oct. 7 to Nov. 6, 1414, see Exch. Accts. 406/26, 29.
[2] Rym. ix. 166.   [3] Rym. ix. 182; Dep. Keep. Rept. xliv. 557.
[4] Dugd. Summons, 537; Cotton, Abridg. 537; Letter Book I, pp. xxiii, 129. Not Sept. 17 as Church, 54, proving that this was not merely an adjournment of the Parliament of Leicester as supposed by Holinsh. iii. 547; Goodwin, 46; Tyler, ii. 23; Kail, xix.

Chamber[1] of the Palace on the opening day, Monday, Nov. 19, 1414[2]. The names of the lords present are identical with those that had met at Leicester in the previous spring[3], except that writs were now issued to the King's younger brothers, the newly-created Dukes of Bedford and Gloucester, and his uncle, the Earl of Dorset, while Richard of York received his first and only summons by virtue of his new title as Earl of Cambridge[4]. The name of one of the judges, John Colpeper, now drops out. He had died about July 1414[5] and was buried at West Peckham near Tunbridge in Kent, where he had previously given lands to the knights of St John[6].

The returns for the Commons show 74 representatives for the 37 counties and 174 for 89 cities and boroughs, making a total of 248. At the opening Bishop Beaufort as Chancellor addressed the assemblage from the text: "While we have time let us do good[7]," pointing out that everything had its proper time. The trees had their times for budding, blooming and bearing; men had their time for peace and war, and the king meant to do some good now that he had his time. The bishop then showed how Henry had set his mind to recover the inheritance and the right that belonged to his crown, though it had been withheld during the reigns of his three predecessors, and he pressed upon his hearers that they must fight for justice and follow what is just, even if they died for it. For this purpose three things would he required from them, viz. wise counsel, strong help, and plenteous grants of money[8]; so let them put in their petitions without delay and choose their Speaker and present him on the morrow. Thereupon the Commons retired to the Frater[9] in the adjoining Abbey

---

[1] Chambre de pinetas, Cotton, Abridg. 538.

[2] Rot. Parl. iv. 34; Stat. ii. 187; Letter Book I, 135. Not Nov. 1, as Brougham, 97; nor Nov. 18, as Tyler, ii. 87.

[3] Dugdale, Summons, 394.   [4] Page 326.

[5] For his will dated at West Peckham and proved at Lambeth, see Genealogist, v. 327.

[6] Foss, iv. 203; Wylie, ii. 489, note 4.

[7] Dum tempus habemus operemur bonum, Gal. vi. 10; Nicolas, 5. Called "work well" in Brougham, 97. The bishop also quoted Ecclesiasticus iv. 33 [28]="till deith strive thou for righteousness," Ramsay, i. 188; Radford, 42.

[8] Copious subside daniers, Rot. Parl. iv. 34.

[9] Une maison appellee le Froytour dedeins l'abbaie de Westm', ibid. The Gascony petitions were as usual (i.e. since 1344, Rot. Parl. ii. 47, and *passim*, ibid. vii. 986) considered by the Triers in the Marcolf Chamber, ibid. iv. 35. This name

and chose Thomas Chaucer, one of the representatives of Oxfordshire, as their Speaker for the fourth time[1]. On the following morning[2] he was presented to the king and advised him in the name of the Commons that, before embarking on a hostile campaign, he should first send ambassadors to France to do him right, if possible by peaceful means[3].

Little is known as to the deliberations of this Parliament. The writs of expenses have not been preserved[4], and it would appear that little contentious matter was introduced. The King took steps to secure that the belongings of the earldoms of Hereford, Essex and Northampton, to which he had succeeded by right of his mother, Mary de Bohun, should not be merged in those of the Crown[5], but remain a separate possession of his family like those of the Duchy of Lancaster[6]. It was also enacted that henceforward no one should be appointed a Justice of the Peace unless he actually resided in the county for which he was commissioned, exceptions being allowed in the case of Justices of Assize and the Chief Stewards of the Duchy of Lancaster[7]. The Parliament was dissolved on Dec. 7, 1414[8], and the members departed to their homes after having granted a double tenth and a double fifteenth[9] payable in equal

does not occur among the list of rooms in the palace in J. T. Smith, pp. 55, 69; or Walcott, 210–218.

[1] Wylie, iv. 308.

[2] Not Wednesday, as Cotton, Abridg. 539.

[3] Nicolas, Agincourt, App. 50.   [4] Prynne, 509, 512.

[5] Rot. Parl. iv. 46; Baines, i. 130.

[6] Cal. Pat. H. IV, i. 188, Oct. 14, 1399; Loftie, Savoy, 82, 255; Wylie, i. 66; iii. 235. Cf. "mine heritage of Lancaster," Wills of Kings, 242; Kal. and Inv. I. p. xcix.

[7] Rot. Parl. iv. 51; Stat. ii. 187.

[8] Usk, 124, 305; Ramsay (i. 189) thinks there is no evidence as to the duration of this Parliament.

[9] For two-tenths and two-fifteenths granted anno 2, see Rec. Roll 3 H. V, Pasch., July 17, 1415; Iss. Roll 3 H. V, Mich., Oct. 30, 1414; Rec. Roll 4 H. V, Pasch., Apr. 20, 30, 1416. For writ dated Dec. 22, 1414, for collecting in London, see Letter Book I, 132, where it is called pro decimâ levandâ. For tenth and fifteenth "darreinement grantées," see Ord. Priv. Co. ii. 148, Feb. 1415; Sloane MS. 4601, f. 99, where it is used for paying the garrison at Harfleur, Jan. 11, 1416. For two-tenths collected at Oxford, see J. E. T. Rogers, 101; see also Church, 54; Kingsford, 116, who thinks that this was the Commons' reply to the Dauphin's "ill-timed jest." Called "a soleyn subsidie to susteyne his werres," Crowned King, 525. Mazas (Vies, v. 558) thinks that this Parliament (which he calls the Parliament of Leicester, where no subsidy at all was called for, see page 323) only voted half the subsidy that was asked for and that the word "France" was not mentioned because the Commons regarded a war with France as unjust. Rapin (iii. 437) supposes that the grant amounted to 300,000 marks. For "double-tithe," see Beazley, iii. 454.

halves at Candlemas next (i.e. Feb. 2, 1415) and the Candlemas of the year following respectively[1], though the towns of Newcastle, Alnwick, Warkworth, Berwick, and the whole of the county of Cumberland were to be excused from payment on account of their losses due to raiding by the Scots[2].

The Convocation of the Province of Canterbury had already met in St Paul's on Monday, Oct. 1, 1414[3], to arrange for sending delegates to the Council at Constance and had doubled their usual grant of a tenth[4] to the king, but the York clergy did not meet till Jan. 10, 1415[5], when they voted a similar sum[6], but only after the usual "much altercation." A century later these large grants were regarded as "such a sum of money as never by no spiritual persons was to any prince before given or advanced[7]," but this statement is only a part of the apocryphal story of how Archbishop Chichele guarded the blow at the Church's goods with a silver buckler[8], already dealt with in a previous chapter[9], though singularly enough the only contemporary reference to the archbishop's influence at the time is a growl at him from St Albans for showing his spite[10] against the clergy by attacking the privileges of those religious houses that were exempt from his jurisdiction.

---

[1] Rot. Parl. iv. 35. For payment of messengers sent to sheriffs to proclaim statutes passed in this Parliament, see Iss. Roll 3 H. V, Pasch., May 1, 1415.

[2] Cal. Doc. Scot. iv. 172, Dec. 8, 11, 1414.

[3] See pages 282, 405. Called synodus praelatorum, in hâc synodo, in concilio nostro, in convocatione cleri Cantuar. provinciae, Conc. iii. 358, 360, 369; Rym. ix. 159; Wake, 351; grande cleri concilium, Otterbourne, 275, though called "*cunctos regni proceres* et praelatos," and "grande concilium" in Wals. ii. 302; Hypodig. 452; Monstr. ii. 302; Chron. Lond. 98 (where Oct. 1 is called Sunday); Holinsh. iii. 547; not 1415, as Parker, 277.

[4] Usk, 124, who notes as an irregularity that these grants were made before the grants of the laity. For the first tenth of two-tenths granted by the clergy of the province of Canterbury *ultimo* (i.e. in 1414), see Pat. 2 H. V, iii. 13, Feb. 13, 1415; also Rec. Roll 3 H. V, Pasch., July 17, 1415. For one-tenth granted by clergy in convocation at St Paul's, see Claus. 3 H. V, 5; Speed, 772. For the second of two-tenths granted by clergy anno 2, see Rec. Roll (Auditors), 3 H. V, Mich., Jan. 30; Feb. 11, 17, 25, 28; March 18, 1416; Rec. Roll 5 H. V, Pasch., Apr. 21, May 3, 1417.

[5] i.e. Wednesday after Epiphany, Conc. iii. 371, as certified by the Archbishop of York on Jan. 20, 1415, with the king's writ of summons, dated Jan. 9, 1415. For a previous meeting on Nov. 6, 1414, see Conc. iii. 370.

[6] For two-tenths granted by clergy (York), *anno secundo*, see Rec. Roll 3 H. V, Mich., Nov. 4, 18; Dec. 23, 1415; Kitchin, Records, 135, where the sitting is dated Jan. 6, 1415.

[7] Halle, 52; Holinsh. iii. 546; Henry V, Act I. sc. i. 79; Biondi, 109; Goodwin, 43; Rapin, iii. 437; Tindal, i. 510; Yonge, 267. "An incredible masse," Martyn, 178; "une somme inouïe," Michelet, vi. 15.

[8] Fuller, Worthies, ii. 172.   [9] Page 390.

[10] Ut manifestaret bilem suam, Wals. ii. 302.

Fortified with these large prospective grants the king straightway made haste to resume the thread of his negotiations with France[1]. The chief envoys were again Bishops Langley[2] and Courtenay[3], but this time they were accompanied by the Earl of Dorset[4] and Lord Grey of Codnor[5], together with two knights (viz. William Bourchier and John Phelip), William Porter, esquire, and Masters Philip Morgan and Richard Holme[6]. These were commissioned

[1] Rym. ix. 183, 184, 185, 187, 206; Carte, Rolles, ii. 217; Dep. Keep. Rept. xliv. 558.

[2] Not the Archbishop of Dublin, as Trussel, 98; Barante, iii. 135, which is a mistake for Durham. For the manors of Harlow, Latton, Matching and Netteswell on the border of Essex and Herts. assigned to him for his harbourage on Dec. 12, 1414, see Rym. ix. 191.

[3] For a reference to a vicar in spirituals acting for the Bishop of Norwich *in remotis agente*, see Pat. 2 H. V, iii. 9, Feb. 17, 1415. For account of his expenses as ambassador to France, see Add. MS. 24,513, f. 68, quoted in Dict. Nat. Biogr. xii. 342, i.e. £364. 3s. 4d. from Dec. 20, 1414 (called Dec. 12 in Mirot-Déprez, lxi. 28), to March 29, 1415, journeying to Paris via Dover and Calais, Exch. Accts. 321/26.

[4] Called Comte d'Ourset in Monstr. 354; not the Duke of York, as Le Fèvre, I. pp. xvii, 211; Ménorval, ii. 57, who imagines that he was brother to Henry V. For £183. 6s. 8d. paid to Bishop Courtenay for this embassy from Dec. 14, 1414, to March 29, 1415, see Iss. Roll 3 H. V, Pasch., April 11, 1415; Ramsay, i. 193, from For. Accts.; Iss. Roll 4 H. V, Pasch., July 8, 1416. Choisy, 315, quoting MSS. de Rousseau, Reg. 59, supposes that the embassy consisted of the Duke of York and the Earls of Dorset and Salisbury, thereby confusing three separate transactions. Usk, 125, 306, adds Lord Scrope. Gilles (ii. 61) gives the Duke of York, the Earl of Dorset and the Archbishop (*sic*) of Winchester. For an action brought by John Kenyver, an esquire living with the Duke of Exeter, against Sir John Cotiller, parson of St Andrews, Lewes, for an assault committed on him and his servants at Lewes when going with the ambassadors to France in 3 H. V, see Early Chanc. Proc. i. 37.

[5] Called Comte de Grey, Amiral d'Angleterre in Monstr. 354; Barante, iii. 135; cf. Wylie, i. 173; ii. 306, note 6. For his account for going to France from Dec. 14, 1414, to March 27, 1415, see Exch. Accts. 321/29, 30; Mirot-Déprez, lxi. 28, showing 30 horses and men crossing in the *Julian de Winchester* (probably Winchelsea), 16 in the *Davide Conkett* (i.e. Le Conquet), and 19 in the *Laurence de Lacechio* (i.e. Lequeytio in Biscay, Wylie, i. 381).

[6] For £166. 13s. 4d. each, paid to the Earl of Dorset and Bishops Langley and Courtenay as envoys to Paris; £100 to Lord Grey and £50 each to Sir William Bourchier, John Philip, kt., William Porter, esquire, and Master P. Morgan and Richard Holme, see Devon, 336, Nov. 3, 1414. For £50 paid to Bourchier, as one of the retinue, from Dec. 10, 1414, to March 13, 1415, see Devon, 340 (May 18, 1415), where he is employed "on secret matters,"—not from Dec. 10, 1413, as R. H. Mason, 216. For Richard Holme's account, see For. Accts. 3 H. V, showing that he left London on Dec. 14, 1414, his six horses crossing to Calais via Winchelsea, and that he was back again in London by March 17, 1415. For £47 paid to John Philip, kt. and £29 to William Porter, esquire, for embassy to France in comitivâ of Bishop Langley, from Dec. 14, 1414, to March 10, 1415, see Iss. Roll 3 H. V, Pasch., April 12, 1415. Both of these latter had specially distinguished themselves in the fighting at St Cloud in November 1411, Wylie, iv. 62. For Wm Boucer's (i.e. Bourchier's) acct. (£100. 0s. 8d.) from Dec. 14, 1414, to March 13, 1415, see Exch. Accts. 321/23; Mirot-Déprez, lxi. 28, where he sails from Southampton to Harfleur and returns by Calais and Dover, shipping 21 horses in the *Julian of Dover*, 21 in the *Margaret of Dover* and four in the ship in which Thomas Chaucer's horses went. For William Porter's account, £62. 6s. 8d. from Dec. 14, 1414, to March 10, 1415, see Exch. Accts. 321/24, 25, showing that he sailed from Southampton to Harfleur in the *Marie de Sebastien* and returned from Calais to Dover in the *Trinité de Cales*.

on Dec. 5, 1414[1], to treat with the King of France for a final peace, but while always insisting on the restitution of King Henry's right to the French crown, they were empowered to arrange independently for the marriage and the dower. It was afterwards represented that Henry offered to forego a great portion of his claim to the French throne[2] and it is certain that his council advised that there should be some yielding in this direction[3], and as the truce would expire at Candlemas[4] and little time would therefore be left for arranging details, they were authorised to prolong it to any date that might be agreeable to both sides.

The official expenses of the envoys are reckoned from Dec. 14, 1414[5], but they certainly did not all start on that day, for at least two of them, viz. Bishop Langley and the Earl of Dorset, were still in London attending a council which met at the Black Friars in the month of February following[6], and communications must in the meantime have been passing with reference to an extension of the truce, for a document is in existence showing that on Jan. 2, 1415[7], the French council in Paris sanctioned a prolongation of it in the absence of the king, and this was more formally agreed to on Jan. 24[8], when it was agreed to prolong it till May 1, 1415, in order to give time for the many profitable meetings and conferences that were to come. On the very day before the above agreement was signed King Henry wrote to the Jurade at Bordeaux that he was in hopes that he would soon be in ease and comfort in view of the coming restitution of his inheritance so long unjustly withheld by his enemy in France[9], and so promising did

[1] Rym. ix. 183–188, 205; called before the Peace of Arras in Larrey, 808, i.e. before its final ratification on Feb. 23, 1415, see page 438.

[2] Nicolas, Agin., App. 50.

[3] An offre that were moderyng of youre hole title, Ord. Priv. Co. ii. 140–142; Nicolas, Agin., App. xvi.

[4] Page 156; Rym. ix. 205, 206.   [5] See page 435, notes 4, 5, 6.

[6] Ord. Priv. Co. ii. 145. In Rym. ix. 209, Bishop Langley and the others are envoyez en France *au mois de fevrier*.

[7] Cotton MS. Calig. D. v. f. iv (5).

[8] Traictiez et communications proffitables sont à avoir, Rym. ix. 207, 209; Report on Foedera, App. D. 78. This was confirmed on June 1, 1415, Rym. ix. 262. For a copy of the trève générale, dated London, Jan. 24, 1414 (see page 179), with instruction to commissioners, Feb. 13, 1414, in the archives of the Count of Armagnac at Montauban, see Maisonobe, 42.

[9] En droyt l'approchement de las heretatges nostres et vestres que par noz adversaries ont esté ja pieça detenuz et a grant tourt occupez, Jurade, 138, written Jan. 23, 1415.

the outlook appear that by March 13 it was believed in Bordeaux that the marriage question had been definitely settled[1] and that there was reason to hope that the Earl of Dorset and the Constable Charles d'Albret were about to make a joint visit to Guienne to secure a peaceful settlement there also[2].

All preliminary difficulties having thus been cleared away, the English envoys finally made their way across to Paris where an influential group of Frenchmen had been appointed[3] to enter into negotiations with them. These were Guillaume Boisratier[4], Archbishop of Bourges[5] and Chancellor to the Duke of Berry[6], Pierre Fresnel, Bishop of Noyon[7], a strong Orleanist[8] and an old diplomat[9] who had already visited England and Scotland[10], Charles, Count of Eu[11], and Guillaume Martel, Lord of Bacqueville[12].

This letter was read in Bordeaux on April 10 and again at the meeting of the Three Estates of the Bordelais held in the Chapter-house of St Seurin on May 4, 1415, Jurade, 152.

[1] Es deyt que lo maridatge de la filha de Franssa es feyt am lo Rey, Jurade, 125.

[2] Benen ensempo part dessa et sere bon esperar lor binguda, Jurade, 125.

[3] i.e. on Jan. 24, 1415, Rym. ix. 206, 207 (not Jan. 24, 1414, as Tillet, Guerres, 111 a).

[4] Not Bouratier, as ·Duchesne, 821; Goodwin, 56; Sveyro, ii. 122; Milner, i. 30; Portal, 79; Strang, 68; nor Bourratier, as Dupleix, ii. 711; nor "Bourretier," as Durham, 40; called "Mr William Boare" in First Life, 24. For his signature "G. Boisratier" in Cotton MS. Galba, B. 1 *passim*, see Roy. Lett. i. 313, 381, 396; ii. 27, 47, where he is a negotiator with the English in 1404, 1405.

[5] Page 155.

[6] He was a member of the Grand Council in 1411, Valois, Conseil, 121, 122. For account of him when he was Master of Requests to the King's Hostel and Chancellor to the Duke of Berry, see Chenu, Archiepiscoporum, 93; Godefroy, 675; Raynal, ii. 481; Guiffrey, i. 297. He had studied law at Bologna, Bononiae leges doctor utrasque legens, from his epitaph in Chenu. For 8 frs. per day paid to him as Chancellor to the Duke of Berry, also 1000 livres tourn. en pension and 225 livres tourn. for robes, see Toulgoët-Treanna, 87. For presents from him to the Duke, see Guiffrey, I. p. xlvii. For a fine copy of Froissart which he gave to the Duke on Nov. 8, 1407, see Froiss. iii. 383; Guiffrey, i. 258. It contains the Duke's signature "Jeanh" and that of Nicholas Flamel, and is now in the Bibl. Nat. no. 8318; called 3318 in Raynal, ii. 510, though neither number corresponds with the catalogue of 1739. For his deposition in the Fusoris case, see Mirot, 155, 222.

[7] Reading "noviomensis" for "norvicensis" in Rym. ix. 226. He was Bishop of Meaux from Nov. 20, 1391, to Aug. 21, 1409, when he was translated to Noyon, Gall. Christ. ix. 1020. He was present in the Council in Paris on Sept. 7, 1415, Moranvillé, 423; also in 1406, etc., Valois, 111, 115, 121, 123, and was killed in the massacre in Paris on June 12, 1418, Gall. Christ. xi. 791.

[8] Valois, Conseil, 115.

[9] He took part in the transfer of Genoa to French rule in 1397, Gall. Christ. viii. 1638; and was present in the Chancellor's house in Paris when the treaty with Owen Glendower was signed in 1404, Rym. viii. 367; Wylie, i. 455. For further reference to these transactions, see Report on Foedera, App. D. 308, 353, where Owen is called "Onuinnus" or "Cuminis," Griffith Yonge is "Griffironges" and Hanmer "Hanguier." He attended the Council at Pisa in 1409.

[10] e.g. as a negotiator in 1388, when he was a canon of Rouen, Gall. Christ. viii. 1637.

[11] Reading "Augae" or "Augio" (see Basin, i. 23) for "Ange" in Rym. ix. 226.

[12] See page 393.

The English representatives arrived in Paris on Feb. 9, 1415[1], where the Dauphin, who was now Regent of France during his father's disablement, had given orders that they should be magnificently received[2]. They were met at the gates by the Counts of Eu, Vertus and Vendôme[3], together with a group of archbishops, bishops and prelates, the provost and skevins of Paris, and the leading citizens, and as their brilliant cavalcade of over 600 mounted men rode through to their lodgings[4], the populace that thronged the streets looked on with amazement and delight[5]. The envoys were entertained at dinner by the king at the Hostel of St Pol, where they saw the Princess Catherine, bringing away with them her portrait to show to their king when they returned home[6].

On the next day (Feb. 10) began a three days' fête[7] in celebration of the general amnesty that followed on the signing of the Peace of Arras[8], during all which time

---

[1] Sequenti die Sabbati, St Denys, v. 408, i.e. Saturday after Feb. 7, 1415. Not 1414, as Brougham, 379; cf. J. Meyer, 244 (with enclosure). Not in January, as Cagny, 193; nor Jan. 29, 1415, as Mirot, 152; nor about the end of January, as Duchesne, 821; nor the beginning of February, as Bourgeois, 644. Cf. "comme Bruma declinast" and Phoebus began to approach the Ram (le cornu mouton), Pastoralet, 756; "ou temps diver," Mirot, 174; modicum ante carnisprivium, ibid. 235.

[2] Magnificé, St Denys, v. 408; grande chère et reception grandement festoyés, Juv. 501; Monstr. 359.

[3] For the Counts of Eu, Vertus, Alençon, La Marche and Vendôme, present at a council in Paris on Dec. 29, 1414, together with the Dukes of Berry, Bourbon and Orleans, see Cosneau, Connétable, 484. For 16 counsellors sent to meet them at La Chapelle, see Mirot, 146, quoting Baye, ii. 190.

[4] i.e. in the Hostel de Clisson in the Rue Vieille du Temple (on the site of the present Archiv) and the Hostel de Navarre (now the Marché St Germain) on the other side of the river et ailleurs, Mirot, 152, 173, 178, 190, 193, 196, 197, 235. Called the Hostel du Temple in Duchesne, 821. For account of the Temple, with pictures of the tower, see Lacroix, 339; Hoffbauer, ii. 1, 3, 9, 11, 12, Plates I, V, VI; Lavallée, Paris, 276; Guilhermy, Itin. 253; H. Legrand, 54; Belloc, 256–260. For picture by Jean Fouquet, see Gruyer, 150; also Leroux de Lincy, 586, from missal of Jean Juvenel. For picture in 1660, see Zeiller, Pt. I. p. 51; Bournon, 36. For picture of the Prior's Hostel, see Gazette des Beaux Arts, xvii. 355. For the Duke of Berry's Hostel du Temple, see Toulgoët-Treanna, 111.

[5] Juv. 524; Monstr. 354.

[6] Quandam imaginem ad similitudinem dicte domine depictam, Mirot, 153, 272, 274.

[7] Called eight days in Waurin, i. 165. For medal representing it, see Mézeray, ii. 567; cf. dured the feast 8 days, Melusine, 243; at 15 dais and cessed the festing, Coudrette, 97.

[8] See page 398; i.e. on Feb. 23, 1415 (not at Arras, as Aubert, Comp. 202). Baye, ii. 210; Dumont, II. ii. 21; Finot, Paix, 5; Coville, 397; Cartellieri, Beiträge, iii. 13; Daniel, iii. 866, quoting Inventaire des Chartes de Bourgogne, iv. 1111; Guizot, ii. 253; Black, ii. 276. Called Feb. 24 in St Denys, v. 422–436; Monstr. 354–359; D. Sauvage, 234; Le Fèvre, i. 200; or Feb. 25, Lavisse-Rambaut, iii. 137; and again in the Parlement de Paris on March 16, Sismondi, xii. 460; also at Tournai on April 1, Vandenbroeck, 120 (where the people are summoned au son de la bancloque et par cri

the streets were flagged, the courts were closed[1], and the whole population rollicked in the open amidst eating, drinking and dancing[2], the bourds[3] being heightened by the news of the recent reconciliation of the Dukes of Orleans and Burgundy[4]. In the jousting in the Rue St Antoine[5] the feeble king[6] broke a *lance d'estime* with the newly-created Duke of Alençon[7], the Duke of Brabant (brother to the Duke of Burgundy) tilted right cordially[8] with the Duke of Orleans[9], and the Dauphin let off some of the strength of his most gracious youth[10]. But sterner stuff was provided by the presence of a band of Portuguese champions[11], who had come to challenge any Frenchmen that dared to meet them. On Feb. 21[12] three of their picked men entered the lists to do their deveer[13] to the death against three Frenchmen with lance, sword, axe and knife[14], and as the English were

public, ibid. 60); called April 2 in Pays-Bas, 352; and at Amiens on April 18, 1415, in the presence of Charles VI, Duseval, i. 275. The peace was sworn in Paris on March 1, 1415, Finot, Paix, 48, 100; called March 3 in Daniel, iii. 866; and a ratification followed on March 14, 1415, Plancher, iii. 419; Barante, iii. 131. For payments made on Feb. 16, 1415, to the Duke of Burgundy's envoys in Paris through Dino Rapondi, see Coussemaker, 105; Plancher, iii. 416.

[1] At St Jean d'Angély the mayor's court was closed for eight days pour cause de publication de la paix de nos seigneurs de France, Aussy, Reg. iii. 128 (April 13, 1415). It was sworn to in Paris by the Duke of Burgundy on March 13, 1415, Caillet, Traité, 222, 224, 234; Cartellieri, Beiträge, iii. 14.

[2] Boires, mangers, joutes, danses et autres ébattements, Monstr. 354.

[3] Hardyng, p. xi; Kingsford, Hard. 748; Godefroy, Cotgr., s.v. *Behourdes*; Murray, Dict., s.v. *Bohourts*; Lhomel, Edits, 69; Nicolas, Chron. of Hist. 110.

[4] Waurin, i. 165.   [5] Bourgeois, 644; Mirot, 152.

[6] For his earlier achievements in May 1402, see Beaucourt, i. 4.

[7] Created a Duke on Jan. 1, 1415, Anselme, iii. 255; Cosneau, Connétable, 37; Cagny, 93, quoting Ec. des Chartes, xlix. 421. For account of him, see Belleforest, Chroniques, 320. For text of the grant registered in the Chambre des Comptes on May 13, 1415, see Bry de la Clergerie, 316. Called May 15 in Anselme, iii. 255.

[8] Moult cordialement, Monstr. 354; Le Fèvre, i. 211.

[9] For plates for armour and un harnois de lecton (i.e. laton) argentie of the Duke of Orleans at the jousts qui ont esté faictes en l'hostel de St Pol a Paris en ce present mois de Fevrier, see Roman, 181, 187, dated Feb. 12, 1415.

[10] Evaporavit robur gratissime juventutis, St Denys, v. 408.

[11] For their doings at Arras, Bar-le-Duc, Lens and St Omer, see Le Fèvre, i. 179, 206; Bourgeois, 620.   [12] St Denys, v. 410; Bourgeois, 59 (644).

[13] Lydg. Min. Po. 51, 122. Did her devir, N. Moore, Foundation, lxxxviii; his dever gan do, Coudrette, 183, 213; did hys devoyre, Melusine, 40; lete runne your horses and doo your devoyre, ibid. 82; York, 97, 108; endevoyred themself wel, Melusine, 150 (i.e. en fist bien son devoir, Arras, 165); cf. Faictes nostre debvoir, Floquet, 159 (from the Costumier de Normandie); to do theyr dever full trewely they ment, Kingsford, Chron. 113; do my devoyre, Brett, 47; done is dever, Krapp, 70; Wylie, iii. 108. For devoir, see Ord. Priv. Co. ii. 249; Mann. and Meals, i. 161, 162; Stengel, 23; "do his duty," Capes, 158; did his dever dewe, Lydg. Troy Book, 9, 189, 241, 359.

[14] Juv. 501; Wylie, iii. 108; Gardiner, 297; Carysfoot, Pag. xiv. For horsemen tilting with lances and daggers carved on a capital in the Abbey Church at Boscherville, see Deville. Cf. but thei lepe up and fauzt on fote, Laud Troy Book, 445.

allies of their nation they were conducted on to the ground by the Earl of Dorset and others of his party who showed much indignation and annoyance at seeing them one by one unhorsed and at the mercy of their French antagonists when the king cried " Ho[1]!"

But all through the festivities there were frequent conferences as to the subject-matter of the mission and at length the English envoys presented their case in official form before the Dauphin and the Princes of the blood on March 12, 1415[2], in the Great Hall of the Palace[3]. Bishop Courtenay[4] was again the spokesman and preached from the words of Hezekiah : " Let but peace and truth be made in my days[5]." He was glad to find so great a wish for peace on the part of France, but he worked up a number of moral tropes to show that there could be no real peace without justice. He fortified himself with many quotations, relying chiefly on the Revelations of St Brigit, who had always urged a marriage between the royal houses of France and England as a remedy for the existing deplorable strife[6]; but whichever way he started, he always came back to the same old point, that Peace could only stand if she were ushered in by Truth and Justice.

On the following day, March 13[7], a paper was put in signed by all the six English envoys embodying their case. It was sealed with a round seal in red wax bearing the figure of an angel and three fleurs-de-lys[8], and a French translation had been made of it[9] at the request of Bishop Courtenay, who at that time had expressed himself as confident of the prospect of a successful issue to the negotiations. On the question of "justice" the English

---

[1] Juv. 501; Bourgeois, 643; Lecesne, 141; Wylie, iii. 109. Cf. Er he fele het y rede say hoo, Kail, 4, 62.

[2] En present sont venus les Angloiz veoir le Parlement, Baye, ii. 210; Bourgeois, 59 (644). De mense martii jam instantis convenientes, Rym. ix. 209.

[3] Aubert, Org. 397.

[4] Vir nobilis, staturae procerae (cf. Wylie, iii. 113), excellentis ingenii et non minus summae eloquentiae et litteraturae quam caeteris de nobilioribus naturae dotibus insignitus, Gesta, 27; Chron. Giles, 24.

[5] Isaiah xxxix. 8.   [6] Juv. 501; Wylie, iv. 36.

[7] Rym. ix. 213; Tillet, Guerres, 111; Report on Foedera, App. D. 77.

[8] Flores liliorum, Rym. ix. 208.

[9] i.e. by Jean Fusoris, who had studied the heavens as to the likelihood of success, Mirot, 153.

still held to their old demands[1], but they now agreed to consider the marriage question separately without prejudice to the question of territory[2]. They began by asking two million crowns as dower with the Princess but soon showed that they would be prepared to accept a million and a half, and after much bargaining ultimately came down to an even million as their last word[3], the King of France to find suitable jewels, ornaments, dresses, and everything for the young lady's chamber against the wedding, and as a final concession, as time was pressing for their return, they urged that if the marriage should come about and two boys should be born, the second of them should have his rights restored in the bailiwick of Montreuil[4] and the county of Ponthieu[5], i.e. the district between the Canche and the Bresle, which had come to Edward I by his marriage with Eleanor of Castile and which should have returned to the English crown by virtue of the Treaty of Brétigny[6].

The French on their side declined to admit any of the English king's pretensions to rights in France. They were quite wishful for the marriage[7], but could not consent to be dismembered of the richest of their provinces[8]. They agreed however to return the specified portions of Aquitaine which had been recovered from the English during the previous reign[9], but which might now be taken to extinguish the claim for the remainder of King John's ransom[10], and

---

[1] Not that "the claims over Normandy and Maine were entirely abandoned," as Turner, v. 393; Lingard, iii. 484; Church, 55.
[2] Dupleix (ii. 706) thinks that the French refused the marriage proposals par une générosité vrayement française.
[3] Pour le dernier mot, Report on Foedera, App. D. 77.
[4] i.e. Montreuil-sur-Mer for which Edward III did homage to Philip VI in the cathedral at Amiens in 1329 as inherited from his mother, Isabel of France, Harbaville, ii. 158; not "Monstreville," as Goodwin, 51. For seals, see Lhomel, Bailliage, 64.
[5] Juv. 500; Monstr. 359. For the five tailliages which made up le Ponthieu, see Belleval, Lettres, 4. Charles VII was called Monseigneur de Ponthieu or Count of Ponthieu in November 1403, i.e. six months after his birth; cf. Baudot de Juilli, 1. Preface, a, iiij; Vallet de Viriville, i. 4; do. Extraits, 241, 242, 243; Beaucourt, i. 7, 9. For an English landing and fight at Mers (near Tréport) in Ponthieu, on July 20, 1407, see Louandre, i. 275. On May 7, 1406, they had fired the county of Eu and none dared to put to sea against them, Fréville, i. 255; ii. 280.
[6] Rym. vi. 220; Juv. 500; Tyler, ii. 74; Louandre, i. 262; Harbaville, ii. 158.
[7] Zantfliet (406) represents that the French refused the marriage because Catherine had taken the veil at Poissy, which is a confusion with her sister Marie, Wylie, iii. 51.
[8] Uberrimam partem regni, scilicet Aquitaniae ducatum, St Denys, v. 408; tanto membro privari, ibid.
[9] Quamvis justé et rationabiliter, ibid. For 1500 places in Aquitaine lost to England since the Treaty of Brétigny, see Monlezun, iv. 160; Wylie, iii. 71.
[10] Report on Foedera, App. D. 77.

they were willing to put up the dower to 800,000 crowns and do the necessary clothing and jewelling[1] of the bride, but they said nothing as to the question of Ponthieu. These points were all entered up in a schedule to which the French king set his seal on March 14, 1415[2]. The English replied that they had no power to conclude on such terms[3], so the French suggested that they should send further envoys across to England and see if the marriage could still be negotiated in some other way[4]. Then after receiving many valuable presents[5] the English took their departure homewards, reaching London on March 29[6], where they reported that their mission had met with no success[7], although they had agreed to abate a large portion of the demands which their king had always regarded as his strict due[8].

We fortunately still possess a little evidence of the spirit that prevailed in the minds of the English envoys, related by a French advocate named Pierre Deley, who was in Paris during their visit. Shortly before the envoys departed[9] he noticed an English clerk, who was one of the embassy suite, strolling in the nave of the church of Notre Dame and got into conversation with him, in the course of which the Englishman expressed surprise at seeing so many monks and other men of religion abroad in the streets of Paris. In England, he said, this would not be allowed, but they would have to keep within the walls of their houses. Deley explained that this was probably because they were scholars[10] pursuing their studies at the University and that there were other reasons why this must be so, and then they got talking about the embassy. The Frenchman said

[1] Vestir et enjoyeler, Tillet, Guerres, 111; Champion, Vie, 138; Rym. ix. 214.

[2] Rym. ix. 214; Goodwin, 52; Tyler, ii. 86.

[3] Report on Foedera, App. D. 77; Pastoralet, 757.

[4] Per aliam viam, St Denys, v. 408; si traitté se pouvait trouver, Juv. 501.

[5] For a diamond given by the Duke of Orleans to a servant of Bishop Courtenay, see Champion, Vie, 137, where the Duke also entertains Sir J. Colvil, Maître d'Hôtel to the Duke of Clarence.

[6] Page 435, notes 4, 5, 6.

[7] Sans aucun exploit reporter de leur ambassiate, Nicolas, 50; Ord. Priv. Co. ii. 150; sans riens besoignier pour les grandes demandes qu'ils fairoient avec la dicte dame Catharine de France, Le Fèvre, i. 212.

[8] De lasser grande partie de ce qu'a lui de droit en ce las appartient, Ord. Priv. Co. ii. 150.

[9] Called about Easter, which fell on March 31 in 1415, in Mirot, Fusoris, 214.

[10] In Paris they were vêtus d'un habit long, grise et sombre à la façon des clercs, Collas, 327, 329.

that the English envoys had been made so welcome because
they had come about peace. "But," said the Englishman,
"your late mission to England was mismanaged, being left
too much under the control of a very bad man[1]," against
whom the French would have to be on their guard. When
pressed for the name he refused to give it, but said that he
was a tall man with a long dark face and a master of the
University. Asked what were the chances of peace he
said that the French king must be prepared to do his duty.
"In what way?" said his questioner, and the answer was
that he must give us what is ours and not his, by which
was meant Normandy, and he proceeded to tell the story
of William the Conqueror and his successors to four or five
generations[2]. Deley said that it was too late to talk in
that way, the demands were unreasonable and there would
be no peace if they were to be pressed. To which the
Englishman replied that all England was prepared for war
(*ordené à guerre*) if the demands were refused, adding that
they had better not talk further on the subject as he was
sure they would never agree. Then the Frenchman pressed
again for the name of the "bad man," and at last found out
that it was a Lombard physician named Pietro of Milan[3],
who had gone over to make his way in England at the
invitation of Bishop Courtenay with whom he was on very
friendly terms[4]. He had had several distinguished patients,
including King Henry, his stepmother Queen Joan and
Lucy, Countess of Kent, who was herself a Milanese[5],
besides Bishop Courtenay himself. Pietro had been living
in London or Westminster for several months[6], where he
had often been nearly killed and the king had to give him
special protection in his household (*comme son familier*).
The Englishman said solemnly that he was a traitor but
when asked for particulars he would only repeat (speaking
in Latin) that on his conscience Pietro was "nequissimus
homo." What he had really done nobody knows, but that
he was clearly suspected by the English is proved by the

---

[1] Un bien mauvais homme, Mirot, 216.
[2] Jusques a quatre ou cincq lignes, ibid.
[3] In Mirot, 211, he is *Maistre* P. de Milan.
[4] Habuit cum episcopo magnam familiaritatem, Mirot, 253.
[5] Mirot, 198; Wylie, iv. 128.
[6] i.e. Oct. 1414, page 425; Mirot, 188, 195, 196.

fact that in his own words he tells us that when Queen Joan told him she would like to consult him again next Easter, he said that he dared not come unless there was peace[1], so in Feb. 1415 he returned to Paris with Bishop Courtenay, whom he attended all through the negotiations[2].

The second embassy had altogether failed, but nevertheless the form of friendly conference was still kept up, and in view of the expected return visit of the French it was deemed advisable again to extend the truce which would otherwise expire on May 1, 1415[3]. Even while the negotiations were going on in Paris a French lawyer, Master Jean André or Andrieu, was commissioned[4] to act in this matter, and on April 13[5], Master Philip Morgan received instructions to meet him on King Henry's behalf, and as a result an arrangement was come to at Calais on April 24[6] that the truce should be prolonged till June 8, 1415, and on May 31 two French experts were deputed to arrange for a further extension, in order that the French envoys who were coming to England might have time to complete the suspended negotiations. On June 5 William Lisle and Philip Morgan were nominated to treat with them, and after several meetings at Leulinghen an extension was arranged to last till July 15[7], and as further time was still required this date was subsequently altered to Aug. 1, 1415[8].

And yet within a fortnight from the day on which he

---

[1] Mirot, 196.

[2] Pour le fait de phisique, ibid. 197.

[3] On May 5, 1415, the King's Council met in the Chapter-house of St Seurin at Bordeaux to consider the expiration of the truce, Baurein, iv. 290. At this there were present the Archbishop of Bordeaux, the Seneschal (i.e. Galhar Durfort, Lord of Duras and Blanquefort), the Constable (William Clifford), the Juge de Gascogne (Bertrand d'Asta), the Deans of St Seurin and St André, the Procurator Fiscal of Guienne and several lawyers.

[4] i.e. on March 13, 1415, Rym. ix. 226.

[5] Rym. ix. 221, 225, 227, 259; Jurade, 163; Ord. Priv. Co. ii. 153; Report on Foedera, App. D. 78.

[6] Rym. ix. 225, 226, 227; Tillet, Guerres, 111a; Jurade, 163, with order dated Paris, April 30, 1415, to publish it at La Rochelle.

[7] Rym. ix. 262, dated Calais, June 10, 1415; Cal. Dipl. Doc. 317; St Denys, v. 510, where the name of the month is omitted.

[8] On the strength of a letter from Charles VI, written in Paris on May 13, 1415, reported by the keeper of the royal seal at La Rochelle to the Jurade at Bordeaux, Jurade, 163, May 29, 1415. For letters of Henry V, dated April 16 and June 15, 1415, granting extensions of the truce which would end on May 1 and June 8, 1415, respectively, see Tillet, Guerres, 123; Vaissète, iv. 437. For truce expired on August 2, 1415, see Dupleix, ii. 711; Deseilles, 416.

had signed the confirmation[1] of the first extension of the truce King Henry was making his final arrangements for "resisting our enemies on the sea," on the ground that they were raising large fleets of war-ships munited with men-of-arms in vast numbers for the invasion of England[2], a phrase which *mutato nomine* exactly describes his own action in regard to France, and when the second extension was still under consideration, a shrewd observer writing in London reported that it would probably be for another month, "and then by God's grace the King will be ready[3]."

It must not however be assumed that King Henry had a monopoly of the deceitfulness that was working beneath this mask of smooth-faced diplomacy, for while the English envoys were in Paris two prominent Welshmen were also there on a diplomatic mission from Owen Glendower to cause embarrassment to him at home in case he should proceed with his aggressive policy abroad. These were Owen's Chancellor[4], Griffin Yonge[5], who had negotiated the alliance with France in 1414, and Philip Hanmer[6], a relative of his former colleague in the same transaction. But Owen's help was now a broken reed and nothing came of this final effort at intrigue, of which indeed we should have been in entire ignorance but for the mention of a gift of 100*l.* made to these Welshmen in Paris on Friday, Feb. 22, 1415[7], while they were waiting for the French king's reply. Owen died, as we have seen, in the following year[8]

---

[1] i.e. Feb. 17, 1415, Rym. ix. 201.

[2] Rym. ix. 202, Feb. 28, 1415.

[3] Lo Rey sera prest am la gracia de Diu, Jurade, 193, from a letter of Benet Spina, written in London on June 8, 1415. Before the second embassy started, Pietro of Milan had been told by the Countess of Kent in London that the King estoit prest et preparé en armes, but that if there were peace he would do fealty for the lordships and lands which should be yielded to him, Mirot, 199.

[4] Wylie, i. 447; ii. 15, 171. For account of him, see Matthews, 123; for his seal, ibid. 121.

[5] He is still called Bishop of Bangor (see page 113, note 7), though the de facto bishop was Benedict Nicole (see page 253), who had been appointed by Gregory XII, on the removal of Lewis Bifort (Papal Letters, vi. 137, dated Lucca, May 1, 1408), who is now stated to have no prospect of being restored, ibid. vi. 502, dated July 28, 1414.

[6] Not Haunier, as H. Moranvillé, 420; Matthews, p. xxxix.

[7] Not 1414, as Matthews, pp. xxxviii, 110, 118. This gift was actually granted on Dec. 3, 1414, Wylie, iii. 270.

[8] Page 111, note 7. For a statement that he disappeared on Sept. 21, 1415 (not 1416, as Matthews, p. xxxix), see Welsh MSS. i. 847; ii. 831, which adds that from thenceforward it was not known whither he had vanished, many saying that he was dead, which the prophetic bards denied. The document, which dates from the middle of the 16th century, appears to be merely an echo of the haunting date Sept. 20.

and Griffin Yonge, who had previously renounced the Roman obedience[1], very soon afterwards abandoned Pope Benedict and was made Bishop of Ross[2] in Scotland by Martin V[3], who arranged a maintenance for him and afterwards appointed him to the see of Hippo[4] in Africa.

[1] Page 112, note 9. In reckoning 2 archbishops and 14 bishops to the English Church in 1459 the Welsh bishops are not included in Débat, 38; Pyne, 68, 113.

[2] Though in Eubel, i. 446, he is Bishop of Ross on Feb. 14, 1414. Not "Ross and Finlay," as Matthews, 125, which is merely a misreading of Papal Letters, vii. 6, "Finlay of Albany" being the name of a Dominican who became Bishop of Argyle, ibid. vii. 69; Eubel, i. 251, and was sent with Griffin Yonge to Scotland on Feb. 24, 1418, to receive the submission of adherents of Benedict XIII.

[3] But it is evident that the former could not obtain actual possession of the see of Ross, as he had recognised Pope Martin V and found himself opposed by Benedict's nominee, John Bullock, and had to be provided with funds from other quarters until he obtained the temporalities of Ross "which he has no hope of doing soon," Papal Letters, vii. 119, Sept. 15, 1419.

[4] i.e. on Feb. 1, 1423, ibid. vii. 287; Eubel, i. 446; though he was still Bishop of Ross on June 29, 1430, on which day he was sent as an envoy to the Duke of Brittany, ibid. vii. 19.

CHAPTER XXV

INDENTURES

ON April 26, 1415[1], it was asserted in an official document that the French king had heard that Henry was collecting a large fleet and army, and the Dauphin was appointed Captain-General to make arrangements to resist him. The huge preparations already described[2] could not in fact be concealed and there was no evidence of any slackening, for all the recent outward friendliness. On Sept. 22, 1414[3], Nicholas Merbury[4], as Master of the Ordnance[5], had been commanded to secure stonecutters, carpenters, sawyers and all necessary workmen for the manufacture of guns and engines, together with supplies of iron, timber and other requisites. Four days later[6] orders were issued forbidding any trader to export gunpowder[7] from any English port, and by the end of October

---

[1] Transcr. For. Rec. 135, from Trésor des Chartes. For an order dated April 19, 1415, sent by the French king to the bailiff of Rouen to prepare against a landing of the English, see Champion, Vie, 139.

[2] Pages 159–163.

[3] Rym. ix. 159.

[4] Page 321, note 10.

[5] Wylie, iv. 144, note 3. For his account as magister armatur' regis, see Exch. Accts. 407/1. It shows basinet' cum visers, pallett, gorgett, stuffat' cum satin boker' et canab' sent to Normandy p. William ffosse, under signet of Dominus de Fitzhugh, Camar' Regis, Feb. 28, 1420; also 1 basinett cum 2 visers, 1 barell de osmond', 1 oz. de tissat' s^d ic' (or sur icelle), 3 covlett', 3 testers fac' de worstede, 3 par blankett' fact', de panno blanket curt', 3 par linth' de tel. lin. brabant. For payments to him for iron wheels as Master of the Works of the King's Ordnance, see Iss. Roll 4 H. V, Pasch., July 24, 1416. Cf. wyth gunnes gret and other gret ordinance, Pol. Songs, ii. 152; your ordynaunce of gunnes that was cheff, Archaeologia, xxxiii. 132; Brut, ii. 583.

[6] i.e. Sept. 26, 1414, Rym. ix. 160.

[7] For £73. 19s. 0d. paid to Paul Milan for saltpetre, see Rec. Roll 3 H. V, Pasch., July 17, 1415. For £13. 11s. 2d. paid to Thomas Gray, citizen of London, for 406¾ lbs. of saltpetre (i.e. at 8d. per lb.), see ibid. July 9, 1415; also £31. 10s. for saltpetre, bought of William Lynn, grocer (Letter Book I, 268, which refers to his will, dated Aug. 6, 1421), ibid. June 25, 1415; also £8 for gunpowder bought from William Woodward, founder, farmer of the manor of Bobbingworth or Bovinger, near Chipping-Ongar; £420 for saltpetre bought from Thomas Burton, grocer (Letter Book I, 203, 229), and collector of the subsidy of wool in London, Rec. Roll 3 H. V, Pasch., June 4, 14, 1415. For £31. 8s. 6d. paid to William Founder for grinding (super triturâ salpetir et sulphur vivi), Iss. Roll 3 H. V, Pasch., Apr. 24, May 1, 1415. For payments to Thomas Chalton, mercer of London, for eight cannons, saltpetre and other necessaries of war, ibid. April 26, 1415.

10,000 gun-stones[1] had been forwarded to London. On Jan. 30, 1415, orders were given for seven of the king's ships[2] to be manned each with about 200 sailors[3] besides their master, constable and carpenters, and at the council held at the Black Friars in London in the following month[4] it was arranged that four large ships, each with a portage of 120 tuns, and ten barges of 100 tuns (each ship and barge carrying 48 sailors, 26 men-of-arms and 26 archers), and ten balingers (each manned by 40 sailors and carrying 10 men-of-arms and 10 archers), should guard the sea from Plymouth to the Isle of Wight and from Orford Ness to Berwick during the king's approaching voyage, so that he might leave the country with an easy mind. This squadron, it was calculated, would require a total force of 536 sailors and 504 fighting men, while provision had also to be made for stationing 300 men at Berwick and in the north, 210 in Wales (i.e. 90 at Cwn-hîr and Bala and 120 at Ystradflur) and 1200 in Guînes and Calais, and all this in the face of a statement by the Treasurer recounting requirements for the royal household, chamber and wardrobe, though at present no one knew where a penny was to come from till the Treasurer had made his statement as to the condition of the revenue[5]. It certainly did come from somewhere however[6], for before the end of Feb. 1415[7] £2000 in cash

---

[1] For £66. 13s. 4d. paid on this account, see Devon, 336, Oct. 30, 1414.

[2] i.e. the *Thomas de la Tour* (William Hore, master), the *Trinité* (J. Kingston), the *Marie* (Richard Walsh), *Philip* (Robert Schedde), *Katherine* (J. Mersh), *Gabriel* (J. Arnold), *Le Poul* (Richard Neal), see Pat. 2 H. V, iii. 8 d, Jan. 30, Feb. 19, 1415; Cal. Pat. H. V, i. 294, where all these are "*de la Tour.*" For sailors to go over sea in a ship de guerre called *Gabryale de la Tour*, see Pat. 1 H. V, iii. 6, Oct. 24, 1413. At this date Thomas Talbot is Admiral of England, see For. Accts. 8 H. V, m. 29 (Catton's account), where he is with the king's ships *le grande Marie de la Tour* and the *Thomas de la Tour* which were driven back from the Isle of Wight to Winchelsea per rabiem venti on Dec. 30, 1414. Also on Feb. 20, 1415, the *Mary* of Rye, a balinger with a portage of 24 dol' and a crew of 33 + 4 (*sic*), John Brymme being master, is in comitivâ of Thomas Talbot, Admiral.

[3] For sailors wanted for the *litel Marie de la Tour* for Bordeaux, also for the *Trinitee de la Tour* and *Thomas de la Tour*, see Pat. 1 H. V, v. 27 d, Feb. 13, 1414. On Jan. 2, 1415, sailors were to be impressed for *la Rude* (i.e. red, Wylie, ii. 86) *Cog de la Tour* (Hankin Pitman, master); also May 3, 6; June 4, 1415, for the following ships (*naves*), viz. *Katherine de la Tour* (John Kingston), *Nicholas* do. (William Robinson), *Trinité Royale* do. (Stephen Thomas), *La Petit* (sic) *Trinité* do. (John Piers), *La Gabrielle* do. (William Richeman), *Petit* (sic) *Marie* do. (John Haterell), Rym. ix. 238, 239.

[4] i.e. Feb. 1415, Ord. Priv. Co. ii. 145.

[5] Ord. Priv. Co. ii. 148. See App. D[2].

[6] Monstr. (362) says that as much as 500,000 English crowns (i.e. £166,666) was collected en monnoie et vaisselle.

[7] For £2000 paid to them for this purpose, see Devon, 340, Feb. 27, 1415; Tyler, ii. 78; also £433. 6s. 8d., Rec. Roll 3 H. V, Pasch., June 8, 1415, and £2166. 13s. 4d.

had been handed over to two esquires, Richard Clitherow and Reginald Curteys, who in a short time crossed over with it to charter additional ships in Holland, where the Duke had been sounded by two English envoys[1] in the previous summer, and the money was now spent in bargaining with the masters and owners of ships in Holland and Zeeland[2] to come over with their vessels as soon as possible to London, Sandwich and Winchelsea and take service with the English king across the sea. On June 8, 1415[3], it was reported in London that 700 ships were on their way from Holland, while we know that others were purchased from Brittany[4] and in response to messages sent to the Mayors of Hastings, Winchelsea and Rye a fleet of vessels from the Cinque Ports had assembled at Dover by May 18[5], to convoy the Dutch ships over to Southampton.

Besides the Dutch it was believed that one of the sons of the King of Portugal was about to join the expedition with galleys and men[6], a rumour based apparently upon the

+£449. 6s. 9d., Iss. Roll 3 H. V, Pasch., April 26, May 18, 1415, a l'oeps de divers marins from Holland and Zealand. For 166 qrs. 2 bushels of wheat at 6s. the quarter, delivered to them as part payment of their wages, also wine at 53s. 4d. the cask (*tonel*), see Exch. Accts. 406/29. Exchange was effected at Middelburg through John Victor, a Florentine merchant. For 400 marks advanced by him on June 6, 1415, see Rec. Roll 3 H. V, Pasch., June 6, 10, 1415. For order dated March 18, 1415, for Richard Clitherowe and Simon Flete to cross to Holland, see Rym. ix. 215; Nicolas, 6.

[1] i.e. Philip Morgan and John Hovingham, page 414. For a baron from Holland who had before been a Carthusian monk but had obtained a dispensation from the Pope to abandon religion, see Tit. Liv. 7; Vita, 35; Kingsford, Biogr. 76. Called "Landinus" in Harpsfeld, 588; "the apostate Olandinus," Kingsford, Biogr. 82, or "Olandyne," Nicolas, Agincourt, 35. He offered his services with 20 armed followers to King Henry at Southampton who indignantly told him to return to his vows, whereupon he took service with the French and was killed at Agincourt. For £100 paid to Her fflorens van Alcmaede, knight of the county of Holland, retained in the king's service for life, April 26, 1415, see Sloane MS. 4600, f. 274; Exch. Accts. 45/5, where he is called Floricio van Alkemade; called Florys van Askemade in Nicolas, Agincourt, 94, where his retinue = 5 + 15. In Iss. Roll 3 H. V, Mich., Feb. 8, 1416, he receives 100 marks per annum.

[2] Monstr. 362; Waurin, i. 168; Rym. ix. 217; J. Mayer, 245; Guérin, i. 322.

[3] Jurade, 193. On July 10, 1415, it was reported in Venice by a courier or rider who had left Bruges on June 18, that Henry had collected a fleet of 125 cogs (*choche*) and several other ships large and small, amounting in all to 306 sail, Morosini, ii. 19.

[4] For £500 paid by Richard Buckland, fishmonger, one of the collectors of tonnage and poundage in the port of London, to three men de Insula de Daces (Ile de Batz) de partibus de Gerand (i.e. Guérande) in Britann. for a ship called St Nicholas de Geraunde, see Iss. Roll 3 H. V, Pasch., Apr. 24, 1415.

[5] For £140 paid to Richard Weavill, esquire, Lieutenant of Dover Castle (possibly the same as Richard Wayvelt, who was placed on a commission of array for Kent on May 29, 1415, Cal. Pat. H. V, i. 408), to pay the wages of crews of Cinque Ports' vessels for this purpose, see Iss. Roll 3 H. V, Pasch., May 18, 1415.

[6] Jurade, 193; Morosini, ii. 20, though the original word is "Chades," i.e. Cadiz, not Cales or Calais. The news had reached Venice on July 10, 1415.

fact that King John of Portugal[1] with his three sons Duarte, Pedro and Henry the Navigator[2], was at that very time collecting ships[3] at Lisbon and Oporto and no one knew exactly whither they were bound. Some said they were going against Holland[4], others against Granada[5], others against Aragon[6] (i.e. Catalonia), others that they were bound for Provence either to protect Pope Benedict at his expected meeting with Sigismund at Nice[7] or to seize the deposed Pope John XXIII and carry him off, or to help the Duke of Anjou to recover his hold on Naples, and there were plenty of other rumours. But all were agreed that something big was astir and that it would be a bad thing for the loser[8]. In the end however the great Portuguese fleet of 225 ships with 45,000 fighting men[9] on board, including many English, set sail from the

[1] For permission, Sept. 20, 1414, for João de Vasquez, knight, to export 400 lances from England for the King of Portugal, see Ewald, xliv. 549.

[2] For permission, July 12, 1417, for Pedro Lobato, ambassador from Portugal, to export 300 lance-staves, three palfreys and a suit of armour for Infante Henry warring against the infidels, see ibid. xliv. 598. For Prince Henry at Ceuta, cf.
De Ceita a Maura tumida vaidade
Primeiro entrando as portas de cidade.
Camoens, 134 (Canto VIII);
Weber 177. For Prince Henry of Portugal, born at Oporto, May 4, 1394, see Major, 24; Nordenskjold, 117; C. P. Lucas, 17; Azurara, I. i; II. 11, with map of Africa (1351), from Medicean Library at Florence. For portrait of him in Paris MSS. Port. 41 f., see ibid. I. xi; Denis, Portugal, 54; Major, Frontispiece; do. Discoveries, Frontispiece; Veer, Frontispiece; Beazley, 258; Oliveira Martins, 58; Historians' Hist. x. 460, where it is "from an old print," though there is no ground for the supposition that the black head-dress (called a barret-cap in Major, Discov. viii, though "barrette" is a high cap in Quicherat, Costume, 255) is an indication that he was in mourning for his brother, Ferdinand the Constant, who died May 20, 1449. For a painting of him in the corridor of the extinct monastery adjoining the Church of St Vincente de Fóra in Lisbon, see Azurara, I. xi. For death of Prince Henry at Sagres, Nov. 13, 1460 (not 1462 or 1463, as Galvano, 74), see Azurara, I. xxvii, lvii; Nordenskjold, 120; Beazley, 305. For his tomb at Batalha, see Major, 302. For figure of him over the gate of the monastery at Belem near Lisbon (i.e. Bethlehem, built in 1500, Grande Encycl. xx. 321), see Major, 311; do. Discov. 244; Azurara, II. Frontispiece. For his signature "I. D. A." (i.e. Iffante Dom Anrique), see Azurara, II. cl; Major, Disc. 299; Pereira, 260; Oliveira Martins, 206; Pina, 210 and *passim*; Veer, 268. For his collar as K.G. now in the possession of the Earl of Clarendon, see Major, 305; Beazley, Frontispiece.

[3] Morosini, ii. 64. For Biscayan vessels with the expedition, see Duro, 181.

[4] Neale, 80.

[5] Pisano, 29.

[6] Ibid. 24.

[7] Morosini, ii. 36.

[8] Sera qualche gran trato per cuy perdera, Morosini, ii. 40.

[9] Sanuto, 898; Morosini, ii. 54. Other estimates, as at Valencia on July 13, had placed it at 150 cogs and 20 galleys (ibid. ii. 36), or 130 coche + 20 fustz de galée, reported at Bruges, June 18, 1415, to be gathering at Cadiz in hunion con lo re d'Engletera (ii. 20); or 150 nefs (ibid. ii. 64). News of the gathering reached Venice by courier on July 10, 1415, Morosini, ii. 20. In ibid. ii. 66, note, the real figures are given as 27 galleys, 32 fustes, 133 cogs and ships + 120 of smaller size. Called 50,000 fighting men + 30,000 mariners in "Q," 216.

Tagus[1] on July 24, 1415[2], doubled Cape St Vincent
and reached Lagos on July 27, where they stayed till
Aug. 7. But their destination was plain[3] when they
passed eastward through the Strait of Morocco[4] and
sailed into the Bay of Algeciras on Aug. 10 and two
days later set sail for Ceuta[5]. Being struck by a storm
they put back for shelter under the Rock of Gibraltar[6],
but quickly reforming were soon again at sea. Ceuta was
captured by assault on Aug. 21, 1415[7], and the victorious
Portuguese were back at Tavira in Algarve on Sept. 2[8],
where their Prince Henry was created Lord of Covilhã[9]
and Duke of Viseu[10].

The fall of Ceuta struck a resounding blow through
Europe[11]. It drove the Moors from their own most
threatening stronghold, smoothed the way for African
trade[12] and led to the immense developments of the most
glorious age of Portugal's colonial history[13]. It proved
indeed, as had been predicted, a bad thing for the loser
and may be regarded as an instructive parallel to the contemporary happenings in England, both from the point of

---

[1] Not from Seville, as Morosini, ii. 54.

[2] Pisano, 32, 38. Called 25 in R. H. Major, 31, 42.

[3] A letter written at Valencia on Aug. 18, 1415, received in Venice on Sept. 14, announced that they were making for Ceuta, Morosini, ii. 54.

[4] For l'estroit de Maroc, see Bouvier, Descr. 124; Strictura de Marot, or Maruec, ibid. 188, 189; or "Marrok," Cal. Pat. H. V, 90.

[5] Called "Sunt" in Wals. ii. 314; or "Septa," Wolkenstein, 58; Pisano, 21, where the name is derived from septem montes called septem fratres; see Azurara, viii. 203; Historians' Hist. x. 455; cf. "Cepta," Zantfliet, 407; Eubel, Bullarium, vii. 537; Bouvier, Descr. 188, 189; "Cepte," Chastellain, ii. 154; "Seps," Korner, 393; "suste," Bouvier, Descr. 126; "Cente," Niem, 35; "Setta," Sanuto, 898; "Seta," Morosini, ii. 64; "Cette," La Marche, i. 116.

[6] Gibillthar, Gibaltar, Bouvier, Descr. 189.

[7] R. H. Major, 29; Azurara, I. 17; Noggler, Reise, 8, 9, quoting Schäfer, Geschichte von Portugal, ii. 283; not 1412, as Navarrete, i. 369; Duro, 181; nor 1411, as Weber, 179; Wurzbach, lviii. 64; nor 1408, as Villari, 34, 36. See App. E[2].

[8] Morosini, ii. 66.

[9] Or Covilham, i.e. Covilhão in Beira, Azurara, I. 3, 17, 30; II. p. viii; Cat, 58.

[10] R. H. Major, 41. Called "Viseo" in La Clède, i. 400; Faria y Sousa, 271.

[11] There were many Genoese merchants living at Ceuta who helped the Portuguese to get into the town under promise of favourable treatment. The news reached Genoa viâ Montpellier on Oct. 17, 1415, and was known in Venice on Nov. 2, Morosini, ii. 64, where 20,000 were reported killed. It was known at Constance in the same month, Viem, Vita, 35, who calls Ceuta, civitas magna fortis et potens...magna ad instar Bononiae, ut fertur, with 3 arces or fortalicia.

[12] De qua ficus, racemi, vina condita (i.e. sweet wines, Du Cange, s.v.) et mala punica ad occiduas diriguntur nationes, Zantfliet, 407, who calls the King of Portugal, Ferdinand. He is called Stephanus in Korner, 393.

[13] For further Portuguese conquests in North Africa (1416–1419), see Morosini, iv. 271.

view of the restless preparations which preceded it and the swiftness and sharpness of the sudden success with which it was carried through ; for while Portugal was gathering her vessels for this great *coup*, England was glowing with the radiance of her own coming fight[1], and her king, in the words of his enthusiastic biographer[2], had an eye everywhere about, repairing walls[3], forging guns and armour, building ships, pardoning the past, scorning ease and never weary, whether mounted or afoot ; but when he adds that he hoarded only to be ready to defend his country's rights in hope of peace through strength for war[4], we feel that the eulogist's judgment has been warped by the drum-head inflammation of his time.

Yet during all this time negotiations never ceased with France. The Earl of Dorset and his colleagues had scarcely returned to report themselves in London when King Henry wrote to the French king, expressing his surprise that he had heard nothing further about the envoys that he had been expecting and asking to be furnished with their names. This letter was written on April 7, 1415[5], and there is plenty of evidence that the French were quite serious in their desire for an accommodation, for the letter can scarcely have been despatched when Jean André[6] arrived at Westminster[7], bringing the very information asked for, and in the afternoon of April 12[8], the council met at the Black Friars. Archbishop Chichele was present, together with Bishops Langley and Beaufort[9], the Dukes of Bedford and Gloucester, the Earl of Dorset

---

[1] Militiae radiis populus jubilando nitescit, Elmham, Lib. Metr. 102.

[2] Vita, 28 ; cf. Capgr. de Illustr. 114 ; Wals. ii. 305 ; Hypodig. 455.

[3] For murage at York, see Pat. 1 H. V, v. 25, Feb. 6, 1414. For new postern at Moorgate, where the common latrine was "drawn down and set on this side of the more," with a "scluys" or "speye" to carry off the filth (p. fimis evacuand'), see Letter Book I, 137 ; Riley, Mem. 614–616 ; Chron. Lond. 99 ; Stow (Kingsford), i. 32 ; ii. 274.

[4] Vita, 11. Cf. Ende of batayle bygynneth pes, Kail, 12 ; The ende of bataile is peace sikerly and power (not povertee, as Pauli, Hertzberg, 62) causeth pease finally, Pol. Songs, ii. 202.

[5] St Denys, v. 498, where the letter is said to have been carried by Dorset herald.

[6] Page 444.

[7] For a letter written by Henry V at Westminster, April 11, 1415, see Jurade, 185. Cf.

> Our Kyng at Westminster he lay
> And hys bretheren everych on. Nicolas, 303.

[8] Ord. Priv. Co. ii. 153.

[9] For £40 paid to him for the support of Henry, son and heir of the Lord of Beamond, then in his custody, see Iss. Roll 3 H. V, Pasch., April 12, 1415 ; i.e. Henry,

and John Prophet, the Keeper of the Privy Seal. Here
it was resolved that letters should be sent to the King
of France and the Duke of Berry by Master Jean André
who was then in London, and on the following day[1]
safe-conducts were made out for Archbishop Boisratier,
Bishop Fresnel, who had been translated to Lisieux[2], Louis,
Count of Vendôme, and William, Count of Tancarville,
together with five knights and two lawyers, including Jean
André and Gautier Col. All these were coming across
with large retinues to continue the negotiations that had
been begun in Paris ; their safe-conducts were to last till
June 8 and by a subsequent order this date was extended
for another month[3]. On April 15, 1415[4], King Henry
wrote to the King of France urging that neither of them
should seek to circumvent the other's rights by crazy
fooling (*obliqua deliramenta*) or tricky light-fingered
chicane (*prestigiosis cautelarum arguciis*) but both join
hands to come to the help of their weeping mother the
Church, who had born them again into the light of day.

But though Henry uttered these fine sentiments, he
was very far indeed from attempting them in practice.
On March 10, 1415[5], he was at the Tower, whither he
summoned the Mayor, Aldermen and some of the most
substantial of the London citizens and told them that he
had decided to cross the sea with a large army to reconquer
lands belonging to the English crown which had long been
kept from it by enormous wrong[6], but that his plans could
not be carried out without money and that he proposed to
send his brothers into the city to see what was to be done.

Lord Beaumont, who died June 14, 1413, Dugd. Bar. ii. 53, where his son is called John
(born 1409); cf. Comp. Peer. i. 285.
   [1] Rym. ix. 219; Ewald, xliv. 559; Carte, Rolles, ii. 219.
   [2] He was translated from Noyon to Lisieux on Jan. 28, 1415, Gams, 566; Eubel,
i. 317; not Feb. 1417, as Baye, ii. 255, note, where he has to pay for dilapidations to his
successor at Meaux.
   [3] i.e. till July 7, Rym. ix. 221, dated June 6, 1415. For further safe-conducts for
them, dated June 29, 1415, see Rym. ix. 282.
   [4] St Denys, v. 510. Oman (Pol. Hist. 242) considers this letter as "strangely hypocritical."
   [5] Letter Book I, pp. xxiv, 135; Riley, Mem. 603; Besant, Survey, i. 107.
   [6] In official documents the purpose of the expedition is described as pro recuperatione
jurium coronae nostrae a diu injuriose detentorum, Rym. ix. 253, 256, 306. Cf. contra
jurium invasores et detentores, Add. MS. 24,062, f. 147; contra Deum et omnem justitiam
Gallorum violentiâ detentus, Gesta, 10; Chron. Giles, 10; agonizantem pro justiciâ,
Gesta, 57; Francorum violenta manus, Elmham, Lib. Metr. 104; rebellionem Gallorum,
Vita, 34.

Accordingly on March 14[1] the Dukes of Bedford, Gloucester and York, accompanied by Archbishop Chichele and Bishop Beaufort, presented themselves at the Guildhall, where they were saluted with due reverence by the Mayor and Aldermen, for such a visit was one of the most notable events that London had seen for many a day. A question of precedence at once arose which was settled by the Mayor occupying the chief seat, with the bishops on his right hand and the dukes on his left[2], and before the distinguished visitors took their leave the city had agreed to advance them 10,000 marks[3], to be secured on the customs on wool of the port of London[4] and repaid by New Year's Day, 1417, the King's Treasurer depositing with the Mayor a large gold pusan[5], or collar, made of crowns and antelopes and enamelled with SS, as a gage for punctual repayment[6]. Having obtained this loan the king issued a proclamation on March 22[7] commanding that all knights, squires and varlets who owed service by virtue of fiefs, wages or annuities granted or confirmed since the beginning of the reign of Edward III should hasten to London by April 24 to receive their marching orders. On April 11[8] an order was issued to impress every ship with a portage of 20 tuns and upwards that could be found in any English haven from Bristol round to Newcastle and to have them collected

[1] Letter Book I, 135; Riley, Mem. 603–605.
[2] For a reference to this precedent in 1670, see Letter Book I, p. xxiii.
[3] Letter Book I, pp. xxiv, 143, 144, 158; Riley, Mem. 613. Not 20,000 marks, as Besant, Survey, i. 106, who supposes that they subsequently added 5000 more and £2000 on the security of a valuable sword.
[4] Letter Book I, 142, 158; Rym. ix. 298, 299.
[5] Probably so called because it came from Pisa, Aubrey, ii. 54. For a "pusan of gold called the rych collar," valued at £2800, pledged in 1440, see Bayley, 180. For gorgerette pisaine (i.e. Pisan), see Godefroy, vi. 176; called "pesan," Wylie, iv. 357; throzhe ventaille and pusan, Stratmann, s.v. *Pusane*; pisan, Kempe, 18; pesyne, Romania, xxxii. 58; gorgerete pizaine, pusane, trois coleretes pizaines, bascinet cum pusano, Kelly, 464.
[6] For indenture dated June 16, 1415, see Letter Book I, p. 143; Riley, Mem. 613; Rym. ix. 405.
[7] Letter Book I, pp. xxiv, 134.
[8] Rym. ix. 218. For money paid to John Everdon, war-clerk (clericus guerrae Regis in presenti viagio), see Iss. Roll 3 H. V, Pasch., May 18, 1415 (*bis*), sending John Wenslowe to pay wages of masters and sailors to be impressed (arrestand') in ports from the Thames northwards, to be at Southampton with all possible speed, see Iss. Roll 3 H. V, Pasch., April 27, 1415; also Rec. Roll 3 H. V, Mich., Dec. 13, 1415; Exch. Accts. 44/27, 28, where Everdon is clerk for paying wages of war. In Rec. Roll 3 H. V, Pasch., July 17, 1415, John Everdon is an auditor of the Exchequer. In Pat. 8 H. V, 15, Oct. 17, 1420, John Draper is appointed to a prebend in St Stephen's Chapel, formerly held by John Everdon *dum vixit*.

at London, Sandwich, Winchelsea and Southampton by May 8 at the latest. The customers and controllers of the ports had been summoned to be at the Exchequer at Westminster by Easter[1], £10. 5s. worth of parchment[2] having been bought at the haberdasher's to be used for the approaching business, and on May 1 the king's voyage was spoken of as expected " within a short time[3]."

But very much had yet to be accomplished before a start could safely be undertaken. On April 16, 1415[4], a great council[5] was held in the Palace at Westminster, at which the Dukes of Clarence, Bedford, Gloucester and York were present, together with Archbishops Chichele and Bowet, eight bishops (including Beaufort, Clifford, Courtenay and Langley), the Abbots of St Albans, Gloucester, Waltham, Colchester and Reading, nine earls and fifteen barons.   To these the Chancellor (Bishop Beaufort) formally announced that the king had resolved to cross the sea to recover his heritage and asked their aid in carrying out his plan.   On the next day[6] they were told that the Duke of Bedford would be the king's lieutenant[7] during his absence from England and that he would be assisted by a council of nine members with Archbishop Chichele and Bishops Beaufort and Langley at their head[8].   The levies of Cumberland,

---

[1] For payments to messengers sent to Hull, Lynn, Melcombe and Exeter, see Iss. Roll 3 H. V, Pasch., Apr. 27, 1415.

[2] See App. F[2].

[3] Infra breve, Iss. Roll 3 H. V, Pasch.

[4] Ord. Priv. Co. ii. 150, 155; Rym. ix. 222.   Not March 15, as Waurin, i. 165.   For £23. 12s. 1¼d. paid for dinner to the Duke of Clarence and other lords in the Palace at Westminster, see Devon, 340, Apr. 19, 1415.

[5] Consilio et assensu *procerum* regni nostri, Add. MS. 24,062, f. 147, written on the return of the Earl of Warwick from Constance.   He was at Bruges on May 1, 1415, on his way back, Gilliodts van Severen, Invent. iv. 332.   Called a Kriegs-u.-Reichsrat in Niethe, 12; not a parliament, as S. Turner, v. 393; Michelet, vi. 13; Sismondi, xii. 459; J. S. D. Scott, ii. 415; principes magnates et proceres, etc., Vita, 35.

[6] April 17, 1415; Ord. Priv. Co. ii. 157; Rym. ix. 223.

[7] Son lieuteñ eñ sabsence, Ord. Priv. Co. ii. 168.

[8] Rym. ix. 224; Ord. Priv. Co. ii. 158.   The others were the Earl of Westmoreland, Lords Grey of Ruthen, Berkeley, Powys and Morley and the Prior of the Hospitallers at Clerkenwell, i.e. Walter Grendon, who was appointed Prior by bull of the Grand Master Philibert de Naillac, dated Rhodes, Oct. 18, 1400, Bedford-Holbeche, 187.   He was previously Preceptor at Halston near Oswestry (Lewis, s.v.; not in Norfolk, as Monast. vii. 802; viii. 1728).   He is mentioned as Prior in August and October 1401 (Bund, 380, 381); also on Dec. 4, 1401, Jan. 19, 1405, Oct. 16, 1407 (Holmes, Reg. 17, 58, 70), where he presents to the living of Halse-Priors near Taunton, Collinson, iii. 528.   He is Prior in 1408 (Monast. vii. 799), in 1409 (Cal. Pat. H. V, i. 35; Pat. 3 H. V, ii. 42; Priv. Seal Writs, 1423/383) and Feb. 20, July 5, 1416 (Pat. 3 H. V, i. 12d; do. 4 H. V, 20 d).   He was succeeded on May 24, 1417, by William Hulles, Bedford-Holbeche, 187; Rym. ix. 455; see Guthrie, ii. 457.

Westmoreland, Northumberland, Durham and York would remain available in the north to check any possible inroad by the Scots and these would be strengthened by a force of 600 men-of-arms and archers[1], while Berwick was to be provisioned[2] and wages were to be paid to the garrisons at Roxburgh[3] and Carlisle. Three hundred men were considered sufficient to protect the whole of Wales[4] whither the Earl of Arundel[5] was to go to hold a muster and report, while 450 each were to be allotted to the defence of the march of Calais[6] and the safeguarding of the sea[7] respectively.

The temporal lords[8] who were present at the meeting agreed to serve if a quarter's wages were paid to them in advance and the payment for all their subsequent service made at the end of the second quarter, but as these terms were too onerous, they agreed a few days later to accept payment at the end of each succeeding quarter as the time came round, pledges being previously given for prompt payment. At the same time the bishops and abbots agreed to make immediate cash advances, which would be repaid as soon as the grants recently sanctioned in Convocation should actually fall in. It was calculated that the king might be away for a year and it was now agreed that

---

[1] Rym. ix. 327. [2] Rot. Scot. ii. 214.
[3] For £628. 19s. 10d. paid to Robert Umfraville, kt. for keeping the castle of Roxburgh, see Rec. Roll 3 H. V, Pasch., July 27, 1415; Ord. Priv. Co. ii. 179 (i.e. from June 24 to Dec. 31, 1415).
[4] For payment to William Butler for convoying certain sums of money to be paid to troops in South Wales, see Iss. Roll 3 H. V, Pasch., May 18, 1415. For £18. 12s. od. lately sent to Wales, see ibid. For £1136. 6s. 8d. + £255. 5s. 7d. paid to John Weele (or Wele, or Weole, Wylie, iii. 267), Thomas Straunge and Hugh Say (Captain of Welshpool in 1411, Wylie, iii. 268, note 1), see Rec. Roll 3 H. V, Pasch., July 17, 1415, where Thomas Walton is Chamberlain of North Wales. For payment to a messenger, carrying a letter with the king's signet to John Grendor, knight (i.e. in South Wales, Wylie, iii. 111), see Iss. Roll 3 H. V, Pasch., April 19, 1415. The following payments were made for the garrisons, etc., viz. £546. os. od. to Thomas Straunge and others from March 25 to June 24, 1415, for North Wales, 60 + 122; £970. os. od. + £930. os. od. to John Merbury, Thomas Straunge and others from June 24 to Sept. 29, 1415, for North and South Wales, 100 + 200. For £282. 14s. 6d. paid to Thomas Straunge for custody of North Wales, see Iss. Roll 3 H. V, Pasch., April 24, 1415; for John Norreys, Captain of Conway (1 + 9), Sept. 24, 1413, see Sloane MS. 4600, f. 267, not Courney, as Nicolas, 382; John Salahel, Constable of Harlech (1 + 12), Sept. 24, 1413, Sloane MS. 4600, ff. 267, 268, 279, 280 (al. Salthagh, Ord. Priv. Co. ii. 336; or Salghall, ibid. iii. 61); Nicolas Saxton, Captain of Rothelan (Rhuddlan), Sept. 24, 1413, Sept. 29—Dec. 31, 1414, Sloane MS. 4600, ff. 268, 280; Ord. Priv. Co. ii. 179. For Rhuddlan castle, see Morris-Jordan, 216.
[5] For £6. 13s. 4d. paid to him before he started, see Iss. Roll 3 H. V, Pasch., April 27, 1415.
[6] See App. G². [7] See App. H².
[8] Called "half civilized chiefs" in Brougham, 99, 105.

during that time each duke who served with him should receive a mark (13s. 4d.) per day, and each earl a noble (6s. 8d.), while barons, knights (or bachelors), squires[1] (or men-of-arms) and archers would be paid at the rate of 4s., 2s., 1s. and 6d. each per day respectively according to a scale fixed more than a century before[2], the rates being much lower if a whole year's pay was received at once, and specially tempting terms being offered if service should be required in Guienne[3].

The days of feudal military service had by this time completely passed away in England[4], and the wages of every man that took part in the coming campaign had to be paid in cash. Moreover the king had to find transport for every horse and every man and to pledge his jewels or plate as a guarantee of payment wherever the money for wages was not immediately forthcoming. On the other hand, he was entitled to claim one-third of all "gains and winnings of war[5]," and if the King of France himself or any of his sons, uncles, nephews or other relatives should be taken prisoner, they were to be his with their accruing ransoms[6]. All other prisoners were to be at the disposal of their actual captors, and the indenture of service contained a distinct proviso that a record must be kept of all prisoners, money, gold, silver or jewels captured over 10 marks in value. But, in any case, if troops were wanted for service abroad, they had to be paid for it and the scale

---

[1] The Sqwyers toke her harneis, Laud Troy Book, 423, 485.

[2] i.e. in 1300, Stubbs, ii. 307; also 1346, Morris-Jordan, 236. See App. I[2].

[3] For les gages de Guyenne, viz. 40 marks and 20 marks to men-of-arms and archers respectively, for a year's service, see Rym. ix. 258. For Gascon arblasters à cheval at 9d. per day, do. à pee (6d.), see Sloane MS. 4600, ff. 274, 284.

[4] H. Hall, Antiquities, 25; Wade, 79, who adds that the horse had to be supplied by the contractor, but the equipments by the king.

[5] For "wynnings of werre," see Archaeologia, xvii. 215; Nicolas, App. 34; gaynes and wynnynges, Rym. xiii. 328. Another one-third might be claimed by the captain (cf. pay his thriddes to his lord, capitene or maister, Black Book of Adm. i. 288, 290, 463), and a further ninth-part by the actual captor whatever his rank, cf. tierces et tierce de tierce et autres gagnes de guere, Rot. Parl. iv. 320, 321; Nicolas, App. 56; parte tertiâ redemptionis (or lucri), Upton, 139, 142, 143; lucrationis guerrae, Exch. Accts. 46/15, 19, where William Mounteney receives 16d. as the third of a third of 12s. from the redemption money of a French prisoner captured by one of his three archers. Also 4s. 5d. as one-third of 13s. 4d. for another Frenchman captured by one of his men-of-arms loco dicti Willelmi. Exch. Accts. 47/13 shows 291 crowns paid by divers prisoners of France (no names) of which the king's share (reckoning 6 crowns to the £, page 407, note 9) = £48. 10s., and Thomas Lord Camoys receives £16. 3s. 11d., which should be £16. 13s. 4d. if worked out as one-third of one-third; see also W. D. Cooper, 133.

[6] Faciendo rationabile aggreementum, Exch. Accts. 45/7, and *passim*.

of payment was certainly regarded as remunerative by the captains who undertook the obligation[1].

It used to be imagined that the troops that Henry V took with him over to France consisted of "a feudal levy[2]," whereby all tenants in chief[3] were originally bound to bring up their armed vassals and serve the king when called upon, free of wage. But one of the inherent weaknesses of the feudal obligation was that it was strictly limited to 40 summer days[4], and since the commutation of the liability to personal service into a money payment or scutage[5] in the time of Henry II[6] it had become necessary to find wages[7] for troops of all arms according to the scale above quoted[8]. All troops serving under these conditions entered into a contract of their own free will, binding themselves under indentures[9] to serve for at least three months on condition that their wages were prepaid for that period[10]. For many generations England had practically been an armed nation[11], the ordinances of Henry II[12] and the

[1] Jähns, 846; J. S. D. Scott, i. 271.

[2] Strickland, ii. 117, 119, who supposes that "extraordinary methods were taken to induce them to tarry beyond the 40 days they were bound to attend." Towle (287) thinks that Henry "ordered every county to furnish its quota," though called "the great barons with their respective quotas," ibid. p. 293.

[3] For tenants in chivalry, see Stubbs, i. 658. For lands held per servitium militare, see Pat. 8 H. V, 3; par service de chevaler, Gaunt Reg. I. pp. xvii, 83. For tenants by serjeanty, see Round, Commune of London, 61, 183.

[4] Lingard, iii. 119; Stubbs, i. 491, 660; ii. 302; Köhler, ii. 362.

[5] Stubbs, i. 661; J. S. D. Scott, ii. 401; Fortescue, i. 16; Lloyd, 56. For earlier examples see Encycl. Brit., s.v. For scutage (or escuage, Hallam, 87) used to pay mercenaries, see Köhler, ii. 357. For the great scutage of 1159, see Baldwin, 3, 21, who calls it "one of the greatest anti-feudal influences," ibid. 63, 110. For the statute of 1346, see Rot. Parl. ii. 160, 170; Rym. v. 489, 490; Lingard, iii. 120; not 1345, as Wrottesley, 1. By this all holders of land or rents yielding 100s. per annum must provide one archer, do. £10 one hobeler, and £25 one man-of-arms. London found 100+500 de unâ sectâ, New Rymer, June 1, 1359, pp. 22–26, 37–41.

[6] Called Edward I in J. E. Morris, 36, 69; Morris-Jordan, 213.

[7] Ad vadia nostra (1297), Stubbs, ii. 309; Lingard, iii. 120, 122; "at your wage," Rym. ix. 883.   [8] Page 457.

[9] For service by indenture since the time of Edward III, see Stubbs, iii. 583; Oman, in Traill, ii. 327; Kingsford, 198, 205. For contracts indents temp. Ed. II, see Fortescue, i. 21; not that the system was instituted by Henry V, as Towle, 287, nor that by this arrangement the statute against liveries was "entirely ignored," as Airy, i. 143, for that statute expressly provided for the wearing of liveries out of England and in presence of the king or in time of war, Stat. ii. 113; Wylie, i. 69. For a specimen indenture with James Clifton (6+18), dated April 29, 1415, see Musgrave, 269; also Beamont, 231, from Rym. ix. 233.

[10] For indenture of prest, i.e. money in advance, see Beamont, 232.

[11] Sont tous gens de guerre, Bouvier, Descr. 119, where the English are cruelz et gens de sang.

[12] i.e. the Assize of Arms (1181), Stubbs, i. 662; ii. 301, 304, 305; do. Select Charters, 153; Translation, 54–56; Tout, 124; Lingard, iii. 122 (1251); J. S. D. Scott, i. 254; Fortescue, i. 11; Green, 106.

legislation of Edward I[1] having compelled every man in the community to provide himself with arms and armour varying according to his degree[2] and the amount of his belongings.

Thus every able-bodied man between 16 and 60 years of age[3] in every town, village and hamlet could be furnished with a quilted jack (variously known as an acton, hauberk, hanselin, paunce, paltock, pilch, purpoint, gambeson or wambais), a basnet (or kettlehat), and gloves, and for attack a sword, a dagger, a pole-axe (otherwise called a gisarme or besegewe), a stock of arrows, a quiver and a bow. In the case of well-to-do persons this outfit was provided at the wearer's own expense and remained his personal property, being kept at his own house and produced for inspection twice a year at a view-of-arms[4] as required by statute[5], though there is evidence that in some cases the articles belonged to the community and had to be re-deposited at a public armoury when the required 40 days of service came to an end[6]. These troops, which were known as the fencibles[7] or the people's array[8], were always

---

[1] i.e. the Statute of Winchester (1285), which re-enacted the Assize of Arms, Rym. (edit. 1821) II. ii. 900; Stat. i. 97; Stubbs, Select Charters, 469–474; Grose, Mil. Antiq. i. 12; Lingard, iii. 120; Stubbs, ii. 116, 304; Green, 166; Tout, 185; Köhler, ii. 370; Jähns, 846; J. S. D. Scott, i. 255; Fortescue, i. 16; Bateson, Leicester, ii. 45.

[2] Armyd and arayde as langys to thair estate, Rym. ix. 883; solonc son estat et facultee, Gaunt Reg. i. 107; secundum cujuslibet gradus et status exigentiam, Cartellieri, Beiträge, iv. 8, 21. See App. J[2].

[3] Rot. Scot. ii. 220; Wylie, iii. 110.

[4] For "muster or view," see First Life, 30; la visitation de l'arnois, Aussy, Reg. iii. 98, at St Jean d'Angély. Cf. quod omnes soldarii in monstris ostensi suam propriam armaturam ostendant, Upton, 137. In 1415 the Londoners crossing to settle at Harfleur were to come "with all manner of clothing, armour and artillery," Letter Book I, p. 161. In Letter Book F (1337) a man-of-arms of the City of London was armed with a haketon, plates, bacinet with visor, and gauntlets of plate. At Orleans, the harness of a townsman consisted of heuque with a girdle (*ortie*, see Godefroy, s.v.), casque de fer sans visière et gorgerin, Lotin, i. 184, where they carry bows, crossbows, swords, guissarmes (*sic*), haches, pics and mallets de plomb. Cf. "wherewith to bie hem bowes, arroes, jakkes and other armour of defence," Fortescue (Plummer), 137, 283; Kingsford, 201. In 1421 an inventory of the belongings of the Dean of the Cathedral at Troyes includes: 1 hauberjon de plate maille sans colet, 1 paire de brasselez à oreillez, 1 do. gantelez, 1 bassinet à camail garny de visière, 1 petite espée à ung plomeau ronc garnie de gayne, 1 hache de noire, 1 petite pique, Arbois de Jubainville (1873), p. 397.

[5] i.e. the Statute of Winchester, 1285, Stat. i. 97, 98; Lloyd, 57. Called 1270 in J. S. Gardner, Foreign, 8, who thinks that the armour was to be "kept for the king's use at a reasonable valuation."   [6] Hutchins, i. 249 (1323).

[7] Omnes homines defensabiles, Rym. ix. 253 [255]; armati, hobelarii, sagittarii et alii homines defensabiles, Rot. Scot. ii. 226; Lansdowne MS. 1054, f. 53; toutes maneres de gentz defensables sibien gentz d'armes hobelers et archiers come autres, Gaunt Reg. i. 107.

[8] Laraye du poeple, Ord. Priv. Co. ii. 167. For the feudal array as contrasted with the national militia or *fyrd* (called wahre Volksbewaffnung in Assmann, iv. 102), see Stubbs, i. 493.

at hand in their own locality and could be called out at any time by the sheriff's hue and cry for the defence of the country. When so arrayed they were classed as men-of-arms[1], hoblers[2] (i.e. lightly armed men who acted as scourers[3] mounted on hobbies[4]) and archers[5], all of whom were mustered and officered in thousands, hundreds and scores[6].

But during the French wars of Edward III great changes had come over the fighting force of England and with the development of the system of service by indenture had come a great advance, especially as regards the armour of defence. The chain mail, with which the fighters of earlier days had clothed themselves from head to foot[7], had gradually given place to less cumbrous[8] and more

---

[1] For homines ad arma, armati et sagittarii, see Daumet, 163; Wrottesley, i. 2, who considers that the first group alone were mounted and that the rest were infantry, Köhler, ii. 354, 371. For a list of burgesses at Troyes in 1404, fit to bear arms for the defence of the town, see Boutiot, iii. 309, where they are divided into (a) hommes de fer (i.e. armed with cuirasses); (b) hommes de pourpoint (artisans) with vêtements de toile ou de cuir armed with a plombier or mallet de plomb. For "men-of-armes," see Secreta, 170, 209; homines armorum, Upton, 136; Chron. R. II–H. VI, 47; Laud Troy Book, 67, 86, 99, 115, 255, 275, 349, 393, 499; Lydg. Troy Book, 176, 403; York, 35; Kingsford, Chron. 77; Nicolas, App. 36; Harflet, 71; Lydg. Burgh, 76; Brut, ii. 383; Caxton, Fayt, Bk. II. chap. 28; Pol. Relig. Po. 24, 31, 34; Crowned King, 528; Halle, 69, 70; Holinsh. iii. 554, 555; J. Coke, 95, 113; homines ad arma, Exch. Accts. 46/25, where the list includes 2 "gentilmen"; "hommes d'armes," Petit, 50, 61, 96, 131, 138; or gentz d'armes, Leroux de Lincy, Chants Hist. 34; Black Bk. of Adm. i. 290, 457, 465; "men-at-arms," Drayton, 43, 64, 66; Speed, 772, 776; but both forms in Trussel, 101; "knightes, squires and yomen," Lydg. Min. Po. 143; called cavalcados (hommes à cheval) in Provence, Fervel, 78. For picture of homme d'armes (1486) with axe, sword and baton, see Leroux de Lincy, 304. J. E. Morris (51) regards the homines ad arma as heavy cavalry and armati as light cavalry, the serviens ad arma being a mounted soldier. Among the garrison at Harfleur (1415), the men-of-arms are divided into mounted and foot, apart from the knights and the archers.

[2] For William le Hobelur, see Exeter Deeds, no. 28.

[3] Scourrers à cheval, Sloane MS. 4600, f. 265; called eine leichte Reiterei, Jähns, 845; "a corps of vedettes," J. S. D. Scott, ii. 26. Köhler (ii. 366) supposes that the hoblers were freeholders and the archers yeomen.

[4] Hobi, steed and good rounci, Laud Troy Book, 192; Kempe, 18; cf. upon his hoby swyftly ran, Pol. Songs, ii. 155; "hoby," G. H. Radford, 23; Meyrick, in Nicolas, App. 44, 46; Kingsford, 203; Murray, Dict., s.v. Hobbler. For Irish hobbies, see J. S. D. Scott, ii. 24; Minsheu, 238. For Hob as the name of a horse, see Drayton, Oldcastle, 333. Called "demilances" in Wrottesley, p. 3, who identifies them with mounted archers. For a "ryght fayre hoby," see Archaeologia, xxvi. 277; Tighe and Davies, i. 369; called "little nags" in Lloyd, 63; supposed to be Irish in Morris-Jordan, 231.

[5] For hommes de trait et de manoeuvre, see Aussy, Reg. iii. 237.

[6] In millenis, centenis et vintenis, Rym. ix. 350, 793 (1419); Gaunt Reg. i. 107 (1372); under the command of constables, centeners and vinteners respectively, Wrottesley, p. 4; Harl. MS. 782, f. 68; Halliwell, i. 238. For "millenars," see Lloyd, 57; Murray, Dict., s.v. *Milleniers*.

[7] For picture (circ. 1250) of a knight in chain mail laced down the leg, see Villard de Honnecourt, 177, Plate XLV. For archers and crossbowmen (temp. Ed. II) fully clad in mail, see Meyrick, i. 175. For specimens of links in chain mail, see Brett, 6, 72.

[8] J. S. D. Scott, i. 201, 211 thinks that plate armour was less cumbrous because the quilted gambeson below the hauberk was no longer necessary.

showy plates[1] of burnished steel, which could be hinged
and buckled round the vulnerable parts and easily put on
and off in sections[2] as required.   Many monuments and
brasses still existing[3] bear witness to the gradual working
of this important change.   The head was protected by
an iron basnet or head-piece[4], the body was covered back
and front with a corslet of plate reaching from the shoulder
to the thigh, the arms were guarded[5] with vambraces and
rerebraces[6], the legs with greaves of plate or querbole[7],
and the feet were shod with steel sollerets[8] articulated like
lobster shells to give free play to the necessary movements,
and we may take it that the men-of-arms who followed
Henry V were armed in plate from head to foot, though
chinks of chain survived at the joints and other flexible
portions of the body, the only remnants of mail being
found in the camail which was fastened by rings to the
basnet to protect the neck and throat and a fringe of it
that hung from the base of the corslet[9] about the loins to
allow of ready movement when in the saddle.

From the fact of Henry's troops being paid a wage
their service has led a modern writer to describe them as
mercenaries and the captains as "hired condottiere[10]," but

[1]   An hol brestplate with a rere-doos
                    Behynde schet or ellys on the side.
                                        Lydg. Troy Book, 396.
                    And wolde have of plate a bavior
                    That on the brest fastnyd be aforn. Ibid.
[2] For "pieces of harnys," see Melusine, 262; "armed of all pieces," ibid. 251, 301, 360. For la coste d'acier, le pan, la piece et les harnoys de jambes as a complete suit, see Arras, 79.
[3] See App. K².
[4] Nicolas, App. 36; Black Book of Admiralty, i. 457.
[5] For 655 paire de gardebras (1382), see Bréard, 150.
[6] J. S. D. Scott,·i. 209.
[7] Querboyl, Lydg. Troy Book, 366; curboille, Baildon, Inv. 172.   His jambeaux were of quyrboilly, Chaucer, Sir Thopas, 13,804; Brett, 75; Halliwell, 285; J. S. Gardner, 41; Ffoulkes, 34. For greaves of "quirboill" (1365), see Hewitt, II. pp. xv, xvii, 231, 237; Wylie, iv. 359. For cuir bouillé, see J. S. D. Scott, i. 222; cur bulhit, Lamothe, ii. 423; cofre lonc de curbulhit (to hold deeds), Charrier, i. 215; page 143, note 6; coffin de fer blanc couvert de cuir bouly, Pannier, xxvii. 34.   For a case of quyrboilli for a psalter (1397), see Dillon-Hope, 280; called "tanned part-boiled leather," Long, lxxxiv, 466; or tanned leather, Strang, 94; gepresstes Leder, Hefner, ii. 28.
[8] Brett, 80.
[9] For chain mail showing beneath the taces or tasses (i.e. thigh-pieces), see Meyrick, ii. 127; Hewitt, ii. 314 (xvii); Lacrosse, 399; Boutell, 37, 38, who supposes this to be part of a light hauberk, or perhaps a skirt of mail, see Steyert, Aperçu, 29; but it is more likely that it was merely pour garantir les parties de l'armure ne joignant pas suffisament, as Steyert, ii. 607. See also the effigy of John de Montacute, Earl of Salisbury (d. 1389), in the nave of Salisbury Cathedral.
[10] Aubrey, Rise, ii. 13.

no name could well be more misleading[1], for the numerous existing lists which give the actual names of the details that made up the force show that all, from earl to villain[2], were out-and-out Englishmen interspersed with a few Welsh, and were obviously drawn from precisely the same classes as those that were liable to be called out at the sheriffs' levies for home defence. A recent writer[3] has supposed that the two groups were wholly. distinct and unconnected with one another and it is still a matter for further investigation how far the new principle of contract between leaders and followers was independent of local and personal attachment. A perusal of the muster-rolls proves conclusively that they were by no means always, or even chiefly, drawn from the tenantry of the captains whom they followed to the field[4]. Some of the existing lists[5] would seem to show that the difference is merely nominal and that the feudal lord still led his own tenants as before, but in one case it is certainly possible to bring the matter to an exact test owing to the preservation of documentary material of a peculiarly valuable kind.

One of the captains who crossed to France with the king's second expedition was William Bourchier, who took with him a retinue of 40 lances and 124 varlets (*vadlet'*) or archers, all of whose names are preserved in the great muster-roll of 1417[6]. At this time he was lord of the manor of Great Waltham near Chelmsford and from the Court Rolls of that manor, which are still extant, we fortunately have an unusually full account of the names and condition of his tenantry. Four years after his crossing to France the manor came into the king's hands, and on July 16, 1421, the whole of the copyhold tenants (162 in number) renewed their oath of fealty and every one of their names[7] is accordingly entered on the manorial

---

For soldarii ad lanceam, see Upton, 142. In Claus. 4 H. V, 13, 15, archers are called solderii. Cf. sowdyour, ibid. 17 d; Wylie, ii. 130, note 13; iii. 97, note 8; sawdyours for silver for to take sawdes, Melusine, 149; pour estre soudoiez pour argent, Arras, 163; soudyours sustenyd by mony, Secreta, 208.

[2] Laud Troy Book, 490.

[3] Oman, 594.

[4] In the retinue of Sir William Butler, only one of the 10 lances (viz. John Orford) seems specially to belong to the locality, Beamont, i. 232; Exch. Accts. 47/8.

[5] e.g. W. D. Cooper, 123–137.

[6] Exch. Accts. 51/2, m. 23; Wylie, Notes, 117.

[7] Waltham Rolls, Dr A. Clark's Note Book B, p. 49.

roll at that date. Yet not a single one of these names
appears on Bourchier's muster in 1417, which contains
many distinctly Welsh or west-country names such as
Ap Thomas, Fairclough, Groyn, Luttrell, Pensax, Poyntz
and Skydmere among the men-of-arms, and Greynder
and Hobledod among the varlets, though Bourchier held
no land in the west country at all[1]. On the other hand
we know from other sources[2] that besides franklins, yeomen
and husbandmen plenty of tradesmen such as butchers,
barbers, drovers, dyers, fishmongers, skinners, and smiths
left their ordinary occupations and flocked to the levies
whenever money was to be got. But though, like everything else in that age, the spirit of military service was in
a transition stage and soldiering under the indenture system
was tending to become a profession[3], yet it is certain that
King Henry's soldiers were thorough Englishmen serving
under captains who were identified heart and soul with
what they believed to be England's quarrel and often
longing to return to their English homes and, as such, far
removed in spirit from those denationalised " companies[4],"
whose brutal brigandage made the very name of soldier
a terror and a by-word throughout Europe[5].

Still, side by side with this, it must likewise be borne in
mind that King Henry's soldiers did not serve for love, but
must not only be paid but pre-paid handsomely[6] for their
pains, and these prepayments had to be punctually made
through their captains[7] if the men's services were to be

---

[1] His own estate in Inq. p. Mort. iv. 48, is limited to Bildeston, near Needham
Market in Suffolk (which came to him by his marriage with Eleanor, daughter of John
Loreyn), and Easton-at-the-Tower, near Dunmow in Essex; i.e. Little Easton, so called
because the church had a tower, Great Easton being called Easton ad Montem, Morant,
ii. 431.

[2] e.g. Fr. Rolls, 4 H. V, 3, 4, 15; Carte, Rolles, ii. 234, Feb. 28, March 3, 9, 10, 12,
13, 19, 20, 1417.

[3] Called "the nearest approach to a standing army," J. S. D. Scott, i. 282; "national
armies of paid soldiers," Lloyd, 56.

[4] See Quicherat, 14; compaignes et gens d'armes nommez escorcheurs, Lannoy,
Oeuvres, 292; duas banderias peditum, Sathas, ii. 123 (for the protection of Modon).

[5] Niethe (57) attributes the defeat of the French to the fact that their army was
a "Lehnsheer," while the English were "Söldner des Königs."

[6] Ransom (p. 144) thinks that Henry had no difficulty in getting troops as the ordinary
wages of labourers was at this time 4*d.* per day, but the archers were not on the same
social level as a labourer. They are more accurately called "substantial yeomen" in
W. D. Cooper, 124; Köhler, ii. 366. Cf. Lord, Knight and archere, Pol. Songs,
ii. 124.

[7] Cf. mighty captayns and knytis in the feild, Pol. Relig. Po. 24; les chieftains
retenuz devers le Roy, Ord. Priv. Co. ii. 231; capitanei seu ductores, Claus. 4 H. V, 21 d.

retained. In a large proportion of cases the captain himself had to find the money in the first instance, relying
upon promises and pledges as his security for ultimate
repayment from the royal Exchequer. On signing his
indenture the captain covenanted to bring a certain number
of men-of-arms and archers, who should parade, or show
themselves (*monstrare*), properly armed and equipped on
a given day at an appointed place usually near the port
of departure. Both day and place were fixed by the king[1]
who undertook no responsibility for the payment of wages
until the men had satisfactorily passed a muster (*monstratio*[2])
held by one of the officers of the Exchequer, who was sent
down to verify them individually by means of a schedule
of names with which he had been previously supplied.
These schedules, together with the original indentures,
were then filed each in a separate pouch or bag of soft
sheepskin drawn together at the mouth with a thong made
of the same material and docketed on the outside with the
name of the official[3] who was concerned with the checking.
The pouches were then hung up on the walls of the Exchequer at Westminster[4], so as to be readily accessible for
reference as required and the whole of the details were
then engrossed on a parchment roll which was preserved
among the official records. The payment of wages by
the Exchequer began as soon as the muster was passed,
however long afterwards the actual start was delayed, and
besides the wage the king provided transport both for the
outward and the return voyage[5] and undertook to repay
the value of any horses[6] that might be lost in the campaign,

For two knights called sub-capitanei in the Earl of Northumberland's force, 1416, see
Claus. 4 H. V, 15.

[1] Le jour de la monstre a faire au lieux q' de par n'seigneur qu'sera assignez dedeinz
le moys de May, Exch. Accts. 45/8.

[2] Nicolas, App. 33. For personation and other frauds at musters, see Cotgr., s.v.
Passe-volant; J. S. D. Scott, ii. 337 (1406); Lavisse, 95; Wylie, iii. 60. Cf. no man be
so hardy as have other men at his moustres, otherwise mostre or mustre, Black Book
of Adm. i. 287, 463.

[3] e.g. "Everdon," Exch. Accts. 44/30, i.e. John Everdon, who was an Auditor
of Accounts in the Exchequer, Iss. Roll 4 H. V, Mich., Dec. 14, 1416.

[4] Aubrey, i. 457; Wylie, Notes, 108. For bags, pouches and hutches (*arks*) at the
Exchequer, see H. Hall, Studies, 16. For the Exchequer buildings at the north-eastern
angle of Westminster Hall, see H. Hall, Antiquities, 28.

[5] Outre double eskipeson, Ord. Priv. Co. ii. 158.

[6] Vickers, 19, refers to Edward III's liberal compensation for losses incurred in his
French wars, "even to the length of paying for horses lost in action." But this was no
new thing, see Edward I in Scottish wars, fr. Cal. Rot. Scot. 258.

the amount claimable in each case being fixed by a mark made on the animal's thigh[1], all else in the way of horsemeat and mansmeat being found by the captains themselves.

As to the armour[2] that Henry's soldiers wore the expert now-a-days will not be satisfied without a minute knowledge of the size, shape, name and function of every piece as vouched by existing museum specimens; but as fashion in armour was as transient as modern dress and varied greatly in different countries, it would be useless to attempt minute descriptive precision. It will be sufficient to note that for this particular expedition the fighting force was classed in two distinct groups, viz. (*a*) men-of-arms, otherwise known as "lances[3]," "spears[4]" or "glaives[5]," and (*b*) archers, known as "bows[6]" or "footmen[7]," the whole of the former and large sections of the latter[8] being mounted for purposes of mobility, though the actual fighting was at this period all done on foot. The men-of-arms usually brought two or more horses to the field each managed by a page, groom, varlet, henchman or custral, all of which appear to be only varying names indicating body-servants[9]

---

[1] Restauro equorum; cf. restour, J. S. D. Scott, ii. 339–341.

[2] For armour, see Weiss, i. 152–186. For armeurie in 1396, i.e. bacinez, heaumes, pièce d'acier, harnois de jambes, visières, haches, espées, fer de lances, dagues, cameaulz, see Trémoille, 83. In Caxton, Dial. 33, the armourer sells a plate, a bacenet, habergeon, gorget, and gloves of iron. For man-of-arms (1441) with basnet or salade (with visor), spear, axe, sword and dagger at the waist (usually hanging at either side of a belt), see Archaeologia, xvii. 215. For hauberks, plates, palettes, espees, bokelers, arkes et seetz et autres harnois, see Rot. Parl. iv. 92; haberions, palettes de ferre, arcuz, seetez, espees, bokelers et daggers, Baildon, 83, 84, 92; arcs et setes, ibid. 98. Meyrick, in Nicolas, App. 46, describes the man-of-arms as clad in complete armour from head to foot, including a shield, the face being covered with a moveable ventail attached to the basnet, a lance in the hand and a sword or dagger and mace in the belt or at either side of the saddlebow.

[3] Cf. de suo solidario ad lanceam vel sagittario, Upton, 143; lanceis et sagittarii, Rot. Parl. iv. 320, 321; Nicolas, App. 56; Exch. Accts. 46/36 and *passim*; lanceis sive militum triadibus, Tit. Liv. 31. For lancegays or lance-de-gay, see Raleigh's Hist. of the World, Book v. chap. iii, quoted in Hunter, Encycl. Dict., s.v.; Halliwell, ii. 503.

[4] "Sperres," Ralph Brook, Harl. MS. 782, in Nicolas, 367; First Life, 33; G. Scrope, 30; cf. men-of-armys with pollax, spear and sheald, Pol. Relig. Po. 24, 33; Melusine, 89, 92, 110 and *passim*.

[5] Jähns, 753; Gleven oder Lanzen, Hegel, III. clxxi; glavis et lansas, Lamothe, ii. 420; "gleaves," Drayton, Bat. 65; Holinsh. ii. 954, quoted in Murray, Dict., s.v. *Glaive*.

[6] G. Scrope, p. xxx; "speres and the bowes accustumed," J. G. Nichols, Fastolfe, 117, 118, from Caxton, translation of *De Senectute*.

[7] First Life, 33.   [8] See App. L[2].

[9] In 1414 the Duke of Burgundy's army at St Denis consists of bascinets, archers, arbalestiers et valets, D. Sauvage, 226; cf. her zomen and her knaves, Laud Troy Book, 423, 485.

or personal attendants, though there is clear evidence that in many cases the varlet was identical with the archer[1].

I have already given on a previous page[2] the rate of payment that still ruled in regard to each of the various ranks that undertook foreign service, but these amounts had to be supplemented by a bonus known as a "reward[3]," the payment of which was practically no longer an incident of each man's earnings, but a claimable and customary addition to them which could not be avoided, the bonus being at the rate of 100 marks per quarter for every 30 men-of-arms employed[4], though this did not apply to the archers.

Before the end of April 1415 indentures had been signed, whereby many leading Englishmen undertook to bring forces into the field varying in number according to their position in the country. Several of these indentures are still extant and were signed at Westminster on April 29, 1415[5], and subsequent dates. They exhibit the utmost

---

[1] For valetti or vadletti and archers in separate groups, but all included as archers in the indenture, see Exch. Accts. 45/18; also in the retinue of William Mounteney with three archers, each of whom is called "valettus," and the whole are grouped as *sagittarii*, ibid. 46/18; also of Thomas Corbet with three archers (Nicolas, 378), whose names are given in ibid. 47/22, where they are called *valetti*, though described as *sagittarii* in the indenture of service. The *sagittarii* are occasionally subdivided into varlets, archers and pages, see John Waterton's list in Exch. Accts. 45/1. In most of the existing muster-rolls of 1415, the terms varlets or archers are used indifferently, as distinguished from the "lances" or men-of-arms, though in those of 1417 the division is into lances and archers, Exch. Accts. 51/2. For three archers to each man-of-arms qui passaient pour leurs valets, see Baudot de Juilly, I. Preface. In Exch. Accts. 44/30 (1), the names are grouped as knights, squires and *valetti*, none being called archers till near the end, from which it might be inferred that the varlets included the archers. A few pages are named, and in one portion the knights and squires are called "gentilez" as opposed to "valettz"; amongst the former are included two chaplains, a herald and two "trumpeys."

[2] Page 457.

[3] Vadia et regarda, gages et regard, Du Cange, s.v. *Regardum*; ovesque regard accustumez, J. G. Nichols, 114, 126 (1421); regardis, Rot. Parl. iv. 320, 321; Nicolas, App. 58; Exch. Accts. 44/27; regardum consuetum, J. S. D. Scott, i. 279; ii. 415; W. D. Cooper, 127, 128; Hunter, 6. Called "prime supplémentaire," Belleval, 18. For "regards" paid to bell-ringers at a progress to visit New College property, see Rashdall, 250; pro rewardo fistulatoribus et palustribus (*sic*), i.e. wrestlers at Reading, see Hist. MSS. Rept. XI. vii. 173; cf. "ffeys rewardis and annuetees," Excerpt. Hist. 26. In Exch. Accts. 47/1 a draft written on paper gives a detailed statement of wages for the retinue of the Duke of Clarence (240+720), in which the totals with corrections generally work out right, e.g.

	£				£		
per day=	31	18	0+regard' 115*d.* (=9*s.* 7*d.*)				
per week=	£ 223	6	0+	,,	£ 40	5	0
month (4 weeks)=	£ 893	4	0+	,,	£ 161	0	0
quarter (13 weeks)=	£ 2092	18	0+	,,	£ 533	6	8
half-year (2 quarters)=	£ 5805	16	0+	,,	£1066	13	4
year=	£11643	10	0+	,,	£2133	6	8

including £31. 18*s.* 0*d.* for extra day.

[4] Exch. Accts. 49/12; juxta afferentiam, ibid. 45/7 and *passim*; Beamont, 231.

[5] Rym. ix. 227–238; Wylie, Notes, 108.

diversity in regard to numbers but in all other respects
are strictly uniform in terms and conditions. Thus the
Duke of Clarence[1] bound himself to bring 240 men-of-arms
and 720 archers, the Duke of York[2] 100 + 300, the Earl of
Dorset a like number[3], the Earl of Cambridge 60 + 160,
the Earl of Salisbury 40 + 80[4], the Earl of Huntingdon
20 + 60, Gilbert Lord Talbot 30 + 90, Thomas Gray 24 + 48[5],
John Fastolf 10 + 30[6], Thomas Tunstall 6 + 18[7], and so on
down to such diminutive retinues[8] as three archers brought
by one of the king's physicians[9] or surgeons[10]. All had to
come provided with a horse, including even the archers.
Every squire or man-of-arms must bring his four horses,
and every knight six, while bannerets, earls and dukes
each brought 16, 24 and 50 respectively[11].

To pay this host there was immediate need of cash,
and claims for any other purpose must necessarily be set
aside. In June 1415 two envoys from Count Louis of the
Palatinate were in England asking for payment of 8000
nobles still due as the dowry of the Princess Blanche, but
the only reply that they could get was a polite acknowledge-
ment of the king's indebtedness though he was for the
moment quite unable to meet it on account of the heavy

---

[1] For letters of protection dated May 8, 1415, for him and the Duke of York for one
year going across the sea in comitivâ regis, see Rym. ix. 239.

[2] For letter of the Duke of York, dated London, Feb. 10, 1415, acknowledging
receipt of 450 crowns in full payment of 500 francs (= 1500 souds esterlins, or 75 livres),
per Richard Makanam (Brutails, Bordeaux, 130, 239, 271, where his wife is Marie de
Saint Avit; or Makenan, Wylie, iii. 82, note 9) of Bordeaux, see Jurade, 189.

[3] For his account, see For. Accounts 10 H. V, 7, where he is bound by indenture,
dated April 29, 1415, to serve from July 4, 1415, to Jan. 4, 1416.

[4] For indenture signed in London, June 1, 1415, between the Earl of Salisbury
and William Bedyk, see Rym. ix. 258. For William More, bailiff of liberty to Earl of
Salisbury in Hunts., see Rec. Roll 3 H. V, Pasch., April 30, 1415.

[5] Rym. ix. 259, June 4, 1415.

[6] Rym. ix. 270, June 18, 1415.

[7] Nicolas, App. 8.

[8] Cf. "his retenewe," Brut, ii. 552.

[9] e.g. Master Nichol Colnet. For his receipt for £3. 6s. 8d. at the rate of 40 marks
p. a., see Rym. ix. 261.

[10] e.g. Thomas Morsted and William Bradwardyn, Nicolas, Agin. 387.

[11] Ramsay, i. 200; see App. L[2]. In Exch. Accts. 46/36, the Earl of Oxford
has 12 horses with 11 "hinkismen" or "henksmen," also 6 horses for his cariage (sic)
with 6 men a mesme la (sic) cheval et son harneys, i.e. a total of 18 horses, also 37 lances
and 31 pages, each lance having 2, 3 or 4 horses, and 1 or 2 archers + 1 page; also
84 archers, 37 of whom have 1 horse each and the rest none. The total money claim is
given as 100s. at the rate of 2s. per horse, but the total number of horses is given as 108
or 109 and the amount does not work out correctly either way. In Exch. Accts. 49/12,
William de la Pole, Earl of Suffolk in 1417, has 24 horses, each of his knights has
6, each man-of-arms 4, and each archer 1.

burdens at present on his shoulders[1], and they were referred to the Bishop of Norwich[2] for consideration and with that the Count must be content. As supplies from ordinary sources were altogether insufficient, the king put out an urgent appeal for prests[3] (i.e. ready money loans), wherever ready money was to be had. For this purpose messengers[4] were sent about the country bearing writs sealed with the king's signet and addressed to any layman or churchman who had any money or land, and John Pelham and William Sturmy[5] were authorised to receive any sums so raised and give a guarantee for prompt repayment. Many of these loans were certainly very soon refunded[6], but before the expedition started much of the royal plate and jewels had to be hypothecated[7] to many lords and knights as pledges for the payment of various amounts due to them under the terms of their indentures[8], it being understood that these

---

[1] Propter onera varia nostris humeris incumbentia et praesertim expedicionis militaris quam in nos suscepimus, Add. MS. 24,062, f. 147, where the envoys are a canon, Henry de G., and a knight, Dietrich K.

[2] Der sendboten van herzogen von Heidelberg bryve sulde der bischoff von Norwiez entrichted, Hanserecesse, vi. 140.

[3] Par voie d'appst., Ord. Priv. Co. ii. 205; "apprestez" (i.e. advanced), Rym. ix. 460, 461; "a prest of money," Davies, York Records, 118; Halliwell, iii. 644; "de prestito," Exch. Accts. 48/21; for roll of imprest (prestita), see ibid. 328/6. Called "imprest" in Blunt and Cowell, see Murray, Dict., s.v.; cf. prest and debte mot be yelde againe, Lydgate, in Monast. iii. 369 (1773); rendre convient debtes et prestz, Dufour, Archbishop. See page 458, note 10.

[4] For 40s. paid to Richard Norton, John Sewale and Hankyn de Mitton, messengers for this purpose, see Iss. Roll 3 H. V, Pasch., May 1, 1415.

[5] In 1414 he was elected at Wilton M.P. for Wilts. (i.e. to the Parliament that met at Westminster), Hoare, vi. 112. He was also M.P. for Wilts. in 1389, 1393, 1399, 1401, 1417, 1422, Return Parl. i. 239, 246, 259, 261, 285, 290, 304; Cotton MS. Cleop. F. 6, quoted in Collins, viii. 103; not "Esturing," as Goodwin, 55; Guthrie, ii. 457. In Pat. 2 H. V, ii. 38 d, June 20, 1414, William Sturmy, knight, is on a Commission of Enquiry in Gloucestershire. On May 29, 1415, he was a commissioner for arraying the king's forces in Wilts., Rym. ix. 253 [255]; see also Wylie, i. 469; ii. 71. For payment to a varlet of the Duke of Bedford as Custos of England, bearing a letter to William Sturmy, kt. from the king in Normandy, see Iss. Roll 5 H. V, Mich., Oct. 4, 1417. He appeared in the Chancery at Westminster on March 3, 1418, Close Roll 5 H. V, 1 d, 2 d, which has: by Sturmy vocat' Whetham in Hampshire. For land in the Pays de Caux in Normandy, granted to William Sturmy, May 18, 1419, see Bréquigny, 95; Charma, 7; Ewald, xli. 783; Carte, Rolles, i. 307.

[6] e.g. the Earl of Arundel (treasurer), £766. 13s. 4d. lent June 28, repaid Aug. 3, 1415; the Prior of Christ Church, Canterbury, £100 lent June 6, repaid June 25, 1415, Rec. Roll 3 H. V, Pasch., June 7, 1415; William Lord Ferrers of Groby, £333. 6s. 8d. lent Sept. 2, 1415, repaid next day; Richard Whitington, £466. 13s. 4d. do. do. Rec. Roll 3 H. V, Pasch., Sept. 3, 1415.

[7] For jocalia impignorata, 3 H. V, see Sloane MS. 4600, pp. 250-254; Nicolas, App. 13-18; diverses joialx en plegge pour lour severalx guages, Rot. Parl. iv. 320.

[8] For 135 indentures of jewels dated at Westminster, June 3, 5, 6-8, 12-19, 21, 23, 1415, and at Winchester on July 5, 6, 8-10, 12-15, 20, 1415, see Exch. Accts. 45/20, 21, 22, 23; 46/2, 10, 11. For Thomas Chitterne, Clerk of the Jewels, April 29, 1415, see L. T. R. Misc. Enrolled Accts. 6/7; also Dec. 19, 1415, Kal. and Inv. ii. 100.

articles would be redeemed by cash payments before New Year's Day 1417[1], though in a large number of cases the redemption was not effected till many years later[2].

On May 27, 1415[3], the Duke of Bedford and Bishops Beaufort and Courtenay were commissioned to deal with this branch, and all manner of articles were brought into the deal, such as swords, spurs[4], girdles[5], hawks-bells, gipsers[6], reading-desks[7], almsdishes[8], rosaries[9], and relics. Among the most notable pledges were a sword valued at £21 garnished with ostrich feathers that had belonged to the Black Prince[10], a gold collar known as "Ikelington's[11]" collar which had belonged to the king

[1] Rym. ix. 285, 288; Rot. Parl. iv. 320. For orders to Bishop Courtenay as Keeper of the King's jewels, dated May 30, July 12, 1415, see Rym. ix. 257, 280; dies circumcisionis domini, L. T. R. Misc. Enrolled Accts. 6/6, where the holders are bound to keep these jocalia absque brusamento or debrusiamento (or fractione) seu pejoracione. For order (1416) that pledges should be brought to the Exchequer to be redeemed, see Baines, i. 130, quoting Claus. 4 H. V, 11 d.

[2] e.g. anno 4, 6, 7, 8, 9, 11, 22 H. VI, Nicolas, App. 14, 15, from Sloane MS. 4600.

[3] Ord. Priv. Co. ii. 167.

[4] For one paire desporons dez tissues rouge pledged to Sir Thomas Hauley, see L. T. R. Misc. Enrolled Accts. 6/10, where the "tissues" weigh 8½ oz. troy. In the same account are one cingli de auro le tissu nigro, where the tissu weighs 2 oz., also one other cinclo de auro le tissu embroudez. For tissue=riband, see Cotgr., s.v.; Halliwell, s.v. Not "tyssers," as Nicolas, App. 17. Called "typers" in Turner, v. 397; or tysters (i.e. straps) lanières, Belleval, 21.

[5] One cinctor' (i.e. cinctorium) le tissu toto argent. garnisat' de auro, Misc. Enrolled Accts. 6/7; "god embroidered girdles," Exch. Accts. 46/15; seinture, ceinctor', ibid. 47/16. For girdles of gold and silver, see Lhomel, Edits, 114; Abram, 164, 308.

[6] i.e. pouches, Ashdown, 91, 138. For "ung gevessier" (i.e. gibecière), see Bruel, 41; not "typsere," as Nicolas, App. 18; gipsere de velvet de colore purpur' hernesat' cum auro, Kal. and Inv. ii. 100; Delpit, 218; returned to the Exchequer by the executors of John Attilbrigge, Oct. 31, 1415.

[7] For a silver reading-desk pledged to John Cliffe, minstrel, see Nicolas, App. 18; Belleval, 21.

[8] Wylie, iv. 333. For pot a aumones, see Bourassé, Châteaux, 65.

[9] e.g. one pair of paternosters containing 12 gold knopps or gaudies (Wylie, ii. 357) redeemed Oct. 31, 1415, from the executors of John Attilbrigge or At Bridge, Usher of Black Rod, see Kal. and Inv. ii. 100; Nicolas, App. 18, where he is going versus Hareflete in comitivâ regis. For unes paternosters de geest (7s. 6d.), see St Germain, 450, 456 (1412); p. uno magno pari de patnosteres de corallo cum nigris gaudees de achate (i.e. agate, Halliwell, s.v.) or jet, Harcourt, 445; unes paternostres de coral à un bouton de perles, Garnier, Invent. 616 (1415); do. d'or, Collas, 310; gaudes esmailles de vert, Baildon, Inv. 170; Rot. Parl. iv. 225; five grains rons de patenostres tailliez et emailliez de roge cler, Tremoille, 64; two paire de patenostres de gest, ibid. 62; une patenostres d'ambre blanc, Tuetey, Test. 581; bedes de cristall, of ambre, of glass and of horne, Caxton, Dial. 46; one peir Bedes de geet, Rot. Parl. iv. 227; paternoster over-gilte when he saithe Our Lady Sawter on hem, Fifty Wills, 58. For paternosters of coral, white and yellow amber, gold and silver, see Rossignol, i. 30 (1406); Rym. ix. 276; also of chalcedony, jet, jasper, crystal, green serpentine, glass, Job's tears, &c., Champion, Vie, 473.

[10] L.T.R. Misc. Enrolled Accts. 6/10, where it is valued at £21 and pledged to Sir John Hauley.

[11] See page 27, note 4. Called "Ikelton" or "Iklynton" in Coventry Leet Book, i. 60, 70; probably John Ikelington, who had been Treasurer of Henry's Household when he was Prince of Wales, page 27, note 4; Wylie, iv. 247; Rym. ix. 357; Pat. 4 H. V,

when Prince of Wales[1], and which was set with rubies, sapphires and pearls and valued at £300[2]. It was pledged together with other collars[3] from the Jewel Tower[4] and with them, in accordance with many precedents[5], were included the royal crowns[6], foremost among these being the "Henry Crown[7]," otherwise called the "Great Harry"

[1] 17, June 1, 1416. On April 18, 1413, he handed over to Thomas More, Treasurer of the King's Household (page 50, note 11) a quantity of chargers, dishes, salsers, spiceplates, silver potellers and galloners (*oll' arg' alb' de lagen'*), one cipp' with lid inlaid (*granat'*) with three leaves, sellars, colliar', chandelers, basins, &c., Exch. Accts. 406/16, where he is *late* Treasurer of the Household to the Prince of Wales. He was Rector of St Andrew, Holborn, from May 13, 1392, also of St Mary Abchurch in London from Feb. 7, 1397, to 1398, Hennessy, lxii. 90, 296. He held the prebend of Yetminster Secunda (Salisbury), ibid. He was Rector of Bridport from Aug. 19, 1394, to Oct. 1397, Hutchins, ii. 30; Papal Letters, iv. 645, and Archdeacon of Wells in 1398, Le Neve, i. 160; also July 16, 1407, Holmes, Reg. 69. On March 30, 1413, he was appointed a chamberlain (*camararius*) of the Exchequer *vice* John Legbourne (see Wylie, ii. 119 n.), Pat. 1 H. V, i. 37; Cal. Rot. Pat. 244; Cal. Pat. H. V, i. 2, 336, 365. In the heading to Iss. Roll 1 H. V, Mich., Sept. 29, 1413, John Ikelington is Camar' Regis. For 8*d.* per day paid to him and Master John Oudeby (page 2, note 4) as camararii of the Exchequer, see Iss. Roll 1 H. V, Pasch., July 14, 1413. In Pat. 3 H. V, i. 5, ii. 32, July 6, 1415, John Wodehouse is appointed a chamberlain of the Exchequer in place of John Ikelington. For four ships with 3300 poisson salez valued at £5 per 100 belonging to Richard Ikelington of London, captured by Flemings on June 6, 1412, see Gilliodts van Severen, 483. [1] Kal. and Inv. ii. 129.

[2] Nicolas, App. 13; Kal. and Inv. ii. 129, where it is handed to the Bishop of Worcester (T. Peverell), the Prior of St Mary's, Coventry, and the mayor and commonalty of that city as security for repayment of £500 lent by them to the king, see S. Turner, v. 396. On Feb. 17, 1424, it was in the custody of the Mayor of Coventry, who handed it together with a "nowche" and a jewel called "Cournall" (Coventry Leet Book, i. 70) to the Prior of St Mary's in return for 550 marks in cash, Devon, 402; M. D. Harris, Story, 104. For a piece of gold called "Iklyngton Collar" in 1440, see Bayley, 179, 181.

[3] For a gold crown and two colers d'or pledged to Ralph Shirley, July 6, 1415, see Kal. and Inv. ii. 106.

[4] It was built about the time of Richard II and is still standing in a mews off Great College Street, near Westminster Hall, Walcott, 209; Dasent, 7. For pictures of it, see ibid. pp. xxxviii, 8, 10, 12.

[5] For Edward III pledging his crown for 50,000 crowns, see Ruskin, Val d'Arno, 127, quoting R. Henry, Bk. IV. chap. i. For great crown pledged to Londoners by Richard II for £4000, see H. Hall, Antiq. 42. For the crown of France pledged to three bankers of Lucca and redeemed for 2030 liv. tourn. Sept. 17, 1414, see Pannier, 169. On Sept. 16, 1411, the Duke of Burgundy pledged la couronne de sa bonne fleur de lys to a Genoese merchant in Paris for a loan of 3000 francs Arras, Gachard, 108; Mirot, D'Orgemont, 140, 144. For Marie, wife of Robert Duke of Bar, pledging her crown to raise his ransom money (60,000 crowns) when imprisoned at Metz in 1372, see Renard, 87; Clouet, iii. 571.

[6] For a crown that had been Richard II's pledged to the Abbot of Westminster, see Nicolas, App. p. 13. For a crown pledged to the Duke of York in 1415, see York, xxiii; = 1 corone auri garnis' environ le chapelette with 4 gross ballys (*sic*) and sapphires and emeralds, L.T.R. Misc. Enrolled Accts. 6/3. For a corone d'or garniz enorrez le tussu (i.e. the fillet) de soy noir, see Kal. and Inv. ii. 106; un veil corone d'or debrusez, L.T.R. Misc. Enrolled Accts. 6/9. All the royal crowns of England were destroyed during the Commonwealth, none of the existing ones being earlier than the time of Charles II, Devonport, 4.

[7] "le Corowne Henry," Rym. ix. 289; also in L.T.R. Misc. Enrolled Accts. 6/1, where it is pledged to the Duke of Clarence and is called la corone de Henr' faite des oveignes de fleurs de lys garnizez le principal fleur dun tres grand balys weighing 1 oz., 1 esterlyng moyns (i.e. minus 1 dwt.), one rubie, one balys, three grosses saphyrs, 10 gross

or the Lancaster crown[1], which was pledged in sections[2], it being a common practice in those days for goldsmith's work to be made so that it could be taken to pieces[3] for convenience of cleaning[4], or to reduce risks in carrying it about[5]. Another precious wed[6] valued at 500 marks was the "pallet of Spain[7]," a head-piece[8] with a crown that had once belonged to Don Pedro the Cruel, King of Castile, and had been brought to England by his daughter Constance, the second wife of John of Gaunt[9].

What exact amount of money came in as a result of the appeal for loans we cannot now tell. The French believed that the total reached 500,000 nobles[10] and some English writers place it at 100,000[11], or even 800,000 crowns[12].

p'les (pearls) and dusze mendres. There are seven fleurs de lys, each of them being separately described et p'enter les fleurs de lys sont toute foitz assises oûaignez faitz a la man' dun pinnacle. For a crown with four fleurons en forme de fleurs de lys ornées de cosses de mouron, see Mirot, Trousseau, 128.

[1] It appears on the effigy of Henry IV at Canterbury, Weiss, i. 129, 135; Encycl. Brit. vi. 620; Aubrey, ii. 8; W. Jones, 37; Wylie, iv. 117. In Harl. MS. 4205 (written temp. H. VI) all the Kings of England wear it; also Cotton MS. Julius E. iv (circ. 1432).

[2] Strickland, ii. 117. For a fleur de lys of it pledged to John Colvyle, a pinnacle each to John Pudsey, Maurice Brune and John Staundish, with fragments redeemed in 1430, 1431, see Turner, v. 396; Nicolas, App. 15; W. Jones, 37. For John Pudsey, esquire, with retinue at Harfleur, see Nicolas, 383; Belleval, 361. For John Pudsey, kt., of Bolton, mar. Catherine daughter of Ralph Eure, see Purey-Cust, i. 38.

[3] Cf. argent rompu, Rym. ix. 798; vessel d'argent rumpitz, Rym. x. 319; depeased, First Life, 65; una chapa unius pugionis (dagger) fistulat' cum uno folio et alio auro fracto, Harcourt, 445. For "broke silver," see Benham, 66. For one chalys of silver broken (d'arg' rumpuz), see Baildon, Inv. 173 (1419); or rumpuz, Wylie, iv. 196.

[4] Cf. toute icelle couronne (i.e. the copper chandelier in the Sainte Chapelle at Bourges) clouée et attachée à viz en sorte que si on veut icelle nettoyer et polir les ouvriers la peuvent mettre toute par pièces et les rassembler en rechef, Chaumeau, 230.

[5] Cf. grand nef d'or rompu et mise en pièces pour porter plus aisement de Blois à Paris, Roman, 175; nostre bonne couronne a esté demembrée et les fleurons d'icelle baillés en gaiges, Pannier, 317, from ordonnance cabochienne, Art. 119. When the Duke of Brittany visited Rouen in March 1419, King Henry presented him with a large gold cup qui se met en trois pièces, probably the foot, the bowl, and the rim, Lobineau, ii. 922. For the Iron Crown of Lombardy now in the cathedral at Monza, see Stacke, ii. 175; W. Jones, 22, where it is enclosed by six equal plates of beaten *gold* joined by close hinges. Amongst the trousseau of Isabella, queen of Richard II, were two crowns each made in eight pieces, as well as gold chaplets in eight or ten pieces, and gold girdles in 12 or 16 pieces, Mirot, Trousseau, 128, 129, 139, 140, 141.

[6] Kingsford, Chron. 54, 55, 58, 119; Halliwell, ii. 920. Cf. be wed and borugh (=par gage et plegge), Blk. Bk. of Adm. ii. 6, 9, 93, 155; put to wedde, ibid. ii. 133; "deil a wadset," Heart of Midlothian, 26; "wadsetting (i.e. mortgaging) his lands," Hist. MSS. Comm. (1902), p. 259.

[7] Nicolas, App. 14; Belleval, Grande Guerre, 573.

[8] Stratmann, 467; Halliwell, ii. 599; Dillon, Besague, 16. Cf. "a prikyng palet of plate," Lydg. Troy Bk. 347; cum palettis in eorum capitibus, Conc. iii. 387.

[9] Strickland, ii. 119; H. Hall, Antiq. 44.

[10] Monstr. 362; Le Fèvre, i. 215; Waurin, i. 168; Nicolas, 24; Lingard, iii. 486.

[11] Holinsh. iii. 547; Stow, 345. Called £200,000 in Brougham, 101; or 300,000 marks, First Life, 27.

[12] Echard, i. 182.

Official records show that very large sums were received in the Exchequer especially in the month of June 1415. The loans were accepted from all sorts and conditions of men. Archbishops[1], bishops[2], abbots[3], priors[4], deans[5], cathedral chapters, friars[6], lords[7], knights[8], squires[9], merchants (both foreign and English), barons of the Cinq Ports, private citizens or burgesses[10], in short everybody who had anything to lend[11], and one of the strangest things about the entries is the evidence they afford that many of the advances were actually repaid within a few days or even on the very same day as that on which they had been received[12] and in some cases lent over again a second time, so that it is impossible to arrive at any reliable conclusion as to the gross total yield. The largest recorded item is for £10,936. 3s. 8d. received from Roger Salvayn[13], the Treasurer of Calais, on June 21, 1415, and not repaid to him for some considerable time[14]. We have a record of

---

[1] e.g. Archbishop Chichele lent £200, Pat. 3 H. V, ii. 43, July 23, 1415.

[2] Bishop Repingdon (Lincoln) lent £400 secured on the customs of Boston, Rym. ix. 268, June 16, 1415. Bishop Beaufort (Winchester) lent £666. 6s. 6d., Pat. 3 H. V, ii. 43, July 8, 1415; he also lent £1963. 6s. 8d. on June 8, 1415, which was returned to him on the same day. Bishop Mascal (Hereford) £100 (ibid.), which was repaid Feb. 23, 1424, Rec. Roll 3 H. V, Pasch., but this seems insufficient to justify the statement in Michelet, vi. 74, that " L'Eglise en faisait la banque," adding "voilà sans doute pourquoi les évêques suivaient le camp *en grand nombre* (!)."

[3] The Abbot of Waltham lent £66. 13s. 4d. on June 6, 1415, repaid June 22, 1415, Rec. Roll 3 H. V, Pasch. The Abbot of Gloucester lent £20, June 6, 1415, repaid July 8, 1416, ibid.

[4] The Prior of Durham lent £66. 6s. 6d., Pat. 3 H. V, ii. 43, July 23, 1415.

[5] The Dean of St Paul's (Thomas More) lent £40, Rec. Roll 3 H. V, Pasch., June 7, 1415.

[6] e.g. Friar Henry Cronnale lent £200, June 8, 1415, Rec. Roll 3 H. V, Pasch.

[7] e.g. Thomas, Lord de la Warre, lent £133. 6s. 8d., ibid., and Hugh Lord Burnell £200 on June 6, 1415, which was not repaid till Nov. 20, 1424, ibid.

[8] e.g. John Arundell, kt., lent £133. 6s. 8d. June 6, repaid June 6, 14, 1415, ibid. John Lilling, kt., lent £40 June 6, repaid June 25, 1415, ibid.

[9] e.g. William Brancepeth, John Phelip, John Aske (page 23, note 2), John Pillington, William Bradshaw, John Chenduyt (Wylie, iii. 297), Thomas Corbet and R. Bruce, Nicolas, App. 18; also John Burgh of Surrey £100 on June 8; John Craven of Suffolk who lent £150 on July 6, 10, 1415, Rec. Roll 3 H. V, Pasch.; Pat. 3 H. V, ii. 40; John Darell and Valentine Baret (both of Kent) lent £40 and £13. 6s. 8d. respectively on June 6, ibid.

[10] John Harreys of Cambridge (per Richard Merlawe) lent £100 June 7, 1415, repaid July 5, 1415, Rec. Roll 3 H. V, Pasch.; John Rowley of Retford, £40 lent June 6, 7, 1415, repaid June 27, ibid.; John Whitwell of ffelingham (? Fillingham, Lincs.) lent £10 June 8, repaid July 17, 1415, ibid.; also Stephen Turnbone £50 on the same day, ibid.; and Roger Swylyngton £33. 6s. 8d. on June 6, 1415, repaid July 23, 1416, ibid.

[11] Ad quemcunque pecuniosum, Usk, 124, 306.

[12] e.g. on June 7 and 16, 1415, the loans received amounted to £2806. 13s. 4d. and £2796. 13s. 4d. respectively, but these items were all repaid in various amounts on June 10, 14, 21, 22, 25, 27; July 3, 4, 5, 8, 1415, Rec. Roll 3 H. V, Pasch. Cf. page 148.

[13] See page 41. For supposition that his wife " managed the finances of the fortress in 1417," see Pall Mall Gazette (23/6/13), p. 3.

[14] viz. £4800 + £2329. 8s. 11d. + £1806. 14s. 9d. on June 14, 1416, July 8, 1416, and Oct. 29, 1421, respectively, Rec. Roll 3 H. V, Pasch.

£573. 6s. 8d. received from Devonshire in April 1415[1], including loans from the Dean and Chapter of Exeter (100 marks), the Mayors of Exeter (100 marks) and Plymouth (30 marks), the Abbots of Buckfastleigh[2] and Tavistock, and the Priors of Launceston and Plympton (100 marks each), besides several from private individuals[3]. In all these cases the advances were amply secured and the same messenger that brought the money from Exeter took back with him from London pledges[4] in plate and jewels to the value of 860 marks to be retained by the lenders until they got their money back. The archbishops were to arrange for loans from the clergy to be certified in the Treasury by July 3, 1415[5], and we have plenty of instances where parish parsons put in quite substantial sums[6]. Loans from towns and cities were numerous but not always large, though usually well secured on the port customs. In the lists Bristol figures for £582, Norwich for £333. 6s. 8d., Lynn for £216. 13s. 4d.[7], Newcastle for £216. 13s. 4d.[8], York (£200), Boston (£80)[9], Beverley, Canterbury, Exeter, Northampton[10] and Nottingham[11] (£66. 13s. 4d. each), Bridgwater[12] (£50), Gloucester, Maidstone and Sudbury[13] (£40 each), Bury St Edmunds[14]

---

[1] Rym. ix. 285; Devon, 340, April 19, 1415, records payment of £10 to John Copleston, junr., probably a son of the mayor of Plymouth, for bringing the money from Devonshire to London and taking back the jewels with him.

[2] Called Bugfasta, Bufestre, Buckfast', Bucfestre, Buffestr', Bustr', Monast. v. 384–387.

[3] e.g. Robert Cary (100 marks), Alexander Champernoun and John Bevyle (each 60 marks), and John Copleston (10 marks).

[4] Including a large silver-gilt tabernacle set with pearls and sapphires that had belonged to the Duke of Burgundy, pledged for 18 months on July 14, 1415, Rym. ix. 285; Hist. MSS. Rept. Var. Coll. iv. 41, 83, showing that it was still unredeemed on June 13, 1423.

[5] Iss. Roll 3 H. V, Pasch., May 1, 1415.

[6] For 13 parsons in the diocese of Durham lending £20 each, see Pat. 3 H. V, ii. 43, July 23, 1415. The parsons of Harpley (John Drewe) and Sall (John Baxter) in Norfolk lent 40 marks and £40 respectively, Rec. Roll 3 H. V, Pasch., July 7, 8, 1415; also John Lincoln, parson of Hadleigh (near Sudbury), 100 marks, and William Shyrymton (or Sheringham, Blomefield, ix. 399, where his will is dated 1421), the Rector of Holt-market (? Holt near Cromer), £20.

[7] Rym. ix. 286, where Master William Westacre lends 40 marks, William Walton 20, and Nicholas Scounfet 10, all of Norfolk. Walton died in 1444, Inq. p. Mort, iv. 22.

[8] i.e. £83. 6s. 8d. lent June 6, 1415 + £133. 6s. 8d. lent June 8, 1415. Both sums were repaid July 17, 1415, see Rec. Roll 3 H. V, Pasch., June 8, 1415.

[9] Rec. Roll 3 H. V, Pasch., July 5, Sept. 2, 1415.

[10] Ibid. June 18, Aug. 17, 1415.   [11] Ibid. June 8, Aug. 3, 1415.

[12] Ibid. June 6, July 1, 1415.   [13] Ibid. June 10, 1415.

[14] Ibid. June 6, 1415.

and Faversham[1] (£33. 6s. 8d. each), Plymouth (£20) and Dartmouth (£13. 6s. 8d.). Many of these sums were lent on June 6th and 7th, 1415, and were repaid within a month, their moderate amount contrasting strangely with the magnificent 10,000 marks that the city of London had just produced[2] at three days' notice.

There seems no reason to suppose that any compulsion was brought to bear upon English lenders, but it was certainly different with foreigners resident in London. For when loans of £200, £1000 and £1200 were demanded from certain Lucchese, Venetian and Florentine merchants and refused by them, 12 partners in these companies were summoned before a council that met in the Black Friars on May 25 and committed to the Fleet Prison[3] though it is evident from other entries that all were not equally recalcitrant[4]. The great London mercers came forward as usual with long or short accommodation; Richard Whitington with £700[5], and John Hende with £4666. 13s. 4d.[6] Executors advanced money from dead men's estates[7]; collectors of customs[8] and escheators of

---

[1] Rec. Roll 3 H. V, Pasch., June 7, 25; July 1, 5, 8, 1415.

[2] For account of persons lending money to King (Henry V) in aid of wars from the Hundred of Ossulston (i.e. Holborn, Finsbury, Tower, &c., Lewis, iii. 304), see Hist. MSS. Comm. Rept. iv. p. 196, where it is assigned to Henry IV.

[3] Ord. Priv. Co. ii. 165; Abram, Life, 108, 309, who wrongly dates it in 1412.

[4] e.g. Philip and Thomas de Albertis (or of the Societas Albertinorum) lent 200 marks on June 6, repaid July 3, Rec. Roll 3 H. V, Pasch., July 3, 1415; also Laurence de Albertis, merchant of Florence, lent £666. 13s. 4d., repaid Sept. 3, 1415, ibid. Paul de Melan (or Miliam or Meleany, ibid. June 6, 22, 1415) lent 200 marks, having already an outstanding account of £478. 18s. 8d. due to him for cloth of gold and other stuffs secured on the customs of Sandwich and Southampton, Rym. ix. 271, June 22, 1415; also Nicholas de Malyn et socii sui mercatores de Venice, lent 1000 marks on June 6, 1415, Rec. Roll 3 H. V, Pasch., June 6, 14, 1415, secured on the customs of London, Rym. ix. 284, July 11, 1415, where the collectors are Thomas Burton and John Botiller. On June 6, 1415, John Victor of Florence lent £266. 13s. 4d., repaid June 6, 10, 1415, Rec. Roll 3 H. V, Pasch.

[5] Fox-Bourne, 58.

[6] Lent June 6, repaid June 8, 1415, Rec. Roll 3 H. V, Pasch., June 7, 25, 1415.

[7] e.g. Roger Rye lent £66. 13s. 4d. on behalf of the executors of Seman Tonge, a baron of the Cinq Ports, ibid. For will of Semanus (probably Seaman) de Tonge dated at Faversham on Aug. 3, 1414 (when he was 40 years of age), proved at Lambeth in the same year, see Genealogist, v. 224. For his brass in Faversham Church, see Gough, ii. 354; Lewis, 10, with inscription:

Hic probus et dignus vir honestus amans que benignus
At vere scitus Semanus Tong sepelitur
Hic vir opportunus baro de portubus unus
In Thruckleigh natus fuit in Fevershamque moratus,

i.e. in the neighbouring parish of Throwley, Hasted, ii. 584, 606; iii. 192. For Semannus Champagne of Winchelsea, see W. D. Cooper, 125.

[8] e.g. Nicholas Blackburn, senr., a citizen of York, lends £100 on June 8, 1415. It was secured on the customs of Hull (for which he was collector in 1405, 1406, 1409,

counties[1] from dues not yet accounted for, and royal officers[2] from monies already earmarked for other purposes[3].

Some writers have imagined that among his other preparations for the coming war King Henry had amassed vast sums of money in his Treasury[4]. But if there be any truth in this, the money must have been soon spent, for as early as May 11, 1414, preparations had been in hand to pledge all the available articles of which the king was possessed. Not only were the cupboards and buffets ransacked[5] but inventories were drawn up of all the valuables[6] in the chapel of the royal household at Windsor which might be parted with to raise the necessary funds, and the king, whose veneration for the externals of religion is so highly praised by the churchmen of his time, was preparing to pawn the most sacred of Church fitments to carry out his plan of invasion; such as buckets, censers, chalices, coffers, cruets, ships, lecterns, holywater stoups, sprinkles, portable organs, processional and other crosses, tablets, tabernacles, ampuls, crucifixes, paxes, sconces, lamp-harness, reliquaries, beryls, and ciborios. Nothing was to escape and the list includes pieces of the Holy Coat and the True Cross, images of the Virgin, the Trinity, St Thomas (in a coffin), Edward the Confessor (minus his sceptre), St Michael (fighting a dragon), St Martin (on a silver-gilt foot), St George (without his shield), kneeling figures of St Catharine and St John, a sepulchre, a head of one of the 11,000 virgins, relics of St Christopher, St Thomas of Canterbury and St Chad, divers relics in a round beryl, a silver stick for the holy candle used at Candlemas and much more.

All these pieces were duly entered up by Edmund Lacy[7], the chapel dean, and handed over to Bishop

Wylie, ii. 422), but was returned to him on the same day, Rec. Roll 3 H. V, Pasch., July 11, 1415. For suit by Nicholas Blackburn the younger against a tailor of York for half a ship called a keel, see Early Chanc. Proc. i. 46; also by Nicholas Blackburn against his son Nicholas Blackburn, sheriff of York City (i.e. in 1427 or 1437, List of Sheriffs, 230), re sureties for the peace, ibid. i. 51.
[1] e.g. Peter de la Hay lends £40, Rec. Roll 3 H. V, Pasch., July 17, 1415. He is Escheator of Yorks., ibid. Pasch. and Mich., Apr. 22, Oct. 25, 1415. On May 29, 1415, he was a commissioner to array the forces of the East Riding, Rym. ix. 253.
[2] e.g. the Earl of Arundel, who was Treasurer of England, advanced £766. 13s. 4d. on June 8, 1415; John Spencer, Clerk of the Wardrobe, lends £267. 11s. 6d. on June 6, 1415, repaid on June 4, 1416, Rec. Roll 3 H. V, Pasch.   [3] Pat. 3 H. V, ii. 30.
[4] See p. 471.   [5] Strickland, ii. 117.   [6] See App. M[2].
[7] For release granted to him Oct. 3, 1415, for having delivered divers indentures to Richard Courtenay, late Bishop of Norwich, see Memoranda Roll K.R. 3, 4 H. V, m.

Courtenay on June 1, 1415, some of them to be broken up and all of them to be pledged away in payment of soldiers' wages. On June 13 a quantity of articles such as basins, cooking-pots, ewers, cups, hanaps, goblets, jars (both galloners and potellers), masers, saucers, skillets, scummers, spoons, standing-cups, bowls, plates, dishes, chargers, chafers, spiceplates, funnels, saltcellars, flaskets, ladles, gridirons, and candlesticks were also turned over from the stores of the royal household together with gold chains, ouches, bracelets, bells, mirrors and such curios as two silver stags, a silver church, a small gold purse, a brooch made like a royal trout, hanaps, gardeviances and ewers that had previously been received as presents[1] and even the lying-in gear and other child-bed paraphernalia that had been used at the birth of royal babies[2]; and when the royal jewellery[3] (*vessellamenta*) was inventoried at the opening of the next New Year[4] the items show but a meagre list of 44 silver chargers, eight dozen dishes, eight basins[5] and a paltry residue of pots, four ewers of which three have lids, some saucers[6] and 19 spiceplates, one with a gold swan belonging to it, and one broken maser, the rest being scattered in the hands of large numbers of captains who still held them in pledge till they were re-couped for their outlay in paying the wages of their men.

---

[1] e.g. from the Dukes of Berry and Burgundy, Exch. Accts. 45/22 (2). For gifts from Queen Joan, the Duke of York and Drew Barentin, pledged with Thomas Lord Camoys, see W. D. Cooper, 134.

[2] e.g. one large potte pour la gesyne, Exch. Accts. 45/9. For bed-room scene (gesine), see R. H. Mason, 231 (from Harl. MS. 2278, i.e. Lydgate, St Edmund, circ. 1433); Besant, Survey, i. 249; Ashdown, 160; Abram, Life, 180, 320; also Harl. MS. 7026, f. 29, where the mother is naked in bed. Also in windows in the cathedrals at Laon and Le Mans, Mâle, 247, 249. For accounts for gesine of Anne of Cyprus, Princess of Piedmont, mother of Amedée IX Duke of Savoy, Feb. 1, 1435, see Bruchet, Ripaille, 480; see also Wylie, iii. 88, note 4; Servion, i. 12. Also at birth of Philip (Count of Vertus), son of Louis Duke of Orleans in 1396, Collas, 242, including la cuve a boigner.

[3] Cf.   Coupes of gold and silver vessels
            Clothes of gold and other jeweles.
                                                    Laud Troy Bk. 372.

[4] i.e. Jan. 1, 1416, Exch. Accts. 406/23, 27; L. T. R. Misc. Enrolled Accts. 6/8; Wylie, Notes, 114; i.e. indenture showing the vessellamenta aur' et argent' handed over on Jan. 1, 1416, by Roger Leche, kt. to his successor John Rothenale, kt. as custos garderobe. +one magn' discus silver gilt cum uno pede et two aquile deaurat' in fine dict. disc + 58 disci (dishes), 35 salsars of which 24 are signat' cum touch de London, + 17 oll' with or without lids. For picture of a goldsmith's shop (temp. Louis XI) with ewers and plates, see Willemin, ii. 170.

[5] These are marked with the arms of England and France quartellat' in unâ rosâ, or with a crowned swan, a crowned leopard or a rose on the bottom (in fundo), two of them being pounss' (i.e. pounced) en les swag.

[6] For discus cum salsario (1307), see Ellacombe, p. x.

It is usual now-a-days to look upon these great pledging transactions as evidence of a lack of enthusiasm for the expedition[1]; but in themselves they tell us nothing as to the general feeling of the people; and so far from being humiliating or degrading expedients, as has been sometimes supposed[2], they are really nothing more than a portion of a well-recognised system of public borrowing which had by that time become quite firmly established in the practice of the Exchequer. We do however get a glimpse as to the feeling of the country and the spirit that was palpitating behind these interesting loans, by a glance at the rich manufacturing city of Salisbury, or New Sarum[3], which was then famed for its fabrics of blanket and motley[4].

Amongst the list of lenders Salisbury appears as advancing £100, with the significant addendum that this money was procured through the mediation of Bishop Beaufort and the Duke of York[5], and a peep into the earliest of the Ledger Books of the corporation discloses some singular facts in regard to the transaction. As far back as June 1413 a letter[6] was sent by the king to the citizens asking for a loan for his proposed expedition across the sea. The request was by no means enthusiastically received, but after petitioning and beating down it was at last agreed to lend 100 marks (£66. 13s. 4d.). The money was to be raised among 85 of the wealthiest burgesses but it was a long time before it was actually forthcoming, one of the contributors who was put down for 6s. 8d. refusing altogether to pay up his share till the mayor had to seal up his house, whereupon he shamefully cursed the mayor out loud and only narrowly escaped getting sent to prison[7]. When at length the money was ready, one of the representatives of the city in the Leicester Parliament named

---

[1] Ramsay, i. 194.
[2] "*Even* pawning the crown jewels," Oman, Hist. 222; J. S. D. Scott, i. 280, who considers this to be humiliating in a monarch. Cf. "extremities so degrading to the kingly office," Musgrave, 271.
[3] Called Nova Sarisburia in Black Book of Adm. i. 364, 376.
[4] Hoare, vi. 113.
[5] Hist. MSS. Var. Coll. Rept. iv. 193. For references to this on Feb. 25, March 2, 1415, see Salisbury Ledger A, f. 54, where the Council agree to lend £100.
[6] It was read at a meeting of the Town Council at Salisbury on June 9, 1413, Hoare, vi. 111; though called 3 H. V (i.e. 1415), ibid. 112.
[7] Hoare, vi. 112, from Corporation Ledger Book A, B, where the recalcitrant is called Thomas Pistour.

Walter Shirley[1] presented a request to the Council as to the security for repayment but could get no satisfactory pledge, being told that he must wait till the king was in the neighbourhood. This may perhaps refer to a plan that Henry had formed of personally visiting some of the hesitating towns in order to stir up a little more enthusiasm, though he appears to have got no further than Reading[2], when he had to confess that the game was not worth the candle. Shirley reported the position at Salisbury on June 17, 1415[3], and retained the loan money in his hands for the present, but shortly afterwards when the king came to Winchester he went over and had an interview with the Chancellor (Beaufort) who promised a temporary assignment of the customs on wool at Southampton, adding that if the loan were not forthcoming, the town would be liable to the king's displeasure. This threat was enough. Shirley paid the money and reported the result at Salisbury on July 3, 1415[4]. But the citizens were in no compliant mood and there would appear to have been little keenness for the coming venture, for a month later[5], when a body of Lancashire men under the command of Sir James Harrington[6]

[1] Or "Shirle." He was mayor in 1416 (Hoare, vi. 695) and represented the city in the parliaments of 1414, 1415, 1417, 1419, 1420 and 1421, Return Parl. i. 282, 284, 290, 293, 296, 298, 301; Hoare, vi. 112. In Pat. 3 H. V, i. 25 (July 11, 1415) he is civis et mercator. For muster of Ralph de Schirley (or Shirley), July 6, 1415, see Kal. and Inv. ii. 106; L.T.R. Misc. Enrolled Accts. 6/1; called Sir Raulfe Shyrley in Brook's list in Nicolas, p. 54. For his indenture of jewels with 6+18, dated Winchester, July 6, 1415, with list of securities for payment of his second quarter's wages (= £86. 2s. 8d.) returned May 30, 1422, see Kal. and Inv. ii. 106; Mély-Bishop, i. 169, who wrongly describes it as a list of jewels taken to France by Henry V.   [2] Page 481.
[3] Hoare, vi. 112, where Bishop Beaufort is described as "Cardinal"; but "Cancellarius" in the original, i.e. Ledger Book A, f. 55.
[4] Salisbury Ledger A, f. 54 d, where the amount is £100.
[5] i.e. on Sunday, Aug. 4, 1415, Hoare, vi. 113; A. R. Malden, 26.
[6] Dominus Jacob' Haryndon, Salisbury Ledger A, f. 54 b; not John Harpyndon, as Hoare, vi. 113. Called Sir James Harrington in *Collection of Remarkable Events*, p. 1, where the date is given as 1421, which is certainly wrong, as Levesham was not mayor in that year. For the retinues of "Sire de Harington" (i.e. John, Wylie, Notes, 131) and Sir William Harington, see Nicolas, 341, 362. For that of James Harington, knight, ibid. 380. For Monsr. John Harpeden in the retinue of Sir John Cornwall, see Nicolas, 361, 380. He was the fifth husband of Joan widow of Sir John Oldcastle, Rot. Parl. v. 397; Wylie, iii. 291, note 7. Not that he was called Richard, as Waugh, 656, where he is "of Oxfordshire," possibly because he owned land at Harpden (i.e. Harpsden near Henley), Inq. p. Mort. iv. 182, 467, though said to be "of Hertfordshire" in Archaeol. Cant. xi. 99, connecting him apparently with Harpenden near St Albans, for which there seems no authority, see Cussans, Dacorum, 349. For his brass (d. 1437) in Westminster Abbey, see Gough, iii. 43, 103, 182; Moule-Harding, 25; Stanley, 179; Lethaby, 341 (who calls him "Harpenden"); F. Bond, 259 (where he is called "Harpedon"); also M. Stephenson, 224; Druitt, 169. For Jean Harpadane, lord of Montaigu in Poitou and of Nuaille in Aunis, see Aussy, Reg. ii. 261; called "Harpedenne" in Gaunt Reg. i. 2, where he is

on their way to the muster at Southampton halted at Fisherton (or Fisherton-Anger) on the opposite bank of the Avon, it did not take much to bring about a collision on the bridge, during which the troops shot at the towns-folk with their arrows and struck them with their swords. The town bell was then tolled and the citizens rushed to arms. In the fray the mayor (John Levesham[1]) lost his hood "in defence of the town," four of the townsmen got killed and 14 other persons were thrown over the bridge into the river, but in the end peace was patched up by a Welsh minstrel who got the mayor another hood and Harrington's troops passed forward on their way.

Midsummer day (June 24, 1415) had been originally fixed for the great muster at Southampton[2], but on April 29 the date was altered to July 1[3] and there was still a vast deal to be done in the way of preparation. Mustering had already been going forward at Dover[4] and on May 29[5] orders were sent to the sheriffs to have all the fencibles arrayed and similar orders were sent to the bishops[6] to array the forces of the clergy by July 16, 1415. Beacons

---

Seneschal of Saintonge, Sept. 25, 1371. For account of him, see Montandre, 16, where he is lord of Belleville in Poitou. He died before June 14, 1406. In Jan. 1410, Jean de Harpedanne is lord of Montandre, Aussy, Reg. ii. 281.

[1] Not "Lewisham" as Lansdowne MS. 1054, f. 53; Nicolas, 286.

[2] Wals. ii. 305; Hypodig. 455.

[3] Harl. Chart. 43, E. 39; called Aug. 1 in Brut, ii. 375.

[4] For orders dated May 16, 1415, to William Massy and Richard Wydevylle, esquires, to report on the following musters at Dover on May 25, 1415, see Gesta, 9, quoting Priv. Seal 3 H. V, viz. five knights, John Holand (24+72), Reynold Gray (20+60), John Popham (30+90), John Gray (40+120), Godfrey Hilton (40+120), and eight esquires, John Burnham (2+6), Geoffrey Writington (6+18), Esmon Cheyne (14+42), John Watford and Robert Wolf (1+9), William Laurence (5+15), Thomas Langford and John Clayton (10+30). None of these appear in Nicolas' list of retinues.

[5] Rym. ix. 253 [255]; Kingsford, 119.

[6] For the order dated May 28, 1415, see Rym. ix. 254 [256]; not May 8, as Goodwin, 54, quoting Claus. 3 H. V, 21. In Ancient Corrdce, lvii. p. 259, the actual numbers in nine dioceses are given as follows:

		hobelars		archers
50	Lincoln	292	+	3632
40	York	250	+	—
54	Exeter	204	+	1200
38	Winchester	85	+	618
52	Wells	70*	+	830
45	Ely	47	+	279
49	St David's	40	+	200+124 fencibles non arraiatos.
62	Llandaff	Total = 230 personarum ecclesiasticarum cum familiaribus assistentium, including 24 competentur armati.		
61	Rochester.	Assembled at Dartford, but names and number of separate schedule are not now preserved.		

* i.e. 60 de clero + 10 mixti seu neutri vulgariter dicti hoblarii.

were to be in readiness for signalling on the usual heights, and all the clergy without exception were to be armed to defend the kingdom and the Church of England[1] against the machinations both of Lollards at home and invaders from without and their names were to be notified to their diocesan before July 16[2].

While these necessary precautions were being taken to defend his doors from the dog[3], the king pressed forward preparations with hot haste for his departure. On April 12, 1415[4], he had sent for the mayor and some of the leading aldermen of London for an interview in the Tower at which he told them that the high prices ruling for armour must be reduced and required an order to that effect to be issued within three days. Before May 18[5] the Treasurer and others met at Westminster to arrange for the quicker despatch of gunners and others to cross with the king, and a letter written in London on June 8 states that guns and bridles[6] were being shipped there every day[7]. Orders were sent to the ports to stop the passage of foreigners[8], and assizes, whether general or special, were to be suspended during the king's absence as so many residents would be away from their homes on foreign service and unable to look after their own interests[9]. On May 16, 1415, an order was issued that smiths and carpenters were to be ready for the journey with carts, iron and timber[10]; wine was to be prised at Winchelsea[11] and Southampton for the king's use[12]; messengers were despatched to the sheriffs of the southern counties[13] to have cattle collected and sent into

---

[1] Page 304, note 3.

[2] For order to the Dean (i.e. John Macworth, 1412–1451, Monast. viii. 1268; not 1457, as Wylie, iii. 50) and the Archdeacon of Lincoln (i.e. Henry Wells, 1406–1431, Le Neve, ii. 45) to repair to their cathedral and defend it, see Rym. ix. 254 [256].

[3] Henry V, 1, 2, 218.   [4] Ord. Priv. Co. ii. 154.

[5] For 10s. paid for their breakfast, see Iss. Roll 3 H. V, Pasch., May 18, 1415.

[6] Or brides, see Littré, s.v.

[7] Se carguan totjorn, Jurade, 193, i.e. in a letter from Benet Spina, see page 128.

[8] Extranei, Iss. Roll 3 H. V, Pasch., May 18, 1415, which shows payments to the messengers.

[9] Pour l'aide et indempnitee de touz noz foialz liges, Ord. Priv. Co. ii. 166, May 26, 1415.

[10] For order to Robert Hunt, serviens cariagii hospitii nostri, see Rym. ix. 248.

[11] Not Winchester, as Ord. Priv. Co. ii. p. xi. For payment to a messenger bearing a writ under the king's signet to the mayor of Winchelsea, see Iss. Roll 3 H. V, Pasch., April 19, 1415.

[12] Ord. Priv. Co. ii. 159.

[13] Iss. Roll 3 H. V, Pasch., May 1, 1415. For orders to sheriffs of Kent, Hants., Wilts. and Oxon., dated May 26, June 20, 1415, see Rym. ix. 251, 252; Kingsford, 118.

Hampshire, and by June 25 great herds of calves and bullocks[1] had been collected at Titchfield, Farnham, Southwick, Alresford, Romsey, Beaulieu, Lymington and other places within easy distance of Southampton. Baking and brewing were ordered to be constantly continued up till Aug. 1 at Winchester, Southampton and all the towns and hamlets round about, so that there might be no lack of bread and beer against the king's arrival[2], and all the mills in England were reported to be at work providing flour enough to last through the winter[3]. One hundred of the best masons to be found in the home counties were ordered to be in London with their tools by June 17[4]; on May 1[5], 25 London cordeners were engaged to serve for six months at 6*d*. a day; farriers were secured with the tools of their trade[6], together with 1200 turners and carpenters, 40 smiths and 60 carters with reins, hooks, collars and leathern piping (*pipes de corio*), and wages were found for 15 of the king's waits[7], including a trumper and several fiddlers and pipers, and when the date fixed for sailing drew near the king made ready for his departure.

On May 9, 1415[8], he was at the Palace at Westminster and on the following day we find him at Reading[9], whence

[1] Cf.
          With salt befe and fat hoggis
          With many a bole and wilde bore,
          Unto her schippes myzt holde no more
          Of corne and flour and gentil wynes. Kempe, 21.

[2] Rym. ix. 253. On May 27, 1415, the Treasurer of England, the Treasurer of the Royal Household and Mons. Johan Rothenhale were appointed to arrange a provision of victuals near the place where the king would embark, Ord. Priv. Co. ii. 167.

[3] Jurade, 193, written June 8, 1415.

[4] Rym. ix. 261, June 6, 1415.

[5] i.e. under George Benet whose account is given in For. Accts. 10 H. V, F., where their pay is to date from July 8, 1415. In Brook's list (p. 59) Benet is called "cordewener de roy."

[6] For order dated May 25, 1415, to Stephen Ferrour serviens ferrurae to provide smiths with iron and all necessaries of farriery, see Rym. ix. 251.

[7] For "les waytes" among the king's officers at Harfleur, see Exch. Accts. 44/30 (1). For their names see Rym. ix. 253 [255]. They include John Cliffe, not "Gliff" as Mazas, Vies, v. 561, who calls him un poète troubadour, see Nicolas, 389; do. App. 18; Hunter, 52. He died before 12 H. VI. For his receipt for prepayment of wages dated July 1, 1415, with seal attached (lion rampant), see Exch. Accts. 44/28. For the second quarter beginning Oct. 8, 1415, he received pledges including a gridiron, a scummer, a ladle, three candlers with spikes and a piece of a by, ibid. 47/23 where he is dead and Henry Jolypas is his executor. For une porc' (i.e. portion) dune by, see ibid. 406/24 (of the livery of the Earl Marshal). Four of these waits, viz. John Cliff, Thomas Norris, William Baldwyn and William Halliday, had been among the minstrels of Henry IV in 1404, receiving 8*d*. per day, Wylie, iv. 245. They now received 12*d*. per day, Nicolas, App. 101.

[8] Rym. ix. 241; Rot. Scot. ii. 213.

[9] Rym. ix. 241; Goodwin, 55. For picture of the ruins of Reading Abbey in 1762,

he issued his urgent appeal for loans[1] to enable him to pay
the second quarter's instalment of wages before embarkation,
as he had covenanted to do.   But this matter would not
brook delay and the captains had to be satisfied, as we have
seen, with pledges many of which were not redeemed till
well into the succeeding reign.   But if wages had to wait
it was otherwise with the wine and sweetstuff, for spice and
confectionery were bought in amazing quantities[2] to be sent
over for the use of the king's household and £1214. 1s. 1½d.
was paid to Thomas Chaucer for wine for the voyage[3].

see Grose, Antiq. Vol. 1; Craik-Macfarlane, i. 419; Macfarlane-Thomson, i. 232.   For
present day, see Hurry, *passim*.   In 1465 it was described as coenobium amplum et
elegans, Rożmital, 45.   For catalogue of 228 books in the library see Engl. Hist.-Rev.
iii. 114, 117–123; Monast. iv. 38.
    [1] See page 468.
    [2] For William Burton, sergeant of the king's confectionery and spicery, see Iss. Roll
3 H. V, Pasch., May 18, 1415.   For £400 paid to Thomas Chalton, mercer of London,
to provide spices and other necessaries for the voyage, and £100 due to him for linen
cloth of Reynes (i.e. Rheims, Wylie, ii. 445; not Rennes, as Tighe and Davies, i. 370;
M. A. E. Wood, i. 99; Archaeologia, xxvi. 279; Amyot, 275; R. F. W. Williams,
i. 221; Abram, Life, 181), and other parcels of mercery, also £4000 paid to the Earl
of Arundel for spices, also £100 for spice as part of £4316. 13s. 4d. paid to Roger
Leche, kt., to provide victuals and other estuffamenta for the voyage+£71. 4s. 11½d.
+£359. 10s. 1d., see Iss. Roll 3 H. V, Pasch., April 26, 1415.   For £99. 3s. 6d.
paid on this account to William Lyme and Richard Loxley, grocer (Letter Book I,
p. 199), see Rec. Roll 3 H. V, Pasch., July 8, 1415; also Iss. Roll 3 H. V, Pasch.,
May 18, 1415, where J. Longevile or Langevile is clerk of the spicery, cf. Nicolas,
App. 91.
    [3] Rec. Roll 3 H. V, Pasch., June 14, 1415.

CHAPTER XXVI

WINCHESTER

THE king's presence at Reading on May 10, 1415, gives us a welcome clue to his whereabouts during the remainder of the month, which would otherwise be shrouded in obscurity. He was really on his way to make a pilgrimage before embarking on his voyage. During the early days of May he was visited by two envoys from the High Master of the Teutonic Order, who reported that after their first interview he took the road from London on a pilgrimage[1] of which his stay at Reading appears to have been the first halt. From Reading he seems to have travelled to Shrewsbury and thence to have passed on to visit St Winifred's well at Holywell, doing the whole of the latter part of the journey from Shrewsbury on foot with great devotion[2].

All preparations being now complete, the king at length set out from London to join the fleet at Southampton. On June 16[3], he took a formal farewell of Queen Joan[4],

[1] Dornach reit der Khoning von Lunden in betevart, Hanserecesse, vi. 148. Cf. regiis peregrinationibus devotis praehabitis, Tit. Liv. 7; First Life, 23.

[2] Usk, 129 [313], who seems to place this after the return from Agincourt; also Brut, ii. 558, which says "*after* he rode about in the land on pilgremage." For an indication of the king's presence at Southampton before May 1, 1415, see page 108, note 3.

[3] Usk, 125 [307]; called June 18, in Kingsford, Chron. 70; Chron. Lond. 100; Grey Friars Chron. 13; Caxton, 225; Fabyan, 578; or June 15 in Greg. Chron. 108; not "vere ineunte" as Pol. Verg. 442. For letters dated at Westminster Palace, May 31, June 18, 1415, see Jurade, 232, 239.

[4] And took his leve ful hendely (or "reverentlye," Vitel.), Harflet, 305; not that she was Regent, as Halle, 11; Holinsh. iii. 548, who calls her Henry's "mother-in-law" (i.e. stepmother); Stow, 346; Speed, 774; Trussell, 98; Goodwin, 55; Brougham, 101; Baildon, Inv. 167. On April 1, 1415, he had granted to her 1000 marks per annum for life instead of a large number of alien priories (see Wylie, ii. 285, note 8), which had been given to her on Jan. 27, 1414, but which he had since resumed into his own hands, Cal. Pat. H. V, i. 165.

who was to reside during his absence at Windsor, Wallingford, Berkhamsted[1], Hertford or Langley[2] as she thought fit. The sum of £200 was distributed "by way of rewards" in largess amongst the pages and boys (*garceons*) of the royal chamber[3] and household. The king then attended a solemn service at St Paul's, where he made an offering[4]; after which he passed through the city accompanied by the Duke of York, the Earls of March, Dorset, Arundel and Oxford, the young Lord Roos, Sir John Cornwall and Sir John Holland[5]. The mayor, aldermen and 340 of the citizens[6] rode with him across the bridge past St George's Corner[7] at the junction of the Kent Road with the High Street of Southwark (where he made another offering) and out on the coast road as far as Kingston[8]. Here the king took leave of them and blessed them in his own name saying:

---

[1] For John Atkyn appointed keeper of the park at Berkhamsted, see Pat. 1 H. V, i. 23; Priv. Seal 658/20, May 10, 1413. For John Ashall, appointed janitor July 14, 1414, see Pat. 2 H. V, ii. 32; Hugh Stanley, appointed Receiver of the castle July 18, 1414, ibid. ii. 35. For the office of porterwick of the castle granted to Roger Bigge, see Priv. Seal 658/30, May 21, 1413. In Pat. 5 H. V, 22, July 13, 1417, Wenslow Dorsteyner, kt. is constable, and in Pat. 4 H. V, 3, Feb. 11, 1417, John Purchas is appointed Receiver of the castle.

[2] For the manor of Langley granted to Queen Joan in exchange for the castle of Hertford (see Wylie, ii. 284) on June 30, 1415, see Cal. Pat. H. V, i. 351. For wine left en le Seler de Chilt^n Langley apres le deptm de nous for use of the queen and her household there, see Exch. Accts. 406/29. For a letter from Queen Joan (not Henry V, as supposed in Cotton Cat. p. 485) to the Duke of Bedford, written at Langley Nov. 10 (1415), in which she appeals to the Duke as guardian of England to pay his fee to John Faringdon as "our attorney general" and "our very good friend," see M. A. E. Wood, i. 89, 91.

[3] Sloane MS. 4600, f. 272, June 16, 1415.

[4]
> To Seynt Poulys he held the way
> He offered there full worthyly.   Harflet, 305.

Locis sacris per eum primitus quam devote visitatis, Usk, 125 [307].

[5] Waurin, ii. 177.   [6] Chron. R. II–H. VI, p. 150.

[7]
> To Seynt George he com in hye
> And there he offred that iche tyde
> And other lordys that weren hym bye.   Harflet, 306.

Called St George's in the Fields in Nicolas, 24; Ramsay, i. 195. Cf. ab angulo S. Georgii in Suthray (i.e. the limit of the jurisdiction of the Mayor of London, Lansdowne MS. 1054, f. 53), Nicolas, 287. For the cage, pillory, stocks and whipping-post opposite St George's Church, see Benham-Welch, 42. For sanctuary at St George's Church, Southwark, see Stow, Bk. iv. 44. For St George's corner, see Noorthouck, 698; Allen, iv. 434; Littlehales, 1; also Ogilby's map in Beryn. For the bishop and clergy of London meeting Richard II there in 1392 on his way from Sheen viâ Wandsworth, while the citizens met him at London Bridge, see Allen, i. 141; also Henry V after Agincourt, ibid. i. 152.

[8] Stow, Chron. 346. Not Blackheath, as Greg. Chron. 108; also Sharpe, Lond. i. 258, who sets great store by this account because Gregory "was an eye-witness of much that he relates," but he does not begin his personal entries till 1441, and was only about five years old in 1415, Greg. Chron. xvii. For £400 paid to John Spenser (Clerk of the Great Wardrobe, see page 28) for delivering the king's harness extra London, see Rec. Roll 3 H. V, Pasch., July 5, 1415.

"Christ save London!" and charging the mayor to go back and keep well his "chamber[1]" till he should return[2]. Travelling on, the royal party reached Winchester on June 20[3] where the king was lodged in Wolvesey Castle[4], which was the episcopal palace on the south-eastern side of the city, in readiness to receive a last deputation of French envoys, who were on their way from Paris charged with issues of momentous import.

The embassy consisted of seven members, the principal of whom were Guillaume Boisratier, Archbishop of Bourges[5], Pierre Fresnel[6], Bishop of Lisieux[7], the Count of Vendôme[8],

[1] Greg. Chron. 109; cf. Brut, ii. 382; Gesta, 109, of the king's departure in 1417. For London as the "King's Chamber," see Sharpe, London, i. 258. Cf. otherwyse cleped youre chambre, Kingsford, Chron. 114; Chron. Lond. 237; L'Estrange, Greenwich, 72; Fairholt, xxiii. The kyngis chambre off custume men the calle, Kingsford, Chron. 115. London the most precious place and as it were the chamber of his realm, Hist. MSS. Comm. Rept. xv. Pt. v. p. 93 (1599). For Carcassonne called "cara camera nostra," see Ordonnances, x. 493; Mahul, v. 354. For Tournai as "chambre royale," see Vallet de Viriville, Valentine, 77. For Cadiz = his port that he thought as safe as his chamber, see Monson, i. 353.

[2] For writ dated Westminster June 20, 1415, to the mayor, sheriffs and aldermen of London that all notable persons necessary for the good government of the city should return to London and remain there during the king's absence abroad, see Letter Book I pp. xxv, 138.

[3] Not 30, as Oman, Hist. 244. For documents dated at Winchester June 16, 20, 21, 24, 25, 26, 29, 30; July 1, 2, 5, 6, 7, 13, 18, 20, 1415, see Rym. ix. 252, 280, 282, 283; Cal. Doc. Scot. iv. 173; Kal. and Inv. ii. 106; Ewald, xliv. 566, 570, 572; Pat. 3 H. V, i. mm. 1, 3, 4, 11; ibid. ii. 39, 40, 43; Exch. Accts. 45/21, 71, 76, 77; Memoranda Rolls K. R. 3–4 H. V, m. 69; Jurade, 232; Nicolas, App. 16; Belleval, 26; Hunter, 44; Ancient Corrdce, vii. 49. Called "a kind of progress through the southern part of the kingdom" in Guthrie, ii. 457. In Pat. 3 H. V, ii. 42; Cal. Pat. H. V, i. 352, is a document dated at Winchester *June* 5, 1415, but this is probably a mistake for *July*. In Pat. 2 H. V, iii. 11, one is dated apud Winton June 26, 1414, which should probably be 1415, see Cal. Pat. H. V, i. 283.

[4] L'hôtel episcopal, Mirot, Fusoris, 157; l'ostel de l'evesque de Vicester, ibid. 180, 184; hospitatus in domo episcopi civitatis, ibid. 240. For account of Wolvesey, see Grose, Antiq. Vol. II (with picture of the ruins in 1780); Milner, i. 300, ii. 132; Woodward, i. 93; Shore, 113, 201; Lestrange, 114; Warren, Winchester, 97, 98, 121, 125; Victoria Co. Hist. Hants. v. 4, 8, 13 (with plan). Cf. "in palacio de Wolvesye," Wills of Kings, 341; "the castell or Palace of Wolvesey," Lel. Itin. iii. 84. It was partly destroyed by Henry II but patched up for use as a palace for the bishop, Shore, 114; though called "a strong castle" in Bishop Wickham's time, in Leach, 112. It was finally dismantled in 1646, Moberley, 237. For plans of Winchester in 1350 and 1611, see ibid. 233; Vict. Co. Hist. v. 2.

[5] See page 437. Berthier, xix. 413, quoting Mart. Anec. ii. 1618 (which however does not bear him out) supposes that he was at Constance on May 5, 1415, which probably means Nov. 1417, Gall. Christ. ii. 86.

[6] Called "Franel" in Monstr. 363; or "Frennel" in first printed edition (circ. 1500), Goodwin, 56; or "Perie Frennall," Stow, 345. Not "Fremel," as Halle, 58, Grafton, i. 510; Redman, 370; Holinsh. iii. 547; Duck, 66; Milner, i. 30; Portal, 79. Nor "Jean de Beuil," as Mazas, Vies, v. 562.

[7] See page 453.

[8] Choisy, 317, quoting Besse, 108. Not *Duke* of Vendôme, as Cassell, i. 526. Writing in London on June 8, 1415, Benet Spina reported that the Duke of Lansson (i.e. Alençon) and other great lords of France deven arrivar en Angleterra, Jurade, 193.

and Charles Lord of Ivry[1]. Escorted by 500 mounted men[2] they had started from Paris on June 4, 1415[3], travelled by St Denis, Amiens, St Riquier, Montreuil and Boulogne to Calais[4], where they were met by a great English dignitary[5] who accompanied them across the Channel. Five barges[6] were awaiting them, in which they crossed the strait, landing at Dover on June 17[7]. Here[8] the archbishop specially cautioned the members of his suite that they were not to have any private conversations with the English, not to leave the high roads nor wander about the country spying out routes or castles or fortresses, if they had any regard to their personal safety. At Canterbury[9] they were met by Sir John Wiltshire[10] and an escort of the king's men, who conducted them on by Rochester to London.

When Henry was informed of their arrival in the capital, he at once sent word to bring them to his presence for a personal interview. They reached Winchester on June 30[11], where they were met about a mile outside the city[12] by

---

[1] Not "Yary," as Dupleix, ii. 711; nor Pierre d'Orgecy, as Beaucourt, i. 259. He was Lord of Oisery, i.e. Oissery near Meaux, Boulé, i. 431. He is supposed to have been killed at Agincourt, but he was a prisoner at Marck near Calais on Nov. 19, 1415, Baye, ii. 224. He died in 1421, Anselme, viii. 879. For a gown given by the Duke of Orleans to the Baron d'Iviry in 1395, see Roman, 71, where he is called Ambroise de Lore, also a robe of black English cloth, Add. Ch. 2393 (Apr. 26, 1402), where he is Charles Sire d'Ivry, chamberlain to the king. He was Lord of St Sauveur-le-Vicomte till 1419, Delisle, St Sauveur, 244. He and his brother Jean d'Ivry were present with Isabel at Ardres in Oct. 1396, Mirot, Trousseau, 158. For his "virtuous reply":

Quant est de moy, ne suis pas de ceulx
Car je me tieng et me tendray a une (i.e. dame).
see Cent Ballades, 221.

[2] Morosini, ii. 34. For 112*l*. 10*s*. paid to Robin de Serigny, esquire, by the Duke of Berry for horses and good clothing going to England with the Archbishop of Bourges son chancélier, see Toulgoët-Treanna, 134.

[3] Beaucourt, i. 259, 260; Morosini, ii. 36 note; Mirot, 157, quoting Besse, Recueil de Pièces servant à l'Histoire de Charles VI, vi. 94. Not April 27, as Guizot, ii. 254; R. Black, ii. 277; nor June 30, as Vickers, 14.

[4] St Denys, v. 512; Monstr. 363; Duchesne, 821.

[5] Unus magnus Anglicus, Mirot, Fusoris, 250.

[6] Ibid. 157, 250. [7] Juv. 502.

[8] Mirot, Fusoris, 224, 239, the same cautions being also given when they arrived at Boulogne and Winchester.

[9] Monstr. 363.

[10] See Wylie, ii. 335. He is called Dominum Johannem de Villequier in St Denys, v. 512; Goodwin, 56; Mazas, Vies, v. 565. For £200 paid to John Wiltshire, knight, in regard to embassy from France coming from Dover to the king at Winchester, see Iss. Roll 3 H. V, Pasch., May 18, 1415. He is called governor of Montivilliers in 1416, St Denys, vi. 794. Fusoris says that the expenses of the embassy were paid from their arrival at Canterbury till their return to Calais, Mirot, 266.

[11] Kingsford, 120. Not June 26, as Mazas, Vies, v. 562; nor June 27, as G. Dupont, ii. 510; nor July 18, as Juv. 502. For belated safe-conducts for them dated at Winchester June 29, 1415, see Rym. ix. 282; Church, 55.

[12] Mirot, Fusoris, 268.

Bishops Langley and Courtenay and the Earls of Salisbury and Dorset[1], and lodged at the Grey Friars[2]. The interview took place in the Bishop's Hall at Wolvesey Castle[3]. The king leant against a table[4], bareheaded and clad from head to foot in cloth of gold[5], with a chair placed beside the throne which was splendidly draped with gold trappings. At his right hand stood his three brothers together with the Duke of York, Sir John Holland and others and on his left was the Chancellor, Bishop Beaufort, together with Bishops Courtenay and Langley who introduced the envoys, all of whom knelt as they entered. Archbishop Boisratier then presented letters from the King of France and his master the Duke of Berry[6], which King Henry kissed and handed to the Chancellor asking kindly after his cousin's health. He then gave a gracious welcome to the Frenchmen, took wine and spice with them and invited them to dine with him on the morrow, when they should have a public audience with the lords and bishops then present. The next day (July 1), after attending a solemn mass at which 28 chaplains assisted, he received the envoys in his chamber seated on a throne beside the royal bed.

Then Archbishop Boisratier, as the leader of the embassy[7], spoke from David's salutation to the churlish Nabal: "Peace be to thee and to thy house[8]!" praising peace in general terms and telling how all men ought to long for

[1] Not Dorchester, as Goodwin, 56.
[2] Mirot, Fusoris, 157; in quodam monasterio, ibid. 219, 250.
[3] Halle, 58; Grafton, i. 510; Kingsford, 120; Vickers, 14; Radford, 46; called dans la salle du capitre de la petite église in Champion, Vie, 139. Not in Winchester Castle, as Milner, i. 300; Lestrange, 20; Portal 129. For pictures of it adjoining the west gate, see Grose, Antiq. Vol. II; Milner, i. 432; Portal, 1; Warren, Winchester, 100; Macfarlane-Thomson, ii. 297. For the great hall completed by Henry III, formerly supposed to have been a chapel, and now used as the County Hall, see T. H. Turner, i. 176; Kitchin, 79, 115; Woodward, i. 295; Portal, *passim*; Warren, Winchester, 102; Lestrange, 28; Sergeant, 127. Not that the interview took place at Westminster, as Mazas, v. 562, 566.
[4] Called "on a cushion," Goodwin, 56; or "negligently," Echard, i. 183; reclining on a dais, Kingsford, 120; Belleval (23) thinks this was because he was "un peu souffrant."
[5] Cf. in clothes of gold as kynges be cladde, Laud Troy Book, 17; semely dyght in golden wcde, ibid. 182.
[6] Page 437, note 6.
[7] Souverain de l'ambassade, Waurin, i. 172. Called "the Embassadour of Burges" in Fam. Vict. 28, who puts in the Duke of Burgundy as a member of the party, which he supposes to have been sent by Charles VII (p. 29).
[8] 1 Sam. xxv. 6. Brougham (102) seems to confuse this with the speech attributed to Archbishop Chichele.

her[1]. Bishop Beaufort replied that the king was very pleased with the speech and glad that his cousin desired peace, but complained that his delays were doing much harm and urged that he should act with greater promptness for the future. Then all went to a banquet[2], Archbishop Boisratier and Bishop Fresnel being seated on one side of the king and the Duke of Gloucester[3] with the Count of Vendôme and the Lord of Ivry on the other, many bishops and knights being placed at other tables in the hall. After dinner the king conversed graciously with the envoys, saying that he was glad that they had come, as he understood that they would really work for peace.

On July 2 they met the Chancellor in the Chapter-house, who asked for more detailed particulars of their proposals and gave them till Saturday, July 6, to pronounce their final reply. The archbishop appealed to the judgment of all Christendom that the French king had hitherto desired to secure peace "by way of justice," offering to give up cities, counties and domains of priceless worth in Aquitaine, together with 800,000 gold francs[4] with his daughter Catherine, a larger dower than any princess had ever before brought with her from her father's home, but he claimed in return that Henry should disband the army which was said to be gathering at Southampton for a hostile descent on France[5] and he asked if these conditions would be accepted. The English replied[6] that their king could

---

[1] For an imaginary edition of his speech dilating on the horrors of war, see Redman, pp. xiii, 33. Halle's version (p. 58) is translated from Monstr. 363.

[2] Called "a week of festivities" in Belleval, 24, who thinks that the discussion did not begin till July 11.

[3] Called "Winfroy" (i.e. Humphrey) in St Denys, v. 516.

[4] It was believed to be four or five million ducats in a letter written at Sandwich on July 18, 1415, Morosini, ii. 36, which is a great exaggeration, as in 1414 the value of the gold franc only exceeded that of the ducat in the proportion of 11 to 10, ibid. ii. 10 (where 1 gold franc = 1 ducat 6 groats and 200 gold francs = 220 gold ducats). At Conflans in Barrois in 1405 the franc d'or = 18 sous estevenans and the livre = 20 sous; also in 1416, 8 gold crowns (French) = 10 gold ducats (Italian), i.e. 1 gold crown = 1¼ gold ducats, ibid. ii. 98. For 800,000 francs as the *dot* of Isabel at her marriage with Richard II, see Mirot, Trousseau, 126. Called 800,000 crowns in Champion, Vie, 139, who supposes this to be a dower "inouï dans l'histoire."

[5] Monstr. 363. Cf. la descente que l'en disoit que le roy d'Angleterre voulloit faire, see letter of Charles VI dated July 12, 1415, in Chéruel, Pt. II. p. 2.

[6] Through Archbishop Chichele, according to Monstr. 363; Waurin, i. 171; Le Fèvre, i. 216, followed by First Life, 25; Halle, 58; Grafton, i. 510; Holinsh. iii. 547; Stow, 345; Speed, 773; Duck, 67; Collier, iii. 311; Lingard, iii. 486; Church, 56, 58; Towle, 293; Yonge, 268; Lestrange, 20. Redman (34) supplies him with a speech in which the editor (p. xxiii) finds "one feature of probable genuineness," viz. the fact that it contains "no heathen philosophy or classic lore," forgetting that Redman himself

abate nothing of his demands, that his cousin of France had written last year that he would send envoys to discuss the "way of justice" (i.e. his rights over Normandy) as well as an alliance and marriage, and that it was understood that they would be authorised to offer more than they had yet done. Then the discussion developed heat. Boisratier denied with some warmth[1] that such a thing had ever been thought of, or that his master's words meant anything more than they actually said, though in the end he offered to undertake that the Princess should be sent to England with the richest jewels and dresses. On the following day (July 3) the conference was resumed, when the English announced that their king would agree to reduce his demands from a million to 900,000 crowns, but Boisratier still held to 800,000 francs, though he yielded so far as to agree to reckon the francs as crowns[2], thereby raising the total by about 40,000 francs. He then asked what allowance the English would make to Catherine after she was married and in reply they offered 10,000 marks (£6666. 13s. 4d.) per annum, which was the usual allowance of the queens of England[3], and he found it was useless to try and get any more. So after dilating on the Princess' high birth and the advantages that would accrue to England from the union, he at length gave it up and the marriage question remained undecided.

On Thursday, July 4, King Henry personally summoned the envoys and himself broached the question of "justice" in the presence of Bishops Beaufort, Courtney and Caterick, the Duke of York, the Earls of March and Huntingdon and

admits that he is inventing (nisi me forte propter benevolentiam in nostros homines fallit). Cf. mit unzweifelhaft-erdichteten Reden, Pauli, v. 99. Belleval (25) attributes the speech to Beaufort (not Chichele), but dates it on July 16. But Chichele was present at two Councils at Westminster on June 19 and 24, 1415, Ord. Priv. Co. ii. 170, 171; Hanserecesse, vi. 149, and did not go down to Southampton to bid farewell to the king till Aug. 10, 1415, Dict. Nat. Biogr. x. 228.

[1] Assez aigrement, Monstr. 363; not "maigre," as Waurin, i. 165. Cf. multa acriter dicta, Pol. Verg. 440.

[2] Not that this was impossible, as Nicolas, 27. Both francs and crowns were called denier d'or, but the value of the crown exceeded that of the gold franc in the proportion of about 11 to 10 or 21 to 20, Grande Encycl. xv. 532; xvii. 958. In 1415, 10 crowns = 10½ francs, Mirot, Fusoris, 274. In the accounts of the Hôtel Dieu in Paris in 1416, 12 crowns = 10 liv. 16s.; 18 francs = 14 liv. 8s.; 22 crowns = 19 liv. 16s.; 50 crowns = 45 liv.; 100 crowns = 90 liv.; 24 crowns = 21 liv. 12s., Brièle, Doc. iii. 24, 26, 44, 49. For the écu d'or of Philippe VI (1328–1350) and the franc d'or of Charles V (1364–1380), see Lacroix, 345.

[3] Wylie, i. 311.

many other lords. In his gentlest manner[1] he invited farther explanations and Archbishop Boisratier promised to throw in the seneschalcy of Limoges[2] with the towns of Limoges and Tulle, over and above the seven counties with their 15 towns already offered, and to raise the dowry to 850,000 gold crowns[3], with which the English king appeared to be well satisfied, only taking time to discuss the matter with his council.

When the day appointed for the final reply arrived (i.e. Saturday, July 6, 1415), the Frenchmen all dined with the king[4] after mass, and when the meal was over the last stage of the proceedings began. Bishop Beaufort first asked that a date should be fixed for bringing over the Princess Catherine with her jewels and the 850,000 crowns on condition that a 50 years' truce should be entered into on both sides without prejudice to Henry's claim to rights in the French crown. If within that time no final peace should have been established, the domains were to be restored subject to sufficient caution[5]. In the meantime he agreed to wait for another month and to send one of his secretaries to France to arrange details, while the French envoys would remain in England until his return. But to this the Frenchmen demurred and an animated discussion ensued[6]. The English proposed that Catherine should be brought across by Nov. 30 and the Frenchmen objected that the time would be too short even for coining the money required; besides, they were not sufficiently informed as to how the domains were held, whereupon Henry showed temper saying that he was the rightful King of France and that he meant to have the crown of the fleurs-de-lys[7], to which Archbishop Boisratier retorted that he had not even any right to the crown of England[8] and that

[1] Dulciter, St Denys, v. 518.
[2] Called "a poor country which it would not be worth while to accept," Church, 56.
[3] Transcr. For. Rec. 135/12; Beaucourt, i. 259, quoting Besse, Recueil, 163.
[4] Mirot, Fusoris, 242.
[5] It was reported at Sandwich on July 18, 1415, that Henry was likely to give way and that peace would be assured, Morosini, ii. 36.
[6] Aliqualis argumentiva negacio, St Denys, v. 516; verbalis disceptatio, ibid. v. 518.
[7] Juv. 503; Waur. i. 171.
[8] Et vous encore moins, Juv. 504; Orig. Lett. II. i. 49; nimis petulanter se gerens in praesentiâ regis, Wals. ii. 305; Hypodig. 456. Villaret (xiii. 343) thinks that if he said this, "il abusa de la dignité de son ministère." Cf.

Anglica non debes sic pabula jure tenere
Et tamen es vicii feritatis nominis haeres
Et privandus eras, Henrice, bonis et honore.   Blondel, i. 86.

they ought really to be treating with the heirs of Richard.
At this the king broke out in a storm of rage, telling the
Frenchmen to be gone and that he would soon be after
them, and then abruptly left the room[1]. Bishop Beaufort
next read out to the envoys a written declaration[2] in which,
after rehearsing the previous negotiations, he told them that
it was evident that their king did not really want peace
and that King Henry must therefore have recourse to
other means[3]. His ultimatum was that if the French king
would not give up all Aquitaine, Normandy, Anjou,
Touraine, Poitou, Maine and Ponthieu, King Henry would
go on with his fixed resolve to recover them all and even
seize the crown of France by dint of sword[4], calling God
to witness that this course was forced upon him by the
long delays and the denial of justice that he had found
in his cousin's dealings. At this the archbishop lost
his self-control[5]. Did they suppose, he said, that all
these offers had been made because the French were
afraid? No! Let Henry come on and he would either
be driven back or killed or captured[6], and so all chance

> Nullum titulum, nullum jus praetendere possent.
>   Ibid. i. 259, 445.
> Dont tu, Henri, deuss es estre
> Privé de succession toute
> Le royaume angloiz que tu tiens
> Te vient-il de bon droit? Nenny! Ibid. i. 131.

Cf. Perfidus iste tyrannus (Henry IV) et sua proles...progeniem e corrupto sanguine
editam, ibid. i. 258.

[1] Fut tant mal content que merveilles, Juv. 503; male contentus recessit, St Denys,
v. 522; alto turgebat fastu, Chenu, Archiepisc. 93; Redman (pp. xiii, 16) invents a highly
moral and dignified speech for him. Goodwin (60) thinks that "their Behaviour was
extreme (*sic*) rude and their language inexcusably insolent," but that "the just and
moderate king bore with great Temper all this storm of words"; also Echard, i. 183.
Lingard (iii. 487) thinks that "the king did not resent the freedom of the prelate," and
for his answer refers to Thresor des Chartres, 79; also Church, 57. Radford (47) thinks
that Henry intended the negotiations to break down.

[2] Called "a hypocritical speech" in Strang, 67.

[3] Ad alia remedia evolara, Transcr. For. Rec. 135/12.

[4] Harflet, 302; Holinsh. iii. 546, 548; Fam. Vict. 36. Cf.
> Raptum nobis aut redde Britannis
> Aut ferrum expectes, ultrices insuper ignes.
>   Ocland in Holinsh. iii. 547.

[5] Vir verbosus et arrogans sed parum disciplinatus, Wals. ii. 305; Hypodig. 456,
where he is called Archbishop of Sens. Not that these words refer to Bishop Fresnel,
as Vickers, 15. In his epitaph in the Cathedral at Bourges, Archbishop Boisratier is
called "eloquio clarus studioque et floribus," Gall. Christ. ii. 87. In Halle, 59, he is "an
unnurtured, unmannerly bishop," or a "proud presumptuous prelate," Holinsh. iii. 547;
"a proud and eloquent man but no diplomatist," Kingsford, 112; a "man of spirit,"
Cassell, i. 526.

[6] Ou tu y seras prins ou mort, Monstr. 363; Le Fèvre, i. 211; Waurin, i. 172; Chenu,
Archiepisc. 94.

of reconciliation vanished in a hurricane of bluster and brag[1].

After receiving their reply in writing[2] the French envoys took their departure on July 7[3] and two days later the customary gifts of diplomatic courtesy[4] were sent after them for their acceptance. Not venturing to appear in London[5] they passed it by and arrived at Canterbury on July 12, where the townsfolk made a brave show and turned out the watch in great force to give them an impressive reception[6]. Thus far the party had held together, but as there were only three barges available at Dover they had now to break up. In these the principal envoys were accommodated and conducted across to Calais on July 14[7] by the same high official that had met them before, many of the members following afterwards in other vessels and paying their own fare over[8]. The envoys reached Paris on July 26[9], where they at once gave an account of their mission in the presence of the king and the council in the Hostel of St Pol. They reported that they had found the English intractable and that King Henry, although he offered peace in honeyed words, had gathered troops from every

---

[1] In convicia erumpunt et irrisum, Tit. Liv. 6; Vita, 30; "after certeine brags blustered out with impatience," Holinsh. iii. 547; "gallant bravadoes," Speed, 773; "ces rodomontades," Dupleix, ii. 711; "much impaciency," Biondi, 112; "with more freedom than consisted with the character of an ambassador," Duck, 68; "a provoking reply," S. Turner, v. 397; "exceeding the bounds of decency," Collier, iii. 311; "language somewhat more violent than might be expected from ministers of peace," Brougham, 103. On the other hand Duchesne (822) thinks that he acted "fort prudemment et courageusement"; cf. "sut conserver dans cette occasion la dignité d'un envoyé de France," Mazas, Vies, v. 564; "avait noblement soutenu l'honneur du royaume," Barante, iii. 137; "in würdevoller männlicher Rede," Pauli, v. 99.

[2] Dated July 6, 1415, Tillet, Guerres, 123. Called Abschrift, Rolls House France Pflio iii in Pauli, v. 99, from Paris Archives J. 646, no. 14; Report on Foedera D. 79.

[3] Mirot, 267, 268; said to be on July 8, dy woren mit dem Koninge czu teydinge wol 9 tage, Hanserecesse, vi. 150.

[4] Grands dons, Monstr. 363; i.e. three days before they sailed from Dover, Mirot, 160, 184.

[5] N'estoyent osez entrer dedans, Mirot, 191.

[6] The Prior of Christ Church and the Abbot of St Augustine's contributed lances and archers (viz. 16 + 24 and 9 + 24 respectively) to swell the numbers, Sumner, i. 148; do. App. p. 64; Hasted, iv. 554, who supposes that the envoys were returning from Southampton.

[7] In Exch. Accts. 406/29 their expenses are paid till July 14, 1415, though Jean Andrée who was with them says that they sailed circa principium mensis Augusti, Mirot, 218. Not that they were kept in England over three months, as Haggard, 109.

[8] Solvit nolagium bargie in quo (*sic*) rediit, Mirot, 250.

[9] Called July 27 in Beaucourt, i. 260. News reached Venice between Aug. 16 and 25, 1415, that the negotiations had failed and that the envoys were back in France by Aug. 1, Morosini, ii. 42, 46. On Dec. 21, 1415, Archbishop Boisratier celebrated mass at the Hôtel Dieu in Paris, Coyecque, ii. 51.

part and was undoubtedly bent on destroying their country[1].

And indeed, even as they were delivering their report, he was actually penning one more bland letter[2], which he dated at Southampton "upon the seaside" on July 28, 1415[3], and despatched to France by a herald[4]. In this letter he declared that he had all along acted with a sincere desire for peace and how by the law of Deuteronomy[5] every one who was preparing to attack a town ought first to offer peace; so although he now said: "Friend, pay that thou owest[6]," yet in the spirit of the Gospel he was still willing to accept the latest offers of the envoys and even to yield in regard to the margin of 50,000 or 60,000 crowns that now divided them, but his conscience would not let him give up the claim to his rights in France, lest he should thereby disinherit his successors for ever.

Some modern writers have been so puzzled with this singular document that they pronounce it at once to be a forgery[7], while others see in it nothing but "a letter of defiance[8]" designed to show that there was now an end to all negotiations[9]. Whatever its intention it certainly had

---

[1] Not that the English forces had been disbanded, or that King Henry had been killed by the conspirators at Southampton, as Speed, 775.

[2] In salbungsvollen Worten, Pauli, v. 99; "in the loftiest terms of self-righteousness," Kingsford, 122.

[3] St Denys, v. 526; Juv. 504; Laboureur, 1000; Halliwell, Lett. i. 78; Nicolas, App. p. 5; Towle, 289-291; Goodwin (63) thinks that the fact of dating it from Southampton was a plain hint that he was ready to embark. For French text of the letter, see Norm. Chron. (Hellot), 11, 191; not that it was dated August 5, as Monstr. 365; Waurin, i. 174; Le Fèvre, i. 219, 221; First Life, 30-32; Halle, iii. 548; Speed, 774; Duchesne, 822; Daniel, iii. 869. Nicolas (36) doubts this date "as Aug. 5 was the day of the execution of his most intimate friend."

[4] Called "Chester" in Juv. 504; "Chestic," Norm. Chron. 14; "Exeter," Monstr. 365; or "Antelop, his pursuivant-at-arms," Halle, 59; "Antylopus," Redman, 38. For heralds accompanying the king to France at 1s. per day (i.e. Leicester, Guienne and Ireland, Kings-at-Arms) and Hereford (Marshal-at-Arms), see Nicolas, 387; Hunter, 57. For Henry Greve (alias Leicester King-of-Arms), see Pat. 3 H. V, i. 33; Cal. Pat. H. V, i. 299. For Richard Brugge or del Brugge alias Lancaster King-at-Arms del North, see Pat. 3 H. V, i. 16, May 9, 1415; Cal. Pat. H. V, i. 71, 326. For John Kiteley or Kighley (Cal. Pat. H. V, i. 297, where he is in Ireland on April 20, 1415), a herald in England appointed Ireland King-at-Arms by Henry V at the suggestion of James Earl of Ormond, see Lodge, Peerage, iv. 11; Gilbert, Viceroys, 316. The title was changed to Ulster King-at-Arms temp. Henry VIII. For Rouge-Croix, herald with Henry V at Rouen Sept. 7, 1418, see Rym. ix. 620; Bréquigny, 363.

[5] Deut. xx. 10; Chron. Giles, 19; Gesta, 21.

[6] Matt. xviii. 28. Redde quod debes, St Denys, v. 528; whose evangelical doctrine willeth that you ought to render to all men that which you ought to do, Halle, 59; to render him that which was his owne, Holinsh. iii. 548.

[7] Diesen erdichteten Brief, Kabel, 19.

[8] Carte, ii. 678.   [9] Guthrie, ii. 458.

this result, for the French king's reply written on Aug. 23, 1415[1], sounded no note of any spirit of conciliation, but merely repeated the flourish of his envoys at Winchester that Henry might come if he liked and that Frenchmen would be ready for him if he came.

While the French representatives were chaffering with the king, an envoy from Michael Küchmeister[2], the High Master of the Teutonic Order at Marienburg[3], was present at Winchester on another errand and has left us a highly interesting description of his experience, though unfortunately he has very little to say as to the last stormy interview at Wolvesey, the probability being that he did not really know what had passed. But at any rate it is worth recording what he has to say as to his own immediate business, falling as it does at so exceptionally critical a time.

It will be remembered that at the death of Henry IV the High Master had large claims against England amounting to over 10,000 marks, the payment of which had been repeatedly promised and as repeatedly postponed[4]. But plague, dearth and floods had brought the Order into the direst straits[5] and, for all their coinage debasement, they were unable to find money to meet the attacks of the Letts and the Poles. So on March 27, 1415[6], the High Master despatched two envoys to England to press for payment of his claim. These were Hans Covolt[7] of Danzig, who had been in London on the same errand three years before[8], and Peter Benefeld, who himself wrote the descriptive despatch now before us. Remembering how his previous emissaries had been at a great disadvantage in England

---

[1] St Denys, v. 530; Daniel, iii. 869; Mazas, Vies, v. 566; or Aug. 24, Juv. 504; Norm. Chron. (Hellot), 13; Orig. Lett. II. i. 49.

[2] i.e. of Sternberg, Lelewel, 18; Lindner, ii. 275.

[3] For plan and description of the castle, see Planen, *passim*. For seal of Marienburg with the Ordenshaus, see Vossberg, Münzen, Plate v. xiv. It became the headquarters of the Order in 1309, Lodge, 457. S'i tient le hault maistre de Pruce, Bouvier, Descr. 81, 117, where the knights are vestus de blanc à une croix noire, and are called le plus grant ordre du monde hors prestrise.

[4] Wylie, iv. 11–21.   [5] J. Voigt, Marienburg, 300, 311.

[6] Hanserecesse, vi. 148. Their commission was dated at Marienburg on Jan. 12, 1415, ibid. 147.

[7] So he signs himself in Stieda, 81; cf. Hanserecesse, vi. 116, 147. He is otherwise officially called John Kavolt (Bunge, v. 177); or Kavold (Wylie, iv. 19); or Kovolt (Hanserecesse, vi. 274); or Cobold (ibid. vi. 148; Stieda, 66, 72, 76, 78).

[8] Wylie, iv. 19, 21.

because they were regarded as "too small," the High
Master started with apologies for not sending men of
more standing on account of the distressful condition
of the Order. Arriving in London when preparations
for the attack on France were in full blast, Benefeld and
Covolt were taken in hand by Hartonk van Clux[1] and ten
days after their arrival they had their first audience. After
this the king was so busy that three weeks elapsed before
they could see him again and when at length they did
secure an interview in the Privy Chamber at Westminster
he could only promise to give them an answer the first
time he could[2]. Then came the pilgrimage to Holywell[3],
on the return from which they saw the king again in the
presence of his brothers and much gentry[4], when he said :
"You see we are busy just now," but he promised that they
should have an answer through the Council. They said
they understood that he would soon be going away and

[1] He is so called in Iss. Roll 7 H. V, Pasch., Apr. 20, 1419, which refers to £40 per
annum granted to him by Henry IV, see Wylie, iii. 42 ; but "Here Thank van Clux" in
Iss. Roll 6 H. V, Pasch., June 1, 1418; Hortonk van Clux alias Voncloix, Cal. Pat.
H. V, i. 98; Here Tank van Clux, Exch. Accts. 45/5 (4). For account of him, see Wylie,
iii. 402. He is called "Sir Hertenke van Cloup" in Gesta, 275; "her Hartung Clux,"
Windecke, 87; HR. vi. 148; Hartungoo, Hertangus, Hertungus van Clux, Bekynton,
i. 86, 96, 160, 167, 187, 245; Hortong van Clux, Rym. x. 769; Mons. Heer Tanke Clux,
on the 9th stall-plate of the Garter in St George's Chapel at Windsor, Bekynton, ii. 408 ;
Ashmole, 710; Beltz, clx; Hope, Plate XXXVIII; Hertank van Clox, Carte, Rolles, i.
260, 290 ; Ewald, xli. 742, where he receives a grant of the castles of Creully and
Courseulles and other lands in Normandy in 1418; Hortank wan Clox, Bréquigny, 26;
Hartung von Kluks, Allgem. deutsch. Biogr. xxxi. 508, where he is sent by Sigismund
to Austria with Caspar Schlick in 1436; Hortank van Clox, kt., Carte, Rolles, i. 290;
Ewald, xli. 742; Sir Heer Tanke or Hartankleux or Hortonklieux, Stow, Lond. iii. 5 ;
do. Kingsford, i. 243; also Hortaux de Vauclox, Hortassa Van Clox, Bréquigny, no. 176;
Hortant Vanclox, Vautier, 32; Heurtangle or Heurtaux de Vancloux, or Vanclos, Postel,
10, 68; Sir Henry Tanclux, Halle, 80, who calls him an Almaine; Sir Hartung Glux,
Wratislaw, 159; Sir Hartank van Clux, Kingsford, 166, who calls him a Silesian.
He appears at Constance as Georius Harttung de Lotz in Mansi, xxviii. 644. In Brook's
list he is at Agincourt as "Hartanke" with a retinue of 100 lances, Nicolas, 357,
but his retinue at Southampton was really only 3 + 9, ibid. 385; Hunter, 34, where he is
called Hertuk van Clux. For his arms, see Richental, Sorg, 218. He died in 1445 or
1446 and was buried in the church of St Michael Paternoster in the Royal, Stow, Kingsford, i. 243, where he is said to have been "borne in Almayne." For continuance of
grant of 40 marks per annum to him, see Iss. Roll 1 H. V, Mich., Dec. 1, 1413; do. 5
H. V, Pasch., May 6, 1417; called £40 in Pat. 1 H. V, iii. 15; Wylie, iii. 402, note 9.
For £20 per annum granted to him from revenues of the alien priory of Llangennith near
Swansea (Wylie, iii. 403), see Pat. 1 H. V, iii. 14; Cal. Pat. H. V, i. 100. On May 26,
1414, Henry Gwyn is occupator at Llangennith paying £20 per annum and Richard
Morgan had recently been elected Prior, Pat. 2 H. V, i. 20. In Rec. Roll 7 H. V,
Pasch., May 12, 1419, Henry Guyn (i.e. Gwyn) pays £8. 13s. 4d. for the custody of the
priory.
[2] Als her eerste möchte, Hanserecesse, vi. 148.
[3] Page 483.
[4] Vele herschaft, Hanserecesse, vi. 148. Cf. the genterie of myn auncestors,
Secreta, 153; gentrie wolde, ibid. 163; this grete Ientrie, ibid. 191.

asked if they should go with him to get his answer but he repeated that they should receive it through the Council. So afterwards they went before the Council[1] where the Chancellor (Bishop Beaufort) expressed surprise that they were so pressing when they saw that the king had so much to do. To which they replied that the High Master had not been aware of that, but that it should be remembered that he had often urged this matter before. The Chancellor answered that the king quite meant to pay and that they should certainly have a letter soon with which the High Master was sure to be satisfied, and with this he left them and would say no more[2]. The next day however they saw him again, but he only said that the king's secretary would write out the letter for them and then he mounted his horse and started off for Winchester. After he had gone they had two interviews with the secretary, who told them that it was a matter for the Privy Seal, and the next day they saw Privy Seal[3] himself, who told them that he had no instructions but referred them to the Clerk of the Council[4]. The Clerk of the Council kept them waiting for two days and then said that he could not find any record, and when they came before the Council itself on the following day, Bishop Langley told them that this was a matter that must be referred to the Chancellor. So the persistent Peter rode down to Winchester, a distance, as he calls it, of 54 English miles. Here he saw the Chancellor (Beaufort), who said: "Aren't you settled yet? I'm exceedingly sorry, but I'll see about your letter to-morrow"; but when Peter went

---

[1] The usual meeting-place of the Council was the recently built hall overlooking the river at Westminster Stair. It was begun by Edward III in 1346. For details of expenditure, see Baildon, 27, where it is nova domus juxta Receptum; cf. pres de la Recette, ibid. 9. It was also known as the Star (or Starred) Chamber, in all probability because it was ornamented with stars; Camera stellata, Chaumbre des estoilles, Chaumbre du Conseil estoilles, Sterne Chamere, Starred Chamber, the Sterne Chamber, see Rym. x. 658; Shillingford, pp. xx, 6; Bruce, 348; Baildon, 8, 9, 36; Baldwin, 15. Its predecessor was called the Chaumbre du Conseil pres de l'Eschequier in 1344, Rot. Parl. ii. 154; not that the earliest mention of it is 1372, as Brayley and Britton, 231. For account of it, see Stow, vi. 50; do. Kingsford, ii. 119, 377. For pictures, see Knight, London, vi. 128; Cassell, ii. 576; Baildon, Frontisp. 7, 18. For star over the entrance carved in 1602, see Baildon, 6; for fanciful derivations, see Archaeologia, viii. 404. Its position parallel with Westminster Hall is well shown on Aggas' map (1578) in J. T. Smith, ad finem; Baildon, 5. It was demolished in 1834, Besant, Westminster, 55; Wright and Smith, 24, 34, 545.

[2] Und wolde uns kheyner rede mey pflegen, Hanserecesse, vi. 149.

[3] i.e. John Wakering, see page 278.

[4] Czu dem scrybere von des khoningis rothe, Hanserecesse, vi. 149.

again the next day he only got put off for eight days longer. And then one morning Bishop Beaufort walked along with him for about a mile and talked over the quarrel with Poland and the deposed High Master, Henry of Plauen[1]. Peter told him all about it quite nicely (*gelympf-lich*) and then the Chancellor asked for three days more, so that he might see the secretary and the Keeper of the Privy Seal. Accordingly Peter rode back to London, saw the secretary and asked him when he would be joining the Court. "In three days," said the secretary, but he told him that the matter would really be settled by the Council and that he had better see the Archbishop of Canterbury about it. So the two envoys saw Archbishop Chichele, who could only say that the king acknowledged the debt but had given no further instructions, and Privy Seal said the same thing. Then Peter rode down again to Winchester in company with the secretary, only to find that the French envoys were there and that it would be quite impossible for the king to attend to him for the next nine days. At last when the Frenchmen had left he got an audience with the king, who beckoned the Chancellor and the secretary aside, after which the former told Peter that the king had said that he would write a friendly letter to the High Master that could not fail to please him. The next day Bishop Beaufort rode back to London with Peter

[1] He was deposed Oct. 13, 1413, Wylie, iv. 18; or Oct. 14, Voigt, Namencodex, 2; Lindner, ii. 275; called Oct. 11 in J. Voigt, Marienburg, 294, who gives a list of his belongings when he removed to Engelsburg as commodor on Oct. 15, 1413; Lelewel, 18; Dlugosz, xi. 347. Cf. Der von Plouwen der waz ein landesherre und ein Ritter, Windecke, 22. He had been Kompthur of Schwetz near Kulm, Ranke, iv. 453; Lindner, ii. 274. For his connection with Eger, see Gradl, Gesch. 330. After his deposition he was made Commodore of Engelsburg, Voigt, Namencodex, 29 (called Engelsbergk in Vossberg, Banderia, 44, Plate V; or Ingleberck, Lannoy, 28; Lelewel, 19, 48), a post which he held till May 22, 1414, J. Voigt, Namencodex, 30, when he was made Commodore or Warden (Pfleger) of Lochstädt (in oppidum Lochstat detrusus, Dlugosz, xi. 347) on the Frisches Haff near Pillau, J. Voigt, Namencodex, 91. This office he gave up in the same year, but resumed it again on May 25, 1429, and died there in the same year, J. Voigt, Marienburg, 296, from his epitaph in St Ann's Chapel at Marienburg; not that he died in 1416, as Wylie, iv. 18; nor 1426, as J. Voigt, Marienburg, 294, who says that he was at Brandenburg till 1425. For his attempts to reform the constitution of the Order, see Nitzsch, ii. 333; Lelewel, 19, who supposes that he was charged with Wicliffry; also Higgins, ii. 46, 151; Lannoy, Œuvres, xiii, where the Order is plus guerrier que religieux; cf. le palais couvent, ibid. xiv. For stories of his misery (pressura) during his seven years of imprisonment at Danzig, where he had no beer to drink and only black bread to eat which he had to pay for out of his own pocket, see Dlugosz, xi. 347. Cf. pour le visiter en sa misère dont je euz grant pitié, Lelewel, 19, 48. For his banner, see Vossberg, Banderia, 22, Plate II. For a gulden (or ducat, i.e. the same as the Hungarian gulden) and schillings with a figure of him in armour, see Vossberg, Münzen, 78, 79, Plate VI.

in his company and four days after their arrival in the capital there was another interview, at which the Chancellor said that, if the money was to be paid, the High Master must be prepared to take it in small instalments and at long intervals, and then Peter wrote home his report in which he told the story of all this circumlocution with phlegmatic dulness unrelieved by a single spark of irritation or disgust, and in this form it may be seen among the archives of Danzig to this day[1].

The above account may also be rounded off by relating a hitherto unknown incident, which for a moment lets in a curious side-light on the private doings of some of the chief actors in the momentous drama enacted at Winchester. Accompanying the French embassy was an eminent savant named Master Jean Fusoris[2]. His father had been a tinkler[3] or coppersmith[4] in the county of Rethel[5] and he himself had started life by following the same business[6]. But he had shown a bent for higher work, and had studied in the University of Paris, where he had qualified in medicine and was now in high repute for his knowledge of mathematics and astrology[7]. His skill in this respect brought him to the notice of Charles V, who took a special interest in the subject[8], and at various times in his career he made clocks, spheres and astrolabes for the great ones of the earth, including John I, King of Aragon[9], Louis Duke of Orleans[10]

---

[1] Hanserecesse, vi. 150.

[2] i.e. Le Fondeur, but he is always called Fusoris in the Procès, Mirot, *passim*; Champeaux-Gauchery, 126, 131; Dufour, Famille, 127, 160; called "Fuseris" in Baye, ii. 237, 308; not "Furoris," as Girardot, 9 [13]; nor "Fusons," as Douet d'Arcq, i. 377, quoting Reg. xiii du Cons. X, 1480, fol. 42.

[3] For "tinker," see Letter Book I, 275; Wylie, iv. 278.

[4] Poterius seu operator stanni, Mirot, 230; potier d'estain, Champeaux-Gauchery, 133; Toulgoët-Treanna, 113; Chabeuf, 195; Lhomel, Edits, 108, 111. For their ordinances at Troyes (1413), see Boutiot, ii. 340. For the Company of Founders or Coppersmiths in London, see Hazlitt, Companies, p. 488. For high repute of the copper produced at Dinant (Namur), see Mirot, 230; Wylie, ii. 267.

[5] Fusoris was born at Giraumont in the Ardennes, Mirot, 142, 173, 279.

[6] Ad faciendum vasa stannea, ibid. 231.

[7] Excellent en la science de géometrie et grand astrologien, ibid. 142; astrologue rêveur, Mirot, D'Orgement, p. i. For connection of medicine with astrology, see page 140.

[8] Qui delectabatur in talibus instrumentis astrologie, Mirot, 231; Wylie, iii. 231, note 5. For treatise *De Sphærâ* from his library at the Louvre, now at St John's College, Oxford, see Delisle, Recherches, i. 266; also a large number of books on astronomy, including six copies of Ptolemy's Almagist (Wylie, iii. 415) and works on the Sphere and the Astrolabe, Delisle, Recherches, ii. 96–118. For Liber Almagest at Avignon (1435), see Nouv. Rev. (1891), p. 79.

[9] Mirot, 231, where Fusoris does not remember his name, but describes him as ille qui decessit in venatu, i.e. from a fall from his horse, May 19, 1395.

[10] For his clocks, see Wylie, iv. 283.

and Pope John XXIII at Bologna[1]. He held canonries at
Rheims and at Notre Dame in Paris as well as the living
of Jouarre[2] on the Marne above Meaux, and Bishop
Courtenay, when in Paris in the autumn of 1414, had sent
a message that he would like to see him. Accordingly he
called on the bishop at the Hostel de Bourbon[3] and had a
long conversation with him on "the science of astrology[4],"
by which we are not to understand merely forecasts of
events, but a scientific study of the motions of the stars so
far as that generation understood it, for Courtenay had been
three times Chancellor of the University of Oxford[5] and
was keen for every genuine extension of knowledge. As
a result of their talk Fusoris sold him seven instruments
for 400 crowns[6], and as the bishop had to leave Paris the
next day he asked him to have a copy of rules written out
for him showing how the instruments should be worked,
and to call on him at St Denis for the money. On the
following day Fusoris attended at the sign of the Sword which
fronted the Abbey at St Denis[7], where he dined with the
bishop and began to draw up the "practice[8]" as requested,
but as it was already late he was asked to stay the night
and go on with the English as far as Pontoise, where he
would certainly receive his money. As the party rode
along to Pontoise on the next day, the conversation turned
on the burning question of the famous thesis of Jean Petit[9],
as to which they were not all of one mind, and Fusoris, who
had strong Burgundian leanings[10], did not like the flippant
and insulting[11] way in which some of them spoke of the
University of Paris. He stood up for the honour of his
University and brought down upon himself some very
threatening language from the Lombard physician, Pietro

---

[1] Mirot, 143, 144, 182, 231.
[2] Joyrre-les-nonnains, Mirot, 142, 203, where he is maître-ès-arts et en médecine,
bachelier en théologie.
[3] Page 418.   [4] Champeaux-Gauchery, 131; Mirot, 173.
[5] i.e. in 1407, 1411 and 1412, Le Neve, iii. 466; Wylie, iii. 113, 443.
[6] Mirot, 150, 173, 266.
[7] For plans of St Denis in 1704 and modern, see Bournon, Frontispiece, and
pp. 29, 124.
[8] Practicam seu canones illorum septem instrumentorum, Mirot, 232; Champeaux-
Gauchery, 131. Cf. "a canon sufficient to teche the maner of the working of that
same conclusioun," Chauc. (S.), iii. 177; "the verrey practik of the forseide conclusions," ibid.
[9] See page 176.   [10] Multum favere partem Burgundorum, Mirot, 222.
[11] Trufabantur et deridebant, ibid. 234.

of Milan[1], who was crossing with Bishop Courtenay to England. At Pontoise the bishop paid Fusoris 100 English nobles, which in the ordinary course should have been equivalent to 200 crowns[2], but in this case they only realised 167 on the Paris exchange[3]. For payment of the remaining 200 crowns he had to be put off again, as the bishop had already spent so much in books, mirrors, jewellery, vernigals[4] and other goldsmith's work[5] that he had had to borrow in order to pay his way home.

When Courtenay was again in Paris in the spring of 1415[6], Fusoris called on him at his lodgings in the Hostel de Navarre[7] where he sold him some books, and when the bishop had presented the English demands[8] Fusoris consulted the figure of the heavens and assured him that they would probably be successful, and once over the dinner table the bishop told him how much King Henry would like to make his acquaintance as he took great interest in astrology[9], and having with him the astrolabe and an almanac[10] which he had bought of him at the time of the first embassy, he asked his visitor whether the king's proposed marriage with the Princess Catherine would be good for England, whereupon they looked up the figure and found that it was good. Then they said: "Let us see whether the marriage will be accomplished in this embassy," and they found that the figure was not good. They then fell to talking of astrology and Fusoris said that there were certain judgments that might be sustained, as for instance about bodily illness and such like, but that others which had to do with events depending upon man's free will were uncertain and had no sound foundation. Then Courtenay told him that he was getting alarmed about King Henry's health, for if the king should die it would be a great blow to his fortunes as he had always been a good and gracious lord to him[11], and with this he took Fusoris aside and showed

---

[1] See page 443.   [2] See page 407.   [3] Mirot, 151.
[4] Unum vas gallicè dictum vernigal, Mirot, 274; Godefroy, s.v.
[5] See page 425; Mirot, 147, 187, 272, 274, where the payments are made partly *in auro* and partly *in monetâ*.   [6] i.e. on the second embassy, see page 438.
[7] Mirot, 245.   [8] Page 440.   [9] Mirot, 233.
[10] Cf. "almanacks which be called Ephemerides," Murray, Dict., s.v. Cf. every day after thy almenack, Chauc. (S.), iii. 177.
[11] Mirot, 236. For estre bon seigneur, see Rym. ix. 625; de vous monstrer bon seigneur, Ord. Priv. Co. ii. 263, 265; hee wolde stand mi gode lord, J. M. Neale, 135; shewing himself hevy lorde, Anjou Letters, 37.

him the king's nativity[1], asking whether he was likely to live long, but the Frenchman was cautious and said that he was not good at that kind of knowledge[2] and that it would take him more than a year to find that out.   As to the debt of 200 crowns the bishop was again obliged to ask him to wait, but he pressed him to come over to London with the next embassy that was to be arranged, holding out a prospect to him of an appointment as physician to Queen Joan as they had no good English doctors, and promising that he would procure for him several large benefices[3].   He hoped that he would stay at the court for at least three or four months and he must be sure and bring with him or send, if he could not come himself, the "practice[4]" that he was making for the astrolabe[5], together with a sextern of puzzles[6] or problems (*ludos*) in geometry, and a composition of the solid sphere[7] and of the seven planets, all these being intended as a present for the King of England[8].   So Fusoris returned to Paris, where he made the compositions and problems in a plain fashion[9] with a demonstration at the end of each chapter, and waited for an opportunity to cross to England himself.

In May 1415, hearing that the French embassy was soon to start, he approached Archbishop Boisratier as to the possibility of his being allowed to join it as a member of his suite, giving as his reason that his only purpose was

[1] La philosomie (i.e. figure) et aussi la manière de la nativité du roy, Mirot, 186.

[2] Non bene dispositus nec pratticus ad hoc sciendum, ibid.

[3] Mirot, 151.

[4] For a treatise on the astrolabe and a "practique de géometrie" translated by Fusoris for Pierre d'Evreux, Count of Mortain (page 173), see Mirot, 144.

[5] For pictures of an astrolabe, see Vallet de Viriville, 24, 25 (16th cent.); Chauc. (S.), Vol. III; see also Wylie, iv. 168.   For an astrolabe said to have belonged to Jean de Béthencourt now in the Musée d'Antiquités at Rouen, see Grande Encycl. vi. 521; cf. astrolabium meum, Tuetey, Test. 326.   For an astrolabe used for measuring the heights of buildings, see Vallet de Viriville, Instruction, 50.   For the astrolabe in Pekin, see Marco Polo, i. 399.

[6] Enigmata id est ludos geometrie et astrologie, Mirot, 237; sixternam de enigmatibus, ibid. 243; Champeaux-Gauchery, 133; cf. reperitur in secundo sexterno, Rym. ix. 610; Du Cange, s.v., where it is compared with quaternum or cahier (i.e. quire or quair). For a book called *De Utilitate Particularum* left to the Faculty of Medicine in Paris by the Dean and used by the masters *per sisternos*, see Tuetey, Test. 508.

[7] For livre de Spera belonging to the Duke of Berry, see Guiffrey, i. 233; cf. "celestial hevynly spere," Coudrette, 222.   For *Tractatus de Sphæra* by John de Sacro Bosco (i.e. of Holywood or Halifax) who died in 1356, see Dict. Nat. Biogr. xxvii. 217; Barnard, 314, where he is called a 13th century Scotchman; Vidal, Perpignan, 287, where he is Johannes de Sancto Paulo alias de Sancto Bosco.

[8] Qui composuit instrumenta *vestra* septem planetarum, Champeaux-Gauchery, 133.

[9] In plano stilo, Mirot, 254.

the recovery of his 200 crowns. But the archbishop refused to be compromised about this, knowing that Fusoris was something of a partisan[1] of the Burgundians and fearing that he might be talking too much about the divisions that existed in France. Then he applied to Bishop Fresnel but with no better success. At length however, having bought a couple of horses which cost him about 80 crowns[2], he induced the archbishop to give way at the last moment as the numbers in his suite were not quite made up, and so with one attendant[3] he found his way across to England. But the archbishop could not get over his suspicions, for Fusoris was always talking with Englishmen[4], was often late at meals and sometimes absent from them altogether. For this he was reproved, but only mildly, for it was thought he might after all be getting useful information out of the English which he would afterwards communicate. The archbishop never knew for certain that he received anything from the king, though he mentions that he had heard it said that Henry had given him 40 nobles[5]. He understood that Fusoris never talked with the king personally, but that all communications between them passed through the Dean of the Royal Chapel.

Every day during the week spent at Winchester, when the envoys attended the Council at Wolvesey[6] where the court was lodged, Fusoris went with them as far as the door of the Council Chamber and waited about for his chance of seeing Bishop Courtenay[7]. He often saw him passing to and fro, but it was not till the middle of the week[8] that he got an opportunity of speaking with him. On that day the bishop shook him by the hand and said in

[1] Aliqualiter esse parcialem, Mirot, 222; se monstrabant ambo partiales (i.e. Fusoris and his servant), ibid. 225.

[2] He sold them for 40 crowns on his return, ibid. 248.

[3] i.e. Jean du Berle or Johannin du Belle, ibid. 175, 182; unus parvus clericulus, ibid. 254, who only knew a little table-Latin (*latinam de mensâ*) just enough to ask for the bread or the wine, ibid. 267.

[4] Though this is denied by his servant, ibid. 270.

[5] This is admitted by Fusoris, ibid. 160, 168, 175, 176, 183, 184, 219, 253, 269, showing that his servant counted them, together with the 100 nobles that he received from Bishop Courtenay in payment of his debt.

[6] See page 485, note 4. Ad palatium, Mirot, 224, 226; ad curiam regis, ibid. 243.

[7] For Bishop Courtenay at Winchester on July 6, 1415, see Kal. and Inv. ii. 106, where he is Tresorer del Chaumbre du Roy et Gardein de ces (*sic*) joialx.

[8] i.e. three days before the departure of the envoys, Mirot, 219.

his genial kindly way[1]: "You are welcome, Master John[2]!" but did not pay him his money.   On the following morning[3] (i.e. the day before the final rupture) he went as usual to Wolvesey accompanied by two French squires, and as they waited in the hall they were accosted pleasantly[4] by an English doctor in theology who told them that they were a little late as the king was in council, and as they would have some time to wait he invited them to have a drink, which the two squires refused.   Fusoris, however, accepted and as they chatted over the wine, the English doctor spoke of a certain college in Paris where two English students could be taken in on condition that the like terms were allowed to two French students in some college in England, but that all would depend upon whether peace was arranged. He then asked if there were many astrologers in Paris, to which Fusoris replied that it was not a science that paid[5], though there were many like themselves who were keen on the science of the motions[6] without meddling with judg-ments[7], whereupon the Englishman took a sextern out of his gown containing many figures of the heavens and re-volutions of years since King Henry's nativity.   Fusoris would have liked to see it had there been peace between the two countries, but as it was, he would not look at it, as he had now no hope that there would be any treaty at all.   Then the doctor said how much he would have liked to spend a year or two in Paris "if only your ambassadors had come sooner[8]," for then he thought the marriage might have been arranged, though he still had hopes that another English embassy might be sent after the army had crossed the Channel.   This inquisitive visitor appears to have been the Dean of the King's Chapel[9], but Fusoris had been quietly taking his measure, and when he reported the con-versation to Archbishop Boisratier he told him that his questioner was called an astrologer, but that he was really ignorant of the very elements of the science and could not

---

[1] Multum affabilis et gratus homo, Mirot, 230.
[2] Ibid. 240.   [3] Ibid. 241.
[4] Unus gratus homo, Mirot, 243; bene sufficiens clericus, ibid.
[5] Scientia lucrativa, ibid.
[6] Cf. "the moevinge of the celestial bodies," Chauc. (S.), iii. 177.
[7] Mirot, 174.   [8] Ibid. 160.
[9] i.e. Edmund Lacy, page 475.

understand even what was told him[1]. Then the Frenchman rejoined his compatriots in the hall and after some further waiting he saw Bishop Courtenay coming down from the king's room towards the chapel where he was due to say mass. Fusoris passed into the chapel with him, and while the bishop was setting the altar[2] they had a few minutes conversation together[3]. About the money the bishop said that the reason why he had not paid it before was that he could not get a dependable messenger to send it over with to France, but "Master John," he said, "you shall have your money though at present I have not got a penny with me in the house[4]," meaning that after the king had gone he would be turning out into other quarters of his own and would then see that the money was paid. He then asked Fusoris if he had brought anything good with him, who said that he had brought the compositions and the other things they had agreed upon. The bishop asked if he had them with him, but finding they were at Fusoris' lodgings he told him to bring them to-morrow morning at mass when he would present him in person to the king. Fusoris sought to be excused, for he foresaw the rupture[5] and knew even before the ambassadors themselves did that the expedition would certainly go forward[6], but the bishop said that the king would particularly like to see him as they had so often talked about him together.

So early the next morning his servant Jean du Berle put up the astrolabe and the book and the other things in bags[7] and he and his master went together to Wolvesey for the last time. The French ambassadors were closeted with the king in his room but all their attendants stood about in the hall[8]. Fusoris waited till Courtenay came down, and after bowing to him followed him into the chapel. When the mass was over Courtenay signed to him among the crowd of onlookers[9] and they went together into the king's

---

[1] Mirot, 219.

[2] Preparabat altare, ibid. 243; ad parandum capellam et altare, ibid. 268.

[3] Quasi spacium dicendi semel septem psalmos, or bis vel ter Paternoster et Ave, ibid. 268; called "long espace de temps" by Jean du Berle, ibid. 184. For "half an Ave Maria while," see York, 100.

[4] Sed non habeo intus aliquod denier, Mirot, 241.

[5] Non sperabat pacem tunc tractari posse, ibid. 243.

[6] Indubitanter, ibid. 219.   [7] In suis bougis, ibid. 245.   [8] Ibid. 267.

[9] Propter multitudinem gentium ibidem existentium, ibid. 244, 268.

pew[1]. The bishop introduced him, saying : "My lord, this is Master John Fusoris that I spoke of, who thinking there would be a treaty of peace, has brought with him a composition for your solid sphere, another for an instrument wherein may be seen the motions of the planets, their conjunctions, oppositions and aspects, together with a figure of the heavens at all hours, a small astrolabe[2] with a practice[3] and a sextern of problems[4], which he offers to Your Majesty," and therewith he presented the various articles one by one. The king merely said in Latin : " Thank you, Master John[5] !" adding "Grans mercis!" in French, to which Fusoris replied : *"Ad bene placitum vestrum serenissime princeps,"* and the interview was at an end[6]. While it lasted Fusoris had stood with bent knee and he was one of the guests at the king's dinner afterwards before the final answer was given to the French envoys on that fateful day.

Of the angry outburst that is reported to have occurred on the receipt of that answer he tells us absolutely nothing, though we know that he was present when it was delivered[7], but when the interview in the chapel was over he had a talk with Courtenay, who shook him by the hand and said that he really believed that if the French envoys had come sooner the marriage might have been arranged, adding that he had not yet given up all hope about the treaty. To which Fusoris answered that as to the marriage it rested with the English, for the usual amount of money

[1] Oratorium, see page 189. For altare de closetâ nostrâ, see Rym. ix. 291; cf. "in myn inwerd hertyly orratorye," Lydg. Min. Po. 78, 122. For Pierre Salmon's conversation with Richard II in 1397 tout seul avecques lui en son oratoire in which there was an altar, see Salmon, 45, 46; cf. " where he had knelyd in a closet," J. Page, 28; " not to speke with hym tyl that hys messe were done," Melusine, 343. For oratoire of Charles VI on the right side of the altar, see Champion, Vie, 131.

[2] Mediocris quantitatis, Mirot, 243; Champeaux-Gauchery, 133; cf. "an instrument portatif," Chauc. (S.), iii. 177. Archbishop Boisratier had one that he wanted to bring with him but it proved too heavy to carry, Mirot, 225. Among Henry V's effects at his death in 1422 is one Asterlabe d'argent valued at £3. 5s. 9½d., Rot. Pat. iv. 225. Fusoris valued his at 28 crowns. He had lately made it and he had recently sold others at 24, 28 and 30 crowns, Mirot, 245.

[3] L'astrolabe et le livre de la pratique, ibid. 161, 177, 265; compositiones et astrolabium, ibid. 265.

[4] Fusoris took the compositio and the enigmata back to Paris with him, leaving the solid sphere which he valued at 10 crowns with Henry, ibid. 245.

[5] Magister Johannes grates vobis.

[6] One of the envoys, Jean André, asserted that Fusoris had also had an interview with the king on the previous afternoon lasting from two hours after dinner till supper time, ibid. 219, and so also said Bp. Fresnel, ibid. 226. But Fusoris denied this and maintained that he had only spoken with King Henry once, ibid. 254.

[7] Mirot, 246.

had been offered as dower, but they had put forward such large demands besides as could not in his judgment be conceded. Then Courtenay went on to praise the king. He was, he said, a good man (*probus homo*) and he did not believe that he had once broken continence since he came to the throne[1], and he asked him what he thought of him himself now that he had spoken with him personally. To which Fusoris made no reply, though he tells us what he really thought without actually saying so out loud, viz. that Henry had great stateliness and the fine manner of a lord, but that he considered him as more suited for the Church than for war[2], for which his brother the Duke of Clarence seemed to him the better man[3]. That evening the king left Winchester to join the fleet, and when Fusoris returned to his quarters for the night and found that the French ambassadors were preparing to depart on the morrow, he told his chief that Henry could not have started on a more unlucky day, for the moon was combust[4] and it was common knowledge that no one could look for a happy issue for any business begun in the crook of the moon[5].

On the departure of the king Bishop Courtenay removed from Wolvesey to a house in the town, where being anxious about his money Fusoris and his man called on him quite early the next morning only to find that he was indisposed and not yet out of bed[6]. Next door to the bishop's lodging was a tavern, and as Fusoris had to wait he went in there for a drink of malmsey or vernage with a priest and a merchant from Harfleur whom he had met as an old acquaintance[7]. Then, as he had soon to start with the envoys, he sent his man to get ready the horses and bring them round, while he himself paid a last visit to the bishop.

Returning to the house where Courtenay was lodged

---

[1] See page 200. Insolentias et lascivias juventutis deferens, Kingsford, Lit. 277.

[2] Cogitabat intra se quod habebat pulchrum modum domini et magnum statum, Mirot, 243; melius dispositas ad ecclesiam quam ad guerram, ibid.

[3] Ibid. 160.

[4] i.e. in conjunction near the sun, Chauc. (S.), ii. 226, 478; iii. 192; luna erat in conjunctione combustâ et inchoare tunc aliquam rem communiter non habebatur inde bonus effectus, Mirot, 246; combustio lunæ or luna erat in combustione, ibid. 175, 224, 226. On July 6, 1415, it was new moon at 2 p.m., Guinness, ii. 507.

[5] Chron. Lond. 109; Gesta, 145; Brut, ii. 441.

[6] Male dispositus, Mirot, 246; infirmus, ibid. 247, 270.

[7] Ibid. 251, 269.

he was admitted by a servant, who took out 100 nobles from a coffer[1] and gave them to him in payment of his claim, together with a schedule by means of which he would be able to get them changed in Paris, but when he said that he had lost 33 crowns in changing the first 100 nobles some months ago, the servant explained that these were all good. Hearing that the bishop was still in bed he left a message that it would be better for him not to cross with the king if he could avoid it, but if it could not be helped he had better put it off as late as possible. Meanwhile his man had come round with the horses and the two rode after the ambassadors and set their faces towards home.

Three days after leaving Winchester the whole party arrived at a country town[2] whose name is not given. Here they stayed for the night, and after supper an English squire rode up to the Count of Vendôme's[3] inn bringing cups and other presents for the leading members of the embassy. At once the news spread, and it being still light, everybody went to the inn to see if there was anything for them, but Fusoris could not get near for the press. However he fell in with the squire, who gave him 40 nobles from the king and Bishop Courtenay, with thanks for the books and the astrolabe. As they walked along together towards the conduit (*fons*) in the main street, the squire asked why the French envoys had been so late in coming, and he replied that he had been told it was because there had been one embassy already, but that in any case the marriage would have been better than a war especially for King Henry, who would then have been secure on his throne, and if he had wanted armed help in future he could easily have got it from France, as he understood that he had several rivals and that a large part of the country favoured either his brother the Duke of Clarence[4] or the Earl of March, and that like Richard II he would find that there would be a rising against him while he was away, however good a

---

[1] Scrinnum, Mirot, 160, 176.
[2] In quâdam villâ campestri, ibid. 247, 269.
[3] He was grand master of the French king's household, Rym. ix. 283; Mirot, 247.
[4] Moult estoit aymé pour sa prudence et vaillance, Monstr. iv. 39; Waur. ii. 360; Le Fèvre, ii. 35; moult biau prince, Fenin, 153; ensample of gentilesse of freedom called the verray exemplaire, Lydg. Min. Po. 25. In Kirkstall Chron. 284 Henry is crowned king ex consensu *majoris partis* omnium dominorum regni.

lieutenant he might leave behind. If he meant merely to make a short raid into France and return with nothing to show for all the expense the country had been put to, he would not meet with much of a welcome when he got back, while if he stayed two or three months in France he would find the armed forces of that country gathered against him and that they were much better drilled (*exercitati in armis*) than they used to be, that the French lords were bound to make up their differences, and when they did King Henry would be in great danger, and this was what the English themselves were most afraid of, remembering that they had done simply nothing when they had been in France before[1]. To all of which the squire could only reply that under God there would be a good peace yet[2]. Three days later the party reached Dover, and in a short time Fusoris crossed the Channel in company with Jean André and Gautier Col, but one of his horses went lame[3] at Montreuil, where he had to hire another as well as a man to lead the lame one, and owing to this delay he did not reach Paris till Aug. 1[4], summing up his impressions in a sentence, viz. that England was a good place to have been in but a bad place to go back to[5]. Six weeks later[6], as we shall see in the sequel, he was arrested in Paris charged with being in treasonable correspondence with the enemy, and it is from the depositions[7] sworn by many witnesses in his long-drawn-out trial that we are able now to piece together with unusual certainty the details of many of the happenings in the Winchester week.

Several of Fusoris' friends[8] who fell under the like suspicion were similarly charged and imprisoned in the Châtelet, and while the English were besieging Harfleur the accused were brought up and judicially examined[9]. In the case of all the others explanations were accepted

[1] i.e. in 1412, Wylie, iv. 76.　　[2] Deo duce esset bona pax, Mirot, 249.
[3] Clochoit, clopidabat, ibid. 203, 270; equum infirmum, ibid. 250.
[4] Called Thursday at the end of July, ibid. 161, 203.
[5] Ibid. 253.
[6] i.e. Sept. 6, 1415, ibid. 161; A. Martin, Patriote, 13.
[7] In Arch. Nat. L.L. 85, where they fill 62 folios, now published by Mirot, pp. 173-279.
[8] Among them was Peter of Verona, librarian to the Duke of Berry, Mirot, 192; Guiffrey, i. 286.
[9] i.e. Sept. 7 and 14, 1415, Mirot, 161, 173; Champeaux-Gauchery, pp. 126-131.

and they were released on their caution[1]. But Fusoris did not escape so easily. Being a canon he was handed over to the Chapter of Notre Dame on Jan. 24, 1416, and kept in their prison[2] for several months. On March 26, 1416[3], he was again interrogated, and on May 31[4], application was made that he might be removed to a more pleasant and wholesome place, such as one of the houses in the cloister, but this was not allowed. At length on July 24, 1416[5], he was rusticated to a semi-banishment at Mézières on the Meuse in his native county of Rethel, where he had studied grammar and logic as a boy. In 1418 he was allowed to reside at Rheims (where he still held his canonry) or anywhere within 10 leagues of it, and five years later[6], when he was nearly 70 years of age[7], he was employed to repair the great clock which still stands at the western end of the nave of the cathedral at Bourges[8].

The clock had been constructed as a gift from the Duke of Berry in 1372[9], but large repairs were now required, for the superintendence of which Fusoris was engaged as the most expert horologist and mechanic of his day, and there is an extremely interesting account still extant[10] showing the payments made during the progress of the repairs, which lasted about nine months[11]. The works were enclosed in a case or house (*domus*[12]) which was fixed into the stone-work above the pulpit[13] with huge nails two or three finger-lengths

---

[1] e.g. Peter of Verona was released on Sept. 18, Mirot, 202. For baille caution, see Lhomel, Edits, 92.

[2] Mirot, 166, 211. For position of the *Queue de Renard*, see Mirot, D'Orgement, 115.

[3] Mirot, Fusoris, 167; Champeaux-Gauchery, 131; Baye, ii. 237, 308, quoting Arch. Nat. 188, f. 59; A. Martin, Patriote, 13.   [4] Mirot, 266, 271.

[5] Ibid. 169, 279; A. Martin, Patriote, 13.   [6] i.e. in 1423, Mirot, 170.

[7] Ibid. 142, 230, though he is called 10 years younger in the indictment, ibid. 173.

[8] See App. N².

[9] Raynal, ii. 403, 408; Champeaux-Gauchery, 20, 194. For his collection of clocks and dials, see Guiffrey, i. pp. cxxiii, cxxv. For the cathedral clock at Angers in 1384, see Joubert, Invasions, 117, quoting Revue Archéologique, Tome xi. pp. 174, 453. For orlogeur summoned from Poitiers in 1378 pour faire certaines ouvres à la grant orloge at Angers, see Port, 179. For a gold clock given by Henry V to the Emperor of Turkey in 1421, see Lannoy, 45.

[10] Girardot, 9–12 [13–16]; Dufour, Famille, 125, 162; Champeaux, Meuble, 99.

[11] i.e. from March 6 to Nov. 1, 1424, Girardot, 9.

[12] For picture (circa 1250) of a "maizon d'ierloge" (called "cage d'horloge," Omont, p. 6; or "boîte," Viollet-le-Duc, Album, 105), i.e. a wooden erection in three separate storeys for the bells, the dial and the figures, see Villard de Honnecourt, 79, Pl. xi; Willis, 41; Revue Archéologique, année iii. part ii. Plate 3.

[13] Dufour, Famille, 127, where a mason (*lathamus*) is paid pro perforando rotam pulpiti subtus horologium; not "au sommet du grand pignon" above the principal porch where the patriarchal cross now stands, as Raynal, ii. 408.

long. The "house," which was painted by John of Orleans[1], was fitted with doors, bolts, hinges and a ceiling with a gilded sun and moon and revolving planets[2], and chimed with cymbals of different sizes struck with little hammers. Payments appear in the account for cart-loads of coal, for copper, tin, solder, iron and lead, for willow wands to tie the stobils[3] (*stabliamenta*) and counterpoises[4] (*contrapensa*), for newbottoming a pan[5], for steel levers and iron wire to work the hammers, for a linensmith (*linifaber*) working inside the "house" lining the top with towel and stopping it with tow. Fusoris' personal share in the work is specified as distilling lead, making the counterpoises and tuning the chimes, but beyond refreshments in the form of bread and pears and a better quality of wine when he came over to inspect we know nothing of what payment he received in cash, for the bill is totalled at 394*l.* 18*s.* 8*d.* with a footnote: "*dont rien pour le savant Fusoris*," who was now very near his end. In 1428 he resigned his Paris canonry, which during his absence had been managed for him by the famous Nicholas de Clamenges, but he lived till 1436, in which year he died[6], being then over 80 years of age. In 1507 the clock was removed from its old place above the pulpit and fixed in the nave at the foot of the western tower, where it remains to the present day[7].

[1] For his family name (i.e. Jean Grancher, or Granchier, of Trainou near Orleans, L. Jarry, 517; Dufour, Famille, 127), see Guiffrey, I. lxxvi; Lethaby, 241, where he is pictor Regis (1361–1408). For a chasuble in samite in the Louvre painted by him circ. 1374, see Lafenestre, 21.

[2] Cf. 20*d.* pro unâ rotellâ pro planetis, also 11 francs of old gold pro deaurando celum lune. The sun and moon were repaired in 1520, Girardot, 12, where la table des cadrans (i.e. dial-plates) is re-done in blue.

[3] For the wire of the stobil in the clock at Westminster (1427), see Archaeologia, xxxvii. 25.

[4] See Du Cange, s.v. *Contrapesium*. For 70 lbs. of lead pour le contrepois de l'auloge of the church of St Maclou at Rouen in 1436, see C. Beaurepaire, Notes, iii. 323. For 100 sols paid in 1435 for ung orloge de petite essence de cuivre doré avec le contrepois, see ibid. iii. 336. For scopæa plombia for contrapondera for the clock on the Cathedral Tower at Clermont-Ferrand, Oct. 30, 1407, see Savaron, 538, 539. This tower was known as the Bayette, ibid. 544; Delarbre, 141. For pictures, see Laborde, II. cxl, cxli; Loth, 94.

[5] Pro fundo cujusdam pelvis.

[6] Mirot, 171.

[7] For a picture of it see Dufour, Famille, 161.

CHAPTER XXVII

SOUTHAMPTON

TOWARDS sunset[1] on Saturday, July 6, 1415[2], the king mounted his horse and with the rest of the royal party left Winchester for Southampton[3], where the forces had been assembling since the beginning of the month[4], and the appointed officials had been kept constantly busy holding musters of the retinues at Wallopsforth[5], Swanwick Heath[6], Southampton Common[7] and in the fields around Portsmouth[8], so that (including many Welsh and Portuguese) there was now assembled a stronger fighting force than

---

[1] Circa crepusculum, Mirot, 219; circa solis occasum, ibid. 246; in vespere, ibid. 268.

[2] Page 492.

[3] Not that he paid "a brief visit to London" after the French envoys had departed, as Vickers, 15; Strang, 68. Nor that he arrived at Southampton on Aug. 1, as Brut, ii. 552. Nor that the whole army about 60,000 strong marched through Winchester, as Portal, 129. For men at Southampton by July 1, 1415, though wages did not begin till July 8, see Exch. Accts. 46/29. Most retinue accounts say that the men were ready at Southampton by July 8, ibid. 46/38. For view of Southampton (1793), see S. E. Harding. The French believed that he left Winchester on July 7 or 8, i.e. the day on which the French ambassadors left, Mirot, 224, 226. For documents dated at Southampton July 20, 23, 24, 25, 26, 27, 28, 31; Aug. 1, 2, 4, 5, 6, 7, 8, 14, 1415, see Rym. ix. 287, 288, 293, 297, 299, 300, 301, 302, 303; Rot. Scot. ii. 214; Cal. Doc. Scot. iv. 173; Dep. Keep. Rept. xliii. 581; xliv. 569, 571, 573, 574; Letter Book I, 163; Pauli, v. 98, from Priv. Seal 3 H. V; Bibl. Top. Brit. iv. 24, 87; see also Pat. 3 H. V, i. 1, 8, 11, 14; ibid. ii. 34, 38, 39; Chancery Warrants, Ser. 1. 1364/20; Belleval, 26; Woodward, ii. 251. For an itinerary from June 25 to Aug. 14, 1415, compiled from documents in Rymer, see Nicolas, 25.

[4] Page 479.

[5] e.g. the Earl of Oxford's men, on July 6 before Lord Harington and John Rothenale, kt. as controller of the Royal Household, Exch. Accts. 46/36.

[6] Near Titchfield; e.g. on July 14 before Hugh Mortimer and Robt. Castcll, ibid. 45/8, with names of the retinues.

[7] Called the Heath, see Davies, 55; e.g. on July 13 before John Rothenale, kt. and John Strange, clerk, Hunter, 33, 35, 40. For order (July 20, 1415) to Richard Redeman, kt. and John Strange, clerk, to hold a muster of the Duke of Clarence's men, see Rym. ix. 287. For lists of names present at these retinues, see Exch. Accts. 44/30 (2).

[8] For troops collected by Aug. 1, 1415, and mustered in campo juxta Portesmouthe cum armis equis et victualibus, see Strecche, 266.

any English king had got together before[1]. The king took up his quarters at the Bishop's manor at Waltham[2] or at the Abbey of the White Canons at Titchfield[3], where he had transcripts made under the seal of Archbishop Chichele of the agreements entered into between his father and the French dukes during the intrigues of 1412 as to Aquitaine, from which they had now receded. These copies he forwarded to Sigismund and the Council at Constance as well as to various Princes of Europe, to prove that he was driven into this war against his will by the duplicity of the French[4]. From Titchfield he removed to the castle at Porchester[5], passing frequently to Portsmouth[6] or Southampton, and from these places he kept a vigilant eye on all the movements and preparations that were going rapidly forward. The Council had met at Westminster on June 19 and 24, 1415[7], to settle the financial details, and on July 24[8] the king was able to issue an assurance that sufficient arrangements had been made for the payment of debts

[1] Nullum praedecessorum ferunt tantas copias militares vallidioremque sagittariorum manum contraxisse, quibus et Portugalienses Walensesque auxiliares sibi tunc confederatos junxisse, St Denys, v. 498; Tit. Liv. 7; Vita, 35. Hunter, 11, thinks that "probably a host so well appointed never before left the shores of England." Not that it was a "Bauernheer," as Bullrich, 5; nor "mit dem schlechtgerüsteten Heere," "einem armlichen Volksheere," as König, 16.

[2] For documents dated at Waltham July 17, 22, 23, 25, 28, 29; Aug. 9, 10, 1415, see Pat. 3 H. V, i. 31, 33, 43; Ewald, xliv. 571, 572; Rym. ix. 304; Memoranda Rolls K.R. 3–4 H. V, 77; Belleval, 26.

[3] For the king staying aliquandiu at Titchfield, see Lel. Itin. iii. 95; Woodward, iii. 68. For a document dated at Titchfield July 17, 1415, see Exch. Accts. 46/3 (13). For the White Canons or Praemonstratensians at Titchfield, see Monast. vi. 931, where it is called "Tychfeud" in a charter of Edward II. It is variously called "Titchford" in Pat. 4 H. V, 16, July 12, 1416; or "Thichefeud" (1280), Archaeol. Inst. (Winchester), 136; or "Tycliff" in Iss. Roll 1 H. V, Mich., Feb. 20, 1414; not "Tinchefield," as Goodwin, 61. For their library, see Gasquet, Libraries, 6, 14, from Harl. MS. 6602–3, f. 3; J. W. Clark, 24 (i.e. Catalogue dated 1410).

[4] Invitus et involuntarius, Gesta, 10; Chron. Giles, 10, showing that copies were kept in a book inter evidentias regias et recorda; also Goodwin, 61, 63, from "Arch. Reg." See Wylie, iv. 64, 68, 69, 70, 80, 84; Letter Book I, 103; Hist. MSS. Rept. iv. 194. Called May 12, 1412, in Boutiot, ii. 336; or May 20 in Rym. ix. 669; Dep. Keep. Rept. xlv. 319. Called the Treaty of Bourges in Loserth, Gesch. 548.

[5] For documents dated at Porchester July 29, 31; Aug. 5, 7, 8, 9, see Rot. Parl. iv. 65; Pat. 3 H. V, i. 11; ii. 35, 36, 42; Ewald, xliv. 573; Rym. ix. 304; Chancery Warrants, Ser. I. 1364/21; Pauli, v. 98; Belleval, 26. For description of Porchester Castle, see R. Warner, ii. 88; L. Allen, 185–192; Hookham, i. 266; Woodward, iii, 322; Hartshorne in Archaeol. Inst. Winchester (1846), pp. 28, 29; Hewitt, I. pp. xii, 189; Vict. Co. Hist. (Hants.), iii. 152, 154, 156, 158; Wylie, ii. 410. In 1220 it was a royal castle, but in the fifteenth century it passed from the crown to the Priory of Southwick, Hartshorne, 34, 38, 41, 42.

[6] For a document dated Portsmouth Aug. 11, 1415, see Rym. ix. 305; Belleval, 26.

[7] Ord. Priv. Co. ii. 170, 171.

[8] Rym. ix. 290.

incurred in connection with the defence of the Marches of Scotland, Ireland, Wales, Calais and elsewhere.

But, though his departure from London had been trumpeted with enthusiastic acclaim, yet there were silent currents still at work below the surface, of which no hint was given till the mine was almost ready to explode[1], though the French, as we have seen[2], were certainly counting on the danger he would run by absenting himself abroad when his throne was threatened by plotters at home. The actual prelude to the outbreak is shrouded in much obscurity, but there is no need to look upon it, as many writers do, as " incomprehensible[3] " or " a mystery which it were hopeless to attempt to understand[4]." One fact about it however is unquestionable, viz. that no far-reaching public principle was for a moment put forward in palliation of the abortive effort, which never rose above the scrape and scrawl[5] of sordid family ambition[6], as a pent-up echo of the Percy and Mortimer failures of the previous reign. It was indeed merely another weak attempt to kill the worm in the broomcod[7] and set up the Earl of March in his stead.

The centre of intrigue was the newly-created Earl of Cambridge[8], Richard of Conisborough, younger brother

---

[1] Une monopole et soubdaine conspiration, Waurin, i. 177.

[2] Page 507.

[3] e.g. Oman, Hist. 245, who also calls it " a singularly ill-arranged and hazardous affair." Cf. " as ill-constructed as it was wicked," Cassell, i. 527; " one of the most absurd and hopeless plots on record," Nicolas, 44.

[4] Woodward, ii. 251. "A mysterious plot manufactured under the eyes of King Henry," Tytler, Worthies, ii. 284. Raine, North Durham, 327, finds it "impossible to ascertain the motives," etc. Absicht und Mittel sind unbekannt, Leo, Lehrbuch, i. 809.

[5] Famous Victories, 23.

[6] Ambitionem et regni cupiditatem, Redman, 41; Halle, 61; Grafton, i. 512. "A purely dynastic business," Oman, Hundred Years War, 108.

[7] For the broomcod, see Anstis, i. 114; Nichols, Observations, 41, who points out (p. 45) that it had long been the badge of the kings of France. Cf. one coler de Brome-coddes, Rot. Parl. iv. 225, or peascod in Hoccleve, Min. Po. 23; Anglia, v. 36; James, 158; Purey-Cust, Collar, 16; cf. " peskodde," Form of Cury, 36; pesecoddys grene, Lydgate-Burgh, 44; branches de genestes semées de feuilles et de cosses d'or, Pannier, xxvi. 220; xxvii. 35; colliers ornés de cosses de genêt, Mirot, Isabelle, xviii. 550. For order founded by St Louis with broomcods on collar, see Roman, 26. For the gosse de genest as a device of Charles VI, see Thibault, 122, 153; cf. branche de genet, cosse de genestre, Mirot, Trousseau, 127, 129, 130, 140, 141; do. Isabelle, xix. 76, 79; livérée de broincoddes, do. Trousseau, 137, which should probably he " bromcoddes," see P. Meyer, Entrevue, 219, where it is curiously supposed to mean " brown cloth." For a houppe-lande de geneste of Louis Duke of Orleans in 1392, see Roman, 33; also yosses or cosses de genet, ibid. 26, 43; fleurs de janettes, ibid. 37, in Godefroy, s.v. *Geneste*, where it is called narcissus; un collier d'or rond à petites cosses émaillées given by Louis Duke of Orleans to his wife Valentine in 1396, Collas, 280; fleurs de genêt, Champion, Vie, 17.

[8] For supposition that he was the rightful heir to the throne, see P. Bernard, 242; or that he wanted the crown for himself, see Larrey, 810; or for his children, Collier, iii.

to the Duke of York[1], who had married Anne Mortimer[2], the elder sister of Edmund[3], Earl of March[4]. She was his junior by some 14 years[5], and on her death, which had only recently happened, he had married as his second wife Maud Clifford[6], whose brother John, Lord Clifford[7], had married Hotspur's daughter Elizabeth Percy[8]. After the failure of the plot the Earl of Cambridge said that he had been drawn into it by "the stirring of other folk egging him thereto[9]," but there can be little doubt that the official estimate is correct in designating him as the chief instigator[10] of the whole affair. To all outward appearance he was in hearty accord with the policy of the new king. He accepted the earldom conferred upon him at Leicester in the spring of 1414[11], and when arrangements were making for the descent on Normandy in the following year he

312; Rapin, iii. 441; Guthrie, ii. 459, who thinks that he meant to put the Earl of March to death. For his arms, see Portal, 129.

[1] Kirkstall Chron. 288. Not elder brother, as Belleval, 30; called il fratello del Duca di Jorch in Sanuto, 897.

[2] Brut, ii. 589; Monast. viii. 1601.

[3] Not John, as Mazas, Vies, v. 553.

[4] Wylie, ii. 35. Not sister to King Richard II, as Mézeray, ii. 565; nor to Roger Mortimer, Earl of March, who was killed in Ireland on July 20, 1398, as Purey-Cust, i. 227, who thinks that he died in Trim Castle where he had been imprisoned for 20 years; nor sister to Edmund Mortimer, who was captured by Owen Glendower in 1402, as Mirror for Magistrates, 307.

[5] She was born on Dec. 27, 1388, Monast. vi. 355; Dict. Nat. Biogr. xxxix. 146, and died after 1412, Comp. Peer. ii. 120. For supposed identification of her remains with those found in the tomb of Edmund Duke of York at Langley, see J. Evans, 317.

[6] Doyle, i. 294; Comp. Peer. ii. 120; Purey-Cust, i. 345. For £100 per annum granted to her after her husband's execution, see Claus. 4 H. V, 22, March 30, 1416. She died in 1446, Hunter, South Yorkshire, 113; Bonney, 78; Whitaker, Craven, 316, who gives extracts from her will dated Aug. 15, 1446, proved Sept. 4, 1446. Her father Thomas, 6th Lord Clifford, died in 1391 or 1393, Comp. Peer. ii. 290. Her mother Elizabeth (Comp. Peer. vi. 84) was a daughter of Thomas, 5th Lord Roos of Hamlake, Whitaker, Craven, 310; Comp. Peer. ii. 290.

[7] Cf. The Lord of Clyfort that never wolde fayle, Harflet, 315. For his retinue (30+90), see Rym. ix. 260, June 5, 1415. For his arms as a Knight of the Garter, see Ashmole, 710 (edn. 1672). He died on March 14, 1422, Beltz, clviii (not 1421, as Hoccleve, Min. Po. xxv). For Clifford arms, see Purey-Cust, i. 99, 220.

[8] Kirkstall Chron. 282; Whitaker, Craven, 310, 317; Comp. Peer. vi. 84; Wylie, ii. 277; iii. 153, note 1. She afterwards married Ralph, 2nd Earl of Westmoreland (who died Nov. 3, 1484, Doyle, iii. 631, who dates his birth circ. April 1404, but this is probably wrong as he was baptized April 4, 1406, Holt, 14, from prob. ætat. 7 H. VI, 80), Hoccl. Min. Po. xxv; Doyle, iii. 632, where the marriage is dated "after 1437," but Elizabeth herself died on Oct. 26, 1437.

[9] Rym. ix. 301; Orig. Lett. II. i. 48; Nicolas, Agincourt, App. 19.

[10] Principalis imaginator, Rot. Parl. iv. 66. Fuller, Worthies (ii. 495) says that he was "fixed betwixt an Antiperistasis (=contrast, Murray, Dict., s.v.) of Royal Extraction," being the grandson of one king (Edward III) and the grandfather of another (Edward IV).

[11] Page 326.

entered into a bond to serve the king with a force consisting of two knights, 57 esquires and 160 mounted
archers[1].

It was during this season of universal reconciliation
that a solid effort was at length made to pacify the north
by the restoration of Hotspur's son[2], young Henry Percy,
who was now 21 years of age[3] and had been kept a prisoner
in Scotland since his grandfather's flight thither 10 years
ago[4]. Negotiations had been long proceeding for the
release of the Duke of Albany's son Murdach, during
which arrangements had been also made that Henry Percy
should be well tended in Scotland[5] with a view to his
speedy liberation also[6]. On May 12, 1415[7], safe-conducts
were issued for a very influential group of Scotsmen, who
were coming to England about the release of Murdach[8].
These were his son Robert[9], his brother John Earl of
Buchan, George Dunbar son of the Scottish Earl of March,
William Lord of Graham in Kincardineshire[10], John Stewart
Lord of Lorne and Innermeath[11], Robert Maxwell of Calderwood[12] and Master Andrew Hawick, parson of Kirkliston
and secretary to the Duke of Albany[13]. Ten days later[14] an

---

[1] Orig. Lett. ii. i. 49; Nicolas, 373; Hunter, 17; though called 3+6 in Nicolas, 339; Belleval, 346; see Wylie, Notes, 137. For his indenture of jewels, see Exch. Accts. 45/22 (1), with his seal (broken) attached showing the arms of England with a label with ostrich plumes, in a border charged with 12 lions rampant, see also Doyle, i. 294.

[2] Not "son of Henry Percy Earl of Northumberland," as Goodwin, 38.

[3] He was born Feb. 3, 1394, Dict. Nat. Biogr. xliv. 405; not 1393, as Comp. Peer. vi. 84, 230. On Nov. 11, 1414, he is deinz age et detenuz en Escosse encontre son bon gree et volontee, Rym. ix. 242; cf. Rot. Parl. iv. 37; Ewald, xliii. 581; Cotton, Abridg. 540; Fonblanque, i. 243, 536.

[4] Ibi dimisso in pignus, Usk, 104; layde in hostage by his grandsire's foly, Hard. 373; Kirkstall Chron. 283, 285; Wylie, ii. 264.

[5] Honorificè in Scotiâ tenebatur, Scotichron. iv. 1183; Buchanan, 107. He witnessed a charter at Stirling on Jan. 18, 1413, Hist. MSS. 4th Rept. (1873), p. 470, App.

[6] For negotiations for his release conducted by Sir Robert Umfraville, see Hardyng, 373. For his commission to treat with the Scots dated May 9, 1415, being then Chamberlain of Berwick, see Rot. Scot. ii. 213; also p. 328, note 2.

[7] For safe-conducts to last till August 1, 1415, see Rym. ix. 244; Rot. Scot. ii. 213; Menteith, i. 222.

[8] Pro deliberatione Murchowe de Fyffe, called Murthowe in Rot. Scot. ii. 213. For seal of Murdach (the same as his father's) to a document dated at Inverkeithing Aug. 19, 1423, see Anderson, Diplomata, Plate LXIV.

[9] Called Robert Stewart of Fyfe. He died before July 1421, Exch. Rolls Scot. iv. pp. clxxviii, 225, 245.

[10] Menteith, i. 246. He was present at Perth on June 22, 1415, and died in 1424, Exch. Rolls Scot. iv. pp. clxxiv, 234.

[11] Ibid. iv. p. clxxxvi; Wylie, ii. 374.

[12] For his previous employment as envoy, see page 55.

[13] Exch. Rolls Scot. iv. 208, 214, 234, 240, 241, 267.

[14] i.e. May 24, 1415, Rym. ix. 250. Not May 4, as Cal. Doc. Scot. iv. 172.

order was sent to the Constable of the Tower directing him
to deliver Murdach into the charge of two squires named
John Hull[1] and William Chancellor, who were to conduct
him to Newcastle, where arrangements would be made to
forward him on to Berwick as soon as the Scots were ready
to complete their part of the bargain.   According to an understanding already arrived at, his ransom money amounting
to over £10,000 was to be paid by the Scots before Midsummer Day[2], and when this transaction was completed
he would be transferred to the border and exchanged for
Henry Percy[3].   But already envoys from the court of
France had found their way to Scotland[4] and produced an
immediate change in the outlook.   Instead of the ransom
money being paid the English envoys were seized and
held as prisoners, and the English king sent a reproachful
letter to the Duke of Albany declining to consider any
further extension of the truce as he could scarcely trust
any Scotchman, seeing that however peaceable their words,
their deeds did not at all correspond[5].   Moreover, other
things had happened to check the hopeful prospects of
pacification.   As the two English squires were making
their way north they were set upon at Kippax near Leeds
on May 31, 1415, and Murdach was forcibly taken out of
their hands[6] by an armed band headed by a squire named
Henry Talbot of Easington in Craven[7].

While these events were happening, a Northumberland

---

[1] For instructions to Hull and Chancellor June 18, 1415, see Ord. Priv. Co. ii. 160.
For £6. 13s. 4d. paid to John Hull for expenses of the Earl of "ffith" in the Tower
+£11. 6s. 8d. for expenses till May 27 next, see Iss. Roll 3 H. V, Pasch., April 22, 1415;
Cal. Doc. Scot. iv. 173.

[2] Add. MS. 24062, f. 145, which shows that letters to this effect had been brought
from the Duke of Albany by Robert de M— (i.e. Maxwell of Calderwood) and John de
Busby, chaplain to the Duke of Albany; see page 55; Wylie, ii. 399, note 5; Rot. Scot.
ij. 208.

[3] For a letter to the Warden of the East March dated June 18, 1415, to hand over
"Murduk" to Henry Percy at Berwick after Percy had paid £10,000 as his part in the
transaction, see Ord. Priv. Co. II. pp. xii, 162.

[4] Exch. Rolls Scot. iv. 238.

[5] Add. MS. 24062, f. 145.

[6] For commission dated from Winchester July 6, 1415, to the Earl of Westmoreland,
ex-Judge Gascoigne, Richard Redman and six others to empanel a Yorkshire jury to
inquire into the late felonious capture and abduction of Sir Moreducus de ffyte, see Pat.
3 H. V, i. 3 d; Cal. Doc. Scot. iv. 173; page 17, note 11.   For tomb of Richard
Redman at Harewood see Whitaker, Loidio, 170; Purey-Cust, Collar, 24.

[7] i.e. in the Forest of Bowland, Add. MS. 4601, f. 103 (135); Otterbourne, 277;
Goodwin, 168.   He was evidently connected with the Talbots of Bashall-Eaves and
Slaidburn near Clitheroe, though not included in the pedigrees in Whitaker, Craven, 32,
37.   See page 34.

knight[1], Thomas[2] Gray of Heton[3], Constable of Norham Castle[4], arrived at the Earl of Cambridge's castle at Conisborough[5] near Doncaster. Gray was now 33 years of age[6], and being a cousin of Hotspur[7], he was interested in the fortunes of the house of Percy[8]. Like many others he had been up to London binding himself to supply a retinue of troops[9] for the coming expedition to France

[1] Militem borealem, Wals. ii. 306; Hypodig. 457; militem famosum, Gesta, 11; Church, 65. Not Comte de Northumberland, as Rapin, iii. 441 (corrected in Tindal, i. 511); Villaret, xiii. 344; nor Thomas Comte de Grey, as Duchesne, 823; Daniel, iii. 870. Called "Milord Grey" in Mézeray, ii. 565; "Lord Grey de Northumberland" in Sismondi, xii. 473; or "Thomaso Graco" in Doglioni, ii. 306. His name (i.e. Thomas Graie) reads backwards in the acrostic:

EIA Ruit GenS Avita Malis Opus Hoste Triumphat,

Vita, 377; Fabricius, vi. 252; Lib. Metr. 105.

[2] Not Henry, as Tit. Liv. 8, where he is called consiliarius in miliciae dignitate notabile constitutus. Cf. "one of the king's privie council," Holinsh. iii. 548; Rapin, iii. 441. For "Greis" on Roll of Battle Abbey, see Brut, ii. 536, where the name is taken from a hamlet near Bayeux. Called "Graye" or "Grai" in A. E. P. Gray, p. 17.

[3] Not Heson, as Bonney, 77. He is called Thomas Grey, *knight*, of Heton in Early Chanc. Proc. i. 28, where John Grey, knight, brings an action in regard to messuages at Newcastle-on-Tyne formerly belonging to him against John Welle a Newcastle merchant. For an account of Heton Castle on the Till, see Bates, Border Holds, 329. Gray was also Lord of Wark on the Tweed (Wylie, i. 81) and of the Towers of Wark-on-Tyne and Nesbit in Glendale, as well as Constable of Bamborough, Bates, 13, 18, 252, 329, 341; do. Northumberland, 194; Mazas, Vies, v. 565, who wrongly supposes that he was a K.G.; Portal, 130. In Pat. 3 H. V, i. 20, May 24, 1415, Richard Arundel, kt. gives up Bamborough Castle, which had been granted to him on Nov. 10, 1404, in succession to Thomas Gray of Wark who had held it since Aug. 25, 1404, Pat. 3 H. V, i. 17; 9 H. IV, ii. 12, where Arundel is called "our cousin." In Bates, 252, quoting Ancient Deeds, Ser. B. 3515 in P.R.O., Thomas Gray receives wages from the Earl of Westmoreland from Aug. 6, 1404. In Iss. Roll 3 H. V, Pasch., May 13, 1415, he receives £120 in compensation for giving up the castle of Bamborough. On May 29, 1415, Alexander Lound was appointed Constable of Bamborough Castle, Pat. 3 H. V, i. 13; Cal. Pat. H. V, i. 328. For order (June 12, 1416) to him as Constable of Bamborough to secure ships for victualling and safeguarding the castle, see Pat. 4 H. V, 23 dors. On April 1, 1418, he was on a commission of array for Northumberland, Pat. 6 H. V, 31 dors. For John Gra, kt. of Lincolnshire in the king's service at Harfleur, who takes proceedings *re* lands in Toulston (Yorks.) circ. 1421, see ibid. i. 36.

[4] For picture, see Raine, North Durham, 284; Craik-Macfarlane, i. 540; Macfarlane-Thomson, i. 418, from Buck (1729).

[5] For account of Conisborough Castle with plan, see Archaeologia, vi. 234-247; Hunter, i. 101; Purey-Cust, i. 283; G. T. Clarke, i. 431. For pictures, see Craik-Macfarlane, i. 624, 628 (with fire-place); H. E. Smith, 11, 21, 45, 49, 53, 73.

[6] Wylie, ii. 59 note, though he is said to have been born at Alnwick on Nov. 30, 1384, and baptised on the same day, Raine, North Durham, 327. For his arms, see T. Gray, Frontispiece; Portal, 130. For pedigree, see Raine, North Durham, 327; Courtenay, i. 174. He was the grandson of Thomas Gray of Heton (d. 1369), the writer of the *Scalacronica*, Bates, Border Holds, 299; edited by J. Stevenson, Maitland Club, 1836, who gives an account of the family of Gray.

[7] He had married Alice, daughter of Ralph Lord Nevil of Raby, and was therefore a nephew of the Earl of Northumberland, Raine, North Durham, 327; French, 104.

[8] Kingsford, 123. Church (65) thinks that he was "probably the intermediary of the king's enemies on both sides of the Scotch border."

[9] i.e. 24+48 by indenture dated June 4, 1415, Rym. ix. 259; Nicolas, 379; Belleval, 359; Wylie, Notes, 136.

and was on his way back to his home on the border to make final arrangements for the muster. On June 17, 1415[1], he had an interview at Conisborough with the Earl of Cambridge, who told him that Murdach had been secured a week ago[2], producing at the same time a letter which purported to come from the Duke of Albany, in which it was understood that Henry Percy and the impostor[3] who was personating King Richard II would be given up as soon as Murdach was restored, but that if this plan should fail the latter might be liberated alone in exchange for any one of 18 prominent persons whose names were listed in a schedule, the best known of whom were Bishop Courtenay, the Earl of Westmoreland, Drew Barentin[4], Richard Whitington and Robert Waterton[5].

Just how these influential loyalists were to be got into the conspirators' hands does not appear, nor is the problem made clearer when we know that the "maumet[6]" had been, or was supposed to have been, dead for about a year, and that the Duke of Albany was unable to recover his out-of-pocket expenses incurred for the maintenance of his deceased "brother[7]." However, the plan was—to get possession of Henry Percy somehow and thus raise the north, to spirit the Earl of March away into Wales[8], and then proclaim him king in case it should turn out that "yonder man's

---

[1] Sefen neghte befor missomer, Dep. Keep. 43rd Rept. p. 582.

[2] A sefen neghte after that Murdok of Fyche was take away, ibid.

[3] Called Thomas de Trompyngton de Scotia ideotam in Rot. Parl. iv. 65; Letter Book I, p. 165; or Trumpetone, ibid. p. 94. Not Richard, as Mowbray, i. 113; nor John, as Wylie, i. 403.

[4] See page 22.

[5] This I take to be the meaning of "Robert of Watton" unless it is one of the Wattons of Ridley near Meopham in Kent, Hasted, ii. 226; iii. 544; Inq. p. Mort. iv. 351. On May 29, 1415, Robert Waterton was commissioned to array forces in the North and West Ridings of Yorkshire, Rym. ix. 253 [255].

[6] See page 34; Wylie, i. 269. Not "mamuet," as Tit. Liv. 99; Rapin (Tindal), i. 520; nor "mamnet," as Orig. Lett. Ser. I. i. 1; nor "manuel," as Speed, 788. He is called a "phantom chief" in Goldwin Smith, i. 245. Lang (i. 186) thinks that he "could hardly be called a pretender; he was idiotic." Cf. "a false Richard," Fletcher, 308. Macdonald (i. 140, 167; ii. 493, 494) thinks that "there is in reality no reason to doubt the story" that it was really King Richard who appeared at Finlaggan Castle in Islay before Margery Bisset the wife of John Mor, Tanist of Dunnyveg (or Dunowaig, called Dunvegan in Oman, R. II–R. III, 175, or Dunnyweg, Macdonald, i. 142, 167; ii. 493), brother to Donald Macdonald, Lord of the Isles (see Wylie, i. 267). He pronounces the Bissets to be "of Greek extraction" who came over with the Conqueror. For a long argument against Tytler's identification of him with Richard II, see Riddell, 1–77.

[7] Ultimo defunctus 1414–15, Exch. Rolls Scot. iv. 213, 289. For his supposed death at Stirling in 1419, see Tytler, i. 351, 430; C. Rogers, 4.

[8] Rot. Parl. iv. 65.

person which they call King Richard should not be really alive[1]." With this view a proclamation had been prepared ready to be cried in the name of the Earl of March when the proper moment should arrive, in which the king would be styled: "Henry of Lancaster, usurper of England." Robert Umfraville[2] and John Widdrington[3] had lately been at Conisborough where they had sworn in the chapel that they would rise against Henry and let in a band of Scots[4] to blow up the storm; Davy Howell had promised[5] to do his part in capturing castles in Wales; and when all this was well a-foot, Oldcastle[6] and Glendower would re-awaken into activity, the Lollards would rise under the lead of 40 "coat-armours[7]" who would desert from the muster at Southampton, and the Earl of March would unfurl a banner with the arms of England and display the crown of Spain on the pallet[8] which had recently been pledged[9] to the Earl of Cambridge, together with a spice-plate as security for the payment of £805. 3s. 4d., which would be claimable for the second quarter's wages of his troops in the coming French campaign.

In order that Gray might satisfy himself more fully as to the chances of the plot, the Earl of Cambridge invited him to remain at Conisborough till the Thursday following, when he would meet Lord Clifford whom the Earl represented as sworn to live or die with him in furthering his plans. Gray however was unable to wait, and so he went

[1] Rym. ix. 300; Nicolas, App. 19; Tyler, ii. 139.
[2] His complicity is further proved by the fragmentary hint that "Robert Domfrevile" was "to look how he may laws (? loose) them without Murdok of Fithe," Dep. Keep. Rept. xliii. 586. He was in charge of Harbottle Castle and the Tower of Otterburn in 1415, Bates, 14.
[3] Called Johannes Wodrington chlr. in Bates, 19, where he is in charge of the castles of Widdrington, Swinburn, Beaufront and Haughton in Tynedale in 1415.
[4] Dept. Keep. Rept. xliii. 588.
[5] "Made me behoft," Rym. ix. 300. Not "be host," as Tyler, ii. 140.
[6] Called "Seigneur de Gobehem" in Waurin, i. 177; or "Cobein," "Gohem," or "Golhen" in Le Fèvre, i. 222, 223, where he is confused with Sir Thomas Gray.
[7] Dep. Keep. Rept. xliii. 590.
[8] Positam super unum palettum, Rot. Parl. iv. 65; Rym. ix. 300; Nicolas, App. 19; Tyler, ii. 140; Dep. Keep. Rept. xliii. 579, 586; Holinsh. iii. 549; Stow, 346; Speed, 774; Hunter, 17, where the pallet weighs 8½ lbs. and is valued at £166. 13s. 4d. Called "the table and stools of Spain" in Musgrave, 264; or "a cushion," Strickland, ii. 119, who supposes that it was to pass with the common people for the crown of England and that the Earl of March was to be crowned with it; also W. Jones, 38.
[9] Page 471. Isabella, daughter of Pedro King of Castile, was the wife of Edmund of Langley Duke of York and the mother of the Earl of Cambridge. She is called mulier mollis et delicata in Wals. ii. 215; domina carnalis et delicata, mundialis et venerea, Ann. 169.

on his way homewards charged with treasonable messages to Umfraville and Widdrington in the north.

But in the meantime a new development had been imported into the case, for a week[1] after Murdach had been captured in the interest of the conspirators he was recaptured in the interest of the king. The rescue was effected by a Craven squire named Ralph Pudsey[2], who was rewarded with an annuity of £20 from the customs of Hull granted to him on June 25, 1415[3], and Murdach was hurried on to Warkworth[4], where he stayed for some time as a prisoner, while Henry Percy still remained a captive in Scotland, and the great scheme perforce hung fire.

For in counting on Robert Umfraville the conspirators had clearly mistaken their man. The Scots, it is true, did actually invade; but instead of letting them in, as he had promised to do, Umfraville followed them up and smote them hip and thigh as soon as their entrance was effected. On Maudlin Day (July 22[5]) he came up with a large force of them[6] at Yevering or Yeavering[7] near Kirk-Newton in Glendale. He had only 400 men with him, but he is said to have killed 60 of the Scots[8], capturing 400, and chasing the rest for 12 miles back across the border. After this he returned to his command as Warden of Roxburgh[9],

---

[1] Add. MS. 4601/103 (135).

[2] Qui recepit comitem de Fyfe, Rym. ix. 280; Cal. Doc. Scot. iv. 173; Menteith, i. 253. His name appears amongst Yorkshire gentry in 1433, Fuller, Worthies, ii. 523. In 1425 he held fees under the Duke of Bedford in Bereford and Rowtheton (or Heton Parva) in Yorkshire, possibly near Richmond in the North Riding from the mention of Aske and Egglestone Abbey near Barnard Castle, Inq. p. Mort. iv. p. 169. For John Pudsey, see page 471, note 2.

[3] Cal. Doc. Scot. iv. 173.

[4] Ord. Priv. Co. ii. 160, 162; Menteith, i. 247–250.

[5] Hardyng, 373; Echard, i. 183; Brougham, 105; Ramsay, i. 199. Not 1414, as Speed, 773.

[6] Innumerabilem multitudinem, Redman, 37; Stow, Chron. 346, where he is said to have been helped by Lord Scrope and Ralph Lord of Greystoke, who died April 6, 1417, Comp. Peer. iv. 116.

[7] For memorial column erected there, see Wallis, ii. 481; Hodgson, II. i. 52, where it is called "a huge basaltic pillar"; Mackenzie, i. 375; Tate, 1; Sparvel-Bayly, 11, who dates it in 1414. The place is called Getering or Greterig in Ridpath, 384, who failed to locate it. For suggestion that it might be Catterick in Yorkshire, see Brougham, 105, who rejects this as too far south. The word is variously spelt, e.g. At Geberin, Adgebrin, Bede, in Wallis, ii. 481; At Gevrin, Tate, 5; Gevera, Hodgson, II. iii. 152; Gevern, ibid. 273; Geteryne, Tate, 45; Gederyng, Halle, 59; Grafton, i. 511; Holinsh. iii. 548; Stow, Chron. 346; Goodwin, 55; Gertering, Bates, 15; Godering, Biondi, 113.

[8] Halle, 59; Redman, 37. More probable than 600 as usually given.

[9] Hardyng, 373; Wylie, iii. 280. He is Warden of Roxburgh on July 17, 1414, Cal. Doc. Scot. iv. 172, though called *Gilbert*, ibid. July 19, 1414. For £300+£333. 6s. 8d. paid to him as Warden on Feb. 26, March 2, and July 12, 1415, see Cal. Doc. Scot. iv. 173.

though soon afterwards he gave up the charge of the castle
with its artillery to the Earl of Westmoreland[1] so that he
might join the expedition to Harfleur, and he was definitely
succeeded as Warden at Roxburgh by Richard Berehalgh[2],
whose appointment is dated Sept. 2, 1415.

Thomas Gray in the meantime had reached his home,
made his retinue[3] and started south again to join the army
at Southampton in terms of his bond.   When he reached
York he was accosted by a man named Skranby, who
brought him an autograph letter from the Earl of Cambridge, which he tore up after reading it and then threw
it into a gong[4].   At York he also had a conversation with
one of Henry Percy's tenants named Creswell, who showed
him a copy of an agreement entered into with Sir Robert
Umfraville as well as two letters that he was carrying to
Lord Clifford and the Earl of Cambridge, and when Gray
said that it would not do for the king to know of these
things, Creswell said that Percy would soon come into
England with a strong hand to help King Richard.   At
length on July 9, 1415[5], Gray reached London where he
stayed about a week.   On July 18 he slept at Kingston,
and on the next day as he was riding along the road to
Guildford, he was overtaken by a stranger named Luce or
Lucy[6], who turned out to be a devoted adherent of the
Earl of March.   After passing a few road-side compliments
the two got into conversation together and Lucy asked the
news about Henry Percy and King Richard, to which Gray

For his retinue (20+40), probably as Warden of Roxburgh, Nov. 17, 1413 (not 1415, as
Nicolas, 385), see Add. MS. 4600, ff. 267, 280.   On June 28, 1415, he was continued in
his command as Warden of Roxburgh for three years with an allowance of 1000 marks
or £1200 per annum in times of peace or war respectively, see Add. MS. 4600, f. 275.

[1] For order to this effect dated Southampton, May 5, 1415, see Cal. Doc. Scot.
iv. 173.

[2] Or Berell, see Wylie, iii. 277, note 6.   Not *John* Borell, as Cal. Doc. Scot. iv. 173.
For £333. 6s. 8d. paid to him as Warden of Roxburgh, see Iss. Roll 3 H. V, Pasch.,
Sept. 2, 1415.

[3] Waleyway ye tyme of yat retenumakyng for hit has broghte me to yis shame and
undoyng, Dep. Keep. Rept. xliii. 582; Vickers, 16.

[4] I redde hit and rofe hit and kest hit in a goonge, Dep. Keep. Rept. xliii. 582.   For
the "gonge" (Greg. Chron. 68) or "reredortour" at St Osythes and St Albans, see Walcott, Osyth, 2; also Wylie, ii. 256, note 2, 407, note 2.

[5] Dep. Keep. Rept. xliii. p. 584.

[6] He may possibly be either William de Lucy of Bodenham near Hereford (Inq. p.
Mort. iii. 239) or John Lucy of Dorsetshire (ibid. iii. 241), both of whom appear as
tenants of Roger Earl of March.   For Master Walter Lucy, haberdasher of London, see
Hoccl. Min. Po. lix, lxiv, lxv.   For arms of Lucy in York Minster, see Purey-Cust, ii.
205.   For "Lucy" on Roll of Battle Abbey, see Brut, ii. 536.

replied that Percy would never come in that way. Whereupon Lucy told him that the Earl of March had been making him huge advances[1] amounting to as much as 500 marks, and as the conversation waxed familiar he spoke out all his mind. The Earl of March, he said, was a pig and a fool for not challenging his rights himself. The Earl of Arundel and Lord Scrope had done well for him and had given him a good time[2], especially the latter when he was Treasurer[3] of England. For the last three years they had been sworn together to help him, and the latter had recently written to say that he would be his liege if he would put his hand in now, urging him either to cross to France or Flanders[4] and work up the Percy interest there, or to escape westwards and join the disaffected in Wales, or to remain behind on the plea of health[5], and when the expedition had sailed without him his friends would rise and make him king[6]. In any case whether he gaed or bade[7] the king was certain to be undone. Primed with these weighty secrets Thomas Gray made his way steadily on to Southampton. On July 20 he lodged at Hambledon[8], half-way between Petersfield and Fareham, and by the following day he was fairly launched in the full vortex of intrigue.

Of all who joined this puzzling plot, the part played by Henry[9] Lord Scrope seemed to his contemporaries the blackest perfidy and ingratitude. He was the Judas[10] whom the king had trusted with his whole heart[11], and who knew

---

[1] Hoge chefesaunz, Dep. Keep. Rept. xliii. 584; cf. Murray, Dict. ii. 332. Called an agreement in Cotgrave, Blount, Halliwell, Johnson, s.v.; lequel contrat (i.e. usury) ils appellent eschange ou chevisance qe plus verroient serroient appelle mescheaunce qar ele perte lonhour et lalme de chevisour et ravise les biens de celey qui semble estre chevyz, Lib. Alb. i. 368, 399, 400; iii. 303. Cf. chevance, Rot. Parl. ii. 173; iii. 280; chevancia, Rym. ix. 301; Dep. Keep. Rept. xliii. 584.

[2] Gefen hym gode dais.

[3] i.e. from Jan. 6, 1410 (not 1409, as Purey-Cust, i. 93), to Dec. 16, 1411, see Wylie, iv. 310.

[4] For the Earl of Northumberland and Lord Bardolph staying at Bruges where he was admitted a *frater ad succurrendum* at Eeckhout in the winter of 1406 before crossing to Bramham Moor, see Usk, 106, 287, who was also there at the same time.

[5] Fust par maladie ou aultrement, Le Fèvre, i. 222.

[6]　　　　　　　And purposed therle of March to croune
　　　　　　　　King of England by their provision. Hardyng, 374.

[7] Whether he bade or zede, Dep. Keep. Rept. xliii. 585.

[8] Hamulton, ibid. The indictment charges him with conspiring on July 20, 1415, Rot. Parl. iv. 65; Holinsh. iii. 549.

[9] Not Thomas Scrop, as Tit. Liv. 8.

[10] Gesta, 11. Cf. he that bore the Bagge betrayed him, G. Daniel, iv. 125.

[11] In cujus fide totus animus regius requievit, Wals. ii. 305; Hypodig. 456, who publishes the names of the three chief conspirators with great reluctance. On whom the

the very bottom of his soul[1]. The king's father had made him Treasurer of England[2] and a Knight of the Garter[3], and he himself had kept no secrets from him whether in his private or his public life[4], ever seeking his advice and following it like an oracle from Heaven, and even as late as July 22[5] he had entered his name among the list of trustees whom he appointed to administer his private estate in the event of his non-return from the coming expedition. Such strange requital was explained by some as a trial sent by God to buffet his elect as with a whirling hammer[6], while others said that in his recent embassies Scrope had smelt the sweetness of a bribe[7] and had sold his king to the French for a million of gold[8]. His own account is that

kyng trosted moost and be whos councell al thing was doo, Capgr. Chron. 309. Inter regis conciliarios in magnâ reverentiâ reputatus et ipsi regi in magnâ fiduciâ proximus et praeclarus, Vita, 36. On March 21, 1413, he was appointed a Justice of the Peace for Lincolnshire, Essex and the North and West Ridings of Yorkshire, Pat. 1 H. V, i. 35 d. On Feb. 19, 1414, he was about to be made a member of the Council with 200 marks per annum, Iss. Roll 1 H. V, Mich. For the manors of Hampstead and Hendon granted to him for maintenance while attending the king in Parliament and other councils, see Rym. ix. 13, May 23, 1413. For his attendance in Parliament till Nov. 1414, see Dugd. Summons, 394; Cotton, Abridg. 537; Rot. Parl. iv. 35.

[1] Henry V, ii. 2. 96.

[2] Not that he was still Treasurer, as Godstow, 211; Chron. R. II to H. VI, p. 40; Chron. Lond. 100; Brut, ii. 375; Caxton, Chron. 144; do. Polychron. 224; First Life, 30; Fabyan, 579; Rastell, 248; J. Major, 126; Redman, 39; Holinsh. iii. 548; Stow, 346; Woodward, ii. 352; Bonney, 77; Trussell, 99; Sandford, 279, 384; Guthrie, ii. 459; Nicolas, 38; Tyler, ii. 132; Beltz, lvi; Towle, 294; Belleval, 30; Mazas, Vies, v. 569; Dep. Keep. Rept. xliii. 579. Nor that he was the king's chamberlain, as Airy, i. 143. In Scrope and Grosvenor, ii. 135, he is born in 1373 or 1376.

[3] Anstis, i. 14, 16, 22; Beltz, lvi, clvii; i.e. on the death of William, 5th Lord Willoughby, who died Dec. 4, 1409, Wylie, iii. 288; not Nov. 30, 1409, as Beltz, clvii. For his stall plate, see Hope, Plate xx, in which he is "le s^r de Wylogby William." For his brass at Spilsby near Horncastle, see Macklin, 144.

[4] De sibi magis domesticum et qui secretis regiis vix fuit alicui tertius in regno, Gesta, 10; Chron. Giles, 11; lequel couchoit toutes les nuits avec le roy, Monstr. 366; Le Fèvre, i. 224; Waurin, i. 179; Rapin, iii. 441; Tindal, i. 511. "The man that was his bedfellow," Henry V, ii. 2. 5; Drayton, Oldcastle, 332, 342; "his companion in the chase," Ling. iii. 487; Mazas, Vies, v. 569, calls him one of Henry's compagnons de débauche, and Belleval (30) thinks that he was the only one of Henry's bad companions that was not dismissed.

[5] Cal. Pat. 1 H. V, i. 356.

[6] Tundi etiam alio dirae turbationis malleo, Gesta, 10; Chron. Giles, 11.

[7] Gesta, 11; Elmham, Lib. Metr. 105; Otterbourne, 276; Capgrave, De Illustr. 114; Dugd. i. 660; Comp. Peer. vii. 90; Gollut, 1011.

[8]
  Lordys of this land oure kyng gan there sell
  For a milion of gold (not "goods," as Evans) as y herd say.
                                      Harflet, 306; Durham, 42.
Kabel, 7, who calls this a "fable"; pro uno milione auri, Bodl. Rawlinson MS. C. 398, in Gesta, 11, i.e. Chronicle to 1437 a quodam Ricardo Rede compilatum teste Jo. Foxe, see Coxe, Catalogi Bibl. Bodl. v(ii). 182, also Chron. Peter. 487; Brie, 98, 100; "for lucour of money a million of gold," Claud. A. VIII. 1, adding "and that there was proved openly," Nicolas, 43; Chron. R. II to H. VI, p. 40; Croyl. 500; Godstow, 211; Brut, ii. 376; Caxton, Chron. 145; "mylyant," Bodl. 71; in magno redimerunt auro,

he was approached by the conspirators "because of his uncle[1]," and it may well be that the memory of the dead archbishop made him an irreconcileable at heart, while his wife Joan[2] probably used her influence to draw him into the toils of her stepson the Earl of Cambridge[3]. At any rate he gave no outward sign of any treasonable attitude, for he went repeatedly on secret business for the king both to the Duke of Burgundy[4] and to the court at Paris[5]. His brother Stephen, the Archdeacon of Richmond, lent money[6] to forward the war preparations and he himself brought a large retinue[7] to join the muster at Southampton, and

---

Usk, 125, who supposes that the conspirators treated with the French envoys at Portsmouth; grandi pecuniâ, J. Meyer, 245; a right greate somme of monie, First Life, 30; called 500,000 crowns in Drayton, Oldcastle, 331, 339; or "a M¹ (i.e. 1000) pounde of gold," Brut, ii. 553; "the gilt of France," H. V, ii. Prol. 26; "the golden earnest of our death," ibid. ii. 2. 169. The story began to be doubted in the early part of the 16th century, e.g. "some writers affyrme," Rastall, 248; "alii existimant," Redman, 41; "as it is reputed," Speed, 774; but it still went on, as in Major, 288; Pol. Verg. 442; J. Major, 126; Halle, 60, 61; Grafton, i. 511, 512; Holinsh. iii. 548; Rosières, 430; Adams, i. 212; ce qui ne doit pas paroître étrange, Rapin, iii. 441; Tindal, i. 511. The story is rejected by Biondi, 113, who thinks that "it is not possible that the King of France should have paid this money, for if so it would have been found after the delinquent's death"; also in Guthrie, ii. 459, who however thinks that Scrope was "immeasurably covetous and immensely rich"; and Villaret, xiii. 344, who adds: "de semblables faits destitués de preuves deshonorent tout écrivain quelque intérêt de nation qui l'anime"; Brougham, 109, thinks that it "appears to be without any foundation"; "un faux bruit," Michelet, vi. 14; "ohne Frage eine Erfindung," Pauli, v. 102. For supposition that the conspirators themselves invented the story and "stained ourselves to save our friend [i.e. the Earl of March] from blame," see Mirror for Magistrates, 308.

[1] Dep. Keep. Rept. xliii. 590; Wylie, ii. 195, 197. To the list of writers who suppose that the archbishop belonged to the Bolton branch of the Scrope family add Stonehouse, 137; French, 62; Oman, Hist. 216; do. Hundred Years, 101. For suit concerning charters, &c. relating to the inheritance of Richard le Scrope, kt., late of Bolton in 1420, see Early Chanc. Proc. i. 14. For £100 per annum granted to Isabel (d. of Sir Maurice Russell, Doyle, iii. 673, widow of William Scrope, Earl of Wiltshire) by the Coventry Parliament in 1404, see Rec. Roll 3 H. V, Pasch., July 1, 1415; Iss. Roll 4 H. V, Pasch., July 13, 1416; do. 7 H. V, Pasch., Mich., May 27, 1419, Jan. 17, 1420; do. 8 H. V, Pasch., May 23, July 3, 1420. In Purey-Cust, Walks, 51, Henry is rightly called "a scion of the branch of the house of Masham," see Wylie, ii. 197. In Antiquary, xli. 426, he is called a Scrope of Danby, where it is supposed that his father was Chancellor temp. Richard II (meaning apparently Richard Lord Scrope of Bolton, Wylie, ii. 197) and that the archbishop was himself Chancellor or brother to the Chancellor, as Keble, 6.

[2] i.e. Joan Holland, second wife of Edmund Duke of York (Doyle, iii. 742), by which marriage Scrope became "step-great-uncle" to the king, Purey-Cust, i. 97; cf. Ord. Priv. Co. ii. 183; Ramsay, i. 198; Wylie, iii. 284, note 5. She was Scrope's second wife and is called "Duchess of York" in his will, Rym. ix. 272, his first wife Philippa daughter of Sir Guy de Brian having died in 1406, Purey-Cust, i. 93.

[3] Dict. Nat. Biogr. li. 13, where the suggestion that possibly he resented his deposition of the treasury (i.e. from the treasurership) two years before is based upon a mistake, see page 14, note 4.

[4] Pages 149, 414.

[5] Page 15.

[6] e.g. £66. 13s. 4d. lent June 8, 1415; repaid Aug. 3, 1415, Rec. Roll 3 H. V, Pasch., June 8, 1415.

[7] i.e. 30 + 90, Rym. ix. 230; Nicolas, 374; though called 6 + 14, ibid. 344.

when he made his will there on June 23, 1415[1], he provided for masses to be said for the king and his father, leaving to the former as a personal memento a golden image of the Virgin garnished with pearls and balais, and praying that he would be good lord to his wife, his mother and his son when he himself was gone.

No sooner had Gray arrived at Southampton than he entered into communication with Scrope, and on Sunday, July 21, the two jointly had an interview with the Earl of March, who said that his heart and will were full thereto, if only he had the power[2]. The three talked the matter over more fully at supper at the Earl's place at Cranbury[3] near Otterbourne, a little to the south of Winchester; on the following Thursday the Earls of March and Cambridge met Gray at Hamble[4], and on the day after Scrope and the Earl of Cambridge had a talk together at the Itchen ferry[5] just under the walls of Southampton, at which it was suggested to set fire to the ships in order to wreck the expedition. Gray likewise discussed this with them at the Grey Friars[6] near the godshouse and then rode off to his lodgings at Otterbourne, whither he was followed by a messenger bearing a letter from the Earl of March complaining that he had just had an interview with the king, at which they had fallen out[7] over some payments required

---

[1] Rym. ix. 272–280, with extracts in Scrope and Grosvenor, ii. 142–147. Amongst many legacies is one to his gardener at Fifhide (i.e. Fifield near Chipping Ongar), Inq. p. Mort. iv. 71, 372. The will was written out by John Bliton, clerk, to whom he left 40*s.* (Rym. ix. 278; Morant, ii. 124) and who afterwards remained Clerk of the Kitchen to his widow Joan, Ord. Priv. Co. ii. 183.

[2] Though Gairdner (95) thinks that he "seems hardly to have countenanced the attempt." Oman (Hundred Years, 108) calls him "a harmless and unenterprising young man" and thinks that he "had no part in the plot," being "simply unaspiring" (do. Hist. 245). Tout (264) thinks that he "repaid Henry's generosity by refusing to join the conspirators." Cf. "whether knowing of the scheme or not," B. E. Warner, 146.

[3] Called Cramboru or Cranborgh in Dep. Keep. Rept. xliii. 586, 591. For Cranbury and Otterbourne then belonging to the Earl of March, see Inq. p. Mort. iv. 87; Woodward, ii. 94; Warren, Kebleland, 94, 96.

[4] "Hamull in ye Hoke"; called "villa Hamel in the Hoke in the Rys" in Rym. viii. 174; or Hamele-en-le-rys, now Hamble-le-Rice (i.e. on the Rise) or the Hook opposite to Calshot Castle, Woodward, iii. 69; Kirby, Hamble, 252, 262. It is called "Hamel-hok" in Walcott, Prices, 88; or "Hamulryse," J. S. Davies, 240; also in Lel. Ttin. iii. 93; Camden, Britannia, i. 134. In 1347 Hamil Hoke furnished seven ships, Brie, 340. It is probably the same as "Annothe" in St Denys, iii. 320; not Havant, as Wylie, ii. 327.

[5] "At ye fere of Hickys," Dep. Keep. Rept. xliii. 585. Called "Hichin Ferry" in Lel. Itin. iii. 94. Cf. "Hichin village that stondith on the farther side of the Fery," ibid. 95. For Itchen Ferry, see Englefield, 78; Woodward, iii. 67.

[6] Monast. vi. 152; Davies, 63, 442.

[7] How foul ze king had faren with him, Dep. Keep. Rept. xliii. 585.

for his approaching marriage with Anne[1], daughter of Edmund Earl of Stafford, who had fallen fighting on the king's side at Shrewsbury[2]. Another meeting followed at Hamble and a further one was to be held in the night at Beaulieu[3].

But Scrope was at the best only half-hearted in the business. He was a zealous churchman[4] with a deep hatred of Lollards, but they had not dared to tell him that Oldcastle was being worked as a factor in the plot[5], and as soon as this portion of the scheme came to his ears he "wondered such draughts were not left." Going straightway to the Earl of March he questioned him closely about his coming proclamation[6], but getting only evasive answers he warned him that if he drew to Lollards they would subvert the land; if he went to Wales he would be enfamined and lost, while if he took to the sea he would be captured by vessels of advantage[7] and instantly undone. Having thus put the pretender into a proper state of apprehension and extracted a promise from him that he would not be stirred further, he worked upon the fears of the other leaders such as the

---

[1] She is called "my lady Marche" by Lydgate, who wrote the Legend of St Margaret for her, Lydg. Min. Po. 176; Horstmann, ii. 371; D.N.B. xxxiv. 318; MacCracken, xxiii; supposed to have been written in 1429–30, Lydg. Temp. cvi. After the death of the Earl of March on Jan. 19, 1425 (Doyle, ii. 470) she married John Holand Earl of Huntingdon (d. 1447, Doyle, i. 712; ii. 230). For a letter (Dec. 1426) from Pope Martin V to the Duke of Bedford stating that his request for a dispensation for this marriage has been referred to the cardinals, see Haller, 297. Anne died in 1433 (11 H. VI) and was buried in the Chapel of St Catherine's Hospital by the Tower, Comp. Peer. v. 244. For 10,000 marks (£6666. 13s. 4d.) to be paid by the Earl of March for permission to marry, of which £2000 was paid in 1415, see Rot. Parl. iv. 212; Ramsay, i. 311. For £2700 received from him de fine pro maritagio suo, see Rec. Roll 3 H. V, Mich., Oct. 30, 1415; Feb. 19, 1416. For £1412. 16s. od. on the same account paid over to the Earl of Arundel for wages for his troops on June 6, 1415, see W. D. Cooper, 127. For a letter of Pope John XXIII dated Constance Jan. 17, 1415, referring to this coming marriage, see Papal Letters, vi. 456. For statement that Prince Henry bribed Queen Joan to induce Henry IV to consent to it, see Yonge, Cameos, 250. In Pat. 4 H. V, 17, Aug. 16, 1416, and Priv. Seal 664/680, are grants to Edmund Earl of March and Anne his wife of all goods from a ship called Le Marie de Villa Le Port in Portugallia (i.e. Oporto) which had been confiscated because shipped at Galway for Zeeland, Middelburg, Flanders or Harfleur instead of at Calais as required by statute.

[2] Wylie, i. 362; ii. 285. Bower (iv. 1193) says that he, as well as the Duke of York and the Earl of Arundel, had promised to desert and cross over to Hotspur in the night.

[3] "Bwlawe," cf. Beaulieu-Selde, Davies, 105. For seal of the Abbey, see Vict. Co. Hist. (Hants.), ii. 140. For picture of the refectory (1766), see Macfarlane-Thomson, i. 731.

[4] For his legacies to abbeys, priories, monasteries, colleges, hospitals, parish churches and shrines as well as to 18 anchorites, recluses and hermits in various parts of the country and to any others who should apply within three months after his death, see Rym. ix. 273.

[5] Exsept he (Gray) noumd nought Oldcastell, Dep. Keep. Rept. xliii. 590.

[6] Page 519.   [7] i.e. swift, Godefroy, i. 510.

Earl of Cambridge, Lord Clifford and the Earl of Devonshire's eldest son, Edward Courtenay[1] (who was married to
the Earl of March's sister Eleanor[2]), as well as Gray and
Lucy, pointing out to them the folly and peril of the venture
they were in, till they one and all took the alarm also and
promised to leave such works henceforth. Whereupon he
seems to have thought that the matter was at an end and
might be left to die down of itself.

Such an assumption however was mere simplicity, for the
Lollards had already resumed their activity several weeks
before. In order to disarm them, if possible, by a stroke
of generosity before hostilities with France had actually
begun, a proclamation had been issued on Dec. 9, 1414[3],
offering a general pardon to all rebels who should sue for
it before Michaelmas next. This proclamation appearing
likely to have little effect, a further one was issued on
Feb. 18, 1415[4], warning Oldcastle that in his case at least
this offer would be withdrawn if he did not submit within
a fortnight of the ensuing Easter. It was however renewed
on March 4, 1415[5], but wholly without effect, and no sooner
had the king left London[6] than a paper appeared on the
church doors pointing out that the time for revenge had
now come when their "utter enemy" was away[7]. Oldcastle was in hiding near Malvern[8], whence he sent a
threatening message to Lord Abergavenny[9], who however
collected a force of 5000 or 6000 men from Worcester,

[1] The erlesone of Devensher, Dep. Keep. Rept. xliii. 591; Cleaveland, 207. He
died in 1418, ibid. 209, and the title to the earldom passed to his younger brother Hugh,
who was 26 years old at his father's death on Dec. 5, 1419, Dugd. i. 640; Comp.
Peer. iii. 104; Doyle, i. 576.

[2] Wylie, ii. 35. In E. Hardy, ii. 70, the two girls are called Joan and Joyce, the
former being the wife of John Gray of Heaton.

[3] Letter Book I, 132.　　　　　[4] Ibid. pp. xxi, 133; Sharpe, London, i. 256.

[5] See page 277, note 3.

[6] Not after he had sailed, as Gairdner, Lollardy, i. 84.

[7] Wals. ii. 306; Hypodig. 458; Capgr. Chron. 369. Turner (v. 395) thinks that the
plot "*may* have sprung from the resisting spirit which Henry's religious persecutions
occasioned," though Tyler (ii. 133) thinks that "no resisting spirit on the ground of
religion had manifested itself."

[8] Called "his own country" in Workman, i. 267.

[9] Called "Bergayne" in J. Page, 12; or "Bergeyn" in Wals. ii. 306; Snow, 55.
Not "Burgoyne," as Tyler, ii. 389, i.e. Richard Beauchamp (b. circ. 1397; killed at
Meaux April 16, 1422, Doyle, iii. 718). He was made Earl of Worcester in Feb. 1421,
Doyle, iii. 718 (called 1420 in Comp. Peer. i. 15). His father, William Beauchamp, died
on May 8, 1411, Beltz, clvii; Wylie, ii. 173, note 3. For Joan, his widow, who has
custody of William son and heir of Richard Mutton, kt., see Rec. Roll 8 H. V, Mich.,
Nov. 18, 1420; also of the son of Richard Arderne, kt., *defunctus*, ibid. Dec. 14, 1420.

Pershore, and Tewkesbury[1] at Hanley Castle[2]. Whereupon Oldcastle withdrew again to his den in the west where no man was able to catch him[3]. A priest however who favoured him was captured, and under his guidance a house was searched with the result that some arms and money were found enclosed in a secret cavity between two walls, also a banner showing a cross with the spear, the scourge, the nails, and a chalice[4] with the Host. On hearing this news several of the king's advisers gave way to panic and urged him not to sail till the mischief was over[5], but he merely placed some of his most faithful adherents in every county to be ready in case of need and went forward with his foreign plans undismayed. He knew that the Lollards were now a broken meynee that had lost its pith[6], that their tail was docked[7] and their captain flown, and that if an earth-clod[8] were slung at their heads or a little rod of twigs lifted against them[9] they would slink back into their holes and never dare show their faces again[10]. Any cause indeed

[1] Towle, 273. Workman (i. 260) seems to think that they all came from Kemerton.
[2] Wals. ii. 307; "Haneleie," Holinsh. iii. 549; not Haneley, as Tyler, ii. 389. It came to him through his marriage on July 27, 1411 (not July 21, as Wylie, ii. 39, note 2), with Isabel (or Elizabeth, Worcester, Itin. 353) daughter of Thomas le Despenser Earl of Gloucester, Inq. p. Mort. ii. 78; Nash, i. 557; Comp. Peer. i. 15; Priv. Seal Writs 1423/245; page 325, note 4. She bore him a daughter at Hanley on Sept. 16, 1415, Lel. Itin. vi. 79 (not Dec. 16, as Dugd. Bar. i. 242; Comp. Peer. i. 16). Isabel afterwards married Richard Beauchamp, Earl of Warwick (Carysfort, Pag. liv; Oman, Warwick, 31; Wylie, ii. 39), who repaired the castle at Hanley, Worcester, Itin. 353, who records the fact that their daughter Anne, who married Richard Neville the Kingmaker, was born at the manor of Caversham near Reading; cf. Lel. Itin. vi. 80. Isabel died Dec. 26, 1440, and was buried in the Abbey at Tewkesbury, Comp. Peer. i. 15. In 1428 Richard Beauchamp, Earl of Warwick, visited St Albans with his wife Isabel and his son Henry, Amundesham, i. 60, where he is called vir vitae venerabilis. For his first wife Elizabeth, daughter of Thomas, Lord of Berkeley (d. July 13, 1417, not 1416, as Doyle, i. 172; Wylie, ii. 34), see Early Chanc. Proc. i. 11; Doyle, iii. 584. She was born in 1386 and died in 1422, and was buried in the Cistercian Abbey at Kingswood near Wotton-under-Edge which, though locally in Gloucestershire, was part of the Hundred of Chippenham in Wilts., hence called "in agro Wiltonensi" in Monast. v. 425. See Atkyns, 259, where "Bellamont" probably means "Beauchamp." For her epitaph, see Comp. Peer. viii. 50.
[3] Capgr. Chron. 309.
[4] There seems no ground for supposing (as Oman, Pol. Hist. 260) that the Hussites afterwards copied the chalice from this banner on the report of "some English visitor to Prague."
[5] Gesta, 12. Ac Veteris Castri plura pericla trucis, Elmham, Lib. Metr. 166.
[6] Hoccl. Min. Po. 20; Anglia, 34; James, 155. Figgis (42) thinks that "Lollardism was soon emptied of its political and social force and only in isolated individuals did the ideas survive."
[7] Pol. Songs, ii. 244.
[8] "An erth clot," Laud Troy Book, 201; "a clot of clay," ibid. 504.
[9] Hoccl. Min. Po. 23; Anglia, 36; James, 158.
[10] And durst nat come and shewe thy visage, Hoccl. Min. Po. 24; Anglia, 37; James, 160.

that now bound itself with them would make but a quaint array[1]. Oldcastle might fill his banner with the Church's most sacred emblems[2], but none were so blind as not to see that his followers were only waiting to cast his net to catch the Church's fish[3]. His old friend and former admirer Thomas Hoccleve now urged him to repent, for he had been too long out of joint; some of his feathers had been lately plucked and more would soon be, if he did not purge him of his trespass. Why should he lie as a lurker[4] in skulkery[5], when every honourable knight was labouring with the king[6]? It was but the cursed fiend that had changed his guise[7]. Let him therefore now come forth as the champion of Christ[8], or he would certainly ere long feel the sore in the fire[9].

But even if this unholy alliance had not been in itself sufficient to wreck the scheme, yet the king had his spies all about[10] and the suppers at Cranbury and the talks at the Hook, at the Ferry, at the Friars and in the streets of Southampton would assuredly not go unobserved, while,

---

[1] Harflet, 306.

[2] Ad seducendum simplices, Wals. ii. 307; "to mislead the ignorant," Collier, iii. 312; "to attract the common people," Waugh, 652.

[3] Hoccl. Min. Po. 22; Anglia, 36; James, 158.

[4] Hoccl. Min. Po. 9, 11, 14, 16; Anglia, 24, 26, 29, 30; James, 140, 141, 147, 150. Cf. "and carefoly away to crepe," Pol. Songs, ii. 244; "and hevely his hede to hide," ibid. 246.

[5] Cf. "not to ligge thus in scolcurye," Laud Troy Book, 480; Kempe, 24. For "skolkorye" or skulkery, see Laud Troy Book, 224, 246.

[6]
> Look how our Cristen Prince, our lige lord
> With many a lord and knight *beyond the see*
> Laboure in armes and thouw hydest thee.
> How can a knyght be out of thonour of this rial viage?

Hoccl. Min. Po. 24; Anglia, 37; James, 180. The poem is supposed to have been written when the king "feust à Hampton sur son primer passage à Harflete," but this colophon was evidently written after the death of Henry V in 1422 "que Dieu pardoint" and is not quite accurate as the king was already "beyond the sea," Hoccl. Min. Po. xx. 8; Anglia, 23; Mason, 11; James, 138; Baeske, 16, 19.

[7]
> Sum tyme was no knyghtly turn no where
> Ne no manhood shewed in no wyse
> But Oldcastel wolde his thankes be there.

Hoccl. Min. Po. 24; Anglia, 37; James, 160. Cf.
> I trowe there be no knizt alyve
> That wolde have don so open a shame. Pol. Songs, ii. 245.

[8] Hoccl. Min. Po. 10, 80; Anglia, 45; James, 143. Not that this "bad poem" was called forth by the *burning* of Oldcastle, as Pollard, xxv.
> And but yee do God I beseeche a boone
> That in the fyr ye feele may the sore. Hoccl. Min. Po. 18.

[10] For playnly ye hadde men on every syde to aspy swilche maner of governaunce, Dep. Keep. Rept. xliii. 591.

to crown all, the Earl of March[1], finding that the toils were closing round him, himself disclosed the whole story to the king[2] on the very eve of the day fixed for the assassinations, which were to have been carried out on August 1[3]. The king immediately wrote to the Mayor of London informing him that a treacherous plot had been discovered[4], but before this letter could be received in the capital the danger was over and the conspiracy crushed.

When the treason was revealed the king was at Porchester, and with his usual promptness he took in the situation at a glance. Dissembling his real feeling[5] he

---

[1] Not the Earl of Cambridge, as Duval-Pineu, ii. 186; nor Scrope, as Tyrrell, 289 [169], who thinks that he was "animated by feelings of honour that did him infinite credit"; nor Sir John Oldcastle, as Drayton, Oldcastle, 339 [written in 1599, Dict. Nat. Biogr. xvi. 10, in collaboration with Robert Wilson the younger (b. 1579, d. 1616, Dict. Nat. Biogr. lxii. 125), Richard Hathway (fl. 1602, do. xxv. 157), and Anthony Munday (b. 1553, do. xxxix. 293)]. In Greg. Chron. 109, "God sende warnynge to oure kyng."

[2] Per comitem Marchie detecti, Usk, 125; Kirkstall Chron. 288.

The Erle of Marche the sothe to say
That is grasyous in all degre
He warned the kyng, that is no naye,
Ho he was solde certanly. Harflet, 306 [Vitellius only].

Per quel dito de la Marzia, Morosini, ii. 46, from a letter written at Bruges Aug. 18, 1415; Gesta, 11; Monstr. 366; Le Fèvre, i. 222; Waurin, i. 178. Echard (i. 183) thinks that he "generously revealed" the conspiracy "foreseeing the dismal consequences to the nation"; Rapin (iii. 441) that he was convinced that the movement was not really caused by any feeling of justice or affection for himself and that he revealed the plot on the very day on which he was approached to join it; also Tindal, i. 511; Guthrie, ii. 459; or "probably revealed," Henry, v. 34. Nicolas (45) thinks that "presumptive evidence justifies the opinion" that he revealed the plot. Lingard (iii. 242) thinks that "this inference is not warranted"; Church (66) that it may be "safely disregarded." Strickland (ii. 119) calls him "really a highly moral young prince," and credits him with a romantic refusal to dispossess his friend (i.e. Henry V). Stow (346) thinks that he did it to escape from the conspirators, who had threatened an hour before to kill him if he did not swear that he would take the crown. Belleval (31) thinks that "ce point n'a jamais été entièrement éclairé"; Adams (i. 212) that he had refused to promise secrecy when approached and asked an hour for consideration during which he disclosed the plot to the king. Yonge (Cameos, 256) thinks that he "loved Henry too well to consent" to join the plot. Oman (Hist. 233) that he "remained a loyal subject all his life." Fletcher (319) calls him "a meek and perhaps a sensible man who had no wish for a crown."

[3] Non cognovit Rex traditionem usque in articulum temporis quo erat mare transiturius, Capgr. De Illustr. 114. The information was lodged on July 31, Stow, 346; not on July 20, as Kingsford, 124; Strang, 68; Radford, 47; nor July 21, as Brougham, 109; Towle, 294.

[4] i.e. on July 31, 1415, Letter Book I, pp. xxv, 140, which contains the mayor's reply dated Aug. 2, 1415, assuring him that the city would be kept safe on his behalf; see also Sharpe, London, i. 258. A further letter under the Privy Seal was sent to the mayor from Westminster on Aug. 12, 1415, charging him to cause absent Aldermen to return to the city for the preservation of the peace, Letter Book I, pp. xxvi, 183; Rym. ix. 306; Riley, Mem. 654, where it is referred to 1417.

[5] Mist les choses en terme par manière de fictions, Le Fèvre, i. 223; Waurin, i. 178; statim, tacitè et sapienter, Gesta, 11; qui moult estoit subtil, Waurin, ii. 182; ung des sages princes du monde, ibid. i. 173; sage et ymaginatif, ibid. i. 178; Le Fèvre, i. 223; cf. Wylie, i. 325; iv. 140, note 3; wysse and manly playnly to termine, Lydg. in Greg. Chron. 53.

summoned all the notables that were at Southampton as if to a council in Porchester Castle, and there informed them that he had heard rumours of a plot[1], though he could not himself believe it, and he asked them accordingly to advise. There was no need for the hell[2]. The Earl of Cambridge, Scrope and Gray were ready with confessions on the spot[3], and were at once removed for safe custody to the new tower[4] beside the Godshousegate at Southampton, where they were placed under the charge of Sir John Popham[5]. No time was to be lost, for the summer was running out and a peremptory order had just been issued[6] requiring all to hasten to their ships in readiness for embarkation not later than the 1st of August[7]. A commission of ten lords and others was at once appointed[8] and a jury of 12 Hampshire men[9] impanelled,

[1] For imaginary speeches by him, see Pol. Verg. 442; Halle, 61; Redman, 39, 40; Holinsh. iii. 548. Turner (v. 394) thinks that he wept on discovering the treason.

[2] Sans guaires grans langaiges et sans gehine, Le Fèvre, i. 223; sans jehynne, Waurin, i. 179; sans gehenne, Lavirotte, 156; cf. tirer en la gehenne, Ableiges, xix; questionné et gehenné, Paradin, 620; mettre en gehine, Coville, Recherches, 396; gehaines, Floquet, Echiq. 130; la violence de la gehenne, Maillard, 72, 74, 75, 82; gehinez, serez, et tirez, Deschamps, viii. 184; gehinez, Cordeliers, 225; qu'il le missent en gehaine, luy firent monstrer les habillements de gehaine, et fut questionné, La Barre, Mem. i. 276; quelque mal et tourment, ibid. 277; mis à la question, Douet d'Arcq, iii. 127; mettre à question de fait, Vandenbroeck, 156. For picture of a torture-chamber, see G. F. Warner, Val. Max. p. 12. For tormentor questioning, see Marks, 35.

[3] Not that they were arrested at Winchester, as Portal, 129, 130.

[4] For picture of it as rebuilt in 1377, see R. Warner, ii. 176. For position and description, see Englefield, 72–75; Davies, 63, 82; Shore, Guide, 48. For £100 paid for repair novae turris prope portum (*sic*) vocatum Goddeshousgate, see Pat. 5 H. V, 25, July 11, 1417; Priv. Seal 5 H. V, 836. It still stands at the south-eastern angle of the walls and was long used as a prison. For picture of the walls of Southampton on the waterside, see Woodward, ii. 342.

[5] Rot. Parl. iv. 65.

[6] Dated Porchester July 29, 1415, Rym. ix. 298.

[7] Caxton, 225; Brut, 375. At Lammas on St Petrys Day, Harflet, 304; i.e. St Peter's Chains, Chron. R. II–H. VI, 40; on the 30th day of Juyl, Cotton MS. Julius B. i. 37, though not in Chron. Lond. For wages paid to masters of ships for six weeks from Aug. 1, 1415, see Rym. ix. 315, 316.

[8] viz. the Earl Marshal, the Earls of Salisbury, Suffolk and Oxford, Lords Zouche, Fitzhugh and Camoys, Sir Thomas Erpingham and two regular judges (i.e. William Lasingby and Robert Hull), Rot. Parl. iv. 65, where the date is July 21, 1415 (repeated in Vickers, 16), but the real date is July 31, as in Pat. 3 H. V, ii. 34 d; Cal. Pat. H. V, i. 409. For payment (Feb. 7, 1418) made to Robert Hill (or Hull), justice for gaol delivery, of the Earl of Cambridge, Lord Scrope and Thomas Gray at Southampton, see Ord. Priv. Co. ii. 207; Tyler, iii. 134, where he receives 100 marks for this and for holding sessions in South Wales. In 1408 he was a serjeant-at-law (Wylie, iv. 190) and was appointed a judge of Common Pleas on May 14, 1408, Foss, iv. 326; do. Dict. 346, who quotes his oath "By God!" from Year Book 2 H. V, page 5 b, as the only oath recorded on the bench. He settled at Shilston in the parish of Modbury near Plymouth, Prince, 267; Polwhele, Devon, 464.

[9] See their names in Rot. Parl. iv. 65. They were selected from a list of 24 men from every hundred and 12 from every city and borough in the county who had been summoned by the sheriff, John Uvedale.

before whom the accused were brought on Friday, Aug. 2[1], in the castle at Southampton[2].

The proceedings were short, for by this time each of the three had made a complete confession and thrown himself abjectly upon the king's mercy, pleading piteously for life. These confessions are still extant[3], though in a fragmentary and (in places) illegible form, but they shed the only broken patches of light that can now be brought to bear on the tangle of difficulties in which the whole story is involved. The Earl of Cambridge[4] and Sir Thomas Gray admitted all, including a charge of conspiring to kill the king and his three brothers. Scrope, while denying all knowledge of this latter count, admitted that he was privy to the rest of the plot, but pleaded that he had merely wormed himself into the conspirators' confidence in order that he might know their malice and bring it to an end; but the plea was idle, inasmuch as he never denounced them of his own accord. Gray was at once condemned to death as a traitor, but the other two claimed trial by their peers. This constitutional difficulty however proved no serious bar, for almost all the dukes, earls and barons of England[5] were then present in the streets and inns of Southampton. Twenty of these[6] were immediately got together[7], and it is little short of amazing to find among them the names of the Earl of March and Lord Clifford, though, in the case of the former at any

---

[1] Rot. Parl. iv. 65; Harcourt, 402. Called "at Lammas" in Hard. 374; not Aug. 5, as Oman, Hist. 246; nor Aug. 6, as Stow, 346. Scrope's goods were confiscated on July 31, 1415, For. Accts. 6 H. V, 20.

[2] In Lel. Itin. iii. 92, "the glorie of the castelle is yn the Dungeon." For the castle of Southampton granted to John Popham, kt. Oct. 27, 1418, see Carte, Rolles, i. 269; Ewald, xli. 702; Dep. Keep. Rept. xli. 702 (i.e. in 1408). For property granted to him in Paris temp. H. VI, see Longnon, pp. viii, 297, where he is called "Poupan" or "Popeham." For inquisition as to property of Henry Popham, esquire, deceased, in Southants. and Wilts., see Claus. 6 H. V, 13, 14, Nov. 1, 1418, where his widow is called Margaret.

[3] Dep. Keep. Rept. xliii. 580; Rym. ix. 300, 301, from MS. Cotton Vesp. C. xiv. f. 39; F. iii. 7; Speed, 774; Guthrie, ii. 459; Nicolas, App. 19; Tit. Liv. 100; Tyler, ii. 139.

[4] Called "a submissive and pathetical letter," Echard, i. 183; "a most suspicious kind of historical proof and no legal proof at all," Brougham, 107; "dessen Wortlaut für uns die Sache nur noch dunkler macht," Pauli, v. 101.

[5] "Practically the whole available peerage," Ramsay, i. 199.

[6] i.e. the Dukes of Clarence, Gloucester and York, the Earl Marshal, the Earls of March, Dorset, Huntingdon, Arundel, Salisbury, Suffolk and Oxford, and Lords Clifford, Zouche, Gilbert Talbot, Harrington, Willoughby, Clinton, Matravers, Botreaux and Bourchier, Rot. Parl. iv. 65.

[7] "Anon right in hast," Harflet, 306.

rate, it is certain that his name was actually included in the indictment[1]. The Duke of York was also one of the commissioners, but his brother had taken pains in his confession to explain that he had never let him know[2]. The commissioners sat in the castle at Southampton on Aug. 5[3], where the Duke of Clarence, speaking in their name and as vice-gerent of the king[4], pronounced the doom. The accused were sentenced to be drawn, hanged and beheaded, but, by the king's special grace, the infamy of hanging was remitted[5] and Gray[6] and the Earl of Cambridge were further spared the ignominy of the hurdle[7]. Scrope alone was drawn through the streets[8] from the Watergate to the Bar[9] on the north, where all three were beheaded[10] with several others[11] without the walls[12].

Forty-five years later the sentences were annulled in the first Parliament of Edward IV, who was the Earl of Cambridge's grandson, and from that time down to the present day all writers who have dealt with the subject

---

[1] Unde indictatus reatatus et appellatus existit, Rym. ix. 303.

[2] Never let the Duke of York wete, Dep. Keep. Rept. xliii. 586.

[3] Rym. ix. 300; Cal. Pat. H. V, i. 409; Chron. Lond. 100.   Not July 29, as Caxton, 225; Fabyan, 579; nor July 30, as Kingsford, Chron. 70.

[4] Harcourt (190, 191) notes that he did not preside as Steward of England.

[5] Tyler (ii. 135) calls this "a most rare instance of mercy in those days."

[6] Rot. Parl. iv. 66; Nicolas (40, 42) dates his execution on Aug. 2 or 3.

[7] Cf. He drow him at his hors tayle as he hadde ben a cut-purse, Lydg. Troy Book, 439.   Not "a sentence of torture," as Towle, 295.

[8] Lingard, iii. 488; Nicolas, 41; Dict. Nat. Biogr. li. 13.

[9] Englefield, 8.   Then called the Barred- or North-gate; cf. "Barre Gate by North large and welle embatelid," Lel. Itin. iii. 91; "the Northgate of Hampton," Peter, Chron. 487; Chron. R. II–H. VI, page 40.   For picture, see Roujoux-Mainguet, i. 423; Woodward, ii. 330; Aubrey, i. 252; McFadden, page 5.

[10] For pictures of public executions where the victim kneels on a table or on the ground with eyes bound and no block while the headsman strikes at his neck with a sword, see Cutts, Middle Ages, 499, from Harl. MS. 4379, f. 64; Lacroix, 448; Wallon, 205; Hanotaux, 262; Lafenestre, 62, from Cathedral at Aix in Provence; Froissart (Johnes), ii. 195; Humphrey, Froiss. I. Pl. XXII; De Witt, 93; Cassell, ii. 43; also Foucquet's picture of the execution of St James the Greater, Gruyer, 132; Foucquet, i. 171; also of SS. Cosmas and Damian by Fra Angelico in the Louvre, Lafenestre, Richtenberger, 74; also MS. Reg. 1 E. ix. 72; 20 C. vii. 30; Sarrazin, Rouen, 163, from Coutumier de Normandie, 1460; G. F. Warner, Val. Max., Plates I, III, V, VI, VII, IX; Add. MS. 29,704; Schultz, 42 (1468), 44 (1512); H. Martin, Boccace, Pl. LVI; Omont, Merveilles, i. Pl. XX; Villard de Honnecourt, 191, Pl. II (1250), where the headsman seizes victims by the hair; also Revue Archéologique, année vi. Pt. II. p. 99.   For executions with axe and block (i.e. a bench), see Sercambi, ii. 410; MS. Reg. 20 C. vii. ff. 112, 133, 134, 139, 140, 203.   For a collection of executioners' swords (16th to 18th century) chiefly of German make, see Brett, Pl. LXXX.

[11] Con moltry altry che ièra chou loro, Morosini, ii. 50. For arrest of John Foxholes, Thomas Blase and others who had lived in the same house as Scrope, see Devon, 342, Oct. 15, 1415.

[12] "Without the Northegate," Brut, ii. 376; but called "without the Southgates," ibid. ii. 553.

have echoed the charge that the proceedings were irregular, unconstitutional and illegal[1]. But there seems little ground for these strictures. It was a matter of course that the Yorkist Parliament of 1461[2] should call the Southampton sentence "an erroneous judgment" pronounced in a "pretended session" and confirmed in a "pretended parliament," but these are merely the partisan expressions of a later date uttered in a moment of victorious political reaction. The Southampton proceedings were the only possible course in a crisis of emergency and they received their formal confirmation at the earliest opportunity when the Parliament met at Westminster three months later[3].

The body of the Earl of Cambridge was buried "head and all[4]" in St Julian's Chapel in the godshouse[5] near the waterside at the south-eastern corner of the town. Eight months later[6] his little son Richard, a boy of four years of age[7], who became Duke of York[8] and the father of two English kings[9], was transferred to the manor house at Methley near Pontefract to be brought up under the charge

---

[1] e.g. Carte (ii. 679) thinks that this form of trial was adopted "for a show of respect to the privileges of peers," but he shows plainly that he thinks the whole charge was trumped up, though he does not deny the existence of a conspiracy. Hume (iv. 48) thinks the proceedings were "every way irregular and unsatisfactory"; Hallam (553) finds "no sufficient motive for such an irregularity"; cf. "a most irregular and indeed wholly illegal proceeding," Brougham, 109; "höchst unregelmässig und hastig," Pauli, v. 102; "a sort of court-martial," Strickland, ii. 119; "privilege of trial by their peers was very insufficiently granted," Courtenay, i. 177; "les formes légales ne furent nullement observées," Roujoux, ii. 242; "a mere direction to the peers to condemn the two," Ramsay, i. 199; "the proceedings were so unconstitutional and irregular that they had to be specially legalised in the next parliament," Plummer, in Fortescue, 8; also Vickers, 16, but this is scarcely borne out by the words: "ut judicia affirmarentur et pro bonis et legalibus judiciis haberentur et tenerentur in perpetuum," Rot. Parl. iv. 66. Radford (47) thinks that the sentence was "based upon the finding of a local jury."
[2] Rot. Parl. v. 484.　　　　　　　　[3] i.e. in Nov. 1415, ibid. iv. 66.
[4] Stow, Chron. 346; head and body, Sandford, 385.
[5] Hospitalis S. Juliani Suthamptonie Domus Dei nuncupat', Monast. vii. 673, 675; Davies, 455. A tablet erected in the chapel by John, Lord de la Warr in 1766 records that all three were buried "near this place," but only the burial of the Earl of Cambridge is proved, Davies, 459, 470; Shore, Guide, 48; Portal, 130. For picture of the remains of the godshouse, see Englefield, 48; Woodward, ii. 282; Clay, 78. For St Julian's in Winkle Street, see McFadden, 11. For the Godshouse Tower, see Vict. Co. Hist. iii. 502.
[6] i.e. March 9, 1416, Exch. Accts. K.R. 49/17; Rym. ix. 318.
[7] Not 14, as Tyler, ii. 133; Yonge, Cameos, 256. He was born on Sept. 21, 1411, Comp. Peer. viii. 214; Dict. Nat. Biogr. xlviii. 176; called 1412 in Dugd. ii. 157; Doyle, iii. 745.
[8] Claus. 4 H. V, 3, March 8, 1417. Duke of York by discent of his fadir And had Marchis londis by right of his modir, Monast. viii. 1601, where his arms are given with those of Dame Cecily his wife, daughter of Ralph Nevil, Earl of Westmoreland. He was knighted at Leicester on May 19, 1426; not 1425, as Sandford, 383.
[9] For his children, including Edward IV and Richard III, see Fabyan, 582.

of Robert Waterton, who received £100 per annum for his maintenance[1]. The heads of Lord Scrope and Sir Thomas Gray were sent north, the former to be fixed on the Mickle-gate Bar at York[2] and the latter on the Tower at Newcastle[3]. What became of their bodies is not known, but it is likely that they were buried in the godshouse at Southampton, though when Scrope made his will on June 23, 1415[4], he had expressed a wish to be buried in York Minster[5], where he desired that he might be laid in a tomb which was to be erected in St Stephen's Chapel between two pillars on the north side of the choir, to the rebuilding of which he had contributed £20[6]. His body was to be set down before the High Altar[7] covered with a white woollen cloth and a red cross, and no hearse, torches, lights or ornaments were to be used at the funeral, save one candle burning at the head and another at the feet.

The goods of all three of the conspirators were confiscated, those of Gray being placed in the custody of his brother John[8] during the minority of his son Thomas[9], and those of Scrope being duly valued and held at the disposal

---

[1] Iss. Roll 6 H. V, Mich., Nov. 28, 1418. For £116. 13s. 4d. paid to Robert Waterton for his expenses, see Iss. Roll 5 H. V, Mich., Nov. 15, 1417; also £135. 11s. 2d., Iss. Roll 7 H. V, Mich., Jan. 20, 1420; also £9. 13s. 4d. for custody of the Duke of York and other prisoners, ibid. 8 H. V, Mich., Jan. 21, Feb. 27, 1421. In Rec. Roll 7 H. V, Mich., Jan. 18, 1420; 8 H. V, Mich., Feb. 27, 1421, Robert Waterton farms the manor of Soureby (? Sowerby, Yorks.) for the support of the Duke of York.

[2] Stocks-Bragg, 69.

[3] Raine, North Durham, 327. For order dated Aug. 8, 1415, for heads of Scrope and Gray to be fixed on the gates of York and Newcastle, see Tyler, ii. 136, quoting Claus. 3 H. V, 16.

[4] i.e. at Southampton, Rym. ix. 272–280; Dep. Keep. Rept. xliii. 593. On Oct. 31, 1415, the will was not to be found, but it was then guessed that his copes large and small would total to about 120, and his silver vessels would not exceed six dozen, Ord. Priv. Co. ii. 183. For a copy of the will in the Public Record Office (Misc. Exch. Treas. of Receipt $\frac{22}{23}$), see Genealogist, N.S. i. 266, where it is dated June 3, 1415.

[5] Raine, York, 83.

[6] Cf. Wylie, ii. 207. For his arms carved in York Minster, i.e. the Scrope band with a lion shaded, cum umbrâ leonis in le bende (cf. Murray, Dict., s.v. *Entrailed*, *Umbrated*), see Purey-Cust, i. 82, 96, 99, 100, who thinks (i. 95) that the third window in the clerestory may have been given by him.

[7] Ante autenticum altare, Rym. ix. 273.

[8] Raine, North Durham, 327.

[9] Pat. 3 H. V, ii. 35, 43, Aug. 8, 1415; Nicolas, 175. For commission dated Dec. 7, 1415, to enquire into his lands in Northumberland, see Pat. 3 H. V, ii. 20 d, where there is a reference to his wife Alice and his son Thomas with his wife Isabel, one of the commissioners being Sampson Hardyng, who was M.P. for Northumberland in 1395, 1399, 1403, 1414 (Nov.) and 1421, Return Parl. i. 250, 259, 265, 283, 297; also Escheator for Northumberland in Rec. Roll 8 H. V, Pasch., Mich., July 7, Oct. 15, 1420, though not in List of Sheriffs, P.R.O. p. 98. He was on a commission for gaol-delivery at New-castle on Nov. 3, 1416; March 11, 1417, Pat. 4 H. V, 13 d; Feb. 24, 1418, do. 5 H. V, 1 d; see Wylie, ii. 260, note 1.

of the king to be drawn upon from time to time as security when money was wanted for the payment of wages to the troops engaged in the operations in France. His lands and manors in Richmondshire and other parts of Yorkshire[1] passed to Henry Lord Fitzhugh[2], who also received a grant of his London hostel near Paul's Wharf[3]. His lands in Lincolnshire[4], Suffolk and Essex[5] were likewise granted away, among the recipients being William Porter[6], John Phelip[7] and Joan de Bohun, Countess of Hereford, the king's grandmother[8]. His family charters and muniments were at first deposited with the Warden of St Leonard's Hospital at York[9], but subsequently removed for safer custody to the Treasury at Westminster[10], though it is

---

[1] e.g. the manors of Masham, Burton Constable, Ainderby-Steeple (= Aynderby-with-the-Stepyle), Pat. 5 H. V, 19; Priv. Seal 5 H. V, 828, June 10, 1417. For the executor's account of his property in Yorkshire, including the manor of Upsall, see Claus. 3 H. V, 5, Feb. 15, 1416.

[2] Pat. 3 H. V, ii. 26, 35, Aug. 6, Nov. 22, 1415, with side-note = "vacat quia aliter inferius"; Cal. Pat. H. V, i. 360, 372.

[3] It was granted to Fitz-hugh on Aug. 8, 1415, Pat. 3 H. V, ii. 34, with a side-note showing that the hostel was taken over by the king on Nov. 20, 1416, but regranted to Fitzhugh at the same date; Pat. 4 H. V, 9; Claus. 4 H. V, 11. See also Priv. Seal 5 H. V, quoted in Gesta, 12; Rot. Parl. iv. 213; Dugd. i. 660, for 15 of his Yorkshire manors granted to Fitz-hugh, which were afterwards exchanged by him for an annuity.

[4] Granted to William Clifford, Constable of Bordeaux, for life, Pat. 5 H. V, 20, May 24, 1417.　　　　　[5] Ad Quod Damn. 370.

[6] Page 345, note 6; Stocks-Bragg, 70, 71, 78, 79, where he is "armiger" in the first grant and "chivaler" in the second.

[7] Pat. 3 H. V, i. 14; ii. 34, Aug. 6, 1415, where his manors of Nedding and Ketelberston (i.e. Nedging and Kettlebaston) near Ipswich are granted Johanni Phelipp and Alicie uxori ejus (with a side-note = "vacat quia aliter in hoc anno"); repeated in Pat. 4 H. V, 25, with side-note altered to "anno tertio"; also Rec. Roll 7 H. V, Pasch., May 1, 1419, where his wife is called "Alicia Phelip."

[8] For custody of lands of Edward Duke of York and Henry Le Scrop granted to her, see Rec. Roll 6 H. V, Pasch., July 16, 1418. For her receipts from custody of lands of Edward late Duke of York, see ibid. Mich., Dec. 2, 1418, also from Roger (? Robert) Waterton, ibid. Nov. 28, 1418. For grants made by her to the Prior of "Lyes" in Essex (i.e. the Austin Friars at Little Leighs near Chelmsford, Morant, ii. 100; Monast. vi. 552), see Ad Quod Damn. 370 (3 H. IV); do. Lists, ii. 743. For money lent by her in Feb. 1417, see Iss. Roll 4 H. V, Mich., Feb. 20, 1417, where she is called Johanna Bohoune. In Rec. Roll 7 H. V, Pasch., July 8, 1419, she is *defuncta*. For her death April 17, 1419, see Wylie, ii. 282. For executors of her will, see Iss. Roll 7 H. V, Pasch., July 3, 1419, where she is comitissa de "Hested," afterwards correctly written as "Heford." For £442. 17s. 5d. advanced to Robert Darcy, esquire, one of her executors for the purchase of live and dead stock, see Devon, 366 (Feb. 27, 1421); Tyler, i. 18; see also Iss. Roll 8 H. V, Pasch., May 24, July 12, 1420, which records £73 paid for books and other things bought from her executors. For a sercle (i.e. circlet or girdle) valued at £236. 10s. qui jadis fuist a Madame de Hereford with balais, emeralds, sapphires and pearls among Henry V's possessions at his death in 1422, see Rot. Parl. iv. 214. For her missal and portos, see Wylie, iii. 328.　　　　　[9] Pat. 4 H. V, 24 d, June 24, 1416.

[10] For. Accts. 5 H. V, shows £9. 0s. 22d. (*sic*) paid to Edward Hastings, sheriff of Yorks. (i.e. 1416, 1417, Sheriffs' Lists, p. 162), for carrying charters of Henry Scrope from St Leonard's Hospital at York to the Treasury at Westminster in a cart with 12 mounted men, including the purchase of chests, coffers and boxes. For 2s. paid to labourers for carrying three chests of the muniments from the Exchequer of Receipt to the Treasury

certain that the king was much troubled in his mind at
having granted away these entailed estates[1], and in the
case of Fitzhugh we have evidence that the manors were
soon afterwards surrendered in return for an annuity[2]; but
all the dead man's personal effects[3], his masers, horses[4],
copper-gilt coffrets, tapets of ruby and black worsted, arras,
worsted beds[5] with silk celers, testers, counterpoints, sheets
and napery, his green tartrin cushions with silk borders
worked with crabs[6] and carbuncles, his scarlet gowns
with tartan sleeves and bodies of double carde furred
with brown-grey miniver and old marten, his plate,
jewels, gold and silver vessels, saucers, dishes, paternosters,
amber beads, breviaries[7] and chapel furniture were im-
pounded and placed in the hands of the Mayor of
London[8], those from Yorkshire being forwarded down
by Robert Waterton from Pontefract[9]. His wife Joan

---

in the Abbey at Westminster, see Devon, 350, April 29, 1417. For 40s. paid to J. Grene-
wode valectus to J. Marshall, late Receiver of Henry Scrope, ordered to come to London
with all evidences as to the value of Scrope's manors, etc., see Iss. Roll 3 H. V, Mich.,
Nov. 11, 1415. For £8 paid for bringing goods and jewels of Henry Scrope, Lord of
Masham, from York to London, see Devon, 361, Oct. 27, 1419.

[1] Moeuz et troublez grandement en sa conscience, Rot. Parl. iv. 213, 287; v. 41;
Plummer, in Fortescue, 278.

[2] Page 536, note 3.

[3] Mublez. Cf. my goods moeble, Wills of Kings, 238; gold and mebles, Lydg. Troy
Bk. 285; meoabylle godys, Greg. Chron. 72. For articles forfeited by Henry Scrope,
see Rot. Parl. iv. 224, 233, 235, 239, 240; Scrope and Grosvenor, ii. 141.

[4] For six of his palfreys and one courser with their names, see For. Accts. 6 H. V,
19; Exch. Accts. 106/24 (1). For four of the Earl of Cambridge's horses forfeited,
see ibid.

[5] See App. T.

[6] For a crab as the probable origin of the family name, see Wylie, ii. 192; Foster,
Feud. Arms, 220. Cf. le Scrap, Purey-Cust, i. 82.

[7] He left a portos to Bishop Beaufort and a book of meditations each to Bishop
Langley and the Earl of Dorset, Rym. ix. 276. For a Latin breviary (circ. 1322) with
arms of Scrope of Masham, see Stow MS. 12 in Warner, Series II; also Palaeographical
Soc. Ser. II. Plate 197.

[8] Pat. 3 H. V, ii. 23, Dec. 1, 1415; Cal. Pat. H. V, i. 378. For £458. 0s. 20d. (sic)
received from Thomas Fauconer, Mayor of London (see page 242), on account of some
of these vessels, see Iss. Roll 3 H. V, Mich., Oct. 9, 1415; also £100 paid to him from
Scrope's money found in the hands of Richard Throkenold, fishmonger of London, Rec.
Roll 3 H. V, Pasch., Sept. 3, 1415. For value of Scrope's gold and silver vessels in
Fauconer's hands, see Rec. Roll 3 H. V, Mich., Oct. 9, Nov. 27, Dec. 3, 1415. For
£266. 13s. 4d. paid by the king per manus John Merbury p. Wallent' (? valentia, see Du
Cange, s.v.) de denar' Henrico Scrope per Robertum Cliderowe, see Rec. Roll 3 H. V,
Pasch., June 8, 1415. For Robert Cliderowe, yeoman of the king's chamber, sent to
Southampton to seize Scrope's goods, see Cal. Pat. H. V, i. 378.

[9] For letter of King Henry in Nov. 1415, to Robert Waterton, governor of Pontefract,
to send up goods of late Lord de Scrop, see Gesta, 101, from "MS. Donat" (? = Sloane
MS. 4601, art. 161). For payments for carriage of them from Pontefract to London and
money realised from the sale of them, see Iss. Roll 3 H. V, Mich., Nov. 6, Dec. 20, 23,
1415; Pat. 3 H. V, ii. 20 d, Nov. 21, 1415. For enquiry as to some of them concealed
in Yorkshire and not given up, see Pat. 4 H. V, 19 d, July 13, 1416. For some of them

Holland[1], daughter of the Earl of Kent[2], now thrice a widow[3] and certainly no longer young, soon afterwards married Henry Brownflete[4], or Bromflete, of Malton in the North Riding of Yorkshire, whose father, Sir Thomas Brownflete[5], had been Chief Butler to Richard II[6] and Controller of the Household under Henry IV[7].

still in the hands of his mother Margaret, see Pat. 6 H. V, 7 d, Feb. 9, 1419. For £10. 6s. 8d. received in the Exchequer from Geoffrey Le Scrop as price of certain cloths and chattels belonging to Henry Le Scrop in his manor at Faxfleet, see Rec. Roll 8 H. V, Mich., Jan. 30, 1421.

[1] For her marriage with Henry Lord Scrope, Sept. 1411 (not 1410, as Wylie, iii. 284, note 5), see Scrope and Grosvenor, ii. 141. For her dower, i.e. one-third of the liberty of Tynedale, see Early Chanc. Proc. i. 33. She died April 12, 1434, Scrope and Grosvenor, ii. 141; J. Evans, 318; Comp. Peer. vii. 90.

[2] Doyle, iii. 742; Rot. Parl. iv. 375 (1431), where she is called Duchess of York, sister to Margaret Duchess of Clarence (see Wylie, iv. 76) and Edmund late Earl of Kent (d. 1408), Wylie, iii. 104.

[3] Wylie, iii. 284, note 5.

[4] J. Evans, 317. He is called H. Bromflet de Vesci, kt. in 1449, Dugd. i. 95; ii. 234; where his will is dated May 21, 1466. This title came to him from his mother Margaret St John, granddaughter of William de Aton (? Ayton) Baron of Vesci, Banks, ii. 16, 61; Comp. Peer. ii. 30; viii. 32. For pardon to him (Aug. 14, 1416) for marrying Joan Duchess of York (see page 524, note 2), late wife of Henry le Scrop, without the king's consent, see Pat. 4 H. V, 18; Rym. x. 316. For his retinue (12 + 36) at Southampton in July 1417, see Gesta, 269. For letters of attorney (Jan. 22, 1420) in the names of Thomas Bromflete and others for Henry Bromflete being with the king in Normandy, see Ewald, xlii. 339. He died Jan. 16, 1469, Comp. Peer. viii. 32.

[5] Dugd. ii. 234. For £20 left to Thomas Brounflete, kt. in Scrope's will, see Rym. ix. 280. He was Sheriff of Yorkshire in 1400, 1401, 1414, 1419, Sheriffs' Lists, 162; Drake, 352; Rec. Roll 3 H. V, Pasch., Mich., July 9, 17, Nov. 4, 1415; Pat. 4 H.V, 4; Ord. Priv. Co. ii. 204, 206, Feb. 15, 1417, where he is *late* Sheriff; For. Accts. 4 H. V, 13 d; Rec. Roll 8 H. V, Mich., Oct. 15, 1420, where he is called "Bromflete," but "Bronflet" in Pat. 8 H. V, 22, or "Brounflete" in For. Accts. 8 H. V, 1. The name appears to be derived from Bromfleet or Broomfleet near Hull (cf. "brom-bred," i.e. brown bread, Mann. and Meals, i. 320). For his connection with the manors of Acaster, Copmanthorpe and Skelton near York, see Early Chanc. Proc. i. 9. For Thomas and Henry Brounflete on various commissions in Beds. and Yorks. in 1423, 1424, 1426, 1427, 1429, see Cal. Pat. H. VI, i. 424, 459, 474. For Joan, daughter of Thomas Bromeflete of Londesborough near Market Weighton in the East Riding, see Purey-Cust, ii. 165, where she is said to be the widow of Sir John Colvil who was executed in 1405 (Wylie, iv. 277) but there must be some mistake, as Joan was not born till 1405 and is said to have been an idiot from her birth, though she afterwards married William Nevil, son of Ralph Earl of Westmoreland. For Thomas Bromflete, knight, of Malton (Yorks.), see Comp. Peer. viii. 32.

[6] He was appointed July 23, 1395, Cal. Pat. Rich. II, v. 608 and *passim*, till April 9, 1400, do. H. IV, i. 252; but *late* Chief Butler May 11, Oct. 29, 1400, ibid. pp. 280, 489. Not that he was cupbearer to Henry V, as Antiquary, viii. 1.

[7] Appointed May 28, 1401, Cal. Pat. H. IV, i. 445. On Dec. 18, 1422, he is Treasurer of the Royal Household (see page 50, note 11), Cal. Pat. H. VI, i. 14, which continues to him the parkership of Folly John in Windsor Forest. He died Dec. 31, 1430, and is buried beneath a brass in the church at Wymington near Higham Ferrers, see Hewitt, iii. 433; Macklin, 147. In his epitaph, for a copy of which I am indebted to the kindness of Rev. C. E. Drew, he is described as:

Regis R ex donis Pincerna fuit regionis
Hujus...fit tresorer hospitiique
H. quarti sibique quia verax vixit ubique
His Rex jussisset ut Thesaurarius isset
Anglis mansisset ex sensu in renuisset.

For Thomas Bromflete, possibly his son, sheriff of the city of York in 1427 and 1458,

Two days after the executions the Earl of March received his pardon[1] on the ground that the others had practised on his innocence[2]. He afterwards continued to receive grants and other evidences of royal favour[3], and little trace remained of the really formidable shock that had threatened to undo at one stroke the costly preparations of two crowded years.

As the time for sailing drew near the king took the usual precaution of making a will[4], in case he should never return to his country alive[5]. The will had been really drafted in London before the second English embassy had started[6] for Paris, but was not finally signed till six months later. In it he trusted that he would be received into Abraham's bosom, not for any merit of his own but through the prayers of Mary[7] the High Mother of God, the angels, archangels, apostles, patriarchs, martyrs, confessors (especially St Edward and his own peculiar patron St John of Bridlington[8]), matrons (including St Brigit[9] of Sweden)

who died Oct. 7, 1458, and was buried with his wife Alice in the church of All Hallows in the Pavement at York, see Drake, 296, 352, 362.

[1] i.e. on Aug. 7, 1415, Rym. ix. 303; not Aug. 8, as Tyler, ii. 136.

[2] Cujus innocentiam tentassent, Gesta, 11.

[3] For grant to him of goods valued at 800 marks forfeited by merchants of Galway, see Priv. Seal 4 H. V, quoted in Gesta, 12. In his will dated July 24, 1415, the king left him a bed embroidered with lions and roses, Rym. ix. 291.

[4] Not that this was in consequence of the alarm caused by the Scrope conspiracy, as Pauli, v. 103. For infamy attaching to intestacy, see Grose, 121.

[5] For other wills made about the same time, see those of Henry Lord Scrope, June 23, 1415, Rym. ix. 272; Thomas West, Aug. 1, 1415, Dugd. ii. 140; Richard de Vere Earl of Oxford, Aug. 6, 1415, Dugd. i. 196; Morant, ii. 213; Test. Vet. 192; Genealogist, vi. 225, from Chichele Reg. P. i. 304; Hunter, 26, proved Feb. 28, 1417 (not 1416, as Gough, ii. 50); William Lord Botreaux, July 20, 1415, Dugd. i. 630 (though he did not die till 1462, Comp. Peer. i. 389); Test. Vet. 191. For knights' wills proved at Lambeth in 1415, see John Clynton, Leeds, Genealogist, v. 327, in retinue of Duke of Gloucester, Nicolas, 333; Thomas Dutton, Genealogist, vi. 24 (for his retinue 9 + 30, see Exch. Accts. 45/5 (4); Nicolas, 378); William Faucon, Calais, Geneal. vi. 25; John Fitzrauf, ibid. vi. 25; Robert Tye, Banham, ibid. vi. 224; cf.

> For he (the lawyer) hath now no bus'nesse at the Barre
> But to make Wills and Testaments for these
> That were for France their substance to dispose. Drayton, 23.

We bachelors bid our friends scramble for our goods if we die, Drayton, Oldcastle, 333.

[6] Pietro of Milan heard this from Bishop Courtenay and regarded it as bad news and not a sign of peace, Mirot, Fusoris, 199.

[7] She was the special protectress of England which was regarded as her dower, cui dos Anglia stat, Elmham, Lib. Metr. 106; quam propensius veneratur Rex Angliae, Wals. ii. 329; Save Ingelond for Mary sake, Harflet, 301; Ramsay, i. 310.

[8] Wylie, iii. 336; be swete Seynt John, Harflet, 303. For St John of Bridlington as a guide in St Patrick's Purgatory in 1409, see H. L. D. Ward, ii. 485. For a chapel dedicated to him in the church of St Michael, Wood Street in London, see Sharpe, Cal. ii. 417.

[9] For one crois d'or ove reliques de Seint Brigit, see Rot. Parl. iv. 219.

and virgins, among whom he named St Barbara, St Catherine, St Ursula and her 11,000 companions[1]. He then prayed that God would guard his successors against all dissensions and divisions and all the wiles of heretics. He directed that his body should be buried in the Abbey church at Westminster with a raised place to hold the relics of the saints above his tomb, which was to be approached by steps up and down at either end[2] and furnished with an altar in honour of the Annunciation at which three masses[3] should be celebrated each day by priests so placed that they should be in full view of all. For these masses £100 per annum was to be set aside as a permanent endowment, and 300 marks were allotted for providing vestments, chalice, paten, bell, pax, cross, cruets and other altar requirements[4]. He desired that all reprehensible extravagance[5] should be avoided at his funeral, but 30 poor men[6] were to be clothed and fed for a year on condition that they should repeat every day: "Mother of God, remember thy servant Henry who placed his whole trust in Thee." Besides this he arranged for 20,000 masses to be sung as soon as possible after his death, specifying particulars as to numbers and titles of each, such as the mass of Christ's wounds, of the Five Joys, of the Blessed Virgin, the Nine orders of Angels, the Three Patriarchs and so on[7]. He gave 1000 marks each to the building funds of the Carthusians at Sheen and the Bridgettines at Syon[8]. He left a jewelled sword to King Sigismund, beds[9], cups, ewers, crosses, coursers[10] and

[1] See page 475. For St Ursula, see Lydgate, Min. Po. 178.

[2] For account of Henry V's chantry, see Lethaby, 254; called a "high chantry" in Feasey-Micklethwaite, 98, 102; "a watching loft," F. Bond, 49, 50, 192, 230, 231, 238; do. Guide, 21, 45, Plates XIX, XX. For view of it, see Le Keux, Frontispiece, pp. 30, 36, 40; Craik-Macfarlane, ii. 52, 232; Bradley, Guide, 65, 78; T. Wright, Views (from the North Ambulatory); Besant, Survey, ii. 133; Knight, ii. 52; do. London, iv. 142; Hiatt, 73. It was enlarged and furnished with statues and iron gates by Henry VII, Sandford, 288; though Neale (ii. 86) thinks that these were included in the iron-work ordered on Jan. 28, 1431, Rym. x. 490. For a chantry called "le Rode Loft" in St Nicholas church at Calais, see Rym. x. 32.

[3] For particulars of these as the mass of the Assumption, the Resurrection, the Salutation, the Angels, etc., see First Life, 21.

[4] See page 475.

[5] Damnanda superfluitas, Rym. ix. 289.

[6] For cloaks and hoods for poor men as torch-bearers at funerals, see Bournon, 54.

[7] Rym. ix. 290.

[8] For his obit in August in the Syon Martirologe, see Add. MS. 22,285; Whitford, xxix.

[9] e.g. a red velvet bed, embroidered with an oak tree in the middle and oak leaves round it, to the Duke of Gloucester, Rym. ix. 291.　　　[10] "Courciers," ibid.

money gifts to his brothers John and Humphrey, and the Earls of March, Dorset, Warwick and Westmoreland with mementos to his grandmother Joan de Bohun[1] and his aunt Joan Beaufort, though it is remarkable that his brother Thomas, Duke of Clarence, was altogether overlooked. To Archbishop Chichele he left a red broidered velvet gown which he had bought of Richard Clitherowe[2], with missals, portoses[3] and a closet-altar[4] to Bishops Beaufort and Langley. He remembered likewise many humbler persons, such as his chamber-ushers and body squires, leaving £10,000 to be divided amongst his household servants, and £200 amongst the clerks of the Royal Chapel[5].

This will was witnessed at Southampton on July 24, 1415[6], and subscribed in his own hand[7]: "R.H. Jesu Mercy and Gramercy[8]. Ladie Marie help," in presence of Bishops

---

[1] i.e. a cup, Tyler, i. 18.   [2] Page 278, note 1.

[3] For portiforium, see Raine, Durham, 100; Wylie, iv. 358. Called portose in Littlehales, xliv; Caxton, Dial. 38; portoos, Rock, iii. 43; portuus, Hoskins, xvii; portaffis, Boys, 384; portisforium, Bibl. Top. Brit. II. App. no. x. 71, 74*; Freshfield, 1; portiphery, Worthy, Wills, 302; portevoire, Benham, 58; quemdam librum Portiforium quo servivit de matutinis et aliis horis canonicis, Test. Ebor. iii. 56; my portoos to say his service thereon, Fifty Wills, 59. For a portos valued at £3. 6s. 8d. see Cambr. Antiq. Soc. Vol. II. pp. xiv, 17. For a clerk at Maldon sued for debt (40s.) in 1436 distrained on his portiforium, see Essex Herald, April 14, 1905.

[4] For super-altare or portable altar, see Lee, 22; cf. altaria viatica seu portatilia quae superaltaria vulgariter appellamus, Holmes, 17. For office for the consecration of a portable altar (benedictio lapidis portatilis seu lapidis itinerarii) with three shown in a miniature, see York Pontifical, xl. 124; Barnes, 39. For portable altars granted to various persons, see Papal Letters, vii. 334, 533 and *passim*. For specimen of a Trag-altar at Melk near Vienna, see Kraus, II. i. 463 = altaria portabilia, gestatoria, itineraria. For autel portatif given by the English to the cathedral at Chartres during the occupation circa 1420, see Mely, 57 (with picture); Bulteau, 128. For aultier portatif de jaspre, de marbre, de porfide, see Guiffrey, i. 52; ii. 60; Fagniez, Invent. xxvii. 397; Gazette Archéologique, xiv. Pl. 24; Noces, 520. For a portable altar for the Fraternity of St Nicholas at the end of the Grande Salle of the Palais in Paris sans qu'il soit attaché au pierre ne en plastre, see Delachenal, 38, 409. For one granted to Thomas Strickland by Pope Eugene IV (Jan. 24, 1431) super quo in locis ad hoc congruentibus et honestis positis per alium sacerdotem ydoneum missam et alia divina officia facile celebrari, see Nicolson and Burn, i. 95. For evesques portatifz, see Delachenal, 320; also avocat portatif, ibid. 319.

[5] Rym. ix. 292, x. 506; Cal. Pat. H. VI, ii. 350; Wills of Kings, 243.

[6] Rym. ix. 293; not July 27, as Mirot, Fusoris, 158.

[7] For his signature "R. h." from Vesp. F. iii. no. 7, f. 5; do. xiii. 37, f. 27, see Wills of Kings, 242; Nichols, Autographs, A. 3; Craik-Macfarlane, ii. 130; Netherclift, 3; Hume (1854), ii. 345; Knight, ii. 56; Towle, Frontispiece; Aubrey, ii. 36; also in Chancery Warrants, Ser. I. 1364/36, 38, 44, 59; Nicolas, Agincourt, 34.

[8] For Gramercy, Graunt Mercy, see Hartlet, 304, 305, 306, 320; Melusine, 9, 30, 41 and *passim*; J. Page, 21, 27; Lydg. Min. Po. 10; Anjou Lett. 39; Grant Mercy, Coudrette, 190; Arras, 38, 49; "Gran mercy God," Collins, viii. 106; seyth "Jesu Mercy," Lydg. Min. Po. 101. For "Jesus Mercy" on brass of Sir John de Brewis or Braose (1426) at Wiston near Steyning (Sussex), see Macklin, 153; Horsfield, ii. 237; also of Wm. Chichele at Higham Ferrers, Macklin, 165; Wylie, iii. 136; iv. 118; also

Caterick and Patrington, the Earl of March, Sir Thomas Erpingham and several others[1]. The original of it appears to be now lost and we only know of its existence through a copy of it which was made in the 16th century and is still preserved in the library of Gonville and Caius College at Cambridge[2]. In it the king appointed as his executors[3] Bishops Beaufort, Courtenay and Langley, and the Earls of Westmoreland and Dorset[4], while Henry Lord Fitzhugh, two knights, viz. Walter Hungerford and John Rothenale[5], who was Controller of the Royal Household[6], and two squires, viz. John Wodehouse[7] and John Leven-

---

fragment of a brass at Wappenham near Towcester, D. Hudson, Pl. 13; and brass of Judge Billing, temp. Ed. IV, at Wappenham, ibid. Pl. 15; Cutts, Slabs, 57.

[1] Rym. ix. 289–293.

[2] i.e. in Vol. II of Collections of Robert Hare (d. 1611) who was Clerk of the Pells from 1560 to 1571. For earlier extracts from the original will, see Harpsfeld, 584, who gives a further extract from a will made in 1418, but the extract is identical in terms with the opening words of the will of 1415 in Rym. ix. 289.

[3] Cf.   L'executeur le pourra faire
            Tel qui luy plaira adviser. Regnier, 122.
For "secator," see Wright, Songs and Carols, 4; "seketour," Wylie, iii. 235, note 5.
            Litel while the mon be myst
            So the executours wol say.
            They rekene his richesse what it amountes
            Ete and drynke synge "hay yol haye"
            The while the fende hys synnes countes
            And brynge to hym the countertayle. Kail, 22.
For dinner of executors charged to an estate at Troyes, see Assier, 45. Cf. executors be covetous and kepe all that they fynde, Clutterbuck, iii. 538; Cussans (Odsey), 136; J. Evans, 316, from epitaph (1433) in the church at Kelshall near Royston in Hertfordshire.

[4] Called Duke of Exeter in the will, but Earl of Dorset in the body of the text, Rym. ix. 291, and in Cal. Pat. H. V, i. 356; Rym. ix. 293, though he was not made Duke of Exeter till Nov. 18, 1416 (page 120, note 3). This singular anachronism together with the gift of a sword to Sigismund as the champion of the Church against heretics (i.e. Hussites, Pauli, Bilder, 301 [335]), raises a doubt as to the accuracy of the transcript.

[5] Otherwise called Rodenale (Iss. Roll 1 H. V, Mich., Oct. 2, 1413); Rodenhale (Inq. p. Mort. iv. 174, 187; Wills of Kings, 242; Cobbett, 226); Ruddenal (Hunter, 33); Rothenhale (Inq. p. Mort. iv. 47). He was a Norfolk man, Blomefield, iii. 528; iv. 88, and the name probably originated at Redenhall near Harleston in Norfolk, Inq. p. Mort. iv. 149, 170, 172, 315, 422.

[6] Sloane MS. 4600, f. 16, June 16, 1415. Called keeper of our wardrobe in our hostel, Iss. Roll 4 H. V, Pasch., April 30, 1416; do. 5 H. V, Pasch., Apr. 21, 29, May 6, 1417; Ord. Priv. Co. ii. 205, Feb. 15, 1417; Devon, 348, 353, Aug. 10, 1416; Nov. 15, 23, 1417. For grant to him of the alien priory of Hayling near Portsmouth, April 1, 1415, see Pat. 3 H. V, ii. 26; also of the domain of Old Shoreham (Sussex) in lieu of the offices of scribe (cirograffarii) in the Court of Common Pleas, water-bailiff of Wiggenhall, gauger of Lynn and Constable of Launceston, Pat. 3 H. V, i. 29, April 17, 1415.

[7] For grant to him of the alien priories of Wells-next-the-Sea (in Norfolk) and Panfield near Braintree (in Essex), see Pat. 3 H. V, i. 2, April 1, 1415; Goodwin, 41. For his signature to a document dated Norwich, March 22, 1419, see Ord. Priv. Co. ii. 248. In Pat. 3 H. V, i. 5; ii. 32, July 6, 1415, he is appointed a chamberlain of the Exchequer in place of John Ikelington (see page 469, note 11) and his name "Wodehous Camar'" appears at the foot of Iss. Roll 7 H. V, Mich. and at the head of Rec. Roll 7 H. V, Mich.

thorpe¹, were specially charged with the detailed work of administering the estate.   The king's three brothers (the Dukes of Clarence, Bedford and Gloucester) were named as supervisors², together with Archbishop Chichele and Bishop Hallum, though the latter was still absent at the Great Council which was then sitting at Constance.

Two days before this will was signed the king had conveyed all the castles, manors, &c. belonging to him as Duke of Lancaster, together with all the other property that had come to him from his grandfather³, Humphrey de Bohun Earl of Hereford, to Archbishop Chichele, Bishops Beaufort, Langley and Courtenay, and other⁴ feoffees to be separately dealt with "simply and without condition." These included the Earl of Arundel, Henry Lord Scrope, Roger Leche, Walter Hungerford and John Phelip, knights, and Hugh Mortimer, esquire, who do not appear as executors under the will of July 24.   But as a matter of fact the will was never really acted upon.   It was superseded by another which was made at Dover on June 10, 1421⁵, just before the king's departure for his third expedition to France, from which he never returned alive.

(1419).   He is called "Groom of the King's Chamber" in Nicolas, 168, where his descendants are said to have taken "Azincourt" as their motto, not their war-cry, as Belleval, 91.

¹ See page 22, note 6.

² Cf. "surveior," Fifty Wills, 54, 62 ; surveiur, Wills of Kings, 227.

³ For annexation of this property to the Duchy of Lancaster on Nov. 19, 1414, see Rot. Parl. iv. 46 ; Baines, i. 130, quoting Coke, 4th Institute, p. 210.

⁴ See Cal. Pat. H. V, i. 356, 357 ; ii. 4, dated Southampton, July 22, 1415, Wills of Kings, 236, 238.   See p. 523.

⁵ Rot. Parl. iv. 299, 399 ; Ord. Priv. Co. iii. p. ix.   Cf. testamentum prius in Angliâ circumspecté conditum, Vita, 333 ; now lost, Champion, Vie, 175.

INDEX